ICANCHU'S DRUM

ICANCHU'S DRUM

An Orientation to Meaning in South American Religions

LAWRENCE E. SULLIVAN

MACMILLAN PUBLISHING COMPANY
NEW YORK
COLLIER MACMILLAN PUBLISHERS
LONDON

Copyright © 1988 by Macmillan Publishing Company
A Division of Macmillan, Inc.

Macmillan Publishing Company
866 Third Avenue, New York, NY 10022

Collier Macmillan Canada, Inc.

Library of Congress Catalog Card Number: 87-22879

Printed in the United States of America

printing number
1   2   3   4   5   6   7   8   9   10

Library of Congress Cataloging-in-Publication Data

Sullivan, Lawrence Eugene, 1949–
    Icanchu's Drum / Lawrence E. Sullivan.
       p.   cm.
    ISBN 0-02-932160-3
    1. Indians of South America—Religion and mythology.   I. Title.
F2230.1.R3S85 1987   87-22879
299'.8—dc19   CIP

The map at the end of this book reproduced with permission from "South American Indian
Languages" in *Encyclopedia Britannica*, 15th edition (1974).

The map on the endpapers reproduced, with permission, from pages 914–915 of Felipe
Guaman Poma de Ayala, *El primer nueva corónica y buen gobierno*, edited by John Murra
and Rolena Adorno (Mexico City: Siglo XXI Editores, 1980).

For Lesley

After the Great Fire destroyed the world and before the little bird Icanchu flew away, he roamed the wasteland in search of First Place. The homeland lay beyond recognition, but Icanchu's index finger, of its own accord, pointed to the spot. There he unearthed the charcoal stump that he pounded as his drum. Playing without stopping, he chanted with the dark drum's sounds and danced to its rhythms. At dawn on New Day, a green shoot sprang from the coal drum and soon flowered as Firstborn Tree, the Tree of Trials at the Center of the World. From its branches bloomed the forms of life that flourish in the New World.

Adapted from the Mataco myth of the Cosmic Fire

CONTENTS

PREFACE

I offer heartfelt thanks to those friends, family members, and colleagues who helped me create this book. Above all, I thank my wife, Lesley Antonelli Sullivan, whose anthropological expertise and editorial skill graced each step of this work. Her encouragement and affection enabled me to persevere to its end. Along the way, Mariangela, Lawrence, and Carolyn brought new life to the effort. My parents, my eight sisters and brothers, and their families furnished welcome living quarters as well as office space and equipment in several ports of call during periods of research. Professor Davíd Carrasco, director of the Mesoamerican Archive and professor of the history of religions at the University of Colorado in Boulder, raised critical questions, while at the same time confirming the general course of my inquiries. Dr. Robin M. Wright, professor of anthropology at the Universidade Estadual de Campinas, offered fruitful suggestions during a season of study at the Tozzer Library of the Peabody Museum of Anthropology. Dr. John Carman, director of the Center for the Study of World Religions, made it possible to conduct investigations in Harvard University's special collections. Clair J. Carty and Jerry D. Weber helped to prepare the index. Trish Love of the Religious Studies Department at the University of Missouri in Columbia shepherded these materials through the stages of their transformation and performed the feat of typing several drafts of the entire manuscript. I gratefully acknowledge research support received from the Marsden Foundation, the Provost and Graduate Research Council of the University of Missouri in Columbia, and the National Endowment for the Humanities. Guaman Poma's world map, which appears in the endpapers, is the first of its kind drawn by a native South American historian and is reproduced, with permission, from pages 914–915 of Felipe Guaman Poma de Ayala, *El primer nueva corónica y buen gobierno*, edited by John Murra and Rolena Adorno (Mexico City: Siglo XXI Editores, 1980). The map at the end of the book is reproduced with permission from "South American Indian Languages" in *Encyclopaedia Britannica*, 15th edition (1974).

São Paulo, Brazil
26 March 1987

Lawrence E. Sullivan
The University of Chicago

PART ONE

ARCHAEOLOGY

THE MEANING OF THE BEGINNING

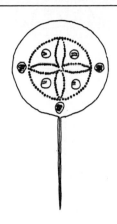

CHAPTER 1

INTRODUCTION

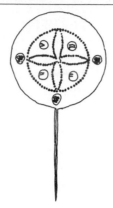

Understanding South American religions is an urgent task for modern people, if only because misunderstanding them shapes our vision of reality. We face our world and reflect on our human condition by primping ourselves with illusions about others. Tortured images of the spiritual life of South American peoples lie at the foundations of the modern self-understanding that has been conjured up since the Age of Discovery.[1] Theories of superstition and animism have maligned the myths and obscured the rites of most of humankind. Suppositions about prelogical mentality, infantilism, and primitivism are revealing poses of modern thought and deserve no depiction here. They mirror back to us the illusory self-definitions that flaunt a fragile, even wistful, hope for a privileged place in human history. These diverse methods disclose a yearning to discover how the investigating culture (through its theology, science, social organization, economic system, technology, or art) might transcend "inferior" expressions of humanity, especially by its power to investigate, theorize, and record history, and to survive in it. In this respect, native South America is shadowed by the same investigative cloud that obscures the religious heritages of Africa, Oceania, and Asia, where religious experience flourishes beyond the doctrinal systems elaborated in written texts. Such misconstructions of the religious lives of others do not contribute to a fertile rendering of the human situation in our day, for these cultures are equally heirs to human nature and have responded with stunning originality to the emotional, aesthetic, and intellectual capacities of being human.

Understanding South American peoples not only requires that we change a few ideas about them but that we dismantle the foundations of who we ourselves are. Perhaps this is why there is no book that systematically scans the broad sweep of South American religious life from beginning to end.[2] Terrifying or liberating, the work of understanding is unavoidable. We cannot rediscover our own creative place in history without uncovering the creative role of South American religions in our common human history. By acknowledging, in our own experience, the agency of South American peoples in fashioning the world in which we live, we become subject to their meanings and capable of responding with deliberate interpretations of our own. Such a self-conscious responsibility to the broader horizons of human creativity shapes and befits our situation in history.

At the turn of the century, the humorous caricature of the "armchair anthropologist" unseated the thinker who reflected on foreign cultures at a distance and enthroned the fieldworking researcher. The rationalizations created for fieldwork grounded a new and fruitful encounter with "other" cultures during the colonial experiment. But the criticisms of reflection-at-a-distance stemmed from a conviction born of, and confirmed in, the alternating rhythms of field expedition and university residence (for writing and lecturing) that constitute field anthropology. Native thought in the field was on the "first level of reflection" and worthy mostly of ethnographic reportage. Informants provided reliable data, the "givens" that were described as if they were the thoughtless behaviors of laboratory subjects and that were carted home as raw materials for subsequent production. At home, meanwhile, academics and literati—poets, social scientists, mathematicians, physicists, and musicians—produced ideas worthy of critical reading, sensitive listening, and even philosophical reflection. To this haven of reflection, fieldworkers returned to "theorize" about their "data" and to "demystify" religious symbols in terms of the socioeconomic self-understandings of the academic community.

This dichotomy between peoples who practice and those who theorize, or between those who supply data and those who reflect, has come under attack.[3] Critics are seeking to uncover credible grounds for reimagining the common creative capacities of the human species, grounds that can accommodate the array of creative experiences evident in the plurality of cultures. To these efforts belongs that of rethinking human history in terms of the uniquely human ability to evaluate existence in time.[4] Mircea Eliade offered a forceful gloss on these attempts:

> If there really has been an original or important discovery made in our time, then it is certainly that: the unity of history and of the human mind and spirit. That is why I do not want, or try, to "demystify" things. One day we shall be blamed for our "demystification" by the descendents of those we once colonized. They will say to us: "You exalt the *creativity* of your Dante and your Vergil, but you *demystify* our mythologies and our religions. Your anthropologists never stop insisting on the socioeconomic presuppositions of our religion or our messianic and millenarist movements, thereby implying that our spiritual creations, *unlike yours*, never rise above material or political determining factors. In other words, *we primitives* are incapable of attaining the creative freedom of a Dante or a Vergil." Such a "demystifying" attitude ought to be arraigned in its turn, on charges of ethnocentrism, of Western "provincialism," and so, ultimately, be "demystified" itself.[5]

The brunt of the blame for misconstruing South American religions should not fall on the last generations of ethnographers, who filed mountains of reliable field reports based on clearly identifiable premises. The fault lies rather with philosophers, historians, and interpreters, who shrink from their vocation to reflect on the full dimensions of human experience in the contemporary world. By pushing South American and "other" religions to the far margins of awareness, workers in the humanities came to embody defensive and sterile stereotypes that they reproduce in the routinized practice of their craft.

Sensitive to the needs of several publics, this book will introduce any reader to the rudiments of religious life in South America. Naturally enough, the book directs itself to historians of religions, who interpret humankind's religious life, and to anthropologists, whose training in religion generally lacks the thoroughness accorded the study of kinship, general linguistics, or social theory. But these constituents represent the smallest part of the book's audience, for it is intended to speak especially to creative artists who have discovered that South American religious life is a worthy subject and stimulus for literature, music, drama, visual design, painting, and sculpture. I hope in this volume to encourage this aesthetic interaction by setting South American creativity in its religious context. Journalists, philosophers, theologians, ethicists, sociologists, jurists, and historians are conspicuous in their lack of interest in South American religions, as well as in the religions of Asia, Africa, and Oceania. This is unfortunate, since their interpretations of reality exert a formative influence on the shape of modern cultures. I hope to excite their interest, enticing and enabling them to look into the religious views of reality put forward by their neighbors. This chapter invites readers to plunge into this preliminary survey at its beginning and to follow its course to the end. By explaining the subject matter, the approach, and the organization of the book, I shall, in the following pages, offer the general reader several more reasons for reading an introduction to South American religions.

South Americans offer original appraisals of the experience of being human. Nowhere is this more evident than in their religious life, which is the foundation of South American cultures. Despite the onslaught of Western culture and its historical and scientific analysts, South American cultures persevere in viewing themselves as people whose significant processes arose in the very beginning from sacred events and from the actions of sacred beings. Mário Juruna, a Xavante chief from the village of Namunkurá in the Mato Grosso of Brazil, played a key role in the Fourth Russell Tribunal convened in Rotterdam, the Netherlands, in 1980 to judge crimes against the native peoples of America. In pleading his case, Juruna emphasized the complete penetration by religious experience of the material and social existence of South American peoples. No single facet of their lives can be grasped without taking hold of all the others.[6] Religious expressions, including art, architecture, and symbolic action, are the most brilliant and ebullient expressions of South America. By refusing to come to grips with these accomplishments, one avoids being impressed by what is singular and startling about the creativity of South Americans.

SUBJECT MATTER: SOUTH AMERICAN RELIGIONS

This book treats the religions of South American peoples, taking the subcontinent as a whole, both spatially and temporally. It presents and discusses the religious ideas of peoples as geographically distant as the Cuna, who inhabit the base of the Colombian-Panamanian Isthmus, and the Yahgan of Tierra del Fuego. It relies on reports filed from the sixteenth century to the present day. Understanding the ways in which traditions change over time (and the ways in which they remain the same) is never a simple matter. Some of the archaeological research of the nineteenth and twentieth centuries relates to religious artifacts and practices that are thousands of years old, evincing a temporal complexity that illustrates a general and fascinating difficulty in the study of religion. Ideas and practices are older than the records in which they first appear, and they bear a complicated history that, while opaque, is essential to the task of understanding them.[7]

South American peoples living in the period since the sixteenth century have played a part in forming the modern world. In studying the religions of South America, we do not reach back into an archaic past, but rather we explore *modern* religious experience: our endeavor parallels, for example, the study of the history of the Protestant experience in Europe since Luther's reform. We are not used to thinking in these terms about South American peoples in the postcontact situation, and we still must learn what it means to do so. But the effort is necessary and rewarding, as André-Marcel d'Ans affirms:

> I declare that I am convinced of the historical value and of the *modernity* of our Amazonian contemporaries. They are not . . . the ancient vestiges of an overthrown past. In an epoch concretely dominated by the effects of western thought, they are moving witnesses to a different way of apprehending the world and others. . . . That is no doubt why they pay such heavy tribute to a History from which, not having been its accomplices, they stand to gain no benefit.[8]

But how can one arrange the coverage of the religious traditions of the whole of South America so that treatment is both coherent and congenial to the religious nature of the data? Commonly, scholars have chosen to organize data along linguistic and geographic lines, but these schemes have proved to be based on troublesome hypotheses. Along linguistic lines, reports Juan Adolfo Vázquez, "It is practically impossible to estimate the number of tribal groups living at present in South America. . . . Modern linguists estimate that there may be around 1,500 different South American languages present or extinct."[9] Jorge A. Suárez grumbles, "Great anarchy reigns in the names of languages and language families. . . . At present, a true classification of South American languages is not feasible, even at the family level because . . . neither the levels of dialect and language nor of family and stock have been surely determined."[10] Suárez nevertheless outlines eighty-two language groups and singles out eight as the most important.[11] On his ethnographic map entitled "Indian Tribes of South America," John Howland Rowe charts the affinity of groups "whose languages are supposed to be related." Rowe lists fourteen principal linguistic classes to which dialects may be affiliated.[12] Bracketing the issues of grammar and vocabulary (as areas complicated by historical interaction), Tadeusz Milewski proposes a threefold typology of languages (Atlantic, Pacific, and Central) based on phonological analysis. Yet another classification suggests three different megacategories for all South American languages: macro-Chibchan, Andean-Equatorial, and Ge-Pano-Carib.[13] If we base our study of religion on a shaky linguistic classification scheme, whether a plan with 1,500 linguistic divisions or only three, we risk mistaking linguistic pattern for religious experience and of viewing religious creativity as a function of language, narrowly construed.

A similar danger attends the classification of religions by geographic area, although many such schemes exist. The most typical of these includes, as distinct regions, Tierra del Fuego, Patagonia, the flatlands of the Pampas, the bush and grass steppes of the Gran Chaco, the vertical steeps of the Andes, the Highlands of Eastern Brazil, the jungle and savannahs of the Orinoco and Amazon Basin, and the tropical forest along the Caribbean coast. This long-lived system, with its several variations, locates people in their geographic habitats but tells little about the nature of their religious ideas.[14]

The problem is that myths and religious practices escape the bounds of these classificatory schemes. On the one hand, similar motifs and symbols appear in the religious life of South American peoples who are linguistically, geographically, and sociopolitically far apart. On the other hand, groups that are near neighbors in all these respects often manifest striking differences in religious expression. The heart of the difficulty is that there is nothing inherent in peoples' religious lives to warrant their division into language groups or geographic areas.

We must look for something in the nature and practice of religion to guide the order of our divisions, keeping in mind that it is unreasonable to expect all South American religious ideas to conform to a few neat principles devised by outsiders. Each South American people has its own history and set of cultural impulses; each must deal with a unique set of ecological variables; and each possesses its own genius and authentic values. One must turn to these factors to uncover ordering principles adequate to the religious materials.

A number of obstructions block the clear view we desire of South American religions and values. Contrary to general impression, South Americans' ideas about themselves are not the biggest problem. Their imagery, unfamiliar to us, does not obscure South American religious life; it *constitutes* it and, therefore, remains the only true source of its clarification. Rather, our own interpretive constructs stand in the way of understanding. To come into the light that South Americans themselves shed on their experience of humanity, we must first inspect our own way of thinking and the shadowy concepts that undergird it. For instance, no people refer to themselves as practitioners of South American religions in the way that others identify with Buddhism, Christianity, Sikhism, Islam, Judaism, or Hinduism.[15] *South American religions* is a category constructed by outsiders who, in a way that calls for critical scrutiny, actually constitute the religious situation described by the term.[16]

What Columbus and other Europeans "found" in the Americas had already been invented, to a great degree, in European culture's demonologies, heresiologies, and legends of a paradisal golden age.[17] The very idea of "discovering" peoples and exploring "new" lands, with the understanding that these realities were thus opened to human history and brought into the light of rational knowledge, exposes the status accorded the human beings living in "newly found" worlds. "Discovered" peoples were believed to live a kind of antihistory in legendary island paradises and Edenic gardens, Amazon-inhabited forests, kingdoms of El Dorado, lost worlds of Atlantis, or lands where lay the fonts of eternal youth. Ironically, the aboriginal inhabitants of the New World incarnated all that European civilization could now reckon it was not. The messianic expansion of European history into a new world and a new age was an immense labor of the imagination that peopled the New World both with monsters from apocalyptic bestiaries and with angels from paradisal revelations. South Americans were, at one and the same time, primeval but timeless, uncivilized but noble, naked but shameless, ignorant but cunning, indiscriminate in eating and aesthetically tasteless but sources of new culinary delicacies, and technologically backward but fabulously wealthy. And they were considered as living far from the "center" even when the lands expropriated from them became, or continued to be, the throbbing capitals of the New World. Reports of the New World brim with contradictions because, deep in the European religious imagination—the generative foundation of its culture—the experience of "discovery," the encounter of contrasting modes of cultural being, was one of disturbing ambivalence. Modernity still shapes its self-conceptions around the responses to this religious situation.

We must stay cognizant of the fact that contact with native American peoples has never been neutral, fair, or peaceful. The severity and violence of the encounter affect every appraisal of South American reality. As Davíd Carrasco has written, "Between us and the pre-Columbian . . . symbols stand not just time and wear, distance and cultural diversity, and renewal within a tradition of wisdom but also the conquest and the invention of the American Indian."[18] The ideology of conquest permeates every image we possess of the people of the New World, and, since the Enlightenment that occurred during the Age of Exploration, has even shaped the way we think about knowledge. Just as European explorers set out to conquer the chaos of barbarity and the unknown, so cartographers, taxonomists, and intellectuals divided into categories the indeterminate worlds of space and history, the myriad "new" peoples, the "new" species of plants and animals, and other constructs of the imagination. By conquering (or simply avoiding) the obscurities of the "savage mind" and by classifying the contents of the wild worlds where these "savages" lived, the "enlightened" forms of knowledge (especially archaeology but also the social and behavioral sciences closely bound to ideas about natural history) created a new religious stance. "These ideologies of the 'otherness of the New World' created taxonomies, theories, and speculations that more often than not confused the data and mesmerized the student of these cultures. The very history of interpretation . . . is a methodological circumstance, a formidable fact." [19]

These obstacles prevent us from opening a study of South American religions with descriptive "data" about them. We must call attention to the historical context, the imaginal experience, where the meaning of those "facts" initially appeared. By pointing to the experience of contact and conquest that first shaped their significance, an archaeology of the data uncovers the meaning of their beginning, the conditions under which these facts could appear in the so-called Western history of ideas about culture. The Conquest is the source of new and significant categories (religion, culture, nature, myth, rite, symbol, society) that preside over the construction of the data. The invention of these new terms to describe reality represents the need, experienced by conquistadors, missionaries, scholars, tourists, and other social actors, to make sense of the newly discovered world. Moreover, contact created a structure of roles to police the manipulation of those categories and the interpretation of that encounter: explorer, conqueror, colonial administrator, missionary, anthropologist, informant, native chronicler, investigator, fieldworker, visitor, tourist, guest, economist, political scientist, historian of culture, and so on.[20] The proclivity of such policymakers to "discover" and mine "elementary forms" exclusively from their own cultural imaginations continues in the paradigms of the social sciences and the schemes of developmental history. But the spiritual universes of the indigenous peoples of the Americas remain to this day largely unexplored by outsiders. Although the geographic territories are often visited, those of the human imagination remain unfamiliar.

For this reason, I have chosen to carry out an exercise in history and to look upon the whole of the South American continent and its peoples with a fresh eye. We must let it confront us as something whole and new and let its unfamiliarity strike us even to the point where its otherness threatens to overwhelm. We must postpone seeking refuge in the divide-and-conquer explanatory stratagems furnished by the canons of cultural relativism, whereby, one by one, each language group, culture, or village is detached from the company of its neighbors and forced to face alone the alien interpreters who exhaustively account for its creativity in their own terms.

Instead of using linguistic, geographic, or socioeconomic blueprints, this comparative historical presentation is constructed in accordance with the mythic structures within which many South American peoples evaluate their existence in time, beginning with the times of creation, heroes, and ancestors and moving toward the end of the world.

Beyond the quality of documents and the historical nature of the facts they present, another obstacle to understanding South American religions is the sheer paucity of information. "Of all the primitive tribes of the world, we know least about those of South America," wrote Ruth Benedict in 1941.[21]

This continent, with its wide diversity of cultures, has remained a black hole in the knowledge of the "modern" world. In his preface to the third volume of the monumental *Handbook of South American Indians*, published in 1948, editor Julian H. Steward mourned the inadequacy of sources. "Not over half a dozen of the hundreds of tribes have been described with the completeness demanded by modern ethnology. Information is largely from random travelers' observations—mention of a lip plug here, a cultivated plant there, a house type elsewhere. Compilation of all the information from the many scattered sources leaves the tribal pictures overloaded with minutiae, usually of dress, ornaments, and weapons, while the essential outlines of the cultures are not even suggested." [22] In addition to the desperate need for fieldwork of every sort, Steward wisely foresaw the need for new comparative studies that would lead to syntheses not only along historical and ecological lines but in terms of "configurational factors." [23] In 1974, Patricia J. Lyon still explained as a "simple fact" the subtitle of her volume *Native South Americans: Ethnology of the Least Known Continent* and lamented that "our knowledge of the continent is still very poor and in many areas virtually nonexistent." [24]

The religious life of South America, more than that of any other area, is unknown. Scholars complain that the problem is cumulative: investigators go into the field without orientation to the religious ideas of the continent and, as a result, are either bewildered, then uninterested, or they report banal generalities that cast little light on the religious life of the particular peoples they visit.[25] Egon Schaden calls for long-term field studies of religious systems by competent ethnologists as well as for comparative syntheses of vastly different religious systems. Both kinds of study mutually depend on one another and, just as important, indicate one another's limits.[26]

APPROACH: MORPHOLOGY AND THE GENERAL HISTORY OF RELIGIONS

Although the scope of this book is ample, its purpose is modest. Each chapter orients readers toward one of the cardinal points (such as creation, space, or death) that define any religious horizon. The volume landscapes a broad panorama of religious ideas from across South America without trying to describe exhaustively the religious life of any single tribe. It neither details the history of language groups nor tracks the development of cultural, technological, economic, or political systems in geographic areas. Symbolic expressions (myths, rites, beliefs, practices) are chosen for their exemplary clarity. They are not compared on account of their historical or geographic proximity but are juxtaposed when the meanings they convey, in their proper historical contexts, can be fruitfully related to interpretations of similar imagery elsewhere. Through sweeping comparisons, the book maps a background against which one may subsequently draw the uniqueness of each tradition with another sort of precision. By creating a place from which readers may view the breadth and height of South American religions without suffering vertigo and by assuming a stance that acknowledges South Americans as creative agents of the modern situation of meaning, the book develops a posture for more sustained reflection on cultural particulars.[27]

DOCUMENTS

The documents on South American religions impede the study of these traditions. One often finds only passing mention of religious beliefs and practices in administrative memoranda, colonial files, adventurers' memoirs, and scientific field notes. Available information lies scattered in books and articles of limited circulation. This reckless strewing of their religious ideas mirrors the territorial dissipation of South American populations. Both aspects of exile echo the loss of "their rich symbolic universe . . . that constitutes an unrepeatable existential and ideological experience for humanity . . . and that seems so irreducible to ours, not because it is archaic but rather because it is parallel to ours." [28]

Consequently, one objective of this volume is to gather and describe South American myths and symbolic acts in an ordered fashion and in some detail, quite aside from an analysis of them. This purpose puts me deeply in debt to travelers, wanderers, explorers, archaeologists, administrators, missionaries, and anthropologists who left, as residue of their passing presence among South American peoples, a bewildering array of records. The volume does present what they have reported as so many empirical facts about religious life, but what they observed cannot simply be taken for objective qualities directly grasped by the senses of the reporters. As Claude Lévi-Strauss points out in relation to the observable movements and characteristics of the sun and the moon, there for all to see, "These properties are abstracted from experience by the labor of understanding." [29] If this is true for the obvious motions of visible heavenly bodies, how much more does it apply to the moves, moods, and motives of the human imagination and its cultural expressions. Culture is a way of sorting out and interpreting material from a variety of sources that test one's faith in reality: revelations, insights, eyewitness accounts, hearsay, and gossip. In this sense, as the book wrestles with its source documents and the fundamental understandings that shaped them, it not only interprets culture but becomes an exercise of it.

HISTORY OF STUDY

This volume takes its place in a line of interpretations put forward during the past five centuries. Ever since the first explorers' accounts, outsiders have had to interpret South American religions. More than of any other dimension of South American life, the fabulous descriptions of religion testify to the need for making sense of the strange experience of contact and conquest. To grasp the meaning of meeting the different expressions of humanity in the New World, adventurers and chroniclers evoked apprehensive images of the spectacular and the fantastic. Contemporary researchers cannot start afresh by unburdening themselves of this legacy of conquest — the first impressions of soldiers, missionaries, and colonials who were utterly unprepared to write interpretive histories of South American religions. The conquerors' experiences comprise an ineluctable patrimony that not only furnishes the earliest written documents but records the first appearances of points of view still influential today.[30]

Theological training and historical interest grounded the more systematic assessments of the differences between native peoples of the New World and those newly arrived there. Early systematic studies include works written by native historians.[31] The tradition of missionary ethnography continues to the present day and offers many valuable studies of religious life.[32]

With the invention of a natural history modeled on images of geological strata and unilinear evolution, a new school of investigators treated South American religions as fossilized behaviors left from an earlier stage of human development. While nineteenth-century surveyors inventoried the natural resources and raw materials of the new Latin American nations, they made romantic but "detached" observations concerning the "noble" or "savage" customs of peoples far removed from the passage of historical time and untainted by civilization.[33] The habit of making random remarks on incidental customs overemphasized the seemingly bizarre and prompted comparative study of sensational themes such as ritual combat, sacrifice, festive intoxication, orgiastic dance, scarification, and ingestion of relics of the dead.[34] These themes constitute *how* we know South American peoples and, therefore, they continue to preoccupy contemporary researchers.[35] Indeed, they must reappear in any thorough treatment of South American religion, but the crucial point, now, is whether the representation of these symbolic forms can transfigure the modern imagination. Without such transmutation there is no creative understanding of these issues. But when we acknowledge the power with which these images bear down on any attempt to comprehend South America and when we recognize how we undergo their meaning, they impress us with their significance and transmute our understanding. The startling appearances of South American religious life can transform the ways we think about ourselves, others, and our world, just as they did when South American and European peoples first encountered one another.

The last eighty years have seen the idiosyncratic report yield to the conventional anthropological monograph that reflects more standardized forms of knowledge, education, and procedures of inquiry.[36] The organization of such monographs typically progressed from introductory sketches of general ecology, linguistic affiliation, and comprehensive social unit (tribe, phratry) to analyses of kinship and social organization (genealogical, marital, descent, and inheritance patterns; age sets; moieties). A monograph ordinarily included detailed discussion of the residence unit, the hierarchy of political authority, the economic life and patterns of exchange, the relations within the domestic unit, and the schedule of daily activities, as well as a description of the life cycle within the particular culture under study. If religion were not subsumed as a function of one or several of these headings, it received treatment in a section on "intellectual life" or "ideology".[37] Under the influence of French sociology, emphasis fell on delineating the social *systems*, evident in collective representations, which underlay "life on the ground"[38]; and, in keeping with the case-study method of British social anthropology, the village became the most typical unit for research. The genre has proven flexible enough to absorb influences from textual criticism and dialogue theory and has made room for the play of intersubjectivity. Such monographs, together with journal articles that reproduced their forms of anthropological knowledge, contain the bulk of what we know of South American religions during the last century. In many ways, this volume pays homage to ethnographers in its reliance upon those excellent ones who, at their best, borrowed freely from the cultures they visited.

A number of reporters have escaped the confines of standard ethnography. Curt Nimuendajú, Ettore Biocca, Karen Hissink, Egon Schaden, Darcy Ribeiro, Marc de Civrieux, and Gerardo Reichel-Dolmatoff, for example, have provided sustained descriptions of myths, rites, and religious ideas. And developments in what is called ethnohistory, as practiced by the likes of Maria Rostworowski de Diez Canseco, Juan Ossio, R. Tom Zuidema, Gary Urton, and Alejandro Ortíz Rescaniere, have pushed ethnography into a confrontation with history in the fuller sense of the word. By forcing field-workers and textual critics to face the meaning of existing in time and to use a culture's own temporal terminology in the analysis of that culture, ethnohistorians of different methodological persuasions make way for the construction of new genres adequate to the new tasks of interpretation.[39]

Although village studies overshadowed comparative work, they could not completely eclipse it. But broad, cross-cultural studies showed no stomach for interpretation and ceased to ruminate over the meaning of religious images, except as functions of social life. Instead they built taxonomies of the so-called formal features of symbolic life.[40] The penchant for classification drew strength from the popularity of Emile Durkheim, Marcel Mauss, Franz Boas, Paul Ehrenreich, Adolf Bastian, Adolf Jensen, and their followers. The explicit assumption during the era of the monograph has been that cultural meanings — archetypically represented in religious ideas — are derivative, superstructural, or surface features. Since these features are relative and, therefore, not comparable, the argument continues, they are unlike deep linguistic structures, or the resources and relations of material culture, or even the givens of ecological habitat.

In general, systematic studies of classification fall into three groups, depending on the source of the features classified. None of these efforts has won the day in regard to South America. Writes Egon Schaden, "More than any other region of the globe, South America presents the ethnologist a situation that defies every effort to classify aboriginal cultures."[41]

The first group recognizes human *mentalité*, a defining aspect of human sociality, as the generative source of classification and order. This group declares language itself and, by analog, all the symbolic codes that order the universe and natural history to be foremost among the cognitive orders imposed on nature by the structure of human (always social) rationality.[42]

A second group of comparativists stresses the historicity of human existence. Over time, this group claims, humans leave the distinctive marks of human order on matter. These distinctive features of material culture (art, architecture, economic practice, cultigens, tools) are the surest guide to an objective ordering of the patterns of culture, which is essentially historical. Analysis of cultural traits reveals the classificatory order inherent in historical and material existence.[43]

The reconstruction of South American cultural history has proved more difficult than first investigators anticipated. Wilhelm Schmidt's work typifies the failed efforts of early enthusiasts. His opening move, one still popular today, separated the "superior" cultures of the Andes from those of the lowlands and tropics. Next, he grouped peoples into historical divisions based on an analysis of cultural traits such as totemism, matrilineality, typical cultigens, systems of exchange, features of boys' and girls' initiation, the role of the hereditary chief, exhumation of bones for second burial, modes of water transport, the shapes of oars, and the distinctive features of bows, arrows, slings, clubs, and shields.[44]

The difficulty of reconstructing the chronological history of South American peoples and the level at which such hypotheses dwell is illustrated by the work of Jacques Lizot.[45] Lizot sounds a methodological call for the analysis of minute detail: "One must . . . reconstitute each particular history [of each ensemble of communities and of the ethnic group as a whole] with *minutiae* and integrate [that particular history] within a larger totality where it takes on its true meaning. This is the price of an exact understanding of social, political and economic life."[46] Lizot scours the demographic and cultural data on population shifts from 1880 to 1980, hypothesizes about the movements and motives of local Yanōmami groups, and, on that basis, generalizes about the reasons for the rapid numerical and geographic expansion of peoples in the native Americas in the last 40,000 years.[47] Such an earnest effort is exhausting as well as exhaustive, yet it is sometimes a fruitful species of historical reconstruction. But one should not mistake Lizot's method as the only possible procedure, for no understanding of history has ever waited for the final assembling of accumulated "facts," and no gathering of "facts" yields understanding without the nature of these facts being questioned. By advancing other evaluations of what history (existence in time) might mean, one subjects the "facts" to alternative methods of interpretation.

Should Schmidt or others have succeeded in their grand task, the question of the meaning of this history of the material expressions of human culture would still face us. The meaning of the material situation in which humans find themselves cannot be exhausted by an account of its historical development even though the reconstruction of such changes would be of immense value in interpreting religious life, since every religious experience is a historical expression.

A third group gives primacy to the ecological base on which a community depends for subsistence and reflection. The weather and climate, the soil, and the flora and fauna of an ecosystem possess an order which preexists the human presence and to which, in thought and deed, the human community must attune itself. The distinctive habitats of the Amazon rain forest, the vertical steeps of the Andes, and the treeless plains of the Pampas provide, so this group claims, the surest ground for comparison of the life systems that thrive in these environments, including the life of human societies.[48]

Ecologically based studies tend to deal only with single eco-niches and to avoid wider comparison of the imaginative lives of human societies. But the limitations of this centripetal tendency are revealed when one considers the religious picture, for "even the phenomena [myths, religious concepts and practices] which one might consider typical of one region or another are not circumscribed by that area alone. We find them among populations whose territories and languages are far apart and whose economic systems and social organizations are palpably different." [49]

A quite different motive propels the cultural studies of a number of Latin American scholars. Although they follow closely the developments of anthropological theory based on linguistic, historical, or ecological premises, their main interest is to explore the historical roots of their own cultural situations and to discover the indigenous sources of their cultures' creativity. Their scholarly investigations of myth, rite, and religious folklore stimulate their creative writing and interpretive readings of Latin American history. These intellectuals and artists are not merely searching for source materials for reflection but are intent on finding their own place in the living indigenous tradition by uncovering its meaning.[50]

One should neither exaggerate the differences nor distinguish too sharply among these strategies for systematic comparison of South American religions.[51] Although they begin from distinctive perspectives, the best investigators proceed to a consideration of elements important to the other theoretical positions. Each view attempts to encompass all the data.

METHOD

It is common in introductions to studies of culture to present one's method, its premises, its procedures, possibilities, and limits. This necessary and worthwhile concern for method should be well situated, lest it appear misplaced and bloated. Interpretive methods are not tools wholly describable and accounted for outside of one's data.[52] In the human sciences, interpretive methods are ways of engaging the investigator's whole being with the expressions and processes of culture, the condition peculiar to human beings. The so-called objective methods of the social sciences are no exception, but they allow one to imagine one's own absence and to fancy what cultural life might mean to another, if one could withhold oneself from total engagement and stand back objectively. Through a powerful feat of fantasy, "objective" scientists have bracketed the fact that cultural existence is never carried on in a vacuum but always in the historical presence of others.

The reasons for attending to one's method are not new. Understanding what is strange — especially humans whose goals, beliefs, personalities, and social constitutions appear *other* than one's own — draws one toward the purpose of the human condition and toward the foundation of its creative impulse.[53]

My perspective is that of the discipline known as the general history of religions.[54] There is no need to be shy about claiming descent from James Frazer, Carl Clemen, Raffaele Pettazzoni, Gerardus van der Leeuw, or Mircea Eliade,[55] because no compulsion drives one to apply their schemes to South American materials. Their theoretical foundations and specific interpretations are dated in many cases and are problematic or unacceptable in others, yet the diversity of their approaches puts us at ease. This diversity illustrates a remarkable freedom of theoretical approach in a field where dissimilar methods and discordant hypotheses have sparked keen, original insights. These scholars are exemplary primarily because they set the question of the general history of religions in proper perspective. They knew that understanding any particular instance of a religious expression would require a total hermeneutics of the religious condition of humankind. To their minds, not only would comparative history amass the evidence of religious life, but it would occasion a sharp reevaluation of human existence through scholars' sensitivity to the way in which their own categories create "facts" and shape them into specific forms of understanding.

Emboldened by this tradition and refreshed by recent criticisms from and innovations in the cultural sciences, especially anthropology, I shall raise general questions and draft broad hypotheses about South American religions, and I shall suggest working generalizations on thorny issues in the study of South American religious expressions.[56]

IMAGINATION AND UNDERSTANDING
Although I have researched materials in their context with care and concern for objectivity, this volume is not a detached work of analysis. I have tried to respond in kind to the creative character of South American religions in the hopes of contributing to the understanding that shapes my own culture, conscious of the need to transfigure the cultural preconditions that make it difficult to understand the full range of human experience. From the time of the Conquest forward these preconditions, prejudices, biases, and inadequacies have devalued and even obliterated whole worlds of meaning.[57] If they do not fall into total oblivion, the ideas and practices with which people have constructed their lives may remain strange and impenetrable caricatures, foreshortening our understanding of human nature and dimming the achievements of human striving in history.[58] In light of the general history of religions, shed especially by cultural heritages once deemed obscure, the study of South American peoples provides an unprecedented opportunity for human beings to forge new cultural values by reappraising imaginal existence in time.

The role of the imagination in the formation of culture remains a constant concern in this volume. Only with awkwardness do interpreters of religion escape their responsibility to be imaginative resources for their own culture. The play of imagination in the interpretive process has been variously perceived. In the view of Gilbert Durand, interpreting cultures involves the comparison of one mode of being with another and, therefore, requires imagination, which is

> the mark of an ontological vocation. . . . The imaginary [condition] is manifest not only as an activity that transforms the world, as in the creative imagination, but above all as a euphemising transformation of the world, as an *intellectus sanctus*, an ordering of being for the better. . . . [It] permits an evaluation of the states of awareness and . . . of the faculties of the human spirit. . . . The imagination is the faculty of the possible, the power of the future to be contingent. . . . [Not only] does this imaginary bond fasten and refasten the world and things in the heart of awareness . . . but even human death is absolved by images.[59]

Understanding is always a cultural act; the process of understanding *is* the cultural situation of humankind, for the struggle to understand is the work of imagination, a uniquely human mode of labor. One's own self-understanding suffers change in the process of understanding. There is, then, a profound truth in the insistence that one should attend to one's method. In order to offer an authentic interpretation of another cultural condition, one must be sensitive to changes in one's own being, which transformations are necessary to understand another world of meaning. This is why historians of religion insist on the value of hermeneutics, the knowledge that comes from the act of interpreting. Hermeneutics is the willingness to treat the attempt at interpretation as a peculiarly instructive cultural process affected by both the subject and object of understanding. In an authentic interpretation, one's method cannot stand objectively apart from one's data; it must become subject to the data in order adequately to grasp what one engages in the act of understanding. The process of interpretation must continually be reexamined in the light of one's attempts to understand. In this light, the up-front confession of one's method often appears simplistic and ill timed, for one cannot so quickly dispatch with the self-awareness that genuine understanding requires. The categories that assemble one's facts and the terms, procedures, and "conclusions" that explain them must remain problematic and subject to question throughout the course of the inquiry. How do one's own forms of knowledge reshape and reveal the meaning of another's thoughts or acts, and vice versa? Understanding is a creative process, and, when it is performed well, the nature of that creativity is itself assessed in the act of interpreting culture.

RELIGION AND HISTORY

This book is about religion. Orienting itself toward South American realities, it reappraises the meaning of religious experience and of symbolic life in general. By offering a rendering of the South American religious imagination, it constructively criticizes the categories with which it must work ("imagination," "religion," "South America," "culture," "symbol," "meaning"), terms often invented to avoid confronting the full, creative presence of

South American cultures, and others, in history. In addition to information on South American religions and interpretations of their meaning, basic questions about our own categories appear throughout the book. What is the sacred? What is the meaning—especially in cross-cultural context—of terms such as myth, ritual, cosmos, space, time, organization, society, creation, and death? What is meaning and how may it be described or apprehended? What is the meaning of religious experience? I have no desire to dismiss these fascinating questions in a preface by defining a few key terms with the help only of Western philosophies or social sciences and unaided by guideposts provided by other cultures. That way of philosophizing no longer uncovers truth in a world where the so-called Western tradition is only one among many forms of historical consciousness. I shall stick close to the methodological concerns that provoke a profound critique of modern assumptions and self-understandings, and I shall cast my reflections on these matters onto the materials of study, hoping thereby to make every interpretive move visible and questionable. This way of integrating general reflections with descriptions of cultural practice not only avoids tedious abstraction; it also reminds us that these myths and rites are always historically conditioned.[60]

Every myth or set of religious symbols relates, in some way, to the political, social, and economic life of the community from which it springs, for religious symbols evaluate every experience of existence. The historicity of all religious experiences, however, cannot absolve us from the responsibility of questioning the nature and meaning of particular historical situations if we wish to understand them.[61] The myths and rites of the Taki Ongo religious-dance uprising, for example, defy, escape, or re-create their own initial historical setting in the sixteenth-century Peruvian Andes. Not only by their periodic reappearance in Andean history but also by their appearance in ethnographies and in our own imaginations, these images transcend their original situation. Their presence among us in the twentieth century makes them and their meanings part of our own historical situation in a way that must be reckoned with. Thus the nature of history proves as slippery and complicated as the human condition itself.[62] That is why, in the study of any culture, we are bound constantly to wrestle with history's nature and with our own process of understanding history. We cannot settle for any quick-fix doctrines of cultural relativity that hide from the real labor of understanding by clinging to the belief that religious documents reflect only their immediate historical circumstances.[63] Without a doubt, cultural context is the place to understand religious symbolism, but "historical circumstances" in the narrow sense do not exhaust the sorts of cultural context in which truths are relevant. Cultural views of reality also stand within the context of culture in the wide sense, that is, the human situation in the world. All peoples are entitled to reflect on this human condition, and any serious anthropology must take these reflections into account when interpreting the symbols that construct culture. Doctrines of cultural relativism may salve the discomfort Western people feel in coming to grips with the significance of their own symbolic life, but the alienation from symbolic meaning so aptly illustrated by the modern social sciences may originate precisely in their avoidance of any serious confrontation with the realities of the many cultural mythologies that have flooded Western awareness since the Age of Discovery. Be that as it may, "We must not confuse the historical circumstances which make a human existence what it actually is with the fact that there is such a thing as a human existence. . . . [T]he historicity of a religious experience does not tell us what a religious experience ultimately *is*." [64] In threading our way between historical circumstances and the general religious condition of humanity, myth is key. Myth not only shapes and explains social, economic, and political orders, but, above all, it reveals the imagination itself, the human ability to draw together disparate experiences into one imagic reality, a world of relations, apprehension, emotion, speculation, reproduction, and judgment.

Because religious beliefs and symbolic acts and imagery enjoy a rich and complex existence in multiple kinds of time, one must ask how to apprehend the truth about humanity which appears in the histories of specific cultures and one must inquire about the relationship that truth bears to what is sacred. [65] For this reason, we should not attempt as a first move to place the study of South American religions on the footing of geography, linguistic affiliation, social organization, or ecology. If we were to begin from those premises, the study of religion would only confirm what we already think we know about the nature of religion, and we would forfeit the chance to make a new contribution to knowledge. The study of religion must be carried on in a way appropriate to its subject matter. This is not a cry against reductionism, for any interpretation of symbolic life must reduce meaning to its scale and purposes. Rather, it is a reminder that social values and functions, which are never absent from or irrelevant to symbolic action and belief, are themselves symbolic of the religious need to encounter what is sacred and to know what is true in order to ground every aspect of life on what *really is*.

Divine beings and sacred sounds, colors, foods, gestures, and words partake of the reality they signify, making religious symbols powerful and effective expressions. As Gary Urton has remarked in relation to ritual dancers who impersonate imaginary beings, they "do not 'symbolize' anything; rather, they *are* that thing." [66] Notwithstanding the helpful distance imposed by historical (including social scientific) and phenomenological methods, we must at some point confront and even reimagine whatever is real in our own world through the imagery provided by South American cultures. [67]

COMPARISON

Why include areas as remote from one another as the Andes and the South American lowlands, or the Amazon and Tierra del Fuego, in the same work? First of all, by setting all areas of the continent on a par for the purpose of preliminary study, one can reappraise their differences, highlighting them in a new way. Though comparison is often taken simplistically as a way of establishing similarities and defamed as facilely settling for superficial likenesses, the real goal of comparison is to discover, and even to create, firm ground for revealing and evaluating significant differences. Besides, it is time to reassess the differences that stand in our interpretions as hidebound fixtures and to treat them as the tentative hypotheses they once were. Thus, Alfred Métraux, who set the pace for evaluating Inca ritualism as different from the "animism" of the Amazon and the "simple theism" of Tierra del Fuego, also confessed that, "in terms of religious life, the contrast among these peoples is not as profound as it may appear." [68] A resurgence of comparative study is the surest way to reevaluate the fundamental concepts that have sustained cultural studies since the last wave of comparison at the turn of the century. "[A]s Boas himself suggested, once culture history had begun to become established as a valid discipline, as it now has for more than half a century, the comparative method might once again reach fulfillment. It would then rest upon a broader and sounder basis in fact. The time to contrast the cosmological systems of ancient civilizations seems now to have arrived." [69] In general, however, regional studies set a premium on the celebrated differences among regions and take a dim view of the comparative enterprise. [70]

The historical complexity of any community, especially evident in its religious worldview, impels one toward comparative study. "It is no longer possible to separate the Indian, Portuguese, African and mestizo cultural traits that have, over the course of time and space since the conquest, dissolved into one another. In any case, they are not separately maintained antagonists but form one single magic mind-set, a whole, a religion." [71] Even a village study is comparative, if it is broadly based, for it calls upon the testimony of lay people as well as specialists, the uninformed and ignorant as well as the cosmologists, medical practitioners, physicists, historians, and repositories of local lore. The varieties of religious experiences, accounts, and opinions in any single human setting raise the same interpretive problems and possibilities inherent in comparison on a wider scale. [72]

There are more philosophically secure reasons for carrying on comparative study. All understanding passes through the travail of comparison, conscious or not. [73] That is, cultures are the matrices of understanding and are therefore inherently and intrinsically comparable, for they are constituted in the experience of comparison and contrast between one people and another, one phoneme and another, one mode of being and another, one idea and another, one pattern of relations and another, and so on. To arrive at new understandings, we must consciously compare a variety of South American views regarding, for example, mythic figures such as the jaguar or the divine twins or religious themes such as the origin of fire, the wearing of masks, the playing of flutes, or beer drinking, rather than only subject the ideas of a single tribal village, through unconscious juxtaposition and comparison, to the judgments of Jean Piaget, Louis Henry Morgan, Vladimir Propp, John F. MacLennan, or Roman Jakobson.

ORGANIZATION OF THE BOOK: AN ARGUMENT OF IMAGES

This book is an argument of images about the integrity of religious life and, therefore, the possibility of a disciplined study of religion. Since the book is argumentative, the reader will miss key developments by wading in at random. This work is neither an encyclopedia nor a collection of ideas, and the case is constructed cumulatively, so that each addition builds on foundations laid in preceding sections.

The goal has been to lay bare a number of cultural axioms—not to explain them in terms of unquestioned scientific principles but to make them visible. Bringing these axioms to the foreground displays the coherence of South American cultures, which does not depend on "deep structures" accessible only to the wizards of transformational grammar. This coherence inheres in South American forms of knowledge, in South Americans' religious practice, and in their own explanations of its meaning.

The discovery that religious symbolism is meaningfully patterned (and the realization that order itself is an imaginative process of signification) spares us the exaggeration involved in accounting for religious life exclusively in historical, political, economic, or social terms.[74] The symbolic context of the human imagination lets one study religious thought and practice in their own right, comparatively and historically. Because symbolism is a species of meaningful and ordered context, one can compare religious ideas even when historical contact between them is unclear or nonexistent.[75] This reevaluation of symbolism questions some long-held dogmas of the human sciences and opens the human sciences to new kinds of experimentation.[76]

In the spirit of experiment, this volume proposes a morphology of South American religious life. *Morphology* literally means an order *(logos)* of forms *(morphē):* in this case, an order of relationships among religious phenomena based on their symbolic forms and meanings. The edification of a morphology of the sacred, the construction of a coherent system of symbols inventoried from among many religious systems, is a deliberate act of interpretation aimed at probing the specific character of religious experience.[77] One can build such a morphology because manifestations of sacred realities conjoin a quality of being which appears in the human imagination with the symbolic structures of human experience and with the cosmic elements in which the sacred appears.

A morphological method is an empirical procedure that is ordered by the very forms it studies. In the short run it forgoes the goal of writing chronological history, stressing similarities and contrasts among symbolic forms rather than the chronological relationships between them.[78] The ordered elaboration of forms clarifies the meaningful connections between different symbolic complexes, and it elucidates, within each complex, the imaginative ties among levels of significance. Unlike the structuralism of Claude Lévi-Strauss, for example, this morphological method does not draw connections at the level of structures abstracted from what lies beyond (or below) the semantic level, but it makes connections precisely at the level of meaning recognized by the cultures studied.[79] For all that, morphology is not a naive attempt to present a series of "native exegeses," pristine and undisturbed by interpretation. The very attempt at arrangement, the choice of subjects, and the inclusion or exclusion of data is the interpretive work of the author, who reduces meanings to a finite and ordered arrangement and makes them intelligible to cultural worlds other than the ones from which they come.

A morphology is not a tree graph of types nor a model of essential structures lying behind all variable features.[80] Typology succeeds best where sets of mutually exclusive features can characterize different types.[81] From our perspective, however, symbols (and their meanings and relations) seldom appear mutually exclusive. The transformative capacity of their forms and the transmutability of their meanings are essential to their character as religious symbols: they transcend their forms.[82] The meaning of a symbol branches out from the mythic complex where it first appears (as, for example, with the primordial hunt that destroys the world discussed in chapter two) to heave into sight again in another symbolic order (when, for example, the animals slain in the first hunt become the constellations whose regular "death" and reappearance establish the temporal order in the fruiting seasons, astronomic calendars, and beer festivals considered in chapter 4).

As it is not typology, neither is morphological method phenomenology (to which it could, however, lead in the construction of an anthropology), for it employs historical materials to lay out a series of meanings arranged in order according to their outward signs.[83] Lévi-Strauss makes clear, for different purposes, that meaning is never without form. We might add that a religious symbol is never without meaning, nor is its meaning exhausted by any single one of its historical expressions. For that reason, the act of constructing a morphology takes the interpreter on a journey through time. The endeavor is historical in the wide sense of the word.

The morphology proposed in this book maps the relationships among religious images in which reality first appeared to South Americans. None of these forms is "archaic" in the brute chronological sense, since few of them date back before 1500 CE and most come from the last generation or two. These ideas of our contemporaries are primordial and archaic only in the weighty sense in which all images of origins are: they are forms of awareness and experience that account for the appearances that make realities knowable and recognizable *in the first place*.[84] When examined in the different contexts of dream, ecstasy, rite, and myth, religious symbols exhibit meanings that complement one another and fall into a pattern. "We do not manage to decipher everything that such a pattern presents . . . until, after having 'decoded' its particular meanings one by one, each in its own frame of reference, we take the trouble to integrate them all into a whole. For each symbolism is a 'system' and can only be really understood insofar as we study it in the totality of its particular applications."[85] The completed mosaic, whose outline is sketched in the table of contents, not only pictures religious life in South America but serves as an edifying device composed of concrete images and directed toward understanding the symbolic life of humankind.

In sum, morphology, as applied in this book, elucidates at least four levels of the imaginative process of culture: it provides empirical descriptions of manifest forms appearing in the imagination, elaborates the structures of an awareness that acknowledges links among the meanings of those appearances, develops an interpretation of religion based on the first two levels, and adumbrates a systematic hermeneutics of the interpretive nature of human existence.

MYTH

The argument for the integrity of the religious condition takes its cue from myth.[86] Myth is the religious reality that allows for an ordered comparative study of religion. In myth one finds the separable forms and moments (creation, cosmos, humanity, eschatology) on which to build a morphology. Myth exhibits an integrity on many levels. Sometimes this wholeness is manifest even as a literary need. Thus Nimuendajú found that, no matter what episode was the focus of attention, the Tupi-Guaraní always wished to tell the whole creation narrative by starting at the beginning, proceeding through the episodes of cosmic destruction, and continuing right up to the consoling reunion with Ñandesý ("our mother") at the end of time. The desire to tell the whole story was so constant, no matter how streamlined various aspects became for the occasion, that Nimuendajú treated the entire tale as an aesthetic pattern that satisfied not only the storyteller but also "the greatest literary demands." [87] Robin M. Wright encountered a similar insistence on relating the entire story of the mythic epoch among the Baniwa. Even when the subject of discussion was a much later episode in mythic history, the narrator always began at the beginning and provided a quick outline of the essentials before taking up the subsequent matter.[88]

Myth does not simply denote a species of narrative; literary or oral genres are only symptoms of myth. Myth is not a form of lore but a quality of imaginal existence. Myth is the imagination beholding its own reality and plumbing the sources of its own creativity as it relates to creativity in every form (plant and planetary life, animal fertility, intelligence, art). Myth reveals the sacred foundations and religious character of the imagination.[89] Mythic symbols signify the possibility, variety, and meaning of cultural imagery. Myths are paradigmatic expressions of human culture; as significations that reveal the nature of significance, they make effective metastatements about imaginal existence.

STRUCTURE OF THE BOOK

The four parts of the book represent the cornerstones of religious life: archaeology, the condition of beginning; cosmology, the experience of a world; anthropology, the specificity of the human condition and the meaning of the changes that define its peculiar creativity; terminology, the manner in which terminal conditions affect significant existence (this use of the word

"terminology" is explained in Chapter 8). Each part's chapters compile understandings of specific issues such as creation myths, episodes of primordial catastrophe, cosmic space, time, religious authority, and death. One may
think of each chapter as an essay on a fundamental theme. Chapter 2, on
creation and destruction, takes its charge from the prestigious place these
events hold in South America and is the most essential section of the book. It
describes not the familiar and active world of human society but the mythic,
ethereal universe of the gods and the fabulous times of heroes and monsters.
As a first step into unfamiliar worlds — both that of South American myth and
of the style of this comparative study — chapter 2 may demand the most
concentration from the reader, but from the fantastic moments it reports
derive the vital rhythms of cultural life. South American peoples return again
and again to these first moments as sources of their creativity. A careful
screening of the myths of creation and destruction is the surest preparation
for the interpretations of boisterous drinking, festal dance, human growth,
and social upheaval that follow in subsequent chapters.

The notes to each chapter, which are gathered together at the end of the
book, aid those who have more than passing interest in particular issues
mentioned, or arguments made, in the text. In general, the notes suggest
additional literature on South American religions or draw out at length
inferences implied in the text and do not reconstruct the forces that shape my
own intellectual history.[90]

One by one the chapters build up a vocabulary for talking about religion.
The defectiveness of terms employed in studying religion has been exposed
even in the endless search for words to categorize the religions of peoples of
South America, Africa, Oceania, and Asia: savage, primitive, tribal, traditional, nonliterate, oral-aural, animistic, prehistoric, ethnographic, and so
on. None of these labels distinguishes the realities of a people's *religious* life.
None grounds the study of religion in anything intrinsic to the nature of
symbolic life. The vocabulary that accompanies the understandings of issues
in each chapter of this book is not a technical jargon, but rather it consists of
common words that acquire an increasing semantic load as one progresses
through the work. Rather than coin new words or use arcane jargon, I ply
ordinary words (beginning, appearance, cutting, division, primordial, crisis,
fabrication, consumption, closure, clothing, ending) to sound the depths of
common language, which grows deeper under the influence of the meanings
of South American symbolism. A fresh look at everyday vocabulary effects a
critique of language (in the wide sense of creative expression) and scrutinizes the nature of reflexivity, since the language we wish to examine (that of
religious symbolism, myth, and rite) already speaks of creativity.[91] As a by-
product of this approach, homely words such as brew, dance, seal, sucking,
sound, opening, and end are enlarged and embellished so that they once
again become suitable vehicles for talking about profound realities.

CHAPTER 2

COSMOGONY

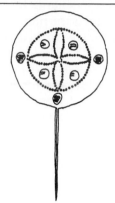

PRIMORDIUM: THE MEANING OF NONSYMBOLIC BEING AND THE RISE OF MYTHIC SYMBOL

At every significant point, this volume will make recourse to the mythic time of creation. The creative period is the wellspring of the human imagination. Its imagery flows through the discussions of human life, death, drink, musical instruments, cosmic space, calendric time, farming, and feathers. Subsequent chapters display these contents of creation, showing how human nature, for instance, is described not only as day-to-day behavior but also in *fundamental* terms, that is, as symbolic of some primordial reality, a species of being that must have appeared for the first time. In myth (that is, in the structure of the imagination), human nature is able to present itself for the first time and come to grips with its appearance. In its primordial appearance human nature makes known *that* it is and, by its very particular mode of existence, reveals itself for *what* it is.

Each of the chapters that follow delves into the creative period and the imaginal condition called myth. This essay as a whole is organized according to mythic time, whose events stretch from the dawn to the twilight of reality, so that each of its sections discusses the bearing that mythic realities have on such mundane subjects as food, feasts, or funerals. South American religion is approachable in this way because the religious life of South Americans is ordered through primordial imagery. The symbolic appearances of mythic tradition exhibit apparent, and not just deep, structures. There is a narrative progression and integrity to the religious imagination that is meaningful and coherent at the level of "surface" symbolism. The integral order of myth, then, challenges the making of too rigid a distinction between surface and depth in attempting to fathom the intelligible meanings operative in culture.

Reliance on myth to interpret the behaviors of South American peoples is the surest way to avoid a premature imposition of categories that obscure the view people have of themselves and the world. Careful examination of fundamental mythic categories at every turn minimizes the risk of foreshortening the full range of human experience available to us as a resource for the study of culture, for it is in myth that South American peoples assay the nature of culture and the value of history. The dismissal of South American religious strategies for understanding the world, whether through our ignorance or because of the imperious categories of academic knowledge, impoverishes our ability to understand ourselves.

From the overwhelming testimony given by South American cultures to the importance of the primordium, one signal rings clear: understanding a reality requires that it have a beginning. Understanding South American religions demands a fresh start, allowing a new symbolic order of reality to appear rather than simply pouring one culture, as "data," into the preexisting classificatory schemes of another. Genuine interpretation itself must be a creative resource for a new expression of culture, a living interpretation of reality that is made in light of all that has appeared about human and cosmic life in manifold cultures.[1] Given the devastating effects of colonial and postcolonial contact, suffering the changes required to understand South American religions (especially the mythic histories, where basic values unfold), is a peculiarly modern possibility and need, and it takes a powerful imagination.

In exploring the myth-based astronomy of American Indians, Anthony F. Aveni and Gary Urton have pointed up the need to forge "a new, and in a sense revolutionary, set of assumptions" to understand Amerindian culture: "Today, working in the field with a different set of theoretical assumptions, we are able to see that the 'fragmentary' nature of American Indian cosmology is perhaps only an artifact of our incomplete understanding of the principles along which indigenous populations of the Americas organize phenomena perceived in their environment."[2] Reconceiving South American religions must include a critical appraisal of its misconceptions, a rereading of the historical, economic, and sociopolitical experience since the Age of Discovery. In order to take their own creative place in the world, contemporary men and women on all sides of cultural contact must begin to create novel interpretations of the recently "discovered" plurality, the multiple cultural understandings that, during the last several hundred years, have come to construct the modern world. Reimagining South American religions is part of that effort to begin laying a new foundation for culture.

COSMOGONY: THE REAL CHANGE

Fundamental conditions are conceived in terms of the beginning, the first order, the primordium. The basic structures of appearance, hiddenness, inchoateness, differentiation, uniqueness, multiplicity, language, gesture, stasis, and change provide footholds for the imagination. By their very presence in the imagination and in the beginning, these principal realities, envisioned in particular symbols, condition all subsequent forms of contingent being. As a foundation for the imagination, the concept of the beginning makes apparent those qualities and images of being that are inescapably determinative and ceaselessly influential. The picture of primordial being delimits what is really possible. Images of the beginning circumscribe what *in principle* (that is, in relation to what is known to be real, to have appeared from the beginning) can be acted upon.

Like the imagination itself, the universe has an integrity of its own because its presence first takes shape in the images of the beginning. The creative primordium is an ordered progression of powerful events that effect the most significant change ever wrought: the appearance of the world. By depicting the greatest contrasts in modes of being, creation reveals what change means. Cosmogonies provide the terms with which to recognize and reflect upon the passage from nothingness (or chaos, prime matter, indistinction, the indiscernible) to the multiple beings, times, and spaces characterizing the present world. Creation accounts provide the basis for imagination, thought, and reflection — that is, for the ordering processes that make the cosmos a home to humankind. Moreover, narrative draws all these contrasting qualities of being into relationships that may be described as temporal, spatial, formal, significant, and so on. The simplicity of the cosmogonic narratives can belie their importance as well as the utter change in being effected by the described events. Since the balance of this book details the ramifications of the mythic era, the following paragraphs present three main kinds of creation scenarios with a minimum of analysis: creation from absolutely nothing, creation by transforming or rearranging elements of a preexisting condition, and creation of this world through the total destruction of an earlier one.[3] These three scenarios also offer an opportunity to discuss several supernatural agents, each of whose appearance as a creative subject is an active ingredient in creation, the appearance of the primordial world and its objective constituents.

CREATIO EX NIHILO AND THE IMAGINATION OF BEING

A number of accounts describe the creation of the world from nothing (*creatio ex nihilo*). Supreme beings figure largely in cosmogonies that begin with an absolute and presymbolic state prior to any created condition. For instance, according to the Ona (Selknam) of Tierra del Fuego, the eternal supreme being, Temáukel, created the flat earth and the sky. The sky that he created was unmarked by the passage of time. It possessed neither stars nor planets. Similarly, the earth was an undifferentiated space without mountains or rivers. The temporal markers of the sky and the spatial markers of the earth were formed later by the culture hero, Kenós. Kenós likewise created the animals and meteorological phenomena that filled the differentiated earth and sky.[4]

Absolute beginnings become focal images for the anxiety associated with unconditioned states of being. According to one cosmogony of the Tehuelche of Patagonia, Kóoch ("heaven"), the eternal and all-powerful supreme being, lived in the dense darkness at what is now the junction of the sky and the sea. He was so oppressively lonely that he began to cry. His tears formed Arrok, the primal ocean. Watching Arrok grow, Kóoch ceased crying and heaved a sigh: the Wind, who dispersed the mists of darkness. Thus was born the clarity of the first day.[5] It was Kóoch who created the sun, Cháleshen. Emerging from the first darkness and waters, Kóoch withdrew some distance into space in order to see better his surroundings. In the process, he scratched (and, therefore, divided) the darkness; a spark followed the arc of his scratching hand. This spark was the sun, Cháleshen, who is responsible for the origin of the clouds. In versions of the Tehuelche cosmogony reported by Llaras Samitier, Kóoch created the birds, animals, insects, and fish on an island that he had brought up out of the depths of the primal sea. Later he sent forth all these creations under the direction of Elal, the culture hero, who set up residence in a new earth, Patagonia.[6]

Before the beginning, indivisible states such as unbounded water, breath, darkness, or divine preconsciousness reign undifferentiated and unimagined.[7] These formless conditions are themselves the images of chaos, unfamiliar and uninhabitable. However, by transcending the knowable world, the religious imagination provides a basis for that world. Myth and rite function to establish a place on which symbolic processes of culture—including economic, aesthetic, noetic, and sensory orders—can stand. Once, when the ethnographer Curt Nimuendajú was discussing with some Guaraní Indians the mythology of their Kaingáng neighbors, one of the listeners made a disparaging remark about a Kaingáng myth. Immediately, the Guaraní shaman Ñeengueí reprimanded the listener, saying, "No, history always has its foundation!"[8] At the outset, an image of what is *in se* unconscious and unthinkable appears in the mythic imagination and gives rise to history, that is, to conscious cultural existence in time.

In fittingly paradoxical language, the ambivalent nature of omniscient supreme beings, supremely imaginative and thoughtful, becomes a match for the unimaginable quality of being of which they partake and from which all images of creation flow. For example, the Guaraní mythic accounts of the supreme being during *iñypyrū*, the beginnings, are indispensable for understanding Guaraní thought because they describe the foundations—the prehistory—of Guaraní thinking and reveal the meanings of elementary and creative symbolic processes, of which thought is but one expression.[9] In the beginning, the Guaraní creator, Ñanderuvusú, lived alone in the middle of darkness. There he kept vigil while primordial bats fought with one another in the darkness. The creator bore a light in his breast. He set in place a beam of wood running from east to west, then placed another beam, which ran from north to south, across the first, and so fashioned the eternal cross that supports the world. Standing at its center, he began to make the earth on top of it.[10] The creator had with him a companion named Ñanderú Mbaekuaá, to whom he suggested that they find themselves a woman. To that end, the creator fashioned a clay pot and sealed it completely. Then he sent his companion to fetch the woman from the pot. The creator had made his home in the very center of the cross supporting the earth. Both he and his companion had engendered children, one child each, in the womb of the woman. When the woman, taking her basket, went to the garden that had been newly fashioned by the creator, he was incensed because she would not believe that he had made food grow so quickly, and he left the earth and ascended beyond the sky, climbing along the trail of the eternal jaguar.[11]

The supreme beings, all-absorbing sources of their own light, see everything, even when there is only nothing to see. Once their omnipotent imaginations give rise to the thought and image-words that call forth beings, supreme beings withdraw — ironically obtaining a better view — in order to keep omniscient but relatively inactive watch over the vital forms that they have generated. Accounts of the withdrawal of supreme beings and other supernaturals do much more than explain the dearth of fully manifest supernatural beings in South American mythologies. By reporting the adieu of the gods, myth engenders images, symbolic processes, and their meanings. Myth steadily relays the message that, when they departed, the divine powers, whose active presence in the beginning conditioned all of creation, left only symbolic vestiges of their once fuller presence.[12] Because the exit of supreme beings thus generated symbolic life, the very fact of their absence guarantees the possibility of human knowledge and human creativity, for these activities are essentially symbolic processes.

THE UNDREAMED DREAMER: TEMPORAL BASES OF CAUSALITY   To imagine an absolute beginning seems to require extraordinary, even supreme, effort — a kind unparalleled by any subsequent act of a created being. There is nothing like it. In fact, nothingness is one of the images associated most directly with the power of the supreme being who creates the absolute beginnings of reality. Descriptions of the nothingness prior to creation are understandably brief. They are also dreadful: the possibility of unimaginable nothingness lurks in the background of being as an unfathomable abyss, a constant, unknowable reality. Difficult to sustain as lengthy narratives, the earliest stages illustrated in myths of creation-from-nothing are mystical, poetic, or speculative. The first acts of such creations are achieved by supernatural beings of a special kind. The drama is surreal, not action packed. The very fact that mystical images appear in the mind of the creator already precipitates the existence of a world.

In a report made by K. T. Preuss, for example, the Witoto of Colombia reported that in the beginning absolutely nothing existed. That is, only "mere appearance" existed. It was "something mysterious." Moma ("father"), the supreme being, somehow touched this illusion, this phantasm. Moma has close connections with the power of ritual words and chants. He calls himself *Nainuema*, "he who is, or possesses, what is not present" — that is, illusive appearance. By means of a dream, Nainuema "pressed the phantasm to his breast and then was sunk in thought."[13] This mystical creation of existence from thought, mere appearance, and illusion continues: "Only through his breath did Nainuema hold this illusion attached to the thread of a dream." Plumbing the dream-contained, breath-held illusion to its depths, Nainuema discovered that it was empty. With a dream-thread, the creator secured this empty phantasm and pressed a gluelike substance on it. Finally, the creator stamped on the bottom of the illusion and thus came to rest on the earth. He spit out saliva to make the forests rise, and he covered the earth with heaven.

Through their intention, dream imagery, sound (word), or longing for being, creators-from-nothing overcome the unconsciousness of the absolute state. The least gestures or passing thoughts of supreme beings become the first perceptible forms of order. Through the power of their imaginations, supreme beings create symbolic life by uttering words, having dreams, coming up with ideas, and expressing thoughts. Finally, they withdraw from the worlds they have created. Creation is the work, the manifest power, of the imagination of those divine beings who are most difficult to imagine because they are not, at first, symbolic. Ironically, the meaning of nonsymbolic existence comes clear in the dense, multivocal, and paradoxical symbols of absolute beginnings: chaos, nothingness, impenetrable darkness, and the ambivalent imagery of the supreme beings themselves (for example, the original changeless and imminent sky), who often withdraw on high, ceding their creative role to culture heroes, or who deputize transformers to do the fine brushwork once they, the creators, have imagined and blocked out the large canvas of creation. Before they undertook their brief but fundamental imaginative activity, supreme beings were often unconscious, unimaginative, inactive, unapparent, and, expressive of all of these, unknown. Consequently, many cultural traditions contend that one cannot know precisely the state of being that prevailed before the appearance of the images that the supreme beings generated.[14] Their primordial creativity, bringing forth being from nothing, defines for each culture the meaning of mystery — the ceaseless appearance of new realities from an infinite and unfathomable source.

THE FIRST CONSCIOUSNESS OF BEING   The first stages of the creation myth of the Desana of southern Colombia, recited on nearly all the festive occasions when groups of people gather to drink and dance, are quite mysterious. The myth is recounted dramatically by individuals or, sometimes, by groups whose members chant in unison. Dancing must wait until the recitation has ended.[15] The first creative moment remains inscrutable — an enigma accomplished by the Sun, but not the sun that is visible. The Creator Sun is an invisible supernatural force that preexists all form, including his own. Paradoxically, in this domain of being, before the appearance of any knowable form, the invisible Sun is omniscient, omnipresent, omnipotent. The paradox continues throughout creation and into history. The uncreated Sun was a supreme state of being consisting of light that the Desana refer to as "yellow intention."[16] Ironically, the very first instant of creation emanates from the yellow intention "without any fixed purpose guiding this act." In a sort of unplanned, or spontaneous, ejaculation, yellow intention seeped out of the supreme being unintentionally. "But once the yellow light had completed this act, the Sun set conditions for his Creation."[17] From that moment on, the Sun Father (Pagë Abé) began to make a perfect world in which he planned every detail: the earth, the forests, the rivers, the animals, and the plants. "To each one he assigned the place he should live." [18]

How the Sun accomplished this creation is not well detailed. Indeed, the point of the Sun's involvement in creation seems to be to underline the omnipresence of the "state" of being called "yellow light." It is upon this emanation of his own creative being that the Sun establishes the regular processes of life and the institutional norms of society. "The Sun was thus an organizer and a legislator." [19] Indeed, Gerardo Reichel-Dolmatoff's informant asserts that the Sun's role was to "stabilize" or "establish" creation. "The Sun created all of this when he had the yellow intention—when he caused the power of his yellow light to penetrate, in order to form the world from it." [20] As a result, every level of being is embued with "yellow purpose," a solar semen that fills the universe in its many forms: the rays of the sun, which penetrate space; liquids like saliva and honey; crystal and quartzite; yellow-colored animals; fibers of the *cumare* palm; and so on.[21] The universe is full of life because at every level of its existence it is inseminated by the creative intention of the Sun Father of all life.

Eventually, however, the Sun cedes his active role to other supernatural characters. He creates intermediate beings who govern the sky and the rivers, as well as masters of the animals of the forest and of the fish. Although mention is made of several male beings created by the Sun, no account is provided of the creation of his daughter, whose fertile imagination (the source of the conditions of culture) is inseminated when the shaft of her father's light penetrates her eye. Neither is mention made of the creation of the Daughter of Aracú Fish, who emerges from the primordial waters when she espies the light of the fire set by the primordial males. Soon after spilling his light and setting the creative process in motion, the invisible Sun departs, leaving the more dramatic transformations to these female culture heroes, the major protagonists in early Desana mythology.[22] Their actions account for the transformation of animals into those forms in which they are known today, as well as for the invention of the techniques of economy, ritual, and art. A great deal of transformative "creating" is left up to these intermediate figures and is described in greater and more captivating detail than is the creation of the universe by the Sun.[23]

After creation was completed, the Sun left the world and returned to Ahpikondiá (the Milk River, house of breast milk, the cosmic uterus), the region whence he came in the very beginning. He is now represented in celestial form by the visible sun that provides light, heat, protection, and fertility during the day[24] and in terrestrial form by the supernatural jaguar, who protects the earth by "covering" the earth as one body covers another during coitus.[25] The Sun commissioned a being named Pamurí-mahsë to conduct human beings to earth in a large canoe. We shall have occasion later to follow the Desana drama of creation through the time when the world was overcome by the chaos of night, destroyed by fire and flood, and reestablished in an orderly fashion. All this happened after the first beings arrived on the earth.[26]

    Creation from nothing calls to mind images of indivisible and formless primary conditions. The first changes initiated by supreme beings, frequently without their fully conscious knowledge, often stream from the divinities' own virtual being in the fluid form of tears, saliva, urine, or semen, or as breath, unbroken light, or all-encompassing sound. Light, fluid, dream, thought, and sound[27] all betoken the supreme being's new state of consciousness. The issue of this first undifferentiated and unreplicable currency amounts to a one-time-only creative exchange and trades one total condition of being for another. This movement of the divine economy marks the inchoate appearance of a new kind of presence, the incipient world itself. In the cases where a supreme being creates from nothing, the awareness of reality (i.e., its appearance, its creation) is itself a divine accomplishment for the first mythic images of creation (divine light, tears, word, dream) are, literally, expressions of the sacred. And these mythic symbols remain sacred, for they spring from the powerful imagining of the divinity. Human culture is a continuing symbolic experience or experiment, begun by imagining sacred beings, the first forms of awareness ever to appear. In some cases, the quickening of the consciousness of being appears as a crossing of the threshhold of personality, the transition from the impersonality of absolute beginnings (a form of emptiness or of chaos unordered by any subjective agent) to the personal being needed to create the meaningful world. Such appears to be the case of the extraordinary supreme being, named Pillán, of the Mapuche of Chile and Western Argentina. He exists on the very verge of apparent form for, in some sense, he can be said to have no form at all. *In se*, Pillán exists as an impersonal, formless, and primal power, but he can assume form and even put in personal appearances (as, for example, the god of thunder). He embodies a mode of being on the edge of conscious form, or consciousness.[28]

    The concept of *supreme being*, especially of the divinity who withdraws from creation after initiating its existence, is of primary importance to the comparative study of South American religions — but "primary" should not be taken in a statistical sense. The supreme being is not the kind of divinity most frequently met with in South American myth; nor are supreme beings the divinities most regularly celebrated in ritual. In fact, there are many societies that either maintain no tradition of belief in a supreme being or have adapted (or even adopted) their beliefs in a supreme being only in response to contact with historical monotheisms.[29]

    While it is true that individual cultures place more or less emphasis on supreme beings, the concept is crucial to students of religion, for it helps them gauge the outermost parameter of the religious imagination. Descriptions of supreme beings let the scholar get a fix on the most sublime end of the spectrum of divine forms. By describing in concrete terms the most remote, transcendent, invisible, or intangible reality, cultures offer to scholars historical expressions of that experience of being that, by definition (the definitions of the cultures in question), most fully transcends the senses. The myths of supreme beings are culturally creative metastatements about the nature of creativity itself; these sublime images provide information about the subtlest powers and the most rarified possibilities of the religious imagination.

Investigators need no longer fear that a serious look at supreme beings will set in motion a theological reductionism that declares there to be, universally, a single monotheistic notion of God. Rather, this outer edge — this most transcendent form — of the imagination presents itself in an astounding variety of guises even in cases where supreme beings bear the stamp of heavy missionary influence. Ethnographic evidence presents us with innumerable images of the nearly unimaginable. In cultures that keep records of such divine appearances, one usually finds evidence of a complicated history of reflection on many different "outside" ideas, of which the input from monotheistic traditions is only one of the most recent.[30] By denying the authentic existence of these divine forms, investigators have denied to the subjects of their inquiry the ability to exist, as imaginative beings, within a history full of dynamic change, and they have also denied to history, existence in time, the creative status of myth.[31]

A WORLD OF UNIQUENESSES   The extraordinary association of the first forms (light, liquid, sound, dream image, thought, etc.) with the very substance of supreme being makes for an early world with a univocal character, for the supreme being is, no matter how described, by definition one of a kind. The unicity of their being overwhelms the qualitative differences among the realities of this first phase. In a world of fully apparent being, everything simply is as it appears. There can be no place for subtle change. The condition of absolute manifestation displays the meaning of eternity, a state which suppresses difference so that even opposites coincide: omniscience meets unconsciousness, self-sufficiency gets lonely for company, necessity needs contingency, total, self-contained light lives in utter darkness, omnipresence absents itself from any one place. Even the flow of primordial fluid becomes a kind of stasis, since it never ceases to give evidence of change: beginning, middle, and end are inseparable moments. Under such circumstances, change itself is unique, for there has been only one real change — the very appearance of being, which has altered forever the quality of reality and exhausted the possibility of any kind of change other than that based on appearance.

This quality of existence Pierre Clastres has captured in a phrase in which he calls all the beings of the Guaraní primordial age "fabulously indistinguishable." After the Guaraní creator, Ñamandu, made his own appearance, he created the gods and goddesses and the first human prototypes. Creator and created lived a remarkable and strangely unified existence, for the divisions between separate kinds of being had not yet become firm.[32] All imaginable kinds of beings lived together in the same world and shared the same conditions of existence. In a world with neither reproducible divisions nor periodic change, uniqueness overcomes difference.

THE NATURE OF TRANSFORMATION   Creation from nothing by supreme beings is not the only means of producing the universe attested to in the mythic traditions of South America. In fact, it would be misleading to give the impression that most South American peoples describe the cosmogony in this way. They do not. In the myths recorded to date, the majority of South American cultures show little extended interest in absolute beginnings. The Akwẽ-Shavante, for example, show little concern for the ultimate origins of the universe. The kind of creation that interests them is the transformation of primordial creatures and the first disclosure or attainment of "creations" by a shifting succession of heroes.[33] The Akwẽ-Shavante offer an example of one such transforming hero who momentarily occupied the creative stage. The allusion made by David Maybury-Lewis to the creation of a human ancestor intimates that this Akwẽ-Shavante ancestor emerged from the earth with three wives and two children — probably a reference to the origin of the three clans and two moieties. The ancestor emerged from the earth when it was "truly empty." Then the East, the place where the sky begins, and "both sides," meaning North and South, were made. As Maybury-Lewis writes, "Various mythical heroes are thought to have been creators in the sense of transforming the world, creating its fruits, and so on."[34]

Taking note of the relatively small number of cosmogonies that narrate creation from its absolute beginnings, Alfred Métraux demonstrated that most South American cosmogonies begin with some prior, although perhaps undescribed, state of affairs, which then undergoes transformation in the course of creation. Even though these latter cases do not describe the absolute origins of being, Métraux concluded that they are sufficient explanations of the current state of the world. In his opinion, this was the principal *raison d'être* of myths of origin.[35] The same point is made by A. Jiménez Núñez as a conclusion to his comparative study of creation myths in South America: "No absolute states exist."[36] Everything is subject to change, metamorphosis, and redefinition.

MATERIA PRIMA Transformation of a formless prime matter is a frequent theme in South American creation stories. According to Toba cosmogonic accounts, God created the world from a lump of earth, which, in the beginning, was tiny ("like a pebble"), and which stood quite apart from God's own being. In the darkness of that primordial age, "God made this lump grow to the earth's present size."[37] After this, God created Metzgoshé, the first human being, and then the sun, moon, and stars. During the first primordial age, there was poor light, for everything was full of smoke "like fog," and the first human could only hear animals but could not see them.[38] Rafael Karsten had recorded a different origin myth among the Bolivian Toba, in which the good divinity Peritnalík created all things and offered them to human beings. The Christians willingly accepted them all. However, the Toba refused these gifts. "This is why the whites now have so many useful animals, whereas the Indians have only some few of them by buying them from the whites."[39]

Creation myths of transformation provide an occasion for a general observation about the nature of myth. Creation myths are more than rational explanations of first causes of physical processes or justifications of existing social conditions. It is of course undeniable that myths can be blunt rationalizations of prevailing cosmic, sociopolitical, or existential orders. However, such an appraisal of myth is overdetermined insofar as it focuses on only one of myth's functions, and it therefore cannot give a complete account of the nature of myth. Nor does it put a finger on myth's specific difference from any number of ideological expressions. Law, science, theology, canons of artistic form, political process, military exercise, revolutionary rhetoric, and historiography can all buttress existing forms of thought, action, and explanation because they all function as parts of a given worldview. The self-evident world of society and cosmos needs no mythic demonstration to justify or make clear its existence.

What myth must make evident is the *meaning* of the world's appearance, that is, the meaning of the very fact that the world has *appeared*. For reasons provided in myth, that kind of meaning is no longer self-evident or fully apparent. It must be made perceptible through myth in order to clothe fully apparent and mundane affairs in some measure of reality. Here is where myth finds its proper place, subtly related to an explanation of everyday events: myth explains that whatever is (whether it be oppressive or liberating, a historical or a future event) has meaning. Concerning itself with the tiniest details of natural and economic history, myth offers an explanation for the fact that every aspect of the world is epiphanic and that the everyday appearance of things is actually significant of reality.[40] Myth is an integral part of reality not because it describes the world which is self-evident but because it characterizes and even directly participates in the imaginal world of beginnings, a world no longer apparent and, as such, the *real* world where the meaning of all apparent signifiers must now reside. Although significance is intimately bound up with forms of appearance, meaning can no longer be fully self-evident in this world except in a mythic way, for meaning is wrapped up with the world of the beginnings.[41] Myth uncovers the first motives of being, which is disclosed in its first appearances.

The accounts of creation through transformation clarify the nature of myth because meanings that are no longer fully apparent can be explored only if the nature of transformation is made evident. In order to do that, the mythic history of transformation, the first appearance of change, must be recounted. Herein lies the importance of cosmogonies of transformation. They not only justify the way things are (a point made in various ways since Malinowski), but, more importantly, they tell of the nature and meaning of transformation itself, the process that, by changing the first appearances of primordial forms, alters their relationship to reality and to their true meaning. Were it not for myth, this true meaning would remain lost, stolen, or hidden in the new signs.

The Hohodene Baniwa of the upper Río Negro recount the myth of the cosmogonic transformation of the world because creation's original form and meaning are hardly recognizable as such in the contemporary appearance of the world. The earth was originally a pebble excreted by the hero Kuai at the time of his birth. Yaperikuli, a supernatural jaguar closely associated with the Primal Sun, had engendered Kuai with his thought. In the role of creator-transformer, Yaperikuli played the jaguar-song on his trumpet over the excreted stone. This deep, resounding bass note, the voice of the jaguar, made the earth open "like a balloon" that grew larger with each note of the song.[42]

> When this Kuai is born, for him our father Yaperikuli of always,
> At his birth, so little, so little is his child.
> Then he shits, he shits, he shits . . .
> This earth, his shit, Kuai's shit is this earth.
> It grew a little, like so little it was, thus we saw the earth long ago,
> The world began for us.
> His earth then, our father-of-always: a rock, thus it was a rock,
> A rock was his village.[43]

Thus Yaperikuli, whose village was a rock (the rock now located at the center of the universe—the rapids at Hipana, where Kuai was born), obtained fertile ground, excrement, from the son he produced with his thought. Once the organic earth had grown to its proper size, it was entrusted to the primordial gardener, Kaali, who taught agriculture and who produced manioc when he instructed his son to burn his (Kaali's) body.

All of Yaperikuli's creative acts are in the form of payments of vengeance rendered against the primordial beings who slew the undescribed being from whose bones Yaperikuli originally emerged in the form of a cricket. Actually, Yaperikuli is, at his origin, a collectivity of three crickets who transform themselves into a woodpecker. The original creative act, preceding the existence of the transformer-creator Yaperikuli, is never explicitly described. It is clear, however, that there had been some sort of primordium before the arrival of Yaperikuli. During that time, *doimeni*, the undifferentiated human-animal beings who lived in the unordered forests of the first time, killed everyone. A bone from one dismembered victim was thrown away into the middle of the river. A "grandmother" fetched it back and placed it into a gourd, from which songs and sounds came. The emergence of the transformer from the bone of a previously dismembered being implies a cosmogony through dismemberment, for the world of Yaperikuli comes to form the head that lies at the top of the universe, a universe that has the shape of a body.[44] The path back through the labyrinth of transformative body-parts, excretions, and sounds would remain indiscernible, and the meaning of reality would be lost in the ordinariness of its everyday appearances (excrement, stone, river rapids, bone, trumpets), were it not for the myths of creation through transformation.

CREATION THROUGH PILGRIMAGE AND MINSTREL WANDERING   Everywhere they go divinities, culture heroes, and, especially, human ancestors wander across the face of the unexplored, primordial earth, altering the world's appearances and thus changing it forever. Such supernatural transformers may directly impose their intentions on the material universe by blowing on it, naming it, responding to questions about it, physically remodeling it, or by performing music, having sex, or making utterances in it. The Inca creator divinity, Viracocha, for example, wandered with his two heroic companions from the southeast to the northwest part of the Inca universe, calling forth new forms of life from their places of origin by naming them. The whole tour was planned by Viracocha on the island in Lake Titicaca where, using painted images, he rehearsed the creative walk with his helpers.

Often, interest in the creator god is surpassed by fascination with the transformative pilgrimages of ancestors. Tukano mythology pays little attention, for instance, to the creative role of Yepá Huaké, a Tukano divinity preoccupied with orchestrating the wanderings of the primordial ancestors, who transform the world through their misadventures. In the beginning, Yepá Huaké intended the Tukano to live forever. When the miscreant ancestors refused to bathe in the waters of immortality to which he dispatched them, and when they refused to eat from the pot of coca to which he directed them, death entered human experience. However, the earth itself was never affected by this introduction of mortality. "I am going to give you earth, and this earth is for all of you. And this earth will never die." [45] Yepá Huaké created the earth in a miraculous way. After having set trees upon it, he made the earth descend below this world. (The earth of that primordial world became the underworld of today's universe.) "And that is why there exists under this earth an underground river which is called *Uamedia*." [46] The universal river system was navigated and transformed by the ancestors. Yepá Huaké also created the wind in a miraculous way. This wind swept away to heaven the bench on which several ancestors were seated. En route, they instigated marvelous transformations, which changed the appearance of the world forever.

The Campa of the eastern Peruvian forest appear to be less interested in the creation of the universe and the absolute beginnings of the cosmos than in the latter stages of the primordium peopled by their ancestors. [47] Indeed, their creation story is a history of transformations that change the earth and its inhabitants into their present form. The Campa recognize a time when realities were in such flux that, when a thing was named, it became something else. [48] Indeed, naming an object seems to be a variation of a transformative blowing which is the main mode of creation in the cosmogony of the Campa. Singing, ritual chanting, and naming—all forms of performative utterance—may be conceived of as variations of the act of creative and transformative blowing. Speech and song are really controlled (that is, ritualized) ways of blowing. They are stylized methods of transformation by aspiration. These models of aesthetic transformation are set up for the Campa by the first supernatural beings.

Each of the sudden transformations of geography and animal species "marked the metamorphosis of a member of the original human—that is, Campa—stock into the first representative of a particular species of animal or plant, or into some feature of the terrain." [49] Human beings are the *materia prima* from which were made the distinctive features of the earth. The ultimate origins of time and space do not seem to interest the Campa. When their accounts concerning Avíreri, the Great Transformer, begin, it is clear that time is already flowing. Avíreri appears on the scene with his grandson, Kíri (obviously the product of several generations). He does not create *ex nihilo* but transforms what he finds. Creation is a process of analogical imagining. In his travels with his grandson, Avíreri "transformed Campas encountered along his route into whatever they resembled, or whatever resembled them." [50] Thus, human beings were transformed into insects, bees, rocks, monkeys, arboreal termite nests, and so forth. Avíreri seems to have planted the original wild fruit trees.[51] Although he is clearly a transformer figure, he often effects these transformations through some form of performative utterance, a form of creativity usually associated with supreme beings. During his wanderings, Avíreri transforms his younger relatives and other human beings in response to the questions of his inquisitive grandson, Kíri. The transforming grandfather names the objects that the grandson points to and thus alters them.

> They moved on, they went on, they went on, (when) he (Kíri) suddenly saw them our fellow tribesmen, they had been climbing in vain. Well, they flattened themselves in vain, they became silent in vain. "What is it there, grandsire? Look at them!, grandsire, they who are fastened there." He looked. "Ha, all termite (nests), grandson." He (thus) transformed them (to) termite (nests). They moved on again.[52]

Avíreri frequently transformed things into stone by calling them stone (mápi).[53]

In keeping with their humanistic explanation of the origins of things, the Campa explain the origins of the alteration of night and day and the seasons as having been created out of products of protohuman culture — in this case, music. In the course of instituting the original festivals, Avíreri dances and plays panpipe music appropriate to the nighttime. By playing the music, he in fact creates the night.[54] The panpipes become "instruments of darkness." Likewise, when he plays certain kinds of music he brings on the dry season, and then the rainy season. The powerful Campa ancestors are also responsible for features of the terrain, and so the distinguishable features of the landscape also become witnesses to the powerful transformative actions of supernatural beings at the beginning of time.[55]

Upset by his transformations, people attempt to do away with Avíreri. In particular, his brother-in-law and sister conspire to trap him in a hole from which he is unable to escape. In retaliation, he transforms them into an armadillo and a flowering tree, respectively. Unable to emerge from the hole into which he has fallen, Avíreri burrows through the earth, making a tunnel that extends to the easternmost point of the rim at the world's edge. "There a strangler vine wraps itself around him and Pačákama [a god who stabilizes the earth] invites him to help sustain the earth." [56]

The Machiguenga of eastern Peru hold beliefs in a similar supernatural being, called Yabíberi, who converted many Machiguengas into animals. After having eaten a large meal of toasted maize kernels, he escapes from an underground hole in which he has been trapped. He travels eastward, and, as he travels, he "sows" the maize kernels in his stool wherever he passes. Yabíberi dams the world-river in order to drown the Machiguenga. When his father tries to intervene, Yabíberi changes him into an armadillo. Finally, another powerful being carries Yabíberi away to the eastern end of the earth. There he is nailed to some tree trunks. Ever since he was nailed down, the Machiguenga have experienced sickness and death.[57] Today he is alive but nearly immobile; he feels no pain, but when he does move, the earth shakes.

Primordial transformers need not always be deliberate agents of change; often their presence alone, their appearance, is enough to provoke it. Rather than create through direct action, they transform indirectly through passion. For instance, merely watching the first act of sex performed by the Desana first woman, Daughter of Aracú Fish, transformed primordial beings into the various species of animals. What they "saw" became an indelible part of what they "are," or, rather, what they appear to be: for example, certain animal species acquired the coloration, shape, or smell of the penis and vulva of the first sexual performers.

DEATH AS THE CREATIVE ACT   Among the great transformative passions of super-natural beings are their deaths. By ensuring that the divinity, hero, or ances-tor suffers the total experience of existence, the death of a primordial figure also guarantees the total transformation or transignification of reality. Each death produces enduring elements of cosmos or culture.

Kíri, the grandson of the Campa transformer Avíreri, for example, goes in search of his missing grandfather, who has burrowed his way to the edge of the earth. In his quest, he plants maize (but not in his stool, as is the case of the Machiguenga hero). Kíri attempts to block the world-river and to create his own easternmost point of the world's edge. When the human beings who are pursuing him discover Kíri at this task, they attempt to shoot him with arrows, but they only succeed in shooting one another until he instructs them as to how they might kill him. "By driving a spike down through his head and body into the ground. This they do, and he is transformed into the palm tree kíri."[58] We will encounter this theme of the impaled hero else-where. Particularly striking is the mythic complex in which the hero's head and/or body is nailed to the earth in such a way as to delineate the four quarters of the earth or to create an *axis mundi* (in this case the *kíri* palm), which reaches into the heavenly plane. As this tree, Kíri produces fruit and instructs people how to transform this fruit into beer. The fruit and beer become a constant reminder of the great being Kíri. In fact, consumption of this fruit and drink becomes a way of communing with Kíri's substance as well as of marking the passage of time through fruit season and fermentation cycle. Having orchestrated his own sacrifice, Kíri instructs birds to bathe once in his blood. Those who do are sacred and emerge with beautiful plumage, but some birds, rather than follow Kíri's instructions by bathing once, greedily immerse themselves in his blood a second time and emerge with ugly plumage.[59]

In the early part of the narrative, Kíri's curious questions transformed fully manifest being by calling the attention of his grandfather's analogical imagination to forms whose meaning was not entirely clear. He has over-tones of a chaotic flood-monster, who controls the waters, occasionally stop-

ping up their eternal flow to give rise to intermediate gradations of river and
rain levels. Through his death, however, Kíri becomes the basis of the fertile
and periodic forms of abundance, such as fruit and maize, as well as of the
patterned markings of multiple species distinguished by the diverse body
markings and coloration of their kind.

Death is one instrument of creation, the other being sexual generation,
in the creation narratives of the Waiwai, a Cariban group from the Serra
Acaraí in the upper reaches of the Essequibo and Mapuera rivers. In these
stories one cannot clearly distinguish a mythical epoch or "time of the
grandparents," as one can in the case of other cultures (for example, the
Canelos Quichua); nevertheless, Waiwai creative murders often involve *chacha*, mythical grandmothers. *Chacha* figure as protectors of the first ancestors; they hide them, advise them, and plot for their survival and salvation.[60]
Nevertheless, not all creative murders and deaths happen to ancient grandmothers. For example, various animal species, especially species of birds,
owe their existence to the bloody death of a mythical anaconda. When the
monstrous anaconda Petali was cut in half, the river flowed with blood.
Various bird-people bathed in the blood, and their shapes and markings were
transformed. These transformations of the outer body caused inner changes
responsible for the creation of the various species.[61] Other creative murders
involve the opossum-hero, Yawari, who dies so that the Waiwai can learn
about yams. Yawari is killed by a *chacha* and resuscitated by her son, who
receives vital instructions from him.[62] Finally, mention should be made of
the instructive case of the Waiwai harpy-eagle – hero, Yaimo.[63] Yaimo directs
his own murder by disclosing to human beings the identity of the one person
who can successfully kill him with arrows. Through death, the unreplicable,
unique bird brought about the creation of the many kinds of hawks and
eagles: his breast down reappeared in the form of hawks and his wing
feathers as eagles.[64]

DIRECTNESS OF RELATIONS   Whether myths describe creation-from-nothing or
the transformation of prior conditions, the primordial world is one of fully
apparent and immediate reality. At first there are no betwixt-and-between
conditions, no intermediate states, no intervening symbolic distances. The
immediacy and directness of fully apparent being finds expression not only
in ready transformation from one form to another but also in the first beings'
willingness to eat whatever there is — including cannibalism and the direct
consumption of earth or other raw materials — and in their practice of indiscriminate sex and incest.

The Campa say that before the moon provided people with manioc,
human beings ate earth.[65] They did not eat earth "at one remove" — that is,
the "fruits of the earth," which are alienated from the earth by time and
space — but devoured the earth itself, immediately and directly. Kašíri, a
supernatural being who would later become the moon, had at that time the
form of a human being. Kašíri would go on hunting trips in order to murder
and eat his nephews. To this day, Kašíri remains cannibalistic. As the moon,
Kašíri provided the first manioc by blowing on earthen termitaries. He also

engendered the sun and originated the painful process of birth by inseminating the Mother of the Sun while she bathed in the river during her menstrual period. With great irony, the Campa view the moon, a cannibalistic and devouring lecher, as the author of life (in the form of the sun), of the sustenance of life (in the form of manioc), and of the birth process, which gives regenerative life to human beings. Also ironic is the fact that the sun, Pává or Tasórenci, the great and good transformer, is the author of death, for at his birth he scorches his mother, who is thereby the first being to die. The brilliant appearance of his fiery life consumes hers.

The origins of manioc, food, menstruation, sexuality, birth, and the moon are all intertwined in the same episode of the cosmogonic myth. Now, people no longer grind up the earth in the form of termite nests as they once did. To appreciate the directness of relations in that first age, one should note that the Campa conceive of termite nests not only as the first food of human beings but as the origin of human beings themselves, as well as of manioc. When the moon soared vertically down from the sky, he blew on earth that had been boiled and wrapped in leaves. In this way, the moon created manioc even as he dismantled the first menarche hut.[66] In the first age, when everything (manioc, food, menstruation, sexuality, birth, dismantling of the first menarche hut) could be experienced immediately, unseparated by the symbolic structures of time, everything seemed to happen at once, in a single but all-embracing event.

THE FIRST SEXUAL INTERCOURSE   In a world of direct relations and fully manifest beings, the differences among species are no obstacle to the sexual unions of primordial progenitors, whose coupling produces creative transformations. The Waiwai, who claim to know nothing about the ultimate origins of the world, allude to a time when heavenly beings lived on earth as people.[67] The Waiwai assert only that the "world has always existed." [68] The creation that interests them is the origin of human beings and of human customs and social phenomena. Waiwai accounts of the preconditions of man's creation provide the most outstanding example of creative transformation by mythical progenitors.[69] Before human beings existed, paired heavenly spirits roamed the cosmos in animal form. There was one pair of each kind of animal, and each of these pairs constituted the prototype of an animal species. (They now exist in a heavenly plane in an existence parallel to life on earth.) In addition to the heavenly spirits in animal form, there were tortoise-people (wayam-yenna), who were not heavenly spirits (kakenau-kworokjam) even though they had animal form. The tortoise-people were "real animal people" from whom both true animals and true human beings would eventually derive. In this sense, the tortoise-people were like human beings. The creation account opens with a wayam man futilely attempting to climb a tree in order to collect fruit. The man can only get halfway up, but his wife ascends the tree successfully with the use of a rope. She discovers that the "fruits" are actually the male animal sky-spirits. Evidently, this tree reaches to their heavenly abode, where the sky-spirits have been unable to reproduce themselves because they have no women. When they see the wayam woman they all shout, "Here is a woman, here is a woman with whom we can lie." [70] She takes refuge in the tree until a grasshopper splits the tree and has intercourse with her. Subsequently, she eats the yellow fruit of the tree and begins to wander, straying to the house of the jaguar-people. An old grandmother (chacha) hides her under a clay vessel. [71] Eventually, the woman is discovered and killed.

The contents of two of her eggs (she is, remember, a tortoise-woman) are placed under a clay vessel. [72] The old grandmother had broken the eggs and extracted the tiny (male) children before placing them under the large clay vessel for three years' time. They came into full maturity during those years, emerging bearded and with body hair, though they wore no clothing or ornaments. After inventing the bow, arrow, and other cultural items, they went hunting.

At first, the tortoise-woman's children had no sexual organs, but then they licked a forest plant and fell into a sleep during which each grew an extremely long penis in the form of a forest plant. [73] When one of the young men, Mawari, tired of gathering roots, he complained to the jaguar grandmother. She produced cassava from her excrement. Since this proved to be an unsuitable species of cassava, the grandmother permitted herself to be burned. "From her burnt bones other cassava plants shot up of the type used to this very day." [74]

In the meantime, having grown penises, the young men began to experience sexual desire. They both tried having sex with an otter who had been caught in a fishtrap, penetrating the otter through its eye. The otter encouraged them to find a real woman for sex. Mawari fished for the woman in a river and, on the fifth try and after having dredged up articles of feminine culture, he fished up a woman of the anaconda-people (okoimo-yenna). Mawari bathed his wife in strong-smelling banana liquid in order to bring the toothy fish out of her vagina. He then had to cure his brother, who had been foolish enough to attempt sex with another woman before taking these preventive measures. His brother's penis was considerably reduced in size.

The offspring of Mawari and his wife all die, with the exception of one pair of brother and sister, who marry to produce the Waiwai. When their daughter reaches puberty, they put her in an initiation seclusion-hut, where she is kept from looking at the sky for a month, lest it fall. Finally, because all their children are dying, Mawari and his wife angrily disappear by ascending to heaven on a chain of arrows. [75]

PRIMORDIAL INCEST   The remarkably direct relations typical of the creative period stand out clearly in the generative acts of mythical incest that transform the appearances of the universe. The Canelos Quichua, not overly interested in the absolute beginnings of the universe, speak of a mythic time — "before creation" or "before the flood" — that was already peopled with beings. Most important among these beings is Quilla, the moon, who commits incest with his bird sister (or daughter), Jilucu. Their sexual union produces the stars, who exist as people in the earliest mythical times. [76] In a kind of act common in many myths, Jilucu smears her unknown lover's face with *genipa* juice during a nocturnal rendezvous, leaving the incestuous lover forever marked with shame and introducing into the world intermediate hues as well as transitional states of being. In a beautiful elaboration of this widespread mythic theme, the stars, the children of this union, mark their own faces with *huiduj*. The children of the moon, painted with his dusky tone, weep as one "collective sister of the moon." [77] Their dark-stained tears sow the earth with the seeds of the *huiduj* tree. The unbroken weeping results in flooding rains, earthquake, swollen rivers, the eruption of volcanoes, and the appearance of new high hills. (Here is a reworking of the widespread theme of the crying child of primordial time who produces transformation in the weather, the seasons, and cosmic periodicity.) The beings of the earth are caught up in a great river, which sweeps them toward the sea. From the river rises the sun, whose regular course reinstates order. Day is now separated from night, whose lights (which were the first ever) have been darkened by the paint of incest. Eventually, some stars fall to earth in the guise of white grubs. These celestial beings inhabit logs or the earth itself until one of them is transformed into the first and most beautiful woman. People become separated one from another and wander through the world on mythical adventures. They have no manioc, and so they eat raw mushrooms, lichens, and animals. [78]

CO-CREATION: ANOMALY AND ANOMY

Creation need not be the work of a single powerful divinity. Creative collaboration often occurs, especially in cases of cosmogony through transformation, where sexual partners, heroic deputies, and supernatural sidekicks lend aid or even take over the process. Through cooperation or competition, the demiurges, culture heroes, tricksters, and ancestors vie with one another or with the supreme being to complete creation by carrying out or thwarting one another's plans. As always, the meaning of such mythic accounts is intended to bring to light the meaning, the sacred origin, of each aspect of creation. Frequently the cooperative venture includes a being who appears to be evil because he introduces processes that counter the efforts of the supreme being. However, these processes stimulate the conditions in which life, in its new multiplicity of forms, thrives by periodically renewing itself. Days, months, years, and even growth itself could not accumulate over time if perpetual light had left no time for darkness or if eternal darkness had saved no room for light. Ceaseless flow without stagnation had created no rhythms of rising and falling tides, and eternal life had offered no opportunity for death and change. The accumulation over time of regenerative life in abundance demands the existence of real change, alienation, and death.

One Campa person told the ethnographer Gerald Weiss that the creation of the universe was a collaborative effort of two powerful divinities. At the very outset an unknown divinity provided Koriošpíri, the Father of Demons, with some earth, from which Koriošpíri made the universe. Koriošpíri is not a full-blown demiurge, since he was created by the good celestial being Pává. The neighboring Machiguenga possess a more rigorous dualism, in which the evil being Kientibákori, an uncreated co-creator, exists in the bowels of the earth, where he creates sickness and other evil things.[79]

Accounts of co-creation frequently clarify how meaning consists in the simultaneous existence of anomalous or contradictory states of experience: virtues and vices, happiness and misery, abundance and dearth, sickness and health. The Toba told Rafael Karsten that Kaloaraík, "the evil one," created the world so as to afflict it with the woe that the Toba now suffer.[80] The good deity Peritnalík created heaven, earth, the planets, and fruit trees, as well as human beings. However, even the story of creation by the good deity has a decidedly pathetic tone, for Peritnalík distributed goods inequitably. Through their ignorant choices, the Toba forfeited the possession of fire-arms, various domesticated animals, and crops. These were given entirely to the Christians. Eventually, Peritnalík conquered and killed the evil creator Kaloaraík. Nonetheless, the debilitating conditions initiated by Kaloaraík have lasting effects. For that reason, the good deity taught the Toba the art of magical chanting, which allows them to overcome evils in the world.[81]

MAKING ROOM AND HOISTING THE SKY   The creation cycle of the Makiritare of the Orinoco valley in Venezuela, recorded by Marc de Civrieux over a period of twenty years, also recounts an elaborate cooperative creation that deals not only with good and evil but with all the multifaceted realities of life. The emphasis in the cycle of stories falls on the earnest attempts of some super-natural beings to establish "good people" on earth.[82] In the very beginning, only sky and eternal light existed. Shi, the invisible Sun (whose name also refers to the visible representative of the Sun seen in the sky), had already created Wanadi, the heavenly creator, by blowing on quartz crystal. Wanadi is the wise one whose knowledge, tobacco, maraca, and song created "the old people," who existed long before the people of today.[83] During this first period, "the Sky had no door like it does now," for there was no separation between sky and earth.[84] Wanadi was bright, and he shone everywhere.

The drama of creation began when Wanadi wished to make houses and to place good people in them, in imitation of the light-filled houses already existing in the sky. Although Wanadi in his fullness always remains in heaven, during the course of creation he dispatched three aspects of himself—his *damodede*, messengers or spirit-doubles. Seruhe Ianadi was the "first Wan-adi" to descend to earth. He is closely associated with the origin of fleshly life. Unfortunately, he buried his placenta in the ground, where it rotted and gave birth to an evil being, named Odosha, who went on to thwart every creative effort and to introduce sickness, suffering, and death. Seruhe Ianadi re-treated to heaven after changing the first people into animals, the quintes-sential embodiment of corporeal life.[85]

The "second Wanadi," Nadeiumadi, was sent to earth to show people that death is not real but rather a trick of Odosha. Nadeiumadi is closely associated with dream, song, and tobacco. He dreamed his mother into existence: "He gave birth to her dreaming, with tobacco smoke, with the song of his maraca, singing and nothing else." [86] His mother would die and come to life again as his dream-thoughts shifted from death to life and back again. It was to be demonstrated that dream is the true power of reality and that the distinction between life and death is an illusion. Nadeiumadi transported unborn good people to earth in Huehanna, a stonelike egg ("a great ball, huge and hollow, with a thick, heavy shell as hard as stone" [87]). *Huehanna* is linguistically related to the mythic gray tinamou *(Huenna)*, from whose beautiful egg hallucinogenic *kaahi (caapi)* is drunk in Heaven.[88] *Huehanna* was filled with the "noises, words, songs, laughter, screaming" of good people, who could not be seen but only heard.[89] It was intended that they be born on earth; however, through the treachery of Odosha, circumstances intervened to prevent their birth. Still encapsulated and waiting in the stonelike shell, the people-sounds were hidden by Wanadi on Mount Waruma Hidi. "It's waiting there, in peace, since the beginning of the world, and it will stay there till the end . . . the good people inside haven't been born yet. They haven't died either. They're waiting there in Waruma *hidi* for the end of the world, for the death of Odosha." [90]

The third *damodede* of Wanadi to descend to earth was Attawanadi ("house Wanadi").[91] Attawanadi specialized in constructing enclosures. It is he who succeeded in creating the enclosed stratum called earth. Arriving on the scene after the destruction and darkness brought on by Odosha, whose actions provoked the retreat of the sky to a place now out of sight, Attawanadi made a new and visible sky for this enclosed cosmic layer called earth. In the new sky he placed the visible sun, the moon, and the stars. Among the Makiritare, the *atta* ("house" or "village" — since the whole village lives in the same large conical house) is an exact replica of the universe itself.

On Mount Wana Hidi, Attawanadi and Odosha, each in his own house, compete in creating things by the power of their ritual dreams, whose occurrences are prepared for with fasting and by assuming ritual postures.[92] Time once again proves a crucial factor. Attawanadi announces, "I've got to do everything fast before Odosha spoils it." [93] Odosha is victorious, and Attawanadi moves away to Truma Achaka, where he goes to the home of Wade (the sloth who is the most powerful ancient shaman), which is located at the foot of Mount Marahuaka ("little gourd").[94]

In order to drive away evil, Attawanadi disguises himself, a trick that Odosha has been using for destructive purposes. Odosha is undone by trickery, beaten at his own game, and Attawanadi's successful performance is not without important repercussions for cosmic history. The way in which Wanadi appears is changed forever: from now on, Wanadi never goes out as himself but always assumes an unlikely form. "And so he fooled Odosha. Odosha went the other way, looking and looking. He didn't come back again." [95] In order to alienate and to drive away evil and illusion from the world, Wanadi himself assumes elusive guises (including destructive ones such as that of the hunter), which makes it impossible to know him when you see him. Here is a profound statement about the nature of religious symbolism and forms in this world: one needs some special awareness in order to see supernatural reality behind tricky guises. The destructive tendencies of obscurity and disguise turn on themselves, becoming a kind of "happy fault" that destroys destruction and obscures darkness—negates the negation. Religious symbolism, the appearance of supernatural and transcendent realities in this world, involves a negative dialectic of the sacred, which human consciousness is privileged to grasp. Odosha, on the other hand, not knowing where to look, is still lost and fooled. "Now Attawanadi made lots of houses and good people." [96] Later, he fishes Kaweshawa, his wife and the daughter of the master of the fish, out of the river. With the help of a couple of supernatural friends, Attawanadi extracts the teeth of the piranha fish which breed in her vagina and so prepares another enclosure, her vagina and womb, for the entrance of human life. [97]

The mythic history of the Makiritare primordium typifies transformation of the first state of being into something less immediate through the creation of "the house": the gateway, door, enclosure, or wrapping of symbolic life. Since myth is exemplary history (what happens is what must always happen), the primordial world must be closed out or kept at bay through some manner or means. Symbolic life, the very existence of mythic knowledge itself, demands that some expression of remoteness intervene among the overly direct relations of the first, cannibalistic, raw, orgiastic, incestuous world of uninterrupted light or darkness. Symbolic space is created by establishing apprehensible difference in form and perceptible distance in time and space. As in the case of Attawandi's creation of the house-world, one arrives at symbolic closure. In myths of creation, including many of those already mentioned, this rending of difference is often accomplished by lifting up the sky and thereby installing the primordial image of transcendence. The sky on high becomes the ultimate paradigm of distance and difference.

Since the primordial sky is so often the object of the first real separation, it betokens the very possibility of distance between one kind of being and another; its continued transcendence guarantees the symbolic life it signifies. This must be the reason underlying the real anxiety, expressed in myth and rite throughout South America, that the sky will fall. [98] It is a fear of the collapse of symbolic possibilities, for if the sky, the reality transcendent above all others, cannot stay at a remove, no symbolic distance of any kind can be guaranteed; representational life will fail. The basis for life in this world as it is known (indeed, as it can be known) no longer holds. Related to this are expressions of alarm that something dropped or lowered from on high (a rock, hard fruit, food, lightning, feathers, crystals) might destroy life or fracture key symbolic bonds on earth (for example, by killing or maiming an affine).

Fear that the sky might fall becomes more plausible when it is realized that only symbolic measures, the elementary images of space and time, mark off the distance of heaven from earth. Religious worry that the heavens will fall is a consequence of remembering that the world system is a symbolic arrangement, a fragile order that was created as distinct modes of sacred being, through the very forms of their appearance and acts, revealed the imaginable and, therefore, imaginary nature of time and space. The sky rests on the sacred structures appearing in the imagination, a mythic mode of apprehension in every sense of the word: understanding, arrest, and dread.

Such is the case among the Wayãpi of Guyana, for whom the earth is as round and flat as a manioc pancake. Its condition is a result of the actions of the two teams, heavenly and earthly, of ancient architects who fashioned the universe.[99] Before creation began, the earth was a world of larvae, mildew, and mushrooms. Its dark and chaotic condition threatens to reassert itself during lunar eclipses, for which reason men must keep vigil during lunar eclipses to prevent themselves from being transformed into mushrooms.[100] The earthly architects, who were already ancient when they set about their task, said, "Let the earth be flat." And so it was. Their principal task was the installation of four posts that were placed under the outermost edges of the earth in order to stabilize it and to provide it an axial order.

The team of heavenly architects worked in an identical manner. "Let heaven rise up," they said. They then shored up the heavenly vault with four posts. The posts that support heaven and earth are of utmost importance. They were placed there "from the very beginning" and "they exist forever." "It is because this was done in this manner that the Earth exists forever; and it's for this reason that there is the sky." [101] Dance played a crucial role in the constructive transformation of the Wayãpi universe. When the architects of heaven first set the sky in place, it was too close to the earth. They raised it higher by dancing while wearing ceremonial ornaments made from the tail feathers of the red *ara* and other birds. "Dancing for the sky" helped it climb up to a great height. After setting the sky on high, the team of terrestrial architects called upon the celestial ones to make light appear, and the heavenly team created all the stars of night.[102]

The great cosmogonic preoccupation with raising the sky, or "roof" of the first living space, emphasizes that only by maintaining transcendence can the religious imagination uphold the distance between kinds of being. As a mythic experience and as a concept, transcendence makes symbolic life possible. Transcendence is the recognition that difference exists, that separate forms represent fundamentally different modes of being. Awe and symbolic understanding are bound up with one another in bolstering the possibility of transcendence, the fundamental underpinnings of the universe in which mythic reality, the life of the imagination, participates in a fully creative way.

Failure to hold up reality (at a distance but also to plain view), that is, to *represent* reality, can bring the whole symbolic world crashing down, crushing the forms of life by obliterating the communicative and regenerative systems of signs upon which life in the present world is based. The symbolic life of the heavens and of all transcendent beings is maintained by the ritual acts (such as dancing), aesthetic codes (such as feathered ornaments and song), and social structures of the symbolic life's own making. That is why, as we shall see, the cosmogony becomes the model for the significant actions that constitute human culture. This is another way of saying that religious symbolism is efficacious: its very first appearance creates symbolic existence, the universe, through its own significations. For this reason symbolic knowledge is ineluctably fearful: failure to represent primordial reality, to act symbolically by imitating the creative acts, would bring the universe down like a house of cards in an instant. The ability to grasp the nature of symbolic knowledge depends on the frightening awareness that symbolic experience, the way of knowing available to creatures in the symbolic world, is not the only way of being. There is a primordial mode of being that utterly transcends this world and that, if restored to its fully apparent condition, would destroy it. Mythic history testifies to this ever-present possibility by recounting occasions when the sky fell, flattening the symbolic world and pitching it back into the chaos of full manifestation. Understanding the nature of symbolic life demands an awareness of how it teeters on the verge of collapse, how its foundations lie on the extreme edge of what is imaginable. "Chaos is not only the reverse of the cosmos, it is also its condition and foundation." [103] The firm hope that symbolism offers for a stable, certain, and secure existence rests on the unsettling and awesome realization that symbolic life itself depends on the greatest contingency and the only real change that utterly transcends human control: the appearance of meaningful being in the first place.

CLOSING THE CREATION ACCOUNT: WITHDRAWAL OF PRIMORDIAL BEING

Removal of the sky from earth is not the only means of imposing symbolic distance on the world and of clarifying the estrangement of primordial reality from mundane existence. Part of the responsibility of myth is to account for the displacement of the first forms of being by explaining that they are no longer the same, no longer fully recognizable. One by one the primordial actors exit the mythic stage. The ways of dispatching mythical characters are myriad. The details of their departures are as revealing as the description of their manners of arrival and of their prodigious actions during the mythic interim. They take their leave through ascent, descent, destruction, or disappearance; they are burned, broken, buried, bottled, drowned, dismembered, devoured, disrobed, flayed, exiled, expelled, painted, pierced, or petrified. Each process is important, for it not only succeeds in dispatching a fully apparent mode of being to some unmanifest condition but also clarifies the symbolic meaning of that transformative process itself. For example, the mythic fire that burns up primordial beings and changes them into spirits explains the meaning of fiery transformations in contexts such as daylight, seasonal temperature, cooking, smoking, cremation, the men's hearth, poisoning, feverish sickness, and "hot" emotional states.

In his sketch of the creation story of the Avá-Katú-Eté of eastern Paraguay, Miguel Alberto Bartolomé gives careful attention to the goings as well as to the comings of each kind of mythical being. Indeed, the matter of their disappearance is of ultimate concern since the destiny of the universe and its creatures is linked directly to the destiny of supernatural beings. The processes of symbolic transformation by which the primordials are dismissed after their last full-scale appearance also mark the first appearance of aspects

of the contemporary world. In the beginning, the world is created by Nanderú Guazú, who then places the universe on a cross made of wood. When
this act has been accomplished, the creator and his companion, Nanderú
Mbaé-Kua'a ("our great father who knows all things"), impregnate the first
woman. She becomes Nandé Cy ("our mother").[104] After creating maize, the
creator withdraws from the earth in a fit of anger because Nandé Cy refuses
to believe that he can cause the maize to germinate in a single day. Nanderú
Guazú and his companion forsake the earth in order to take up residence in
the heavenly heights. Eventually Nandé Cy gives birth to twins, the sun and
the moon. She is then devoured by supernatural jaguars. Taking up residence
at the entrance to the Land Without Evil, she eternally awaits the coming of
her children. The sun and moon carry out a series of epic adventures that
transform the earth and make the elements of culture (game animals, fire,
the hunting bow, plants, and the rules of social order) available to humankind.[105] They ascend into heaven along a chain of arrows. Origin myths that
recount the beginnings of a number of plant and animal species complement
the adventures of the twins in this cycle. The origin of stars and constellations
is also sacred, and their beginnings, their connection to humankind, and
their transformation while moving into the starry vault of heaven are recounted in myth. Thus, "each Avá-Katú-Eté lives in total awareness of the
sacred nature of his environment and his sociocultural order"[106] because he
knows the entire mythic history of each one of its forms.

The withdrawal of primordial beings has a telling effect on the nature of
the physical universe and its material and organic contents. In their version
of the creation of the world, the Campa describe a universe and a time when
the earth and sky were close to one another and were connected by a sky-
rope-vine. At that time the sun (Pává), referred to here as Neháronci, resided
on earth with his children. When he desired to transfer his residence to the
sky (for reasons which are not explained), he enlisted the aid of the smallest
of the birds, the hummingbird Neorónke, who succeeded in carrying the
sky-rope-vine to the highest level of the universe. During the migration of
Pává into the sky, a number of significant transformations, which account for
the present condition of nature, occurred. Many beings, which at that time
were in the form of human beings, were transformed into animals such as the
tapir or the mouse, who kept some kernels of maize hidden in his mouth. For
this reason that primordial plant still exists on earth. Certain trees and
flowers by which time is measured throughout the year were daughters of
Pává, who originally had human form. The calendrical trees are the former
"clothing" of those daughters, clothing which they stripped off and left behind when they migrated to heaven. When the sky-rope-vine was thrown
down to the earth, a number of beings fell onto the earth with it, including the
porcupine, the sloth, and the wasp.[107] It is significant that the vast majority of
important beings who existed at the beginning of historical time all had to
ascend into heaven from their place as human-form beings on earth. The
single exception might be the moon, Kašíri, who, it is said, "returned" into
the heavens. Although they are celebrated in myth, very little attention is paid

to the transformative beings in ritual. Informal ritual attention is paid to Pává. For the most part, the highest echelon of supernatural beings is entirely neglected in Campa ritual.[108] Significantly more attention is given lesser spirits in festivals such as the Ayahuasca ceremony.[109]

The withdrawal of primordial beings is essential to the life of the religious imagination; it is a part of every complete corpus of myths. Since every reality appearing in the time of beginnings is total (a complete expression of being, fully apparent, an absolute statement of its kind), every change that mythic events provoke is also absolute and permanent: a total eclipse or disintegration of some primordial form. This retreat of nonsymbolic reality, most vivid in the death, transformation, or withdrawal of individual supernatural beings into the heights or margins of the cosmos (such as, for example, forest or underworld), is true of primordial existence as a whole.

AGES OF THE WORLD: THE CATASTROPHE OF DESTRUCTION

Why should the perfect and powerful primordium fall prey to disaster?[110] What force could undo realities so powerful they were the first beings ever to manifest themselves and to alter the very quality of being? Before returning to these questions, I shall present two different accounts of the violent destruction of the primordial world, the most important event in South American mythic history. An elderly Pilagá man named Daichiki told Enrique Palavecino the story of the cosmic flood. Taking the form of a mangy dog, the celestial being named Lapichí descended to earth during a rainstorm. Because no one recognized him or offered him shelter, Lapichí caused the flood rains to continue for five years. Only an old man and his family were saved, by repairing to a dugout canoe that floated up to heaven, where they met Lapichí in all his glory. He offered the survivors the choice of returning to earth or remaining permanently in heaven. When the old man chose to return to earth, Lapichí made the flood waters recede instantly by driving a cane into the earth.[111]

Like many South American peoples, the Pilagá betray a certain dissatisfaction with any single account of creation and tell of several such destructions through various means. Palavecino felt that the story of a cosmic fire that ravaged the entire primordial world was the most typical destruction myth of the Chaco area. When the world was consumed by fire, protohuman beings tried to hide in the bottom of a lake. However, the fire made the water boil, and young and old people alike floated dead in the water. Everything burned. The only survivor of the cosmic fire was a small bird. This beautifully colored bird began to dance and sing without cease. As a result of his performance all the kinds of trees were, one by one, reborn and began to grow again. The periods of their growth, flowering, and fruiting created the differentiated and orderly time periods that mark the progression of time in this world.[112]

The Pilagá also recall another total disaster in which absolute darkness filled the earth, obliterating every appearance of reality. People hid in caves until the first *algaroba* fruit ripened and fell. Then the sun reappeared and people emerged. As they did so, most of them were transformed into animals.[113] The Pilagá describe other catastrophes as well. These include a period when the sky fell. Only one family was able to save itself by taking refuge beneath the lone tree that withstood the crushing weight of the heavens. The tree became the generative center of the new world; by prying apart the heavenly and earthly modes of existence, it also served to connect them, joining one world to the next.

A second set of accounts of cosmic destruction comes from the Makiritare, who, like the Pilagá, describe a number of universal devastations. Each myth narrates the origins of specific items or processes that help constitute today's world: magic quartz crystals, food and food processes, agriculture, the river system, and so on. Whether these are different renditions of a single cosmic catastrophe that affected every object or whether each item met with its own trouble while coming into the new world cannot be decided from the mythic accounts. What can be said with assurance is that a thorough destruction of the primordial condition of existence was needed to make way for the particular forms in which life now appears. Each reality had to assume new form (destructible, consumable, replicable) before it could appear in a new world.

The colonial realities of the Makiritare world also had their destructive origins in the mythic period. In fact, the appearance of the colonial world and its agents distinguishes an epoch of mythic time, a period dominated by the greedy *fañuru* (from the Carib word *pañoro*, derived from Spanish, *español*), who ascended the rivers on an epic journey in order to murder and eat people, rape women, and kill Wanadi, the creator god, on a cross. The successful Makiritare rebellion against the Spanish in 1775 is barely recalled as such by the Makiritare. However, it is remembered vividly that, sometime during the mythical age when the *fañuru* appeared along the rivers, a powerful shaman named Mahaiwadi once went into ecstasy while playing his maraca, singing, and smoking. While lying "dead" in his hammock, he sent his *damodede* (spirit double) out of his body. It went to call forth enormous supernatural anacondas from the water domain. They ate the *fañuru* after overturning their canoes. Continuing to lie in his hammock like a dead man, Mahaiwadi "went out in a new body, like a jaguar" to devour those *fañuru* who were in the forest. A few surviving *fañuru* buried gold at the foot of Mount Wana Hidi and turned into poisonous stones. The jaguar now called forth the people from the caves where they were hiding. " 'The Fañuru are in my stomach. You can come out of your caves now.' "[114] When he had thus recreated and repopulated the world, Mahaiwadi awoke and his *damodede* flew away to heaven in the form of a bird, singing "free, free, I'm free."[115] His skull and bones remained behind to help cure the sick.

What point is there to recounting details of the primordial world when, almost invariably, it is annihilated only to begin again? Why not begin with

the creation that succeeds without fail? The mythic accounts of cosmic destruction attempt no satisfactory answers. On the contrary, they preoccupy
themselves with revealing good ground for the questions. Universal cataclysms uncover the primordial origins of a dissatisfaction with any sort of
being that appears exhaustive, total, or absolute. Why was the fullness of
being destroyed? The myths of destruction appear to say that, apart from any
single answer, *the question is real:* that is, that because the puzzlement concerning primordial being and its disintegration arises from sacred events of
the very first order, that puzzlement is a recurrent reality that must be con-
fronted again and again. The status of absolute, eternal, and indestructible
being is questionable. It can be subject to critical thought because it has
proven vulnerable to cosmic crisis. Destruction through flood and fire offers
ontological proof that the first world remains open to the critical questions
associated with the appearance of this transitory world through the demise of
the primordial one. More importantly, myths of catastrophe provide the
symbolic language with which to conduct such a critique.[116]

THEORIES OF MULTIPLE EPOCHS AND DESTRUCTIONS

Accounts of the appearance of multiple worlds envision distinct universes,
each populated with its own characters, characterized by its own sets of
relations, and punctuated by destruction. Even where those accounts appear
quite random and disjointed, they testify to the ability of the religious imagination to grasp reality from more than one perspective. For example, the
Gran Pajonal Campa "know that the universe has been created, destroyed,
and recreated various times."[117] According to Stefano Varese, the Campa
believe that "white people are the precosmogonic chaos and the chaos at the
end of each cosmic cycle."[118] One sure sign that the end of this world *(kipátzi)*
is already approaching is that there is a rank odor in the air because the
divinity, tired of holding things together, is letting the cosmos go to rot
(omóyeka). Soon an earthquake will pitch over the foul-smelling world. Then
the underworld will have the chance to rise up closer to the celestial divinity
and to renew itself.

   In some accounts the relationship of multiple epochs to one another
appears rather vague. Except for the important temporal marker that allows
the Waiwai, for instance, to speak of the time "before the flood" and "after
the flood," most allusions to early primordial epochs lack precise terms of
temporal reference. Rather, the succession of Waiwai ages is spoken of in
terms of different modes of being. Thus, the world itself, heaven, the sun, and
trees are most ancient. Later, these spaces are peopled with heavenly spirits
(kakenau-kworokjam) and "real animal people" *(yenna)*, from whom real
animals and real human people would eventually emerge. Human beings
then enter the scene in the person of Mawari, the human progenitor. When
human beings die, their souls *(ekati)* are transformed into ghosts, or former
souls *(ekatinho)*, which may in turn transmigrate into animal soul forms
(ekatinho-kworokjam).[119] Without systematically clarifying the succession of

ages, the Waiwai nonetheless remark that there is a "history" of forms that proceed from one another and from the succession of mythical events that bring on their origin.

A sequence of mythical destructions also sets off the unfolding of the mythic history of the Siriono of Eastern Bolivia. The Siriono say that at the time when Yási (Moon) lived on earth "there was nothing but water." [120] At that time there lived a species of hostile beings whom Yási wiped out. Today long arrows are made from the several kinds of reeds that appeared in the watery marshes where Yási destroyed groups of those primordial beings. Consequently, these long arrows serve as mnemonic markers, perpetuating the memory (and, so, the presence) of the various categories of beings who preexisted the present world.

SYSTEMATIC HERMENEUTICS OF HISTORY

Cultures often coordinate multiple ages and calamities in a systematic history. The existence of separate worlds, along with the distinct modes of being present in each, creates a modal series of existences. In his comparative model of South American cosmologies, Peter G. Roe mentions the widespread belief in the existence of other worlds that preexisted the current one. He calls them "cyclic variations." Each variation contains a number of worlds in the spatial scheme of the cosmos. Each successive world is imperfect and suffers destruction by flood, by fire, or through petrification. Roe sees an oscillation between terrestrial flooding and celestial fire, which extinguish life in successive attempted universes. [121]

However, these world systems are never simply hypothetical; each one leaves a discernible residue of consequences in subsequent worlds. Such is the case for the Tehuelche, who distinguish at least four epochs to which they dedicate different cycles of myths. The first cycle describes the creation of the world and its fundamental elements (water, wind, light, and the cosmogonic island on which the supreme being does his creating). The second cycle narrates the birth of the culture hero Elal, who reshapes the world into its present form. The third cycle recounts Elal's arrival in Patagonia and describes his cultural instructions to humans, especially concerning hunting. The fourth cycle describes Elal's departure from this world and his installation in the starry heavens, where he now resides. [122] Because of their continuing influences on the present world, the multiple ages and their consequences make this contemporary cosmos a complicated historical entity. Each successive world is understood in temporal terms: that is, it represents a mode of time. And each cataclysm exterminates a specific quality of time, for after each destruction comes a new age. The Canelos Quichua, for instance, reckon that there has been a succession of at least four ages: the Ancient Times, the Times of Destruction, the Times of the Grandparents, and the Present Times. [123]

Most often, because each of the various primordia reveals its own mode of time, the succession of ages moves from the perfect stasis of the past (e.g., a time of total rain or absolute drought or of total day, total night, or perpetual twilight) to the dynamism of human history, which is calibrated in terms of all the accumulated varieties of time that have come into existence — the alternation of days, nights, and seasons and the transitions and changes of sun, moon, and stars. Because each unit of measure (sun, moon, stars, rains) was destroyed in the past, each of these modes of time now has termination or disappearance built into the manner of its contemporary appearance. The sun disappears each evening and may "die" during eclipses or winter solstices; the moon perishes each month; the stars vanish each day; rains stop from time to time. Through the mythic accounts of their origin and demise (images which reveal the meaning of time), all worlds, including this one, find places in the schematic history of being from its earliest imaginable stirrings to its final eclipse. According to the investigations of Núñez del Prado B., Quechua mythology recognizes three ages of the universe: a dark Era of the Spirits, lit only by the moon; a rebellious Era of the Ñawpa, who are blinded and dried by the newly risen sun; and the Era of Man, which provides a range of vacillating lights in a full range of tone, color, and intensity, such as that found in the stars, in rainbows, in minerals and gems, and in woven textiles.[124]

The Andean people of Pinchimuro, in the district of Ocongate (Quispicanchis, Peru), offer subtle nuances on this theme. They recognize a progression of five overlapping epochs presided over by the three persons of the Holy Trinity. The first is the cosmogonic epoch, during which order is imposed on chaos. God the Father created the world (other divinities, mountains, rivers, humans, and animals), gave it over to the safekeeping of Pachamama and the Apus, and then withdrew to a place of supervision. In the second period, the ancestral ñawpaq machula, self-possessed and long-lived giants, lived in a state of perpetual darkness. The moment the sun began to shine for the first time, these beings fled with their animals to the forest. Many of them were either consumed by the fire of the sun or transformed into stone.[125] Their world was destroyed. Many ñawpaq machula now serve as beneficent powers of fertility, and they are celebrated in an annual dance. On the other hand, some of the beings from the age of machula giants were never consumed; they linger on today, preying on the carnal and sensual life of human beings by devouring them with disease. The evil spirit Soq'a Machula, for instance, emits a pathogenic vapor in the vicinity of ancient cemeteries and sickens people by sneaking into their homes at night to have sexual relations with them. In such cases, the prognosis is usually death, although "sometimes a sick person is able to be healed by drinking a tea of crushed soq'a bones. Eating the soq'a who is trying to eat the sick person is the way one may be cured."[126] That is, if such pathogenic "leftovers" (literally translated from the Latin superstitio) can be consumed, as they were not by the cosmic destruction that brought their world to an end, they can be transformed and dealt with symbolically. These superstitions are forced to assume forms more properly suited to life in this world when they are devoured or destroyed. Human consumption, then, continues and extends the devastating process that brought the human cosmos into being. This is why eating sustains life in this world: it keeps the forms of this world in existence because it imitates the processes of primordial destruction that initiated it. Cooking spreads the conflagration; eating devours and annihilates the plant, animal, and mineral beings from the worlds that preexisted this one; preparing and drinking beverages swell the cosmic flood. Through art, ritual, economy, and other symbolic expressions, human beings create a world by reenacting processes that altered primordial modes of being. The symbolic relations that human beings have with the material reexpressions of supernatural beings from annihilated worlds constitutes spiritual life in the present epoch.

The third age is called the Golden Age of the Inca. This age, presided over by God the Son (Dios Churi), was one of great scientific advancement. It ended with the European conquest of the Inca, who, as supernatural powers, took refuge in the remote areas around Lake Titicaca or in the forest, and who now work for the well-being of the local people. Many hope for the future return of the Inca. The fourth age constitutes the history of events following the Conquest until the present day. It is a period of continual decline and degeneration, both of society and the order of the world. "All agree that the fourth epoch will end soon. Some say, 'when the snow disappears from Ausangate.' " [127] The fifth age, to be presided over by God the Holy Spirit, is not clearly delineated. It will come into existence when this, the fourth age, ends. The ethnologists Rosalind Gow and Bernabe Condori found the people they interviewed confused about the shape and meaning of the age to come. Some of the elders in the community held that the world would return to its state during the period of the Inca, the golden age. Younger people often looked toward the future epoch as a time of independence and financial progress. Some contended that there would be a final judgement during the fifth epoch. In short, although all agreed that there would be a new era in the future, there was no consensus about what it would be like. [128]

THE TENDENCY TO END AND THE TELOS OF SYMBOLIC LIFE

In the beginning of this book a question was posed about primordial being, the kind of being and question that must appear in the beginning. The postulate, already stated, that the status of mythic being remains, in a fruitful way, *questionable* finds support in the history of the world as recounted by South American peoples. As we have seen, they describe a series of ages each of which ends in the destruction of the beings who appear in it. Without anticipating the ensuing closer look at cosmic disintegration and its aftermath, we can already delineate several generative tendencies visible in theories of multiple aeons.

First, being is inclined to move away from the condition of stable perpetuity toward the changefulness of life of this world. The case of the Shipibo is typical. The Shipibo allude to an epoch, before this present age, when the sun stood still in the east. People did not then possess fire. There was only one source of light, fire, and color and it stood immobile. The uniqueness of the first age is construed as a selfish, private or deprived existence, for Ŝhäno Inca ("bad Inca"; also called Yoashico and identified by Roe as the moon) kept fire and food (manioc) to himself. In the static world of uniquenesses there was only one exclusive form for each mode of being, so there could be no overlapping or shared quality of being between any of them. A new age began when a bird stole a coal of the unique fire and attempted to set a tree ablaze. When Ŝhäno Inca tried to douse the fire with a tempest of rain, change was introduced (the rainy season). However, a number of birds protected the fire with their wings. When they divided the burning coal among them, the sun began to rise. A new age, peopled with transitional beings, dawned.[129]

Successive ages rework old forms to create new appearances. The propensity of the images of creation to divide and replicate in interesting ways has played a part in generating the form of this book. By constantly returning to primordial imagery, I hope to put forward a stable and sustained analysis of basic themes in South American religions. By periodically returning to the stability of primordial imagery, I hope to offer an interpretation that is consistent and systematic. At the same time, as the images of the primordium fan out in increasingly complicated ways over the course of their development in time, each chapter of this present volume will likewise address a new development. Each episode will speak about new appearances and will adjust to new rhythms.

A second trend of being is noticeable in the unfolding ages of the world. This is the move from direct communication to indirect, symbolic knowledge. This important development is evident in several ways, including the increasing loss of immediacy on linguistic, cognitive, and physical planes. Direct communication between different modes of being passes away in favor of symbolic language, codes, and signs. The River Campa offer an example. They mention ages which preexisted the historical age of their ancestors, and they order these mythological accounts by referring to events of terrestrial transformation, celestial transformation, or the history of humankind.[130] The greatest of earth's transformations was the passage from the time when the earth responded to Tasorenci's creative questions to a time when it ceased to answer. Stuffed with generations of dead bodies, the earth has gotten literally fed up with human life and lies weak and inert. "According to the informant Sariti, it is because the Campas die and are buried that the earth has suffered and no longer speaks, at least within the confines of Campa territory. In describing the universe, however, it is not unusual for a Campa to impute the power of speech to the ground underfoot where the good spirits live at the end of the earth and in the sky."[131] Because of death, the earth and the creator no longer create by speaking directly to one another in this world. Many material forms are mute or opaque, and their meanings are no longer clear.

The drift from immediacy is also evident in cognitive terms. During the "ancient times" described by the Canelos Quichua, for instance, all beings enjoyed full knowledge of the meaning of reality and communicated directly with Sungui, the master of the river spirit-people, and Amasanga, the master spirit of the forest. During this time "before the flood,"[132] the meaning of all things was immediately clear. This was the time of *unai*, when all spatial domains and forces of being were in direct relationship with one another. All celestial and underworld people lived on the earth "as people," because the sky, the earth, and the underworld were united.[133] The world was inhabited by beings called *tayaj rumi*, rock-souls that existed side by side with the other beings who lived during that time. There was little need for work. This time had always existed. Reality was marvelously united and undifferentiated, for other times, other forms of being, had not yet appeared. Animals possessed all knowledge. Since that time, obviously, different species of beings have found it increasingly difficult to communicate with one another and have come to do so through the media of symbolic life: dreams, visions, rites, and hallucinations.

Indirectness also appears in the increasing absence of immediate physical relations with primordial beings. The Waiwai did not report to Niels Fock any systematic theory of the succession of primordial epochs. They pointed out, however, that there had existed a period "before creation." At that time, heavenly beings walked the earth as *yenna* (people).[134] Withdrawn on high, they left only symbolic residue within physical reach.

Third, we might say that every image tends toward integrity, wholeness, or closure, and that in this regard the experience of primordial being is exemplary. The fact that primordial being, the real world, has an end sets the stage for the disintegration of the present world or of any other entity that hopes to be real. Thus, for example, the Shipibo contemporary age will itself end when demons swallow human beings.[135] The reality of termination provides South American religious life (that is, the interpretive life of South American cultures) with an integrity that is evident, within the mythic accounts, from the beginning. All symbolic life associated with South American religions respects that wholeness and acknowledges its end. That is why this book, itself a symbolic form or arrangement of symbols associated with South American religions, suggests that to end some ways of interpreting South American religions might be a sign of a new beginning, constitutive of an integral cultural order better suited to the present age.

This volume does not set itself the agenda of installing such a new climate of human interpretation; that must be the collective venture of many hands and the fruit of many kinds of cultural experience. For the moment, the tendency of everything that begins also to come to an end, apparent time after time in theories of multiple mythical epochs, has immediate bearing on the symbolic structure of this book, which begins with creation and terminates with the end of the world. The symbols of the beginning and end—of the gods, of the universe, of the village space, of the calendar year; of human life, flesh, and bone and of the stages on life's way; of food supplies, songs, and mythic narratives; of legitimate authority, political regimes, and networks of trade—the beginnings and ends of all these realities lend this book and each of its parts a certain wholeness. By positioning the symbols of creation and termination at either end of the volume, I hope to ensure that the whole work of fracturing mythic narratives into images that reappear in separate chapters not only has an end but also a creative *telos*, an outcome directly related to the book's beginning with sacred beings, the first to appear in the human imagination.

MODES OF DESTRUCTION

Scenarios of destruction reward a closer look. This conviction endures among South American peoples who reflect on the deluge or the world conflagration in their myths and rites. Taking its cue from this abiding fascination with primordial devastation, the balance of this chapter provides detailed images of cataclysm, the conditions provoking annihilation, and the consequences of universal ruin.

An enormous number of narratives of catastrophe appears across the continent. Within a single community, there sometimes exists a variety of stories about the cosmic flood, fire, drought, earthquake, putrefaction, or petrification.[136] The forms of destruction need not be exclusive: different calamities may decimate one world after another, or the same form of extermination may revisit itself on creation. For instance, after the Ava-Katu-Eté creator made the world and then abandoned it in anger, the earth was destroyed either by a cataclysmic flood or fire or by both. In some versions the creator himself destroyed the universe by overturning the wooden cross on which he had placed it.[137] Toba myths describe a quite different situation. Before human beings knew how to control fire, an enormous snowfall came from heaven. After falling for successive weeks, snow covered the whole earth. Human life was destroyed. The Tobas who died in the cold took on a transformed life in *piyím* (heaven) as ostriches, sheep, and goats. "Only in one house one man and one woman of the Tobas and likewise of other human races remained alive." [138] In this way human life was preserved.

The myriad details of multiple accounts defy reduction to a single set of structures. The following sections briefly outline a few reports of universal flood, fire, and darkness. Before any one of them is decoded, the multiplicity of mythic disasters sends a message of its own: creation suffered a disaster so total, no single account can describe it adequately. Like every manifestation of sacred being, devastation remains a total event, never able wholly to be accounted for. Because the origins of failure are inexhaustible, they continue to appear in new mythic expressions as well as in the real tragedies of daily life. The dissatisfaction with any single mythic account describes an existential restlessness with the singular and the unique. Not only do the narratives sketch the fracturing of the unique primordium to reveal the uneasy landscape of existence, but the myths themselves suffer modification to appear as multiple variants. The interminable need to retell the events in new ways reveals the uncomfortable situation of human beings as they confront sacred realities, the beings first apparent in the structures of the imagination.

FLOOD: THE LIQUIDATION OF DISTINCT FORM

Formless, primal chaos returns in the image of the universal flood, which submerses nearly every mark of distinctness in the created world. By obliterating almost every sign of difference, the deluge makes itself the great divide, the principle marker disjoining antedeluvian existence from life after the flood.

Frequently, an aquatic monster provokes the cosmic flood by trying to block the eternal flow of life-giving waters. The result is the appearance of periodic life, ebbing and spurting in halting rhythms. Not surprisingly, the marine dragon can be a close associate of the creator even if their relationship is an antagonistic one. Such is the case in a narrative told by the Tukano. Sé, the flood-being, is consubstantial with the supreme being, for he is fashioned from the left arm of Yepá Huaké, the creator. The universal deluge occurs when Yepá Huaké ascends into heaven. At that time Sé causes torrential rains to deluge the world by damming up the river which runs "up above." The intimate relationship of creator to water-monster does not end with the origin of Sé. After sixty days of continuous, destructive rain, Yepá Huaké kills Sé to save the world from perpetual annihilation.[139]

Slaying the monster of chaos to mark the beginning of a new creative epoch is a recurrent theme in many South American mythologies. The alternating manifestations of power by a creator (or transformer) who withdraws and a water-monster who appears in the resultant void is tantamount to a cosmic battle of order and chaos.[140] These shifting appearances of formative and formless modes of supernatural being create the rhythms of periodic time, the succession of primordial ages. A widespread Araucanian flood myth, for example, describes the universal struggle between two unformed serpents. A primordial serpent named Caicai makes the waters surge up at the same time as another primordial snake, named Tentén, causes the mountains of the world to rise at the same rate as the waters. Since both powers are coterminous and coextensive, simultaneity and indistinctness rule the day. Earlier, Tentén had warned humankind of the impending catastrophe and encouraged them to save themselves by coming to the mounting hill. However, the protohumans paid scant attention, and only a few sought out the hill's summit at the last moment. On the other hand, a large number of animals did seek refuge. As the waters overtook them, some animals became fish and sea animals; "others turned directly into rocks."[141] The contest of primordial serpents finally forced the emergence of definite form in the shape of a mountain that rose decisively above the destruction. Eventually, the mountain, also called Tentén, ascended as far as the sun in order to outdistance the floodwaters. Only a few humans and animals avoided death in this cataclysmic battle between the snake-floodwaters and the snake-mountain.[142]

Total chaos is inherently incapable of revealing its own limits or structures, hence the need for struggle between the ordered and unordered modes of being. According to the Apinayé, for instance, the shape of the marine serpent is not something intrinsic to it. The serpent is amorphous. The Apinayé deluge[143] occurred when the gigantic snake Kaṅẽ-rōti rose out of the limitless sea to form the Tocantins and Araguaia rivers. His appearance changed the state of being in the universe. "The whole world was flooded." [144] Separation became the key strategy for the survival of life forms and the creation of new imagery. The land, standing separate from the river water, gave lifesaving definition to the serpent's body. The division of water from land was only one kind of parting. Groups of people also diverged and survived this cosmic flood. The first group, fleeing to a mountaintop that rose above the flood, gathered palm sprouts and nuts. The second group floated on the flood in three gigantic gourd bottles, into which they had put manioc cuttings, maize, and other seeds. These people became agriculturalists. Members of a third group, who had scaled the tall *jatoba* trees, became bees and termites. Today, each group maintains its own language and lifeways. The flood accounts for the separation of languages, the variety of symbolic systems, and the diversity of customs.

Like Kañẽ-rōti himself, meaning, matter, and time threaten to remain essentially featureless because of their intrinsic boundlessness and indivisibility. The lesson of the flood, however, is that chaotic formlessness is divisible; it is bounded by whatever it is not. The monstrosity of the virtual becomes defined by whatever remains external to it, whatever resists being inundated by indeterminacy. The very possibility of another image of being vanquishes the infinite possibilities of virtuality and amorphousness. The imagination permits differentiation. In the face of the flood, the survival or appearance of other forms of life (of diverse ecological niches such as mountains, trees, and interfluvial land; of language and culture) conquers the chaos of infinite possibilities. Similarly, the period of time characterized by the presence of the flood-monster gets defined only by its outermost limits, that is, by the order imposed by the forms and images of the worlds before and after the deluge. Since the recession of chaos in the face of form remains an intrinsically unaccountable event, the recurrence of chaos remains an everlasting threat and, at the same time, a constant source of new forms as well as of the renewal of the imagination itself. Chaos makes it possible to separate what comes before from what comes afterward. In turn, these two modes of being, ordered through the imagery of their temporal expression, limit and specify chaos by setting it within temporal boundaries. Chaos becomes the bounded condition of passage betwixt and between separate modes of being.

Because the flood effects a radical change in the mode of being present in the world, it marks the transition from one aeon to another. In the face of the separation that the waters impose between primordial and cosmic modes of being, every other kind of difference becomes relative and subject to the limits of space and time. Thus, for instance, the central event delineating the succession of temporal stages in Waiwai primordial times is a great flood. [145] Unfortunately, only abridged versions of the narrative exist. The Waiwai flood story explores the problem of boundedness by centering its drama on an adolescent girl. The serpentine flood-monsters relate directly to the openness of this young girl (her eyes, her vagina) and to the penetrable closure of her vessel of salvation, a clay pot. When the girl looks at the middle of the river during her first menses, she arouses the anaconda-people dwelling there. They flood the land. Placed in a clay vessel by her *chacha* (grand-mother), the girl remains there until discovered by a giant armadillo who burrows through the earth and penetrates the floor of the hut where the vessel was stored. Water begins to seep, and eventually to flood, in from the hole in the ground directly under the girl.[146] The girl's grandmother helps her to flee into the forest, and, at the same time, the old woman saves certain key items of culture from the flood.

The fate of the aquatic dragon can reflect the need to abolish chaos. The drama of the flood often results in the monster's death and dismemberment, and the divisibility of the water serpent assures the discreteness of form. This becomes clear in the creation cycle of the Makiritare. Nadeiumadi, an earthly aspect of the Makiritare creator, had brought a stone-egg, Huehanna, from heaven. In it were contained all the invisible sounds of future life-forms and species. Since the conditions for life were not propitious, he hid the stone-egg on the heavenly mountain. Nuna, the male, cannibalistic moon, stole Huehanna with the intention of eating its contents, the potential life of the world. In order to save the beings (the invisible sounds) contained in it, Nuna's sister Frimene hid the stone-egg in her vagina. During the night her brother stole into the place where she was lying and, forcing her legs apart, thrust his hand into her vagina in search of the stone-egg of sounds. Frimene escaped from her cannibalistic and somewhat incestuous brother by turning into Huiio, the mistress of water and the anaconda rainbow-serpent. The future multiform life of the universe seemed to have fallen into an inextric-able quandary: the invisible sounds of people were encased in an impenetra-ble (i.e., nongrowing, timeless) stone-egg, which was now enveloped in chaos, the body of Huiio. The solution was found in Huiio's death. When she appeared in the sky as a rainbow, a numberless horde of hunters shot arrows into her. After she fell, each being ate a mouthful of her flesh and washed in the river of her blood. A flood now inundated the entire earth.[147] At the same time, Huehanna fell from Huiio's formless body and crashed on a rock in the river. All the sounds inside of it became creatures of the domain of water except for two tiny eggs (the twin heroes) that survived intact. The dissoluble nature of an indivisible world was overcome by penetration, brokenness, dismemberment, and separation. Each process allows one mode of being (e.g., the periodic) to trespass on another (e.g., the eternal) and thereby to extract form from formlessness. Their violent collision established prece-dent-setting distances and boundaries between modes of being: the diverse habitats and languages of separate species, the disjunct worlds of the moon and rainbow, the distinctness of ethereal being (e.g., sound) from incarnate form, the discrimination of all other carnal relations from those restricted by the incest taboo.

REFUGE FROM IMMEDIACY   The theme of junction and disjunction finds expres-sion even where no aquatic monster figures in the flood scenario. Sometimes a cosmic tree is the crux of the matter. Appearing during the flood, such a medium both separates heaven and earth at a proper distance and conjoins them in a suitable place. This image of distance and differentiation offers refuge from the flood. In some cases, the tree is called into being for the occasion, its growth having been prompted by rhythmic noise, song, or some other sign of the passage of time. It is in fact the passage of time, the appearance of a new form of being, that calls the cosmic tree into existence; the tree is the effective sign of transition in space between entirely different modes of being. The Chiripá myth of the primordial grandmother, Chary Piré, was recorded by León Cádogan. When the earth was deluged completely in a flood, Chary Piré sang a sacred song to the accompaniment of her *takuapú* (rhythm stick). As she sang, an eternal palm tree grew out of the waters. Taking her son with her, she ascended to its heights. This same tree now acts as a bridge connecting the sky and the earth; it also keeps them at a significant remove from one another.[148] By obliterating the primordial epoch, the flood effects in temporal terms the same passage from one mode of being to another and makes way for the appearance of a new age.

Without the cosmic tree to separate the celestial from the terrestrial mode of being, all hope of distinguishing between qualities of being disappears in the flood. When the properly calibrated connection between heaven and earth is severed, being plunges into the chaos of immediacy. Using the familiar imagery of sexuality, tunneling, dangerous penetration, dismemberment, and destruction, the Pemón myth of the flood underscores the inevitable crisis that occurs with the recognition of more than one mode of being (celestial, earthly; male, female; near, far; contained, boundless). The Pemón Indians of Venezuela are descendants of the sun. A long cycle of their myths describes the adventures of the first *makunaima* ("children of the sun").[149] The *makunaima* chop down Wadakayik, the tree of life, which connected heaven and earth and provided nourishment for animals and people. "When the tree falls, a river of water and fish runs from the trunk, flooding the earth."[150] The Pemón make clear that the ax used to fell the tree is a kind of penis. In fact, it "deflowers" the tree trunk–womb, which then gives birth to fish and regenerative waters. The cataclysm marks the beginning of a new epoch.[151] It is important to note that, in the Pemón view, the multiplication of species and the regeneration of life on earth through cosmic waters are obtained at the cost of severing the easy communication that had been enjoyed with celestial life in the earliest times. New life is obtained only by giving up immediate relations with old life-forms and powers. Henceforth, intimate communication between realms of the cosmos will be much more difficult. A more or less violent transition—an antagonistic conflict inherent in the relationship of one mode of being to another—serves as the basis for the reproductive life of multiple epochs and multiple generations.

Often the instrument of mediation between heaven and earth, and, therefore, the medium of salvation from the indistinctness of the flood, is not a tree but a mountain. The Selk'nam of Tierra del Fuego, for example, recount the episode of a cosmic flood that inundated all the earth, covering even the mountains. Those beings who saw the flood coming ran to take refuge in the highest cliffs. During their flight they were transformed into wolves and birds.[152] Rodolfo M. Casamiquela recorded a similar myth of primordial deluge of Pampa (Ranquel) origin from the Río Negro area. At a time when it was always dark, a ceaseless rain fell down from heaven. The first humans and animals took refuge on a mountain. The spatial image of the mountain was not the only mediating form to result from the flood. When the people and animals beseeched the sun to light their way during the long night, the sun sent his wife, the moon. This periodic form of temporal mediation lights up the night and drives evil spirits away from the "corral of the deceased." Although the moon carried fire during the night of the deluge, she was drenched with rain and, consequently, her light remains cold. Eventually, the floodwaters subsided and people dispersed to the pastures of rheas and guanacos.[153]

Religious language can also be a form of mediation, providing a means of sorting out the differences between one mode of being and another. A Mapuche flood story was recorded in 1973 among the Paraje Atreico in south Neuquén, Argentina.[154] The myth describes the time when the "earth turned around and there was much water." The earth became restless and shook every day. The "great people of before" sought out the *machi*, a female shaman-savior who knew the powerful words to stop the waters.

PASSAGES: TICKING, TRANSITION, ORIFICES   The disaster of the universal flood brings to the fore a number of different kinds of passages, through which chaos is escaped by effecting transition from one condition of existence to another. The Guayakí of Paraguay recount that the earth and its inhabitants were destroyed by a cosmic flood of red water. Only one man and one woman escaped by scampering to the top of an old and enormous palm tree. There they wept while the flood waters continued to rise and all life was swept away below them. The palm tree in which they took refuge stood firm. Spanning heaven and earth, it served as the means of ontological passage, which it signified in spatial terms. Eventually the man and woman took some fruit from the tree and dropped the fruit below them. The splashing sounds of falling fruit ticked off the time of destruction. When some mature fruit fell with a thud upon stone, they knew that the waters had subsided. The maturation of the fruit and the noises made when the fruit fell signified in sound the passage from one mode of being to another and from one time to another. The Aché (a subgroup of the Guayakí) who had been swept away in the flood were transformed into animals. These souls of the ancient Aché now live in water in the form of capybaras.[155]

During times of important transition marked by the flow of blood or significant life-bearing fluids, the Aché take special precautions to stave off a repetition of the cosmic flood. For example, when a child is born, a new fire is lit inside the parents' home. Then a young girl takes a flame from this fire and extinguishes it in a bowl of purified water. This prevents a return of the "red water" of the universal flood. Similarly, special precautions are taken during the menstrual period, when women avoid unnecessary and direct contact with water. The same restrictions apply to a murderer *(brupiare)*, who must not come into direct contact with water. If a murderer were to drink by pouring water directly into his mouth from a gourd, his action would precipitate a deluge similar to the one which swept away the first ancestors. In order to drink, the murderer uses a tiny brush called a *koto*.[156] In effect he quenches his thirst through the controlled symbolic act of staining or painting. Kept at a remove from free-flowing liquid by an instrument of art, the murderer is marked by his thirst. In this way he and the world are removed from the flood that his bloodletting threatens to bring on.

Because the flood eradicates entire forms of existence, the imagery of universal deluge carries with it the power to begin a whole new kind of time and to effect passage between different conditions of being. For that reason, many different meanings of the word *passage* cluster around the symbolism of the flood. Included are images of body passages (mouth, eyes, vagina, ears, wounds), passages opened in the earth, passage from one place to another along an axis, the passing away of one form as another appears, and so on. The Yąnomamö provide a case in point. They recognize a succession of primordial ages, but they do not seem interested in presenting these as a systematic theory of epochs. The major primordial time-marker is a cosmic flood, which divides mythic episodes and beings into those that came before the flood and those that came after.[157] Two mythical brothers murdered the jaguar that had devoured their mother. They developed an unquenchable thirst soon after having satisfied their sexual desires with a girl whose vagina subsequently grew teeth. When a third hero attempted intercourse with the woman of the toothy vagina, he lost his penis. At this point, the mythical brothers tunneled a hole in the earth, from which poured forth a cosmic flood of water. The great beings of the first times were drowned in the flood, and, from that day on, things are different in the world.

Since the flood effects the passage it signifies, flood imagery *en miniature* frequently reappears during the transitions from one age to another on both the cosmic and the personal scale. Significant liquids can be tokens of the flood, of change. Thus, for example, the appearance of the first rains to swell the rivers after the dry season signals the beginning of a new annual cycle; the immersion of initiands in water accomplishes the transition to a new stage on their life's way; the flow of semen into the habitable womb generates new life-forms; the flow of menstrual blood and amniotic fluid marks the passage of time from one generation to another. The flow of drink into the thirsty mouth signifies the openness of human life to the liquidated world and the vulnerability of human life, thirsty for changes in mode of being, to liquefaction. David Maybury-Lewis provides summaries of mythic accounts of an Akwẽ-Shavante cosmic flood.[158] These myths are the explicit foundation for the meaning of immersion ceremonies during initiation. As soon as a boy's ears have been pierced, he is considered capable of a productive act of sexual intercourse, for "the cylindrical plugs are said to pierce the lobes of the initiate's ears just as his penis may now pierce a woman."[159] In fact, the creations and transformations that characterize this world first appeared during the time of the cosmic flood. The cause of the flood is not entirely clear. In one variation of the theme, reminiscent of stories in which the passage of time is tapped out with a rhythm stick or falling fruit, a mythic hero, Tpemra, struck the ground and causes water to cover the earth. Tpemra remained in the water with his wives and "created many things." In another variant, the hero S'ribtuwẽ incestuously devoured his mother's vagina. Having destroyed the orifice-instrument of passage, he lived in the undifferentiated waterscape of the flood. Among other things, he created women there and married them. A third mythic testimony to the Akwẽ-Shavante cosmic flood features as instruments of passage the body orifices of the creative hero Prinẽ'a, who lay down on the savannah while hunting jaguars because he felt a terrible thirst. "Water poured out of his nostrils and covered the earth." [160] This permitted his hunting companions to quench their thirst.

INDISCRETION AND INDISCRIMINATENESS   Many flood myths suggest that the openness associated with appetite and need threatens to destroy all discreteness between separate forms. The gaping openness of bodily orifices satisfies many kinds of desire, such as curiosity and the need to speak, as well as hunger, thirst, sex, and excretion. However, that permeability, symbolized by the yawning chasm of passages of every sort, literally runs the risk of inundating experience. Utter openness, symbolized by the unchanneled flood, implies an undifferentiated state of being where the borders between things, between inside and outside, remain unimaginable. For this reason, the ability to maintain closure focuses on bodily openings (ears, eyes, mouth) and depends upon the appearance of primordial distinctions in the imagination: the distinction between what should be listened to (obeyed) and what should not, what should be seen and what should not, what should be said and what should not, what should be eaten and what should not, what should be kept closed and what should not. The criteria of ascetic life, the decrees discriminating moral from criminal existence, and the fundamental features of the cosmos are contiguous with the discerning powers of imagination, just as is the possibility of meaning. All these levels of discernment are subject to dissolution in the flood of indiscriminate openness.

For the Kari'ña of Venezuela, hunger and curiosity played key roles in the flood that destroyed the world and its life-forms. The universe had already been desiccated because of disobedience of the rules pronounced by a *kaputano* (heavenly being) named Tumön'ka (the Pleiades). The flood episode of the Kari'ña cosmogonic narrative tells how the *kaputano* was attempting to bring a comestible fish to earth by carrying it in a gourd full of water taken from heaven. He covered the gourd and instructed human beings not to look at the fish. Eventually the beings on earth, driven by hunger, opened the gourd and attempted to catch the fish. When they tossed the water from the gourd onto the earth, Tumön, the heavenly sea who is the source of all fertile waters, flooded the world. The catastrophe was repeated even after the supernatural being recollected the waters and placed the gourd of waters deep in the earth.[161] No form of enclosure or seclusion proved impermeable.

In the primordial world of absolute and total manifestation, establishing closure presents special difficulties because the useful device of periodic time is not yet present. A reality is either open or closed; one cannot decide to close one or another passage for a while. Any change effects total change, passage to an entirely different state of affairs. The role bodily passages played in the primordium explains why they remain effective instruments of change. Nowhere is this more explicit than in the mythic narratives of the Baniwa. As their mythic hero, Kuai, lies high in the *uacú* tree and becomes "drunk with smoke" from a fire that is roasting his body, which is in the form of *uacú* fruits and *pacú* fish; his body parts and passages open and sing uncontrollably, and his "spit falls like rain from all of the orifices of his body. The spit comes out in a loud, onomatopoeic, watery sound." Kuai descends and "calls rain . . . a Great Rain, Huge Waters!! . . . then he lay his mouth down on the ground: huge!! A HUGE rock cave!" [162] In order to save them from the flood, he swallows into his cave-mouth three of the four children who have been sitting and eating at the base of his tree. He swallows the tree (or the fruit of the tree). Then he regurgitates each of these items into its proper basket, that is, into a container that provides a separate enclosure for each of the discrete subjects and objects of appetite. The three children have been marked by a new kind of openness to periodic time and space, for when they were engulfed in Kuai's monstrous mouth, the *uacú*, the fruit-bearing (i.e., seasonal) tree growing at the center of the earth "made holes in the children's chests." [163]

The deluge portrays the universe as subject to liquefaction, but being seldom appears totally homogeneous even in the state of chaotic change. Something salvageable always stands apart from the flood. In the flood narratives, the theme of separation, isolation, or dissent rises above all others since some place of refuge, a place set apart, usually offers salvation. Vessels of salvation are of two kinds. The first type is a container (a clay pot, a floating gourd or log, a canoe, or a mountain cave) that acts as a vehicle of passage while keeping the flood at bay. The container affords its contents the possibility of future life of a new kind. The second kind of refuge cuts through chaos, penetrating the waters to rise above the flood. The top of the cosmic tree or mountain best typifies the place of transition, which transcends the chaos of the deluge.

Both places of salvation stand for, *pars pro toto*, the entire world that has disappeared. For the first time, a reality that is no longer distinctly visible must be represented. The vehicle of salvation, whether container or pinnacle linking earth to heaven, is the first great symbol. The possibility of life, meaning, and knowledge in this world depends on the existence of the symbol. Standing apart at the center, where life is regenerated, the symbol of salvation and separateness offers its representative character to the new world taking shape around it, a world in which the primordial realities, no longer fully manifest, must be represented symbolically.

The myths of deluge dramatize the tension inherent in symbolic life. In the first place, the recognition of different modes of being implies a crisis, an imaginative separation between kinds of reality. The place where one mode of being yields to another and the time when the manifest world gives way to the unmanifest are chaotic and monstrous. In the second place, the center of symbolic life, having remained or emerged during the flood, never partakes fully of this world but instead possesses some share in the mode of being that has passed away. The ambivalence of religious life is embodied in the tree, mountain, or vessel of refuge, which symbolizes primordial existence even while it centers the new world order. These most sacred images become marks of distinction because, by their very nature, they stand apart from any of the worlds in which they appear and *make a difference*. They are thoroughly negative, wholly other: they exhibit the power to leave behind the primordial world, transcend the chaos of the deluge, and stand apart from mundane existence. They remain distinct, not belonging to any of these worlds. Primordial distinctions in time, space, and meaning appear in the imagination along with the chaos of flood, the event of separation that introduces the first genuine division into the "fabulously indistinguishable" world of the beginnings.

FIRE: FAILED CONTAINMENTS AND THE CONSUMPTION OF SEPARATE FORM

The cosmic conflagration demonstrates the absolute spirituality of matter in the primordial world and shows that being in all its forms is susceptible to total spiritualization. No cozy blaze, the cosmic sea of flames, like all mythic realities, is a full manifestation of a primordial mode of being. Unique and undivided, cataclysmic fire reveals a condition of complete and unbridled consumption, the raging, roaring violence of the ethereal condition of sacred matter, all-consumed and all-consuming. In keeping with the uncompromising paradoxes of chaos, the cosmic fire remains intrinsically formless while taking life and form from what it consumes, thereby introducing the meaning of sustenance. More than any of the consuming and consumable forms to which its presence and extinction subsequently give rise (e.g., separate species of animals, plants, and cultural spectacles), fire *is* what it eats.

Given that cosmic fire is a form of chaos, myths of conflagration bring to light the concerns about openness and closure that are also found in the flood episodes. The failure properly to contain the power manifest in fire opened the primordial world to the possibility of extinction. The Apinayé cosmic conflagration, for example, came about during the adventures of the sun and the moon, who were obtaining brilliant headdresses from a celestial being, a mythical woodpecker. The sun had already received his headdress, which "was like real fire." [164] In keeping with the consumptive character of this "fire", the sun used his flaming headdress only for hunting and only during the day. At night he kept it in a gourd. One night when the sun was away, the moon put the headdress on and danced in the house. He then pleaded with the sun to help him get a fiery headdress of his own. When the woodpecker let fall another headdress, the moon, for fear of the fire, let it drop to the ground. "At once the entire grass of the steppe was aflame." [165] Even the moon came away from the cosmic fire "blackened by the smoke and with his hair singed off." [166] For this reason the moon is dimmed and spotted to this day. "Weeping, he declared he would nevermore take out the headdress without permission." [167] In place of the absolute darkness and absolute brilliance that had contained perfectly one another's full manifestations, there now existed a full range of colors, light tones, and darkened hues.

As an instrument of consumption, the mouth, when properly controlled, can serve as a container of fire.[168] Toba myths describe in several ways a cosmic fire that destroyed the whole earth. The first such cosmic destruction occurred at a time before the creation of any human beings. Eventually, a Toba man emerged from the earth and seized a firebrand. When the earth was threatened with a second cosmic catastrophe through conflagration, a Toba man succeeded in averting destruction by employing magical songs that had been taught him by the good creator deity, Peritnalík.[169] Speech and song, ritual forms of opening and closing the mouth in prescribed order, effectively demonstrate the containment of consumption by fire.

Sound is a symptom of openness and consumption and can be associated with the cosmic fire. Control over sound, either by observing silence or by making deliberate noise, curbs the total appetite of primordial consumption. According to the Cubeo, the cosmic fire took place immediately after the moon "died." The conflagration destroyed the whole forest that existed at that time, leaving nothing standing. Today, when there is an eclipse of the moon, it is said that "Avwa [the moon] is dying." In order to revitalize him and help prevent another universal forest fire, the Cubeo make loud noises, shout, and fire gunshots into the air.[170]

Differences in sound betray degrees of restraint over openness. In addition to music and speech, laughter and flatulence help define the nature and limits of consumptive processes such as appetite, insubordinate speech, humor, and anger. In 1970–1971 the Mataco of the Tachos'nai group reported that the world was once destroyed by fire when the "father of fire," Itaj Asla, "shot fire out of his ass."[171] "Itaj Asla was a very refined man" who countenanced no speech or laughter in his presence. He was always sure that people were laughing at him. Nonetheless, he gathered large crowds of people around him wherever he went because he could drive away wasps from their nests with his smoke and flame by shooting fire out of his ass. In this way he helped people find honey to eat. Once, when Itaj Asla was shooting fire and smoke at a hollow tree trunk, Oven Bird laughed uncontrollably. This angered the prepotent father of fire, who scorched the earth to cinders. Only three beings escaped the conflagration: the trickster hero Tokwaj, the *icanchu* bird, and the *chuña* bird. Ironically, the conflagration sparked by the primordial intolerance of contradiction and contrariety, burned itself out. Whereas this absolute fire roared on to its extinction by leaving nothing other than itself to consume, occasional outbursts of humor and flatus triumphed in the end in the body of the trickster. Tokwaj's exploits, motivated by appetites for food and sex, center on his exorbitant body passages (mouth, anus, eyes, ears) or the appendages with which he penetrates the passages of those whom he meets. His occasional urge to consume or to excrete and his burning lust make for a cycle of humorous adventures wherein he obtains boons for humankind and stimulates reproductive life.

The mouth and anus are not the only orifices associated with consumption. When associated with other bodily openings, the cosmic fire enlarges notions of consumption to clarify the myriad ways in which all forms of being are consumable or already consumed. In particular, the appetite of curiosity, visible in the desire to see and in the power of vision, lets one "take in" separate forms of reality. The myth of the cosmic fire is extremely important among the Mataco, the Eastern and Western Toba, and the Pilagá of the Gran Chaco. In most of the cosmic fire myths of the Toba, people take refuge in the earth when they are forewarned of the fire. Those who fail to heed the warning about the fire and to contain themselves in the earth are consumed and became spirits. When the smoke clears, the survivors emerge in a pre-scribed way (at the proper time, with guarded vision, in a fixed order) through an open hole. Those who fail to observe restrictions on behavior while emerging from the earth are transformed into the various species of wild animals.[172] (For example, to open one's eyes prematurely bears the same consequences as the uncontrolled raging of fire, and so the open-eyed folks are transformed into edible game animals.) Humans are those who maintain control over what they see, what they "take in" through their eyes. Humans emerge with cloths covering their eyes. This symbol of binding establishes separation of form in a couple of ways. First, it hems in human power, preventing it from escaping through the orifices of the eyes. Curiosity and vision are not dissipated. Like all ritual enclosures, the cloth, an article of culture, imposes its nature on the being it contains or envelopes. But, sec-ond, the cloth also screens something out: namely, images, those first and lasting impressions that put their stamp on the inner character of human beings. In a very deliberate manner far removed from the indiscriminate chaos of random or unbridled seeing, the blindfold is taken off so each person's vision first falls on a boy who is like a god. He instructs them how to behave properly. What they see and when they see it are of utmost impor-tance.

Direct openness of one mode of being to another, a characteristic fea-ture of primordial destruction, makes way for passage between them or for change from one state of being to another. In short, the combustibility and comestibility of modes of being create the need and preconditions for new kinds of time. The appearance of multiple modes of time and the passage from one time to another are symptomatic of the appetite for primordial being, the hunger to consume its various modes. The fact that a chaos of consumption ended the primordium guarantees that an ultimate separation of forms is impossible. All that can be hoped for is that new modes of differ-ential time, by staggering their appearances and disappearances, will protect the forms of being from another simultaneous extinction through total con-sumption.

In this connection, each image of openness associated with primal fire, each orifice and passage, releases a new mode of time. For this reason, one frequently encounters a riot of redundancy in full accounts of cosmic incin-eration. In the Makiritare creation cycle, for example, consumption by fire is associated with burning urine excreted through a bodily orifice and spewed out of the mouth of a gourd. The matter does not end there. From the gaping mouth of a medicine pouch oozes forth the magical darkness that, in its turn, had once contained the light of dream-images. Furthermore, the consumption of fire and death are linked to the open, squawking mouth of a bird and to the openness of inquisitive eyes. In the end, death itself, brought on by the cosmic fire, is seen to be a form of excessive openness, for the flesh burns away to expose the bones once contained within it.

The Makiritare recognize a succession of epochs that begin in mythic times and eventually continue into the periods of colonial history. During the earliest epoch there was only continuous light in the sky, the only place which existed. There Wanadi, the creator who had been made by Shi (the invisible sun), remained on high. However, as I have already recounted in the section on "making room and hoisting the sky," Wanadi wanted to send aspects of himself to earth to order the world. The original plan was that dreaming, a form of light, would be the most powerful reality able to overcome the illusion of death. By placing his head inside a dark medicine pouch, the aspect of Wanadi called Nadeiumadi intended to effect the resurrection of his mother by dreaming her back to life. As his mother began to sprout from the ground, a noisy parrot called Nadeiumadi to come running "to see what his new mother looked like." [173] Due to the sudden noise and his overpowering curiosity to see, he forgot to close the pouch containing night. At the instigation of the evil being Odosha, night escaped from the pouch and darkened the Earth. In the meantime, Odosha caused a gourd of his urine to spill on the tender shoot, Nadeiumadi's mother, which was still sprouting from the ground. Odosha's urine was like fire, burning the flesh off the female being's bones. The destruction by the burning urine took on cosmic proportions and left only "darkness, ashes, bones, cinders," silence, and an open medicine pouch. [174] The earth now closed and kept the dead.

AN END TO RAW CONSUMPTION: CONSUMING THE POWER TO CONSUME AND FEEDING THE FIRE The conflagration suggests that the life of the cosmos is deeply associated with food, that, in fact, the cosmos's existence is that of food. In many cases myths portray the earth as a griddle. Relying on information obtained in 1933, Alfred Métraux reported that the Toba universe had once been completely destroyed by a cosmic fire. "At one time in the past it ate the men and animals and consumed the plants right to their roots. Only one couple survived." [175] Since that age of destruction, the cosmic fire has withdrawn to the horizon, where the world ends. There, enormous pots full of food are set to cook over the fire. However, if anyone speaks too loudly about meadows high with thick grass, the cosmic fire is liable to overhear him and devour the universe once again. [176]

The catastrophe of fire "cooks" existence to render primordial reality consumable and to make this world an endless cycle of consumption in which all is food; i.e., subject to a consumptive power that manifests its presence as spirit. [177] The conflagration spiritualized the universe. That is, reality ultimately proved itself to be transcendent, able to sustain life beyond the forms of its primordial appearance. In a sense, universal destruction by fire "creates" the spiritual world by rendering it ethereal and invisible. Because they were totally consumed, the first beings have become spirits. Their transformation or spiritualization is equivalent to a kind of depletion, exhaustion, or consumption. Each being took on a consumable, material form representing its new spiritual condition and fate.[178] In the Pilagá versions of the cosmic conflagration, celestial jaguars (spirits of the dead) were responsible for the fire, for they ignited fire on earth when they set about consuming the moon (causing an eclipse). Pieces of the moon's body fell to the earth and set it ablaze. In vain the first beings tried to save themselves by plunging into the boiling water of lagoons. Only those who stayed among the bulrushes survived. The rest of the decayed corpses were transformed into birds.[179] Through the splintering of the moon and the multiplication of animal species, consumption and spiritualization destroyed the unique world and created replicable life.

Indiscriminate and random consumption—the bad eating habits best typified by the cosmic fire itself—brought on the existence of good food and spiritual sustenance. Destruction by fire is one of the most common themes in Baniwa mythology. A few examples illustrate its importance and pattern. Yaperikuli, the creator-transformer, once destroyed the chaotic beings of the primordial times with fire because these *doimeni*, undifferentiated animal-people of the forest, had been killing and eating people randomly.[180] Likewise, to make the first gardens, the hero Kaali is consumed in a cosmic fire set by his son at Kaali's own instruction. The fire scorched the entire earth. Soon manioc plants began to sprout from Kaali's dead body, which remained rooted in the soil. In a third instance of cosmic destruction through fire, the body of the hero Kuai, son of Yaperikuli, is burned at the center of the earth. In the course of the conflagration, Kuai is burned, but he does not die forever. He is soon reborn into immortal, or everlasting, forms, including the multiple forms of musical flutes and trumpets and of the sounds that generate the distinctions between species of animals and people (linguistic groups). After the fire that destroys his unique body and creates his new, multiple bodies, Kuai lives immortally in a state of permanent ecstasy: "Kuai's spirit lives an immortal existence in the Other World, while Kuai's body is represented in the sacred flute, *Kuai*, which men play today." [181] The theme of cosmic conflagration is also found in the millenarian expectations preached by Baniwa messiahs. At the end of the world, they say, this "world of pain" will be destroyed and purified.[182]

The periodic rhythm of appetite and satiety is a meaningful expression of time as it relates to matter. This rhythm carries with it the idea of change and of the spiritualization of matter. The *materia prima* which was consumed left sustaining signs of its passing. However, if the cosmic fire renders the consumptive consumable, what remains uneaten by the fire may linger as disease, an undevourable devourer. These untransformed prime matters stubbornly resist the ravages of passing time. In 1938, for example, people of the southern Andean community of Kauri (Peru) maintained that, at one time during the first creation, the sun, identified either as Inti Huayna Ccapac or

Jesus Christ, burned to a crisp the original, mountain-dwelling beings of that first world. The primordial beings (including certain species of winds and waters) who survived that catastrophe untransformed (by hiding in *chullpas*, or rock cubicles) have become ambivalent bringers of diseases.[183]

Cosmic fire deals directly with bodies, the instruments and objects of consumption. Conflagration delineates the processes underlying the sculpting of bodies, their ornamentation, spiritualization, replication, affliction with consumptive disease, restoration to health, and ultimate transformation at death. The universal fire incinerated primordial life to produce fleshly species, which are marked with signs of primordial appetite and consumption. Many myths recount how some animals (e.g., red-throated birds) obtained their bright markings when they swallowed bits of the fire and how others received their dark colorations when singed by its heat or blackened by its smoke. External form and inner appetite, the presence of spirit, are contiguous.

The cosmic fire was the total, simultaneous manifestation of all consumptive processes. As an absolute presence, raw consumption destroyed itself at the beginning of time. However, the division of the cosmic fire into partial appearances, such as the colorful body markings of animals, the bodypaint of humans, or the periodic hunger of bodily appetite, renders life replicable. After the universal incineration, the "firing" process appears in multiple and partitioned forms (sun, hearth, burning fields, cooking and eating, kiln, sex, gestation, life cycle, and ceremony); these processes of partial destruction effect transformations over and over again without totally obliterating existence. Once purely appetitive, but now competitive, repetitive, and, in this sense, self-perpetuating, the power of consumption spreads across generations of time and splinters throughout space in a hierarchical manner via the bodies in the food chain, the cycle of prey, the sexual links forming the chain of procreated generations, and the series of social feasts centered on the separate fire of each ranked and replicable unit of consumption. In other words, the cosmic fire is the unique and nongenerative version of all of the appetitive "firing" processes that, now apparent as a spectrum of changes (in time, in form), transform and sustain life.

In a sense, after the cosmic conflagration all creation exists in order to perpetuate the destruction by fire (that is, in order to continue the process of spiritualization), for, ironically, something must be saved from the fire in order to feed the fire in the future and to keep alive the insatiable appetite for other modes of being, which appetite acts as an instrument of transformation into spirit. By destroying the primordial eternity and generating time, the openness (consumability, combustibility, comestibility) of one form of being to another emerges as a solution to the problem of the extinction threatened by the propensity for general consumption that forms the ubiquitous basis of spiritual existence. The passage of time, the existence of multiple ages and generations, allows everything to become consumed, *but not all at once*. After the cosmic fire, being arrives at a compromised state never before imaginable: it can be all-consumed and all-consuming even while it maintains itself as an array of genuinely distinguishable separate forms. In this way, existence retains both time and eternity, having its cake and eating it too.

OCCULTATION OF PRIMORDIAL LIGHT AND LIFE: DARKNESS AND THE ECLIPSE OF IMAGINATION

The flood that liquidates all discrete forms and the fire that consumes them are not the only events responsible for extinguishing the primordial world in the mythologies of South American peoples. Absolute darkness also succeeds in blotting out the first appearance of being. In impenetrable darkness no discernible difference exists between one form of being and another. Invisible reality remains indivisible. Where all meanings and images merge, no relationship or value emerges to rule over others. Anything is possible; absolute creativity, unconstrained by any manifest form, works under cover of mysterious darkness and is capable of anything.

According to the Guayakí, for example, the original state of the world was one of continuous and unbroken sunshine, which warmed the earth. One day a man, walking with his uninitiated son, encountered a supernatural container, the great kettle of Baiö. The father warned his son not to touch it, but, disobeying him, the boy bashed the pottery with his cudgel. From the broken pot poured a flood of ashes, forest birds and animals, and a permanent night. The world remained in darkness.[184] Only when some wax of the *choa* bee was thrown on a fire did the day return, enticed by the pleasant odor of the smoke. Unlike the first world, where the absolute containment of darkness broke down, the new world was ordered in a regular rhythm of daylight and night. From time to time (for example, during eclipses) a blue jaguar threatens the new existence by trying to devour the sun or the moon. Should the celestial beast succeed, human beings would once again be plunged into a state of eternal darkness or, perhaps, eternal light. One of these days the jaguar will triumph. When he does, the world will end.

That the primordial world fell victim to destruction suggests the possibility that the world ends from time to time. Historical circumstances, the actual and lived state of being in the world, can exhibit clear signs of catastrophe. An honest reading of the colonial situation drove many cultures in South America to the conclusion that chaos had returned, bringing with it the close of an entire mode of being. For example, the Andean myths and legends that describe the demise of the Inca Atawallpa are often descriptions of the passing of a cosmic epoch.[185] The decapitated body of the royal Inca is buried deep in the earth (in some versions of the story, all Andean peoples migrate into the underworld to join him). The violent removal of the sacred king from this world to the world below this one carried cosmic consequences: Pachakuti ("world upside down") reigns. The guiding light of this world has descended into the realm of unimaginable, primordial darkness. The sun is dimmed by smoke. Black rainbows yield to eclipses, hailstorms darken the world, and life itself goes into mourning, a state of dormant occultation.[186]

What rainbow is this black rainbow that rises? . . .
[E]verywhere a sinister hailstorm strikes.
The sun, growing pale, leads the night. . . .
[A] river of blood flows forking and forking without end. . . .

They say that the clouds descend bringing with them the night;
that the mother moon grows pale, diminishing in size; and that
everything goes into hiding, suffering.

They tell that the earth refuses her womb to her master,
as if ashamed of wanting his body,
as if fearful of devouring her owner.

And the rocks shake for their lord, singing mournful chants;
the river also roars from pain, swelling,
and intermingling with the tears. . . .[187]

As in the mythic past, however, the utter ruin of the universe brings with
it the chance for new life. The tragic demise of a cosmic epoch raises, at the
same time, the possibility of renovation when this tragic episode of chaos
comes to a close. The same logic at work in the stories in which universal
destruction by flood and fire brings about new forms and conditions of life
applies to the historicized myths of the Inkarrí (from Spanish, *Inca rey*, "Inca
king"). The Inca's head, buried in the darkness of the ground after his deca-
pitation, is growing a body. The darkness signals the presence of the same
mysterious processes of primeval creativity that transformed primordial
being. "When the body is complete, Inkarrí . . . will return to preside over
the final judgement and to restore cosmic order." [188]

STATE OF AFFAIRS BRINGING DESTRUCTION

Rather than dwell on defensible explanations that show the cause of the
universal destruction, myths of primordial catastrophe merely proclaim that
something happened, that change occurred, and that particular modes of
change were once totally manifest at the beginning (that is, that change is
real). Although the myths do not justify the obliteration, one can extract from
them a few characteristics of the state of affairs that led to destructive change.
In light of the subsequent history of the world, one may view this state of
affairs as a set of problems, contradictions, or enigmas that inevitably make
for crisis and for recreation in the form of a new epoch. The difficulties
center on the immediacy of primordial being. The full and direct character of
the first age is the heart of the matter. Omnipresence (fully manifest presence), absoluteness, uniqueness, and infinity prove to be problematic and
ambivalent modes of presence, for they resist change even as their appearance impels it.

THE VORACIOUS SENSE OF SELF AND UNBOUNDED SEX

Ferocity, arrogance, and fighting ruin the mythic epoch. Tukano speakers, as
reported by Marcos Fulop, attribute the destruction of multiple epochs of

creation (through rain, fire, and darkness) to this belligerence. The divinity Yepá Huaké tells the primordial ancestor that "I made this world for you. All peoples will fight with one another for three years, and thus in this way the world will be ended." [189] For their part, the Cubeo contend that the flood was sent to destroy the earth because *abuhuwa*, cannibal monsters of the forest, were killing people. Many of the *abuhuwa* were destroyed; only a few survived by taking refuge on a hill.[190] In yet a different account, the Yąnomamö explain that, after the flood, extremely savage men were born from the blood of the spirit of the moon.[191] These early males were so fierce, especially where the blood of the moon fell thickly on the earth, that they soon exterminated one another. Their destruction, then, came about by virtue of their own intrinsic character; they were so ferocious that they did themselves in. Despite their catastrophic end, however, these nonreplicable beings (they were all male) account for the conditions of being which the world now enjoys. These earliest mythic heroes brought stone axes, fire, and other essential items of culture. In addition, the fierce beings born of the blood of the spirit of the moon still comprise the ideal model for the Yąnomamö warrior.

The Quechua-speaking people of the Andean community of Qotobamba present a different picture of disastrous hubris and warfare responsible for the passing of one era and the beginning of another. The second mythical epoch is inaugurated in reaction to the arrogance or sinfulness of the *ñawpa machu* ("ancient old ones"), who were powerful enough to move rocks through the energy of their own wills. The Era of the *Ñawpa* opens with the creation of the sun by Roal, who, in his annoyance at the *ñawpa*, orders the sun to rise into the sky in order to blind them and to dry them with its heat. The outcome of the punishments sent by Roal is never finally decided, for the *ñawpa* prove to be incorrigible and, in one form or another, impossible to destroy utterly. They take refuge in stone houses that protect them from the punishing rain of fire sent by Roal, also known as God *(Dios)*. In one version the era of fighting ends with the crucifixion of Christ, "who belongs to the lineage of the ñawpa." [192] Some of the *ñawpa* took refuge in springs. Those who survived now appear as *soq'a*, earthbound creatures who appear at sunset or during the new moon and who afflict people with consumptive diseases.

In all cases of this sort indiscriminate fighting, battling without end, devastates the primordium. When unbridled fury, like all primordial conditions, obeys no limits and becomes a totally manifest reality, it is time for a change. By the logic of its own significant appearances, the primordium can no longer endure. By becoming an end in itself, unmitigated hostility puts an end to itself.

A lack of observed limits and a boundless openness of one being to another are also at work in cases where mythic incest (or promiscuity among all species of beings) sets in motion the events of destruction. The Most Ancient Times of the Canelos Quichua, by way of example, apparently ended with a great flood brought on by the tears of the stars, who wept at the discovery of their incestuous conception. The stars are the children of the brother-sister (or brother-daughter) union of the moon and the mythical bird Jilucu. The deluge of the stars' tears all but obliterated the knowledge of the meaning of the universe.

Incest between sacred beings not bound by the rules of human sexuality also figures in the ending of the Waiwai primordium. There was a time, described in Waiwai myth, when the moon lived on the earth and had incestuous relations with his sister. However, because the earth was a place of mortality and death, and because the moon did not wish his children to die, he moved with his sister-wife into the sky.[193] The absence of the moon and of the other primordials who withdrew on high changed the face of the earth.

Since each primordial being reveals its own kind of time, the coupling of mythic beings results in the multiplication of times; that is, primordial incest generates various periodic expressions. In their account of the creation of the world, for instance, the Desana distinguish several stages. At the earliest stage, the details of existence are shrouded in mystery. Although it appears that the moon may have once had a place of greater prominence (for during the primordium, the moon is divested of his privileged feather-crown of primacy by the creator, Sun Father), few details of this earliest stage of existence are provided. Creation began with an emanation of seminal light ("yellow intention") from the invisible and formless Sun. This was the brilliant age before night existed. After the intercourse of the Sun Father with the Daughter of the Sun, during which she was inseminated with his light through her eye, creation went to ruin. The act led to a dramatic tension between the two rival suitors, the sun and the moon, who separated to follow separate courses: the lunar and solar rhythms, each with its reckoning of months and years, punctuated by eclipses, solstices, equinoxes, and disappearances. The divine incest changes not only the forms of the sun and moon but also alters the body of the Daughter of the Sun, who begins to lose blood each month, thus establishing another cosmic rhythm, a female time-line marked by periodic menstruation.

DISOBEDIENCE AND DIN; PEEPING AND INDIVISIBILITY

Tumult and din, as well as disobedience (in the literal sense of faulty listening), bring early creation to a screeching halt. Ungoverned sound bespeaks uncontrolled openness between kinds of realities. On the one hand, since each sound reveals the presence of a distinct mode of being, excessive noise causes one mode of being to impinge on another in a simultaneous medley. Separate kinds of reality no longer remain distinct. No longer static or contained in a single place, being runs riot; medley becomes melee. Furthermore, one kind of being overhears another, a meddling invasion of privacy akin to stealing. In the time leading up to the destruction of the Desana creation, monsters and demons filled the world. They coupled in exorbitant ways and multiplied so that they rampaged wildly through the universe, carting people off from their proper places to the forest, where they were sexually violated by the monsters and left for lost. These acts spawned a glut of lecherous beings who were violent and incestuous. They wantonly penetrated people sexually in the same way that unguarded sound penetrates bodily passages (e.g., ears). Primordial horseflies were typical of this sort of demonic monster. They buzzed around people's heads like bull-roarers. Their incessant noise stung and penetrated people without regard for boundaries.

Further aggravating sonic disorder, these noisy monsters illicitly eavesdropped. "They were always near the malocas, listening to what was said." [194] That is, they overheard and therefore experienced or participated in realities unfolding beyond their assigned habitats. Both forms of boundless sound (unguarded noise and overheard speech) dislocate being and create chaos. As a result of this degeneration, the sun descended to earth and ordered a catastrophic flood, in which all the demons were drowned. Once the flood had subsided, the Sun had the earth consumed by fire. Only the armadillo and a tiny songbird were saved. "Then life returned again." [195] In the new world a solution to these "sound problems" was found in the form of invocations, that is, the controlled, ritually ordered sounds of sacred speech and song. These acts of ordered speech secure the confines of being laid down by the sun. They protect the *maloca* (the communal dwelling) from invasion by demons by casting a net of reticulated and regulated sound around it, a protective shield that reinforces the boundaries of the unique order of creation and the intentions of the creator-legislator.

Unguarded vision and uncontrolled openness associated with the eyes also proved to be a major cause of disaster. In the case of the Canelos Quichua, tears streamed from the weeping eyes of the stars to cause the deluge. Their eyes had been opened by the knowledge of their incestuous origins. In Waiwai mythology, the glance of an adolescent girl in menarche fell on the middle of a river and caused the anaconda-people to rise up and flood the earth.

Furthermore, the question of disastrous sight is complicated by the active, passive, and reciprocal aspects of vision: being seen can be as much a problem as seeing. This is true not only for the marine monsters already mentioned but also for those mythic beings whose destiny is thwarted because the hidden process of their regeneration is interrupted when someone steals a look at them. Such was the case of the dead and buried mother of the Makiritare creator. As she sprouted from the ground in the form a new plant shoot, her eternal son interrupted his re-creative dream of her to gaze upon her directly. The result was catastrophic darkness, flood, fire, and interminable death.

Similar disasters resulted from unrestrained gawking during the primordium of Kayapó mythic tradition. In the earliest days of creation, the Kayapó lived in the sky layer called *kaikwa*, a state of unbroken daylight. At that time, Nhyborway, a being who lived on earth, kept darkness in a gourd. One day Nhyborway's son Joipekrõ visited the daylight land in the sky where the Kayapó lived. He taught the men the way to journey to the house of his father, the keeper of the Gourd of Night. The people wanted darkness in order to sleep and also because night is an important element in ceremonial life. Unfortunately, the men who were given the Gourd of Night did not obey orders. They were told to bring the Gourd of Night back to their own place and were admonished not to look inside it. Instead, they were to let Joipekrõ open the gourd. If he had been allowed to this, night would have been an unambiguously good reality. As it turned out, though, the Kayapó ancestors impatiently opened the gourd before arriving back in their home village. Because of their impatience, night is noxious, invasive, and penetrating. Describing night in a way reminiscent of the Desana horseflies and their sound, the Kayapó say that the darkness of night now "stings." Like the glances, which first stole a look at it, night is uncontrollable; it has spilled out everywhere.[196]

In keeping with its fabulously indistinct character, the primordium, on the eve of destruction, was indivisible. Only the creation of a mediated state, a symbolic world, was able to extract multiplicity from unicity through death and regeneration. Darkness contributed to this indivisibility. In the Peruvian community of Qotobamba, for example, the first epoch is known as an "era of the spirits," a time when only the divinity Roal and others like him existed. The sun did not exist; the earth was poorly lit only by the moon. Roal made the earth, stars, the spirits of the mountains, and the ancient beings called ñawpa machu. This was a time of unbearable contradiction: on the one hand, a number of supernatural beings, each one of a kind, manifested fully their different modes of being; on the other hand, the darkness brought to light no real distinctions between them. Rocks and willful powers illuminated only by the cold light of the moon soon yielded to another episode of time.[197]

Darkness is not the only image of indivisibility. In some mythic worlds, plenipotential beings existed who embodied in one organic whole all the realities that in this world are thought of as distinct. One such being is the Baniwa supernatural Wamūndana, who is perhaps an aspect of the culture hero Kuai, the embodiment of all sounds, musical and linguistic. Wamūndana was a person who had the body of an animal, or, rather, whose body joined together many kinds of animals in one being. "*Wamūndana* lived in the sky as a spirit, but when it descended to the earth and walked with humans, its spiritual existence assumed the bodily shape of the collective animal but person."[198] The body parts of this animal-person corresponded to all the species of animals and their languages as well as to all musical instruments and their sounds. From this compound body also came what are now distinct ritual objects, fruits, and foods. Before Wamūndana's destruction through fire, all these orders of being—consuming bodies and plants, the sounds they produced, the offspring and fruits they generated, and the matter they consumed and excreted—were indistinct, embodied in a simultaneous experience and single expression of appetitive existence.[199]

THE INSIGNIFICANCE OF ABSOLUTE BEINGS

Each picture of primordial reality carries with it a specific image of infinity. Unmediated and boundless, life without limits played the prelude to disaster: eternal light, uncontained darkness, unstinting noise, unclothed vision, unrestricted consumption, ceaseless rain, loose talk, or unbridled sex.[200] Additional negative valences such as omniscience and omnivoyance (experience and sight which knew no bounds) led to a final and damning negative assessment of the primordium: interminable existence proved inadequate in the sense that none of its manifest expressions could equal its infinite reality. Without adequate measure no manifest condition, whether of sex, sound, shape, color, or hue, could be either encompassed or contained. For the intrinsic reason that all these fully manifest forms could not coexist without overrunning, penetrating, or shattering one another, these primordial states of affairs had to come to a close through withdrawal, disappearance, or destruction.

Total destruction is not only teleological, accomplishing a certain goal, but entelechial, inherent in the very nature of first manifest being. Total darkness and total light, for instance, were bound to run into one another sometime.[201] Thoroughgoing consumption had to meet up with absolute consumability somewhere. Each absolute manifestation demanded infinite expression. It could neither yield nor find common ground for coexistence. The infinity of primordial being in multiple modes can only appear at the brink of chaos. The appearance of more than one kind of unbounded being signaled disaster.

Infinity, the absence of limit or the want of an ending, became also the manifest need for termination, if only to demonstrate the everlasting meaning of transcendence. Without new expressions, without true change, transcendent and infinite forms exhausted all their manifest possibilities in their very appearance. De facto, such absolute conditions proved unable to sustain themselves. Life without limits had its limit. Any change in an absolute world required absolute change. Where order existed, imposed by a legislative creator such as the Sun Father of the Desana, it proved intractable. Once the beings of one spatial domain or maloca invaded the space of another through illicit penetration, encroachment, eavesdropping, dislocation, or voracity without dietary restriction, prime order was no longer recuperable without the intervention of the kind of periodic change to which the first world could never accommodate itself.

The state of affairs that ushers in destruction reveals the paradox of the plenipotent primordium: although full of meaning, the precondition and potential for significance, primordial reality in se remains insignificant. The heart of the paradox is that the first, absolute appearance of reality is conditioned only by itself. A primordial reality is all that it appears to be, an exhaustive expression of its own mode of being. It cannot point beyond itself. It cannot signify something else for which it stands as an outward expression, for it is itself; it is the fully manifest form, without limit, of that kind of being. Consequently, there can exist no significant order of sound — only different kinds of sound, which, taken together, become noise. Nor can there be any significant order of sight — only voyeurism and indecent exposure. Nor of body openings — only wanton sex, gluttony, and excretion through all orifices, as well as promiscuity among all species; nor of bodily integrity — only violent dismemberment of primordial bodies or killing, rape, and burning consumption of separate forms. No symbolic conditions exist to regenerate order or to sustain life through change. Ultimately, the nonsymbolic world must end to make room for a universe in which nothing lies beyond symbolic expression. The total destruction of the first world initiates an existence where nothing, not even transcendent reality, remains without significance.

DISASTROUS RESULTS: REPLICABLE DIVISIONS AND GENERATIVE REMARKS

Before drawing general conclusions about the nature of the difference between the worlds separated by cataclysm, this section will provide a close-up view of several aspects of the new age that appears on the heels of disaster.

THE SACRIFICE OF INSIGNIFICANCE DISPELS CHAOS

A sacrificial death often causes the fire to burn itself out or the flood to recede. The dismissal or demise of primordial characters puts an end to destruction, as the beginning of a new age implies the end of the old one. The fate of the jaguar, the aquatic dragon, protohuman ancestors, the primeval bird, the all-being who encompasses every species, or some other mythical being embodies the demise of the first aeon. The cataclysm dispatches these excessively manifest modes of being, whose nature is inherently related to the chaos that does them in. That is why their dispersal or disintegration, in turn, brings an end to the destruction provoked by their unbounded presence. The disappearance of the primordials amounts to the first sacrifice; it creates the possibility of a new, sustainable order and reveals the creative character of destruction. Just as the unique beings lent character to the first epoch, the manner of their extermination sets the stage for the new era. By appearing only from time to time and in transformed guise, their creative presence sustains life.

Burned, transfixed, fractured, crushed, dismembered, frightened to death, left to rot, or turned to stone, primordial beings take on hidden, partial, or periodic form. They reappear in the temporal expressions of lineages, stars, lunar phases, and rainy and dry seasons, of the home fires of each social unit, of the dance lines and body ornaments of new generations, and so on. The piecemeal state of primordial being ends the univocal world and creates the puzzle of multivalent existence and symbolic life. The great divide of flood, fire, or darkness creates the new divisions of replicable time, which are needed to regenerate and sustain life in multiple forms.

The death of a monster from the water domain (anaconda, frog) or the destruction of the primordial jaguar helps gain control over the formlessness of fire, flood, sound, consumption, and wind. In Makiritare accounts, for instance, Huehanna (the heavenly container filled with sounds), fell from Huiio (the rainbow serpent's slain body) and crashed on river rocks.[202] Two eggs from inside the stone-shell were taken by Kawao, the mistress of fire. She generally kept the fire in her stomach, but she would blow it out of her mouth from time to time in order to cook food. This was her great secret, for she would retrieve the fire from under the cooked food with her tongue and restore it to her stomach. Using her hidden fire she hatched the two surviving eggs and they became two boys, the twin heroes Iureke and Shikiemona. The twins grow up to avenge the death of Huiio (their mother) by killing Kawao, the toad, and stealing her fire.[203] They dismembered Kawao and tricked her husband, Manuwa (the jaguar), into eating her. Because they divided fire and hid it in two trees — half in the tree called Wishu and half in Kumnuatte — fire jumps out when the wood from these two trees is rubbed together and reunited.[204]

Manuwa, the Makiritare primordial jaguar, was also done away with, and with him went the vine connecting heaven and earth. Manuwa was tricked into swinging on this enormous vine while breaking wind on a cosmic scale. His flatus propelled him further and further into the sky. "He swung out and back. He liked it. 'New air!' they said to him. 'You're getting new power!' . . . He went way high up. . . . He flew way out, hanging on the vine. Now they raced up the palm tree [from which the vine was suspended]. They cut the vine from above. He just took off and flew. He didn't come back again." [205] Manuwa was catapulted, blown away by the aftereffects of his carnivorous voracity, to the edge of the earth, where he fell and broke all his bones. "He never came back." [206]

Myths in which a primordial jaguar is gotten rid of in order to make way for the present world are among the most common in South America. The model for the transmission of Canelos Quichua female soul-stuff, for instance, is drawn from a myth similar to the widespread story of the boys who kill the supernatural jaguar to avenge abuses heaped on their mother (or even her death). The Canelos Quichua myth tells of a wandering pregnant woman who meets a black jaguar. This ancient jaguar is known as Apayaya ("grandfather, he who transmits female human soul-substance"). He protects the woman from his fellow jaguars, extracts the child (or twins) from the woman, and raises her child as an Apayaya puma. Eventually, this young puma, also called a grandfather jaguar, grows up to kill the ancient jaguar who had captured his mother. The young jaguar-man comes to reign over the animal world.[207] Eventually, the first woman is instructed by Nunghuí, the female spirit of pottery clay and garden soil, to separate the domain of the wild forest from that of cultivated fields of manioc. When jaguar- and cougar-boys protest in favor of maintaining the uniform domain of the jungle, all but one of them are devoured by caimans. In the death of the jaguars are found the origins of lineages and the generation of social structure.

Among the Kamaiurá of the upper Xingu area of the Amazon, the sacrifice of several kinds of primordials ends an all-devouring chaos and instigates the ordered transitions now characteristic of the world. On the one side, the sun and the moon, embodiments of recurrent periodic order, slay the supernatural jaguars who attempted to devour all the first people. On the other side, a young girl dismembers the primordial snake who was swallowing all the first people. These same myths of sacrifice describe the origins of ritual order (e.g., of the ear-piercing ceremony and of the men's house, where body painting and ornamentation are carried on),[208] which effect the transitions of social and individual life cycles.

At times the victim of sacrifice is a protohuman being. "In some versions, the [Tehuelche] flood is stopped by a human sacrifice of the son of one of the surviving couples." [209] A dramatic episode of the Mapuche cataclysmic flood resolves itself in the same way. At one point the Mapuche flood becomes a contest between two supernatural hills that speak their own names, magically affecting the level of the waters. One hill is called Tren-tren ("up-up"); the other is called Kai-kai ("down-down"). [210] When Kai-kai speaks the world becomes increasingly immersed in rising waters. When Tren-tren speaks, a hill grows above the waters. "The *Machi* [shaman] savior penetrated the interior of the hill with the knowledge [of her powerful spirit-words]. For that reason that hill grew, and where Tren-tren was, there was everything." [211] Eventually, at the advice of the *machi*, the heart of an illegitimate boy was touched to the central pillar of the cosmic hill and to the four posts that supported it from within. The sacrifice made the hill grow in such a way that it decidedly outdistanced the rising floodwaters. "[T]his is how the people were saved and the animals and the creatures." [212] Also at the instruction of the *machi*, a rooster was sacrificed to divine that the flood had ended.

Sacrifices of this sort help one to imagine the conquering of chaos and indistinctness. By penetrating bodies, breaking bones, slicing flesh, and lugging the guts from the center to the periphery of the primordial world, sacrificial acts rupture and break up the homogeneity of primordial space. Death through transformation, absence, growth, incineration, disappearance, and massacre cause some places to stand out above others as remarkable for difference and change. The high-water marks of destruction leave indelible signs where being passed from one mode of manifestation to another. These new signs condition the new world of significance, memory, and symbol. The end of the Waiwai flood myth, previously related, is a time of such creative sacrifice, in that the slaying of the anaconda-monster and the birds' action of bathing in its blood marks the transition to the appearance of separate species of true birds. [213] The origin of the Shokewika festival, in which Waiwai marriage alliances are formed, occurs shortly after the separation of humans from animals, that is, after Mawari, the primordial jaguar, leaves the scene and after the murder of the bloody anaconda-monster. [214] In Waiwai mythology there appears to have been a valiant Time of Grandparents, especially grandmothers *(chacha)*, who provide key items of culture and who protect the male and female heroes who establish culture. Many of the staples of human culture come into existence with the death of one or another grandmother. In many instances, the grandmother offers herself for sacrifice or directs the killing of a being whose death results in the advance of culture. Death of "the one," the fully manifest primordial form, is needed in order that the unique being take on many partial forms across many spaces and times. [215]

Some primordial beings meet their deaths through petrification; they are turned to stone when they run from the limitless menace of unbroken light or noise, obliterating flood, limitless voracity, or perverse sex. The nature and destiny of the first era becomes crystallized in the lot of this first community, which scatters during the fearful flight. Spread across the face of the universe, these petrified ancestors or primordial progenitors now stand stony and silent in various marked places of the world, such as the rocks at the center of the earth, the boulders with glyphs that stand at important river rapids, cliffs on the margins of known space, or even the constellations of the starry night. Like a fast-action photo showing the concentric waves produced by a raindrop on water, the current locations of petrified primordials allow one to see lines of force in the helter-skelter and to discern the center from which the now-immobile immortals were fleeing when frozen with fear. The *ñawpa*, supernatural beings of the primordial age of ancient Andean mythology, for example, became motion set in stone. *Huacas*, petrified divine beings who are now holy sites, dot the Andean landscape; the rocks are memorials to the last fully manifest act, the last fleeting moment, of the primordium. For that reason, they forever evoke fear and awe; they are that ultimate experience of primordial being.

In the case of the Inca, the orientation of the separate *huacas*, the direction of their movements, and their precise location within one or another of the four quarters (*suyus*) of the universal empire revealed aspects of the impelling force at the singular center from which they came. The point of their origin, inferred from their relative positions and the myths that described how they arrived at these places, marked a center of time and space, the most important center being the capital city of Cuzco.[216] The fate of this primordial community of *huacas* epitomizes the lot of the first age: what was once unique has suffered division. The pell-mell scattering of the first community generates the ordered divisions of species and the multiple units of carnal and astronomic time which measure off abundant life. Because of their associations with the creative powers of the beginnings, the dispersed sacred sites serve as the regenerative centers of life for various kinds of time (solar, lunar, sidereal), groups of human beings (lineages, language groups, local residence groups, ritual groups, foreigners) and species of animals. By crystallizing the destructive instant, petrification permanently marks the points where one mode of being became another, allowing cultures to discern the orders of geographic space, astral movement, calendric time, animal taxonomy, and social hierarchy. By originating the conditions of intelligibility, the primordial experience of fear, a stony form of sacrifice, is the beginning of wisdom.

The sacrifice of primordial beings accomplishes and conditions the appearance of this world: its colors, shapes, sizes, smells, tastes, sounds, and textures. The end of full manifestation may be violent, as when the loss of the primordium occurs through flood, fire, blood sacrifice, devouring, or rotting, or more subtle. Withdrawal and disappearance are less coarse but equally efficient ways of dispatching sacred beings, especially those supreme beings who dominate the primordial scene with overwhelming thought or blinding light rather than with dramatic action.

In either scenario, the sacred beings who appeared in the first times and who transcended every boundary fall subject to the strictures of space and the passage of time. Primordials retire, in ignominy or majesty, before the coming into existence of the multiple spatiotemporal aeons. Their disappearing act sacrifices (from the Latin *sacer facere,* "to make holy") the absoluteness of their first-order appearance. That is, their dismemberment or retirement makes other forms holy. These sacrificed beings become broken and sacred expressions conditioned by time and space. These relative and partial forms of sacrality, such as festival days or ritual places (dance plaza, shrine, or shaman's bench), render primordial beings present again but in less absolute guise. Primordials no longer appear as they are, boundless in meaning and power. Rather, their appearances in the new world become partial *signs,* which represent a once self-evident but now darkened, inundated, or consumed reality.[217]

The following sections show how the ordered appearances of this world (food chains, cycles of prey, the Milky Way, political offices, sounds of languages) arise from the nature of significant (partial, bounded, multivalent) imagery. The various symbolic orders result from the sacrificial experience and sacrificed expressions of primordial beings who, at the beginning, were total and nonsignificant. The destruction of the primordium is the sacrifice of that lack of signification.

Because reality after the catastrophe no longer discloses itself in full but only in fragmented forms in the imagination, every appearance can be significant of the whole. With every image, the religious imagination testifies to transcendence and significance — to presences and meanings no longer fully manifest. It thereby renders all apparent forms potentially sacred. For this reason, the religious imagination may be said to be a sacrificial mode of existence. As the paradigmatic sacrificial process, the imagination becomes the condition of reality in the new world. Through it meaning and power assume new expression. The new and imaginative forms of experience, knowledge, and order are grasped as expressions of sacrifice, the process that has made them sacred and, therefore, intelligible as the symbolic representations of a primordial meaning that appeared fully at the beginning.

HEAVENLY BODIES AND THE CALENDAR

Universal catastrophe and disaster gave rise to astral life, an order constitutive of the new world. In some cases, the first beings ascended on high to get out of harm's way, as in myths of cataclysmic flood or fire. In other cases the astronomic order emerged as primordial beings were hunted down, exterminated or dismembered. In South American mythic traditions, stars often result from the chasing, maiming, slaying, partial consumption, or division of primordial game. This is not so surprising when one keeps in mind that our word *zodiac* derives from the Greek word *zodiakon,* meaning a collection of small animals. The Inca and other Quechua-speakers, as well as peoples throughout South America, also recognized a "zodiacal" system of celestial animals. The chronicler Antonio de la Calancha, writing of Indian groups of Pacasmayo (Peru), contended that "every star in the sky had a corresponding animal below."[218]

This zodiacal system is, however, more than a taxonomy of mythical beasts. The symbols of mythical animals, supernatural beings of the primordial age, play a primary role in a system of correspondences that includes not only the animals themselves but also the cardinal points and intercardinal axes, the zenith and nadir of the universe, colors, shapes, sounds, weather, plants, and relations among the first beings. The myths of the origins of these symbolic forms reveal their essential relatedness as orders generative of multiple kinds of being. Because different symbolic orders originate in the same mythic events, they can orient the universe into a coherent system, a whole.[219] The order of the stars and the integrity of spatial and temporal life appear as figments of the religious imagination, a mode of being rooted in creation and catastrophe, appearance and disappearance.

Conjoined as different moments of the same event are the disaster caused by excessive openness (unguarded sight, openmouthed eating or singing, open or weepy eyes), the disappearance of primordial supernatural beings, and the rise of the stars in their rhythmic procession. According to an Izozog Tapuí (Tapiete) myth, for instance, a primordial drinking feast was the occasion that prompted the ascent of the stars into the sky, marking the beginning of a new cosmic age. Originally, the stars were the children of the beings who lived on earth. During a drinking bout, one little girl saw her mother drinking *chicha* (maize beer).[220] The angry mother punished her child. In response the girl, her brothers, and their friends "with deep sadness . . . began to sing, taking one another by the waist and forming a long infantile line. While they sang, they insistently looked to the sky, as they quietly and with firm slowness ascended." [221] Transformed into *yasitáta* (the stars), the children, linked as an endless chain of dancers (probably the Milky Way), illumine the dark night sky. "The parents could only cry for the loss of their children" and now look toward the heavens with "bewildered and inconsolable eyes." [222] The event that originates the passage of time and the reckoning of time by the movement of the constellations is an irreversible tragedy of cosmic and human existence.

South American myths consistently link the death of primordials (later known as animals), the cataclysm, and the first ascent of the stars. A Barasana myth, for instance, describes the origin of the star cluster we know as the Pleiades (Opossum) whose first appearance follows on the death of the mythical Opossum. When Opossum dies, the sky darkens and torrential rains fall to flood the world. This first fertile rain is the menstrual blood of the supreme being of the sky, Romi Kumu. The death of some primordials and the fatal catastrophe provoked by other mythical beings creates the year's cycle.[223]

THE DISMEMBERMENT OF TIME: TRYING TO REMEMBER THE PRIMORDIUM   The dismemberment of the primordial water serpent during the flood marks the demise of chaos and provides the fundamental conditions of order. In a Baniwa account of the origin of constellations, the stars ascend into the sky after the great water serpent Iniriferi ("mother of fish") is slain and dismembered by the culture hero Inapirikuli. The water serpent had come onto land and devoured the son of the Pleiades, who, at that time, lived on earth.[224]

Frequently, pieces of the primordial monster or of its swallowed victims (who are then excreted or disgorged in the sky) become various species of animals, or the spattered blood, feces, colors, or body-patterns of this monster become the distinct features of each species. Portions of the single inchoate being who interrupted primordial time to demarcate a new age often become animal constellations, whose appearances and disappearances in the sky divide time into epochs of passage measurable as astral units.

The body parts of primordial monsters or slain primordial game serve as metronomes. They create temporal and spatial units of measure by revealing something of the nature of the light, time, and space they first inhabited. Not only does each animal in the sky manifest its own kind of time, expressed in its breeding, gestation, growth, and molting cycles,[225] but the unique movements of their limbs and body parts, amputated while dancing or running in full stride, mete out forever a variety of qualities of time, each unique. Partial and periodic units of temporal measure (synodical rhythms, lunar phases, Venusian cycles, annual circuits of stars), like the amputated limbs of primordials, are differential aspects of a time that was once an organic whole. That is why these separate rhythms may be coordinated into a megacycle, or calendar. Together they form one cosmos. The universe, however, is never just the sum of its parts, for it now must include the reality of destruction. The whole of reality always transcends the parts since the primordial wholeness, the fullness of time, was lost, maimed, stolen, or destroyed. What remains is a ceaseless recycling of the broken parts, which, taken together, imply a glimpse of the whole, a composite afterimage spread throughout periodic time.

Thanks to the research of Robert Lehmann-Nitsche, Alfred Métraux, and Buenaventura R. D. Teran, Toba mythology offers up many fine examples of star origins. In Napalpí, near Quitilipi in the eastern Chaco, the Eastern Toba groups draw a direct connection between the establishment of the order of heavenly bodies and the universal destructions through flood and fire.[226] In cases of universal conflagration, a number of beings ascend to the sky to save themselves from the fire. The order of their ascent is important, as is the position each assumes in the heavens relative to the others.[227] Characters that at first appear as incidental "extras" in the cosmic drama, prove to be important stars, planets, constellations, and the dark nebulae of the Milky Way. Several versions of the universal-flood story also provide origin myths of the ordered stars of heaven. In addition to the scenarios of chaos (through flood or fire), one other kind of primordial mythic drama is responsible for the position of heavenly bodies. This is the mythic depiction of the primordial hunt that takes place across the face of the cosmos. In the case of some of the Toba accounts, a young hero, who later becomes χ Centauri, with his dog (β Centauri) pursue a rhea into the sky. The head of the rhea becomes the dark nebula near the Southern Cross that is known as the Coalsack; its body and wings become the constellation Ophiuchus; and its leg, stretched out in full flight, becomes the section of the Milky Way that extends downward from the center of *Scorpius*.[228] In some cases, heavenly bodies are the transformed pieces of animals that were hunted, killed, and dismembered or amputated.

Such is the case in the story of two children who were lost on a mountain while searching for honey. They passed the night in the branches of a tree, under which stood a ferocious feline who wished to devour them. It went away when they urinated on its face. These children later burned two old women who possessed fire and who had wanted to keep the young people in servitude, hauling wood for them, forever. Before burning the old women (who later became nameable stars of Ursa Major), the children cut off a breast from each of them. These became a male and female pair of hunting dogs, the ancestors of domesticated hunting dogs. Then these first dogs ascended to the sky to become α and β Centauri.[229] In Toba myths of these three kinds (flood, fire, and first hunt), Lehmann-Nitsche was able to recognize stories of the origins of more than thirty heavenly bodies.[230]

Bodily mutilation, especially through cutting, slicing, and tearing open, will take its meaning from incisive primordial events that fracture or dismember the primordium (whole, total and absolute space, time, light, or darkness) to create new states of being marked by the rhythmic spaces, times, and lights of the new world. For instance, the Kamaiurá account for the origin of the stars in a myth that describes a hunt for and dismemberment of a tapir. The animal is hunted by a number of boys who, after the kill, climb up into the sky with their roasting rack and roasted meat.[231]

The myths of Pie'temü (Orion) and Tumön'ka (Pleiades) among the Kari'ña illustrate how destruction by cutting and slicing is suffered not only by animals but by primordial trees and vines as well. All primordial reality suffers division; all the consumptive, divisive, and destructive aspects of cosmic, social, and individual life come into being at the cataclysm: food, social divisions by sex, language, and labor. At the time described in the myths of the origins of Orion and the Pleiades, primordial beings had no food. The tapir was the only one who knew how to nourish himself on the fruit of Allepántepo, the tree of all foods and fruits. One day the other beings followed him to find out his source of food and then distracted him by asking him to use a sieve to fill a calabash with water. This kept him busy for a long time. In the meantime the other beings cut down the tree of life, from whose trunk there issued a flood of waters. In a slight variation, the beings who discover the tapir at his food-source are the divine twins Pia and Makunaima. They decide to kill him, but, during the chase, one brother inadvertently amputates the leg of his other brother. They eventually rise into the heavens where they assume the forms of Orion and the Pleiades. The tapir, owner of all foods, becomes the Hyades. Here, once again, the events of the flood and the establishment of the food chain are linked to calendrical time, which is marked by the megacycles of the zodiac.[232]

A Makiritare flood story dramatically illustrates many of the connections between universal catastrophe, the death or dismemberment of primordials, the first appearances of heavenly bodies, the origin of replicable divisions, the orders of periodic time and bounded space, and the processes of sustenance. The deluge occurs in connection with the myth of the ascent of the stars, led by Wlaha (the Pleiades). They were forced to ascend on high by Kuamachi, the Evening Star, when he avenged the death of his mother.[233]

Kuamachi and his grandfather enticed Wlaha and the other stars *(shiriche)* to scale *dewaka* trees to gather the ripe fruit. (To this day the rearrangement of the space of the heavens and their stars takes place at a particular time, the time now marked by the ripening of the *dewaka* fruit). "Kuamachi climbed up a tree. He picked a fruit. He dropped it down. When the fruit fell, water came out. It spread. It flooded the forest." [234] With his thought Kuamachi created a canoe in which he and the grandfather escaped. En route, they created the deadly animals of the water domain: anaconda, caiman, piranha, stingray. Among these were the *mawadi*, the terrifying supernatural anacondas who cause floods, overturn canoes, steal women away, and live in river rapids. [235] One by one, Kuamachi shot down the stars of heaven with his bow and arrow. They fell and were devoured by the water animals. The water ran red with their blood. "Caimans, Anacondas, legs, heads, they were all floating and tossing around together." [236] Wlaha, who had not been shot out of his tree, took his seven *damodede* (messenger aspects) from his body,[237] and, calling forth from the water the "gnawed, gored," and "half dead" survivors, ascended into the sky on a ladder of arrows, the seven-runged road to Heaven. One by one the stars, all maimed by Kumachi's arrows, took their proper places and began shining. Ahishama, the brilliant orange troupial (the planet Mars), flew up first, carrying a "long, long vine" [238] to which the seven rungs of the ladder of heaven were attached. [239]

At first they believed they had ascended to heaven, but they soon discovered that, because "they had killed" and "had eaten human flesh," the Scissors Master would not let them pass through the door to the realm of true light, Kahuña (the "sky place"). They live instead in the visible sky of night. "It's not the real one. It's fake. Just like the one we see during the day . . . we can only see the things of this world. The real Sky (Heaven) is invisible. There aren't any stars there, just Wanadi, shining alone." [240] Since the stars share the life of this imitation, this symbolic world (they are consumable, transitory, representative of another reality), they too will die.

The interdependence of all forms of partial and periodic being is a measure of reality. Changes in the appearance of the sky, in animal and human form, in seasons and weather, mutually affect one another, for the reality of all these changes derives from the same mythic events. In his work on Mocobi astronomy, Lehmann-Nitsche refers to an early eighteenth-century report concerning the mythical event of the world's destruction when the sun and the sky fell. The people of that mythical age managed to shore up the sky by placing wooden supports under it. For one reason or another, however, the sky fell once again and the earth was overrun with rivers of fire. Most of the earthly beings who fled the flood of fire were transformed into animals, especially capybaras and caimans. Only two people managed to escape by climbing the highest tree. There they were scorched by a flash of lightning, which turned them into the first monkeys. [241]

ANIMALS IN MULTIPLE, MULTIPLYING SPECIES
Not all of the beings that appear after the flood are heavenly bodies. The animals rising into the sky as stars manifest distinct times, spaces, and de-

grees of light. Their ascent parallels the appearance of separate species on earth at the moment of catastrophe. The biorhythms, ecocycles, habitats, and coloring of distinct animal species also reveal new aspects of time, space, and light. All these outward signs of their distinctness are fragments of the primordium, as are their odors, textures, and sounds. According to the Selk'nam, for instance, animals, stars, lunar periods, and distinct features of the landscape as they are known today came into existence with the demise of primordial life. During the *howenh*, the mythical time of the beginning, all important forces, including stars and primordial shamans, lived on earth. As the mythical disasters unfolded, however, primordials were changed into animals, especially birds, as well as plants, mountains, hills, valleys, lakes, and the rainbow. Death came into existence along with these transformations. So did night. Three primordial male beings, who later became three different kinds of bird, stole a look at the female beings' celebrations. They discovered that the females were not really supernatural entities or spirits but merely women impersonating spirits. Matan, one of the female beings, was attacked while dressed in her ceremonial garb. She became Kom, the black-throated swan, whose markings are similar to the designs that were painted on the body of the primordial being (i.e., Matan). At this moment of confusion and violent chaos the moon was pitched into a fire by her husband. She managed to save herself only by leaping far above the earth forever. She still bears the scars of that catastrophe.[242]

The destruction at the beginning of time — whatever its form — broke up the uniqueness of primordials so that they became the many species of animals, who have multiplied and filled the earth. Animals figure significantly in the development of multiplicity itself: multiple body forms, generations, days, nights, seasons, social units, food groups, and so on. In Shipibo mythology, for example, animals are the mythic beings who help establish the movement of history by stealing fire. Once the primordial fire is stolen (and replicated), the multiplication of nights and days and of the social units associated with fires and the reproduction of food in the form of manioc and plantains commence. In addition, animals embody fire in a multiplicity of ways by assuming the color of fire in their markings. This is especially true for birds, who shelter primordial fire under their wings; even their dark feathers are iridescent, because they embody fire. The colors of nature are associated with the acquisition of fire, the movement of the sun, and the death of Yoashico (the primordial fire), whose blood colors the brilliant wings of birds. The destruction of the unique fire produces "body paint," the stunning plumage of nature.[243]

The introduction of periodic time through destruction, death, and disappearance subjects primordial uniqueness to symbolic guise. Significant distinctions symbolic of primordial space (e.g., bodily shape, habitat, spoor), time (e.g., molting cycles, mating, estrous, and gestation), light (coloring), sound, and smell mark each species of the multiplying forms as unique. Furthermore, a species' typical markings may combine in unique ways to identify each individual of the species. The symbolic features that distinguish one animal species from another often figure in the origins of the generative differences (language, dress, life-style) between human social groups and between the sexes. The origins of both animal mating and human marriage are involved with the primordial destruction, disappearance, and death that created the new situation of periodic existence, spatial dispersal, and the need for regeneration. Recreating uniqueness becomes the work and privilege of bodies, animal and human, through the unique features of symbolic life: gestures, physical features and adornments, languages, and the spatial arrangements that change according to the signs of changing time (time of day, seasons, feasts, menstruation, life cycle). After the Desana cosmic destructions of flood and fire, and after the appearance of men on earth, the first woman, the Daughter of Aracú Fish, emerged from water. The yellow light of the men's fire and the dancing of their feast attracted her to land.[244] She fell in love and copulated with the first Desana man. A number of animals watched this first act of human intercourse, and, as a result, the animal bodies were transformed. The turtle took on the color of a vagina; the curassow, who saw the man's penis, now has a red neck. Later, when the Daughter of Aracú Fish gave birth, other animals watched the parturition and were transformed. These were noxious spiders and insects, who licked the blood of childbirth. All this happened in the age before the invocations of childbirth and the postpartem ritual bathing were known.

Body-related symbols, such as dances, disease symptoms, or the shape-changing that occurs during growth, become configured in distinct and meaningful arrangements at the fall of the primordium. The passage of primordial time, brought on by destruction, gives meaning to all other forms of passage and renders particularly significant the symbolic orders associated with bodily orifices: sound, speech, song, wind instruments, foods, excretions, visual expressions. For instance, the Baniwa conflagration burned the unique body of the supernatural being named Kuai. From the consumed body parts, which hissed, whistled, and hooted as they burned, came the various animal species, which are differentiated by their sounds, as well as the various sacred flutes played now by the separate sibs of the Baniwa people. "There is a progressive differentiation among [animals, people, and spirits] in the course of the story and this would have importance for how we might consider related developments, such as phases of the life-cycle."[245]

The Baniwa myth of Kuai's burning accounts for the generative transitions and passages associated with the life of the body. Among other orders, these include the reproduction of generations through menstruation, birth, growth, initiation and death; the different languages and musics of distinct human groups; the symptoms of illness and its remedies; and the symbolic orders of rituals. The variety of human speech and music originates in the melodic speech patterns of primordial animal-beings (wamūndana). These animals were originally a single collectivity, part of the body of Kuai, who is both all sound and the all-animal; however, just as sounds became fractured, so did the all-animal break apart into separate species, each with its own language. Symptoms, sicknesses, and antidotes came into existence from the substances of Kuai's body (e.g., from the fur of his animal-body image or from the splinters of his paxiuba-palm-tree-body image). Venom poured from his orifices as he smoldered; it now causes diseases. Shamans cure by procuring the spirit of Kuai, the "owner of sicknesses." The carefully controlled symbolic orders of rituals emerge from the paradigmatic events of Kuai's burning.[246]

The meaningful existence of the body appears as primordial reality disappears. It is evident in the significant arrangement of the body's senses and in the fruitful expressions of its orifices. Body passages create the replicable signs (speech, offspring, food, social interaction) that sustain life.[247] Bodily expressions are significant and efficacious markers of differentiation in space and transition through time because they signify the demise but also the transformation of primordial meaning. Nowhere is this sustenance of primordial life more apparent than in the ordered relations of the food chain.

THE FOOD CHAIN AND THE MEANING OF ORDER IN NATURAL HISTORY

The appearance of animals and plants is no more random than the appearance of the stars. Disappearance is part of the constitutive nature of stars because they came into existence as the primordial scene passed from view. Taking advantage of the periodic time to which they are now subject, the stars exploit the death that has been an inherent part of their character from the moment of their origin. They spread their disappearances throughout time. One by one, the stars rise in a linked procession that sustains heavenly life through the orderly arrangement of the disappearances that brought the stars into existence. The demise of each in turn gives way to the life of other lights just as the extinction of the primordium gave birth to them all.

Fleshly bodies also manifest an ordered arrangement of destructions responsible for sustaining earthly life. Kaingáng myths report a chaotic war of the primordial animals, which breaks out at a festival during which there is intense singing, dancing, and drinking. There is a peculiar seating arrangement among the animals attending the feast. Each positions himself next to an animal that he intends to murder. From that time on, relationships in the animal world are those of hunters and prey.[248] Such a scenario also seems to underlie the Yukuna myth that tells of the rise of hunting relations between men and certain animals. In fact, the order of animal bodies (the ways they dance and the shapes of their paws, hoofs, legs, and bodily orifices) dictates the order of those relationships in which they are game and human beings are hunters. Before they leave the primordial scene, the first Yukuna beings — mythical animals — hold a feast. Each species sings in its own language a song whose words indicated the manner in which it can be successfully taken in the hunt. For example, the rat, alluding to the trap now used to capture it, sings, "break the branch, kill my leg."[249] While the various game creatures dance, the culture hero Kawarimi looks up their anuses to take note of their distinctive kinds of stool. He also remarks on the paws and the tracks they make as well as on the distinctive cries made by each animal as it dances. These shrewd observations of the instruments and signs of passage make

game hunting possible. The diluvial rain began to fall. With his clumsy dancing, the tapir shattered the "bells" made of seeds and forced the primordials
to move off to dance elsewhere.[250]

The total demise of primordial being gave way to the serial and staggered
deaths of the food chain and to the cycles of prey, but also to revenge, feud,
war, and ritual sacrifice among human beings. The order that comes into
being after the Kari'ña deluge, for example, is marked not only by the four
winds and their center but also by an ordered food chain that is coextensive
with the organization of the animal kingdom and hunter-prey relationships
and with restrictions surrounding eating and hunting. Likewise, when the
flood recedes there comes into existence an ordered chain of vengeance
relationships associated with the spatial distribution of the different species
of being.[251] Along with these established orders comes sickness, which is the
bodily repercussion of infringements on the order of relations. Food restrictions and hunting restrictions as well as prohibitions of certain relationships
and behaviors are related to the way in which the first spirits, the *tamurü*,
who could assume any form at all before the flood, incorporated themselves
as distinct *wara*, species of distinct sounds, each of which assumes only one
bodily form after the flood. They assume these forms if they are called by their
proper names (sounds). For this reason, proper phonetic order, displayed in
ritual pronunciations of sacred names and in ritual animal calls, is a prerequisite to good hunting.

All forms may still consume one another, as was the case in some scenarios of catastrophe where being was all-consuming and consumable. However, periodic existence scatters that consumption, in a life-sustaining manner, across the passing times of generations and life cycles and across the
differential spaces fashioned by the shapes and locations of animals, plants,
and human beings. For the Wayãpi, for example, the food chain is established
during the time described in myth. This basic relationship of humans to
animals is mirrored in the symbolic order of meaningful sounds, especially
the system of names that human beings acquire throughout their lives. In the
mythic time, when humans, by virtue of the powers of their own self-consciousness, separated from animals, a hierarchy of being and a cycle of
consumption were established according to a set of resemblances such as
sounds and other features (e.g., tracks, leavings) but generally excluding
brute physical form.[252] In a similar way, the food chain of plants was set up
immediately after the flood when a primordial grandmother orchestrated
her own fiery death at the hands of her son-in-law. From her body, which had
previously given off manioc beer in the form of pus from boils, issued all
manner of cultivated plants. The taxonomy of plants reflects the integral
order of her body because separate species sprang from her distinct body
parts. When she offered her own substance to her son-in-law she also instituted another body-based principle of order: the bond of marriage alliance.
In this story we once again see the association of sacrifice, consumption
(especially of festive drink), marriage alliance, and sustained, regenerated
life made present through death.

The taxonomic order of trees, plants, and flowers also emerges from catastrophe. The Mataco offer an example of the way total destruction gives rise to a new and ordered plant realm. After the conflagration but before changing into birds, two Mataco bird-beings, Icanchu and Chuña, traveled ceaselessly in search of their original homeland. However, since the whole universe had been transformed by the fire, they found their place of origin difficult to recognize. It was Tokwaj, the trickster, who instructed them how to find their place of origin by pointing their index fingers straight ahead of them. When their fingers turned downward by themselves, said Tokwaj, they would find themselves pointing to the spot in which they originated. Icanchu and Chuña roamed through the burnt wasteland. In their quest for food they unearthed a piece of charcoal, which Icanchu used as a drum. "He danced and danced all day. On the next day at dawn, he went to look at the charcoal and saw that already a shoot was coming out." [253] The shoot grew larger each day, and it soon provided shade for the wandering pair. Eventually, the piece of charcoal grew into an enormous tree with a different species of tree for each branch. Shamans' helper-spirits travel to this Firstborn Tree (also called *aya ute*, "test tree") when shamans go into hallucinogenic trance.[254] Icanchu threw stones at the tree, breaking off the branches. They crashed to earth, where they gave rise to every known species of tree. When all the limbs had fallen, the *hataj* tree *(Piptadenia macrocarpa beuth)*, the source of hallucinogenic agents, sprouted from the center.[255] Here in one complex are a number of symbolic associations frequently found together: the destructive passing of a cosmic age and the regeneration of a new order of life, beginning with the cosmic tree at the center of the world; the regenerative order of sacred sound; the subsequent serial order of destruction (the breaking of limbs one by one), which sustains life; and the sacrificial character of the new world, centered, in this case, on ordeals and sacrifice. Each appearance of ordered, multiple forms develops out of the destruction of unique forms, including, in turn, the primordium itself, the one tree, and each of its singular branches.[256]

The serial deaths of this world can be set in order and rendered comprehensible by referring them to the total destructions of primordial life reported in myth. When seen as partial and relative reflections of the great disappearance, deaths become symbols of a real and sacred event. By linking everyday death to mythic catastrophe, the language of revenge helps clarify the meaning of death. Retribution for some catastrophic event of the past explains an individual death and justifies further taking of life. Insofar as they remain reflections of the great chaos that gave rise to ordered existence, vengeful and avenged deaths can sustain the life that appeared after the cataclysm and can perhaps even redeem the life destroyed by it.

Makiritare myth depicts vengeance as a way of ordering bodies through the images of destruction, primordial and mundane. At the first Makiritare feast, the heroic twins reconcile their differences, which arose in a squabble over the younger one's wife. They reunite for food and drink, which the younger twin, Iureke, literally "dreams up." [257] In order to paint their bodies for the feast they go to get the gourd of *shimi* (palm oil and pigment) from the house of the water mother, Huiio, at the bottom of the river. They carry the gourd to the earth and spill out its contents. "The rivers overflowed. Now it began to flood all over."[258] Dama (the sea) flooded the land and had no shores and knew no bounds.[259] The twins attribute the deadly return of watery chaos to the punishment due all creation for the slaying of their mother, Huiio, the primordial anaconda-monster. Deaths linked in an endless chain demonstrate that every cause has an effect. However, to make death creative and, ironically, life-giving, the endless chain must become a cycle of punishment and vengeance. Like every other absolute manifestation of the primordium, death must undergo destruction and transformation. The linear series of deaths must be disrupted in order to close the circle and turn death back on itself, lest it remain infinitely destructive. In the case of the Makiritare accounts, most creations bring on a cycle of vengeance. Events involving death produce items of culture (yucca, the *iukuta* festival brew, the blowgun cane, etc.). Later in time these deaths are avenged through others, which also produce conditions of culture.[260] Because all deaths reflect the death of Huiio, mistress of the water domain, and the deluge which avenged her, they find a place in the ordered cycle that constantly regenerates existence in this world. Primordial death, in the transmuted forms of revenge and punishment that subject infinite mortality to the recurrent periodic conditions of this world, therefore forms part of the life-sustaining process.

Once established, the cycle of prey and its analogs can organize the wider universe. Fundamental distinctions and relations are applied on a general scale. The arrangement of space in the Kogi universe, for instance, may be seen as a cycle of prey, for the world's existence is consumptive. "The North is associated with the marsupial and his spouse the armadillo; the South with the puma and his spouse the deer; the East with the jaguar and his spouse the peccary; and the West with the eagle and his spouse the snake." The division of the Kogi macrocosmic egg into these articulated spaces gives rise to a series of abstract concepts, ordered according to a hierarchy of values. These orders are associated with mythical beings, animals, plants, colors, winds, and minerals.[261] "In other words, the ancestral couples form antagonistic pairs in which the 'male' animal (marsupial, puma, jaguar, eagle) feeds on the 'female' animal (armadillo, deer, peccary, snake) and marriage roles prescribe that the members of a certain patriline must marry women whose matriline is associated with an animal that is the natural prey of the man's animal."[262]

In some cases the various taxonomic orders of animals, foods, and elements spring from the same universal catastrophe or set of catastrophes. That is why all significant orders cohere. At base, all symbols potentially point to one another because each reveals an inkling of the first mythic reality, the fabulously indistinguishable world of absolute manifestation. Thekla Hartmann has ably illustrated the interdependence of various Boróro classificatory schemes. Thus, for example, the Boróro distinguish botanical categories from one another by using criteria drawn from animal categories, divisions in the order of space, and the ritual names of humans, weather beings, and supernatural entities. They associate most plant categories with categories of animals. They distinguish plants by using the names that distinguish insects, for example, from four-legged animals, from birds, from reptiles, and from bees and wasps. Alternatively, they separate plant categories according to the animals to which they "belong," or they name plants after distinctive features of animal anatomy or physiology or after the offspring of an animal.[263] In short, the various symbolic divisions of classificatory schemes imply one another. They arise from the deluge, the great divide.[264] Division at one level implies the possibility and existence of division at every other. Paradoxically, the transitivity of these separate symbols (the interdependence of their meanings) implies their permanent relationship within a whole.[265] The primordial world, revealed in myth, offers access to the meaning of the whole and, therefore, to the significance of any one of the fractured or transformed parts that appear after the passing of the first creation.

THE END OF PRIMORDIAL DIN: GENERATIVE PHONETICS AND THE ORDER OF FRACTURED SOUND

After the image of uproarious chaos puts an end to unbridled din, sonic order can appear. It breaks up primordial noise for organized distribution into intelligible sounds. The ceaseless, fully manifest, singing or hubbub of the first world is divided up by means of the images that periodically appear to bring it to an end: stops, silences, interruptions, and restraints in volume, place, and time. In this way speech, sound, and music, like the heavenly and earthly bodies of the new world, become replicable instruments of multiplying and abundant life. The Kamaiurá account for the origin of languages in a myth of primordial sacrifice. The birds of the world wished to kill Avatsiú, a being who was "exceedingly dangerous" and who was constantly singing and dancing. One day Avatsiú was lifted into the air by a number of eagles. They carried him into the sky. He was still singing and shaking his gourd rattle. "I have an enemy with great talons who is going to kill me," sang Avatsiú, in a sense directing his own death.[266] "When the boy and the eagles were very far up, they let go of Avatsiú, and he fell, till he smashed on the ground below."[267] Immediately all the birds of the world were invited to a bloodbath festival to celebrate the being's death. Until then, all species of birds had spoken the same language. Now, however, "with Avatsiú's blood, they were going to make new languages for all of them. The first to get their own language, drawn from the blood of Avatsiú, were the *Iapacaní* and the *Uapaní* eagles. . . . [One by one, each one in carefully marked order] the guests kept coming, taking some of the blood, and using it to produce new languages."[268] Thus equipped with its own form of speech, each species of bird waited for the ordered rhythm of time in the cosmos to come into motion: "[W]hen the day breaks, we will sing, and it will be beautiful." One by one, the bird species divested themselves of their symbolic plumage, giving their feathers to a young boy. They taught him their various languages and dances by singing to him their accounts of this event. Human ceremonial languages and symbolic acts are therefore imitations of the birds' imitation of Avatsiú's eternal but fatal singing. Birds and human beings, however, employ these symbolic languages only occasionally (at the transitional times of dawn, twilight, and festivals), in keeping with the periodic rhythms that maintain the world. Languages are a controlled expression of the chaotic and deadly nature of bodily life.

Sound in this world becomes a pervasive image of separation. Each species of being makes its own separate sound: falling water, squeaking trees, blowing wind, rumbling thunder, chirruping crickets. Animal calls and diverse human languages arise from catastrophe, the deafening noise of the flood, fire, or mayhem that introduced separation into the world by rending an ontological difference between primordial and mundane being. For example, the Juruna myth of the flood opens with an account of a roaring fire that destroyed Sucuri, a large snake who had lived under the earth and who had once dragged all the people into a river, where it noisily gulped them down.[269] "Out of the burned sucuri all kinds of plants [began] to spring up: manioc, potato, yam, corn, pumpkin, pepper, everything was bursting forth from the ashes of the sucuri." [270] In a related mythic episode, the Juruna recount the cosmic flood, in which Sinaá, the culture hero, saved people and plants in his canoe. People became separated from one another, taking refuge in the faraway hills. "At the time of the separation, Sinaá gave each group that was leaving a different language and a piece of string, which he went along cutting and handing out." [271] Sinaá ranked the linguistic groups, arranging them along a river from headwaters to mouth. Sinaá then moved far away downriver. Divisions of all kinds — geographic, linguistic, material — are materially or metonymically related as parts of a single whole.

Because of the authentic divide of cataclysm, imitations of it, signaled in sound, can generate further distinctions. This is why, at every level of significance, language bespeaks division. Not only do the separate orders of animal and human speech arise after the tumultuous demise of pandemonium, but sentences separate into words, words divide into syllables (often ceremonially performed as such), and syllables fragment into phonetic bits of sound, invisible breath partly eaten by the tongue and teeth. Because this fractious existence results from destruction, language consists of signs and symbols.[272] The Kari'ña recognize a link between the division in primordial time and space made by the flood, the multiplicity of kinds of beings, and the orders of separate and bounded sounds apprehensible by humans. It was only after the Kari'ña deluge that human beings descended to the earth.[273] Unfortunately, there were as yet no animals to hunt, no fruits to eat, no fish in the sea. In fact, people did not eat. They did not know how; they lacked understanding because of their unwillingness to "blow" magically and sing. At this point, Tumön'ka (the Pleiades) decided to "blow" and sing. He filled the world with tropical palm trees, animals, and rivers running with fish.[274] Then Tumön'ka told the human beings that they would no longer receive foods prepared by the spirits in heaven but must instead work by ritually singing and by hunting for their sustenance. The supernatural beings who exist in the form of invisible sounds and who escaped the destruction of the flood can assume the visible forms of the many animal species, each of which possesses its own language and wisdom.[275] Each animal form has its own kind of sound-magic. Listening (obedience), the kind of hearing that garners wisdom, is seen as being in a consumptive relationship to sound. By capturing and slaying (i.e., imitating and reproducing) their sound, the Kari'ña can transform the primordials into game animals. This sort of consumptive listening, the beginning of profound knowledge, originates with the deluge. The act that ended the mythic era by forcing primordials to assume new forms is repeated in the Kari'ña father's ritual hunt for a sound (a voice) for his newborn child. Installed in the throat, the instrument of ordered consumption and passage, the voice-sound makes calls to attract supernaturals who now exist in the animal forms of pets and food. That is why the human voice, a fraction of primordial sound, generates wisdom.

The imitative sonic order is expressed not only as speech but also as music, which comes into being with the transition from one kind of world to another. Kalapalo sacred music is inextricably bound up with passage from one mode of being to another, from a unitary (or, today, communal) condition to one of differentiation.[276] For the Kalapalo, the careful ritual orders that emerge from the boundless time *(titehemi)* of the primordial period *(inilano)* are reflected in the primary reality of the order of sound. In fact, music is not seen as an accompaniment to festival action. On the contrary, since sound (of music and myth) is the primary reality, "the movement of tones [is] accompanied by movement of the producers of those tones." [277] Ordered tones produce the ordered conditions of existence. Musical performance merges the performers with the origin of the sonic order that produced them. Kalapalo myths of primordial beings invariably describe them as manifesting in a musical way their power over creative sound.[278]

HUMAN APPEARANCE: "DRESSING TO KILL"

After the flood, the Makiritare creator, Wanadi, decided to make houses and "new people." [279] Wanadi is not the only creator to have made human life appear after universal destruction. For instance, in the Quechua-speaking community of Qotobamba, the Era of Man comes after the universe has endured two earlier destructions. This third age, in which human beings now live, opens with the creation of humankind either by the divinity Roal or by Christ. In one version of this myth,[280] Inkarrí and Qollari are the first man and woman to appear on the depopulated and inactive earth.[281] Although many mythologies point to the existence of some protohumans or primordial ancestors in the time before the disaster, human life as it is known today generally appears as part of a re-creation operation after the cataclysm or after the withdrawal of primordial life. Once its death or disappearance occurs, body forms (the vestiges left over after the death of primordial life) can appear. The traditional chicken-or-egg controversy is here complicated and rearranged. Death becomes a part of the very constitution of bodies that, in some cases, are refashioned or regenerated from residue remaining after primordial destruction (eggs or embryos, muddy slime, ashes, smoke, rot-

ting wood, blood, bones, or flotsam such as gourds). Once death of the sort
that is periodic or recurrent appears, so can things that are mortal, corrupt,
putrifying, or rotting. Their constitutive mortality, the trait that defines them
over against the unchanging supernatural beings of the first time, comes into
existence first. Death defines the nature of their form.[282] Once it exists, so can
mortal nature.

The entry of humans into the postmortem world sets the stage for the
symbolic orders of action and relationship in human communities: speech,
social process, rite, etiquette, history, art, forms of knowledge. What the first
humans look like, the order in which they appear, and the way they behave
become criteria for authentic human existence. Like the stars and animals
after the close of the primordial age, humans are significant beings: they
constantly signify what they mean through their changing symbolic life. To
put this another way, the meaning of human beings can never be exhausted
by any one of their appearances. The only exhaustively meaningful appearances were the full manifestations of absolute beings who have now disappeared or transformed themselves. Consequently, significant human life
must, to one degree or another, be imitative of the supernaturals who preexisted it. In this respect, human life shares the signifying and imitative quality
of the entire new world. Because cosmic process is a symbolic performance,
a creative restyling of primordial being, it is noticeably repetitive, even redundant. That is why symbolic life is regenerative and endlessly creative,
recurring over and over in the forms of astral years, generations of animal
species, meals of consumptive life, and festivals of the calendar. Since the
disappearance of the first beings, all subsequent appearances are partial. The
"mere" appearances of this world, including human lives, participate in
reality only to the degree to which they are symbolic and imitative of sacred
beings and events.

Symbolic life requires separation, the distinction of one quality of being
from another — primordial from mundane, celestial from terrestrial, animal
from human, one species from another, and so on. In their account of the
origins of symbolic life after the deluge, the Waiwai are most interested in the
mythic period during which the various tribes and animal species originate.
That is, they are fascinated by the history of peoples and animals since the
"fall" that divided primordial being and time from history.[283] After the fall
and flood, the ontological division introduced by destruction affected every
sort of reality. Human beings and animals separated into species and tribes;
time itself fractured so that certain species, or qualities, of time came into
being in the form of crop cycles and special festivals, which latter stand apart
from one another as well as from ordinary, nonfestal time. Sacred ornaments
and symbolic items also appeared, set apart from the other implements of
culture that came into existence in this period. The flood was caused by the
glance of an adolescent girl, which aroused the anaconda-people. After the
supernatural flood monsters retired from sight, human beings tried to imitate the "true" decorations of the anaconda-people. The genuine fish eggs
worn by the anaconda-people were imitated with beads. The anaconda-

people's necklaces were made of genuine flatfish, but now an imitation plate had to be used. After the flood, people used feathers to approximate the real ornaments worn by the ancestors who lived at the time of the flood.[284]

It is after destruction that the first humans appear in all their symbolic array. Inca creation myths, for instance, place great emphasis on a postdestruction anthropogony and/or sociogony that is symbolically elaborate enough to allow for highly differentiated social groups and classes.[285] In an example cited by the chronicler Cristóbal de Molina, human beings emerged from the earth immediately after the cosmic flood. Prior to the cataclysm they had taken refuge in a box carried by the wind to the place called Huanaco (Tiahuanaco). There, the creator modeled them in clay and decorated them with paint. "Those that were to wear their hair, with hair; and those that were to be shorn, with hair cut; and to each nation was given the language that was to be spoken, and the songs to be sung, and the seeds and food that they were to sow."[286] The divinity then breathed life into the clay figurines and sent them beneath the earth to the places where he directed them to emerge: caves, mountain springs, trunks of trees, and so forth.[287] Before the flood the ancestors were without the symbolic trappings of differential order. After the flood they made their first appearance on earth bedecked with their new significations.

Everything about the first human beings establishes precedent for the symbolic order through which life endures. The human being is *homo simbolicus*, whose every aspect is a signification, just as is every feature of the new cosmos. Not only are their looks and manner of appearance significant but so also is the order in which humans show up. The Tapirapé, for example, consider themselves to be living in the third epoch of the universe. The first two epochs were destroyed by flood and fire, respectively.[288] After the destruction by fire, beings emerged from different places. For that reason today's society is divided into eating groups, each of which is named after the place (*tantanopao*, "place of the fire") where its mythical ancestors first emerged from the earth. Other social divisions are named after paired classes of birds that survived the flood. These groups formed the bird societies into which the Tapirapé divide themselves for ritual and for competitive teams in collective labor and hunts.[289]

In Baniwa accounts also, humans emerged from holes in the ground, coming from *wapiná-koa* (the "World Below") after Yaperikuli, the transformer-creator, had burned the earth. Standing over the emergence hole (in some versions, blowing tobacco smoke from his cigar into the hole), Yaperikuli passed a finger around the edge of the hole. Then a sib ancestor arose from the hole wearing a sacred flute on his head and chanting the name of his sib.[290]

The appearance of humans, the beings in the world who are both thoroughly mortal and self-consciously symbolic, helps regenerate and sustain the cosmos. Symbolism curbs the excessively manifest and purely self-referential mode of being of the primordium: maintaining ritual custody over one's vision, speech, or knowledge and observing prescribed ritual order check and control openness. The case is made clear in the Toba story of the destruction of the world by fire after the creation. The Toba managed to escape destruction by taking refuge in an enormous pit dug in the earth. They plastered the inside of the enclosure with clay.[291] There they remained without food for three days. A small boy first emerged from the pit to survey the world above. "The boy was like a god and instructed the others how they had to behave."[292] Covering their eyes with cloth lest they be turned into animals, all the Tobas emerged from the pit unharmed. On the scorched earth only one being had remained alive, a small bird called Guessal, who planted different species of tree and fruit. Then the good deity Peritnalík brought down additional human beings (the Christians and the Chiriguano) from heaven, along with foreign food plants such as watermelons, maize, and pumpkins.

HUMAN HISTORY AS A FORM OF SUSTENANCE Yąnomamö human beings, generative and multiple, could only come into existence after the early ages and destructions by flood and fighting had subsided. Women were born from the left leg of the hero Kanaboroma. Men, more timid than the fierce mythical beings made from the flood of moon's blood, were born from Kanaboroma's right leg.[293] As people multiplied and time began to be measured by the passing of human generations, mythic epochs faded, replaced by the rhythms of human history. The beings of the first times became spirits, *yai*.[294] For one group of Yąnomamö, the Waika of the upper Orinoco, the flood made possible the existence of the soul-elements without which there could be no truly human being. For the Waika, the present-day human being consists of post-cataclysmic components that, before the destruction, were part of a single, unified kind of being, which disintegrated into the animals of the food chain, spirits, and human soul ingredients.[295] Only after this disintegration was it possible to begin human history.

Memory, the symbolic repetition or continued repatterning of images from a transcended sacred age, makes for historical existence, the self-aware evaluation that one lives in reflected conditions of time. Human self-awareness and ability to reflect are character traits that derive from the nature of the time in which human beings live: disrupted, symbolic, ordered, periodic, and recurrent. Reflective awareness of one's own existence in time is a suitable definition of history, the human situation. Historical order, like the order of stars and of the food chain and the cycle of prey, is a means of sustenance. Through historical experience even primordial time is able to be recovered in the fragmentary events of communities and individuals. Historical existence, as an ordered life-form, shares the character of the cosmos; the new world is one that recovered itself after the passing away of the genuine article. That recovery act continually renews itself through the symbolic devices of historical reckoning: divisions of labor in subsistence and ritual, divisions of the sociopolitical order, lineages and paths of descent, patterns of residence, and so on.[296] Through history the cosmos sustains itself by undergoing the meanings and order manifest in human significations, the distinguishing marks of human physical and cultural life.

History, the cumulative recovery of experiential knowledge of primordial being, becomes the order of symbolic existence after destruction. According to the Canelos Quichua, for example, after the Age of destruction and the loss of knowledge of the meaning of things, there commences a period that lasts from the beginnings of creation to the present time. This epoch opens with the "creation" of men and women.[297] Ever since the Canelos Quichua Age of the Grandparents, which followed the deluge, the Apamama Grandmother, a mythical being, has maintained her position as the vehicle through which the primordial realities reappear, throughout history, in the symbolisms of human lineages. The transmitted primordial reality is the inherited soul. *Apamama* is the kinship term applied to that woman who gives birth to a man's inherited soul: his father's father's wife. Typical of all realities in the postdestruction age, the soul appears in staggered, sustaining form throughout the generations and across the sexes. If one is a male, one's own *apamama* substance (the ancient grandmother soul-vehicle that one needs in order to have access to other realms) passes through one's own wife, who is preferably a female in the line of his father's father's wife's uterine relatives.[298] A woman of the present time, who inherits a female soul from her mother's mother's husband (*apayaya*, "grandfather"), likewise invokes an exemplary model from the Times of the Grandparents.

Born in disaster, the images of historical time can signify and sustain a tragic mode of existence.[299] The Mashco story of the flood illustrates how myths of catastrophe allow for adaptation to postcolonial change without disrupting the knowledge that life is a symbolic imitation of the sacred. For example, iron tools, a relatively recent introduction to Mashco culture, have their origin in mythical time. During the cosmic flood, human beings saved themselves by scaling Wanamei, the cosmic tree. They descended from the branches of the tree on *wámbo éme* (New Day), the first day of the new age. Standing at the center of the world on that precedent-setting day, each human community declared itself in possession of specific cultural relationships and objects. The Huachipaire and Zapiteri peoples declared that they would receive iron goods from the *amiko* (Europeans and Andeans). The myth accounts for the sacredness of iron implements, the trade through which they are obtained, and the restrictions set on their use.[300] Everyday existence both manifests an order based on its outward expression and reveals a meaning proper to primordial realities no longer fully evident. Every aspect of historical life can be symbolic, for it relates to the beginnings. For the Mashco, not only do iron tools exist as part of the modern order, but their mode of existence, replete with the changes and relations they create in the world, has authentic meaning.

Separate symbolic orders relate to one another through the meanings they signify, for they arise from and point to a single set of events, the withdrawal (consumption, occultation, liquidation, or petrification) of the first supernaturals, the beings whose meaning was fully evident. Primordial destruction promotes the apparent absence of fully manifest beings. Thus, for example, a month after the deluge of Tukano mythology, when the rivers had returned to their normal water level, Yepá Huaké, the creator, returned to the sky.[301]

The end of mythic narrative signals the end (in both senses) of the mythic age and the purpose of myths of extermination. Episodes in the Baniwa myths about the culture hero Kuai, for instance, are punctuated with sounds and closed with narrative indicators that say that the point of separation between animal, person, and spirit is irreversible. Robin M. Wright terms the moments "watershed moments" or "critical separations" marked by "ending" — words such as *pikétem!* ("the last, no more return!") or *kamets' Hapeken!* ("that's truly all!").[302] Myths are self-destructive; they climax with the end of the mythic epoch.

The poignant mythic descriptions of the first end have left their mark on South American folk culture. Such is the case in the region of the Río de la Plata, where the theme of the withdrawal of supernatural beings has made its way from indigenous myths to contemporary Argentine folklore. The last calls of primordial heroes, transformed into squawking or crying birds who ascend on high, linger in the air as contemporary folksongs or festive whoops; their last steps on earth are traced in the patterns of modern dance movements.[303]

Because humans appear after the disappearance of primordial reality, their life is full of the replicable divisions of significant existence. In the mythic pictures of catastrophe, South American religions present motives and meanings for a human existence that is mortal, partial, imitative, symbolic, cyclic, multigenerational, socially divided, linguistically fractured, ritually restricted, and historically lived (i.e., evaluative of its own symbolic existence in periodic time). Myths reveal that the separate forms of multiple human experiences, actions, and knowledge are one in meaning even though, given the damaged circumstances of the cosmos, that meaning cannot be made perfectly clear in any single expression. The condition of meaning mandates change.

CHARACTER OF THE NEW WORLD: THE RELIGIOUS VALUE OF CHANGE

This chapter has presented several scenarios of creation and destruction, of the state of affairs that provokes the demise of the primordium, and of the orders that result from catastrophe. The time has come to assess the nature of the new world. In contrast to the primordial worlds that passed away, the current age is above all one of abutments, junctions, and disjunctions. It is a fractured existence, where transitions of space and time constantly occur.

PARADOX: THE DANGER OF SYMBOLIC VEHICLES IN THE PREPOSITIONAL WORLD

After a comparative study of myths of the cosmic flood, François Berge concludes that the most notable difference between the world that existed before the flood and the contemporary cosmos is that the former is undifferentiated whereas the latter is differentiated.[304] Citing the flood story of the

Ackawoï as a particularly clear example, Berge points out that, before the flood, all vegetal life and all water creatures existed in a single space: the trunk of the world tree. When Sigu, the culture hero and transformer, wanted to separate one form of life from another, he cut down the cosmic tree and flooded the earth. From that day on there existed sharp distinctions between animals, men, and gods, as well as between the realms proper to each.

For Berge, the universal cataclysm is a "breaking into images" as well as an image of destruction. Thenceforth begins the history of separate peoples, species, rivers, and mountains. Humans and divine beings must establish new kinds of relations through the deliberate action of rituals and through the knowledge of symbols. He calls the myth of the deluge "a symbol in action" because it puts into play, into human history and culture, the "symbolic value of all the elements" of creation. For this reason, he considers cosmic disaster, especially the flood, an "essential moment in the history of the cosmos."[305] It wiped out the primordial age of undifferentiated form, which seemed bent on its own destruction, and brought into being the world in which humans now live. It accounts for the absence of primordial form and is responsible for the images that now symbolize the presence of supernaturals.

The prepositional world of transitions from, to, in, over, under, around, and through disjointed spaces and times is filled with danger. Transposition from one state to another, like the catastrophe itself, is a form of death. The new world is death-ridden with paradox.[306] Ceaselessly deciphering their way in order to survive in a symbolic universe, its inhabitants must reckon with the meaning of constant change in the weather and in crop cycles, in the spoor of prey, and in the life of dreams, exercise of memory, performance of myth, and celebration of history, and of the continual fluctuation evident in the quirks of human personality, the infinite generativity of language, the symptoms of sickness, and the appearance of new generations. The difficulty is that, on the one hand, each significance in this world can mean many things and, on the other hand, the meaning of any single sign can be lost in chaos (through inundation, consumption, and so on). The significant actors of this world are caught in the bind of transitions and in the double-bind of ambiguous meanings upon whose interpretation they must act even though, by definition, meaning is no longer fully apparent. As they tentatively, doubtfully, and hypothetically decode the signs of meaning in the symbolic universe, they construct and reconstruct their own semantic ambience in a state of creative puzzlement. These sustaining acts of interpretation are either redundant replications of the first mythic creation or reinitiations of the universe, reenacting the first world's destruction in order to begin this world over again.[307]

Symbolic existence is death-dealing even while it is life-sustaining. To effect transition from one state to another and to understand the connection between realities in a prepositional world (connections such as those between signifiers and what is signified or between the sexes, the generations, or the classificatory categories of kinship) involve the danger and violence of symbolism, the imposition of difference and distance. The age after the flood, for example, is known by the Canelos Quichua as the Age of the Grandparents, but it is important to point out that women and men perceive their history from distinct points of view: Canelos Quichua men refer to this period as the *apayaya rucuguna*, the Times of the Grandfathers, whereas women speak of *apamama rucuguna*, the Times of the Grandmothers.[308] In one myth the Apamama Grandmother is a caiman who comes to rescue two brothers stranded on a great rock in the middle of a mighty river — a situation reminiscent of the great flood. The caiman carries the brothers toward the bank until one of them opens his eyes, falls into the water, and is carried away. This lost brother later reappears in the form of a mushroom, *ala* (a word that can mean "mythic brother," a term that Canelos Quichua males use to address one another).[309] In another version of this myth, the caiman-grandmother is called upon to carry the two brothers across a wide lagoon. Once again, the younger brother opens his eyes before touching shore. The Apamama Grandmother chomps off the young man's right shinbone (the right shinbone is the locus of a person's soul). Eventually, the caiman is killed, the lost soul is retrieved, and the brothers continue to wander. The caiman-grandmother acts as a helpful but dangerous vehicle of transportation, which is achieved at some cost in a transitional world that suddenly requires mobility in order for entities to communicate. In the course of such movement between different domains, the symbolic vehicle itself endangers and devours the soul. This accounts for the soul's periodic disappearance and reappearance over time through a linked network of lineages.

Symbolic existence is often a heroic accomplishment. Before they withdrew and even through the extraordinary acts of their death or disappearance, mythic heroes established the grounds for symbolic existence. Their behavior, bodies, or guises became the symbolic connections effecting the transitions or passages that sustain life. The lives of heroes are reminders that elements of symbolic existence, especially memory (which ties the meanings of the past with the images of the present), are inevitably associated with passage, ordeal, and pain. Wahari, the central figure of Piaroa mythology, is one such culture hero who creates through transformation. Acting on the mythic stage during the creation, a time of immense transition, he himself undergoes several changes, appearing under the forms (i.e., wearing the "masks") of various animals.[310] With the passage of time Wahari recognizes the intense need for memory as a basic condition of human culture and spirit. To aid people's memory, Wahari creates disease-bearing animals, which, when hunted and consumed, cause people to remember the creator of these illnesses. After his death, Wahari's spirit enters into the tapir.[311]

Symbolic existence requires that certain spaces, times, sounds, smells, tastes, and textures exhibit a surfeit of clear meaning, a perceptible complexity, or some such manifestation of extraordinary power marking them as distinct from all others. A couple of fleeting examples can illustrate how time and space in this world are marked by paradox.

MARKING TIME: THE PARADOX OF COMMENCEMENT AT THE END A major paradox of the time in this world is that it begins with an end. Today's universe started with a big bang—the last gas passed by the disappearing jaguar who dominated the first age, or the crunch of his breaking bones—or at least a dull thud heard when the sky fell or a stone or some fruit dropped from on high to mark the close of the primordial age and to tick off the beginning of a new one. Cosmic catastrophe ravaged time, leaving it scarred, tattooed, and scored with the past. As vestiges of the first world, cuts, stains, burns, punctures, high-water marks and other residue found on this world's landscapes and body-forms are not only marks of destruction but also signs of orientation to meaning in the new existence. By bringing an end to the unbounded time of the primordium, these same signs make all time re-markable with the same signs and, therefore, terminable; that is, all periods grow or move toward determined ends. During the heroic adventures of Yukuna mythical times, for example, a number of irreversible events, which marked off the passage of time, occurred. These events were betokened by the fall of ripe fruit, an act equated with death. The fall of each piece of fruit marked the event and made possible the recurrent passage of time symbolically associated with it.[312] Until the great feast when the animals first danced,[313] there was only one tree. Its four branches contained all the different fruits. All red fruits came from one branch; yellow from another; green from another; and black from the fourth branch. But once the fruit fell and the eternal and unique tree was exterminated, growth took place everywhere. The fruit, the sounds of its fall, and the colored stains of death became replicable markers of change throughout the world.

The end of time recurrently marks periodic times of change. Temporal transition is predicated upon termination. Each stage of new growth includes the loss of a prior condition or at least the loss of its signs. For this reason, living in this world implies ordeal. One paraphrased version of the Mapuche flood myth adds this telling detail: "It is very sad when the change of the year comes, it is very sad. It is very painful." [314] Passing from the old year to the new parallels the destruction and recreation of the world as it happened at the beginning of time. Since the destruction of the primordium is the fullest manifestation of ending, its imagery serves to mark all other kinds of transitions. The succession of the ages of the world in Shipibo mythology, for instance, become the model for other kinds of periodicity— wet and dry season, menstruation-receptivity cycles in women, night and day, and so forth.[315]

MARKED SPACE: THE PARADOX OF THE CENTER OUT THERE Cosmic destruction puts an end to the pointlessness of primordial space. The world after catastrophe orients itself toward fixed points in the celestial vault, the horizon, or the terrestrial plane. Henceforth creative wandering is no longer the aimless stroll of the creator nor the epic wandering of heroes and ancestors. Movement in space assumes symbolic value; life becomes a pilgrimage whose direction and pattern can be reckoned in relationship to specific points and ends appearing as fragments in time. Life in space becomes centered—not around a single center but around the multiple symbolic places, purposes, and understandings related to the supernatural events of the past and to the multiple species of being.[316] Each mode of existence in the complicated world has its own center. Moreover, each period of growth is centered on a space befitting that stage of development.

During the cosmic flood, for example, the Yąnomamö mythic beings escaped into the mountains of the interior. Foreigners, babbling in strange tongues, floated away on logs and in canoes to the margins of the world. The mother of the girl with the toothy vagina (who had sex with the mythical twins) became Rahara, the serpentine monster of the watery underworld who devours Yąnomamös who attempt to cross rivers. In short, the world fragmented into foreigners, enemies, spirits of sickness, monsters of the river depths, and so on. All lived in realms centered on their own modes of being. The time of beginnings was lost and gone forever.[317]

The Yąnomamö description of the differential physical universe alludes to a process of historical unfolding that is not drawn in a systematic way. The universe did not always exist in four planes. Now, however, there are two levels of the universe above this layer. In fact, this layer is a fragment from the level above, which, at some unspecified time, broke off to form the present-day earth. At some later time, another fragment of the level above broke away and fell clean through the earth to form the bottom layer of the universe.[318] The Yąnomamö universe now stands as a series of separate places that are related and ordered by the accounts of their origin.

During the course of universal destruction, one place often stands out above all others. Rising above the flood or offering insulation from the fire, a mountain or tree, vessel or trough, rattle or flute, hole or spring, spindle or crystal, plant or vine remains rooted in the primordial world or appears fortuitously in the midst of devastation. This place, representing primordial reality *pars pro toto*, becomes the ambivalent center of a new existence. On the one hand, its shape, texture, smell, color, and sound symbolize the world that was left behind in fire and flood or that withdrew of its own accord. On the other hand, the place of refuge marks the generative origin of a new kind of life.[319] In fact, the center maintains contact with every form of being that has ever appeared and, therefore, offers access to all realms that transcend this world.

For the Kari'ña, the four winds assume their prestigious positions (associated with the four cardinal points) after the deluge. These four helper-spirits, the *tavopoto*, are installed and kept inside the shaman's rattle, which is the center of the earth—the place where the four winds and four directions meet. Ironically, the center is the single locus of the beings marking the outermost margins of the horizon. As the symbol *par excellence* (that which most evidently represents the withdrawn primordial existence), the center is at one and the same time the efficacious mark of convergence of all symbolic realities and also the effective sign of differentiation among all species of being in the new age. From the Kari'ña rattle, held by a human shaman at the center of the world, the four invisible winds take their separate directions; through it they gauge their relationship to one another.[320]

TRANSFORMED PRESENCE OF PRIMORDIAL POWERS

The symbols that dot the spatial landscape with remarkable ambiguity and that riddle the passages of time with memorable paradox represent the transmuted presence of primordial being. Life in this symbolic world is imbued with realities that don't quite fit. These signs disguise primordial existence even as they perpetuate it. According to the Canelos Quichua, for example, the souls that were acquired by ancient peoples have continued to live after their deaths long ago. For that reason primordial knowledge is retrievable, even today, through dreams and through the people of the forest. During the Times of Destruction, the intimacy of being, the direct communication between all things, and the knowledge of the meaning of all things were lost.[321] Today this knowledge may be reacquired, however, and the Ancient Times may be "entered by song, by night dreams, by graphic design, and by ceremony." [322] The eternal souls themselves are contained within the human shinbones, within the clay of pots and in their decorations, within animals, within the sounds of snares on drums, and so on.

Throughout South American cultures primordial being continues to exist in the symbols of this periodic world: flashes of eternal light (dreams, daylight, firelight, brilliant colors, radiance of feathers, hallucinations), fragments of darkness (night; the inside of the body; blotches on animals' coats; drab colors; the dark lines that etch every image, including the individual physiognomy of each person's facial or bodily image), snatches of unlimited sound (songs, instrumental music, language), durable pieces of petrified reality (rock, crystal, hard wood, bone), soft refuse of putrefaction (animal and human skin or flesh, vegetal pulp). Sparks of cosmic fire remain present in the transformative powers of the mouth and in the culinary and consumptive processes that nourish and sustain life (food preparations; colorful ceremonies of song, music, and dance; speech; sex) as well as in cooked and consumable entities. Splinters of unique modes of being, these features of symbolic existence make differentiation possible and thereby effect the generative passage of being from one form to another.

The Baniwa provide an example of the way in which all remarkable forms can symbolize the supernatural powers that disappeared in the catastrophe as well as the events that initiated and accompanied it. Music of the sacred festival flutes *(kuai)* came from the hissing and whistling body of the hero Kuai, who crackled in the cosmic fire. "Thus all Baniwa sibs and phratries who today have ancestral flutes in some sense share in the one single body from which the flutes came." [323] The music of *kuai* was carried across the universe by a parade of female beings led by the primordial serpent, Amaru. The sounds produced the geographic features of the world: headwaters, hills, and rapids, as well as the consumable fruits (plants, animals, fish, people) that come from each distinct ecological niche. Music, then, is the tangible and efficacious sign of separation, the transitive state that constitutes this world's existence. The audible by-product of death through cosmic fire remains in existence in the world as a power that, through the symbolism of its effective sounds, ironically prevents the permanent alienation of separated spaces and times from one another. The primordial sound was broken up only to become reembodied in separate instruments and sounds, which can be brought together again, in an orchestrated, nonchaotic way, as a single ensemble. Musical sound, a vestige of the primordial unity, holds separated things together across time and space.[324] The ensemble re-members Kuai.

Fire itself leaves a vestigial presence of primordial beings. Kuai, while being burned, speaks in musical sounds from within the fire to point out that "You cannot kill me . . . the fire is my body, this fire is Kuai's body." [325] Then he lists some of the elements that compose his body and that become, in this world, everlasting transformations of his fuller mode of being before the fire:

> His body is wood . . . it does not die.
> His body is stone. It does not die.
> His body is the quartz pendant. It does not die.[326]

The list continues by mentioning iron, clubs, guns, and sickness (hiwiathi). Kuai's speech and musical sound become a sickness-giving venom that remains in this world as his presence.[327] All material reality bespeaks the presence of Kuai and his tragic mythic history.

For that matter, chaos itself, also a primordial appearance, is never utterly destroyed, nor does it totally disappear with the dawn of the new age. Rather, it too is parcelled out, destructured so that it appears subject to periodic time. Some form or other of primal chaos can become a definitive part of every image that is bounded and knowable; the chaos that brought an end to absolutely manifest being rings the contours of every comprehensible experience. Rupture, interruption, break, disintegration, penetration, darkness, stone, and light prolong the presence of primeval chaos and the disorder of infinity in the world. These partial images of total chaos inspire a continuing need for creativity and for fresh expressions of the primordial impulse that brought order to the first chaos and that reestablished order after the primordium was destroyed.[328]

Primordial reality proves inextinguishable. Its life has not ended, but rather it has changed. Symbols, the transformed presences of primordial realities, continue to reveal the meanings whose appearances once created, and now order, the universe. The sacrifice of primordial appearance gives rise to the symbols that make life holy, ambiguous, paradoxical, and significant.

HIERARCHIES OF VALUE IN SYMBOLIC CODES: VARIABLE APPROXIMATIONS OF MEANING

Because of the way the primordium was devastated, the fractured qualities of symbolic orders are rarely equal. Not all lights (sun, stars, moon, paint, feathers) are of similar intensity; nor are all appearances of light (lunar phases, days within the year, astral years marked by the risings and settings of constellations) of uniform measure; neither are all sounds of identical volume, pitch, tone, timbre, or duration.

Hierarchies are the orders of inequalities that appear after the destruction of the world. The birth of hierarchies from catastrophe makes plain that, although their fragments may represent primordial realities, the rank orders of symbolic forms arise from violence and tragedy. Spatial, temporal, astronomic, gastronomic, economic, and political orders prolong the tragic circumstances of a postprimordial existence that is scarred by calamity. Because knowledge of mythic meaning is unevenly distributed, it sets the foundation for a hierarchy of religious power.[329] After the Kari'ña flood, for example, ritual (good order and reflection upon it) and respect *(nendo)* protect humans from harm. Although this order of being and respect has visible effects in social behavior, its principles rest on invisible meanings revealed in myth. This prescribed order, together with its effects and premises, is called *o.ma* ("way, path").[330] *O.ma* is used to refer to oral traditions, teachings, customs, wisdom, good conduct, and so forth. It is transmitted and influenced by *emeri* (a word that means both "tradition" and "extended family"). This historical mode of transmission accounts for local variations in the meaning and knowledge of symbolism. Linguistic analysis reveals that *o.ma* is, at root, the way (both in a sense of manner and path) of the original mythic beings, a road opened or revealed by tobacco smoke and saliva, which transform the human beings into a spirit identified with a primordial being through the sonic order of their name. The highest levels of knowledge and the most intense and prolonged experiences of human identification with the way of primordials are reserved only for shamans. For powerful shamans, *o.ma* is a condition of omniscience made available by the practices and techniques that were demonstrated for the first time by the mythic beings who showed human beings "the way." [331]

Several recent structural analyses of myths of the origins of the Inca capital, dynasty, and state underline the importance of the emergence of structural hierarchies after the catastrophes of flood or petrification into stone.[332] Inca myths of origin point time and time again to the ways in which death and destruction put an end to the chaos of the static worlds of darkness, of eternal light, and of perpetual stone. These cataclysms left Inca leadership in charge of the dynamic order of the universe. As Bernard Mishkin writes,

> One Incaic view of creation might be summed up as follows: the Sun created the world but left it in a very imperfect state, and its people in the pit of extreme savagery. The Incas were specially created by the Sun to continue primary creation, and add the touches of perfection, to bring civilization and enlightenment to the world, to contribute the spark of human character to its inhabitants, to give them laws and teach them agriculture.[333]

All hierarchical orders — especially the symbols manifest in water sources, irrigation systems, residences, land, social divisions, crops, herds, wool, and textiles — were organized according to the distance from the center and the altitude of the *huaca*s, that is, of the petrified supernaturals. Inca hierarchies, in force at every level of material and social existence, were also coordinated with the movements of the stars. All these systematic orders of inequalities culminated in Inca hegemony.[334]

Myths of destruction and its aftermath make clear that inequities are real. Hierarchies of inequality reveal meanings that disclose the various and incommensurate religious situations in the world. Originating in the violent and tragic moments when sacred realities passed away, the ranked symbolic forms of knowledge, appearance, status, accumulation, distribution, and action reflect the shattered condition of primordial power. Because of the nature of their origins it becomes difficult for such hierarchies to pose as permanent. On occasion (e.g., succession of leadership, the onset of a new year, the military takeover of power or territory, the initiation of a new generation) the community must return to a state of chaos in order to renew the images in the hierarchy. Remaining latent in such periodic events is the hope that the return to chaos can undo the postdeluvian (or postconflagratory) history that accounts for the prestige of existing hierarchies of privilege. The occasional return to chaos offers the possibility that hierarchies of the status quo can be obliterated in favor of a totally new order.

ENDING THE BEGINNING

Symbolic existence is the consequence of the violence and negativity that affect all creation. The crimes perpetrated by and against sacred beings in the beginning offer grounds for discrimination and discretion and criteria for order and judgement. The extinction of dragons or monsters who dominated the primordium produces tinctures of color from their blood, fur, and feces. The marks become the symbolic distinctions between species of animals, social groups, and ceremonies. The awesome and devastating events of the first world provide every reason for apprehension, in all senses of the word. The catastrophes that sliced, scribed, dismembered, riddled, and divided primordial life into the replicable forms of appearance, experience, and knowledge provide the model for the contemporary sciences (forms of cutting, of knowing, of remembering). The scorching and scoring of the primordial earth gives meaning in today's world to scarified flesh and slashed land, which produce in manifest ways the creative conditions they signify (e.g., knowledge, fruitfulness).

The myths of creation followed by the disappearance or total disruption of the first world present fundamental cultural outlooks that are vividly critical of the *status quo entis*. The crumbling or occultation of the first kind of being permits South American cultures not only to face change with courage but to welcome and instigate it as a part of their religious responsibility for continued creation. Renovation and innovation become the principal forms of creativity sustaining cosmic existence. The images of primordial crisis equip South American peoples not only for critical thought, but for

critical existence, that is, for symbolic life. Chaos impresses on the symbolism of South American cultures the marks of destruction and withdrawal
that are integral to the process of sustenance. The world is essentially a
violent state, a condition of protracted or serial catastrophe. While this conviction often underlies uneventful transitions of power or seasons, and while
it more rarely leads to unprecedented and even revolutionary change, it
usually clarifies the meaning of suffering existence, of undergoing change.

By gathering together a number of issues regarding creation, destruction, and multiple ages of the world I have not argued that all cosmogonic
and cataclysmic myths resolve these matters in the same way.[335] The nature
of being, its epiphanic condition, the questionable nature of eternal or fully
manifest being, the character of first appearances and of sublime and transcendent being, the inevitability of crisis, the absence or relatively unmanifest presence of supernaturals, and the symbolic nature of critical existence
are concerns pressed to varying degrees and in different directions by South
American mythologies. Each culture faces these fundamental issues of the
religious imagination with unexpected and unpredictable creativity. I have
tried only to scrape out a place in which to stand and from which to begin
looking over the rich variety of approaches to these issues. For that reason
this beginning must remain tentative and open-ended; any apparent absoluteness of description or interpretation tends to open itself to question as time
goes on. Most of all, the lesson of the beginning is that one must expect these
first appearances and first impressions to subject themselves to criticism as
time goes by, for crisis and change are built into the very nature of symbols,
the multivalent and fragmentary signs that point to a beginning that can no
longer be fully manifest in the episodic structure of this world (or this book).
This book is not only full of images and symbols originating in South America
but, as a written corpus, it represents a powerful and symbolic mode of being
in both literate and nonliterate cultures. A book becomes a world unto itself,
where meanings appear for the first time in specific guises and relations. If it
hopes to be a genuinely critical work of interpretation, science, or fiction,
the meanings of the world from which it arises and the universe of meanings
it creates must undergo change before coming to an end, a conclusion.

The following chapters divide up, dismember, or analyze the images
which have already made their appearance in the beginning: space, time,
human being, death, and termination. Chapter by chapter these issues, dismantled and rearranged in more precise and ordered expression, reappear
in a series of periodic returns to the mythic origins portrayed in South
American myths and to the interpretive language used in beginning this
book.

PART TWO

COSMOLOGY

CHAPTER 3

SPACE

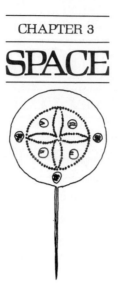

THE DIFFERENT QUALITIES OF SPACE AND THE SEPARATENESS OF SPACES

Every form of existence takes place in a space appropriate to its nature. Whether a being is eternal, invisible, or mortal, it is coinvolved with its own space in such a way that the two realities reveal one another's character. The space of the universe is not vague and undefined but structured and knowable. Not every space in the universe is the same. Each culture identifies several kinds of space, all of which have come into existence since the demise of the primordium or since the withdrawal of the full manifestation of primordial beings. The cosmos's differentiated spaces are not, however, abstractions detached from their inhabitants. Different qualities of space render viable a variety of specific life-forms. Heavenly realms, earthly worlds, watery depths, mountain heights, darkened forests, fruited gardens, and even human bones map religious geography, which is not an objective geometry but rather an imaginal territory as essential to existence as are the beings located in it. The structures of the participatory universe are essential and vital; its different places form a modal set of existences, the multiplicative fruits of the cataclysm that destroyed indistinctness and of the sacrifice that conquered chaos by marking off the homogeneity of primordial space.[1] Before choosing several kinds of spaces for special consideration, I shall in the following paragraphs survey the landscape of mythic geography by describing the variety of spaces recognized in several cultural systems.

The universe may consist of a differing number of significant levels.[2] For example, the Pemón conceive of the universe as having three different levels. Good and evil may exist on any of these strata.[3] The Tapirapé, according to Herbert Baldus, acknowledge the existence of four levels in the cosmos: a

112

highest level, "near the wild banana plants," is known only to shamans; below that lies the level called the "sieve" (Urupema); still lower is the earth, where the Tapirapé live; and, finally, there is an underworld.[4] The Waiwai cosmos exists in five different planes.[5] Each level has a *terra firma* and forests as well as an opening that provides access to the other tiers. Each layer contains a different mode of being.[6]

The Warao also acknowledge five important levels in the cosmos: the flat dish of the earth's surface; the cardinal and intercardinal mountains on the horizon of the world; "the imaginary belt mid-high around the bell-shaped cosmic vault; the center of the world at its highest point, bell-shaped rather than rounded like a dome; and, finally, the underworld below earth and ocean."[7] Each cosmic zone is inhabited by different kinds of supernatural beings.[8]

The Yukuna universe contains a still larger number of spatial structures. The earth is a flat circle with a bottomless hole in its center. The seven levels of heaven above the earth are peopled with mythic heroes and spirits of the dead. In the underworld live spirits of living beings. The underworld is an exact temporal opposite of this world; its midnight is earth's high noon, and vice versa.[9] The entire universe is bounded by a universal stream, which bears the boats of the sun and the moon.

There are nine different levels of being in the Kógi world system. They extend from the zenith to the nadir of the cosmos. The Kógi universe is shaped like a spindle and is centered on an all-important vertical axis. The central circular plane of the universe is the earth of human beings. Its orientation in space is "defined by the intercardinal directions of solstice sunrises and sunsets and link the horizon to the primary world axis."[10]

The participatory universe is an imaginative existence. In each spatial dimension life is imagined; that is, a set of perceptions constitutes the mode of being in each realm. For instance, for the Campa of the eastern Montaña of central Peru, the universe consists of a series of strata. The inhabitants of each level experience their world as possessing firm ground *(kipáci)* underfoot and a wide sky *(henóki)* up above. However, the solid qualities of the earth and the fluid qualities of the sky are perceptions. What appears to human beings to be the sky is solid ground for those beings who live in an upper realm. Similarly, the earth of human beings is seen as infinite sky by those in the levels below the earth.[11] The Campa insight is a profound one, for it indicates that symbolic knowledge participates in creating the cosmos. Religious imagination is the symbolic basis for spatial existence.

Cosmic planes are not the only significant spatial features of the universe. Within each layer or between levels are structures that have special shapes and important functions. For the Chiripá, for example, earth is now separated from the level of heaven. The two realms are connected by an eternal palm tree, which sprang up when the universal flood destroyed the earth.[12] This *axis mundi*, a symbolic feature connecting (and, at the same time, separating) heaven and earth, is a widely recognized feature of the religious landscape.[13] The fragility of communication between cosmic realms is often symbolized by the difficulty of maintaining the *axis mundi* intact. For instance, in ancient times the world-tree of the Shipibo was cut down, and the waters in its trunk flooded the world.[14] This myth and its widespread parallels are not merely quaint accounts. They deal with the profound spiritual challenge at the center of human existence, a challenge posed by the religious imagination, which risks undoing itself and under-mining its integrity through the richness of its own possibilities. The very symbolism which provides access to transcendent realms of meaning func-tions to separate worlds and epochs. Maintaining unity among all imagina-tive existences requires constant attention to the full range of symbolic life.[15] Wholeness demands the spiritual exercise of the process of metamorphosis, the redemption of meanings alienated in the symbolic process of fabrication. Diverse spatial realms and geographic features comprise one universe be-cause, no matter what the differences among them, they are all symbolic realities; that is, they are significant because they reveal the meanings of specific sacred beings and actions. Since no single symbolic expression can exhaustively reveal its own meaning, symbolic life generates different strings of meanings. Even within a single culture, perceptions of space shift as the meaning of the sacred, over the course of time, changes aspect.

As in all mythic geographies, every place described in the Desana cosmos is an essential place, and each contains its own kind of being. Every aspect of cosmic space has a meaning.[16] Not all spatial images are distinct shapes: color, for instance, may be a dominant way of symbolizing the mean-ing of separate spaces in the world. For the Desana, the three levels of the universe are color-coded according to how intensely the sun's energy is present and manifest at each level. In other instances smells, sounds, degrees of temperature, and humidity are markers that indicate differential qualities of space. This is because different kinds of life are possible in, and are condi-tioned by the meanings of, different kinds of space.

When viewed in the light of the comparative study of cultures, no aspects of space are unimportant. In addition to the entire universe and the gross units of its spatial domains, the Canelos Quichua recognize several other important kinds of spaces, especially rocks, the family house, pots, and the bones and cavities of the human body. The house and the human body are microcosmic spaces; they integrate all the forces of the Canelos Quichua universe and generate new relationships and meanings.

Every point in mythic geography is essential, and the involvement of life and understanding with the specific imagery of spatial systems explains their durability in the face of competing or oppressive alternatives. Cultures cling tenaciously to the fundamental spatial schemes by which they traditionally have understood their existence and history. For example, after a study of communities in southern Peru, Juan Víctor Núñez del Prado B. concludes that the space of the supernatural world is ordered by the same principles and symbolic fixtures that ordered the Inca empire. "The surprising thing is not, however, that the supernatural world has changed, but rather that it has not disappeared entirely, considering that the culture under investigation has coexisted for 400 years with another that has constantly tried to eliminate native beliefs and replaced them with its own." [17] Religious borrowings from Christianity are seldom received in a passive way; rather, they are reworked, reshaped, and reinterpreted creatively when brought into the local systems of belief.[18] The adaptability and tenacity of imaginative frameworks that organize multiple qualities of space point to their importance in the survival and continued creativity of culture.[19]

The multiplicity of world-planes and of qualities of space indicates the richness of manifest being. It demonstrates that known existence cannot be rendered by any single image. More important than that, this multiplicity proves that space itself is, in its essence, a manifestation of the meaning of existence in whatever form.[20] Furthermore, the variety of perceptible spaces shows that human awareness, enriched by the imagination, can encounter multiple kinds of beings on its own terms. The following sections provide a brief overview of several spaces: heavens, underworlds, peripheral realms, and this world.

HEAVENLY SPACE: REMNANT OF THE AGE OF UNIQUE BEING

The upper world is a one-of-a-kind world. As is the case for each of the cosmic tiers, no other time and space has precisely the same qualities. In the case of the heavenly world, however, this exclusivity is a symptom of the fact that it is *in se* an existence of uniquenesses. From the time of the primordium forward, the beings whose existences unfold in the heavenly realm are unreplicable, one-of-a-kind beings. In retrospect, the exclusive and unreplicable quality of heavenly beings can be expressed in the temporal terms of the contemporary epoch: the primordial beings who inhabit the heavenly realm were the *first* of their kind. Because it is conceived as one and indivisible, the existential form of any of these beings is, at any moment, the full manifestation of its complete essence: there is no need for growth or change through time for the full contents of its being to be revealed. For this reason, in contrast to this world, the upperworld most nearly transcends imaginable qualities; it is indivisible, unique (without analogy), infinite, unbounded, omniscient, omnipowerful, eternal, omnipresent, and so on. To gain a clear grasp of these meanings, it may be necessary to be transported beyond this world to the spatial and temporal conditions of the heavenly realm. By situating one within the utterly different conditions of the heavenly world, rapture and ecstasy render apprehensible in image the realities of the upperworld. Heaven bespeaks transcendence and reveals its specific cultural meaning. The upper realm is the quality of existence that prevailed when being was manifest in only one kind of place and time. Heaven is a remnant of the unique age, the unique world — the one world of oneness. It is a principle of identity, a nonsymbolic reality where what appears in existential form is identical to what is in being. In South America, two images of uniqueness and indivisibility frequently recur in descriptions of the upper world: light and liquid.

HEAVENLY LIGHT

Celestial light encompasses both the brightness of the sky and the lightness of weight manifest in the immateriality of substantial light. Not weighted down in the way that incarnate beings are, the disembodied brilliance of the sky reveals the meaning of the heavenly heights. The ability of birds to soar like heavenly beings is frequently attributed to the radiance of their feathers. Unlike hair, which burdens land-bound beings with weight, feathers' brilliant colors and iridescent light lighten the bodies of birds. The rustling noises of wings, like human ritual songs, are audible imitations of the sound-forms of heavenly beings.[21] The principal manifestations of these heavenly sound-forms are the visions of light that appear in dreams and hallucinations. Because feathers are expressions of the sound and substance of light, they buoy up the bodies of birds.

Many of these themes are brought together in the Waiwai description of upper realms. Above the level of the earth inhabited by human beings exist three heavenly layers collectively termed *kapu* ("sky") by the Waiwai. The first of these heavenly levels is the domain of the *maraki-yenna* (hawk-people). It is to this happy place of light that the eye-souls of the dead repair after death (and after having become disembodied by having their material substance devoured by ants). Only the eye-soul's power to perceive light remains as the defining quality of human existence after death.

The next heavenly level of the Waiwai universe is the dwelling place of *kakenau-kworokjam* (disembodied sky-spirits who were once animals on earth). This is the realm of the shaman's helper-spirits. These spirits can be dangerous to the uninitiated. When one of them is called down to help a shaman, "there is always the risk that other *kakenau-kworokjam* will slip through the hole in the layer at the same time."[22] The sun and the moon, although not helper-spirits, are *kakenau-kworokjam* who move between these first two heavenly layers.

The highest heavenly plane is inhabited by *kurum-yenna* (buzzard-people). These beings look like ordinary Waiwai. One Waiwai man told the ethnologist Niels Fock that there may indeed be more distant levels of heaven, but he did not yet know of them. Prototypes of every animal and plant on earth have a parallel somewhere in the heavenly layers. These prototypes once lived on "earth" before any other realms existed and the universe was one place.

The Desana use colors to distinguish the qualities of heavenly light. The uppermost stratum of the Desana cosmos is the locus of the visible sun itself (the invisible Creator Sun has withdrawn from the cosmos to live elsewhere). This solar region possesses three gradients of color in descending order, beginning with the outermost: white, yellow, and orange.

The sky was once very close to the earth. Only later did these layers separate from one another.[23] The separateness of heavenly space in today's universe betrays the fact that its primordial condition was disturbed by an event, the appearance of change, that set the plane of eternal being apart from the transitory conditions of this world. The substantial form which celestial beings enjoyed became detached from their essence, and since that time their immateriality has been described in negative language: something is missing. Symbolic form is now distinguishable from the significant reality to which it points. The inaccessibility of the heavenly plane reveals the fact that "something" happened.

Accounts of the separation of sky from earth provide a number of reasons for the division. Whether depicted as abandonment, withdrawal, or absence, the very concept of separation is what is revealed by the sky realm in comparison to all other planes. That is, the idea of separate times, natures, beings, histories, and spaces is first revealed in the separateness of the sky. The corollary of this truth is that "firstness" and uniqueness are inherently related to the meaning of absence and separation. For instance, the Yạnomamö universe exists in four strata. The highest stratum, Duku Kä Misi (the "tender" level) is devoid of being even though many things originated there before descending to other strata.[24] This upper level is now referred to as an old and infertile woman or an abandoned garden.[25]

There seems to be an intimate connection between the fully manifest quality of the heavenly world, its unreplicability, and its lack of transitivity, which is described in terms of the exhaustion of its function once the creative era closed. Once unreplicable being reveals itself, the show is over. Although the meaning of its appearance may be inexhaustible, the form of its appearance can only be repeated without change. Instead of new generation of multiple forms, the celestial realm offers reappearance and eternal return. Descriptions of the eternal and unchanging space of heaven become difficult to distinguish from the stasis of boredom. Although it includes all possibilities, in the light of the realization of history the space of heaven discloses otiosity, abandonment, and void. The celestial world is an alien existence of alienated realities whose exhaustive nature, like that of the null set or zero-concept, makes possible the generative systems of this multiplicative world. The realm of total, invisible, and indivisible light gives rise to the possibility of colorful, brilliant, radiant, and visible forms.

HEAVENLY LIQUID

Along with light, heavenly fluids frequently manifest the indivisible life-conditions of celestial space. Unmarked by notable change, their ceaseless flow manifests eternal life: perpetual renewal without the perceptible decline that characterizes true change. The word used by the Campa to designate the sky is inkíte; inkíte consists of an indeterminant number of heavenly levels with no specific names.[26] All the various levels of inkíte are inhabited by henokinírì (sky dwellers). Hananeríte, the river of eternal youth, flows through the sky. Although it remains invisible to mortals on earth, many good spirits rejuvenate themselves by bathing in its waters.[27] The Campa do not identify the river of eternal youth with the Milky Way, as do their neighbors, the Machiguengas, who call the heavenly river of eternal youth *Meshiaréni* (the "river where one's skin is changed"). The name of this celestial river derives from the word *mešiá*, a tree which loses its bark and grows a new "skin" *(omé-šina).*[28] The Machiguenga believe that good spirits shed their skins and regain their youth when they bathe in the river. For the Campa, the river of eternal youth remains invisible.

Above the Machiguenga earth (inhabited by mortal beings) there exists a "region of the clouds," which only Machiguenga shamans can see. This region is drained by a tributary of the Milky Way and is inhabited by a species of demonic beings. Above the level of the clouds lies the sky, *inkíte*, which is crossed by Meshiaréni, the Milky Way. This river flows from the sky to a point at the end of the earth, where all rivers terminate and where it merges with the earth in a landslide. When shamans are entranced, they see the place where the rivers end, from which point a trail begins to ascend to the sky.[29]

In heaven, water or some other liquid is often geographically central. Instances of rivers running through the center of celestial planes have already been provided. For the Makiritare, Lake Akuena, a placid lake of unchanging water, lies at the center of heaven. Beings immerse themselves there to become rejuvenated.[30]

Participation in the life of the heavenly world frequently requires immersion in the life-giving waters of heaven. Bathing in springs of heavenly liquid renews the bather because the waters obliterate all trace of change (e.g., aged skin, memory, or affinal relationships). The wanderings of Tukano ancestors were a ceaseless search for the waters of immortality.[31] Their pilgrimage peopled the entire earth. When they found the spring of life, circumstances prevented their bathing in it. For this reason, earth is separate from the heavenly realm of the divinity Yepa Huaké.

For some South American cultures, to cross through the celestial river or to bathe in the central lake of heaven changes one's existence; immersion in heavenly fluid is an initiation, which, like all acculturations, alters the conditions governing the meaning of one's senses. For the Quechua of Qotobamba, for example, immersion in life-giving waters is required to gain full participation in the life of heavenly space. The universe exists in three cosmic realms. The upper world, called Hanaqpacha, can be reached only after life. It is peopled by God, Christ, the Virgin Mary, and those of the dead who have been washed in the waters of Baptism. Around its periphery is Limpu (Limbo), the place where unbaptized children's souls reside. Also on the periphery of Hanaqpacha are zones where animal spirits go after death.[32] The Quechua disposition of heavenly space reflects the fact that initiated humans are the beings whose life-condition and ultimate destiny are shaped by the manipulation of water. Such control is evident in the symbolism of ritual washings, in irrigation technology, in ritual beverages, and in cooking. Through the symbolic manipulations of ritual and technology, human knowledge affords control over items that originate in and that define the nature of heavenly space. Like the possession of celestial fire and heavenly plants, the human ability to manage life-giving waters stems from the symbolic foundations of human knowledge. Such knowledge, based on the meaning of sacred symbolism, sets human beings apart from animals in the zoning of residential space in heaven.

The liquid in the center of heavenly space exhibits the constancy and eternal fullness of celestial life. When from time to time these fluids seep through the boundaries between cosmic layers and appear in this world, their radically different nature threatens to inundate the structured, periodic order of this world. The fullness of the heavenly tier would flood the earth in chaos by submerging the markers of space and time, the symbolic structures that channel the fluids of this world, and the meaning of such spatiotemporal symbols would disappear below the level perceptible by human awareness. The life in heavenly space is therefore not readily comprehensible to the consciousness accustomed to the structures of life in this world.

Nonetheless, the celestial fluids that do trickle down from the upper-world make new life possible. Several examples illustrate the creative ways in which cultures make this statement. Yąnomamö men, for instance, tie up their penises in such a way as to catch drops of rain in their foreskins. The rain flows from the lake of blood located in the center of the moon; it enables men to procreate children. The Desana offer a second example: in the upper region of their universe is the Milky Way, an enormous river of semen. This important celestial structure circulates throughout the biosphere, comprising a zone where earthly beings may communicate with supernatural beings. In sexual terms, this exchange parallels the fertilization of all things, since life depends on contact with the supernaturals.[33] The Waiwai furnish a further example. In their spatial arrangement of the universe, heaven is a large rock in the form of a cassava pan set on three upright stones. Rain falls through holes in the pan to renew life on earth.[34] To cite a final instance, in the Andean community of Misminay, near Cuzco, the Milky Way is also viewed as a seminal river that flows through the center of the sky at the proper time in order to bring on the rainy season. Within the river of semen are specks of earth, dark-cloud constellations that are believed to be bits of female being. These are the mothers of the various species of animals on earth. During the rainy season, the androgynous river fertilizes the earth and renews each species of creature.[35]

The eternal and indivisible life of liquid located in the space of heaven expresses itself as fertility when subject to the conditions of earthly space. Celestial seminal fluid and heavenly blood, when channeled into symbolic space, not only become the fertile flow of rain, rivers, semen, and menstrual blood but they also produce the spatial configurations of domestic units grouped in residences, lineages paraded in ritual, crops planted in gardens, and fermented brews contained in drinking vessels.

From the examples of light and liquid it is clear that the spatial structures of the heavenly plane house unique modes of being. When subject to change they generate not only the material abundance of crops and animal species but also the fertility of the human imagination. In ritual, art, and technology, human beings experiment with the uniqueness and indivisibility of sacred light and liquid. In the separate space of this world-plane, where multiple forms thrive, human consciousness creatively contrasts the reproductive processes of divisible units of cosmic space and social organization with the nonreplicable and indivisible ones of heaven. Such comparative evaluation of the relationship among heterogeneous kinds of space amounts also to a self-consciousness that promises the total transformation of the human condition itself through exposure to celestial light and immersion in heavenly waters. The re-creation of human being effects either a transportation of human life to the heavenly plane[36] or a renewal of the face of the earth on the model of celestial space.

In either case, the acquisition of the state of being that is found in heavenly space is tantamount to obtaining salvation. In accordance with the prestige given heavenly liquid and light, the salvific state can be glimpsed during the "death" of drunken visions or the "blindness" brought on by brightness. According to the Makiritare, all of existence was originally just one single place called *Kahu* ("sky"), which was filled with infinite light. It was there that the invisible Sun (Shi) created the creator, Wanadi, by blowing on quartz crystals, the substantial and powerful images of eternal wisdom and light. Heavenly beings drink a celestial liquid (*kaahi,* related to the word *kahu,* "heaven") out of the stonelike egg of the tinamou (*huenna*). *Kaahi,* a hallucinogenic drink, is prepared from a vine that grows on the banks of Lake Akuena located in the center of heaven. It was Wanadi's intention to build "good houses" in which to place good people. The creator sent unborn people to earth in Huehanna, a stone-egg likened to the *huenna,* the container of heavenly liquid. The first attempts to do this were futile. Darkness and death filled the space of earth, which was ruled by a being named Odosha, who had been born of the rotting placenta of one of the aspects of Wanadi who had previously been sent to earth. In some accounts, Huehanna was shattered to bits, each fragment becoming a species associated with the water domain. The true sky retreated on high, to a place now out of sight.[37] Today only *huhai,* shamans, drink *kaahi* in order to travel to the invisible world of heaven.

SKIN AND AMBIVALENCE

In closing this consideration of the upperworld, it is worth calling attention to two features of the sky: its association with skin and the ambivalent nature of the life it contains. Heaven is the place of changing skin. This is not an accident. Skin is the container of space. It conforms to any shape and has no inherent form of its own. Radiant skin betrays the character of the being contained by it. The seamlessness of the sky's skin is identical to the unique and infinite mode of being it contains. Where once the sky lay close to the earth, the withdrawal of the constant life of heaven, symbolized by the aloofness of its skin container, heightens the contrast between invisible and visible reality. The loss of the sky's skin, or its withdrawal from full manifestation into invisibility, establishes the meaning of clothing, the richly ornamented spatial life of other cosmic planes. Visible but sloughable clothing, when understood in contrast to the sky, becomes an important statement of the symbolic nature of space and life, the condition which veils all finite containers of being in guises, disguises, markings, and boundaries. A remnant of the first age, the seamless skin in the sky is forever young. Its constancy, once removed on high, becomes the basis for the meaning of renewal. For the Barasana, the sky itself is skin that periodically renews itself during the rainy season. The renewal of cosmic life is a by-product of the renewed skin, the shining face or gleaming womb, of the sky.

The spatial imagery of the upperworld expresses the meaning of ambivalence. The quality of being in heaven is imagined as quantity or duration in the terms of this world's space. Unreplicable spatial features reveal a constancy that is grasped as regeneration. Changeless life is described as ceaseless renewal. Uniqueness is seen as plenty or superfluity. Fullness of life is described in ways that make it difficult to distinguish from stasis. The omnipresence at the beginning of time of what is now the upper plane is intrinsically related to its nearly total withdrawal from other kinds of space in the contemporary cosmos. The fully manifest character of heavenly space during the primordium accounts for its invisibility today. These ambivalences are expressions of the nature of the upper realm. One achieves knowledge and experience of the upper realm by passing through and beyond the condition of paradox and opposition.

UNDERWORLDS

The presence of liquid often characterizes the underworld as well. But the waters of the underworld are not the same life-giving waters that determine the nature of the upper world. For example, a river of death runs throughout Gabáironi (or Gamáironi), the lowest level of the Machiguenga world. Gabáironi, a dismal realm of dead bodies, was created by the evil being Kientibákari. The next level above, Kamabiría, also has a river, a tributary of the great river of eternal youth, running through it.[38]

In the Campa cosmos, two additional levels of space, Kivínti and Šarinkavéni, lie below the earth. Kivínti is the home of good spirits who visit other regions of the world. In contrast to the Machiguenga, the Campa make no mention of a channeled river flowing through this lower plane. Instead, the river that flows through the center of the earth-plane eventually falls into Kivínti at Ocitiríko, a point at the easternmost edge of the world. Below Kivínti is Šarinkavéni, the lowest level, where Koriošpíri, the lord of demons, lives.[39]

In the underworld, life (as it is known on earth) ebbs away or drowns. If the waters of the upperworld disclose the sense of abundance, those of the underworld reveal the significance of "inundance." The withdrawal of the upperworld gives rise to the myriad forms of symbolic life; the underworld is populated by forms weighed down by reified meanings and by appetites.[40] Exhausted and no longer capable of absorbing the world around it, the human body is drawn down, never to rise again. As the waters of the underworld flow, they take life with them.[41] This explains why submersion in pools, springs, whirlpools, and rivers provides access to the underworld. The process by which one travels there is akin to drowning. For instance, in order to descend into the Canelos Quichua underworld, one must first transcend the watery domain of Sungui. His domain is entered via a whirlpool *(cutana)*. Once having entered the water-world, one may continue along an underground river to reach the domain called Ucupachama, an underworld inhabited by tiny people and animals. These beings are powerful shamans who test the sincerity of human beings by questioning them.[42] Similarly, access to the Shipibo underworld is gained by passing through deep pools of water. One may also enter the Shipibo underworld by entering caves and penetrating mountains.[43]

In contrast to the lightness required for life in the upperworld, access to the underworld demands weight. The lower world is constituted by the appetites responsible for weight gain. The sheer bulk of its own accumulating weight often accounts for the underworld's position in the cosmos. For example, the Yąnomamö underworld was once a part of Hedu, the level above the earth. In ancient times (but after the earthly portion had fallen from Hedu), a fragment of Hedu fell clean through the earth and came to form Hei Tä Bebi, where live cannibalistic demons left over from primordial times. They send spirits onto the earth to kidnap elements of children's souls, which they devour.[44]

Participation in the life of the underworld calls for the heaviness that drags one into the watery deep and prevents one from rising to the surface. With its ponderous bulk, the underworld anchors the universe by creating a sense of gravity. For example, under the earth and the ocean of the Warao cosmos is a rectangular underworld, the home of Hahuba, the serpent-goddess of the nadir. This threatening monster "looks like a wide-open fish mouth that devours navigators." She pulls them down into the waters of the sea. Hahuba also seeks to devour women heavy with their first child.[45]

In contrast to the world of heaven, the underworld is clearly a place of weighted bodies. Thus Hahuba, the Warao monster, keeps watch over animals' bodies.[46] Likewise, the third and lowest zone of the Desana universe is Ahpikondiá, the cosmic uterus from which all embodied and carnal life comes. It was from here that the invisible Sun, the creator father, came at the beginning of the world; and it was to this place that he returned after finishing his creation. Male human beings also emerged from this place and traveled to earth in a snake-canoe. The emphasis on carnal life of the body in the underworld lends itself to sexual depictions of that space. The root meaning of *Ahpikondiá* involves symbolisms from the physiology of sexual reproduction.[47] Reichel-Dolmatoff translates *Ahpikon-diá* as "river of milk," referring to maternal milk. This lower zone of the cosmos, the uterine paradise, has a tripartite structure. The emphatically feminine river of milk *(Ahpikon-diá)* is counterbalanced, complemented, and fertilized by the "land of milk" *(Ahpikon-yéba)*. Both of these structures are enveloped within the "house of milk" *(Ahpikon-vi'i)*, which is imaged as a placenta. "It is there the souls of the dead go, returning again to the maternal womb and the uterine paradise."[48] This lowest plane of the universe is said to be a place of hunger. The entire lower zone of the universe is the green color of coca, whose consumption dulls the pangs of hunger.

The proclivity of the underworld for sucking weight down into it and for centering itself on the gravity of the body is brought out by a tale from Wayãpi mythology. The Wayãpi say that knowledge of the world below was acquired when two men went out to hunt birds. They had positioned themselves in a tree when a *woo*, a sluggish and dangerous giant who lives in the underworld, appeared and cast a glance at one of them; the victim's head immediately rolled to the ground. The *woo* then carried the headless body into the under-world. The dead man's comrade, surreptitiously following the *woo*, was sucked head first through the passage that traverses the distance from this world to the next. The consciousness of beings in the lower world is body-centered. This is reflected in the way they perceive reality. In his adventure in the Wayãpi underworld, the man in the Wayãpi story learned that the creatures there classify humans only by their animallike bodies and regard human beings as kinkajous. He also acquired an instrument that allowed him to decapitate *woo* merely by pointing it at them.

The ranking of upper to lower worlds is often iconically represented in the kinds of body-forms characteristic of the distinct levels. The scheme of the world planes may amount to an animal taxonomy. For the Waiwai, for example, the upper units of the cosmos are associated with the bodies of specific birds, bearers of light in their feathers. Below the Waiwai earth is the level of the *taritari-yenna* (the cicada-people).[49]

Several general points can be made in closing this brief treatment of a few South American underworlds. The underworld houses the nadir of the universe, a point toward which human life, despite considerable resistance, is drawn. It may be the *terminus a quo*, the outermost limit of human perception, even if it is not the *terminus ad quem* sought by human beings. If the upperworld highlighted the meaning of ambivalence, the lower world manifests the significance of ambiguity. One is led there by the sheer force of the underworld's gravity.

The ambiguous pull of the underworld is related to another of its characteristics: life there is often the reverse of life on earth. Such is the case, for example, in the Canelos underworld described above. Furthermore, the reverse life of the underworld is serially related to existence on earth. For instance, according to the residents of the Andean community of Qoto-bamba, the tiny people and animals that inhabit Ukhupacha, the lower level of the Quechua cosmos, live an existence that mirrors that of people on earth. Ukhupacha is the least known of the three spatial worlds. Its inhabitants, notwithstanding their small size, cause harmful earthquakes and electrical storms. Ukhupacha is also the dwelling place of Supay, the Devil.[50] Night falls there just as dawn arrives for the human inhabitants of Kaypacha, the earth. The underworld is the reverse of this world in such a way that the two planes complement each other in a kind of hostile, or fearful, symmetry. The incomplete existence of the one implies the incomplete existence of the other. The serial relationship between the levels turns cyclic: one begins where the other leaves off, and the other brings to an end what the one begins. In this relationship of hungry symmetry, each world devours and undoes the other even while it complements and completes it. This relational quality has enabled Claude Lévi-Strauss brilliantly to analyze the "science of the concrete," that is, the repetitive formal relations embedded deep in the structure of myth as well as the serial presentation of these formal relations in mythic narratives. After the passing of the unique primordial world, and despite replication, reversibility, inversibility, and all the other formal relations between images, different cosmic levels can never quite mirror one another perfectly. The mirror image is marred by time. The spatial and temporal constraints of mythic narrative, to which the meaning of images must frequently be harnessed, testify to the imperfection of space in time. Narrative is a temporal condition constraining the meaning of primordial realities and subjecting them to the serial condition (the story line) of life in this world. Only the unreplicable forms of the upperworld were totally self-referential, and they were so only at the time when the celestial space was the only space. Now forms crave completion, and their dissatisfaction with incompleteness —the ambiguity inherent in all formal relations—inspires the incessant need for a denouement that can never come.

It is impossible to "live" in both worlds at the same time. They are temporally and spatially exclusive, and they exist together within the same experience only in an ambiguous and negative way.[51] Entry into the underworld demands a kind of death to life in the other realms. It is significant that the earth, the middle world of human life, separates the upperworld from the lower. Human existence (imaginative, cognitive, embodied, regulated, and so on) separates one construction of cosmic life from another. Therefore human life situates itself ambiguously. In the very act of separating categories and modes of being, the human religious imagination constructs a cosmos and, in coming to know something of the "others," constitutes its own specific difference, the human quiddity, which is drawn to them all.

THIS LAYER, THE EARTH

Human life always occupies the space at the center of the universe. For example, the Shipibo earth is situated in the middle of the cosmos. Above and below the earth are several other strata.[52] The space of human life is a flat disk across which rivers run. The celestial vault is curved over the flat earth.[53] (It is not entirely clear whether the earth is quadrangular, modeled on the Southern Cross, or whether the midpoints of heaven and earth are connected by a stairway.[54]) Similarly, at the center of the universe as described by the Quechua people of Qotobamba is the cosmic region called *Kaypacha* ("this world"). It is like a ball floating in space. Here one finds the divinity Roal, the earth in its fullness replete with mountain spirits, living animals, plants, humans, and, in the opinion of one investigator, the heavenly bodies of the moon, sun and stars.[55]

The central world, the world of human life, is a place of food and the means of its preparation. According to the Wayãpi, the earth is round and flat "like a manioc plate."[56] Yaneya created it in such a way that there are heavenly realms both above and below it. The central world-space is also the place where fertility takes on special meaning, not only for food plants but also for animals, plants, fish, insects, and human beings. For this reason, the spaces of the earth are often sexualized. For instance, the earth is the second level of the three in the Desana universe. It is a single plane between the upper, male world and the lower, female world. For the Desana, all creation is made of four fundamental elements: land, water, air, and the energy which infuses them.[57] Land is principally a masculine element; water is a female element; and air is an asexual medium of communication between the two. Every aspect of ordered creation participates in a life-process wherein masculine power fertilizes the feminine element of the world. Masculine solar semen pervades every aspect of creation. Nevertheless, "seen in its totality [the world], as a field of creation, . . . has primarily a feminine character over which the Sun must exercise its power."[58] The earth and its biosphere are identified with the color red, the color of life, blood, and sexuality.[59]

The nature of its food and fertility contrasts this world to the upperworld. Each is a space of consumption and multiplying life-forms, of incompleteness and change. For example, the Yąnomamö earth, called Hei Kä Misi ("this layer"), was once a fragment of Hedu, the plane above it, until it fell to its present position.[60] The fragmentation and consumption characteristic of the central world link food, sex, destruction, and death, which fit together, like pieces in a puzzle, to depict the space of the central world. The Warao, for example, hold that the earth of ancient times was flat, circular, and divided into four parts. The southwestern quadrant is the place of origin of root crops and maize. This farming area was presided over by a tree-frog–woman, Wauta, who tricked the culture hero Haburi into committing incest with his mother. Haburi had been escaping from the southeastern quadrant, where his father, a peccary hunter, had been killed by an evil ogre. Haburi and his mother escaped to the northeastern quadrant, the land of Nutria, a land inhabited by fishermen. This last, northeastern, quadrant is the land of origin of the Warao. It is covered by the sea and tidal swamps.[61]

The puzzle of fragments that depicts the central world requires piecing together. For the Canelos Quichua, the earth is divided into forests and water. The symbolic life of Canelos Quichua dreams, songs, art, and rituals unites these spatial domains. Human life does not stand apart from the space in which it is contained: puzzlement and edification are existentially bound up with one another. The awareness of fragmentation and the construction of a cosmology are part of the same imaginative process.[62] The initial pattern designed by a creator or culture hero serves as the model for the ritual arrangement of human space at the center of the central world. Ritual arrangement of space by human beings maintains the fragile but fruitful order of space established by primordial beings. For example, Attawanadi ("house Wanadi"), the third aspect of himself sent to earth by the Makiritare creator, succeeded in establishing ordered and habitable space in the universe. Attawanadi created an enclosed stratum, earth, and made the visible sun, moon, and stars. Originally they were like people. Attawanadi placed them in a new sky, which he created especially for the earth. "The real Sky couldn't be seen anymore," according to the Makiritare narrative.[63] The earth was also given its own sun; Shi, the original Sun (the original Sun-creator of Wanadi), is the true Sun and remains forever unseen. "You could see a sky above the Earth again, the Earth's own sky," the myth continues. "You couldn't see Kahuña, the real Sky, any more, like in the beginning, nor the Kahuhana, the ones who live in the Sky. Now the earth has its own Sky." [64] Now the old people who had hidden in the ground during the times of destruction, and who were unable to see, came forth with courage and vision to take up their place in existence. By arranging a symbolic place, an ordered space *representative* of the true structures of being and light, which cannot be seen, Attawanadi makes human life possible. We may say that Attawanadi actually institutes "religion" by creating symbolic life, which, through the indirect route of image and representation, achieves contact with sacred realities that are no longer fully manifest or directly accessible.

The proper disposition of earthly space can be imagined in different ways. In the Chiripá view, the earthly level possesses three qualities of space: the forest, the cleared and cultivated fields, and the spaces cleared for human residence and travel.[65] The proportions among these spaces are maintained by means of work and ritual that follow heroic examples and that are performed at proper times.

Brief mention should be made of spatial worlds that exist on the margins of the earth. These are of several kinds. Most familiar are the forest and water domains. For instance, Dauarani, a female deity who lives at the edge of the Warao world, is the "mother of the forest." Her soul lives on the world-mountain at the intercardinal horizon on the southeast; her body remains in a mountain dwelling at the southwest intercardinal point. "The locations of these intercardinal mountains seem to coincide with the observable points of midsummer sunrise and sunset, respectively." [66]

The Kaingáng of the Brazilian Highlands divide the forest into "clean places" and "dirty places," depending upon the amount of light they contain. In the clean places there are no vines, thorns, or bamboo bramble. The Kaingáng refer to these as "pretty" places. Opposed to these are the "dirty places," where growth obscures light.[67] Similarly, at the western end of the Desana earth-plane is a "dark region" governed by the "night people." It is a zone of pathogenic "residues."

In general, the Canelos Quichua forest is the realm of Amasanga, the soul-master of forest beings. He knows everything about the forest. Amasanga and his wife Nunghuí, soul-mistress of pottery clay and garden soil, are important sources of knowledge and protection for the Canelos men and women who consider themselves to be people of the forest. Opposed to this realm of forest and soil is the world of Sungui, master of the water spirits, who lives with his wife, Yacu Supai Huarmi ("the continuity of water life"; also known as Yacu Mama). Long ago, Amasanga and Sungui agreed to respect the boundaries of their separate realms.[68] Hills *(urcu)*, replete with jungles and rivers of their own, constitute yet another separate domain within the Canelos Quichua cosmos. The hills possess rivers that flow into the sky-world and caves that descend down into the underworld.[69] This world is inhabited by Amasanga and the cannibalistic Juri Juri, a furry monster associated with monkeys. Given their relationship with Amasanga, the hill-worlds appear to be a part of the domain of the forest.

RELATEDNESS OF SPACES: THE SYSTEM OF THE UNIVERSE

The paragraphs above illustrate that there are different kinds of space in the universe and that each kind of space conditions the status of beings that reside within it. The matter does not end there. None of these separate spaces exists solipsistically: the disjunct planes of being are systematically associated with one another in such a way as to constitute a whole. At root, complete systematization is possible because all spaces were, in primordial times, inherently related. Their unity of being is revealed most clearly at the time of their origin. Systematization of the spatial universe becomes a way of thinking about being's essential integrity, as revealed in myth. Examination of the systemic processes of connection and separation among levels of space clarifies the very nature of disjunction and conjunction, concepts essential to the formation of the separate categories used in thought.[70] Their status is essentially imaginative; that is, the consciousness of primordial images allows for the construction of a system of symbolic correlations.

The spaces of the universe may be integrated by means of a wide range of imagery: color coordination, animal relations, grades of metals, and so on. Not colors themselves but their meanings understood symbolically become principles of universal organization. In the midst of his ongoing research in the meaning and use of toponyms in the Bolivian community of Chuani (Province of Camacho, Department of La Paz), Gabriel Martínez has put forward some stimulating hypotheses about the ways in which different spaces relate to one another. The differences between places appear to be linked to the distinctions between different metals, colors, and waters. Each of these media serves as a model for a distinct symbolic code. However, each differentiating system makes clear that all distinctions can be obliterated in favor of an essential unity of being. All differentiated colors, for example, are believed to merge in *kürmi*, the rainbow. Similarly, in mythic times, all animals were members of a single species of being, that of the mountain divinities. Martínez tentatively outlines the extraordinarily subtle cognitive bases that allow for distinctions between symbols that are essentially related, whether they be symbols of place, space, color, water, metal, or animal taxonomy. The basis for the epistemological distinction of essentially related beings must be found in the relationships portrayed in myth between creation, destruction, disorder, and recreation.[71] The rainbow, from which all colors derive, is considered to be a kind of degradation of the primordial colors. It is an articulation of separated, degraded colors that allows them to become recollected and reordered in a conjunction that is no longer truly possible in this world. The rainbow "conjoins the 'unconjoinable,' that which is not able to be directly joined; it has a function which is doubly dangerous since, in allowing for the joining together of separated things, it achieves the shattering of this world in which 'we' live and brings about the elimination of differences and the loss of identity." [72] The word *k'isa* ("conjunction") is ironically defined as the place where two symbolic realities (e.g., colors and places) separate from one another at the same time as they merge into the kind of unity they enjoyed before the creation of this prepositional world. *K'isa* is as much the disintegration of unity that must occur at the borders of every separate category as it is a distintegration that took place in "time" as the primordial epoch gave way to the age of this cosmos. At the same time, it is, as Martínez demonstrates, a category that conditions the symbolic operations of human consciousness. Martínez finds that all symbolic distinctions (spaces, metals, colors, animals) point to a single manifestation of the sacred: the *achachila-wak'a* complex of sacred space, centered on the river of "all color" or the mountain of "all metal." In such circumstances, every symbolic category (the color red, for example) rests upon the double application of a negative dialectic involving the relationship between *allqa* (disjunction) and *k'isa* (the conjunction that marks the separation between disjoint symbols). In this world, both concepts exist without canceling one another out. All of the symbolic relations are tied directly to the place where they all relate: the center *(taypi)*, visualized as a mountain that contains all metals, animals of all colors, and rivers of all kinds of waters.

At times, the relationship between spaces is organic. Separate places are parts of a cosmic body. Such is the view of the people in the community of Kaata in the Bolivian Altiplano. The mountain-body on which they live extends through all three cosmic zones, from the head in the upperworld to the toenails in the lower plane.[73] In a different image of the cosmic body, the Baniwa describe the universe as a world-system of separate planes, each one of which has its own history of mythic events. Each cosmic level has at its center a different supernatural mode of being, which includes the chief protagonists in the mythic accounts of life on that level of the cosmos. For example, Yaperikuli (or Inaperikuli; at times also called Jesu Cristo) is the earliest being whose actions help create the world. He lives in the highest heaven. Beneath him is the level of his son, Kuai. Passing through the sky-door below Kuai's village, one comes to a series of other worlds located in the sky. Below them is the world trail, which leads to this world (Hekoapi). One could continue to descend to the "world below us" (Wapinákoa). Below that, in the depths of the cosmos, one finds the mirrored reflection of the Sun.

All of these separated worlds are systematically linked together to form the outline of a human body in which Yaperikuli's village is part of the head and the "world below us" forms the genitals (the locus of the unborn). This tubular body, like a bone container, is curved in some way so that the reflected sun at the bottom is connected to the top of the universe where the true Sun is.[74]

Drawing from body imagery, many South American cultures cast the relations of the different spaces in terms of relations between the sexes. The sexualization of spaces accounts for their separation as well as their relation. Spaces, like genders, are viewed as different qualities of being. The Guayakí, for instance do not distinguish between forest and village *per se*. Rather, they conceive of the spaces they inhabit as having a sexual opposition. The productive space of the forest, furnishing game animals and honey, is masculine; the consumptive space of habitation is feminine.[75] The two separate spaces of the Guayakí universe, together with the tasks of men and women, which are symbolically associated with each of those spaces, are referred to as "the bow" and "the basket." The opposition between bow and basket is maintained in spatial, sexual, and economic terms. These two symbols become principal ways of defining the human being. Women are forbidden to touch the bows of hunters, just as men are forbidden to touch the women's baskets. One of the most profound separations of space and sex is manifest in the separate songs and singing styles of men and women. In the proper spatial setting, men individually improvise the *prerä* (hunting song). Women are said not to sing; rather, they perform a "weeping of lamentations" *(chenga ruvara)*. Each style of song corresponds to a specific expression of space and "expresses a different mode of existence, a different presence in the world, a different system of values." [76] The separation of sexualized spaces is systematically apportioned to accord with the sexual division of labor, ritual performance, and property.

In a similar way, the spaces of this earth have a sexualized valence for the Chiripá. The forest is unknown and mysterious. Men often absent themselves and withdraw into the forest for days at a time for purposes of hunting and trapping or to seek special construction materials or engage in trade. The domestic residence-space is properly the domain of women and children. The spaces cleared for planting and the cleared areas around the house are spaces shared by men and women.[77]

The sexualized system of the universe serves as a reminder that significance of sexuality is bound up with the meaning of space. On the human scale, the meaning of space is manifest in sexually differentiated female and male body-spaces and the different experiences and qualities of being they betoken. The relations between the sexes, which generate the human condition, parallels and participates in the relations among cosmic spaces, which form an integrated universe.

In Canelos Quichua culture, cooperation and complementarity between the human sexes helps fuse the separated domains of water, soil, and forest. The process is a deliberate one based on cultivated wisdom and knowledge of symbolic realities (dreams, songs, souls), which are experienced differently by men and women. After several feast-days of preparation during which firewood and manioc are gathered for the principal Canelos Quichua ceremony, the women paint the men's faces black, induce the men to drink heavily, and then put red paint on the men's faces.[78] The men are then dispatched to fish and hunt for a week or even longer. The men seek foreign people's souls by killing monkeys. They look for stones (often in the form of hairballs or bezoars) that contain souls. They shoot birds whose plumage is valuable for ritual dress. Not only is the larger Canelos Quichua community partitioned into two ritual groups during their principal feast, but there is a ritual separation of men and women for much of the celebration. Ordinarily, Canelos Quichua houses are divided into male and female spaces.[79] However, while men are absent on a ritual hunt during the semiannual Canelos Quichua festival, the house of the female *chicha*-givers *(asua mamas)* takes on an entirely female valence. Furthermore, although the women as a group maintain their solidarity in the central area established for the ceremony, the men are further separated into ritual hunting parties. In spite of the ritual formations, which crosscut those mundane divisions of day-to-day life, the ceremony stresses the idea of the common descent of all the participants.

THE CENTER

The existence of a center is essential to the possibility of a meaningful universe. In cultures where the universe consists of multiple planes of being, the center is the place where these planes intersect. Here the qualities of being that are manifest in space encounter one another and, therefore, appear most fully. All essential modes of being converge on the center, where communication, and even passage, between them is possible.

Existence of a manifest center permits the establishment of a world-system of interrelated symbolic realities. Ironically, the center's relevance to the meaning of all space in the universe depends on the sacred quality that sets it apart.[80] At the center one obtains the most direct contact with the sacred. The existence of a sacred place demonstrates that not all space is the same; a space may stand apart from another based upon the quality of being it manifests. In other words, space is symbolic. It opens out from one level of meaning to another. The significance of space, revealed in the quality of being at its center, permits one to view the universe as a system.

"When a Warao baby emerges from the womb of his squatting mother, he falls right into the heart of the universe."[81] The Warao believe that humankind occupies the center of the earth, which is a saucer-shaped disk surrounded by water. The Warao baby is born at the foot of the world-axis, which joins the earth to the highest point in heaven.

The belief that the center of the universe is the locus of human life is found throughout South America. Proximity to the center makes *human* life — as opposed to the kinds of existence possessed by animals and by the monsters who live on the margins of the world—possible. The Kayapó (Xikrin) are a typical example. They situate themselves in the center of the universe, halfway between heaven (*koikwa*, "sky") and a lower world. They are also centered between east (*koikwa-krai*, "root of the sky") and west (*koikwa-enhôt*, "top of the sky").[82] The Campa, too, live at the center of the earth, which is a flat surface that is itself the central stratum of the universe. The center of the earth is divided by a river system whose point of origin lies at the southernmost tip of the earth.[83] The river's origin is called Intatoni. After flowing through the center of Campa territory, the river passes to the east, where it falls through a hole in the earth. This place, at the edge of the earth's rim, is called Ocitiriko. Both the point of the river's beginning and the point of the river's end are inhabited by good spirits.

The centrality of human existence is often a condition achieved by primordial beings who first created the order of space. These creators or heroes have disappeared from the world. For example, the Kaborí, a Makú subgroup, place themselves at the center of the world because it was here that the culture heroes called the Itaáp, two mythical brothers, lived in primordial times. Although they had human form, they were actually made of stone. At some point, the two brothers began to quarrel and separated from one another. Their adventures that followed their separation brought about the world as it is now known. One of the brothers went upstream to live on a high mountain at the source of the river. According to the Kaborí, there, in the land of Nadöb and beyond, live the "mothers" of various animals. Eventually, the world ends in that direction at a rocky cliff where the one stony Itaáp brother lives. Downstream, where the second brother journeyed, one finds the lands of settled cities and of beings who eat flesh and drink blood.[84]

In Yukuna mythology, two heroic brothers measure the earth; that is, they mark off a portion of *esawa* (the uncharted forest), beginning with the bottomless pit at the center of the world.[85] They begin this act of orientation at that instant when the sun is in the center of heaven. Only then, and for an instant, does light penetrate into the hole of the agouti (a passage to the other world), which is filled with winds and is called the "funeral trench." A replica of this funeral trench is dug in the Yukuna longhouse itself at the time of funerals.[86] Along the same lines, Viracocha, the Inca creator, and his two heroic companions walked along the spine of the Andes from southeast to northwest. Passing by Cuzco, Viracocha journeyed along the Vilcanota River. His procession through space oriented the spatial divisions of the Inca empire and its capital.

THE AXIS MUNDI
The center is the place suitable for human life because its symbolism provides access to other cosmic realms of being. The center of the world is manifest in a range of symbols: cosmic tree, mountain, ladder, vine, pillar. Each of these central images functions as an *axis mundi*, the "hub" or "axle" of the universe. The image of the *axis mundi* symbolizes communications between spatial planes. The term refers to the function and meaning of the

place, to the experiences associated with it, and to the images of the communication that takes place there.[87]

The experiences of ascent and descent that characterize the center entail a concept of verticality, for knowledge of the universe implies experience of the upper and lower worlds.[88] For example, *ucumu* ("straight down") and its opposite, *cusca* ("straight up"), give definition to the relational center of the Canelos Quichua universe, which is referred to as *allpa*, "the dividing point of straight up and straight down."[89] As Norman Whitten writes, "The very center of the Canelos Quichua house symbolizes the center of the universe." Straight up and straight down are discerned from the central point of the house. It is here that men and women sleep and dream, here that they hide special stones. Here souls leave the body during the life-cycle rituals, life-crisis rituals, shamanic voyages, and dreams. From here, one gains access to the whole universe.[90]

The world-mountain at the center of the world establishes the axis that opens the earthly realm to the celestial; it is the highest point of the universe. Here creation first began. The mountaintop breaks the plane of heaven. Conversely, the summit is the point where the heavenly realm of the primordium first extends downward from the plane of the upperworld into earthly existence. The Mapuche are among the peoples who center their life on such a cosmic mountain. The continuum of Mapuche time stretches vertically from the historical present to the mythical past along a cosmic vertical axis that ascends the mountain of being. At the top of the mountain, the summit of being, dwells the supreme being, Ngeñechén; there the beginning of time perdures, for Ngeñechén is the first being and the creator. This summit and origin of being is accessible only through the special category of sacred songs that are performed ritually. Only sacred sound allows one to scale the axis, the time line that runs through the center of the universe and that takes on historical expression at the "lower" end of the continuum, in one's own patriline.[91]

There exist many images of the axis mundi other than the cosmic mountain. Gerald Weiss found that the Campa and Machiguenga[92] used the image of a sky-rope connecting heaven and earth. In subsequent research he traced the appearance of the sky-rope not only among the Arawakan-speaking Piro but also among many lowland tribes.[93] Another common image is that of a cosmic tree or cosmic pillar stretching from earth to heaven. Peter Roe contends that the Shipibo world-tree of mythic times now serves as a central pillar, supporting the world and upholding the cosmos. The world-tree grew when a tapir kicked a *guayaba* tree and it turned into an enormous *lupuna* tree. The tapir remains the guardian of the world-tree.

Just as the cosmic mountain was the origin-point of life, so also the sky-rope may be a vehicle of refuge and the cosmic tree a source of life. For instance, connections between the three realms of the Pémon cosmos are effected by a cosmic tree, Wadakayik, which stands in the sacred center of the universe. Wadakayik produces a variety of fruits that are used as food by animals and people ("children of the sun"). At some point during the primordium, this *axis mundi* was cut down. From its trunk flowed fish and floodwaters, the sources of a new, regenerated life.[94] Its roots may descend into underworlds or may be doubly rooted in heavenly soil as well as in the earth. The branches spread throughout the world-planes.

THE VESSEL AT THE CENTER

A vessel frequently serves as an *axis mundi*, that is, as the symbol of communication between realms. The English word *vessel* denotes both a container of liquid and a vehicle through which liquid is carried: in both senses the center-as-vessel, set apart by its own self-defined limits, serves as a shaped and bounded space over and against the paradigmatic image of fluid formlessness. For the Pémon, the trunk of the cosmic tree contained waters that, when released, flooded the earth. I have already mentioned above that, for the Shipibo, the cosmic tree was a vessel containing poison.

Frequently a vessel that contains a beverage is installed at the center of a ritual space. During the Chiripá festival called the Prayer of the Forest, for instance, a ceremonial-drink trough, made of sacred cedar, establishes the center of sacred action. Situated in front of a building known as the "house of dances," the trough is shaped like a canoe. In front of this canoe-trough stand three cedar posts. The central post is the *kuruzú* ("cross"), a replica of the structure on which the creator placed the world during creation. Beside the cross is placed a small arrow, which is associated with the adventures of the sun and moon, twins who ascended into heaven along a chain of arrows. All of these objects are covered with feathers. Facing the trough and posts and sitting in a single row with the women standing in a line behind them, the men chant throughout the night. Over the course of the ritual's first eight days, the participants gather in increasing numbers while additional drinks, honey *chicha* and a beverage made from sugarcane, are prepared.

The other sense of *vessel*, that of a vehicle, can also be found within the imagery depicting the *axis mundi*. (As the Chiripá canoe–beverage-trough illustrates, both meanings of vessel can be exhibited at the same time.) The establishment of spatial order achieved by the journeys of heroes (and the knowledge of the universe gained thereby) is not limited to ascent and descent along a fixed passageway. Heroic and creative movement, which established the bounds of order, was imitated by human ancestors and continues to be reenacted by pilgrims, travelers, and adventurers during their wanderings. As an *axis mundi* situated in the sacred center of human culture, the symbolic vessel of magical transport — the tree-canoe, the drum, the gourd-rattle or flute, the shaman's bench or cigar-holder — provides a bounded refuge. It safeguards the human capacity for consciousness and rescues the possibility of understanding in a supernatural world inundated with meaning.

Functioning as an *axis mundi*, the central vessel offers controlled contact with the formless chaos symbolized by liquid. The movable central vehicle carries culture through the fluid, undemarcated outer space. The vessel that holds sacred drink contains and shapes the otherwise formless liquid. It is this liquid that, in ritual drunkenness, transports one to a different quality of space, where images blur in such a way as to signal to the senses that one is out of this world. Both kinds of vessel safely transport one to and from the emergent being of primordial times.

The image of the *axis mundi* as a vessel intensifies the intrinsic semantic connection between, on the one hand, travel to all realms of the universe and, on the other, the convergence of diverse forms of being from distinct world-planes.[95] The link between realms and forms exists at the level of human experience, which remains essentially a unified one, despite the differences among beings encountered in alien conditions of space. Even more fundamental is the implication that the unity of human experience is grounded in a quality of space shared by every form of manifest being: its relationship to a sacred center and, therefore, its potentially symbolic status. The world of outer space and the potentially chaotic reality of inner space are related. As a vessel, the center represents the containment of chaos, an imaginative check against the boundless symbolism of unorder, whether it be located inside or outside the container. Drinking and control over travel are both symbolic strategies for containing potential chaos, which threatens to drown articulate experience, while gaining knowledge of forms of existence in other realms.

The musical instruments used in ritual are also important spatial images often associated with the center of the world. Frequently they are constructed of materials (e.g., wood or gourds) taken from the *axis mundi* (e.g., the cosmic tree). Rattles, for example, often contain quartz crystals or seeds obtained in an ascent of the cosmic mountain, or they are fashioned in the image of the *axis mundi* itself.[96] Musical instruments associated with the center of the world can be understood in some of the same terms as the vessels just discussed: that is, as means of transition that, through controlled ecstasy, transport the performer from one cosmic zone to another.

REPLICATION AND INTERCHANGEABILITY

The interchangeability of one image of the *axis mundi* for another, even within the same culture, seems characteristic of the symbolism of the center. No single image — mountain, tree, pillar, gourd, vessel, musical instrument — can exhaust its meaning. The enrichment of significant imagery at the center contributes directly to the edification of a symbolic universe. The elaboration of symbolic forms extends the sacrality, power, and meaning of reality that is found at the center. A fine example of such multiplication of imagery of the center is furnished by the Makiritare. The earth connects to heaven at several important points, and these serve as markers of the ordered space of the Makiritare universe. All these sacred places represent the communication between realms of the cosmos. The center of the Makiritare heaven is marked by Lake Akuena. It was from this lake that waters poured down through the cut trunk of Marahuaka, the tree-mountain that grows on earth but that is rooted in heaven.[97] Lake Akuena contains Dama, the sea that once flooded the entire earth when it poured through the trunk of Marahuaka. Discussion of the center of heaven raises the interesting issue, to be taken up shortly, of the relationship of center to the periphery, for it is said that Lake Akuena, located in the center of heaven, also "circles the entire Earth from east to west and west to east." [98] Coming into existence with the great flood provoked by the heroic twins, Dama (the sea) at first covered the earth but then receded. Now it surrounds the earth, and underground river-ways on earth connect this encircling sea with Lake Akuena in the center of heaven.[99] On the earthly plane, the matter of the imagery of the center is more complicated and enriched. For example, there is the "tree of refuge," where Attawanadi, the creative culture hero, and his wife Kaweshawa, flee-ing in the form of a woodpecker and a frog, saved themselves and turned into the first forms of man and woman. This tree reaches all the way to heaven. Today it is seen as a mountain.[100] Similarly, Marahuaka, the unique tree that first gave forth every kind of fruit, was rooted both on earth and in heaven and connected the two realms. When it was cut down to form the first garden, a flood issued from heaven through Marahuaka's trunk.[101] Today, the remains of that primordial and unique tree may be seen as Mount Marahuaka, the "Little Gourd," the 8,500-foot mountain that rise between the Padamo and Kunukunuma rivers in Venezuela. Another mountain, Kushamakari ("home of Kuchi, the Evening Star"), is said to be the central pillar of the universe-house. It supports the heavens.[102] It was on Kushamakari that an aspect of Wanadi, the creator, first lived on earth, and it is to this mountain house that Wanadi's spirit will return after his crucifixion, when only his body remains hanging on the cross.[103] Kushamakari is shrouded in mystery. Its very exis-tence was a secret until Wanadi's aspect had left the earth:

> No one knew about it. Only he did. No one else. He didn't say anything. . . . It was hidden deep in the mountains . . . hidden in the headwaters. . . . It's very hard to get there. Lots of rapids for canoes. Lots of mawadi [enormous supernatu-ral anacondas] living there to guard the way. You have to sing a lot to get there. You can't eat meat or sleep with women either. A huge bat guards the cave. . . . Only powerful, good beings live there . . .[104]

The identification of so many symbols with the meaning of center en-ables the construction of the world-system. This becomes clear when one looks at the Baniwa conception of the universe, in which the center is the prestigious place. The center is imaged in a bewildering array of symbols: tree, mountain, cave-vessel, musical instrument, navel/umbilicus, village, and human body. Each plane of the cosmos has a center that is occupied by beings who have "the greatest living immediacy" for the mode of being characterizing that level of the universe.[105] The Baniwa themselves live at the center of the earth, the level of the universe that they call the "place of pain." They, unlike the other groups and tribes who live around them, are the perfect expression of humanness. On the level above this earth, Kuai, the supernatural culture hero, lives at the center of his sky level. Around him are located the souls of the dead human beings who, on this sky level, must inhabit the margins of existence. In the center of the disk that represents the topmost level of the universe, the highest level of the sky, lies Yaperikuli's village. Movement from one level of the universe to another is always from center to center along the *paxibua* palm tree located at the hub of the world. The tree, called "Kuai's navel (or umbilicus)" and "sky navel/umbilicus" *(îiepolepi-ēēnu)*, is said by some to have leaves of gold at its top. A sky-door is constantly opening and slamming "like a scissors," making the passage from earth to heaven a perilous one. Kuai, from whose burning body came the sounds of animal species and the languages of human social groups, had once been in the center of this earth. Kuai rescued three children from the flood by swallowing them into his mouth, a cave. When he vomited them up, they were transformed, for holes had been made in their chests by the fruit tree located in the central cave. They were forever marked by this spatially centered index of seasonal time. At the center of this world is also a musical instrument (or, rather, *all* musical instruments, for they all come from Kuai's body-tree after his death). Today the sound of the *axis mundi* is best embodied in the ensemble of ancestral flutes.

The tendency toward replication of the image of the *axis mundi* on the multiple scales of the village, house, ritual space, human physiology, musical instruments, art, personal ornaments, and cooking utensils organizes the world which humans live in. At every level the cosmos is the space set apart from and opposed to the chaos beyond, behind, or outside it. That chaotic state of being was never ordered by supernatural beings nor consecrated in rites imitating the primordial creative acts. The cosmos, centered on human culture but including the order of nature, is a refuge, a vessel of salvation, for it is protected by the imagination, that is, by the image of a center. The imagination is centered on the image humankind possesses of sacred reality, and all other orders are generated from this. Replication of the center through formal and informal acts of consecration identifies the fullness of sacred being that is characteristic of the center with the universe as a whole. Replication and imitation guarantee that human existence, even at the level of everyday gesture, maintains contact with reality in its fullest manifestation.

The richness of meaning found at the center and the elaboration of its symbolic forms make the human imagination adventuresome. The appearance of reality at the center of earth is reassuring. The knowledge of the center inspires confidence, emboldening human beings to experiment, to apply the center's sacred meaning to a wide range of existential situations. Because the center is the image that unites universal order with the destiny of humankind as well as with the individual, knowledge of it has immense impact on the formation of cognitive and existential processes. Johannes Wilbert attributes the high level of intellectual activity and social adventuressness of the Warao to the sustaining knowledge that one "can live safely at the center of his universe." Wilbert writes,

> On their journeys across the sea the Warao could always remain in the center of the universe as the circle of the horizon traveled with them, and, if need be, they could establish a new home wherever two mountains could serve as the poles of their earth and the abode of the two earth-gods. . . . the movable center [of the Warao universe] could have been taken along in the minds of the navigators, who

would enjoy the security of always being physically and psychologically in the middle of the world and of residing close to the tidal heartbeat of the Snake of Being.[106]

It should be clear by now that the center is not a purely geometric concept. Defined by a unique relationship to the sacred, multiple "centers" of the world-space exist in any cosmos or microcosm. The center is not a locus in Euclidean space but in mythic geography, that is, in the imagination, which is able to distinguish and evaluate qualities of being. As such, the center is not a detached abstraction but a symbolic depiction of what appears as real, essential, and knowable about space.

The examples presented thus far have emphasized the way in which the center connects the earth to upper and lower levels of the universe. However, the center not only relates cosmic planes to one another but also brings horizon and zenith into relationship. This is especially evident in astronomic systems. Azimuths calculating the relationship between heavenly points are determined by scrutinizing the horizon. While doing so the astronomer stands on a line passing through a specific center (used as a "backsight" or "foresight") of earthly observation. The earthly center mirrors the zenith-center of heaven. Anthony Aveni reminds us that South American cosmologies are constructed from experiences and observations of the universe within particular geographic conditions. In particular, he is interested in the way in which astronomic observations are applied in the construction of a world view. In the lower latitudes of the tropics, writes Aveni, "the horizon and zenith seem to be the underlying principle of the symbolic and organizational expressions of every system. . . . In the higher latitudes this is not always the case." [107] Aveni believes that, for geographic reasons, tropical peoples place an emphasis "on the vertical, zenith-nadir axis." [108]

Another clear example of the ways in which the complex image and dynamism of the *axis mundi* relate the center to the cosmic boundaries on the horizon comes from the Desana. The Desana concept of the center is keyed to the organization of earthly territory as well as to the order of the sky. It accounts for the structures of existence as well as the outermost boundaries of creative energy. The Desana cosmos took shape when the Sun imposed a willful order on the cosmic prime matter—the "yellow intention" that had emanated from him in the form of solar semen.[109] The center of the universe was formed when the Sun Father sought a place to put his upright staff, his bone-penis (go'á-mëe; ve'e go'á, tubular bone). It was filled with the yellow intention, the yellow light of the invisible Sun. The Sun Father wished to set it erect in a place where it would cast no shadow; he found such a place where the womb of the earth was open. In that whirlpool he impregnated the earth, and it was from that cosmic uterus at the center that the Desana men came forth in anaconda snake-canoes. "[T]he shaft of light from the zenith sun fertilized the earth with procreative energy" and defined the center of the universe. The semen of the sun, celestial yellow intention, spilled onto the earth in the form of hexagonal quartz crystal. This hexagonal shape, the solidified manifestation of the expressed contents of the center, is the ordering principle of all the spaces of the universe. The universe itself is bounded by six mythic anacondas. Each one is stretched out at length so that together they form the hexagon that defines all sacred space.[110] The structure of the sky is that of an enormous celestial hexagon centered on Orion's belt. Where the six stars of the hexagon create corners, the earth touches the sky. The places are marked by six waterfalls streaming from the heads of each of the six primordial anacondas who occupy the bounds of the world. In the image of the Sun Father's penis, the *axis mundi* transfixes all zones of the universe through their center, joining all cosmic planes into a dynamic universe whose components are united in a continuous act of intercourse. The center is a vessel of solar semen. It conducts the "yellow intention" of the creator into the cosmic uterus, Ahpikondiá ("river of milk") from which all life comes. Ironically, the creative act that marks the center, the penetration of the earth by the celestial creator, is now said to occur at the edge of the universe, at the corners of the hexagon, where the sky cohabits with the earth.[111]

AMBIVALENCE OF THE CENTER

All the images of *axis mundi* express ambivalence. For instance, Quechua speakers regard the mountain Ausangate as an all-powerful being in its own right. Although Ausangate is a violent being, especially during the time of the carnival feasts, his waters are essential to life. The waters are nonetheless dangerous, since they attract murderous beings who may "tempt [human beings] to sell their souls in exchange for food, animals, and power." [112] Another example, already presented, showed that the Shipibo portray the central tree as a vessel that helps to contain chaos but that also contains poison.

Further indications of ambivalence derive from the symbolism of the center itself. The *axis mundi* conjoins planes of being, but, at the same time, its images are visible signs measuring off the gulf that separates the different realms. The ubiquity of the replicated image of the center suggests easy access, but the dangers surrounding it can render it unapproachable without arduous ritual preparation. Roe isolates a pattern of forms which associates the world-tree with a devouring dragon, a frog (a lesser form of the dragon), the poison of tree frogs, and fish poison.[113] Roe gathers together myths portraying the world-tree as thorny. These spines protect its hidden fruits. The world-tree facilitates communication between various regions of the universe, but its inner nature is noxious.

Although the *axis mundi* unites the universe, many myths paradoxically depict its destruction. It is severed, chopped down, or fractured. The brokenness of the *axis mundi* is linked with the need to rupture existential planes in traversing it successfully. Paradox, experience of a different order, is demanded in order to make the passage available at the center of the universe. In this way, the ambivalence of the center reveals itself as a central quality of religious experience. On the one hand, the journey to the center, the achievement of other states of existence, is a dangerous task, requiring a complete transformation of one's spiritual being. Acquiring a new state of being means "death" to one's ordinary state. On the other hand, communication with essential realities, which are spread throughout the universe, is everywhere possible. This easy access is a reminder that, in the primordium, all forms of being communed effortlessly. Somehow the essential unity of being may still be centered within its multiple forms or, at least, in the human experience of them. The destruction of the primordial *axis mundi* emphasizes that the connection among realms of being is now achieved in the religious imagination. On every plane of space, the meaning of the symbolism of the center of the world emphasizes that the heart of existence consists in an experience and a quality of being different from the ordinary world around it. Paradoxically, it is from this central conjunction of different qualities of being that the reality of the universe derives.

PERIPHERY, BOUNDARY, CLOSURE

The first sentences of this chapter pointed out that every form of existence appears in a space appropriate to its condition of being. The corollary of this is that every being whose meaning can be articulately known is contained. For example, over the course of a lengthy Tukano narrative, it is made clear that all important and potent items are enclosed in their proper containers, that is, in spaces that present themselves as ordered and integral and that bespeak a uniqueness of purpose as well as a particular mode of being.[114] Furthermore, each mode of being requires its own contained space. Human beings, for example, need a *maloca*, a communal longhouse, or else they will die.[115]

The manner in which Canelos Quichua describe this idea of power-in-containment is quite different. For the Canelos Quichua, rocks *(rumi)* contain transformative substances. A rock is called a "flowerbud" *(tutu)* because it is a hard and silent soul-enclosure. All rocks and stones possess the power to enclose ancient souls.[116]

The principle that each quality of existence is contained within its proper space explains why some peoples, such as the Yawalapíti, contend that all growth and new knowledge come during seclusion in a ritual container. Each new container is a source of new power and consciousness. The Waiwai observe the same logic in their practices of ritual confinement. In addition to cosmic spaces, the Waiwai observe that certain forms and shapes of space, certain enclosures, are especially important and powerful. Thus, a shaman performs his magical "blowing" while singing powerful songs over a magical stone in his mouth. These performances take place in three different kinds of space. The first is the open air, in which the shaman performs rites to invoke the sun, bring on rain, and ensure good hunting. The second place of performance is within the confines of the communal house, where blowing is performed to help cure mild illnesses. The third and most important space of the shaman's practice is the *shutepana*, a conical hut that is entirely covered with palm leaves so that it has neither door nor windows. At night, in this enclosed hut, the shaman will send forth his soul to fetch back the souls of the seriously ill.[117] The *shutepana* must be reconstructed every twenty-four hours and may not be used for more than one soul-flight.

For the Waiwai, as for the Tukano and the Canelos Quichua, the very idea of containment derives from the mythic era; the power of various Waiwai containers is related to their sacred origins. At the close of the mythic first drinking festival, after they had bathed in the blood of the slain anaconda-monster, the various bird species took refuge in specific enclosures in order to protect themselves from the rain. The birds were transformed — the species' differentiation by body forms and colors was effected — by the enclosures they built. The change in body markings signals a change in mode of being.[118]

The periphery is frequently defined by the appearance or movement of being at the center. Thus, in Desana culture, "the word *béro* means circle, but the verb *vabéri* is to dive, to move the water."[119] The relation between the circumference of the circle and its center is intrinsic: the circular shape is produced as a ripple by an object plunged into the water. Only time marks the difference between the center and its outward-bound expression. They are distinguishable moments in a dialectic. As a related pair of symbolic expressions, the center and outer circle constitute a feminine space for the Desana. In dances they are combined in the symbolism of the dance shield *(vabéro)*, which the Sun Father carried when he created the universe. The circle and center embodied in the dance shield are usually conjoined with the stick-rattle, the image of the *axis mundi* — the phallus of the Sun Father, which inseminated the uterus of the universe with light and sound.

There is something about the boundary that is continuous with or identical to the center. Some of the materials already explored in this chapter offer ample illustration: the Campa center is crossed by a river whose beginning and end mark the outer limits of the cosmos; the Kaborí center is built by mythical brothers who now reside "upstream" and "downstream" on the outermost margins of earth; the central post of the Canelos Quichua house is hung with trophies, the bodies of dead "foreigners" (monkeys obtained in the ritual hunt that demarcates the outermost boundaries of a new territory).

The nature of the center to which the periphery is related determines the character of the boundary. This discovery that the outer margin expresses in altered form the same values found in the center was a fertile theme in the work of Victor Turner. For Turner, the values manifest during the central ritual processes of a society were ontologically related to those manifest on society's margins. Such values are expressed symbolically in such a way that they create an "arena," a space within which new relations can form and old ones dissolve. Within this frame, society and individuals can make symbolic, emotion-laden statements in such a way as to reshape the social and moral order.[120]

The existence of an imaginative frame, whether demarcated as a spatial boundary or as a first premise, makes communication possible. By circumscribing relations, an imaginative boundary, or "limen," allows them to

rebound reflexively.[121] In this way the image of the limit, the liminal experience, generates a system of symbolic relations that open the way to self-consciousness.[122] As already demonstrated, the center represents the "break" in
the planes of the universe, the rupture in the uniform quality of being. Ironically, the place where spatial closure dissolves makes for a boundedness on a
new scale. This dynamic dialectic between center and periphery opens one
to the larger and enriched symbolic universe. The periphery of a universe
manifests closure, which makes understanding possible, and reflects the
knowledge obtainable in limit-situations. That is, the periphery of the universe, fashioned simultaneously with the center, reveals the meaning of
being, as being is defined by its limits.

The periphery of the world is frequently understood in terms of the
points on the horizon, the cardinals and intercardinals, which coordinate
with one another through the center. The Canelos Quichua, for instance,
mark east and west by the sun's rise and setting. However, the cardinal points
of north and south are recognized by the Canelos Quichua in a much more
general way, being referred to as *chimbajta* ("either side").[123] The nadir and
zenith define the orientation of vertical space. The Canelos Quichua sky,
usually referred to with some form of the word *jahuama* ("high"), joins the
earth at the cardinal points. "The center of the sky is 'straight up.'" [124] Oftentimes the horizon is inhabited by beings who, in mythic times, occupied the
center. For example, at the four cardinal and four intercardinal points of the
Warao world are mountains that once were enormous trees. Petrified, these
trees have become the mountain homes of the *kanobotuma* ("our grandfathers").[125] Overlap and contrariety are latent in the points that define the
horizon; they are not absolute markers but relative ones. In this respect, the
horizon is like the center: it reveals the meaning of irony and contradiction.

At times the periphery of the world is a boundary made of water. The
periphery holds at bay, on the margins of the universe, the formless being
that threatens to flood the world. For instance, immersed in the seas that
make up the Warao horizon is the monstrous Snake of Being, who encircles
the entire earth but whose heart beats at its center. Rivers also encircle the
Shipibo earth.[126] In a slightly different vision of things, there exists among the
Campa a widespread belief that in the place called Ocitiríko, the "river's
end," dwells an enormous crab, whose movements affect the level of the
river and who could even bring a great deluge upon the earth by stopping the
river entirely.

The boundaries of space provide images for a limit-language, the terminology of word and deed with which a people perceives and understands
itself. The periphery — the experience of contact with other kinds of beings
and the spaces proper to them — reveals the meaning with which a culture
defines the character of its own world.[127] The image of the periphery becomes reflexive in language, the self-referential acts of gesture and speech
that are generated in the internal relations imposed by symbolic closure.
Playing with the images revealed in and bounded by the space of the universe, language is thus capable of describing truths whose character is con-

sonant with the outer limits, the axiomatic images, of the system. The images of the limits of space define the power and intent of language.

MEDIATING ELEMENTS, OPENINGS, AND PENETRATIONS

To say that the center and periphery are related is to underline the fact that the universe is a dynamic — not a static — image and that it is participatory. The universe is *one* place because its various structures come into existence as dialectical expressions of one another. All mediating elements are associated with the center. Mediating elements pass through the center of the zones they enter since, by the definition employed in this chapter, the center is the opening that makes penetration of the space possible and through which passage and communication occur. In the Warao universe, journeys between cosmic zones and the cardinal and intercardinal points are effected by means of bridges, ropes, and slippery paths that lead out from the center of earth or from the central zenith-point of heaven. In fact, travel along these mythical media becomes an ordeal that can be successfully undergone only with the help of spirit guides, shamans, and initiatory training.[128]

Moving water and light symbolize passage between spatial structures. Frequently there is a marked tension between distinct mediating elements. The opposition is symbolized by the contrasting directions of the path of the sun and the flow of mediating waters. For example, the Canelos Quichua world consists of opposed spaces or cardinal directions, which are in continuous communication with, and even transition into, one another. The Canelos Quichua recognize an east-west axis marked by the terminal points of the sun's journey. Indi, the sun, rises in the direction called *urai* ("downriver") and sets *janaj* ("upriver").[129] All the parts of the universe are therefore related in special ways and comprise a single whole, consisting of parts in dynamic relationship. The same opposition between movement of the invisible or visible sun and the waters that pass through the center is found among both the peoples of the Andean highlands and the peoples of lowland South America.[130] Once upon a mythic time, the current of primordial waters may have moved both upstream and downstream at the same time; the sun may have stood still.[131] However, neither of these primordial conditions any longer obtains. Mediation in the contemporary universe is a two-directional movement, the expression of two different qualities of being, water and light, which exist in creative tension.

Light itself possesses gradient expressions, intermediate forms that carry on a mediating function in the universe. Stars, for example, are muted or mutilated forms of light.[132] Gary Urton has shown that contemporary Quechua speakers regard the light of the stars in the Milky Way as a gleaming river of semen, a stream of fertilizing waters that mediates between the center of earth, the coordinates on the horizon, and the zenith.[133] The dynamic order of the Milky Way accounts for the intercalation of all the life-cycles of species. For the Machiguenga as well, the Milky Way seems to be a network of tributaries that connect all cosmic zones.[134]

Colors, when seen as intermediate grades of light, likewise fulfill a mediating role in the universe.[135] For the Desana, the Milky Way is the path of visions and hallucinations induced by *viho* (*Piptadenia* peregrina) powder. The Milky Way is a neutral blue, an ambivalent color. During trance, one can move from one cosmic level to another, carried along by the circuit of the Milky Way. The Milky Way is an ambiguous structure, for it is also the abode of diseases that were expelled from the earth in primordial times. As a muted tone of light, the Milky Way also mediates between the manifest and the unmanifest aspects of being.[136]

Meteorological beings frequently play the roles of spatial mediators in the universe. They move from one level to another to lend their dynamic and fertilizing powers to all the creatures of the cosmos. Immediately above the Campa earth, but below the vast reaches of the sky, lies the level of clouds (*menkóri*). At this intermediate level one finds a group of good spirits who act as interstitial go-betweens. It is also the abode of air and wind as well as other meteorological phenomena such as rain, lightning, and thunder.[137]

Weather beings are only the most prestigious of cosmic mediators. The Canelos Quichua sky and the earth are in continuous interaction with one another thanks to the intercession of a number of entities. Fog transports terrestrial life into the sky, while rain brings celestial life down to the earth. The Milky Way is the "fog" of the star people.[138] Like weather phenomena, birds serve as intermediaries, carrying songs between the earth, the sky, and the underworld. Women send their own songs and the songs of spirits from the world of soil to the world of water. Sky-rivers then sweep songs to their destinations.[139] Thus fog, rain, women, rivers, birds, and spirits traffic between beings and between places of the universe. In addition, *amarun* beings (snakelike beings, such as the anaconda, the boa, the rainbow, and so forth) link the forest domain of Amasanga and the water realms of Sungui. Thus, Sungui appears in the form of a giant anaconda (which can also span the forest realm in the form of a rainbow), whereas Amasanga possesses a boa-skin crown and journeys across the water's surface on a boa.[140]

Intermediaries are noted for their association with change, especially the potentially violent changes associated with fertility and growth.[141] According to the people of Pinchimuro in Quispicanchis Province, Peru, certain lakes came into existence on account of a flood sent either by God or by evil spirits. They are the locus of hail and wind, which originate in other cosmic levels but appear in this one in order to make human beings, animals, and crops fertile. Certain classes of religious specialists receive knowledge and inspiration through the mediation of these sacred lakes, the same lakes that may strike other travelers with sickness. Some lakes are said to be filled with the bodies of dead soldiers who were destroyed by powerful *apus*, mountain-dwelling divinities. In fact, the rivers which stream from springs on Mount Ausangate, the snow-covered mountain peaks which serve as the homes for the most powerful *apus*, share the very "elements," the sacred substance, of the *apus*.[142]

Divinities of weather are not the only beings to link cosmic zones in mythic times. The mediating element may be the adventurous hero or human ancestor who wanders through all levels of the cosmos. In this case, an "ethnogeography" is mapped by recounting the momentous journey of the mythical ancestor.[143] Ancestors and sacred music are the principal mediating elements of Baniwa cosmic space. Ancestors, as well as sacred flutes and their sounds, are one and the same being, Kuai; *Kuai* is both the name of a hero and the name given collectively to the set of ancestral flutes. Sacred geography is established by Amaru, the primordial serpent, and her female followers, who wander across the face of the earth blowing trumpets and flutes made from the pieces of the body of Kuai, Amaru's son.[144] They wander from the center, where Kuai was burned and where his ashes sprouted in the form of a *paxiuba* tree that spanned heaven and earth. Throughout a whole night during the closing ceremonies of initiation, elders now sing the sacred geography of the whole world and of its food products while they blow spells over the pepper pot, thus rendering food edible, just as at the beginning. They relive the wandering of the Ancestor-flutes. As Robin Wright relates,

> With tobacco they blow the words of their spells into the bowl. With tobacco they "think of" *(napinieta)* Kuai: in their thought they make a journey, as recounted in the myth of Kuai, to all the known places in the world (rapids, hills, rivers, every foreign land) where Amaru and the women took and played Kuai as Yaperikuli pursued them. According to the myth, it was Kuai who first performed these spells in the first initiation rites. . . . In the approximately fifteen sets of chants, the chanters name an incredible number of places, which they must do exactly. They cannot say only half of the places, or mix up the order. They travel in their thoughts to all the ends of the world, remembering the sacred music of Kuai. Then they return to the center of the world at Hipana coming back on tobacco, the means by which their souls travel.[145]

By becoming their ancestors—the flutes that, in the myth, are played against the lips of Amaru and her female disciples—and by "thinking to Kuai," the contemporary Baniwa fertilize the mothers of every place, people, and species throughout the world. It was thus that Yaperikuli's "thought" impregnated the primordial Amaru while he pressed the outline of an opening, traced on the crown of his head, against what was to become her vagina. The sounds of the music are the fertilizing thought-soul of Yaperikuli whistling in and out of his son Kuai's body orifices, the sacred instruments. These instruments open every matrix of fruit, animals, and people for fertility and birth. It would be difficult to find a clearer example of the intercessory role of the wandering mediator who effects transitions and passages by overcoming the distance between the center and all other marked places. Here, the establishment of sacred geography through sound and ancestors is also control over the food chain ("blowing," or blessing, the food is a chantlike form of breathing). Food is made safe, and the world is made edible, open to consumption and available as sustenance.

Links between places reveal the nature of dynamism, fertility, and consumption. Some Tukano accounts of the wanderings of the first ancestors present a long series of important spaces visited by these primordial beings. The chief of the ancestors, Yúpuri Baúro, alone or in company with his sister or other beings, travels along riverways in a boat or bench. At each *maloca* he procures powerful items of culture: tobacco, coca, painted ritual belts and garters, pieces of seeds, and so forth.

Ultimately, human beings themselves become the principal moderators of space in the universe, whether they imitate mythical beings or assume unprecedented mediatory roles of their own.[146] For example, the Canelos Quichua husband and wife travel at night to other realms of the universe. They awaken some hours before dawn to explain these vision-voyages to one another and to interpret them together. Their dreams and interpretations merge to make a meaningful whole of their experience and, in this way, join together the separate spaces of the universe.[147] In other cultures it is encumbent upon ritual specialists to mediate between the spaces of the universe. For example, in his ecstasies, the Waiwai shaman *(yaskomo)* travels between cosmic spaces. Three places are particularly important. He sends his soul to *kapu* (any heavenly layer, but especially the level of his helper-spirits); to the great rock-cave in the big mountain of wild pigs, where the Father of Peccaries dwells; and to the world of anaconda-people (the riverine and underworld areas).[148] His intercession in space is needed to bring insight, fertility, and health to his people.

The establishment of a symbolic space for ritual and the ritual rearrangement of spatial indicators become the conditions ensuring growth. Ritual control over spatial mediation is most clearly visible in the regulation of symbolic openings, closings, and penetrations. Thus, for example, practitioners of the Afro-Brazilian religious tradition known as Candomblé approach and enter places of passage with special care. A devotee would not step into the sea without first addressing Ìyá Olóòkun with respect and asking her permission to enter the waters. Similarly, since the streets of the city of Bahia (Brazil) belong to Èṣù, one invokes his presence with sacrifices at intersections.[149] In the same way, all the bridges of the city of Bahia are sacred for Candomblé adherents and are identified with Èṣù. Since all places are manifestations of specific beings, passage from one place to another requires that one be conscious of the act of intercession one is performing. Ill-managed crossings can lead to pathogenic invasions of powerful beings into places where they do not belong. The penetration of space in these cases leads to disease or even death.

The dynamism exhibited by mediating elements points to the importance of time in the imaginative construal of existence. Concepts of time help sort out and evaluate the experiences of order and disorder in space. The mediating elements of space introduce a context conducive to the discussion of time. Acts in which objects from one cosmic domain penetrate into another are associated with the dynamics of fertility, sickness, health, and death. Traffic from one space to another has temporal consequences.[150] It engenders time lines associated with the markers of the solar and lunar cycles, and with seasonal variations in the weather, as well as with conception, gestation, birth, the life cycle, and multiple generations. The rupture of planes marks a beginning, a moment for reckoning.

SPACES THAT CAN NOW BE UNDERSTOOD

Three spatial expressions of meaning contribute to the understanding of space on other levels of human existence: 1) the meanings of the center, connected with the first appearances of mythic reality; 2) the significance of the periphery, providing a culture its images of introspection and reflexivity; and 3) the dynamism of mediating elements, revealing the generative power of symbolic action. Cosmic symbolism is especially prominent in the sacred places set aside for symbolic action. For example, before 1925, when most of them still lived in houses deep in the forest, the Warao gathered for ritual at ceremonial sites that consisted of clearings that had a temple or shrine on the eastern side and a row of houses on the western side. A large platform on which symbolic movement — ritual dance — was performed mediated the space between the shrine and the houses.[151] At the center of the temple was a sacred stone which represented the severed head of the child of the Toad God, Butterfly God, or the Bird God—whichever was the patron of the particular community. The rock was taken in a basket to any location to which the community moved. "The highest-ranking priest-shaman is considered to be the father of the rock spirt. He addresses it as his son, whereas the congregation calls it 'grandfather.' "[152]

The impressively detailed temples of the Kógi exemplify structures built on the model of the cosmos. For the Kógi, the universe is like an immense whirling spindle, weaving life from its male and female elements. The hard central shaft of the spindle is male. Penetrating the female whorl, it spins the thread from which the universe's fabric is woven. As the central shaft of the spindle traverses the universe vertically from top to bottom, it passes through the nine disk-shaped layers of the cosmos, which correspond to the nine months of gestation. The Kógi religious specialist first locates the center of the site where the temple will be constructed. Then, with a measured cord, he designs the layout.[153] "Although they build only the conical, above-ground section, . . . they think of their temple as continuing in mirrored segments," extending into the earth to the bottom of the universe and also into the heavens to the zenith of the cosmos.[154] The earthen floor corresponds to the earth itself, the central disk of the universe. Every beam and rafter of the frame corresponds to a structure of the upper part of the universe. The circular outer wall demarcates the circumference of the earth's disk. Pairs of posts mark off the cardinal directions; four wall posts sit at the intercardinal directions; four hearths, set at the intercardinal positions, represent the positions of the sun in its solstices. An opening at the top of the temple admits light from the sun when it is at its zenith. The beam of light that, over the course of the year, is cast onto the floor of the temple through the roof hole is considered to be the pattern of life woven by the sun in the universe. "Through the year, as the sun moves north, south, and north again, it is said to spiral about the world spindle. It weaves the thread of life into an orderly fabric of existence, and the cyclical changes of the sun's daily path are transformed into a cloth of light on the temple floor." [155] The sun is the male shuttle penetrating back and forth into the north-south warp of the female earth. "This pattern [of cosmic order based on the movements of heavenly bodies] is perceived in the mind, remembered on the loom, and played out in the temple, where the visible signs of celestial order make the space sacred." [156]

The patterned significance of space delineated in this chapter should not imply that all space has the same purpose or function. The richness of being characteristic of the center and the multiplicity of substitutable symbols that appear there encourage different spatial expressions of sacred places.[157] An elaboration of function and form may be found even within a single religious tradition, as is testified by the variety of Waiwai ceremonial enclosures already described. Afro-Brazilian traditions provide an additional illustration. Candomblé cult spaces highlight how strictly space can be associated with mode of being. The *ilé-ibọ-akú*, the house of worship of the dead *lẹṣẹ̀ òrìṣà* (sustainers of the divinities), is completely different from the *lẹ̀sànyìn*, the house of worship of the *egun lẹ̀sẹ̀ egun* (the sustainers of the *egun*). In the first space, the *ilé-ibọ*, the spirits of the *adóṣù* are worshipped. The *adóṣù* are priestesses who had been initiated into the cult of divine beings *(òrìṣà)*. In the *lẹ̀sànyìn* are worshiped the *ará-ọ̀run* (the ancestral spirits), the nine sons of Ọya and Ṣàngó, and Ọ̀run, which "is an abstract concept of an infinite, wide and distant place" inhabited by ancestral spirits and those who had been initiated into the mystery of the *egun* (ancestors who take on bodily forms.)[158] To each of these separate cult spaces is attached not only a separate mode of being (divinities versus ancestors) but a different hierarchy of ritual leaders (predominantly male in the first case and female in the second), a different technique of communication with the supernatural realm (as reported by Juana Elbein Dos Santos and Deoscoredes M. Dos Santos, possession is not used as a medium of communication in the *egun* cult), as well as a different set of rites and songs and a different calendar of feasts.

The act of consecration systematically replicates the symbolism of cosmic space. It reenacts the powerful acts of primordial beings, whose first appearances in space afforded the possibility of meaningful order. That is, consecration represents events occurring at the center, the place defined by the rupture of planes and the convergence of diverse modes of being. Consecration sets a place apart in the same way as the center was set apart by the appearance of powerful reality.

Replicated and generalized by means of the dispersal of sacred sites, specific symbols of sacred reality become central to the places where people live and to the reflexivity that makes for human creativity. Waldeloir Rego argues that the *òrìṣà* of Candomblé and the religious outlook of Afro-Brazilian religions in general are rooted in the sacredness of local places for historical reasons. He contends that the African cults from which these religions derive were location-specific, especially attached to the royal cities of West Africa.[159] Rego presents an analysis of the quarters and neighborhoods of the city of Bahia, detailing their religious meaning and history. Each section is under the patronage of a sacred being or beings and specializes in particular religious functions.[160] Before any gathering for worship can begin, a suitable place must be consecrated and an *ilé òrìṣà*, House of *Òrìṣà*, must be constructed. The *òrìṣà* will choose the place and make its will known. A seat is prepared for Èṣù, the "porter" or "doorkeeper," who will guard the entire area. Next, the house of the deity is constructed. Finally, an inauguration ceremony is conducted for the *ilé òrìṣà* (otherwise known as *roça*, Candomblé, *axé*, *casa de santo*, or *terreiro*). Once this sacred center is established, acts are carried out to extend the sacrality of space to the rest of creation, with special attention given to the rivers *(odò)*, the sea *(òkun)*, springs and wells *(ibu)*, and the firmament *(òfuurufú)*. As a result, virtually all important places become sacred to one degree or another.[161]

Space is shaped by the imagination's response to the appearance of meaning. Consequently, even houses in which people live out their everyday lives embody the sacred meanings revealed in universal space. For example, the Yekuana subgroup of the Makiritare construct their roundhouse in the same manner that the creator, Attawanadi, made the cosmos—that is, the first roundhouse. He began by setting the central post in the center of the universe. In this way, he linked together the realms of earth and heaven. Built into the structures of Attawanadi's house are places for the primordial sea and land and for the underworld of darkness and the dead. After establishing the center, Attawanadi set crossbeams oriented to the four cardinal directions. The beams set in a north-south direction are called *adämniädotádi* (the Milky Way). The sky is supported by the studs of the outside wall; these are called *shidichääne* ("pillars of the stars"). The joints of the beam structure mark the points of the solstitial sunrises and sunsets.[162]

In a rich comparative study, Johannes Wilbert points out the structural, cognitive, and mythical similarities between the Yekuana roundhouse and the structure of the universe among the Winikina subtribe of the Warao. He compares the physical and supernatural properties of the directions, the seasons, the shapes of space, the rays of the sun and the movements of the winds, skylight, the constellations, and so on. In addition to similarities, Wilbert stresses important differences that forestall diffusionist conclusions, which, he says, always have "a tinge of triviality." Instead, Wilbert concludes that "the correspondences together with the differences of Warao and Yekuana cosmological beliefs point to a larger cultural tradition of which these tribal ones are just two surviving examples. . . . Continental, but also insular and possibly Circum-Caribbean, elements were amalgamated over time, giving rise to local cultural variance with a common denominator." In particular, Wilbert stresses that both cosmologies, manifest in the universe and in the house, "recognize the squaring of the circle archetype as the organizing principle of personal and societal identity."[163]

This patterned structure is extended further. The Makiritare house is called *atta*. The *atta* houses the entire community. As with the Yekuana subgroup, the first *atta* was built by Attawanadi in such a way as to replicate the very structures of the universe. The name of the communal roundhouse also denotes "village," since the entire community lives in the single house. The house, the village, and the universe possess the same set of enduring structures, created by Attawanadi in order to make existence habitable for human beings. Within these sacred structures human beings can assume their position, their creative and courageous stance. The festival of Atta Ademi Hidi ("to sing house") recounts the first house construction and the arrangement of proper space in the human universe.[164]

The extension of the patterned meaning of space has endless possibilities. Reichel-Dolmatoff illustrates in striking detail the extent to which the same mythic image brings order to all significant spaces in Desana culture: the universe, the longhouse, the celestial vault, the hills (where dwell the master of animals and his charges), the skull (which houses the human brain), spider webs, tortoise shells, honeycombs, and so on. All of these spaces are ordered by the same supernatural forces that they contain. They are broken down into ordered compartments transected through their center by the cosmic anaconda with hexagonal quartz crystals of semen at her mouth. For example, the Milky Way, which bisects the celestial vault, is formed by two intertwined serpents, male and female.[165]

The place where sacred being first appears, whether the upper realm or the "first place" of life on earth, becomes the model for innumerable constructs of space in cultures throughout South America. It provides the model for the normative relationships among meaningful qualities of being expressed symbolically in the living space of the domestic unit; in the residence space of the community; in the spatial fixtures of the shrine, sanctuary, temple, or ceremonial plaza; or in the city, the empire, or the "world."

MODES OF BEING AS SPACES

Space is the appearance of being in imaginable, apprehensible form. It is the expression of the encounter of primordial being with human imaginative being. Images of space reveal necessary qualities of existence. Spatial existence enables human beings to live life surrounded by expressions of significance and value. Perception, understanding, evaluation, and judgment are possible and valid because of space's affinity with being. For good or ill, space shapes and guarantees the immersion of human life in reality. The Quechua world, for example, is full of powers (both beneficent and pathogenic) that are associated with the geographic features of the earth. Certain valleys are the homes of the evil spirits of hail and winds. Quwa, for example, lives in the wind and appears in many different forms, transforming himself as his need for escape arises. He brings sickness, paralysis, and death.[166]

The human imagination is central to the universe. Human life would not be the same in any space other than that of the center. To see reality from a different perspective is to be different; to enter another condition of space is to become transformed. This is demonstrated in accounts such as that of the

Wayãpi man who once took up residence in the underworld where the sun shines during the time called night in the upperworld. The children of the sun kept the human as a pet monkey in their house, where he lived for an entire month. At the time of the new moon, the moon came to visit his brother-in-law, the sun. At the moon's insistence, the sun presented the human being – monkey to the moon as a gift. "Then the moon carried the man to earth during his voyage at the time of the first quarter." [167] Only then was the man able to reassume his true shape and destiny.

Space is always dynamic. The significance of space is disclosed by the acts that take place there. Seen in this light, space is linked to historical action and to memory of it. The Akuriyo of southeastern Surinam are a nomadic people who do not have bounded, fixed territories. Trails are the important spatial markers with which they orient their world, both physically and metaphysically. Trails are esteemed because they are the loci of sacred events. "For the Akuriyo a trail is not just a path, but a cultural phenomenon; not just a geographic feature, a line connecting more or less useful things, but an ongoing series of historically related *events*." [168] The Akuriyo use these trails on their long treks. "The trails — chains of broken, bent, or twisted saplings, occasional ax cuts in the bark of a tree, emptied bee nests, and old campsites — can easily be recognized by a practiced eye." [169] Peter Kloos found that the Akuriyo use the trails, the geographic features, as mnemonic devices for ordering and recalling information that is extraordinarily rich in history and significance.

Understandably, spatial expressions bear a complicated relation to temporal expressions of being. Canelos Quichua spaces (e.g., *rumi*, "soul-stones") are entities that encapsulate mythic time. A different view, described in accounts from the Andean highlands, attributes the ubiquity of sacred spaces to the appearance of diurnal time. Stones are the dwelling places of dangerous Quechua ancestors, the Ñawpaq and Inca, who now have assumed the form of enormous monoliths. Once upon a time, the sacred stones tried to flee the central area around Lake Titicaca in an effort to avoid the dawning of the first day. They preferred to live in a state of permanent darkness. As the Ñawpaq fled to the peripheral forest, scattering themselves across the Andes, the sun appeared and immobilized them wherever they stood. As a result, "each group of houses possesses its own sacred stones to which offerings are made." [170]

The dynamic qualities of being revealed in any static space may be temporalized: that is, they may make periodic appearances elsewhere in the universe, thus spreading themselves across time in expressions of growth or abundance. For example, the Mataco say that a miniature version of all the summer fruits exists in the constellation Orion, the heavenly dwelling of Potsejlai, who is the Mataco master of wild fruit. Healing specialists visit this realm by riding on the backs of supernatural birds, which they call forth from their breasts with their sacred songs. [171] When an ecstatic curer visits Potsejlai, the healer gazes on the "still life" of fruit to determine whether the coming summer's crop will be plentiful or not.

By definition, all forms of manifest being pass through the center in order to appear in this world. This succession of apparent forms creates a procession of being. The center is held by one form of being after another. The order of their appearance, as reckoned in mythic narratives, defines the temporal order of feasts in the sacred calendar. The Tapirapé are a good case in point. Not only do the Tapirapé associate different cosmic spaces with different modes of being *(anchunga)*, but each spirit takes up residence in the center of the universe, the *takana* (the men's house, in the center of the village), for a fixed period of time during the year. The *anchunga*, represented by pairs of masked dancers, are mostly animal spirits of the primordium who now reside in the far-flung zones of the universe. Two by two, the *anchunga* appear in the men's house during the marked moments of the year. The masked dancers "sing" by making shrill cries that are the sounds of each spirit animal (fish, eel, pig, and so on). Such "song" periodically makes the *achunga* present in the center of the human world.[172]

The dynamism of space may be temporalized in still another way. Space may be arranged in such a way as to form a hierarchy expressed as a temporal order. In other words, the hierarchical arrangement of space expresses the order of time. The Inca empire, the most immense spatial organization in South America, stretched for some 4,300 kilometers along the west coast of the continent. "This vast territory, which the Inca called Tawantinsuyu, or 'Land of the Four Quarters,' was the largest empire ever formed in the native Americas, and probably the largest ever formed anywhere on a 'Bronze Age' level of technology." [173] Mercedes López-Baralt has carefully demonstrated the continuity of the basic categories of thought that underlie Andean images of space. The relations of objects in the mythic geography permit one to think in terms of evaluations of space, time, sexuality, and hierarchies of being.[174] For instance, the organization of space in the Inca empire and capital not only stood for the organization of modes of being,[175] but for the order of time as well. The Inca set up vertical pillars *(sucanca)* to mark the sun's position on the horizon at significant points during the year. Several of these important observation pillars were located on lines radiating out from the center of the city. Apparently, the pairs of pillars framed the sun at crucial moments of the agricultural year, providing indications that the planting season was approaching or that it was nearing its end.[176] Some lunar observations may have been coordinated with solar sightings.[177] There is little doubt among investigators that Inca concepts of time were embedded in the Inca's organization of space. But the interpretation of this interplay is an arduous task. As Aveni writes, "Sadly, the old historians paid too little attention to the sophisticated calendar system that was written in the landscape of Cuzco, under their very feet." [178]

SOME IMPLICATIONS

The symbolisms of the center, of the periphery, and of the mediating elements of space include one another. They are not evolutionary developments, one out of another, but rather are givens of the spatial universe; their relationships are dialectical. The nature of revealed reality and the nature of human imagination underlie the relatedness of the different qualities of space, which together make a universe possible.

Symbolic processes and human consciousness are inseparable. The meanings of different spatial structures are aspects of the human awareness of being. "Members of our species are peculiarly festooned with prepositions, with relational and functional connectives. . . . We are for, against, with, toward, above, below, against, within, outside, or without one another." [179] The center is of fundamental importance, for the appearance of being in symbolic guise permits humans to apprehend its meaning in the first place. The revelation of reality at the center calls the imagination, the specifically human mode of being, into existence and displays its fundamental structures. Human culture situates itself here. The center is primordial, for it is here that being first appears before the imagination. The distinctness that renders the center separate and knowable holds out the promise that the rest of space may exhibit distinctions that might reveal its meaning as well, since, by extension, it also can become symbolic.

The images of the periphery make limits and reflexivity possible. Consciousness, quickened by the appearance of reality at the center of the universe, can also turn toward itself. The symbolism of boundary betokens the processes of introversion, reflection, and reflexivity. These experiences of closure are responses to specific symbols of supernatural being that appear at the center of existence and are mirrored on its periphery, and such responses shape the identity of individuals and groups. The nature of space in the universe reveals that imaginative existence is self-conscious.

The mediating structures of space underscore the moving and dynamic aspects of being. Understanding is never a settled affair; rather, it is an ironic mode of existence: explicit meanings are juxtaposed in such a way that new meaning is revealed by their conjunction. Understanding dynamic being requires irony and paradox, for symbolic meanings overlap. The different symbolic orders of time evaluate and unfold the contrariety inherent in symbolic space. In this world-epoch, the full dynamism of space can be grasped only as a temporal expression. It is therefore to the structures of time that we now turn.

CHAPTER 4

TIME

BEING AND TIME IN THE POSTCOLONIAL WORLD

A glance at any culture reveals that all peoples use concepts of time to comprehend the world around them and, more especially, that people understand themselves as existing in time. This is true whether the significant temporal setting of culture arises principally from human agency or desire (as may be the case in certain notions of history or *samsara*) or from the movements of cosmic or supernatural powers. In either case, time becomes a principal instrument of understanding the properly human place in a world of heterogeneous spaces.

A basic observation opens this consideration of time in the religious worldviews of South America: every culture exists in *times*. Each society apprehends several, perhaps many, temporal orders, including day and night, solar and lunar years, astral calendars, biological cycles and rhythms, personal life cycles, and sociostructural schedules. There exist wholly different kinds of time: mythic, historical, lineage, vegetal, animal, mineral. These are religiously significant in degrees and for motives that vary from one culture to another.[1] Time in cosmos and culture is not, indeed cannot be, uniform in shape, homogeneous in texture, or univocal in meaning. The multiple modes of time cherished and reflected upon in every culture mirror the complexity of human experience. For those trying to grasp the function and significance of time in culture, this relativity raises several pressing questions.

What is time? What range of cultural choices confronts us in answering this question? Why do all peoples recognize the existence of plural times? Are they indeed all recognizing the same things? What does the fact that time always has cultural significance mean in understanding human being? Is the recognition of any particular concept of time essential to the human condition? Is time a human discovery, an invention, an extrapolation from natural rhythms and clocks, a cultural construction, being in itself, or a revelation? Is there any sense of time common to all its multiple manifestations?

Several of these questions fall outside the scope of this investigation and are the business, rather, of philosophy or phenomenology. Nevertheless, it is worthwhile to pose them explicitly, since they hover in the background of any cultural study. In the past one hundred years, scholars of culture (ethnographers, ethnologists, linguists, historians of religions) have attuned themselves, as everyone does, to the understanding of these issues embodied in their own traditions. Traditional images of time set the tone for fundamental evaluations of history, causality, morality,[2] and work (the labor time of political economy). The explicit and implicit temporal notions embedded in academic culture have affected the interpretation of South American religions. Consequently, those students who wish to make a serious exploration of South American cultures need to be self-conscious about the foundations of their own intellectual heritage.

There is also a deeper reason for posing the questions above. Failure to confront cognitive and existential issues while studying South American cultures must lead one to depict native concepts of time as simplistic adherence to the raw rhythms of nature or, at best, unreflexive conformity to ritual or mythic models.[3] Or it may cause one to exaggerate the differences between history and cosmic symbolism in a way that obscures their essential similarity. Because the symbolic nature and performative quality of narrative history and of other constructions of "ethnographic" time have been ignored, we have fallen into the familiar distinctions between kinds of peoples: historical (we latter-day "moderns") versus "primitive" (literally, the first peoples) — that is, those who hail from "primal," "prehistoric," or "microhistorical" societies. Their different grasp of time and, therefore, their distinct location in it has meant, for academic researchers, that "traditional" peoples are not "progressive," as are those in historical civilizations. Primitive temporal notions, when described empirically (like trilobites in amber), have been deemed immobilizing and nonreflexive constructs embedded in nature. According to such interpreters, these intellectual fossils have provided a glimpse into nonadaptive cultural forms, unfit to survive the cultural evolution that led to the industrial clocks of historical societies. Suspended in static equilibrium, primitive societies remained unable to use self-criticism in ways that would have made them agents of self-directed change. This distortion of perspective has been augmented by the fact that, while the contradictions of temporal experience in the investigators' culture (the time of Newtonian or Einsteinian physics, the time lines of geological strata, the time of European history, the varying atomic half-lives of different elements, the conflicting reckonings of Jewish, Christian, and Muslim calendars) were respected as depictions of the complexity of Western history, similar contradictions on the part of "primitive" peoples, whose temporal symbolisms include mythic and historical meanings of sounds, stars, plants, fragrances, and colors, were dismissed as garbled thought, lack of curiosity, or slow-witted indifference to inconsistency. Because hermeneutics of history and phenomenologies of time have begun to redress these exaggerations, they are important to the ethnographer. They demonstrate how history and cosmic rhythm can serve equally as instruments that satisfy the cultural demands for precision and as highly interpreted symbolic systems that allow a culture to evaluate its existence in time.

Too strict a separation of Western philosophies (worthy of reflection) from native concepts (fit mostly for ethnographic reportage) not only prejudged considerations unjustifiably, it implicitly condemned to oblivion the fully human dimensions of local philosophies and phenomenologies of time or history.[4] Cognitive, existential, and introspective aspects of temporal symbolism faded from view when scientists of culture overlooked its subtle reflexivity. A genuine and contemporary philosophy of history (or phenomenology of time) demands coming to grips with the complexity of cultures constituting the current global scene.[5] Dissemination of technology and the independence of postcolonial nations leave less room for manipulating temporal notions (e.g., unilinear evolution, the chronology of imperial history, or cultural relativism) in order to sidestep the confrontation with a plurality of self-conscious cultural histories.[6]

Would it be too much to claim that the foundations of a forward-looking philosophical anthropology must include the temporal constructs that have supported South American standpoints on human life? Ironically, even as they threaten to annihilate alternative cultural forms, the economic, political, and intellectual ponies (international trade, market, and monetary systems; multinational alliances and forums of sovereign states; ethnographic museums and academic ethnology) that pulled the colonial cart return home as Trojan horses, bearing oppugning ideas back into the center ring of "modern" history. From Africa, Oceania, Asia, and the native Americas come dissimilar existential responses to human existence, ironically recorded in writing even as (in some cases) the oral transmitters fell silent through extinction at the hands of the scribes. Whether alive or fossilized in ethnographic literature, these ideas form part of the reality of the world in which philosophers now find themselves and in terms of which reflective thinkers must seek to understand the truth of their own situation in history.

DIFFERENT STRUCTURES AND QUALITIES OF TIME

Before plotting a systematic analysis of the temporal materials, it behooves us to survey the terrain before us. Every group in South America marks off time into basic repeatable units.[7] The structures of these integers differ from one another. These lengths of time, measured with more or less precision, include the cycle of the year, the division of the year into seasons, lunar phases, day and night, and so on.[8] The day could be divided further. For example, the Nambicuara recognized six stages of the day; the Yahgan viewed the day as a succession of four-hour periods; the Araucanians reportedly broke the day into ten, twelve, or fifteen segments.[9]

South American cultures also recognize varying kinds of times. For example, the time lines governing the celebrations of the Quechua-speaking people of Pinchimuro, Peru, are of three different kinds, each one basing itself on a different manifestation of sacrality: cosmic life, the life of Christ, individual life.[10] Outstanding in this regard were the Kaingáng, who possessed a complicated system of semantic categories to express different qualities, including major paradigms, of time: "specific time," "time depth," "general time," "sequential time," "attitudinal time," "aspectual time," and "subjective time."[11] In addition, the Kaingáng distinguished a succession of units of time, some of which possessed a distinctly moral character. Given the complex breadth of the Kaingáng's temporal notions, Ursula Wiesemann's conclusion is all the more striking: "History was not one of their interests."[12] She writes that "before the conquest . . . the Kaingáng did not seem particularly interested in pinpointing events in time."[13]

Many reports make the same point. South American cultures recognize multiple kinds and units of time without using the unilineal variant of chronological history, which is predominant in dynastic genealogy, biblical account, the structures of written narrative, or industrial clock-time, as a primary measure of difference. David Maybury-Lewis points this out in regard to the Akwē-Shavante. They have a cyclical age-set system, which would allow them, using it as a mnemonic device, accurately to date past events. However, they choose only to demarcate three aeons: duré-hẹ (distant past), duré-iri (not-so-distant past), and nimõtsi (recent past).[14] "This lack of historical interest is at least partly explicable on structural grounds. With the possible exception of the age-sets themselves, the Shavante have no relatively stable corporate groups whose history might be remembered."[15] For example, the Akwē-Shavante "men's council" ordered and directed the hẹmono, the occasional communal hunts associated with important ceremonies.[16]

The realization that time is heterogeneous marks the starting point for any consideration of its religious meaning. Each quality of time reveals its proper meaning, the basis for its evaluation. People do not remain indifferent to the distinctness of times whose variable values order the cosmos, society, and the individual. Different times call for action appropriate to their character. For example, Candomblé practitioners in Bahia avoid being in the street at midnight, a dangerous hour of transition from one day to the next. They prefer to step into a building and wait for the first few minutes after midnight to pass by. Conversely, particular activities require suitable temporal conditions. Thus Candomblé festas de barração, in which the sacrifice of birds (bichos de pena) or four-legged animals (bichos de quatro pés) is a fixture, are public rites which must take place at night.[17] This is the case even though Candomblé ritual offerings (called oro in Yoruba or obrigação in Brazilian Portuguese) may be either cyclical or spontaneously required by the divinities. In quite different cultural milieux times manifest propitious conditions for variable activities. Night, for instance, is the only time when the Kari'ña celebrate both categories of their dances. Both in group choreographies and more powerful individual performances, Kari'ña dancers seek to embody the first beings who danced at the beginning of time. For the Kari'ña, night is the time most propitious for passing from one kind of existence to another because darkness lowers the marked distinctions between forms.[18]

The distinction that is essential for understanding the religious experience of time is the fundamental difference between mythic and other kinds of time, which latter flow from the transformations that brought the primordium to a close (the separation of darkness from light, sun from moon, upstream from downstream, and rainy from dry season; the appearance of irreversible death or of menstruation; and so on). The Canelos Quichua, for example, observe this basic distinction between the present and the time of "beginnings" (callari).[19] In the Time of Beginnings, the callari rucuguna, the ancient people were more knowledgeable than present-day people. All subsequent times are marked by a loss of that knowledge. These ages of imperfect knowledge began with the incestuous intercourse of the moon and his sister, the bird Jilucu. The subsequent flood brought on by the crying of their children, the stars, swept beings away from the intimate relation they once enjoyed with the world and set them within the moving world of star-time. During the annual rainy season, water streams down from the sky at the time when the Milky Way, the procession of star children, crosses it.

The thought of the Mapuche concerning the differential qualities of time provides an instructive addition to our survey. Diverse qualities of time are associated by the Mapuche with various manifestations of light. These gradations of clarity (anti) include, in order of descending value, morning (epewun), midday (rangin anti), twilight (kirinif), darkness (pun), and midnight (rangin pun). Each species of light-time has social, spatial, mythical, genealogical, moral, and theological correlates that find expression in ritual paraphernalia such as drums, rattles, bells, costumes, tree branches, and tree-trunk ladders, as well as in sounds and acts.[20] In the Mapuche view, ceremony does more than punctuate the flow of time into units. Throughout the years and across generations, ritual symbols shuttle strands of separate times back and forth so that they crisscross one another. Ritual life weaves the temporal filaments of myth and patrilineages into a multidimensional web, the matrix of human existence. At dawn on each of the three ceremonial days of the Mapuche fertility feast, special supplications are made. In order to understand the meaning of these supplications and the source of their power, one must understand the Mapuche concepts of sacred time. Basically, the Mapuche recognize two dimensions of time, two ways in which the luminous species of time may intermesh. Alün is the historical time marked by the individual and four preceding generations of ancestors. Events in this period of time may be spoken of in common speech. This kind of speech, dungulún (introspective speech), uses the first person singular. Events in this historical period may be related in improvised songs called *kantún*, which are nonritualized performances in which anyone may participate.

In contrast, mythical time *(alüaluntu)* embraces all the beings and events beyond the four generations of historical time. "In order of ascending importance and power, this domain comprises a group of overseers of natural phenomena (rain, clouds, volcanoes, rivers, mountains, etc.), four old couples responsible for the four cardinal points, the keepers of cosmological order (F'ta Chau and his wife, Ñuke Mapu), and the head of the universe (Ngeñechén)." [21] Communication with the hierarchy of beings who exist in mythical time can only be realized by using a special mode of discourse, the *lukutún*, for which there are special texts and melodies. Since the performance of the *lukutún* places the performer in another time-space context, that of the supernaturals, it is always ritually performed by specially prepared individuals.

The ritual transportation of the historical participants into mythical time by means of the symbolic vehicle of the Mapuche fertility feast underscores the fact that these two dimensions of time, *alün* and *alüaluntu*, "are indispensable to each other." [22] Just as the historical time of the individual flows back into the powerful ancestral period in order to prosper, so the divine couples of the mythic age continue to manifest their power in their historical descendants. This is graphically portrayed in the construction of the human person who, at birth, possesses two souls, which function as temporal organs. One is a purely individual entity, the other is shared by all the members of his or her patriline. The various kinds of time support one another, and even make each other possible, intelligible, effective, and significant.

The interpenetration of times effected in ritual is possible because ritual symbolism reenacts the beginnings, the period before time lines and cycles definitively separated from one another. Symbolic return to the time of unitive being and meaning makes imaginable the restoration of the integrity of time. In turn, occasional experience of that temporal condition *(illud tempus)* loosens the bonds of the imagination, too often tied up with single threads of time (historical, personal, patrilineal, and so on). By reminding the imagination of the fullness of time, ritual empowers it to reunite essence with existence, being with becoming, is with ought, freedom with history, beauty with truth, and truth with ritual method. This is why so many cultures insist that the religious experience of ritual time be normative for the aesthetic, intellectual, and moral life. [23]

Spatial symbols frequently negotiate the interpenetration of times. As vehicles of time, symbolic spaces communicate the idea that temporal meanings coexist. This is one conclusion of Jean-Paul Dumont's study of the Panare Indians of Venezuelan Guiana. The Panare realize that the sun, the moon, the Milky Way, the rainbow, and the stars reveal that "repetitive time and cumulative time coexist and mediate one another. By means of an astronomical code, the Panare — excellent philosophers ready to reconcile Zeno and Heraclitus — express the paradox of time." [24]

Because the Panare sun and moon are an incestuous brother-sister pair, time is given a bodily image and a sexual valence. All temporal differentiations — the daily movements of the sun, the nightly and monthly wanderings of the moon, and the movements of the stars — must derive from an initial unity of all temporal being, for the sun and the moon, as body-spaces, were once joined in an incestuous union. This is why all series of times, no matter how differently reckoned in the contemporary universe, are essentially one. By spatially embodying the image of simultaneity (for example, when incest images the union of heavenly bodies), the religious experience of space conveys in one symbolic vehicle the meaning of temporal relations that inhabit several different levels of signification.

Punctuations basic to the temporal rhythms of South American cultures are myriad: moments of death, destruction, change, disappearance, or occultation (of beings, flowers, fragrances); striking noises or sounds reverberating in the midst of silence; dance movements strutted in a static world; and so on. In their first appearances, these markers of time break into the status quo in ways that insert new conditions of existence into the world. Mythic events — first appearances, withdrawals, and transformations — punctuate time. Myths describe the creating moments that stand out from all others. Myth is essential to an understanding of the meaning of times because the mythic images of powerful moments signify the qualities of existence and the time-lines they instigate.

COSMIC CYCLES

Cycles are fundamental temporal structures. These symbolic complexes make time apprehensible. The meaning of a cycle is enmeshed in its symbolic expression (sounds, smells, colors, textures, fruits, etc.); cycles of time are the symbolic predicaments of specific existential meanings. Cycles based on the alternating appearances of sun and moon, day and night, or rainy and dry seasons signify perfection in a world steeped in transition. On the one hand, cycles respect the permanent character of being. Remarkable moments in a cycle, such as the first flowering of a species of fruit, return eternally, because whatever has been in some sense always is. The first appearance of this remarkable moment has made it part of the condition of being itself. On the other hand, cycles disclose the ephemeral nature of a world whose temporal structures cannot abide incompatible states of concrete existence. Cycles derive from the encounter of two unlikely modes of temporal being: the transitions of earthly existence and the fullness of mythic being cannot accommodate one another. Cycles have the best of both these worlds.

Each symbolic mode of being (e.g., celestial, lithic, aquatic, igneous) has imperial designs on meaning. Each tends to seize the center of the imagination, explain all of existence in terms of itself, and leave no room for other significations. However, ultimate symbols (the symbols in terms of which all else is understood) come full circle upon their own destruction.[25] By becoming ends in themselves such symbolic terms bring an end to themselves. For example, to understand being only in terms of water yields a flood that leaves no other forms visible or intact; or to understand all being in terms of fire gives way to drought and conflagration, which destroy all other meaningful symbols. Forcing a single dominant symbol to surrender its position to other expressions of meaning subjects it to the transitory structures of existential time, which alternates between appearance and occultation. In this way, every meaning has its proper time and every symbol brings its peculiar temporal meaning into existence.

Various origins account for the cosmic perfection, the programmed completeness, of cyclic time. Cycles may commemorate episodes in the life of a divine being or the lives of supernaturals. One cycle of Quechua feasts, for instance, underscores the sacredness of the structures of the cosmos and its rhythms. These feasts celebrate the acts of Pachamama, the holy mother earth who is the source of all life, and of the *apus*, mountain-dwelling divinities responsible for generating life in humans, animals, and fields. During most of the year Pachamama is peaceful and dormant, receptive to seed and growth. On special feast days, however, she takes on the active physical and emotional life of a woman. From 1 to 6 August, from 25 December to 1 January, and on the Feast of Saint John (24 June), Trinity Sunday, and Holy Tuesday, she receives offerings of food and drink. She is alternately annoyed and joyful; she speaks and she cries.[26] The cycle of cosmic feasts follows the fertility cycles of livestock: "alpacas and ewes during the carnivals and the feast of St. John, bulls and cows on Trinity Sunday and at the equinox of St. James."[27]

Similarly, the actions of Avíreri, the Campa culture hero and trickster, create cycles of time. He brings about the seasons and the night by playing music and dancing dances appropriate to them. Urged on by his curious grandson's questions, Avíreri becomes very drunk and happy and begins, for the first time ever, to play the panpipes. "It was he who showed it, therefore, all festive activities also."[28] Today river water levels rise and fall to mark changes of the Campa seasons because Avíreri once played powerful panpipe music to bring on the rains. The rainy season is called Kimohánci, from the word which means "big water." The dry season, Osarénci, serves as a way of measuring years, which are reckoned by dry seasons, or "summers." The Machiguenga reckon time in two seasons, rainy and dry,[29] in ways noticeably similar to their Campa neighbors.

The Apinayé also attribute the origin of time cycles to events in the lives of supernatural beings. The lunar cycle depends on the adventures of the moon, the brother of the sun. Special songs are sung by the Apinayé during lunar eclipses, when men fire burning arrows at the moon and an elder holds up a girl shouting, "Look, here is your wife! Don't die!"[30]

The constant reappearance of moments of time affords access to the modes of being they signify. For example, the time of transition from night to day is recognized by the Canelos Quichua as the period when the present merges with the mythical past. At that time, souls can leave their bodies and wander through the domains of the universe, where they acquire soul-substance and new knowledge of the meaning of the universe. Dreams are ways of circling, of backtracking, into the mythic past. Dreaming is the proof of the existence of soul-substance. *Muscuna*, "to dream," also designates visionary experiences with hallucinogens (*Datura spp* or *Banisteriopsis spp*). Dreams and visions of the primordial past account for and effect the reality of the diurnal present. The cycle of day and night assures that nothing is lost and highlights the essential relatedness of both qualities of time: knowledge of the past reveals the meaning of the present.

CYCLES OF STARS

The perfection of each cycle has its own story. The origin of the stars, for example, brings to light meanings of existence that shimmer differently from one culture to another. Unlike the brilliant sun, with its easy perfection, or the inconstant moon, with its dazzling but fallen aspirations, the stars twinkle back from the sky every halftone of fractured light. Their lackluster life is of a betwixt-and-between sort, an overlap of splendor daubed with darkness, shade suffused with light. Stars being to light the indiscretion of time, that is, the forbidden union of prescriptively discrete qualities of time. According to the Panare, *tyakun* (stars), whose sexuality is not very well defined, spring from the incestuous union of the sun and his sister, the moon. The appearance and disappearance of the Pleiades[31] often serve to divide the circle of the year into two equal halves. Other stars are characteristic of the dry or rainy seasons, and their appearances and disappearances mark midyear points for other cycles that begin and end at different points on the calendar's yearly round. Consequently, "there is a brief overlap in each season of the stars conceived of as belonging to the opposite season."[32] The Panare look upon these "overlapping seasons" as separate and distinct periods, "which in themselves form an opposition to the seasons proper."[33] The interseasonal periods are marked off by four movements of stars: the appearance of the Pleiades and appearance of Orion's Belt delimit the first interseason, and the disappearance of the Pleiades and the appearance of Antares mark the outer limits of the second interseason. The conjoined meanings of incest, generativity, multiplicity of times, and death also flicker in the Panare origin myths of the Milky Way's nameless stars, the burning souls of the dead.[34]

In the Canelos Quichua mythic origin of the astral cycle, the moon, in an incestuous union, fathers the stars and thereby peoples the realm of the sky. Knowledge of their origins besmirches the stars' once radiant splendor. In fact, all celestial bodies are brilliant suns of the night (*tuta indi*). They glitter dimly because they smeared *genipa* paint on their faces as a shameful sign of their incestuous origin. Glistening in the dark, the stars follow the irregular habits of the moon — with the exception of the Evening and Morning Stars, whose appearances accord with the regular movements of the reliable sun.

The fact that astral cycles rhythmically follow the cadence of fate fosters a sense of security and predictability. By locating events within the revolutions of time as these are marked by the acts of supernatural beings, cultures understand and evaluate their changing historical destiny. As suggested by the origin myths, however, such security carries with it an undercurrent of tragic irony.[35] The cycles of stars reveal the meaning of past events, whose effects are inescapable because they constitute the present conditions of existence. For example, when Bartolomé Ruiz led his men and horses onto the coast of Ecuador for the first time, the Inca Huaynacapac received word from the coast that "the waters had disengorged marine monsters, looking like men, who move on the sea in huge houses." Aides reminded the Inca that an astrologer foresaw this event in the stars as early as a year before it happened.[36]

The sun, moon, and stars, and the colors of seasons and species, illustrate degrees to which celestial light, the substantive being of the primordium, has assumed cyclic structure and persevered even under cosmic conditions of time. Every gradient on the spectrum of light has a beginning and an end, a rising and a setting. Day, night, month, year, Venusian and synodical cycles, molting and foliage seasons—all spangle a universe darkened by the withdrawal of fully manifest being and expose the meaning of primordial light, now appareled in guises that are better suited to worldly existence. Nonetheless, abundant life still depends upon the presence, *mutatis mutandi*, of primordial light, whose multiple and colorful appearances now end and recur, obedient to the constraints of symbolic existence, wherein nothing can be totally apparent.

SWATCH-TIME AND THE ECO-NICHE

Light is not the only recurrent form. There exist other kinds of life-giving compromises between mythic permanence and cosmic transitivity. These are the cycles of fragrances, flowers, fruits, and honey, as well as the cyclic comings and goings of insects, and their buzzing noises and of migrating fauna and their calls. Sounds and smells are not abstract measures standing apart from the meaning of the time they signify. They are tokens of the temporal conditions marked by regular appearance.

CYCLES OF SOUNDS   Gary Urton describes how the cycle of daily tasks and of seasonal divisions and activities in the Quechua community of Misminay revolves around sound. "[A]round 4:00 a.m. . . . the village slowly comes to life through sound"—the whistle of *pichiko* birds, the crowing of roosters, the flapping of hens' wings, and the braying of a burro all processing toward dawn.[37] "[T]he greatest amount of noise in the village occurs at dawn and dusk: unnecessary noise, even that of animals, is not easily tolerated at any other time. . . . Noise marks the transition from day to night and from night to day," whereas deliberately controlled sound orders the rest of the day and night.[38] Distinctive sounds also mark the rainy and dry seasons: drums and *quenas* (flutes) are associated with the rainy season; *pututu*s (wooden or, in some communities, conch-shell trumpets) are associated with the dry season. Even these seasonal instruments resound with respect for the daily sonic epicycles. Men play the drums and flutes, for example, only during the hoeing periods during the wet months of November and January. They do so exclusively in the late afternoon, "between sunset and darkness," when they return single file from the maize fields after a day of reciprocal labor *(ayni)*.[39] Soft at first, the music continues until nine or ten o'clock at night, building to a crescendo during the drinking of fermented *chicha* at the home of the owner of the field. Urton was told that "the drum and flute music helps the maize grow."[40] The *pututu*, in marked contrast, may only be blown outdoors in the morning during the wheat harvest, which occurs in the dry months of April and May.

Examples abound of time-specific sounds, for no sound in this world is constant and unbroken. Therefore, each sound can become the best measure of the period defined by its duration. Sound-specific times and the sounds that characterize them are perfectly consonant. During Carnaval at Juncal in the highlands of southern Ecuador, for instance, performers play certain musical instruments that must not be heard during any other time of the year: the *pingullo*, a flute made from the bone of a condor, and the *caja*, a small tom-tom. These were the instruments played by the mountain-being, Táita Carnaval ("Father Carnival"), when he came to open the mountains with musical sounds and distributed to the people the goods that were contained inside.[41]

The role of sound in the construction of a world-order enlarges our concept of what a cosmology is. The world, perceived as a unified order, is not spread out before the eyes in full static view but, like sound, is "dynamic and relatively unpredictable, an event-world rather than an object-world, highly personal, overtly polemic, fostering sound-oriented" structures, which are in constant process.[42] In addition, perception of the universe as a dynamic event of sound recognizes that the world is a powerful presence: "Sound signals the present use of power, since sound must be in active production in order to exist at all. . . . Hearing registers force, the dynamic."[43] Furthermore, the presence of the universe, betokened by sound, is always personal: "[V]oice is for man the paradigm of all sound, and to it all sounds tend to be assimilated. We hear the voice of the sea, the voice of thunder, the voice of the wind, and an engine's cough . . . , an unpredictable and potentially dangerous dynamism. . . ."[44] When looking at the world as a sonic event, a set of voices, cosmology becomes a theory for ordering the relationships among personal beings. The senses of sight, taste, smell, touch, and hearing are grounds from which such correlations arise. Cosmic order, however, is not rooted exclusively in any single sensory soil. Rather, it is embedded in the whole experience of existence, an integrity created in the imagination.

CYCLES OF FRUITS, FLOWERS, AND FRAGRANCES   Every species of fruit and food-crop brings a new cycle of time into existence. Human time-lines may conform to specific vegetal cycles, singled out for their religious meaning. The fruit festivals of the northwest Amazon are famous. There the rhythm of individual life cycles and of generations is tied to the initiation of age groups during the propitious time for specific fruits. For example, the sound of red fruit as it falls punctuates Baniwa mythology. This percussion first creates the cycles, which continue to mark time forever. Not only do the sounds of falling red fruits establish the cycles of the fruit season of ripening and rotting, but, in the case of the myth of the celestial divinity Yaperikuli, the same sounds and fruits establish cycles of menstruation, birth, and initiatory rebirth.[45]

Vegetal time can become the predominant temporal measure used in evaluating human existence. Curt Nimuendajú alludes to the vestiges among the Apinayé of an annual ceremonial rhythm that began with clearing ground for planting. Lifting seeds to the rising sun, a representative from the upper moiety planted the first clearing. Following his lead, the entire community sang to the sun while continuing the sowing. Next, there followed the Čwỵl-Krõ to celebrate the moon.[46] The community then went on trek until harvest time. During the trek, two guardians (one from each moiety) presided over the growth of the "children," the fruits of the garden. Because the sun and moon created humans from gourds, cucurbits receive special attention. The guardians measure the length of these gourd-children and promote their growth by song and magic. For example, the guardians are required to sleep with their bodies straight so that the gourd-children will grow to full length within the proper time.[47] Eventually, when the time for the harvest arrives, one of the guardians brings mature fruit of the garden to the hunters' camp. After one last communal hunt, the trekkers log-race their way back to the village. "This marks the opening of the great ceremonial period." [48]

In a similar way, the ceremonial cycle in the mining community of Pataz (Pataz Province, Department of Libertad, Peru) is anchored to beans. The community's largest feast is held toward the end of April. It lasts five to eight days and honors the patron saint of the town, Santo Toribio. The principal activity is the parading and processing of the statue of the saint throughout the whole area. For the occasion, the saint's effigy is dressed up in the clothes of a traveler. Everywhere he passes people play music, set off firecrackers, dance, and drink.[49] The procession of the saint reenacts the moment, in 1605, when Archbishop Toribio de Mogrovejo visited Collay. During the time when the Saint is on display, the mood is one of wild euphoria. The parish priests are always prevailed upon to allow Santo Toribio to stay out a little longer. Although it commemorates an historical event, the feast always coincides with the blooming period of the greatest number of brilliantly colored flowers. More specifically, its timing coordinates with the appearance of the first fruits of an unspecified bean plant. In fact, during the procession, people frequently leave the parade route in order to attack, in mock destruction and despoliation, the seed beds of these beans.[50] Several of the important festival songs link the patron saint with the beans: "Santo Toribio, green sombrero [which he wears during his travels], each time that you come my beans [habas] are destroyed." [51] As the saint is carried throughout the environs, newly ripened food products (sugar cane, fruits, and so on) are heaped onto the platform on which it is mounted. Eventually, the saint is returned to his place in the church. His peasant traveling clothes are once again exchanged for the dignified dress of a bishop, and he waits there until his voyage at the same time next year.

Le Ahuno is the principal feast marking the festival cycle of the Waica. It is held during January and February. The timing of the celebration is dependent upon the cycle of *lasha*, the fruit of the peach palm *(Guilelma utilis)*. When the ripened fruit appears, the Waica gather it for the feast. The Witoto also mark their festival year by the appearance of the same fruit.[52]

The flowering of specific trees during the wet and dry seasons marks off periods within the Campa and Machiguenga year.[53] "When a visit is planned or an engagement made, the time is fixed by the blooming of a certain flower."[54] Within the flower cycles, shorter periods of time are calculated by observing the moon and the sun.

The appearance of flower fragrance or animal musk does not occur *at* a time that stands independent of it. Like a swatch of fabric that actually is the material it represents, the floral or animal essence *is* that time, which cannot be accounted for in terms of any other kind of clock. The aroma of seasonal flowers or the odor of estrus constitute a determined order of time because their redolence is symbolic; that is, they *are*, albeit in a limited way, the very powers they give off. Being a unique mode of existence, each scent exudes a specific temporal condition, a remarkable moment whose fading and return form a cycle. Perfume not only marks special occasions but makes times special.

CYCLES OF ROT, CONSUMPTION, WASTE, DECAY   Each cycle depends on contradictory states of being distributed in time: ripening and rotting, birth and death, solid and hollow, wetness and drought. Claude Lévi-Strauss has drawn together a large number of such conditions recognized in South American myth, which he terms the "science of the concrete."[55] The alimentary cycle, for example, revolves through the conditions of hunger, consumption, satiety, excretion, and renewed hunger. Periodic existence accommodates ontological contradiction and allows even mutually exclusive states to cohere in a single integral experience within the imagination. Although there may be many of them, cycles are relatively simple units of time based on disappearance and reappearance. The diverse cycles are the ways in which each species of creature replicates the disappearance of the supernatural world at the close of the primordial age and its occasional reappearance in the symbols of subsequent epochs.[56] The primordial roots of symbolic realities account for their power to return eternally. From time to time, the cycles of stars, fruits, flowers, and fragrances manifest that same sacrality. It explains their dynamism and relentlessness.

To exist within a cycle of time means to have a beginning. Cycles celebrate creations and beginnings. It must also be said, however, that cycles have their ends. Temporal cycles of any kind, such as the solar year or the fruit or rainy seasons, imply annihilation of time's unbroken and homogeneous flow. They must end in order to begin again. In fact, any temporal marker (e.g., the New Year's feast or the appearance of the Pleiades) entails disruption of some sort (e.g., cosmic flood or fire, the withdrawal of a supernatural being into the sky, the petrification of primordials).[57] The brokenness of marked temporal orders favors the observation that there exist symbolic identities among different realities and different symbols for identical realities. Recognizing temporal similitudes is a reflexive act that grounds the human condition: one turns back to the time whose meaning is always the same but whose concrete conditions of appearance, in some ironic sense, can never again be fully manifest. Symbolic life reimposes the existential distance it promises to overcome. On the one hand, it takes one back to the moment of rupture that marks time — for example, to the primordial first feast of mythic animals, the slaying of the aquatic dragon, the emergence of the ancestors, the falling of the first fruit, or the first rising of the sun. On the other hand, the insurmountable nostalgia that provokes continual symbolic return to the origins of time induces the self-conscious realization that there can be no going home. Cyclic ceremony periodically retrieves and relives the meaning of all the human experiences of that "same time." This ritual exercise in the hermeneutics of time steeps humans in a profound appraisal of their existence. Through recollection, people grasp their own situation in a critical way.

Marked by ripening and rotting, flowering and fruiting, percussions and interruptions, consumptions and excretions, appearances and occultations, cycles depend on recognizing the *significance* of apparent breaks in the flow of time. The cyclical nature of time in this world is being's concession to the transitory nature of cosmic existence. Human senses are organs for adaptation to these changing conditions of meaning. Urton writes,

> It is important to note that the divisions and passage of time are related to the different crops and activities, and that these in turn are related to the different senses. Since the astronomical reckoning of time depends primarily on vision, the above material suggests that the total perception of time and space will involve the union of all sensual perceptions of change in the environment.[58]

Cyclical existence accompanies the realization that comparable and contrastive meanings present themselves in semblances, resemblances, simultaneities, and analogies. By recounting the first appearance of temporal markers, myths identify the symbolic guises of their times and display their meanings. These mythic similitudes provide a warrant for all temporal cycles and guarantee human life against an endless succession of dissimilar, unique, and dissembling experiences. Insofar as it is cyclical, then, symbolic existence becomes the repository of verisimilitude; that is, the constant return to meanings apparent in mythic beginnings makes truth a central human question. This explains the privileged status of mythic time in establishing the foundations of culture.

CALENDAR OF SACRED FEASTS

Calendars are complex devices. They respect the multiplexity of human experience. They function negatively to overcome the hegemony of any single quality or symbolism of time. They also operate in a positive way. Throughout various courses — rotating episodes suited to the impulsive senses of human beings, whose interest soon flags — calendars nourish people with a well-rounded diet of temporal experiences. The variety of temporal treats reflects the multiple realities that appear in the mythic period, at its demise, and in subsequent history. Calendars insist that cultural experience be real and full. All that has ever come or gone finds its point on the calendar round, which reconstructs and maintains the delicate web of existence. Because calendars emphasize the value of experiencing incompatible modes of time, they embody contradictions. Because they reenact the establishment of the conditions of fruitful existence, the calendar of rituals keep life creative, abundant, and ordered.

Conversely, failure to carry out calendric ritual in the proper fashion can have cataclysmic results. For example, an eclipse of the sun, with its drastic consequences for the life of beings in the world, is thought by the Panare to be the result of a poorly performed ritual, "a bad dance" at the peak of the dry season.[59] The Panare are not the only South American people who know that ritual performance maintains the order of the universe. Symbolic action upholds or, in some cases, redefines the fragile web of multiple spatial relations, periodicities, and life-forms characteristic of the cosmos.

MYTHIC EVENTS FOUND FEASTS

Rituals maintain the arrangements of time because they reenact the events that created temporal orders in the first place. For instance, four annual feasts were celebrated by the Witoto during 1969–1970. The unfolding of each feast, from the very beginning of its preparation, is marked off into episodes by an extremely solemn recitation called the "word of the father." Although no mythic narrative is recited on these festive occasions, the "word of the father" is a formal list, in eleven sections, of the fundamental concepts of the world; it is enunciated in such a way that "the very order in which [the fundamental concepts] are evoked retraces the unfolding of the first stages of creation." [60] In a different case, many Makiritare festival games and dances are modeled on the strange courtship behavior of Attawanadi, who structured time and space on the model of the first communal house, and Kaweshawa, the daughter of the master of fish.[61] Similarly, the Waiwai order the progress of their year around mythic events. They observe two major festivals. Unfortunately, the ethnographer Niels Fock was able to observe only one of these, and the more important feast, the two-month-long Yamo Dance, has never been witnessed by an anthropologist. It celebrates the time when anaconda-people rose up out of the river (due to an adolescent girl's glance) but were defeated by her patience, strength, and endurance. At the direction of her grandmother, the girl controlled herself and sat still for a longer period of time than the anaconda-people were able, while awaiting her appearance, to keep dancing. Her motionlessness overcame their powerful movements simply by outlasting them in time. Ultimately they retired, leaving their ceremonial decorations in her house; the girl immediately emerged from the seclusion of her clay vessel and fled from a cosmic flood in the company of her grandmother, who carried with her into the forest key items of culture, including the Yamo Dance costumes left by the anaconda-people. An adolescent girl's power to endure and her grandmother's wise directions had defeated the anaconda-people once and for all.[62] This mythic drama marks homologous moments in personal, social, and cosmic time: individual female adolescence, group celebration of a new generation of women, and the beginning of a new season.

In the same way, Mapuche rituals interweave mythic threads to merge the time of an individual lifespan with the times of the growth of crops, the breeding cycles of animals, human lineages, seasons, and day and night. The Mapuche celebrate a fertility rite, the Ngiyipún, usually in March or April.[63] It lasts three days and two nights. The purpose of the ceremony is to augment the harvest and increase the herds. To guarantee this increase, the Mapuche consider it essential to invoke a certain quality of time, a mythical past. In fact, it was Ilche Wentrú and Ilche Domó, the mythical first couple who populated the earth, who taught the ceremonies to human beings "so that we might see the things of the past."[64]

In rituals that bind and loose diverse qualities of time, recollection is key. The abundance of Mapuche herds and the prosperity of individuals depend on the memory of the *witakultruntufe*, a female ritualist who presides with her song. It is essential that she recall the entire *tayil*, the time-transcending lineage-soul that conveys prayers to the supernatural beings who act in mythic time. She does this by solemnly singing the genealogies of the men who form the core of the patrilineal residence group. In the same way, female adults, prepubescent boys, and certain ceremonial animals chosen for sacrifice have their *tayil* performed. All the time-lines are gathered by name and merged to recreate the wholeness of mythic time. Then the act that ended the flood and closed the mythic era is restaged: ewes are sacrificed by having their hearts removed and tied to two apple branches at the center of an altar.[65]

The ways in which mythic precedents symbolically reappear in the feasts they found can vary. During the most important of their yearly feasts, Canelos Quichua women and men recreate images and acts of the Ancient Times. While men are away on a ritual hunt, women haul pottery clay into the house. They then work for many uncomfortable hours forming ritual pottery trumpets, figurines, drinking and storage bowls, and so forth. Through their "think-singing" of spirit songs and through their designs and decorations, women impart souls to these pottery vessels. During this intense pottery-forming time, the women recite myths to one another, stressing the episodes and themes associated with their pottery designs. "Each woman is molding a special created mythic universe segment, to combine into a ceremonial whole with the other female-produced segments."[66] Through their designs and shapes, the potters recreate figures from Ancient Times and from all epochs of myth and history. Norman Whitten calls attention to the many two-sided figurines, such as the one with a *jilucu* bird, who is the moon's sister and sexual partner, on one side and an eagle-owl soul of a shaman on the other side. Indeed, the universe is reintegrated in a new and creative way through these individual women. For nearly a week men are absent, and culture (the whole house and, symbolically, the whole universe) is entirely *female* as it replicates an Ancient Time. During this time men are "gone." In their production of world-items and in their singing of the primordium, the women celebrate a ceremony within the ceremony. Whitten observes how each woman enacts a

> personal integration of design, life, spirit, and soul substance. The mutual, collective endeavor of graphic portrayal generates an intra-ceremony female universe symbolizing, among other things, temporal and spatial reintegration and ayllu continuity. Women excitedly watch and listen to one another as they work along on their own projects. Individuals sing songs, and older women sometimes help out younger girls, even imparting small secrets to them.[67]

During the men's absence, the women also prepare as much as four hundred gallons of *chicha* for each ceremonial house. During the preparation of this manioc brew, the women think-sing songs of Nunghuí, as well as other songs with mythic themes. The women beseech the birds and the rivers of the sky to transport their thought-songs to the men, who are hunting far away. During the night, when the women dream, they are able to observe the fate of their song flights. In their dreams they receive songs sent by the hunting parties. During this period of ritual separation, then, songs and dreams (carried by birds and rivers) connect the sexes as they reenact the first times.

Apinayé feasts frequently reenact the achievements of the sun and the moon. During the third day of the Apinayé harvest feast, a man from the "lower" moiety, with his face blackened, attacks a wasp nest in such a way that he is stung very badly. This celebrates an ancient mythic event in which the sun tortures the moon by causing wasps to sting him. However, the moon succeeds in obtaining special medicine from the sun in this way. In fact, each of the various travails of the Moon (he is mocked and made to stumble and fall, his testicles are pinched, his hair and skin are singed, and so on) succeeds in obtaining a boon to human culture (the arrangement of domestic space in the house, ceremonial ornaments, honey, game, and so on).[68]

Afro-Brazilian festivals frequently celebrate the acts of supernaturals or the descent of mythic kings to earth. The Candomblé festival of Osala, father of all the gods, commemorates his creation of all things. In Bahia it extends over a three-week period. The festival begins on a Saturday night with the celebration of Água de Osala; the feast of the First Sunday of Osala is celebrated throughout the next day. It is on this First Sunday that Osala appears, dancing to his songs. He is welcomed as an honored guest. On the Second Sunday, Osala again returns to his people, this time in a solemn procession below an *àlà* (ceremonial white cloth). On the Third Sunday of Osala, known as the Pilão de Osala, he distributes his special foods to the participants.[69]

A twelve-day set of rituals likewise celebrates the mythic adventures of Şàngó, the god of fire. Ìyá Mase (also known as Dada or Bāyànní), Şàngó's mother, is goddess of the vagina—the keeper of the gate through which all human life must pass to enter this world. Şàngó's father is Oronyòn, a former king of Oyó, a royal city of the Yoruba peoples of West Africa. These figures of the fire god's birth and youth reappear throughout the days of the ceremony. They play key roles in restaging the outstanding moments of his divine life.[70]

Symbolic actions that mark time base themselves upon sacred events that established new temporal orders. Ritual and myth become the responsible ways of reacting to symbolic life. Both genres possess narrative and performative qualities; that is, both frame reality within the temporal conditions of plot, story line, and episode by which drama unfolds. Both ritual and myth maintain critical and reflective awareness of the sacred realities whose emergence transformed existence in time. The symbolism of those apparitions generates imaginative connections, calendric webs of meaning that intercalate the world's delicate movements. In this universal ecology, human acts carry cosmic consequences.

Calendars of feasts coordinate into a single system all the time cycles revealed by the appearance and disappearance of primordial beings in the mythic world. Unlike cycles that focus exclusively upon the appearance and disappearance of a single entity, calendars include the appearance of all significant qualities of being, each one of which asserts the existence of a unique imaginable mode of time. Just because complex temporal systems are essential to and ubiquitous throughout all cultures, however, they should not be taken for granted. The simplest calendars reflect great subtlety. The axiomatic function of the primordium displays a sophisticated irony: the inordinate power of extraordinary beings makes calendric order imaginable. Mythic events impose meaning on the unbroken flow of experience in such a way as to organize a temporally heterogeneous cosmos. Each event or appearance in the mythic world literally *makes time* for a new mode of being. The present-day world experiences these different ontological states only as separate, serial, periodic, or ironic moments.

In order to perdure through time, cultures are forced to react creatively to sacred appearances; cultures must remember and transmit sacred meanings in a manner befitting their character.[71] Subjected to the creative imagination of human culture, the realities of the mythic world become different lengths of time, jointed together to form one body of moving parts, rhythmic limbs stretched out as moments in the festal calendar. Calendars license distinct ritual reactions to symbolic life and coordinate them. A calendar cycle variously displays, commemorates, reflects upon, rediscovers, covers over, or redefines symbolic meanings. In short, by manipulating the sensual symbols (sounds, smells, sights, actions, etc.) that constitute cycles, calendars experiment with the sacred realities whose appearance first structured existence in time. Through calendars, cultures redesign the meaning of their universe and keep intact their experience of it.

DESTRUCTION OF THE PRIMORDIUM: WHEN EVERYTHING IS TIMING

Cycles conjugate to produce a calendar. Given the fundamental role of the disappearance of primordials in forming each of the interlocking cycles, it is not surprising that the most important festivals allude to the great chaos that dissolved the entire primordial world. Dance ornaments, undertones of forbidden union, ceremonial space, ritual competitions, chaotic noise, special songs, fires, drink, and darkness can refer to the moment of cosmic destruction, when the old world passed away.[72] The great Makiritare garden festival, for example, celebrates its own beginnings and includes the recitation of its origin myth. Associated with the adventures of the supernatural twins, the story is a variant of the universal flood. At the first feast, the brothers spilled a gourd of oils used in body-painting. The container had been taken to earth from the house of Huiio, the water-mother, which lay at the bottom of the river. When it spilled on the earth it caused a flood. The body-paint oils used during the Makiritare drinking feast bring to land again the liquid of the aquatic monster's domain, a world made real both by painted skin and by the intoxication produced in the carousers by the fermented brew they imbibe. The body-paints are temporal markers, not only because they signal a stage in the festival, but because they coat bodies with chaos, the unmarked reality whose appearance from watery depths washed time itself, flooding and submerging primordial life. The palm tree in which the twins took refuge from the flood becomes a key marker of the temporal order in an otherwise unmarked world. As the twins consumed its fruit, consumptive time began to meter existence, and the sea receded to its proper place at the edge of the Earth.[73] Fruits of the Makiritare garden continue to furnish the stuff of festive consumption for the feasts that fuel the march of calendric time.

Festivals frequently make symbolic allusion to the sacrifices of primordial beings, whose deaths brought order to life in this world. The Waiwai, among other groups in South America, celebrate a rite in which women symbolically slay "animals" imitated by men. As Fock points out, "The dramatic representation of a hunt and the ordering of a number of the most important food animals must be assumed to have a magical significance, though its importance is to some extent forced into the background by the sporting and amusement aspects."[74]

Destruction becomes the key moment, generating multiple (and multiplying) times. Disappearances of primordial conditions become turning points to new stretches of time, new qualities of existence. The point of passage, of destruction, assures that calendars are built on a paradoxical experience of time, wherein the end becomes the beginning and the celebration of the beginning marks an end to what has already unfolded. In order that life press on, time renews itself by returning to its source.

CALENDARS INFOLD DIVERSE CYCLES

Calendars gather cycles together at impressive cusps of time, intants of disappearance and reappearance for distinct conditions of existence. Turning points of this sort, often accompanied by vigils and fasting followed by feasts, incise time. Because they bring contradictory states of being together in one moment, feasts are anomalous. They nourish existence in time by consuming it; they restore time by taking time; they renew time by sounding a knell at its passing. The megacycles of the calendar explore such breaks in every plane of time and logic. The calendar round frees consciousness from fixating on any single time cycle and enriches experience by opening it to multiple dimensions of time. The paradoxical symbolism of calendar celebrations unites the infinitesimal moments of human life with the nearly infinite movements of the universe.

THE INCA CALENDAR: MOVING HIERARCHIES OF SPACE THROUGH TIME

No calendar in South America has received more post-Conquest attention than that of the Inca. This is probably why Wendell C. Bennett concluded his study of South American time-reckoning systems with the opinion that "few groups besides the Inca and Aymara can be said to have true calendrical systems." [75] For him the Inca calendar was a combination of agricultural and ceremonial temporal reckoning. R. Tom Zuidema has brought new understanding of the Inca calendar through his investigations of Inca myth, art, astronomy, economy, city architecture, textiles, social structure, and rituals.[76] Zuidema centers his study on the Inca capital of Cuzco, where the calendar integrated the movements of people in space with their positions in social hierarchies and their loci in genealogical and dynastic history. Framed between the Huatanay and Tullumayu rivers, which join to become the Villcanota River, Cuzco was divided into two halves: Hanan-Cuzco (the upper half, lying to the northwest) and Hurin-Cuzco (the lower, southeastern half). Centered on Cuzco, the Inca empire was divided into four quarters, each of which was ranked and its resident population divided into *ayllu*s, residence groups with rights to land. Zuidema contends that the Inca used hierarchies to organize space (e.g., altitude, imperial extension, distance from administrative centers, direction relative to the capital or to the equinoxial and solstitial points on the horizon) across time. The Inca calendar intercalated hierarchies of divinities, of spaces, of colors, of social groups, of animals, and of textiles. For example, each of the twelve months called for sacrifices that were coordinated with the need for rain and the growth patterns of crops. Long-haired white llamas were offered to the sun from September to November (the period framing the equinox), the time before the heaviest rains. At harvest time (March to May, framing the fall equinox), specific groups in the social hierarchy provided multicolored llamas for sacrifice to the god of thunder. The periods around both solstices were marked by sacrifices of brown huanacos (wild llamas) to Viracocha, the creator. One hundred animals were sacrificed in each of the twelve months.

The population of the valley in which Cuzco lies was divided into twelve groups, each of which was in charge of the rituals held at a specific sacred site *(huaca)* during the month after which the group was named. The spatial position of the sun and stars and the direction and distance from Cuzco at which each community lay served to coordinate the rotations of ritual presidency as well as the locations and timing of the rites. These rotations were announced with sounds and trumpets, a fact reflected in the extraordinary variety of Inca musical instruments.[77]

Genealogy also played a role in determining the ritual responsibilities that revolved through the rank order of those groups with noble Inca lineages (the ten "royal" *ayllus*). To each royal *ayllu*, depending on its direction from Cuzco, corresponded a plebian group of nonroyal lineage and ranked groups of local (non-Incan) peoples who had been conquered by the Inca overlords. Although the royal *ayllus*, called *panacas*, lived on land throughout the entire valley of Cuzco, they symbolically identified themselves with Hanan-Cuzco (the upper half of the city, which included Chinchaysuyu, the northwest quarter, and Antisuyu, the northeast quarter). The nonroyal *ayllus*, which were likewise scattered throughout the valley, prescriptively identified themselves with Hurin-Cuzco (the lower half, comprised of Collasuyu in the southeast and Cuntisuyu in the south and southwest). The calendrical ranking of the four quarters crosscut the hierarchical ranking of the two halves: Chinchaysuyu (northwest) ranked first in order; Collasuyu (southeast) ranked second; Antisuyu (northeast) came third; and Cuntisuyu (in the south and southwest) fell fourth.[78]

Panacas, whose ritual responsibilities were activated at precise periods throughout the calendar year, were not only administrative units and lineage-based residence groups. Their rank order also reflected altitude, as well as distance and direction from the capital. Specific *panacas* were associated with particular monthly periods. Through a complicated calculus of these features (descent, distance, rank, mythic origins, altitude, color, month, and so on), the *panacas* arranged the approximately 328 to 408 sacred spaces (*huacas*) within the *suyus* (quarters) into various calendrical sequences.[79] Such sequences could endow the shifting relations of the social groups that presided over specific *huacas* with astronomic values, which were reflected in terms of aphelionic and perihelionic half-years, sidereal periods of seventy-three nights, sidereal lunar years (formed in terms of double sidereal lunar months intercalated with the solar year to comprise what was perhaps an exclusively female calendar), Venusian cycles (of ten Venusian years, equated with sixteen solar years and ten double lunar cycles), and so on.[80]

Zuidema has hypothesized that such units are connected with the disposition of social groups and *huacas* on the landscape of Cuzco and its environs. The *huacas* were arranged to form some forty-one lines (*ceques*) radiating from the Temple of the Sun, at the center of Cuzco, toward the horizon.[81] The *ceques* allowed for an intricate and systematic numerical intercalculus of social and astronomic time. The Inca used these lines (apparently in combinatory groups formed by factors of three), the numbers of *huacas* that lay along them, and the shifting rank order of communities responsible for ceremonies at the shrines to calculate varying time-units in overlapping cycles and megacycles. Zuidema further demonstrates that Andean textiles encoded these unit-measures of time in repetitive sequences of colors, figures, and patterns. The typically mirror-image textile pattern with 5, 8, and 9 rows or figures of 73 units each, for example, would thus represent the 365 days of the solar year, the 584 days of the Venusian year, and the 657 days of the double sidereal lunar year, respectively. Since the activities of the *suyu*s also corresponded with the seasons (e.g., Chinchaysuyu with the months from December through February), peoples (and the places where they lived or prayed) whirled through the cycles of time, propelled by the power of sacred beings and ordered in accordance with cosmic forces. Thus, for example, the ninth mythical king-hero, Pachacuti ("he who turns time-space"), founded the *panaca* that presides over January, the second month of boys' initiation. During his own, legendary initiation, Pachacuti saved Cuzco from the destruction of a flood brought by a giant. Through his initiatory ordeals and feats he caused the sun to "turn around"—that is, to run another year's course after it had reached the end of its road at the December solstice. The principal feasts *(raymi)* of the Inca calendar followed the two solstices and the two equinoxes. The lunar cycle was also factored into their timing because the ceremonies began with the first new moon of the period.[82]

Although the Inca calendar had complex astronomic values, nonastronomic and nonagricultural measures were essential to its existence and operation: economic, political, and social units, together with their locations, sounds, and ritual activities, became principal symbolic coordinates in the calendar. Furthermore, by describing the original appearance and disappearance of supernatural beings associated with particular spaces and of genealogical founders whose symbolic acts and trappings constitute determined social units, myth provides the fundamental significant language of spatial meaning and rank order, the marks used to evaluate existence in time. Even in the case of the Inca, the precise intercalation of large numbers of cycles into orders of startling complexity does not depend on the predominance of mathematical or astronomic language.[83]

BEYOND THE INCA

Let us look more closely at the various ways in which calendars enfold distinct symbolic cycles. Cycles of labor, shifting resources, and crop growth figure largely in the Akwẽ-Shavante worldview. Important Akwẽ-Shavante ceremonies were coordinated with the calendar of economic tasks; for example, the two important stages of initiation coincided with the maize harvest and with the later harvest of beans and pumpkins.[84] Consequently, the community treks, during which materials were gathered for ceremonial regalia, and the months-long tedium required to manufacture dance masks and ornaments had to be coordinated with the calendar of shifting ecological resources and the calendar by which social relations and divisions of labor were coordinated with those changes. Such calendrical coordination of tasks and people was the task of the council of mature men (who were subject, however, to the advice and vetoes voiced informally but forcefully by women from their huts). Since the proper timing and aesthetics of ceremony are the symbolic instruments that effect the cultural order and the artistic pleasure they signify, it was imperative that Akwẽ-Shavante festivals be celebrated at their proper time. Given the immense set of complicated chores associated with important festivals, the correct timing of a set of feasts during the year (or during the important five-year cycle of an age-set) required considerable perspicacity. For example, the closing, climactic stages of initiation had to be celebrated at the appropriate time, the height of the dry season.[85]

The Apinayé calendar of festivals draws together crop cycles with solar and lunar periods, as well as with the times of day and night. It also coordinates times manifest in human beings: age-sets and the rhythmic movements of the body in time-factored dances. Apinayé celebrations honor the sun and the moon. Just before planting begins, the sun is invoked to protect crops.[86] Another important dance-feast in honor of the sun is celebrated at harvest time. It should be mentioned that the circle of houses and the dance plaza in Apinayé villages represent the sun.[87] During this four-day harvest feast, dancers paint themselves with *urucú* stripes and dance in three concentric circles, one for each age-set. The middle circle moves in a direction counter to the innermost and outermost circles. The concentric-circle dance lasts all day for each day of the festival.

The round of Guayakí feasts conjoined cycles of honey production, of the appearances of species of insects, of changes in temperature and winds, of colors of flowers, of the human life-cycle, of the gestation and birth of plants, and of the cyclic time of the dead (people of the past, whose existence was believed to characterize the future condition of the living). Once a year the Aché Gatu (a subgroup of the Guayakí) celebrated an annual feast of honey, the Tö Kybairu (from *tö*, "human heads," and *kybairu*, "new honey").[88] The feast was actually celebrated by the four or five bands that composed the Aché group that was called Iröiangi, ("strangers") by the Gatu band. These were groups with whom the Gatu group could form marital, economic, and military alliances. The festive reunion occurred toward the end of the month of June. Pierre Clastres witnessed the celebration in 1963. (The 1963 festival lasted for an entire month. Clastres believed that it was the last time the feast was ever celebrated.[89]) The beginning of the feast was signaled by the arrival of *duy pute* ("extreme cold") and by the transformation of the color of the flowers of the *kymata* liana from bright yellow to red. Seen as an aspect of the supernatural power of the red-flowered liana, the cold was said to "avenge" the liana. Vengeance *(jepy)* was considered a restorative process. The cold and the red flowers signaled the time when the universe itself moved to correct and reorder deviations, corruptions, and deformations that had seeped into the cosmic process during the year. Their appearance therefore signaled the propitious moment to reinstate the intended order of things.[90] The *kymata* liana was said to be pregnant and ready to give birth to her child: the honey of the *myrynga* bee. The feast was a celebration of the new year, a celebration of new fragrances and also of new sounds (from bird chicks). Tö Kybairu was celebrated by adults, who retired into the forest to consume the new honey communally. This ritual was the only gathering of the tribe as a whole; during the rest of the year, people gathered in groups no larger than the band. The cold and the wind were seen as forces of the souls of dead Aché and testified to their presence. They were said to descend from heaven to participate in the annual honey-feast.

Afro-Brazilian traditions link the cycle of time that is based on the condition of the dead to crop cycles, to the times of creation and mythical lifetimes of ancient divine kings, to moments of the living body's life cycle (e.g., birth and initiation), and to time-factored musical instruments and sounds.[91]

The Chiripá provoke signs of propitious timing for their feasts by inducing symbolic manifestations of flower and insect cycles. On the ninth day of the Chiripá Prayer of the Forest feast, the second part of the drinking festival begins. It is short-lived but intense and festive. This part of the festival starts with an incantation by the shaman. He then breathes onto a small quantity of drink, which is presented to him in a gourd. "In the case of honey chicha, a bee should fly from inside the 'cup.' In the case of cane chicha, a white flower should appear. These signs mean that the sacred part of the ceremony has been successfully performed, since they are signs of the deity's pleasure." [92] After the shaman has taken the first drink, the whole community joins together in intense dancing and drinking.

Fluids are especially malleable symbols of time. As seen in the case of the honey beer employed by the Guayakí and Chiripá, beverages can encode many kinds of temporal cycles and even symbolize the contradictory evaluations of time that undergird the anomalous character of calendric feasts (e.g., time is poured out and flows even while its institution and restoration are being commemorated). As a result, drink is frequently a prominent feature of calendrical feasts.

Canelos Quichua culture conjoins the cycle of fermented mash with the timing inherent in the human digestive process as well as with cycles of songs, flowers, spatial domains (water, soil, forest, the male and female bodies), and insect sounds. During the principal drinking festival, Canelos Quichua women think-sing songs of the manioc flower. The symbolic singing effectively opens women to female-power spirit bees, which communicate between domains in the universe.[93] The Canelos Quichua make *chicha* with three ingredients: manioc mash, water, and "women's substance." This last ingredient is introduced into the mixture after the women have held portions of manioc mash in their mouths for an hour or more, that is, until the mash has begun to ferment.

The fermentation of drinks made from specific seasonal fruits is a key calendrical device for the Toba. The fermentation includes the timing patterns of the ripening of *algaroba* fruit, the digestive process, the qualitatively different times marked by the rhythms of sacred gourd rattles, the birth and the life cycles of particular spirits, and the temporal conditions of the celestial life of the dead. The drink used in the Toba feasts is prepared in a ritual way. *Algaroba* fruit is collected by women. Then old women and old men chew the mash and mix it well with their saliva. The fermentation process is likened to the birth of a *peyák notta*, a benevolent spirit who ripens fruits and who serves as an individual helper to curers.[94] The time of fermentation is filled with danger. The chewed mash is placed on a large hide or in a wood trough. During the night, groups of men arrive bringing their sacred rattle gourds, which are inhabited by their helper-spirits and decorated with powerful signs. Sitting around the hide or trough the men intone a wordless song to the rhythm of their rattles. Their ceremony, called Niapilák Map ("to hurry on the algaroba"), drives away harmful spirits, who would spoil the beer and prevent the successful birth of the *peyák notta*. The singing and rattling continue throughout the whole night.

In fact, the *peyák notta* are beings who inhabit *piyím*, the highest heavens, where the souls of the Toba dead return after death.[95] The process of fermentation brings this class of heavenly beings "to its highest point of development" and influence in the concrete and manifest world.[96] It is in this most fully manifest form — that of an intoxicating beverage — that the Toba ingest the sacred being. The sacred beings literally incorporate themselves by entering the fleshly bodies of the Toba celebrants. Through the medium of fermented brew, the divine spirits incarnate themselves and take on human form. The same vigil of fermentation and consumption of drink is celebrated in lesser ways throughout the year, especially in healing ceremonies and at the time of initiation. Each feast is timed to coincide with a turning point in the brewing process. Fermentation extends the process of ripening in order to bring the fruit to new birth — to take it to an ultimate point of development, one that lies just at the edge of rot and decay, when it would "turn bad."

The power of a sacred event reveals the connections among distinct qualities of time: solar and lunar cycles, rainy and dry seasons, flower cycles, the cycles of songs and sounds, the human life-cycle (viewed as an unfolding floral bud attracting droning beings), and periodic manifestations of emotions and colors. Reappearing temporal conditions establish cycles that check and balance one another. Conjoined in the calendar, interlocking cycles become visible expressions of the dialectic relations among differential qualities of existence. Through the symbolism of the calendar humans are able to live more than one kind of existence. This accounts for the dynamism and creativity in culture. Calendars are strategic devices, existential mechanisms that offer the community a full experience of being through the rotation, alternation, and overlap of cycles (of fruit, sound, stars, etc.) and temporal moods (e.g., the prescribed festive euphoria, rage, fear, or nostalgia symbolic of events of the mythic age).

MUSIC AND DANCE MAKE CALENDARS POSSIBLE

In order to understand how rituals define and order time into a calendar, we shall look at the function and meaning of the key festival elements of music and dance. Why are they ubiquitous? In what ways are they inherently temporal? Whence derives the symbolic force with which they order cultural experiences of times and bend all cycles to themselves?

CALENDS, CALLING, AND CLAMOR: MUSICAL PROCLAMATIONS OF TIME

In Aymara-speaking communities of the Andes, the round of festival and economic year is marked off into episodes and tasks by the complex cycle of musical instruments. The intruments, their sounds, and their players are coordinated with the seasons, the weather, and the feasts, as well as with specific dances, costume designs, tasks, and so on. For instance, in the community of Irpa Chico, on the eve of the Feast of Saint Andrew, five-stop flageolets *(pinquillos)* are played by merchants who trade in pears.[97] Such sonic calendrical markers have endured a long history in the Andes. Pan-pipes, for example, are played by contemporary Andeans to mark the onset of the agricultural season, the time when water runs in the irrigation canals. Such is the case, for example, in Chuschi, the capital of the southern Andean department of Ayacucho, Peru. There Quechua-speakers celebrate the Yarqa Aspiy, the feast of the cleaning of the irrigation canals (*yarqas*), at the time of the September equinox. Musicians playing *chirisuyas*, paired wooden reed instruments, accompany the people who gather from the diverse communities of the mountains' upper slopes. They descend the mountainsides by following the irrigation canals. Musicians always play in pairs, perhaps reflecting the dual system of irrigation canals as well as the moieties into which the society is divided. The pipes and the scraping of the canals celebrate the marriage between Máma Pacha (mother earth) and her two grooms (one from each moiety), who are lake-dwelling mountain divinities (*wamanis*). The seminal waters of the *wamanis* and the sounds passing through the aerophones flow down along the canals into the open fields to impregnate the fertile earth mother.[98] Ideally, the reed in the pipes is a feather from the tail of a condor.[99] Zuidema alludes to the antiquity of panpipe playing to mark the beginning of the agricultural season in September. The practice was observed by the Inca and the Mochica (among whom the instrument was played by the dead in conjunction with ritual drinking) and in Nazca culture (where the pipes were played by an earth deity) and Huari culture, which absorbed the custom from Nazca but emphasized its association with war.[100]

Musical instruments, melodies, styles, and arrangements do not only accompany the moments of the calendar; seasonal music actually orchestrates the passage of time. Musical performance modulates the shifting relations among entities, a variability that is implied by temporal change. In creating audible symbolism from instruments and song, music induces perceptible physical rearrangements in the body and among bodies. These movements of muscles, breath, teeth, tongue, and limbs are symbolic of the changing structures of time as it passes. Each festive moment of the calendar calls for special music so that the community may grasp the meaning of the particular quality of time through which it is passing. For instance, after the aggressive tickling contests that open their annual festival, Guayakí men wash off their body paint and the women chant ritual greetings appropriate to the occasion. A pig is set on the grill, and *daity*, bamboo-weave baskets sealed with wax, are filled with fragrant honey. When night falls, warriors recount their exploits in special song, emphasizing the greatness of their skills as bowmen and hunters. Using a piece of bamboo to beat the earth in the steady rhythm characteristic of the festival, the women listen to the men's songs. Then, accompanied by the music of whistles fashioned from vulture bones and played by the eldest women, the women sing songs which mark the occasion. In accordance with the responsorial genre of song typifying this feast, the young men then respond to the women's songs.[101] The music creates a complex orchestration of symbolic structures (emotional, rhythmic, antiphonal by age and sex, etc.). In a way suited to life's seasonal expressions, the orchestration orders the process of reflection upon contradictory existential values (masculinity versus femininity, hunting versus basketmaking, youth versus age, life sustained by food versus death perpetrated in killing and consuming game, and so on). These are ordinarily serial and separate experiences; however, under the special conditions of time created by seasonal music, they are recollected and made accessible to the reflexive experience of all.

As part of its function in calendrical ritual, music imitates the sounds of the mythical acts commemorated by particular feasts. Musical symbolism represents the conditions of an event in mythic time. The presence of that mythic quality of time periodically interrupts mundane time and marks the calendar with sound. The participants in Piaroa masked festivals, for example, identify themselves with mythical animal masters, reproducing their sounds in order to induce them to multiply and make life continue. Women and girls are not permitted to prepare or to use the ritual objects and musical instruments. When the Piaroa masters of animals chant their sacred narratives, only the mythical animals represented by the masks themselves can understand what is said. In fact, an esoteric language is used so that only the initiated can follow the ritual songs.[102]

The Campa provide a different estimation of the temporal dimension of festival music. Their culture hero created the seasons of time by playing the music appropriate to them. Consequently, special panpipe music, sacred songs, and dances distinguish the Campa *masato* festivals, during which, at dawn and at midday, the pipes are sounded in honor of the sun.[103] The Let'ére ceremony of the Apinayé, to cite another case, commemorates episodes in which the moon taught humankind six special songs. One song compares the moon to an armadillo, who disappears for a time only to reemerge later. Another song was chanted by the moon when he left the earth. The songs return the community to the conditions that obtained during primordial comings and goings. The Apinayé perform the songs in such a way as to make the festival's episodes coincide with lunar movements (beginning with the new moon). Through song, cosmic and social time are brought into alignment with primordial conditions.

According to an analysis made by Jonathan Hill, Kamayurá flute music possesses the ability to coordinate the order and meaning of social, cultural, and temporal categories of experience[104] because each kind of flute corresponds to a different supernatural being. For example, the *jaqui* flute is associated with the *mamaé*, the spirit mothers of fish; the *tarawí* flute is associated with spirits who either afflict or cure disease; and the *uruá* flutes are associated with the myth of the origin of women and death. In short, the different kinds of music demarcate—and intercalate into a calendar—

entirely different qualities of ordered time: the ecological time of the seasons, the structural time of society's life-passages, and the personal time of
death.

The way that primordial sound is reproduced at festival times has repercussions for life far beyond the strictly musical sphere. The modes of musical
production become models for social organization and cultural activity. For
the Canelos Quichua, "mythic time or structure can be entered by song." [105]
The unified state of mythic existence arrived at through song becomes the
goal of all Canelos Quichua cultural life (art, dream, ritual), which is directed
toward drawing together the separate domains of forest, water, and sky. By
recreating the unity of the mythic world, festival music renews the community's contact with the sources of creative action. The order manifest and
experienced in ritual music is a moral imperative grounding the achievement of aesthetic and social norms.

This explains why, for the Tapirapé as well as for other South American
peoples, "music is a central focus of their culture." [106] Charles Wagley regards vocal music as the focus of all Tapirapé ceremonies; he writes, "One
cannot exaggerate the role of singing in Tapirapé life." [107] Nonetheless, the
meaning of song texts is unintelligible; the songs either have no words or
have texts consisting of gibberish.[108] The meaning of the songs *(kaó)* is perfectly clear, however, when set within the mythical context. Myths recount
the origins of the sounds of mythical beings, especially birds. The sounds of
these mythical proto-animals become the model for the *kaó*.

Myth locates the meaning of festive sound for the Kalapalo as well.
Ritual music and dance are part of the same act.[109] The music, gestures, and
dance of performance are considered to be one complex symbolic action
performed by an *itseke* ("powerful being") during *inilano*, the mythic time of
the beginning. During the performance one not only sings and acts like a
powerful being, but one also acquires the intense feeling which existed when
the *itseke* performed their powerful acts. Ellen B. Basso treats these musical
rites *(an)* as symbols of culturally significant psychological states. The music
both achieves and symbolizes the transition into a different state of being:
". . . the name for this kind of performance is 'birding' *(itolotepïgï)*." [110] The
songs are in fact "pure" singing and have "virtually meaningless song texts."
However, the meaning of the music is clear to those who know the myth
relating the event in which the song was invented. The music is a symbolic
means of communication with the powerful beings of the beginning. However, "one might say that communication occurs not by singing *to* a Powerful
Being, but by singing it *into being*." [111] Songs are essential to the celebration
of calendric feasts because their sounds *are* the very events that they reenact.
Their meaning does not have to be translated in order to be clear, for they are
the acts themselves. They are what they mean.

WHEN EVERYTHING SOUNDS THE SAME

The paradoxical capacity of calendrical sound to mark moments of change
with a resounding similitude, a regathered mythic moment, rewards a closer

examination.[112] Several cases will help us to explore the meaning of this calendric ability to instigate change by periodically annihilating sonic difference. For example, the most important and most sacred period for the Makiritare is the Adahe Ademi Hidi ("to sing garden"), a three- to five-day festival held between the time of clearing new garden land and planting it. Since the mythic events that it celebrates involve, among others, the creation of humankind, it is appropriate that initiation of young men and women take place at this time.[113] During the feast, sacred songs called *ademi* are sung in an esoteric language originally spoken by the *sadashe*, animal masters and prototypes of species.[114] The feast originated during the mythic times of creation, when the *sadashe* made the first garden by cutting down Marahuaka, the tree of life, which is now a mountain called Little Gourd. This allowed the various plants and fruits that grew on the tree-mountain to be reproduced in garden soils. The tree had been rooted in both earth and heaven. The heavenly trunk gushed forth a flood of waters from Lake Akuena, situated in the center of heaven. The waters, the static center of the heavenly and unchanging world, created the flowing, living, moving rivers and rains of this world. This same mythic episode accounts for the separation of heaven and earth by the severing of Marahuaka, which had up until then, because of its rootedness in the soils of both realms, provided a firm connection between them. In its place now is the rainbow-serpent, an aspect of the mistress of the water domain. At the end of the first great garden feast, while the supernatural beings and masters of species sang and danced themselves into an ecstasy that transported them to heaven, the great snake Huiio leapt from the earth's rivers and passed through the air at the very moment that the brilliantly colored beings who had prepared the first garden were ascending into heaven, leaving their feathers and bird-bodies on earth.[115] The rainbow connection between heaven and earth is the spatial effect of this moment in sacred time; it has a vastly different nature from that of the unique tree, Marahuaka. The rainbow, an ephemeral aspect of the water domain (a realm of chaos and formlessness), now connects the human life-realm to the eternal realm of heaven.[116]

Success of the festival depends upon the mastery of song, the exact repetition of the sounds made by the *sadashe*. The *sadashes'* renewed presence in song and esoteric sound reactivates the power of these essentially sonic beings to destroy the stasis of primordial realities and to set loose patterns of change (the rainy season, the growth cycles of crops, the life cycles of humans, and so on). These sonic beings had promoted the separate spaces of this world, making the distinctions necessary for the temporal movements of passage from one state to another; to imitate their sound, therefore, is to recapture their presence at the very moment when their reality violently marked time with creative change.[117]

Kari'ña festival music reproduces mythic realities in a similar way. The Kari'ña refer to the very beginnings of existence, the time of myth, as *upa.poro* ("the ancient dance").[118] There are two forms of dance (*uba*, "existence provoked by sound-reality") based on bird models: group dances, which are social and public, and individual dances, which are esoteric, sexual, and shamanic. The Kari'ña never tire of observing and imitating the sounds and movements of birds and snakes, which are the visible forms, left on earth by the heavenly heroes, of perfect primordial sounds. The *puidei* (shamans) of ancient times had learned to sound their rattles with the rattlesnakes, to sing with birds and to dance with both of these magical "races." In this way, they acquired their wisdom and their language in strict conformity with the *eti.mpo* (whistle, original sound), the *derü.mpuo* (primitive language), and the *upa.poro* (ancient dance, mythical existence) of the gods and mythical animal masters.[119]

The sounds of various species — their true invisible and celestial forms, which reverberated at the first celestial dance — together with the procession of certain constellations through the sky and the fertility cycles of terrestrial animals are coordinated by the Kari'ña in a seasonal calendar. Certain frogs and toads, which belong to the water domain (governed by the great anaconda), are linked with specific seasonal cloud formations, with rains, with the initiation ceremonies of hunters, with the Pleiades and the Belt of Orion,[120] and with fertility and Heaven. "Their night singing in choirs is extremely powerful." [121] It is this power that allows it to become an ordering factor in the calendar of heavenly and earthly rhythms. Similar zodiacal, calendrical, and life-cycle coordinates are made for other noisy animals, including crickets, grasshoppers, wasps, bees, and so forth.[122]

Festival music "cuts" two ways. On the one hand, it once disrupted the primordium, introducing change; on the other, it now offers human beings a return to moments that are always the same. In either case, sacred music has a disruptive character. In order to re-create the mythical past, festival music must do violence to the mundane experience of time. Its destructive capacities undid the primordium when the realities there broke into song or when they withdrew from the world, leaving music or sound as a vestige of their passing moment. Mapuche ceremony shows how both these incisive aspects of music simultaneously come into play in festival. The Mapuche distinguish ordinary song from *tayil*, the musical manifestation of an inherited patrilineal soul. *Tayil* is the only material manifestation of this invisible reality, which stretches back into mythical time. Mapuche festive sound is fully calendrical. It infolds varied cycles of time. For instance, *lukutún*, the special discourse used during Mapuche fertility feasts, is essentially a litany of supernatural names, beings of the primordial time whose sounds are uttered in a fixed order that respects the chronology of mythic history. The diurnal timeline also finds its way into the sonic symbol. As the sun rises, and to the accompaniment of special dances, each male adult recites his litany while pouring libations of prescribed fluids in prescribed places. Then a female musical specialist, the *witakultruntufe* ("she who carries the drum"), performs her essential task of calling the roll of patrilineal souls and making present each man's *tayil*, "the only tangible facet of a lineage soul [that can] transcend the boundaries of time and gain direct access to the beings of *alüaluntu* [a mythical time that embraces all the entities and events that lie beyond the four generations of historical time]." [123] The *tayil* of each man is identical with the sounds of a mystical text. In fact, the sound (both syllabic and melodic) of the *tayil* is the shared soul of a patrilineage. "The texts carry no lexical meaning in everyday speech; they arise from a patrilineal continuum spanning past and present time." [124]

The Mapuche performance of the *tayil* is called Entún Kuifí ("pulling the ancestors"). During the performance, the *witakultruntufe* pulls the patrilineal soul from the mouth of her husband and his relatives and fuses it with the soul-stuff of the deceased members of the patriline. The performance is viewed as an extraordinary physical feat, requiring enormous strength. The *tayil* has four phases that correspond to an actual movement of the performer through time and space. The performer must move into the mythical world of the first ancestors. [125] She can sing the *tayil* in its entirety only if she is able to think/see the various realms through which she pulls the spirit of the lineage. She "cuts" her way through these space/time realms with her sacred song-speech. For this reason, she forces the air through her clenched teeth: she "cuts the air with the knife" of her teeth. [126] In this way, she both imposes a cutting edge on her speech and prevents evil from entering her mouth. As Carol Robertson describes this performance,

> By performing through clenched teeth and with minimal lip movements, women ensure that the deities and ancestors being addressed will not confuse *tayil* with song. Song cannot reach the realm of ancestral or past time; but if for some reason songs were to cross the time barrier, the deities would pay them no heed. On the other hand, *tayil* demands explicit cosmological attention; it cannot be ignored. [127]

Cultures may apply the cutting capacity of music and sound to open the spatial world to the times of abundant life. Constructing a symbolic universe and manipulating instruments that reproduce primordial sounds, festive revelers march across ritual space, thereby subjecting the microcosm to time and change. Musical instruments render the earth's spaces fruitful and multiplicative. The Baniwa carry sacred flutes "all over the world" to activate every species of fruit and other food. Their festival processions, now conducted only by men, mimic the worldwide parade of primordial women who, led by the female water-being Amaru, first played trumpets to open all the spaces and wombs of the universe and thus activate the species of plants and animals. [128]

The festival sounds expressed by discrete spatial entities (human and animal bodies, whistles, rattles, aerophones, falling fruits or stones, the creaking of wood, and so on) subject all spaces to one another's time. Sound penetrates space: for the period of its duration it opens the being symbolized by one spatial mode to the cross-fertilizing presence of another resonant space. In that respect, music furthers the intermingling of sexualized spaces and distinct shapes. [129] Using differently shaped spaces as instruments, sound penetrates distance to create the new tempos of generation, growth, fruitfulness, and descent for each species. Music becomes the effective symbol of complex time, transforming static spaces into dynamic containers of changing life.

The strolling musicians of festival processions reproduce the acts and sounds of the wandering primordial minstrels who transformed the space of the earth. Amaru and her band of female followers set the precedent for the Baniwa parades. Romi Kumu, the celestial divinity of the Barasana, also toured the world with her all-female band of trumpeters and flautists. Men pursued Romi Kumu:

> They went round the edge of the world and then down the middle but they could not find her. . . . They chased after her, following the sound of the *He*, but each time they got near she ran off again. She walked along the rivers and one can still see her footprints. . . . The men punished *Romi Kumu* and the other women by making them menstruate.[130]

Today only men play the trumpets and flutes while parading out a choreographed imitation of the ancestral entourage. The sounds and dance steps of the *He* House and Fruit House festivals mark moments both in the yearly calendar (when fruits ripen) and in the megacycle of human life (when a new generation appears during boys' initiation).

In a similar way, the dancing adventures of the Yukuna hero Kawarimi, in which he establishes the food chain of animals and plants, produce the musical sounds that mark off the annual Yukuna calendar of breeding, hunting, flowering, fruiting, collecting, and celebrating.[131] Kawarimi's wandering is narrated as a tour of the spatial world, but his gallivanting through mythic space creates the sounds of a dance-drum and, therefore, also generates the passage of time on all levels. Plants, sprouting from a grain taken from the upperworld, begin to grow. Kawarimi's tour of that upperworld, where he joins in the festival of game animals, is, at one and the same time, the sound of his own primordial dance act, a promenade through the entire spatial world, the ritual dance processions performed in the central area of the *maloca* during the year's festivals, and the round of the calendar of each species of fruit. The most important Yukuna feast is a dance in which, through the use of a center ceremonial pole under which is set a sound box, the *maloca* itself is turned into an enormous musical instrument. On top of the pole is set a seed-bell that vibrates to the proper rhythm. The *maloca*/world emits sound heard at a great distance.[132] In the symbolism of the musical hero, calendric performances unite in the imagination the various material, intellectual, cognitive, and sonic (as well as spatial and temporal) aspects of reality.[133] The places of the world become instruments of its ordered passage through time.[134]

Festival music marks the changing moments of the calendar with temporal similitude, songs and sounds that are ever the same as they once were. Sacred music attempts to annihilate difference with the same violence with which its primordial appearance eliminated homogeneity. However, the creativity of holiday musical performances—a creativity called for by the character of the mythic times they represent—provokes nostalgia. Notwithstanding the appeal of sonic icons of another time, there's no going home anymore. There can be no final return to the fully manifest primordium as long as this world endures, as long as myriad cycles of periodic appearance and disappearance continue to unfold. The transitory nature of sound and song, their intrinsic relationship with the passing of the primordium, renders them wistful. Festival music guarantees that return to an eternal life can only be approximated through eternal return, the continuous passing of calendric moments, which cluster together the cyclical qualities of transient existence.[135]

FESTIVAL DANCE

The human body comprises one set of instrumental places whose movements and relations mark off calendric time. Body parts are rearranged and moved through space to form configurations that suit and signal qualities of time, seasonal as well as rhythmic. Dance is an important, often essential, element of festival. Why do peoples mark time by dancing? A closer examination of the meaning of calendrical dances may expose dimensions of calendric time. The symbolism of dances is enormously complex, reaching into every realm of life. "The majority of dances can only be explained through mythology," writes Herbert Baldus.[136] In a comparative study that draws together many important reports on South American dances, Baldus mentions some of the features which disclose the mythic meaning of a dance: the relative roles and movements of the sexes; the choreography of the dancers, their gestures, their order of appearance and relationship; the style of the dance; the songs that accompany the dance; the instrumental accompaniment; the time of the year; the time of day and the duration of the dance; the place of the particular dance in the order of dances on that occasion; the animal associations and the symbolism of imitative sounds; the language employed; the meaning of the costumes, masks, and ornaments and of the materials from which they are made; the significance of spaces on the dance floor and the cosmography of the plaza or village. In the light of myth, all these elements become symbols whose significance helps uncover profound cultural values.

Festive dances embed such a wealth of religious meaning because they are calendrical. The calendar, focused on the complex of festival dances, transmits an entire culture. The extent to which dance can form a center of religious life is well-illustrated by the case of Candomblé. Under the guise of weekly entertainments (weekend dances), African religious traditions were maintained and embellished in the Christianized environment of the Americas. In the opinion of Pierre Verger, this ritual heritage, with its social organizations and cross-cutting ties, has been the vehicle for the profound influence of African values on coastal Brazil.[137]

The role that festive dance plays when it serves as a focus for cultural creativity and the transmission of tradition explains why good dancing can become a major goal of social existence. For example, Timbira dance, if analyzed in all its symbolic complexity, brings out—one could even say instigates — the full range of cultural and social constructs which integrate Timbira society. What is more, it is the way in which the Timbira view their own social organization: not as an abstraction that takes on flesh at various occasions, but as a community whose divisions of labor and symbolic properties exist in function of the dance. The aspirations of Timbira social existence are subsumed under the supernatural goal of ecstatic dancing. Dance provides power and justification for the calendar. The realities manifest in dance coordinate the seasons of fruit and flowers, the orders of colors, the cycles of sounds, and the divisions of labor that are part of the dance ceremony.[138]

From all that has been said about the relationship of calendric holidays to the crumbling moments of the primordium, it will not be surprising to discover that festival dances often reenact moments of destruction and the violence of change. The Apapocuvá offer a clear example. "In practice there is no religious dance which makes no reference to Mbaé Meguá [destructions of the world] if it is not itself the occasion for the dance." [139] This is so because, in the Apapocuvá view, the destructions by fire and flood were the movements that, par excellence, effected change in the world. Festival dance and song are imitations of those powerful movements. Since, "in general, the Apapocuvá know only of dances and songs which are religious and do not know of any profane dances and songs," every performative movement is sacred, and all are related to those transitional movements of disaster, the origins of movement itself.[140] Furthermore, song, dance, and prayer are, for the Apapocuvá, one single conception in which the spirit is modulated through changes in movement and sound.[141]

The violence of change is frequently the explicit occasion for the celebration of dances. Primordial destruction licensed and necessitated the formation of a calendar in the same measure that it instituted the diverse movements and symbols of the festival dances, which demarcate the jolting passages of time. During the Waiwai Yamo Dances, which last about two months, men dance wearing costumes and performing movements that imitate the anaconda-people's dance around the silent and hidden adolescent girl who, in an act that ended the primordium, had let her glance fall on the river waters. The anaconda-people rose from the waters to flood the land, forever altering the relations among peoples and among species of animals.

Since mythical times, new dance steps and instruments have been added to the Yamo celebration. These have originated during shamanic spirit-journeys into the underground world of the anaconda-people, where they still maintain the primordial condition of life. Watching the anaconda-people dance, one such shaman was shown some new steps and given musical whistles with the warning not to show them to women.[142] During the first month of the dance festival, the whistles are used. Consequently, in imitation of the opening scenes of creation, women are not allowed near the dance area. Men dance with their faces masked and their bodies costumed in palm leaves. They are completely disguised and anonymous. During the second month of dancing, women may participate, since the whistles are not used.

The dancing men sound a rhythm with their rattles. The women, like the adolescent girl of the flood of mythical time, sit motionless in the middle of the communal house. Male dancers perform in pairs. In between dance sets, young men dress up as Yamo clowns and spit water, an allusion to the way in which the anaconda-people still threaten to flood the earth if looked upon by an adolescent girl. From time to time, women chant invitations to the Yamo dancers to join them as sexual partners *(wayamnu)*.[143]

The link between dance and the passage of time explains its prominence in the messianic and millenarian movements that have appeared from time to time throughout the continent. In these cases, dance has been used not only to act out the mythic foundations of indigenous culture but also to hasten the destruction of the historical situation in favor of the paradisal conditions of the world to come — either a returned golden age or a new eschatological condition. Dance played the central role, for example, in movements as geographically distant and differently focused as the Taki Ongo revival in the Andes and the Guaraní messianic revolt led by Oberá, both of which occurred in the sixteenth century. In the first case, divine beings seize people, forcing them to dance in order to rid the world of the Spanish; in the second, Oberá, "son and radiant splendor of God," ordered his followers to sing and dance without cease until the arrival from on high of the promised liberation (which was to come in the form of an enormous comet that the messiah kept in a container).[144]

Dance masks themselves can be calendric instruments. Since each mode of being manifests its own proper time, a mask may coordinate, in one aesthetic and seasonal object, features that, *pars pro toto*, represent diverse qualities of time. When masks combine colors, feathers, gourds, teeth, hair, and other materials symbolic of different orders of mythic and natural history, their festive appearances help compose a calendar that coordinates the realities of nearly incompatible life-forms — human lineages, social groups, and sexes; birds, vegetal matter, stone, animal and insect species. For example, the most important feast of the Piaroa of southern Venezuela is the Warime, a set of masked ceremonies during which masked dancers and chanters represent the "lords" of the peccary, the monkey, and the wild bee.[145] Each mask is a composite of temporal features. Taken together, they make for moments heavy with mythic, historic, and species-particular time. In other societies, the passage of calendrical time is signaled by the periodic appearance of various masks, each one a time device, whose symbolism effects the passage of time and the continued existence of the social order.

Dance and festival movements coordinate diverse temporal cycles because the entire human situation, especially the human body, stands as a time signature for the cosmic composition. In his explanation of the function of the gourd rattle, Karl Gustav Izikowitz makes clear the fact that the power of musical sounds is not to be separated from or abstracted from the movements of body parts, from the breathing of the dancers and players, or from the instruments that produce the sound. Neither does that power stand apart from the forces inherent in the physical properties of the materials from which instruments are made or the physical attributes of the people who fashion and play them.[146] Rafael Karsten provides an example of such interplay when he relates how necessary and effective is the rattling of gourd rattles, at the time when *algarobo* beans are ripe, for brewing sacred beer, gathering wild fruits, pulling in large catches of fish, and so on:

> It is difficult to make out exactly the train of thought underlying this curious custom . . . [T]he very movements, together with the "power" emanating from the magical instrument, are evidently believed to exert a direct, mysterious influence upon natural processes and even upon human thought and feeling.[147]

Furthermore, the circumstances in which the instruments are manufactured — including the seasonal time in which the instruments, or their components, are prepared — may contribute supernatural properties to the performance. The whole complex of materials, gestures, and sounds compose the significant symbol of musical dances. Together, they create a complex species of time, the festival calendar — that is, the time of human culture. Symbolic existence, the human capacity to see nature and history as signs of sacred life, enables cultures to pull the separate movements and conditions of existence into fruitful relationship with one another. Above all, it is because human life is symbolic of sacred being that dances "have a magico-religious efficacy and are executed to influence supernatural beings or to coerce nature." [148] This "coercion" is nowhere more apparent than in the festival-dance calendar. Through its instruments, ornaments, gestures, foods, and songs, it directs the entire cast of symbolic realities to make their appearances in accord with the performances of human culture.

EMOTIONAL TIME, RITUAL DANCE, AND MORAL ACT: CUTTING A GOOD FIGURE

The dance calendar demonstrates that existence in time is emotional and that emotions are symbolic statements of value that have temporal aspects. Like any other condition that comes and goes, an emotion betokens an ephemeral state of being whose reappearance establishes a cycle. Prescribed festive emotions such as merriment, nostalgia, or fury immerse the community in specific qualities of time and, by providing normative experiences, allow for an evaluation of existence. "Dance is a powerful, frequently adopted symbol of the way people feel about themselves." [149] Because calendric ritual dances place one within time in a deliberate and measured way, emotionalism is essential to a self-critical moral life. "Like all expressive forms, dance provides a concrete, condensed, exaggerated projection of the values, world view, and life-style of the performers. . . . Within a neatly demarcated frame of time and space, it encapsulates the critical elements of an entire culture." [150]

Ritual dance, in its moral aspect, is neither a method nor a set of principles and rules that stand apart from the existence it evaluates. Sacred dance is not a technocratic response to a problem. It does not address the question, What policy of action should we adopt to solve the conflict facing us because of our anomalous existence in time? Rather, it answers the question, How are we to behave in the midst of this mystery, this epoch of paradoxes? The answer to this question sprouts from ground shared by ethics, ritual, and dance—forms of action whose value depends upon coming to grips with the meaning of symbolic existence. The ritual answer is both moral and aesthetic: behave properly and stylishly; that is, make the right move with good timing and in due time. To accomplish this goal, moral life requires scrutiny of the significance of symbolic experience. The calendar of feasts furnishes symbolic experiences that are normative because their meaning has been clearly revealed in their mythic origins. Festival dance and music and their symbolic accoutrements and emotions serve as moral bench marks for evaluating the more inchoate experiences of mundane time. The controlled and meaningful movement of the body in space during ritual dance becomes a paradigm of human existence in time.[151] The moral imperative of dance (to dance, to dance in time, to dance well) serves as reminder that what "is" in the calendar (space, times, supernatural life) is grasped representationally —that is, it is literally "figured" out, acted out. Moral life has an aesthetic base; it requires cutting a good figure.[152] Good style guarantees that what "is" can be experienced forcefully enough to compel an "ought." Stylish dance represents in clear figures the power and grace of existing in time.[153] By calculating with these figures, cultures not only mark off the calendar with feasts but also establish guidelines for acting morally throughout existence in time.

The meaning of time and of the mythical events that found calendrical existence also underlies the performative dimension of human action and creativity. The same mythical events that created the calendar are reenacted constantly in the dramatic moments of human culture. These dramas transform community life into a re-presentation of powerful beings and acts. Community life, insofar as it is conscious, powerful, and creative, takes on the quality of a performance. Every human gesture becomes potentially symbolic and sacramental. Awareness of the sacramental quality of one's acts brings everyday gesture closer to the arena of ritual drama. The knowledge that mythic events are their proper models draws all actions into the moral realm, which is centered on the paradigmatic acts of mythical beings. Moral acts are ones whose experience is properly ordered, that is, ordered fundamentally by the actions of divinities and culture heroes "in the beginning." Morality is always dynamic; it is based upon the experience of order in motion. Morality continuously expands awareness of the significance of one's everyday actions by evaluating their creative and destructive possibilities against the background of acts of supernatural beings who created or transformed space and time. This is why Baldus could say of the Tapirapé that " 'moral' behavior in relation to the supernatural world is singing and dancing in order to defend the community against unknown dangers and to increase fertility in the world of nature." [154] It is not the brute singing and dancing alone which make actions moral but the performance coupled with full awareness of the meaning of the events the performer is imitating. Morality, then, probes to the basic and normative foundation of the dynamic order of existence. It grounds one's knowledge and awareness of one's own actions in the fundamental actions of being.

HUMAN LIFE AS A CALENDRICAL EXISTENCE

The calendar is a mode of existence, a way of living exposed to and aware of complex matrices of time. To that extent, the calendar of sacred feasts is a form of knowledge on the basis of which cultures assume an intentional stance in the world. In his analysis of Canella social and cultural life, Izikowitz insisted that "life among all peoples follows a certain system of time or perhaps we may say, falls within a certain rhythmic system. . . . As a matter of fact every rhythmic structure is built up of several coordinated systems." [155] The ensemble of rhythms recognized and coordinated by a society reflects the values that predominate in the culture.[156] By reveling in and feasting on symbolic expressions of time, cultures express and evaluate their intrinsic ontological ties with fruits, flowers, fragrances, insects, spaces, stars, sounds, animals, colors, and all other apparent forms. All these features share this in common: the different times of their appearances and disappearances also symbolize another kind of time, whose being they share through their origins. This primordial dimension of time, revealed in the symbolism of cycles, enfranchises calendrical existence.

The Canelos Quichua concept of the present, for example, seems to be defined in relation to a temporalized state of knowledge, the degree to which one has reentered the wisdom of Ancient Times. Consequently, "the concept of 'present' is modified according to the speaker's age, knowledge, and sex and is always considered in the plural, for there are as many 'now times' as there are people in specific localities with specific histories. There are no present times, in the abstract, which do not involve some aspect of continuity with the past." [157] Men and women accumulate and acquire soul-knowledge by acquiring ancient souls, with their independent histories, in different ways. Furthermore, over the course of his or her lifetime, a person accumulates and acquires more souls and soul-knowledge. Understandably, then, since the "present" exists in relationship to the Ancient Times of the beginnings, and since people's knowledge and relationship with Ancient Times is also relative, it stands to reason that there are many "presents" or "now times" *(cunan).*

Social structures reflect qualities of time ordered in the calendar.[158] Calendrical existence offers a range of temporal qualities that social groups may embody. That is why, during the blending of times that occurs at feasts, mundane structures are dissolved and then resolved in new ritual formations. Rituals offer societies possibilities for critique and creative change because they experiment symbolically with alternate forms of social action. Victor Turner referred to this phenomenon as the "anti-structural" aspect of ritual processes. Its intrinsic relation to change lets ritual shape history; rituals refashion the meaning of existing in time. These kinds of temporal-structural choices are available, for example, to the Guayakí during *Tö Ky-*

bairu, the annual honey feast, which is named after a kind of ritual game in which both men and women place their heads close together in imitation of the cells of a honeycomb, "a metaphor for society." [159] The festival is a conjunction of all sorts of temporal qualities manifest in the annual cycles of seasons, honey, and flowers and in the growth of human hair, the adolescent maturation of unmarried persons, the conception of a new generation, the fermentation of drink, and so on. *Tö kybairu* is celebrated when yellow liana flowers are slain, turn red, and are "avenged" by the cold. The feast emphasizes courtship and lovemaking. Special care is taken to make oneself, especially one's head, look beautiful. Hair is shaved in a ceremonial way, excess hairs are depilated. Head ornaments are made from jaguar skin and coati tails. Each man outfits himself as a great bowman, a true Aché, in order to be attractive to women. Amorous liaisons are arranged for married individuals, and marriage exchanges are negotiated for those who are single. In some sense, the whole festival is seen as a movement of men to women, through whom (or, literally, in whom) lie ritual ties that crosscut the normal structural patterns of residence groups. [160] It is a curious paradox, in keeping with the anomaly of calendric existence, that the "metaphor for society" acts out the destructuralization of social order and its reformation along alternative social lines.

Calendars constantly run communities through permutative social exercises. For example, the Akwẽ-Shavante divide their time, their year especially, in such a way that they "no sooner complete one ceremony or ceremonial series but they start planning for the next." The age-set institutions are the key coordinating elements in the endless cycles of ceremonies and their preparations. [161] Although the Akwẽ-Shavante appear quite conscious of time and systematically shape their social life to its contours, they do not concern themselves with dating historical events.

The Tapirapé illustrate another way in which the festal calendar rings the changes of social forms. They not only organize themselves according to kinship categories based on the temporal concepts of generation and descent, [162] but, from time to time, they reconstruct their society along two crosscutting ritual lines associated with different modes of sacred time revealed in myth. These are the Bird Societies and the Feast Groups. The Bird Societies are men's secret societies in which members are grouped into unnamed ceremonial moieties, each of which is further divided into three classes according to age. Throughout the year, which is marked off into serial units of time, paired sets of masked dancers sing the songs and perform the dances of mythical birds. [163] During the same annual cycle, each ceremonial division "hosts" its mythic animal beings and constructs masks to represent them. [164] I have already alluded to the fact that the calendar temporalizes modes of being that can also be expressed in images of space. It is worth noting in this connection that the Feast Groups divide the Tapirapé society into eating groups named after *tantanopae,* "place of the fire"—the places where mythical ancestors first emerged from the earth immediately after the destruction by cosmic fire. [165]

Even dream life, when brought before the evaluative tribune of awareness, can become calendrical. The power of primordial dream images can be used to calibrate the complex cycles and rhythms of the cosmos. For example, the timing of Avá-Chiripá drinking festivals is set by interpreting images from the dreams of the highest ranking shaman, who also leads the ritual. Such festivals celebrate the harvest or the appearance of seasonal fruit. They can also function to mark the rhythms of life cycles or to forestall cycles of degeneration (e.g., as prophylaxis against epidemic disease).[166]

CALENDARS AND THE OTHER INHABITANTS OF WORLD-SPACE
Calendars are ecumenic devices. The calendric nature of human existence forms the foundation for tolerating contradictory worldviews. Since cultural existence is already calendric, this precedent for accommodating incompatible conditions of existence can serve to intercalibrate additional orders of religious experience within a single culture. For example, in addition to the cosmic calendar based on the seasons, weather, and solstices, a second sacred calendar of the Quechua follows the cycle of feasts associated with the cult of Christ (e.g., Holy Week) and the Virgin Mary. These sacred beings are understood in Andean religious terms. The feasts center on celebrating the miraculous appearances and acts of the *apu* Ausangate and of Pachamama, "Holy Mother Earth." The principal feast in the cycle is that of Señor de Quyllur Rit'i, which draws ten thousand pilgrims a year to the sanctuary where this lord appeared in the guise of a common peasant. The place of the miraculous appearance is an ancient sacred site. It is a place of power where the *apu* Ausangate heals through the medium of holy snow and the lord cures with his holy water.[167] Sacred waters are taken home, for they are thought to have the power to fertilize. "There are many who think that the Lord also may desire human sacrifice. It is thought that the feast has been a failure if no one dies during the celebration."[168] It is said that the lord himself, after his appearance, disappeared into a rock now found at the shrine. The Feast of Señor de Quyllur Rit'i, celebrated the week before Corpus Christi, is orderly, solemn, and respectful even though some twenty different groups of dancers and musicians — pilgrims all — take their place one after another to honor the lord for his suffering and compassion.

A different atmosphere prevails during the Feast of the Lord of Piñipati, a lesser feast wherein the emphasis falls on drinking large quantities of *trago* (cane alcohol). The feast is often peppered with disputes that sometimes escalate into fights between entire communities.[169] The Feast of the Lord of Piñipati is celebrated on the feast day of the Sacred Heart of Jesus and is a local celebration.

Three other feasts celebrated in this Andean-Christian calendar center on Pachamama: the local version of the Feast of the Immaculate Conception (8 December) and the feasts of Christmas and New Year. The earliest of these feasts focuses on the fertility of the fields. Food and *chicha* beer are ritually exchanged during this well-organized festival, which actually lasts from 7 to 10 December. Few people actually go to church. Contemporary celebrations of this feast have been marked by drunkenness, a fact credited by some elders to be the cause of recent failures of the potato crop. At Christmas and New Year, which also honor the earth mother, "offerings are made in the four quarters of the field . . . [T]he offering determines the lot of the field throughout the length of the year." [170] During the time of these festivals, the earth is alive and open.

A third cycle of Andean sacred times is related directly to the life process of the individual person. It follows the moments of birth, ceremonial haircutting, confirmation, marriage, and death. All of these religious time cycles find their places on the megacycle of the calendar. Together they form the complex religious *oikoumene*, the world that houses whatever forms of being there are in the universe.

Temporal constructs do not always encourage accommodation of diverse worldviews, however. Certain notions of time, notably religious and political histories in the narrow sense, can license intolerance by becoming imperial, that is, by refusing to give ground to the complexity of human existence in time. Such, for example, may be the nature of the concept of unilineal evolution that underlies accounts of modern history or of the notion of salvation history that underlies those religious philosophies of mission that are predicated on exclusive adherence to a single worldview. Accounts of modern nation-states in Latin America, for example, almost never successfully integrate national histories with Amerindian evaluations of existence in time (so-called mythic history and ethnohistory).

LAST ROUND: CALENDARS, CYLINDERS, AND RECALLING THE ROLL OF BEINGS

This chapter has resisted looking upon calendars as technical achievements of "science" in the sense of a method that stands apart from the existence in time it observes. It avoids a too-detached notion of calendrical data because it wished to encounter the human motivations for observations of time and to uncover the cultural purposes that govern the assignment of value to the calendric process. Furthermore, these considerations have sought to scrutinize the intended cultural outcome — the aesthetic (i.e., sonic, colorful, dramatic, beautiful, and entertaining) evaluations of experiential knowledge that are derived from celebrating the recurrent moments of the calendar. Assigning calendars a primarily quantitative or astronomic basis makes their appearance in cultures unduly "sudden" and inexplicable.[171] This analysis prefers to view the usually strict sense of calendar as but one manifestation of a temporally multiplex existence. The so-called astronomic calendar is one kind of ordered reckoning of the human situation, which must recognize itself as subject to multiple, even myriad, qualities of time.[172] The calendars I have described illustrate that cultures recognize, know, adapt to, and manipulate multiple evaluations of temporal existence. Human beings live in the conjunction of multiple existential conditions, and creative cultural existence demands a calendrical sense not unlike the sense of balance that assists orientation in space. Such a calendrical sense operates only through image, a function of the imagination.

Human culture stands at the center of time, just as human being stands at the center of space. That is why times encircle human being within recurrent cycles. The calendar is a centering device: it guarantees that human culture will situate itself at the center of *all* recognizable cycles of time, that is, within the dialectic of disappearance and reappearance of all significant supernatural beings. One by one, or in coordinated groups, the calendar roll calls all remarkable beings into the arena of human culture, the center of time. The human imagination is the locus of this ontological dialectic wherein rupture marks the center. The center of space was a place of intervention, a breaking of planes; the center of time is one of interruption. Festal moments reenact events that disrupted the primordial quality of existence, and those events continue, from time to time, to intrude upon cosmic life. Destruction plays a key symbolic role in locating or establishing a center of space and time. Disintegration breaks up homogeneous existence. For this reason, sacrifice lies at the heart of the human world; it reinforces, or reenacts, the differentiation of places and times that is reflected in the organization of ritual spaces and calendars. Through sacrifice, a mode of being implicit in the constantly disappearing moments of the calendar, human life maintains the center's existence as well as human culture's proximity to it or even identification with it. Sacrifices, offerings, and consumption, by reenacting the withdrawal of fully manifest primordial being, set apart as sacred certain places and times, which symbolic structures are consecrated by the immediacy of their connection with supernatural beings. The calendar and the coordinated spatial system of the cosmos constitute a sacrificial mode of existence by which human life is identified with the symbolic process at the center of the universe.

The meaning of cultural performance connects directly with the symbols of time that human beings use to evaluate their existence. Specific concepts of time inform the quality of knowledge that serves as a context for performance and that sets performance apart from mere behavior.[173] The ethnolinguist Dell Hymes characterizes this conditioning knowledge as a deep concern, not with "something mechanical or inferior, as in some linguistic discussion" of rules or structures but rather with "something creative, realized, achieved, even transcendent of the ordinary course of events." [174] These terms well describe the mythic events that found the passing moments of time and that therefore institute the calendar of festival performances. The knowledge undergirding calendric performances is not merely cognitive or epistemological. It remains open to other dimensions of creative concern and has values that might be called psychological, aesthetic, political, existential, moral, and philosophical. Awareness of time, in specific cultural configurations, grounds human action in all these spheres and establishes a basis for rituals that reflexively evaluate those aspects of existence in time.

In their aesthetic and public life, human societies and individuals bear the ornamental marks of calendric existence. The recognition of various cycles, their calendric order, and their meanings, saves human action from being nonsymbolic. The consciousness that human culture is founded on sacred acts occurs retrospectively during the festival recollections of temporal cycles. Knowledge of the origins of existence in time redeems human behavior from insignificance.

DRUNKENNESS AND VIOLENCE OF FEASTS

In Chapter 3, after delineating some structures of spatial organization and their meaning, I turned my attention to applying those principles to particular cases (shrines, villages, cities). In a similar way, at this point in the consideration of concepts of time, I shall apply the temporal complex of cycles, calendars, music, dances, and founding feasts that I have outlined to the features of festal drinking and violence that are prominent aspects of many South American religious festivities. A closer look at the underlying symbolic constructs of time pulls into sharper focus the meaning of these symbolic actions. To provide a feel for the issues at hand, the section begins with several brief descriptions.

The Shodewika dance festival, held at least once a year, is celebrated by the Waiwai more frequently than is the arduous, two-month-long Yamo. Fock reports that these "dance festivals could equally well be termed drinking festivals, for enormous quantities of beer are consumed. The Waiwai say themselves that they only dance in order to drink." [175] Beginning at sunset, a visiting group paddles to the landing of their host neighbors. There they don dancing costumes (capes of palm leaves, which completely cover the dancer's body) and bark armbands. [176] The festival calls for intense dancing and singing over a period lasting from three to seven days, depending on the amount of drink available. During that time, there is constant drinking. Indeed, one has the distinct impression that the men are drinking up a "flood" brought on by the women. Not only do women prepare the ritual drink for the festival, but it must be remembered that it was the glance of a young woman that created the drinking feast when it caused the anaconda-people to rise out of the water and flood the land.

The Canelos Quichua recognize two kinds of festivals. Both involve ritual drinking. The first is the *huasi* (household) power ritual, a spontaneous musical drinking bout instigated by the man of a household and carried on by neighboring men and women, who join in the festivities. [177] Whitten describes a spontaneous *huasi* power ritual that began with a man making a headpiece during his return from the hunt. Arriving home, he began to play his private soul-song on a transverse flute while striking a drum so that its snare "sang" a soul-dream sound *(muscuyu)*. (The beating of the drum is Amasanga's thunder, and the buzzing of the snare is the drone of the spirits who bring dreams.) The man circled his house, listening to the songs of animal souls. Women forced *chicha* down his throat and danced with him.

(The *chicha* is the rain that accompanies Amasanga's thunder.) Other musicians joined the circling ensemble. More souls of animals and spirits were freed by this festive behavior and joined the circle. The circle then pivoted, its members marching in the opposite direction so that the monkey-skin drumhead with the fiber snare now resounded outward toward the forest and the peccary-skin drumhead faced the household. When two or more gallons of *chicha* were forced down the throat of the instigator and his companions, he beat a path to the next household, where women forced more *chicha* down his throat — even dousing his head with *chicha* — and said, "One who walks like thunder must experience rain." [178] The spontaneity of such festive moments makes them difficult to sustain.

Ritual drinking is also a prominent part of a more formal Canelos Quichua ceremony, an annual or semiannual celebration that is staged by a residence group and that centers on a core of kin. Late in the afternoon of a certain day, after beer and pottery have been made by women and after all the hunters have returned, an officiant begins to beat a drum and to march in a circular direction. The men shout out *parihú, parihú, jistata ranuuuuuu*, "togetherness, togetherness, the ceremony is constructed." [179] For three days women force men to drink *chicha* in impossible quantities.

As the men are forced to drink at the chaotic climax of this principal Canelos Quichua festival, the women release streams of *chicha* from fingerholes which they have secretly made in the pottery. They douse the men with brew. "Some women even put round pottery snakes . . . on their heads, dancing until they fall off and break." [180]

It has not been easy for ethnographers to ascertain the nature of the religiosity in drinking bouts.[181] Descriptions of the so-called Festival of the Full Moon among the Campa, for instance, are confused and conflicting on this point. Weiss concludes that the celebration of manioc beer festivals merely coincides with the full moon's appearance but does not involve worship of the moon in any way.[182] Nevertheless, he does not dismiss entirely the ethnographic reports that ascribe a sacred character to these drinking festivals. The problem lies in locating a source of sacrality with intrinsic relationship to drink.

Equally troublesome for interpreters has been the staging of ritual violence. For example, to prevent epidemics after an eclipse, the Panare community practices self-flagellation, *otnyepa ipumowon*, "to club the Panare," a phrase that also applies to the act of clubbing to death an incestuous human couple.[183] In a quite different case, Nimuendajú mentions the existence of ancient masked dances among the Apinayé in which performers imitated anteaters that were "clubbed to death" at the end of the ceremony.[184]

The analysis in this chapter suggests that temporal constructs rooted in the primordium and its demise bring into relief the connections between drink, violence, festive consumption, dance, and the calendar. Ritual drink highlights cycles of rain and drought, of stars and fruit, of ripening and rotting. For example, starter mash is prepared from vegetables or fruits that are harvested at the proper point in their ripening cycles and is then held partially consumed in women's mouths. On the cusp of decay, it then re-emerges, as in a process of rebirth. It instigates a new kind of life: one that is not simply biological but festive, cultural, and reflexive. Fermentation marks a calendrical node where various time-cycles can be gathered symbolically. Furthermore, fermentation is a deliberate process by means of which human beings, imitating the actions of sacred beings, subject cosmic times to cultural artifice.

DESTRUCTION: THE NEED FOR A BREAK

The origin of any of this world's temporal cycles implies some kind of rupture, or interruption of a preexisting temporal condition. This destructive capacity of time takes visible form in the drinking feast. The Waiwai drinking festival, for instance, celebrates the mythic event that marked the separation between real animals and real human beings. At that time, a shaman and his helper-spirits (in the form of otters) succeeded in cutting in two a monstrous anaconda named Petalï, who had devoured a local woman. When Petalï's blood flooded the riverbanks, various species of animals, especially birds, bathed in the liquid and were immediately transformed into separate species. The festival now celebrates the productive differences between the kinds of peoples, for it is celebrated in view of marriage alliances.[185]

If the Waiwai Shodewika drinking festival lasts for a long while, and people run short of food, a break will be taken, during which people go into the forest in order to hunt. When the festival resumes, a number of animal imitations are performed. Significantly, it is the women who usually "murder" the animals that the men or young boys imitate.[186] The women carve up the corpses of "*pakria*" and strike off the long snouts of another of the species of anteater being imitated. The women also slaughter a number of "tortoises" with knives[187] and throw lumps of hardened beer mash at "howler monkeys," which have scampered up poles to sit in the communal-house rafters. The women continue to throw the lumps until the monkeys fall down "dead." A number of other animal species are treated in the same way. Thus women "kill" "anteaters" who fall to the ground and roll in the vomit of tired celebrants.

Ritual drinking has the function of restaging the transformative acts that originally marked off time. Drinking feasts therefore frequently celebrate the origin of the separate forms of animal species, whose distinct markings betoken the existence of unique breeding and life cycles. This connection between time, drink, and animal form shows clearly in the only Siriono myth reported by Allan R. Holmberg. In describing the origin of the drinking festival, the myth relates an episode in which animals are transformed to their present shapes. The moon, Yási, arrives at a place where animals are celebrating a drinking feast called Héri Héri. The moon is enraged because Yakwa, the jaguar, has killed the moon's child. The sight of the drunken animals heightens his anger, and in a frenzy the moon twists the necks of the celebrating animals into their present shapes, places spines on the porcupine, and forces the tortoise to walk slowly. Thus, the death of the moon's child, the celebrations of drunken feasting, and the transformation of animals into definite species based on body forms are mythically conjoined. Dancing and drinking feasts are celebrated by the Siriono only on brightly moonlit nights.[188] They make present again the moon's fierce and creative anger, which gave rise to separate time-cycles, and they reestablish the temporal order, which is built on destruction.

Death and destruction can underlie festival drinking in a more subtle way. Since many of the plants used to concoct fermented brew originated from the bodies of slain or dismembered mythic personages, the preparation of the drinks by crushing or chewing such plants is tantamount to sacrifice. Pierre Grenand reported such a view among the Wayãpi, for whom manioc beer is accorded the status of meat in ceremonial meals because the manioc plant originally derived from the flesh of a supernatural old woman. Manioc beer oozed as pus from the boils that covered this "grandmother." [189]

INTEMPERANCE: UNDER THE INFLUENCE OF IMMODERATE TIME

The destruction that is alluded to by drinking festivals is often the catastrophe (most notably the cosmic flood) that destroyed the primordial world. Such is the case for the Avá-Chiripá feast called ñemboé kaagüy, the "prayer of the forest." This drinking festival is the principal ritual — and only common assembly — of the Avá-Chiripá. It celebrates the myth of Chary Piré, who was able to escape from the universal flood by pounding her sound-stick and singing her sacred song.[190] The Chiripá receive their sacred names at this sacred feast, which is celebrated in the center of the village in a structure known as the "house of dances." An enormous trough containing chicha is placed in front of the ceremonial house.

The cosmic catastrophes of flood and darkness likewise provide the backdrop for Mataco drinking feasts. At the beginning of a new moon, the Mataco celebrate the Atj, a ceremony in which Nowenek, a good spirit who inhabits the bodies of human beings, is entreated to bring forth carob beans, fruit, and corn. A more important aspect of this festival involves curing specialists called aiawu, who carry out elaborate performances aimed at dispelling evil and epidemic disease.[191]

The Atj ceremony is performed in order to make contact with the powerful beings who control the forces of the cosmos. Mataco myths show that the world can be destroyed if such contacts are not maintained: "The sun can stop shining and leave the world in darkness. Pejlai, the master of rain, can pour a huge amount of water and produce a flood. The Itoj Ahla, or men of the fire, can burn the forests." [192]

Commemoration of universal catastrophe does not prevent the destruction of drinking feasts from taking on personal scale, sometimes effecting the ceremonial death of the participants. The greatest feasts in the seasonal cycle of the Toba Indians offer illustration of this. Toba drinking bouts are held during the season of algaroba fruit. Algaroba originally descended from heaven along with other useful plants after the world was destroyed by a cosmic fire. At the height of the Toba drinking festival, the men dance around all the women of the village. The dance, called Nahót Dónnaran, is held for several nights running. When it reaches its noisy climax, the women fall to the ground, "dead." Each one in turn is then attended to by the curer, who leans over her, recites magical words, sucks on her breasts in two places, and blows on her. The dancing men shake their rattles violently and stamp on the ground while they yell. One by one, the young women, whose faces have been painted with special magical designs, are revived. These acts protect the whole community from the epidemic arrival of the evil spirits who attack women at the end of the dry season. Karsten mentions a significant detail:

> Whilst the dance went on another peculiar ceremony took place: a fire-brand was swung around in all directions on the place of the dance. A man took the brand and carried it far into the forest chanting loudly, made a big circle and lastly appeared again on the scene of the dance, chanting incessantly.[193]

In fact, this is a ceremonial repetition of the actions of the first human being, a male who emerged from the earth and seized a blazing brand from the cosmic fire that had consumed the world. He then carried the blazing brand to all the places of human habitation.[194] Soon after that, women appeared in the world. Although they descended from heaven in an enclosure, the men cut the cord from which the enclosure was suspended. The enclosure then plummeted to earth and from inside of it the women called out, "Who wants a good wife?" The men dug the women one by one out of the earth and brought them into the light. Taking the women as wives, the Toba produced offspring. When one considers that, according to Toba mythology, women and fruit trees came to the earth in the same way (both descended from heaven), the relation between the principal ideas behind the Nahót Dónnaran — to prevent women's sickness and to hurry on the ripening of the *chañar* fruit, the staple food which matures in October — becomes clear. Clear also is that dancing and firebrand ceremonies allude to the myths of the destruction of the world, the emergence of man, and the descent of women to earth from heaven.[195]

That drinking-feast participants die to one form of time as they reenact the first violent appearance of another can be shown in a multitude of ways. In any case, drink itself is the reappearance of a destructive or deadly mode of being that manifests a unique temporal condition and marks a certain cycle of time. At their dancing festivals, the Kari'ña consume a fermented drink called *sakura*, a word also used to designate the venom of the coral snake, *sakurakura*. The word *sakura* also refers to the supernatural substance of wisdom. The root word, *sak*, denotes a magic sound that calls beings to it. During festivals, people drink until they are drunk (*ti.mi*, a word that can also mean "to carry to that which is invisible, to become powerful, to amaze or astonish, to terrify").[196] The connection between "drinking until drunk" and "to carry to that which is invisible" is made by use of the root *e.ti*, meaning "sound, noise," for sounds are the invisible and true forms lying behind all imaged and bodily appearances. The wisdom and death brought by *sakura* in both of its forms (drink, venom) are irresistible. Human beings invariably succumb to the death it brings (either physical death or death to profane existence when one is transported into the world of invisible realities), and it invariably entices the spirits who are the sources of wisdom.

[The bite] of the coral snake does not immediately produce pain or local swelling but a strange neurotoxic poisoning which is generalized throughout the entire nervous system [and which] is reminiscent of a strong alcoholic intoxication. It appears to be unrelated physically to the bite; it rather seems to constitute an enchantment [or spell, *hechizo*]. It is believed that *sakurakura*, when it bites, astonishes—or frightens—the companion spirit (shadow-soul) of its victim, pursues it into the savannah and forces it to drink enormous quantities of an invisible *sakura* in order to change it into a coral-snake spirit and take it away to the house of coral snakes. If the snake succeeds in its purpose, within a few hours the man who has been stripped of his soul will sicken and die.[197]

THE RETURN OF ANOMALY: MONSTERS, THE DEAD, AND ECCENTRICITY

Allusions to violence during festivals represent a break in the plane of ordinary time, a temporal interruption provoked by the appearance of a new form of being and, concomitantly, a new expression of time. Periodic drinking feasts reenact the effective return of destructive events and of monstrous beings, especially aquatic monsters, whose very forms embody formless chaos. For instance, at the end of the main festival celebrated by the Canelos Quichua, a ten-foot bamboo pole (with four notches in it) is erected. It is said to be the giant anaconda form of the master of water from the Ancient Times. In each of the four notches, copal torches are set burning, their red color representing the rainbow. Directed by a powerful shaman, four ritual dancers, called *lanceros* (inmarried foreigners whose dances imitate the threat gestures of a mythical deer-warrior), perform dances choreographed in a quadrangular pattern.[198] Participants pick up the body (*churana*, literally, "dress") of the giant anaconda-spirit and encircle the central plaza. In theory, the ceremony ends with the commemoration of this period when the ancient water serpent "dominates the land, flooding it with ancient water power."[199]

The aquatic monster is not the only being whose return abolishes the normal structures of time and whose death establishes new symbolic orders and periodicities. Other kinds of sacred beings, long since withdrawn or banished to the margins of the cosmos, make their reappearance in the ritual center of the universe. During the Canelos Quichua festival, Amasanga, the master of souls of the forest, visits the men, and Nunghui, mistress of garden soil and pottery clay, visits the women. Other spiritual visitors include souls of the dead, of animals, and of important spirits.

The return of the dead figures largely in South American drinking festivals. The Kaingáng, for example, celebrated a drinking festival to remember their dead. Dancing in a circle, singing, and drinking heavily, the participants wept as they recollected with song the memories of their dead relatives. According to the report of Jules Henry, these drinking feasts traditionally resulted in murder: "[They] used to be almost always the forerunners of raids on the Brazilians or on vendetta enemies."[200]

The great Toba drinking festival of ripe *algaroba* fruit is marked by a special set of dances, called *nomí*, which are performed each day during the ripe-fruit season (from November through January).[201] During this time the spirits of the dead return. Although it is a happy and joyful time, it is not without ambivalence. The drinking, which makes the dead present, is offset by the dances, which keep the invisible shades *(kadepakál)* of the dead *(ilúh)* at a distance. The dances are prophylactic; they prevent the dead from entering into personal relationships with any individuals. The *nomí* is the only dance performed during the daytime. Begun one month before important fruits ripen, it is danced only by young men and is associated with their courtship. The performance of the *nomí* dance during the daytime is associated with the daylight appearances of the dead. Ordinarily, all dances are performed at night as, at all other times, spirits appear only at night. The season of ripe fruit allows for both the visit of spirits by day and for group performance of daylight dances. The same *nomí* dance may be performed in times of communal crisis — during the time when a council of elders deliberates about war, or in preparation for battle, or when the chief's wife is sick in childbed. The Toba case suggests the combative function of drinking festivals, a theme I shall explore shortly.

For the moment it suffices to call attention to a striking set of cases wherein the dead return in association with fermented brew. The death symbolism inherent in drinking feasts comes into sharp focus in the ritual consumption of ashes of deceased relatives mixed into ritual beer. After cremation, which occurs during primary or secondary burial, the semicalcinated bones are pounded into a fine powder and placed in a fermented drink such as *chicha, masato,* or plantain soup. This practice of communion with the dead has enjoyed a widespread distribution.[202] The ashen, twice-consumed substance of the dead is folded into a process of fruition and fermentation. The temporal cusp of ripening and rotting, of death and re-birth, constitutes the proper moment for consuming the dead. The medium of brew recontextualizes the matter of human death. It takes a material swatch, representing the terminal moment of the human life-cycle, and blends it into the fruitful tokens of recurrent cosmic time-lines. Drinking the dead closes the circle of human consumption, bending it back on itself while setting it in the fertile frame of the eternal return of cosmic life.

SYMBOLISM OF PROMISCUITY AND INCEST: OVERCOMING GENERATIVE DIVISIONS THAT RESULTED FROM NOW-FORBIDDEN UNITIES

Festivals return the community to a time and condition of being that is no longer accessible, or even licit, under mundane conditions. The imagery of illicit sex is reminiscent of a time before the strict differentiation of forms. The sexual union of representatives of social units that are now held apart as normatively distinct (e.g., lineages, residence groups, nuclear families) recreates the state of affairs that obtained in the time when supernatural beings merged in unions that were unrestricted by social sanction. Those sacred beings were laws unto themselves. Their acts gave rise to the social divisions whose ritual mimesis of cross-fertilization regenerates society in each sacred season of festival time.

Festival promiscuity is an exemplary relaxation of the normative social frame. For example, one of the culminating and central acts of the Guayakí new year honey feasts involves a tickling game called *proaä mata*, "seizing the bean." [203] A man or woman places a large bean under the armpit or in a closed first. The other participants throw themselves on the bean-holder and tickle him or her in an attempt to make the bean-holder relinquish the bean. The game can become rather violent and loud and is restricted to adults. Tickled by dozens of hands, the holder of the bean rolls on the ground and is kept from escaping. This game, one of the principal rituals of the feast, provides married people with the opportunity of finding extramarital sexual partners and gives young singles a chance to declare their passionate interests.[204] Everyone in turn submits to the tickling. By relinquishing the bean under the touch of a particular chosen individual, the bean-possessor can make a symbolic declaration of love: "I let you have the bean so that you let me have something else." [205] Direct physical contact, ordinarily avoided, is so generalized during this feast that Clastres reports that "the *tö kybairu* is the festival of the body. Any pretext at all will serve for touching it." [206] By ritually abandoning social norm, Guayakí society renews itself.

Symbolic reenactment of primordial incest is one of the most striking and powerful images of the festal annihilation of separation. An Apinayé ritual, for instance, celebrates a mythic event in which a group of boys had intercourse with their sisters. During the ceremony, young males pierce a banana tree with their arrows. The tree is dressed as a human being. Eventually the effigy is chopped down with an ax and "blown" with tobacco smoke.[207]

Incest often becomes the predominant image for the transmutation effected in festivals: the merging of human being with sacred being, a union of forms that has been impossible ever since the withdrawal of the primordium and the initiation of social history. The Akwẽ-Shavante, for example, live a social life dominated by binary oppositions, which are adapted to every level of factional division.[208] However, the Akwẽ-Shavante mythical image of incest dissolves the separations that uphold social life. As David Maybury-Lewis reports, "The Shavante term for incest *(tsiwamnâr)* is interestingly enough the same word as is used in Shavante legends to refer to metamorphosis, usually when people change into animals or vice versa. Their notion of incest is thus clearly that of passage from one state to another or confusion of statuses." [209] Given the fundamental importance of the distinction between the categories of kin and affine, the prospect of confusing them, entertained in Shavante mythic symbolism, is serious. "[T]here is a terrifying monster which appears in Sherente stories and is referred to by them as a *romsiwamnâri* from *ro* = countryside, creation, things in general +

siwamnãr = metamorphosis, confusion, incest. This monster is the spirit of confusion; he has everything mixed up." [210] Through their myths, the Shavante draw a connection between incest, creation "of many things," and immersion in the primordial water which flooded the earth.[211] The unity of these symbolic themes is made explicit in the ceremonies when young men are initiated, especially during the episode when their ears are pierced and they undergo an ordeal of immersion in water.

Since each mode of being (e.g., stars, sun, moon, humans, animals, plants, stone) is understood and evaluated in terms of the temporal order it reveals, incest imagery lets incompatible temporal horizons reconverge in imaginative experience. Separate kinds of time-being are collapsed together in favor of the primordial being that they somehow shared before it withdrew at the moment of their appearance as diverse forms. Moments of illicit merger mark time with the return of precosmic conditions. The calendar can offer human culture a modicum of symbolic control over the potential threat this condition poses to the ordered progress of the human life-cycle. For example, *towömuku* is the word with which the Panare designate both incest and an eclipse of the sun. During a solar eclipse, the sun and the moon resume their incestuous activity. Their violation of the established spatial expressions of their different temporal periodicities carries with it serious consequences. After the eclipse-incest of the sun and moon, the Panare feel themselves threatened with epidemic disease and death. Once differentiation of being and time has become part of existence, return to unity of being is dangerous to the multiplicity of life forms now in existence. Only through ritual or myth should one obtain the power that is acquired in contact with the fullness of being found at the beginning. For the Panare, eclipses, which reenact the incestuous union of sun and moon at the beginning, threaten disaster unless they are made subject to ritual. Return to the fullness of being can, with impugnity, only be achieved in carefully prescribed ways, with powerful sacred techniques.[212] According to Panare belief, the power of the original fullness of being should be appropriated only symbolically — that is, through the effectiveness of symbols — through the indirection of the dry-season ritual, for otherwise to attain fullness of being as it existed in the beginning (here, through the incestuous union of the sun and the moon) would obliterate the world of multiple life-forms, which the union of sun and moon originally produced.[213]

Incest imagery has a direct bearing on understanding drinking festivals. Mythical incest not only manifests the metamorphosis of temporal horizons, the reentry into primordial time that undergirds all calendric feasts, but it also relates significantly to ritual drink. The Tukanoan-speaking Desana offer one instance of the connection between incest and ritual drink. Reichel-Dolmatoff has pointed out that their Yuruparí festivals, although essentially male fertility rites, find their mythic origins in the account of the incest of the Sun-Father with his daughter. "The *yajé* [hallucinogenic drink] child is the offspring of a divine incestuous union." [214] Furthermore, the notion of incest is linked to the concept of visionary "drowning"; one's life is suffocated by realities that enter one's eyes during ceremonial visions just as the daughter of the sun was impregnated with the yellow light that streamed through her eyes. In his analysis of the figures and designs seen in Tukano hallucinogenic visions, Reichel-Dolmatoff helps us understand the link between visions and sex. During hallucinations, the Tukano invariably see beings belonging to the generative time of creation. It is this generative power of the beginnings that enters the body of the viewer through the eyes (as color, shape, and light), mouth (as liquid), and ears (in the form of ritually controlled sounds). Vision and *yajé* are the same creative being, and each symbolic figure, sound, and beverage can be identified as a being who was active in the mythic world of beginnings.[215] This "drowning" can also refer to orgasm, the sensation produced by the sexual expression of the generative act.

Most drinking festivals contain subtle symbolic cues that draw together the meanings of distinct times, primordial incest, drink, and consumption, merging these images in ritual visions and mimetic metamorphoses. The Canelos Quichua celebrate an annual or semiannual ceremony that involves traveling back in time, that is, having visions *(muscui)*.[216] This ceremony celebrates and reenacts the incestuous union of the moon and his sister-bird, an act that brought people into existence. Through alcohol, sleeplessness, and music, a visionary experience is produced that "spans and integrates jungle, water, and soil domains, the sky and the underworld, and opens the entire sequence of linear time to enduring mythic structure."[217] This ceremony, divided into male and female halves, celebrates the mythic event that accounts for the origin of the star-people, from whom the first human women were made.[218] The whole community is redivided during the festival into two ritual parts, the Jilucu *jista* (named after the sister-bird) and the Quilla *jista* (named after the moon). These two ritual groups are considered united by both consanguine and affinal ties, as were the moon and his sister. Opposed to all these related participants are four foreigners, who act as ritual warriors. These men, called *lanceros*, are usually men who have married into the group from outside.[219]

During their main feast, Canelos Quichua women force *chicha* down the throats of the men.[220] "Sometimes four or five women converge on one person, each continuing her pouring as the selected receiver gulps, blows out liquid, and even stands on the bench in an effort to avoid the inevitable chicha shampoo."[221] Drummers beat two-sided drums. They circle first one way, so that the monkey-skin drumhead's resounding snare (which brings dreams) buzzes in the direction of the house; then they circle in the opposite direction, so that the buzzing carries out toward the forest and the peccary-skin drumhead faces the house. The drummers call in women to dance. Other dancers join the group, bringing drums and transverse flutes with them. The dancing men and women think-sing songs to Nunghuí and Amasanga. The songs are said to come from an ancient soul. Men are dressed as animals and birds, whose souls accompany the men and merge with them during their dance. All the spaces and times of the universe mingle and merge in the dance circle.[222]

During the night, the group representing the moon's sister visits the group representing the moon. These visits, replete with dancing, singing, forced *chicha* drinking and shampooing, continue until the middle of the night. Even after that, care is taken to keep vigil for fear of losing one's soul lest it stray during a dream,[223] for there are too many strange souls in the neighborhood.[224] The yellow color of the flowers brought by the guests commemorates the incestual affinity of the moon-bird union that produced the first people. After holding vigil, the group splits into parties that ceremonially visit the other houses in the area. Continuing to drink, dance, and make noise, each party brings yellow flowers to each of the houses it calls on. Perhaps in recognition of the "many" that originated from the incestuous union, the visitors' movements reproduce the segmentation and replication of *tuta indi* ("the suns of night," i.e., the stars), the celestial nighttime suns who are said to be yellow people.

It should go without saying that ritual imagery of incest should not be confused with a disregard or ignorance of a primary social prohibition in human culture. All the cultures who use the image in connection with notions of time and drink observe the so-called incest taboo, often in rather demanding extensions that prevent even symbolic intercourse such as common eating, work, or conversation between prescriptive kin. The incest under discussion here is a symbolic reference to the actions of sacred beings. As Irving Goldman has observed, genuine ritual is not a childish return to these origins. Mature individuals of any culture realize that "there is no going back" and that ritual must be a careful mimetic encounter with powers that are made present through symbol. Ritual incest should be seen as a sophisticated anamnesis/mimesis; participants are aware of the ritual's imitative character and are conscious of the dangers of an overly naive, direct, or literal return to the fullness of being.[225] Incest and the fusion or confusion of different forms is reenacted in a reflexive way in order to prevent chaos from happening again. Like the blurred vision that results from deliberate intoxication, incest symbolism achieves a metamorphosis, a merging of forms that have been separate since their primordial differentiation. The irony and paradox underlying all calendric celebrations are put on parade here: incest is *acted* out precisely to prevent its destructive consequences from recurring. Celebrating the unity that all beings share below—or before—the separate forms of their appearance, symbolic incest honors the origin of the differences which gave rise to symbolic life. Festival time celebrates itself, its own differentiation, the beginnings of change. For this reason tension is in the air. It is the excitement of the first rending. By alluding to primordial incest, drinking festivals transport revelers to a pristine condition of time, a unitive mode of being, a fluid state not available in this world of distinct periodicities, normative social divisions, and exclusive existential situations.[226] The religious imagination of the realm of sacred beings forms the baseline of meaning for the symbolic world of human culture, which, by contrast, signifies differentiation.

THIRST, FLOOD, AND RECREATIONAL DRINKING

Ritual processes associated with fermented drink carry within them long histories of social and religious meaning.[227] For the Chayahuita, *masato*, fermented manioc beer, is not only a dietary staple but also a central ingredient in the economy of social relations. *Masato* plays a key role in the development of Chayahuita social roles and in cultural exchange. Since the responsibility for preparing *masato* falls upon women, Carole Daggett suggests that an examination of its use provides an important way of evaluating the impact that women have on the construction of networks of social relations.[228]

In fact, women feature prominently in drinking festivals.[229] Women frequently play a crucial role in both the myths about ritual drink and in the actual preparation and consumption of fermented brew. Numerous cases already cited describe a mythic drama in which a young woman, just coming into child-bearing age, serves as the literal center — the generative locus, the beginning — of culture and society. In myths describing the origin of drinking feasts, the young woman is surrounded by chaotic forms, anaconda-people or aquatic monsters, who rise up out of watery depths. Drinking feasts celebrate the return of the chaos first set loose by an adolescent girl's excessive openness (her first menses, her unguarded glance, her breach of food taboos, etc.). They also celebrate her triumph over chaos. With the aid of a mythic grandmother or elder female, the girl remains motionless or enclosed (e.g., under a clay jar). Through her fixity she defeats the serpents of chaos or brings them to heel, thereby establishing the possibility and the space of human culture. In contrast to the miraculously acquired magical weapons of epic heroes, her principal instruments are intrinsic to her character: blood, skin, patience, endurance, long-suffering, and, above all, closure. Closure and containment, which seal individual character and give rise to the closed symbolic system of human culture, are evident in the custody of her eyes; in the control she acquires over the openness of her vagina by shutting herself in menstrual seclusion when her womb is "open" or by observing sexual mores, which subject penetration of her womb to cultural will; in the mastery of her mouth through silence and fasting; and so on. For her pains, culture is provided decorations (e.g., necklaces left by the anaconda-people) that mark the human body, the ultimate cultural container and symbol of closure.

During drinking festivals, when the order of culture temporarily relapses into the chaos of primordial destruction, women, who ordinarily are "closed" in defense against the deluge, release a flood from within their own being: the festival drink, which is primed with women's saliva. In making the starter-mash for fermented brew, women's substance flows freely. Ironically, the flood is drunk up by the men. The men become containers of women's substance. In contrast to the primordial flood, which was warded off by female closure, men defeat liquid chaos with their openness, absorbing all the liquid foisted on them by the women. Men guzzle up the flow of life that streams from the orifices of women's bodies, the paradigmatic enclosures from which human life comes. The process is the complementary inverse of sexual intercoure, during which the seminal liquid of life spills from the bodies of men and is drawn into the body-containers of women in order to impose spatial form (a new child's body) and temporal order (a new generation) on the fluid experience of human life. In both drinking and intercourse, the sexes collaborate to give bodily containment and fixed cultural form to the fertile flow of inchoate life.

Throughout South America there are endless and important variations on these themes. No attempt is made here to contend that all drinking festivals reenact the same myth or convey precisely the same values. Rather I am trying to ferret out a nexus of meanings that can be variously construed and significantly rearranged in creative ways as we interpret the interplay of calendrical existence, the girl at the center and origins of culture, the flood, destruction (through death or disappearance), water monsters, seclusion, closure, bodily ornaments, drunkenness, and so on.

For example, the Shipibo call their main festivals "Big Drinks." These festivals not only mark off the passage of time during the calendar year but also affect temporal passage in the lives of individuals. It is during these drinking bouts that the Shipibo initiate girls, investing them with a superabundance of ornamental clothing. Furthermore, the Big Drinks are timed in accordance with the cycles of the moon.[230]

The mythic background of rituals helps to make the meaningful connection between drink, women, ornaments, and time. Peter Kloos reports a Maroni myth that binds together drunkenness, the festal celebration of girls' initiation, and the presence of a menacing water spirit. During her first menstruation, a Maroni girl ignored her mother's warnings to stay in seclusion and was seduced into a river by the water spirit who appeared in the guise of a strange man who offered her a necklace. When the man sent the girl back to her weeping mother, the girl's friends made her drunk and compelled her to speak of the supernatural being whom she had seen. Unfortunately, the water spirit had instructed her to say nothing. As a result of her telling the tale of her encounter, she disappeared.[231] The myth has a bearing on understanding the drinking and chaos connected with the New Year feast, the most important calendric festival in Maroni River Carib society. It begins around 25 or 26 December and reaches a drunken climax on 1 and 2 January. The major element in the festival is complete drunkenness, which is accomplished by drinking manioc beverages and other fermented and distilled bottled liquors. An uninterrupted celebration begins on New Year's Eve; it ends only when all of the alcohol has been consumed.[232]

According to the reports of Udo Oberem, consumption of extraordinary volumes of alcoholic *chicha* is an essential aspect of all Canelos Quichua feasts, whether informal or formal. As I have already described it, the informal festival is spontaneously initiated by the head of the household, who, returning from the hunt, marches around his family house pounding a small drum. Guests are force-fed *chicha*. If men fail to consume everything that is poured down their throats by the women, the remainder is poured over their heads.[233] The most formal Canelos Quichua feast reported by Oberem is the Christmas celebration, which takes place alongside the Christian Mass and procession. A meal of hunted game is prepared on a long table. Dancing begins — especially the formal dancing of the *lanceros*, who carry iron-tipped spears. Once again, raucous consumption of *chicha*, forced on the men by the women, is the ritual order of the day.

The connection of festival drink with primordial flood draws attention back to the earlier discussion of primordial (now celestial) liquid considered as a fixture of space.[234] Ritual drink is metonymically part of the fluids (heavenly liquid, floodwaters) of mythic time. The eternal or static waters of the primordial or paradisal state of being appeared in this moving world as a destructive flood. The waters of destruction brought new life of a rushing, fertile, growthful, symbolic, and regulated kind to the cosmos. These are the liquids which humans regularly reabsorb during life-giving feasts which mark the passage of periodic time. The beer brings back old times and marks the reappearance of ancient presences. The Maipuri, for example, celebrated a drinking and dance festival called Cheti (literally, "animal"). During the festival, primordial serpents returned to the village to dance with the men. The men consumed fermented beverages, which the mythical snakes brought with them.[235] The women reportedly feared the supernatural beings.

Festival drink, taking its origins from chaotic destruction, is deadly. It brings the "death" that lies at the heart of the creativity and fertile generativity of human culture. The death brought by drink is associated with the life of the mouth, the place of life-sustaining processes of consumption and of the saliva that brings brew to fermented life. This string of meanings comes to the fore in the case of *caguī* (from *ka'u*, "to make drunk"), an Apapocuvá festival drink, which ferments with the help of saliva. *Caguī* is the special water, the life source, that will be consumed at the end of time. At that time, souls are to avoid consuming ordinary water. *Caguī* is associated with the dead, for it is the principal source of nourishment for the dead.[236] Unlike the external floodwaters, which suffocate the senses and drown them in formlessness, the fermenting process, present in the form of this drink that is taken internally, is essential to life in its fullest form.

High alcohol content is not necessarily the most important characteristic of fermented festival drink. For example, for the Tapirapé, who also refer to their maize beer as *caguī*, it is enough that the brew ferment at all. The religious importance of beer lies in its peculiar symbolic capacity. As a symbol, *caguī* bespeaks an essential aspect of human existence associated with the performative capacities of culture, which are founded on the reciprocal creativity of the sexes. From the same root come the Tapirapé terms *kangui* (woman) and *kágua* (man, literally, "my beer"); thus, human beings are those beings who can become drunk, who are capable of making and consuming *caguī*.[237]

The deadliness of ritual, which is linked with the consumptive processes of the mouth, draws it into the net of meanings generated by the primordial destructions of fire and flood. It has become a commonplace in analyzing the origin myths of cooking fire to point out that structured human life can be identified with fire, whose images embody various spiritual constituents of human experience: personality, soul, breath, libido, and so on. These spiritual elements constitute the basis of consumptive processes of production (e.g., appetites for food, sex, land, housing) as well as of processes reproductive of social units (residence groups, lineages, moieties).[238] In a parallel way, ritual drinking can symbolize the capacity to absorb the kind of undifferentiated experience that threatens to drown the senses and to blur the distinctions that ground the relations among the sensuous meanings that lie at the heart of human existence. Ritually to channel primordial being within human culture in the form of drink requires the collaborative capacities of both kinds of human forms, female and male. The connivance (in the literal sense of "closing the eyes") of women and the gulping of open-throated men conspire to contain the destructive powers of regenerative life in ways suited to their respective body forms and demonstrate the relationship of those forms to sensual life-processes of seminal emisson, conception, gestation, and birth.

As ritual drink, primordial liquid is neither completely placid nor utterly destructive. In a way contrary to the separation of spirit from form in the spiritualization effected by fire, the dissolution that occurs in ritual drinking merges separate forms. It overcomes the distance from meaning that is inherent in all symbolic existence.[239] In contrast to immersion in primordial liquid (as in the bath taken in the blood of a slain aquatic monster), which action marked distinctions among animal species and times, the pouring of ritual drink into the body replenishes the senses by obliterating distinctions between forms. Symbolic life is renewed. Meaning, ordinarily parceled out among the separate bodily senses, reunites in its primordial form.

The exercise of containing unbounded primordial liquid offers human culture control over abundant life. The instrument of this control is the human body. By containing primordial forces, the body gives shape to the otherwise undifferentiated forms of free-flowing primordial powers. By marking the center with spatial and temporal aspects of the human body, human culture holds chaos at bay. For these reasons, humans *must* consume enormous quantities of ritual drink; they must force themselves to overreach their fullest capacities. The exercise betokens the struggle of culture to absorb and channel the boundless meaning of sacred life.

This explains the widespread practice of forced drinking. Exorbitant ritual consumption, enacted as a sign of spiritual capacity, must transcend the bounds of personal pleasure, individual preference, and good taste. For instance,

> [I]n the course of the Waiwai Shodewika dance each individual consumes such enormous quantities of drink that it is impossible to hold any more. However, it is still offered to them and it is not good form to refuse; indeed, they even exhort the hosts to bring still more. In consequence one frequently sees a man who just filled himself up quite calmly spit it out or vomit it up in order to be able, courteously, to accept the next time a drink is proffered.[240]

In the scorings of the earth's surface effected by human culture as well as in the incising of the human body, primordial destruction has left its marks. Such markings (the slashing and burning of cultivated fields, the scarification of human skin during initiation) are symbolic tokens of the passage of time.[241] These ritual marks of time help us figure out significant dimensions of ritual drink. For example, an Akawaio woman must be specially prepared to make the fermented festival drink called *cassiri*. Cuts are made around her mouth and on her forearms. The wounds are then injected with a sweet substance (e.g., honey) and a dark dye. But these are only the outward signs of a deeper spiritual experience, for the cuts are said to be the marks of deadly stinging beings, most notably the scorpion. It is this fatal and strong bite that permits the woman to infuse the fermented beverage with the stinging aspect of her own transformed being. As she chews the manioc mash and holds it in her mouth to begin the fermentation process, it acquires not only a sweetness but also a deadliness, which accounts for the "sting" of drunkenness.[242] With their tattoos, women become like the biting spiders or scorpions which scarred them. Women sting men with their venomous drink, their own substance.[243]

Audrey J. Butt draws together similar reports from a number of different Guiana groups. In order to make drink sweeter, for example, the Wapishiana tattooed the tongues of women by allowing a special kind of ant to bite them. Sweet honey was then mixed into the wound.[244] The association of the drinking of alcoholic beverages at festivals with the cutting of designs of stinging and biting beings is not limited to body tattoos. Drinking vessels among the Wapishiana and related groups are frequently decorated with scorpion and snake designs so that the liquor will be "strong and biting." Making ritual drink requires scarification of the land, the utensil, and the body, the alteration of surface that marks the earth, the implement, and the person with the transitive quality of time. This cutting of the skin incises women with the interruptive species of time that destroyed the primordium and brought on time's passage. Through the saliva of scarified women, ritual drink reacquires that same venomous ability to destroy life. The "death" it induces marks the passage of calendrical time with periodic drinking feasts.

Deadly festival drink and the ceremonial body ornaments find a different origin among the Baniwa. They are nonetheless still tied to the meaning of the event that ended the primordial age. According to Baniwa mythology, the original drinking festival was a deadly affair at which the sky-people *(eenunai)* mixed their poisonous hair with fermented beer to produce a venomous beverage. Most of the guests saved themselves by drinking the antivenom, made from *limathoaiya* (a gourd inside which grows a tiny red fruit that induces vomiting) that had been blessed ("blown") by an elderly aunt. Unfortunately, one being, Mawerikuli, did not drink the remedy and died. His death marks the origin of death in the world. From this first drinking feast of death and venom come ornaments used in drinking feasts.[245]

The origin myth of Makiritare festival drink recapitulates or alludes to many of the themes touched upon in connection with ritual drinking: destruction, sacrificial death, incestuous union, obliteration of time, fertility, a central female protagonist who defines the space of culture, rebirth, a serpentine monster, drink as venom, consumption of death in fermented brew, and so on. The Makiritare link festival brew with snakebite venom, which inspired a vicious thirst in a bitten girl, the sister of Kasenadu (lightning).[246] She meets her death by drinking a false imitation of festival cassava beer. In death, she dreams perpetually, remains in an endless ecstasy, and, in spirit form, dwells forever in the Snake House.

It was Kasenadu who had caused his sister to be bitten. Lightning himself slithers through the clouds "like a snake of fire." [247] He asked Ñomo, the snake mistress, to have the girl bitten. Ñomo heals souls of people bitten by her four poisonous snake-children, slaking the victims' feverish thirst with a drink of forgetfulness. When the sister of lightning died of snakebite and the forgetfulness beverage and when her bones were clean, her brother Kasenadu cut her up and instructed her sons how to prepare a proper garden. The authentic festival brew was provided by Kuinadi, the collared trogon (quetzal), who placed the power of *moriche*-palm ashes in a gourd full of cassava beer. He offered the drink prepared from the girl's remains to her son, who was clearing the cassava fields in the manner prescribed by Kasenadu.

Human control over time is manifest in the manipulation of drink and the other waters that offer abundant life. Irrigation, navigation, and festival brew set humans apart from animals and heavenly beings, who have access to fluid but do not control it symbolically.[248] The human calendar, like the ritual drink and irrigation which extend human control over vegetal life and rain, subject cosmic cycles and periodic tempests to the artifice of human culture. The relationship of sacred drink to calendric feasts and rites of passage through time is not arbitrary. It is predicated on the association these events have to sacred beings and events. The Inca chroniclers Guaman Poma and Santa Cruz Pachacuti, for example, describe a special ritual-drinking procedure in which the drinker consumes ritual beverage from one vessel while offering a second vessel to the supernatural being associated with the season. These symbolic actions were carefully calibrated with cosmic time. At the June solstice, clearly associated with fertility, the Inca (i.e., the king) performed this ritual toast to the sun; at the December solstice, drink was offered to the ancestors. Both chroniclers attribute the first such drinking to the mythical fifth Inca (either Cusi Huanachiri Amaru or Capac Yupanqui). Through drink and liquid Inca society and individuals came under the influence of cosmic and mythic time. This same king first brought sacred water to Cuzco from an island in Lake Titicaca and first established the custom of piercing the ears of aristocratic initiates on the day of the summer solstice. The ear-piercing was performed at the source of a river or canal.[249]

Drink is recreational because it recapitulates the time, the quality of relations, that re-created this world. Like all calendric moments of passage, festival drink commemorates a destructive node, a consumptive cusp of change when a primordial state of affairs passed out of existence, faded from view, or assumed new form. In particular, festive brew bears metonymic affinity with the primordial waters of the catastrophic flood, with the venom of deadly beings, or with the incestuous seminal flow which engendered cataclysm.

Ritual drink's capacity to represent the sacred times and mythic events that established culture link it to cultural vision, art, and dream, all of which bring human life into encounter with the same imaginal world. Because it shares with them a common time of sacred origin, drink is brought into relationship with other cultural artifices that order temporal existence, such as the control over space evident in the ritually cleared fields (e.g., in the Makiritare case) and irrigation canals (e.g., of the Incas). Temporally significant control over space also occurs in human bodies, which at symbolically important times are closed to the passage of particular symbolic substances, such as avoided foods, semen, or excretions.[250] The same temporalized control over spatial forms is exercised when throats and birth canals are opened at appropriate times, when the skin is cut or pierced at initiation time, and when the body is decorated with the crystallized moments of change, the symbolic ornaments left by supernatural beings when their departure marked the paradigmatic passing of time in this world. The cultural thirst for sacred brew and for calendric drinking bouts represents a desire for a fresh experience of time, an experience of the moment when time was new. By renewing time, cultures replenish the human senses, blurring images and dissolving distinctions in the return to the primordial source of meaning.

RITUAL COMBAT: DESTROYING DESTRUCTION BY REENACTING IT

Ritual combats, singing or oratorical contests, races, and dance competitions between pairs of antagonistic groups play important parts in many calendrical feasts, especially ceremonies held at the New Year or at the onset of agricultural cycles. In such cases, violent confrontations are integral to the renewal of time, the remanifestation of the creative power which makes a quality of existence begin again.[251]

Ritual combats assume different forms and fill different functions. Several brief examples suggest their variety. Wrestling matches accompany the drinking bouts held by the Siriono during the dry season. This is the time when bee honey is plentiful; it is made into mead. Although drinking bouts appear to begin informally, it should be noted that the mead that will be consumed must be carefully prepared beforehand. A drinking circle forms. Participants sing, heroic accounts are recited, and then the wrestling starts. Frequently the wrestling matches escalate into open brawls.[252] The Apinayé Ro'ród festival centered on log races but included other stylized forms of aggression, such as the sounding of trumpets and flutes; the singing of animal songs; the whipping of boys and girls who exhibited signs of masturbation; the scourging of men, boys, women, and girls; and a final dance with the whip.[253] In the case of the Inca, young warriors (ararihua) were not only responsible for waging wars of imperial expansion and defense but also for driving disease from Cuzco, the capital, in a staged rampage held during the annual feast of Situay. In addition, Inca warriors had the ritual duty of battling the spirits of thunder and hail during the early planting and growing season from September to November.[254]

Mataco ritual combatants fought with celestial beings during the Atj festival. The ceremony is based on a mythic battle during which a healer saved the people, whose enemies has imprisoned them in the trunk of a tree. Taking the form of a wasp *(viscacha)*, the healer led the people in their escape. Then they became eagles. "They fly like birds and so they can fight."[255] Beginning at dawn on the day of the festival, the Mataco religious specialist prepares a ritual space by spreading a deerhide on a grassless spot. The specialist prepares himself by dusting his body with *yulo* feathers. His principal instruments of power are the sacred rattle and whistle with which he performs powerful songs unique to his personality. Taking the rattle in one hand and a bunch of feathers in the other, the specialist spreads his arms wide "to clear the way among the clouds." His singing and whistle-blowing encourage spirits of dead medicine men to reappear and join in the fray.

The battle with celestial spirits rages fiercely. It is the responsibility of the ritual leader to protect the participants in the ceremony—and, in fact, the whole community—from harm. In one reported Atj performance, the ceremony leader, cautious and watchful, caught an invisible arrow which had been thrown by an evil being. "He pretended to introduce it into his rattle, which he later shook as he was blowing his whistle."[256] A report provided by Alfred Métraux highlights the dangerous and warlike aspects of this ceremony.[257] Métraux explains that the ceremony, celebrated to ward off an epidemic, "symbolically fights the spirits or disease demons." As arrows are thrown by evil beings, the Mataco set up a "counter-offensive with magical songs accompanied by gourd rattles." In a state of trance, the leading curer makes a soul voyage to the sky, for the sky is the place of battle between the attacking spirits of disease and the souls of the curers, which have taken on the form of birds. Called forth by the presiding shaman, the spirits of dead shamans battle victoriously on behalf of the living.

The most dramatic annual festival celebrated by the Tapirapé is the ceremonial fight against Thunder. This annual battle against Thunder and his spirit children takes place in late December or early January, when the heavy rains begin again. It is led by the most powerful shamans, who intoxicate themselves by gulping tobacco smoke and then reingesting the nicotine-filled saliva they vomit up. Paired with their wives, they sing and dance themselves into a trance; they fall unconscious, shot by the *topü*, children of Thunder. Their souls then travel to the home of Thunder. With the help of their wives and fellow shamans, they are revived with tobacco smoke and rattling. This spiritual combat widens the distance between the sexes, for the whole community abstains from sex before and during the festival performance. The conclusion of the symbolic struggle signals a resumption of intercourse, so that "many women . . . become pregnant."[258]

Reenacting the violence of the change effected by sacred beings, ceremonial violence at seasonal feasts is essential to the fertility, growth, and health of animals, plants, and humans. The central issue is abundance: the replication of times, the multiplication of crops, the appearance of plenty. Such is the underlying motive for a pan-Andean tradition of festival combat.[259] This tradition of ritual combat (*pucara*, literally, "fortress") extended from Bolivia through Peru and into Ecuador. The ritual battles were often carried out by using *waraka*s (bolas or slings). The details of such a ritual battle, which took place during the feast of Carnaval, were gathered in Juncal, Cañar, in the highlands of southern Ecuador, during the last week of February 1974.[260] The myth of Táita Carnaval is the "essential factor in making people look forward to the festival days." [261] During the festival, Táita Carnaval ("Father Carnival") returns to visit the community as he did once long ago. He may bring the community good luck, but the outcome is never sure, for Táita Carnaval walks in company with Yarcay ("hunger"). Father Carnival plays music on a flute made from a condor bone. He also plays a small drum (*caja*), which is a chest filled with gold and precious gems. With music from these instruments, Táita Carnaval opens the mountains, one by one, allowing access to the riches that are contained within them.[262] Táita Carnaval is thus drawn within the circle of the *wamani*s, the mountain divinities of the Andes, whose mountain dwellings open in February and August to give life to the world of creatures who together form the mountain-body. Long ago, a man who accompanied him into the mountains was told by Father Carnival to do battle with him: "Can you stand up to me or can't you? . . . If you can stand up to me, I shall let you have what I have. . . . If you cannot stand up to me, you will lose everything." [263] Thus began the tradition of ritual combat during festivals. "It was the good luck they were fighting about." During some years, the man from the local community managed to strike Táita Carnaval, win the contest, and obtain good luck for the next year; on other occasions he lost the match.

One entered the symbolic world of the inner mountain after drinking enormous quantities of *trago*, sugar-cane liquor. The ritual battle took place just outside the openings of the mountains and immediately after participants emerged from the inside. It was fought over the goods contained inside. In the past, the ritual battles were indeed contests between teams in which all men participated. Even until the mid-1960s "the Indians feared that the year and the crop would be bad without a ritual combat." [264] In 1974, the ritual fighting seemed to have been a time for settling personal scores and grievances accumulated throughout the year. In any case, "the expressed aim is that blood must be shed and that one party must be proclaimed to be the winner, because luck will follow the winners and leave the losers." [265] In fact, Eva Krener and Niels Fock report that a lot of blood is shed during these days of ritual battle: "if the blood flows from the victim's nose or ears, it is said that the winner will always try to get to drink some of it." [266]

These social antagonisms reinvigorate all of creation and stimulate it to new life. Through the symbolism of the contest, the social group reconnects itself with the powers of the mythical past and renews time. Like the sacred events they restage, the ritual antagonisms have a re-creative effect on crops, animals, and human beings. Victory of new life is guaranteed by the stylized violence just as it was assured in the primordial drama of change.

THE BATTLE OF THE SEXES   The violence is stylized by heightening the symbolic differences between social actors and groups. The symbolic differences between men and women are the ones most frequently exploited in calendric combat. The antagonism of male and female can be obliquely present in ritual combat in cases where opposing teams of men are formed on the basis of the men's different relationships to the same women. For example, the Guayakí engage in an annual ritual confrontation between two opposed groups: women's brothers and their future husbands. The men are painted by women using daubs made from a mixture of smoked wax, powdered charcoal, and resin. During the annual feast the men are decorated in this way with an aim toward making them look terrifying to their enemies. Thus dressed for war, the ornamented warriors face each other as ritual opponents. Women are the hinge of the stylized battle, the link drawing the two groups of ritual warriors into combative relationship with one another. In fact, all this is carried off to accomplish marriage exchanges of women. "One may capture women at the end of a victorious war with the result of transforming brothers-in-law into enemies; or one can exchange spouses in a peaceful way and build an alliance of exchange." [267] This peaceful and ceremonial ritual of exchange of women is in the nature of all ritual behavior, paradoxical: it is "a war which one avoids carrying out." [268] By mimicking the act of war, one paradoxically demonstrates the point that war is not intended. [269]

In keeping with the stylized aggression used to instigate relationships of friendship and alliance, the Guayakí celebrate the ceremonial game of *kyvai*, tickling. Normally, physical contact is scrupulously avoided except in cases of aggression. During the honey feast, however, warriors pair up, seat themselves on the ground, and tickle each other violently. Each tries to withhold his laughter. The tickling can become violent and torturous. The tickling continues until one of the two, suffocating with laughter, begs to have the contest stop. Between the two tickling warriors there is established a special bond of friendship. These tickling contests inaugurate the celebration of Tö Kybairu, the principal drinking feast marking the change of year.

The opposition between men and women in ritual combats that mark temporal passage, foster fertility, and increase life is not usually so subtle. More often, this stylized aggression between men and women is overt. In particular, single-sex secret societies act to heighten the terrifying spiritual relationship between men and women. Symbolic violence between the sexes is inherent in many such societies, for their sacred possessions (e.g., musical instruments, masks, dances, songs), on which the celebrations center, have been forcibly taken from the opposite sex during the mythic period. That primordial aggression remains an efficacious part of the possessions' power today.

Masked dances—to choose one manifestation of stylized terror between the sexes — are performed throughout South America on a variety of calendric occasions. The masks themselves represent a large range of meanings. It is all the more remarkable, then, that so many masked dances represent ritual antagonism and combat. Thus, for example, the masks worn by Ona and Yahgan men in front of the *kína* (men's house) are intended to frighten women. The same purpose lies behind the antagonistic masked performances of the Chamacoco.[270] Theodor Koch-Grünberg provided reports of masked funeral performances among groups of the drainage area of the Caiarí and Uaupés rivers. Mythical animals, present in the form of masks worn by men, attacked the *maloca* (communal house) while the dead man's mother and wife keened in company with other women. Eventually the masked figures, singing ritual songs, burst into the house and performed phallic dances.[271] In girls' puberty rituals (as among the Lengua of the Gran Chaco), young boys impersonating the mythical spirits of chaos and destruction menace the menstruating girl. The boys wear feathers, masks, and deerhoof rattles. They make shrill noises. Mature women protect the young girl by driving the intruders away in a ritual battle.[272]

Women and men deliberately put themselves at odds with one another through the imagery of ritual aggression and dance in order to reenact mythical scenarios whose violence effected significant change and passage of time. Death to a prior condition of existence is a theme intrinsic to such qualitative transitions of being and time. In the violent death of ritual combat, the victim falls prey to a sacred being, whom the actors must impersonate with a force worthy of a supernatural being. Attack by sacred beings is reconstitutive; it brings new life. An important category of Toba dances is the *nahōre*, the "jaguar dance," during which the loins of girls are lashed with cloth by young men dancing in a circle around them. One by one, the young women fall to the ground in the center of the circle. Lying "dead," each girl is attacked by a supernatural "jaguar" (played by a curer who makes the grunting sounds of that wild beast). His attack consists, however, of curing actions: "He puts his mouth to the girl's breast, sucks it on two spots and blows on it, after which he spits out what he pretends to extract. Then he treats the head in the same way, sucking it and blowing on it." [273] In this way, each girl is revitalized. This entitles the women to a ritual encounter with the jaguar, an ambivalent power who is, in the end, a benevolent being. In fact, Toba men are not initiated in any serious way, and it is women, not men, who are most frequently transformed into supernatural jaguars after death.[274]

Festival combat between the sexes exhibits a variety of forms. Aside from masked dances and the mimed attack of supernatural animals, there are rhetorical competitions and bouts of verbal abuse as well as food fights and eating and drinking contests. For instance, toward the end of the Canelos Quichua festival celebrating the incestuous origin of the first people, guests arrive bringing bundles of yellow flowers, which they place in a hexagonal-weave basket. The women pounce on the male flower-bringers, forcing them to drink quarts of *chicha* and dousing their heads with *chicha*, an action "symbolizing the ancient, enduring water system of the rain forest." [275] Later that afternoon, local men return from the forest with palm branches and yellow flowers. The men must stage a forced entry into their ceremonial house. As they do so, women pour *chicha* down their throats and over their heads.

After Sunday Mass, the ceremony's final stage, called the *camari*, is begun. This is a meal during which servers and served ritualize hostile relationships. In fact, it appears to be a ritual enactment of chaotic and destructive relationships. Hosts insult visitors; guests take great offense. If a person does not wish to eat more, soup may be poured down his throat and spilled on him. Even local authorities have *chicha* poured on their heads.[276] The dousing soon degenerates into a general free-for-all, where men and women throw mud, grease, and *chicha* at one another. During this general food fight, insults are made about the meal. Throughout all these belligerent antics, the circular march around the feast table continues to the accompaniment of drums, and "many women dance as a unit, throwing their hair to and fro."[277]

Whitten was told by Canelos Quichua informants that in former times this ritual culminated in war raids against the Jívaro in order to kill people on a large scale.[278] The fact that the festival may have been a prelude to war parties against the Jívaro makes sense of both the escalation to violence that occurs in the very last stages of the ritual and the emphatic rhetoric of alliance engaged in after the close of the present-day ritual.[279]

Orchestral music is an important medium of symbolic belligerence. During calendric feasts, groups of instruments embody sacred characters. Their sound makes the ancient beings present once again. This staged battle of the bands symbolically aggravates the tension between the modes of primordial being represented by the two sexes. Musical flutes (as well as masks) figure largely in Kamayurá festivals in which ritual combats are enacted. In particular, the masked dances and flutes of the Jaqui festival heighten the antagonism between men and women, for the dances and sounds are forbidden to the view and hearing of women. "If a woman breaks this rule, she risks being gang-raped by all the men of the village. . . . The *jaqui* symbolizes a relation of dialectical opposition between the sexes as groups."[280] In a parallel way, the *tarawí* flutes of the Taquara Dance act out a battle between afflicting and curing spirits.

In a version of a Baniwa myth provided by Wilhelm Saake, the myth of the origin of sacred festival flutes also describes the origin of ritual battle along sexual lines. Amaru, the water snake-monster and the mother of Kuai (from whose body the ritual flutes and trumpets are made), argues that she has a right to possess the flutes since they are parts of the body of her son, who had been taken from her. They are her "grandsons."[281] Kuai's father, Inapirikuli, who impregnated her,[282] wishes to keep the flutes from her. A battle shapes up for which Amaru musters up thirty female followers, who rise out of holes in the ground. Over and against these female forces are thirty male beings summoned by Dzuri, the lord of tobacco and shamanic blowing. To the accompaniment of music, the Baniwa sexes reenact the battle over instruments, body parts, holes of emergence, and the fertile places of the earth.

It is a sonic struggle associated with the heterogeneity of space, a battle over those many kinds of spaces that emit sounds or that are filled with sound. The sexual overtones of the battle serve as a reminder that space obstructs the unity of human experience and that continuity of human life, dependent on that unity between the sexes, is the outcome of creative tension between two kinds of space, male and female, which cannot easily be possessed at the same time. Temporal symbolism, especially the imagery of aggression that is built into the complex calendric order, is a necessary device in the celebrated struggle to overcome spatial difference.

Alternation is one temporal device for negotiating differences between incompatible spatial expressions of reality (human bodies, ritual spaces, the sexually valenced places of the world, such as fields, forests, ceremonial plazas, and cooking areas). This appears to be the function of ritual aggression during some Brazilian Candomblé ritual dances: "At rites such as the *Lorogun* the 'male' deities will in some houses contest with the 'female' to determine which will 'rule' during the year ahead." [283] Alternation in time resolves contradictions inherent in a cult space whose meaning is presided over by both of the two sexes.

The symbolism of the calendar and the ritual combats used to pass time at festivals achieve the unity of separate modes of spatial being — male and female bodies — that is essential to continued life. From one point of view, the battle of the sexes is essentially a struggle between types of being understood as spatial ciphers. For this reason, although sexual symbolism looms large in the stylized antagonism of calendric feasts, ritual combat can be waged in terms that are not overtly sexual. Ritual combat between Desana shamans is, as is often the case elsewhere, a competition between types of being. Fittingly, each type of being has an integral space all its own. In the Desana cosmos, all such integral spaces are six-sided (as, for example, the yellow crystal that embodies the creative light, the semen of the Sun Father). Desana shamans carry out violent ritual combat while they lie in their hammocks in a state of ecstasy:

> During these fights each shaman imagines himself as standing encased in a crystal which serves him on all sides as a protective armor. Next to him stands his adversary, also enclosed in a crystal. Both are thought to stand upon hexagonal shields, and the ensuing struggle involves an attempt by each contestant to unbalance his enemy, to knock him over, and to make him and his crystal lose their firm footing on the shield.[284]

Ritual combat is often a response to the existential dilemma of spatial existence. That is why symbolic battle is fought ostensibly over spaces of various kinds (bodies, cult houses, territory of exogamous groups) and extensions of those spaces into time (offspring, quantity of yield from land, accumulated abundance). Through their calendric capacity — the ability to coordinate times into complex rhythms — human beings seek the resolution of the paradox of aspectual life and of many other contradictions generated by the fragmented or prepositional quality of cosmic space. The major forces of Canella existence, for example, are brought together in struggle and competition during ceremonies; these forces are seen as existing in a rhythmical relationship. Izikowitz reports that, among the Canella, "one does not gain prestige or honor if one wins a log-race. I should rather interpret the races as complementary actions. It is a case of two opposites which belong together and interact." [285] The quest for rhythmic synchrony of incommensurable experiences inevitably leads to contact with the sacred beings, supernatural events, and primordial times that form the basis of the calendar.

Festival combat is one of the temporal configurations of change, growth, alternation, destruction, withdrawal, and cyclical reappearance displayed in calendric festivals. By creatively coordinating incompatible spatial existences, stylized aggression and conquest give shape to time; ritual battle changes the course of history, the cultural meaning of existence in time. Because struggle, aggression, and conquest are experiences of space cast into the symbolic terms of reflexive life, they can create new eras, new evaluations of existence in time. Ritual combat is calendric —"historical" in the wide sense — because it temporally enriches and recontextualizes aspectual life. Any single celebration of stylized aggression moves the spatial trappings of culture within the synchronic plane. However, that single dimension can never be the end of the story reenacting a mythical event. Periodic recurrence of ritual battle in the festival calendar carries spatial existence of human culture back and forth along the diachronic plane. In fact, it would be silly to reduce the multiplex experience of time to only these two dimensions. Ritual battle is the struggle to insert the full experience of time, even the way sacred beings experienced time in the primordium, into one passing moment.

The Goajiro battle-dance between the sexes conjoins in a recurrent calendric movement many levels of the conflict operative in ceremonial antagonism: supernatural forces, existential conditions of space (heavens and earth), life and death, movement and stasis, and so on. The Yona Dance is the most popular and most often performed collective gathering in contemporary Goajiro culture. It "acts out a veritable battle between man and woman." [286] In actuality, the couple dancing depicts much more than the battle of the human sexes. They represent the supernatural couple Juyá ("rain," a male being who represents the year demarcated by the rains that fall under the constellation Arcturus) and Pulówi ("earth," the female being of specific locations on earth and their heat). The dancers represent the cosmic forces of life and death and of sickness and health. Both Juyá and Pulówi embody different, alternating aspects of both positive and negative forces. They manifest, for example, alternating seasons, constellations, colors, geometric shapes, height and depth, unity and multiplicity. All of these are symbolized in the dancers' costumes, face paint, and gestures.[287] In short, the dance is intense and appropriate at almost any time because it embodies all the possible relations of different qualities (wild/cultivated, mobility/stasis, etc.), whose alternation, complementarity, or opposition contribute to the vitality of creation.

In cases such as that provided by the Goajiro, ritual combat is itself a visible calendar, not only because it is a choreography danced out in due season, but because it is an inherently temporal expression, a complex of times compressed and compelled to coexist in the stylized movements of coordinated body parts and spatial images. Symbolic battle conjoins separate and unequal spatial containers—and limbs—in a singular ordered experience, the festival year. The syndesmotic movements of the variable measures of existence (different lengths of time and space) are stylish struggles that mark the passage of human culture through different states of being and qualities of relations (dry and rainy seasons, passing generations, seedtime and harvest, rivalry and alliance, consanguinity and affinity).

NOISE: IMAGES OF CHAOS IN SOUND

Several points already touched upon in this chapter help decipher the meaning of festival din. In the first place, a connection was established between the appearance and disappearance of significant sound and the sonic cycles that contribute to the formation of a calendar, and an intrinsic relationship was established among the meanings of calends, callings of the roll of supernatural beings, proclamations of changes in quality of being, and clamor marking the passage of time.

In the second place, it was observed that, by reenacting the chaotic moment of their origins, festival symbols mark the calendar with regular moments of controlled return to an experience of the primordial conditions once enjoyed by sacred beings. In a negative dialectic, the imagery of destruction is employed to undo its own effects. Ritual drink blurs the separate senses into a singular experience of merged meanings, a unitive existence akin to that of primordial liquid. Symbolic incest and promiscuity erase distinctions between normative social categories. Ritual battle struggles to achieve a temporal state which conquers the contradictions of spatial existence. All these symbolic actions issue from the destructive moment of chaos. From that same event emerged another important calendric device: ritual noise, which overcomes the separateness of distinct sounds.

Thirdly, the discussion of ritual combat performed as a battle of the bands illustrated how closely related are the meanings of stylized aggression and musical din. The emphasis need not fall on the belligerence of unfriendly groups of instruments or choirs. Staged tumult—the deliberate swelling of noise—extends the concatenated meanings of clamor, proclamation, calling, and calendar. The confusion of sounds implies pandemonium, a melding of beings and their temporal modes. Ultimately, ritual noise, a clash of meanings signified in sound, represents the attempt to recreate primordial conditions of time. That state of the fullness of time, when all sounds could be significant simultaneously, predates the serial or narrative existence of this world, where formal distinction between sounds and beings becomes essential to intelligible meaning.

In general, there are two kinds of ritual noise celebrated in the festival calendar. On the one side is *racket*, ear-splitting volume of din. The Óyne, the mourning ceremony of the Cubeo, provides an example of this when, after the playing of *xudjíko* horns by the men and the keening of the women, the rite gives way to the hostile masked dances called *hwananíwa* (wild peccary), wherein noisy men, in mock frenzy, attack women and shrieking older women mime high sexual arousal.[288] On the other side lies *babel*, the simultaneous utterance of confused tongues and sounds.[289] The Mapuche offer an example of babel. Individuals sing their genealogical litanies simultaneously, but not in unison. In this way, the recitation of the names of a variety of beings and powers from the mythical past calls into existence the fullness of that powerful time. The two kinds of noise often combine and overlap. Both racket and babel are deliberate sound effects, intentional symbols.

Mataco healers use the babel of songs to summon spirits. In one report of Mataco ritual, dead medicine men and other spirits appeared in response to the curers' sacred songs. The curer offered some *sebil* (hatax snuff) to the spirits, who alighted on a stubble of grass, then collected these spirits by gathering them into his feather bundle.[290] The shifting sounds of sacred songs, whistling, and flapping feathers punctuated the ritual into episodes. Gradually, more healing specialists joined the ceremony. Eventually, twenty-four living and eight or nine dead curers presided. "Everybody stood up and sang at the same time . . . songs were intensified." [291] Potsejlai (the constellation Orion), the master of wild fruit, was called upon at the height of the cacophonous singing. "Songs and the sound of rattles filled the air. . . . a woman became excited and started to tremble. Some sorcerers looked somewhat upset." [292] The moment was truly awesome, for the noise symbolized the plethora of all the spiritual powers known to the participants.

The Toba also use noise as a healing device. In their Nahót Dónnaran ("spirit-singing") dances they aim to prevent sickness or to cure a patient who is ill. The Toba's most dramatic spirit-singing performances occur in October, at the onset of the wet season. Noise is part of a complex of symbolic acts that include drinking, dance, and prescribed aggression. The sick patient is placed in the center of a circle of dancers, who do not join hands. Stress falls on individuality; each person follows his own impulses and no common order is observed. Each dancing man brings his sacred bell-rattle, a habitation of his guardian spirits. Throughout the night, each dancer marks his own rhythm and dances to it in his own way. As the night proceeds, the chanting and dancing rise to a chaotic crescendo that climaxes in loud shouting. The emphasis on individuality becomes increasingly ironic since separate sounds are drowned in the common hullabaloo they themselves create. "[I]n fact, the main principle in the dance seems to be to make as much noise as possible." [293] In the center of the circle a curer quietly mutters his chants and shakes his rattle over the individuals to be protected or cured.

The Waiwai also conjoin the symbols of din and drinking with a danced battle of the sexes. During their Shodewika drinking festival they twist bark into spirals to fashion trumpets nearly a meter long. Early in the evening, the visitors sound their trumpets and enter the communal house of their hosts. The dance leader, who plays a rattle and bark trumpet, chooses the music, the rhythm, and the textual themes. Inside the men's dancing circle, a group of women dance and sing without aid of musical instruments. The women's dance leader chants a different melody and text. Later in the evening, everyone breaks for a meal, which is eaten in silence. Returning to the dance, the participants sing competitively for the rest of the night. The clashing male and female songs allude to lengthy series of mythic episodes. During all this time, the men must drink as much as they can.[294]

The Canelos Quichua also orchestrate sounds as symbolic noise in order to effect a symphonic arrangement of beings. Instrumental and vocal music combine with images of chaos and ancient deluge while men and women perform the roles of ancient star-people. Each powerful shaman plays a six-hole soul-flute called a *pingullu* ("tibia, soul-bone") during the principal drinking feast. The various flutes, drums, and voices, each sounding the song of a different ancient soul, give new meaning to the notion of counterpoint, for not only are sounds woven together from separate melodies, but, in the process, the multiple times, places, and beings of the universe become spiritually attuned, creating a symphony of beings.

Pottery trumpets, ceremonially made by Canelos Quichua women, are played by prestigious individuals of the community during the feast's ritualized hostilities. The woman who made a trumpet fills it with *chicha*, hands it to her husband, and watches him pass it to a guest. The song that the band plays, the song of the trumpeter swan, is said to "torture" everyone. The pottery trumpet possesses three female souls: one from its own maker, one from the household of the maker, and one from Nunghuí. The music of many voices and instruments played together descends into noise. "People begin to wonder if, during this ceremony, . . . the great flood of antiquity will return."[295] Once again, women seem to orchestrate this ritual return to chaos, which is modeled on the descent into the Times of Destruction that followed the act of brother-sister incest of the moon and the *jilucu* bird. At that time the tears of the stars brought a great flood to the world. Now men and women play the roles of those mythic star figures and ancient people. Pottery figurines represent these key protagonists of myth. Women use the figurines to force men to drink.

SOUNDNESS: SONIC WHOLENESS   Ritual clamor is neither random nor accidental. The intense and prolonged confusion of sounds is skillful and purposeful. Its goal is to create a state of soundness and a fullness of being no longer available in mundane circumstances. The Kalapalo use the term *ail* to designate a communal ritual performance in which different kinds of music and instruments and singing are performed simultaneously in one place. *Ail* is a feeling of wholeness, of soundness, "a sense of satisfaction resulting from the resolution of some group problem, or the accomplishment of a difficult task by a group."[296] The simultaneous performance of different musics is an act of collective feeling that, ironically, is translated by Basso as "feeling harmony." She writes, "I don't think it would be going too far to call this a South American version of the experience of *communitas*. It is music as an enacted symbol that communicates, and at the same time creates, that attitude."[297]

The wholeness achieved through the symbolism of sound is not only a symbol of an undifferentiated state of meaning; it is the ultimate reality on which the temporal world is founded. Noise recreates a mythic reality that is wholly concrete and sensual, even if the experience of it be mystical. The fullness of primordial being is organic, and it may even be imagined as a single body. Participation in that mystical body, reconstituted in the symbolism of noise, is a sensuous experience. During the fruit season, for example, the Baniwa celebrate festivals for initiation. While initiates stand blindfolded in a line at the door of the main house, the "grandfather" (elder presiding over the rite) says to them, "When we have finished drinking, then I will summon you." [298] Carrying a pole, the old man sings toward the sacred flutes (the ancestors) at the portal. "You come see your grandchildren," he sings, naming each flute-ancestor in turn. "Heee . . . see your grandchildren, you Kuai . . . Kuai-body . . ." [299] Robin Wright reports that the players "then march up from the port, in a well-ordered file, with a tremendous noise of them playing together. . . . [T]here are upwards of twenty different named pairs, each played responding to each other, each with a distinct melody." [300] Played all at once, with a tremendous noise, the separate instruments sonically recompose the body of Kuai, the "all-sound," whose every body part and orifice emitted a different musical sound at the moment of his disintegration in the cosmic fire. During this time of playing, the initiates are whipped and their wounds are filled with the sound-substance of Kuai and of their sib-founding ancestors (who came from Kuai's body) so that they will know Kuai and will be able to grow and multiply. Following the logic of calendric existence, the spatial containers of the boys' bodies are incised with the event of primordial destruction and their skin is interrupted by the sounds of passing time in order to enable them to change and to reproduce.

THE CALENDAR AS CALCULATED COMMOTION

Ritual racket and babel, like the symbolisms of incest and combat, return culture to the inaccessible fullness of being at the instant when it definitively passed away. At that time, the meanings of separate relations and distinct sounds could be entertained and understood simultaneously. Distance and time were no obstacle to significant experience. True to the logic of all calendric symbolism, promiscuity, noise, dance, and stylized struggle are all forms of commotion, images of movement and change deliberately coordinated with the cataclysm, the first and paradigmatic motion that set time spinning. As symbolic strategies, commotion and chaos aim to attain conditions made illicit or impossible by their own consequences, the temporal structures that normatively order this world.

The calendric propensities of the religious imagination assign responsibility for the continuation of mythic existence to the mimetic skills of human culture in the dramatic moments of festival performance. Overcoming the effects of time by imaginatively regathering or even annihilating its disintegrative consequences, each feast of the calendar returns ritual actors to the cusp of time, when the primordial world ended and cosmic history began.

The religious imagination allows human culture to become a continuation of mythic history, uninterrupted by the catastrophe. Human beings live at least two qualitative modes of existence, reflected in the kinds of time they inhabit. Human history in the cosmos of fragmented times and prepositional places is not the only tale to be told. Human life is also an elaboration of a mythical story that continues, undiminished by the consequences of history, through the sacred powers at work in the human imagination. The cyclic nature of cosmic time guarantees that human beings will live out a sacred story even as they mark off their passage through mundane existence. Even more to the point, the images with which the mythic story is lived out in sacred moments become the measure of meaning and the standard of value for human existence in time.

CONCLUSIONS

At various points, this volume touches upon many kinds of time: the cosmogonic time of the creation and transformation of the cosmos; the time exhibited by each mode of supernatural being, whether divine, heroic, or monstrous; the time manifest in the human constitution; the time of postmortem existence; and the temporal quality of relations obtaining after the destruction of this world. This chapter has explored only one narrow band on that temporal spectrum of the religious imagination: the periodic order of cosmos and culture.

The relatively simple device of the temporal cycle merits particular scrutiny. All replicating vital forms in the cosmos pass through life cycles marked by appearance, duration, disappearance, and reappearance. Significant cycles of time base themselves on the reappearance of stars, flowers, fruits, fragrances, colors, insects, birds, and sounds. Each one introduces a uniquely ordered experience and reveals the meaning of a specific quality of being. Cycles of birth and growth mark time, but so do their complementary negative dimensions: the cycles of rot, consumption, waste, and decay. These cycles of appearance, disappearance, and reappearance become building blocks of temporal existence.

Many feasts celebrate the generative moments of time by reenacting or alluding to the "great disappearance"—the destruction or withdrawal of such primordial forms as the star-people, the sun and moon, supernatural insects, or an aquatic monster. Fittingly, the symbolic consumptions so prominent in feasting highlight the ironic temporal truths of cosmic existence: destruction marks time's continued passage, and the consumption of life-forms sustains life. However, the symbolic capacity of culture, the ability to recognize the sacredness of being in whatever transient guise, rescues the meaning of consumable forms from depletion. Ancient and primordial meanings appear renewed in changing transforms. For this reason, temporal meaning in this world cuts an inescapably cyclic figure that centers on human culture. Life is renewable, replicable, multiplicative, and abundant because the imagination returns culture to its sacred source, inexhaustibly rich in meaning.

Through the calendar, human culture symbolically reflects these recycling forms of the cosmos. The complex human experience of times infolds relatively simple cycles into a temporally complex calendar. The occasional celebrations performed throughout the calendric megacycle are temporal inflections — inflections enunciated, for example, in the cycles of sound and seasonal music that effect the social and spiritual modulations they signify. Like the coordinated movement of a seasonal dancer's limbs, calendars manifest the ability to live a multiplex experience of differential times in an ordered and meaningful way, so that cyclic parts cohere as a significant, graceful, and creative whole. Through properly timed sounds and movements, the calendar reveals that temporal existence has an integrity of the first order. This primordial condition of the religious imagination, brought to the fore during feasts, underlies culture. Through the unity of temporal experience that is made possible in sacred performances, the elements of the dichotomy of disappearance and reappearance central to distinct cycles (e.g., of human generations, fruits, stars, or rains) mutually imply one another. Within the single calendar the many dialectics of creation-destruction and presence-withdrawal entailed in different temporal cycles of beings "express the modalities of life comprehended in rhythm and rotation." [301]

The calendar not only clocks time but also makes a metastatement about the nature and value of temporal existence. More aptly put, the calendar of feasts comprises a metaperformance that comments on the human act of existing in time. In symbolic action, calendric rituals render reflexive and visible the specifically *human* quality of knowledge underlying the performance of cultural acts: the awareness of one's multiplex temporal existence. This way of stating things emphasizes the essential connection between ritual and the meaning of time. Ritual action is time on display, temporal spectacle; symbolic action postures the reflexive nature of human existence in time. Ritual offers access to the first, fundamental movements of evaluable life. Time and rite are basically paradoxical and ironic: human beings get a grip on their own meaning by creatively repeating the acts that generated the conditions of culture — the acts of supernatural beings conditioned by utterly different modes of time. Ritual is a comparative exercise, an interpretation of contrastive modes. By symbolically restaging the mythic acts of creation, transformation, and destruction, cultures compare their symbolic time to the acts of sacred beings in primordial time.[302]

In contrast to the symbolic nature of cultural time, which points to meaning beyond itself, the time of sacred beings was nonsymbolic. Each primordial reality exhaustively manifested its own meaning; it *was* the meaning it stood for. Primordial time was unreflexive and total, exhibiting neither regular transformation nor periodic change. The only change possible for such totally manifest being was total change, destruction.

The rituals of the calendar meld cycles together at celebrations that commemorate their separation and withdrawal from one another. Cycles of rains, fruits, stars, animal breeding, and human age-sets combine at festival commemorations of the primordial events that separated colors into the first rainbow, or dispersed animals into distinct species differentiated by sounds and body marks, or fragmented a serpent into the lineages that descended from its dismembered parts. The calendar's joints are disjunctions: moments of destruction, separation, and withdrawal. That is why I have called the calendar a *syndesmotic whole* — one whose separate periods are joined by breaks. Like the human skeleton, the calendar is articulated; cultural experience is made whole through the movement and meaning of its ritualized disjunctions.[303] In particular, sacred rites are calendric because they re-gather and relive both essential modes — the apparent and the occult — assumed by primordial beings over the course of mythic history. In the ability to mime radically different modes of supernatural being, human symbolic life discovers the power to effect change.

Through the recurrent significations of cosmic cycles, ritual also re-collects human experiences from the scattered experiences of individuals or social divisions. The calendar salvages the unity of myriad human experiences by occasionally remeasuring them against mythic images of eternal duration. Thus human beings come to understand themselves in times that are "out of joint," through the differences that exist between them and the supernaturals.

Prominent ritual symbols are especially apt calendric vehicles. This chapter has examined several. Ritual drink, for example, is a complex temporal reality combining several significant cycles: the cycles of vegetation, digestion, seasons, ripening, and rotting; the life cycle of spirits; the recurrent mythical episode of the flood; the rhythms of the sexes; and so on. In a similar way, symbolisms of erotic promiscuity (or incest), ritual combat, and festival din proved to be temporal strategies designed to reunite the fractured times of the periodic world. They make available a temporal state of affairs to which access is normally forbidden by virtue of the conditions under which human life unfolds in the mundane world. This explains their frequency and important place in the celebrations of calendar feasts. The unified condition they signify returns to become accessible to human experience only through these and other images of anomaly, chaos, monstrosity, or eccentricity.

By highlighting recurrent cycles of mythic origin as the significant markers of passing time, the festival calendar diminishes the importance of exhaustively personal circumstances and their consequences, which resist assimilation to the meaning of mythic events. Contingencies unrelated to the primordium risk falling into insignificance. The calendar trivializes those memories that accentuate the irreversibility of events and that resist being cast in symbolic terms.[304] Human life need not be encumbered by the residue of consequences originating from its own acts. Culture can model itself upon the truly creative acts of sacred and powerful beings. Those happenstances that resist reflexivity and remain unmarked by mythical time, the calendar (i.e., the integral human experience of time) passes over without cultural remark.[305] Reflexivity requires bending experience to image. In the case of religious calendars, reflexivity is linked to mythic prototypes.[306]

The ubiquity of dance in calendrical festivals serves to bring forward the moral imperative of style and the moral dimensions of graceful, prescribed, or normative cultural action. Existence in time requires flair: action properly timed with meaning. The figurations and transfigurations of calendric dances choreograph the ethical disposition of human culture; the reponse to the mystery of existing in time deliberately intends to create a stylish existence. One must *act* in time, behaving properly in the midst of a mystery.

In the final analysis, culture seeks neither to reinstate the unbroken primordial condition nor to maintain an undivided plethora of being. Rather, the religious imagination takes stock of its temporal situation in the world, subject as it is to conditions of cosmic time. Working within the framework of cosmic periodicity, culture combines fragments of time into a calendar that aims at perfection, a shuffled fullness, the stylized arrangement of all possible qualities of being symbolized by times. Each mode of primordial reality makes its return to the center, but only for the calendrical moment that also celebrates its passing. The human appetite for being is satisfied piecemeal, periodically, and cumulatively. On the one hand, the calendric capacity of human culture exploits to the full the transitory nature of this world wherein the capacity of signals to express meaning and of the receptive senses to absorb it can be surfeited or depleted. On the other hand, the significant experience of time takes the steadiness of its beat, the recurrence of its rhythms, from the inexhaustible, eternal character of sacred beings.

PART THREE

ANTHROPOLOGY

THE MEANING OF THE HUMAN CONDITION

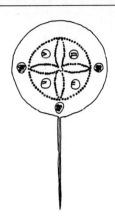

CHAPTER 5

THE HUMAN
CONSTITUTION

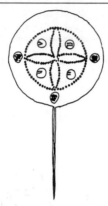

To construct a new anthropology and arrive at a humanism suited to our contemporary world, it is necessary to take into account a wider range of cultural notions about what constitutes the *anthropos*, the human being. The variety of concepts about human being in South America have only recently become available to a global public.[1] The following pages scrutinize South American understandings of the construction and deconstruction of the person. After a consideration of some accounts of human origin, emphasis falls upon the temporal, spatial, and sonic imagery that composes an individual human being. These cultural conceptions are crucial to a proper understanding of the human being. It is no longer credible to think that the unique structures of human being may be discovered if science can only penetrate beyond the contingent images of separate cultures. Culture is not a discardable cloak draped over human nature. Rather, culture *is* the specifically human condition, the way in which humankind understands itself. One cannot be human without being a cultural being.

THE MORTAL ORIGINS OF BEINGS FILLED WITH FIRE

The unique mode of human death accounts for the nature of human growth. Death provides an opening at the heart of human reality which admits human life to other realms. The deadly experiment with other planes of existence accounts for human nature and growth.[2] Few peoples make this point more forcefully than the Warao, who look upon life as a process of gradual dying.

"They have no word in their language for living, only for dying."[3] Indeed, different degrees of vitality are described by using variations of the term *waba,* the stages of death. A cadaver is described as *waba,* that is, "dead." A corpse is buried in a *wa,* a dugout canoe that represents the vagina of Daua-rani, the goddess of the forest, "so that life, according to Warao symbolism, can clearly be recognized as a process of dying by returning to the womb."[4]

It is remarkable how often South American accounts link the origins of human life with death. In many instances, life results from death or follows upon a series of destructions. The mystery and power of death receive nearly inexhaustible application in South America. A later chapter discusses death as a passage beyond life; however, it is fitting to speak briefly of this sense of death in these first considerations of the human being in order to interpret its ubiquity in the accounts of human origins. The confirmed lesson is that mortality initiates a life-condition of transition and metamorphosis.[5] For instance, in the Carajá myth of humankind's origin, human beings originally lived in the underworld, where there was neither sickness nor death. Since no one ever died there, it soon filled to capacity. People died in the very act of emerging from the underworld onto the earth as human beings. Keening accompanies the opening movements of human existence.[6] Death is in the nature of human being and the human epoch *from their beginning* in this world.

Human life releases death in new form — such is the view of the Guayakí. In their myth of human origins, a young boy strikes and shatters a celestial kettle, causing night and a flood of ashes to escape, thus darkening the eternal day of the primordial period. The future destiny of all individuals lies in this mythic kettle of origin, now a funerary urn found in the invisible forest on high. At death, a portion of the Guayakí personality (the soul, *ové*) jour-neys to the celestial kettle of Baiö. The origin myth of human beings is completed by the deceased Guayakí's return to the scene that marked the outset of human history and cosmic time. The quality of Guayakí death maintains life as a cycle which returns humankind to its beginning. The human soul takes up residence in the pottery that had once contained the sea of ashes and night.[7] The fusion of death and birth makes of human life an initiatory existence. Human life, from its inception, requires rebirth.

In the light of these traditions, it would be a mistake to view death primarily as a last chronological event, the terminal instant of life.[8] Instead, the reality of death has always been integral to human existence. This con-clusion is inescapable in, for example, the Selk'nam account in which human existence begins in a state of mourning because during the earliest episodes of mythic time (the *howenh*), the male primordial beings killed all the mature females, who until then had possessed total authority and power.[9]

For the Makiritare, death is housed in humans in the same way that fire is contained in the wood of the two trees from which wood-drills are made. The wood-drill trees are thoroughly filled with fire[10] even before they are con-sumed by flame. Fire assumes the form and meaning it now has in conjunc-tion with wood's consumable being.[11] Death assumes new form and significance within human mortals and in their putrifying world. Tree and human are thoroughly consumable by realities (fire, death) present in their inmost natures, realities that come to light only in consuming them.

THE ORIGIN OF SYMBOLIC EXISTENCE

Death renders being symbolic. The discovery of the meaning of human death is, at the same time, the disclosure of the symbolic nature of human life in a cosmos where reality lies behind or beyond any one of its forms.[12] In death, the Waiwai become linked symbolically to the existence of animals, for the human soul takes on an animal form after death. The bodily ephemerality and spirit life of human beings are full of contrariety, mysterious ambiguity, and overlap with other modes of being.[13]

The Warao view that human beings are, in essence, dead even while they live[14] reveals the essentially symbolic nature of human being as well as the nature of symbol itself, which constantly points beyond its ephemeral form toward its full meaning.[15] Death becomes a major constituent of the socio-cognitive frame that gives meaning to "life" in this epoch.[16]

Death licenses the wandering of awareness necessary for existence in this world. Unlike primordial light or stone, human life sustains itself only as a series of interruptions. It cannot continue in a constant form but must change. Constant becoming means continually quitting what one is. Desana myths express this truth concretely. The first Desana born on earth was swallowed immediately by the Mother of Snakes, who kept the child in her belly below the river waters.[17] She was slain to effect his resurrection. The episode serves as the model for the incessant and overlapping birth-death-rebirth cycles of symbolic life.

By originating the possibility of symbolic life, death gives birth to change and to the range of all growing and consumed realities. Each new form becomes a symbol, the best expression of the implied and unknown whole, which is manifest only in its partial and passing images. For example, cassava and constellations frequently result, in origin myths, from the murder or self-sacrifice of primordial beings, who are dismembered and partially de-voured. The birth of consumable beings is a form of death. For that reason, "the Trio word 'to be born,' *enuru*, is also used to describe fish which flounder the surface when they are poisoned."[18] Consumed objects lend their character to this epoch. Many cultures contend that human life is played out on a gridiron or in a world shaped like a griddle.[19] Noncomestible and eternal items, such as the sacred stones and forest ogres that linger in this world, are strange "superstitions," literally "leftovers" from another time.

From a mythic point of view, the partial forms of this world, including the human, stem directly from the cataclysmic moments that initiated the passage of time and fragmented the universe into generative but separate species of being.[20] Recognizing the deadly nature of this earthly state of affairs, the Campa name the level of the universe which humans inhabit Kamavéni, the Land of Death.[21] Death shatters earthly beings. The human species is, therefore, a composition of parts, often calendrically coordinated, or, at the very least, composed in accordance with the ordered passage of time across an individual life cycle. The essential message is that the human being can be born and grow *because* it is mortal and transitory. In this light, it is not so surprising that the Waiwai call a prepubescent child an *okopuchi*, a word that means "little corpse." [22] Ceremonial operations frequently instigate growth through symbolic means by gathering together the scattered experiences of death. In some cases, symbols of the constant interruption of death take the form of cuts and perforations on the body of the person who is to grow. The human being lives a life sustained on time borrowed from the other beings it kills and consumes — not only in the literal food-process but also in its first mythical appearance and in contemporary musical performances. In this world, life is replenished by death.[23] The symbolic world cannot exist on its own, objective and autonomous. It *subsists*, contingent upon connections maintained between all levels. Even the life of heavenly bodies is exhaustible. The Campa believe that both the moon and the sun were Campas in ancient times. Their existence is contingent and precarious. During a lunar eclipse, the moon, who is a cannibal, has a human being stuck in his throat. During a solar eclipse, the sun runs the risk of being extinguished.[24] Only their cyclic and synodical nature assures their continued existence.

The mortal condition, then, is the condition of the symbol. It exists only within a complex set of meaningful relations, which demand transitional moments that highlight some aspects of meaning while obscuring (killing) others. The symbol consumes past meanings in order to remain vital.[25]

HUMAN ORIGINS

Accounts of the origin of human beings are many and varied.[26] It would be pointless to seek a uniform narrative or plot of human creation in all of South American mythology. Humans are created from a wide variety of substances at the hands of a large number of supernatural beings. According to the Apinayé, human beings were created from bottle gourds *(Lagenaria spp)* by the sun and moon.[27] After the sun and moon had cleared a garden spot and planted gourds, they took the ripe gourds to a deep pool in a stream. Tossing pairs of the bottle gourds into the water transformed them into human beings.[28] After creating a few couples in this way, the sun caused a couple created by the moon to be blind and lame. In retaliation, the moon magically deformed children of the sun. Their tragicomic miscreation of human beings continued until no gourds remained.[29]

The above scenario of human origins is highly dramatic and vivid. Alternately, human beings may appear in this world under mysterious or vague circumstances. Such is the case among the Campa, who recount that the first human beings were made from earth, from termites' nests that were blown upon and transformed into human beings by "someone," an unidentified supernatural being (called a *tasórenci*).[30] That is why all Campas return to the earth when they die. Their myths recount how other beings were made of more durable substances. Equally speculative or mystical is the Siriono anthropogony; they tell of the moon creating human beings by transforming them from a formless state.[31] Formlessness is also the backdrop of the Kaingáng myth of human origins. According to the Kaingáng, human beings first emerged from a boundless ocean at the beginning of time.[32]

In other cases, human beings are descended, derived, or created from stars, or they are formed from the body-substances of heavenly beings — for example, from the light of the sun or the blood of the moon. The Yąnomamö place the creation of man and woman after the cosmic flood, when the spirit of the moon was shot with an arrow. An extremely fierce breed of males was created from the moon-blood as it fell to the earth. These fierce males were so aggressive that they exterminated one another. The legs of Kanaboroma, who was one of the survivors of this breed, became pregnant. From his left leg women were born; from his right leg were born men who were less aggressive than their predecessors. These people reproduced themselves quickly, and, mingling with the few remaining fierce men of blood, they produced the Yąnomamö.[33]

Some accounts report the origin of human beings from the offspring of the union of divine or monstrous beings and animals. According to the Waiwai, human beings originally came from the union of an anaconda-woman and the human progenitor Mawári, himself the offspring of a celestial animal-prototype and an anaconda-person. A brother-sister marriage between the offspring of Mawári produced the first Waiwai.[34]

Widespread and familiar are myths describing how human beings either are fruits of the earth, as in the Apinayé example just mentioned, or come forth from the earth. According to the Guayakí (Aché), the first human beings emerged from the earth at a time when the earth was terrifying and huge. They had to scratch their way through the earth with their nails. Once they had emerged on the land, they, in order to transform themselves into human beings, had first to lift themselves up from the earth and to learn how to stand in a vertical posture. This they did by climbing a wall by using their nails. The first act of "birth" is, then, an act of ascension, or of rising up, which distances people from earth and distinguishes human beings from animals through humans' assumption of vertical posture.[35]

Even in the same culture, distinct accounts may be given of the origins of men and women. Among the Toba, the first man emerged from the earth before any woman existed. After a cosmic fire destroyed the earth, this first man came forth from the ground and seized a firebrand from the conflagration. He carried it away to all the places where human beings now live, which is why people now possess fire. Women, on the other hand, descended from heaven in an enclosure. When a Toba man who was about to fall asleep heard a strange noise above his head, he "lifted up his eyes and saw the women coming down from the heaven like deities." [36] He took the firebrand, setting it upright and hiding behind it because it was black, the same color as his own skin. The women were laughing, shouting, and eating the man's food. Taking a large stick, the man severed the rope that held up the enclosure, and the women plunged deep into the earth. One by one they were extracted from the earth and brought into the light of day. The Toba men married these women, who bore them many children. At first some of the women gave birth only to boys and others to girls.[37] Other variations of the story of the creation of human beings continue to place most dramatic emphasis on the arrival of women from heaven.[38]

The Desana also report a separate origin for men and women. Male human beings descended to earth in a snake-canoe from Ahpikondiá, the cosmic uterus, which was fertilized by the Sun Father's "yellow intention." The first woman, the Daughter of Aracú Fish, emerged from the water when she was attracted by the yellow light of the men's fire, which burned as they feasted and danced. She made love to the first Desana man.[39]

In a parallel way, different origin accounts are sometimes provided for separate language groups, social classes,[40] and exogamic groups. For example, in addition to their account of the origin of couples from gourds, the Apinayé also tell of the creation of inmarrying women. During a hunting trip the sun captured two young dwarf parrots, which he and the moon taught to speak. Out of pity for the sun, the two parrots transformed themselves spontaneously into young girls, who prepared food for the sun and the moon while they were away hunting. "They were very beautiful and of light skin, and their hair extended to their knees." [41] The sun and moon married these young women,[42] thus originating all inmarrying women.

Different races may be ascribed different origins, for all distinguishing characteristics are set in place at the beginning. A striking example of this is provided by the Yupa, who recite three myths to account for the origin of three different kinds of people: dwarfs, whites, and Yupa. In the first of these myths, a Yupa man is trapped in a funeral cave; from there he travels into the underworld, where the dwarfs (pïpïntu) dwell. Eventually he marries a woman of that place. During his stay, in answer to the dwarfs' request, he carves an anus in one of the young dwarf's bodies. Although the perforated boy finally dies, many of the dwarfs continue to ask for the operation, for, without anuses, they can eat only by allowing food to roll down their backs. They die when they try to imitate the Yupa, who puts food into his mouth. Because the dwarfs are without true anuses or intestines, the food they put in their mouths crushes their bodies from the inside, and they die. The dwarf wife of the Yupa man bears him children, the ancestors of the pygmoid Yupa people seen today.[43] On the other hand, whites originate in this world when a girl is conceived in an extraordinary way: her mother masturbates with an artificial, stone phallus. The Yupa then kill the mother and shatter the paternal stone. The girl born from this union decides to destroy all Yupas. She is an evil genius who creates all manner of deadly technologies — machines, iron tools, and guns. She decides to leave for Europe, and, as she walks over the ocean, the sea impregnates her. Once in Europe, she gives birth to the first white man, "whose ancestors include his grandmother, a Yupa; his grandfather, a stone; his mother illegitimate, and his father, the sea." [44] Eventually, the white boy creates offspring by continually impregnating his mother, then his sisters, and finally his daughters. With the European conquest of South America, his descendants have returned to the territory of the Yupa in order to destroy them.[45]

The Yupa themselves were created by God from a tree that spurted blood when it was cut down. God carved two tiny statues of human children and placed them in a box made from another tree trunk. "Then, calling a bird, the woodpecker, he commanded it to sit down upon the figures, closed the box with a cover, and left it in the forest."[46] Eventually, the female companion of the creator heard voices in the box and, looking inside, found the two children and the woodpecker. God let them propagate, then levied a proscription against further incest; finally, he held a great drinking festival before withdrawing from the human scene.

From the variety of myths of human origin in South America, one may draw the following seven generalizations.

1. Although the earth is the proper center for human action in this epoch, there was a time when human life did not exist on earth. For example, in Boróro myths, the motive for the creation of humans is always the same: the loneliness of the culture hero Jokorámo-doguéddu, the monkey. Because the earth was empty of all life except the opossum Kurugo and the parrot Riko (and perhaps a third party, the snake Awagu), Monkey decided to use his magic wand, the *pemo*. He pounded the ground with his magic wand and spoke the names of the different peoples of the earth. One by one, with the pounding and the utterance of their names, they appeared to populate the earth. He used the same procedure to create the different species of trees.[47] One can conclude that human existence is not a given, not an assumed part of the cosmos in which human beings find themselves. The human experience of the world is strange and unfamiliar. From the time of its origins, human life involves the effort to feel at home in this world.

2. The origin of human beings is an event that takes place in time, in this world. It is an *inter-vention*, a coming-among-existing-things. The appearance of human life is an intrusion that changes the nature of existing relations and foreshadows human culture's gradual reordering of nature.

3. The places of human origin are invested with special power and are treated as sources of life.

4. Human beings differ from eternal or primordial beings in that humans are vulnerable to ageing, decay, darkness, and death.

5. The nature of human origins establishes indissoluble bonds, though perhaps indirect and symbolic ones, between human beings and other modes of being (plants, animals, or celestial beings). This is the case among the Canelos Quichua, for whom women descend from larvae that were once shooting-star–people who came down to earth.[48] Canelos Quichua males refer to one another as *alaj* ("my mythic brother"). This form of address alludes to the ancient origins of men because, in the beginnings, a man emerged from a rock in the form of a tree mushroom, *ala*. As long as Amasanga, the master of souls of the forest, permits mushrooms to grow from

trees and rocks, men will continue to exist.[49] In a quite different way, Waiwai origin myths account for the indissoluble bonds between humans and animals and between humans and plants. Mawári, the great Waiwai progenitor, who embodies the carnal life of animals, originally had no sex organs. His sexual organs sprouted in the form of forest plants.[50] Only then could he perform the act of sex that procreated humankind. Mawári's composite nature links human beings with the mortal bodies of animals and the cyclical regenerativity of plants.

6. Human nature is inherently linked with technology. Fire making and the preparation of cultivated food, for example, are "sciences"; that is, they are kinds of knowledge based on the imitation of more powerful forces (e.g., supernatural animals or culture heroes). The ability to know through imitation, or symbolic representation, constitutes the essence of technology and serves, in the forms of art, music, tool use, and ritual action, as the foundation of human creativity and culture. It even underlies the less utilitarian techniques of play. For example, the Kaingáng are divided into five groups, which are distinguished by their body-paint markings. These marks go back to the time of human origins. After a Kaingáng child is "made" in the Waichëdn festival, the parents and ceremonial parents play the game of *kavígn*. They divide themselves into teams distinguished by body-paint design. Fashioning bags from the soft inner bark of a certain tree, they stuff the bags with tree hair. Long bags represent men, and short ones their wives. During the game, people make the sounds of the animals consonant with their body-paint marks. For example, the "dot people" imitate small hawks. That is why, when people join in the fun and throw the bags high into the air while dancing, they shout "catch my animal."[51] The meaning of the game was made clear by one of the Kaingáng when he explained to Jules Henry that the first ancestors, who lived at the beginning, called these animals their own. The primordial game, the body marks, and the primal sounds of the first animals signal that the festival makes the participants the contemporaries of the first beings who emerged from the cosmic ocean.

7. The origins emphasize that the mode of being human is distinguished by sex from the very beginning; i.e., the very consciousness of sex is sacred.

The diversity of accounts should not lead to the conclusion that the imagery of human origins is of little consequence. Neither can a list of abstract shared postulates exhaust the meaning of the origin stories. On the contrary, in each case the substances and processes that first shaped human beings have spiritual value and lasting importance. They become the elements of human character, the stuff of which it is made. They remain valuable indexes of human nature throughout its subsequent history. They impel and constrain human destiny. It makes a difference to the Yạnomamö that they descend from the moon's blood, to Canelos Quichua men that they emerged from a rock in the form of a tree mushroom, and to the Apinayé that they are transformations of gourd containers thrown on the waters by the sun and moon. These images become the focus for reflection and lead to self-understanding. They serve as foundations for taking one's place in the world.

The meaningful web of relations between human and cosmic life is spun from this starting point.

The Makiritare illustrate many of these points in a beautiful account of the origin of Wahnatu, the first man. This event took place toward the close of the first Falling Tree festival, which is associated with the universal flood that streamed from the heavenly trunk of cosmic tree, cut down to clear the first garden plot. The first man was created after the birds, the old people, and the sky people, who had been drinking, had danced themselves into ecstasy and had begun to fly away in a migration to Lake Akuena in the center of heaven.[52] The old people and sky people left bird forms and colors behind them as vestiges, or signs, of their existence. Huiio, the great snake and mistress of the water domain, also ascended from the earth's new rivers and journeyed to the eternally still waters of Lake Akuena. Merging with the colored bird feathers in midair, she left the rainbow as a sign of her passing. The time of the creation of human beings, then, came after the cosmic destruction of the first earthly beings and after "the real Sky couldn't be seen any more."[53] Human creation occurred after a "new sun," "new moon," and stars — the gory fragments of murderous beings — were set in place. In short, Wahnatu appeared only after a new stratum of the universe was organized according to the temporal and spatial conditions that were to obtain during the human epoch.[54]

One of the chief reasons for the cosmic flood had been the creation of gardens (i.e., of cultivated food) and the processes of food preparation. Now that the sky people responsible for these items of culture had ascended into heaven, the creator, Wanadi, fashioned people, who would continue growing crops and processing food. The *raison d'être* of human life is to care for food through knowledge of tradition. Humankind is entrusted with food; human nature takes shape around food. Animals, whose bodies are the vestiges of earlier beings who ascended into heaven, would not know how to take care of food.[55] They had had no experience of cultivation since all food had been provided for them from heaven during the primordial times. Wanadi decided, "I'll have to make another person to stay here on Earth and take care of it."[56] He took clay from Mount Dekuhana, wedged it, shaped it, and fired it; he lit his cigar and sang and blew on the clay. In this way he made Wahnatu, the first human and "grandfather" of all the Makiritare.[57]

The first acts of the first man were to clear a garden to grow food, to make musical instruments (which contained the voices of the masters of all animals), and to undergo an initiation at the hands of the masters of all species, which initiation introduced Wahnatu to mythic history. The first musical instrument he fashioned was the *siwo* horn, which contained the voice of Semenia, the master of bird-people and teacher of agricultural skills. The voice itself *is* Semenia, who calls down from the sky the masters of all animals and birds. They present themselves in their true and invisible forms. They are the sacred sounds of the festival. These masters of animals and birds are the very beings who cut down the first tree when the first garden was cleared. They taught Wahnatu how to make a dance stick *(wasaha)*, and they initiated him as the first songmaster and dancemaster. Just as these beings are the masters of their own species, which they generate by uttering the prototypical sounds of those species, so does Wahnatu become the progenitor of human beings through his mastery of song, music, and dance—the distinctive sound-forms of human culture in the moments when it recreates itself.[58] At the same time, each species-master provided Wahnatu with one of the visible powers of human culture: feathers, palm fibers, seeds, vegetal dyes. Through the initiation he underwent at the moment of his origin, Wahnatu obtained the knowledge to use these powers to construct festival body-ornaments, costumes, and body-paint designs.[59]

Mythic beginnings are the root-stock of human origins. The fundamental character of human being presents a sacred aura. Through the capacity to grasp its original character, through self-consciousness, human life fastens upon its own constitutive ability to reproduce sacred meaning in the works and images of culture.

CONSTRUCTION OF THE HUMAN BEING

The rites that attend the human person's passage through one state after another in the course of gestation, birth, and growth have received close attention from ethnologists since Arnold Van Gennep's study *Les rites de passage*, published in 1909. Van Gennep's fundamental insight may be stated in this way: human beings tend to mark changes in states of being with symbol and image, especially with ritual.[60] Van Gennep's work was a statement about the nature of human perception—about how mind and imagination cope with ontology—as well as a judgment about the inescapably symbolic dimension of social existence. However, subsequent use of his insights tended to restrict their application to transitions in social status, ignoring transitions between other states of being recognized in culture.[61]

The social construction of the person need not always require change in status. Neither must rites of passage be elaborate and dramatic. Breathing over new food before giving it to a child for the first time or passing a child over dead game so that the infant inhales the animal's soul or the power of its smell are scenes played on the back stage of the human drama; nonetheless, they can be important moments in symbolically composing the individual.

FABRICATION AND METAMORPHOSIS: COMPOSITION OF THE PERSON

Two kinds of processes underlie the construction of the person: fabrication and metamorphosis.[62] These two symbolic processes are brought into relief by following the career of the specific, personal elements (e.g., name, dream, blood, skin) that are ritually acquired, embellished, or alienated throughout an individual's life. Eduardo B. Viveiros de Castro, writing about the Yawalapíti, portrays the two processes, fabrication and metamorphosis, as means of producing the human person by arranging the images that constitute an individual.[63] According to the Yawalapíti, making a human body grow requires the exercise of conscious intention. Coitus is only one among many such deliberate acts. In actual practice, the Yawalapíti recognize a large complex of intermediary processes that manipulate the substances that communicate between the body and the outside world: breath, blood, semen, urine, feces, tears, saliva, vomitus, other body fluids, foods, emetics, and tobacco. By controlling the entrance or exit of these substances, one becomes conscious of the body as an enclosure, a being of passages, which through passage masters forces for its own transformation. One becomes self-conscious of the composition of powers and faculties contained in one's body. Bodily changes that are effected by the systematic treatment of such substances can become effective instruments of change in one's social identity as well.[64] Since human nature is constructed by social processes, Viveiros de Castro concludes, "the body is *imagined*, in various senses of the word, by society"[65] and created by social processes over time. The process of fabrication involves the conscious imposition of human intention on matter. Producing human beings involves the subordination of material substances to cultural design and conscious form.

The process of metamorphosis, on the other hand, subjects even the essence of humanity to unforeseen and excessive modification that obscures the boundaries between the human and the spirit realm.[66] The concept is not limited to the Yawalapíti. For example, "the Shavante term for incest *(tsiwamnãr)* is interestingly enough the same word as is used in Shavante legends to refer to metamorphosis, usually when people change into animals or vice versa. Their notion of incest is thus clearly that of passage from one state to another or confusion of statuses."[67] This passage associates metamorphosis with a primordial mode of being and brings out an important dimension of the incest events that occurred during the time of beginnings recorded in myths. This is the period when multiplicity is emerging from unity. From the point of view of contemporary human beings, incest myths return one to that time before clear and separate statuses existed. The acts are not human; they are acts of the gods or supernaturals. The language in which they are related must therefore be one of overlap and contrariety. Consequently, mythic episodes in which primordial beings commit acts of incest mark transitions of the world from one state of being to another. In order to reenter that world, the contemporary human being must pass through a coincidence of opposites, a spiritual state attainable only in that time *beyond* (or before) the metamorphosis into separate forms.

The process of metamorphosis also manifests itself on the level of body form and gesture. In creating the specifically human body, the process of fabrication negates those body potentials that were nonhuman, but the process of metamorphosis reappropriates these nonhuman possibilities without undoing human nature itself. Metamorphosis transcends the fabricated human condition.[68]

Many of the symbols that compose the person cannot be handled in any depth here, although their importance merits attention.[69] Such is the case, for example, with smell. In spite of Lévi-Strauss's suggestions in *The Raw and the Cooked*, there is little comparative data on the subtle olfactory codes that mark the transitions of persons from one state to another. In some cases, there exist calendars of fragrances (of blooming flowers) that are used to mark the proper times for rites of passage. Many rites require particular fragrances provided by incense, flowers, fermenting sour mash, beers, and so on. Unfortunately, ethnologists have not often treated smells as the efficacious symbols they sometimes are. For example, for the Suyá of central Brazil, odor is an important expression of power, force, or danger, as well as of a range of other states. "The categorization of the world in terms of odor provides an important system for the interpretation of Suyá actions and attitudes."[70] Characteristics of smell are used to "classify certain types of persons and transitional periods."[71] The classification of animals and humans by smell differs in one respect: "while animals are permanently classified in a given category (except for the tapir and the porcupine, which change after they are cooked), human beings have different odors according to sex, stage in life cycle, and transition through certain ambiguous states."[72]

TEMPORAL IMAGES CONSTITUTING THE HUMAN BEING[73]

THE SOUL, MYTHIC AND LINEAGE HISTORY

The human soul manifests the full experience of time. The soul is "the whole man in his sacredness . . . constituted by concrete reality, experienced as a unity."[74] The meaning of the soul is unique in each culture.[75] The biorhythms of the breathing, pulsing body may be associated with the soul, which is frequently linked to the body and its physical capacities. "The Carib make no distinction between soul and heart. In Tucano there is but one word for soul, heart, and pulsation. In Witoto the word *komeke* has the meaning of heart, chest, memory, and thought."[76] The association of the soul with the body is not limited to the human being's own body. The Island Carib believed that the soul found in the heart migrated to heaven (to the sky) after death. However, the other souls in the human body (in the head and in the places where the pulse could be felt) transformed themselves into different animals' bodies.[77]

Explanations that appeal to purely physiological processes, however, cannot exhaustively account for the functions of the soul—not even the soul residing in biological tempos. For instance, all Tobas are possessed of an invisible principle of life, which resides in their chests. This is the *kadepakál* ("our shadow").[78] During sleep this soul wanders through the world of dreams; at death it leaves the body forever and becomes a supernatural being, which takes the form of a rhea for men and the form of an armadillo for women. The immateriality of the physiological soul is further illustrated by the Chiquitano, in whose view the person contains three souls, which are connected with different aspects of bodily life: a shadow soul, a blood soul, and a breath soul.[79] During dreams the blood soul *(otór)* can make short journeys while staying close to the body. This accounts for the process of dreaming. However, the shadow soul *(ausípiš)*, which ordinarily hovers in the vicinity of the person, can undertake long journeys, leaving the blood soul far behind. In the morning, the shadow soul returns to offer the other two souls an account of its travels. These long journeys account for deep dreams and trances, which are travels through other realms in space and time. During these long journeys, the shadow soul may visit the future or may travel to a heaven reserved for the preexistent souls of future children. These journeys are dangerous because supernatural beings, called *oboíš*, attempt to capture the soul with invisible cotton threads and to force it to drink a beverage whose ingestion would trap the soul in the other world.[80]

The soul may visit not only the future but also the ancient past. For instance, the Kari'ña soul, which is shaped like an animal, goes forth from the body during sleep at night. It comes to know the invisible world of spirits and speaks with the *tamurü*, who is the dreamer's invisible "grandfather" and the protector of that animal species to which the dreamer's soul belongs. It may also see the spirits of dead relatives or aspects of the dead animal souls that inhabit the earth.[81]

The soul, therefore, reveals human existence as continuous and whole. Such constancy is essential since the collision with many qualities of time fragments human experience. Each kind of time ensnares the individual in different webs of relations with human, animal, and preternatural forces.[82] For example, conception and birth link the Waiwai soul, *ekatï*, to an ancient and eternal category of beings, the *kakenau-kworokjam*, who live in the highest and immutable level of the sky. These celestial beings also possess *ekatï*, a fluidlike soul that extends throughout the body but seats itself in the heart.

The different kinds of time encountered by the soul transcend the movements and changes of the body. While in the body, for example, the soul of a Campa resides in his or her heart. However, even the soul of a Campa infant is only loosely attached to its body. Later in life, the detachability of the soul from the body is exploited in order to extend the spiritual life. Each Campa individual possesses a soul, which can exit the body during dreams, illness, or shamanic soul-voyages. The soul leaves the body permanently in death[83] and survives the disintegration of the body.

Because individuals possess souls, their existence may be seen as a history. The soul is the basis of history not only because it provides a continuous series of experiences that expose one to specific qualities of time but also because it offers one the images needed to evaluate one's existence in these times. For example, their experiences may be bound together as lineage history, the mythic history of ancestors, the epic of heroes, and/or the natural history of elements.[84]

The events of creation may constitute a history, an existence in time embraced by the human soul. Such is the case among the Makiritare, each of whom receives an *akato*, a companion spirit that descends from heaven at the moment of his or her birth.[85] The *akato* is immortal and everlasting. It returns to heaven after the person dies. In fact, the loss of the *akato* is frequently seen as the cause of death. Since the *akato* exits the body at night and travels during dreaming, it is vulnerable to capture by the evil being Odosha, who is master of the earth's darkness, disease, and death.[86] The *akato* is normally beyond the strict control of the individual. However, the shamans, like the creator Wanadi himself, are able to control their spirit-doubles and to send them, under strict orders, as messengers.[87] These messenger-spirits are called *damodede*.

The experience characterizing the soul includes but also transcends the span of the body's years. One of the fullest reports of a South American culture's ideas of the soul has been filed by Whitten in his research on the Canelos Quichua. Canelos Quichua souls are linked in a network that extends back to the ancient times of the beginnings, when souls were first encapsulated in stones by primordial beings. As mentioned above, men and women obtain and care for their souls in different ways. An *apamama* once gave birth to the male-inherited soul. (An *apamama* is a man's father's father's wife.[88]) Therefore, men's souls derive from the ancient grandmother souls of mythical times. The term "father," *yaya*, derives from the word *aya*, "soul." [89]

A woman obtains her inherited female soul from her mother's mother's husband; ultimately, female-inherited souls may be traced back to a mythic *apayaya* ("grandfather"). A woman transmits not only her own female soul but her husband's father's soul as well; she passes this latter soul on to her children (her father's soul passes on to her brothers).[90] As the vehicle and embodiment/locus of soul transmission, a woman's spiritual life is linked to Nunghuí, who is the mistress of garden soil and pottery clay and the wife of Amasanga. Nunghuí empowers and draws together the domains of soul-transmission, food, and pottery for women. Indeed, the continuity of bodily life and soul life depends upon women's work of gestation, parturition, food cultivation, cooking, *chicha* preparation and pottery making.[91]

In other cultures the soul is associated with ceremonial groups based on names, residence, or types of ritual performance, and so its experience may extend across generations. Understanding the nature of the human soul is the key to evaluating human existence, which is ensconced in several qualities of time.[92]

PROPERTIES OF THE SOUL: SPECIALIZATION AND MULTIPLICATION OF SPIRITUAL ELEMENTS

Human encounters with all manner of sacred beings complicate life, bringing modalities of sacred time into human existence. The potentially bewildering richness of spiritual life requires that cultures provide concepts to discern its movements. The soul, the temporal organ *par excellence* of human existence, becomes the focus of a spirituality frequently analyzed by South American peoples as a set of human properties located in specialized elements of the soul. As some of the above examples have shown, some traditions speak in terms of multiple souls comprising the human person. These widespread beliefs warrant closer attention.

The Waiwai propose a construction scheme, according to which the living human being possesses two souls, the *ekati* and the eye-soul. Each of these takes on a different kind of existence after death. During life, the *ekati*'s privileged locus is the heart. When the heart stops, the *ekati* has left the body. However, the *ekati* is a kind of fluid soul-substance that spreads throughout the entire body, extending into even the hair and nails. It is invisible but divisible; portions of it may attach to remnants of chewed food, footprints, and so on. Though insubstantial, the *ekati* possesses some weight, as demonstrated by the fact that sick individuals, who have momentarily lost their *ekati*, are lighter. The *ekati* is somehow associated with breath, for when a child sneezes it runs the risk of losing its *ekati*. To prevent this, parents blow into the child's mouth.[93] The *ekati* takes the form of an individual's body. Its divisible fluid is contagious, spreading from one's body to those things with which one comes in contact. During childhood, the *ekati* is only precariously attached to the body. Consequently, a child is vulnerable to soul-loss until he or she has reached three years of age. Certain religious specialists, called *yaskomo*, may also send their *ekati* out of their bodies at will. The *ekati* of ordinary people may leave their bodies during dreams at night.[94]

At death, the human *ekati* is transformed into an *ekatinho*, a "former soul." It then leaves the body to live an existence on earth in the form of invisible animals created from the souls of the dead. There does not seem to be any question of personal survival of the individual soul, for the *ekatinho* has no memory of its previous existence as an *ekati*. The transmigration of the soul is evident only to surviving relatives. The *ekatinho* inhabits the gravesite of its former body. However, especially at night, it is free to roam through the forest. It is dreaded because it is vengeful and attempts to kill human beings.[95]

The Waiwai eye-soul is described as "the small person one always sees in the other's eye."[96] At death, the eye-soul ascends to an upper level of the universe, called Kapu. There, the eye-soul is subjected to an ordeal, in which stinging insects invade and dismember it, so that it may take on a pure, rarified, and disembodied existence in Kapu, the happy world of light.[97]

DEATH AND THE VISIBILITY OF THE SOUL

As was intimated above in the discussion of Makiritare fire-drill trees, death renders the elements of the soul more "visible." For this reason, those investigators who have probed cultural ideas about death have frequently come upon the clearest articulation of the structures of the soul.

Such was the case in Clastres's inquiries among the Guayakí (Aché). The seat of the soul of a Guayakí woman is located in her basket, which is destroyed at her death. The seat of a man's soul is in his arrows. His arrows and bows are broken and burned at his death.[98] Clastres was able to discern the elements that compose the human soul by examining the separate paths they take when the person disintegrates at death. In general we may speak of *ianvé*, the evil spirit of the dead, and *ové*, an animal double of the dead person. The animal-double of the Aché is the coati. At death, the *ové* makes its way to the realm of the sun. The path it takes is imaged by the smoke from the burning bows or baskets of dead human beings. Supernatural coatis carry the *ové* of a dead human being to the topmost branches of the mythical trees that reach to the heights of heaven. There the *ové* may continue its journey by scaling a liana that unites the lower world with the upper world. At death, then, the *ové* makes haste to return to the "invisible forest," the upperworld. In fact, the *ové* returns to a mythic place revealed in the accounts of primordial events: a mythic kettle from which death and darkness came at the beginning of time. At times, the *ové* of a mature adult is accompanied on the celestial journey by other beings, who are dispatched for the purpose. Ordinarily the coati, emblem of the *ové*, is forbidden as food. However, during initiation, candidates are encouraged to eat the skin and the fat of this animal.[99]

According to Clastres, the *ové* may transmigrate in certain cases. For example, someone may declare, "I am the *ové* of Terygi."[100] The transmigration is effected during cannibalistic rites that take place during funerals. When Terygi died, a woman named Dokogi was pregnant. She was given the penis of the dead man to eat in order that she would give birth to a boy. Even though she eventually gave birth to a girl, that child, named Kimiragi, considers herself the *ové* of Terygi.[101] The postmortem *ové*s of certain Aché become *barendy*s — "luminous beings," that is, stars.[102] Carried by the coati, they mount into the sky along lianas or rays of sunshine.[103]

The second major element of the Guayakí soul is the *ianvé*, the evil spirit of the dead. Unlike the *ové*, which moves toward the realm of the sun after death, the *ianvé* refuses to leave the land of the living. It roams the darkness, hovering close to the earth and frequenting the places where people camp. The *ianvé* attempts to destroy living Aché[104] by penetrating their bodies, rendering them sick, sometimes fatally. It may be driven out of a person's body by burning wax and resin to produce a perfumed smoke, which unsettles the *ianvé*, or by covering the body with ashes and mud.

The *ianvé* desires revenge.[105] There is some sense in which the *ianvé* is a historical entity, coming into being with time. Children do not yet possess it and consequently may be buried close to dwelling places. Adults, however, are possessed of this dangerous soul-element and must therefore be disposed of in quite a different way. In some fashion that is not made systematically clear, the Aché dispose of the dead by consuming them in order to prevent the independent existence of the *ianvé* as a haunting ghost.[106] The idea seems to be that the *ianvé* becomes an evil being once it is liberated from a living body. To prevent the *ianvé*'s complete liberation from a body-envelope, the flesh of a deceased Aché is consumed in order to "re-embody" this soul-element and prevent its transformation into a negative and destructive mode.[107]

The Guayakí contend that the souls of healthy, living people possess *pakryra*, a calm state of physical and psychic health and life.[108] When the souls of the dead attack the living, they are seeking *pakryra*. For this reason, the dead must be devoured. If they do not devour the dead, the living will be plunged into *pakryra-iä*, intense anxiety, or into *pakombo*, a state of palpitating and cowardly fear that leaves one as good as dead.

SYSTEMATIC THEORIES

Some cultures arrange soul concepts, faculties, tasks, and loci very precisely. Such instances permit one to speak of a systematic theory of the soul, which, in turn, coordinates a series of complex spiritual functions and relationships. This is the case with the Yąnomamö. the Yąnomamö recognize that the living human being is composed of at least three important spiritual elements. Each of these constituents transforms itself at the moment of death. The first element, *buhii* ("will" or "self"), appears to consist of a person's conscious ability to choose. When an individual dies, this individuality is transformed into a *no borebö*, which journeys to the realm of the souls of the dead, Hedu. Along the way, it is judged by Wadawadariwä, the son of Thunder. If the *no borebö* is condemned as having made selfish choices during life, it is sent to Shobari Waka, a place of everlasting fire. Few Yąnomamö fear or expect this fate.[109] Instead, they expect to be sent to the happy world of generous and worthy souls in Hedu. Since children do not possess the *no borebö*, one must presume that this character, formed by conscious choices, is the spiritual fruit of experiences of mature people.

Yąnomamö are born with a second soul-element, the *no uhudi*, which is loosed from the body at the moment of cremation to roam through the forest. Dead children invariably assume this form of postmortem existence. When *uhudi* become dreadful and aggressive, attacking victims with clubs at night, they are called by the name *bore*.[110] When listening to tape recordings of their own voices and music, the Yąnomamö describe them as *no uhudibo*, this wandering soul-element.[111]

The third soul-element is the *noreshi*, a twofold phenomenon, one of whose aspects lives within an individual and the second aspect of which, an alter ego, lives in the jungle. The two aspects suffer the same destiny and perform the same actions during life. They are inherited from one's parent of the same sex and transmitted to one's child of the same sex. The *noreshi* may leave the body, and, consequently, it is vulnerable to capture and to loss. The Yąnomamö see photographic images of themselves as aspects of their *noreshi*.[112] Because a Yąnomamö hunter may kill another man's *noreshi* (and thus the man himself) when he kills a game animal, hunting is equivalent to warfare in the Yąnomamö view.[113]

Since 1958, Otto Zerries has provided information about the various souls and soul components that comprise the human being according to the inhabitants of the Yąnomamö village of Mahekodotedi. His reports are a salutary reminder of the variability of soul concepts even in the same "culture." He discovers five different kinds of soul in the Yąnomamö conceptualization of the human being. To one degree or another these components are shared with animals and plants, whose separate species and spirits originated when the primordium was destroyed. The soul, then, is a complex relational system across time. The *mi-amo*, an animal life element, resides in the guts of every living person.[114] The *nobolebe*, the soul of the dead individual, lives out a person's postmortem fate in the afterlife.[115] The shadow-soul (*nonish* or *noneshí*), in animal form (often the harpy eagle), serves as an alter ego.[116] An image-soul *(noúdibe)* is possessed by every being, including plants.[117] The *hẽa*, the symbolic marker of the individual human being, manifests itself as the voice of an animal, especially a bird, or, in the case of approaching enemies, as thunder.[118] The *hẽa* tends to announce itself as sound in the presence of certain animals, plants, and men.[119]

TWO SYSTEMATIC TENDENCIES: PHYSIOLOGICAL AND EPISTEMOLOGICAL

In general, multiple spiritual elements within the individual are systematized along two lines. The first is physiological. This principle has appeared at work in several of the examples above, which picture the soul as a spiritual element or set of elements seated in specific body parts. The elements interact in a way that is homologous to the functions of body organs. The physiological principle is extended to include animals, the bodily creatures *par excellence*, which serve as doubles of or loci of human soul-elements. The physiological basis for organizing the soul emphasizes the relational construction of the human being. For example, the animal-soul's appetite for food relates the human to animals and plants. Similarly, the spiritual element that quickens the appetite for sex relates female to male, affine to affine, and parent to child. The body's senses, physiological concomitants of the soul's capacities for meaning, organize relations with outside realities that are warm, wet, soft, brilliant, loud, and so on. Each appetite manifests its own time (e.g., the periodic appetite for food or sex) and generates other kinds of time in the relations it establishes (e.g., the digestive cycle or the passing of generations).

The second organizing principle of systematic theories of the soul is epistemological. Particular spiritual elements are associated with such specific human faculties as speech, thought, reflection, imagination (dream, vision), memory, insight, will, understanding, and judgment. This view brings into relief a concept of the human being as a self-contained and relatively autonomous being set apart from the objects of its perceptions.[120]

Guaraní groups present several varieties of the epistemologically ordered theory of the soul. His own field research and his scrutiny of other ethnographic documents allowed Miguel Alberto Bartolomé to point out that each of the groups and subgroups of the Guaraní in eastern Paraguay, southern Brazil, and northeastern Argentina possesses its own particular characterization of the human soul. "However," Bartolomé writes, "they all coincide at two fundamental points: the identification of the soul with the spoken word and the existence of an internal duality—even in the tripartite conceptualizations—which governs the cultural definition of behavior as positive or negative."[121]

The Mbyá of the Ivy Pyté (Paraguay) recognize that a portion of the human soul and human personality is a historical entity, a by-product of past existence and a residue of past acts. This is the element called *ang*, "the shadow, the trail of the human being, his echo." [122] The word (*ñeé*, "speech" —i.e., human language) is an indestructible manifestation of the human soul. For the Chiripá and other Guaraní groups (Mbyá, Jeguakává, the Apapocuvá), *ñe'é* ("language") and *ang* ("soul of divine origin") convey precisely the same meaning. In addition, for the majority of Mbyá subgroups, *ñ'eng*, the word for the human voice, is also used to identify the divine element in the human soul, the "vital word" that was the first thing created by Mybá, the creator.

The divine element of the soul, the vital word, is only one component of the human personality. To it is added the *tekò achy kué* ("product of the imperfections"), which grows during an individual's lifetime and accounts for human appetites. This element of the human personality is known as *tupichúa*, the "animal-soul" that encourages transgressions of the social order. [123]

Some Guaraní groups of southern Brazil recognize three soul-components, which exist in the form of shadows (*nane'a*, "our shadow"). In fact, the theory espoused by the Ñandeva group is a striking portrayal of how spatial imagery can be used to order even the human personality:

> Shadows cast in front or behind are called *ayvú-kué-poravé*, "the good word which we speak," and form the soul which returns to its divine origin when a person dies. The shadow cast to the left is the *atsy-yguá*, considered as the biological basis of man and of the "animal" aspects of his behavior. The shadow cast to the right is the *ayvú-kué* [the word which sprouts] and is limited in function to being a sort of companion to the *ayvú-kué-poravé* which it implicitly obeys. [124]

The Apapocuvá and the Avá-Chiripá recognize a dual-component soul consisting of the *ñe'eng*, a divine soul of speech, and the *asynguá*, an animal soul, which perches like a monkey on one's shoulders but which cannot be seen. As in so many other instances, the animal-soul acts as a sort of alter ego and is associated with restrictions (or the breach of restrictions) on food, sexual behavior, and so on. In fact, the Apapocuvá go so far as to distinguish between one soul-element generating an appetite for vegetables and another element stimulating the appetite for animal flesh. Of the two parts, the animal-appetite element causes the differences among individuals. Differences between people are fundamentally matters of taste. Over time, appetites of the soul take on increasing physical, emotional, and social weight by directing one's habits of consumption over time. [125] There *is* accounting for taste in the Apapocuvá spiritual portrait of the human constitution. It is located in the nape of the neck. For example, the larger the animal whose form the soul element *(asyiguá)* assumes, the more evil the person is, for the voracious appetite for evil corresponds to the animal's body weight and capacity for food. [126]

The difference between the physiological and epistemological tendencies[127] is the same as that generally recognized between two kinds of soul: "one or more bodily souls that grant life, movement, and consciousness to the body, and one dream or free soul identical to man himself as he is manifested outside of his body in various psychic and twilight zones." [128] Some scholars of Amerindian culture employ this distinction to categorize every soul concept and element.[129] However, it is preferable to view the difference as occurring at the basic, categorical level at which the elements are systematized: the level of *logical type*. It is preferable to view the two levels of logical type and catalogued element as distinct because the systematic tendency of logical typology highlights the desire and capacity for intellectual clarity and rational order of thought, whereas the soul itself is rarely so restricted in focus. The full range of the soul's experience should not be confused with the theoretical apparatus used to think about it since the soul's elements circumscribe the whole of spiritual existence and not simply rational inquiry.[130] In addition, depending on the type of systematic construal, the same soul-elements may account for both biological as well as psychic movement. In any case, these two typological solutions for ordering the temporal properties of humans, and ultimately for portraying the panorama of the spiritual life in a systematic way, are seldom mutually exclusive. This is clear from Theodor Koch-Grünberg's report that the Taulipáng possess five different souls of increasing lightness. Four of these souls can be seen as shadows. The fifth is unique. It enables one to speak. This "speaking soul" leaves the body during sleep or during fits of sneezing. After death the "speaking soul" transmigrates to the other world, but the other soul-elements either remain with the body or transform into the shapes of animals such as birds of prey.[131]

Each of the two systematic tendencies are "locative" operations of the mind, which "maps," in the space of the imagination, the human soul's ability to encounter multiple modes of time in a symbolic way. That is, the soul's contact with the sacred affords the possibility of systematic reflection on the human capacity for mental, emotional, and physical experience.

The soul is by no means immortal or indestructible. Great care must be taken that it not be consumed or annihilated in its spiritual adventures during life or in its perilous journey to the other world after death. A psychopomp (guide of souls) is frequently a necessary help. Even if the soul is not destroyed, it may suffer tragic metamorphoses that threaten its identity or preferred state of being. With performative movements and symbolic manipulation during its life span, the body aids the soul in achieving its "well-tempered" state. Ritual movements of bodies help intercalate the temporal experiences of the soul with the macromovements of supernatural and cosmic time in the seasons, stars, rivers, plants, and animal cycles. Even so, the full trajectory of human existence, the goal of the soul, is frequently accomplished as a salvation. By guaranteeing the continuity of individual identity in the face of a lifetime's involvement with other modes of being, the soul emboldens the human to experiment with the sacred and so assume responsibility for existence. Knowledge of the symbolic reach of human nature and of its meaning offers the desire and courage to act in a significant way.

CASTING THE IMAGE INTO TIME: THE DREAM-SOUL

"For sociology, interested only in man awake, the sleeper might as well be dead," wrote Roger Bastide in criticism of his field.[132] Nothing could be further from the religious perception of human being among South American peoples. In their view, the individual encounters ultimate reality while asleep. In studying the dreams of the Hopi of North America, Dorothy Eggan proposed two hypotheses that are helpful in understanding the reality that serves as a basis for their view of dreams: first, "The conceptual universe . . . was not delimited, as ours is, by notions of time and space which made of dreams an experience apart from reality"; and, second, there is a continuity, "largely below the level of awareness," between the imagery of dreams and the patterned cultural imagery of rite, myth, and art.[133] In other words, whether conscious or unconscious, a person moves within the same world of meaning—a continuity ensured by the imagination.[134] This continuity is the essence of the soul, as was illustrated in the beginning of this chapter. It is not surprising, therefore, that the soul itself may be viewed as a dream-image of the person or as an element of dream life acquired during maturation. This section does not analyze dreams. It examines theories of dream as they relate to the construction of the human person.[135]

Among the Kagwahiv, dreams are an essential aspect of human existence since they are clairvoyant views of the spirit world. Kagwahiv dreams always to some extent involve the flight of the soul, and "anyone who dreams, it is said, is a little bit a shaman." [136] Dreams represent another dimension of time, another quality of reality. "The psychic state of dreaming is expressed gramatically in a particle, *ra'ú* (related to the word for representation or dream image, *ráúv*), which is used like a tense marker to indicate that the action or experience being related took place in a dream." [137]

In this respect, the Siriono hold a similar view. Dreams occur while the Siriono soul wanders at night. Siriono dreams reveal the future; for example, they predict good luck in hunting or in gathering food.[138] The *places* to which the Siriono soul wanders in dream are other *times*. In nearly the same fashion, the Boróro describe dreams in temporal terms. The soul-shadow *(aroe marigudu)* is a constitutive element of the Boróro person. The soul-shadow is received from a dead person whose bones have already returned to powder and whose breath, no longer enclosed in a body, is kept in a mortuary gourd.[139] At night, when a Boróro dreams, the *aroe marigudu* assumes the form of a small bird and flies silently to faraway places. When it returns to the body, it remembers dreams that portend the future times visited during its voyage.[140]

The meaning of the soul's movement through time in dream cannot be understood unless dream experience is set within the wider frames of existence represented by the meaning of symbolic space and time. These include the spatial symbolism of the house (or other place) where the dreamer lies as well as the mythic times the soul visits. For instance, dreams are evidence of the Canelos Quichua soul's existence and instruments of its growth. Dreams are a species of vision, and both dreams and visions are clarified by myth.[141] During the time when night passes into day, souls leave their bodies to journey through mythic times and spaces. Visions that transport one back in time also occur during large ceremonies. "Visionary experience spans and integrates jungle, water, and soil domains, the sky and the underworld, and opens the entire sequence of linear time to enduring mythic structure." [142]

It is at the center of the Canelos Quichua house that the soul leaves the body, for a dream is the visual narrative of its travels in other domains. At the center of the universe one gains access to these other dimensions of time and space. Husband and wife sleep on either side of the center, and from there the married couple's souls traverse the universe. "One frequently wakes during a dream to mention the soul's movement to the other." [143] In the hours before dawn, husband and wife share the contents of their dreams and work out interpretations. Through their dream life, knowledge of the whole universe and its past may be pieced together and its progressive unification effected. In that sense, dreams fulfill the same function as the other cultural performances that take place at the center of the house: conception, birth, vigils of the dead, healing, and *Banisteriopsis*-induced journeys.[144]

The ritual movements of bodies at the center of space orchestrates time through the manipulation of their symbolic motions. The Canelos Quichua sexual performance at night manipulates the temporal expressions of lineage- and soul-transmission in order to extend them into new generations. Dreams shared in the speech acts between husband and wife in the predawn hours parallel the sex acts shared between them. At work in both actions (as well as in the other ritual acts performed at the center of the house-world) is the same creative melding of supernatural forces that are temporally expressed (as descent of the soul across time in the links established by *apamama* and *apayaya*, in the case of sex; or as the ancient times of myth visited in dream) in order to produce human history. History is always an evaluation of human existence in time. Consequently, the experience of time in dream and myth frequently contributes to a culture's concept of history. For the Canelos Quichua, human history is the sense of responsibility, provoked by the images of sacred and ancestral time, for furthering the dynamism of cosmic rhythms and for uniting the spatial realms of the universe (water, land, forest, sky, and underworld).

THE DREAM-SOUL: THE IMAGE AS AN ELEMENT OF THE SOUL AND THE DREAM OF CREATION

Dream images express both a human attitude toward existence and the sacred realities met in that existence. Among the sacred realities prominently featured in dream experience is the dream-element of the human soul itself. The concept of *karõ* is central to the Krahó concept of person. *Karõ* designates the principle that endures after death. It is also found in living human beings, although it absents itself during dreams or illness.[145] Although it is not identical with the body, *karõ* does refer to the body or to any image of the body (e.g., a photograph). The *karõ* leaves the body definitively when the dead person socializes with the community of the deceased by eating food with them, having sex with them, or participating with them in body-painting or in log races.[146] The images that occur in dreams are considered to be *mekarō* (the plural of *karō*). *Mekarō* may also be met in the forest or beside a river. Once the *karō* detaches itself from the body, it may take on several different forms, and it usually undergoes a series of metamorphoses into forms of ever-diminishing size: "they are believed to be able to die several times and to take on successively the forms of large animals, then of smaller and smaller animals, . . . and finally to end as stones, roots, or tree stumps." [147]

The Apinayé concept is cognate to that of the Krahó. The Apinayé word *me-galō* refers to the human soul, a ghost, a shadow, or a visual image. The word also refers to a bull-roarer. Animals and plants also possess *me-galō*; rocks do not. Human souls endure after death, whereas plant and animal souls do not.[148] Souls appear and wander at night, and so the *me-galō* of small children are subject to loss or even to capture by other spirits when they stray from the body.[149]

For many peoples, existence itself is a dream of the creator.[150] In such cases, human dreams are believed to be contained within the dream of the creator, who is the undreamed dreamer. In essence, both wakefulness and sleep are dream-figments of the creator, and the reality of human dreams is placed on the same footing as that of human action in the waking state.

Dreaming constitutes the central pattern of human existence among the Guajiro, appearing to them to be the best illustration of human nature: ordered yet mysterious, individual yet shared. For the Guajiro, dreams constitute the power of reality because it was through his dream that the creator Maleiwa first experienced, and therefore called into being, the universe itself. The experience of the creator is the model for human existence, for the dream-spirit Apusanai, who brought the dream-state to Maleiwa, also brings the dream-state to each human being. "That is, Apusanai creates the mental matrix for dreaming in which the actual dream itself appears." [151] During dreaming, the Guajiro soul detaches itself from the body and enters the dream-state prepared for it by Apusanai. Dreams bring people a constitutive element of self-consciousness, one that characterized the creativity of the creator god, for "Apusanai reveals himself to Maleiwa when Maleiwa becomes aware of his own dreaming." [152] The self-conscious dreaming of the creator transposed being into a new state of existence, which included human life. That is why dreaming is "an inherent and vital part of human nature." Insofar as human existence is real, it is constituted by the experience of dreaming because dreams "are an image of a larger but very real order of metaphysical reality, of which waking consciousness is but an imperfect reflection." [153] The Guajiro theory of dreaming makes a statement about the fullness of knowledge implied in any experience of symbolic reality: the meaning of any symbolic part or particular symbolic complex is related to, and in some way depends upon, the significance of all being as manifest in its symbolic representations. "The complex interrelationships between natural, human, and supernatural orders, which in effect defines the meaningful totality and unity of all existence, can only be penetrated through the act of dreaming." [154]

Such a view brings home forcefully why it is that dreams perceive reality: dreams called reality into manifest existence in the first place, and/or they identify the heart of the dreamer's consciousness with the creativity of supreme being itself. In either case, there is an unbroken continuity between the reality of the world dreamed by the creator and the world visited by human beings during dreams.

The Makiritare consider the matter from a slightly different angle. Through the images of his dream and the symbolic sounds of his song, Nadeiumadi, the second aspect of Wanadi, the Makiritare creator, accomplished his powerful acts. However,

> he did it to show us that death isn't real. He sat down. He put his elbows on his knees, his head in his hands. He just sat there in silence, thinking, dreaming, dreaming. He dreamt that a woman was born. It was his mother. . . . He made his own mother. . . . He gave birth to her dreaming, with tobacco smoke, with the song of his maraca, singing and nothing else. [155]

Through his singing and smoking, the creator demonstrated that dream is more powerful than death.

Creation *ex nihilo* through thought or word shares a process in common with creation through dream: the world and its creatures arise as perceived images within the creative being. [156] This permits us to understand two aspects of the human dream-soul that appear in the examples above. On the one hand, the human dream-soul (or image-soul) has an eternal nature, and so shares in primordial sacrality. On the other hand, since the thought-image or word-image in the creator's mind is associated with his performative utterance of creative speech, the dream-soul is associated with the faculty of human speech and song. Keeping in mind the view that language is essentially rooted in the images that appear in the primordial world (for example, in the divine mind) rather than in the words or phonemes formed by the human mouth, one may begin to understand that dream, thought, speech, and creativity in every guise partake of the same essential nature as the image-soul constitutive of the human being. This is why, for the Campa, the discovery of the meaning of one's own spiritual existence makes visible the links between levels of reality. The Campa soul resembles the living person. [157] In keeping with their extremely human-centered view of the universe, the Campa believe that many of the significant forms of nature were originally human beings. For example, the deer was once a Campa hunter. He hunted so poorly that he began to bring back strips of his own flesh as game. [158] So, too, the dung beetle was once a Campa who refused to eat manioc and preferred devouring the dung of his wife. In the same way, insects, toads, bats, frogs, and crabs were once human beings. [159] In other accounts, the Campa describe how the tapir, the mouse, the weevil, and calendrical trees were once all beings with primordial human forms. [160] The human image was transformed into all the species of creation through musical performance, through ritual "blowing," or through the performative utterance of a creative "grandfather." The significance of the human image generates a range of symbolic analogies creative of the whole universe. The act of recognizing the human image (the shape of spiritual existence) opens experience to the nearly infinite forms of meaning that the human imagination can handle.

Manifest creations are concrete expressions whose reality and existence depend upon appearance as an image within the creative and eternal being of the primordium. Creative sound (e.g., divine speech) is, at bottom, a symbolic image. This image, inhabiting the soul in the form of either a dream-song element or a divine-word element (or both), is the locus of creative speech. Dream and sound, seemingly quite distinct realities, share primordial image as their common footing in reality.[161] In the primordium both dream and sound exist as sacred image.

INTERPRETING THE EXPERIENCE OF THE DREAM-SOUL: THE SOCIAL CONSTRUCTION OF REALITY

The dream becomes valid and assumes specific value through the act of interpretation. The same logic applies to the dream-soul or image-element acquired or quickened during adolescence or during the call to a vocation. Interpretation of important dreams rarely assumes the form of a detached or objective commentary. More often, interpretation is a socially significant act, a public performance derived from the dream itself.[162] Such valorizations of the experience of dream and image often take the form of song, ritual, or alteration of one's public role and behavior.[163]

For example, the Avá-Chiripá lay great stress on the acquisition of a chant during one's dreams. In order that the chant become effective and powerful, however, one must translate this mystical experience into the mundane world by remembering the chant and reciting it before the community in a session of collective prayer.[164] The song one hears in one's dream is tantamount to an announcement of one's vocation, for the song is sung to the dreamer by a messenger sent from the creator, Nanderú Guazú. In the case of one chief, the dream-song signaled his commission as the creator's envoy on earth. Bartolomé reports the chief saying, "In order that I may know the designs of Nanderú Guazú, I must not eat meat or fat, and I must carry out his orders so that I may care for my people. He made me listen to his prayer so that I could chant it. In my dream he made me listen to it, and so I prepared and made ready my ears." [165] After he awoke from his special dream, the chief's family prepared a space for him to perform the dream-song prayer he heard in his dream. Through dream-song, the god provided both knowledge of and a way of release from the supernatural world seen in the dream. In fact, as Bartolomé points out, the recitation of the dream-song vividly reenacts and revives that moment of contact with the divine messengers. The supernatural world encountered in one's dreams is made present in the public light of day. "The shamanistic chant or prayer is like a bridge which permits communication between the world above and the world below." [166]

A group's description of the dynamics of the soul proves especially illuminating in understanding beliefs concerning the nature of dream and its relationship to performance, especially song. The Apyteré visualize the three souls of the human being as the "good word," the "words placed crosswise," and "the word held in waiting." [167] During dreams, the first soul (the "good word," which is of divine origin) takes flight in company with the second soul-element (the "words placed crosswise," so-named because it accounts for the negative aspects of human behavior). When these two elements return from their night's voyage, they describe in song the "visions, events, and revelations which they have witnessed or acquired." In this way the third soul-element, the "word held in waiting," comes to know the events of the nocturnal journey, and the sleeping individual becomes conscious of his or her dreams. Dreams, then, have a disintegrating function: the personality dissolves to obtain valuable vision-knowledge of realities that transcend its own conditions of being. Chanting and recounting visionary experiences reintegrate the personality by rejoining components of the soul and by transmitting knowledge gained by the traveling soul-elements to the waiting soul-element. [168]

One must resist the temptation to reduce the logic of dream validation to the circular argument that dreams have impact on one's daily life if one acts them out in daily life. The matter is not so simple as the fact that dream can become real if acted out in real life. The world of dream and the world of waking life are both real. If there is a circularity here it is a "hermeneutic circle" shared by all acts of interpretation. [169] The question concerns how to transport the powers of dream reality into the world of everyday existence so as to empower the latter or how to make manifest in both dimensions of reality the meaning of imaged powers who appear most fully in only one of those dimensions. The dream-soul element casts the images seen during its dream-travel into the episodic and narrative rhythms of song, rite, and recited story. The temporal structures of these three genres are consubstantial with the structures of time conditioning this world and human culture. [170] In the same way that temporal structures of cultural performance transpose eternal realities into the rhythms of this world, the symbolism of performative and fine arts translates primordial images into visible and audible expressions. The dream-image soul, by creating an "enchanted" world of imagery in song and story, lends the spatial and temporal extension typical of this world to those realities seen in another kind of time and space.

Dream-derived song is a clue to understanding dream as a species of performance, the *ideal performance* of the sacred realities whose "acts" created reality. Via the dream-soul element, the human being is admitted to the creative scenario as a spectator or even as a participant. Song-images heard in dreams punctuate the dramatic acts of sacred beings in a way akin to the episodic cadence of rituals, the acts of human culture, which are powerful because they replicate the primordial actions seen in the dream-scenes.

The song makes present the powerful images that manifest themselves as the sounds heard in the dream. The ritual song, composed of symbolic (i.e., meaningful) sounds, is a *real presence* that makes authentic performance possible.

ABOUT DREAM

Dream is an essential constituent of the human person because it brings each individual into direct contact with the sacred. This general view of many South American societies calls for close study of specific cultures. But this was not the goal in the section above, which aimed instead to delineate the coherence of complex dream symbolism in the religious life of South America.

In general, South American ideas of the dream-soul reestablish the perspective on the relationship between conscious thought and dream experience. Thought, the deliberate and conscious manipulation of mental images, is but a tiny application, a by-product, of the experience of the imaged world. Without interruption, imaged reality cuts across modes and degrees of human awareness. Human experience of reality continues through the whole range of imaginal existence: dream, ecstasy, vision, myth, rite, art, architecture, as well as the scientific modes of thought that arrange images in astronomy, botany, ornithology, and so on. Even awake, human attention is narrower in focus than the experience of reality: while concentration draws a bead on an object of attention, the larger, peripheral world still impinges on experience.[171] Dreamlike, most of the images of the world are drawn into human perception subliminally as subtle but significant "cues," the background to the world's meaning.

The shapes and sounds of meaning attend the well-lit courtroom of full consciousness in meager numbers. Their ranks swell in the unintended hum, the ceaseless innuendo, of half-heard sounds and visual distractions. The peripheral world is, in fact, more in tune with the true world of power, the primordial world of being no longer fully present in everyday space and time but accessible in dream imagery. The concept of the dream-soul scribes a number of important kinds of images within the same compass: dream, divine word, image of primordial being or even divine being, creation, speech, thought, music, and artistry. All these image-based realities fall as points on the same arc of meaning.

Images testify to the constancy of reality from its very beginning. Dream is never set apart from reality, nor is it used to downgrade or compete with the reality of everyday social existence. Dream is essential to the full range of human experience of reality. True, it does abolish the system of space, time, and relations that conditions human limits. Nonetheless, it opens human being to complementary meanings manifest in myth, rite, stupor, and ecstasy. Furthermore, even though the soul is momentarily freed from the constraints of mundane space and time, human perception is still ordered by the character of the dream- or image-soul, the structure of the imagination. The dream process is patterned because the soul guarantees spiritual continuity in the encounter with every appearance of reality.[172] In particular, the dream-image soul plays a crucial role in constructing the symbolic patterns embracing all levels of existence, including its own individuality.

What is most remarkable is that the element of dream appears in the very heart of the human. It is often, in fact, the element of the soul responsible for human artistry in speech, thought, music, and visual form. The soul's continuity assures that human creativity makes worlds in the image of the sacred world that gave rise to the universe and its creatures.

CASTING A SHADOW INTO TIME: REFLECTION

The description of the soul as a shadow merits special attention, not only on account of its ubiquity, but because of the important values it allows us to see. It invites us to understand the meaning of "reflection," the process by which the soul's shadow is cast, made visible, seen, and understood.

Darkness is the effective symbol of indivisibility of forms, a state of being contiguous with the indistinction of unconsciousness. Nocturnal rites, including dreaming and sex, utilize darkness to merge the universe's varied realities of light seen in the images of dream, vision, and the visible forms of the day.[173] The human shadow-soul cannot be set apart from the meaning of darkness. It is a form of darkness constituting the human soul. On the large and darkened stage of human slumber and inattention, the tiny daytime drama of human awareness is played out. But the darkness of the shadow-soul is a significant portion of the constancy of human nature. Unlike primordial being, whose substance can be light itself and whose dreams or images are shadows cast out as reflections from the primordial world into time, the human being, sleeping unconscious in earth's darkness, perceives even those shadows of the primordial world as so many forms of light.

For the community of Chuani, Bolivia (Camacho Province, La Paz Department), the light in color (and, indeed, all light-forms in this world) originated in a mythic event that occurred near the beginning of time. The world owes its display of lustrous colors to the disintegration of Achachila-wak'a, the being of primordial all-color. Achachila-wak'a manifested a condition of being that included both the brilliance of perfect light and the invisibility of absolute darkness in such a way that there was neither the need for nor the possibility of distinguishing between them. That condition of perfect light disintegrated when all-colorful Achachila-wak'a broke apart. Light and darkness, strewn across one another's apparent forms in this world, are now visible in one another. The iridescent colors of this world's realities, especially rainbows and feathers, reflect the variety of ways in which illumination and opacity, two modes of the imagination of being, relate to one another.[174]

As do many other peoples, the Baniwa project their souls as shadows. Shadows are the active, but relatively separable, spiritual aspects of human beings. Similarly, supernatural beings, such as the fish-people and animal-people, project shadows. However, the shadows of supernaturals are projected as visible and tangible body forms, whereas human shadows are spiritual entities. In the beginning, light and sound were bound together. Sounds are the audible expression of Kuai's (the culture hero's) body parts as he was set alight with fire. The fire was instigated by Yaperikuli, the celestial master of light and fire, whose existence preceded Kuai's. The visible play of shadows and the audible play of musical sounds are the realities cast by the same substantial image of the primordium: Kuai's body. From his body parts were fashioned the various animal species and the sacred flutes whose tones now fertilize the world.[175] The withdrawal of light from sacred matter — the body of Kuai and the primordial world consumed in the cosmic fire — has effected all these animals and sacred flutes. The result is a dual existence of activity, a constant state of separation of form from spirit — a state of suspended ecstasy peopled by the shadowy activity of symbols.[176]

The ecstasy of the universe — that is, the separation of light from other forms of being (animals, humans, etc.) — diffuses primordial being. The withdrawal of light produces multiple *shadows* (the "animal" bodies of supernatural beings, souls of humans, ghosts of the dead, images seen by the soul in dreams or trance, etc.). Separation of light from form or matter produces a whole shadow-world of spiritual life, a world whose every action corresponds to the actions of material forms but whose difference in meaning is marked by its divisibility. Experience must be transitory in order to be equal to the multiplicity of forms. Maturity at initiation consists in obtaining full experience of one's soul, that is, awareness of one's wider spiritual existence and capacities. Such experience and knowledge makes one's life a whole.

The notion of the shadow-soul is a subtle one. Close attention to detail draws out the full weight of its importance in understanding the nature of reflection and the meaning of the temporal imagery that constructs the human person. The Kari'ña case merits scrutiny. The Kari'ña call the human soul *aska*, a word that means "family member" as well as "shadow" or "reflection." This shadow-soul is normally invisible, although from time to time a person may see his or her soul as a shadow cast by the sunlight on the ground. In this case the defining features of the soul-shadow, the face and eyes, are indistinct. Water is a better medium of reflection of the features of the soul-shadow. Mirrors, "magic objects which allow one to see the invisible," provide a clear look at the soul.[177] Human *aska* are nature spirits that belong to species *(wara)* of wild animals, whose forms souls assume when they become visible. Because each person possesses an *aska* in his or her body, every person acquires membership in a second invisible family, the animal species protected by its mythical progenitor *(tamurü)*.[178] These invisible ties between human beings and invisible species branch out secretly, so that the Kari'ña as a people have secret but firm ties with all the families of spirits. They enjoy the powerful protection of the whole range of mythical beings who preside over the mystical species.

The Kari'ña shaman *(puidei)* does not possess the ordinary *aska* shadow-soul; rather, he has a *tamu* ("grandfather"), a celestial spirit *(kapu akarü)*.[179]

This is no animal nature spirit for, unlike the *aska*, it casts no shadow and cannot be subject to the spirits of the earth or of water.

During his apprenticeship, the *puidei* gradually learns to see his own reflection, to know himself, by coming to see his own soul's image clearly. He rubs his eyes with pepper juice and makes ascents to heaven. There, if the supernatural being of the primordial age chooses to help him, a heavenly spirit will gaze upon him. The first act of apprenticeship, therefore, is passive: to be seen by the supernatural being, or, more actively stated, to become an image in the spirit's eye. Eventually, the *puidei* will see his own image, his soul, reflected in the eyes of the heavenly helper spirit. That is, he learns to know himself as he is known—the image in the divine eye. This self-consciousness marks the beginning of his knowledge of all things. Recognition is reminiscent of that form of creation in which the image, arising in supernatural being, passes into earthly existence. Here, however, the direction of that process is reversed so that the earthly being reassumes its primordial manifestation as an image in the mind's eye of its progenitor. Unlike the simple *aska*, the shaman's soul at death does not become transformed into an *akaton* or *ioroskan* (elements of earth, the residue of deceased souls), but returns to its celestial home on The Mountain. The simple *aska* is limited in several ways: it is impulsive, since it will leave the body without reason and control; it is relatively ignorant, since it knows how to change into only one form, that of its own animal species; it can undergo injury at the hands of a more powerful being's bad intentions. In sharp distinction to this ordinary soul, the *tamu* of the shaman exits the body only under strict control during ecstasy and is wise enough to take on any animal form. When it exits the body, it is strong enough to take care of itself as well as to do battle against enemy spirits. The *tamu* comes when it is called. In its very character it is obedient to the will of the shaman.

There appear to be three ways in which the *aska* may be weakened and a person made to fall ill, even to die. The first is when a harmful spirit overshadows the intended victim and obliterates its distinctive outline and features. Identity, an expression of the constancy of the soul, is destroyed. The *aska* becomes terrified and flees to its mountain home, leaving the body empty and powerless. The overshadowing spirit then enters the sick person's body in a form consistent with the domain it governs. For example, the Grandfather of the Earth will overshadow a sick person and, when the *aska* has left, will enter the body in the form of worms, lice, spiders, scorpions, cockroaches, and so on. If the overshadowing spirit is of a species from the water realm, the pathogen will enter in the form of a snake, an iguana, a frog, and so forth. The patient may only be healed if his *aska* is called back to its body with a powerful *aremi* (sacred song; lit., "a call"). If the magic song is successful, the *aska* returns to expel the pathogenic spirit *(piopo akurü)* from his "house," the human body. The *aremi* song is a sound-image that casts the proper human shadow back into the human body.

Second, a soul may be weakened by being captured and taken as a slave to the house of another spirit, a sound-image who casts shadows in the forms of animals other than that of the captured *aska*. In this case, the existence of the shadow-soul's form is not directly threatened. The danger is that the discovery of one's identity, the reflected image of one's soul, serves no purpose in a world where unfamiliar and misbegotten shapes bear no symbolic relation to one's own. Without the possibility of understanding, the soul is enslaved by the forces of a world without meaning. The shaman must invoke the help of one of the four winds, his spirit-helpers, to attack the capturing spirit and release the sick person's *aska* from its confinement in a house of misshapen existence.[180]

The third manner in which the Kari'ña shadow-soul may be weakened or made vulnerable is through soul loss. This occurs when an attacking spirit comes to capture a victim's soul and the *aska* responds by volunteering to accompany the attacker. Occasionally a soul is enticed by food and sex to live with the spirits in this way, and animals and birds are also subject to the same seduction and are never seen again. The problem is that the species of the attacker with whom the *aska* has decided to live is not the species of the *aska* itself. As a result, rather than being protected by the master of the species, the human being and its soul are made the slaves of their host. In such a case, very little is done to save the person who has "left." The person simply spends the rest of his or her life living with spirits. A person lost in this way can only be cured through a very difficult process of soul-hunting directed by the shaman. The matter is complicated since the lost shadow-soul changes form along its way to the home of the spirits and loses its identity.[181]

One temporal aspect of the soul is reflected in the appearance of its individual meaning, the unique features of character that result from the historical process of maturation. The shadow-soul gains its distinguishing features in two ways. First, memories and decisions of the will accumulate as images recollected over time.[182] Second, the soul is shaped by time spent in a life of reflection, which is the process of contemplating one's image when it appears as a primordial being that is cast as a shadow into time. One grasps one's likeness in time as it is projected against a totally other reality.[183] The origin of human reflection, the cornerstone of understanding, lies in seeing that one's essence is a shadow cast by the sacred.

To see another's outward appearance, the defining features of the other's face and eyes,[184] is not the same thing as to see oneself. Reflection is a different process than vision and bears different fruit, allowing one to see a different level of reality. Outward appearance, easily seen, is merely suggestive, a semblance, of the shadow-soul. However, the ability to see the defining features of the shadow, to grasp one's own character, is the culmination of a spiritual process.[185] Once one has arrived on the level of true reflection and is self-aware of the reflected shadow of reality within, the world's meaning is opened up in a new way. This is because all forms of darkness—the darkness of the shadow-soul, the dark areas delineating a figure, the darkness of the primordial night—are one. Each of the world's realities, faces, feathers, figures, and colors, blends darkness and light in its own way. This is not a mysticism founded on inaccessible mystery; rather, it is a mysticism of the obvious. The basis for it is as plain as the nose on your face since primordial darkness is evident and consubstantial with the distinct features of each face.

Reflection on the nature and relationship between shadow and light forms the basis for evaluating reality in many cultural systems. (William Blake insisted that chiaroscuro was a mechanical technique only superficially related to the fact that wise men see outlines and therefore they draw them.) In many South American societies, the speck of soul-shadow, this human heart of primordial darkness, imbues every human perception of reality. This is why the recognition of one's own human semblance, the meaning of one's own image grasped in reflection, permits the formulation of a theory of resemblances embracing the significance of all images of the universe.[186] In the Kari'ña case, the human form is the true form underlying all beings. Kari'ña rituals involve a number of self-cancelling paradoxes: humans become enchanted (lit., "sung") and become birds. That is, they assume the visible animal-form of the true invisible sound-form that constitutes that species. The animal form, however, is merely a transitional object or device allowing the human being to penetrate the original celestial world of sound-forms (the creative word-images of the invisible, species-prototypes). Once there, once having arrived at the world of invisible, primordial sound-form, one "recovers the universal human semblance, the only one which is real." [187]

The existence of the shadow-soul, then, guarantees individuals a direct connection to the world of fully manifest light — the omniscient, omnipresent, and omnipotent mode of being that humans experience in their inner being as a dark absence constitutive of their own soul.

CASTING THE FLOW OF TIME INTO FLESH: THE EXAMPLE OF MENSTRUATION

The soul's epistemological faculties (dream, image, shadow, reflection, thought, will, understanding, speech, and song) do not exhaust the temporal images constructing the human being. As seen above, the epistemological tendency analyzes the soul in terms of the innate properties acquired during the process of maturation and exposes the contents of human individuality. As such, the examination of the soul-elements of dream and shadow accentuated the continuity, or constancy, of a person's existence even while encountering multiple modes of time.[188]

INTERCALATING COSMIC PERIODICITY INTO HUMAN LIFE

Menstruation, on the contrary, is an effective sign of the periodic nature of the cosmos embodied by human existence. Myths of the origin of menstruation frequently make this point. For example, the daughter of the sun, the Desana culture heroine who bestows on humans the possibilities of culture, became filled with the regular periodic nature of her father, the sun, when he had sex with her. He inseminated her with light, his "yellow intention," through her eye. Menstruation is the monthly remembrance of the incest of the sun, the Desana creator, with his daughter.[189] The sun established girls' puberty rituals when he revived his daughter-lover, who had been wasting away, so preoccupied with sex that she would not eat. This brief example already displays the interrelation among several modes of periodic time: the *optimally cyclic nature* of human attention, of successive generations of offspring, and recurrent appetites for food or sex, as well as the cycles of waste, death, and revival. Periodicity conditions all relations in the cosmos. The capacity to relate to things in a proper, periodic way is fundamental to the possibilities of culture. In the Desana case this capacity is an achievement of sacred beings, who transmit their knowledge to humankind.

Menstruation is the clearest image of the periodic quality of time that conditions human existence. It brings forward the changing aspect of the being *containing* human life.[190] In the cyclic expression associated with the vagina, the organ through which life passes in regeneration, the flow of life is, at one and the same periodic moment, the ebbing of life and the loss of life's blood. Each culture states this in the language of its own imagery. In their myths concerning the moon, Kašíri, the Campa draw a pattern of associated images that includes first menses, blood (menstrual blood), the moon (who penetrates the menarche hut, the water's surface, and the surface of the earth with his penis), human penetration into a river for bathing, the origin of manioc as food, the birth of the sun (a Campa), and the death of the first woman.[191] In the Bolivian altiplano, Aymara speakers consider menstruation part of the physiological tempo of the land, the mountain-body, which constantly loses and regains its substance in the periodic celebrations of rituals.[192] The same flow of life manifests itself in the periodic rhythms of the good life, misfortune, and the restoration of vitality. In the Inca view, the body of Pachamama (Holy Mother Earth) opened to manifest itself as fertile during the period of Jujay (July–August), a time for sowing, public festival, and nocturnal astronomic observation conducted to obtain the esoteric knowledge essential to coordinating life with the rhythms of the cosmos. When Mother Earth opened during this period, she became "alive," but, for that very reason, she was also said to be "ravenous," "annoyed," even "enraged." Her openness yielded not only the possibility of new life, but it also cleared the passage for all manner of evils to enter human existence.[193] The cycles of food, stars, fertility, and disease were coinvolved with the periodic openness of Pachamama.

The containers of human life (the body, the womb, the skin, the house) manifest rhythms of their own—rhythms punctuated by the periodic passing of substances such as blood, semen, air, food, and feces in and out of its openings. The openness of the container *from time to time* creates the temporal conditions generative of *relations*—for example, between male and female in sex, between parents and child in filiation, between age groups in generations, between exogamous groups in marriage alliances, between the individual and society in privacy, and so on. The mode of time made manifest in these exchanges[194] is orchestrated into complex rhythms by carefully coordinating them with crucial cosmic cycles that also manifest the same powers of life. The Shipibo celebration of girl's initiation, for example, takes place around the day of the full moon. Few Shipibo can give an adequate explanation of this fact, since the moon does not figure directly as a character or as a recipient of veneration. Peter Roe, who lived among the Shipibo, believes that the moon, a female mythical figure, helps transform girls into women. The Shipibo assert that, in mythical times, women originally had penises. They looked like huge clitorises and, because of them, women succeeded in lording it over men. With the help of a bird, men succeeded in capturing fire from the daughter of Yoashico, a selfish being who had kept fire to himself. Yoashico was killed, and the men bathed in his blood.[195] The Shipibo today seem not to have a clear and coherent explanation of the association of the moon with these rituals. Since a woman's period is known as "the evil of the moon," [196] Shipibo women may perform clitoridectomy on young novices in order to culturally control female bleeding in such a way as to intercalate it into lunar cycles. In so doing, they align the rhythms of female reproductive physiology with the cosmic regenerative power manifest in the phases of the moon. Such a culturally imposed menstrual period is set at the time of the full moon, whom Roe thinks the Shipibo believe instituted the rites called the "great drinking," which are celebrated at the full moon. The *hoboshco*, a drinking cup made to resemble sex organs, dips into the vessels of beer in a symbolic act of intercourse. The novice's mother manipulates the *shërvënanti*, a ceramic pubic cover worn while the girl's wound heals, so that it penetrates the girl's vagina. The possible use of a *bushi* (a ceramic phallus) for similar purposes alludes to a similar desire symbolically to align the timing of penetrations of the vagina with the cosmic power of regeneration manifest in the rhythms of the moon as well as with the regenerative powers of culture displayed in the periodic celebrations of festival.[197] The men, too, desire to be bloody like the girls and at the same moment. While the women perform the operation on the novice, the men engage in a dance during which they score their scalps until the blood runs over their heads and faces. Like the girl novice, the men are drunk.

The temporal constitution of the person allows human cultures to orchestrate the periodic rhythms of the cosmos by symbolically controlling the passages of the body in two senses. First, cultures open and close the body in the symbolic manipulations of toilet training, initiation at menses, and sexual abstinence and orgy, and during fasts or forced feedings of food and drink, in the process of ritual breathing for magic or music, at ear- and lip-piercing ceremonies, and so on. Second, cultures symbolically control the passage of the body parts themselves; that is, cultures deliberately move the body and its parts through symbolically defined space in properly timed ritual and dance movements. These rhythms, manifest in the social relations they generate between individuals and groups, disclose specific forms of periodicity embedded in the life of the body.[198] Though different in tempo, their common periodic nature stands out when set against the kind of time manifest either in the constancy of the eternal dream-image or in the spontaneity of the divine-speech element located in the human soul.

IS FEMALE TO MALE AS NATURE IS TO CULTURE?[199]

Because of their materialist foundations, the social sciences have focused
their scrutiny on empirical social actors, on the movements and interactions
of individual bodies and groups of bodies, and have examined many of these
biologically based relations of "life on the ground." The social sciences have
been determined to see social relations as expressions of "history" [200]—
whether social, economic, personal, or political—and remain unable to
perceive them as existing in any other kind of time or as expressions of any
other temporal imagery that is constitutive of the human being.[201] The inability to view social relations as generated by the periodic nature of the human
being has had two negative effects.[202] First, it has obscured the role that
religious meaning and value play in the formation of social relations. Before
considering the religious meanings specific to any particular historical situation, the foundations of social science exhibit the general tendency to treat
such significance as superstructural ideology that follows upon existing social relations or derives from "deep structures" inherent in the communicative codes reflected in the orders of natural history.[203] The implication of the
expressions "follows upon" and "derives from" is temporal, so the inference
drawn from the relationship between "deep" or social structures of relations
and religious meaning is viewed as one of cause and effect. Even if lip service
is paid to a certain dialectical relationship between religious meaning and
structural relations, religious imagery is seldom examined as possessing an
integrity of its own (as is economic life or art).

Second, the exaggerated importance of material movement through
"history," as opposed to other imaginable forms of time, clouds the relationship of social order to the sacred rhythms of the cosmos. This second incapacity of social science reifies its own dichotomies of value between, say, life
"on the ground" versus "ideology." [204] Two examples, the fundamental concepts of consciousness and culture, show how central such dichotomies of
value are to social science. First, the dogmatic distinction between "conscious" and "unconscious," an intellectual armament manufactured for use
in cultural studies during the colonial experience of the West,[205] empowers
the researcher to affirm the adequacy of his or her science's ontology in the
very act of "accounting for" alternative cultural constructions of the meaning of awareness. "The separation conscious/unconscious, among all borrowed scientific vocables, has probably caused more evil, more malicious
slandering of peoples and traditions, during our lifetime, than any other
methodological approach." [206] In the second instance, cultural anthropology's foundational distinction between "culture" and "nature" is, understandably, one of its most popular reifications of scholarly value wielded to
"explain" the alternative ontologies of native peoples while fending off the
call to rethink its own.[207] However, for many South American societies, as
Terence Turner makes clear for the case of the Kayapó, culture is as much a
given as nature. The items of nature and culture (e.g., fire, the structure of the
family) may be given by or stolen from supernatural beings. Both nature and
culture manifest a similar mode of time as opposed to the primordial beings

now unmanifest in this world. These facts have not stimulated Western science to rethink its categories so much as to dismantle South American ideas into "mythemes" in order to sort them into preordained holes.[208] Not human invention but supernatural being, now unmanifest, caused menstruation and dance forms to exist just as the forces of primordial times shaped the forest and the movements of rivers. Scholarly language, afraid of being converted into religious discourse,[209] clings to impertinent categories of value, such as "nature" and "culture," and thereby finds it difficult to penetrate the meaning of such a statement.

The data do not warrant the conclusion that male is to female as culture is to nature. All humans share the same periodicity manifest in this epoch/world. Without distinguishing "natural" from "cultural" kinds, we see that each kind of being (sun, stars, moon, plants, festivals, males, females) discloses periodicity in its uniquely meaningful tempo. Neither do the data allow the general conclusion that the constancy of the soul represents a male ideology while periodicity discloses a female one.[210] In all the cases cited above in the discussion of the soul's continuity, women have souls. More to the point in this discussion of menstruation, men, from the moment of their conception, are marked by the rhythms, the periodical openings and closings, of their enclosure. This becomes evident, for example, in the behavioral restrictions and food avoidances of a child's parents during gestation.[211]

Throughout their lives men continue to embody the periodic rhythms to which they were first initiated in the womb: in the blood pulsing through the body or spurting from wounds in war or rite, in the tempos of the hunter's life (the periodic fasts, avoidances, and sexual abstentions), in the steady "thump" of one's lineage as it matures and falls as the ripe fruit[212] of a new generation or age-set during the periodic performance of initiation.[213] Guayakí men who are related by blood to a menstruating girl undergoing initiation, or who have had sexual relations with her, become *bayja*, that is, "attractive" (in the sense that a lover is attractive) to beings who threaten their very existence. Among such beings are Memboruchu, the great celestial rainbow serpent and swallower of men, and the blue celestial jaguar, who attempts to devour the sun or the moon and who will attack men in a state of *bayja*. Women's periods and female physiology are strictly bound up with cosmic cycles. They *are* a cosmic rhythm and their motion casts the human beings around them into a motion that must be carefully intercalibrated with the cycles of the sun, the moon, and so forth. If not, one risks returning to the disorder of the flood, of eclipse, or of extinction of life. A menstruating Guayakí girl's body is washed, and every inch of it is scrubbed by two ritual washers using a piece of *kymata* liana. Women sing the ritual lament, the *chenga ruvara*. All who have had contact with the girl, especially her lovers, are similarly washed.[214]

The above-mentioned fasts and sexual abstentions are avoidances (periodic manifestations of "shame" and "respect")[215] related to specific categories of people, food, and actions. They link male life to the periodic cosmic tempos manifest not only in the menstrual flows of women but in all that has a beginning, is born, grows, dies, and has an end: plants, stars, animals, and body movements.

In many cultures both men and women are said to menstruate. It would be crass prematurely to interpret all instances of such a statement as expressions of male jealousy and desire for control. The language of these cultures points in another direction of thought: menstruation is the best statement of the periodic nature of incarnate human life. This periodic flow is manifest both in men and women; thus, both sexes "menstruate." For instance, in the Barasana view, menstruation consists of a changing of skin in the womb of the woman. This new skin makes conception and birth possible. It is its association with menstruation that lends the symbolism of changing skin a primary importance in all processes of regeneration. This same changing of skin is effected for male initiates by shamans at the He House festival. During the closing stages of the festival, the novices are said to be in a state of *bedigɪɪ*, a word for menstrual confinement. "In order to give birth [to the initiates of a new generation], men must first be opened up and made to menstruate." [216] In the Barasana view, the rhythmic existence that renews life periodically by the shedding of skin is not limited to human initiation or menses. The rainy season is the menstrual period of the sky, Romi Kumu (woman shaman), who is the primordial supreme being from whom all life flows.

Women testify to their embodiment of the periodic flow of life in the ebbing of menses. While unique in its meaning and in the kinds of relations it creates, the periodic flow of menstrual blood cannot be understood apart from other periodic tempos of incarnate life — tempos manifest in inhalation, exhalation, alimentation, evacuation, excretion, urination, and sexual intercourse. Each of these acts has rich symbolic value in many South American religions. Each reveals something about the sacred as it flows into carnal life. In Barasana male initiation, the sacred flute (not the vagina) is the instrument through which new life passes; it allows men to "menstruate" periodically in order to produce a new generation of their patriline. Not the controlled periods of flowing blood but the periodic flow of elder's breath creates the passage of human time. The periodic modulations of elder's breath through the trumpets into the body openings of the novices in each generation marks the cadence of human time.

SONIC IMAGERY CONSTITUTING THE HUMAN BEING

When a child is born among the Waiwai, a shaman bears the newborn's soul to the moon. Gazing on the soul-form of the new child, the moon and his brother bestow a spirit name on it. [217] This name forms part of the child's soul *(ekati)*. Another name, usually the name of a dead ancestor, is given by the child's grandmother. [218] This simple naming process clarifies how a religious understanding grounds the importance of the name. Naming is not always as simple as the Waiwai make it. Among the Apinayé the bestowal of a name is an elaborate event. In *The Apinayé*, Curt Nimuendajú describes his own

Apinayé naming ceremony.[219] Body decoration and painting receive great emphasis. Feet are painted red, limbs are doused with latex. Anklets, arm- and knee-bands, sashes, and strips of paty wool decorate the body. After solemn dancing by two lines of performers, one of men and one of women, the candidates face east. Then an older namesake solemnly pronounces all the forms of the individual name.

THE IMPORTANCE OF A NAME: SEEING WHAT YOU MEAN

These descriptions highlight two convictions common to them: that a name is a weighty word, a statement of one's specific presence in the world,[220] and that one's visage (ritually viewed by the moon and his brother, by the sha- man, by the rising sun, or by the namesake at the instant of naming) is a visible image inherently related to a person's sonic structure, disclosed by the name.

Outsiders can barely grasp the religious weight of names in South Ameri- can cultures. This incapacity is evident to Amerindians and is reflected in their evaluation of the power of traditional names and the relative ineffectu- ality of "Christian" names used only to speak of an individual or gain some- one's attention. For instance, in the first decade of the twentieth century, the Apapocuvá still held a night-long, elaborate ceremony during which the soul of a powerful shaman, in a state of ecstasy, journeyed to other dimensions of space and time in order to seek a child's name. The ceremony climaxed at the rising of the sun.[221] "For the Guaraní, the name obtained in this way holds a meaning greater than a mere combination of sounds used to call someone. The name is . . . a piece of the soul of its bearer or is almost identical to it, inseparable from the person. A Guaraní is not 'called' such-and-such a name, rather he 'is' so-and-so." [222] By contrast, Christian names were considered ineffective and unimportant. They were changed often, for the Apapocuvá

> found it extraordinarily ridiculous that the priest, who always considered himself superior to the pagan shaman, during the rite of baptism would ask the parents what name is to be given their child: they present themselves as "fathers" [padres] but are not even capable of knowing the right name for a child! From this stems the low esteem Guarani place upon Christian baptism and Portuguese names.[223]

GIVING VOICE TO SHAPE THE PERSONALITY

Immediately after the birth of his child a Kari'ña father goes on a ritual hunt for an animal. He stalks the *saka* ("voice"); he hunts down the sound of an animal for his child. The following explanations of the word *saka* and its cognates will clarify the meaning of the father's symbolic act. In addition to designating a whistle, noise or name, *saka* also means "help, service, power- gift, teaching." [224] The word *sakura* designates the deadly venom but also the wisdom of the coral snake. In the Kari'ña view, death is part of the imaged symbolic act called knowledge. As a form of knowledge bespeaking the shape of the personality, naming includes death. This is evident in the father's slaying of game. A name, like game meat, is a basic form of nourishment, one's first taste of transitive but sustained worldly existence. Unlike the consumable meat the father will bring home to feed the child later in its life, the name becomes constant food for thought because the "voice," one's name, has the power to call significant beings to it throughout the person's lifetime. One's name draws other beings within the compass of personal experience just as specific food attracts particular species of hungry beings. These encounters with other beings form the foundation of reflection. The name enables the person to take initiative in spiritual life.

Naming includes death for another reason. Through the imposition of knowledge in the form of one species of sound-shape on his child, the father "eliminates"—that is, effectively slays—all other species-possibilities for shaping the personality of his child. Only the captured or slain game-voice lives on in the child's name.

Saka ("voice") is, at root, a sacred sound that attracts and captures spirits. It is for this reason that it forms the basis of wisdom. The invisible saka manifests itself as aska (shadow or spirit companion) "if the father is able to hear, imitate, and respond to the sound [the reality, the true form of a spirit-being]; i.e., grasp it." [225] The saka and aska are, respectively, the unmanifest and manifest aspects of the same reality. The dominated and humanly controlled aska is a reflection or shadow cast by the invisible reality called saka. One says that during this ritual hunt for reality, the father "turns into an ear." The father may hear, for example, a bird, an insect, a mammal, the whistling of the wind in the trees, the scraping of tree branches; he attempts to "answer" the "call" of the first significant sound he hears. He responds to it by reproducing it; that is, he takes possession with his voice of the spirit that has offered itself. [226] Then the father, in turn, offers the spirit to his child's soul in the form of a name. The child now comes under the protection of the master of that wara (the species of beings who make this sound). Far from becoming routine, the importance of name grows as one matures. One not only employs the power of one's own name, but one also takes on spiritual responsibility for the names of others, that is, for playing a part in shaping their existence. For this reason, boys' initiation to adulthood, when they acquire the ability to father children, awakens extraordinary auditory power, "an astonishingly hypersensitive perception of sound" such that hearing becomes the most highly significant and subtle sense. [227] Receiving a name, capturing a sound, calling other modes of being within range of experience, knowing by name, and giving voice to others mold one's entire being to the shape of one's sound.

Names and sounds are constitutive of a person. This much is clear. At the same time, it would be an exaggeration to consider the individual in isolation from the group. On the one hand, names are bestowed and understood by social actors. On the other, taken collectively, the meaning of names helps compose the order [228] and meaning of society. An example from the Krahó makes clear that the individual and society mutually create one another in images of sound. According to the Krahó, blood and flesh wrap up a person's life force. As long as blood and flesh cling to one's bones, an individual exists as an independent biological entity. Once these have desiccated, however, bones and name remain the permanent locus of the personality. Men's names return to the house or residential segment from which they originated. Women's names are transmitted from a kinship classification that includes fathers' sisters. Consequently women's names move from house to house and from generation to generation (i.e., in death) in the same manner that men's bodies physically move during men's lives. Thus, women, who are actually immobile in an uxorilocal system, belong to a naming pattern that circulates from house to house. Men, who must move when they marry, see their names return to their maternal home at death. The transmission of names provides the society with a stable and permanent image of itself.[229] Because the image possesses both static and dynamic qualities, it assures both males and females the fullness of human existence even though social life divides experiences along sexual lines.[230] At the same time, the religious value attached to names in South America impels one to conclude that both society and the individual, each in its turn, merit being called both "the one" and "the many."

THE NAME OF THE GAME: DEAD SHAPE AND LIVE SOUND
Human life sustains itself at the cost of the life of other beings. Like all life forms in this world, human beings exist in a cycle of prey, or food chain. However, in the human case, this nexus of relations is by no means limited to the material consumption of food. In fact, consumption serves as an image of the nourishing involvement with supernatural forces necessary to sustain life[231] even in the womb, when no material food is necessary. The body-image of a Guayakí child's name is eaten by his or her mother while the child is still in the womb. Here, the principle "you are what you eat" (or at least what your mother eats while she carries you) holds. The name of the dead game that the mother chooses ritually to eat becomes her child's "nature." More importantly, the name launches the child into a specific network of alliances with humans and animals that nourish and shape the child's personality; that is why, for the Guayakí, names are the supernatural forces most determinative of the individual personality. The name bestowed on an infant at birth is chosen, before the child is born, by the mother-to-be. Names have nothing whatsoever to do with the sex of a child. Names are not different for men and women. During the final months of a mother's pregnancy, she is brought game by various hunters who are unrelated to her or her husband. She chooses the name (bykwa; lit., "nature") of one of these game animals as the name for her child. The future child will possess the bykwa of the game animal eaten by his or her mother in her final stages of pregnancy. (The suffix -gi is added to the animal name as a signal that the appellation now applies to a human being.) Thenceforward, the hunter who has brought the name-game is bound up in a new and close relationship with the newborn child and the child's parents. The hunter is called chikwagi, a ritual friend with whom a friendly and affectionate alliance opens up a lifetime of mutual trade, advice, and protection. Most Aché (Guayakí) possess several names, several "na-

tures." Apparently, the names are always furnished in the same way, that is, by a hunter bringing the meat of a game animal to a person's mother.[232] In a way more vivid than the Kari'ña father's hunt for a "voice" for his child, the Guayakí associate the name and the "nature" of individuals with death, with a presence whose meaningful form is no longer fully manifest. Largely invisible, the meaning of a person's nature depends on a unique pattern of symbols threaded together by the power of his or her name.

THE NAMING CEREMONY: PLACING SOUND IN THE CONTEXT OF CULTURE

Naming ceremonies offer to the body the order and socially shared meaning of sound. As we have seen, however, the choice of a name usually involves an act of interpretation based on viewing the body or image of the named individual or at least the body of the dead game after which the person will be named. Between the two kinds of structures (sound and person), a relationship exists whose meaning is interpreted and effectively uttered in the chosen name. The name is always an interpretation of culture.[233] The interpretation shapes both realities, individual and society, across time.

CORRELATIVE CONJUNCTIONS

Interpretation lies at the generative heart of culture. The interpretive act of naming contextualizes a personality by placing the human being in a specific conjunction of earthly and transcendent relations. Naming ceremonies make this clear. An Akwẽ-Shavante boy's naming ceremony involves two kin groups centered on his father and his mother's brother (more aptly put, two men who find themselves related as sister's husband and wife's brother). The boy's mother's brother's wife prepares a pie of maize, which the boy's father distributes to the boy's father's sister's household. Then, sitting before his mother's brother, the young boy is dressed in a *sō'brezu* necklet and given a name.[234] The mother's brother and sister's son are now bound in a formal relationship. The boy receives a new name when he enters the bachelors' hut prior to initiation. At initiation, he will take on a third name, and he takes on a fourth name when he assumes the age-set status of a mature man. "Each name is supposed to cancel out previous ones."[235]

An Akwẽ-Shavante girl, on the other hand, does not receive her name in a kin-based ceremony. Her name is bestowed on her by the community as a whole in a public ceremony that makes no reference to lineage divisions.[236] Women generally have one name only, which they receive at a much older age than that at which boys receive their names.

David Maybury-Lewis is unclear as to the function of names among the Akwẽ-Shavante. He notes that names are not heard in everyday use. They do not seem to identify or classify individuals or clan affiliations. Nor do they seem clearly linked to any system of statuses. "Names are not therefore attributes of the person who bears them."[237] In fact, the *process* of giving names is more important than the names themselves, perhaps because "they bring that person into certain relationships with other people."[238] Because of the nature of relationships opened to a named (interpreted) individual, a person who has passed through the naming process is mature, no matter what the functions of the name he or she possesses.[239]

Many cultures recognize that, as a person changes by passing through different conjunctions of relations along the course of life, he or she acquires new names and sheds old ones. For instance, a Bora receives a temporary nickname at birth, a classificatory true name at adolescence (which places a male in metonymic relationship with his clan and his father and a female in that relationship to her paternal aunt). When children are born to them, individuals receive an additional, "less beautiful" name. Finally, in old age, a Bora receives an "ugly" name.[240] The naming feast at adolescence is celebrated with the greatest fanfare: intoxicating beverage, ritual dances and sports,[241] the recitation of myths, and the baptism of children. Deliberately reenacting the gestures of the mythical hero who performed the first baptism, the chief of the *maloca* pronounces each adolescent's name. Family members ceremonially repeat the names. After exchanges and the use of tobacco, powdered pepper, and coca, the participants and guests wash themselves, vomit up tobacco juice, and don new clothes. Dances and mythic songs continue throughout the night. The transmission of names can only take place in the most important *maloca*s, which are called "the houses of the dance floors of *asái*, a kind of palm."[242] The ceremony installs the newly named individual in a symbolic situation of social relations and supernatural forces represented in the items arranged for the occasion.

The conjunction of relations within which one is set during the naming process has moral weight. This conjunction is the normative order of experience, which makes it possible to define, in clearer terms, one's existence in the more inchoate domain of the moral order.[243] Although the Kaingáng clan system was no longer in existence in 1967,[244] Ursula Wiesemann argued that there still existed residual semantic categories that help distinguish the names for the clans of one moiety from another.[245] The term *viji* designates a complex of names given to a child. To each type of *viji* there correspond body-paint markings used on ceremonial occasions. The complex of birth-names and the corresponding markings on the body both bestow certain specific powers on individuals and protect them from forces not in their possession. The *viji* is considered "bad" if it consists of only two names, "good" if it possesses many names — that is, many spiritual relationships associated with avoidances and periods of seclusion. The ritual avoidances, based on the set of particular names, form the foundation not only of proper behavior but of moral choice. A specific quality of reflection must ground all moral action. Action is moral when it is based on knowledge gained from reflecting on ordered experiences, properly arranged in conformity with the meaning of one's name. The order of that experience is normative. Moral discernment applies to the choice of action[246] and the knowledge gained in reflecting on one's normative order of experience.[247] Personal and public morality are inseparable in such a view.

The power of a personal name does not organize the structure of the personality into a static configuration; rather, it launches the individual into the trajectory of relations (mythic, supernatural, ancestral, historical) at the point in time when the cosmic and social forces are aligned in a way similar to the disposition of forces in his or her own personality. The act of discerning this configuration guarantees that a personal name is always an interpretation, an act that gives rise to culture[248] and that therefore shapes the individual just as all acts of culture do.[249] The naming ceremony brings into visible as well as audible being the set of inner correspondences through which the universe becomes accessible even to the most idiosyncratic of personal dispositions.

WHAT'S IN A NAME? THE ACHIEVEMENT OF CULTURE WITHIN THE PERSON

The philosophical status of personal names across cultures is by no means clear.[250] Personal names are not categories, in some cases, but descriptions of subjective states proper to specific moral actors.[251] For instance, the Panare bestow names only on human beings, dogs, and certain celestial bodies.[252] Stars represent the visible aspect of the supernatural realm, whose invisible aspects (for example, the forest spirits) are not named but merely classified. The names of stars are public and comprise a closed set. The names of dogs belong to a private and open set of names. The Milky Way (Toëpinkomune) is a collection of unnamed stars representing the dead in general. The named stars represent individual mythic beings.

There are four sets of human names. They are "the names of the very first Panare who came out from ten caves in the Upper Cuchivero Basin after their creation by the demiurge Manataci."[253] Panare names do not identify individual personalities. Rather, they describe in a general way the social status of the bearer: male or female, initiated or not. The context of the name use will also reveal whether the initiated individual belongs to the category of affines or consanguines. According to Jean-Paul Dumont, the enunciation of one's name "aims at establishing a conversation," which provides further information (e.g., kinship terms or periphrases) intended to clarify individuality. Naming guarantees cultural exchange, conversation, and significance: "The names are used to delimit the frontiers of . . . cultural order."[254]

In many cases, however, it becomes difficult to distinguish between categories and personal names, especially when one takes into account the entire sweep of mythic and historical time appearing in a name. Some patterns of naming, such as the Bororo case below, illustrate how personal names can designate a category that includes heroes, places, mythical actions, body decoration, human individuals, and powers acquired at specific moments of the life-cycle. Although some of these meanings transcend the social order, every item in the category represents the same configuration of forces, moments of similar meaning in the otherwise fluid space and time of being.

The importance of place in connection with name has surfaced already. In the examples presented, name can be transmitted only in the proper place. In addition, the senses of the person's body, the locus of the individual's being in this world, are arranged by the meaning of sound, that is, of the person's name. Furthermore, the body, as the place of the personality in life, is the symbolically structured space within which the name resides. Such is the case in cultures where the name lodges permanently in the marrow of the shin-bone.

The name is associated with place in another, more essential way. The name itself is often a toponym.[255] For example, central Brazilian men's names are not only associated with the ceremonial plaza, the central stage of symbolic life, but "people are said to enter their names when they receive them and to leave them when they pass them on to others."[256] The name shapes the personality because the person is surrounded by the sound of his or her name. Just as a person can be set within a physical space whose architectural structures symbolically order the experiences of the senses, the person is set within the meaning, the configuration of relations, of his or her personal sound, the name. Life is acted out within that presence, the essential sound-structure that is one's constant context.

The practice of naming is an important clue in deciphering Boróro anthropology. The Boróro person is understood to exist in a fluid space-time context that escapes rigid structural models and is best understood through the transformations recognized by the Boróro themselves in their symbolic language.[257] Physiological processes are linked to ceremonial and social processes through ties in the custom of naming.[258]

Boróro personal names are bestowed in special ceremonies whose actions include the protective covering of the body with feathers, the perforation of the lower lip (in the case of boys) and earlobes, and the protection of the soft spots of the head.[259] The naming ceremony takes place at sunrise in the center of the plaza. The names themselves, the *Iedaga-mage*, represent a certain circular and hierarchical order of social roles and prestige. This hierarchy of privileges derives from the association of the names with the actions of Iedaga (lit., "my name-giver"), a Boróro hero responsible for providing knowledge of the techniques of burial, including all forms of festival decorations and body paintings.[260]

Boróro personal names, *Iedaga-mage*, are mythical place names associated with heroic actions. When properly rotated, these place names configure a circular pantheon, which is reflected in the shape of the Boróro village.[261] Individuals, then, are places symbolically named and decorated, the loci of the transformative actions found in myth. In this name (in this mythical place replicated in the space of the body, the house, and the village), women and their husbands procreate children for each hero. Their names allow them to recreate the heroic acts that created culture. Boróro mythical heroes are fabulous hunters who never die because they reconstitute themselves in the places, the living bodies, of their descendants. Conversely, the true identity of the living individual lies within the meaning, the name, of the mythic hero. Thus a Boróro man can exclaim, "I am Jerigi Otojiwu. I am this hero!"[262]

The bestowal of Boróro names is associated with the life of consciousness and with social roles.[263] Consequently, names are associated with language, with reflective thought, with understanding, and with the places where these activities are located — the head, the tongue, the eyes, and the heart. Although time and space are fluid, one's name fixes a person in the dynamic sequence of the heroic events that create culture. In this way, one's name helps one cope heroically with unforeseen contingencies. This explains the great care taken in choosing the right name. For the same reasons, a child may receive several names.[264]

Another important aspect of the Boróro man is associated with the name of the penis sheath. Potentially destructive temporal modes manifest in dreams and in the growth of female hair are offset by personal names. In addition, however, the process of giving names to penis sheaths counterbalances the potentially negative effects of change. Penis-sheath names are associated with certain plants, the sun, and fire. For the young male, the process brings the ability to procreate children.[265] The presentation of the penis-sheath name not only permits one to procreate children and to make cotton strings for one's wife, but it also entitles one to begin learning how to manipulate the souls of humans, animals, and plants. That is, having become one's name (the place where heroes once acted powerfully to create the foundations of culture), one can ceremonially replicate those acts in order to recreate culture. For example, his penis-sheath name spiritually empowers a young man so that he can perform the dangerous but obligatory task of dancing, singing, and eating on behalf of those who have recently died "and who transform themselves into the souls of animals and of plants ceremonially represented during the funeral." [266] For these services the named dancer receives magical items, more personal names, bows, and arrows.

The deceased Boróro's personal names, nicknames, and penis-sheath names are no longer mentioned. Instead, the names of the hunt of the dead, *iebio-mage*, are used. Personal names of deceased Boróro are applied to new living beings only when the dead person's bones have powdered.

To summarize the wealth of meaning invested in names — in the connection of their audible form to the visage of the soul, in the ceremonial process of their transmission, or in their inherent spatial and historical structures — is impossible. By touching upon a few illustrations of names in such a way as to suggest their deep meaning and coherence, this section intends to invite further inquiry. The important point is this: whether it is used as a syntactic element,[267] as an index of social order, or as a conjunction of relations, only the fully religious value of a name in each culture can reveal its true nature. The proper name[268] is a symbol whose most ample meaning transcends the individual. The bestowal of a name is a quintessential act of culture; that is, it is a sacramental interpretation of the sacred.[269] For this reason, the name draws the person identified with the dynamic significance of its sound into a pattern of meaning beyond his or her immediate experience. A name's lexical, social, and psychological power reflect its sacred origin.

SOUND, THE EXCRETION OF PRIMORDIAL BEING

For the Baniwa, sound is a by-product of the first great change. The body-passages of Kuai, the primordial being, extruded sounds as his form altered.

Sound is a vestige of the body of *Kuai*, the first body with passages and, therefore, the first body to pass through birth, growth, and death.

This is the sense in which all Baniwa song *(likaako)* is a distinctive feature of the mythic being Kuai. The supreme being Yaperikuli, who is associated with the celestial realm, "inseminates" the serpent Amaru with his thought. Until that moment, Amaru's form had been undifferentiated; that is, she had been a serpent of water without any opening in her body. No conceptual passage could distinguish her outer form from the omnipresence of her fertile inner reality. Without distinctions of this fundamental sort, neither conception nor the birth of the discrete moments of time that condition cosmic life and human knowledge could exist. Yaperikuli conceived Kuai by placing the crown of his head against the inchoate form of Amaru's body. Kuai is born through the opening that appears where Yaperikuli's head marks the vestige of his being on the indistinct form of Amaru. Much later, at the instigation of Yaperikuli, Kuai's body is burned in a cosmic conflagration. As he dies in flames, Kuai emits songs from his orifices. For instance, a frog song, "a short, tooting 'Moo!'," blurts from his anus at the same moment that a *paxiuba* tree sprouts from his anus (or umbilicus) to connect earth to sky.[270] Another example is the *maliawa*, probably the "white heron song," a male song, which tinkles as *Kuai* urinates. The *maliawa* is always the first animal song performed in any series of songs. The female counterpart of the *maliawa* is the *waliadoa*, the "young sister song," which is the sound of Kuai's tears *(idzake*, "tears" and "rain") and which produces the rain and river water.[271]

Through the meaning of sound, the Baniwa draw together body openings, sexuality, body functions, and modes of wetness into the symbolism of the same passing moment. This entire complex is organically related because it was emitted together with a sacred being's sound, now symbolized by song. Sound is the effluvium from passage, the inner contents of primordial being voided in time through the embodied instruments of change. Imitating the first fanfare of sounds extruded by being as it assumed distinct form in the passages of time, human songs, like the cumulative effluvia of body passages (ear wax, urine, feces), provide demonstrable evidence of change brought on by passing time. More than that, the meanings represented by occasional songs effect the very changes the songs signify since their performance marks the times and places of passage in which culture regenerates itself. The songs of Baniwa cultural performance are effective because they are the by-products of Kuai's body passages while, at the same moment, the burning body itself passes away. Songs performed in ritual are but the insignia of the first accompanying sounds excreted when being passed from its primordial mode to the multiple expressions of existence in the contemporary cosmos. This is why song is the great symbol of human culture. While human lives pass away in constant transition, the orchestration of human passages through the symbolic control of effluvia (including gas, feces, tears, semen, blood, and breath) generates culture, the interpretation of the meaning of the sacred in time.

Wright claims that "a more significant point can be made here," namely,

"that the *songs* which Kuai produces shortly after his birth *express* the reproduction of Yaperikuli's *soul*." [272] Yaperikuli's soul is described as a quality of
knowledge, a species of creativity that, expressed through Kuai, takes the
form of passage and growth. That is, song represents a new form of being, a
spiritual existence, audible but invisible. The meaning of song, spiritual
knowledge, has the power to "open" the body to increasingly profound
experiences of being in the world just as Yaperikuli's knowledge opened the
body of Amaru to conception and the birth of Kuai, the origin of all distinct
forms of existence. Kuai's body opened with sound to produce the earth and
all its specific places, both locales and bodies. In their turn, these localities
and bodies are opened and fertilized by the specific sounds of their inhabitants, human and animal. For their part, animal and human bodies are fertilized, through their opened passages, by the culture- and species-specific
sounds of language and music. Thus, cultural forms and the forms of given
species perpetuate themselves through time, reproduction becoming a kind
of communication of sound through time. Open bodies produce the sounds
of languages and musical instruments, which, in their turn, let humans
create new offspring at the moment of conception and produce a new generation of open offspring at the time of initiation. The sounds also open the
earth, fertilizing fields and wild fruits. In this mysticism of openness, sound
becomes the principal expression of change, the passage through openness.
Together, openness and sound create new, reproductive levels of reality. [273]

In different ways in other cultures, sound is imagined to be a by-product
of the passing of sacred beings. One example from the Ayoreo will be enough
to illustrate the similarity of the idea to that expressed in Baniwa myth and
the contrast of its creative expression with the imagery of the Baniwa. The
Ayoreo of the central part of the Chaco Boreal in Bolivia and Paraguay
recount their origins in myths called *kucáde kíke uháidie*, "the cyclical vestiges of things." Each myth includes two parts: stories *(eró)*, followed by one
or more sacred songs (called *saúde* when used for curing illness and *paraga-
pidí* when used to prevent sickness). The term *kucáde kíke uháidie* underlines the capacity of the song-chants to make present once again the powers
of primordial events and personages. Myth-chants, the debris of withdrawn
beings, are fragments of sacred time, which, by its very nature, is recurrent
and as powerful as it was in the beginning. [274] The ancestors, *nanibaháde*
("ancient men") or *nanibaháde nupabenháni* ("men from ancient times now
turned into dust"), left these myth-chants behind when they were transformed into the various creatures of the earth. Thus, each important animal
species and cosmic phenomenon has its myth-chant that recounts its origin
and leaves its medicinal "vestige" of song. [275] The transformation of the first
beings produced all the creatures that exist in the world. The only primordial
beings that were not transformed were the ancestors of human beings. "The
Ayoreo derive from precisely those mythical ancestors who did not change,
or become metamorphosed, but remained in human form." [276] That is why
humans have no songs of their own, no cyclical vestiges of their transformation. All the songs of human culture are imitations of beings who have trans-

formed into spirits. The myths that recount these transformations are dangerous since the chanter who recounts a myth runs the risk of suffering the same tragic fate as the primordial figures. Only *igasitáde*, persons who are specially prepared, may recount the myths and sing the curing chants.

It is noteworthy that the Ayoreo associate the sacred songs of the primordial beings with their transformation, with change, and, therefore, with the passage of time. For example, at one time the sky, Gaté, and the earth, Numí, lived together. However, because the people on earth urinated on the face of the sky, Gaté separated himself from Numí, saying, "I am going to look for a place to live because I am fed up. People show me no respect." [277] The sky then retreated to where it is found today, "and each one, in his proper place, sang his *saúde* (curative chant)." [278]

The Ayoreo songs, like the Baniwa songs and trumpet music, are the time of change in the primordium. They are the residual traces of primal being left over when sky separated from earth or when effluvia passed from the dying body of Kuai. Their meaning, which once marked off the transition from the primordium to the world of change, now metes out the performances that constitute human life. [279]

THE VOCATION OF BEING AND THE DIRECTION OF SOUND

Sound plays a distinct role in scenarios of creation. It is always distinct. Sound arises from the presence of a specific being, as in the Ayoreo and Baniwa cases. It does not matter whether the being is known or recognized or not. Sound implies that the eventual revelation of a specific being is possible. The first presence of sound is creative in several ways. Essentially an invisible reality, the utterance of sound effectively announces the recital, the audible existence, of its own structure. The sung texts of creation scenarios frequently consist of no more than "I am, I am [the name of the supernatural being], I am." The very fact that the being makes an audible sound reveals its presence. The very sound of the name in song performs the function of a revelation of the nature of the being. It also calls into being a new disposition of spiritual existence, that of the hearer. Perhaps this was the thrust of Pierre Laromiguière's fundamental epistemological hypothesis that "the faculty of hearing is the first faculty of the soul." [280] Furthermore, since audible sound always has the potential of being heard by particular beings, sound always possesses the character of direction. Sound is pointed. It has a bearing, even if that direction cannot always be controlled. [281] For these reasons primordial sound can always be called a vocation, a calling out of being to specific forms of existence.

For the Kari'ña, every sound is a power that constitutes a species *(wara)*. [282] Consequently, every species has a unique sound, its language. This invisible sound is actually the true form of all the particular animals, especially birds, in a given species. [283] It is true that every *wara* (sound-species) has a particular body form, which it will assume from time to time. This form is called *tamu* or *tamurü*, meaning the mythical progenitor associated with that species. [284] The *wara* is called forth from its invisible existence as a symbolic form of sound to live its transitory animal existence as the name-form of a mythical prototype *(tamutu)*, which is taken as game in the hunt. Then it reassumes a "hidden" existence in human form. The *tamurii* (the mythical ancestor who is the master of each *wara*) could assume more than one form at the beginning of time, but today's animals have only one particular manifestation.

The cosmogonic sound, which called the universe and its species into being, is not the only example of a creative call. Many cultures recognize that part of an individual's constitution is called into existence by a unique sound or song acquired as he or she matures to a new state in life. The sound that proclaims a new identity, a vocation, is tantamount to a new act of creation. Anthony Seeger asked himself why both individual and group singing are so important in Suyá society. One important step toward an answer was his examination of the mythic meaning of sound. Both individual songs *(akia)* and group songs *(ngere)* are learned from a specialist who has the power to hear the songs of animals, fish, bees, trees. The teacher sings the songs under his breath in a single, whispered performance. Then, in the case of the *akia*, the individual man who receives the song stands up and sings it. It will always be associated with his name. In fact, he becomes identified by his song. The *ngere*, however, becomes identified not with a name of an individual but with a name-based ceremonial group.

The structure of both sorts of Suyá song is a set of distinct episodes that suggest the plot-outline of a creation myth. Like the chaos of preformal beginnings, the first episode is called *kwā kaikaw* ("without substance"). This part of the song consists of nonsense syllables, *kaikaw-kumeni* ("really without substance").[285] The structure of the song begins to move into a more ordered realm of sound during the next episodic section, which is called *sinti suru* ("approaching the name"). At this point, words are sung and actions occur, but they are not strung together as a narrative. That is, images appear but they do not manifest the temporal mode of a story taking place in consecutive time. "Typically *[sinti suru]* will state an action but will not name the animal or plant that performs the action. It literally does not 'tell the name.'"[286] The next episode is the climax of the song. Fittingly enough, it centers on the revelation of a name and is called *sinti iaren* ("telling the name"). The pronunciation of the name is the central feature of the creative performance. The same is true in creation narratives when the creative word, uttered by a supreme being who evokes the universe or by masters of species, calls forms into existence by name. During this central episode of Suyá song, the name of an animal is pronounced. The song itself is identified by this animal name. The last part of the song structure is the *kuré* (coda; lit., "end"). In performance this entire structure is repeated—a duplication consonant with the dualistic nature of Suyá society, which is divided into two ceremonial moieties.

Music shapes society and its structures because it replicates the sounds of sacred being.[287] Songs and names intoned in ritual performance broadcast the creativity of mythic action. Even in the mouths of human actors, these call-imitations transmit power to evoke the appearance of the forms of social and individual order.[288]

ACCOMPANIMENT: SOUND AND THE AFFECTING PRESENCE OF ANOTHER

Underlying all aural aesthetics is the conviction that sound is a witness to a species of being that is of its own making. Sound makes for company. To hear a sound is to be in the presence of another being.[289] This has already been demonstrated in two ways. First, cosmogonic sound calls other beings into a new state of existence. Second, the intrinsic directedness of sound creates a spiritual disposition, a mode of being in the world, associated with hearing. For this reason, sound becomes the effective instrument for achieving the coincidence of opposites needed to transcend the state of contradiction and enter the plethora of being beyond. By bringing such transitions to pass, sacred sound becomes a key to the experience of the fullness of being.

The Shipibo hear a flute's sound when a soul *(kayá)* enters or exits the body during the night. The *kayá* is a kind of alter ego which wanders from the sleeper's body. While it journeys it continues to play a flute. During the soul's absence, in fact, it is dangerous for the flute not to sound. If the music does not accompany the soul's travel, the soul will be lost.[290] Sometimes a hunter may shoot the soul as it flies through the air. If he shoots with a shotgun which makes a loud report, the soul plummets to the ground in the form of a large stork. "In that case the sleeper will be left a corpse." [291] The Shipibo maintain a stringent association between the soul, the shadowlike image of the body which is present in the body during waking life, and the meaning of air forced through the flute to make sound. Music and the life of the human soul are intimately bound together.

Since all sound in this cosmos is distinct, even if the distinctions may overrun one another and become noise, every sound is the presence of a specific other, potentially recognizable if still unknown. Consequently, every sound offers the possibility of a discovery. For example, each Apinayé *me-galó*, the soul's visual image which wanders at night and is seen in dreams, has a song peculiar to it. A competent person sings the song to lure the lost soul back to the body. When such songs do not succeed in calling back the soul, they become laments, which "are known to the Apinayé in great numbers." [292]

The Canelos Quichua exploit sound's ability to disclose the presence of specific beings. They employ special sounds, particularly the repetitive drone of drum snares, to bring dreams to human beings.[293] Indeed, the helper spirits that live in one's torso are droning insects (like bees). They evoke dream images, powerfully immersing individuals in mythic time.

Because sound is distinct and associated with the presence of a specific being, it can proclaim the revelation of a specific divinity. In the height of possession, expressed in African religious ideas as mystical marriage but in Afro-Brazilian religion as a parent-child relationship, a young girl's body is taken over by an *òrìsà*, a divine being. At the moment when this occurs, the òrìṣà lets out a shout *(ilá)* — a specific cry, unique to each òrìṣà, that permits its recognition. It is a kind of call which demands attention, recognition, and ritual devotion in the form of specific music and rhythms.[294]

SYMPHONIC ARRANGEMENT OF EXISTENCE

The copresence of beings through their sounds allows for compositions of being, unions of opposites, calendars, and other complicated orchestrations of the forms of existence. The symphonic arrangement of existence allows human beings to approximate the fullness of being, that is, to bring the myriad forms of being close together in culture, the creative center of human existence.

Sound possesses a calendrical capacity that industrial societies associate only with mathematical units. This is why music is so effective in properly situating an individual within the flow of time. The calendrical capacities of sound explain why songs offer mastery over the passage of time, especially control of the temporal rhythms of weather manifest in rain, sun, drought, and temperature. Among the Desana, sound has this all-encompassing ordering ability because, paradoxically enough, it is a prime manifestation of the inchoate energy *(bogá)* that pervades every realm of the cosmos. In the form of a serpent-conduit that runs through the center of every conceivable scale of space (from the Milky Way to the brain in the skull), the *bogá* produces perceptible sound waves. Said one Desana, "The sounds want to activate something, but we don't know what it is." [295] The statement is an admirable summary of the association between sound and revelation. Because it is a symptom of all-pervasive energy, sound can orchestrate different orders in ways that are startlingly complex. For example,

> The Desana have some twenty musical instruments, mostly wind and percussion, a selection of which is played on ritual occasions. Each instrument is associated with a certain ritual, a certain time of day, a certain age-group, and a certain animal. Furthermore, the sounds of each instrument are classified by color, smell, and temperature and are said to produce specific types of vibrations which, by affecting a particular part of the brain, transmit to the audience a specific, culturally coded message. For example, a particular large flute is played only by adult men; its long-drawn sounds are said to have a male odor, a very strong yellow color, and a very high temperature; the melody is said to be of a merry kind and is associated with the image of a multitude of fish running upriver to the spawning beds. The vibrations produced by the sounds are said to trigger a message which refers to childrearing, especially to breast-feeding during the first year of life. Another example is this: a small whistle is blown by adolescent boys early in the morning when they bathe in the river before dawn. The odor of the tune is said to be male, the color is red, and the temperature is hot; the tune evokes youthful happiness and the taste of a fleshy fruit of a certain tree. The vibrations carry an erotic message to a particular girl.[296]

EXISTENCE AS WEEPING AND DANCING: THE PROPER RESPONSE TO CREATIVE SOUND

Weeping and dance in South America illustrate the religious foundation of the cultural response to being. Mindfulness of meaning is that proper response, a mindfulness never detached from the meaningful sound to which one responds. Consciousness of meaning is an interpretive act, drawing that reality into cultural life. Culture, the suitable reply to the presence of the sacred in sound, is the performed interpretation of its meaning.

Performed weeping answers to the awareness that emotion is significant.[297] Weeping can be a response to nostalgia or to destructive fury. The first weeping, described in myth, is the reaction of mythic beings to the wholeness lost in the passing of the primordium. Weeping occurs in the hiatus between two realms of being. Accordingly, symbolic weeping by humans is the proper response to the meaning of nostalgia in all its forms. Ritual weeping overcomes the divisions between separate forms of beings by linking divided spaces and times. By responding to the nostalgic image of the integrity of being, weeping recreates, in the significant emotional form which shapes society, the meaning of the wholeness for which it longs.

A few examples make the point clear.[298] The transitional quality of Tapirapé women's weeping originated with the sounds of bird-beings after the cosmic destruction by fire. Women sing lamentations and weep for the dead at sundown. In general, contemporary Tapirapé sing sacred songs of the first birds at transitional times of the day. The *kaó*, festive songs, are sung most appropriately at sundown and sunup.[299] Among the Cuna, both male and female singing and weeping "link and effect transitions between domains that are otherwise quite distinct and sometimes opposed."[300] Women's singing stands out as particularly effective in major rites of passage constituting the person. It is a weepy singing modeled on mourning, the singing that mediates between life and death as well as between heaven and earth.[301] Similarly, the Akwẽ-Shavante mark transitions of status by performing ritual weeping.[302] As Maybury-Lewis observes, "[R]itual weeping in situations such as I have described is a *rite de passage*."[303]

Ritual weeping may be a response to the significance of other emotions, such as blind fury. The separation of forms that occurred at the passing of the primordium is repeated in initiation. Not infrequently, ritual weeping marks phases of the rites. For example, during the Guayakí boys' initiation ceremony, groups of women sing in a mournful way, *chenga ruvara*. The weepy singing drives the fathers of the male initiands into a frenzy of violence, and they attack the choir of women. This reenactment of destruction is essential to the proper performance of the rite. The men are said to be *by-iä*, a state in which their *by* (their "nature," or name) has left them. They no longer possess a name-nature and become dangerous, vengeful. In a rage, they seize their bows and arrows and threaten the lives of young men.[304] Without names, human nature is no longer recognizable. It becomes unbridled, losing its distinctive order. The human order is a response to meaning made present in the sound of names. Without names, that ordered response of culture is impossible. Responding to the significance of catastrophe made present in the weeping songs of women, Guayakí culture symbolically works itself into the frenzied fury of primordial destruction, which made possible the initiation of this world.

During Guayakí initiation, boys sing sacred songs for the first time. The mature men, some distance away, respond with their own chant. Following the logic of copresence, the men's sounds are added to the choral weeping of women, the mothers of the initiates, who sing the sacred *chenga ruvara*. This "weeping greeting" accompanies every important moment of transition from one state of being to another that occurs by means of a symbolic death.[305] The singing contest between the three groups eventually escalates to a climax of violent, cacaphonous chaos.

Dance is the proper response to the significance of movement in space. Specific dances interpret the meanings of particular kinds of movement first made by primordial animals, supernaturals, and other characters of myth. For example, in the Kari'ña view, dance *(u.ba)* is ultimately the state induced by song, the strings of sounds that created the world's entities. The first movements of sound-forms created the bodies that move in space. Humans repeat these creative sounds in ritual songs. This makes clear why the word *u.ba*, "dance," also designates "existence." Thus, *uwa* means "I am dancing," or, simply, "I am." Existence is the inevitable result of the utterance of these creative sounds, the movement of true but invisible realities. Thus, dance (existence) "possesses the power to create forms and to effect the identification of the being who invokes and dances with the being who is invoked and 'danced.' "[306]

For the Kari'ña, the generic supernatural forces of *a.bare* (specific song or power) and *u.ba* (dance, the deliberate moving that is a creative existence in time) "become a particular being of a particular species *[wara]*."[307] *A.bare* (specific song) is the foundation for *ba.ra* ("likeness, identity"), which gives the world a discernible, meaningful order of relations. This audible (but invisible) fixed point provides for the comparison of resemblance and difference. The sound is meaningful and connective of realities because of events that took place in *uba.poro* (mythic time; lit., "ancient dance"). This is why "dance" can express what creative existence is. "This means that the celestial heroes *[uba.porompo;* lit., "ancient dancers"] made everything through the power of their dance . . . and that all visible creation (earth) is the magical work of primordial dancers."[308]

Kari'ña dances and enchantments are only effective in complete darkness, when there is less divisibility between forms. For example, in complete darkness, snakes come onto the land and become venomous, bringing the wisdom with which they poison human beings, thereby effecting the transitions of ritual death. In water, snakes are innocuous, but at night people and serpents take on the forms of supernatural being. The invisibility accorded by darkness is the sacrament of indivisibility, wherein all forms are possible because none is separate and discernible from another.[309]

MARCHING IN TIME TO THE MUSIC

Music, rather than language, is the "primary modeling system" organizing human bodies. This argument, proposed by the musicologist John Blacking, applies to the cases reviewed here. The way music organizes the body, as well as the aesthetic and emotional tones of meaning inherent in the expression of musical order, together constitute a principle for organizing relationships within society. In addition, the model of the musical organization of the body coordinates, on the most general level, forms of symbolic action within society. "Music is a metaphor of feeling that draws on man's own nature for many of its forms. . . . The point is that human feelings are also structured and in the transformation of feelings into patterns of sound and vice versa the innate structures of the body play a part in creation and interpretation." [310] Myth bestows on music a symbolic value and contravenes the tendency of music "not to represent anything but itself." Myth renders music referential, intelligible (even if untranslatable), significant, and revelatory. As a sacred symbol, music possesses the power to represent the supernatural mode of being it signifies. This enables it to serve as the model for culture — as a template, that is, for the generative relations between the forms of animal, plant, human being, space, and time.

In an analysis of two kinds of Suyá song, Seeger argues that music in South American cultures is not primarily aesthetic or incidental, that it "is a fundamental part of social life, not merely one of its options." [311] The performance and structure of *akia* reflect the construction of the individual personality. It has associations with key places, times, and relationships that are instrumental in the construction of an individual's identity. For instance, the *akia* is sung only by individuals to their sisters who are separated from them by uxorilocal marriage; it is sung in two parts in front of the eastern and western men's houses, etc. The *ngere* are songs sung in unison by groups. The groups reflect larger social divisions into ceremonial moieties, for they are never sung by kinship-based groups. In other words, the social structures constituting the individual and the community are reflected in the structures of the music. However, Seeger correctly insists on this important point: the structure of the music is not a simple reflection of the structures in society. "The simple reduction of one domain to another," he writes,

> is always a dangerous exercise and in this case quite wrong. I would argue that it is musical events that create the dualism of Suyá social organization. Suyá moieties are purely ceremonial. They are partly defined through the *ngere* they sing together. The structure of the music, far from being a reflex, is part of the creation and continual recreation of the dual features of Suyá society. Thus the dual structure of music is fundamental, not reflexive. What is expressed by singing is crucial, not incidental. . . . This observation is supported by the universal participation in extended musical occasions. . . . We should begin asking what it is about music-making that is so important in all of these societies.[312]

At one point in Tukano mythic accounts, animals plot to eat people while the people feast and dance. The divinity Yepá Huaké asks Wejké (tapir) how he intends to kill the people. Wejké responds that he intends to kill them with a whistle. When Yepá Huaké asks for a demonstration, Wejké plays, and the earth opens up and nature goes to pieces. Yepá Huaké asks to see the whistle in order to take it away from Wejké. Yepá Huaké announces, "You are not going to eat people, on the contrary people will be eating you." [313] He makes Wejké exchange whistles with Emo (monkey), whose whistle is much smaller. At Yepá Huaké's direction, Emo takes the tapir's whistle and climbs into the heights of a tree. Wejké is left with the tiny whistle, which makes a pitiful sound and causes him to cry. Yepá Huaké banishes Wejké to the forest.

The Barasana recount a similar story of an exchange of musical instruments between animals, the tapir and the howler monkey, and a concomitant rearrangement of the animals' spatial domain. The meaning of sound, revealed by sacred figures and their music, corresponds to the ranking of social groups and ritual roles. The sound of music generates not only the spatial and temporal conditions of culture but divisions of the social order as well.[314] The periodic opening and closing of the animals' orifices (mouth and anus) symbolically orchestrate sounds in relation to specific times (day and night, seasons). In the exchange of voices between sloth and monkey, for example, sound correlates the simultaneous presence of different kinds of being manifest in the meanings of wetness, body openings, human performance, temperature, filth, darkness, height, and the seasons.

A study of lower-class African-American communities in Colombia and Ecuador illustrates how particular music constitutes both specific social contexts and networks of kin and friends which define the individual.[315] The marimba dance (currulao), the wake for a dead child (chigualo), the wake and burial of an adult, the celebration of a saint's feast day, and the dance hall fiesta are characterized by different kinds of music, which serve as focuses for a whole range of symbolic actions that configure quite different relations and attitudes. The choice among musical styles and settings manipulates strategic change so that music creates alternative social forms, encouraging social experiment and change.

LANGUAGE, THE NEGATION OF SOUND; SOUND, THE UNDOING OF LANGUAGE

The relationship between sound and language is a negative one in several ways. Sound is always meaningful and whole. Speech threatens that integrity by fracturing the sound so that meaning is parceled out one syllable, one word, one sentence, or one spoken idea at a time. Sound, a presence that is always meaningful, can be fractured by human language in such a way that a person can even use sound to "speak nonsense."

A second antipathy between speech and sound has to do with their origins. Human speech, insofar as it is significant, consists of sounds appropriated from other beings and animals. Human speech, like fire, is often seen as having once been the possession of other beings. Indeed, the sound of speech was a statement of the meaning of other modes of existence. Human speech alienates the meanings of sounds from their original sacred presence and separates the figures of speech from the sacred realm of primordial images. This is the corollary of the fact that speech implies a copresence. *Aura* is the Kari'ña word that designates human language, originally acquired by human beings by means of the *auran.puo*, the primordial words spoken by the beings who started life and prosperity on earth through the medium of their sound. These *uba.porompo* were celestial beings who descended to earth. Meaningful strings of syllables, the *auranko* (words, myths, discourse and so forth), were fashioned from their original sounds.[316] *Aura* means both human language and wisdom. Every mode of being (*uara; uaran; wara,* sound-species) derives its nature from its own *aura*. Every race and species of living things has its own language and wisdom. The privileged place human beings have in this world is based on *borrowed* power, in this case on the sounds borrowed from primordial beings and elaborated into meaningful strings of words. The power of human beings and their words can be maintained effectively only if the original integrity and meaning of the sounds is properly respected. That is why *nenbo* (obedience to omnipresent spirits) is the highest virtue.[317]

One might raise the question, Since the songs of the masters of animals performed at feasts are said to be *exactly* the same as at the beginning, how is it that they help define *human* culture? The answer must be sought in the quality of knowledge underlying performance. They are symbolic, remembered, mimed. The sounds do not arise from the essence of human being; rather, they are the presence of sacred beings as echoed in human reality. They are reflected in the symbolism of human culture and in the imaginative mode of human awareness. Like ceremonial ornaments imitative of the body marks of primordial dancers, the songs are deliberate fabrications. Fabrication allows for the extraordinary kind of reflection that occurs in religious performance. The senses are rearranged by the songs. People are remade in the image of sound. Human culture is always a performed interpretation of the sacred, creatively absorbing the substance of primordial forms into human existence.

The antithesis of sound and language may be seen in yet a third way. The full meaning of sound can dissolve the fragile arrangement of the separate parts of speech. A number of the above-mentioned religious assumptions about the nature of sound form the conceptual foundations for the widespread use of song for both the construction and destruction of human individuals and groups. According to Clastres, the Guayaki consider song a constitutive part of the human condition. Men and women sing different songs in different styles because male and female modes of existence embody different systems of values and different ways of being present in the world.[318] To this opposition of sexes manifest in sound corresponds an opposition in space and in economic relations as well. Ironically, sound and song are what allow one to overcome the restrictions placed on one's condition by language. Song allows one to dissolve one's separateness, one's assigned status and role in society, through, ironically enough, individual performance. The Guayaki celebrate sound as the negation of language, which separates spaces and individuals.[319]

The power of sound may be applied to the common destructive practice of harmful blowing, a magical technique used to debilitate an enemy. Sound can overwhelm the necessary staccato of human life effectively symbolized in an individual's speech. In such cases sound dissolves the personality by returning it to an inchoate condition. In this inarticulate state of being, like the one that preexisted creation, meaning is undifferentiated, no longer patterned in the ways required for human understanding. Unable to interpret meaning, the articulate structures of the victim collapse into chaos. For instance, the Waiwai couple the solvent power of sound with its specificity and power of approximation in their art of harmful blowing. The process involves singing magic songs that project one's magical blowing, the effective symbol of inarticulate and undivided breath, in specific, intended directions. The song is a compelling and conscious intention.[320] The Waiwai recognize two kinds of blowing, *tono* and *parawa*. *Tono*, meaning "to eat or devour flesh," involves the expulsion of one's breath while singing magic songs. Such action, when performed correctly, will affect the soul of the intended victim. The victim will die because his or her own soul is displaced by the invading and devouring soul.[321]

Parawa is a blowing performed at the time of cremation for the purposes of blood revenge.[322] One blows by imitating an animal sound and by singing a magical song. The father, brother, or spouse of the dead person removes some bones usually thigh- or handbones, from the cremated pile. The avenger pushes heated bones into a hollow bamboo tube that has been blocked on one end, and the tube explodes. The bamboo is then buried in a hole in the ground.[323] The soul of the intended victim hears the animal sounds that are imitated at the same time the blowing is performed. The victim's soul responds with the same sound. Sounds and songs serve as connective instruments between individuals in separated spaces.

In some cultures, speech is the ritual (i.e., the meaningful and controlled symbolic action) of killing sound. In such cases a primordial unison is slain and dismembered to form the phonetic bits that compose diverse sentences and languages. Speaking and sound are accomplished, according to the Kari'ña, through the power of breath, an indivisible and invisible reality. Saliva *(etako)* also figures as an important transformative medium and is likened to venom and fermented brew. Breath and saliva, two formless entities, take on specific form through the vehicle of the mouth. The human mouth during speech is likened by the Kari'ña to the serpent's mouth, whose fangs are the supreme image of wisdom and magic craft (in the sense of power). This image calls to mind the theme of the toothy vagina as the transformative locus where wisdom is available to the spirit who can cope with the treacherous passage through it.[324] The implication is that the words and sentences of speech are the products of an endless number of phonetic initiations, the death and rebirth of sound as its flow is interrupted and renewed in every syllable. Speech is an endless succession of ordeals for sound, which is ritually (i.e., in a controlled, symbolic, and meaningful way) divided into phonemes by the dismemberment of the otherwise formless breath and saliva by the teeth and tongue. The mouth and teeth devour and transform meaning. These instruments of consumption are always transformative. Their sacred role is no different in speech. Like breath and mouth, saliva is essential to the speech process, the image of the process is knowledge. The tooth, the wisdom it embodies, and deadly venom are all elements of knowledge shared with the serpent, the paradigmatic animal of the water domain. Saliva, especially when intentionally spit out, attracts spirits to it because it is a token-portion of their home realm. In Kari'ña parlance, the word *etake* (from *etako*, "saliva") means "by virtue of, through the means of, with the help of, by power of,"[325] showing that symbolic expression, especially language, derives its power from the passage through indivisible and formless conditions, such as the chaotic flood waters betokened by saliva but transsected by the spoken word.

FINAL WORDS ON SOUND

In the religious stances presented, sound is always significant because it originates in sacred beings. Particular sacred beings accompany the hearer. Their sound announces their presence. More than that, their sonic presence symbolically expresses their meaning in such a way that it summons the hearer to a new condition of existence. For this reason, sound always involves transition and change. This is also the reason why visible, audible, and saporous images can share the same structure or even be images of one another: they are presentations of sacred being, the same meaning that gives rise to the separate forms of their appearance. For instance, in Tukano accounts, the sounds made by the first-born mythic child are the tastes and visions of the hallucinogenic drink made from *cajpí (Banisteriopsis caapí),* "for as soon as the little child cried aloud, all the people who were in Diawi became intoxicated and saw all kinds of colors" just as one does when one takes *cajpí.* The divinity Yepá Huaké ordered that the child be ritually dismembered and a piece of his body distributed to each tribe. This is why, according to the Tukano, all neighboring peoples today possess *cajpí.* The various portions received and the rank order in which peoples received them accounts for the ranked divisions of social order as well as the differences in the quality of the color and the vividness of the supernatural images that appear in the visions of different groups.[326] The primordial meaning of being imbues all forms of existence, whether they be emotional, social, temporal, gustatory, fragrant, visual, or musical. At the same time, the inexhaustibility of the sacred origins of the cosmos assures a multiplicity of individual experiences and cultural forms.

Human life is always set in sound; that is, it is always situated in the condition of meaning that we call culture. Specific sounds comprise particular societies. The presences they announce identify and shape a society's values and social forms. Aside from specialized analyses of music and language, the study of values through the analysis of culture-specific symphonies of particular sounds (e.g., industrial sounds, highway noises, farm sounds, foot traffic, the creaking of construction materials, the rustling of wind on culturally prepared materials, the noise of particular machines, faunal sounds, and the culturally heightened sounds of "nature" artificially produced by fountains or pets) has not been a part of the comparative study of cultures. But this is precisely the hermeneutic strategy of the peoples of the eastern montaña and highlands of Peru when they evaluate the complex values of technological society expressed in the noise of industrial machinery. The metallic whining and screeching of heavy industry are the sounds made by the victims of Pishtaco, a supernatural monster who aids industrialists by capturing Indians. He sucks out his victims' body fat, the prestigious symbol of the power of incarnate life, in order to grease the machines of modern industry (airplane motors, car engines, launch engines). The sounds of modern culture prolong the moment of agony when Pishtaco squeezes and sucks the life out of the indigenous populations.[327] As seen in other cases mentioned earlier, this interpretation holds that sound is an embodiment of the violence of transition.[328] Furthermore, it not only identifies the anonymous sounds of industry with personal forces of human action and individual choice, but it offers a moral discernment of the values manifest in the sound.

Just as any profound consideration of the meaning of religious imagery must include an appraisal of the value of image in dream and delirium, so should the interpretion of deliberately performed sacred music be set within the context of an interpretation of all valuable sounds: name, speech, shouting, and din, as well as the subliminal sounds and background noises of a society. Looking at the significance of sound in all its forms, the interpreter may move closer to understanding the specific sonic aesthetic, the meaning of sound, that constitutes an individual of a specific culture.

SPATIAL IMAGERY CONSTRUCTING THE PERSON

Spatial imagery also helps compose the self-understanding that is characteristic and constitutive of human nature because human beings conceive of themselves in the image of space. This suggestion surfaced while analyzing the toponymous aspect of sound in personal names. The present section focuses more directly on spatial imagery that constructs the person. Awareness of the significance of the body as it extends through space expresses itself as a symbol system, a religious language of the body. More vivid is the converse statement: the body, imagically conceived, is a religious language of values used to understand all spaces constitutive of human life.[329]

PHYSIOLOGY AND BODY LANGUAGE

Several investigators of indigenous societies in Brazil have recently argued that the notion of person and the vision of the human body are the two basic paths to understanding the cosmology of these peoples.[330] The unique contribution and creativity of traditional Brazilian tribes is their rich notion of person, which is articulated with special reference to corporeality as a language of symbolic focus. In fact, these investigators insist that corporeality is the prime idiom for what outsiders call religion.[331] The processes of the personality, the physiological processes of the body, the dynamics of names, and the properties attributed to body substances and fluids are the social idiom as well. That is to say that, if one is to understand the logical structure of society, one must turn to the ceremonial or metaphysical plane on which society constructs the person over time.[332]

The body remains the center of mythology, the locus of transformational possibilities. Because of the sacred meaning of their spatial imagery in myth, humans and animals, as embodied beings, cannot be strictly opposed to one another.[333] "For societies like the Tukano, for example, the dominance of a supernatural plane establishes a mediation between Nature and Culture which practically dissolves their opposition." [334] In the light of the supernatural status and, in that sense, the fully symbolic language of the body, the distinction between "nature" and "culture" must be rethought.[335] Like the ceremonial plaza of many central Brazilian societies or the *maloca* of the northwestern Amazon, the individual body becomes the point of convergence for supernatural entities from every cosmic realm.[336] The physiological language of creation myths is applied to the organization and meaning of all created spaces — house, plaza, cosmos, ceremonial space. In short, the language of the body is used to reflect on the relations between all manner of beings within society and within the cosmos.[337] The capacity to reflect on meaning as it is imagined in a spatial mode constitutes human nature. It does not so much set the human body apart from the spatial universe as draw the human into the meaning of creation revealed in myth.

For these reasons, the body, its forms, and its decoration and adornment become a central theme of myth and ritual.[338] These authors call attention to a basic dualism in speaking of the body and those spheres to which body language is applied. This is the tension between the body's internal aspects (e.g., physical reproduction) and external aspects (e.g., ceremonial and social reproduction). They parallel this tension to the basic oppositional structure of central Brazilian (Ge) societies: the periphery of the village, which is the locus of domestic space, versus the central, public ceremonial plaza, which is associated with the activities of naming and performing public roles. The human body, in its internal aspects, is linked to blood, semen, and physical reproduction. Its outside and public aspects are tied to names, statuses and roles, body painting, ornamentation, and songs.[339]

In many cases, it seems unjustified to import too rigid a dualism. For example, the relationship of meanings between the inside (ceremonial plaza) and outside (periphery) of the village is the complementary reverse of that between the inside and the outside of the body. The internal, central plaza becomes the place par excellence of public display, whereas the external periphery is the locus of nourishment and reproduction. Furthermore, notions of the spatial construction of the person bring one into the realm of shared ideas, since bodies are not made simply of semen but of the spatially imaged powers that underlie the symbolic language structuring both person and society.[340] Among these powers is, for instance, the meaning of sound, of personal name. Names are consubstantial with the spaces they configure across time (village space, personal space, the space in which the hunt of the dead is carried on). Over time, the circulation of names throughout all dimensions of imaged social space encompasses both the inside and the outside of the village without rigid distinction between the two. Thus, when the fully symbolic range of meanings of spatial imagery is allowed to disclose itself, it proves unwarranted to make general conclusions about the existence of a single kind of dualism that would oppose all the values of public versus private and plaza versus periphery. The quality of tension and difference varies: from complementary opposites to alternations, reciprocities, simultaneous coincidences of opposites, contradiction of opposites, or other possibilities.[341]

Desana physiology is a language with which to understand the cosmos because physiology is a process common to both the universe and human beings. The universe is filled with semen in the form of the "yellow intention" of the creator, the Sun Father. This energy is present in every dimension of existence. Passing through the divine bone-penis, an *axis mundi* transfixing all the levels of the universe at the center, the "yellow intention" of the Sun Father fertilizes the cosmic uterus, Ahpikondiá.[342] Lightning is envisaged as the fertilizing ejaculation of the semen of the sun. The Milky Way is a wind current, the breath of the universe. The biosphere is essentially feminine, possessing *uhúri bogá*, feminine fecundity (*uhúri* means "to attract with the mouth, to suck in, to ingest something"[343]). The expression includes the magical sucking by which a curer removes sickness from his patient's body. The underlying idea is that the womb and the mouth suck in, or ingest, substances in transformative ways. In the case of the womb, the attraction and sucking of semen brings about a transformation into new life (i.e., conception). The attraction of the mouth of the curer and the sucking he performs draw the pathogen into a transformative enclosure (his mouth), which changes the nature of the illness-causing agent into something harmless or beneficial.

The human body and its physiological processes, then, together make a specific instance of an extraordinary cosmic process. Desana myth makes clear that the human body can serve as a basis for a ritual physiology—that is, a manipulation of body parts, substances, and fluids that transforms social groups and processes. For example, when the water turtle sees the first act of coitus it assumes the color of the vagina. Similarly, when the curassow sees the penis of the first man copulating with the first woman, he develops a red neck. Animal species and body forms are radically changed by the physical procedures of human bodies. It is from these primordial "animals" that the various groups of sibs, phratries, and exogamous linguistic groups descend. To arrange and manipulate animal body-forms in the primordial period is to establish a model of social group relations and an ecological network of relations linking humans to the surrounding world.[344]

People can *be* a category of space. The Panare use the names of headmen and kinship terms to designate space used for habitation. "[T]hey conceive of themselves as coextensive with the category of space."[345] Such a self-understanding is not unique to the Panare. The Toba also see human physiology as a kind of mythic geography. In the center, the chest, reside one's individual guardian spirits. Hair and nails, which grow and are detachable, house special concentrations of power. Heightened powers reside in one's body fluids, especially in blood and saliva. In the cure of disease, saliva is particularly powerful. It acts as an antidote to the evil effect of harmful spirits. Saliva manifests its spiritual power in the magic of fermentation, a process likened to the birth of a powerful and good spirit.[346] The voice is a particularly powerful instrument, regardless of the words it expresses. Song is efficacious. The mythical geography of the human body comes into play in a special way when the curer diagnoses and heals the disease of a patient. Evil is held to be located in certain parts of the body, from which the curer will isolate and withdraw the invading pathogen.[347] A curer's bodily secretions and fluids possess special power. The curer's long-term relationship with his or her helper spirits has heightened the powers present in the normal human physiology.

THE CONTAINER: SPATIAL RELATIONS OF BONE AND FLESH

Physiology emphasizes that the individual is a container whose life processes initiate relations that are organized by the senses, the body's capacities for meaning. During life the body is the spatial container of the soul. For example, the Canelos Quichua person is born with a human soul in the right shinbone, the *aya tullu*.[348] It is, then, significant that in certain myths a caiman chomps off the right leg of one of the heroes. The amputation amounts to a kind of soul loss.[349]

Even when certain faculties of individual life are dispersed because the fleshly envelope has decomposed, bone continues to serve as a container of essential faculties of life until it disintegrates into powder. The bones of the dead Boróro person, once the flesh has worn away after the first burial, are ceremonially cleaned and adorned with feathers. In the final stages of the funeral, they are painted and arranged inside the funerary basket, which is then buried. Only when the bones have powdered may the deceased's name be bestowed on a living person.

The extent to which a culture may view the person in the image of a container becomes clear when a Guayakí dies. It is believed that the *ové*, a particle of the Guayakí soul, prepares the death of a person well in advance.[350] It fashions a large earthenware pot and places in it all the parts of a person—bones, hair, excrement, skull, ashes. Setting the pot on a fire reduces the bones to ashes. When the moment arrives, the *ové* places the pot between the roots of a tree and shatters it. "It strikes, and the ashes of the skull penetrate into the mouth: then death arrives, then mortal sickness arrives." [351] Assisted by the birds of Thunder, the *ové* cracks the pot open, causing the bones, ashes, hair, and excrement to abandon the body of the living person and leave it lifeless. All this takes place "at the heart of darkness," that darkness of ashes first released from the kettle of Baiö at the beginning of time, when human beings were created.

A Guayakí person's bones are the seat and source of life. In one report, it was said about an old man ageing toward death that *ikä mano ruwy*, "the bones are almost dead."[352] Bones, as containers of life, are treated in a special way during funerals (after the flesh has been consumed by the mourners). Mourners burn the bones in a special fire, then ritually smash them to pieces, especially the skull. Lamentations of dead relatives stress the fact that kin properly struck and destroyed the skull with blows from their bow.[353] The words make vivid the image that the bones, especially the skull, have been beaten into the earth.[354] Pierre Clastres points out that this funerary action takes its model from the myth of the origin of human beings, the same myth that recounts the original release of night and death from their container. There, at the beginning of time, a young uninitiated boy smashed the clay pot of Baiö. By breaking it, he flooded the world with the ashes and darkness it contained.

SUCKING AND BLOWING

That bone contained the very first kind of life and is the source of all subsequent life is the view of the Baniwa. Their creator-transformer, Inapirikuli, the culture hero associated with the origin of human beings, was made entirely of bone. He had no flesh, a useless substance; rather, skin was attached directly to his bones.[355] Human beings not only share the substance of bones with their culture-hero maker, but they share speech and word with him. For it was his word that brought everything into being. With it he called into existence two companions, the first beings with bodies of flesh. These were the first two *pajé*, shamans. Each of the two companions embodied an essential power that makes fleshly life possible. Blowing and sucking are the two clearest manifestations of these powers. Dzuli, one of the incarnate companions of the culture hero spoke the proper words over food so that humans could consume food without dying. The second primordial shaman, Mariri, sucked objects out of the body: bones, hair, stones, and tiny bits of wood. In this way he made healthy life possible.[356] Thus the first beings of flesh made possible the sucking that is needed to cure the sick and the blowing that is essential to speaking and eating.[357] That is, the first fleshly beings brought about the two major modes of transformation with which the human container governs its relations with the outside world: expulsion and ingurgitation. These symbolic uses of the mouth can deliberately generate or destroy sets of relations.[358] These two powers over passages not only account for the origins of flesh — the specific form of the human container — but also initiate spiritual processes of meaning, which offer incarnate human life dynamism and self-control.[359]

DISEASE AFFECTS THE BODY

The meaning of the spatial imagery that constitutes the human person makes clear why disease is often associated with physiology, that is, with the container of human faculties. The invasion of beings into the body can provoke disease. The Siriono, for instance, attribute the cause of most diseases to the *abačikwaia*, "evil spirits" who enter the nose and mouth during sleep, especially when a person snores. The soul's absence from the person's own space also may cause sickness. The soul of a Siriono wanders during dreams at night; should it stay away, the individual would sicken and die. The violation of personal space by the breach of food restrictions and other taboos also renders the body vulnerable to penetrating pathogens.[360]

In a similar way, sickness among the Chiripá is caused by the presence of foreign elements inside the body. Foreign elements can be introduced into the body in two ways. Patients themselves may be responsible for the increase of imperfections within their "animal" souls. Because of improper behavior, these negative forces weigh the soul down and must be removed. The second way foreign substances enter the body is through the attack of "spirits of nature" who prey upon souls weakened by lack of piety.[361] In a slightly different scenario, the integrity of the Boróro person can be undone by magically manipulating plants whose souls are carnivorous animals. The animals enter the body and devour the eye, the tongue, and the heart of a Boróro, the loci, respectively, of reflection, speech, and understanding.[362]

The nature of space, especially the space of the body, determines the character of those diseases that are forms of possession. This is why the significance of sickness is so closely bound up with the religious meaning of physiology. If the possessing element principally manifests itself to the healing specialist in a visible way, the pathogen is probably a "superstition," a particle of material power never deconstructed in the cataclysm that closed the primordium. Leftovers from an earlier spatial world, these eccentric elements normally orbit the fringes of inhabited space in a harmless way. Wandering forest ogres, stones from mountains at the edge of the world, and poison ashes or darts [lying on paths in the far-flung forest] are among such elements existing on the distant periphery of this world. During an episode of sickness, however, these beings penetrate the center of living space in this world and become "visible" in the human body. On the other hand, if the pathogen announces itself to the curing specialist primarily in an audible way, then it is possibly the presence of a being whose primordial form of existence was utterly changed, that is, who was totally spiritualized in the process of withdrawal, sacrifice, or destruction. In either type of possession, the power or spirit of the pathogenic being invades the space of the body, the locus of the specific meaning of a person's experience of the world. The possessing agent reshapes, expels, or destroys the contents of that meaning.

PHYSIOLOGY: CONSTRUCTING THE BODY OF PASSAGE BY CONTROLLING THE PASSAGES OF THE BODY

The Yawalapíti techniques for changing the body devolve on the channels of contact and communication between the body and the wider cosmos. Rituals of fabrication manipulate substances that leave or enter the body through its orifices. Symbolic expulsion or ingestion of semen, food, tobacco, and blood, for instance, collaborate in the body's growth and strengthening. By controlling the entrances and exits of these substances, the body itself becomes an enclosure capable of controlling its own transformation. During initiation, youths must retain their semen by abstaining from sex. The retention of seed strengthens them. The construction of a new human being and the promotion of mature adolescents to the state of parenthood, however, requires the emission of semen in the act of sex. In another example, since it is believed that blood can collect in the stomach and make one ill, scarification opens wounds in the body envelope and encourages good health through bleeding. In a slightly different symbolic manipulation, those endangered by accumulation of blood should abstain from eating fish. These include fathers in couvade and menstruating women. The abstention from fish and the use of emetics cleans the body of fish and blood and induces the production of semen.

Every symbolic item passing in and out of the body creates an economy of relations. This is as true of waste as it is of speech. The consumption of food is one of the clearest examples of the way in which symbolic ingestive control fabricates a web of relations. For instance, it is only when a Kaingáng man has become mature (i.e., has "grown for a very long time") that he may eat the meat of the tapirs that he kills.[363] A special ritual meal celebrates this transition from the younger, këlú, status. Significantly, during this ritual meal the food that he eats has first been chewed by someone who loves him and then been mixed with charcoal from the burning of the tapir's bundled heart. Apparently it is quite common in ritual meals for a close blood-relative of the person being honored to chew the food first and then "cough it up" for that person to consume. Birds, in particular, are often eaten in this manner. According to information given to Jules Henry, eating food in this way increases the skill of the hunter. Since the man can eat his own game, he may now separate himself from the group in which he has lived for years and strike out on his own. He receives the license of economic autonomy through the mouth of a consumer who is fed with products from his hunt. Defined by the symbolic gesture of passing food through the transformative opening of the dependent consumer's body, the hunter can now establish an "autonomous" network of economic ties. His economic independence, however, is framed by dependence on consumption and constrained by the meaning underlying the control that defines it. The symbolic meaning of control gives the hunter's life the new value required to make him the center of an economic unit. Previously, no matter how skilled the hunter, he was dependent on others for game-food.[364]

CONTROLLING ONE'S DIET
Nourishment builds bodies as much by controlling the passage of time and space as by placing nutrients in the passages of the body. The mouth, like the womb, is an enclosure that sucks in powers and transforms them into beneficial, body-building forces. This is why the meaning of the symbolic control manifest in passing food through the mouth is a primary means of both physical and cultural construction.[365] The meaning of food, the relations entailed in its production and distribution, and the values manifest in table manners mark cultures as unique and distinguish different modes of being from one another.

According to the Kalapalo, human beings *(kuge)* distinguish themselves from the other categories of *ago* ("living things") by the foods they avoid eating. In fact, diet is an important attribute used to distinguish categories in the Kalapalo system of classification of beings.[366] In general, hierarchies, paradigms, and taxonomies are established by using cosmological terms, drawn from myth, which characterize physiology, states of being, and qualities of relationship.[367] All living beings participate as both consumers and consumed, the dialectical nodes of the food chain. These nodes permit differentiation into the separate categories whose order constitutes the cosmos of this age. "Put differently the consumption of food is given a uniquely Kalapalo meaning through symbols that constitute the Kalapalo world view."[368]

Because the mouth controls contact with the cosmic powers that order one's shape and meaning, the symbolism of diet distinguishes groups and qualities of relations within a given society. The Tapirapé observe a very complicated set of dietary restrictions, which have puzzled behavioral researchers because the actions appear to be "dysfunctional."[369] One's state of being is, to a large degree, keyed to what one eats or does not eat. Shifts in traits of age, sex, and temperament, as well as alterations in one's relationships, tasks, and intentions require changes in select foods and in the social patterns of their consumption. Complicated codes of color, smell, shape, and sound help coordinate these sets of taboos.[370] Some animals are too strong-smelling or loud for consumption by individuals in particular conditions. For example, men setting fish traps in streams cannot eat pumpkins; menstruating women cannot eat fish caught in conical traps. Even the proper functioning of culturally constructed spaces, such as fish-traps, are affected by what they "ingest" or avoid ingesting. If an electric eel is "swallowed" in a trap, the spirit of the trap will fall ill and be unable to make the sound necessary to "call" the proper fish and, consequently, the communal state of health will suffer.[371] Each individual is a finely qualified spatial image containing subtle arrangements of character traits. These arrangements are reflected in the foods that, under specific conditions, may or may not enter the individual body container. The ways one inhabits space — the cultural habits of selecting items for insertion into or exclusion from one space or another — become the marks of taste and distinction.

BUILDING A VESSEL, OR VEHICLE

Since human culture locates itself at the center of the spatial universe, where passage from one dimension to another occurs, the human space must accommodate itself to different species of time. The human being is able to pass through the center to different planes of being, and each passage requires a change of form, a rearrangement of the meaning of one's senses, so that one may survive within the different contexts of space and time. Rites of passage exemplify rearrangement of the spatial fixtures of the body. The body becomes a vessel, a container of life, which is, at the same time, a vehicle for passing through changing times.[372]

The clearest examples of the necessity of rearranging one's spatial image, the human body form, in order to travel through different realms of reality occur in reports of personal existence after death. Several cases make the point clear. For the Krahó, the personal principle that endures after death embraces several *mekaró* (body images). As each of these dies in its turn, it changes spatial form. The *mekaró* may take on the animal shape of the tapir, the deer, or the armadillo. If one of a pregnant woman's kin should eat such an animal, the *mekaró* may reincarnate itself in the child being formed in her womb. This seems to be the only suggestion of reincarnation among the Krahó.[373]

The Campa and Boróro provide further illustration of reconstructed spatial images. After death, a Campa's soul, located in the heart, may assume the menacing form of an animal. Such game animals are called *peári;* they are never eaten. They are, in fact, diseased or sick animals. There is some question whether or not certain groups of Campa believe that the souls of dead people may reincarnate themselves in the form of other animals, especially deer *(maníro).*[374] The Boróro believe the person disintegrates into parts at death. Flesh and skin are eaten by the *bope,* who descend to earth after the first burial. The breath of a dead Boróro becomes the breath in the voice of a soul-shadow *(aroe),* which, in the form of an animal, had once wandered away from the now-dead person's body during a dream. Now the breath of that dream-animal is stored in the mortuary calabash. The soul-shadow of the deceased person also flees into the form of a carnivorous animal.

The specific spatial images that constitute a person must change to make metamorphosis possible. Since flesh contains and defines the nature of human space, changes that transcend the limits of the body break down this human form. Such alterations of fleshly space are symbolized by cutting, perforating, and devouring, as well as by putrefaction and decomposition.[375] The point is not that the body is necessarily the enemy of the individual's spirit, but rather that the body is an instrument of spiritual change. The body is not simply a shell to be jettisoned in favor of spirit. In South American dualism between body and spirit, the dyadic relationship between the two is frequently cordial, even intimate. Precisely because spatial body-form and spiritual content are inseparable aspects of human individuality, the symbolic breakdown and reconstruction of the body is the instrument of meaning enabling a person to understand, and therefore effect, spiritual growth.[376] The body is a vessel of spiritual life, a vehicle of change. Since the very perception of transfiguration is always an understanding of the spirit, the mutation of the body-figure is always the result of spiritual transition. More precisely, the metamorphosis of the spatial imagery of the body and the transmogrification of the spatial imagery of the soul are two complementary ways of imagining the meaning of the same process of change.

SANCTUARY: MAKING THE BODY A HOLY SPACE

Knowledge of one's spatial imagery removes one from random existence. Physiology, a theory of body processes, permits the deliberate rearrangement of individual space through acts of consecration. The alteration of the body during its passage through life is never undirected; the symbolic action of *rites de passage* is goal-oriented. They consecrate the individual as an image of purposeful space. The nature of sacred being itself grounds the purpose of individual space. The meaning that the sacred assumes in each culture defines the goal of the cultural recomposition of individual symbolic imagery. One's consecration in the image of space makes it possible to assume one's proper place in the world and to become responsible for one's own history. No longer passive, one may dedicate oneself to a task or to another being. Knowledge of the symbolism of physiology permits one to become a holy house — or even a body — for a god. In such cases, the goal of spirituality is to receive (or to continue to lodge) the supernatural being within one's own being.

The skull can serve as a specially arranged residence for primordial being. It would be impossible to capture in a brief space the complexity of Desana ideas concerning brain structures and functions. Mythic imagery reveals the structure of the brain, its functions, and its significance. Housed in the skull, the brain is ordered in the way that the supernatural structures of the cosmos are organized. As manifestations of the same primordial forces, brain and cosmos were set in place and in motion just as the Sun Father created the universe. The functions of the two hemispheres of the brain are distinguished in important ways:

> The great fissure [between the two hemispheres] is seen as a deep riverbed; it is a depression that was formed in the beginning of time (of mythical and embryological time) by the cosmic anaconda. Near the head of the serpent is a hexagonal rock crystal, just outside the brain; it is there where a particle of solar energy resides and irradiates the brain. The fissure can also be seen as a stream, a great current of *bogá*, or cosmic energy.[377]

The head is the sacred enclosure *par excellence* because the brain is an image of the perfect container, the hexagonal universe formed by the six outstretched primordial serpents placed end-to-end. Inside them and streaming from their mouths are all the creative forces of primordial being, inseminated by the light-image of the Sun Father.

Devotees of Afro-Brazilian Candomblé take on the shape of the residence-space of the *òrìṣà*, the divine beings. By spending a long time in residence in the cult house, the devotee individualizes in his or her own body (and in this world) that perfect expression of space. Through ceremony and through the powerful presence of supernatural beings manifest in their sounds, the body space is rearranged.

The goal of the *candomblés* of Bahia is to "make a saint," who will protect and empower the devotee.[378] All human beings have a spiritual patron who can dwell within them, "mounting" them just as one mounts a horse. In Candomblé divination ritual, individuals may have their spiritual patron, their *òrìṣà*, revealed. The goal of Candomblé spiritual life is to prepare the devotee to receive the deity within his or her own being. These ritual preparations are directed by the *pãe-de santo* or *mãe-de santo* ("father in sainthood," "mother in sainthood"; equivalents of the Yoruba expressions *babalóòrìṣà* and *ìyálóòrìṣà*). The ritual and spiritual director "acts like one arranging a house for occupation. . . . 'Making the saint' requires time, long residence in the cult house with the devotees, the practice of certain secret ceremonies within the cult house, with a special orchestra of drums and African musical instruments." [379] In keeping with the metaphor of constructing a house, or receptacle, for divine life — a womb, of sorts — Edison Carneiro believes that Candomblé is essentially "a woman's enterprise, essentially domestic, contained within the four walls of a house." [380]

Important theological notions underlie the religious practices of Candomblé in Bahia. *Ase (axé)* is a mystical, magical force that pervades the entire cosmos and takes on particular manifestations for good or ill. As a good force, it derives from the *òrìṣà* and the ancestors *(òku òrun)* who have important involvements in mythic and historical processes. As an evil force, *ase* can be of two classes. The first is a class of beings destructive to the integrity of a person; they cause death, illness, paralysis, imprisonment, and so forth. The second class of evil *ase* consists of *aje*, the force that brings about a total annihilation of the human person.

The *orí*, the head as it is mystically perceived, is the essential part of the head; it is constituted by all the *ase* in one's personal possession, and this concentration of supernatural power composes one's fate, strength, and foibles. This is why the *orí* serves as the seat of the *òrìṣà* who comes to be present in the person. The presence of the *òrìṣà* will depend on the strength of the *orí*, to which the *òrìṣà* is attracted by the force of its *ase*. That is why the *orí* is the most important part of the body *(ara)*.[381]

Depending on the strength and composition of the *orí*'s *ase*, particular *òrìṣà* come to a person. The connection of a person's physiology and personality to an *òrìṣà* has important social and historical ramifications. Not only does each *òrìṣà* bear a mythic and social history, but each one is also connected with the geography of the city of Bahia and the history of its neighborhoods. Each area of Bahia, each street, bridge, and important landmark, is *òrìṣà*-specific. Each *òrìṣà* is connected to a specific location, set of activities, and sociopolitical group in the city. In short, both the city and the human body are transformed into mythic geographies, maps of essential and varied conditions of being, replete with sacred histories that explain powerful events and their meanings by recounting the descent of the *òrìṣà* to particular places on earth and their actions when they arrive. Ritual physiology and the social body-politic are not isomorphic homologies of one another. Rather, each one is a new and creative manifestation, a new moment in the history of the *òrìṣà* powers manifest as *ase*. As Waldeloir Rego reports,

> In the locality once called Quinta das Beatas there is an infinity of cultic places of African provenience from which have derived the names of many streets. Among them is one street called Giri Giri, a name taken from a hymn to Ososi, one of the gods of the hunt. Giri Giri refers to the manner in which the reins of a horse are secured when it is mounted, since one of the images of Ososi is of a king who is

always mounted on a horse. In the locality secularly known as Campo Seco, there are today a large number of Afro-Brazilian cult places. In this area there exists a street named Beru, a corruption of Gberu, the proper personal name of one of the kings of Oyo. It is very common for the people to preserve the memory of kings of those regions from which their ancestors came, especially if these kings were divinities. In the case of Oyo several divine kings are spoken of and revered: Oranyan, Aganju, and Ṣàngó.[382]

In this way each toponym is invested with popular, social, and mythical history associated with the name of an òrìṣà.

One's survival in an afterlife depends upon the head *(orí)*, the seat of one's powers and relationships with supernatural forces as well as with social and historical processes. Consequently, one runs a great risk when one submits oneself (specifically one's head) to the ritual ministrations of the *obrigação*, the ritual acts of Candomblé. Wittingly or unconsciously, another participant could harm or even annihilate one's being in the process. Each participant in the rites places tremendous confidence in the good force and spiritual powers of others as his or her *orí* becomes the seat of a resident *òrìṣà*.

Ase is passed from one body to another. Thus, the hair of both deceased and mourners is clipped at death so that the *orí* (with its *ase*) can be freed from the body and join up with *egun* (soul). It should be clear, then, that *"ori* is the same thing as an *oriṣa*, and behaves like one, even speaking during divination. Our *oriṣa* lives in our *ori."* [383] From the first instant of life the *òrìṣà* [is washed and seated with respect on the infant's *orí*.] Each person, each physiological integrity, is then a shrine, the locus of sacred forces, as well as an icon of sacred history, the powerful acts of mythic and historical past. This enables the person to become a new and creative expression of cosmic force, *ase*.

THE SOCIAL BODY

Images of space compose human nature not only at the level of individual existence but also on a communal scale. Looked at from one point of view, the spatial elements of different individuals, like the particles in different kaleidoscopes, can be arranged in the same order. If several individuals contain the same arrangement of spatial images, to a large degree they share the same organization of experience. They experience the same reality. The symbolic management of meanings, the senses of the body, forms the basis of common self-understanding.[384] Architecture and social space deliberately order the experience of the world by constructing an artifacted world, framed within its essential temporal structures. These symbolic arrangements of space and time publicly impinge, both overtly and subliminally, on the sensations of every member of the group. They impose a stamp of common order on experience. As spatial interpretations of the sacred, they lend effective form to the meanings that generate a community.

Architecture and sacred space are not the only ways to build a social body for communal experience. Cultures work directly with the spatial imagery that structures the individual. The "work" is not just the literal body-work of a trainer or masseur. It is the work of the imagination, which displays, reenacts, and reflects the meanings of spatial imagery. Conditioning the body culturally through the architecture, interior design, and choreography of the symbolic imagination makes self-understanding powerful and creative. That is, the experience of oneself, grasped with the symbolism of culture, conforms to the meanings manifest in sacred beings during the creative beginning. The Kari'ña case illustrates this point. The *wei* (form, appearance, behavior) of a Kari'ña individual derives in large part from his or her place in a particular social group. *Wei* has a social and historical dimension. *Wei* is one's mannerisms *(o.ma)* and style in their particular historical and social manifestation as they are shaped by *emeri. Emeri* designates the extended family as well as the local historical tradition and social experience that have unfolded since the extended family's foundation in mythical time. A *puidei's* (shaman's) *wei* derives from the community of invisible beings with whom the *puidei* is in intimate contact. The shaman's social community is not limited to human beings, and so he may assume an unlimited number of *wei,* forms, appearances, and transformations.[385]

Another cultural strategy provides common experience by making the same body-parts available to different individuals. If people can be made to share the same body parts, they can approximate the same sensual experience of the world, the experience of similarly ordered meaning.[386] Sharing the experience of the same body parts can be effected literally in ritual sex. Such is the case with the Cubeo during the second phase of the *óyne,* the mourning ceremony.[387] The orgy cannot be understood as mundane promiscuity.[388] It is the deliberate imitation of the momentous act that altered the course of the history of existence. If one wants to understand these actions, it is imperative to keep in mind their sacredness. They are a consciously symbolic performance imitative of powerful beings of the mythic era. These primordial beings are made manifest in masks, and the entire house is transformed into the primordial world for the duration of the rites. Both phases of the celebration proceed with apparent spontaneity but are, in fact, carefully orchestrated symbolic acts. One dimension of the symbolism is sexual. This is because the first death and first masked rites of mourning originated when a young man copulated with his sister in her manioc garden.[389] When the boy died after three months of shameful ostracism, the mythical being Kúwai instructed the first people how to perform the masked dances and rites of the *óyne.* Irving Goldman interprets the symbolism as a dramatic enactment of sexual foreplay and climax on a communal scale.[390] He writes,

> If one looks at the *óyne* as a whole . . . and follows the sequence of events from their slow and solemn beginning to their conclusion in a simulated sexual orgy and then a real one, a single main theme emerges, and that is the sexual interplay between men and women. . . . The climax of the first part of the *óyne* is ritual coitus, just as the climax of the second part is sexual license. We can therefore describe the *óyne* in terms of ritualized sexual sequence.[391]

The symbolic performance of forbidden sex, a reenactment of the unlawful sex act at the beginning of time, brought mortality, the human condition, into existence. More importantly, it prompted Kúwai to create masks and dances for humans so that they could appropriate the powers of sacred beings, which powers underpin the very conditions of culture. With simultaneous hilarity and menace the entire irony of this mystery is relived in the *óyne*. Although the act of sex, which physically regenerates human life, brings death, the celebration of death brings continued life to culture.

Sharing the experience of the body's senses through sex need not be a literal orgy. The figurative play of subtle symbolism may also merge body forms into one. For example, Roe mentions special drinking cups used at the Shipibo drinking festival called Ani Ŝhrëati. The first special cup is the *hoboshco*, "a hollow cup in the form of a phallus complete with testicles." [392] The second cup, the *ŝhërvi toncoati* "is a realistic vulva with the vaginal slit forming the opening." [393] Dipping for the drink and consuming it mimics the sexual act, makes the festival a symbolic sexual orgy in which everyone participates, and becomes yet another expression of shared body parts.

SOME CONCLUDING REMARKS

Every physiological system is adaptive to its environment. The relationship between an individual space and the space of its environment is best seen in developmental, historical, and comparative perspective. By arranging the spatial imagery of an individual, ritual physiology is no less involved in the physical and social processes in the world of which it is a part. In fact, ritual physiology appears to be a set of imaginative theories that clarify and systematize the orders of environmental and social processes. It evaluates these processes by assigning to nature and the wider cosmos meanings consistent with human self-understanding. Ritual physiology also appears clearly in comparative study across time: the time of the transmission and acquisition of souls, the time of the circulation of names through mythical epochs (at first) and then through configured social history, and the time of the individual life-cycle marked off by alterations of the body-space. The space composing the human individual is contiguous in meaning with the space of all the realms of the universe. The sacred foundation of the body's spatial imagery links each person to the meaningful taxonomic orders of sounds, animals, and the food chain.

The meaning of space does not stand apart from the sensuous experience of life. There is no body of knowledge apart from the knowledge of the body. This carries with it important implications for understanding religious and medical ethics in South American cultures. In South American cultures there is rarely any suggestion that medicine is, in itself, a collection of protocols or value-free techniques that may be neutrally applied toward either moral or less than moral ends. Rules of ethical discernment do not exist outside the body itself. Ethics must be consonant with the order of sensual experience. Physiology, because it is image-based knowledge, is not a process detached from the body of rational principles. All significant human action takes place in relation to one's spatial imagery, of which the physical body is one kind. The arrangement of physical space in dance and medicine is a moral resource. These symbolic movements are not purely objective techniques in need of moral direction. The spatial imagery of an individual is not an abstract geometry but an ordered mode of existence, which is sensual and, therefore, meaningful. In order to understand the body, and therefore the self, as a physiological system of meaning, it is not necessary to look upon it as a set of mechanical devices or systems (histological, alimentary, glandular, osteological) standing apart from the individual person. The body is the very basis of individuality and morality. Neither the physician's body during procedures of cure nor the patient's during episodes of sickness, neither the eater's body nor the dancer's can function apart from moral action. This is because the body's actions can always be symbolic, always open to the possibility of meaning. Because the individual is composed of significant spatial imagery, ultimately modeled on the sacred beings who reveal meaning, all human acts in space are those of moral actors, inviting understanding.[394]

CHAPTER 6

HUMAN GROWTH
AND CREATIVITY

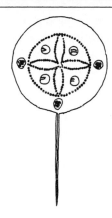

The symbolic elements that constitute the human person can be acquired, alienated, rearranged, or elaborated. Shuffling the recombinant images reveals new personal and social meanings and constantly initiates the process of change. Such alterations in symbolic form as the changing of the voice, the periodic flow of internal substances (excretions, menstrual blood, semen), or the changing space of the maturing, decorated body reconfigure relations among the qualities of being that compose the person. One view of this process is that dramatic events of personal and social life compel and facilitate reinterpretations of an individual's meaning. But since those changes have mythic precedent and are homologous to the great changes of the primordium, another perspective also holds true: one becomes what one means. One is inexorably drawn through the event, which effects what one signifies. Looked at from within this second framework, the dramatic event serves to arouse awareness of the transformative power already present in one's symbolic constitution.

By thus following in the wake of one's meaning, the quest for completeness sets one in pursuit of a condition characteristic of primordial forms, a condition now revealed (but also veiled) in symbols. From symbol to event to symbol, the circle of the conditions of being closes: the pursuit of being constantly and consistently moves one through the significant transformations of this transitory world, where the meaning of existence reveals itself in all its forms. Change and meaning are inextricably coinvolved because the withdrawal of sacred beings into the many significant forms of appearance in this world initiates and drives forward the process of change. Close examination of the process of change exposes the source of contradiction: symbols are themselves transformative events, powerful changes in states of being.

The pull of symbolic gravity in contradictory directions (change prompting new symbolic meaning versus significant meaning sparking the events of change) sets up a dialectic of growth and decay. New life and growth cause a tug-of-war, a violent contest of disparate forces in every domain of human imagery, whether temporal, spatial, acoustic, visual, saporous, or olfactory.[1] The contradiction of meaning on every level and knowledge of its significance for growth comprise a spiritual process of the senses. This multidirectional entelechy, stemming from the creative acts of sacred beings, whose violent transformations originated symbolic life and its fan of meanings, accounts for the drama of rites of passage, the moments set aside to manage and mark growth. Insofar as human life is symbolic, it embodies the changes of meaning and concrete form that were instituted by mythic beings. Movements through conditions of being must be effectively punctuated by symbolic action. In this regard, the so-called Chapacura, who live on the Brazil-Bolivia border, better represent the general rule than the exception when they mark their life-cycle transitions with dietary restrictions, confinements, special body decorations (including lip perforation and lip ornaments), and color codes (e.g., of feathers in one's headdress).[2]

Conversely, shifts in symbolic configuration propel one into and out of ontological states (existential, emotional, and spiritual states as well as social ones). Such life-passages stand out as important symbolic occasions for both a culture and an individual. In fact, Udo Oberem found the rites of passage that conduct one through the culturally recognized growth-spurts of the life-cycle to be among the most stubborn and enduring of the symbolic complexes in a culture. They withstand hundreds of years of foreign influence. The outward signs of once elaborate rites of passage still can be seen in the symbolism of special foods, drinks, songs and musical instruments, dances, games, colors, clothing, divisions of labor, calendrical timing, and other symbolic features.[3]

In order to highlight the religious importance of rites of passage in their capacity to orient human life to meaning, this chapter briefly examines a number of transitional moments (viz., conception, birth, initiation, marriage)[4] and the processes that constantly underlie them: spiritual companionship, knowledge, and creative labor.

CONCEPTION

To treat successful conception exclusively in terms of the beginning of a life occasions misunderstanding.[5] In reality, conception is as much a denouement as a beginning, or at least should be. It ought to result from deliberate symbolic actions performed at the initiations and marriage of the parents as well as from their own conscious acts of dancing, singing, decoration, fasting, hunting, gardening, eating, foreplay, intercourse, and avoidance of specific foods and behaviors.[6] From the outset, in other words, an individual does not fashion his or her own signifiers, their incarnate life. The signifiers that constitute new life must be the fruit of the significant acts of others (of supernatural beings and others working within the cultural tradition). Conception is the outcome of a powerful process of experiential knowledge that is both spiritual and carnal.

The Baniwa, for example, attribute conception to the power of the highest celestial being, Yaperikuli ("our father"). The mechanics of conception involve the father's blood (*lirana*, or *likai*, "sperm"), which makes up the blood of the infant. Yaperikuli, however, produces the child's soul and furnishes its bones and organs as it grows in the womb of the mother.[7] Just as Yaperikuli's "knowledge" impregnated Amaru, the primordial water serpent, during the first conception, so also human knowledge, a spiritual awakening through intimate contact with the sacred, is necessary for proper conception. The reason is because male menstruation *(kewiken)*, the opening of the male sexual orifice, takes place during initiation, when the young man comes to "know" Kuai, the culture hero/ancestor/flute, who is the fruit of the union between Yaperikuli's thought and Amaru's containing form.

Ultimately, the symbolic logic of conception, which begins with the premise that no human individual is the author of the significations that engender his or her own conception, pushes back toward the original situation of human beginnings. The conclusion is that another condition or kind of being, primordial and supernatural, originates the meaning and symbols that generate new human life. These may be creator gods, culture heroes, founders of lineages, owners or curators of species, lords of the dead, masters of the domains of the heavens, forests, rivers, and so on.

According to the Tapirapé, successful conception occurs when the soul of a child enters the woman's womb and decides to stay. The soul is an independent supernatural entity, the offspring of primordials. During his dream-trance, a *panché* (shaman) brings the spirit-child of certain supernatural animals, fish, or thunder to the desirous womb prepared by the procreating couple.[8] The spirit child responds to the call of the shaman and accompanies him on a visit to the prospective abode. However, the child reserves the right to decide to whom it will be born. For this reason, the Tapirapé consider one act of intercourse insufficient preparation for conception. More semen must be deposited in the woman's womb in order "to build the flesh of the child," which the abiding presence of the willing spirit-child will quicken and shape. It is possible, then, to have several father-genitors, although care should be taken, for the sake of the child's health, that the child not have "too many fathers."

A similar dependence of successful conception is acknowledged in the Andean community of Amaru, located along the Chongo River. Conception is viewed as the planting of a seed in the woman's womb.[9] A woman takes care during her pregnancy to remain in a correct relationship to the supernatural forces contained in ancient mummies (*machus, gentiles,* or *soq'a*); otherwise, they may overpower the woman's spirit so that she dies in childbirth or may possess the life force of her child so that it is stillborn *(machu q'apirapusqa)*.

That conception is the culmination of a cyclic logic of symbols, which originates in the primordium and spins through the generations, can also be discerned in the symbolic acts of birth control, the attempts to derail the efficacious process of signification (e.g., of supernatural heat, or primordial fertility of the land). During their investigation of women's life and ideas in two Peruvian towns, Susan C. Bourque and Kay Warren found that women attempt to control fertility by "throwing the placenta into the river after childbirth instead of burying it in the fields as is customary."[10] It is generally assumed by these townspeople that women who have only two or three children control their fertility either by disposing of the placenta in a river or by entering a river themselves in order to "cool their ovaries" to prevent conception. Water symbolism figures largely in notions of women's fertility. A menstruating woman may find that her menses stops and her stomach fills with water if she crosses a river during her period. As a result, during the first day or two of a woman's period, her work centers on the land, on tasks associated with the field. Individual women, in the reports given to Bourque and Warren, do not affect the fertility of the fields directly with their behavior during menstruation, pregnancy, or parturition. In addition, premature babies who die and stillborn children who have not been baptized "are buried in pools of water in the river." [11]

Bourque and Warren bring home the important point that relations with supernaturals, which relations are crucial to the process of conception, are negotiated symbolically. Behind the symbolic management lies a knowledge of the significance and power of symbolic life and the symbolic possibilities of everyday gesture. During pregnancy a woman takes care to avoid circumstances and actions that could adversely affect the developing fetus. Supernatural sounds of the *abuelos* ("ancestor spirits") are dangerous because they may penetrate the woman's body when she becomes frightened by them.[12] Sound is also associated with another source of magical fright, *susto*, which is the sound of thunder during heavy storms. The danger is most acute during the summer months and in the higher altitudes,[13] but dramatic stories are told of how lightning attacks pregnant women who are in the fields from November to February.[14] A woman frightened by lightning may give birth to a deformed child. However, this need not be the necessary outcome. In fact, in keeping with the ambivalent nature of the sacred beings involved, even the birth of healthy children is associated with lightning: "Women who have given birth to healthy children recount escapes from lightning in a light-hearted fashion while noting that they took the threat seriously at the time."[15]

Finally, during pregnancy, women in these towns guard their behavior toward animals lest their actions adversely affect the personalities of their children.[16] For example, "Little pigs are thought to be very nervous and bothersome. When a baby is nervous, continually turning its head from side to side, it is likened to lambs. When infants behave in these ways, their mothers' actions toward domestic animals during pregnancy are said to have influenced the child." [17]

Through symbolic interventions, the channels of encounter with supernatural beings, community, and parents induct a new human into life. Symbolic induction is a species of inducement. To risk stating the issue in its most extreme terms: rites of passage are not merely ornamental trim celebrating changes that would take place without them; they are acts of coercion, inducing change by manipulating symbols of sacred powers in such a way as to reveal a presence or relationship whose meaning imposes itself to determine the course of events. Symbolic acts of the life-cycle create the significant states of being into which ones passes.[18]

That is why the decorative trappings and gestures of mature men and women, acquired during their passage into the active symbolic life of the community, play decisive parts in conception. Successful procreation among the Akwẽ-Shavante, for example, is aided by the father's red earplugs.[19] Just as earplugs penetrate the earlobes of a mature man, his penis is able to penetrate a woman to good effect. The fetus is fashioned by the man through repeated acts of intercourse. By the fifth month of pregnancy, the child is fully "made." The symbolic gestures of the father, which shape the child, do not end there. Fathers observe restrictions of diet and behavior before a child's birth.[20] In many other cultures, both parents curb their appetites and behavior in deliberate ways. Once the Waiwai infant's soul is present (probably from the moment of conception forward[21]), the parents begin their careful pattern of avoidances. In order to protect the child's soul, the symbolic pattern is firmly in place by the last trimester of pregnancy.[22]

It becomes increasingly clear that the stirring of new life in the womb not only results from the symbolic performances of primordials and human beings but also bears repercussions of its own in the supernatural world, repercussions that manifest themselves in symbols. The symbolic aftereffect may be as unobtrusive as sleep. Such is the case for the Siriono, for whom conception and pregnancy are often announced to a woman in dreams, during which her soul enters the world of supernatural realities. One woman reported to Holmberg that she knew she was pregnant because, in her dream, she saw a small child inside herself.[23] On the other hand, conception may carry more dramatic and powerful consequences. For the Guayakí, for example, conception brings hope of supernatural cure of illness. While in the womb, fetal children, like the supernatural twins of the mythic age, advise their mothers by speaking of realities no longer manifest in this world. Receiving such wisdom, pregnant Guayakí women become particularly good healers. Drawn from the inhabitants of the dark and aquatic domain of the womb, their power is concentrated in their saliva.[24]

In any case, because of the nexus of supernatural relations it embodies, a new child, from its conception onward, creatively reorders the world around it, an effect reflected first in the symbolic acts of parents but later rippling outward, life-passage by life-passage, to include ever wider social circles. More importantly, an individual's life of transition, symbolically most visible in initiation, begins with the actions surrounding his or her conception. Those ritual acts comprise an essential moment in the religious progress through life because they institute a sacredness that is characteristic of human being. Without that symbolic affiliation with sacred being established in conception, further religious involvement in the creative life of culture would be neither possible nor thinkable.

BIRTH

The rites of birth are generally quite simple. The plainness of biological birth is strikingly ironic since the drama of conception, gestation, and birth serves as model for the more elaborate celebrations of cultural and spiritual rebirth held during the transitions of the life-cycle. No matter how streamlined, the acts of birth bear important consequences for individual, family, and cosmos because, on account of the new presence manifest in the child, they are actions *performed for the first time.* The delivery of the child from the womb to the world, the physical disposition and cleaning of the infant, the disposal of the afterbirth, and the supportive actions of assistants may seem only unadorned necessities. Expedience and economy of motion rule the day. However, when regarded in their fully symbolic light, the requirements of biological life signal fundamental messages about the full reach of existence in the world.[25] Birth practices and beliefs underscore the capacity of even so-called functional behaviors to reveal meanings that affect the texture of existence and, indeed, effect life itself. The practical movements of the birth process launch the child and the constellation of relations centered on it into a symbolic trajectory with long-term effects for the destiny of all parties concerned.

The very existence of an opening into life is the achievement of mythical beings. The Aguaruna attribute the origins of parturition to the advice of a mythical rat, Katíp. Until that time, men had opened up their wives' wombs often killing their offspring in the process. One women sent her husband off on a ritual hunt and then talked the mythical rodent into instructing her. The little rat gave her good obstetric care.[26] South American mythologies give considerable attention to the fashioning of the first birth canal. Opening the first threshold of transition is often seen as the work of mythical beings, who later leave animal forms behind as symbols of their primordial existence. The woodpecker, for example, frequently opens a way to the womb by pecking at an impenetrable female being made of wood. The sound creates transition in the form of the vaginal passage.

Since the opening of the first birth canal can serve as the model for all transitions, it is usually accomplished, as in the case of the woodpecker's sound-image, through knowledge associated with the power of symbolic life. For the Baniwa, all life passages are associated with Kuai, whose body is full of passages that emit subtances and sounds generative of growth, life, and change. Yaperikuli engendered Kuai by impregnating Amaru with his thought. She had no birth canal, so had to be opened for the first birth, Kuai's birth. "At the birth of Kuai, there is no explosive sound; rather Yaperikuli opens Amaru by encircling the crown-point of his head, where 'knowing' is located, and puts the elliptical shape on the place where the child is to leave.

Through this action alone, Amaru is opened." [27] Knowledge of symbolism, at once carnal and spiritual, is essential to the human kind of being, whose existence is assumed by crossing over a threshold. Human life first appears in transition and, therefore, embodies the essentially betwixt-and-between meaning of the exemplary experience of its first moment.

The acts of birth must properly introduce a child to the new condition of space. A guide acts as spiritual companion, leading the new being out of the old realm and into the new atmosphere. In some cases, a shaman accompanies the child's soul from another world to this one. Among Makuna, for instance, a shaman presides over the rituals of birth. A newborn is identified with its grandparent of the same sex (that is, a classificatory grandparent). During the birth ceremony, the shaman conducts the soul of a dead person of the grandparent's generation from the house of the dead into its new "house," the newborn baby. [28]

In many cases the transport of the soul from one place to another is a spiritual function of the midwife, who, in the same act, delivers the child's body into this world's space. Apinayé grandmothers act as midwives during delivery and continue to enjoy privileged ritual ties with their grandchildren. They symbolically rearrange the body-space of the child to suit its new spatial conditions by painting it with rubber pigment and decorating it with ornamental bones, seeds, and bits of wood. These spatial ornaments help the infant grow and protect the child from harm. Other spatial preparations are made for the transition: an Apinayé child is born in a conical hut of palm leaves. Only women are present at the delivery. Parents observe a period of restrictions against cutting their hair, painting their bodies, and eating certain foods. When the father goes to hunt a rhea and then a deer, the child is painted with red *urucú* to prevent it from crying when the game is killed. "[T]he mystic bond uniting the bodily welfare of parents and children persists throughout life." [29]

The importance of the child's posture at birth reflects the long-lasting importance of its first moment in the space of this world. For the Candomblé tradition in the city of Bahia, the instant of birth and the first experiences of the new body in this world affect the particular expression of *ase* (mystical force filling the cosmos) that a person will relate to in his or her own unique way for the rest of life. The most minute circumstances of birth will affect the way in which the person and his or her fate are constructed in subsequent ritual life. Girls born in a particular posture, for example, belong to Iya Mapo, to whom rites are celebrated in order to prevent such girls from becoming lesbians. [30]

Birth is an important spatial installation. For the first time, a new person takes his or her *place*, a situation that defines the person's relationship to the shaping influences around him or her. In the case of the Chiripá, just as the gods Nanderú Guazú and Tupá ride the winds seated on their *apyakás* (zoomorphic stools), so too human beings take their proper places in the world (that is, become incarnate in body form) when they "take a seat" among humans. [31] During the Chiripá naming ceremony, the mother of the named infant weeps ceremonially while the child is sprinkled with sap from a sacred cedar tree, the same tree from which the *apaká* is fashioned.

Frequently the first acts of a new child are made to conform to the first acts of human beings at the time of their appearance on earth. The child is immediately a ritual actor, its life in this world a performance of sacred moments. Assisted and washed by ritual companions, the child reenacts the gestures of ancestors bathing in the waters of the receding flood or in the pools of emergence. The child's head is shaped, or its body is adorned with ornaments: acts that not only draw it within the aesthetic circle of culture but that, through these sacred symbols, also put it into contact with supernatural life. Parents and neighbors act in prescribed ways in order to represent sacrifices, weeping, or sounds that successfully accomplished transition to new life during the primordial catastrophe. Every proper birth of an Aché, for example, repeats the first act of standing upright. The ritual of birth includes two moments; *waa*, a "falling" from the womb to the earth, and *upi*, a "lifting up" by a ritual parent, the *upiaregi* ("she who has lifted up").[32] The birth process itself begins with the "fall" of the body to earth from the mother's womb. To give birth *(waa)* is to cause a person "to fall."[33] This act introduces one into the condition of incarnate existence, which is shared by human beings and animals. The process of birth cannot be complete, however, until a being is "lifted up," an action that, for the Aché, distinguishes human life from that of animals. This act requires the assistance of a ritual companion. Every action in the birth process is ritualized and carried out in solemn silence. The *tapave* ("she who takes the child in her arms") is given the ritual role of the *upiaregi* ("she who has lifted up"). The title derives from the verb *upi*, which denotes the specifically human part of the birth process.[34] The emphasis on "raising up" in order to be born a full human being derives from the origin myth of the Guayakí, in which the primordial ancestors emerged from the earth and set themselves upright upon it.[35]

The child is then handed to a man who plays the ritual role of the *jware*, who holds the infant in his arms and bathes the child for the first time. Beginning with this moment, great care is taken of the person's body, for it serves as the focus for a multitude of supernatural (and, therefore, social) forces and processes. The bath waters parallel the first waters, present at the emergence of people in the beginning of time. The *jware* molds the child's skull into a round form, which is considered beautiful. Eventually, other people from the residence group aid in shaping the child's head. The placenta is buried in order to rid the world of the spiritual menaces that derive from the forces at work within the woman's body during pregnancy.[36] The day after a child's birth, its father, who has not yet seen the child or the mother, leaves the encampment on a ritual hunt. He is in a state called *bayja*, a spiritual condition that "attracts beings."[37] Among the beings attracted to the father in his present state are game animals, which present themselves in great abundance.

The state of *bayja* brought on by the birth of the new Guayakí child endangers the father's life in more than one way. Not only do supernatural jaguars seek him out, but the rainbow serpent, *Membroruchu* (who is a double serpent, one snake enclosed within another), attempts to attack him in his state of *bayja* in order to swallow him whole. The presence of this rainbow serpent in the heavens presages death because, by dividing the sky, *Membroruchu* makes it possible for supernatural jaguars to rend it asunder and destroy it completely. *Bayja* not only threatens human beings but the very order of the cosmos itself.[38] The jaguar attempts to devour life as it is known in this world, bringing on (for instance) an eclipse of the solar or lunar rhythms that mark the passage of time. A blue jaguar appears to devour the sun or the moon. The ritual hunt seems to satisfy the jaguar's hunger for life (i.e., death) which accompanies the birth process.[39] For it is not, after all, the jaguar who is slain during a hunt—any other game animal is.[40]

As is usual in moments of significant change from one state of being to another, the Guayakí birth process, especially the purification episode carried on for the whole community through a ritual washing with *timbo* (a vine that produces a soapy foam with hallucinogenic properties), is accompanied by women's lamentations. These are ceremonial songs, which mark transitions, and "crying greetings," which are performed on occasions of arrival and departure.[41] A ritual flame is extinguished in a specially prepared vessel filled with water in order to prevent a repetition of the cosmic flood that once destroyed the world.[42]

The ritualized acts of the birth process often bring the newborn child into intimate association with the earth. Mothers gave birth while deliberately in contact with the ground, or deliver the child onto the earth, or have the child deposited on the soil by an assistant. In the same exemplary moment that the child is born of woman it is born of earth. The mystery of birth and of feminine fruitfulness is linked to the fertility of the earth just as the new life of the child is likened to a plant or vine freshly sprouted from earth's life-giving womb. The studies of Billie Jean Isbell and Ana Maria Mariscotti de Görlitz, for instance, point out that, in the Andes, the earth (Pachamama) gives birth to humans just as she does to plants.[43] The holy and primordial fertility of Mother Earth is assimilated to woman. In the Andean towns studied by Bourque and Warren, although a child is born on a cloth covering the ground, a relative carefully buries the placenta in a field close to the place of birth. The act of placing the placenta in the earth is not only essential to the health and growth of the child and the community but also to the continued fertility of the mother, animals, and crops. Concern that the birth process conform to the expectations of symbolic action may explain why women in these towns prefer to give birth at home, under the ritual presidency of a local midwife, rather than in a hospital.[44]

The symbolic actions of the birth procedures can be of utmost importance. When a child is born in the Andean community of Amaru, it is said that it has been "saved," for a successful birth is the result of powerful ritual behaviors carried on since (and including) the moment of its conception.[45] When the placenta is expelled from the womb it is wrapped in a cloth of clean, white wool. Then, in order to preserve the life of the mother, the whole bundle is burned. Because the birth requires these procedures, "it is inconvenient to give birth in a hospital." [46] When the stub of the umbilicus, the outward sign of the voyage from one kind of being to another, has dried and fallen off, it is kept as a powerful object, which, when placed in an amulet, brings spiritual aid to travelers.

The ritual role of midwives, relatives, and sponsors is indispensable for proper birth, for they guarantee that the biological functions of human parturition are also cultural acts, meaningful interpretations of the sacred. In addition to the biological parents, therefore, the child is frequently provided a pair of ritual parents who preside over his or her birth to culture. Immediately after a Kaingáng child is born, for example, a ceremonial father *(kôklá)* and mother *(mbë)* are appointed at the rite in which the placenta is disposed of in a little basket and sunk in a stream. The basket is fixed to the stream bed with a stick. [47] Shortly thereafter, during the newborn ceremony, the ritual parents wrap the infant's ankles with loose cords. During this feast the parents, who play host to a large group, do not eat. Men sing as the women remove the cords, which are then thrown into water with a small piece of the umbilicus attached to them. After this, the child may receive a name. [48]

The actions of the natural parents must also be raised to the level of visible symbolism in order to make clear, for their own safety and that of their infant, their relationships with the forces that have come together in the person of their child. For example, fathers often practice the couvade, taking to bed as if bearing the new child and observing avoidances and purifications. [49] The presence of the powers that produce new life calls for response. The symbolic actions are not only prophylactic; at times they are tantamount to salvation from disintegration. Especially in the beginning of life, the constitution of the newborn's life forces is unsettled, a tenuous and uneasy combination of spiritual elements. For the Waiwai as for many South American peoples, the newborn child's soul is seen as being in the following predicament: clinging precariously to its body in the early stages of growth, the soul stands in need of protection, especially through lullabies, which keep away the stray spirits who want to enter the child and force out its unsettled soul. [50] In its early life, the child's soul journeys back and forth between its mother and father. Consequently, they are required to stay close together so that the soul does not become lost by having to wander over great and unfamiliar distances. The child is protected by its parents' behavior. After the child sneezes, for example, they restabilize the soul by blowing into the child's mouth. They refrain from many kinds of activities and foods in order to protect the child's soul. For example, a father will not dig a posthole for fear that the baby's soul will enter the hole and the child fall ill. If, inadvertently, this should happen, the father splashes water on a heated stone. The child's soul rises up with the steam, is grasped by the father, and is saved. [51]

In any case, the vulnerability of a child's invisible soul and hidden life forces demands that parents perform publicly or curb their behavior in publicly prescribed ways. Such is the case when a Toba child is born. Its cord is cut with a shell and kept until the navel wound is healed. The new mother abstains from eating meat and fish. Her husband begins a drinking-bout ceremony by chanting to the beat of his gourd rattle (the habitation of his guardian spirits) throughout the evening after the birth. Dangerous spirits are present in the first days after birth. They arrive in the form of invisible snakes, and the wind tries to carry them into the house and into the body of the mother.[52] Every action that the parents do or undergo will affect their child. If twins are born, the second of them is usually killed.

Though their requirements for new parents differ from those of the Toba, the Siriono demand that parents perform publicly and toward the same end. For them, birth is a public event carried on before groups of women and children who gather together and entertain themselves but who do not in any way assist the woman in labor. The father of the child, however, departs on a hunt in order to seek a name for the child. After the birth, the father returns and bathes. Then, properly purified, he cuts the umbilical cord with a bamboo knife.

After birth, Siriono parents continue to be "intimately connected" with their child. The parents' action profoundly affects the child. Consequently, for a period following the birth, parents do not move at all.[53] The parents of a newborn child have their legs scarified; an eyetooth of a rat or squirrel is used to draw blood. This rids the body of old blood, which could harm the child. The day after its birth, the child's eyebrows are painfully depilated, as is the hair on the crown of its head. This hair is worn in a necklace by the child's mother to make the child's hair grow.

On the second day after birth, Siriono parents are adorned with feathers and *urucú* paint. The time of the parents' seclusion ends when they scatter ashes and kindle a new fire. Filling new, miniature baskets with the ashes of a dead fire, a new mother places her child in a new carrying sling for the first time. The father marches down a trail into the forest, carrying his arrows and bow and warding off harm from the child. With the child in her sling, the mother carries the basket of ashes and a calabash of water. She scatters the ashes along the trail. No one speaks. After a short time the group stops and the mother weaves a new basket from palm leaves while the father seeks firewood. They return home and kindle a new fire. The child is washed with water from the calabash.[54]

Physical birth is a paradigmatic moment of transition and, consequently, serves as a baseline for symbolic dramatizations of many other moments of passage in life, which become interpreted as moments of symbolic rebirth. Although few additional theatrics compound the urgent life-and-death drama of delivery, birth is not without symbolic meaning and religious significance. In fact, it is the result of an intimate encounter with creative forces, sacred beings of the primordium, during the initiation and marriage of parents, the festivals of the year, in dream and song, and so on. The symbolic acts surrounding birth are incipient attempts to grasp the meaning of those powers and to discern the repercussions that encounters with them will bear for individuals and groups. Birth is first and foremost an appearance, an epiphany of supernatural forces at work in the life of the parents and the community and embodied in the infant. The parents and community structure their existence around these powers, which are composed, signified, and revealed in the incarnate form of a new person.

INITIATION

Initiation should be understood in light of the entire spectrum of symbolic life, for it is a process coextensive with the human condition. The common mistake of considering initiation as an occasion that stands on its own, separate from all others and complete in itself, may be opposed on several grounds. In the first place, in addition to forming the experiences of the novices, who occupy the limelight, every initiation rite generates teaching and learning roles played by other social actors of varying age and status: parents, ritual sponsors, food preparers, ritual decorators, instrumentalists, cantors, dancers, mask-makers and mummers, stylized warriors, and honored guests. A lifetime of such shifting participation allows a person to see a series of mythic and ritual revelations from many angles, so it can be said that initiation never ceases. It remains an ongoing instrument of maturation. A principle benefit of initiation for novices is that it opens for them a lifelong and ordered progression of roles, allowing them to experiment with modulations of the sacred.

Because it places sacred realities at the disposal of human understanding for the first time, initiation can be a most dramatic moment in human culture. Knowing the meaning of the sacred through a mature encounter with its symbolic expressions is the central event of culture. Initiation, then, serves as a reflexive gathering point for all similar moments of breakthrough, when human understanding penetrates through symbolic expression to new revelations of meaning. This is a second reason for looking upon initiation as a constant process of spiritual regeneration. Such instants of insight mark new beginnings because the significance of human life changes hue in the light of new signifiers and new understanding. Experiences of this sort are, in the full sense, processes characterized by an initiatory structure. Formal initiation ceremonies celebrate all such experiences of individual transition from one state of meaning to another and lend them primordial power and enduring significance by relating them to mythic models.

In the end, to cite a third reason for the constancy of initiation, one may even say that initiation cannot be set apart as a moment separate from others because it celebrates an essential quality of human being: the whole of human life is an initiatory existence. The human being is constantly ending and beginning again: sitting, standing, stepping one footfall after another, sleeping to wake, working to rest, and passing from one phoneme to another or from speech to silence, from one meal to the next, one generation to the next, from birth to death to afterlife. Being human is itself a crossing-over, a betwixt-and-between condition. The profound realization that being human is situated in the transition of ontological conditions occurs when even the most basic of human behaviors are understood as symbols: eating, excreting, procreating, working, trading, making noise, feeling pain, and dying. The discovery that human life is initiatory is the flip side of humans' disclosure of themselves as symbolic beings whose self-understanding and comprehension of the world involves their own symbolic capacities. During formal initiation, cultures insist that individuals make this discovery. In order to face the world with creative confidence, novices are forced to confront their own symbolic nature and capacity for understanding. These link them to the reality of their world.

Novices learn that human beings apprehend their world in symbolic terms. The cosmos gives up its order and meaning to their creative machinations when its outward expressions are taken as signifying some force, nature, or relationship that is not fully apparent. With admirable consistency this reflective logic is applied to the very process of human understanding during initiation. The symbolic quiddity of human life is grasped through its own signifiers, through human existence beheld as a cipher of initiatory meaning. For this reason, the great truth of initiation becomes the self-assertion that, because it is symbolic, human life is an initiatory condition, a transition between states. By orchestrating and exegeting a dramatic experience of paradox and contradiction, initiation teaches novices that, on the one hand, human symbolic life makes humans live two conditions of existence at any given time. By acting in one set of events, humans signify another realm of reality. On the other hand, initiation instructs novices that human beings can never fully manifest either of the states of being they signify without interruption (i.e., apart from symbolic life and the meaning of initiatory experience).

In the rites of initiation examined here, cultures publicly proclaim the world to be a set of significations of a sacred reality. Furthermore, through human ability to imitate sacred beings and events, initiation rites effectively demonstrate that, by acting as a human, one culminates the ways in which the world can symbolically reveal sacred space and time.

FEMALE INITIATION

Women's initiation highlights the ways in which the human body serves as an instrument for transforming not just the individual human character but humanity itself. Indeed, time and again, the origin myths relived in women's initiation dramatize how the mature female body, as a manifestation of primordial character, subdues and governs inordinately powerful cosmic forces. During the mythical destruction brought on by an exchange effected through one of her body openings (menstrual flow, a glance, intercourse, eating), a goddess or supernatural heroine seals herself in a container or turns her own body into one by controlling the openings of her eyes, mouth, ears, and vagina. She thereby establishes a locus that is generative of new life; that is, she installs culture in the image of space. Withstanding the buffets of overwhelming supernatural forces (often with the help of a mythic grand-mother, who scampers away from the flood with cooking utensils, musical instruments, or fire), the heroine saves the very possibilities of culture from destruction and allows the flooded or crumbled cosmos to pass through a time of chaos into a state of fertile regeneration. On their bodies, especially in their skin, initiated girls bear the scars or the decorative souvenirs of that cosmic battle of resistance.[55] Tattoos, bite marks, stamped designs, or orna-ments commemorating the turning of the tides of primordial time are the punctures or impressions of body parts (teeth, nails, stingers, or penises) or the anatomical designs of the monsters that the primordial female subdued.

Several brief sketches from different cultures will illustrate the general features of women's initiation. The most central issues evident in women's initiation are seclusion, the containment of openness and flow, propriety (hygienic and moral), invisibility (darkness), and display. One should assess the presence, weight, and meaning of these symbols in the historical context of each of the particular societies in question since they are never precisely identical. Although examples are mentioned in connection with only one of these features, the quick summary of symbols makes clear that each could illumine many other issues discussed elsewhere in this section.

SECLUSION: ENCIRCLED BY GRAND TOURS, RINGING TONES, SWADDLING BANDS, LAST ROUNDS, AND WINDING SHEETS

Girls are secluded during their initiation. Whether shrouded away in a meta-phoric tomb or womb, the ubiquity and importance of concealment makes it a striking feature of female initiations. During Baniwa girls' initiation, the body of the adolescent candidate is covered with heron down and red paint. Baniwa boys undergo similar "seclusion" through decoration or investiture during initiation, but girls are subject to more hiddenness than that pro-duced by codes of dress. The girl is placed inside a basket. During formal delivery of advice to her,

> she is supposed to stand on the inside of the basket *(walaia);* she has another turned upside down and put over her head. This one might be decorated with feathers. After the speeches of counsel, the elder whips the initiate; then and *only* then are the baskets removed. Finally, after the elder gives the initiate pepper, touching it to her lips, then a small hole is made in the dirt floor, and she is instructed to spit in it.[56]

Chanting over different kinds of foods blow-blesses these species for her use. The ritual actions are based on the mythic account[57] of the female followers of Amaru, the formless water serpent who was the primordial female being. Amaru and her female band stole the *kuai* flutes from males and initiated their youngest sister by placing her in a basket while they blessed food all night. Several beings called *makulitete* (earthworms or earth insects) tried to penetrate the seclusions of her container-basket.[58] Eventu-ally, a small armadillo *(tatú)* succeeds in burrowing through the earth. He tunnels his way from the riverbank, where the men are, to the center of the women's house. Led by the creator-transformer, Yaperikuli, the males come through this passage.

The blessing of food during that primordial night takes the form of a journey across the face of the earth. Through the powerful sound of the *kuai* flutes, which Amaru and her companions play during their travels, the earth opens and becomes fertile. The cosmic tour marks and opens all the places that give forth life. Each life-giving place originates a species of plants, animals, or foreigners. The youngest sister, who is also considered a kind of place (since she, too, is defined by the process of enclosure and opening) represents the regenerative cultural life of humans. The supernatural females create the entire reproductive universe and make one of their own kind the locus of the replicating processes of human (Baniwa) culture.

On the grandest scale, by circumscribing the universe, their journey literally defines the limits of the cosmos. Their musical road trip establishes the world as a closed symbolic system, a regenerative place whose vital meaning and immutably sacred source are signified in the marked changes of the world's own growth and transformation. This is why whipping to the accompaniment of *kuai* flute music accomplishes a function similar to that of the parade and seclusion. Not only is it part of the same mythical event, but it also bears the same effects. Since whipping marks the outermost limits of the body, it simultaneously defines and opens the container (of fruit, of skin, etc.) and allows growth.[59]

The grand female entourage that marked the outer limits of the world and the succession of grandstand performances around containers of each species along the way (especially around the basket of the youngest sister) rendered the world habitable in general and some specific places fertile in particular. What happened during the grand march is that, from the individual to the cosmic scale, one set of regenerative spaces created and celebrated all others. For the Baniwa, life gestates, grows, and changes in different containers. Insofar as it is constant growth and change, life (both mythic and human) can be seen as a succession of containers, each one of which is closed and opened ritually to effect transfers or transformations from one to another. Each container in the series bestows its character on the living contents.[60]

In contemporary women's initiations, the Baniwa continue the festive process of the mutual and simultaneous creation of all life-containing spaces by touring them.[61] The containers, movements, and sounds of Amaru and supernatural females become instruments of closure that is needed for life to thrive. That is, understanding the fully sacred meaning of the procession and obtaining this knowledge experientially offer the individual woman and her entire community the chance for reflexivity and control over the meaning of change. Through her the community not only grows in the form of future physical life but also regains contact with the sacred foundations of symbolic form itself, the distinguishing mark of human culture — offering it power over its own processes of physical, social, and economic reproduction.

SHROUDED ROUND   For the Yawalapíti, death is the greatest enclosure and the most effective period of seclusion. It is a condition that utterly transforms life, just as all such concealments should, by marking an end to a condition of being. For this reason, the seclusion needed to "make" a girl during her initiation occurs during funerals. For the Yawalapíti, to make (umá-, "to make" in the sense of "to make a child or a person,") is the verb for actions that produce new identities. These key moments in time are marked by the entrance or exit of symbolic substances into or out of secluded space: the seclusion of the mother's womb, where repeated acts of sexual intercourse give seminal substance to the body of a child; the physical isolation of puberty initiations, during which time parents abstain from sex and administer emetics to their sequestered child; the burial-seclusion at death when the body is deposited until ritual exhumation of the bones; and the ritual enclosure in which candidates for shamanism are confined during their initiation.[62]

These moments of the life-cycle are constituted by passage into new states of being. Such a process of passing is not considered natural but is dependent upon the careful intervention of human beings.[63] The new states of being, with their accompanying new social roles, are effected "by means of a technology of the body."[64]

A single mythic model accounts for the affinities of meaning in all Yawalapíti rites of passage and for the fact that all are linked with death. The myth explains why ritual enclosures have such power and how exchanges of symbolic items through their openings can control passage from one state of being to another. In the myths, a demiurge named Kwamuty (or Mavutsinin) transforms large logs into living beings by blowing tobacco smoke on them. Significant for our purposes is the fact that these posts had been kept in an enclosure. One of the posts became the mother of the twins, sun and moon, who provided order for culture and cosmos. Since she was the first person to die, the original feast of the dead was celebrated in her honor. In the straw initiation enclosure, the girls are blown with tobacco smoke, a substance that corresponds to semen. The act transforms them into human beings. This ritual, the Itsatí, is the most important ritual in Xingu society. It is of singular importance to note that the funeral-initiation rites explicitly reenact primordial creation.[65] In the moment when recently initiated girls are presented to the community, "these young girls who come forth from their isolation are seen as the first human being: the mother of men (for their emergence from seclusion coincides ideally with their first marriage)."[66]

BOTTLED UP: CONTAINERS AND VESSELS CONTROLLING OPENNESS AND FLOW   Female initiation among the Maroni River Carib begins at a girl's first menstruation, when she is placed in seclusion for eight days (in former times, one month). In other ways as well, she is spatially hemmed in by symbols of supernatural closure. She scrupulously avoids the river and the forest, for the water spirit Oko:yumo becomes furious at the smell of female reproductive processes. He would carry her away with illness and death if she should venture beyond the bounds of her confinement. Even her body is bounded in a symbolically new way, for the girl dresses unattractively to repel the water spirit.[67]

These are not isolated instances. Initiation of a girl at menarche highlights the fact that the drama of initiatory closure is a response to her openness and the flow of forces. The desire is to construct a more perfect cultural vessel whose biological openness will be one with the power of her reflective will and the support of communal imagery. A Chiripá girl's initiation occurs at the moment of her first menstruation. For the Chiripá, as for many South American peoples, the body must, at some point in its growth, become open.[68] The generative and reproductive system of Chiripá culture, however, demands closure, a necessity dating back to the time of the catastrophic flood that brought closure to the primordial condition and initiated the changing conditions of this world. The deluge gave rise to culture as a symbolic system. Through symbolic life, especially the construction of symbolic containers, culture safeguards the closure necessary for meaning and, at the same time, allows for the periodic flow needed to regenerate life. In order to satisfy these contradictory demands, the key element of a Chiripá girl's initiation remains her seclusion, during which she is kept away from the "spirits of the earth" *(ywy ojá)*, which could possess her during this vulnerable time. With the aid of cultural symbolism she is transformed into a perfect container of life on the model of that which "surrounds" her—namely, culture, the world of mythic realities, symbolic life, her own character. Ultimately, she becomes an embodiment of those enclosing symbols and values; she becomes an expression of creative transformations. The Chiripá primordial heroine was confined under a jar. Ritual seclusion of girls once took place in a palm-branch hut where the girl spent all her time spinning and plaiting fibers of plants. By 1969, however, a place was prepared within the home, usually in a corner of the house.[69]

Looking upon the girl initiate as the symbolic container (at the generative locus of culture) of otherwise free-flowing life brings her into close affinity with the meaning of the drinking vessel, the center of cultural life during ritual drinking bouts. Many South American societies explicitly make this association by drawing the menstrual flow of bleeding girls and the flow of fermented brew into the same arc of meaning.[70] The Tukuna female initiation, staged at first menses, is called the Vorëki Cheii, the "drink of the initiand," since the girl's emergence from seclusion is marked by a three-day drinking bash that is the single most important Tukuna ceremony. Similarly, the Makiritare initiate girls in two phases, the first of which occurs at menarche. At that time the novice's head is completely shaved. When, about three months later, her hair has grown back, she is presented to the entire community as a mature woman ready for marriage. This presentation is made during the Yena Cajodi, an event which commemorates the first drinking festival.[71]

In many cases, bodily mutilations that cut or score the candidate's skin (or hair)[72] deliberately coordinate the discharge of blood with an outpouring of drink. Nowhere is the flow of blood and fermented brew so dramatically linked with girls' initiation than in Shipibo culture. In one violent and dramatic event, the Shipibo set blood and beer flowing from their vessels. The central ceremony of the Shipibo is the Ani Shrëati ("big drinking"), which is celebrated at the time of a girl's initiation. Here, as elsewhere, the prescribed flow of ritual drink is coordinated with the flow of blood from the reproductive parts of the female initiate. However, in this case the candidate's blood is deliberately let, since the most dramatic event of the three-day ritual is the radical clitoridectomy performed on girls before they can marry. It is coordinated with the flow of blood from men's heads and parallels another rite wherein women kill animals so as to create a blood bath.

In structure the Ani Shrëati closely resembles the related drinking celebration held for the ritual cutting of hair, the Bëstëti Shrëati, which is also associated with girls' initiation. The Ani Shrëati institution is of some antiquity since artifacts associated with the rite, the ceramic pieces that cover the vagina after the excision, date to as early as 800 CE.[73] Roe has analyzed the various reports of this "big drinking" ceremony and finds agreement on its episodic structure. However, compared to other South American communities, "as a total configuration centering on the clitoridectomy the Ani Shrëati is unique."[74]

Several girls are initiated at one time, the number ranging from three to eight or more. Seclusion remains the primary instrument for transforming the girl into a container sealed by symbolic openings. After her first menstruation, a girl is isolated in a hut outside her home. This is the pushuva ("house of silence"). There she observes strict dietary restrictions over the foods she may introduce into her body through her mouth.[75] The girls, their seclusion, the flow of blood or beer and their ritual containment, and the ritual foods passed into body-containers at the prescribed times become the focus of culture for years at a time. The whole process takes some two or three years to prepare, since special fields of sugar cane and manioc must be planted and a large house constructed for use during the celebration. More immediate preparations consist of the pressing of sugar cane and the concoction of a fermented cane juice called guarapo and of masato, a beer made from fermented manioc.

When enough drink is prepared and the time for the ceremony has drawn near, some men make thigh-supports of (quënám) light balsa wood. Women then paint designs on these. Eventually, women are sought who will hold the girl down during the operation. It is very important that these assistants be good singers.[76] Carrying guarapo and playing the tiati flute, they go to find the woman who will cut the clitoris. When all the guests have arrived back in the village, the initiates are invited to dance and sing throughout the night. They are made extremely drunk. Only then can the operation begin.[77] The girl is placed on a painted bench and her body smeared with special designs. Her face is dotted with genipa. She has been decorated with special ornaments, including monkey-tooth bracelets and bells, "the seeds that sing."[78] Songs are sung to describe how pretty she is and telling her that she will be so drunk she will feel no pain. With a bamboo knife, the woman chosen for the task performs the operation, and the blood is allowed to flow through a hole in the painted bench.[79] From testimony it is not clear exactly what kind of cutting is done.[80] The bleeding is staunched with water and herbs.

While the girl is being cut, the men, dancing drunkenly in a separate place, menace their fellow dancers and, in fact, cut the crowns of their fellow dancers' heads with sharp instruments so that blood flows down over their faces.[81] The men who are dancing and slashing one another conduct a ritual battle to combat supernatural enemies. This stylized aggression wards off the *joshin*, evil spirits that threaten the girls.[82]

Before positioning the girl on the thigh rests assistants place a *shërvën-anti*, a ceramic cover, over her vagina. One of Roe's informants told him that the *shërvënanti* readies the girl for intercourse, for the girl's mother inserts the ceramic object into the girl's vagina periodically during the time of healing, and pushes it in with the heel of her foot.[83] Participants drink and dance as long as the beer lasts.

After the clitoris has been cut another festival may take place, the Bëstëti Shrëati, or the cutting of hair. This festival follows the same episodic structure as the Ani Shrëati. Inordinate numbers of beautiful clothes drape the candidate, who is overdressed in a way typical of many women's initiations.[84] Enveloped in clothes, colors, beads, and seeds the girl is, in fact, heaped high with death, for the ornaments with which she is invested are the remains, the symbolic vestiges, of primordial beings who once lived but who passed away.[85] Excessive amounts of drink are prepared. Only the participants in the Ani Shrëati may join in the haircutting celebration, a detail that suggests it is essentially a continuation of the same "big drinking." However, added to this festival is a rite which Roe calls the "killing of the pets."

Guests arrive and are welcomed with ritual wrestling. They dance and drink themselves into oblivion and continue to dance all night long. On the morning of the second day the girl's hair is cut. Then the "pets," that is, wild animals that have been raised in captivity since they were very young, are tied in front of a large balsawood cross. These pets usually include the razorbilled currasow, the white-lipped peccary, and the collared peccary. One by one the animals are shot with arrows by the male guests. The men often miss the animals and send their arrows through the elaborately decorated woven garments made by the mother of the girl and her matrilineal kin. The men succeed only in wounding the animals, who writhe on the ground and spurt blood, and it is the women who finally kill the animals by pounding them on the head.[86] The bodies of the dead animals are then placed on special mats and wrapped in special clothes.[87] Songs are sung to extol the beauty of the beasts, and a dance is performed around their bodies. A fire is built up. The women skin and prepare the dead animals. The young girls, standing near the house-posts, watch people eat. These young girls are beautifully dressed and decorated, especially their faces, hands, and feet. Finally, on this the second day, their hair is cut. The girls may now marry. People drink as long as there is beer.

The role of symbolic seclusion in Shipibo girls' initiation portrays culture as a process of containment. Culture, in the person of the female initiate, contains primordial forces through the experience of the symbolic meaning of the girl's own growth processes, whether physical, mental, emotional, aesthetic or moral. Containment cuts several ways: it hems in some symbolic items (e.g., sound, when she keeps silence), shuts out others (e.g., men, forbidden foods, or evil *joshin*) and encases the initiate herself within a macrocontainer whenever symbolic items must flow through her own body openings (e.g., menstrual blood). On the one hand, the process of ritual containment during girl's initiation wards off chaotic forces coming from the outside, thereby establishing an outer perimeter of symbolic life. Beyond that periphery lurk the forces of unbounded chaos. On the other hand, by encompassing the chaos of superabundant primordial life, which is symbolized by fluids like blood and drink, the containers provided by culture (the enclosure, the initiate, the drinkers) establish a center where life, human and cosmic, periodically regenerates itself. When contained within the pregnant womb and bounded by cultural symbolism (avoidances, restrictions, seclusion), the waters of chaos, which threaten to be the menstruum of cosmic life, subsequently serve as a life-giving environment generative of new life. Within that space, controlled by human being, fluids are admitted and emitted on deliberately observed and symbolically marked periodic schedules (menstrual periods, festival cycles, and times of conception, gestation, parturition, and life-passage). As a result protean elements like the flood, the lustful moon, blood, and skin assume their regular periodic forms as flood tides, high-water seasons, lunar cycles, menstruation, and new children. At some point in each one of these cases, its specific periodicity and outward form signifies the meanings of shame (i.e., of change, exchange of one transforming appearance for another).

The enclosure of the girl by means of symbolic seclusion, parallel to the way in which a container prevents the open flow of liquid, concentrates all creative processes in one place. It bends the cycles of ripening and rotting in on themselves, making them reflective. In other words, enclosure renders the process of metamorphosis the girl undergoes during her confinement homologous to fermentation.[88] Stopping the flow, bringing closure to a state of being, introduces the condition of death, decay, rot. This is viewed as the same yeasting process of change, or ferment, which cultures appropriate to regenerate life. Containing and manipulating the process of deadly liquefaction produces new vegetal, human, and spiritual life in the forms of beer, the new woman, her prospective offspring, the spirits reborn in brew, the gods or heroes reincarnate as the drinkers and the candidate. In celebrating both kinds of ferment, drinking festivals and women's initiation effect the regeneration of cultural processes themselves.

Like the ritual shame that publicly and symbolically characterizes the emotional state of the initiand during her seclusion, the cultural process of containment is designed to set up a situation of embarrassment, an encircling barrage, dam, or barricade which obstructs the normal flow of events and relationships during the passage from one reality into another.[89] Openness of the body signalled in first menses, bodily mutilation, or unguarded glance proclaims that human existence, insofar as it is unbounded and undefined, dissolves. The fact that human life opens at all raises questions about the resources that can staunch its flow, prevent it from utter openness and dissolution. Shyness and other avoidances that create ritual seclusion are cultural symbols that protectively embrace the changing individual, who suffers the attack of watery or periodic beings such as aquatic monsters or the lascivious moon. By surrounding or covering a girl with its imagery, this protective mantle of seclusion defines a fixed place and time of hidden change. Ironically, if these processes of change were not hidden, their effects might never be seen. Conversely, by suspending the molten candidate in a cultural chrysalis, society protects itself from deliquescence. By appearing to cover over moments of change, the occluding images of concealment foreshadow the emergence of newly formed symbolic meanings when the veil is lifted.

BEING KEPT IN THE DARK: PRESCRIBED INVISIBILITY OF THE COVERED GIRL Invisibility of the candidate frequently becomes a goal in women's initiation. Symbolic invisibility functions as proof of utter closure. It is a sign that seclusion is successful. The candidate is kept from sight, in both senses of the phrase. She remains out of public view and is prevented from seeing in the ordinary manner. Women's initiation frequently underscores the antipathy between light and the creative transformation of the sort that must take place to change a girl into a woman. The initiand is blocked off behind sunscreens, removed from the full light of day. The girl herself, one in being with her creative womb, which is being readied as a container of life, becomes an "instrument of darkness."

Initiation among the Waiwai, formally held only for girls, makes the girl as invisible as her cervix. The girl spends two months secluded in a hut that she enters at menarche. She is to remain absolutely out of sight until her mother thrusts a long bow through the leaves of the hut and tells the girl to "hold on." At that time, without saying a word, the girl is drawn out of the hut and given a small gourd which she must push up between her legs so that, in the future, her cervix will remain unseen. Like the regenerative instruments of her reproductive anatomy, the girl herself must become a hidden process. Next, she is given a belt full of stinging ants to prevent her from becoming lazy. After receiving instructions from her mother she is redecorated, this time with armbands made of strings of white beads. These are her marks of maturity.[90]

The Waiwai girls' initiation seems rooted in a myth that describes the events of a cosmic flood and the foundation of a dance festival called Yamo. In those ancient times an adolescent girl, contrary to strict orders from her grandmother, stared at the middle of the river and excited the anaconda-people. Wishing to have sex with the young girl, they rose up from the river. Her grandmother hid her in darkness under a clay vessel. For days, the anaconda-people danced around the house where the girl was hidden. However, they never discovered her. The perfect darkness under the vessel and the invisibility of seclusion saved her. Eventually, the anaconda-people tired of the dancing and retired, leaving their ceremonial ornaments and dresses in the house. No sooner had they retired than a giant armadillo penetrated the ground underneath the vessel where the girl was hiding. Along with the armadillo came floodwaters, rushing through the ground and carrying fish and water beings. The girl narrowly escaped in the company of her grandmother, who had the presence of mind to bring with her some of the items of culture from that ancient world, including the decorative ornaments left from the anaconda-people's dances.[91] Indeed, it is imperative that a Waiwai girl be initiated, for if she is not, anaconda-people will spit and cause a flood.[92] In light of the cosmic catastrophe that already occurred in the mythic past, this is no idle threat.

The Toba also insist on making a female initiate invisible by keeping her completely under wraps at all times. Her face is painted or covered, and her body is ensconced in a special hut. Toba initiation is celebrated as a puberty rite for girls, but is not generally celebrated for boys at all. Menses is brought on by a new moon. During her first menstruation a girl is especially vulnerable to the attack of harmful spirits. For five days she is confined to her house and conducts a rigorous fast. Her whole body is covered.[93] On each of these evenings young men assemble to drink, dance, and sing to the accompaniment of their magic rattles. Each day young men perform the powerful courtship dance, the *nonomí*. When the girl's first period has passed, her mother and women friends search for armadillos. The men in the village go rhea-hunting. A feast is held in which each sex consumes the game that it has found. It is important that the men consume a great volume of *algaroba* beer and that they dance in a magic performance around the girl, who, under cover of nocturnal darkness, sits in the center of their circle with her face covered. During the day she has had her face painted with red *urucú*. At the time when a young girl is ready to marry, a young man considered suitable by her parents must prove his worthiness in a ceremonial ordeal. The girl is placed inside a small hut of straw, which is built for the occasion. It has a tiny entrance and a small hole in the middle. Although food is brought to her she is not allowed to leave the hut.

The same ingredients of invisibility and hiddenness from light are important in Guayakí women's initiation, which also takes place when a girl reaches menarche (*pirä upu o*, "the blood flows").[94] Clastres records one such case. The girl fled into the forest at her first menstruation. She avoided letting people look upon her. She was said to be *by-iä*, "without a name, without a nature." Returning soon afterward, the girl seated herself in the hut of her relatives, and addressed her grandmother (the only one to remain in the otherwise evacuated home), saying, "My blood is there." The grandmother had served as the *tapave*, "she who lifted up" her granddaughter from the "dropped" state during the girl's birth ceremony, and had therefore raised her from the condition of a ground-bound animal to the status of a human being. Now the old woman announced the arrival of menses in a loud voice. The girl's mother began to sing a weepy lament. The girl's father cried out that his daugher's blood had fallen on the peccary meat he was roasting. Two old ladies began to massage the skin of the young girl. The grandmother joined in. The girl, lying passive and immobile, with her eyes closed, was massaged and then completely covered over with dried palm branches. To screen out the light of the sun, the girl's father built a shelter called *tapy jyvapa*, a menstrual arbor not unlike the initiation hut made for boys. The girl moved into the hut and was blanketed over with ferns. These symbolic actions accomplished their goal. They rendered the girl *kaku* — invisible, that which cannot and ought not be seen. Nothing else happened that first day.

The next day the ritual resumed at a very early hour. The seclusion hut had been brought outside the encampment area "for there where (the girl) was lying during the night, the space had become soiled, not directly by her blood, but by all manner of things which serve as vehicles for fearful and repulsive beings." [95] The girl's father had gone to the forest to bring back *kymata* liana, which would serve in the ritual purification of all those who had been contaminated by contact, especially sexual contact, with the young girl.

Two fiber cords are tied around the girl's knees in order to make her legs fat, a sign of health and vigor. As she lies flat on her stomach, she is whipped by two old women from her shoulders to her ankles. The fibers are so thin and light that the ordeal is mostly symbolic. The fibers are referred to as the "whips (i.e., penis) of the tapir." They serve the purpose of instilling sexual desire for men in the girl.

The girl is darkened with hot wax. The dark stain takes several days to disappear. Her face is painted with horizontal lines on her forehead, vertical lines on her nose, four marks on her cheeks, and six on her chin. Her chest and back are painted as well. The skin of the young girl's stomach is now subjected to the ordeal of slicing, scarifying and tattooing, the *jaycha bowo*.

SUMMARY DISPLAY   Through the closure and enclosure of her own body, the girl fixes a space marked by a death of some sort: animal sacrifice, the passion of her initiatory ordeals (silence, immobility, scarification, cutting), the passing away of the primordial beings on whom she models her behavior, the occultation of her own body and personality under the "deadly" sign of the cocoon and ornamental trappings of her own transformation. This female container contains the liquefaction of change, the flow of time, to become the generative center of culture. By providing spatial images of closure for the fluctuating currency of existence in time,[96] women's initiation makes space investible (habilitable), decorable, habitable, and able to assume new forms in the shape of a new child in her penetrated womb, abundant crops in opened fields, or culture itself in the interventions of the sacred into the space of the cosmos, interruptions which mark religious celebrations of change.

Women's initiation celebrates the regenerative event that occurred when solvent powers and fluxive properties achieved closure in space. In regard to women's initiation, cultures reenact such closure in several ways: (1) through symbolic *encompassment*, accomplished dynamically by the whirlwind tour or pilgrim's parade around the cosmos; (2) through *enclosure*, a passive approach emphasizing cloister, stasis, fixity, immobility, overshrouding, and overinvestiture; and (3) by drawing lines, that is, by making *sharp distinctions*.[97] Separating one space (or concept, or image, or meaning) from another is achieved through bodily mutilations such as scarification or haircutting, which mark the outer limits of the body, or by means of the staged reappearance of signifiers (the mythic jar of seclusion, the primordial monsters, the flood) whose contradictory meanings (inside/outside, openness/closure, decoration/occultation, attack/alliance, life/death, before/after) shaped culture in the beginning. Above all, the closure accomplished in women's initiation makes possible a new kind of disclosure, a "coming out" that is deliberately cultural. The display of radiant beauty upon emergence is the telos of confinement. The transformed girls are put on parade. The exhibition honors them as effective signs of the mysterious processes and creative forces that transformed them.[98] Because women's initiation collapses the inner and outer realities of space (e.g., the candidates become viable containers of life by being impounded), the ordinarily unseen processes at work in the hidden darkness of women's wombs or in the invisible dimensions of cosmic space are made visible through women's own beautiful and effective bodies, in the products of their craft (basketry, pottery, weaving) exercised during initiatory seclusion, in the eventual fruits of their subsequent labor as farmers and feeders, as well as in the bodies of their future offspring. The display of all these goods reveals the sacredness of women, which undergirds the power of the cultural process. That is, the display of the debutantes and their wares discloses an aspect of the sacred as it impinges on the nature of femininity and its essential role in the generation of culture. Women's beauty, power, acumen, effectiveness, and fertility manifest the forces they encompass, absorb, and embody.

MALE INITIATION

Initiation is essential to being human. The examination of female initiation clarified several reasons for this. Most especially, initiation provides the initiate the awareness that she or he is the product of human culture. People learn to identify themselves as cultural beings. Through experience, candidates suffer the knowledge that, like culture itself, they are fashioned in the image of sacred beings and events. They are, in fact, a summation of values revealed in the mythic beginnings. In order to become fully human, people must pass through the process of initiation, the discovery that *they are symbols*. In becoming themselves, they seize the irony at the heart of the imaginative (the human) mode of existence: each person is always also another reality, a supernatural state of being. This accounts for the negative undertone of denial and ordeal so prevalent in initiatory processes: one must discover experientially that one's life is neither simple nor unidimensional but multivalent. This self-disclosure requires constantly dying to one level of meaning and identity in order to be reborn on several others. The passage from one ontological condition to another, a transience that characterizes human being, demands that a human individual resolve this crisis, this split brought on by the fan of meanings and references that sprout from one's own symbolic nature. The result is that human existence is a ceaseless series of ordeals and deaths, grasped, of course, on the imaginative level since symbolic existence is the heart of the matter. These deaths permit rebirth, a requickening of one's symbolic meaning in a new light, and a redefinition or even resurrection of the self in a new mode.[99] The need for initiation explains why humans must be doubly made, fashioned and then refashioned to conform in mind, spirit, and awareness to supernatural beings.

The initiatory process of being human not only places the reproductive processes of biological, vegetal, animal, aesthetic, and cosmic generation in a new symbolic setting during women's initiation, but also sets within their properly sacred context the reproductive processes of physical and sociopolitical life in which men have enjoyed a high profile.

The Makiritare ably communicate the urgent need for initiation. The first Makiritare man was created at the close of the first New Garden festival, which was celebrated by the primordial beings. However, in order to become a genuine human being he immediately had to be acculturated. He had to be made a particular expression or interpreted reenactment of the divine beings whose acts established the conditions of culture and revealed the profound significance of the reality in which he found himself. Consequently, that first man was immediately "initiated" to the ritual practices and mythic knowledge of the primordial beings, the masters of all species. He was taught how to call down the sky people who instructed him how to fashion musical instruments and sing the unalterable songs that describe the cutting down of Marahuaka, the unique tree-mountain that once connected heaven and earth.

The songs of the contemporary New Garden festival are a self-contained revelation made known, always in the same phonetic form, by the *sadashe*, the masters of species. Through drinking, dancing, and musical stimuli, the initiates are drawn into wisdom and power. Fasting, isolation, and silence precede the more dramatic moments of initiation. Sleeplessness, intoxication, and endless forced dancing break down the normal structures of the body and mind and force the candidate into a strange state of waking dream.[100]

> He must go on dancing and singing and listening, never for a moment losing contact with the spinning world around him. That's the way one learns how to conquer death — entering the collective trance of the dancers, singing, listening, responding, lost in the monotony of movement and song, integrating further and further into the telepathic circle of So'to [Makiritare] in the communion of ritual. Listening to the words of the Master, the dancers' task is to immediately and accurately repeat them. The [master of song], however, sings in such a way as to make the comprehension of his words as difficult as possible. He wants to sharpen the senses of the youths, musicians, and dancers to their absolute maximum. As if absorbed in himself he sings in a very low, almost inarticulate voice. In order to hear the words, the initiates bring the noise of their steps and the sound of their instruments down to a bare minimum, drawing close enough to

the Master to see the fleeting whisper itself escape from his lips. And so they get it and repeat it, just the way the hunter gets and repeats the song of the bird he draws near in order to kill. They open their eyes and ears. They hold their breath. They wait for the words and pry into the mind of the Master. The students' mental concentration now is extraordinary, the repetition unerring, even though in the beginning the sounds were unintelligible.[101]

A new consciousness is needed to understand myth. The rituals of initiation are geared to develop this new consciousness, one possible only in the mature adult, who has developed an increasingly sensitive sense of hearing and ability to understand. The candidate is forced to drink and dance until "he's dead," "*nëumai.*" At the end of the initiation festival, the ornaments are burned and the boys stamp-dance on the embers as a final ordeal — just as did the mythic twins at the beginning of time.

Makiritare initiation drives home the fact that the initiated state is the fully human one because, by making the initiate dead to what has become ordinary, it introduces a new awareness of the sacred world. By prescribing new levels of pain and endurance, initiation rearranges the established order of dormant senses and shocks them into wakefulness. It opens the ears and eyes, quickening the candidates to new orders of intensity and perception so that they hear, smell, feel, and see everyday events as signs of their immersion in primordial reality.[102] Their life, inescapably cultural and symbolic even in their dreams and deliria, is a reenactment of sacred events.

Strategies of male initiation often bear striking resemblance to the symbolic contrivances of female initiation. Symbolic instruments effecting transformation into a regenerative being can be remarkably similar for both sexes: enclosures that represent the tombwomb, shreddable and sheddable skin, smells of rot and fermentation, musical instruments, masks, body decorations, haircutting or hairbinding, gourds and containers of darkness, and so on. This similarity of symbolic strategies has not been lost on South American peoples. The most fascinating explanations for the overlap locate the reason for it in the ancient origins, the mythic history, of these sacramental signs, when males borrowed or stole the powers and instruments of regenerative life from primordial females, who were their first possessors. These myths acknowledge that the strategies of enclosure, encompassment, musical instruments, and masks are most properly associated with feminine sacredness. In the course of mythic history, usually through some act of violence, males expropriated them.[103]

Today men possess external signs (whereas women maintain internalized vestiges) of the reproductive capacities of primordial females. Men exhibit the outward signs in the form of musical instruments or masks periodically displayed in initiation and in the festive, regenerative moments of culture. In menses, pregnancy, and parturition, as well as in other moments of production and reproduction, women periodically display the fact that they have internalized primordial powers that are consubstantial with their bodies. The hiddenness and exhibitionism of the two sexes, therefore, not only follow the different rhythms of their signifiers (their festive sacra and the calendar of their appearances, their bodies, their sacred expressions and discharges) but cause the values of privacy and publicity, occultation and revelation, to change, depending on their relationship to specific modes of reproduction.

In these cases, regenerative life-processes attach themselves to men only through violence and the dynamism of relating to or even expropriating what is strange and foreign. Reproductive processes connect themselves to male sacrality only through the violence of the religious imagination. The mythic theft could be said to describe the violence perpetrated by all images of symbolic affinity. Mythic violence represents the force of imagination required to overcome the tendency toward nongenerative randomness and meaninglessness that is inherent in nonsymbolic life, where there threatens to be an apparent lack of relation in space between objects (e.g., men and the instruments of regeneration; the male body and the bodies of offspring from the female) and an apparent separation in time between distinct events (e.g., intercourse and parturition). The origin myths of male initiatory devices, forcibly taken from females, forge a symbolic link between generative acts and their reproductive consequences in a space and time that are themselves grasped as symbolic manifestations of powerful modes of being. That is, in light of their origin, the instruments of transformation in men's initiation manifest in social form the violence intrinsic to change, especially the changes of meaning endemic to human symbolic existence. The myths of a lost primordial matriarchy connect the violence of men's initiations with this fact: the relationship of primordial males to the power that is able to reproduce life is never intrinsic and apparent, as it is in the case of primordial females. Rather, it is established and maintained through the force of cultural ideas (e.g., theories of conception or the myths of primordial matriarchy). Therefore, in such cases, the male power of reproduction remains an appendage to male sacrality; a cultural construction that appears external, ideological, or instrumental. Due to the male relationship to reproductive processes, clarified in the myths, men's symbolic life is a clearer window on the meaning of violence; it better signifies the force of imagination, which undergirds all symbolic processes comprising culture. In any case, the myths are about a primordial condition and its transformation. They account for the fact that both sexes play a role in the reproductive processes of human life (biological, aesthetic, cultural, sociopolitical) and that their differential roles are a reflection of the various ways in which their bodies and habits serve as signifiers of a sacred history. The patterned bodies, acts, and relations of the sexes are symbolic forms that signal diverse aspects of the history of the sacred.

Among the most fascinating implements used for male initiation are the muscial instruments that are employed by groups in the northwestern Amazon region. In many instances, myths make clear that these sacred flutes and trumpets, embodiments of ancient ancestors or even pieces of the body of a single supernatural being, once belonged to females. For the Baniwa, for example, primordial women, led by Amaru, first used the musical horns that are now sounded during male initiation. Amaru was the first female being to have an opening; the birth canal through which the hero Kuai passed at birth. Amaru and her female band were the first to use the openness of Kuai's body parts (the musical instruments) to open the fertile places (species of trees, animals, plants, language groups) of the earth. Baniwa adolescent initiation, called Kuaipan ("Kuai-house"), is held in coordination with the ripening of certain forest fruits (which fruits vary with the account) and with the appearance of the Pleiades (Oalipere) on the horizon at dusk. It is fitting that this event, which marks the passage of human time, should be a calendrical nexus of cosmic and seasonal times as well. An elder hosts the affair and directs the men who came to participate. Using the strategy of seclusion, they seal every hole in the house wall. Then they gather manioc, tobacco, peppers, ornaments, feathers, whips, and panpipes. The Baniwa attend to all details with consummate care in order that every initiation be precisely the same as the moment when Kuai, the body whose passages make the sounds of the ancestral sib-instruments, passed from this world in a fire.[104]

Essentially, the Baniwa rites of initiation are performed to "open" the candidates just as Kuai was opened to make sounds that fertilized places and matrices (Amaru and her female companions) throughout the earth. The moment also has cosmogonic overtones since it was sound that caused the separation and opening of the earth in the very beginning. As a trumpet was played over the tiny stone (or piece of excrement) that was the earth in the beginning, it began to expand with each note to take on the fertile proportions it now has. So, at initiation, the sacred Kuai flutes "make holes in the initiates' bodies, including the opening of their sexual orifice. They are open."[105] For the Baniwa, possession of the Kuai flutes is essential to the making of people, both in the myth that separates humans from animals and in the process of the life-cycle that "opens" a person. The openness effected by the sound of the flutes is a condition essential to the "knowledge" that makes a person fertile and responsible.[106]

GROWING A CHANGING SKIN

In addition to the musical instruments that reassemble a mystical body in order to open the candidates, there exists the related symbolic device of changing skin. This was the means for utter transformation of being designed for some Tukano-speakers by their creator, Yepá Huaké. The creator had secured the gifts of dream and of night for human ancestors and had them brought to Diawí, a placental world existing in the image of a *maloca*, so that he could ritually bestow on humans the gift of sleep. Yepá Huaké then directed all the people to sleep and to awaken at midnight. Upon awakening at midnight, the people were to proceed to the landing and bathe themselves. Then they were to drink water and vomit it up again. While the chief ancestor was vomiting up the water, two other ancestors should smoke tobacco and knock on the door of Diawí, the *maloca* universe. After knocking on the door, they could begin to peel their skin away from their heads to their shoulders. Later they could continue stripping their skin away down to their belts. By knocking at the door at intervals between these episodes of progressive peeling of skin, they could continue stripping their skin away down to the knees and then eventually peel it off completely. According to the creator's instruction, when all the skin had been stripped off the body of Cajtá, Yúpuri Baúro and all the people would be able to enter Diawí, in the center of which they would find the divinity Yepá Huaké seated with a pot of coca, from which they were to eat before falling asleep again.[107] Unfortunately, the two ancestor-heroes, Cajtá Casóro and Cajtá, did not wake up in time to peel their skin off. However, Tukano tradition preserved the creator's detailed instructions concerning skin change and the obtaining of immortality, and the Tukano-speakers symbolically carry out these acts in order completely to change the being of neophytes during initiation.

Skin change is also part of the mythic foundation of Juruna maturation. A Juruna myth describes the transformation a person had to undergo in order to marry. The story involves a cosmic tour similar to the instances described in the discussion of women's initiations. It recounts the wanderings of an old man, wrinkled and ugly, who thought of nothing but death, although he wished to be married. Coming to a clearing in the forest, he saw a ladder stretching down from the sky to the ground. He ascended to a place where he met Alapá and his four daughters, whom the old man treated with utmost respect. As a reward for the old man's deference to the primordial females, Alapá permitted him to bathe in the celestial waters, which transformed him into a fair youth with clear, new skin.[108]

Shedding skin is tantamount to rebirth. In many cases rebirth and change of skin are not just metaphors of one another but explicitly identified as the same. For example, according to Barasana theories of gynecology and conception, the processes of conception and gestation clothe the substantial elements, powers, and processes (especially evident in blood, bone, and semen) of a new person in an envelope of new skin that grows from the lining of the uterus during the time between menstrual periods.[109] In such an interpretive frame, the acts of clothing, growing new skin, closure of space, and birth of a new person are essentially the same. They are identical to the shedding of the skin of Romi Kumu, the sky, during the first rejuvenating skin-change of the primordium and, subsequently, during each rainy season which renews the face of the earth and the procession of the stars. At puberty the birth-skin that has enveloped an individual from the moment of conception in a woman's womb is split off, molts, or dissolves in order to assume a new, cultural and mature social skin,[110] which is the garment of symbolic meanings that line the matrix of culture.

The symbolism of shedding one's skin in order to be rejuvenated and to achieve or approach that state of being enjoyed by the immortals of mythic times is a common one and is often found in association with initiation, that special time of rebirth to sacred realities. The Barasana of the Pirá-Paraná River (Vaupés River drainage), however, make a startlingly thorough and original application of this pattern of initiation.

The Barasana believe that *He* House, a celebration honoring the *he* (ancestors and the musical instruments that embody them), effects a change of skin.[111] This change of skin accompanies the change in status of the initiates, a process referred to as "changing the soul or spirit" *(ɯsɯ wasoasi)*. During *He* House the initiates are vulnerable to the danger inherent in the ritual objects as well as the danger of attack from shamans and spirits; they are in a state comparable "to that of crabs and other animals that have shed their old shells or skins."[112] The special enclosure built by the shamans for the initiates serves as a kind of protective cultural integument during this vulnerable time.

However, the linking of boys' initiation to the female reproductive process lends the symbolism of changing skin quite a different and original tone.[113] This different emphasis takes its cue from myths about the supreme being, Romi Kumu, who is somehow identified with the sky.[114] She is called Vagina Woman, and her menstrual blood and urine are identified with the rain.[115] Romi Kumu creates the *he* people from her womb; they have no father.[116] The *he* people are like women because they menstruate. It is believed that Romi Kumu becomes old and ugly at the end of each day. But in the morning she bathes, changes her skin, and is rejuvenated. She is able to effect this transformation by means of a gourd of beeswax, which she keeps with her in the sky. Stephen Hugh-Jones illustrates how this fundamental mythical example of the creator – supreme being serves as the model for all regenerative transformations in Barasana life: "To change skins is a way to rejuvenation and hence, to immortality, and this theme is stressed throughout *He* House and the period following it."[117] Likewise, Romi Kumu uses face paint toward the same end. The face paint is believed to be her own menstrual blood. When she removes the blood it takes away a layer of skin, and her face becomes radiant once again.[118] Since menstruation is an internal changing of the skin, women can live longer than men. When the initiates are painted with black paint at the opening of *He* House, the object is to change their skins. The disappearance of that paint, which marks the end of the seclusion, proves that this purpose has been achieved. Likewise, the obligation of initiates to wash their faces and the ordeal of being whipped ought to be seen as growing out of the need to change one's skin.[119]

Christine Hugh-Jones emphasizes the tension that exists between the renewable female cycle and the irreversible progress of male lineage-time. Nevertheless, the Barasana, as she points out, believe that renewal and rebirth for both men and women are inescapably bound up with the primordially feminine process of growing new skin.[120] With the aid of musical instruments and other ceremonial trappings, ancient males appropriated some control over this symbolic technique for change. The Barasana resolve the tension between kinds of temporality, between the sexes, and between biological and cosmic existence by modeling their transformations on the rejuvenating menstrual cycle of Romi Kumu. During *He* House, even men enter a condition equivalent to that of menstruation.

To be sure, allusions to male sexuality are not lacking: the sky-vagina is like a gourd penetrated by the primal sun, *Yeba Hakɯ*[121]; the earth-space is also penetrated from the east by the primordial ancestor anaconda, who swims to the center of the earth; the longhouse interior is penetrated ceremonially by the men's procession of patrilineal kin when they enter the house playing the *he* flutes and trumpets during the *He* House ceremony. From that house, the womb of the sib, will issue offspring of this penetrating patriline. The procession itself is an explicit imitation of the journey of the ancestor anaconda at the beginning of time.

Food penetrates the body space, wherein it is transformed into nutrients for the body. This is analogous to the Barasana belief that semen feeds the growing fetus when the penis penetrates the womb. Thus, blowing through the long musical tubes onto the boys and over the fruit during *He* House and Fruit House ceremonies is likened to the mythic episode in which fruit is inseminated by penetration. Eventually the fruit ripens, matures, and multiplies. One might also see the idea of the penetration of a contained space of transformation in the mythic episode in which *He* Anaconda, when his grandsons see the *he* for the first time in their lives, swallows them and transports them to the primordial Water Door in the east. There they die inside of him. Eventually, however, *He* Anaconda returns to the *maloca*, reliving his first penetrating swim to the center of the earth, where he vomits up the bones of his grandchildren (the bones of the son of the sun) into a special enclosure. It is this very enclosure into which the initiates are delivered during their period of seclusion at the end of *He* House.

In spite of all these allusions to male sexuality, it is made very clear that men also must bear responsibility for the proper opening and penetration of sacred enclosures, especially their body-envelope. They do this through fasting or eating prescribed foods, induced vomiting, aversion of the eyes, control over breathing in playing the sacred instruments, and control over the openings in their musical instruments (both the sound holes and the "bell" of the trumpets and flutes). Above all, men demonstrate their responsibility for and control over their body-envelope when they open the sacred instruments (the flutes and their bodies) only during prescribed periods. Periods of fruiting, like periods of menstruation and musical timing of modulations of sound, become the markers of meaning constructed on a mythic model.

Based on field work in Colombia between 1968 and 1970, Stephen Hugh-Jones's elaborate descriptions not only illustrate the strategy of changing skin but also the initiatory devices of encompassment by cosmic parade, seclusion in initiatory enclosures, and the reassembly of a primordial body of passage (the primordial anaconda whose penetration into the world-space and passage through it marked the beginning of time) through musical ensemble. The Barasana male initiation process extends over a seven- or eight-year period and has two stages.[122] The first stage begins when the boys participate in Fruit House rites for the first time. After dusk they remain in the longhouse interior. At midnight they receive snuff blown through a bone tube; around dawn they are confined, along with the women, in the rear of the house. In the morning, they are washed on the plaza, and tobacco smoke is blown over their heads and hands by shamans. The boys then wash their

faces and hands and paint their legs black. Dressed in garters, white necker-
chiefs, and palm-leaf crowns, they are led inside the house as honored
guests.[123] They play short musical flutes and are offered the ceremonial
cigars, coca, and pink *kana* berries prepared by the shamans. Then they assist
in tipping out onto the floor the fruit that the men had carried into the house.
The youths watch the elders and shamans blow their trumpets, moving the
instruments over the fruit in a circling motion. For the most part, however,
the initiates sit quietly and motionlessly on a mat prepared for them. The
initiates are served drinks of strong *yagé*. When darkness falls, the boys are
whipped (as are other participants, including the shamans). Once they have
participated in the Fruit House for the first time, the boys will continue to
participate in a number of Fruit Houses as each fruit comes into season. The
second stage of initiation consists in seeing the true *he* instruments during
the *He* House ritual after which the initiates observe a two-month period of
restrictions on food and behavior.

Just before the celebration of *He* House rites, a Fruit House rite is held in
which shamans make preparation for the more elaborate ritual. The flutes
are fed tobacco snuff by way of a shaman blowing into the sound holes.
Between this Fruit House and the beginning of *He* House lies a three-day
period during which the initiates observe food restrictions and wake up
before dawn to bathe in the river and vomit. In the afternoon of that third day,
the initiates paint themselves black from toes to chin;[124] the younger men are
painted up to their hips, the elders up to their thighs.

During the period before *He* House, men close up any holes in the walls
of the longhouse. During the first day and night of the three-day rite, the
initiates remain with the women, confined in the rear of the house. Occasionally they flee from the house when the shamans prepare the ritual items
of wax, coca, and red paint, or when, at dawn on the second day, the long
flutes are played into the house.[125] When the sun sets on the second day, the
initiates, whose hair has been cut and whose bodies have been completely
painted black, are carried into the house by some of the older men. They are
placed in a line, linking themselves to one another by their little fingers, and
are given *kana* berries to eat. They are then told to sit in a fetal position and to
remain "absolutely motionless and not to glance from side to side. If they
move, it is said that their backs will break." [126] In this position the initiates are
given the ceremonial cigars, coca, and *yagé*. Then, for the first time, the
initiates are allowed to see the *he*, as each instrument is played and paraded
very slowly before the initiate. The trumpets are held close to the ground so
that the players' knees are not damaged (perhaps because the sound will
penetrate in a transformative way any break, joint, or opening at which it is
directed). The sound of the *he* trumpets is likened to the roar of ancestor
jaguars who wander in the forest and of an ancestor anaconda who lives in
the rivers. By making sound, the instruments breathe and come alive. "The
He instruments, brought from the forest, breathe life into the house. At Fruit
House, this same life-giving ancestral breath is blown from the trumpets over
the piles of fruit so that its soul is changed and becomes ripe and abundant,

and at *He* House, it is blown over the initiates themselves to change their souls and to turn them into strong adults." [127]

After beeswax is burned, two ornamented men play the long flutes known as Old Macaw. The initiates must remain completely motionless; they are not allowed to look at the two figures. These two figures show the initiates how to be fierce, for the flutes threaten to kill people.[128] The rest of that night is taken up with episodes that include sessions of chanting, the ingestion of coca, the smearing of snuff on one's knees, and the whipping of legs, chest, abdomen, and thighs.

Toward dawn, the initiates and young men paint one another's legs and bodies. These body-painters become related to one another in a new way — "like brothers." Then the initiates stand in a line while their G-strings are cut and their penises are blown over with the *he* instruments.[129] At dawn the next day, people go to the river to bathe. The *he* instruments are filled with water so that they can drink and vomit. The initiates drink from the flutes and trumpet. The people wash, using leaves as soap. The leaves are then crushed into a drink that induces vomiting, which ensures that the initiates will become good dancers and singers.[130] After a final meal, the bark wrappings of the instruments are dismantled and the *he* are once again submerged in the river.[131]

Shamans then shut the initiates in a special compartment, and there begins a period of ritual restriction on foods and normal activities. During this period, men are described in terms applicable to menstruating women *(bedira)*. Contact between the sexes is minimized. Each day the initiates must scrub their faces with leaves that whiten their skin.[132] "For the initiates the end of this period is signalled by the total disappearance of the black paint applied to their bodies at the start of the rite." [133] That is, the initiates emerge as new people when they have successfully grown the intended new skin, the changing and sheddable skin that is the outward sign of a symbolic and, therefore, a cultural being.

MASKS, DISSEMBLANCE, AND DISSIMULATION

Musical instruments and changing skin are not the only technology of transformation taken from primordial females and used in male initiation. Masks often reflect a similar mythic history and function. Perhaps the initiatory masks most celebrated in the ethnographic literature of South America come from Tierra del Fuego. They belonged to the Kína and the Klóketen, secret Fuegian societies of Yamana and Selk'nam men, respectively, to which boys were initiated at puberty.[134] Mythic females once used the masked ceremonies to defraud and subjugate men. Together with the secret rites in which they were worn, the masks were stolen by primordial males in a frenzy of violence, in which the men slaughtered the primordial females, who were then transformed into various species of animals. The masks became the exclusive property of men.

Yamana myths of *kína* origins forcefully emphasize the concept of disillusionment, which provoked the symbolic violence associated with the history of masks and the battle between the sexes. A hero's discovery that the masks and the life processes of regeneration associated with them were only a hoax, a facade of the supernatural, provoked the revolt of the men against women. They stripped women of the masks and rites and expropriated them as their own instruments of growth.

In these cases once again, the violence associated with men's behavior, understood symbolically, is directly related to the discovery of the symbolic nature of life. This discovery about the nature of the symbol, this critical awareness that the meaning of a sign is not fully present in its appearance but points to something absent, does violence to existence. In the case of the Yamana, the awareness of dissimulation (the condition of time that makes it possible to be two kinds of being simultaneously) brought closure to Yáiaa-šága, the primordial world presided over by Hánuxa, the insuperable female leader. The discovery of pretense fissured time, closing off the primordial time of matriarchal social order and opening up history, the temporal climate conducive to the growth of human culture. Hánuxa's reign ended in the utter transformation of an entire mode of being through the processes of death (massacre), occultation, change, and the differentiation of species that represent symbolic existence. Masks symbolically bear this history of violence, dissimulation, and disenchantment as symbolic aspects of their regenerative power.

Just as primordial females were stripped of their masks to reveal a hoax to primordial males, so in the men's initiation disguises are often deliberately exposed as ruses to novices. This may occur at a climactic moment of the ceremony, or at the end of the rites (when, for example, mummers are unmasked), or when the sacred costumes are taken off, dismantled, destroyed (e.g., tossed into a fire), or stashed away in hiding. Disillusionment of candidates through the divestiture, symbolic dismemberment, or even through the violent destruction of sacred symbols in male initiation plays a role comparable to the display of the initiate in women's initiations.[135] Both disillusionment and display reveal the creative power of total change; both of these symbolic maneuvers center on the role of absence and occultation. The display of the emergent novice in women's initiations provides stimulating evidence of unseen powers, the transformative forces of hiddenness. However, disillusionment takes a different tack on the unseen winds of change. In the case of men's initiation, ritual disillusionment frequently reenacts the violence that accompanied the discovery that the changing appearances of symbolic life, the highly visible signs required to reveal the sacred foundations of reality, insinuate conditions for deception and occultation of the sacred. "Through initiation culminating in disenchantment, the novice enters religious life in a state of crisis, disappointment, or perplexity about the nature of the sacred. The only thing he knows is that he has been fooled and his sense of what is real and what is not is confounded."[136]

Keeping in mind that initiation marks the beginning of a maturing process, not the full achievement of adulthood as a static state, and that initiation admits a young man to participation in the ritual life of the community, makes clear the cultural intention that, through lifelong symbolic action, the novice will gradually unfold the mysteries and puzzle together the pieces exposed to him during initiation. By glimpsing masks, musical instruments, ornaments, and other cult objects as symbols that point to "an encompassing mystery that is inexhaustible" [137] and hidden under signs of presence, initiation sets novices on their adult quest for a mature understanding of reality. Only through living subsequent life as an outward symbolic expression that disguises inner realities in the very process of resembling them can the sacred become more fully known.

Initiation introduces the novice to a process and to a discovery-procedure full of possibilities for ambiguity, illusion, deception, and danger as well as revelation. The mythic origins of masks, their reenactment in ceremonial mummery, and their deconstruction or disappearance for the off-season portray the tempestuous violence of symbolic life. Disillusionment is an experiential component required for the mature use and understanding of symbols. Masks cannot be taken at face value.

THE RUSE OF REVELATION Considering the many meanings and lessons of masking, it is not surprising to find that it is a central element in initiations — both those that occur at puberty and those that take place during admission into secret societies—for many South American peoples.[138] Among Akwẽ-Shavante, for instance, the very term for initiation (wamñõrõ da) means, literally, "to make masks," for the masks themselves "make the boys mature" (wapté ĩ-wa'ru da). The masks are closely associated with the spirits known as wazepari'wa, fierce and fearful beings who roam at night and who prevent the souls of the deceased from completing their journey to the village of the dead. They live at the end of the sky (the west).[139]

Akwẽ-Shavante initiation takes place in three separate phases over at least a six-month period.[40] This does not include the lengthy period of preparation that boys spend in the bachelors' hut in the age-grade of young men (ritai'wa), who, although ostensibly married, are generally not able to lead the lives of married men.[141]

The period in the bachelors' hut, a time of shared food, work, dreams and songs, is one of frequent athletic rituals (wrestling, dueling with clubs, racing with logs). The athletic rites, dances, song-learning, and preparation of ceremonial ornaments prepare the boys both physically and mentally for the demanding series of physical and spiritual exercises that will be carried on during their initiation.[142]

The first phase of initiation may be of some three weeks' duration. During this time action centers on the immersion of the candidates in cold water, where they splash, jump, and slap the surface of the water to make loud noises.

During the second phase of initiation, the boys manufacture dance masks and the formal leaf capes worn by the ceremonial leader of the running displays held every morning until sunrise.[143] The huge grass capes, called no'oní, are composed of the thin center strands of outsized palm fronds. Every evening, double-barreled flutes are played in the bachelors' hut. The second phase of initiation closes with a dance by a senior ceremonial leader who wears an outsized grass cape and a rattle of deer's hooves. While performing a fierce stamping dance he throws the cape off his shoulders so that it lands between the goalposts at the finish line of the racecourse. Then, after similar dancing by others, the goalposts are tied off, and passage between them is closed.[144]

The third phase of initiation lasts five days. The first day is spent singing, dancing, and completing the dance masks. That evening a vigil procession, led by a capebearer, begins, and it goes on throughout the night. The ceremonial cape is tapped with a wand by a person who whistles ceremonially. Completing the circuit by processing clockwise, the party returns in the opposite direction, stopping in front of every other house and carrying the double-barreled flutes on scarlet poles.[145] The procession continues until sunrise. On the second day, women of a mature age-set paint themselves in male ceremonial style and, separating themselves from the men, sing songs characteristic of the second stage of initiation. In the brush, men who had retreated there watch a masked ceremonial leader dance in a solemn way. Later in the day, the two new ceremonial leaders of the new age-set kneel on a mat in the center of the village. On either side of the mat is a scarlet lance with a double-barreled flute hanging from it. The boys are painted and decorated. The rest of the day, evening, and night is given over to various kinds of ceremonial dances, which last until dawn the next morning. Then, at a given signal, the men, hoarse and tired, rush into their houses to seize the dance masks before the girls can manage to "steal" them. The masks are brought to the mature-men's circle at the center of the village and given to the chief. He, in turn, passes them to those women who participated in the dance.[146] During this third day, a singing-marathon is carried out during which initiates, led by mature men, move solemnly from hut to hut looking neither to the left nor the right. The novices sing until nightfall, when the other men of the village come toward them crouching as if they were stalking game. The novices squat in a straight line in front of their bachelor's hut. A small circle of bast is placed on each initiate's head. All the gathered men then whistle in a ceremonial fashion and the boys go into the hut.

On the fourth day, the newly initiated boys are allowed to kindle their own fire by using a brand taken from the mature-men's fire.[147] Later the age-sets perform a ceremonial run into the village during which each newly initiated boy is accompanied by a group of helpers who "run him in."[148] On the fifth day of the ceremony's third stage, the newly initiated boys prepare the opening of the age-set that is to follow them by cutting and dressing the hair of boys and girls younger than themselves.

Initiation for the Akwẽ-Shavante, as for other peoples, is the most intense social experience of a person's life.[149] The ceremonial activities are, in fact, displays of virtues (literally, "powers"), which are esteemed because they are known, from myth, to have brought about the very conditions of existence and culture.[150] Vanity concerning one's appearance and physical prowess is emphasized, since the novices "embody virtues" and powers that created or transformed the myriad forms of being during the heroic age of myth. That is why they are, by definition, beautiful. They are expected to train themselves to acquire and sustain a state of conscious attention, vigilance and concentration *(warīti-)*. Ceremonial running displays, log races, hunting, dancing, and singing bring about the alertness and vigilance that they signify.[151]

The initiation rituals of the Akwē-Shavante are the primary illustrations of their philosophy that rituals "make one beautiful" and that "to be beautiful" is to "be good." Morality has an aesthetic foundation.[152] Ritual performances, in particular, are those beautiful patterns that have the efficacious power of creating an harmonious whole. When they are "beautiful" and proper, they possess an unimpedable generative power, on the model of those beings who successfully exercised such creative power in mythic times.[153]

Aside from musical instruments and masks, other male initiatory devices may derive directly from primordial females. Such is the case among the Apinayé, particularly in regard to the ceremonial axes and clubs that distinguish between age-grades of initiated Apinayé males. Strategies such as haircutting and decoration are also already familiar and overlap with the symbolic mechanisms of maturation employed in women's initiation. In fact, the first phase of Apinayé male initiation appears to be a long preparation of ornaments for the closing ceremony. Two logs are painted red on the outside and blackened with fire on the inside. Then they are decorated with leaves. After the logs are raced into the village, they are paraded around the plaza. The boy and girl novices then observe a singing-vigil on the logs in the plaza. After two nights of such vigil the male candidates rub their bodies against an old woman, wiping their red paint on to her body. This prevents premature conception of children. Later, at the stream, they rub their bodies against a tree stripped of bark. This gives them strength. They also drink sap from the tree "in order to live long." [154]

The seclusion of the second phase of Apinayé initiation is much more strict, lasting five to six months. Instruction during the second seclusion is more pointed, centering on marriage instruction and on training in the virtues of obedience, chastity, and cooperation.[155] As in the first phase of initiation, an important moment of transition occurs in association with feminine imagery. This time, instead of rubbing against the skin of an older woman, each boy is carried into his mother's house, placed on the platform bed, and completely covered with mats by older men, usually the boy's mother's brother and a "formal friend." From that time forward "the boys are no longer called pebkaág [initiates], but pēb [warriors]." [156]

The novices go on communal hunts. When they return with their game, they are given ceremonial clubs made by their *krạmgéd* (ritually appointed friend).[157] The Apinayé also have a traditional account of a group of foreign women who once enjoyed making love with a caiman. When their husbands returned from a hunt, the men killed and ate the caiman. In turn, the women ambushed their husbands and clubbed them to death. After that event, the women moved off and formed the tribe of Kupē-ndíya—an all-female community whose members "kill all male infants they bear." [158] It is from this community of women that ceremonial anchor-axes, the mark of the warrior age-grade, were obtained.

When they attain the grade of warrior the novices have their hair cut for the first time since entering seclusion, and they log race into the village when an elder signals the beginning of the race by blowing on a *Lagenaria* flute. In the village, they spend the night in vigil, singing while sitting or standing on the logs. In the morning, as in the first phase of initiation, they rub off their red paint against an old woman's body and a stripped tree trunk. However, this time they redecorate themselves and then spend the day standing in the plaza, facing the sun. Then a series of log races is run over a period of days. Each race begins later in the day until, on the last day, the last race occurs at sunset.

Regarding initiation, mention should be made of the Apinayé myth of the jaguar who possesses fire, cooks meat, and teaches a young boy how to hunt. In this myth, the adventuresome boy not only encounters the jaguar but also Megaló-kamdúre, a specter who captures the boy in his basket (*megaló* = soul, soul of the dead, or bull-roarer). Both of these fascinating beings are met during the boy's journey, which discloses the pattern of initiation. [159] That is, the origins of culture (fire, reproducing social units, hunting), spiritual maturity, and knowledge of the afterlife through an experience of death are all part of the same initiation experience.

Enclosure through investiture is also used in boys' initiations. For example, Tapirapé boys' initiation emphasizes body decoration, as its name, *anchin-kungitanchin* ("to tie one's hair and wear a large headdress"), signifies. [160] "Preparing the youth for the ceremonial was a slow and painstaking task, but it seemed to be a work of love. Networks of strings, bird down, sap, oils, hair cords, body paints, wooden blocks for holding the pigtail, bead necklaces, ear pendants and flowers, a lip plug made of white quartz all added up to body ornaments that 'must have weighed about 20 pounds.' " [161] The boys' initiation celebrates the adventure of a mythical hero named Mankanchi, who escaped from the enemies who had eaten his father. "Mankanchi was tied by the arms and legs, and was burdened with a headdress. He was expected to dance before he was killed and eaten. But he worked himself loose from his binding and, freeing himself of the headdress, he ran into the forest where he hid in a hollow log. The next day the [enemies] found only his ankle ornaments, wrist ornaments, and the headdress." [162] The initiatory ornaments are signs of both binding and loosing, of closure to one mode of existence (the childish one) and openness to another (the cultural). Since they are, for example, the bonds that fettered primordials or the vestigial signs of their undoing when they withdrew from the world, wearing them can identify the novice with a supernatural being and liberate the human initiate from his earthly or mortal condition.

Not all initiatory scenarios are elaborate. Nevertheless, even in extremely simple cases, male initiation may be a by-product of the religious life of women. Such is the case for a Waiwai boy, for whom no dramatic rites are held at initiation. Instead, his mother simply gives him an armband at the age of thirteen or fourteen. Then his nasal septum is pierced so that it can hold feathers.[163] These decorations were obtained by the first female initiate, the heroine who defeated the flood of anaconda-people with the help of her mythic grandmother.

The technique of pilgrimage and world travel in those female initiations that reenact the grand tour of the mythic cosmos also appears in male puberty rites. For instance, the initiation of aristocratic boys among the Inca was indeed a spiritual introduction to—in fact a spiritual experience of—the space and time of the universe. During their initiation seclusion, the boys relived parts of the cosmogonic and origin myths of the Inca. They visited the sacred places, the *huacas* of petrified primordial beings, in each of the four quarters of the sacred valley surrounding the imperial capital of Cuzco, the center of the universe. Just as the creator and his emissaries did at the beginning of time, the boys visited the "four quarters of the world" *(tahuantinsuyu)*. For example, in November, on their first pilgrimage to Huanacauri, the noble novices reenacted the journey of their own ancestors, who emerged from the sacred cave of Pacaritambo. They visited the hill that survived the cosmic flood and relived the creative journey of the supreme being, Viracocha, who called forth the creatures of the world after the flood. Indeed, their initiation recreates the initiation of the universe and its peoples.[164]

In many instances, due mostly to a lack of mythic data or exegesis, it is not clear how closely allied the instruments of male initiation are with feminine sacrality or primordial women. Even in these cases, however, the transition from boy to man during initiation may be performed with the collaboration of women from the community, who bring uniquely female symbolic capacity to express meanings of openness and flow. In particular, the prescribed flow of sound from the mouths of lamenting women and the staged stream of tears from their eyes operate as efficacious symbols of openness. These kinds of behavior are often ritually required to effect the change of boys into men.

Such is the case among the Guayakí, whose theory of the supernatural powers of physiology underlies many of the symbolic actions of initiation ceremonies. When a boy considers himself *yma* ("grown and vigorous, attractive to women, knowledgeable of the hunt"), he and his *peperöve* (initiation companions) ask their fathers for *imbi mubu*, the perforation of the lip. The boys and their fathers mutually agree on an *imbimubuaregi* ("the piercer of your lip"). This ritual role is a prestigious one. Under the direction of this leader, a ritual clearing is made and a special fire is lit around which the boys spend the first night they have ever spent alone. This is also their first fast from food and drink and the first time that they raise their voices and open their mouths to sing the *prerä*, the sacred song of men, which they perform shyly and inexpertly. Meanwhile, the men and women retire separately for this, the first night. On the next day, the young candidates continue their fast.

They go into the forest and, with metal axes, they fell *pindo* palm trees and split them open to scoop out the soft marrow. The marrow and the palm branches are brought back to the initiation site. The young men set about constructing an initiation hut while the master of the ceremony, the "piercer of the lip," departs on a ritual hunt for a coati and the candidates' mothers go to the forest to fill their baskets with palm marrow left behind by the boys.

The boys now stuff themselves with coati meat, palm fruit, and marrow from the palms they have felled. During the candidates' period of symbolic death, the coati *(kare)* meat fills them with the supernatural force they need in order to be reborn into a more powerful mode of being.[165] The meal of coati and heart of palm is eaten as the sun rises, and it ends when the sun reaches its zenith, directly over the *enda ayiä*, the sacred space prepared for initiation. This was the position of the sun during the permanent day that reigned at the moment, recounted in myth, when human beings came into existence. "And in memory of that first event in the history of Aché [true human beings], one awaits high noon in order to celebrate the *imbi mubu*, to celebrate the solemn origin of the true Aché." [166] The first ancestors emerge once again from the earth into the light of the full First Day.

The novices' heads are shaved and their lips are massaged to soften the skin. The lip is perforated with the tibia of a monkey. The "perforator" holds the boy's lip with his left hand, looks deep into his eyes, and forces the *piju*, the monkey tibia, through the lip from the outside to the inside. The instrument is then withdrawn. This act is called the *mubu*. An assistant of the perforator then inserts a pointed *piju* monkey tibia, through the lip from the inside to the outside. This is the movement called *kutu*. The bone is left in the lip until it heals and scars over. The boy has now passed beyond the age group called *embogi* ("the penises") and attains the state of a *betagi*, wearer of the lip-plug.[167] The paradox of these shifting names involved in the process of maturation is not lost on the Guayakí. They make it a source of reflection on the nature and relationship of "being" and "having": "One is a penis as long as one does not have one; one ceases to be a penis from the moment a man possesses one." [168]

Just as on the First Night, perfumed beeswax is thrown on the initiates' fire. It was this wax, burning and giving off a pleasant odor at the beginning of time, that instigated the return of sunlight and the beginning of the regular alternation of day and night that now characterizes the order of the universe. This regular order prevents the celestial blue jaguar from devouring either the sun or the moon and upsetting the cosmic rhythm of constant renewal.

Once the boys' lips have been pierced and the wax burned, the chorus of women breaks out again in the lamenting wail of the *chenga ruvara*. The women are attacked by the fathers of the candidates. That is, the husbands attack their wives. The men deliver blows with their feet and hands, and other women rush to the aid of the singing mothers. They throw themselves on the men, trying to calm them down. They rub the men's faces and torsos with hearts of palm. Women blow in the men's ears, but the men are beyond control: their *by* ("nature, name") has left them. The men excite themselves into an unnamed fury. They take up their bows and arrows and begin shooting into the air in a menacing way; the arrows land near the initiation arbor. According to Clastres, the Aché know that this staged rage *(rapa michi)* is more than pretense. "[W]ithout this battle of men against women and the defeat of the latter, without the play of violence, . . . without all that the initiation would not be complete." [169] The master of ceremonies is the one who restores order. He does so by flying into a similar rage and going *by-iä*, "out of his name, or out of his nature." [170] After this violent episode, the people return to their residences and normal routines while the initiates stay another four days and nights in the initiation camp waiting for their wounds to heal. During this time the parents of the boys and the master of ceremonies must avoid sexual relations. The young men may now make their own bows and arrows and hunt in earnest. A young man may now seduce young women, but he will not enter into a permanent marriage until several years, usually six or eight, have passed. During the rites that make him eligible for marriage, the young man's back is deeply sliced and scarred while he remains absolutely silent, embracing a tree felled for the occasion.

The openness of fluxionary women, signified by their tears and the sounds of their voices, provides the climate for the candidates' desired openness, symbolized by the flow of blood from their pierced lips. Guayakí wailers and weepers, accompanied by the staged fury of the male violence they provoke, succeed in bringing closure to the life of boys and, thereby, in giving the boys rebirth as men.

Cases considered thus far emphasize initiatory images of flow from body orifices such as eyes or wounds. In all cases, this is the *first instance of flow*. The fluid, especially blood that is the image of life *par excellence*, flows from openings made for the first time or from openings that are, by their sacred nature or relation to origins, primordial. A phase in the initiation of local (i.e., non-Inca, non-noble) peoples living under Inca hegemony in the Cuzco region illustrates this point very well. In the month of October the Inca celebrated the feast of Umaraymi during which the autochthonous people of the area called Umá (a word that means "head" or "origin" in Quechua, the language of the overlords, and "water" in the local, Aymara language) entered an intense period of reflection; that is, they turned their attention to the first flowing, the beginnings of cosmic time, in several ways. At this time they commemorated their ancestors and initiated young men. The procedures called for a symbolic flow of tears and for the flow of rain from the sky. These requirements were fulfilled by tying a black llama to a stake. Fixed in relative immobility, the animal was prevented from drinking water and eating food. The point was to force the animal to weep in order to bring on the rains. There was a superabundance of symbolism of flow during this period since, in addition to ritual weeping and fertile rains, the river *(mayu)* of stars in the Milky Way and the flow of milk sucked by the constellation called Baby Llama from her mother-constellation appear on the sky's horizon in October. Furthermore, it was at the source of a river that the initiates had openings pierced in their ears for the first time. In spatial and temporal terms, Umaraymi literally marks, on individual and cosmic scales, the beginning of the flow of life.

MATRICULATION VERSUS THE DISTINCTNESS OF MALE INITIATION

This treatment of male initiation has tried to avoid exaggerating whatever is exclusively and uniquely masculine about the symbolic practices and imagery. In fact, by following the mythic history of initiatory processes and by noting the degree to which male and female initiatory symbolisms overlap, one can see how male initiation seems to have stolen, borrowed, or shared the regenerative strategies of females. Even in those cases where females are entirely excluded from men's initiations (as in so-called secret societies and men's clubs), the women's absence is *marked*. That is, the absence of women is a deliberate and strategic symbolic act, performed with reference to specific times and places. It helps to effect and define maturity for men.

Nevertheless, the examples of male initiations cited exhibit some distinctive features due to the differences in the spiritual situation of men and women as revealed in the distinct origins and practices of their ceremonies.[171] More than in the case of women, male initiation introduces candidates to participation in the ceremonial, rhetorical, and sociopolitical processes of the public arena, frequently a cultural space defined by the absence or official silence of women. Women's initiations climax in momentary display of the individual woman as a manifestation of hidden powers underlying reproductive processes. Through the processes of conception, gestation, and parturition carried on in her womb, of farming in her garden soil, of cooking in her kitchen space, and of pottery or other crafts, the initiated woman symbolically expresses her continuing relationship with transformative and reproductive powers. They define her specific sacrality.

Men's initiations, on the other hand, lead to a protracted ceremonial life in which are displayed the regenerative powers who established culture and then withdrew into symbolic appearances at the close of the primordium. Men's initiation takes a different stance toward the hiddenness, dissimulation, and display intrinsic to symbolic knowledge of the sacred. Whereas women's initiation displays the hiddenness and constancy of the powers of dissolution and metamorphosis, male initiation more often highlights the violence of change inherent in all symbolic display. Moreover, male initiation more often widens the gulf between visible signs and their hidden but sacred meaning. In fact, interpreting the distance between appearances and their meaning becomes a major preoccupation of men's initiatory societies. By reenacting myths of origin they focus on and extend into everyday life the absence (or alienation) of meaning and the meaning of absence (or alienation). The images of the sacred associated with personal and historical experiences (the ubiquitously present and inalienably symbolic forms of dreams, deliria, intoxication, hallucination, songs, masks, taxonomies of natural history and kinship organization, and public behavior such as speech, ceremony, and economic life) are represented in ceremonial life in order to discern their relevance for the group. Initiation introduces boys to the work of men: the interpretation of visible signs of the sacred for the purpose of discerning its relative presence or absence in daily collective affairs. This process of reflection is regenerative of human culture and constitutes the public dimension of the sociopolitical process.

In both male and female initiation, a strange, cunning rapport establishes itself between the candidate and supernatural beings who threaten him or her. However, the beings who menace initiates often differ in the cases of men and women. Women are more often menaced by aquatic monsters (anaconda-people) and beings associated with the earth (worms, armadillos) or by irregularly periodic beings (the moon). In men's initiations, generally speaking, celestial or celestial-forest attackers (the mythic jaguar, the sun, the sky, primordial birds) have a higher profile. Women more often come into possession or control of the menacing powers by embodying them within themselves (as the fluids of the womb, sheddable skin of snakes, menstrual blood, hair) or in utensils used everyday (manioc sieves, pots), whereas men instrumentalize threatening powers (feathered ornaments, hair tubes, penis sheaths), frequently in sacred implements that disappear in the off-season (musical instruments, masks).

Men's initiation tends to highlight the imagery of bone (e.g., the bone of the jaguar in myth, the bone used to pierce boys' lips, the bones of primordial ancestors, which become muscial instruments used in the rites). The hardness and durability of bone becomes a virtue with which boys are imbued or transfixed. Races, athletic competitions, and feats of strength — modeled on the achievements of prodigious heroes — more often characterize the kind of endurance desired in men's initiation. Boys often perform rites coordinated with the sun's movements (e.g., sunrise services, high noon observances), whereas girls' initiations shade them from the sun and highlight the role of night and of the periodic fluctuations of the moon. The initiatory rapport with the jaguar reinforces men's powers as predators in hunting and warfare. The jaguar's relationship to fire and the sun affords men control over the symbolism of the replication of social units and processes.

A boy initiate is more likely to be subject to processes that once belonged to the opposite sex than the girl novice, who usually models herself on the actions of a heroine. To this extent, male initiation emphasizes the deliberately imposed distance of cultural reproductive processes from women, either through myths of expropriation or through the staged absence of women from participation in ritual action.

Men's relationship to life processes, the regenerative processes of culture, is an uneasy one in comparison to women's. Whereas women's relationship is intrinsic — that is, part of the primordial condition of the mythic world — men's involvement in reproductive processes threatens to remain borrowed, instrumental, and ideological rather than material. The feminine symbolism of male initiation, especially as embodied in the instruments and procedures taken from primordial females, aims at providing men a fundamental and corporeal relationship to powers of regeneration, growth, and transformation.

Whereas images of death in women's initiation center on liquefaction, dissolution, melting (molting), and languishing in darkness, men's initiatory death more often dramatizes dismemberment and the disintegration of body parts.

ORDEAL: APPORTIONMENT OF INDIVIDUALITY THROUGH PASSION

Before closing this consideration of the initiatory condition, a word should be said about its arduousness. All initiations, male and female, find a place for ordeal, whether passive (immobility, silence) or active (feats of strength). Such trials are not just arbitrary inflictions of discomfort or pain. They are carefully chosen and deliberately applied techniques, tests that stretch the limits of patience, skill, or strength and that aim at a revelation, the critical self-knowledge required for human maturity. This revelation is twofold. On the one side, ordeals reveal what is essential and enduring about an individual character. They make known some truth about the initiate. On the other, they accomplish this self-revelation by making visible one's relationship to unseen powers and supernatural beings, the realities who condition a person's character. Ordeals are proofs of the presence of supernatural powers as well as of the strength of individual character.

Ordeals are fundamental acts of division, in which one is dealt out not only blows and sufferings but one's lot. Ordeal bears striking affinity to divination, for it makes visible one's destiny, the configuration of sacred powers governing one's ceaseless transformations. Ordeals separate one mode of being from another (e.g., the mature from the childish, "the men from the boys," one individual from another) by doling out symbolic pain (not to deny its physicality), which literally signifies one's apportioned uniqueness. One suffers *one's own* pain, and one subsequently bears the psychic and physical marks to prove that, at the hands of culture and on the model of sacred beings, one has suffered the changes required to become a unique individual. One has been dealt one's defining portion, for the ordeal has succeeded in making known in significant and experiential terms the supernatural character of the powers that underlie one's mature being.

WHIPPING, CUTTING, AND PIERCING   A brief mention of the most common initiatory tests (whipping, cutting, silence, fast, custody of sight, marathon dancing, induced vomiting, exposure to water, vigil, and immobility) serves to illustrate their religious foundation. Perhaps the most widespread form of ordeal is whipping. Métraux called whipping "one of the most conspicuous ritual acts in magico-religious ceremonies" throughout South America, but especially in Guiana and the Amazon.[172] Whipping is most notably performed at puberty rites, but it is also performed at war parties and at funerals to give its victim power. It is also common in agricultural festivals, especially in the Orinoco and Río Negro areas.

In ethnographic accounts of Baniwa initiations, the whipping of initiates and other participants has proved to be the most often reported detail. Indeed, for the Baniwa themselves it constitutes a central element of the initiation process. The public display and whipping of initiates while chants are performed and flutes are blown makes them grow. Whipping is equivalent to the mythic breaking of the shell of the first fruits, a breakage that marked the passage of crucial transitions, the first time-markers in the mythic age. A number of homonyms reinforce the connection between whip *(liiyaka)*, fruit shell *(liiya)*, treebark *(haiko-iiya)*, and human skin *(liiya)*.[173] "Kuai's songs are done together with whipping, as a part of 'knowing' kuai." [174] Both songs and whips are "fruits of Kuai." "Kuai's whipping-with-song is thus like striking shells of ripe fruits, which are like striking the skin of a person."[175] Maturity and growth in knowledge, the knowledge necessary to be fertile and to conceive a child, requires the splitting of the container, the opening of the body, to encourage the growth of new skin; that is, it requires the growth of new enclosures that are larger and more open to the powers in the outside world.

The Baniwa initiates are cracked open like shells of fruit. The sounds of song music, first produced by the body orifices of the mythic being Kuai, enter the beings of the initiates through the openings in their bodies: through their eyes, body passages, and the new openings cut by the whipping. Souls *(ikaale,* "souls, heart, souls of the ancestors") now enter the children, who, before this, had no souls. The souls' entrance alters their spiritual faculties and enables the initiates to "think, remember" *(napienta)*.[176] The imposition of the images of breaking and cutting impress on the initiates an effective symbol of a new kind of *closure* that makes memory, reflection, guilt, history, and accountability possible. Now they can evaluate their existence in time. "This 'thinking' is precisely what turns children into reproductive adults, for thinking is one element necessary for the conception of children." [177] The whips are called "whips of the sun," the being who fertilized Amaru, the primordial serpent, with his thought and cut her open so that the first offspring might be born.[178] Openings that ironically allow for symbolic closure by marking the outer limits of the body for the first time, make life conceivable in every sense.

Whipping is not restricted to the northwest Amazon, nor is its meaning always linked to the imagery of fruit. In all cases, however, it draws its significance from mythic history. The fiber whips wielded by women in Guayaki girls' initiation, for instance, are imagined to be the penis of the mythical tapir, the seductive trickster who is an irresistible and lewd adventurer. Clastres interprets the ritual to be a controlled contact with this paradigmatic symbol of male sexuality. He sees this as a first "sexual act" performed in controlled circumstances (although it is clearly not the first intercourse that the young Guayaki girl has had, since she has already had several lovers and a husband).[179]

Whipping in Baniwa and Guayaki initiation breaks the skin and opens the body for the first time to the seminal penetration of cultural symbols (e.g., sounds), tradition (the ancestors embodied in the flutes, the wisdom passed on through instruction delivered while cuts heal), and critical reflection (the memory of sacred beings, which serves as a benchmark of revelation and a guide to proper performance as a cultural being). The cuts that the whip imposes on the skin are effective symbols, signifying and provoking separation on an ontological plane. To that extent whipping shares a great deal in common with other ordeals that mar the skin.

Initiatory measures that cut, scar, pierce, bite, or tattoo the body abound. A key element in Chiripá male initiation, for example, was the insertion of the lip plug *(tembetá)*. When the young candidate fell into a drunken sleep, a shaman punctured his lower lip with an instrument made of wood or deer's horn. The meaning of such an act derives from each culture's notions of the sacred. For instance, the ears of Kamaiurá adolescent boys are pierced during the ear-piercing festival, the *namim* (lit. "ear"). The boys gather for the ceremony in the center of the village. Their ears are pierced with jaguar bones or wooden implements. The occasion marks the beginning of a lengthy period of ritual confinement.[180] The first ear-piercing ceremony was performed by the sun and moon on the occasion when a primordial water-serpent crawled onto the land in order to devour all living beings.[181] The giant snake was eventually chopped into pieces by a young girl. From the pieces came all species of snakes. The sun transformed the girl into a dove. This myth also recounts how the sun and moon slew the primordial jaguars by shooting arrows into their eyes.[182] (In another Kamaiurá myth, describing the killing of fish in the Milky Way, birds celebrate an ear-piercing festival; the birds create the songs now sung during the festival.)

Cutting and piercing appear in both male and female initiations. When a young Aché man has grown a little beard *(buta provi bu)*, his back is scarified. The *jaycha bowo* ("cutting of tattooed patterns") is an excruciating ordeal that the young man must undergo in complete silence. The young man searches streambeds for a stone with a flat surface and a slicing edge.[183] At noon on the day of the ceremony, the young man lies on his stomach on a log from a tree felled especially for this ritual purpose; he grasps it with both arms. With the sharp edge of the stone, deep slices are cut, running down the entire length of the young man's back. The deep furrows are incised by men with strong grips, for the skin resists the cutting. Finally the entire surface of the back, from one shoulder to the other, is covered with deep lines. A mixture of honey and ashes from the *kybai* ("man") tree is rubbed into the wound. This staunches the flow of blood and encourages the formation of thick scars. When he grows new skin, he will be allowed to marry and father children. He is now called *jyvete*, "fierce." [184] The Aché liken the "splitting" of the skin of young men's back to the "splitting" of the earth with axes that was performed by mythic ancestors when the blue jaguar of heaven threatened the existence of the universe. They imposed order on the chaotic form of the earth to bring on the passage of time and transition and to prevent the world from falling into the chaos that had destroyed it in the first time, that of permanent states of being.[185]

After an Aché girl has been stained with wax and painted, she too is subjected to the *jaycha bowo*, the ordeal of scarifying and tattooing. Her male ritual sponsor seeks the appropriate stone. The young novice lies down on her back and allows her skin to be sliced from just below her breasts to her pubic area. The incisions form two arcs on either side. These cuttings, called *jaycha mama*, are intended to bring on conception. The wounds are then filled with charcoal powder. Without these scarifications, a woman would be *gaipará*, dangerous to others. Being so afraid of the process as to refuse it would indicate that the boy or girl had no access to the spiritual powers necessary to overcome dangerous forces.

In both male and female cutting, the initiate's scars are not only mnemonic of a moment of growth in personal history but of a great divide in the history of being itself. From one to three years after her moment of decoration and display, a Tapirapé woman's face is cut and scarred. This is after she has married but before she has a child. The process, called *achahut* ("woman cut"), is extremely painful. A myth describes its origin, and the origin of a lament sung by a species of bird, in an event when a mythic female died while being cut.[186] The woman's face is cut with half-moon designs on both cheeks, and *genipa* dye is inserted in the wounds to give them a permanent dark outline. The woman's husband or brother is cut by the same shaman. With the teeth of a dogfish, the man's arms and legs are cut from shoulder to elbow and from thigh to kneecap. The man must not make a sound during the process.[187]

The cutting of an Akawaio girl's face around her mouth at puberty marks her with the designs of a scorpion bite or snakebite or the sting of an ant or bee. This readies her for marriage. The scarification takes place at the girl's first menstruation (although, by this time, her arms have been tattooed). The cutting is usually done by an older female relative. The girl's entire being has been transformed and made mellifluous. Henceforward the novice can perform the tasks of a mature woman, making a sweet, fermented beverage from cassava, which she chews with her tattooed mouth (even the tongue has been scraped and, thus, tattooed). The sweetness of her character, signified by her wounds, imbues and ferments the drink as she chews the manioc mash, for, during her ordeal, her cuts were filled with sweet honey.[188]

Cutting the body during initiatory ordeals should not be separated from the meaning of cutting in other contexts of the culture in question.[189] A complete study of the meaning of this form of ordeal would examine its symbolic value, for example, in the cutting of the umbilicus at birth; the paring of nails and cutting of hair; the cutting of teeth; the cutting of breath performed by the teeth during incisive speech; the chopping up of a primordial monster (jaguar, anaconda); the piercing of the earth by a mythical being such as the burrowing armadillo; the cutting down of the world tree or vine that once linked earth with heaven but whose fall marked the beginning of time; the cutting of meat, fruit, cassava, or manioc cake; the slashing and cutting involved in groundbreaking for a new garden. Like the cutting of the initiatory candidate, these acts signify shared public understandings and form a systematic complex of meanings related to the same sign.

The myth of the sixth Inca ancestor-king, Inca Roca, for example, connects initiatory ear-piercing with the groundbreaking and sodbusting of new fields in February. When he was a prince, Inca Roca placed his newly pierced ear to the ground. He heard a sound: the rush of an underground river. He plunged his arm through the earth, and fertile waters bubbled forth for the first time. Thus began the flow of irrigation for Cuzco. Inca Roca's piercing of the earth marked the initiation of an essential condition of Cuzcan culture. Initiatory ear-piercing commemorated his actions, channeling the chaos of life's unbroken sound and liquid into the marked and ordered spaces of the body, irrigation canals, and fields as well as into the initiated generations of human time.

Other images of piercing were significant in Inca culture. For instance, when they sowed seeds in the fields (thus impregnating Mother Earth), Inca warriors wore the *casana*, a symbol of piercing, on their shirts. In the chronicle of Guaman Poma, the *casana* is worn by Mayta Capac, the fourth Inca mythical king-ancestor, as he pierces the earth to initiate the first planting rites. Warriors wore the *casana* when they ritually drove diseases threatening fertility beyond the city limits of the capital. Examples could be multiplied.[190] The point is that piercing and cutting mark the initiate with every conceivable kind of time and change—the transformations of being that make creation rich, elaborate, and regenerative.

Cutting the body brings all shedders of blood into the same symbolic orbit. For example, the Tupinamba cut geometric designs into a girl's back at her first menstruation. Similarly, Tupinamba warriors who had killed in battle cut geometric patterns onto their bodies before resuming their everyday activities.[191] Both categories of blood-shedders (both active and passive) passed through a period of behavioral restrictions typical of a rite of passage. The Taulipang provide another case in point. After dancing and singing their victory song, Taulipang warriors were purified by the same ordeals as those undergone at puberty. Men who had killed an enemy were dangerous to themselves and to the community; their purification was effected by ordeals of breaking the skin. "They sat on ants, flogged one another with whips, and passed a cord, covered with poisonous ants, through their mouth and nose. Then they abandoned their village and settled in another site." [192]

FASTING, GORGING, VOMITING   The logic of symbolic control over penetration through cutting and piercing continues in the ordeals of fasting, gorging, and induced vomiting. Like other body passages and cuts open for exchange (of blood, honey, ashes, semen, saliva, waste, sound), the mouth becomes an intersection for symbolic traffic during rites of passage. Fasting and forced eating become visible transactions for accomplishing the less perceptible transition from one state to another. Passage of symbolic items of food parallels the passage of the initiate as a symbolic item through stages of the spiritual economy of a culture. Withholding food during fast helps clarify the nature of the initiate's separation from mundane existence. The symbolism of food embraces an immense range of meanings. Always, however, the fast or feast finds its reason for being in the first events of the primordium. Consequently, the ordeal of fasting can determine one's relationship to the entire cosmic cycle of consumption. For example, when the Tukano ancestors entered the *maloca*-universe, Diawí, at the beginning of time, they were afraid to eat from the pot of coca, as the creator had instructed them to do, because all around its edge were ferocious animals. As a result, the pot of coca was given to animals. Whereas humans did not eat what was prepared for them, thereby forfeiting immortality, animals did eat the creation that Yepá Huaké had made, causing the creator to declare, "The earth, the fields and the stones and all the animals will not die." In response, the earth ominously thundered back at the creator, "We will not die, we will eat the people which you have created." [193] The earth will never die because it consumes the life of the people created by Ycpá Huaké, but, because they refused to eat what was good for them, human beings (the Tukano) are by nature both hungry and mortal. Tukano fasts and coca-consumption during initiation attempt to break the tragic cycle of consumption in which human life is caught and to reestablish the conditions of human immortality intended by the creator. In many cultural cases, the initiates, reliving a primordial condition now no longer obtainable, are permitted and even encouraged to eat foods otherwise forbidden (for example, Guayakí initiates eat coati, an emblem of the mature soul-double; Kayapó initiates are allowed to consume jaguar meat).

Induced vomiting, a common initiatory ordeal, is a powerful expression of the double-directedness of cosmic exchange. Regurgitation signifies the convertibility of consumptive processes, which makes possible the experience of resurrection. Myths of the origins of initiation frequently portray the first novices as beings devoured by a supernatural monster who later vomits them out alive. Consumption of this sort is part of a sustaining cycle of life. By controlled vomiting, the candidate (who has already joined in the more obvious cosmic process in which one form of life devours another) now participates in the restoration of that life. Insofar as it is a deliberate display of resurrection, induced vomiting bears affinity with the dramatic emergence of the candidate from the enclosure where she or he has died in the course of transformation.

SILENCE, STASIS, AND CUSTODY OF THE EYES Some ordeals seem to be attempts to render the candidate partly "senseless", that is, to suppress the use of at least one sense. The suppressed sense varies from case to case: sight, where extreme custody of the eyes is prescribed; touch, in those cases where candidates are not allowed to scratch their own skin; or articulate speech, where aphasia-like silence or senseless babbling is induced by fiat or by overstimulation and exhaustion (as in Makiritare initiation). These techniques aim at calling forth other extraordinary senses or at least new uses, meanings, and hierarchies of the ordinary senses. New sensitivities to the presence of extraordinary and sacred realities that lie behind everyday appearances are necessary for the welfare of the changing individual and for the common good. A Guayakí girl, for instance, keeps her eyes closed during her initiatory seclusion, even when she eats the food brought by her female ritual sponsor. "She must not only keep herself hidden [*kaku*, invisible], but must even avoid turning her face toward others, especially toward men who are neither

her father nor her male ritual sponsor." [194] Were she to look at a man, she would place him in a state of *bayja*, a dangerous vulnerability to supernatural forces that could make him ill or even bring death.

Restricting the sense of touch—even to the point where the initiate is kept from touching his or her own body—is a common initiatory ordeal. The candidates must scratch their skin with an instrument or seek someone else's aid to do so. Such an ordeal demonstrates that the novice's entire being is undergoing change. Ordinarily, only certain parts of the body—notably the places of passage and penetration, such as the mouth, penis, anus, vagina— manifest such evident change as to have important social impact. These loci of transition are socially important and socially governed because the actions and transactions of symbolic exchange (meals, excretions, births, sex) effected by them propel and measure the passage of the whole community through time. Therefore, these highly efficacious chronometers become subject to public control; contact with them is usually kept out of the public eye. They are only stimulated or used at prescribed times and places. These publically controlled actions become either private functions, through the restriction of their transitional impact to the individual scale, or civic moments of community transition and regeneration through regulating and standardizing, according to a mythic model, the measures of change they signal. Either way, they are surrounded with cultural conventions. During initiation, however, the candidate's entire body is changing, especially the outer skin, which becomes a public marker of social change. Even skin and the sense of touch come into the public domain, subject to the action of others.

Ordeals that suppress the senses separate the individual from the ordinary world by breaking down the usual sensitivities and installing a new level of spiritual awareness of one's self and the world. Such ordeals express the desire to restructure the senses in order to attune the body's experience to invisible and intangible levels of reality, to open the senses to the spiritual world that gives rise to reality, and to make the sensual body itself a manifestation of what is sacred.

ENDURANCE TESTS: MARATHON DANCING, EXPOSURE, VIGIL   Other kinds of ordeals also arise from the actions of mythic beings. These ordeals simulate the conditions of the first separation between different conditions of existence. This is true of the trials of extended duration, such as marathon dancing (which may bring on the light of the First Day, the waters of the deluge, or the first ascent to heaven),[195] prolonged exposure to the elements, and all-night vigil. For example, the Akwẽ-Shavante immersion ceremonies, which last some three weeks, are grounded in a mythic event in which heroes, immersed in the floodwaters that covered the earth, could not be persuaded to come to dry land. While in the water, they created "many things," including the women whom they married. In one version of the myth, a hero created the flood when waters gushed out of his nostrils and flooded the earth. This provided drink for his thirsting comrades.[196] The immersion ceremonies take place immediately after the candidate's ears have been pierced, a sign of incipient sexual potency.

In its attempt to conquer sleep, vigil becomes a major symbolic expression of the new spiritual condition of the candidates. Because it signals the degree of wakefulness of the candidate's entire spiritual existence, the quality of vigilance may determine the effectiveness of other initiatory actions. The goal of vigil is to attain the unbroken state of awareness required of mature humans. During adolescence in the Xingu area, for example, boys are given a beverage made from the bark and sap of the *manucaiá* tree, a hardwood known for its height and straight trunk. The liquid is ingested so that the boys will take on the trees' characteristics. What they absorb is the spiritual essence of the tree, for the drink is vomited up immediately.[197] A Kamaiurá myth explains that other ordeals, especially nocturnal vigil, are necessary to become like a tree (that is, like a mature adult). Once, a young man wandered to the center of the forest, where he leaned against a *camioá*, a hardwood tree used as the center post of the house and as a symbol of the dead person during funeral ceremonies. It is from the *camioá* that the first ancestors were made.[198] Expressing the aspirations of novices, the young man addressed the tree, saying, "Tamãi [Grandfather], I would like to become just like you." The tree responded, "You wouldn't be able to stand it, my grandson. To be a tree is very difficult. You have to stay awake all the time. If you fall asleep, you'll die and that's that." [199]

We have used the root meaning of the word *ordeal*, "a division or apportionment," to understand the ways in which the dealing out of pain, discomfort, and restriction separates one from one's prior existence in order to assay the truth (the defining relationship to a unique configuration of sacred powers) of one's new character. Like divination and revelation, ordeals frequently have a negative valence. They explore and extend one's concrete limits of endurance and control. That is, they ring with contradiction (e.g., fasting to sustain life) the boundaries of one's new paradoxical situation, in which rebirth to new life is attained through the deliberate experience of death. Ordeals mark new growth by imposing the limits of failure. In fact, as noted, many ordeals represent the failures of mythic characters to maintain or achieve the immortality of primordial beings through inobservance of silence, fast, correct diet, and so on. Ordeals emphasize the importance of failure, of limits, in achieving new conditions, new beginnings. Not only does this reinforce the integral relationship between negativity and personality (especially when viewed as a set of properties),[200] it underlines the fact that the personality itself is a compound of virtues, powers whose presence and measure is ascertained through a negative dialectic including the experiences of alienation, absence, withdrawal, and death.

In fact, at initiation it becomes clear to what extent and in what manner the individual is a microcosmic configuration of the forces at work throughout the universe since the beginning of creation. The more a person is configured in a way homologous to the universal structures of space and time, and the more one becomes a transparent cipher or simile of the cosmos through knowledgeable imagination and experience of the sacred, the more one needs to regulate his or her behavior through discipline and symbolic control (even if this means stylized frenzy).[201] Openness to growth and maturity calls for a concomitant ability to control the openings of passage and transition between planes and states of being. Ordeals keep individual, cosmic, and mythic conditions separate and orderable. They make sense of oneself.

WRAPPING UP INITIATION

Initiation marks a new beginning. It marks that new start with failure: the failure of primordial being to accommodate a new condition of existence. For that reason, primordial fissures, deaths, and unsuccessful tests are relived during initiation ceremonies. The breakdown is signified in the breaking of skin, the cutting of openings, the need for new kinds of enclosures to contain the signs of spilling life. Through breakdown and dissolution the limits of the primordium make change and regenerative life possible. Origin myths of initiation illustrate the interruption of the birth process through premature ripping from the womb (as in the ubiquitous myths of the divine twins), or premature ejaculation (e.g., of ancestors from their penis-canoe-anaconda before arriving at the headwaters), or the precipitous and unguarded opening of the curious eyes, the speaking mouth, or the bleeding vagina during primordial adolescence. These myths indicate that ordinary life is not what it should be or what it could have been. It never came to full term; never arrived at its intended destiny. The very nature of the temporal conditions required for growth undid the projected perfection. Something leaked, spurted, or broke out before it was time. The very process of becoming renders being vulnerable to immaturity. Existence in time jeopardizes essence.

Initiation redresses this ontological dilemma by exploiting failures and limits and treating them as possibilities for rebirth. Here lies the importance of the symbolism of enclosure. Placed within new symbolic limits, the initiate continues the process of primordial gestation. Because limits exist, the gestating or incubational process of closure can generate manifestations of being on a new scale. Culture is that closed system of meanings that reflect back on themselves to achieve new levels of development, pulled forward by the power of culture's own significations. Through its symbolic capacities, culture recovers and redeems that failed process by making death symbolically equivalent to gestation. The result is the initiatory condition, a state of constant rebirth that characterizes the religious history of human culture and that allows being, by transcending through symbolic death whatever state it is in, to come to full term. For this reason it is important for initiates to learn that authentic human existence must be critical; initiates must experience and locate the reality of the crisis and passion that constitute their initiatory condition. At the same time, however, the initiate is impressed, even transfixed, with the truth that every recognition of cosmic and individual failure signifies the hope of beginning life over again. Even more, when the community reenacts the absolute catastrophes of flood or fire or the deadly ordeal of a supernatural hero, the initiation signals not only the rebirth of the candidate but the transfiguration of the universe.

Initiation exhibits the irony of the symbolic situation, the paradox of growth in a species that is, by nature, a growing kind of being. How can it come to be what it already is? The answer to that question lies on the level of human conscious experience, knowledge of one's own transformative nature. *Human* growth means participatory awareness in the very conditions of one's growth; the imposition, observance, and transcendence of one's own limits through the symbols of discipline, seclusion, controlled exchange, ordeal, death, and rebirth. One enters the mythic ground of one's own being and refashions them. The knowledge of one's own symbolic nature is the critical issue separating human culture from other modes of being. It is to their own critical symbolic life that novices are introduced.

At this point passivity and activity collapse into one primordial experience. To become invisible, one avoids looking. In order to see new realities when emerging from seclusion one is displayed and seen as at the eye-opening moment of birth or primordial emergence. The same rigorous symbolic logic, manifest as the cycles of prey, vengeance, and memory, merges *actio* and *passio* even while images spread out the single reality as though it were a system of separate events in time.[202] To become a vessel, the initiate is contained; to penetrate fruitfully, the novice is pierced; to effect his or her passage, he or she is made open; to mark the separations between categories of being and social statuses that are crucial to cosmic and community organization, the candidate is marked by separation. Having disgorged what one devoured in one's deadly appetite for life, one is vomited out of the jaws of monstrous death and is resurrected.

This is the logic of metonymy, for one participates in the sacred power of one's own creation.[203] Subject and object become cognate and consubstantial. Collapsing action and passion, the initiatory symbols of death and rebirth proclaim that the essential act of human culture is to undergo symbolic existence and suffer one's own significations. Through human growth one comes to critically reflect, and even embody, the powerful cognizance, division, vigilance, dynamism, change, creativity, and sacredness intrinsic to meaning.

RITUAL FRIENDS AND COMPANIONS

A consideration of human growth must mention ritual companionship. Case after case records the presence of some ritual friend, chaperon, sponsor, attendant, usher, or accompanist during moments of dramatized change. One cannot pass through death to rebirth alone because human life, transitory and symbolic from the moment of conception, is always social. Then too, the vagaries of symbolic life, discerned as occasions of maturation or decay, have social impact because the life-in-death adventures of the human spirit structure and transform society.

The social repercussions of an individual's ritual death and resurrection often become visible in a ritually appointed companion. Conversely, the companion represents the shaping force of the group that necessarily conducts the ontological passenger across the floodwaters of change. The roles and images of ritual parents, relatives, sponsors, formal friends, and ceremonial companions vary widely. For obvious reasons, a thorough understanding of the meaning of the ritual sponsor would require careful delineation of the composition and significance of social groups in the particular society in question. This brief treatment limits itself to uncovering the fundamentally religious ground of ritual companionships of whatever sort.

Whether the ritual tie fulfills primarily an economic, psychological, aesthetic, or social function, it springs from deep within the human capacity for relationship to someone else. This ability to relate self-consciously to someone other than oneself lies at the core of the uniquely human version of growth and change. In becoming oneself (as an individual and as a society) one must relate to another. The conviction that identity depends on a relationship to "something other" is based on the paradigmatic relationship of human life to supernatural beings of the mythic world. In fact, most relationships of ritual companionship or formal friendship model themselves on the association of primordial figures such as the sun and moon, the divine twins, the first body-painters (who have in some cases slain a primordial monster to bathe in its blood and the contents of its bowels), fellow travelers through the first worlds, or some other mythic beings who during the primordium mutually effected one another's transformation.

Understanding oneself in relation to others, a prerequisite for mature human growth, is a self-critical symbolic process. To that extent it takes its cue from the primordial crisis that gave rise to symbolism, significant change, and the division of social forms. Scholars distinguish among the many categories of ritual fellows, marshals, friends, or squires. Manuela Carneiro da Cunha and Roberto Da Matta, for example, lucidly separate formal friendship from ritual companionship among the Krahó and Apinayé; Jacques M. Chevalier delineates different sets of relations between traditional Campa trading partners *(ayompari/niompari)*, on the one side, and the system of godparent and co-godparent relationships on the other.[204] This is not the place to reiterate, synthesize, or extend the classifications of ritual helpers. Our purpose is simply to call attention to their existence, their variety, and their religious foundation.

THREE TYPES OF RITUAL ACCOMPANIMENT

On the most general level one can distinguish among three kinds of ritually appointed company. The first category includes all those instances where supernaturals serve as ritual friends to humans. Soon after birth, for example, the Guayakí is given the name of an animal especially hunted for the occasion. The name actually represents the primordial animal into whose guardianship the child passes. The hunter who has slain the name-game remains bound to the child and the child's family in a close bond, which is expressed through the exchange of trade goods. The matter soon becomes more complicated. There corresponds to each *bykwa*, the name-animal possessed by an individual human being, a supernatural forest-companion, the *ijagi*. This is a forest animal of a species different from the one after whom the individual is named. For example, the *ijagi*-companion of the wild pig *bykwa* is the *kweve* bird. In fact, each forest animal that can serve as game for a human name has an animal companion to whom the named human being will also be bound. The mosquito is accompanied by the howler monkey; the companion of the coati is the *pipi* bird. A name is prerequisite to human existence because it draws one into a web of social, economic, nature-historical, and supernatural relations that are not only necessary on the abstract plane but are particular to one's specific, named character (*by*). The unique network of relations emanating outward from one's name (the animal from which it was taken, the hunter by whom it was slain, the mother by whom it was accepted, the forest-companions and their companions) defines who one is.[205]

The second type of relationship consists of humans serving as ritual friends for supernaturals, nourishing their cravings for food, flesh or memory and helping them transmigrate through cycles of forms in the space-time world where humans are at home. For instance, the Warao envision the soul, *mehokohi*, as a light that shines in the chest of an individual. Warao life is orchestrated in such a way as to ensure an existence of the soul in a mythical abode. To that end, human beings and supernatural beings mutually provide for one another's needs. The gods ask for food, especially tobacco; humans aim at gaining protection for their lives and goods and at securing guidance in the realms beyond death. Since human beings are unique in their possession of fire, they are the source of tobacco smoke, desired by the gods as their divine food.[206]

These first two categories of ritual bond, closely related to one another, will be considered in the discussion of tutelary spirits present during possession and ecstasy, where they figure most prominently.[207] The third class of companions is bound by the ritual bond between humans. This category encompasses an immense variety of ritual relations, which form the center of focus in the following discussion. The symbolic nature of all these relationships allows them to be mutually convertible, so they are often understood in terms of one another.

PEOPLE HELPING PEOPLE

Several examples help illustrate the variant forms and functions of human ritual consociates. Since among the Canelos Quichua, the process of maturation and increased knowledge of one's identity is accomplished through experience of one's mystical past, this development is further aided by one's insertion into an institution of ritual or mystical friendship (*gumba*).[208] The knowledge, memory, and wisdom that impel genuine growth require constant transition to mythic domains. In this process the ritual friend serves as a necessary mainstay for the relations that define one's identity.

Similarly, the Krahó maintain an institution of formal friendship. It is an ambivalent relationship of both avoidance and solidarity between two people, and it is actualized in two kinds of situations: physical danger (in moments of burns or ant bites, the formal friend undergoes the same suffering); and during rituals of initiation or the termination of social sanctions against an assassin (when the formal friend facilitates the reintegration of the individual into society).[209] Carneiro da Cunha believes that the concept of formal friendship among the Krahó is centered on the antonymic meaning of symbols. Since the formal friendship has a double aspect of avoidance and joking relationship, it plays with all angles of antonymy: inverting it, contradicting it, negating it, or just being an antonym.[210] Formal friendship is used extensively among the Krahó in order to transcend states of creative chaos and to effect new creative transformations. "[T]he presence [of the formal friend] attests to the dissolution of the personality which accompanies that return to an undifferentiated chaos of liminal states."[211]

The meaning of Krahó formal friendship in rituals and intermediate conditions is most easily understood from the models found in myths. Sun and moon are formal friends and act in this capacity for one another during the myths of creation.[212] During the course of their formal friendship they institute the fundamental rituals of the Krahó. The sun figures largely in the creation of rites of regularity (e.g., log races). The moon, on the other hand, creates disorder and inconvenience (e.g., mosquitoes and snakes). The moon is responsible for the dynamic principle behind creation, and so it is understandable that the moon is the founder both of the rites of childbirth and of funerals. As author of the rites of separation and seclusion, the moon becomes responsible for the cultural processes of creation, which, at the same time, involve the destruction of spaces that are purely personal in favor of space defined by the interaction of relationships.[213]

Just as the Krahó institution of formal friendship corresponds to a radical opposition through which one may be defined, another Krahó institution, that of the "companion" *(ikhuonō)* comes to stand for similarity and simultaneity. The word for a companion is rooted in the word *ikhuoti*, "placenta" — in other words, that is created and born with you. Carneiro da Cunha contends that a person's companion is a mirror image of *action*, and not of body form. By mirroring the person's actions, the companion allows for the reflection that provides a self-image as an acting person. The companion permits one to assume an identity. Carneiro da Cunha points out, however, that the institutionalized companion only reflects what one is as a social actor. It does not allow one actively to gather a notion of one's personhood through creative and transformative processes. This role belongs to the formal friend.

Since Krahó formal friendship is based on a dialectic of alternatives and antonymies, it provides a dynamism for the construction of the person. It is the ritual formal friend who reflects alternate and dynamic possibilities and aids in the construction of an autonomous being with a specific difference from others. On the other hand, as a "placenta," the companion only reflects action that is similar and singular. The ritual companionship is the foundation of the reflexive process that defines one's mature identity.[214]

Ritual company is always an efficacious symbol of socialization. The ritual companion succeeds in resocializing someone by acting as either a protecting chaperon who wards off threat; a consort who shares one's apportioned lot of physical, emotional, or spiritual ordeal; a teacher or an escort who serves as a guide into the etiquette proper to a new situation; a conductor who accompanies the person in ritual, the vehicle of passage; or as a stylized jokester or adversary who, through reverse psychology or a logic of negative coefficience, drives the person to find one's identity on the opposite shore of relations and behaviors. For those, such as shamans, who are joining a supernatural society (and not just visiting it temporarily), the supernatural ritual companion helps make the adjustment.[215]

Because older relatives can be forerunners of the new social climate into which the individual is entering, they often serve as ritual ushers. They are already situated within the nexus of relations to which the transient aspires. The Apinayé grandmother, for example, acting as midwife in the ritual of birth, seems to enjoy a kind of ritual relationship with her grandchild: she not only keeps her grandchild's umbilical cord in her medicine basket, but, if the child should injure himself, the grandmother may visit on herself the same kind of harm. If the child dies, "the grandmother lies down on a mat beside the decorated corpse, resting its head in her arm, and remains in this position throughout the night."[216] Elders are also the ritual sponsors for Baniwa initiation. They teach the initiates the "speech of our ancestors" and, in the case of boys, mediate between the initiates and the "world of beginnings," the sights and sounds of the kuai flutes.[217]

The trials of ordeal, restriction, doctoring, washing, decorating the skin, or cutting (the skin, the hair, the umbilicus) frequently call for the assignment of a ceremonial attendant or nurse. To accompany a young initiate during his ordeals the Yukuna appoint an old man who models his behavior on the myths of the culture hero Kawarimi.[218] In the Andean community of Amaru, as in many others, a relationship of ritual kinship is established for the first time at the rite called chukcha rutuchi, the first cutting of hair.[219] Throughout eastern Peru the importance of compadrazgo bonds at the time of ritual cutting of the umbilicus and ceremonial hair-cutting (corte de pelo or lanta tipina) are noted.[220] In Brazilian Candomblé, the ajibona[221] (also called madrinha or padrinho do santo) is the ritual sponsor of the initiate during her important rites of passage, especially during the treatment of her head. The identity of the initiate is confirmed by revealing the identity of the òrìṣà resident in her orí (the head mystically conceived).[222] The alabé (musical director) induces the òrìṣà to manifest itself by singing songs in honor of the initiate's santo. The ritual sponsor widens the network of spiritual ties and, therefore, of social relations. The sponsor may even come from a cult-group centered in a different house from that of the initiate. The relationship endures after initiation and, if the ajibona should become an important spiritual leader, the bond becomes more intense and important.[223]

The period of enclosure during rites of passage is prime time for appointment of ritual companions. During their seclusion, for example, Akwē-Shavante boys are provided formal friends. The boys' admittance to the bachelors' hut (*he*) is marked by the ceremonial bestowal of penis sheaths and light, wooden ceremonial clubs (*um'ra*), which are painted red with *urucú*.[224] During this time (at least six months) in the bachelors' hut before formal initiation, boys are instructed, mainly through exemplary action rather than oral teaching.[225] The boy is provided with one or two *ĩ-amō* ("my other."), formal friends between whom he sleeps and dances. Those who keep formal company with the boy during the spiritual adventures of sleep and ceremonial dance remain bound in a formal relationship throughout life. These ceremonial partners are usually classed as affines.

The Akwē-Shavante ritual institution of formal friendship finds its origin in the myths associated with the immersion ceremonies performed after the novice's ears are pierced, for, during the flood, the mythical hero transformed his ceremonial partner into an amphibious frog, who was capable of accompanying the hero on both land and water. "[T]he immersion ritual which starts the initiation cycle is intended to endow the initiates with the heroic qualities of their mythical prototype. . . . during their immersions they symbolically reenact the separation of the creator *wapté* from his fellow men."[226] However, through contact with the ritual companion, a living token of social life, the initiates keep in touch with social reality. Social relationship becomes an ingredient of their transformative experience.

TRADING PARTNERS: EXCHANGING ONE MODE OF BEING FOR ANOTHER

Ritual companionship between humans is neither insubstantial nor limited to the realm of ideas or good counsel. For instance, the Cubeo *híkü-híko* relationship of ceremonial friendship, usually between a male and female who form a substitute brother-sister pair, is expressed both economically and aesthetically. Usually, it is not a sensual relationship, for "they forgo the erotic play that even brother and sister are supposedly allowed to indulge in."[227] The relationship is established in a public symbolic act. During a drinking bout, "friends paint one another with red pigment which they refer to as 'blood.' "[228] This is why ceremonial friendship is equivalent to a blood-sibling tie.

The *híkü-híko* relationship endures even after death. The two spirits experience full bliss when they stroll arm-in-arm through the afterlife. The converse situation helps to understand how essential such a relationship is to authentic human existence: whichever party breaks off the relationship will not enjoy a human condition, but will become an insect, in the afterlife.

The spiritual weight of this relationship expresses itself economically, as do the Campa *ayompari/niompari* and the Canelos Quichua *gumba*. The two parties exchange products to which their specific modes of sacrality provide them access. In the case of the Cubeo *híkü-híko*,

> She will provide him with manioc for chicha, if he wishes to sponsor a drinking party, and she will prepare farinha for him which he will use to trade for objects

of white manufacture. He will reciprocate with appropriate gifts and with making household implements for her. When he is paid for his labor in the rubber forests he will surely bring cloth and trinkets for his híko.[229]

The Barasana *henyeri-henyerio* relationship is virtually identical to Cubeo ceremonial friendship. During their initiation the initiates and younger men apply dark body paint to one another's legs and bodies. The painters become "like brothers" and call one another "my painter" and "my painted" *(yıt sïtori)*, forms of address that replace normal kinship terms.[230] However, this lifelong relationship is only a pale reflection of another, cross-sex ritual friendship. At the moment of their emergence from confinement, when the "dirt" of dark paint has been washed off, the initiates are decorated by women, who paint them from head to toe with red paint. "They put strings of beads round their necks and new garters around their legs below the knees and give them gourds and packets of red paints."[231] In turn, the initiate bestows on the woman who paints him the baskets he has woven during his seclusion. "This rite, called taking a *henyerio*, establishes a special ceremonial friendship and trading partnership between the man and the woman who paints him."[232] He calls her *henyerio;* she calls him *henyeri*. It is significant that the ritual items whose exchange establishes the relationship center around the experience of seclusion. This is not only due to the link between painting and the new envelope of skin that the initiates grow from the time when their skin is stained until the new, clear skin appears. The connection is more direct: women give the men garters, ornaments woven especially during menstrual confinement. In turn, men give the women baskets plaited during their period of *bedigıt* (a term that refers both to menstrual confinement and to male initiatory seclusion).[233] Like the periodic cosmos itself, the *henyeri/henyerio* relationship is the product of the hidden creative processes of confinement (a form of created display fashioned with one's own limits). An exchange of the tokens of transition particular to each creature's own sacrality, the trade between the friendship's partners gives each sex a share in the other's most powerful and hidden (because inalienably his or her own) experiences of the sacred.

However, Stephen Hugh-Jones makes clear that this privileged ceremonial relationship is only one of many such ritual friendships. In fact, the experience of formal initiation embeds the initiate in a range of new relationships predicated on and signifying the powerful transformation he has undergone.[234] Furthermore, other transitional moments with relative degrees of confinement, such as birth and first menstruation rituals, achieve the same end, producing ties that dissolve "normal" relations and generate new networks of social links. "It is as if, after initiation, the initiate is reborn with a new set of elementary kin. These ties of ritual kinship cross-cut those between the initiate and his nuclear family and long-house community."[235] Ritual sponsors, friends, and escorts are effective proof that symbolic death and rebirth opens one's social universe and transforms social relationships of every concrete kind. The network of ties in the wider world is negotiable because social forms are ordered by the very logic of symbolic forms whose appearance transformed the maturing individual.

A ceremonial relationship may be a sensual one, quite apart from its economic value. The core of Kaingáng social stability, for example, is a set of patterned friendship relations among men who are hunting companions, sleeping companions, and caressing companions.[236] This prolonged physical contact and companionship help form an ingroup that is protective of insiders and destructive of outsiders. The group is based on a concept of self-love called *waikayú*. Heterosexual relations are considered an obstacle to the development of *waikayú*. Instead, during the young adulthood of a male, physical contact between men is stressed. Men who caress one another and lie together while sleeping establish stable bonds between themselves. Henry found, however, no suggestion of genital sexual relations in these groups of caressing men.

Adoption can be a public mechanism for installing a ritual relationship between individuals. Such a performance creates a new center of meaning in a ramifying field of relationships. For instance, if two Chiripá men or women wish, they may ask a shaman to pray over them, joining them in a formal friendship called *aty'vasá* ("adoptive brother"). This makes the property of one the possession of the other and it initiates a lifelong obligation of reciprocity. "They must respect each other more than brothers."[237] Marriage alliances are often formed between the children of formal friends. Formal friendship among the Chiripá is distinct from the institution of ritual sponsorship. Ritual sponsors act a godparents during baptism. They are obliged to present gifts to their godchild and to bless the child when required.

MARRIAGE PARTNERS AS RITUAL RELATIONS

Ritual assignation of friends, companions, and antagonists moves self-awareness beyond the social ties generated only by personal preference, the nuclear family, and subsistence needs. Ceremonial appointments create new links, and the ostentation of the new tie displayed during ritual and in subsequent dealings can provoke critical reflection on the nature of symbolic action, which regenerates social forms and renders them generalizable. Individuals and groups are configured by symbolic processes and are the outcome of the symbolic existence first generated in the mythic period. That ceremonial bonds often endure outside the rite underscores the permanence of growth. Change continues to have social bearing. One has a companion for life, that is, for one's entire transitive situation in the world, and this companionship has long-term social effect.

Nowhere is this more evident than in marriage, a creative ritual bond between individuals, the groups they represent, and the groups they spawn. Rather than looking upon ritual ties as sublimated homologies of the marriage alliance (or, for that matter, of trade or political alliances, which are often privileged with an undeserved concreteness by notions of reality prevalent in academic culture), it may prove helpful to consider marriage and affinity as a particular form of ritual bond. In this regard, "Rivière . . . argues that marriage as an isolable phenomenon of study is a misleading illusion and that it should be studied as *one* of the socially approved and recognised relationships between the conceptual roles of men and women." [238] In fact, the marriage partner aids in the performance of symbolic behaviors (sex, child-rearing, eating, ritual). He or she functions as a ceremonial partner, friend, collaborator, or adversary whose physical presence serves as an effective symbol of change and growth for both the individual and the social group.

In many cultures, marriage partnerships and other ritual friendships or companionships arise from the same symbolic wellspring of the religious imagination. Among the Barasana, for example, wives, sisters, and *henyerio* partners are the three classes of women who paint the bodies of men in order to effect their transition into the sacred reality made present through dance. Physical links, which, from case to case, are quite different in spatial and temporal expression, function symbolically to bind the man to each of these ritual partners. [239] Hugh-Jones concludes that marriage is only one particular form of socially approved and ritually recognized relationship. [240]

Like other ceremonial relationships, marriage brings together the separate forces of lifetime, history, lineage, cosmic time, bodyspace, residence space, and cosmic space that are embodied in the two individuals and their families. Their partnership ritually coordinates changing economic forces and the creative powers that periodically set in swing the rhythm of a new generation.

There is no point in attempting to survey all the creative expressions of marriage that exist in South America. This symbolic tie, so evidently generative of society and its symbolic forms, can be the focal point of a culture's creativity. When marriage is regarded as a total symbolic fact — when it is set within the full context of all its causes, effects, and extended significations — marital bonds display themselves in myriad patterns in South America. For all that, marriage does not always stand on its own as a remarkable ritual event. Often, marriage partnership is the by-product of other rites of passage prerequisite to it. At times, courtship may require that one accompany one's partner-to-be during the ordeals suffered on his or her path to maturity. This is in line with the role of other formal friends. When a Toba girl is secluded in her initiation hut, for example, her suitor wears a waistband made of the bones of the different animals that he has killed. Outside the girl's hut he sounds a small drum, swaying to its rhythm in such a way that the bones rattle together noisily. The boy's chanting, drumming, and dancing may continue for as long as eight days. He is not allowed to tire or to rest, and he may take a break only for his most urgent needs. "The girl is sitting inside, looking through a hole at her future husband and listening to his chant." [241] The ordeal demonstrates that the young man is able to use the supernatural power of his drum, his dance, his song, and the rattling trophies of his hunt in order to protect his wife-to-be from the harmful attack of destructive beings. Having accompanied one another during their initiatory transformations, husband and wife prove themselves suitable catalysts for a lifetime of such growthful change.

Proof of the ability to change in symbolically controlled ways is often a condition for entering into marriage partnership. Such change is never random; it is defined in terms consonant with the entire symbolic world of value in a culture. This means that the desired change derives its significance from the same primordial world that created the symbolic conditions of culture. For example, in order to gain the handsomeness and strength that will make him worthy of marriage, Mominaru, the young Makiritare mythic hero, must first flee from a jaguar by assuming the form of a crab, a skin-shedding creature.[242] In that form he is saved when he is devoured by an otter who later excretes him. Free but "half dead from suffocation," he ascends to heaven and dives into the still waters of Lake Akuena, which lies at its center. He emerges with another body, handsome and healthy. When the *madi* fruit is ripe, he returns to earth as Kaichama, a spirit who is summoned with ritual flutes *(momi)* to ripen fruit. Only now, having suffered this extraordinary transformation, does he meet the girl he desires to marry. She is out collecting fruit, but she does not recognize him. She believes he had been killed by her father in a wicker fish trap. She takes the handsome stranger home and introduces him to her father.[243] This Makiritare story typifies the mythic accounts of marital origins in which a series of symbolic transformations, magically effecting an entire world, must occur before a marriage alliance can be formed. The marriage bond, like the entire nexus of symbolic relations of which it is a key constitutive element, signifies the sacred reality on which culture, as one historical interpretation of events in the mythic world, founds itself.

Viewing marriage as a ritual relationship, a symbolically guided spiritual adventure, carries with it an important corollary that returns us to the beginning of this chapter. Parenthood is a form of ritual relationship defined by prescribed and meaningful behaviors carried on in relation to one's child. The parents' performance of sex, adherence to food restrictions, and ritual avoidance have symbolic efficacy and result in the successful conception, birth, and growth of a new being. Parents' collaboration forms a new being who combines the creative powers and processes imaged in their blood, semen, flesh, breath, song, dream images, bone, lineage-souls, and their relations to light, water, soil, food, drink, and so on. Ritual parenthood includes biological parenthood. Conceiving and giving birth are symbolic performances, full of meaning in the context of a given society and as efficacious as any other ritual relationships.

ENDING RITUAL FRIENDSHIP
Ritual friends come to the fore in moments of personal reconstitution, which is a process made visible in sonic, spatial, or temporal terms. For this reason, ritual companionship bears close association with changes in the primordial images of sound (name, language, song, instrumental sounds), space (bodily mutilation, growth, or decoration), and time (age, altered or acquired tem-

poral expressions such as the lineage soul, goods fashioned and accumulated over time, and experience of the mythic world). These and other symbolisms of change and exchange alter a persons spatial and temporal expression and so configure processes of growth proper to one's given species. Personal expressions of sound, space, and time are among the images that define one's properly human place in hierarchies of relations and systems of values throughout the cosmic and social worlds.

Individual rites of passage are growth spurts in the spiritual awareness of one's worldly circumstances. Ritual transitions do not leave society unchanged for they profoundly affect the structures and processes of the community by reconfirming, renewing, or revolutionizing them. Human-to-human ritual ties are effective signs of the mutual transformation of individual and society. One may go so far as to say that the ultimate foundation of ritual companionship is the bond between the individual and society, bound to one another through the meanings of their own symbolic expressions: social forms, structures, roles, and organizations, as well as individual creative expressions, choices, personality traits, and bodily and linguistic features. One could construct a complete religious sociology (or a typology of social relations) on the similarities and dissimilarities between symbolic forms, actions, functions, and mythic origins of primordial simultaneity or dissimulation. At every step (i.e., at every change), the inalienable bond between human society and individuality finds symbolic expression in ritual friendship, companionship, advocacy, sponsorship, teaching, guardianship, nursing, protective custody, or antinomy.[244] Viewed from many angles throughout individual life-cycle and social history, the spectrum of human-to-human ritual relationships highlights facets of this social-personal ligament, which is intrinsic to being human.

The bond between individual and community is highly symbolic; that is, it is sacred, as Durkheim made clear in his own way.[245] Both idiosyncratic and group dimensions of human reality constantly recompose themselves in the face of the changing symbolic appearances of sacred and, therefore, enduring primordial powers. Ritual relations further heighten that symbolism in order to reveal to novices (and to impress upon them) the religious nature of their communal bond. Revelation of this kind, *ipso facto*, situates the initiand in wider economic and social networks. Understanding the relations among human individuals, on the one hand, and the relationship between any one of them and the larger human community, on the other, requires an experiential awareness of the supernatural reality from which they all spring.

LIVING WITH MATTER: LABOR AND TECHNIQUE

Significant human growth is not limited to formal rites of passage. Change on the physical, moral, emotional, and cognitive levels occurs daily. It results from the self-conscious, symbolic exchange of body fluids, substances, foods, and sounds and from all the symbolic processes of fabrication and metamorphosis that constitute the individual.[246] These processes not only exist on the personal level, they penetrate every plane of cultural existence. The cycles of work and rest, and the cyclic accumulation, surplus, consumption, and depletion of goods express the same periodic rhythms of symbolic transformation described in myth and acted out in ritual; that is, they are lived out in a certain quality of time. Myth, rite, and work are essentially contiguous cultural performances, interpretations that reshape individuals and societies in the image of revealed realities. All these efforts base themselves on the awareness — a uniquely human quality of knowledge — that the patterned means of producing the changes that sculpt society are skills and inventions achieved by culture heroes or mythic beings in primordial times. To the degree that craft and economic activity follow the same mythic models as rite and art (that is, insofar as they too are the "work of the gods"), they also can be considered the productive work of culture. In many cases, subsistence activities such as hunting and farming are overtly ritual acts.

HUNTING

An indispensable part of hunting is the spiritual fortification or even transformation of the hunter — and the entire hunting context — through music, dance, fasting, continence, and decoration. The mechanisms for changing the hunter are not unlike those used in other rites of passage and growth.[247] For example, the Wapishana scarify the hunter's arm with cuts, into which they rub the ashes (in a wild-honey solution) prepared from selected burned body-parts of desired game.[248] As in rituals of growth, the times when significant items pass in and out of organized space are symbolically marked. For example, the weeping of women, a familiar device in the transformations of growth, occurs in many cultures when a slain animal's body is brought into the village. In the case of the Boróro, crying over a slain jaguar helped regain control over its soul. According to Métraux, Tupinamba women not only wept over the body of a dead jaguar but invested it with initiatory feathered ornaments and armbands.[249] Consonant with rites of passage and recomposition, items that have passed in and out of the body, such as hair balls and bezoars removed from the stomachs, crops, or gizzards of the slain game and, of course, arrows and darts, also receive special care.

Dances reenact the creation of the desired game, the primordial hunts of heroes, or the capitulation of menacing mythic animals who were overcome by magical means. The Chapacura, for example, consider certain songs and dances an indispensable part of their hunting procedures. These *kawaná*, sacred means, guarantee a good supply of game.[250] Choreographed rehearsals and denouements recall the origin of animals and the performance of the first perfect hunt. They stress the performative quality of the actual hunt, which is a dramatization of the first chase across mythic geography.[251] The chase also includes more or less elaborate supplication or propitiation of the supernaturals associated with game. The Piaroa, for example, spend the night before the hunt singing the praises, the origin myth, and the primordial exploits, of the animal they seek to kill.[252] Numerous ethnographic reports describe ritual feedings of slain game with ceremonial food and drink, especially tobacco smoke, fermented drink, or human spit.

Hunting rites also encompass the ceremonial treatment of the hunter's weapons and body as well as of animal bones and fur, and they include litanies of animal names and songs.[253] For instance, among the Siriono, good fortune in hunting may be assured by hanging animal skulls or bird feathers on sticks. This action causes the same animals to return. Siriono hunters also smear *urucú* on their faces to make themselves "attractive" to game.[254] Symbolic flirtation and courtship between hunter and hunted before the climactic penetration of the animal's flesh by the man's weapon is not unprecedented. In theory, a Siriono hunter may not consume the game he has killed lest the animal refuse to return to be hunted again. Such a theoretical restriction is not always honored in practice.[255]

Regarding such restrictions on eating, Herbert Baldus gathered together reports of the custom prohibiting a hunter from consuming his kill. He found evidence of this custom among the Puri (of Minas Gerais), the Krahó, the Siriono, the Kaingáng (of São Paulo, Rio Grande do Sul) and the Shokleng (also known as the Botocudos of Santa Catarina). Baldus makes clear that the custom can only be understood when economic and social factors are set in the light of the supernatural relations that human hunters have with animals.[256] Ordinarily, the abstention of the hunter from the meat he has taken is initiatory; it usually applies only to the first kill of that animal species. Furthermore, mostly young hunters suffer such restrictions, which last only until a short time after marriage. In fact, the young hunter is being treated in a ritual way. The hunter is in the vulnerable state in which initiates find themselves during transition. The body substances and spiritual components of the hunter's person are rearranged, dispersed, and then regathered in new configuration. "[T]he 'strength' of the hunter is going with the arrow or the lance like his 'blood' entering the animal."[257] There is a danger that the young hunter may be so weakened by the spiritual effort of the hunt "that the spirit of the animal could easily take possession of the spirit of the hunter and destroy it if the abstention from eating the meat and ritualistic treatment were not applied to the killer."[258]

The spiritual effects of economic labor ripple through the community along patterned networks of relations, which are made visible through symbolism. Establishment, maintenance, or transformation of such ritual ties is the outcome of careful symbolic action associated with good hunting. The new Guayakí father, for example, scrupulously avoids the kinds of improper and careless behavior that would put him in a state of *pane*, a condition of bad hunting that places its sufferer outside the network of distribution, reciprocities, and optimal relations of exchange in the community. Avoidance of *pane* in the ritual hunt after the birth of his child is a matter of some urgency for a new father, for this ritual hunt is absolutely necessary to save his life. Great numbers of supernatural jaguars stalk him, attracted to a special power within him, *ete-ri-va*.[259] The father must kill game animals before he is taken prey by jaguars. "In order to remain a human being [and not become the animal-like prey of jaguars], the father must be a hunter. [His] choice is to die like an animal or kill like a hunter." [260] If a man is luckless in hunting (pane) on this day, he will die like an animal.

The symbolic acts of women affect the outcome of the hunt. Through hunting men place themselves alongside women as shedders of blood, providers of food, and sustainers of life by means of its transformation. From different perspectives the symbolic aspects of men and women participate in and focus reflection on the mystery of blood, life, and food. For example, Guayakí women are directly involved in both the positive and negative aspects of the hunter's state of being. A hunter becomes bayja, "attractive to beings," when women's sacrality is in motion: at parturition, at the time of his wife's menstruation, at a daughter's first menses, or at the time of his wife's abortions (whether spontaneous or elective). [261] These movements of a woman's reproductive powers endanger men's lives by making them attractive to beings in superabundant numbers. Paradoxically, the very same moments in a woman's cycle may render a man pane, luckless in the hunt. In order not to fall into the state of pane, a man must practice avoidances of women during their powerful periods. In particular, he must neither see them nor eat with them, two ordeals typical of initiatory existence. After game has been taken and after women and men have been ritually washed with timbo, a liana used to both prevent and cure disease of supernatural origin, a normal state of relations among humans, animals, and supernatural forces is restored.

Clearly hunting is a ritual act requiring cooperation from the entire community to orchestrate relations with the visible and invisible powers of the cosmos. The important point to underscore is that there is no overly evident boundary between rite and economic act in the hunt. Symbolic action envelops the whole. The urge to act creatively by interpreting the sacred and the need to subsist find the same expression. Indeed, they spring from the same source. No tear between symbolic and nonsymbolic behavior rends the fabric of culture into divisions between infrastructural economic production and superstructural ritual performance. The contradictions and continuities (that is, the alienation of primordial being represented in myth and reenacted in irrepressibly symbolic action) are as characteristic of the one realm as of the other.

AGRICULTURE

Agriculture, too, is not only an imaginative activity with evident empirical value but also an economic mode with mythological dimensions. [262] The Campa typify the outlook that farming techniques and tools were created for humans. In ancient times, Campa merely initiated the chopping to clear their gardens. They left the rest to their machetes, which finished the job alone. [263] Contemporary practices are but the symbolic vestige of a process whose mystical power is still evident in the myths of origin.

Although subject to altered conditions of time, agricultural tools and practices still possess efficacious power to transform creation in reproductive, life-giving ways. This is because they are the achievement of creative beings, the divinities and cultural heroes of the first times. According to the Desana, for instance, the mythic Daughter of Aracú Fish who taught people how to farm manioc.

It is important to remain cognizant of the sacred origins of gardening. Agricultural labor often becomes a medium of the messages it signifies and the context of their transmission. Apprenticeship serves as a time to acquire tradition along with technology. Such is the case when a Canelos Quichua woman sets a new field. Remaining with her children in the fieldhouse, the woman recounts and reenacts episodes from ancient myths.[264] She may stay there with her children for two or three days, singing songs to Nunghuí, the goddess of garden soil.

Jívaro women also sing to a supernatural female named Nunghuí at the time of planting.[265] Nunghuí is short (about three feet high), very fat, and dressed in black. She pushes up crops through the earth, and she dances at night in cleared, well-weeded gardens, thereby making her dancing partners, the new shoots of manioc, grow. These crops shrink during the daylight hours, so women harvest them in the morning when they are at the maximum size. Nunghuí's power undergirds all fertile feminine forms: the soil, the garden plot, the female souls of manioc and other female plants, and the gardener herself, who honors Nunghuí with rites designed to attract her to the garden and keep her there.[266] Women who know Nunghuí grant her two requests: "to be given a place to dance and to be provided with 'babies'"[267] These "infants" are three red jasper stones (nantára), whose hidden location Nunghuí reveals to the woman in her dreams and hallucinogenic visions, one stone-baby per dream. Nantára contain the blood-sucking female souls of manioc plants. The woman hides the stones under a food bowl at the center of her garden.

In mythic times Nunghuí had given primordial females her own powerful child, who magically accomplished all the tasks of farming with a word. When a woman desired manioc, a garden, a beer brewing jar, or anything else, she merely asked Nunghuí's sacred child. With a word from the mystical child, the desired goods appeared: "Let there be manioc" (or fish, or smoke-dried meat, etc.) One day, however, another child threw ashes in the eyes of the divine child and, contrary to Nunghuí's express prohibition, beat the sacred child when it cried. As a consequence the magic garden disappeared into the earth, the child was spirited away, and people now suffer. Only the contemporary garden and the red stone babies of Nunghuí remain as signs of the paradisal garden. However, the reality of its hidden presence and fertile power still govern the agricultural process.

Special care is taken of those manioc seedlings planted in view of their prospective use at a Jívaro "tobacco feast" honoring a woman. Women gather together to sing or think-sing to Nunghuí while squatting over seedlings. The first manioc cutting placed in the garden is painted red and placed against the gardener's vaginal opening. The woman sits on a tuber of a manioc. "The connection between the fertility of women and the growth of food plants could hardly be more clearly expressed." [268] Once the fields are planted, women dance for five nights in a row to please Nunghuí and enlist her powerful presence as an aid to new growth. If agricultural labor is itself a ritual process, the fully conscious concentration on its symbolic value and the oftentimes tedious compulsion of ritual (with its obsessive attention for detail) may be reserved for specially highlighted moments. Like all ritual processes, agricultural labor is episodic, accommodating itself to the rhythms of the cosmos and of human capacities for reflection. The Jívaro and Canelos Quichua typify the impulse to mark the first planting or first clearing of fields with special rites. Alternately, a major agricultural festival may be set aside to commemorate the first time fields were cleared, planted, or harvested in the mythic era. Such is the case for the Makiritare celebration of the New Garden festival, which occasionally gathers up for reflection the mysteries revealed in the mythic history of agriculture.

According to the Makiritare myths, the development of agriculture happened in stages. In the very beginning, food was sent to primordial beings directly from heaven. That stopped on account of the performance of sexual intercourse, and the first beings found it necessary to eat dirt directly. Next, a slip of the unique Yuca Mother Plant in heaven was stolen and planted on earth, where it became Mount Roraíma. Later, transplanted so as to be closer to human habitation, it became the mountain-tree Marahuaka.[269] In the first period, food was associated with heaven and sexual intercourse; in the second, with earth; and now, in the third stage, it becomes linked with death. For whenever a branch of the tree became heavy with ripe, edible fruit, it fell on top of a being and killed it. The fourth step in the process was orchestrated by a supernatural being named Semenia, the red-billed scythebill. He instructed the first beings how to cut down the Marahuaka tree, showing them how to work in tandem to get their food. Previously, when they had tried to cut down the tree, the notches they cut during the day grew back while they slept at night. Now they divided the labor and rotated sleeping turns so that the notch became increasingly deep as time went on.[270] When the tree was cut through, it still would not fall, for it was rooted in heaven's soil and had to be cut there as well. "Then the great Marahuaka tree finally fell. The entire Earth shook. Branches, fruit, palms, seeds, everything fell. It felt like the sky was falling. It was like the end of the world." [271] Now rain fell through the heavenly stump and formed river systems, which are like snakes traversing the earth. The world bloomed. The one had been destroyed in favor of the many. Today the work must be done in exactly the same way:

> The men clear[ed] the *conuco* [the slash-and-burn garden], like Marahuaka in the beginning. The women plant[ed] and harvest[ed] and prepare[ed] it . . . then the men worked again. They wove baskets, strainers, trays, presses. They carved graters and *kanawa* [hollowed logs used to prepare festival beer]. Those are their jobs. The women harvest, carry, grate, press, cook the cassava. They make *iarake* [festival beer] in the *kanawa*.[272]

After felling Marahuaka, the people celebrated the first great festival, *Adahe Ademi Hidi* (the New Garden festival), at which they played bark horns and recounted everything that had ever happened. "Just as they sang, we sing now."[273] The festival ritual is a part of the very act of agriculture. The effective set of agricultural actions includes singing, dancing, and remembering, as well as slashing, burning, and planting. Like the products of the fields, the feast is a vital sign, a living witness, whose very existence in the world testifies to the constant power of its sacred origins.

Contemporary agriculture, like rituals of other kinds, is the laborious version of sacred processes accomplished with relative ease in the primordium. Because ceremonial and agriculture practices equally symbolize the primordial state of affairs, albeit through the skill and effort of knowledgeable human labor, both can be productive, replicating life in abundance. They do not, however, offer the same kind of eternal, static life as existed during the primordium. Because they are symbolic, they bring into existence life-processes imbued with the death, disappearance, alienation, and withdrawal of primordial forms. Precisely for that reason they can bring into the world life in greater quantitative abundance, an accumulation of numbers of different goods over time, or, alternately, their tragic depletion and exhaustion. That is, meaning and value, the products of the symbolic acts of human ceremonial and economic labor, follow the same periodic life-cycles of surplus, depletion, exhaustion, and revalorization as religious symbols themselves.

SPECIAL CRAFTS

The principal subsistence activities of hunting, gathering, fishing, and agriculture are not the only labor symbolic of sacred realities. In brief sketches aimed at illuminating their religious nature, mention may be made of several crafts, including canoe making, blowgun manufacture, and pottery. In each of these cases, as in many others, myths or legendlike narratives (dreams, visions) describe the sacred basis for the ritual behavior of labor. That is, work is inseparable from the activity of the imagination as it confronts various material modes of being. "In working with a piece of flint or a primitive needle, in joining together animal hides or wooden planks, in preparing a fishhook or an arrowhead, in shaping a clay statuette, the imagination discovers unsuspected analogies among the different levels of the real."[274]

Warao canoemakers, for instance, undergo an apprenticeship that includes a powerful experience of ecstasy. In fact, every new large canoe which a Warao canoe maker crafts is an attempt to reachieve the "sublime blinding moment of ecstasy" he experienced during his initiation. He spends the rest of his life repeatedly trying to return to his supernatural origin, the womb of the great mother, Dauarani, whose vagina serves as the model for the perfect canoe. Far beyond the striving for technical competence and socioeconomic status, this "mystical yearning of the *moyotu* [canoemaker], as he attempts with each canoe he constructs to recapture the light that might once more dispel the 'dark night' of his soul, could well be the most dynamic motivation of them all."[275]

Boatmaking is related to Warao seafaring, which is both an economic activity and a spiritual adventure on the model of mythic heroes. The Warao were seafarers from ancient times. Because of the important position of tobacco in their shamanic complex, their dangerous voyages to Trinidad may have been motivated in great part by their desire to acquire tobacco.[276] The perilous sea voyage was conducted as a ritual on the model of the journeys of the primordial culture hero Haburi's crossing of the sea in his escape to the Father of the Rivers. The bowman now dresses himself as did Haburi in ancient times. Behind him two women chant the *erere*, the songs sung by Haburi's mothers when they escaped in the canoe that eventually transformed itself into the serpent body of Dauarani, the Mother of the Forest. Two invisible gods accompany the passengers to keep the dragon monster from drawing their boat down into the sea. Their invisible servant, Himabaka, drives away spirits of the deep with his sword.[277]

The essential body parts of the butterfly god, Warowaro, are painted on the escutcheon at the bow. While the butterfly god guides the boat to Trinidad, a mythical horse powers the boat from the stern. The captain-shaman feeds his invisible passengers with tobacco smoke from his cigar and placates Hahuba, the sea monster, with his songs. Hahuba is lonely and tries to devour navigators and transform them into pleasant company for herself. When she speaks, her words unleash the winds. Before reaching Trinidad, the southern gods leave the ship and entrust it to a northern deity. They will, however, accompany the boat on its return journey. Upon their return, after a priest-shaman assures himself that the boat is not carrying any bad spirits, the canoe maker, who guides the boat from the helm, is directed by the captain-shaman to bring the boat home. "The expert canoe-maker who, because of his skill, courage, and above all, his esoteric knowledge, had made it all possible, had reached the pinnacle of his career."[278]

Tools, weapons, and other manufactured objects, fruits of the labor of human hands and imagination, become multivalent symbols of all the levels of meaning in which human existence is involved. The material objects of work, foci of hours of human attention, become images economically representing whole universes of force and meaning. The simplest item can irradiate elaborate significances throughout the entire cosmos and its history. For the Makiritare, blowgun cane is a principal item of trade. Nevertheless, it is gathered with ritual care from the sacred places where it fell "in the beginning."[279] These symbolic actions stretch back to the time of origins when the cane first fell to earth in the form of the feathers of the two slain Dinoshi, the fearful harpy-eagle pair who had once terrified the earth. Now, when the Makiritare go to collect it there, when they come to that peak of

Marahuaka ["little gourd," the mountain-tree that once connected heaven and earth], we ask permission from its master, Kahuakadi. We come and we say to him . . . 'We haven't eaten. We haven't touched our women.' As we come upon the blowgun path. We play our flutes. We plant our shoots in the earth when we get there, as offerings to Kahuakadi. We sing softly. We don't shout. . . . [W]e never cut more than four canes together. That way we don't upset the Master.[280]

The religious symbolism of myth and ritual make available for reflection the intimate relations humans have with modes of matter. The forms of human labor become so many ways of assessing and developing that intimacy in a characteristically human way through symbolic action, productive creativity, and the self-awareness that is critical to an understanding of the human situation in the cosmos. In establishing the essential conditions of culture, heroes and gods made sure to provide these means of production and the knowledge of their symbolic meanings. Desana pottery and basketry, for instance, were taught to human beings by the daughter of the sun. It was she who invented fire, clothing, and methods of eating. Among the Jívaro and Canelos Quichua, the goddess of the garden soil is also the mistress of pottery clay and its techniques, especially dreams, which serve as resources for creative designs, and songs, which keep pots from breaking under fire. Through pottery work women maintain human contact with the goddess's sacred powers. When Canelos Quichua women go on soul voyages induced by *Datura*, for instance, their bodies are guarded by women rather than by their husbands. In these visions they ask Nunghuí for knowledge about their own body-souls and they seek ways of merging these souls with their pottery designs. They learn special songs owned by spirits. They are also taught the technique of sending their songs safely to an intended receiver.[281]

During the middle period of the annual or semiannual Canelos Quichua festival that celebrates the union of the moon and his sister-bird, men are absent from inhabited space. The whole house, normally divided into male and female sections, becomes entirely female.[282] During this time women make pots, pottery trumpets, and figurines that depict items found throughout the mythical universe, and they sing songs of the primordial times. The patterns collapse all the times and spaces of the universe into the order of mythic time.[283] Pottery making thus recreates the primordial universe. Among the Kógi, subsistence can be highly symbolic activity. Each action and object can be looked upon from two different symbolic points of view, which are consonant with the two elements that make the universe fruitful and regenerative—femininity and masculinity. Thus, for example, arrows represent the penis, as do spindles and machetes. Small gourds or calabashes represent the uterus, as do traps and snares. As a result, spinning, weaving, and hunting can regenerate and sustain life because they are coital acts of cosmic forces.[284]

Among the Yekuana, similarly, the weaving of baskets is an essential process in the continuation of cosmic order from one generation to the next. The designs on rectangular storage baskets and round trays derive from the acts and beings of the creative times described in myth. It is encumbent upon the basketmaker to make present again, in a graphic way that parallels narrative presentation of myth, the processes of supernatural forces, which created the world and creatively maintain it. It is this link with the creative supernatural beings and the creative continuation of the cosmos that impels the basketmaker toward perfection in his art. Mythic animals (e.g., the aquatic and monstrous water snake, the monkey who originated yuca, the frog who is mistress of the earth and underworld) and constellations, are again made present, as efficacious and powerful as at the beginning, in the images on basketwork and in the human imagination, which contemplates them.[285]

Technology and labor are forms of distinctively human knowledge not separable from religious knowledge, for they also are symbolic actions. Furthermore, the sacred powers they signify are effective. The symbolic nature of productive behavior and the concomitant knowledge of the significance of one's reproductive acts of labor define the uniqueness of human existence. All forms of symbolic self-awareness in technology base themselves on critical knowledge of the past, that is, on knowledge of the sacred origins of the life forms in question and of the primordial crisis that first alienated them from the technical processes that now represent them. Canelos Quichua education, which stresses knowledge of the meaning of one's past as an effective basis for shaping one's future, centers on the meaning of technology, that is, the significance of manipulating mystical substances. A Canelos Quichua youth constructs a micro-universe of mystical substances in a large, dried pod, *misha puru*.[286] The youth learns the meaning of these various substances, as this small universe begins to "grow" within the pod. The different substances and the changes they undergo correspond to the youth's own special spiritual experiences related to dreams and voluntarily acquired souls. Just as the youth opens and unfolds to the dynamics of the spiritual world around him, the tiny flowers in his micro-universe – pod are believed to open and attract bees — a development that parallels the movement of his own bee-spirit helpers, which drone in his belly and bring him dreams. "The whole thing 'ferments' like chicha to produce a living spirit-helping universe close to the youth's own soul substances." [287]

The sources of meaning, according to the Canelos Quichua, hark back to a time that no longer exists — the mythic time when meaning was undifferentiated, fully apparent, and immediately known. The process of maturation, then, is a never-ending search through symbolic means (the techniques of hallucinogenic vision, pottery, agriculture, hunting). The meaning of one's soul is uncovered through the acquisition and knowledge of other souls and is developed through experimental technology, the manipulation of substances signifying the sacred.

URGENCY

Clearly, in such cases as those considered in this section on labor, the economic activities of hunting, fishing, farming and artisanship are also religious acts hemmed in by, imbued with, or identified as ritual action. Control over sound, diet, motion, relations, passages, and body parts is symbolic expression, exhibiting the same logic and intention in hunting, agricultural, or craft rites as do symbolic expressions in the processes of change that constitute the human person and society. Economic action effects serious change in the symbolic composition of individual, the community, the world. The shared, symbolic nature of economic labor and ceremony helps narrow the gap investigators may be tempted to set between diverse ergological expressions: the work of subsistence and the work of interpretation, act and thought, knowledge and theory. Myth (theurgy demiurgy), ceremony (liturgy, dramaturgy) and all other urgent forms of handiwork (surgery), physical labor ("work," orgy), and mental exercise express in equal measure but in different ways the human need to be energetic, creative, and, thereby, productive of culture.[288] Interpreting sacred realities is laborious and coextensive with human relationships to modes of matter. The burden of culture to reenact sacred origins — and thereby to reinterpret them — through the changing expressions of each generation takes concrete form not only in the ceremonial arts but also in crafts and in political economy.

KNOWLEDGE AND SELF-CONSCIOUSNESS AS HUMAN FORMS OF CREATIVITY

The unique consciousness of the human being sets if apart from all other modes of existence. Human awareness is, literally, the most significant element of the growth characteristic of human beings for it is a self-awareness gained through manipulation of and reflection on one's own physical, social, and psychic changes held up as symbols. Many South American cultures recognize the singular role that human knowledge plays in personal and social formation. Human knowledge is a form of creativity directly related to the creativity of the primordium, for human action and interpretation are understood to be symbolic, modeling themselves on mythic events. The Kógi are not alone when they insist that human life should be given over entirely to the acquisition of knowledge,

> a term [designating] the myths and traditions, the songs and spells, and all the rules that regulate ritual. This body of esoteric knowledge is called by the Kogi the "Law of the Mother." Every object, action, or intention has a spirit-owner who jealously guards what is his own, his privilege, but who is willing to share it with mankind if compensated by an adequate offering.[289]

Dedication to knowledge — a way of living life — characterizes the human quality of acting. This section briefly examines several theories of knowledge in order to indicate their sublety, their sophistication, their ability to distinguish among cognitive operations such as memory and reflection, and their connection to the symbols coined in myth.

The process of knowledge cannot be mistaken for simple sense perception. Human perception is always interpretive (a corollary to the fact that, in the symbolic reality humans inhabit, appearances are deceiving). The Wayãpi illustrate that human perception is affected by the mode of human knowing. To the human being (i.e., the Wayãpi), animals look like animals.

By contrast, when animals view a human, they see an animal. Likewise, the sluggish giants who inhabit the underworld, the *woo*, look at human beings and see animals (monkeys). Even the sun and the moon see both animals and men as animals. As Pierre Grenand points out, these observations emphasize the animal nature of the human being.[290] However, an even more important point is made in this way by the Wayãpi. It is a philosophical claim that the essential animality of human beings is transformed in some way by their own self-perception, by the special mode of cognition they enjoy, for human beings *see themselves* as *human* beings. The human consciousness of self and other is different both from that of animals and from that of divine beings. For the human being, the other is an animal but the self is a human — an observation animals cannot make. It is only the self-consciousness of human nature that sets it apart. For the Wayãpi, ontology and meaning are creations of different conscious perceptions.

In his investigations of taxonomies of plants and animals among the Wayãpi, Grenand discovered some fascinating information about the Wayãpi concept of perception and cognition. The human relationship to nature is one of conscious perception achieved simultaneously about the whole and its parts. Each advance on one level presupposes a simultaneous advancement of knowledge on the other. This kind of knowledge is communicated to young people by "reciting *in situ* the most significant stories and legends" concerning plants and animals.[291] The learner is placed in the paradoxical position that "in order to recognize what is essential, one must know everything." [292] Under these circumstances, myth becomes the suitable foundation for human knowledge, for myth accounts for the world as a thoroughly symbolic reality whose parts always signify the whole of meaning as it stood in the primordium.

The Wayãpi symbolic classification of animals places great stress on criteria having little to do with their visual form. Sound (of mammals, birds, noisy insects such as wasps and honeybees) is especially important. In a way unlike what occurs in those taxonomic systems that depend on comparative anatomy, the recognition and classification of these animals in the Wayãpi system depend on recognition of the *living* being by its sound, its tracks, its leavings, or its nests or dwellings, but *not by sight*. Grenand points out that birds, in particular, "are recognized only with great difficulty if they are presented already dead without previous observation by sight while still alive." [293] Fish, instead, are recognized by sight. On the other hand, the vegetal world is known mostly by visual markers with occasional assistance from fragrances.

This fascinating division of kinds of knowledge by symbolic sound (living animals), sight (fish), and appearance-texture-fragrance (vegetation) finds its parallel in the constitution of the human personality and its division into faculties.[294] In myth, language is linked to animals but not to plants. Human names are the various animal names acquired throughout life. By locating an individual in a specific place in the symbolic, sonic world, these important symbols define one's personality and determine the *modus oper-*

andi of personal faculties of perception and cognition, which govern growth. Applied to people, these names set up strings of associations that link one into a world system since animal names are part of the interrelated divisions of sounds, sights, spaces, and times running throughout the whole cosmos.[295]

Bestowing a name, then, cannot be a casual affair for the Wayãpi. Instead, some character trait of the child, revealed by its sound, appearance, or behavior, betokens its place in the order of resemblances that compose the symbolic universe of meaning. What its sound or behavior resembles in animals, however, far surpasses mere appearance. The bond with the name-animal is a profound one, drawing one into an endless set of symbolic associations, which weave their way through the universe. "They think, in effect, that a part of the animal is placed within the human being and influences both appearance and character."[296] In the same way, of course, animals possess capacities associated with human character. It is imperative to keep in mind that the connections in this system of resemblances can only be made at the level of myth.[297] Mythic and ritual performances become the paradigms of significant human knowledge because they signify the creative events of powerful beings whose acts ground the comprehensibility of all existence.[298] This is why myth is essential to knowledge of the universe, both in its parts and as a whole.

COGNITION, TIME, MEMORY

Cognition requires proper relationship to time. If a reality is to be grasped as it is, the act of knowing must be an act of self-realization, bringing the human into proper relationship to the mode of being he or she seeks to understand. Time becomes a symbolic means of negotiating the relationship to different modes of the real in a knowledgeable way. Thus the Campa understand that, for various reasons, the being who created them did not make them like stones and trees, which do not die. One reason for this is that when rocks and trees were queried at the beginning of time, they made no reply. For example, when the creator-transformer spoke to the *mešiá* tree and asked questions of it, it said nothing. Consequently, he did not fashion human beings from this tree, which rejuvenates itself each year when it sheds its bark. On the other hand, earth did respond when spoken to.[299] Because the creator made humans from earth (actually, from earth taken from termite nests), all Campas return to earth; they die. Only prime material able to answer primordial questions is suited for human creation. From the very beginning of human life, human existence is marred by tragicomic flaws associated with the irrepressible urge to respond to inquiry. At least with respect to immortality, there were other options for human existence that were not chosen at the beginning of time.

The Campa contend that human involvement with passing time has its benefits. Campa theories of knowledge as it relates to time are not purely epistemological. Knowlege is a total experience, both aesthetic and physical. Through the passage of time human knowledge improves or makes more durable the relationship between the soul and the body. In addition, transient time can overcome certain innate incapacities of human perception and cognition. For example, the human eye is unable to see good spirits in their true form. However, if one continually ingests sacred substances, (tobacco and *ayahuasca*), one's eyesight will improve. Campa shamans are those who ordinarily are successful in their search for more extraordinary vision.[300] It is significant that, under normal circumstances, human beings do not have full sight of all that exists in the universe. An important and powerful dimension of the universe remains opaque to human vision. It is only with difficulty and with supernatural aids that corrected vision can be acquired and "true" appearances seen for what they are. True knowledge, a state of human action that is physical, mental, and imaginative, intermingles the visible and invisible worlds. Everyday events, their ostensibly arbitrary and random occurrences, can be fully understood with reference to what is invisible and can become visible to the senses of the wise person who, sizing up his or her own transitive state, exploits these conditions of passage in order to enter into primordial conditions of time.

Memory plays a key role in symbolic knowledge because it allows for comparison of different states of time. By recalling to mind other temporal conditions and juxtaposing them with the present, memory permits one to grasp the unique symbolic configuration of one's present situation. It allows one to come to grips with one's own significance. Recognizing the importance of memory in human growth and cognition serves to open an enormous panorama of cultural ideas, for memory takes many different forms. Symbolic representations of the process of memory shape the act of remembering. Memory is a symbolic treasury; how memory is signified (e.g., in weaving, writing, fighting, exchange, or sound) serves as a standard in evaluating other imaginative aspects of knowledge in culture.

Memory is linked to the images of limits and of death. In compensation for human beings' having to suffer the fate of mortality, the Tukano divinity Yepá Huaké offered them the means of remembering their past. White men, personified by the character Alemán, are not able to remember things by memory alone; therefore they receive paper notebooks in which to record the past. Their culture takes shape around the imagery of the written word. The Tukano, in the person of their mythical chief Yúpuri Baúro, have no need of notebooks and paper, for they have the capacity to remember, purely by memory, all that which happens in the world.[301] They do so by restaging the events associated with Yepá Huaké.

The Kaingáng, to cite a different image of memory, take a great interest in recalling their history. Feuds occupy an essential place in the history of Kaingáng relationships. A feud establishes a lasting bond between lineages. Feuds become not only physical exercises but also the premise for spectacular exercises of memory. The details of hundreds of years of feuding are remembered down to the very location of killings and the kinds of wounds inflicted.[302] With the help of feuds and cycles of deadly vengeance, "they know who their father's father's father's son's wife's sister's daughter's husband is down to the last detail of all his names, what he died of, and how many children he had." [303] Henry collected such detailed genealogy to a depth of two hundred years.

Death, as it figures in the symbolism of memory, need not be so literal. Remembering, especially recalling dreams, is a major mode of spiritual consciousness for the Apyteré. Spiritual awareness is the result of a dialectical process of disintegration of the personality into its constituent parts during dreams and its reintegration through recounting the history of spiritual events through song. Memory is the sung account of the dream-world and of adventures in it as performed by the disparate personal elements of the person who dissolved during sleep. Song recomposes the personality through the performance of memory.

At times, what is remembered through religious song is related less to the death or symbolic disintegration of a single human individual and more to the withdrawal of a supernatural being or a primordial state of affairs. Creative musical laments that remember such events are not restricted to the mythic performances of tragedy in tropical South America. According to John M. Schechter's investigation of early chronicles and dictionaries, the two dominant Inca cultural themes were lamentation and memory-retention.[304] To accomplish these goals, the Inca possessed several categories of official historians, who chanted history at the pricipal feasts. They were remarkable for their memories. They performed lengthy historical laments recounting the admirable deeds of their ancestors, military exploits, and the lives of deceased monarchs.[305] These official transmitters of history (quipu-camayocs, amautas, and harahuicus) were honored not only because their memory retention was "a laudable individual characteristic" but because "retention of ancestral memory . . . played a major role in the ethos of Inca society as a whole." [306] The performance of historical laments maintained and strengthened social order through the exercise of memory of lineage and group-affiliation events as well as through the symbolic divisions brought about in the ritual performances themselves. In short, "the bards and the Inca nobility were in a symbiotic relationship whose keystone was memory." [307] In this case we see history treated as a mythic cataclysm leaving its residue of historical song, the lamentations generated by the passing of powerful ancestral beings.[308]

SYSTEMATIC THEORIES OF KNOWLEDGE

Since the knowledge process is recognized as the key ingredient in the growth of human individuality and in the creative changes desired in human society, cultures frequently make knowledge the subject of systematic attention. Examples from the Canelos Quichua and the Desana illustrate the degree to which South American epistemology and analysis of learning experience can be complex and subtle.

Canelos Quichua dreams propel the process of knowledge in two ways: they may proclaim knowledge brought by mythic spirits in the dream itself, and/or they may provoke reflection, observation, and conversation with learned people in the never-ending process of their intrepretation.[309]

For the Canelos Quichua, a ceaseless quest for knowledge *(yacha)* by acquiring souls is essential to human existence. Self-understanding, the recognition of one's own soul substance and its meaning, is an ongoing process of remembering the exemplary past, for one's own soul is ancient and only the knowledge of its past history and transitions will make its meaning clear. Clarification of the meaning of one's own significations is essential to the process of human growth. Such knowledge, and the power that derives from it, can be gained through the acquisition of the souls of animals, the dead, and so on. The living community is linked in an unbroken network of souls, which go back to Ancient Times.[310] Even to become the founder of a household, a Canelos Quichua man must have a Datura vision during which his body "dies" and his soul journeys through the forest.[311] The traveling soul sings a special song, watches flowers bloom as it passes by, and welcomes spirit-helper souls in the form of bees and wasps. His soul not only travels to other spaces of the universe, but journeys back to Ancient Times. He is asked to scrutinize the past life of his souls as well as his dreams for the future and to explain them to Amasanga, the master spirit of the souls in the forest.[312] Amasanga may suck out evil darts from the body of the man. Freed from evil, the male soul is introduced to powerful underworld beings who are shamans. In this way, the man who intends to found a household gains familiarity with curing plants, his own inner being, and the wider spirit world. He returns home "strong, knowledgeable, confident, and brave." [313]

Human memory, stimulated by souls acquired in hunting and visions, serves as a counterweight to the temporal passage begun in Ancient Times. At various periods in life, a Canelos Quichua must reflect on the nature of his or her own soul. Such reflection necessarily requires contemplation of the beings of Ancient Times—a sort of anamnesis. During primordial days, according to the Canelos Quichua, the ancient people knew how to control their souls in such a way that, when they died, the souls would enter rocks or indestructible logs to be reborn when a future shaman liberated them from their confinement.[314] During the Times of Destruction, however, many of these souls were lost, since there were more people in Ancient Times than there are now. Nonetheless, the knowledge these souls possessed may be retrieved because people in Ancient Times knew how to encapsulate their souls in indestructible forms (rocks, logs).

Whereas ancient people could acquire souls from animals, contemporary human beings (Canelos Quichua) both inherit ancient souls at birth and acquire them through techniques that allow one to enter *unai*, the time before creation.[315] As one acquires souls, one's knowledge of mythic times must increase in order to understand the meaning of their power.[316] Consequently, one's growth in wisdom, age, and power draws one increasingly into the Time of the Beginnings and the later mythic epoch called the Time of the Grandfathers, when animal ancestors conferred souls on human beings. By continually reentering the times of myth through dreams and ritual, the "full meaning" of creation and human experience, a meaning available to the ancients, can be reacquired.[317] This process of the acquisition of human knowledge *(yacha)* requires absolute sincerity of heart, a condition that is tested by the master spirit of forest souls, Amasanga. "The ability to understand life's processes, to become integrated with them as an intellectual, questing, creative human is the primary meaning of *Sacha Runa*—jungle person, knowledgeable *(ricsina)* person."[318]

The Canelos Quichua emphasize that to be human is to seek out knowledge *(yachana)* and experience of one's own sacred history. Only in this way can the meaning of one's present being, one's "now time," be understood and effective action in the present as well as transmission of one's soul toward the future become possible. The Canelos Quichua thus maintain a complementary distinction between *yachana*, the knowledge or learning derived from myth and historical legend, and *ricsina*, the accumulating personal experiences, perceptions, and understandings. *Yachana*, cosmic knowledge, serves as the foundation for *ricsina*, knowledge derived from experience of the cosmos. Through their dreaming *(muscuna*, "to see, to dream")* and thoughtful reflection *(yuyana*, and also *yuyarina)* individuals put their personal stamp on the symbolic shape which knowledge assumes in this world.[319]

Canelos Quichua cultures' growth in new knowledge through the creative expressions of knowledgeable individuals *(yachaj*, "one who knows")* appears most evident in male shamanism and in female pottery. The male shaman is at home in the spirit world. He has literally taken his place among supernaturals, for he sits on a turtle *(charapa)* seat of power just as Sungui, the supernatural master of the water domain, and other powerful spirits do. Based on his experience in the exotic worlds of spirits and foreigners, the shaman acquires fluency in alien tongues and spirit sounds. The female potter also recasts cultural imagery in conformity with her knowledge. She stylizes cosmic symbols by drawing designs of mythic beings on her pots in creative images shaped by her personal experiences. For this reason she is called *sinchi muscuj huarmi* ("strong image-shaping woman").[320]

In the Canelos Quichua view, because a culture's tradition of knowledge is shaped by individuals' experiences, and because those personal experiences that shape society are, in turn, based upon the events of that society's unique origins as relayed through the images of myth, different cultural communities develop distinct symbolic forms. The symbolic means (e.g., language, pottery designs) by which one culture transmits its knowledge are different from another culture's as are the meanings the two sets of symbols convey, for both signified and signifier within one culture stem from and share the same creative reality, signified by their symbolic nature. Thus the Canelos Quichua distinguish between *ñuchanci yachai* ("our cultural knowledge") or *ñucanchi risiushca runa* ("our people's perception") and *shuj shimita yachai* ("other peoples' speech, knowledge"). One may venture to say that society—like dream, language, and pots—is itself a form of symbolic knowledge.

The Desana present a quite different cognitive scenario. They center their theory of thoughtful knowledge around the activity of *ka'i*, mind, the complement of the soul. *Ka'i*, like the soul *(simporá)*, is a temporal organ. Important differences, however, exist between them. The *simporá* is a luminous "little cloth" located in the human heart. It flutters when one breathes. Animals possess no *simporá*. *Ka'i*, possessed by all beings that think, is located in the brain. It is intimately bound up with memory, for it consists of the accumulation of experiences. As a consequence, the *kai'i*, unlike the soul, is essentially personal. It begins at birth and continues to grow, existing as a shadow even after the death of the body.[321]

In ways uniquely configured by the personal history of each individual, the processes of memory, thought, and reason are performed by the *ka'i*. The entire operation is essential to the act of mental conception *(pemahsíri)*, the uniquely human operation of the *ka'i*. Conception, a creative human act associated with symbols, is more closely connected with the image of hearing than with seeing. *Pemahsíri* is a compound of *peri* ("to hear") and *mahsíri* ("to know"). Conception of this kind stands apart from the mere act of perception, *inyamahsíri* (from *inyári*, "to see," and *mahsíri*). The eye sees, but the mind *(ka'i)* conceives; that is, it reflects on the echo *(keorí)* of realities.[322] The centrality of *keorí*, the echo, is of utmost importance in probing the Desana process of conception. "The concept of symbolism, of symbolic thought, is expressed then in the word *keorí*, the echo, the shadow, the image, the essence. Used as a verb, *keorí* means to measure or to take the measure of something, and our informant explains that 'the echo is the measure of sound.' "[323]

A Desana individual conceives of the world by "hearing" the unseen image, or invisible essence, of realities as they are echoed within one's memory and as they resound within one's uniquely personal history. That is why the images of reality must change with the changes wrought by growth, and vice versa. The Desana recognize linguistically that the capacity to know *(mahsíri)* is the distinctive feature of the human being *(mahsë*, "the thinker, the knower"): "A man is he who sees and hears the echo and thus knows . . . the symbolism of things, objects, acts, events, and who has the capacity to establish chains of symbolic associations, which become more and more abstract. Conversely, a man is one who can reduce an abstract concept to its simplest symbolic expression."[324]

The symbolic reflection carried on by the mind *(ka'i)* is different from mere understanding *(pesi turage)* or even intellectual gymnastics. Reflection implies hearing the symbolic image in a way that moves beyond understanding to orientation, to taking a firm stand in relation to the meaning one hears. Reflection of this sort includes a judgment and evaluation of the meaning signified by the symbol, the echo. As Reichel-Dolmatoff reports,

> This cognitive act is designated as *pesi k'ranyeári*, a term derived from *peri*/to hear, to understand, *k'rapíri*/to step, and *nyeári*/to seize. Mentally, this expression is accompanied by a fixed image: a man standing upright, firmly planted on the ground as a cosmic axis, stepping firmly. . . . To achieve this state of reflec-

tion, of "stabilization" and equilibrium, is the ideal of a Desana man because only then does he find security through the comprehension of religion and its function in the life of society.[325]

Hearing the echoes of foregone realities and recognizing these symbols for what they are increasingly makes the mind *(ka'i)* what it is: the human capacity to situate itself symbolically in time. With the cognitive instruments fashioned from its own nature (the epistemological imagery of memory, "hearing," understanding, stepping, seizing, standing upright) and made manifest in ritual gesture and dance, the mind reflexively refashions the changing guises in which it appears to itself so that they conform to the images of primordial realities whose echoes the mind hears in the reverberations of its own changing structures. Change and growth are shaped by the images and symbols which human perceptions, cognitions, memories, and reflections must necessarily assume. The meanings signified in the processes of human awareness reconfigure their human agents. Knowledge is the distinctly human process through which humans become what they are.

CONCLUSIONS

This chapter has surveyed several cultural ideas surrounding human change and creativity. Composed of shifting symbolism — names, language or songs, dreams, growing bones, flesh and fluids, sexual parts, hair, changing skin, acquired souls — the human being is as dynamic as its ingredient imagery. Human growth becomes a form of knowledge, for it is bound up with the symbolic constitution of individuals and societies. Insofar as the world and its inhabitants are symbolic, they are knowable; that is, human beings can know themselves as subject to the influential experience of the cosmos and its contents.[326]

Under the signs of growth in the human life-cycle, the ritualized moments of passage lift up the different existential threads that run throughout the entire fabric of human existence. From time to time, the publicly marked stages on life's way pull consciousness into focus from various temporal perspectives. Altered states of awareness at conception, birth, puberty, marriage, parenthood, and death crystallize the constitutive symbolic process of change in diverse, recombinant images of knowledge, a set of processual signs whose sum betokens human nature. Over a lifetime the individual becomes aware of the enduring symbolic value of his or her changes.

Successful conception, for instance, results from the acts of others (e.g., supernaturals, parents). From the beginning, theories of conception remind us, the human individual is not the author of his or her own significations. Blood, semen, bone, water, light and darkness, foods, sounds, and temperatures affect one's defining composition. One's conception and gestation are consequences of the logic of one's signs, postulated by others. In some fundamental sense one's personal destiny remains the outcome of prefigured meanings. Existence is inextricably social; its particulars make sense within the total ontological situation, a society of different qualities of being. Parents, like the other ritual assistants who perform symbolic acts generative of new life, channel cosmic and social forces into new and specific forms.

The imagery of birth demonstrates the human propensity for first performances. The creative need to treasure acts carried out for the first time impels a cycle of growth that reaches to the outermost capacity of one's environment, arrives at full term, and opens one to a new setting in time and space. In the same way, the event of death generates imagery that clarifies how every human experience requires leaving something behind, for no moment subject to the space and time of this world succeeds in capturing the fullest conditions of being.

Maturation reveals what one already means. Bodily change, brought on through biological growth or deliberate mutilation or decoration, is a transfiguration of the human image, enlarging understanding of human life and individual meaning. Equipped with the light of new understanding, one consciously directs change, steering a course in accordance with the beacons of one's own symbolic guises, which are reflected most clearly during ritual moments of passage. Initiation awakens the candidate to the full extent of symbolic life and its repercussions. Because the body is symbolic, for example, body functions such as crying, menstruating, excreting, or eating are exchanges of significant items (tears, blood, waste, food) with economic, moral and cosmic value.[327] Modeled on sacred paradigms, the spatial and temporal regulations of body openings, closings, and transitions cooperate in a symbolic process that interweaves hygienic, ethical, epistemological, and cosmological levels of reality into one system worthy of the reflection that generates it.

Although birth, puberty, marriage, and death appear as cross-over moments from one state to another and as spread throughout an individual's life-cycle, each celebrates a constant of the human condition. The dispersal of these transitions throughout the life-cycle allows the symbolism of time to resolve, at least apparently, the contradictions inherent in human existence: that one becomes what one already means, that change is a constant fixture of the human condition, that creativity demands both performance of acts for the first time and the repetition of primordial events of power, that mature symbolic thought requires revelations tantamount to disillusionment. The various constant truths of being human, highlighted in different rites of passage, appear to contradict one another. In fact, they are paradoxical because they bespeak the human condition. The idea of change becomes a temporal device that permits one to sort out the contradictory meanings of human existence, the symbolic state. Severally and together, rites of passage revel in the symbolic condition of a being whose most spectacular (literally, most visible) creativity rests on the awareness of its own changing significations.

Maintaining the human state of creativity, a calculus of immersion in (but also a critical awareness of) symbolic processes, is a matter of some urgency. Symbolic knowledge is a form of creative work, an encounter of the human imagination with species of matter found in such ergological expressions as hunting, gathering, fishing, herding, farming, thinking, speaking, remembering, and liturgics. The urge to create reverberates in art as well. In pottery, basketry, and weaving, for instance, human craft locates itself on the continuum of world-creating and world-sustaining processes of time, especially the nighttime and other hidden or periodic temporal processes that deliberately control darkness, light, liquid, and sound in containers, colors, or instruments. Human beings recognize themselves as containers whose continual openness to growth offers the constant possibility of new and creative forms of closure, new significations, and new awareness of the sacred origins of their meaning.

CHAPTER 7

SPECIALISTS

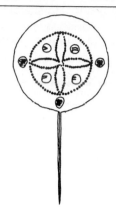

A close examination of the life and ideas of religious specialists is invaluable for the study of religion in South America. The practices and beliefs of the men and women who play special religious roles never account for all the religious expressions of an entire community. Nonetheless, they form an important and integral part of a religious tradition, and no study of religious life could be complete without looking at them. The warrant for study of specialists, however, is weightier than the obsession for thoroughness. Terms employed to evaluate special roles—the imagery of a calling, the evidence of authoritative rapport with supernaturals—provide a relatively systematic account of a tradition's reckoning of the sacred in all its forms. The symbolic life of the specialist is an ordered ensemble of religious ideas shared by the community but perceived from a particular point of view.

The speculative histories, theologies, and systematic ontologies of specialists comprise an elite lore related to hierarchies of privilege and configurations of power. A sociology of knowledge would examine these ideologies in the context of each community and place such knowledge in proper perspective within the sociopolitical praxis of specific groups. Such a social history could show, for example, the different ways in which the claim to special religious knowledge (in societies as different as the Jívaro, the Avá-Chiripá, and the Makiritare) formed a leadership that functioned as a core of resistance against the military, ecclesiastical, and administrative powers of the colonial enterprise. This volume is not a history or sociology of knowledge. Rather, it seeks to collaborate in such efforts by surveying the root meanings of several religious ideas that should be accounted for in such histories. The idea of religious specialization is an important one in any community. In describing the religious ideas of South America, one must neither exclude the specialist nor exaggerate his or her isolation from the community. This chapter investigates what is known of the sacred through experiences that a community recognizes as extraordinary. In particular, it scrutinizes the ways in which human beings can know the sacred and examines what cultures deem to be the outermost reaches of the human capacity for religious knowledge and power. The crux of the issue is this: the community recognizes that some humans, but not all, experience extraordinary rapport with the sacred. In what guises and through what symbolic means do these religious capacities come into play?

BASES OF RELIGIOUS AUTHORITY: POSSESSION, CANON, ECSTASY

The chapter examines the basis of a specialist's authority, the nature and source of his or her special knowledge, and the symbols manifest in the exercise of that authority. There are, of course, several possible foundations on which to establish special religious authority.[1] Without exhausting the list, mention can be made of three bases of authoritative knowledge: the experience of possession, the mastery of a canon, and the experience of ecstasy. Because of its ubiquity and central importance in South America and the wealth of its complicated religious symbolism, ecstatic experience will comprise the bulk of this chapter's considerations. In passing, a word may be said about the other two platforms of religious authority.

During possession, supernatural beings tenant the body and the personality of their host. Vocal sounds, facial features, and physical gestures betray the fact that an inhabiting spirit overshadows the proprietorship of the human soul, which acts as receptionist, faithful servant, or absentee landlord for the visitor. No longer self-possessed, personalities and bodies become instruments of direct communication with the spirit world. Possession is frequently an intensely social drama and not a solo performance. Since the possessed individual is, by definition, out of control, musicians, singers, and dancers frequently accompany him or her. This backup band of sidemen calls upon named spirits by invoking them with specific rhythms, melodies, or words. The accompanists induce trance and try to control the episodic progress of the trance's duration.[2]

Healing is a necessary component of all authority based on possession because of the miraculous healings performed through the agency of the resident spirit but also for another reason: since unabated possession would itself amount to sickness, closing the possessive séance is tantamount to cure.[3] During sessions, the nonpossessed prevent the devout host from becoming a hostage; they keep the supernatural tenant from becoming a tenant for life. In addition, the medium's companions cushion the unselfconscious body from physical harm.

To a degree that varies from one culture to another, religious authority based on possession is invested in the medium,[4] or, since the medium is often out of control during the most revealing moments, in those who control the medium's enthusiasm (music directors, choreographers) or who interview the visiting spirit. In any case, authority derives ultimately from the supernatural being who commandeers the human individual in order to communicate directly with the community.[5] Through the medium of a human personality, "the community transcends the human condition and guarantees its spiritual liberation."[6]

Mastery of a closed canon of revealed knowledge is another source of religious authority. Given the opportunity for schooling provided by social station or special election, the canonist learns a lexicon of taxa and their attached meanings and studies the systematic procedures for their application. This principle of authority finds a wide range of application: ritual presidents, for example, command the rubrical lexicon of liturgy and the calendrical taxa of festival space and time. They exegete the ways in which these taxonomic items coordinate with the structures of the universe (the seasons and animal cycles; the movements of sun and moon or of the stars; the positions of the cardinal directions; the divisions of the sexes and social groups; etc.).[7] Preparation for the priesthood among the Kógi, for instance, calls for eighteen years of arduous training emphasizing solitude and sexual abstinence. (Apparently, the details of this training descend from the ancient Tairona people of the time of the Spanish conquest.[8]) During the years of preparation, the ritual expert *(mama)* learns the ceremonial lore and practices necessary to maintain *yuluka*, harmony or balance, in the universe. The eighteen-year period is divided into two cycles of nine years each. The middle of the training is marked by the candidate's arrival at puberty. The *mamas* learn the ceremonial customs, the mechanisms of confession (the "Law of the Mother"), and the process that moves the universe on its creative course. The "Law of the Mother" is the esoteric knowledge that reveals the relationship among all things and their regulation in ritual as a series of interrelated matrices (generative wombs and spaces). Separated from his natal home very early in his life, the novice studies under a ritual expert in an isolated valley marked by a mythic event (a lineage origin or an heroic adventure).[9] The novice spends most of his time during the daylight hours inside the ceremonial house. He is strictly enjoined to avoid sexual activity with women and contact with the sun: "he should never see the sun nor be exposed to his rays."[10] Similarly, the novice should cover his head with a special basketry tray if he goes outside on a moonlit night. The first nine years of training are especially given over to dietary restrictions; during this time, the novice eats mostly vegetables and fish. After puberty, he is introduced to different kinds of meat. The boys are dressed in an ancient traditional garb of the Tairona. Reichel-Dolmatoff lists the main disciplines of *mamas'* learning as the following: (1) cosmogony, cosmology, and other mythology; (2) mythical social origins and social structure and organization; (3) natural history, including geography, geology, meteorology, botany, zoology, astronomy, biology; (4) linguistics, meaning ceremonial language and rhetoric; (5) sensory deprivations and abstinence from food, sleep, and sex; (6) ritual, dancing, and singing; (7) curing of diseases; (8) interpretation of signs and symbols, dreams, and animal behavior; and (9) sensitivity to auditory, visual, and other halluci-nations.[11] Such knowledge usually comes in the form of a total complex: for example, the novice will be taught to dance and gesture while reciting lore and singing sacred songs or myths.

The essence of the *mama*'s task is to "turn back the sun" when it threatens to "burn the world" or to avert rain when it threatens to "drown it." The Kógi *mama* is essentially a ritualist who regulates the sun, whose movements through space weave the fabric of the universe.[12] "This control of the *mamas*, however, depends on the power and range of their esoteric knowledge and this knowledge, in turn, depends on the purity of their minds. Only the pure, the morally untainted, can acquire the divine wisdom to control the course of the sun and, with it, the change of the seasons and the times for planting and harvesting."[13]

Since there are other kinds of closed taxonomies, ritual presidents are not the only kind of canonists. Diviners frequently draw their authority from their mastery of the system of correspondences obtaining between their symbolic apparatus and the larger world.[14] Herbalists[15] and confessors can function by virtue of their control over lists of pharmacopoeia,[16] protocols of therapy, catalogues of sins, and principles of moral adjudication.

Some canonical authorities serve because they are designated to do so by operational outcomes of canonical procedures. Such, for example, is the religious king or emperor whose election results from the unfolding of a closed genealogical system. Accumulation of wealth (the closed system of symbolic currency) and election (divination through the procedure of prop-erly casting a limited number of lots or votes) can also be magisterial, canoni-cal operations used to bestow special religious authority. Canonical exper-tise has all the earmarks of information science: emphasis falls on the quantity and reliability of data as well as on the skillful mnemonic organiza-tion of an efficient retrieval system. However, discretion and artistic inter-pretation are seldom completely suppressed in favor of rote memory.

All three forms of authoritative knowledge are experimental sciences; that is, they base themselves on experiential knowledge. Personal experi-ence, however, does not play the same role in all three types of authority. In possession and ecstasy, on the one hand, authoritative knowledge flows directly from the individual practitioner's encounter with the sacred. That firsthand experience, the pathos that is part and parcel of the practitioner's personality, is the basis of authority. Possession and ecstasy are empathetic sciences; data are generated in the rearrangement of the authority's physiol-ogy and personality.

On the other hand, the information mastered in an authoritative canon need not flow directly from the personal experience of the practicing author-ity. In fact, since canons are by definition closed, the bounded corpus of traditional lore has already been determined without regard for the pecu-liarities of the practitioner's personal experience. Canonists learn their lexi-con of taxa scholastically even if, during that educational process, they be-come so acculturated to the purity of their academic categories that all reality appears to reflect the structures of their own discipline. In the exercise of canonical authority, experience and experiment enter mostly at the level of interpreting data. For canonists, the application of the fixed body of data, as called for in settling specific cases, remains fairly personal. Religious style and breadth of information, rather than the quality and content of canonical knowledge itself, owe their relative adequacy to the experience and personality of the canonist. Authority itself resides in the canon.

ECSTATIC SPECIALISTS: THE SHAMAN

Because of its influence in South American religious life, ecstasy will be the focus of this chapter's look at the symbolism of religious specialization. During ecstasy, the human soul leaves the body. Sickness or accident may provoke ecstatic experiences. The soul may stray from the body during dream or because of a fright, a fit of anger, a sneeze, or a cough. Evildoers may seduce the soul out of the body or drive it away. Ecstatic specialists learn to control the passage of the soul out of the body. Using special techniques, their souls exit the body at will for various purposes. The shaman is the most important and well-known ecstatic specialist in South America. A general practitioner of the arts of the soul, the shaman not only controls the ecstasy of his or her own soul but specializes in the knowledge and care of the souls of others. Shamanic ecstasies serve the souls of the community. This service requires wide knowledge of spiritual life: the nature of the soul, the times of transition or crisis at which the soul moves, and the contained spaces (body, cosmic realms, ritual spaces) in and through which the soul effects its passages.[17]

ORIGINS OF SHAMANISM

Shamanism arises in the period described in myth. Proto-shamans are frequently deities, cultural heroes, primordial ancestors, or other such sacred beings. Depictions of the origins of shamanic spirituality identify human life with the function and destiny of supernatural beings. The creator god himself may provide the model for the shaman. For the Tukano, for instance, human beings would have become immortal had they bathed in the waters of immortality. When they refused to bathe, they thwarted the intentions of the creator, Yepá Huaké, and death entered the world. In order to compensate for this loss, Yepá Huaké provided the people with shamans (Payé, Yai, and Kumu). "And just as I 'blew' you in order that you should live, the Payé will also 'blow' you and will save you when you are sick. If the wind with which I blew you becomes spent, then the sick will die and the dead will turn into dirt."[18]

Similarly, the apparel worn by the creator god Nanderú Guazú is reproduced in the clothing and ceremonial ornaments used by the Avá-Chiripá shaman in his practice. The creator gave these clothes, together with their powers, to his son, the divine twin and culture hero Kuarahy, who stands as model for powerful shamans. This apparel includes the *mbaraká* (gourd-rattle), the *yasaá* (a cotton sash decorated with feathers, worn on the chest), the *poapi-guaá* (a cotton bracelet decorated with feathers), the *acaan-guaá* (a feathered tiara), and the *kuruzú-ipoty* (a feathered cross).[19]

The origins of shamanism account for the range of the shaman's responsibilities as well as for the power of his or her accoutrements. The shaman's tasks may include weather control, growth magic for crops, providing game animals for hunters, supplying fish, securing names for newborns, presiding over rites of passage, curing illness, accompanying the dead, escorting the souls of ritual offerings to their destinations, and many others. The shaman faces these tasks with confidence, sure in the knowledge that, in the very beginning of time, powerful beings made their accomplishment possible. He possesses these beings' techniques, their power items, their example, and their direct aid. For example, the first Pémon *piache* (shaman) was the father of the culture hero who fertilized the earth with his semen. This hero was a young boy who killed fish when he bathed in the river. Subsequently, the young hero was fatally bitten by the great serpent, the rainbow. When the small corpse was carried home in a basket, a milky, semenlike liquid dropped to the earth, where the varieties of plants now grow. The bones of the boy became mullein, a poisonous plant used for fishing. The boy's father, the first *piache*, gathered all the birds of the world so that they could slay the rainbow-serpent.[20]

Knowledge of the sacred and successful origins of shamanism enables the community and its specialist to face the dangers inherent in the encounter with manifest and unmanifest reality. For instance, the Krahó shaman's experience and powers are valid, legitimate, and powerful because of the acts of the mythical first shaman, Tɨr'krẽ. As Júlio Cezar Melatti reports,

> Since we showed our surprise when the curer Zezeinho told us that a hawk taught him to cure, he queried: "And was it not the hawk who taught Tɨr'krẽ?" as if to say: If Tɨr'krẽ, in whose existence, and the truthfulness of whose story, we all believe, received instruction from a hawk, why cannot the same happen to me?[21]

The power of the shaman need not always be benign. Knowledge of soul travel and rapport with sacred beings may have negative applications. Once upon a time, beings in the Warao underworld had an umbilical-like duct, which drained the blood from the hearts of sleeping people and conducted it to the spirits of the underworld. However, the system broke down, and now death is caused by the dark shaman, who kills his neighbors with magical arrows and transports them upside down to the land of death.[22] The Warao do not bemoan this practice as purely evil, for a world in which everyone continued to live forever would be impossible.

No matter what the mythic shamanic practice, primordial shamanism no longer exists: it serves as a model. Something changed. Present shamanic practice is a symbolic imitation, repetition, or approximation of the original. The Andean community of Pinchimuro, Peru, provides an example. It recognizes two types of religious specialists as particularly important, the *altomisa* and the *pampamisa*. Both types of specialists are called to their vocation by the *apu* (mountain-dwelling divinity) Ausangate with God's permission. The *altomisa* is the more powerful of the two.[23] At one time the *altomisa* had the power to speak directly with the *apu*s, the *rugale*s, and the earth. He held direct conversation with all the gods, with Pachamama, with the rivers, and with ancestors and communicated their wishes to the human community. Consequently, the will of gods and supernatural forces was always clear to human beings. By communicating the desires and knowledge of supernatural beings to them, the *altomisa* could direct human beings in establishing perfect order and balance in the universe. There was neither sickness, want, nor fear.[24]

Unfortunately, the *altomisa*s of the past abused their extraordinary powers and communicated with evil beings. Soon the *altomisa*s became murderers. Their powers degenerated, lasting only three or four months beyond the time of their initial vocation.[25] Eventually, human beings were no longer fit to serve in this office. However, the power of direct communication with supernatural beings endures in the universe. It now belongs to certain birds, who speak with the gods but who are unable to communicate clearly with humans. On occasion, especially in instances of bad luck or death, the birds announce their fatal message by making unclear and fearful noises, which sound like laughter or screaming, at night.[26] The disorder and disease that exist throughout the universe can be explained by the degeneration and eventual disappearance of the institution of *altomisa*. Now that the *altomisa*s, the primordial shamans who originated ecstatic techniques and knowledge of the soul, have passed from the scene, it is encumbent upon their followers in each generation to care for souls by mastering the technics of their own souls' coming and going.

VOCATION (CALLING)

The novice may be called to the vocation of shaman in various ways. For example, among people of the Putumayo area studied by Métraux, the vocation was hereditary. The adult shaman chose the hairiest of his children because "spirits often were pictured as hairy men."[27] In most cases across South America, a supernatural being makes a direct appeal to the youth in a dream, a vision, or a spell of delirium, during which a song is revealed to the novice. Many times, the supernatural call brings on unusual behavior, such as shaking, which confirms the vocation.[28] It was Martin Gusinde's opinion that the shaman in South America is, above all, a specialist in the knowledge of the soul. For this reason, the shaman is sought out for the cure of sicknesses due to afflictions of the soul. The vocation to become a shaman, then, is signaled by some manifestation that the individual's soul possesses extraordinary capacities or that the individual is extraordinarily sensitive to those states and images in which souls manifest themselves (dreams, visions, trances, states of intoxication or concentration, sounds, and so on).[29]

A shaman-to-be may receive his or her call from a supernatural being who provokes ecstasy through sickness,[30] dream, or vision. Or a novice may be chosen for the vocation of shaman by an older shaman. Such is the case among the Avá-Chiripá. One shaman designated his heir by having the candidate sit on a stool made of deerskin strips. The older shaman unfastened the nominee's shirt and, in a breathy fashion, sang a *guaú eté* (sacred "true" song). Acting as if he held in his right hand a "kind of flower" that he passed through the flow of his breath into his left hand, the shaman spread out a sash *(yasaá)*, to which he attached parrot feathers. He breathed on the sash and put it on the candidate's chest, advising him never to part from it. The sash was to be inseparable from the "character" of the new shaman, who was instructed never to have sex while wearing it. During a ritual hunt on the following day, the candidate was advised to "think about the animals killed." The older man then lectured the novice about the greatness and arduousness of his vocation as well as the merits of a vegetarian diet.[31] No matter how individuals receive their vocation to become shamans, they must learn to control their propensities for ecstasy. They must undergo an initiation and serve time in apprenticeship so that they may master the techniques of ecstasy and the ways of the soul.

APPRENTICESHIP AND INITIATION OF THE SHAMAN

Little is known of the training and apprenticeship of shamans in South American cultures.[32] Nonetheless, the information available offers the most vivid and startling picture of South American religious life. These portrayals dramatize a world full of supernatural adventure, power, and danger. The opening phases of the shaman's career display the symbolic processes that will be considered in the next sections of this chapter: soul travel, clairvoyance, magical music, shape-shifting. Before focusing on those particular symbolic complexes and their meaning, however, the following pages describe several schools for shamans. The dedication of a few sympathetic visitors provided the vehicle for this precious information; through trusted ethnographers, local specialists offered outsiders glimpses of their world, a reality ordinarily closed to those who are temperamentally unsuited or spiritually unprepared to enter it.

In a report published in 1936, Gusinde claimed to have been the only European to undergo the rites of South American shamanic initiation and apprenticeship.[33] His experience provided rare details on the training of shamans. Gusinde stressed that, since shamans are specialists in dealing with souls, only specially gifted individuals are suited for this vocation. One can enter the *lóima-yékamuš*, the Yamana school for apprentice shamans, only if one possesses evidence of special sensitivity to the world of spirits, a sensitivity that may manifest itself by the appearance of supernatural beings in one's dreams, the ability to hear voices others cannot hear, and so on. In some cases, an older shaman has a dream that reveals the vocation of a young man whom he knows. As soon as a young man gives evidence of such sensitivity to souls and the spirit world, he places himself under the protection of an experienced *yékamuš* (shamanic practitioner). When the time is appropriate, a conical hut, made of logs nine to twelve feet in length, is constructed for the period of seclusion.

The period of initiation is marked by a series of extraordinary physical ordeals. The young man's body is completely painted with a mash that hardens to a glistening white color. He is adorned with green feathers. His body, especially his face, is painted anew each day. The candidate sits in a prescribed way on a smooth piece of ground within the hut. A bed of twigs is spread out beneath him. Staring straight ahead at a fixed point on the ground, he sits without resting his back against the side wall of the hut, keeping his legs stiff and straight in front of him and his hands straight by his side. He must not move or twitch the least muscle; should he do so, he is hit in the back of the neck with a cudgel. He sits and stares in absolute silence. He is told that he must take his thoughts within himself. His sleep is restricted to about four hours a night. Even this he must do while maintaining his seated and immobile position, although he is allowed to rest his back against the logs that form the wall of the hut. Should he unconsciously fall out of position, the older shamans prop him upright again.[34] Food and drink are severely restricted to a certain kind of mussel and a sip of water in the morning and in the late afternoon. With his body completely exhausted and his nerves frazzled, he learns to master the spiritual powers that appear to him during his hallucinations, dreams, and flights of fancy—in particular, the spirits of dead *yékamuš*, those who existed in the beginning, and the souls of the dead. Special bonds are established with ancient shamans, who act as spirit helpers. Gradually they help the novice gain control over the spiritual world in which his wearied body has left him. According to Gusinde, the candidate's goal is to gain the ability to enter the supernatural realm of images quickly and to embody the wishes and conflicts—as well as give clear conceptual form to the desires and fears—that the soul (his own or that of his client) experiences.

Gusinde's account draws the connection between the powers and adventures of the soul and the manipulation of the body. In addition to the rigorous physical demands already mentioned, the achievement of mastery of the soul and the spirit world bears consequences for the shaman's physical being. During the entire time the novice receives instruction from the experienced shamans and the ancient supernatural shamans (a period of at least six months), he must rub his cheeks, especially his cheekbones, with white clay and the soft yellow wood-shavings of the barberry tree. As the new shaman grows in wisdom, the old skin of his face disappears and gives way to a softer, finer, and shinier skin, which first becomes visible after a few weeks of rubbing and painting. At this early stage, however, it is seen only by experienced shamans during their hallucinations. They take it as a signal that the novice is making definite progress. As the novitiate continues, the rubbing of the cheeks becomes a more and more delicate exercise. If the novice even touches his cheeks, he experiences an intense pain. This mystical massage continues throughout his apprenticeship, until it reveals a third layer of shining skin, more beautiful and tender than any other. Then is the time to bring the seclusion to an end. From that moment, the aspiring shaman apprentices himself to an experienced practitioner. Since the novice has proven himself capable of discerning spirits and mastering his own soul, he may now learn the particular practices and methods employed by a shaman in his medical practice.

The length of shamanic training varies widely from one South American culture to another. Among the Arecuna and Taulipáng, to choose extreme examples, the shamanic novitiate was reported to last from ten to twenty years.[35] As Métraux reports,

> While serving his master as an assistant, the novice learned to recognize the herbs and magic substances utilized in curing. He progressively familiarized himself with the ritual gestures and learned the technical aspects of his profession, such as the imitation of bird and animal calls and, if he had the necessary gift, ventriloquism. To this knowledge he added the memorization of chants, magic formulae, and sometimes the traditional lore of the community. Astronomy could also be part of his curriculum. Shamans emerged from their training period equipped not only with the magic techniques that permitted them to get in touch with the supernatural at will, cure their patients and destroy their adversaries and the enemies of their clients, but also with a fund of practical knowledge. They became acquainted with curative herbs and drugs and were able to perform simple surgery. Their knowledge of natural phenomena helped them to make predictions based on actual observations.[36]

Generally, the time of training was from several months to a few years in length. In any case, since the process of ecstasy brings knowledge, the practice of the shaman is a ceaseless education to wisdom very much in line with all mystical traditions. Spiritual life is not a closed system of information but the penetration of an open-ended mystery that, even with a lifetime of probing, is never exhausted.

Shamanic apprenticeship cannot be equated with education in general. The shaman is a specialist whose experience transcends the ordinary plane. Even if the subject matter encompasses wide areas of learning, knowledge is acquired in a manner that befits the shamanic vocation and the temperament of ecstatics. The school for shamans has a unique, mythical structure derived from the accounts of the first shamans' exploits.[37] Knowledge of the soul and of the spiritual world serves as the foundation for the mastery of the disciplines studied. Basing this conclusion on his earliest visit among the Krahó in 1962–1963, Melatti makes clear that, whatever the unknown details are, "some individuals, if not all, on becoming shamans, relived the myth of Tĩr'krē."[38] Melatti forwards the hypothesis "that apprenticeship among the Krahó . . . is combined with the reliving of the myth."[39] Even the dreams that apprentice shamans receive during their isolated training bear the same structure as the Krahó myth of Tĩr'krē. In fact, Melatti argues, this same myth fulfills an identical function in other Timbira groups, such as the Ramkokamekra and Apinayé.

The Krahó myth of Tïr'krē recounts that he fell sick one day because an ant entered his ear while he slept. Abandoned and forgotten by his community, he lived in isolation until vultures (*urubus*) encouraged tiny birds to remove the pathogenic ant and carried him to the heights of heaven, where a hawk brought him game to eat in the form of a *jaó* bird. Tïr'krē devoured the *jaó* bird raw and vomited up blood. He did the same with other birds, but he refused to eat human feces when it was served to him. In the celestial realms, Tïr'krē learned to change his form into that of an otter, a large ant, a *tututi* bird, and other birds. He returned to earth in the form of a *sambaiba* leaf that had the power to cure and to harm.

Krahó shamans describe their vocation and transformation into practicing specialists in terms of these mythic events. Melatti brings into relief the initiatory, mythic structure repeated in the accounts that various shamans provide about their own vocation. An individual becomes isolated from the human community, usually through sickness. This psychic isolation and illness contribute to the disintegration of the individual's social and psychic being. A nonhuman entity appears to the afflicted individual. Often this being appears as an animal, a supernatural animal in human form, or, in the cases of women cited by Melatti, a plant. The visionary being presides over the cure of the individual, which often involves feeding the patient. The food frequently consists of birds eaten raw. Substances are then taken or forced out in the form of vomit, blood, sweat, fat, and so on. Along with magical foods, the visionary being provides the patient with special magical powers, often introducing them directly into the apprentice shaman's body. In one case, the items inserted into the patient's body included "a radio, a knife, a bowl, rice, [and] the meat of various animals." [40] Next, the cured patient, still in isolation (perhaps in the celestial realms), practices the powers he or she has acquired. The structure of the shamanic curriculum as well as the order of the shaman's experience are shaped by the events of the mythic world. Both the program and the candidate assume a mythic structure. [41]

In this respect, Akawaio shamanism conforms to the general outlines found in the Americas and in Asia. [42] The apprenticeship of a shaman essentially takes place in the spirit world. Consequently, the rigorous fasting, vigil, and physical ordeal undergone by the novice should be seen as symbolic expressions of an activity that, because it conforms to the ideal pattern of myth, need not take place in a literal fashion. [43] Every phase of shamanic apprenticeship and training correlates with ideals expressed symbolically in myth. This assures that the shaman's experience in ecstasy is not absolutely individualistic, "nor is it uncontrolled." [44] Any Akawaio who wishes may become a shaman. Only individuals who show control and progress in their spiritual life, however, succeed in becoming renowned and respected shamans. A dream is often the call to the role of shaman. This vocation sparks the beginning of months or even years of training under the tutelage of a veteran shaman, whether living or dead. The pace of Akawaio apprenticeship depends on the capacities of the individual. A living shaman is not necessarily present at the instruction: his spirit may take over, teaching the novice even when the living shaman is physically absent. In any case, the *ladoi* ("my side") is less a teacher than a partner and ritual companion during the candidate's spiritual experiences. Thus, whether living or dead, the shaman teacher's spirit *(akwalu)* assists and guides the apprentice. The novice enters into a special period of seclusion, *bogoibe* (lit., "being sad, being alone"). Food restrictions play a large role in acquiring the capacity "to see" spirits.[45] The goal is to become thin *(etotsali)* and light so that one can become a support *(yabon)* for the wings *(malik;* lit., "songs") that carry one into ec-stasy.[46] In the 1950s, the seclusion consisted largely of travel away from home. This could last one, two, or more years. Earlier, the seclusion may have been in the mountains or along rivers far from all human habitation. Contemporary apprentices acquire bits and pieces of foreign languages, whose tones and phonetics they reproduce during their séances. Isolation from one's natal group is absolutely essential to heightening spiritual experi-ences of a contemplative kind.

Special tree-bark infusions are taken and vomited out, leaving the spirit of the bark in one's body. This spirit of the bark enables the shaman to rise high into the sky, the spirit world.[47] Another "ladder" spirit is a string plaited from sharp reed grass. The string is drawn through the nostril and out of the mouth in order to clear the passage, the steps or ladder, along which the shaman's soul will climb into the sky during ecstasy. The connection be-tween heaven and earth is envisioned as a tree.[48] If the Akawaio novice does not learn how to maintain that connection, his spirit could remain perma-nently in ecstasy and cause his body to die. Along that same ladder, helper-spirits descend into the shaman's body. All this is achieved by vomiting up bark infusions.

Tobacco is the key element in the Akawaio shaman's paraphernalia. Tobacco is said to originate on the top of Karowrieng Mountain, where it grows from the tree that propagates all fruits and vegetables, whose seeds then fall to earth. The pupil-shaman learns to ascend this high mountain and acquire the tobacco from a spirit there. Such a journey may be metaphorical. Also obtained from the mountain is a tiny gourd *(kasakili)* that holds the spirits of charms and medicines. Tobacco is of great importance because the tobacco spirit makes the shaman's spirit small enough to pass through the cracks of the house to fly into the sky and the various spirit realms. In addition, the tobacco spirit brings down the spirits of the mountain birds, who help the shaman. First among these are the *kumalak*-bird spirits, who assist the tobacco spirit in lifting the shaman's soul off the ground with their songs, the sounds of their wings.

Malik, the songs sung by the Akawaio shaman, are the spirit songs of the mountain-bird beings. Essentially invisible sound-realities, *malik* can mani-fest themselves in forms other than shamanic songs. *Malik* designates the sound of the rustling of the shaman's spirit as it takes off in ecstasy; the term designates the "wings" that the shaman assumes in his trance state, and it also refers to the ceremonial ornaments (called *činik,* "flowers") worn on the shaman's arms and ears during his first public séance.[49] Thus, sound, songs, wings, ecstatic flight, and ceremonial ornaments, as well as "flowers," become manifestations of the same spiritual realities.

Another aspect of the Akawaio shaman's training is the strengthening of his voice. To that end he eats insects known for their strong noise (e.g., cicadas, *wamon* bees). These insects "make your voice come good." Because each spirit has its own *malik*, the shaman must acquire *malik*, song-wings, during his apprenticeship. To do so, he must develop an extraordinarily fine sense of hearing and a voice skillful enough to "catch" the sounds (that is, reproduce them exactly). During an average séance, which may last some three hours, the novice may summon up to forty spirits, "and all of these are 'made to sing,' so it can be appreciated that a shaman has to have an extensive repertoire of songs. . . . [F]or when he flies away he finds the spirits dancing on the mountains and so he learns the spirit songs." [50]

When the apprentice has mastered the sounds of his song-wings and his leaf bundle, he ends the initial portion of his apprenticeship by conducting a public séance. He fills a small drinking barrel with tobacco juice. The barrel is called *koriaĩ*, a word that designates the barrel but also a tree trunk as well as a dugout canoe. The barrel is a container that is also a vessel, in the sense that it joins different spaces together. The apprentice then consumes an enormous amount of tobacco juice and falls to the ground unconscious, in a state of dangerous ecstasy. "He would die were it not that another *piai'čan* [shaman] is present to *piai* [control ecstasy] for him. He is placed in the hammock and looks as if dead. He dies virtually." [51] All the spirits with whom the apprentice has become acquainted during the seclusion have come to feast on the tobacco juice. The spirit of the novice is overwhelmed and flies to the mountaintops, dancing and singing with spirits there. There is a great danger that his ecstasy will become permanent. The novice's shaman-teacher leads his disciple's soul back to its body. The novice is now an autonomous shaman, for he has "died" to his former life and has proven himself capable of dealing with the spiritual world.

THE MASTER

These cases make clear that the presence of a master is essential to shamanic apprenticeship. This cannot be explained only by the need to impose ortho-doxy by controlling the transmission of knowledge to the neophyte. In many cases the master is a shaman who has already died. Sometimes the teacher, although alive, instructs the candidate by sending his soul to the novice's place of seclusion. Although the living master may not be physically present during the apprenticeship, he performs an essential role by preventing the loss or disorientation of the novice's ecstatic soul. The value of magisterial teaching inheres not only in advice on practical matters such as when to sleep, wake, and wash, what to eat, and how to prepare ritual items but also in the spiritual direction that guides the novice through unfamiliar supernatu-ral terrain during ecstasy. [52] The master discerns the spirits who traffic with candidates and teaches novices to probe the nature of their own perceptions. Through a master novices come to grips with the meaning of their own experience of the sacred and examine the nature of their own consciences.

Because apprenticeship has a mythic structure, the ultimate master is the mythical first shaman. For example, before beginning an apprenticeship under a deceased shaman, the Kari'ña candidate must ask the "owner of the mountain," a living *puidei* (shaman), permission to "rattle," that is, to sound the maraca. The master convokes an assembly of spirits and conveys the neophyte's request to them. He introduces the novice to the spirits if they decide to admit him to candidacy.[53] After ritually preparing himself during the early evening in the "owner's" house, the novice is transported, under cover of darkness, to the "mountain" (actually a hill no more than ten meters high). There, he is taken to "the cave" (the opening of a tiny ravine), where offerings of tobacco and alcoholic drink are made. The spirits consume the essence of these gifts.[54] The only authentic and fully knowledgeable *puidei* are the ancient beings of the mountain, who act on behalf of today's ignorant and comparatively powerless human shamans. Contemporary healers are powerful only to the extent that they become totally identified with ancient spirits.[55]

Different types of shamanic vocation exist even in the same culture. The variety of masters of novices reflects the diversity of spiritualities among ecstatics. In a posthumously published report, Enrique Palavecino emphasizes that only a small number of specialists, called *piogonak* by the Toba and *aiawu* by the Mataco, possess the mystical capacities to "bewitch a whole enemy tribe, cure somebody who has been wounded by an arrow of the spirits, return the soul to a sick person who lost it by accident, predict the future, and make rain or stop a storm." [56] Among the Mataco, initiation to the rank of *aiawu* may be obtained in three different ways. The first means is through education and apprenticeship to a master healer, who instructs the novice with song and dance. (The songs and the dances belong to the individual novice.) Alternately, one may become a curer through the inheritance of powers and skills from one's father. In this case, the father trains the son. The third, most dramatic kind of initiation is initiation at the hands of supernatural beings who appear suddenly before the unwitting novice. There are a large number of such supernatural initiators, among whom is one called Noethl, who appears suddenly before a person, makes him a novice, and draws him inside a tree where he bedecks the candidate with ankle decorations made of cloven hooves and instructs him in a sacred dance. Initiators are frequently animals who appear to the novice in their true (human) form. For example, spiders assume the form of children. They then lead the novice into the region below the earth, where they teach him how to dance. When the novice emerges from the earth, he is an expert healer.[57]

ORDEALS

During apprenticeship, the novice must survive a series of ordeals. These range from simple quizzes on matters of fact to demanding physical feats or even harrowing psychological episodes. The ordeals deconstruct fixed patterns of thought and behavior in order to rearrange the novice's sense of things. The meaning of reality is questioned and reconfigured because the candidate's own perceptions are put on trial. Ordeals serve the goal of obtaining a new spiritual state, a new level of encounter with sacred being, or a new quality of spiritual power. To arrive at any of these requires that the candidate be reconditioned. Ordeals undoubtedly possess psychological value. Furthermore, their presence during any initiation may be related to the cosmic ordeal, that cataclysm that deconstructed primordial existence and initiated the symbolic order of this world. At that moment, many sacred beings initiated their prolonged ecstatic state of existence; their spirits withdrew from this world, leaving only symbolic vestiges of their presence: animal bodies, songs, sacred stones, trees, metals, and so on.

For the shaman, however, ordeals have more than psychological or mythic value. They are envisaged as means through which he or she passes into control over the experience of ecstasy and, at the same time, acquires powerful knowledge of the realms visited during ecstasy. Ordeals test the authenticity of the shaman's call and try his or her ability to carry out the role. At the same time, ordeals function sacramentally as an integral part of the initiation process. The tests to which candidates submit themselves establish the worthiness they signify. This is why ordeals are frequently in the image of stations along a path. The path is a succession of trials whose performance is part and parcel of the final goal attained. The accomplishment of each trial moves the candidate along the trail of ecstasy. For example, during his initiation, the Warao priest-shaman must undergo twelve ordeals along the road from Yaukware's house, at the top of the world, to the world-mountain home of Dauarani, the Mother of the Forest, which is situated at the southeastern point of the end of the universe. There the priest-shaman receives six helper spirits who will guide him through life until he eventually takes up permanent residence with his divine patron.[58]

The dismemberment of the shaman's body is a paradigmatic ordeal of his or her apprenticeship. In a state of ecstasy, the candidates watch their own deconstruction and reconditioning: reduced to pieces, they are then reordered and refashioned. Since ecstasy, when the soul departs the body, is an experience of death, the death-and-resurrection experience remains a constant feature in many shamanic ordeals.

Even the introduction of Christian ideas, as incorporated into the indigenous Hallelujah cult, did not disrupt all of the traditional initiatory scenarios of Akawaio shamanism. For example, the Makusi prophet Bichiwung, the founder of the Hallelujah cult, was killed several times by a sorcerer (edodo), but he was resurrected with the help of medicine that he had seen in his journeys to heaven. It is particularly noteworthy that after Bichiwung had been dismembered, he was reconstituted from his parts by being treated with magic oil from the seeds of the crabnut tree:

> The process of chopping up someone seems to have a fascination of its own, for it is related that there was a Makusi shaman called Sonny who, when chopped up, used to put himself together again! It is probable that, as in Bichiwung's case, this process is conceived to be entirely spiritual, as are so many of the shaman's activities, and is not done visibly and in the flesh.[59]

TECHNIQUES

The shaman uses technology to master the movements of his or her own soul. Carib shamans, for instance, employed tightropes. Bound by the hands, they swung through the air and induced vertigo to achieve ecstasy. At times they sat on rope swings suspended from the roof. The ropes were twisted so that the swing whirled when released. In this way, the dizzy apprentice *pujai* was carried to heaven.[60] Songs, fasting, seclusion, and sexual abstinence figure largely in the shamanic repertoire for reasons explored later in this chapter. Shamans in South America, perhaps more than those in any other area, have traveled to other supernatural realms by manipulating the powers of magical plants through music, motion, and mood. The shaman's control of hallucinogens colors and shapes the desired vision of sacred realities.

All technology has an impact on social relations. The systematic science of the soul is no exception. For example, during his apprenticeship the Machiguenga shaman is gradually inducted into *ayahuasca* use. He is led into the experience by an elder shaman and a guardian spirit.[61] The *ayahuasca* visions result in the formation of a "circle of mutual dependence" that includes the novice, his master, his guardian spirit, other helper spirits, and the wives of the shamans. Later, that circle extends to clients, relatives, and neighbors whose behavior and relationship with the spiritual world determines the success, and sometimes even the life and death, of the shaman. Although the shaman's wife's behavior bears directly on his practice and well-being, she is afforded a large measure of prestige and is permitted a degree of license in her behavior that exceeds even her husband's. The shaman's apprenticeship teaches him to live within the new social network that his experience and techniques create.

In some communities, the existence of society itself depends upon the shaman's techniques of ecstasy and knowledge of the soul. For example, the very life of the Tapirapé hangs on the success of the shamans in each generation. A prospective Tapirapé shaman must tend to dream a lot. During apprenticeship, the novice is induced to dream further by "eating smoke," that is, by vomiting and reswallowing saliva rich with tobacco. In his dream adventures, the shaman acquires helper spirits.[62] The point is that Tapirapé shamans not only acquire helper spirits for personal use in their own spiritual careers, but that during their ecstasies they acquire from other realms of being the souls of every individual successfully conceived in a woman's womb.[63] Every human being represents the successful application of the shamanic technology of regurgitating tobacco and of dream control. Furthermore, proper social order represents the cumulative success of shamanic discernment of spirits: choosing the correct realm to visit as a soul-source and conducting back to earth the soul best suited to the social and historical circumstances.

Knowledge of the dream process is a prominent technique of ecstasy in South American shamanism. Control over dream life and its interpretation amounts to coming to grips with the sacred world through which the ecstatic soul wanders. At the same time, dream technology is a process of self-understanding because dream image constitutes the uniqueness of one's soul.[64]

Increasing control over dream life can be essential to apprenticeship. An older Guaraní shaman, for instance, may designate a disciple as his heir, but the candidate will never succeed in his vocation unless he has had a divine revelation in his dreams. During a period of intense dreaming, during which the novice encounters supernatural beings, "he [withdraws] into solitude, he [becomes] extremely grave in character, he [speaks] little." [65]

The initiation period and apprenticeship of the Avá-Chiripá novice begins only after the death of his mentor. Only then does the novice have his first initiatory dream, in which the dead teacher appears and speaks to him. Only then does he learn his first song. This song will be used to invoke the divine soul-element of the dead shaman in subsequent dreams, in order to seek his advice and guidance on dream journeys. The image of the master shaman should be evoked in a deep meditation before falling asleep. Gradually, throughout his apprenticeship, the novice passes through the several stages of shamanic knowledge: acquisition of his master's teaching, which leads to "wisdom" (lightness of weight and purity); the capacity to travel to the land of the dead (ñe'eng-güeri), where the novice acquires the wisdom of other dead shamans; and the stage in which he gains the power to receive visits from the sun's messenger, called Mainó ("hummingbird"). The knowledge transmitted by the hummingbird enables the novice to speak with the spirits of all plants and animals. Finally, the novice acquires the powerful help of a special auxiliary spirit, with whom he enjoys a special relationship. Over the course of this spiritual development, the shaman gains the ability to sleep in an ever more powerful way. Accompanied by his ritual gourd-rattle, the shaman sings his special song "with great sincerity" before falling asleep, and he then discovers in his dreams the correct therapy for sick people in his charge. Here is an instance of sleep therapy; its value, however, inheres in the sleep of the curer, of the shaman himself, and not in the sleep of his patient.

Dream itself serves as an initiation presided over by a master of initiation and psychopomp, the dead shaman. Just as do all initiations, so also dream initiation leads to special "knowledge" and power. In this case, as in so many others, the initiation involves the ordeal of "conquering" sleep. Sleep is "conquered" not by staying awake, as in so many initiatory vigils, but by overcoming the meaningless unconsciousness of sleep, expropriating from it a singular importance and meaning.

In order for one's powerful song, revealed in a dream, to be effective, one must perform the chant powerfully in public. In fact, the song becomes effective and powerful to the degree in which it can reactualize the encounter with powerful supernatural beings met in dreams. Conscious and public ceremonial life, then, become "real" and "powerful" only to the extent and degree to which they are like a dream! [66]

Dreaming may be more than an element of apprenticeship; it may itself constitute apprenticeship and initiation. For example, the Cashinahua huni mukaya, a specialist who cures through "bitter medicine" (i.e., supernatural power obtained directly from spirits), must be a person who dreams a great deal. During dreams, one of the five personal soul-elements leaves the body.

This *nama yuxin* ("dream spirit") makes the acquaintance of a large number and variety of spirits; it also runs the risk of losing some of the *muka,* spiritual power or medicine, that it has gained in other spirit trips. If one wishes to become a *huni mukaya,* one "pursues dreams," trying to "maximize the number of dreams [one] will have in any night." This dream quest has the structure of an initiation, for the excessive dreaming imposes a psychic isolation on the dreamer, who eventually falls to the ground in an unconscious trance state. At that moment he receives *muka* from spirit familiars. During the time of withdrawal leading up to the unconscious trance, the excessive dreamer is listless, withdrawn from human company, disinterested in sex, unlucky at hunting, and seldom hungry. When he attempts to go hunting, animals speak with him in a friendly way. Eventually, the individual is seized by the spirits — the number and variety of which determine the power of the individual. The process of becoming a *huni mukaya* is "dangerous and inconvenient." [67] Although the Cashinahua whom Kenneth M. Kensinger met in 1966 felt the vocation too burdensome, they all agreed "that the absence of any huni mukaya seriously jeopardizes the health of the tribe, since only a huni mukaya has the power to deal with the spirits with relative safety." [68]

Artistry of the soul requires the ability to work in many media. In addition to dreams and tobacco, the apprentice masters the powers of song, stone, and space (through the construction of special enclosures and ceremonial ground). For instance, a Waiwai *yaskomo* (shaman) carries out his tasks with the aid of certain technical tools: tobacco, dreaming, and, especially, magical songs and stones. Before learning how to employ these instruments of his profession, the shaman must receive a call to his vocation in a dream.[69] After reporting the contents of his dream-call to a veteran *yaskomo,* the new candidate continues his education in a specially constructed hut. Here, at night, a magic stone *(ñukwa)* appears in his mouth during a dream.[70] The *ñukwa* is a piece of quartz that belongs to heavenly spirits. The spirit who owns the stone aids the *yaskomo* whenever he blows tobacco smoke over the crystal. Tobacco is not a mechanism automatically inducing ecstasy through its narcotic effect so much as a food-offering for the helper spirit who will guide the *yaskomo*'s soul out of his body.[71] Holding the magic stone in his mouth, the novice learns to sing magic songs *(eremu).* All this instruction takes place in the *yaskomo* hut, called a *shutepana,* "a small conical hut made of posts that meet at a point . . . covered with leaves . . . [with] no opening for door or window." [72] A new hut must be constructed for each twenty-four hours of use. Only one soul-flight may take place in each hut. After careful instruction in magical songs and in their use (for example, certain songs may be sung only on days following particular kinds of dreams), the new shaman is inducted in a public ceremony.[73] The instructing *yaskomo* sings the whole day long in an area near the communal house. The candidate joins him. This is the only Waiwai ceremony that uses a stronger, narcotic tobacco, which is ritually prepared and consumed in large doses. Fock maintains that this final marathon of tobacco and song demonstrates the extraordinary alliances the candidate enjoys with supernatural powers and generates full confidence in the new *yaskomo*.

One of the most important techniques learned during apprenticeship is the ability to return from ecstasy and seclusion. Control over ecstasy demands proof that one can bring the episode to an end. This power is often effectively demonstrated in the public performance that concludes the novices' initiation. The initiation of Carib shamans is a case in point. Peter Kloos separates the apprenticeship of the Carib shaman into five phases. In the first phase, the shaman is called by some supernatural sign, usually a sickness that afflicts him or a family member. After he chooses a teacher, the second phase begins. This centers on the apprentice's consumption of two containers of latex *(ta:kini)* while he lies in the house of seclusion *(to:kai)*. The two small gourds containing the liquid represent man and woman. This sexual union of alkaloid liquid generates a delirium in which spirits visit and speak with the novice. The teacher addresses the spirits and persuades them not to kill the apprentice. During the third phase of apprenticeship, the novice, surrounded by restrictions, learns sacred songs and esoteric spirit-language. During this period of seclusion, the novice acquires spirit helpers. The fourth episode is a large feast, *atuwena:ano*, which ends ecstatic apprenticeship and regurgitates the novice back into society. The symbolism of regurgitation is evident in both the name and behavior of the feast: it derives its name from the verb *uwe:naka*, "to induce vomiting." After being bathed in water, the novice force-drinks enormous quantities of fermented brews and tobacco juice. His master blows tobacco smoke on various foods and reintroduces them to the diet of his novice. In a similar way, the painted and ornamented novice is reintroduced to the world of sexual relations when he is placed in the hammock together with his wife and ceremonially swung to and fro.[74]

HELPER-SPIRIT ACQUISITION

Shamanic apprenticeship fosters special relationships with spirits. On these spiritual alliances hang not only the shaman's knowledge and success but also, depending on the spirits with whom the shaman develops rapport, the dynamics of the shaman's personality, style of behavior, physical appearance, and ultimate destiny. Moreover, the spiritual life and physical health of the community depend directly upon the supernatural helpers with whom the shaman enjoys special ties. Garnering the aid of spirits is a fundamental function of the novice's training. In a comparative study of anthropomorphic guardian spirits in South America, Barbara Chesser divides them into two primary categories: on the one hand are ancestral ghosts and ancestral culture heroes; on the other, spirits of nature.[75] Even this restrictive typology underscores the fact that most of the mythic and created world opens itself to help the shaman. In Métraux's wider analysis, the helper spirits can include the shaman's own soul (sent specially for his vocation), which may assume the form of a bird or supernatural jaguar; the soul of a dead shaman or an animal spirit; the spirits of plants or animals; the essence of breath or tobacco smoke; or the power inherent in mysterious substances introduced into the shaman's body, such as crystals, darts, or other objects.[76]

Among the Waiwai, for instance, the term *yaskomo* (shaman) literally means a being who has special spirit helpers *(hyasi)*.[77] With the aid of his helper spirits (who are all animal spirits, that is, animal prototypes that now have their existence on a heavenly plane although during mythical times they lived on earth), the Waiwai *yaskomo* controls the weather and the supply of game for hunting and provides for the health needs of the community in times of grave illness. His helper spirits also empower the *yaskomo* to perform an essential task at a child's birth: to transport the child's soul to heaven and present it to the moon, who bestows on its soul a spirit name.[78] Although the sun and moon are not among the shaman's helper-spirits, they do belong to the special category of heavenly beings *(kakenau-kworokjam)* with whom the shaman enjoys a special rapport. The *yaskomo*'s helper spirits are all animal spirits who belong to the *kakenau-kworokjam* category of beings.[79] In an important sense, a Waiwai shaman's wife is also a spiritual helper, offering him power.[80] When a shaman's wife dies, it is understood that he has lost his powerful magic and must yield to a successor. The reason for this is not entirely clear.

During his apprenticeship, the Mataco shaman obtains spiritual help from the *yulo*, a mythical bird who was the first shaman. This spirit helper has a complicated history and structure. The *yulo* once danced while drumming on a piece of charcoal left over from the world conflagration. As a result, the cosmic tree shot up from the ashes in the center of the world, and a slip of the hallucinogenic *hataj* plant sprouted from the center of the growing tree. An alkaloid substance extracted from *hataj* stimulates ecstatic trance, impelling the souls of dead shamans to fly forth from the ecstatic novice during the Mataco shamanic initiation ceremony. These souls of the dead are spirits resulting from the postmortem fusion of the three soul-elements that comprise the living person. The souls of dead shamans fuse with the mythic proto-shaman. As a result, a single helper-spirit soul flies forth from the candidate in the form of a *yulo* bird. It flies to the center of the world, where it perches on the branches of the Tree of Trials. There it endures the novice's initiatory ordeals. As soon as it touches a branch of the tree, "its feet become wax. The test takes place as the tree shakes and the *yulos*, due to their weak feet, fall to the ground where they must change themselves into gourds so as not to be eaten by the caymans that surround the tree. The apprentice shamans must undergo this test in order to demonstrate their capacity to perform their duties as such."[81] By inducing ecstatic trance, the *hataj* tree, which was created by the mythic spirit helper, offers the Mataco shaman a chance to visit either the land of the dead, the locus of powerful shamans who once lived on earth, or the land of the sun, the source of wisdom and medical knowledge. The shaman's soul, united with his spirit helper, undertakes such trances in order to diagnose illness and cure disease.[82]

The spirits aid the novice with help that takes the form of a revelation of their sacred names, symbolic forms, and character. Intimate and systematic knowledge (i.e., technology) of this sacred nature is itself an extraordinary power. The helper spirit elects the candidate and freely offers to sustain the shaman's soul with its own supernatural presence. The power of the shaman resides in the nature of his or her spirit helper. Often more than one spirit supports the shaman. The Machiguenga shamans, for instance, possess a two-tiered helper-spirit system. Guardian spirits (*inetsaane*, from the verb "to visit") of the shaman (*seripigari*, from *seri*, "tobacco") are part of a large category of celestial beings, called *saankariite* ("invisible ones"), who assume the forms of animals, especially birds.[83] The spirit helpers, "pets" raised by the guardian spirits, live in stones that must be "fed" with tobacco smoke by the shamans. The helper spirits are bestowed in the form of stones upon the novice shaman by his guardian spirits. When the novice feeds the stones tobacco, they transform themselves into supernatural jaguars (*matsontsori*).

SELF-INTEREST OF SPIRIT HELPERS: THE APPETITES OF POWER

Certain incentives impel spirits to ally themselves with shamans. Spirits may find themselves in the midst of a cycle of transformations that began during the mythic period. They may seek the aid of shamans in order to continue their transmigration. On the other hand, compassion, responsibility for maintaining cosmic order (e.g., protection of game, weather, or crops), the will to save humankind, or the desire to reveal themselves may motivate spirits to aid a shaman. In any case, the spirits' self-revelation discloses not only their power but also their desires, needs, and even their vulnerabilities. In particular, helper spirits frequently make known their need for food for their spiritual bodies. Above all, this food takes the form of tobacco smoke.[84] Since human beings are the possessors of fire during this cosmic epoch, spirits seek out human assistance in obtaining foods, especially tobacco, that are "spiritualized" through consumption by fire.

Acquisition of spirit help requires learning the inner nature and meaning of consumptive processes. Serving food to spirits implies knowledge of spiritual appetites. This is the goal of Chiquitano shamanic training. The Chiquitano *čeeserúš* (shaman) may be called to his vocation in a dream or may simply decide on his own initiative to become a shaman. This call initiates a lengthy period (three to six years) of training under a master shaman. During that time, the apprentice develops a rapport with the masters (*hiči*) of various cosmic elements (mountain, forest, water, pampa, and so on). In particular, the novice must learn the preferred foods of the different master spirits. He discovers that the entire cosmos is a process of supernatural appetites and that the desire to consume is innate to the spiritual powers that govern the dynamics of the cosmos. When he has prepared himself to know the wishes of the *hiči*, the novice shaman presents himself to a master spirit who licks his body from one end to the other. Using the organ through which the world passes in the form of food, the master spirit bestows power on the new shaman, the master of spiritual consumption. In this way, the novice symbolically dies during the rite that closes the apprenticeship and is then resurrected.[85] The novice possesses an insider's view of spiritual consumption.

The connection between spiritual assistance and consumption (both of material and symbolic form) is complex and extensive. On one level, the origins of many spirit helpers lie in accounts of death or destruction in which their primordial form was consumed and they first took on spiritual form.[86] In addition, spirit helpers not only need food; they are *like* food. Spirit assistants may reside in the body of the shaman just as nutrients are ingested and stored in the human body. Meditation on the meaning of his spirit helpers, then, necessarily draws the novice into reflection on the meaning of his own appetites and the way in which they draw him into relationship with all creation. He comes to know himself as a set of relations, a consumer of visible and invisible realities. The training of the Canelos Quichua shaman provides illustration. In addition to the spirit helpers *(putan supais)* that all people keep in their stomachs and whose droning noise brings dreams, the Canelos Quichua shaman acquires special spirit darts. Since all Canelos Quichua acquire souls and mystical substances throughout their lives, the ability to cure and to send sickness into others with the aid of spirit darts distinguishes the shaman from other people who have acquired souls. These darts must be purchased from the proper person. A master shaman offers the candidate instruction in their use.[87] When both shaman and novice have imbibed *ayahuasca*, the soul-master spirit of the forest, Amasanga, appears (in the form of two black jaguars) accompanied by the Sungui, soul-master spirit of the river, (in the form of two anacondas). "[W]ith their help and knowledge, a shaman's spirit-helper dart is coughed up by the shaman from his own stomach. The spirit moves around in the shaman's hand, proving its viability, and the buyer takes it and swallows it." [88] This process of instruction and acquisition of spirit darts continues for several years, during which time the candidate must keep the spirit helpers in his stomach. They accustom themselves to his personality and other soul substances and aid him in diagnosing and curing illness.

The next plateau in a Canelos Quichua shaman's training requires fasting, special diets, and abstention from sex. The transmission of knowledge, power, and spirit helpers appears to be an almost visceral, material process. Ingesting a mixture of bananas and tobacco water, the candidate falls asleep. Spirits come out of him in the form of spirit darts and tempt him to use his power against enemies. The candidate must resist this insuperable temptation and reswallow the spirit darts, for only in this way can he become a successful curing shaman. By reswallowing spirit substances already emitted from the inside of one's own body, one comes to know oneself and the powers of the universe that are at work in one's own, microcosmic, body. Spirit-helper darts will now protect the *cusca yachaj* ("straight up shaman") from spirit darts blown by enemy shamans.[89]

As a Canelos Quichua shaman progressively gains familiarity with spirits through knowledge of their souls and control over their passage through his mouth, he becomes more powerful in the spirit world. One may attain, for example, the status of a *sinchi yachaj*, who learns to acquire and control spirits who possess human souls.[90] Beyond that stage, a shaman may attain the status of *bancu* ("bench, stool"), thereby acting as the seat of certain spirits who "speak directly through the shaman's mouth."[91] The acquisition of souls by Canelos Quichua shamans makes possible the continued existence of society. Furthermore, the way in which they acquire souls and transmit them becomes a foundation of kinship and social structure, for society cannot exist without the powerful and effective knowledge from the past.

Jívaro culture also reflects the connection of spirit help with consumption as symbolized by the mouth. Two kinds of shamanic specialists are knowledgeable in Jívaro realities: bewitching shamans and curing shamans. Michael J. Harner estimates that one out of every four Jívaro men is a shaman. In practice, any adult man or woman may take *natema*, a species of *Banisteriopsis caapi*, under the direction of a master shaman in order to obtain knowledge of supernatural powers. During apprenticeship the master shaman vomits *tsentsak*, spirit helpers in the form of magical "darts," which are then swallowed by the novice shaman. During apprenticeship, the novice gains control over these *tsentsak*. While abstaining from sex and observing dietary restrictions, the novice learns to keep the *tsentsak* in the stomach so that they might be vomited up at will. Although a *tsentsak* emerges from a novice's mouth after one month of apprenticeship, the novice must control the desire to use it in a harmful way. If the novice wishes to become a curing shaman, he must reswallow this first *tsentsak*.

During the period of abstinence from sex (lasting from five months to a year), the novice learns how to transform almost any object small enough to be swallowed (insects, plants, and so on) into a *tsentsak*. These objects appear in their "true" form under the influence of *natema*, when they reveal themselves as brilliantly colored demons who bear different names from those of the material objects with which they are associated. In this form, with new names, the *tsentsak* become spirit helpers "such as giant butterflies, jaguars, or monkeys."[92] These spirits aid the shaman in either bewitching or curing.

The shaman's body, its desires, and appetites become identified with helpful spiritual powers at work in the cosmos. The Yạnomamö shaman, for example, acquires helping spirits in the form of rock-dwelling (or mountain-dwelling) *hekura*, who take up residence in his chest. These are "tiny humanoid beings whom the shamans, shobori, acquire during a period of fast from food and sexual continence." Napoleon Chagnon estimates that "probably half of the men in each village are shamans."[93] Using a hallucinatory plant called *epene* the shaman contacts his *hekura* in order to cure victims of illness or to inflict harm on enemies.

Through the work of his spirit helpers, the shaman's physical and social relations express in this life the reality of the supernatural world. For example, helper spirits inhabit the breast of the Warao light-shaman. He is their "father," and his wife becomes the "mother" of these spirits through a ritual-ized sexual union. Light-shamans and their wives are fed on tobacco smoke offered by fellow shamans on earth.[94] The shaman's body, through the aid of spirit helpers, becomes an instrument of extraordinary knowledge. This special knowledge has a direct bearing on the order and well-being of the community. On the one side, it sets the shaman apart as a specialist, thereby structuring his social and political relations. At the same time, the shaman's knowledge of the sacred, obtained through alliances with helper-spirits, broadens the very meaning of human community by extending intimate social ties into the furthest reaches of the spiritual world. Through the sha-man's spirit helpers, the fate of humankind becomes a function of the super-natural processes of sacred beings.

MAGIC FLIGHT TO FAR-FLUNG WORLDS

The shaman uses ecstasy to gain knowledge; that is, to experience a supernat-ural condition of life. Superhuman conditions exist, in varying qualities, in the heterogeneous spaces that constitute the universe. During controlled ecstasy, the shaman visits these cosmic realms with the assistance of helper spirits. One of the most striking and widespread images of shamanic practice is the ability to fly like a spirit. This should neither be reduced to a flight of fancy nor to a metaphor for the mind's contemplation of eternal truths. South American cultures regard the shaman's flight neither as silly or child-ish nor as philosophical.[95]

Assuming the form of beings in the primordial age, or buoyed up by them, the shaman's soul takes the physical form of a bird, a beam of light, a lightning bolt, a cloud, or a breeze. In a brief but detailed comparative study, Gerhard Baer draws attention to a set of symbolic associations tied to sha-manism in South America. This symbolic complex includes lightning, thunder, rain (and other weather conditions), and stone.[96] Baer believes the complex to be held together by all these elements' celestial origin. Lightning and a kind of transparent stone (which crystallizes heavenly light) become a link with the shaman during his ecstatic journeys to heaven. In addition, thunder and lightning betoken a state of the dead: the separation of body and soul. As such, they are symbols of the powerful state of ecstasy that typifies the shaman's uniqueness and makes his magical flights possible.

In this altered form — the condition of the privileged beings of the mythic age — the shaman takes on autonomous existence in another world. He or she overcomes the gulf of time and cosmic tragedy and reaches heaven. For instance, the Mataco religious specialists (aiawu) use their mu-sical techniques of ecstasy to visit Potsejlai (the constellation Orion). After taking hataj snuff, the aiawu "sings until the moment when something like a figurine comes out of his breast. He mounts a bird, that is a yulo." [97] If the first mythical bird he uses tires, the healer calls forth another.

Having mastered the art of transformation so as to achieve a buoyant form, the shaman's being may fly out of his or her body to soar to other worlds at any time. Shamans need not await death to take on the form of free souls ascending to heaven. They rise at will, and they do so in a concrete and material way. To enter ecstatic states in which they perform cures, for example, Baniwa shamans inhale snuff, said to be the blood *(lirana),* or menstrual blood *(likanüpa),* of the male culture hero Kuai. To begin to understand how snuff bears affinities with semen, one should know that male menstruation is said to be equivalent to masturbation and that male menstrual blood (with which the shaman's snuff is identified) is essential for successful insemination. "After shamans inhale snuff, they immediately open (. . . *liṁeloo)* the Sky-Door above the earth, which separates this world from the unseen 'other' world of Before. In a sense, the shamans 'die' by taking snuff, but it is to make a passage as in the passage at the birth of children." [98]

The reachievement of the full condition of being, the free-moving and weightless state of the first age, is a reminder of the shortcomings of the present human condition. In this age, only human limits, mortal death, can free most human beings from their present state and liberate their postmortem souls to fly to celestial existence, but the shamans' ecstasies transport them beyond the human state. Taking on the capacities of their helper-spirits, shamans crisscross the boundaries of separate qualities of being; they pass in and out of all cosmic realms and between the states normally labeled "life" and "death." [99]

The mythic geography the shaman traverses in ascent underscores the concreteness of the shaman's experience and ecstatic knowledge. Spatial structures (rainbows, mountains, vines, ladders, and so on) provide access to the heavenly realm. By their means, the shaman enters a state where communication with other realms is substantive and concrete and not merely metaphoric. According to the Winikina-Warao, for example, there are three classes of shamans who, through their ecstatic flights, are familiar with the labyrinth of mythic geography: the priest-shaman, the light-shaman, and the dark-shaman. The priest-shaman mediates between human beings and the *kanobo* gods, the "grandfathers" who live at the cardinal and intercardinal points of the universe as well as at the zenith and nadir.[100] Carried away on a winged golden horse, the priest-shaman mounts to the zenith. Later in his ecstatic trip the priest-shaman traverses a treacherous path from the zenith to the world-mountain of the Mother of the Forest and dangles his way across an abyss with the aid of a rope. The light-shaman is marked for a different duty and destiny. He mediates between humankind and the supernatural beings in the Land of Light, the residence place of Kanobo Amawari, which is reached by crossing a bridge bordered with beautiful flowers. This Land of Light was brought into existence by the Creator Bird of the Dawn and is occupied by four powerful beings who chant the songs of light-shamanism.[101] The first light-shaman came to live in this sacred home. Now other light-shamans and their wives follow suit.

The ritual action of shamans often reflects their capacity to fly. Mapuche *machi,* for example, undertake an ecstatic flight to communicate with Nguenechen, the heavenly supreme being. Their ascent of the *rehue,* a ritual ladder made of a thick post of oak, signals the height of their ecstasy. The *machi* dances on top of the *rehue* while her transformed spirit soars through the heavens. Because of its association with ecstatic flight, the *rehue* is "the distinctive symbol of the machi." [102]

The shaman's ability to fly freely to other realms is not restricted to celestial journeys. In order to obtain knowledge, retrieve lost souls, or do battle with disruptive powers of chaos, the shaman may experience the life of the underworld. In some instances the shaman's own helper spirits may inhabit the lower worlds, whose powers the shaman therefore serves. The Warao dark-shaman, to choose but one example, carries on communication between the human world and the land of death. His soul is patronized by the macaw god in the western underworld. The dark-shaman must furnish the food necessary for the survival of the beings in the underworld. To that end, he harvests human life on earth. In his breast, the dark-shaman carries two helper spirits and also a supernatural sling with which he throttles his victim. "The pathogenic bolt is carried by tobacco smoke he blows from his reversed cigar that, searching for the heart, enters the individual's ribcage to perform the sacrifice." [103]

Depending on the construction of the universe and the powers of the individual specialist, the shaman may visit lateral cosmoses, located on the horizons of this world. Here, for example, is the account of a powerful Avá-Chiripá shaman's journey to the land of the dead on the eastern margins of the universe.

"I walk a little way, toward the east, and there I see a beautiful house with its doors all the same. I arrived there, at this place which we call ñe'eng-güeri (country of the dead). It was there in ñe'eng-güeri that I learned my prayer. There I met my brother-in-law and my grandfather. My brother-in-law took hold of my left arm and my grandfather took hold of my right and together they revealed to me the ladder which joins earth and sky. Then I noticed that there was dancing, and the place of the dancing was the beautiful house like a church of the type attended by you (whites). Then I asked what it was and my sponsors told me that it was the place where prayers are learned—I can hardly tell you about these things since merely thinking about them makes me want to weep. As the dancers turned toward us, I noticed that there were no young men or women among them. Therefore I do not like to look at the women when I am praying since, in prayer, we are concerned with things of true worth. After I had seen the men dance, I looked toward the sun in the east. I looked to see if it was going to rain but I knew that it was not going to rain. In the midst of all this, I was taken to a mountain to hear the chant. On descending I saw a dead man in a pit. The body was distended and flies swarmed round his grave. Then my sponsors, who were still with me, said to me, 'Protégé, you are the one who must cure this man,' to which I replied that I could not since I did not know how. Then my sponsors made me listen to the prayer which I had to say [at this point he chants a little and sobs a little, saying that in telling these things, he relives the experience] and made me walk three times round the tomb. I chanted and breathed on him and the man was cured. It had been a man who had been buried there in the forest and he arose and began to speak. Sometimes Our Father, when he hears these prayers, will even restore the dead to life. On the following day, I chanted early in the morning as I had been taught and every night my sponsors showed the remedies by which I could cure the sick. To get this knowledge I went to the east and that is how I know the love of all things." [104]

In the form of a free-moving primordial being, the entire mythic universe is open to the shaman. In Canelos Quichua culture, a powerful shaman gains access to all spaces and times of the universe with the aid of *ayahuasca*, the "vine of souls" that reaches back to the beginnings. With the use of *ayahuasca*, a shaman can maintain communication with any of the spirits that have ever existed. He does this by acquiring and encountering souls from all cosmic domains. [105] In similarly far-flung travels, the Tapirapé shaman *(panché)* voyages in his "canoe" (a gourd used as an eating implement) or in the form of a bird to other realms in the cosmos: celestial realms, faraway places of foreigners, the home of Thunder. "The Tapirapé are thus equipped with a wide range of second-hand experience. They have no concept of a closed or limited universe." [106]

Not infrequently, classes of shamans are distinguished by the cosmic realms they visit and by the worlds from which their spirit helpers come. This is the case in Baniwa culture, where different degrees of power separate the categories of shamans. The most prestigious shamans reach the highest levels of the cosmos and, therefore, perform the most difficult cures. For example, some will reach the height of the mid-sky, where Kuai, "owner of sicknesses," and Dzuliûeri, "owner of shaman's snuff and tobacco," reside. [107] The most powerful of all Baniwa shamans attain the highest level of the universe and become "like Yaperikuli," the creator-transformer associated with the primal sun.

THE ROADS BEYOND DEATH

Ordinary human beings sometimes visit the land of the dead before they actually die, but shamans do it with a difference. Several Machiguenga myths illustrate this so-called Orpheus tradition of South America. Two kinds of Machiguenga myths describe the world and life of those who have died. The protagonists of both kinds of myth are transformed by their journey to these other worlds. In the first case the adventure begins with the death of someone who is then pursued into the underworld by a living loved one. The myth of the husband who follows his dead wife to the land under the earth proclaims that the dead undergo a series of continuing transformations in the next life. The husband also learns the use of magical and medicinal plants. Through these and other initiatory techniques, the husband obtains wisdom, which allows him to leave behind his wife and his longing for death. [108] However, the second kind of myth, the one about the shaman who, in a state of ecstasy, visits the heavenly realm of primordial vultures, betrays a difference that helps us to understand the meaning of shamanism. The shaman is completely transformed by his experience. Even his physical appearance changes, for he takes on the form of a vulture. Baer rightly insists that we not look upon the postmortem narrative as merely an appendix to a hero's adventures. The entire purpose of the shaman's life is to ready himself for this voyage beyond death. To that end he rearranges his physical condition, his pattern of family ties, and his economic responsibilities.[109] For all that, the realm of the vultures attained after death at first appears very similar to human life on earth. On closer inspection, the differences stand out: the vulture people consume their own flesh when they eat, hunt animals that were once carrion, and so on. The shaman and his brother are transformed when they eat food that they have been ordered not to consume. Baer and his collaborator, Gisela Hertle, point out that these myths emphasize the extraordinary ability of shamans to experience a full existence in two different worlds — so full, in fact, that they assume two different forms that make possible the two kinds of experience. Reports of shamans' experience in the vulture world enlighten all Machiguengas about the structure of one part of the cosmos, the postmortem shamanic heaven of the vultures.

Equipped with ecstatic techniques of transformation, shamans practice traveling to the places that ordinary mortals visit only when they die.[110] The Krahó term *akrãgaikrit* ("light heads"), for example, includes both accomplished and potential shamans. *Akrãgaikrit* are individuals who have journeyed to the land of the dead. More precisely, their *karõ*, the "double" or personal principle that endures after death, journeys to the abode of the dead and converses with them. Unlike the *karõ* of ordinary mortals, that of shamans is powerful enough to return to the land of the living.[111] Personal experience of the road beyond death is the basis of shamanic authority.

The shamans' familiarity with the worlds of the afterlife offers distinct advantages. The Warao provide elaborate illustrations of these postmortem privileges. Since the souls of Warao shamans in trance have traveled to various heavens, these shamans remain confident that they will survive the perilous journey to their final resting place after death. On this final ecstatic journey, the Warao priest-shaman hears the golden horse of death approaching him. Astride this winged creature he mounts to the zenith, the home of the god of the center. Traveling like a shooting star or lightning bolt, the priest-shaman smokes cigars that the god of the center has provided him. Dressed in fine clothes, the shaman thunders from the central zenith toward the end of the world, never looking back. An invisible guide takes the soul along the mythical road but leaves difficult decisions to the traveler. The journey is terrifying, and the temptations to be waylaid are many. Eventually, after stepping through a door that rapidly opens and closes, the priest-shaman's soul enters a cave, the mountain home of the Mother of the Forest. In the afterlife there, priest-shamans enjoy one another's company as well as the tobacco provided for them by shamans on earth.[112]

The Warao dark-shaman, smoking a cigar, finds his way along a different path to his eternal rest in the land of the dead. His spiritual helper, the Macaw, plays a trumpet to attract the shaman toward his goal. The stench of coagulated blood and rotting flesh also draw him on. Upon his arrival, the dark-shaman's soul is furnished with human blood, which he drinks from a canoe, and human flesh to eat. Adorned with a necklace of human ribs, "he assumes a body that is half-parrot and half-human, with the tail of a monkey."[113]

The ability of shamans to pick their way through the perils of postmortem existence not only assures their own destiny, it enables them to serve as psychopomps able to guide other souls to their appropriate supernatural destinations or to recover lost souls that have prematurely strayed from their place on earth.

THE MASTER OF FIRE AND THE LIGHT OF A CIGAR

The power of shamans resides not only in the strengths of their spirit helpers but also in the knowledge revealed about the spirit helpers' weaknesses. In particular, the shaman learns the appetites of many cosmic beings. Through knowledge of the hungers of spirits, the shaman becomes a master of consumption. He understands its nature as an expression of the intrinsic relatedness of matter and spirit that has obtained since the passing of primordial wholeness and the appearance of fragmented symbolic life and religious history. The alienation of spirit and form in this spatiotemporal epoch makes the process of consumption visible in fire. As in the cosmic conflagration[114] and the burning of mythic beings,[115] fire produces a spiritual and symbolic world.[116] The shaman, specialist in the care of the soul, must master the processes that produce transformations of spirit, and so becomes a master of fire.

In the accounts of many mythologies, human life, as opposed to the life of animals, plants, and spiritual entities, is characterized by the possession of fire. The greatest importance is placed on the fact that animals and even supernatural beings do not possess fire and consequently are obliged to eat their food raw and pass their nights in cold and darkness. Although mastery of fire (like irreversible mortality) is now a defining feature of the human condition, it was not always so.[117] Fire origin myths testify to the fact that human nature has undergone a profound change — a spiritualization — by obtaining fire. Like all distinguishing transformations that separate one kind of being from another, the acquisition of fire is often closely associated with the myths of cosmic cataclysm.[118]

Control of fire as a technique for spiritual transformation originated with the first shamans of the mythic age. In a Toba-Pilagá myth, for example, a primordial shaman destroys the earth with the heat of the sun. He destroys people because they have stolen from him. Only those who hide underground reemerge after the conflagration. The myth threatens that the shaman may do the same thing again in the future.[119] The Baniwa proto-shaman, Yaperikuli, is a celestial jaguar, the master of consumption and transformation and, most especially, the master of fire, which cannot destroy him but which he uses to destroy the world and mythic beings. His fires are all transformative. They produce a state of undying ("not-dead") existence by rarifying the essence of an entity, separating it from its body form and giving it a new existence in a less destructible (or even an indestructible) form.[120] In the most important event of Baniwa mythology, Yaperikuli destroyed the culture hero Kuai with fire. This conflagration provoked the withdrawal of primordial beings from this world and introduced disease when venom poured from the flaming orifices of Kuai. The venom of disease also came from burning animal hairs and urine, which were transformed into noxious spiders, biting animals, and disease darts. The fire produced a number of different transformative orders over which the shaman, the master of fire, presides: the generative order of physiology (menstruation, birth, growth, death); the orders of speech and music, which produce separate species and human language groups; the orders of sicknesses and their remedies; and the orders of symbolic action, especially initiation rituals.[121]

The mythic scenarios linking primordial shamans with fire differ widely. Although there is no opportunity to investigate all of them here, these differences are of great importance, for they signal the creativity of individual cultures. The Juruna illustrate another point on the wide spectrum of difference that exists among these mythic accounts. From the very beginning the Juruna shaman is a master of fire. Sinaá, the primordial shaman and culture hero, set out on a quest for fire at the instigation of an otter. Paddling a canoe, the culture hero set off to get fire from the eagle. To trick the eagle, Sinaá transformed himself into something dead. At first he became a dead tapir but his lively eyes gave him away, and the eagle would not approach him. In his second attempt, Sinaá partially buried himself in the ground in the form of a dry branch. Seizing the fire of the eagle, Sinaá blew on the eagle and transformed him into an animal. At the moment of his transformation, the eagle wept at the loss of fire. This lamentation became a ritual song, a sonic residue of a primordial being whose material vestige is the body form of eagles seen today. The eagle points to an essential characteristic of shamanism when he taunts the shaman, saying, "You're some shaman, if you can't make fire; without fire, you don't have anything." [122]

The burden of the mastery over fire can be awesome. Responsible for the transformative process burning at the core of spiritual life, the shaman must master the symbolism at the center (the hearth) of the social unit, the communal group, all civilized human life, and the cosmos itself. Mataco shamans, *ayavu*, for example, bear responsibility for preventing any repetition of the primordial conflagration. According to Mataco interviewed by Alicia M. Barabas and Miguel A. Bartolomé, the helper spirits of shamans fly to the center of the world, to the Tree of Trials (or the Firstborn Tree, *ayavu ute*), which sprouted from a piece of charcoal left over from the cosmic fire. This shamanic responsibility began when one of the mythic survivors of the cosmic fire pounded the charcoal like a drum. The survivor, a mythical bird named Icanchu, danced for several days to the accompaniment of his drum rhythm until a large shoot sprang from the charcoal and grew to become an enormous cosmic tree. The shamanic sound that rang from the pounded charcoal reestablished access to the heavenly realm. Icanchu's music and dance become the basis of the rites celebrated to stimulate the growth of the carob tree, a staple of the Mataco's diet from November to February.[123] The controlled growth of forests relates directly to the shamans' mastery of fire. The ecstatic specialists ward off fire by summoning their helper spirits and ordering them to fly to the home of the *itoj ahla*, the "lords of the fire," who live in the bowels of the earth. The purpose of the ritual is to trick the lords of fire by convincing them that no more forests remain on the earth.[124]

BEARER OF THE CRYSTALS OF LIGHT

Endurance of the light and heat of heavenly beings[125] demonstrates and proclaims the shaman's mastery over fire.[126] The Warao priest-shaman is called *wishiratu*, which may be translated "master of fire."[127] The Warao shaman not only masters the fire inherent in poison but controls the fiery heat of the *hebu*, spirits who cause disease when they enter the human body. The shaman counters their pathogenic heat with the fire that he controls in his gourd-rattle. He cures by fighting fire with fire. His gourd rattle contains quartz crystals, which are embodiments of celestial light and heat. The shaman feeds the rattle spirits, embodied in crystallized fire of quartz, by blowing tobacco smoke into the "four mouths," the slits on the gourd. Tobacco-smoke food is itself a product of the consuming fire that the shaman controls with his cigar. Once the "head" of the rattle is fed with tobacco smoke, it "wakes up."[128]

The Warao shaman's mastery of fire is not an adjunct position. It is linked in an essential way with the other distinguishing features of the shamanic vocation, namely, his ability to communicate directly with the celestial realms of primordial heat. Furthermore, in shamanic experience the ideology of consumption is inextricably associated with the experience of ecstasy. Consumption by fire becomes a means and a sign of the death brought on by supernatural powers. The trance of ecstatic death dispatches the soul on a voyage envisioned as a spiritual "awakening." Being consumed by divine powers and simultaneously feeding them with etherized substance produced by fire is to be transported to another state of consciousness, an awakened state. The Warao shaman travels to this awakened realm of heat along the central shaft of his rattle. It is the axis of the universe itself. The shaman fashions it from a wood used to kindle the ritual fires from which the shaman lights his cigars. The lighted cigars "feed" the spirits who transport the shaman into ecstasy. The central shaft of the shaman's rattle, like the lit cigar, *contains* fire. "As with fire-containing poison, fire is believed actually to be burning within this wood."[129]

For the shamanic master of fire, the symbolism of fire centers the world. The *axis mundi*, the means of connecting all realms of the universe, is an expression of burning desire—the cosmic process of consumption contained and controlled by human culture.[130] The human experience of passage from one symbolic realm of the imagination to another brings all realms of time and space—and all modes of being—into relation with one another. The shaman masters this process of mystical transition that constitutes human life and maintains the universe.

Control over fire surfaces during medical applications of shamanic

power. Control over fire is useful in the diagnosis of disease and the preparation of medicines. Disease is frequently a form of burning present in the body
as a consumptive intruder or a poisonous product of primordial fire. The
shaman uses knowledge of heat and fire, in all its symbolic guises, to overcome sickness. For instance, the Chiquitano *čeeserúš* performs his massag-
ing cures with a cigar in his mouth. Placing the lighted end of the cigar inside
his mouth, the shaman bathes his patient's body in smoke. Dipping his hand
in oil, the *čeeserúš* strokes the sick body, extracts the pathogen from within it,
and burns the sickness in a fire that is kept burning nearby.[131]

PYROTECHNICS OF THE ECSTATIC SOUL

Shamanic mastery of fire extends to dazzling displays that provide entertainment and magical demonstrations of power. The emphasis in these cases
falls on spectacle rather than on any specific religious or healing function.
The Machiguenga shaman *(seripigari)* is a master of heat and light. He glows
in the dark. When in an ecstatic trance, singing and wearing his feather
crown, "a shaman who really knows his business can give his guests light in
the house [at night] by singing." [132] Because his guardian spirits are like
lamps "bright as day" when the shaman sings, the room fills with light.

Entertaining demonstrations of fiery heat and light spur reflection on
their nature and on the power of the human specialist who "knows" them
intimately. Before the eyes of awed spectators, Guajajara shamans, for example, eat hot embers from the fire when they are protected by the frog spirit.
Boróro peoples attributed to their shamans the ability to drink boiling water.
"Fire walking was a common performance by shamans in the Chaco and
Tierra del Fuego." [133] The Campa of the montane of eastern Peru recognize
several different kinds of religious specialists. Among them are shaman
souls, which are good spirits. When shamans of the category of shaman souls
travel to other worlds at night they can cause their souls to flash in the form of
lightning *(ipóreki,* "he flashes") for all to see. Traveling shamans visit the
supernatural swineherd, *Tasórenci*, in order to request the release of wild
pigs from his corral in the mountains.[134]

The shaman's cigars, sometimes several feet in length, manifest the
ability to maintain and control the fire-process that fuels the life of spirits.[135]
Investigators draw the enormous cigar holders used for ritual smoking into
the same symbolic complex of meaning as the shaman's bench.[136] Like the
shaman's bench, an image of the center and a vehicle of access to all cosmic
planes, the cigar holder is frequently carved and painted in a way that makes
it a symbolic microcosm: its prongs are an *axis mundi*, transfixing the levels
of the universe; its pointed base passes into the underworld. Although used in
other rituals, the cigar holder is preeminently the instrument of the shaman,
the traveler through cosmic realms. This connection between the cigar
holder, cosmic structure, and the shaman is strengthened in myth. Günther
Hartmann considers the Tukano-speaking peoples to present the clearest
example of the connection between carved cigar holders and the shaman's
bench. Among Tukano-speakers, rituals manipulate these shamanic para-

phernalia in a similar way. For example, for ritual smoking, both items are set up in pairs facing one another.[137]

THE PHYSIOLOGY OF THE ECSTATIC SOUL

During ecstasy shamans pass out of their bodies to assume new forms. Control over passage through the openings of the body is essential to shamanic practice. Because the shaman's experiences of other worlds are concrete, the shaman's body can be no ordinary one. His entire being, including his physiology, accommodates itself to new conditions of space, time, sound, light, heat, and so on. Maintaining sensual perception, consciousness, and sensitivity to meaning in these circumstances requires metamorphosis of some kind. The shaman's physiology assumes cosmic proportions and becomes an extraordinary vehicle for his transformed soul. The body of the shaman is part of his technology, a controlling instrument of transition for his entire being.

Apprenticeship rearranges the shaman's body. In some cases, the experience of the shamanic call and training dismembers the body and reassembles it with new parts. Experiential knowledge reconditions the order of the senses, the meaning of the body's perceptions. Frequently, the transfer of power from master to disciple is visceral. The Apinayé master *vayangá* (shaman) transfers power to his apprentice by stroking down along his own arms and torso and up along his pupil's. Control of body form, crucial to the *vayangá*'s practice, becomes evident in other techniques. Novices learn to transform their bodies into those of mammals, birds, and reptiles.[138]

The body of the shaman acquires mystical but concrete extensions. Sacred stones acquired during a novice's apprenticeship seem to form a part of his physiology. Stones containing spirits are absolutely essential to the shamanic vocation among the Machiguenga. The stones are obtained from a celestial invisible being who appears during the novice's early *ayahuasca* hallucinations. Gerhard Baer and Wayne W. Snell believe that the bestowal of stones culminates the Machiguenga novice's initiation.[139] "Although the novice's physical organs are neither changed nor renewed at initiation, . . . the *stones appear to be in a sense organs removed* to the outside, since they are always carried on the body and since their loss leads to death" (emphasis in original).[140] In addition, the stones must be "fed" regularly with tobacco smoke. When they are nourished in this way, they become the bodies of arch-consumers, jaguars *(matsontsori)*. The stones become an extension of the shaman's mystical physiology.

Examination of the shaman's physiology reveals the concreteness of the shamanic passage to another world. During ecstasy, a substantial form passes out of the shaman's body. The ability of shamans to pass concrete items in and out of their bodies demonstrates the substantiality of their experience even while it exercises their dominion over the passageways of their bodies. The Krahó myth of the first shaman and the personal accounts of the Krahó shaman's vocation lay great store in the ability to cause objects to enter in and pass out of the body, whether the body of the mythical being Tĩr'krẽ, of the apprentice shaman, or of the patients upon whom shamans practice their skills. For example, a fish appeared to one sick apprentice in order to cure and teach him. This miraculous fish produced "from its own body, a table, tablecloth, spoon, plate, rice, beef, chicken, and even coffee." One by one, these items were introduced into the body of the patient by the fish-teacher. They constituted the service for a copious meal.[141] In the Krahó view of things, human beings obtain such marvelous powers over substantial passages of this sort only if they relive the myth of Tĩr'krẽ.

The power objects of shamanic craft and the weapons for struggle with cosmic processes are introduced into the novice by the master shaman or helper spirit, who injects these invisible darts, needles, stones, splinters, thorns, or bits of bone or crystal (etc.) into the novice's body. For example, a Toba master would wallop his novices with a club that entered into the body and remained there.[142] The Barama River Carib shaman put a spirit-stone in his novice's mouth. Then he would drag the spirit-stone through the body of the young man, making it pass from the throat, through the neck, and into the shoulders and arms in order to create an opening through which pathogenic projectiles could be shot at will.[143] Such preparations enable the shaman to draw magic substances from his body in order to heal or to harm. In many cases, the power that infuses a shaman's being and resides in his body is identical with poison capable of killing.[144] The Chiquitano shaman, for example, was able to kill his enemies by injecting them with a black substance that he kept in his stomach at all times.[145]

The ability of shamans to control their physiology gives way to magic display, spectacle, and sleight-of-hand performances. Thus, Bororo shamans chewed up tapir bones. Apapocuvá shamans extracted honey from within closed sections of bamboo. "Tereno *piai* extracted feathers from their skin, swallowed arrows, and even 'removed' limbs."[146] The Selk'nam shaman housed inside him a three-meter-long rope, which he could yank out of his mouth at will and reswallow again in the blink of an eye.[147]

Extraordinary power can reside in specific parts of the shaman's body. The physiology of the Toba *yeyátten* reflects the strength he derives from a spirit who inhabits his body. The specialist's blood, saliva, sweat, and other secretions, as well as his hair and nails, are special concentrations of the *yeyátten*'s sacred power.[148] In a similar localization of power, the Tapirapé shaman cures fever by spraying a mixture of water and honey from his mouth over the house of the sick person and its occupants. The honey and water alone would never do the trick, "but sprayed from the mouth of the *panché* [shaman] it drove away fevers."[149] In many societies the shaman's mouth holds special power, manifest in sacred song and esoteric speech and in the ability to suck and transform pathogens and to blow with magical effect.

The power to pass the substances of spiritual life into the body links the shaman to food. Learned in the ways of food through contact with the spirit world, the shaman knows the forms of edible species of animals and plants. A Kaingáng shaman, for instance, divided every animal species into supernatural, untouchable members and natural, touchable (consumable) members. The shaman was able to recognize the untouchable members of the species as actually being supernatural children of his "friend," his helper spirit. The consumable members of the species were a gift of food from this helper spirit.[150]

The shaman identifies edible foods by discerning relations in the spirit world. Consumption of food is an essentially spiritual process. This is the corollary of a conclusion reached earlier: the shaman's helpers show that the spiritual life of the cosmos is consumptive. The shaman's experience of cosmic spirituality enables him to identify the levels at which eating and the body are one. The spiritual power of food fortifies and changes the body. The materiality of food changes the soul. Eating is an important threshold experience, a rite of symbolic passage in which important changes of form occur. Eating affects the whole substance of a person (body and spirit) just as it substantially changes the form of food in the process. In this connection, the shaman may undertake ritual action to help in hunting, gathering, or growing food. In addition, the shaman may prepare food (e.g., by blowing on it) or prepare the eater spiritually for new foods. The shaman's connection with eating does not end there. Among the Wayãpi, for example, sickness is generally due to breaking a hunting restriction or consuming forbidden game.[151] With his rattle, the shaman (paye) cures the sickness caused by the penetration of improper animal forms into the body.

The shaman's mastery of physiology and knowledge of animal forms directly ties in with shamanic expertise in spatial forms in general, a knowledge based upon the shaman's penetration of cosmic spaces during ecstasy. That experience of elementary forms and the grueling analysis of his or her own perceptions of their meaning performed by the shaman during apprenticeship reshapes the shaman physically and orients him or her to the spiritual order. Dealing in a relatively controlled way with the chaotic fullness of spiritual life requires the power of discretion, that is, the ability to experience the cosmos as a variety of discrete and ordered spaces (e.g., cosmic realms and the bodily forms of animals). The Pemón piache's concern with body forms goes back to the times of myth and stems from the slaying of the primordial rainbow-serpent: "the piache summoned all the birds to select their coloring from the snake's cadaver. Those who did not respond to the summons to paint themselves remain black to this day."[152] Similarly, land animals were called to the snake's cadaver by the piache. The four-footed animals, who were first to arrive, "utilized all of the bones from the serpent's cadaver to form horns and antlers."[153] The body forms of various animal species became spaces with distinct markings.

CONTROL AND MEDIATION

The separation between spaces is heightened and controlled through the regulation of eating, a process in which one spatial form enters (or is ingested by) another. The great Tapirapé culture heroes were all great shamans. These primordial, ancestral shamans of the Tapirapé destroyed various kinds of demons, frequently demons of the forest, who had exaggerated physical features and appetites. In particular, they eliminated, or at least pared down the number of, beings who were aberrant in regard to sex and who had appetites for blood as food. They thus set the model for order and control in the realm of the physiology of sex and hunger.[154]

The conquering of chaos through the ordering of discrete spatial forms (by mystically passing from one to another under strict control) prepares the way for the specialists' knowledge of elementary spaces. Techniques of control distinguish the shaman. After a careful comparative study of Mapuche shamans, one Chilean psychiatrist concluded that all the ecstatic trances of the Mapuche *machi* (shamans) were accomplished under strict control. This control exercised itself no matter what circumstances or techniques prompted ecstasy: revelatory dreams, hallucinations, ecstatic trance, catalepsy, or the direction of some other *machi*.[155]

Even though the behavior and techniques of ecstasy and the episodes of trance for shamans are striking and, at times, disturbing to the spectator, the element of rigid self-control in dealing with the supernatural is essential to the vocation. Surveying shamanism in history and across cultures, Peter T. Furst considers control one of the overwhelmingly obvious traits of shamanism:

> It is clear from a wealth of solid, firsthand, anthropological observation all over the world that far from suffering serious mental illness or other pathological impairment, shamans as a rule are strong and healthy in body and mind, highly intelligent individuals, possessed of admirable self-control, strength of will and of character and in general capable of intellectual effort far beyond that of the collectivity.[156]

Shamans may help a society maintain control of itself in the face of the colonial encounter with "other" kinds of beings whose reality is conditioned by "other" kinds of space. In particular, Furst points out that South American communities with a strong shamanic tradition have been better able to maintain their physical and metaphysical equilibrium and "have fared psychologically far better under the ideological and material impact of encroaching white civilization than those among whom the traditional shamanistic system had already been weakened or otherwise deteriorated."[157]

Because shamans use their techniques of ecstasy to accommodate themselves to multiple modes of existence, they serve the community as mediators between worlds and they function as psychopomps and guarantors of threatened souls. At funerals, the Guaraní shaman used the sound of his rattle and song to guide an element of a dead man's soul back to the realm of divine being whence it came. However, even in the first reports on Guaraní shamanism by André Thevet, Jean de Léry, and Hans Staden,[158] these shamans were shown to be religious and political leaders who managed people's relations with all outside worlds, both human and transcendent. They organized resistance to colonization and missionization at the same time that they led messianic migrations toward paradise. In death some of these powerful figures lived on as deified or heroic "saviors."[159] There are even reports of the worship of the bones of dead shamans.[160]

Bartolomé points out the parallelism between the healing function of a shaman and the role of the shaman in integrating society: "[T]he society becomes the shaman's *collective patient*. . . . [T]he shaman mediates with the sacred; he heals and is the ritual mediator in his dual sacred and social role. This is why tribal communities which lose their shamans (through plagues and so on) tend to disintegrate for the lack of someone to give a sense of cultural values."[161] The shaman is an important political individual for religious reasons. "The individual's and the society's relation to the forces which govern their destinies always seem to be united in the person of the shaman."[162] In addition, in the case of Guaraní, since the phases of agriculture and hunting are determined by the shaman's dream songs, his ecstatic passage into the realm of the sacred becomes an important instrument in the local economy.[163]

In summary, techniques of ecstasy offer the shaman control over passage to other realms of the cosmos: heavens, underworlds, inner worlds, and the domains of forest, water, and mountain. The shaman's physical form accommodates itself to the traffic of his or her soul, offering instrumental control of cosmic appetites and consumptive processes that substantively transform the spirit. In this sense, the shaman's body is like the fire or poison whose consumptive process he masters to produce changes in spirit. As bearer of the cigar and crystals of light, the shaman acquires or harnesses the heat of supernatural existence, transports it into human existence, and maintains it, protecting it against the ravages of time in this world. These techniques ensure that the shaman's passage to other realms is concrete — a transformation of his entire condition of being. Able to accommodate himself to the inaccessible reaches of the universe, the shaman is the ideal mediator between incompatible modes of being. The specialist's familiarity with the spirit world offers control, poise, and orientation in circumstances that defy the ordinary imagination. This is why the shaman in South America can act as a psychopomp to guide souls from life to death; as a curer, returning lost souls to the land of the living; and, at times, as political leader interpreting the encounter with colonial beings whose reality is shaped by other conditions of time and space.

CLAIRVOYANCE

Shamans possess extraordinary vision. The ecstatic passage of the shaman not only lightens the body so that it soars as a primordial being, weightless and free, but it also enlightens the sight of the shaman. Shamans see spaces and times no longer fully manifest.[164] Henry reported that Kaingáng shamans could constantly "see" certain spirits. This clairvoyance marked them as specialists. The spirits they saw were Fish, Wasp, Howler Monkey, and so on — the beings of the first age. As usual, the specialist's skill served the community. Shamans pointed out these spirits to others so that they, too, might thenceforward maintain a relationship in which these spirits served as their guardians.[165] In fact, by the time (1932–1934) of Henry's visit, all the shamans had died and the Kaingáng were left without visible means of introduction to their protecting spirits. Henry was able only to gather reports of what had once been the shaman's function. The people attributed the disintegration of their group to the loss of shamanic clairvoyance.

Shamanic "seeing" is a total experience. It cannot be understood as the functional exercise of a single set of independent organs. To see in a new and extraordinary way means that the shaman must assume a new, extraordinary form of being. As the shaman is immersed in pure light, unimaginable colors of sacred realities suffuse his entire substance or concentrate themselves within him as crystals. Experience of heavenly light and supernatural apparition (in dream, trance, ecstasy, and stupor) sharpens and reshapes perception. The supernatural light remakes the "eye" and offers it an acuity, a focus penetrating the heart of invisible realities. Gone is the darkness that marks the distinctions between forms and separates them from one another. Shamans see reality in its immediate state. For example, the central concept of Akawaio spiritual life is *akwa* — "light, brightness, life" — found "in the sun's place." [166] *Akwa* is a state of being for which the sun stands as a symbol. Based on one's relationship to *akwa*, one takes on a supernatural condition as either an *akwalu* (a spirit; lit., "a kind of light") or an *akwalupö* (a ghost, or shade; lit., "without light"). It is the shaman who sees, and therefore experiences, the realm of light, of true life. These basic concepts of Akawaio culture were not lost as these Carib-speakers absorbed beliefs and practices of evangelical Christianity to create the Hallelujah religion. The prophets and founders of the new religion are portrayed as powerful shamans who made ecstatic journeys to the sky. The clairvoyance of the Makusi founder of the Hallelujah religion permitted him to have direct knowledge of God without need of any intermediary.[167] Likewise, the Akawaio founder of Hallelujah, Abel, fell asleep while praying. His spirit *(akwalu)* wandered from his body to heaven where it saw *akono* (from the English word "archangels"), and *engelö-dong* ("angels"), as well as sacred food and drink.[168]

Clairvoyance overcomes distance. The shaman recovers that condition of knowledge that existed before separation intervened. Such is the case with the Jívaro shaman. Essential to his tasks of harming and healing is the supernatural ability of the shaman "to see" things hidden to normal human vision. The harming shaman sees his intended victim at impossible distances and sees the spirits who will assist him in his menacing task. For example, he sees *wakani* ("spirit") birds, to whom he entrusts *tsentsak*, magical darts regurgitated from his stomach. These *wakani* then perch near the intended victim. If the victim is cured by a healing shaman, the *wakani* bird throws a new *tsentsak* into the victim.[169]

Just as their being overcomes space and time to enter other cosmic realms, the vision of shamans penetrates matter in the same way as primordial light. Solid mass presents no obstacle. The sight of shamans overcomes the distinctness of corporeal forms. They see into bodies with the power of the inner light that shapes their new being. The Krahó shaman, for example, sees at enormous distances, or sees hidden things. Concealed objects include pathogens that a helper spirit, appearing in a vision, inserts into bodies so that the apprentice shaman may practice finding and removing them.[170] By the authority of their own visions, Krahó shamans also become experts on the land of the dead and the nature of the afterlife.[171]

The reciprocity between supernatural light and the shaman's ability to see is extended even further. Seeing realities no longer fully manifest in this world is related to the shaman's invisibility. The connection with light and vision explains why the most important power that the Kari'ña *puidei* possesses is the ability to become invisible.[172] This power is based upon the *puidei*'s supernatural ability to see his own reflection in the eyes of ordinarily invisible supernatural beings. Clairvoyance and invisibility are achieved as part of the same process of gradual transformation that occurs during the shaman's initiation. Initiation is carried out under the direction of ancient dead shamans who are mountain spirits.[173] The *puidei* begins his career by making nocturnal journeys to the mountain twice a week. During this time, he continues to work and relate to the people around him in a normal way during the day, although he does observe some restrictions, abstaining from meat and sex. In past times, the isolation of the shaman was more marked: he remained in seclusion, smoking tobacco and eating only cassava and fish. Before ever seeing spirits, the novice prepares for his nocturnal journeys by rubbing his eyes with a tobacco and ginger mixture during the late afternoon. Once visions begin to happen he will prepare for his journeys by rubbing his eyes with a *Capsicum* pepper mixture. It is worth noting that his eyes are treated with substances used normally to stimulate the mouth; that is, his vision is somehow connected with actions (eating and producing ordered sounds) normally associated with the mouth. At first he sees spirits only as dark shadows, for they are wearing "masks" that prevent a clear vision of their eyes. Because *their* eyes are covered, *he* cannot see well. "When the candidate *puidei* succeeds in discovering the eyes of his teacher *(maware)*, he then glimpses this 'little man,' the Celestial Spirit, and thus comes into possession of him."[174] The spirit will not see or recognize the candidate until the candidate sees him, a fact that explains the eye preparations and the ceaseless insistence on the phrase chanted during this stage of initiation (and later as well): "Me, me, here I am."[175] Invisibility and intangibility of the shaman's existence demonstrate his intimacy with supernatural realities. He gains sight to the degree that his whole being is transformed by the heavenly realities he sees reflected in his own heightened vision.

SEEING SUPERNATURAL LIGHT WITH SACRED PLANTS
The desire for a complete transformation achieved through the experience of extraordinary light and signaled by the capacity to see sacred realities renders magical plants an important part of the shaman's technical repertoire. Rubbing tobacco or *Capsicum* peppers on his eyes sharpens the Kari'ña shaman's sight. But the matter hardly ends there: South American

cultures, perhaps more than those in any other region of the world, make religious use of plants that spark luminous visions. Knowledge of hallucinogenic plants controls the encounter with figures of light. The power of these sacred plants rearranges the shaman's entire sensible being and lifts him or her to another plane of unearthly light. Often, for instance, Mataco *aiawu* make spirit journeys to the sky, especially to Orion, with the additional aid of snuff of *hatax* (cebil, *Piptadenia macrocarpa*).[176]

Visions of supernatural realities induced by the ingestion of sacred substances do not appear through a simple and automatic chemical process. Every step of preparation, both of the infusion and of the participants, is ritually controlled.[177] Sexual abstinence, fasting (which produces a state of dehydration), vomiting and prescribed diarrhea, choices of time of day, the position of the participant, and so on are all carefully controlled because they contribute to the experience. Whether one sits in darkness or close to the fire is a matter that is controlled by the shaman. As Reichel-Dolmatoff reports,

> Acoustical stimulations are said to be of importance. The sudden sound of the seed rattles, the shrill notes of a flute, or the long-drawn wails of the clay trumpets are said to release or to modify the luminous images that appear in the field of view after a few drinks of the narcotic potion. As a matter of fact, the entire ritual is *orchestrated*, so to say, in a very complex fashion, and no sounds, movements, or light effects are quite arbitrary occurrences, but obey an overall plan of well-defined and predetermined sensory signals.[178]

The shaman both orchestrates the hallucinogenic séance and defines and interprets the graphic symbols that constitute the experience.[179] The Tukano-speakers, for instance, recognize that the state of being one enters in hallucination is arrived at and understood in successive and guided stages that are determined by the particular kind of plant, the details of the ritual setting, the state of the individual's personal preparation, and the situation of the community as a whole. The ability to travel and to see other realities involves one's entire physical, social, and spiritual being. Intellection alone cannot bring one into the supernatural world and it cannot make one see. The shape and color of designs and figures seen in trance reveal the degree to which one has successfully entered the various degrees of knowledge and reality.[180] These designs cover the Tukano bodies, houses, pottery, barkcloth aprons, masks, stamping tubes, and so on. Art, a representation of the supernatural realities seen in visions, gradually transforms the communal setting so that it looks like the spheres of reality glimpsed during hallucinogenic journeys.[181]

Based on his field work among the Jívaro in 1956–1957 and again in 1964, Harner provides vivid descriptions of the light-reality that shamans see. Through the use of hallucinogenic plants, the shaman completely and concretely enters another, normally unmanifest, dimension of existence. His vision effects his primordial intimacy with sacred beings. Harner writes,

> He had drunk, and now he softly sang. Gradually, faint lines and forms began to appear in the darkness, and the still music of the *tsentsak*, the spirit-helpers,

arose around him. The power of the drink fed them. He called, and they came. First, *pangi*, the anaconda, coiled about his head, transmuted into a crown of gold. Then *wampang*, the giant butterfly, hovered above his shoulder and sang to him with its wings. Snakes, spiders, birds and bats danced in the air above him. On his arms appeared a thousand eyes as his demon helpers emerged to search the night for enemies.

The sound of rushing water filled his ears, and listening to its roar, he knew he possessed the power of *tsungi*, the first shaman. Now he could see. Now he could find the truth. He stared at the stomach of the sick man. Slowly, it became transparent like a shallow mountain stream, and he saw within it, coiling and uncoiling, *makanchi*, the poisonous serpent, who had been sent by the enemy shaman. The real cause of the illness had been found.[182]

According to the Jívaro, only in the controlled circumstances of ritual performed with the aid of sacred hallucinogenic substances may the shaman see the real forces that underlie the illusion of conscious life.[183]

The place of hallucinogens in shamanism should neither be exaggerated nor isolated from other features exhibited during the call, training, and practice of this specialist in the human soul. Shamanic ecstasy by no means depends on hallucinogenic plants in all cases, not even in South America.[184] In any event, neither possession of the plant as a piece of property nor the privilege of ingesting it distinguish the shaman. Rather, the shaman's knowledge of the symbolism and meaning of the plant stands distinct because it bases itself on controlled, ecstatic intimacy with the sacred realities revealed in the myths of a given culture. The power to discern spirits, which is based on the shaman's metamorphosis during ecstasy, distinguishes the specialist's control over hallucinogenic techniques as it does his control over other forms of knowledge. Clairvoyance is a function of changes in the physiology of the shaman's soul. The shaman's material senses adjust to his existence in the realm of clear light. There, where invisible beings see all creation, the shaman develops a glance that penetrates both material and unmanifest form with perfect clarity.

MASTER OF SONG AND SOUND

Shamans are masters of music because of their intimacy with the powerful sounds of the primordial world. The noises of mythic beings were instruments of the world's passage into its present shape. Their groans, roars, squeaks, and tinkles created and transformed the world, which is why these sounds serve as the bass line for magical music. By creating variations on the primordial theme, the shaman replicates these sacred sounds to evoke a new way of existing.

THE GOURD-RATTLE

The rattle is the most important sonic emblem of the shaman in South America.[185] Métraux esteemed the gourd-rattle as "the most sacred object" among the tropical tribes of South America. He considered it the instrument *par excellence* of the shaman,[186] for it provokes and controls ecstasy for shamans across the face of the continent. Its origins and symbolism offer deeper understanding of the shaman's view of the world.

The South American shaman's gourd-rattle forms part of a large mosaic of use for sacred gourds. The composite includes the gourd found in myths of the creation and divination as well as the gourd used as an amulet, as a container of medicines, and so on.[187] The religious complexity of the gourd rivals its antiquity. The *Lagenaria* bottle gourd, according to Carl O. Sauer, "is often cited as the one cultivated plant common to both the Old and the New World."[188] It must be cultivated in order to be preserved. It has been found in Peruvian gravesites and, especially in Nazca, served as a model for ancient pottery.[189] That it never served as food is noteworthy. Nonetheless, native trade carried it further than pottery.[190] Donald Lathrap hypothesizes that the white-flowered bottle gourd *Lagenaria siceraria*, holds the key to agricultural and cultural systems in South America. "[M]etaphorically the gourd is a womb. . . . [I]t is the whole universe, or, stated more simply, the universal womb, . . . the womb in which all more elaborate agricultural systems developed."[191] He continues, "The artificial propagation of the bottle gourd and certain other technologically significant crops such as cotton and fish poisons imposed particular disciplines on man and in the context of these behavioral patterns all of the other nutritionally significant agricultural systems arose."[192] We cannot rule out of consideration the religious motivations that prompted the dissemination of this plant. In every place where we know something of the cultural values assigned to it, it looms large as a sacred instrument.[193]

Karl Izikowitz once outlined a symbolic complex associated with the bottle gourd *(Lagenaria vulgaris)*, which includes its use as a container for alkaloid solvent, its carved star-shaped lid, its use as a container of magical sounds (e.g., "insect musicians"),[194] and ceramic imitations of these gourd-boxes.[195] Gourd containers are among the earliest doctor's accoutrements found in South America. A polished *Lagenaria vulgaris* gourd, covered with red and yellow windings of yarn, was found in a Tiahuanacoid tomb in highland Bolivia dating from approximately 650–850 CE.[196]

The power contained in gourds and gourd-rattles was more than medicinal. For instance, in the 1920s it was reported that the Chaco (Lengua) of Paraguay carried a gourd-rattle during journeys to strange places. Should an unfamiliar being or animal be seen, its image was engraved on the gourd, which then exerted control over the spirit of the new entity.[197] Métraux reported that people in the Pilcomayo River area used a gourd-rattle filled with sacred beetles on many different kinds of occasions when supernatural powers were needed: "to keep evil spirits at a distance, when [a man] wakes up after a bad dream, when some danger threatens at night, to gain the favor of a girl, to bring good luck to women who collect fruits, to ensure a big catch of fish or game, and to help the fermentation of algarroba beer."[198]

"I consider the *mbaraká* [gourd-rattle] the symbol of the Guaraní race,"

declared Curt Nimuendajú.[199] The gourd-rattle is indispensable for the sha-
man-led dances of the Apapocuvá (for example, during the Nimongarai feast,
when it is ceremonially painted). "It seems to me," wrote Nimuendajú,

> that its holiness and magical power reside especially in its "voice," i.e., in its
> sound. . . . [A]s soon as the *mbaraká* sounds, serious and solemn, it seems to
> invite one to present oneself before the divinity; at times it sounds strongly and
> wildly, transporting the dancers toward ecstasy; later, smooth and trembling, as
> if the desire of this tired race for its "mother" and for the repose of the "Land
> without Evil" was crying inside of it.[200]

From the very beginning of Avá-Chiripá shamanism, sound and power
have been intimately linked with one another. The gourd-rattle is the paradigm of that sacred sound. Kuarahy, the divine twin who is the sun, used
shamanic techniques to communicate with his father, the creator-god Nanderú Guazú. Fashioning himself a rattle *(mbaraká)*, he danced himself into
ecstasy "until his father [took] him away with him." [201] Because of Kuarahy's
success through the sound of his rattle, the *mbaraká* has remained the basic
shamanic tool according to all reports of Guaraní culture. In the earliest
reports of the Tupinambá, the ritual rattle was made of a gourd transfixed
with an arrow. Its sound was a direct communication of the supernatural
being dwelling in it. Four hundred years later, Bartolomé reported that the
Avá-Chiripá, who transfix their gourd-rattle with a wooden rod decorated
with feathers, listen to the rattle for the sounds of a spirit who calls other
spirits from inside the rattle. The sound is produced by a tiny fruit whose
truest form is to be found in *oka-vusú* (paradise).[202]

Sound is a suitable symbol of the shaman. Like the shaman's soul, emitted sound has an ecstatic existence. The sound of primordials assumes an
autonomous life outside and beyond them. Thus, for example, the sound of
the master of an animal species, according to the Kari'ña and others, takes on
new, distinct form as the animals of the species that makes that sound. From
the perspective of human beings, sound is perceived as a reality *expressed* (or
expelled) from the inner being of primordial masters of animals. It takes on
independent existence as an audible form. Sound comes out of some being
or body (the mythic figure, the rattle, or the shaman) and stands as a well-defined, concrete presence of its own. Sound is like the shaman's soul in
ecstasy. The Baniwa explicitly identify the rattle with the ecstatic soul. The
Baniwa shaman's rattle represents his soul, which travels throughout the
universe during his ecstasy. The rattle, image of the shaman's soul, is called
"the companion of snuff," the menstrual blood of the celestial male culture
hero, Kuai. The shaman may also use his rattle for cures that require sucking,
for the rattle extracts the pathogen.[203]

Alternately, the rattle may be a metonym of ecstasy, a substantial token
of the ecstatic state. According to Daniel de Barandiarán,[204] for example, the
Sanemá-Yanoama shaman journeys to the clouds where Lightning lives and
receives the gourd-rattle from his hands. The shaman fills the rattle with

elements he collects in subsequent voyages to the heavenly dwelling place of the supreme divinity, Omao.

There is still another direct relationship between the rattle and ecstasy. The rattle of a divine being may provoke the human soul to exit the body. Among the Tapirapé, for instance, the supernatural being Thunder is extremely powerful and dangerous. Thunder's rattle is particularly dangerous to the shaman, for it induces in the shaman who touches it a permanent state of ecstasy (i.e., death). Each year the Tapirapé shamans stage a four-day ceremony to fight with Thunder and the *topü*, Thunder's children, who shoot lightning into the shaman's body. "When a shaman is shot by *topü*, he falls screaming upon the ground, writhing and shaking, and then becomes unconscious." [205] In this trance, the shaman's soul wanders through the cosmos and visits the house of Thunder. If he touches Thunder's rattle he will remain in ecstasy; he will die. Usually, however, he is revived with blowing of tobacco smoke. The shaman's own rattle is also dangerous. Only he, as master of heat, may touch it without expiring. [206]

The Kari'ña shaman's ritual *maraka* is different from the sacred dance rattles used on ceremonial occasions. The rattle of the Kari'ña shaman repeats the first rattlesnake's sound, its essence. The primordial rattler originated a sacred dance at the beginning of time. The sound and body-rhythms of the dance held the secret power of attraction that enables one to kill enemies and to attract women. [207]

The structure of the Kari'ña shaman's rattle gathers the powers active throughout the cosmos. The construction of the rattle and the composition of its elements amount to a creation of the cosmos. Near the top of a calabash the shaman burns four large holes (the four winds), which form a cross marking the four directions. In addition to these there are four rows of holes with four holes each emerging from the center to form a crisscross through the intercardinal axis-points. [208] Inside the rattles are two handfuls of seeds and four stones. The seeds are the voices of many different spirits, who are called on to cure specific diseases, and the pebbles, found on the mountain at the center of the universe, are the principal spirits of the mountain (i.e., the four winds) converted into stone. They are the four great "fathers," the primordial *puidei* who created and control all the other spirits. They manage the *maraka*. Power enters the *maraka* when the shaman sucks tobacco smoke into his lungs and then blows it into the *maraka* through the four large holes. The four winds enter in the prescribed order in which their names are blown. The wind spirits are enticed by the attractive smell of tobacco smoke in the *maraka* and respond by leaving their home on the mountain and entering the *maraka*. [209] One by one, as their song is sung, they drift out through the holes with the tobacco smoke, which is their "clothing." [210] The first and most important wind-spirit appears in the form of a cloud of smoke hovering over the rattle. He sings the songs which call the three others. Together with the shaman they chant the sacred songs *(aremi)* of all the spirits called to the rattle. Shaking the rattle makes audible the "sound" of these helper spirits' voices while they consume tobacco smoke, the symbolic form of their own appearance. "You know nothing," explained one Kari'ña shaman concerning the powers in the rattle, "but they know on your behalf and with them you call upon their offspring, all the spirits you want, those spirits of all the seeds in the maraka." [211] The seed-spirit sounds are able to cure.[212] The four main spirits of the winds are the ones dispatched to do harm.[213]

The structures of the Warao shaman's rattle also embody the dynamic forces — symbolized especially in fire, light, and poison — of the entire cosmos. As master of the gourd rattle, the Warao *wishiratu* (shaman) is a master of fire. The Warao look upon the shamanic gourd-rattle as an instrument of fire, for it is fire that empowers it. The gourd contains yellow crystals, which are hot and bright celestial spirits. With the gourd-rattle, the shaman fights the *hebu*, the spirits of heat and fever. The Warao rattle originated when a primordial shaman ascended to the celestial realm to visit the spirit of the south, who handed his guest the *hebumataro* ("spirit calabash").[214] The Warao shaman's rattle is the center of the universe. Its handle is the vertical path that rises to the celestial vault. Along this road the ecstatic shaman's soul journeys to heaven. After death, the *wishiratu*'s soul enters the yellow crystals in the rattle and ascends into heaven as bright heat in the form of a shooting star, a comet, or a lightning bolt.

The Warao rattle is constructed in a way quite similar to the Kari'ña rattle. The ritual of constructing the instrument that defines the center of the universe is a cosmogonic act. After selecting and preparing the appropriate gourd (a fruit of the *Crescentia cujete*), the shaman cuts four "mouths" on the rattle's "head." Designs represent teeth. The head is filled with yellow quartz crystals, embodiments of spirits who are fed with tobacco smoke. These are the "family" of spirits who protect the shaman. Fastening the handle to the head represents the joining of male and female elements in the universe, an act of fertilization that makes the sounds of the instrument effective and creative. A ruffle of feathers (described as "hair") is attached to the tip of the rattle. The rattle is kept in a temple hut, guarded by supernatural jaguars.

The Warao shaman uses his rattle's fire to fight the fire of poison and fever in his patients. While the shaman sings and rattles himself into ecstasy, the gourd actually showers a rain of sparks. "[T]hrough rapid rotation and shaking, the pebbles within the calabash shave off a fine meal from the highly combustible wood of the central shaft. These particles ignite in the heat generated by the whirling crystals and fly out as glowing sparks through the rattle's four mouths." [215] The calabash is nicknamed the "wand of Canobo" (Canobo is the supreme being). It is brought down on the patient's body like a club which beats away the hot spirits of disease.

These detailed reports begin to clarify why the shaman's rattle is of unsurpassed sacredness in so many South American cultures. Through its sounds, its fixtures, its inhabitants, and its ties to the shaman's ecstasy, it represents the sum total of the sacred forces of the cosmos itself. Because the rattle's various parts symbolize the structures of the world, making a gourd-rattle recreates the universe and situates the human being at its center. Cutting mouths into the gourd reinstigates the cosmic hunger for being, which even spirits experience. By means of the rattle the shaman feeds the spirits tobacco spiritualized through fire and maintains the physical well-being of the community. Safeguarding the rattle and playing it properly during ritual fulfills the destiny of the human spirit to sustain the order of existence.

MAGIC SONGS AND MUSIC

The shaman's mastery of primordial sound is not limited to the noise of the *maraka*. Shamans cultivate song and other forms of music. Their acquisition of melodies and rhythms and the ends toward which they apply them remain consonant with shamans' ecstatic vocations. According to a study of the Mapuche by Mariani Ramírez, music is the fundamental technique for entering into the ecstasy central to several shamanic rituals: *ñeicurehuén*, celebrated to cure a sick *machi* (shaman); *machitún*, for diagnosis and cure; *rehuentún* (or *machiluhun*), the initiation of a *machi;* and *nguillatún*, prayers offered to the supreme being, Nguenechen.[216] The ceremony called *ñeicurehuén* has three purposes: the cure of a *machi*, the instruction and partial initiation of new novices to the state of *machi*, and the renewal of the *rehue*. The *rehue*, or *prahue*, is a trunk of oak thick enough for a *machi* to dance on top of it and thus communicate with the spirits. It has at least five notches cut into it and is surrounded by lances, thick branches of the cinnamon tree, and vessels that contain the blood and hide of a sacrificed lamb.[217] The shaman's music controls the entire ritual sequence. The ceremony is marked into episodes by the kinds of instruments played, the rhythm and melodies chosen, the dances used to accompany the songs and so on. The principal instruments are the *cultrún*, a drum made in the form of a truncated cone decorated with symbolic designs and colors especially associated with the rainbow that connects heaven and earth; the *cascahuilla*, a metal bow hung with bells; and the *huasa*, a calabash gourd-rattle. Over a long period of time, the music and dancing led by the oldest female shaman induces a deep trance state in which, one by one, all the *machi*s faint dead away on the ground. They fall in a row facing east.[218] They are revived by drum-playing *machi*s, who spray them with water squirted from their mouths. All during this time wooden whistles are blown at full force by two individuals who face each other directly. One plays a high note and the other a low note. The fainting and reviving episodes continue until a strong emotional climax is reached. At that point, the *machi*s ascend the *rehue* and, having arrived at the top of the post, stare off into heaven in a state of ecstasis. A young lamb is then sacrificed by extracting its palpitating heart, which is passed around the circle of *machi*s so that they can leave their teeth marks in it. The face, head, and breast of a sick *machi* is smeared with blood from a piece of the sacrificed lamb. Music and fainting spells continue, as do the showers of water produced by spraying out mouthfuls imbibed from a ritual gourd. At this point, the words of the songs describe the renovation of the *rehue*. Holding hands, the *machi*s form a circle and dance around the new *rehue*. Before the sun sets, the old *rehue* is carried away.[219]

The shaman's songs replicate sounds heard in other worlds during ecstasy. For example, the chant of the Warao dark-shaman imitates the crying of the infant son of Soul-Hoebo at the zenith of heaven. When the novice makes his first journey to that height, he pledges to bring his share of grisly food to feed the hungry child.[220] Warao shamanic songs become instruments of the ecstasy they signify. Thus, for instance, when the *wishiratu* (the Warao priest-shaman, helped by his celestial *hebu* spirits) sings, he is no longer an ordinary human being. "[T]he shaman becomes the spirit about which he sings."[221] Singing is the principal efficacious gesture of control over the spirits — so concluded the investigator Dale Olsen: "Is it possible that music alone, without the aid of hallucinogens, is capable of causing the religious leader, the shaman, to reach an altered state of consciousness in which he has contact with the supernatural world? I believe it is, at least within the curing context of Warao shamanism."[222] The total involvement with the supernatural world that occurs during the shaman's ecstatic trance "is unthinkable and indeed impossible without music."[223] The very structure of shamanic curing songs among the Warao possesses a dramatic-plot quality, a mythic-narrative structure in two parts. The first part is the melodic "naming" section, which identifies the pathogenic spirit.[224] This first episode is marked by a melodic expansion of the tones sung, from the normal spread of a fifth to intervals of minor and major sixths, minor and major sevenths, an octave, or even a minor ninth. The second movement of the curing songs indicates the presence of a supernatural or mythological character who loosens, removes, or devours the pathogen. The episode is distinguished by an "upward drift" of the singer's tones, "a gradual and continuous microtonal rise in pitch."[225]

The songs of the shaman do not merely serve to control the shaman's own ecstasy. As the specialist himself does, the melodies affect the wider community. They are the fruit of the shaman's altered being. The Toba *yeyátten*'s voice, for instance, is particularly efficacious. Quite apart from the words he sings, the specialist's songs work wonders. His musical instruments are similarly powerful objects.[226] All across South America, shamans perform music on behalf of the sick.[227] The Mataco provide a fairly typical illustration. The most potent possession of the Mataco shaman is the sacred song he uses during his healing rites. "The song, obtained by revelation rather than by instruction, is his own property."[228] Indeed, the song seems to form part of the curer's mature personality. The musical instruments of the Mataco *aiawu* "have a power and almost a life of their own."[229] It is important to note, however, that this power is not simply an automatic mechanism associated with the musical instrument. Rather, it is a sacred power acquired by degrees as the specialist practices his art. The power of the music inheres in the personality of the performer; that personality, in turn, is shaped by his enduring ties with the spirit world. As the specialist uses his rattle over time, he learns to communicate more effectively with his deceased colleagues and develops a better rapport with beings in the supernatural dimension. The instrument gains in power as the shaman develops progressively better relationships with powerful beings and gradually acquires the professional knowledge communicated by them. The power and personality of these Mataco specialists is so intimately connected with music and sacred song that when an individual terminates his apprenticeship, the proper expression is, "This one already sings his song." [230]

Songs of shamans sometimes form the heart of the political community. Among the Piaroa Indians of the forests of southern Venezuela, the shaman is the *menyerua*, the "man of the songs" who also serves as head man of the local group.[231] The *menyerua* helps ward off disease from the community and cures the sick. He recounts the mythical traditions, prepares ritual objects, presides over initiations, and organizes the most important of seasonal festivals, the Warime. His most powerful religious tools are chants, which he sings almost every day. The chants have an epic quality. They describe the stalking and killing of the mythical animals who existed at the beginning of time. When the *menyerua* sings, everybody hears the supernatural beings, for the slain mythical beasts are actually "the narrators" of the magic epic-songs. The sound of the shaman's voice assures the Piaroa that the mythic characters continue to be present in human affairs. The songs compose the totality of a rich and complex reality.[232]

Curing and healthy political life are not the only goods accomplished through shamanic music. With their songs, shamans bring favorable weather or plentiful game to their communities. For example, the Waiwai *yaskomo* summons game from the "fathers" *(yin)* of various animal species. Peccaries are attracted to the stone that the shaman holds in his mouth while he sings the wild-peccary song. As the animals come through the forest toward him, his residence-mates take their prey. However, the *yaskomo* can neither kill the animals nor eat the meat taken in this way.[233]

For several reasons, deciphering the meaning of shamanic songs has been slow and difficult. For one thing, their focus on the role of words has — given the unintelligibility of the language in shamanic songs — distracted investigators and led to misunderstanding. Convinced that the meaning of the songs lay in the words, many visitors found the lyrics inarticulate expressions of a trance state. Henry, to choose a typical example, found the Kaingáng curing songs meaningless because the words made no sense. He admitted, nonetheless, that "the symbolism of the song and cry is transparent to the Kaingáng." [234] Some investigators concluded that shamans sang in archaic languages unfamiliar to the investigator.

Also, attempts to delineate the aesthetic criteria that set shamanic melodies or rhythms apart as a distinct musical category failed when judgments were made solely on the basis of acoustical data. The formation of aesthetic categories and genres is not external to their religious meaning. The origin of the songs in the realm of space and time visited by the shaman during ecstasy and the symbolism that links the sounds to primordial events form essential features of their aesthetic and musical character. The tone and rhythm of a chant revealed in dream-sleep are more important than the unintelligible words. Such is the case for the Guaraní shaman, who accomplishes his indispensable services to the community because of the power of his dreams and the strength of his songs. If he is indeed powerful, his songs reactualize in all their potency the supernatural forces he encounters in his dreams.[235] Based on this criterion of power, Bartolomé distinguishes several categories of Avá-Chiripá shamanic songs. His first distinction is that between sacred songs *(guaú)* and profane songs *(koti-hú)*, which latter cannot reactualize supernatural beings. A further distinction is made between true sacred songs *(guaú eté)*, which are more powerful, and little sacred songs *(guaú aí)*, which are less so.

Every Avá-Chiripá human being may possess a personal song for his or her lifetime. These songs appear to fall into four categories based upon the degree of power they contain. Healing shamans possess the most powerful chants, for they can represent and recreate the very divinities seen during the dream journeys of song acquisition. "The shamanistic chant or prayer is like a bridge which permits communication between the world above and the world below." [236] Every person sings his or her song to the supernatural being or divinity that reveals itself in that individual's dream. The names of these divine beings figure prominently in the performance. The most powerful shaman's songs mention Nanderú Guazú, Tupá, Kuarahy, and Yacy.[237]

Avá-Chiripá shamans sing the "true sacred songs" in words that are completely unintelligible and may reflect the vestiges of an archaic sacred language.[238] Even the "little sacred songs" are sung in an archaic form of Guaraní, which makes agreement on their meaning quite impossible. For example, a great many of these songs consist of a single word, *engay* ("yearning"). "This word is repeated continually but with great changes in rhythm and melody in each individual case." [239]

UNINTELLIGIBLE SOUND, BLOWING AS SILENT SOUND, AND APPROXIMATING THE MEANING OF ABSOLUTE SILENCE

The unintelligibility of powerful shamanic songs leads in two directions. The first ends in the suppression of articulate phonemes, reducing singing to whispers, murmurs, or inarticulate blowing. The second ends with the development of an esoteric language, a set of distinct sounds intelligible only to the initiated. In both cases, the shaman remains the master of sound.

In the execution of Kari'ña harmful magic, blowing "silent" sounds through tobacco smoke attracts and captures a victim's soul. These sounds of silence underline the fact that "sound" is, first and foremost, an image, an intelligible and communicative expression common to all being. All existence has a sonic structure that, given certain levels of perceptive consciousness, becomes audible. Magical "blowing" invokes precisely the same reality as sound, except that only powerful shamans and spirits with extremely subtle senses hear it. In fact, acts of "silent" blowing are to sound what invisibility is to sight: the form that the most potent entities assume. For example, one of the most intense acts of the Kari'ña shaman, the master of sound and speech, is the silent strutting he performs while breathing across a wad of tobacco and saliva. His strutting is a deliberate imitation of the "silent sounds," the irresistibly attractive call, of the heron's mating dance (an intense, precopulatory, ecstatic dance performed by both the male and female heron).[240]

Although Akawaio practices of ritual blowing are many and complex, the Akawaio theory of ritual blowing, *taling*, is comparable to that of other South American societies.[241] Ritual blowing, as opposed to unconscious breathing, is a performance, not merely a behavior. Effective ritual blowing relies upon deliberate, conscious knowledge of one's action. Consciousness and deliberation are signified and effected by fixed-form word charms interspersed with sudden expulsions of breath. The words of the charm express specific intentions or commands, which are carried out by the blower's vitality, which detaches itself from his or her body. A person's breath is intimately linked to, though distinguishable from, the person's spirit, or supernatural essence. This spirit of a person, *akwalu*, is in contact with *akwa*, the light and essential life of the sun. For this reason one's own spirit, embodied in breath, can be sent forth as an effective power.[242] Spirits as well as human beings may perform *taling* and apply it to good or evil ends. Evil blowing, used to sicken or kill a person, is performed by blowing tobacco smoke on an object that is then thrown in the direction of the intended victim. "It is the spirit of the object which goes out, enters the victim and makes him ill." [243] The most powerful sickening objects are spirit stones— quartz crystals, possessed by shamans, that house strong supernatural beings within them. "[T]he theory of blowing postulates two important principles — the efficacy of charm words and the power of the spirit associated with the breath." [244]

The relationship of blowing to spirit sound allows for interchangeability and creativity along the entire acoustical spectrum. Every spirit summoned to an Akawaio curing ceremony blows on the patient. The shaman must master each one of these blowing sounds. In the past, the Akawaio shaman learned during apprenticeship to construct and use the *maraka*, the gourd-rattle with seeds and pebbles inside. He used the *maraka* to imitate the blowing sounds of these spirits. However, in the 1950s the rattle was replaced by the *piai'čan yale* (shaman's leaves). These are gathered for the shaman by a person who must maintain vigil during the séance in which they are used. If the person who gathered the leaves should fall asleep, his or her spirit will block the way of the shaman's soul and prevent his ecstasy.[245] The novice shaman must learn to control all the subtleties of the leaves' sounds. The blowing sounds made by the rustling leaves effectively manifest the beneficent presence of the spirits. The sounds themselves are important and powerful. "According to one spirit song, the leaves give the shamans spirit wings (the *malik* . . .) to enable him to go to the mountains and under the ground." [246]

ESOTERIC LANGUAGE

Opposite, yet similar to, the indistinctness of blowing is the unintelligibility of the lyrics of many shamans' songs, whose meanings are deliberately couched in a language known only to the initiated. Occasionally the secret speech is an idiolect known only to the shaman and his spirit helpers. For example, Piaroa magical chants *(menye)* are described as so many "pearls on a necklace," which the religious specialist strings together into mythic epics. He sings them in an esoteric cant sometimes understood only by the mythical animal "narrators" whose mask the singer wears.[247]

In some respects, shamanic secret idioms can be fruitfully compared with other kinds of elite languages. The Warao, for instance, employ elite argots that serve to distinguish social statuses in Warao society. These means of communicating hide their true meaning from untutored hearers behind metaphors whose connotations cannot be known by those outside the group. They also foster prescribed and preferred interactions within the group. They encourage a density and intensity of communication in the group while lowering the incentive for communication with outsiders. To this extent, they also play a role in courtship and marriage alliance. At its deepest level, the meaning of an elite language (conveyed in tales about the use of the language) "carries a transcendent message for a Warao youth."[248] The lesson learned from its fathoming is that there is an entire world of meaning, "a metaphoric snare that lies out there in a foreign group or band, threatening to entangle him."[249] One needs to know more than the *words* that compose speech. To avoid disorientation in the network of meanings that composes reality one must master the significance of images and symbols and the wide fan of meanings they connote. In other words, the language that orients one in this life transcends speech to situate one within the creative powers of the imagination.

The function of shamanic secret speech goes beyond that of an elite jargon that serves to define exclusive groups and offer individuals poise. The purpose of the hidden language of shamans is to communicate with spirits in another realm. Its strangeness testifies to its efficacy: it makes sense only in another condition of existence. "According to Carib tradition, the first *piai* [shaman] was a man who, hearing a song rise from a stream, dived boldly in and did not come out again until he had memorized the song of spirit women and received the implements of his profession from them."[250]

Familiarity with secret language bespeaks the shaman's acculturation to the spirit world. During the seclusion of his apprenticeship, for instance, the Maroni River Carib shaman, whom Peter Kloos views primarily as a medical practitioner, learns the esoteric spirit cant of shamanic songs (*ale:mi*, "old songs"), which enables him to speak to the various categories of spirit helpers.[251]

As usual, the shaman's talent for esoteric talk serves the entire community. For example, the Makiritare shaman controls the ecstasy of every new generation by communicating with the spirits who transport the initiates' souls to other realms. He does this in his capacity as the *adehe ademi*, master of songs. His songs are sung in an esoteric language intelligible only to the initiated. Under his linguistic direction during sacred festivals, the Makiritare sing sacred songs *(ademi)* taught them at the beginning of time by the *sadashe* (masters of animals and prototypes of species), who cut down the tree of life, survived the subsequent flood, cleared the first yuca garden, and celebrated the first new garden festival:

> The sacred songs sung in the *Wanwanna* [sacred festival dances] are in a strange language very different from the everyday speech of the Makiritare. These ritual orations, called *ademi* or *aichudi*, belong to the language of the *sadashe*, the primordial spirits and masters of the tribes. The *ademi* were given for everyone at the beginning of time and cannot be altered in any way by men. Nevertheless, their semantic uniqueness does show signs of certain simple tricks of human origin: archaic words, others taken from neighboring tribes, more or less phonetically deformed, complicated ritual endings concealing words from normal daily usage, refrains with no definite meaning, inarticulate vocables, onomatopoeias, whistles, jungle and water sounds, animal movements. As the initiate begins to understand this language, he immediately grasps its phonetic essence, its music, without paying any attention to the meaning of the individual words. Those who still don't understand it, perceive no more than incoherent madness.[252]

The *ademi*, the sacred songs, must be repeated in the exact phonetic pattern in which the *sadashe* revealed them. The sound *is* the power. To change any of the sounds would not only deprive the sacred moment of its potency as a performative utterance to effect the initiation of the dancing candidates to a new social status "but also of its ability to communicate with the spirit world and thus influence it." [253]

Few studies of shamanic esoteric language are more precise or penetrating than de Civrieux's report on the Kari'ña theory of language. A presentation of some details of this theory gives some glimpse of its subtlety and sophistication. De Civrieux's data on shamanic language illustrate how the various capacities of the shaman (e.g., magic flight, mystical physiology, clairvoyance, and mastery of smoke, consumption, and sound) inhere as intrinsically related branches of a single complex of specialized knowledge.

The Kari'ña shaman is called a *puidei*, a clairvoyant who has mastered the speech of all forms *(dei)*, especially the sacred power-sounds of animals. Although human beings are ignorant and frail, they may obtain wisdom and power because of the primordial *puidei* who were able to communicate with animals and receive their powers during the times described in myth.[254] Of all the animals, birds occupy the central place in acquisition of knowledge and speech. The *puidei* is able to "see" sounds since he "sees" the true form (*tamurü*, "sound-name"), that is, the substantial wisdom and power, of every species (*wara*, beings with the same sound or language). He "sees the invisible." What he sees, in fact, is another *time*, since the sound-form of every species exists in true form only in the time of mythical prototypes.[255] Animals are simpler expressions of more complex celestial models *(kaputano)* existing in the *uba.poro*, the time of myth (lit., the "ancient dance" of the mythic beings).[256] By transforming himself into an *akurü*, a spiritual member of an animal *wara*, the shaman enters the time of true forms in "heaven." The idea of "seeing sounds," the normally invisible, true forms of all existence, is directly connected with dreaming, *enu.menka* ("to see the invisible").

Puidei are "masters of speech" because they know the deep meaning of certain elemental sounds, especially consonants, which may be interpreted on many different levels of reference. De Civrieux speaks of "a kind of Kari'ña Kabbalah." [257] The *puidei* may assume an unlimited number of aspects (*wei*, "forms, appearances") because, through the effective speech that allows him to make connections between all realities at their deepest level, he has moved out from under the influence of a narrow *emeri* (the extended family, the tradition which accounts for the shape of physical features as well as mannerisms). He joins the community of first beings, who could achieve any physical transformation and whose identity exists essentially in sound, invisible form. This community of powerful spirits gradually becomes the defining *emeri*, the community or historical tradition that shapes a shaman's *wei*, outward appearance and behavior. This is why a *puidei*'s technique is associated strictly with sound and why the shaman erases the lines between species and between humans and animals. *Weitopo* (from *wei*, "form," and *topo*, "technique") refers to the magical art of transformation, "that realm of forms [which exists] by virtue of the voice, of music, of dance." [258]

Both snake's venom and shaman's wisdom are transmitted through, literally, mordant speech (that is, speech which is incisive). Shamanic initiation is likened to a bite because the ancient wisdom shamans acquire is called *dyerü.mpuo* ("primordial tooth"), a name applied to the esoteric language sung by shamans, the masters of speech. The word *ekako*, which means "bite" and "puncture" but also "speak" and "explain," is the imperative form.[259] The physical organs of speech and knowledge are also the implements of consumption. The shaman knows the teeth, lips, mouth, and tongue both inside and out. He can speak food for thought because, like the living word, he has been bitten and chewed.[260]

The word *aremi* designates a special category of Kari'ña ritual songs, which act as irresistible calls to powerful spirits.[261] In fact, the *aremi* are nonreplicable beings, the very powers of the primordium. An *aremi* may not be improvised or composed but must be performed as a reenactment, a re-presentation in exactly the same form in which it existed at the beginning of time. This form which must be reproduced exactly is the song's *etiska*, the precise and original phonetic arrangement — the pronunciation that has been its sound-form since *uba.poro*, the beginning. *Etiska* ("pronunciation") is a compound word formed from *e.ti* ("sound, voice, call, whistle, name")[262] and *aska* ("soul, spirit").[263] The sounds are a repeatable and inexhaustible power, but they are not replicable. They do not generate more of themselves. They are always themselves as they were sung for the first time by mythical beings.

The secret language of Kari'ña shamans is called *derumpuo* and is the quintessence of the languages of all spirits and animals.[264] Since the power of each species *(wara)* is identified with its *aura* or *e.ti* ("voice, sound, way of singing"), each category of spirits is invoked in its own language. Although this is not a language of precise and concrete analytic and mutually exclusive words, de Civrieux concluded that it is indeed a language that "obey[s] the norms of well defined communication."[265] Any imprecision in this secret language appears to be linked to its ability to elaborate associations that are rich with meaning. Each word "means many things and can be translated in diverse ways."[266] The esoteric language of shamans is used only in strictly controlled circumstances wherein *puidei* identify themselves with their spirit helpers for positive reasons or to seek vengeance. "The *derumpuo* language does not express complex ideas so much as a mental state, psychic and obsessive. It has the monotonous and morbid character of an hypnotic litany and induces a heaviness and lethargic sleep."[267]

In *derumpuo* secret language, the *aremi* are called *avare*, ("call, invocation"). "In the *avare*, the sung voice of the *puidei* is accompanied by the 'voice' of his maraca (the voice of the *yakuari*, the helper-spirits who can be invoked). A 'dialogue' is established between the two until, finally, a perfect consonance and syntony is achieved between the human voice and the maraca. This reflects the union of the *puidei* and the spirit."[268] Throughout the *avare*, the *puidei* blows tobacco smoke, which attracts the spirit to his singing mouth. The shaman's "blowing" *(blolë)* is equated to the wind, power, or spirit that brings life to the tobacco whose names and fragrances attract the *yakuari*, the helper spirits. The *blolë* especially entices the spirits of the four winds to take up residence in the shaman's rattle, which is also filled with tobacco smoke. The overall goal of the *aremi* is to capture "the voice," the true invisible power, of spirits.

In esoteric language, a recurrent refrain of the *aremi* is the word *sepuedai*, the same word the *puidei* uses when directly addressing his spirit helper. The name is a variation of the word *puidei*, the ordinary term for a shaman. A second constant refrain in the *aremi* is "de edee edee," a group of sounds that derive from the word *de*, or *deri* ("tooth"), the root word that underlies the term *derumpuo*. *De* refers to the sharpness, knowledge, and powerfully wise tongue of the curer. Since curing and battle (struggle on the spiritual level) are the same thing, an important aspect of all *aremi* is the *puidei*'s declaration of his good intention *(iuspun)* to cooperate with *kurano*, constructive therapeutic power. Even *aremi* performed for vengeance are viewed as constructive and good intentions directed toward the elimination of evil, that is, as acts of justice. There seems to be a complete identification of the shaman's personality with the invoked supernatural power: "I am *kurano*, I am cure, the power to cure *(kurano au; kurano awa)*."[269] In what way techniques of ecstasy are at work here needs further clarification since "in magic language, *awa* and *au* indicate possession."[270]

The *aremi* open and close with special sounds or whistles that call and dispatch the desired spirit. Each *aremi* is the reenactment of events performed by mythical beings with whom the *puidei* becomes totally identified:

> Ededee edee, ededee edee [tooth, sharpness, wisdom, esoteric curing language]
> I am the same as you, I am spirit now, spirit *[sepuedai]*
> A bird am I, a white heron
> Just as I am a spirit . . .[271]

Once identified with the mythic being, the *puidei* takes its voice, its secret language, and the words that constitute its true and invisible being. These are the powers of cure. In identifying himself with a mythical sound which has an animal form, an *aremi*, and a dance, the *puidei* likewise identifies himself with the heavens and a particular constellation of stars.[272] Sounds ordered in ritual speech and movements ordered in ritual dance are coordinated with the ordered experience of time in this world-epoch, which is marked by the ordered procession of constellations through the sky.

There exist contemporary *aremi* sung in Spanish and based on a Christianized "neomythology" of Dioso, a god miraculously conceived in the womb of a girl by the snake master of the water domain. Dioso is eventually murdered in the battle he wages against demonic beings, but he rises from the dead in the form of the constellation Orion. These *aremi* ward off evil coming from *pañoros* (creoles) since they are sung in the sound proper to their species.[273]

SOUND AND SPECIAL VOCATION

Shamans' mastery of sound and song sets these ecstatics apart in the same way that all their knowledge does. Secrecy and specialization are not simply functions of information that they keep hidden from others. A shaman's mastery of sound requires a fundamental rearrangement of his or her being. The fact that this experience is not the vocation of the general public isolates shamans from the group.[274] The physiological changes of apprenticeship prepare shamans to learn the secrets of nature. Nowhere is this intimacy with the cosmos more apparent than in the fluency shamans acquire in esoteric languages of primordial animals and spirits. In learning to speak with the sounds of a rattle, feathers, leaves, wind, water, stones, or birds, the shaman understands the meaning of the paradisal life that existed before the world's catastrophic division into separate kinds, babbling and senseless. In the sound of its shaman, the human community learns that the cosmos makes sense. Humankind can live and communicate freely with being in all its forms.

FORM-SPECIALIST: TRANSFORMATION

The shaman specializes in the knowledge of other forms, other kinds of space. A number of factors contribute to the shaman's close association with the bodily forms of animals. Chief among these are intimate knowledge of the secrets of nature; transformed physiology, which, at times, assumes the form of primordial animals; ability to "know" (i.e., experience) life as it is conditioned by other kinds of space, including bodily shape; and expertise in consumption, which provides familiarity with the dynamics of the food chain.

The large jaguar *(Felis onca)* is the most dramatic and widespread form in which South American shamans appear. In his study of the ubiquity and meaning of the shaman-jaguar identification, Reichel-Dolmatoff identifies the heart of the issue:

[I]t is thought that a shaman can turn into a jaguar at will and that he can use the form of this animal as a disguise under which he can act as a helper, a protector, or an aggressor. After death, the shaman may turn permanently into a jaguar and can then manifest himself in that form to the living, both friend and foe, again in a benevolent or malefic way, as the case may be. . . . [T]he connection is so close that shamans and jaguars are thought to be almost identical, or at least equivalent, in their power, each in his own sphere of action, but occasionally able to exchange their roles.[275]

The identification of shamans and jaguars appears in the earliest reports of colonial chroniclers and continues into contemporary ethnography for the entire continent without respect for ecological, cultural, or linguistic barriers.[276] The predominance of the shaman's jaguar-transformation has been accounted for in various ways: the adaptability of the jaguar to all ecological zones (the water domain, land, and the "upperworld" of trees), the way in which its hunting behavior resembles that of humans, its admirable but fearful aggression, its reputed sexual prowess, its thunderous noise (tying it to violent weather), its involvement as an eponymous emblem in sociopolitical codes of descent, its moral ambivalence (expressed in symbolic links to incest), its capacity (as a symbol) to represent psychic experiences exacerbated by hallucinogens, and so on.[277] For the moment, it suffices to underline the complexity of jaguar imagery. This entanglement should be treasured and understood, for it testifies to the ancient and sophisticated history of religious ideas centered on shamanism. This thick knot of complex ideas should not be unraveled in favor of simple strands pulled from studies of natural history, chemical neurophysiology, or psychology during the last several decades. In assuming the form of a jaguar, the shaman also assumes the burden of a religious history that goes back to the primordium. The religious symbolism of the jaguar is already an interpretive gathering of ideas, practices, arts, and experiences with psychological, economic, and social value. Above all, by nearly every community in which shaman-to-jaguar transformation appears, it is regarded as a reality that is out of this world, a description of an entire condition of being that only specially transformed human beings can accomplish.

The total transformation of the human condition is an immense achievement, a conquest carried off by the human spirit. Everything ordinary about the human condition of the shaman is devoured, digested, and left behind as waste. The shaman's initiation, modeled on the events of mythical shamans, effects this total disintegration and metamorphosis. In this connection, the jaguar is the consummate consumer, the devourer of his prey. Given the insight of the apprentice shaman into the nature of consumptive processes as revealed in fire, in helper spirits, and in the images of ecstatic death, his identification with the arch-eater links him more surely to the cosmic processes of transformation. Consumption by the jaguar, parallel to the process of consumption by fire, produces spirit.[278] The shaman's mastery of jaguar form, like his control of fire, assures human control over the changes that make up the spiritual life. Through the shaman-jaguar complex, the spiritual significance of appetite (for food and sex), spirit-transformation, fire and light, death, generation, and rebirth are creatively cross-threaded, elaborated, and rewoven in unique cultural patterns.[279] Because the spiritual life enlivens all social and psychological reality, these same images appear in myths about the foundation of social units, the ordering of sexual mores, the institution of economic practices, and so on.

At times, the shaman's control over jaguar form is portrayed as an act of vanquishing supernatural jaguars. Primordial shamans may have conquered, banished, dismembered, or tamed mythic jaguars. Alternately, the battle may still rage on today. The Campa, for example, distinguish between their good shamans and the evil shamans whom they call *maníti* ("jaguars"). These jaguars are the souls of jaguar-shamans, transformed into felines when the shamans died.[280] The jaguar-shaman also presides over a number of jaguar "children." The valences of celestial and terrestrial realms are made clear in encounters between good shamans and jaguar-shamans: "the good shaman challeng[es] the jaguar to follow him in the form of a lightning flash, knowing that the jaguar can only run along the ground." [281] In keeping with the Campa notion that each realm of being has a different perception of the universe, it is said that jaguar-shamans see human beings in the form of peccaries and the dogs of the villagers as coatis. Jaguar-shamans, then, hunt human beings as if they were game animals. A good shaman can turn this fact to his advantage. In fact, jaguar-shamans are disposed of by trapping them in large pits in which they think they will find their favorite game. The hole is covered and the jaguar dies inside.[282] Another way of disposing of jaguar-shamans is for the good shaman to carry them beyond the eastern edge of the world's rim to a place called Impírani, where the jaguars themselves are consumed by fire.[283]

More often than battling jaguar adversaries to acquire power over them, shamans ally themselves with or become jaguars. Such is the case, for instance, among the Kari'ña, who make clear that the shaman's control over jaguar transformation is consistent with his general mastery of forms and spaces that contain different modes of being. The spirits of the four winds, pebbles in the Kari'ña shaman's *maraka*, may be sent in the form of jaguars who destroy enemies. The *puidei* sends them by singing while seated on his oak bench, which is carved in the form of a caiman with two heads, one male and one female. "With his *aremi*, with the power of the voice of the jaguar, the *puidei* himself is changed into a jaguar and devours the evil spirit." [284] This transformation is necessary for certain categories of affliction—for example, if the afflicting spirit is the Grandfather of Deer.

Evils are destroyed by being devoured. Different "domains" of evil require different song-spirits to consume them. The afflicting forms associated with the domain of earth are flies, worms, insects, and rats. Snakes, frogs, and fish are associated with water. The principal sources of affliction associated with the mountain domain are human beings themselves; these humanly generated diseases must be consumed with the help of heavenly constellations of stars and supernatural jaguars. Heaven is governed by various species of birds that may cause and cure affliction; the birds that can cure the afflictions of heaven are those which consume other species of birds.[285] The theoretical foundation of Kari'ña medicine is the cycle of consumption — a food chain that consumes all species of being and, paradoxically, sustains existence at the same time. To follow the cycle of consumption in the correct manner is to follow the ritual food and hunting restrictions that provide proper sustenance for each kind of being. To reverse the cycle of consumption is equally possible. However, this reversal would set into motion the negative and nonsustaining "consumption" of disease, which, because it is a nonreplicable power of consumption, would, if not controlled, eventually exterminate the transitional and sustained form of life of this world by returning it to the unitary state of being that existed before the appearance of human life. As master of consumption, the jaguar-shaman directs the dynamic of spiritual life and maintains its proper order. By embodying the power of consumption on behalf of his community, the shaman guarantees the existence and the viability of spiritual transformation.

BIRDS, SNAKES, AND OTHER ANIMAL FORMS

The shaman's special knowledge of other forms and spaces is not restricted to the privileged form of the jaguar. The discussion of ecstatic flight has already stressed the importance of the shaman's transformation into a mythical bird (often a raptor). In this free condition, unfettered by darkness and weight, the soul soars through the world of the beginnings of time.[286] The shape of social life itself may depend on the shaman's ability to become more than one kind of animal. The power of shamans to assume different animal shapes and the variety of souls and knowledge that they acquire in doing so form the basis of Canelos Quichua kinship and social organization. Shamans are the key nodes that make possible the outward ramification of the consanguinal and affinal chains of Canelos Quichua kinship.[287] The shaman plays this role because he forms a link to the Ancient Times, a link that makes knowledge and the continuity of generations possible. Contemporary shamans are able successfully to act because shamans in Ancient Times were powerful and effective in both acquiring and transmitting souls. In particular, these ancient shamans knew the art of *sumi*, by which one could transform one's body into that of an animal (especially a jaguar), and they knew how to project their souls into indestructible containers, especially stones or large tree trunks.[288] When ancient shamans died, they sent their souls into rocks and indestructible logs, from which other ancient shamans could acquire them by drinking a secret substance. This second set of shamans, now possessing acquired souls, could patiently practice the art of *sumi* so that they might eventually send their own souls into stones. In the meantime, the soul acquired from the original shaman soul-stone was liberated to enter the body of an owl or harpy eagle *(apapa)*. "All owls and eagles are ancient souls." [289] Eventually, the soul moves from the defunct *apapa* into the form of a polished shaman's stone *(yachaj rumi)*. Here is evidence of a complicated system of metempsychosis wherein the soul moves from ancient shaman to stone *(aya rumi)* to harpy eagle or owl to *yachaj rumi*, the shaman's stone.[290]

It should be noted that bodily transformation, the changing of body-space, is connected to transition through time. By means of this technique, Canelos Quichua shamans have been able to recover some of the knowledge lost in past times. During the epoch called the Times of Destruction, many of these soul-stones became lost and took on unfamiliar animal forms in unknown locations. In some cases, for instance, the rock-enclosure of the soul (called *tutu,* "flowerbud") changed into a toad, which hopped away carrying the souls of dead ancient shamans. The continuity of life and society itself depends upon the shaman's recovery procedures of animal transformation, for all Canelos Quichua adults descend from an *apayaya* ("grandfather"), an ancestor shaman existing in animal form.[291]

Snakes feature prominently in many shamans' practices. Poisonous serpents are alleged to be the especially close friends of the Apinayé *vayangá* (shamanic healer), for "every incipient *vayangá* is supposed to be bitten by such a snake and even at that stage of his career is able to overcome the effects. Then the snakes become his friends, lying in wait for him in order to converse with him." [292] One *vayangá*, carrying a snake in such a way that its head rested on his shoulder, insisted that some women paint the serpent with the *genipa* dance paint that they were applying to themselves.

One of the Kari'ña shaman's special tasks is to deal with the power of venomous snakes, especially rattlesnakes, who, like shamans, sound their rattles at night. A *puidei* attempts to imitate and to identify with the snake so that he will have as effective a "fang," a symbolic embodiment of wisdom and magical knowledge. The rattler's mouth, like the shaman's chanting mouth, possesses deadly wisdom and knowledge, expressed as speech, sound, song, venom, saliva, and so forth.

Kari'ña shamans are instructed and aided by supernatural jaguars *(kaikuishi)*, on the one hand, and by snakes and other sharply intrusive beings that can penetrate the body harmfully, on the other. Serpents, stinging insects, invisible spirit arrows, thorns, needles, and darts: all insert their substance into the body by means of their sharp bite.[293] They are classified by the Kari'ña as "water people" under the tutelage of Akodumo, the great anaconda.[294] Each of the two supernatural domains (of jaguar and anaconda) requires a different bodily transformation if the shaman is to acquire its power. Powerful shamans allow themselves to be bitten by serpents in order to obtain wisdom. They learn how to sustain life by experiencing this form of death.[295] Power and knowledge are transmitted in the form of venom *(sakura).*[296] This compound, *sakura,* is formed from *sak,* a root designating sacred sound, incantation, or magical calling,[297] and the Kari'ña word for therapy, *kuru,* which also designates a magic drink consumed at festivals. *Sakura* refers to the venom of the coral snake, *sakurakura,* who both poisons and cures and is associated with the daily water-therapy ablutions that give protection from the dangerous realm of water, the domain of snakes.

Each animal with which the shaman identifies has a power and a meaning revealed in myth. The Yukuna shaman, for instance, is a master of many animal forms because the mythical shaman Maotchi transformed himself into various animals during his heroic adventures, saving himself each time he was trapped in an impossible situation. The shaman not only imitates Maotchi's transformative abilities but appropriates the salvation available in experiencing Maotchi's great escapes.[298]

Familiarity with changes of form can make the shaman an expert in costumes and disguises. The Piaroa shaman directs the construction of masks and musical instruments as well as their use during the course of the seasonal ceremony that is held to further the fertility of the "lords" of animals. The man-of-song's position as master of ceremonies is seen to be a logical extension of those shamanic powers with which he controls the processes of nature.[299]

The shaman's interest in experiencing other kinds of body forms need not be limited to appropriating animal bodies. Living the bodily experience of the opposite sex follows the same logic and motivation as other kinds of bodily transformation. For instance, although most of the reports of contemporary Araucanian *machi*, shamans, describe them as women, Gusinde reported that in the past they were almost exclusively men who, however, dressed and acted as women. In fact, ritual transvestism and homosexual experience was a prerequisite for the office of *machi*.[300]

ANIMAL BODIES: SPECIES OF SPACE

It should be clear that the power of shamans to transform (or even to assume) the bodily shape of mythic animals is directly related to their power to penetrate and endure the conditions of other kinds of cosmic spaces. In ancient times, for example, a young Waiwai *yaskomo* resuscitated the culture hero Yawari (opossum). The ancient shaman revitalized the dismembered and rotting corpse of the culture hero when he set about to cut out its tooth and blow on it. For his troubles, the ancient *yaskomo* was shown three types of houses.[301] On another mythic occasion, a *yaskomo* led an attempt to conquer a giant anaconda who had devoured some human beings and who was threatening to devour all. Aided by otters who contained the serpent in one part of a river and then penetrated the serpent by entering its mouth and exiting its anus with the bones of one of its victims, the *yaskomo* cut the snake in two pieces. The *yaskomo* was able to enter the anaconda house by singing a magical song (*eremu*).[302]

The Waiwai shaman carries out his practice in three different spaces. In the open-air space at the center of the village, he may summon the master of peccaries by singing this spirit's song while holding his magical stone in his mouth. He may also use the open air as the place to invoke spirits to help him bring on rain or sunshine, provide animals and fish for the hunt, ensure abundant harvests, and so on.[303] The shaman copes with cases of mild illness within the space of the communal house, singing magic songs and performing acts of curative blowing assisted by his helper spirits.[304] In cases of serious illness, however, the shaman retires to the isolation of his special *yaskomo* hut, the *shutepana*, from which, during the night, his soul journeys to the proper spirit realm. With the help of dreams, the *yaskomo* tries to discern what kind of clothing the patient's lost soul is wearing. In this way, he can tell to what zone in the cosmos the soul has strayed in order to follow it there. Completely sealed inside his conical hut, the shaman sits on a stool and summons his spirit helpers by blowing on special whistles. The whistle is itself a space used to manipulate and transform breath. All Waiwai laymen may perform acts of magical blowing, but only the shaman uses magical whistles to summon helper spirits. "This use of an implement has presumably replaced the simpler form of ordinary blowing from the mouth." [305] Efficacy is bestowed on breath in a new way by introducing it into a different container. The use of the whistle, then, is a more effective and magical variant of blowing one's breath.

The shaman's management of space, embodied in the imagery of mythical beasts, helps situate the entire community in proper relation to the powers that define its territory. For instance, a Canelos Quichua shaman usually attains powers to communicate with other spirits through the intercession of Amasanga, a *Datura* spirit, who introduces the shaman to spirits of the underworld who are also powerful shamans. Only then is the human shaman powerful enough to establish a new area for swidden horticulture for an inmarried group because he is now powerful enough to drive out *Juri Juri*, a supernatural monster who inhabits wild, unclaimed, and unpeopled areas of the forest. The animal's bodily form marks the boundary between human space and the wild. Exemplifying the logic of consumption ("you are what you eat"), this two-faced monster devours people with his rear face and monkeys with his forward face. By driving out the *Juri Juri*, the shaman explores and extends the imaginative and physical limits of culture.

BODY SPACE AND HUNTING IMAGERY

It is safe to say that, in part, shamanic intimacy with animals reflects a religious ideology developed during the long period when hunting and gathering were humankind's chief means of sustenance. Given the long sweep of human life on earth, the period during which settled agriculture has been practiced represents only a tiny fraction of human history. Shamanism presumably represents some of the religious reflection that preceded the religious revolution brought on by agriculture. Even if this hunting ideology has been greatly reworked, it has not been entirely annihilated. For instance, animals are the key links in Wayãpi cosmic life. Their sounds, tracks, names, spatial locations, and behaviors are multivalent symbols organizing social life and human self-understanding. In fact, for the Wayãpi, living as a true human being (that is, as someone conscious of the connections in the universe) requires hunting. Naturally, such momentous behavior is surrounded with rules prescribing specific actions. The shaman is the guide to relations with animals, relations that govern symbolic life. For example, an individual's failure to observe food restrictions concerning certain game may cause sickness, which the shaman must diagnose and cure. [306]

Lingering hunting ideology surrounds the shaman's involvement with the hunt itself. The esoteric way in which Kari'ña shamans deal with the animal forms of spirits is essential to good hunting. Not only does it fill the forest with game, it becomes the model, for example, for the exoteric sound magic used by Kari'ña hunters. The shaman may not himself hunt, but he does make the secret sounds that are the invisible and true forms of supernatural beings. Naming them, he calls them into existence; he transforms them into the animal form of prey. The next step in the procedure, finding and shooting the game, requires that hunters pursue their prey, the transformed spirits, in a ritually controlled manner.[307] As de Civrieux reports,

> The Kariña hunter, when he pursues animals, acts in a way very similar to the *puidei* who cures the sick. Proceeding slowly and with great caution he keeps quiet and opens his ears to the maximum in order to hear *(e.kanopi)*. He learns to identify the calls or names *(eti)* of animals and imitates them. The calls of attraction are used by the hunter, just as by the shaman, to entice and capture the animal, to become the master of its body or of its spirit, as the case may be. The hunter practices an auditory and vocal magic, enchanting his prey by using their own languages.[308]

If the hunt can take on the proportions of a shamanic cure, so the shamanic shooting of a pathogen into the body of a victim can, conversely, perpetuate the spirituality of the hunt. Shamans perform this operation in several different ways. At times, the shaman deputizes his helper spirit, who assumes the form of an animal that then introduces the pathogenic agent into the victim. In other cases, the shaman may dispatch his own soul to throw the spirit dart.[309] In the Kari'ña case, four pebbles (the spirits of the four winds in the shaman's rattle) are used as spirit-darts. Putting the pebbles in his mouth, the *puidei* blows smoke over them while uttering curses. Then, placing them in the crook of his elbow, he "shoots" them by pointing in the desired direction. The stones disappear, for they enter into his "powerful arm" and exit from the invisible hole between his fingers. This "strong-arm" tactic is fatal if the spirit-dart travels clear through the victim and returns to the *puidei*'s *maraka*.[310] If, on the other hand, the dart sticks in the body of the victim, it becomes a pathogenic object (dart, thorn, hairball) or animal (worm, mosquito, fly, spider, toad, snake), which a curing shaman may suck out.[311]

The shaman utilizes the powers of space that he comes to know and understand during his ecstatic travels.[312] In some way, he is transformed into those spaces; he assumes their conditions of existence as his own. This makes the shaman a specialist in forms and an expert in the process of transformation. Because his knowledge of space is always existential, he not only sees what is in other forms, he *becomes* other shapes. Foremost among the shapes he becomes are the mythical animals (the jaguar, the harpy eagle, the snake, and so on) that dominate the domains he visits. By living their experience, he acquires their wisdom and makes their power available to the wider human community.

PLANT AND VEGETAL FORM ASSOCIATIONS

Although shamanism's roots may lie in the hunting heritage of human history, it would be a mistake to exaggerate shamanism's relationship to hunting and gathering as a system of economic subsistence, especially in South

America. Romanticizing the alleged influence of ancient hunters is a kind of historicism that will not help one to understand shamanism as practiced in the last several centuries, for this interpretive frame overlooks the thorough integration of shamanic ideas into the religious existence of the farmer in South America. Quite some time ago, Claude Lévi-Strauss responded to a suggestion by John Cooper that the cultures of the tropical area of South America should be divided into those groups basing their economy on farming and those basing their economy on collecting. Lévi-Strauss responded, "Irrespective of the usefulness of such a classification for practical purposes, it is necessary to keep in mind that farming always accompanies, and is never a substitute for, the exploitation of wild resources." The tropical forest culture, "based altogether on farming and on the exploitation of wild resources, which requires as much skill as farming, is the only genuine culture of tropical South America." [313] Wild plants are exploited not only for raw economic purposes but also for their manifold symbolic value as ornaments, body decorations, and ritual items, as well as for their "power," best known to the shaman, as poisons and medicines.

In light of some of the earliest evidence of shamanic practice, it is clear that the shaman has always possessed special knowledge of plants, especially plants that alter the status of the soul. The so-called Niño Korin site discovered in highland Bolivia by Stig Rydén[314] is a tomb in which, among others, a medicine man was buried with his implements. The tomb and the burial are dated to about 650–850 CE.[315] S. Henry Wassén considered the collection of objects found there to be a "medicine man's laboratorial and medical outfit." [316] The collection of implements included wooden snuff trays (containing incised decorations with figures familiar in Andean religious art) and a snuff tube. Other bamboo tubes served as containers. There were also containers made of fruits and gourds. Animal pouches, probably made from the South American deer, contained vegetal materials, possibly *Nicotiana*. There were a number of reeds that Wassén believes were part of enema syringes as well as a variety of spatulas and a mortar and pestles made of wood. In addition, there were several bunches of leaves from the *Ilex guayusa* covered by a leaf of *Duroia*.

The properties of plants, especially magical plants offering supernatural sight, are part of the shaman's technology of ecstasy and control his clairvoyance. Aided by the power of plants, he can safely see sacred beings, see what is wrong inside a patient's body, or even find lost items. The Juruna tell a myth that explains the importance of a beverage they make of tree scrapings. In order to become a shaman, the mythical figure Uaiçá fasts, sleeps, and dreams underneath the sleep-inducing tree. Here he sees the primordial shaman, Sinaá, who instructs him how to use his visions and dreams to cure, to procure animals for the hunt, and to find lost articles.[317]

The shaman's knowledge of plants comes to the fore in medical practice. Normally, powers of the vegetal world intervene to drive off diseases brought by beings from the animal, human, or supernatural world. For the Wayãpi, for instance, each pathogenic failure to observe correct hunting and eating procedure has a corresponding vegetal antidote.[318] The effectiveness of plants in curing disease is not a function of impersonal chemical properties. The use of plants widens the sufferer's network of spiritual relationships. The power of the plant introduces the patient to new alliances and advocates. For example, after an Avá-Chiripá shaman has diagnosed the cause of illness by sleeping on the matter, he attempts treatment with herbs. This therapy is effective because the culture hero Kuarahy taught humans the meaning and power of certain therapeutic plants. The healer must intone invocations to the spirit of the healing plant that he gathers. During these chants, the plant's spirit is incited to do battle with the spirits of disease.[319] Illness and cure, then, are a spiritual process, a spiritual combat with organic manifestations.

The spiritual alliances that the shaman instigates with the plant world can benefit the entire community and spur the growth cycle of the plant world itself. In addition to private sessions of healing, a special class of Mataco curers called *aiawu* presides over a public ceremony called Atj, celebrated at the beginning of a new moon. The feast-ceremony entreats Nowenek, a being who resides within the human body, to provide an abundance of carob beans, fruit, and corn. The ceremony puts harm and disease, especially blight and epidemic disease, to flight and assures the fertility of crops. Atj is portrayed as a battle, played out in the air, between good and evil spirits.[320]

In their dealings with plants, shamans remain true to the vocation of the clairvoyant who specializes in undergoing or instigating transformations of the spirit. These spiritual changes may be manifest in the growth of plants or in the ailments of the human body.

SHAMANIC CURE

As a specialist in space, especially the space the soul inhabits during ecstasy, the shaman cares for the health of the body, the home of the human soul. His own mystical physiology affords knowledge of the inner workings of the human body. When acting as curers of the seriously ill, shamans restore well-being by reinstating lost souls to the body or by extracting from the inner space of the body pathogens that only they can see. Shamans cure by replacing things in and taking things out of the body. By using their ecstatic ability to penetrate all the separate planes of existence, shamans safeguard the good order of cosmic spaces—keeping souls and pathogens in their respective places. As curer, the shaman directs cosmic traffic and polices the various, qualitatively different areas of the universe. The shaman-physician maintains the relations between cosmic spaces and the space of the body. This knowledge of physics guarantees the significance of human physical existence in the universe when human beings are threatened by the disorder of disease.[321] As Bartolomé explains, Avá-Chiripá shamans' cures are usually effective, and failures are very few because the goal of therapy is not only to cure but to give meaning to sickness. Through the therapy the patient becomes aware "that the whole cosmic order is acting on his behalf." [322]

The precedent for shamanic cure is usually set by a mythic shaman. On the one hand, the Avá-Chiripá shaman's treatment of illness by breathing is powerful and effective because this was the way in which Kuarahy revived his brother Yacy, the moon. Yacy had been devoured by supernatural jaguars, but Kuarahy prevailed upon the jaguars to leave the bones intact. He then took the bones of his dead brother into the forest and breathed upon them. "He breathed until flesh returned to Yacy's bones. His flesh returned again and, with it, his life."[323] When the shaman breathes on the spot on the upper part of the head, where the soul enters, a special power leaves the body of the shaman and enters that of the sick man. This magical power will wrestle with the pathogenic spirit and force it to leave the sick man's body. Treatment by shamanic chant, however, is the most powerful form of Avá-Chiripá medicine because this was the way in which Kuarahy sought to raise up his dead mother, the great earth mother, Nandé Cy.[324] Curing with song may be seen as an extended form of treatment by breath. The chant calls down the power of the shaman's helper spirit, the divinity who granted the healer his vocation.

FINDER OF LOST SOULS: RESTORING SELF-POSSESSION

Healing a patient suffering from loss of soul may require dangerous travel for the shaman. Lost, stolen, or gone astray in other cosmic domains, the wandering soul must be freed from the forces that ensnare it and guided back to its place in the body.[325] Powerful shamans, helped by the techniques with which they control the movements of their own souls, can undertake such journeys whenever the need arises. The most important task of Baniwa shamans, for instance, is curing the sick. As masters of fire, they are also masters of the soul that has separated from the body, in the same way that the spirit of the proto-shaman Kuai separated from his body as it was consumed by fire in mythic times. The curing session begins with the narration of the mythic account for the origins of illness, that is, a narration of the myth of Kuai.[326] The recitation of the myth begins with the creation and proceeds to the accounts of the origins of disease and cure. In cases of disease caused by soul-loss, it is believed that the being Kuai, now living in the zone of the midsky, has embraced the victim's soul in his arms. The patient brings offerings for the shaman to transport to Kuai in an ecstatic flight so that he will relax his embrace on the soul. The shaman returns to earth with the soul and blows it back into the patient's body with tobacco smoke.[327] The shaman blows tobacco smoke over the patient's extremities and in this way binds the soul of the patient to the center of the patient (i.e., to his heart).[328] For shamans, this act is equivalent to that that ended the long night of eternal darkness and terminated one of the primordial worlds. At that time, Yaperikuli, the proto-shaman, transformer, and master of fire, made the sun return through song. The soul, in the shamanic view, is parallel to this light of the dawning day of the new world. The shaman, master of fire and therefore of the soul's light and heat, is able to cure the loss of the light and life-heat of the soul.

Ecstatic flight, song, sound, and light (of vision or of fiery heat) continue to be principal elements in the shamanic cure of soul-loss. These items never have precisely the same arrangement of meaning in any two cultures. They always reflect the mythic origins and religious creativity of historical communities. In ways quite different from the Avá-Chiripá and Baniwa cases, two further illustrations, from the Shipibo and the Apinayé, show how the images and meanings of shamanic cure, while still remaining an integral symbolic complex, can ramify in different and unique directions.

The Shipibo recognize two kinds of shamanic specialists, the curing shaman and the bewitching shaman.[329] During his curing ritual, the former journeys to the realm of the sun, accompanied by light-colored birds. A great crown of hummingbirds surrounds the shaman as he journeys along the "way of great light" to the sun.[330] It is said that a good shaman must always wear his *tari* (cotton poncho) during the night. It is heavy with special supernatural power. He also wears this *tari* when he cures his patients.[331] Roe associates the good, or curing, shaman with light-colored birds and the powerful hallucinogenic liana *Banisteriopsis caapi*, called *nishi* by the Shipibo. Only good shamans use this vine. The Shipibo do not, however, place great emphasis on the role of narcotic plants.[332] The *nishi* spirits do not obliterate the shaman's lucidity. Under the influence of *nishi*, the curing shaman is able to carry on conversation even if he may occasionally drift off into falsetto songs. Shipibo shamans often sing in a pseudo-Quechua. During a curing ritual, a shaman may sing for three successive nights. Often other shamans will join in the song.[333] The curing shaman will blow tobacco smoke over the patient's body so that his curing songs may be effective. As Roe relates, "It is a powerful and moving spectacle as late at night a moon-bathed plaza resounds with the shaman's unearthly falsetto while bats flit past broad, swaying banana leaves and from the nearby lake the curiously human coughing of the freshwater dolphins expelling air from their blowholes drifts toward the huddled circle of people."[334]

The Apinayé *akólo-čwųdn* is a *vayaṅgá*, a healer instructed by spirits of the dead, whom he invokes with the songs they have taught him. He need not wait for the helper souls to come to him with advice. In order to fetch back a patient's lost soul, the *akólo-čwųdn* visits the village of the dead in the guise of a kind of black snake that devours venomous snakes.[335] The specialist uses tobacco to dispatch his transformed soul to the realm of the dead. At night, in front of his home, the *akólo-čwųdn* faces east and smokes tobacco until he collapses in a trembling heap. His assistant guards the prostrate body while the specialist's soul, in serpent form and using serpent language, confers with the spirits of the dead. "The assistant blows tobacco smoke on his own hands and places them on the medicine man's, thereby reviving him. On waking up, he allows tobacco to issue from his mouth."[336]

THE WOMB OF THE MOUTH: SUCKING, BITING, EXTRACTING, REGENERATING

Erwin Ackerknecht, the renowned historian of medicine, listed the most common characteristics of South American theories of illness and techniques for its cure as these: the concept of disease as an intrusion into the body; shamanic sucking accompanied by ecstasy, singing, smoking, and massage; prescribed bleeding, enemas, or restrictive diets; piercing of body parts (lips, ears, etc.) or decoration of the body as preventive medicine. The shamanic attributes examined in earlier sections explain how these techniques are intrinsically related to an ecstatic vocation and why immense social prestige is acquired by the shamanic healer.[337] At this point, it pays to look more closely at scenarios of shamanic cure.

When a patient is sick because a harmful object has penetrated the body, the shaman usually removes the pathogen through massage and suction.[338] In this respect, notwithstanding the variety of spiritual afflictions and their many interpretations, "the treatment of the sick [is] practically identical from the West Indies to Tierra del Fuego."[339] Kaingáng shamans, for instance, specialize in extracting pathogenic projectiles (thêyê) sent by the supernatural monsters Yunggi or Pain. The shamans who perform these cures, at least in the accounts provided by Henry, are all women. Integral to their curing technique is the power of song. Normally, for example, a Kaingáng curer will wash the patient, massage the patient's body parts, force the pathogenic projectile into one location in the body, and bite out the projectile, seizing it in the teeth and pulling. These techniques of cure by biting, spitting, blowing, and singing were obtained by shamans from the nggïyúdn, the myriad spirits of nature.[340]

Sucking cures provide moments of high drama in the community. The tension and excitement has not been lost on visitors.[341] Among the Tapirapé, for example, when someone fell ill because of a pathogenic fish bone, worm, arrow, or some such object inserted by a sorceror, the shaman cured by blowing with tobacco smoke and sucking. Obviously affected by witnessing one such operation, Charles Wagley offered this description:

> The shaman squatted alongside the hammock of his patient and began to "eat smoke"; that is, he swallowed large gulps of tobacco smoke from his pipe. He forced the smoke with great intakes of breath deep into his stomach; soon he became intoxicated and nauseated; he vomited violently and smoke spewed from his mouth. He groaned and cleared his throat in the manner of a person gagging with nausea but unable to vomit. By sucking back what he vomited he accumulated saliva in his mouth. In the midst of this process he stopped several times to suck on the body of his patient and finally, with one awful heave, vomited all the accumulated saliva on the ground. He then searched in this mess for the intrusive object that had been causing the illness. . . . Sometimes, when a man of prestige was ill, two or even three shamans would cure side by side in this manner and the noise of violent vomiting resounded throughout the village.[342]

Noteworthy here is the theme of multiple consumptions. For example, tobacco smoke, from tobacco already consumed by fire, is ingested, vomited and reswallowed; saliva is gulped down, regurgitated, and reingested. This process of refinement utilizes consumption to attain the rarest "essence," the purest and most powerful form of distilled spirit.

The spirit darts and other intruding objects extracted by sucking are, in almost all cases in South America, similar to those that were passed into the novice's body during apprenticeship and initiation. They are so linked with the body's inner area (and, in many cases, with specific organs) that the cure by sucking and extraction may be seen as an extended variation of the shamanic initiatory experience of evisceration and/or organ replacement. For example, among the Cubeo, a powerful supernatural force takes up residence in the body of the shaman during his apprenticeship. This happens when the master shaman puts small pieces of crystal into the head of the novice; these crystals are said to eat up his brains and eyes, replacing these organs and becoming his "power." [343] The counterpart of this experience, from the patient's point of view, is seen most clearly in the practice of the Araucanian shaman, who dances and drums himself into an ecstatic trance during which he "extracts" the patient's viscera. [344]

The great emphasis on sucking as a curing technique goes hand in hand with the South American religious emphasis upon the body as a microcosm. During episodes of soul-loss, the South American shaman, like shamans in other religious traditions, cures by means of ecstatic journeys through the cosmos. However, in South America great emphasis is placed on the passage of supernatural elements through the human body. If shamans in general familiarize themselves with the complex mythical geography of the macrocosm, the South American shaman is particularly knowledgeable of the ways of passing in and out of the realms of the body, the microcosm. In his own apprenticeship, he practices control over such passage and, in the widespread techniques of sucking, he harnesses this knowledge in the interests of therapeutic cure. The efficacy of sucking cure is directly related to the shaman's mystical physiology, especially the ability of his mouth and stomach to engulf, transform, and extrude spirits appearing in the form of physical objects (tobacco, hallucinogenic beverages, stones, splinters, snakes, insects, songs, etc.). [345] Swallowing and vomiting are parts of the sucking operation. Together they clarify a spirituality of cosmic matter centered on the transformative locus of the shaman's mouth.

The Jívaro help us understand the spirituality of the mouth in sucking cures. The powers of the Jívaro curing shaman complement those of the bewitching shaman. The healing shaman swallows the hallucinogenic drink *natema* and other narcotic substances, such as tobacco juice, in order to "see" into the body of the patient "as though it were glass." [346] The healing shaman works in company with the darkness, for he cures only at night and in a dark place in the house. Only at night can he "see" the supernatural forces that afflict the patient. Darkness subjects the outer world to the same conditions that obtain in the inner world of the body; it unites the two worlds. As the sun sets, the shaman whistles his curing song until he breaks into full-voiced song. Then he vomits two *tsentsak*, spirit darts, from his stomach and positions one of these magical darts in the front and the other in the back of his mouth, blocking his throat. When he sucks out the pathogenic dart lodged in the patient's body it becomes trapped between these two *tsentsak* of his own. "He then 'vomits' out this object and displays it to the patient and his family saying, 'Now I have sucked it out. Here it is.' " [347] In the opinion of the shamans, the material object produced is not nearly as important as the supernatural essence of the pathogenic magical dart he has removed from the patient. However, "to explain to the layman that he already had these objects in his mouth would serve no fruitful purpose and would prevent him from displaying such an object as proof that he had effected a cure." [348]

The magical darts which the Jívaro curing shaman regurgitates from his own stomach must be identical to the kind of magical dart afflicting his patient. The shaman must already "know" the disease; that is, his body must already possess an experience of it.[349] Consequently, the most powerful curing shamans possess a large quantity of powerful *tsentsak*, perhaps even hundreds of them. As Harner writes,

> His magical darts assume their supernatural aspect as spirit helpers when he is under the influence of *natema*, and he sees them as a variety of zoomorphic forms hovering over him, perching on his shoulders, and sticking out of his skin. He sees them helping to suck the patient's body. He must drink tobacco juice every few hours to "keep them fed" so that they will not leave him.[350]

The success of the healing shaman's practice also depends on his ability to "see" the *pasuk* and *wakani* spirits that have collaborated with some bewitching shaman to afflict the patient. As a result, not only is the space of the patient's body cleaned by noisily sucking out pathogens and regurgitating them with deep dry vomiting, the curing shaman also cleanses the patient's house by using his mouth to "blow" it free of all afflicting spirits and elements. Through the powers brought into the mouth, all "dirtiness" *(pahuri)* is removed from both of these integral spaces, the body and the living space.

The sucking cure is directly related to the shaman's expertise in ecstasy. In Wakuenai shamanic cures, the shaman, in order to suck out disease successfully, must control *two* aspects of the pathogenic object that is sickening his patient. The first aspect is internal to the patient: the intrusive pathogen, which is the cause of a specific sickness. This object is a particular historical manifestation of disease. However, the pathogenic being itself is actually in an ecstatic state because its generic spirit roams the skies even while its internal and specific aspect lodges itself in a particular patient's body. In order to heal the patient, the shaman must overcome the pathogen's ecstatic state by restoring the unity of manifest form and spirit. He does this through sucking. Armed with the feathers of his rattle, his singing, and his clairvoyance, the shaman recaptures the generic external spirit of the pathogen and scoops it into his mouth just after he has sucked out the internal aspect, the physical intruder, from his patient's body. The separated parts of beings whose ecstasy provokes disease are reunited in his mouth, where cosmic forces come together in transformative ways. Through the mystical physiology of the shaman, sucking amounts to a kind of restoration of the soul, but, in this case, the shaman retrieves the lost soul of a pathogenic object. "The purpose of his actions is to link together the external and internal . . . causes of sickness inside his own body so that both disease-causing agents can be vividly expelled into the bushes through vomiting." [351] The shaman brings an end to the dangerous ecstasy of the pathogen only after the members of the patient's family have confessed their faults.

Extraction of a pathogen by sucking with the mouth cannot be understood in terms of a mechanical process for eliminating an inert substance. It is a cosmic drama in which the shaman enlists the aid of all the ecstatic techniques and spiritual powers with which he is acquainted. The entire universe may be mobilized in the microcosm of forces at work in the sick body of the patient and the mystical body of the healer. This becomes clear in the case of the Canelos Quichua. If a sick person is afflicted with spirit darts, a Canelos Quichua shaman may use *ayahuasca* to help effect a cure. When the *ayahuasca* liquid is prepared, all women depart except for two who help the shaman, usually his wife and daughter or some female relative of the patient. The women make cigars and a tobacco-water concoction. These are used to clarify visions and to clean objects. Seated on a stool shaped like a turtle or caiman, the shaman blows tobacco smoke into his bowl and whistles a special song; he thinks of the words to the song and consumes the *ayahuasca* served by his female assistant. The men present now drink *ayahuasca*,[352] continuing to imbibe while the women assistants drink a tobacco concoction through their noses. Then "the earth trembles and . . . a great waterfall . . . comes down around the house." [353] This is an ancient waterfall, not one of those found in the contemporary forest. If the participants contain evil within them, they now vomit it up. The spirits that appear are identified by name. The identification is confirmed or corrected by the shaman and his female assistants. Within the house where the *ayahuasca* curing rite is performed the participants watch souls emerge from within their bodies, and spirits come from faraway spaces or times to glow before the spectators.

Within this context of the awakened universe, the Canelos Quichua shaman searches for the cause of the patient's illness. His spirit helpers arrive in the form of "bees, butterflies, fireflies, and sparks." [354] The shaman is "opening" like a *Datura* flower, attracting these beings. Like insects, the spirits, souls, and powers fly toward him, called by the music he plays on the violin or whistles while thinking the words, "Datura is flowering and wants its bees." [355]

The female helper now brings the shaman his curing-leaf bundle, which he cleanses with tobacco smoke. The bundled leaves appear as a flickering of snakes' tongues with three tips. This is evidence of the medicine-poison in the bundle. Ayahuasca Mama, "the giver of the vine of souls," now brings a boa- or anaconda-person to examine the shaman's torso-innards for any evil substances. If any evil is discovered, the shaman will vomit it up.[357]

The shaman now turns his attention to the patient, who is covered only with a sheet. He blows tobacco over the patient's body and shakes the curing-leaf bundle from head to feet. He sings intercessions on behalf of the patient, pleading to forest monsters and powerful shamans to recall their spirit darts. Those spirit helpers, recalled by their powerful masters, are placed on leaves and carried outside the house. Having eliminated this general malaise, the shaman can zero in on the specific spirit darts remaining.

He drinks tobacco water through his nose and lights another cigar. "The embedded darts appear in their real form — poisonous snake, lizard, spider, water toucan, machaca moth, ball of hair, black stone, or any of dozens of other *supai* [spirit] manifestations." [357] Aided by the shaman's instruction, the other participants in the curing session behold the spirit darts in the body of the patient, "glowing a brilliant blue under the skin, in the stomach, or in a vein or artery." [358]

Drinking tobacco water and blowing smoke on the affected area of the patient's body, the shaman

> places his mark completely over the area, and his own spirit helpers come up into his mouth to help him. He sucks noisily and the *supai* is removed from the victim and taken down into his own stomach for identification by his spirit helpers. Then the shaman places both hands on his head and vomits the foreign spirit up into his own mouth; he *retains its own acquired human soul.* He then moves to the side of the house . . . and blows the spirit dart with a *shuuuj* sound outward toward its *ayllu* of origin. He repeats this process for half an hour to an hour until all *supai birutis* [spirit darts] are removed.[359]

MYTHIC MODELS

Ordinary humans could never perform such sucking. Successful control over cosmic processes requires superhuman power. Obtaining this power for the first time was the achievement of mythic beings. The Avá-Chiripá shaman's remedies have a heroic model in the actions of the mythological twins, the sun and moon. The shaman is able to cure people by sucking out the pathogen because Kuarahy, the sun, had once upon a time revived dead mythic birds in the same way. He placed them in a basket made of philodendron, and, taking them out one at a time, "he sucked their throats and the birds revived." [360] These kinds of cures must be carried out in conjunction with special dreams, which the healer experiences on the eve of the curing session. The dream brings the shaman into the mythic world of the beginnings and allows the healer to diagnose the cause of illness.

Shamanic sucking is able to save a patient because it once saved the world itself. The Baniwa shaman's sucking cure is modeled on the mythic moment when Kuai, the culture hero, was smoked by a fire that raged at the foot of the tree in which he was staying. Great streams of saliva poured from all of his orifices. His saliva flooded the world as a great rain. In order to save the children who were tending the fire at the foot of his tree, he transformed his mouth into an enormous cave and swallowed three of them. Then he vomited them up. This is held to be the moment when the sky and earth came together, united by the water from his mouth. In shamanic sucking-out (*watsūtsū*, a word related to the musical sound of the falling saliva),[361] sky and earth come together again because, although appearing to remain on earth, the shaman is actually on an ecstatic journey in the sky.[362] For this reason, when shamans succeed in sucking out pathogens, they are said to possess "the mouths of Kuai," which enable them to extract the venom of Kuai's animal fur, his poisonous saliva, or the spirit-splinters from his tree-body and, "with great streams of water coming from their mouths," to vomit them up together with the pathogens.[363] The shaman's mouth, like the mouth of Kuai, embodies all the transformative processes that make life in this world possible. The Baniwa shaman's rattle, the embodiment of his soul and "the companion of snuff," is a similar kind of transformative container; it, too, sucks the disease-objects from the patient's body.[364]

THE OPERATING THEATRE

Shamanic cure is deliberately histrionic. As operatic entertainment, the medical spectacle not only eliminates the suffering of an individual but fosters the good health of the entire community. Public display of the sick and dramatic celebration of the triumph over the forces of disease are, in themselves, acts promoting health. The cure of the sick becomes a sacrament of well-being. By focusing communal reflection on the normative shape of the cosmos, curing rites dramatize the meaning of order and disorder. Put on stage in this way, episodes of sickness publicly puzzle out the relations of the cosmos, the body, and life itself. Sickness becomes a kind of divination, where, for a little while, the multivalent and ambiguous possibilities of the symbolic universe become clear signs of the way cosmic processes relate to individuals. The shaman leads the community through a cosmological exercise. The operating theatre is staged as a battle, bringing the hidden to light and disclosing what lurks unknown. The episodes of cure develop a plot with the same revelatory structure as myth. Uttering sounds that recreate primordial conditions, the shaman searches out the origins of sickness, discovers and pronounces the name of the afflicting or recuperative power, and displays *sacra* that include the shaman's power objects as well as the extracted pathogen. As he does so, the origins and destiny of the individual and the community reveal themselves.[365]

For example, the Toba *yeyátten*'s most common role is to perform as a curer, extracting pathogenic beings from his patient's body. He draws out spirits in the form of splinters. "To 'draw out the splinter' *(nakát kaipák)* is the ultimate aim of the medical art."[366] The cure is divided into four episodes. The first is called *empaché*, or *pionák* ("to chant"). It begins shortly after nightfall. Using his sacred rattle and a leather belt to which a number of small bells are attached, the *yeyátten* sings over his patient. His "voice is by itself supposed to have a magical efficacy."[367] Locating in this way the seat of the evil spirit, the curer shakes his rattle close to that part of the patient's body, spitting and blowing on it. The second episode begins when the curer spits and blows on the patient. This action prepares the place for the extraction of the pathogenic splinter. During the second episode, the *tok tolýgin*, "the magical power which is inherent in the whole body of the medicine man also manifests itself in his saliva and his breath." During the third stage of the cure, the *hayeyátten*, the curer invokes his good guardian spirit. He does this without the assistance of his sacred rattle. Leaning close to the patient he chants in a very low voice, "Come, good spirit, from the heaven to draw out the splinter! Yes, he is coming, he is coming!"[368] The fourth stage of the cure is the propitiation of the harmful spirit, *jamaranyín peyák*.[369] The afflicting

being is drawn out of the patient's body in the form of a splinter that is held up
for all to view. However, there is a danger that this afflicting being will
repossess the body of the patient during the night. To prevent this, the curer
enters into a "negotiation" with the pathogenic spirit:

> Turning away from the patient and pretending to hold the spirit in his hand, the
> medicine-man converses with him in a low muttering voice, directing, as it
> seems, various questions to him. . . . "Do you want tobacco? Do you like to
> smoke a pipe?" The medicine-man himself as well as the surrounding men an-
> swer these questions — on behalf of the spirit — through a nod of the head and a
> low mumbling.[370]

Then tobacco smoke is offered to the spirit in thick clouds, which the curer
draws from his pipe and blows around his patient. The Toba shaman's actions are always powerful and effective. "The failure of his operation is only
regarded as a sign that this time the 'good spirit' did not allow the sick person
to recover but had decided that he should die."[371]

RIGHT BEFORE YOUR VERY EYES: THE PUBLICITY OF SHAMANIC CURE

Unlike the medical protocols of the herbalist and the bone setter, the shaman's cure is miraculous; it is a deliberate exhibition of normally invisible
powers. It aims to astonish spectators, and it compels them to admire what is
real and, therefore, life-giving. Miracle publicizes realities ordinarily housed
in unseen realms of the universe or stashed beneath the limen of awareness.
Truth-telling in shamanic medical practice requires that the performance
amaze the audience with a startling demonstration of that truth. The shamans' understanding of the patient's condition is founded on their clairvoyant penetration of the spirit domain. To communicate truth of this kind,
shamans must make the audience see what they see. Just as importantly,
miraculous performances help the viewers see reality reflexively, the way the
shaman sees it.[372]

The Kari'ña shaman, for example, acquires a mode of self-reflective
consciousness that transcends mere self-consciousness. He comes to see the
true spirit world when and to the degree that he sees himself being seen in it.
One is ready for instruction when one "sees in the dark," clearly beholding a
small man (the reflected image of the reflecting candidate) in the irises of
disincarnate and invisible *mawáre*, the teaching-spirits of dead *puidei*. This
man is the powerful "heavenly soul."[373] Here we see a mystical, but nonetheless systematic, conception of the way in which one's own self is composed of
reflection on transcendental as well as historical forces. These forces are the
invisible but real source of the heightened degree of self-consciousness
needed to obtain the power that cures and controls evil. By reflecting on
one's ability to reflect and to be reflected in consciousness and by doing so
against the backdrop of different kinds of time and history (dead shamans
and mythic beings), one attains creative knowledge of unsurpassable power.
The shaman sees transcendental realities in the degree to which he envisions
the range of his own spiritual possibilities. Conversely, sacred beings be-

come visible to the extent that their eyes mirror the "corrected" spiritual vision of the shaman. Tracking the course of his own soul's transformations sharpens the shaman's focus on the wide screen of spiritual existence itself. In shamanic ideology, certain diseases alter the spiritual condition. Miraculous cure takes changes visible only to the clairvoyant shaman and makes them available to the naked eye.

This miracle play must effect the appearance of sacred powers, change supernatural conditions in a perceptible way, and restructure the world in order to move the patient and the audience into a healthier state. Discovering a cure means disclosing unmanifest forces by embodying them. In order to remedy the condition of his patient, the shaman acts out the supernatural state that conditions his own body and soul. Pierre-Yves Jacopin insists that the shaman's power does not consist in uttering mechanical magical formulae.[374] The Yukuna shaman's efficacy, for instance, requires an entire ensemble of sounds and symbolic gestures, songs, and dances. These are the effective outward manifestations of the secret knowledge that composes the shaman's existence; they are symbolic expressions that betoken an entire, extraordinarily powerful state of being. This state of powerful existence is sacred, for this quality of existence was achieved for the first time by the mythical hero Kawarimi (or some other mythical being).[375]

The performance of cure, which reenacts the gestures of mythic protoshamans, provides for the public what ecstasy provides for the shaman: a visible encounter with the forces at work in other planes of existence. The community needs this existential knowledge, mediated by the shaman, in order to sustain well-being.

Much of shamanic medicine, whether sucking or soul-restoring, involves the personal engagement of shamans with the forces of sickness that afflict their patients. In some sense, the curers themselves fall prey to the disease insofar as they step into the path of the attacking spirit to battle it — either during apprenticeship or in the healing séance. This means that the shaman can use his own extraordinary physiology on behalf of his patient in order to thwart and defeat the sickening spirits. The ordinary human, vulnerable and unprepared, need not face these powers: the sufferer has a champion who suffers for him. "One of the great merits of homeopathic magic is that it enables the cure to be performed on the person of the doctor instead of on that of his victim who is thus relieved of all trouble and inconvenience while he sees his medicine man writhe in anguish before him." [376] The care-giver needs the ritual opportunity to suffer publicly and symbolically in order to see and to understand what sort of realities confront him as he tackles a patient's disease.

The passion of the shaman and the drama of cure restore the optimal conditions of creation. In moments when order breaks down, communities discern, through negative example, the outline and spiritual meaning of the proper cycles of prey, penetration, intrusion, and consumption — the cycles that fuel the dynamics of the cosmos. Through ecstasy, the shaman already knows — indeed, in his mystical physiology he embodies — the invasive, intrusive interaction that occurs between realms of being; he has himself suffered such ruptures of plane while encountering the sacred at work in all dynamic processes. The shaman is an intercessor, specially equipped to cope with disorders due to soul-flight or the unseen presence of intrusive supernatural powers. Since an episode of sickness and recovery often launches a shaman's career by signaling his vocation,[377] it is not surprising that the shaman remains involved with illness as it afflicts those less fortified to combat it. By summoning the spirits and powers with whom he is familiar, the shaman enables the community to return to good health, that is, to resume its properly creative human stance in relation to divine beings, sacred space, and sacred time. As an antidote to sickness, shamans prescribe experiential knowledge of one's relationship to the sacred and, in the performance of cure, they dose it out through the miraculous intercession of their own bodies.

CONCLUSION ABOUT SHAMANISM

The diverse techniques and talents of the shaman form a vast symbolic complex at the center of South American religious life. The peculiar nature of the shaman's ecstasy causes these elements to cohere as a whole. Techniques of ecstasy transform the shaman's entire existence into that of a free spirit; that is, the shaman gains concrete experience of the primordial world. In new form, rearranged and adapted to supernatural conditions, the shaman maintains possession of the senses that ground his autonomy. He maintains mastery over his own meaning. Called and transported to other realms, the shaman clairvoyantly penetrates dazzling spaces far removed from the mundane world. During initiation, cut off from the rhythms of his historical community, he suffers the dismembering experience of living disjointed qualities of time. The ecstatic's experience of time is out of joint with the temporal rhythms of this world. Hearing the first creative sounds uttered in the primordium, the shaman acquires facility in the cognate languages of created nature: bird song, animal calls, rustlings of the wind, and the voices of seeds and stones.

The shaman is *made to understand;* his soul is physically refashioned for knowledge. Although his senses are reorganized into a physiology that is acclimatized to new kinds of meaning, he remains in control of himself when confronting sacred beings. He even takes possession of spirits so that they serve as his helpers. It is true that authority based upon ecstatic knowledge is not the exclusive prerogative of the shaman and that other specialists base their skills on the experience of ecstasy. However, these other types of ecstatic specialists do not become meta-ecstatics, do not use their ecstasy to specialize in the knowledge and practice of ecstasy itself as it applies to the general theory of spirits.[378] The shaman practices ecstatic transformation in order to recognize the changing spiritual world in all its apparent shapes: song, sound, smoke, consumptions; penetrating arrows, stones, and darts;

the hot light of crystals, fire, and feathered wings; the dark inner spaces of animal bodies.

Special knowledge sets the shaman apart from his peers. At the same time, in his pursuit of special knowledge, he does not forsake the community. Mastery of spiritual existence remains not only an elementary form of social life but also an essential ingredient of cosmic physics as well as of physical change in people, crops, and game.

THE RELIGIOUS AUTHORITY OF CONTRACTS AND CONSENSUS

Thus far, this chapter has discussed religious specialization as it inheres in persons who possess authoritative knowledge deriving from very different qualities of religious experience. The first sections briefly touched upon the possessed medium and the canonist (both the scholastic and the person magisterially designated for authority by canonical procedure), and the remainder profiled the experience of the ecstatic. It would be incorrect, however, to leave the impression that all religious authority is personal or individual. The authority possessed by binding contracts and consensus formed in group parleys also has a religious foundation. Ceremonial dialogue is one such parliamentary procedure.

The custom of ritual dialogue is widespread in South America. Brief descriptions of several cases will sketch some of its common features. The Akwē-Shavante practice a typical kind of formal dialogue in which each short phrase is pronounced rapidly and a "replier" responds antiphonally. For example, when a new person arrives in the community he must stand facing the chief and act as the formal "replier." [379]

The features of formality, exchange, and confrontation go hand in hand with the length of the proceedings. The Ranqueles welcome visitors and inquire about the purpose of their visit with solemn ceremonial dialogue. The adventurer Lucio Mansilla had ample opportunity to witness these traits in action; on the basis of his experiences among the Ranqueles, he distinguishes between two applications of the ritual speech: parliamentary speech and the solemn dialogue used at meetings. In both cases the structure of the ritual speaking is similar. However, in parliamentary speech, the proceedings are more structured than in the second type of ritual speaking, where there is more room for spontaneous interjection by the spectators. The ceremonial dialogue is invoked when there are at least two sides of opinion regarding an important issue. Two groups, each representing a particular perspective, put forward their best orators. [380] The orator for one side begins presenting his case by listing, one by one, the reasons why his group takes the position it does. Each reason is given in a formulaic, rhythmic way, chanted in a monotonous tone at a rapid pace. At the end of each briefly stated reason, the orator throws his voice into an interrogative tone, turning the statement into a rhetorical question that is answered in the affirmative with a chant from the group. When the first orator has finished his first round of reasons, the second orator immediately holds forth with a longer list of his own. Eventually, concessions are made, consensus arrived at, and contractual arrangements drawn up.[381] As one may surmise, such solemn dialogue is generally protracted to extreme length. Says Mansilla, "It lasted long enough to annoy a saint."[382]

The *oho* chant of the Waiwai is a highly stylized ceremonial dialogue. The exchange takes place between two people who squat on separate stools and chant archaic ceremonial dialect in a rhythmic fashion and in a high tone of voice at great speed. They avoid eye contact. A large part of even the content of their speech is stylized and formal, including lengthy opening sections of self-deprecation. The exchange may be extreme in length. "There is even an example of an Oho which went on for 26 hours without any interruption. . . . [D]uring this time the two chanting persons did not eat or move at all."[383]

Since the practice is generally directed toward the reconciliation of conflicting requests and claims, Fock considers the ceremonial chant a judicial institution. Requests or claims are pronounced in short sentences with distinctive tones. After each phrase the opposing claimant responds with a barely perceptible "oho," meaning "yes." The two participants alternate in taking the roles of principal litigant and affirming respondent. The practice is employed for marriage negotiations, trade, appeals to communal work, invitations to feasts, defenses against accusations of evildoing by "blowing," and lamentations before and after cremation, among other purposes.[384] In the example provided by Fock, the main section of the text is made up of nonsense phrases repeated over and over again.[385]

Fock contends that binding agreements are arrived at more through aesthetic means than through the content of arguments:

> The means to these important ends [solidarity and limits to conflict] is the speaking grace you must grant your opponent, who can propound his arguments unexposed to violence. The speaking grace is assured by the strict formalism and ceremonialism expressed in the sitting posture, the dialogue, the stereotyped chanting tone, the quickness, and the dialect words. The whole ceremony so completely binds the two implicated parties that the result of the Oho is not determined by public expressions of sympathy or the like, but is exclusively realized by the two parties involved.[386]

In his comparative analysis of this ceremonial institution, Fock observes that the area of its distribution seems to be mutually exclusive of that area in which the "weeping greeting" occurs.[387] Fock maintains that similar forms of ceremonial dialogue were practiced by the Trio, the Macusi, the Tauli-páng, the Yekuaná, the Achagua, the Cuna, the Cáua, the Siusí, the Jívaro, the Wapishana, the Nambikwara, the Witoto, the Boro, the Cagaba, the Paru-kotó, and the Yurakare, among others. The institution is thus found among several different language families including, the Chibcha, the Arawak, the Carib, the Tukano, and the Jívaro.[388] Fock suggests that it originated in sub-

Andean chiefdoms of Colombia, from which the practice spread to other areas. He believes that the institution reflects the administrative structure of societies that were more socially stratified than that, for example, of the Waiwai. He therefore concludes that groups such as the Waiwai have borrowed from differently organized, neighboring cultures.

PARLIAMENTARY PROCEDURE AND MYTHIC STRUCTURE: THE CREATION OF ORDER AND THE ORDER OF CREATING

On closer inspection, ceremonial dialogue in many cultures may be seen to derive its binding efficacy from its association with the power of myths. In some cases, the connection is formal: myths are delivered in the same way as ceremonial dialogue. Myth takes on power and contractual speech becomes binding through the performance of the same kind of speech-act. For the Kaingáng, for example, *wainyêklâdn* (ceremonial dialogue) is a singularly important institution. In this form of solemn ritual speech, "two men sit opposite each other and shout the myths at each other, syllable by syllable, very rapidly, while they swing their bodies back and forth to the rhythm of their shouting. One man shouts a syllable and the second man repeats it; then the first man says the second syllable, and the second man repeats it." [389]

The acts of myth-telling and parliamentary speaking are both oppugnant existential stances. They come about because of deep contradictions inherent in life. Their performance publicly manifests the combativeness needed to sustain human culture. They call into question present reality by creating a new quality of relations and a new kind of being, which ceaselessly confronts everyday existence. The new conditions can be understood and endured only if old ways are left behind. [390] Myth and ceremonial dialogue are not only creative but persuasive. In their very performance, they must create the motives of credibility and the conditions of plausibility for accepting new lifeways and abandoning old ones. For example, the Kalapalo perform their myth recitals in the manner of a ceremonial dialogue. The narrator is accompanied by a focal listener called the *tiitsofo*, the "what-sayer." [391] At each pause in the narrative, the *tiitsofo* inserts a responsive expletive such as *eh*, "yes." [392] Through these responses, the ceremonial listener orchestrates the content and emotional intensity of the narrative. A good performance makes the *tiitsofo* "see" the mythic events that the narrator "sees." The successful performance of narrative depends on the verbal competence of both performers as well as on their powers of concentration, for they must move simultaneously through the flow of matching mental images. Ellen B. Basso reports that, "as performance, Kalapalo narrative de-emphasizes the boundaries between individuals, perhaps more so than any other speech event. During the mythic narrative, the speaker attempts to create or enhance certain images in the mind of the listener, images that will, with skill, begin to approximate his own very closely." [393] Basso emphasizes that, "rather than ambiguity, there is a sense of a submersion of concrete individuality into a larger whole (the narrative event), together with an experience of concreteness and individuality through heightened cognitive work, by thinking about what is being said in a way that might not occur in casual speech." [394]

CONTESTATION

Shared structure, style, and ability to merge the images of separate world-views betray the fact that more significant connections exist between myth and ceremonial dialogue. They both owe their power to the creative speech-acts of sacred beings during the primordium. For example, the Trio, Carib-speakers living on the Brazil-Surinam border, maintain a rather complicated institution of ceremonial dialogue. Peter Rivière refers to it as a form of verbal dueling whose function (of simultaneously provoking fission and fusion) is similar to that of feuding in some other societies. [395] The Trio distinguish several different kinds of ceremonial dialogue. The "strongest" forms are the most formal. They are stylized ritual competitions between men. The competitors in the "strongest talk," a form of oppugnant rhetoric called *nokato*, reenact the origin myth of the dialogue. It talks about itself. Aside from the issues under discussion, the dialogue is powerful because it restages the moment of its own beginnings. In vivid image and gesture, the primordium itself is presented as a credible witness to the creative power of litigation. Contestants seat themselves on stools in imitation of eternal and mythical stone stools. [396] The most solemn ceremonial dialogue receives its urgency, its life-and-death efficacy, from its foundation myth in which there transpires a dialogue between a mythic figure and a piece of wood. The primordial dialogue should have been carried on with a stone, whose sound responses would have brought into this world the eternal and unchanging qualities of the stone's own character. Instead, the series of assertions and responses performed with the log (a being subject to rot and decay) brought death into the world.

Similarly, Tiriyó ceremonial dialogue bases itself on the conversation between the culture hero Pereperewa and the first woman, Waraku, whom he fished out of the river. [397] Spoken between two mythic characters from entirely different realms of being, their colloquy overcomes their differences and creates a whole set of new relations. The exchange also generates new items of culture, especially fish and other foods. Pereperewa (who is probably the supreme being of the sky) utters creative words that instigate a dialogue with the principal being from the realm of water (here called the first woman). This dialogue produces the human soul as well as human incarnate life. [398] For these reasons, ceremonial dialogue, the imitation of the creative encounter between entirely different qualities of supernatural being, is a suitable ritual behavior on those occasions when different social or linguistic groups must merge their cultural perspectives or self-interests creatively. [399]

Forensics and social contract derive their structure, efficacy, and binding authority from primordial speech, contests, and acts of creation. [400] Dramatically restaged in the lengthy proceedings of parliamentary debate, the original powers of ceremonial dialogue and legislative hearing appear in cameo as living witnesses to the effectiveness of the contestants' speech.

RELIGIOUS FOUNDATIONS OF SPECIAL AUTHORITY

This chapter has touched upon several kinds of specialization, both personal and institutional: medium, ritualist, diviner, shaman, and member of parliament. By unearthing the fundamental forms of knowledge that undergird these specialists' authority, it has exposed four kinds of religious experience: possession; ecstasy; scholastic inculcation of a structured, canonical lexicon of items; and faith in formal argument's power to create new solutions to conflicts between incompatible forms of existence (as happened at the beginning of time). The religious bases of specialism should not be confused with the functions to which they are applied. Any of the four forms described in this chapter may be applied, for example, to healing or evildoing.

The close study of the shaman illustrated to what extent the symbolism of the specialist's career depicts the religious world of the community. Not even the tiniest images (e.g., whistling, the seeds in the rattle, the light of the cigar) are trivial. Together they form a coherent symbolic complex whose elements are related by the meaning of ecstasy in that community's religious grasp of existence.

In all instances of specialization, public performance is crucial. All authority, even if self-appointed, must gain the recognition of some constituency in order to become effective. Performance renders the alleged basis of a candidate's authority visible and open to communal scrutiny. Legitimate authorities must make public appearances. By symbolically demonstrating intimacy with supernatural powers, a persuasive performance moves the community toward the conviction that the specialist's authority is credible. The admiration of the community does not always equal approval. Specialists in evildoing, for example, use their powers in unacceptable ways. Nonetheless, seeing the effects of the performance prompts belief in the power on which the evildoer's knowledge rests. For all that, publicity may weaken an authority's credibility. The necessity of staged performance always lays the practicing specialist open to the charge of hypocrisy, mere acting.

From the symbolic complexity of all the examples reviewed, it is apparent that separating specialists from laypeople takes a powerful imagination. To remain set apart by symbolic investiture from the rest of the community, specialists must maintain the vitality of their symbolic gestures, ornaments, and instruments of power. The exercise of their special role serves as vehicle for renovating contact with the sacred and thereby reimbues the community's imagination with power.

PART FOUR

TERMINOLOGY

THE MEANING OF THE END

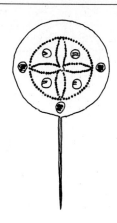

CHAPTER 8

DEATH AND THE
END OF TIME

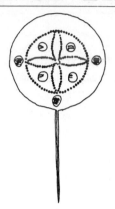

Termination is a significant and constant concern in human life. The closing part of this study deals with deliberate attempts to accomplish a proper end. The meaning that effects *termination* discloses itself through symbols associated with the death of an individual, in funeral rites and after-life beliefs, and the end of the world, in eschatologies. These beliefs and practices display the quest for a living language that must also function as a *terminology*, that is, as a set of signs capable of signifying an appropriate closure to meanings revealed as nearly infinite in number throughout the course of existence and as infinite in kind in the primordial beginning. Through the vivid symbols that mark the end of earthly life, cultures not only recall the *terminus a quo* of each form of existence but uncover the *terminus ad quem* of cosmic and personal life itself.

Endings are intrinsically probative. They take the measure of a reality, sound it out, and put it to the test. Death, for example, often comes about in the context of a trial: it is the result of failure to pass a test or to undergo an ordeal. In the beginning, according to the Tukano, Yepá Huaké, the creator, miraculously produced a pot of coca mixed with ashes, in which were concealed a serpent, spiders, and other frightening animals. The creator commanded Yúpuri Baúro, the chief of the Tukano ancestors, to eat this mixture, but he was afraid of the animals and refused. Because of his failure in this ordeal, death entered human experience.[1] Yepá Huaké then told some animals to consume the coca; because they obeyed him, these animals never die, but simply change their skins or shells. Corresponding to the ordeals of destruction and withdrawal undergone by sacred beings in origin myths of this kind, death and eschatology are the final strain gages of human and worldly significance. These endings test language, trying to the limit its capacity to reveal and communicate primordial meanings. Whereas myths of creation and origin reach toward the imaginative limits of primal chaos or sublimity, images of demise measure language against the final, outer reaches of experience and against the very end—both termination and *telos* —of meaning itself. Subjected to this end, the creativity of first appearances goes on trial; the meaning of death and the end of time subject signification to its ultimate test. Can symbolism completely account for itself by revealing the meaning of the end? Because death renders a judgment on the value of symbolic expression, the merits of all significant aspects of life hang in the balance. But where does the meaning of death manifest itself? To answer this question, we begin with a study of the signs of death as they appear in myths of its origin, accounts of its bodily symptoms, funeral practices, notions of decomposition of the deceased personality, and of the geography and life-style of postmortem existence.[2]

ORIGINS OF DEATH

Even the end is caught up with the beginning, since death originates at the dawn of time. To study the end, we must begin at the source of all significant imagery, the ceaselessly creative, mythic mode of being that characterizes origins. Myths of the origin of death do not generally rationalize death or show just cause for its appearance. Rather, in light of the fatal consequences, the explanations appear trivial, absurd, or ludicrous. The capriciousness of death's origin matches the freakish whimsy of its intervening presence. The images of death's origin reveal the significant ways in which death is real and has meaning; the first deaths serve as the frames of reference for all subsequent funeral procedures.

INFANT MORTALITY AND THE FRUITS OF THE MORTAL WOMB

In the primordial world, many supernatural beings suffered momentary and reversible deaths. They died or disappeared only to return soon after to fully manifest life.[3] Final, irreversible death frequently insinuates itself into the cycle of conception, gestation, and birth and becomes inherent in the process of regenerative life through the death of the first child or the first conceiving mother. Thus, according to the Desana, the first being to die was a male child of the daughter of the sun, whom she had conceived in an incestuous union with her father, the creator. The child was one of two sons, both of whom strove to become *payés* (shamans). Unable to take his mind off women, this son wasted away. No invocations could cure him. His symbolic trappings both signaled and effected his end: "His copper earrings, which were like grooves, like halves of a tube, turned so that the concave parts were toward his face, indicating that life was not with him."[4] After her child died, the daughter of the sun instructed the people how to conduct funeral rites, which would henceforth be necessary.

The death that arises in regenerative life often appears as part of the experience of the first mother.[5] Ironically, since it is the regenerative womb that spawns death, the first fruit of the womb may be an immortal hero. Once the immortal child is born the mother retroactively becomes mortal: death reveals itself in the mother, showing itself as an element of the matrix, the consumable and devourable flesh that gives birth to life of the same kind. The Chiripá trace the origin of mortality to the death of Nandé Cy ("our mother"), who bore the heroic twins Kuarahy (sun) and Yacy (moon). When Nandé Cy was devoured by supernatural jaguars (who are the masters of the destiny of the postmortem soul), her heroic sons tried to bring her back to life and almost succeeded. For the Chiripá the fate of Nandé Cy, whatever it may be, is that of all human beings.

> Then Kuarahy spoke again: "We shall try once more. I am going far away from this place while you must stay here quietly praying. When she begins to get up, pay no attention. Remain quietly where you are and do not call out 'mother!'" But hardly had the flesh begun to develop on the bones, than Yacy ran toward them shouting, and the bones again fell to the ground. It is because of Yacy that we, too, are unable to rise up. It is Yacy's fault that we cannot live forever nor remain eternally young. Because of Yacy, Kuarahy could not raise up his mother. If he had succeeded in doing so, we should not have to die. It is because of Yacy that life comes to an end.[6]

For the Chiripá, death enters the world, then, not through human action but through a divine drama. It is particularly noteworthy that death comes through a naming process that involves the moon. Tension between the intentions of the sun and the moon, these two powerful periodicities, is settled by the moon's effective control over the power of a name.

The irreversible death of the primordial mother introduces a new quality of time, one that reveals the dissoluble condition of mortal being. All changing and corruptible matter — blood, flesh, wood, humus — reveals this condition at some point in its cycle, a condition that is inert, dormant, decomposed, opaque, chaotic, and fertile with possibilities of new life.

In cases where it originates from the first placenta, death appears as an afterbirth, an element of the material matrix of regenerative life. In Makiritare myths death originates in the first placenta, the locus of first regenerated life, and becomes irreversible through the death of the first mother. An aspect of Wanadi, the creator, sent to earth to make houses and good people, committed the mistake of burying his placenta. Eaten by worms, the placenta gave birth to Odosha, a humanlike creature covered with hair.[7] The growth of this evil being in the rotting placenta brought death into the world. Wanadi, a being of perfect light, intended to unmask death as a dark illusion. In the light of his wisdom, death should have been revealed as unreal, a mere trick which could be countered through the power of dream, song, tobacco smoke, and *maraka* playing.[8] To prove death's illusoriness, an aspect of the creator put his head inside the darkness of his medicine pouch. There he dreamed his mother into existence, dreamed of her death, and intended to go on to dream of her resurrection. However, before death could be overcome by resurrection, the "hidden sleep" that was kept in the medicine pouch was released through Odosha's ploys and the screeching of a bird. The noise interrupted the life-restoring dream of the creator. Darkness of night drove away the luminous wisdom of Wanadi: "Sky hid itself."[9] Death and darkness are now fixed conditions of this world-epoch. But unborn, immortal beings are waiting to appear at the end of time, when the perfect light that is now invisible will return.[10] Death is a humiliating consequence of material existence, turning one into humus, the decayed and dissolute condition of prime matter rich with the possibilities of new life.

THE WRONG SIGNAL

At first, death was reversible and resurrection was the norm; a tragic mistake made death a definitive condition. An eastern Boróro myth about the origins of death and resurrection centers on Ari, the moon. Whenever Ari died, he was brought back to life by his older brother Meri, the sun, who would build an effigy of Ari out of wood and leaves, using a termite's nest for the head. Ari would soon awaken from his sleep, sit up, and finally stand up, fully restored to life.[11] Similarly, according to the Kamayurá, the creator of humans originally intended them to live forever. When they died, he cut sections of logs and, through the ministrations of funeral ceremonies, tried to revitalize them by transforming the logs into living, breathing flesh. However, the process was interrupted before it could be completed, and death entered the world.[12]

Regenerative life takes place in the symbolic world, the partial and fragmentary existence born in the wake of primordial destruction.[13] Often, a miscue, an ill-timed signal or incorrect sign, provokes death. Such was the case with the inward-facing earrings of the first Desana child, and the premature mention of the title "Mother" by her sons in the Chiripá myth. Unlike that of the primordial world, symbolic existence is a replicable and self-sustaining form of life. Mistakes made under such regenerative circumstances are irreversible and repeat themselves time and again. The Selk'nam relate that, in the beginning, when the culture hero Kenós lived on earth, people followed the example of Kenós and his companions when they grew old and feeble. He went to the north and lay down on the ground in his mantle with three other companions; after a few days of deep sleep they arose as rejuvenated, lively beings and had their bad odor washed off by Kenós. Those who did not wish to rise up rejuvenated became mountains, birds, winds, or animals.[14] It was Kwányip, a proto-shaman (*xon*) born of an incestuous union, who provoked symbolic life by distinguishing one expression of primordial being from another, thus creating a representative world of bounded, finite parts. He separated night from day, and he first definitively distinguished life from death, making them effective signs of separate modes of existence. When his elder brother lay down "dead" in order to rejuvenate himself, Kwányip sang powerful songs constantly and thus prevented his brother from rising from the dead. "Thus he remained dead until this day. . . . [E]ach person now remains forever dead."[15] The death provoked the withdrawal of several supernatural beings. Kwányip painted himself red in mourning and is seen as a red star in the sky.

In a symbolic world of subtle distinctions, meaning expresses itself in fatally complicated ways.[16] Significant meaning requires careful coordination of symbolic orders of space, time, light, sound, movement, and so on. The wrong signal, emitting the wrong one of its many possible meanings at the wrong place or the wrong time carries irreversibly fatal consequences. Any symbol can be deadly: ornaments, clothing, gestures, spoor, smells, tastes, colors, or sounds. According to some Baniwa mythic accounts, death should not have been a permanent condition, for the culture hero Inapiri-kuli, "he who is entirely bone," intended that skeletons be reinvested with flesh and take on life once again. This plan was frustrated by a mourning widow, who, disobeying the divine admonition, looked into the grave of her husband before the four prescribed days had passed. Instructed by his skeleton to coat him with a red color, taking care to smear the paint in one direction only, she failed to observe these directions and rubbed him the wrong way. In other Baniwa accounts,[17] the creator-transformer, Yaperi-kuli, intended that Mawerikuli, the first man to die, should rise anew from the grave, but the woman who was painting him for his "coming out" feast turned the stroke of her hand the wrong way and Mawerikuli dropped to the ground. The heap of bones fell with a thump, an irreversible, terminal noise. The wrong signal (the inappropriate movement of her hands, the incorrect design, the sound of his fall) had deadly effect; death is now an irreversible state.[18]

DISOBEYING ORDERS: FATAL CHOICE, BREAKING RANKS, AND DEVALUATION

Typically in these myths, an act of disobedience, often involving sound, is the cause of permanent death. The Ayoreo of the central Chaco Boreal trace the origin of death to the failure of their ancestors (*nanibaháde*) to obey (to listen effectively to) one supernatural being exclusively. In the earliest times the ancestors had to choose whether to obey the tapir, Dahusúi, who promised to make them grow fat, or the moon, Gidosíde, who promised immortality, an immortality consonant with the moon's own experience of ever-resurrecting life. "If you obey me," said the moon, "then you will never die. In truth, you will die as I do, I who come back after three days."[19] The *nanibaháde* chose to obey the tapir who, in the end, tricked them, since today there are both fat and thin Ayoreo. When the origins of death are traced to a fatal choice made during primordial times, the choice is often between a sensuous but mortal life and an eternal but static one.[20] For the Ayoreo, however, the choice is between a single, sensuous life of prosperity and a cyclically renewed life punctuated by death, which is never final.

Generally, the supernatural command that it is fatal to disobey is one that imposes a negative existence on creatures. Divine or heroic commandments surround existence with negative assumptions founded in the negativity that typically frames symbolic life. The symbolic is a paradoxical condition in which contraries overlap and coexist: nothing is exhaustively what it appears to be, and no appearance totally exhausts the meaning it signifies. Hence, injunctions take two characteristic forms: proscriptions imposing avoidance ("thou shalt not . . . ") and exhortations stipulating exclusivity (thou shalt only). Exhortation takes several forms, commanding people to act, speak, eat, dance, and adorn themselves only in such and such a way and no other or to regard certain entities (kin, allies, affines, enemies, supernaturals, cardinal points, colors, plants, etc.) as privileged and to relate to them or value them in such a way as to exclude from that position of privilege all other people, substances, objects, manners, and emotions. Proscription directly establishes negative relations, imposing absolute distance and separation by explicitly forbidding stated categories of act, thought, sound, time, food, or relationship. Exhortation indirectly imposes a network of negative relations, since the demand for exclusive ties with one kind of food, place, being, or activity implies a relatively negative evaluation of all other kinds.

Both types of negative command are intended to sort out and maintain communication, the condition of meaning in a postcatastrophic world. They switch open certain signal-paths by closing off other relations. If the commandments had been strictly observed, they would have maintained the patterned conditions conducive to perfect symbolic communication. In the beginning, all important signals could have remained unimpeded, distinct, and ranked in good order around the primary and unambiguous markers of social, dietary, sexual, territorial, periodic, and other taxonomic orders. The commands cautioned creatures of the new world against acting like primordial beings, the nonsymbolic and fully manifest realities who performed acts of sex, noise, consumption, dance, and travel with blatant disregard for where, when, and with whom they acted. The new creatures of the symbolic world were told that, if they wished to perform such wanton acts, they should at least refrain from doing so in the absolute manner of primordials and instead confine them to proper symbolic settings or times. Thus, breach of symbolic closure (of the womb, the mouth, the eyes, the season) is the key issue in "disobedience" myths of the origins of death and mourning.

Kamayurá myths of the origin of death, indispensable for understanding the behavior prescribed for Kamayurá funerals, treat this theme of preserving enclosure with high drama. In the beginning of time, Mavutsini(n), the creator of the world and of human beings,[21] intended to bring the dead back to life; to do so, he went into the forest and brought back three logs of wood. These he decorated with ceremonial ornaments and body-paint designs, the same patterns used in body tattoos today. He ordered a pair of toads and a pair of agoutis to sing near these decorated logs, called *kwarup*s. Forbidding the people to weep, Mavutsini(n) insisted they sing and play their *maraka*s without ceasing. This lasted the entire first day of this first ceremony, during which there was no weeping. On the second day Mavutsini(n) gave the order not to look at the *kwarup*s. At midnight the logs began to stir. "The cotton thread belts and the feather armlets were trembling, the feathers moving as if shaken by the wind. The logs wanted to turn themselves into people."[22] As the *maraca-êp*s (the toad and agouti singers) sang their hearts out, the *kwarup*s began to rise up out of the holes where they were buried. From the waist up they had taken on human flesh and features; only their lower halves were still wooden. Mavutsini(n) repeated over and over again that people must not look at what was going on. Around noon on the third day "the logs were nearly real people. They were all moving around in their holes, more human than wood."[23]

Mavutsini(n) had by this time ordered people to control what passed out of the opening of their eyes (by not weeping), what passed into the opening of their eyes (by not seeing), and what passed out of the opening of their mouths (by continuously singing and shouting). Now he escalated the degree of control required over openings: every entryway in every house was to be covered and shut tight. All the people were to enclose themselves in the houses, while he alone remained outside, beyond every form of closure, to watch the transformation. He promised the people that, when the moment was right, he would bid them to stream out of the houses shouting with joy and laughter. Only one other kind of control over openings had to be negotiated: "Those who had had sexual relations with their women during the night ought to stay inside."[24] At his signal, the people rushed out of the houses; the transformation was nearly complete. But at that final moment of victory over death, tragedy struck and human destiny was altered forever. The one man who had had sex with his wife could not contain his curiosity, "and after awhile he came out too. In that very instant, the *kwarup*s stopped moving and turned back into wood."[25] In a fury Mavutsini(n) condemned subsequent humanity to irreversible death. The *kwarup* logs would not only be used in festivals commemorating this fatal event. Mavutsini(n) prescribed that after each festival the *kwarup*s should be thrown into the water or disposed of in the depths of the forest.

Disobedience results in poor symbolic performance. Faulty signification introduces death. A Goajiro hero who visited the land of the dead was sent back to Juyá, the land of the living, and told by the divinity of the rains that are associated with the constellation Arcturus (that is, of the "year" marked off by the cycle of that constellation) that he could escape irreversible death on two conditions: he had to prevent his female relatives from greeting him with the ritual lamentations (ayalájakat[26]), and he had to keep secret all that he saw in his travels to the land of the dead and to Juyá. The hero did succeed in keeping his female kin from weeping when they greeted him, but unfortunately, he could not keep his mouth shut. "One day he recounted where he had gone. When he finished his story, he died."[27] He had seen the reality of death but was forbidden to communicate any sign of it on earth. Now the myth of the origins of death is itself a violation of this command. The hero's tale of his travels in the other world *is repeated in the act of deadly tale-telling that the narrator now performs for the ethnographer*. By virtue of the narrative human life becomes utterly transformed by the presence of permanent death. The performance itself makes death present. Other myths convey the same point: response, weeping, singing, and recitation are performative utterances that transform human existence, as did the sacred beings represented in them. Performing acts that signify the deadly quality of being dissolve human life and render it mortal.

Myths of the origin of death demonstrate how the efficacy of signs in this world eventually impedes the clarity of their meaning. Once one emits the efficacious signal of death, whether through unguarded speech, the inadvertent misdirection of body paint or earrings, or deliberate disobedience, mortality enters the world in the form of interruption, opacity, and noise.

DEADLY SOUNDS

Any inopportune signal suffices to bring death into the world. Of such signals, sounds (percussion, loud reports, cries, noise) are the most striking in the myths of the origins of irreversible death.[28] A closer look at the scenario in which the mother of immortals dies accents the role of sound in her passing. The Yamana report that death became a permanent condition when the mother of the mythical Yoálox brothers died. She lost her strength and fell into a deep sleep so that she was no longer moving. The two brothers began to cry. After she had been buried for a while, however, her voice was heard outside the hut. The elder brother stopped his crying and went out to see her. The younger brother, who wished her to remain dead, stayed in the house "and shouted furiously at his mother: 'Why are you coming back here? Leave us at once and stay away forever!' Then the mother retreated very slowly, never to return again."[29] The noise made by the younger brother, his curse, becomes the instrument of his mother's permanent condition of death. Although the fatal sounds in this case were distinct words, death-dealing noise need not be intelligible speech.

CRYING
Exploiting the mythic tendency toward redundancy, many accounts of the origins of death play with sounds. Not only do speaking, yelling, shouting, and onomatopoeic noises resound prominently in the oral recitation, but music and the sound of crying also figure in the story as instruments of death. According to the mythic accounts of the origin of the Mataco, for example, the first people did not die forever. Instead, the culture hero Sipilah gave instructions on how to bury people temporarily. Above all, he forbade people to cry over the dead. "[H]e would not allow tears, saying: 'don't cry, for in five days he'll be alive, and then he'll be young again.'"[30] Death was made a permanent condition through the treacherous actions of the perverse trickster, Tokhuah, who believed that "when someone died it was better for him to disappear completely." For this reason, "he told the relatives of the dead man to cry, for they had really lost their old father" And "instructed them to beat a drum and cry loudly all night after the burial."[31] Henceforth, percussive music became the efficacious instrument of death and the marker of transitions. In this way, Tokhuah gradually eliminated the deceased from the population of the living and had them admitted into his own village of the dead, where they live lamentably, in almost complete nakedness. Their bodies are bloodless, and they can no longer communicate directly with the

living. The dead usually journey to the postmortem village after five days in the grave. It is reported that once a dead man attempted to return to the land of the living in spite of Tokhuah's wishes, but the trickster "frightened him so badly by yelling and shouting at him that the man ran away and never came back. Then the people stopped reviving after death."[32]

WRONG ANSWERS

Creative relationships in the primordium were frequently contestatory: heavenly beings strove with earthly beings; the terrestrials or celestial birds battled with aquatic dragons; one kind of mythic animal preyed upon another. Through the precedents set by their outcome, the first oppugnant relations affected existence forever. Sound is an important ingredient in these adversary proceedings. The rapid-fire staccato of questions and answers during primordial interrogations, the rhythmic patter of antiphons recited by alternating mythic songsters, and the uproar of pitched battle are matters of life and death.[33] In myths of death, contestation frequently occurs in responsorial form, and, in a world where symbols are efficiacious, if the respondent fails to produce the proper password, countersign, grip, or high sign in the prescribed manner, death is the result.

Responding incorrectly is a sonic form of failing the test of death. The Apinayé believe that death entered the world when their wandering hero, a boy who ought to have been long-lived, ignored the instruction of the primordial jaguar. The account is set within a larger and important mythic narrative in which the young boy and his community obtain fire from the primordial jaguar. When the boy complains to the jaguar who has captured him that the jaguar's wife is threatening his life, the jaguar furnishes the boy with bow and arrow and instructs him to kill the wife if she menaces him again.[34] At noon the next day the boy is hungry, and he shoots the jaguar's wife. She falls down "with a roar. For a while he heard her roaring, then nothing was to be heard."[35] Unperturbed at the news of his wife's death, the jaguar feeds the boy roast meat and gives him directions back to his home village, warning him to be on guard during his journey home:

> [I]f a rock or the aroeira tree calls him, he should answer, but he was to keep still if he heard the gentle call of a rotten tree. In two days he was to return and fetch the fire. The boy moved along the brook. After a while he heard the rock shout and answered. Then he heard the call of the aroeira and again answred. Then a rotten tree cried out, and the boy, forgetting the jaguar's warning, answered it too. That is why men are short-lived; if he had answered only the first two, they would enjoy as long life as the rocks and the aroeira trees.[36]

Sound, as the quest for a song or name during initiation and the music or din during festivals show, is an essential marker of the transitions of human life.[37] Choosing the right sound for a given transition requires a calendrical calculation, and it affects one's destiny by situating one within the subtle modulations of space and time that make up cosmic existence. During the transition-initiation of death, it becomes supremely imperative to find the right voice, bringing the right supernatural presence into the order of time through sound, for one's whole destiny depends upon it. By replying wrongly (to the rotten tree, for example, rather than the stone), the losing contestant locates death improperly within the tense relationship between contradictory states of being, the struggle of signs that constitutes symbolic life. The sign of death misses its cue; its utterance is irrevocably mistimed and misplaced.

ANSWERS AS MATTERS OF LIFE AND DEATH

The origins of death are not simple, nor should the scheme of this section create the impression that the meaning of fatal sound is easy to identify. Even groups that speak the same language and share the same mythic corpus can show considerable divergence in their myths about the origin of death: sound may variously signify excessive openness, recklessness, antagonism, disobedience, inattention, ignorance, sadness, or some other condition. The multiplicity of myths of death and the many sounds that figure in these stories leave one with the impression that whereas each mythic variant brings a kind of clarity, none is wholly satisfactory. Taken together they appear to represent the profound cultural conviction that continued creativity and multiplicity are ways of grappling with or, perhaps, finally overcoming the meaning of death.

Staying with the theme of contest, let us examine briefly the wide range of variants possible in even a small sample from a single group. The Warao account for the origin of death in different ways, but principally by ascribing it either to sound or to female reproductive physiology. In one Warao account, shortly after the world was made, two spirits were to pass over the people on earth, who were to maintain a vigil throughout the long night. The first being to pass over would be death, to whom no response should have been made. Instead, people were to answer the call of the second, good, spirit of life. Unfortunately, a young man, who had fallen asleep, "awoke with a start and answered the voice . . . the call of Death."[38] In a nearly identical account, reported by Basilio de Barral, the animals and people of that time were promised that if they kept vigil and refused to respond to the call of death, they would not die, and that if they responded to the good spirit, they would live. "When our earth was profoundly silent, the animals, the felines and the people listened with a great deal of attention."[39] However, a young man, as in the other account, made the fatal response. That is why people die and animals, if they are not killed, do not.

The origin of death is associated with female reproductive physiology in a Warao tale of a man who married a water spirit. Against her instructions, but at the insistence of the other women, he sent her to the women's menstrual hut. There she died. Ever since, her father, also a water spirit, sends death upon the people when they go to sea during women's menses.[40]

One Warao myth of the origin of death combines the themes of female physiology and sound. According to this account, people descended from the sky world in the beginning of time. They left the first world behind by passing through a hole. Unfortunately, a pregnant woman got stuck in the hole leading from the sky, plugging it up before the *wisiratu*, the great proto–priest-shaman of the heavenly world, could descend through the opening. (The woman who had stopped up the sky-hole was the wife of the *wisiratu*.) Stuck in the sky-world, he "began to pace the firmament of the sky, shouting and stomping."[41] If anyone were to answer his ranting calls, all on earth would eventually die. If they refused to answer his shouts, they would live. At first, only the beasts of prey responded and became mortal. Eventually, after a long time, a human being responded and brought death into the world. Bringing new generations of life into the world is part of the same process that ushers in death; it is a process of transition, change, and passage. Only the *wisiratu* remains immortal, makes no transition from one place to another, is incapable of passage into the realm of mortal beings.

In all Warao accounts, the sound of a voice — either as a response to the call of Death or a curse that causes death — plays a role in making and marking the transition that is death. We cannot understand the religious meaning of the variant origin-stories, however, by reducing them to their common structure. In general, although helpful for uncovering the logical, aesthetic, linguistic, psychological, or sociological values of a people, to focus solely on common structures impedes close engagement with the divergent modes of mythic discourse and ritual symbolism. The religious value of myths appears precisely in the significance of their multiplicity; their multivalence is directly related to their capacity to depict the real and to reveal the ambivalent, ambiguous, and contradictory. Their religious value resides in the imagination, which spawns significant contradictions, puzzling and clashing images of what is real, accompanied by signals that the full meaning of these symbols transcends any single representation. As exemplified in such mythic variety, the religious imagination creates a perpetual need for new experiences and expressions and is constantly preoccupied with the conditions of creation and creative transformation. If one wishes to understand religious life, one must interpret the mythic mode of being evident in symbolic details and images; that is, one must do more than simply to *explain* a single story or set of narratives.

IMPORTANCE OF PROPER NAMES

Failed interrogation and improper response are not the only audible signals of death. Naming, too, can play a key role in death's origin. In several stories, use of the proper name at the proper time could have prevented mortality. Use of the wrong name for beings who are periodic (that is, who experience death from time to time) can cause the irreversible separation of life from death. The Cashinahua associate the origin of death with the origins of the moon, menstruation, the rainbow, and conception and birth. The hero Yobwë Nawa Boshka used to sneak into his sister's hammock under cover of darkness, which hid him from her sight, to have incestuous sex with her. After she smeared him with *genipa*, revealing his identity, he wandered in disgrace through the world, hunting with his brother-in-law. He returned home as a rolling head, and his mother suggested that he transform himself into something else. He decided to change himself into the moon by ascending into heaven along a pathway of six colored threads linking heaven and earth. He said goodbye to his family, predicting that they would see him again three days later, when he would appear in the sky. He gave them instructions not to offend him by crying out, "There's an entirely new moon appearing!" Instead, they were to call him by name saying, "Look at that. There is Yobwë Nawa Boshka renewed and appearing in the sky." He also forewarned them not to point a finger at the rainbow and say "There's the rainbow." He ascended along the "road of all colors" and took it with him into heaven, where it became the rainbow. Contrary to his instructions, a young girl, whose breasts were just beginning to swell, called out when she saw him, "Look. There's an entirely new moon appearing!" Immediately her vagina began to bleed—the first menstrual period ever. Now all women have periods. Apparently the first girl was stung by the tail feather of a red *ara* bird. From that day on, women began to conceive children. On the following day the rainbow appeared for the first time in the sky. Contrary to the hero's instructions, the first person to see it could not stop himself from crying, "There's the rainbow!" and pointing a finger at it. From then on, Cashinahuas began to die, something that had never happened before. "In fact, before all this happened, no one was born, women did not bleed, no one died, and neither the rainbow nor the moon existed."[42]

THE FIRST SIGNS OF DEATH: THE RECOGNITION FACTOR

All myths of death's origin illustrate that the meaning of death, in whatever image it first appeared (darkness, noise, moldering decay, faulty gesture or decoration, offspring or generative womb), has never been sufficiently recognizable for what it is. In particular, its consequences have never been entirely clear. That is why its noise, opacity, and disorder continue to obscure meanings needed to negotiate one's course through symbolic existence today.

The self-consciousness of mortals helps sort out the process of signifying and communicating primordial meanings in the symbolic world. Self-consciousness is predicated on the clear sense that one's existence is symbolic.[43] Awareness of one's own meaning, founded on a full experiential knowledge of one's own significations, contributes to the reestablishment of authentic communication in the cosmos. The fact that humans die becomes a key to this kind of knowledge. The self-consciousness of humans is exercised and developed through rituals that manipulate alienation and ceremonial death during transition from one state to another. Undergoing the symbolism of death, the great divide, cultures re-sort signs and analyze (break up or factor) noises into the separate sounds of music, language, speech, dance, color, design, and the other symbolic codes whose meaning is evident. That is, only by making sense of this new signal, the sign of death, and coming to grips with its obscuring effect does primordial meaning regain the clarity that maintains significant order in the cosmos.

Symbolic languages are a *"terminology"* not only because they must prove adequate to the meanings and ends of death; they must include the reality of termination at every turn. Symbols make metastatements about the ends and purposes of all bounded forms: speech units, such as inarticulate yelling, syllables, sentences, curses; hand movements, such as the direction of body-paint strokes; decorative articles, such as earrings; dance patterns; social statuses; weeping; and so on. Since every symbol includes and is predicated on its finiteness,[44] symbolic expressions must remain true to their overall end (the meaning of death, of depletion, and of the demise of time) at every finite moment right to that end. The intimate tie between symbolic life and irreversible death replicates the values and functions of termination at every level of structure and meaning. The following sections scrutinize symbolic life as it tests the power of its own imagery. During its most trying moment, the language of regenerative life confronts death in its most telling form.

FUNERARY RITES AND BELIEFS

Full reports of funeral procedures are rare, for death is not usually a programmed event, and investigators cannot time their visits to communities to coincide with death. Funeral arrangements, unlike scheduled festivals, tend to be notoriously ad hoc, taking unpredictable directions depending on the economic, physical, geographic, political, and other circumstances of the deceased, his or her relatives, and the community. Not knowing quite what to expect next, visitors who wish to record the proceedings often find themselves at the wrong place at the wrong time: with the family while the grave is being dug or with the gravediggers while the family mourns.

The following outline of topics should not suggest that peoples throughout South America, or even in the particular communities mentioned, follow the same rubrics at every funeral.[45] The few significant moments and acts presented do not represent a typical historical case, but rather provide the elements of an argument to the effect that death, when appraised through the symbolic acts, emotions, and beliefs attendant upon it, becomes a drama of human life, revealing in an extravagant way the nature of the sacred and the meaning of symbolic life itself.

THE MOMENT OF DEATH: PHYSIOLOGY AS AN ICON OF CHANGE IN MEANING

The instant of death signifies a profound change, one whose nature and effects are revealed in the shifting images of the dying body. New relationships with other dimensions of time and space provoke the individual's death by recomposing his or her physiology.[46] At the instant of irreversible death, or at some definable point of no return in the process of dying, the person's body manifests signs of the reconfiguration of the powers that constitute him or her, and this disposition of the soul or the spiritual elements is a prime factor in defining death.

Spatial indicators are of special importance at the moment of death. The body is, after all, a space. At death the elements of personal and social life no longer congregate in a viable way, for the space of the body no longer symbolizes their full presence. Most frequently, the soul, the organ of mythic and human history, abandons the space of the body, thereby also losing its accustomed place in all the spatial worlds that converge on the body. The moment that a body becomes a corpse, the spaces of the house, village, and universe come to signify a different meaning; they betoken not life but death.

The Makiritare offer a striking image of this shift in the meaning of space. The community is known as an *atta*, or *ëttë*, a word that refers not only to the community itself but also to the house in which it lives and to the cosmos, which has the same essential structures of habitable existence. The *kahityana*, the political chief of a Makiritare community, is the soul of the *atta* in every sense. He is the link with every dimension of its history since the beginning of time. He is the one who directs the construction of the village house, a process that reenacts the creation of the world. When the *kahityana* dies, the life goes out of the *atta*. The corpses of both are abandoned. That of the chief is interred at the foot of the center of the dead world, the central post of the house, where the life of the universe originated at the first instant of time. The house too becomes an empty husk, a shell of death, for the community immediately abandons it. The *atta* has died.[47] Thus, at the moment of death, space becomes an indicator of one's changing relationship to the diverse qualities of time.

Since change is constant in the transitional world of symbolic life, death cannot be defined by change alone. Death is change of a particular sort. A new kind of change — an irreversible one — effectively signifies death. At the moment of death, attendants commonly look to the cessation of breathing as the most evident sign of the passing of life. Throughout one's life, a ceaseless series of reversible transitions sustains life and induces growth. On the communal level these transitions, periodically carrying the group back through symbolic time, occur in festivals that reenact mythic events and the recurrence of the seasons; on the personal level, transitions in and out of death and other temporal dimensions happen during initiation, ecstasy, trance, ceremonial death, ritual drunkenness, and sacred song. On the physiological level, there exist a number of recurrent transitions in the form of ingestions, excretions, speech, hearing, weeping, and vision.[48] But it is the ceaseless series of reversible transitions of breath in and out of the body that most typifies the passages which sustain life, passing personal elements back and forth from one realm to another. Once reversible transition ceases, signified by the cessation of breath, so does life in this world. Since life in this epoch is a series of momentary deaths, care is taken to assure the community that this time the deceased has finally and irrevocably died.

The person who serves notice of death, whether a relative of the deceased, a neighbor, or a ritual leader, is not merely a medical examiner but a discerner of spirits. The disposition of a person's entire spiritual composition, manifest concretely in breath, muscle tone, pulse, color, smell, temperature, and sound, defines death. Death is a condition of the whole being; an expert reads the physiological signs as evidence of irreversible spiritual change. For the Krahó, for example, the stopping of the heartbeat and breathing indicate that the body has entered into the state of a cadaver (*ratek*). In a living person, wind (*khwôk*) enters the throat, proceeding all the way to the heart (*itoto*), and then leaves the body. "This vital breath is directed by the heart which also controls all one's movements, feelings, and thought."[49] However, the state of death brought on by the cessation of breath governed by the heart may be only temporary, merely indicating that the *karõ* (the soul-double of a person, which may be seen at times in photographs or reflections) has left their body. With the help of a curer, the *karõ* may be found and reinserted into the body of the "dead" person in order to restore him or her to life.[50] During this state of transitional death, the *karõ* may visit the village of the dead. However, the state of death becomes irreversible if the *karõ* enters into the communal life of the dead: eating with them or enjoying sexual relations, body painting, or log races with them. From this moment when the social, emotional, and physical aspects of life relocate themselves in another quality of space and no longer sustain themselves by periodically returning to the heart, their center in this life, wind never again passes through the throat.

For the Krahó, as well as for the Makiritare and others, the space of the village is consubstantial with the space of the body. As the body gives signs of the impending irreversible passage of the person from one condition of being to another, the Krahó individual makes a last passage through the geographic space of the world. The dying man makes every attempt to die in his maternal home, even if this requires a painful journey. In this uxorilocal society, a man's life emerges from the space of his mother's womb into the enclosed space of her family home on the periphery of his maternal village. This home furnishes individuals to the community, both the living community, which is sustained by the rituals performed at the center of the circular village, as well as the community of the dead, which exists beyond the periphery of civilized space. Just as he emerged into life in the maternal enclosure, the Krahó man should breath his last there, signifying his one-way passage into the new condition of death and prefiguring his emergence as a corpse. The cadaver belongs to the maternal home. The place of the womb that bore him is also, ideally, the material matrix of death. Symbolic actions related to the Krahó corpse make evident that this kind of death, different from the transition at parturition or the ritual death of ceremony, is a mode of being irreversibly separate from transitional life: once the gravediggers have torn the body from the possession of its kin, those kin must never touch it again.[51]

Exhalation of breath is an effective sign of transition. Although the final exit of air in the dying person's last gasp, sigh, or rattle helps effect death, it is not only that person's breath that contributes to the proper accomplishment of the change. In many cases, the breath of those present accompanies the breath of the deceased. The mourners' breath is symbolic, and, therefore, ordered. Song makes audible the symbolic order of their escaping breath. The Apapocuvá take full advantage of the idea that song is an effective sign of passage, the excretion of one mode of being into another.[52]

The Apapocuvá face death peacefully. A shaman keeps watch over the subtle physical changes of the dying body. As long as the dying person has breath, a choir of neighbors and kin continues to sing the special songs acquired in the life-sustaining transition of initiation.[53] Once the fatal outcome is clearly determined, however, the chanters start singing a different tune. From then on the desire is that death should come as soon as possible in order that the reincarnated elements of the individual's soul may again join the company of the living in different form. The whole process of dying is ritualized, guided by the president-shaman, who leads the assisting company in song. The melodies and rhythms change as the shaman observes the different stages in the dying process. Thus, taking its cue from bodily changes, the ritual of dying is marked off into episodes by variations in music. Scrutinizing the head of the dying person, the shaman watches for the instant of death. When it occurs, he leaves aside all strong rhythms and accelerated song and begins to intone the solemn *Ñeēngaraí*, the clear sweet melody with which the shaman accompanies the deceased soul on its path to the other world.[54]

Cultures may orchestrate the final exhalation of breath in other ways in order to control the effective sound that accomplishes death. Those present may induce the dying person to deliver a few last words to them. Or they may compel the dying body to give a clear sign of transitional life's irreversible departure by forcing the issue of breath from the lungs or bones in such a way as to emit the audible signal that executes the final passage. Among the Aónik'enk (Tehuelche), for example, the diagnosis that someone may be dying begins when someone falls unconscious or stops eating. This is a sign that one has an evil entity inside. Since the origin of death has always been associated with persons, however, the assistance of ritualized human agency will intervene before life ends in order to help accomplish a fitting end. When the time is right, the heaviest women of the younger generation, the largest daughters and daughters-in-law, sit down hard on top of the sick person's body. The patient's groans and moans are the sounds of the evil spirit's breath leaving the body. As C. Onelli reports,

> When the sick person, half asphyxiated, stops groaning, then one finishes him off by folding him doubled over with his chest over his knees. The daughters and daughters-in-law, ample and heavy as they are, seat themselves on top of him until a strange crackling noise of shattered ligaments indicates that the spinal column has given out and that the body has been reduced to a tiny bundle.[55]

Just as the transmogrified forms of mythic beings transformed primordial meaning at the demise of the first world, the physiology of human death modulates meaning in this world. The concrete changes of the body, most notably its sound (including its deadly silence), not only modify a human being's appearances but symbolize the altered conditions of significance itself as a being passes from one mode of presence into other qualities of space and time.

THE INQUEST

The causes of death are often taken into careful account because their significance can affect death's meaning. Among the Sanemá-Yanoama, for instance, death must have a reason. A death whose causes cannot be discerned or one that is provoked by sickness and fever without evident origin is nonsensical and gives rise to accusations and hostilities until a reason is found. As a result, it is incumbent upon the mourners to uncover the true causes of death.

The reasons for an individual's decease are often plain. For example, the Akwẽ-Shavante usually attribute the death of a mature adult to the malevolent manipulation of *wede-dzu*, a kind of sawdust often used to powder the hair of a participant during a ceremony. The evil manipulation of such powder constitutes sorcery (*simię-di*).[56]

Postmortem inquest amounts to a reconstruction of an individual's history, a biographical process. The signs of the deceased's existence in time are interpreted. When they begin such a historical hermeneutics, for example, the Toba already know that death occurs after a pathogenic spirit has entered the body. It is the specificity of a death that concerns them — death as it has appeared in a particular individual. They seek to uncover how the spirit took such strong possession of the body that it caused the person's soul to leave permanently.[57] Their inquiry displays and validates the history of this spiritual process. History is vital to the Toba. The danger of death is that the spirit may gain such total possession of the afflicted body that the victim may identify with the death demon and become a destructive spirit. Consequently, the distinction between disease- and death-spirits, on the one side, and the spirit of the deceased person, on the other, cannot always be clearly drawn. As a result, a person who was loved during life may be perceived as dangerous after death. The inquest leads beyond an identification of the historical facts to an evaluation and judgment concerning these facts' meaning for the future life of the community. On these historical judgments rest fundamental distinctions between respect, love, and fear of the images that appear in one's memory and patterns of avoidance in one's behavior or relations.

The history retrieved during an inquest is not merely an evaluation of existence in the time signified by the deceased's life span. A full inquiry into the causes of death often considers the clash and contradiction between other modes of time pointed to by the entire symbolic existence of the dead person. These include mythic realms at the beginning of time as well as marginal or anomalous worlds contacted by the deceased, his acquaintances, or enemies. Don de M. le Marquis de Wavrin reported in 1930 that the

Jívaro attributed the immediate causes of fatal sickness to "sorcerors" who sicced powers of affliction on their enemies. Ultimately, however, the cause of death was a supernatural water serpent named Pangui.[58] Through dreams, fasting, and ritual acts the Jívaro learn the lessons they need to know from history; they discover the specific ways in which primordial chaos has insinuated itself into social and personal life.

More disturbing than cases where the causes of death are known are the cases where the motives for death are less clear, such as untimely death through accident, sickness with anomalous symptoms, illness of unknown origin (such as epidemic disease brought by colonists), or suspicious circumstances. To clarify matters, relatives or neighbors conduct an inquest, using special heuristic techniques or consulting a coroner or diviner adept at bringing the hidden forces of death to light.[59]

Death is not generic. Each death exhibits a unique conjunction of realities, which accounts for its presence in this person in this moment, place, and manner. An individual's situation may portend his or her death and lead to the development of a prognostic system. The Kaingáng believe that certain omens may foretell death. These foretokens are often particular to groups of people. For example, those who ceremonially decorate their bodies with line patterns are those whose origin, at the beginning of time, was the boundless ocean to the east. For these people, rain and flooding rivers foretell death. However, for the people who decorate their bodies with dots during ceremonies (whose ancestors emerged from over the dry mountains in the west), dry river beds predict death.[60] The images of their original transition into life characterize the instruments of their dispatch from it. The efficacious symbolism of the one limen, the outer margin over which one crossed in the beginning, must be evident also in the limen at the end.

A more mysterious cause of death among the Kaingáng is intercourse with particular supernatural monsters or ghosts. The supernatural being seduces its victim at night, leading it away. After succumbing to temptation, the victim falls ill and bleeds to death or goes insane.[61] Widows and widowers are especially vulnerable to this kind of seduction by the ghost of their former spouse.[62] Ghost-souls love and long for the company of the living. If they can, they will take living souls with them into death so that the living will not suffer by mourning their absence. In short, one death can precipitate an enormous migration of the living into the realm of the dead.[63]

Bringing to light the supernatural seductions that cause deaths of this sort is necessary and difficult. The way in which the cadaver burns helps reveal the cause and meaning of death for the Kaingáng. The ultimate cause of death is the total loss of the soul, which has been enticed away either by the good hunting or good sex offered by supernatural beings, the *nggïyúdn*. If the soul has copulated with *nggïyúdn*, death is inevitable and the victim will rot inside or go mad. In such a case, the corpse will be slow to burn or will explode. On the other hand, if there has been no prior sexual contact with the spirits, death is due entirely to the *nggïyúdn* devouring the victim from within.[64]

The inquest is a hermeneutics of retrieval motivated by suspicion. It does not seek to create a meaning but rather to decode and identify the devastating presence already announced in the peculiar signs of a particular death. The coroner's report, like history, is the outcome of a process of recognition or even of revelation. It may attribute blame, but it does so only by recognizing a presence announced in the residue of terminated acts that determined final meaning. Unlike myth, where the beginning appears first and whose interpretation amounts to repetition or imitation of the acts that constitute the creative foundations of culture, historical inquest reads the past from its fatal consequences, reconstructing unique interpretations of irreversible events in order to avoid a repetition of their deadly effects or to transcend the signs of their endings. Incumbent on the postmortem inquiry is the creation of an *interpretation* that can serve as a criterion for evaluating future behavior, imagery, memory, and other forms of the reflective life. Inquest about death becomes an exemplary moment of the examined life.

SYMBOLIC HARDWARE OF AN UNDERTAKING

Burial presents special opportunities for understanding religious life in South America. Evidences of the special care exercised in disposing of the dead, along with tools for hunting and weapons for taking life, are the earliest evidences of human life in South America. Unfortunately, without our being able to see the symbolic action, to hear it explained, and to acquire knowledge of the mythic world it signifies, the meaning of burial and death remains virtually impenetrable. In Venezuela, for example, there is evidence of a pattern of skull burial in which the skull was placed carefully and precisely between two vases bearing polychrome designs. Archaeologists have found the same disposition of materials in several sites which bear no relation to the cultures known to have occupied the area during historical times. José Maria Cruxent suggests that the evidence points to an as yet undiscovered cultural complex in the region of Lago de Valencia.[65] The motives behind the care given these remains will in all probability remain unknown. Once the funeral performance is over, burial places signify the state of being they represent: opacity of meaning to those living in another condition of time.

For this reason the following discussion relies on several detailed descriptions of funerals set within the context of the significant imagery, beliefs, and practices of the cultures in question. These symbols and their mythic meanings help reveal death as a fully symbolic fact, that is, as a meaning whose reality helps interpret every aspect of human and cosmic existence. The focus falls on several images, ideas, and practices that often punctuate funeral proceedings, including the following: covering the cadaver with shrouds, ornaments, or some other wrapping (e.g., a pot, coffin, or leaf-bundle); ritual strife and morbid humor; images of cutting and separation; ceremonial feeding; burial; and cremation.

SYMBOLS OF CLOSURE

In many myths, excessive openness and imperfect closure brought death into existence. During ceremonial death, especially at moments of transition through life, ritual seclusions enshroud space in order to define times of change.[66] The ambiguous imagery of enclosure surrounds death to the end, for the dead are often enveloped in containers during their disintegration, their permanent state of dissolution. Because all containers hide signs of life, they can be instruments of transformation and change. The precise nature and meaning of that change depend on the meaning of the transformative enclosures appearing in the primordium. Those first pots, bundles, gourds, and graves revealed the powers that fill all the bounded spaces inhabited by transient life forms. Funeral enclosures (casket, grave, body wrappings) are part of the same continuum of meaning. For example, even the gourds ordinarily used as containers in Kamayurá household processes are placed beyond use during the funeral period. All Kamayurá containers are linked together by myth. The calabashes of ordinary household use are identified as part of the symbolic spectrum of transformative enclosures, which also includes the mats and netting that enshroud the corpse. All of these containers are expressions of the primordial container, the mythic gourd in which the supernatural heroes Kwat and Yaiì incubated, gestated, and came to term and from which they were born after they had been torn from the womb of their slain mother. "[T]he mat of buriti palm which surrounds the dead person in his grave from the feet up is made of the same material and is placed in the exact same position as the ritual enclosure which isolates those who are hidden away for ritual purposes in the outer world — in precisely the same way that the calabash gourd isolated the two heroic twins."[67] When empowered to do so, all Kamayurá containers are instruments of passage and transformation of life, able to bring death to existing conditions. That is why even domestic jars and gourds cannot be used at this time.[68]

Redundancy reveals the centrality of closure. Funeral proceedings multiply the images of enclosure. In the same funeral the cadaver may be covered with paint; wrapped in leaves, ferns, or vines; surrounded with mats; and put in an urn, which is then placed in a hole. The deceased's body passages may be tamped up, the mouth and eyes deliberately shut before rigor mortis sets in, and the arms and hands folded or otherwise arranged to signal closure. Among the Guayakí, the ceremonial weeping of women announces death. Then the undertakers enwreathe the cadaver with vines, binding it into a fetal position. Interred in a deep pit, the bundled body kneels, facing the sun. Placed all around it are mats, which protect it from the earth. The hands of the dead person are wrapped across the face with the fingers arranged against the temples. Spread and bent, the fingers "reproduce the claws of the jaguar," into whose "hands" the deceased is forever commended.[69] Images of enclosure continue to multiply. Earth covers the whole complex carefully and lightly, and, to top things off, when all these enclosures are formed, a miniature replica of the seclusion hut (tapy) used during life-cycle transitions is constructed over the grave.[70]

CLOTHING AND CLOSURE
Prominent among methods of achieving closure and concealment is the use of clothing. Clothing accomplishes the occultation of enclosure. Usually, the

wearing of ceremonial attire and accoutrements is restricted to the festivals that renew the signs of life by bringing closure to the seasons, those qualities of being manifest in temporal imagery and marked off into the periods of the festival calendar. Ordinarily used only for festival, the commemoration of a primordial time set apart from mundane time, party clothes and liturgical wear are taken off and put out of sight (or even destroyed) after the "time out of time" ends. When it adorns the corpse, however, festive garb signals irreversible closure, buried with the dead body, it shrouds it forever. Reporters of Araucanian burials have remarked that corpses are dressed in colorful new attire, which the mourners bring to the funeral to deck out the deceased with unprecedented elegance. Also notable is the Araucanian custom of *echol*, in which the deceased is furnished with grave goods essential to ceremonial and economic life after death: weapons and hatchets for the men; woolen textiles, spindles, pots, and broken grindstones for the women.[71] The outfitted corpse is hidden away in much the same way as liturgical wraps, sacred masks, and ritual ornaments are cached during the off-season, with the difference that the condition of occultation is periodic in the case of ritual clothing but perpetual for the corpse. Graveclothes indicate a closure of a different order from the recurrent transitions that sustain life, one that excludes further change; the wrap does not come off. Personal property, too, becomes a token of death. Permanently enveloping their possessor, the goods accumulated in passages and exchanges over time become signs that this final transition is for keeps. One's fate is sealed.

Death is an occasion for the display of closure in its most conspicuous forms, and its finality is vividly exhibited in these multiple wrappings and seclusions. The occasion of death gives manifest form to closure through consummate finery. The Kamayurá carry this costumery to the limit.[72] Pedro Agostinho delineates the Kamayurá funeral process, paying particular attention to the rites surrounding the death of the morerekwat, the village headman.[73] The body of the corpse is painted for the last time. The funerary decorations and body painting are quite elaborate and distinct, as are the many ceremonial decorations placed on the body. The corpse is dressed up as for a feast, with cotton bracelets, feather ornaments, belts made of cotton thread and shells, beads, garters and legbands, earrings, and special necklaces. This list barely begins to describe the careful and detailed ornamentation of the cadaver, which adornment represents the consummation of the dead person's symbolic life. An emblem of the sex of the cadaver is placed in each hand. Women hold a spindle in one hand and in the other an *uluri*, "a small triangular vaginal ornament of whitish bark which is attached to a palm-fiber belt and worn just above the labia by the women of the Alto-Xingu."[74] Men hold a bow in one hand and arrows in the other. If the deceased is a shaman, he is also supplied with some of the trappings of his office, such as his rattle, an emblem specifically related to his particular helper spirit, some tobacco, magical herbs, and so on. The corpse and its accoutrements are wrapped in a network of swaddled matting so as to form a careful series of designs from head to toe. These windings are arranged to correlate with the identical body-paint patterns with which the mourners, using *genipa* paint, have darkened their own skins. Images of real death, the signs enwrapping the dead body, mottle the decorated mourners.

The wrappers of death can provide the opportunity for closures of other sorts. The Kamayurá funeral rites celebrated for someone of the village-headman (*morerekwat*) "class," for example, are an essential precondition for the celebration of Kwarìp, the principal festival cycle of the Kamayurá and other groups in the Upper Xingu area.[75] The Kwarìp ceremonies are the source of fertility and new life in the world. In other words, prominent death helps terminate the periods of time between the celebrations of the important Kwarìp festivals.

By bringing an end to the current epoch, village, and world, death surrounds the Kamayurá community with the quality of mythic time that is commemorated in festival. The closure marked by an individual's death, evident in the heavy decorations, renews communal and cosmic time by returning community and cosmos to their beginnings. Every move is governed by myth, for the Kamayurá funeral proceedings and even the structure of the graves go back to the very first times.[76] That is why, from the instant of death onward, the actions of the participants are highly stylized and carefully orchestrated.[77] They reenact the parts played by the supernaturals when they created their masterpiece of cosmic and social life. At the moment of the *morerekwat's* death the people of the village gather at the house of the deceased leader. To some degree, the whole community enters the state of occultation and ritual enclosure. All the mourners bring ceremonial ornaments and darken their bodies with paint. They raise a din, keening and crying. After a brief time, a number of men, having obtained permission from one of the *yayat* (lit. "gifts of the dead," classificatory kinsmen who act as directors of the funeral), dig a grave in the center of the village plaza. When a headman dies the funeral rites begin with the ceremonial construction of the *apenap*, a temporary enclosure made of very short lengths of wood, which completely encircles the gravesite. This usually occurs some three days after the body-paint of mourning has been reapplied, resealing the bodies of the mourners and the gravediggers with a new coat of paint.

THE WOMB AS THE SIGN OF MORTAL CLOSURE

The end of any particular mode of life suits that mode of being and, consequently, is determined by the nature of its beginning. From its origins, fertile life is wrapped up with death. That is why final closure represents a return. The condition of being that snuffs out regenerative life has been an occult part of life from the moment of its conception in the dark place of the womb. Death, the final condition, fulfills and completes all the partial appearances of mortality (prenatal life, passage out of the uterus at parturition, disposal of the placenta, the excretions through bodily orifices, the detritus of one's life, the ordeals of sickness and transition). It should not be surprising, therefore, to find the enclosure of death likened to or associated with the womb.

Gertrude E. Dole has described an Amahuaca funeral rite in which a child's corpse was folded up and sewn into its mother's skirt. While the mother keened over the bundle a young man dug a shallow grave in the center of her house. The corpse-bundle was placed in a large cooking pot and lowered into the grave, where it was covered with another large pot and palm-leaf mats. Then the grave was filled loosely with dirt. Materials that had come in contact with the dead baby were destroyed. The mother then used a smooth stone to rub and pound the grave's surface until it was completely flat and solid.[78]

While the tomb may represent the womb, the material substance of this final womb is different from the natal one. Once one took on carnal life in the fleshly womb; now, other sorts of transformative containers influence one's future condition: earth reduces one to prime matter; gourds initiate one to the dissolute state of vegetal rot; and so on. The precise meaning of the transformation inheres in the mythic power of the particular symbolic container (e.g., fired clay pot, leaf bundle, traveling vessel, wreath of ferns or greens, textile mantle, wooden crate, fiber net).[79] This meaning must be regarded in the light of its cultural context. For instance, among the Canelos Quichua, the corpse is placed in a container, which symbolizes a canoe, along with food, drink, and effects, and the "canoe" is buried along a cardinal axis. A plantain stem is planted near the head of the corpse.[80] Before being placed in the ground, the soul leaves on its journey to the sky-world and underworld. It may eventually enter another being or become a star. The dead Warao (Winikina) boatmaker is also laid in a canoe, but for the Warao this action represents his being placed in the vagina of the goddess Dauarani, from whom regenerative life came in the beginning. While he lived, the artisan had seen the goddess during an ecstatic journey he made to her home on the horizon. There, during a passing moment of ritual death, he took the measure of her parts. With every boat he built, the craftsman experimented with the image of perfect closure, the final container of death. Now, in death, the canoe becomes what it has always signified: a vessel of one-way transport to a new world and the womb of rebirth to a new, supernatural life.

Mythic conceptions of the tomb-womb vary widely. The traditional manner in which the Shipibo and Conibo disposed of their dead, for instance, consisted in bending the corpse into a kind of fetal position and placing the body in a burial urn. The urn was actually a very large cooking pot, deemed to "correspond to a kind of ceramic womb. Thus the very act of burial also was an act of impregnation of the earth with the spirits of the dead, who were going to be born again."[81]

The nature of the mythic image used to achieve closure reveals the specific values of death, the transmutation of incarnate existence. Because death is the ultimate ritual seclusion, it effects the passage from transitory existence to the domain of postmortem life. Funeral enclosures accomplish the complete transfiguration of the dead person. By irreversibly dissolving or occluding the significations that marked the deceased in this world (physical features, personality traits, social statuses, change, and growth), these final seals foreshadow and make room for a new kind of appearance under utterly new conditions.

FEARFUL RESPECT FOR THE DEAD

The act of sealing the dead from sight by bedecking them in their finest array unveils a fundamental ambivalence toward death. Ironically, high visibility and conspicuous display also cover over a mysterious mode of existence. At its final passing, human life, relatively at home in the symbolic world, now assumes a fully supernatural expression, the unmanifest condition of sacred beings. That is why the dead become objects of fear and awe, dread and attraction. Although mortal remains take up space, all signs indicate that the meaning of the dead being has no place in this world. The deceased becomes unfamiliar to relatives and dangerous to have around, even if remembered with fondness and longing. Memory, dream, and image become sources of danger and dis-ease. It is certainly true that discomfort with death has what might be called psychological and sociopolitical value. But what is more interesting for our purposes is that funerals and mourning reveal death-related ambivalence to be a religious situation.

At times the ambiguous attitude toward the dead expresses itself in downright contradictory behavior. Loved or esteemed until their moment of passing, the dead are quickly set apart from the living even though the community mourns their loss and seeks signs of their continued presence among them. After a Shipibo individual dies, the body is removed from the house. However, ashes are scattered behind it so that the footprints of the deceased person's spirit, as well as the tiny footprints of the demonic being who killed him (if the patient died due to witchcraft[82]), may be seen in them. Thus even while all signs of the dead are disposed of, ambiguous preparations are made to preserve every last trace of them: ashes are even spread over the covered grave to protect survivors against death.

Explicit fear of the dead often emerges swiftly. The community takes immediate action to protect itself by dispatching the deceased and his or her effects. Such is the case with the Kaingáng, whose funerary rituals are the most elaborate ones they possess. Through the rites the spouse (thûpáya) and the whole community are protected from the ghost-soul (kuplêng) because the rites destroy all contacts with the deceased.[83] Since they are pathogenic and lethal, all items belonging to the dead person are disposed of. "Every death can be explained in terms of a ghost that has followed the owner of some bit of property that belonged to it while it dwelt in a living body."[84] Dogs are also killed and great emphasis is placed on the destruction of pots from which the deceased had eaten. The spouse, in order not to see the bones of the dead, leaves for isolation before the cremation and burial. The spouse is not allowed to eat food cooked in a pot until all the death rituals are over. Eating food cooked in a pot would cause death from heat. Nor does the spouse eat any meat during this period.

The Kaingáng offer one of the most touching images of ambivalence toward death. The surviving spouse sleeps with his or her arms wrapped about the stems of a large *nggign* fern, just as he or she once clung to the deceased. This same fern plant, used to ferment beer, also lines the grave and enwreathes the deceased's cremated bones. The fern is an ambiguous presence, both a marker of death and a sign of the new, festive life that ferments after liquidation. Rounding out the fern's role as a sign of the condition of total and all-encompassing respect (including the sense of honor and avoidance) is its power to frighten away the *kuplêng*.

That death, for the Kaingáng, is a paradoxical condition of being is also evident in the redoubled reversals of the funeral rites. Mourners perform special funerals songs and circular dances around the seated widow or widower. Dancing with rattles, whose noise keeps the *kuplêng* away, the mourners succeed in frightening themselves quite badly. Although they dance ostensibly to protect the widow, "they are afraid of the woman because she used to live with her husband . . . that is why they dance the woman."[85] To complicate contradictions even further, for a period of time, public roles and symbols are deliberately reversed. Body-paint marks belonging to one group are worn by a different group. Women, who usually serve drink, are given drink instead. Children, contrary to normal custom, get up in the morning before their widowed mother rises. Vessels belonging to particular individuals are exchanged in order to confuse the ghost-soul.

In the presence of death, ambivalence reveals itself as a total condition, akin to primordial chaos. Conditions that ordinarily are opposed to one another, such as fear and fascination, longing and dread, or love and hate, appear in an absolute and unbounded form. Their unbridled coexistence creates a single existential situation that is overwhelming and consumptive.[36] This does not mean that the experience is unimaginable; it is figured in the image of universal catastrophe. Cataclysmic fire, flood, darkness, stone, and rot reappear in forms of funeral pyres, weighty memorial stones, durable bone relics, bonfires or flames, all-night vigils, libations, toasts, heavy drinking during wakes, watery graves, and so on.

For the Campa of eastern Perú, for example, fearful respect for the dead soul is a prime consideration in the disposal of the corpse. The body is usually thrown into a river after being weighted with a stone.[87] Alternatively, the body may be set adrift on the river after having been tied to a raft. In some cases, the body is slung from a pole and then carried to a place where it is either buried or abandoned. The corpse may, in rare circumstances, be buried in the house. Weiss also reports the practice of cremation. "In any case, the settlement ordinarily is abandoned" and the house burned.[88] The house-burning is a prophylactic against the demonic activity that caused the death of the victim. The River Campa, according to Weiss's report, have no formal period of mourning or expression of grief.[89] It is understood that the victim will soon be followed by those who are burying him. When a corpse is pitched into a river, the Campa exclaim "Go ahead! Watch for me, I [also] will die, I."[90]

Nevertheless, the Campa do observe certain customary symbolic actions at death, which reveal a fundamental ambivalence. The day after someone's death, the surviving relatives ingest substances that induce vomiting. The vomiters include members of the immediate family.[91] If a child has died, the child's father seeks a tree noted for its poisonous sap. He shoots his arrows into the tree and leaves them there with his bow so that demons will not take the child's soul. This action also protects the father's other children. The members of a dead person's immediate family have the hair cut from their heads, an action believed to prevent the early death of other family members. According to some of the Campa, shaving the head insures "that the ghost of the deceased will not recognize the survivors and carry off their souls."[92]

At the time of the death of a Campa child, immediate family members remove armbands and legbands and exchange their clothing with others in the community. For perhaps two months they do not wear their own clothes. This action prevents the ghost of the child from recognizing them. Strips of cotton function symbolically as snakes, which protect against the appearance of the ghosts of dead people. If a community does not move after a death, such cotton strips are strewn on the paths leading to the community residence. The siblings of a dead child have strips of cotton attached to their necks to ward off the ghostly soul.[93] Many Campas also abstain from spinning for a few days after a death, fearing that the spun thread may become the dead person's intestines.[94] The practices of the neighboring Machiguenga people show more explicitly how creative processes are associated with chaos in situations of ambivalence. They remove their armbands lest they be transformed into the veins of the dead person and cause death to the wearer. The women stop spinning after a death because threads would be transformed into the intestines of the deceased, attach themselves to the intestines of the living, and bring about the death of the community.[95]

BREAKING AND CUTTING
Prominent among symbolic attempts to penetrate ambivalence of death are images and acts of mutilation, slicing, biting, gashing the skin, and gnashing the teeth,[96] whereby mourners can cut through the unbroken continuity of ambivalence. Funerals frequently include acts of self-injury through scratching, scourging, splitting the skin, tearing out one's hair, or tearing one's clothing or ornaments. Orestes Araujo gathered several reports of finger amputation by widows or close relatives of a deceased person during the period of mourning among the Charrúa of Uruguay.[97] Cutting, breaking, and biting leave impressions, mark fundamental distinctions, and reimpose symbolic order on chaos just as some form or other of sacrifice, by dispelling absolute darkness or deluge, divided the primordial from the mundane mode of being to initiate life in this world. The mutilations of mourners make visible the process of symbolic existence, which imposes distinctions between modes of being, sorting out fear from fascination. For example, during the Siriono mourning period, which lasts about three days, the mourners cut

their legs with the eyetooth of a rat or squirrel, smear their faces with *urucú*, and decorate themselves with feathers. These are precisely the steps taken by parents at the birth of a child.[98]

Breaking skin, rending garments, smashing utensils, and destroying ornaments or personal effects overcome chaos by rending differences in a sacred, fundamentally seamless, reality. Because they confront the inordinate (irrational, undifferentiated, indistinct) condition of primordial being in order to dispel it, the mutilations of mourning must be impressive. The Tehuelche, for example, cut themselves, making their blood flow throughout the funeral rites. Men mutilate their feet and women scarify their cheeks, and both sexes cut their hair, the women in the front and the men at the nape of the neck. The dogs of a deceased man have their throats slit; his horses are hung and consumed by the mourners.[99] In the chaotic presence of death, these actions express the desire for an experience of division that will not only separate death from life, conceptually and existentially, but restore the possibility for all the distinctions that make symbolic life possible. These acts subject death to sacrificial existence, they make death holy by making it a symbol of the sacred, which withdrew or was dismissed at the end of the primordium. With contradiction and paradox, funeral performances reenact that ambiguous act of dismissal and abandonment, which dispatches the chaotic presence of death.

According to Allan Holmberg, the Siriono try to avoid paying attention to a dying individual. Eventually, however, relatives of the dying person gather around to watch his last gasp.[100] Before the moment of death, they take him from his hammock and place him on a mat of *motacú* palm. Women begin to mourn and keen. Men smoke tobacco in their pipes or, if a renowned hunter is dying, probe him with questions to hear the last word on places to find the best game. The corpse is not buried but is placed within two mats of *motacú* palm and laid on a platform in the house. The house and the personal belongings of the deceased are then abandoned. There is a danger that the ghosts of the dead may become either *abačikwaia*, invisible and formless evil spirits who bring bad luck, sickness, and death, or *kurúkwa*, visible monsters whose ugly, black, and hairy shapes resemble human beings. *Kurúkwa* lurk outside the house at night. "Before leaving, the men shoot arrows in all directions through the house to drive out the evil spirits."[101] For the Siriono, ambiguity toward the dead remains even after the flesh rots off the bones. All the bones except the skull are buried. This interment prevents the soul from wandering as an evil spirit or a monster. The skull, on the other hand, is kept as a relic. Fearful of but fascinated by the skull's supernatural power, the Siriono keep it in a special basket near the hammocks of close relatives.[102] Although there is no elaborate cult of skulls, they are said to protect one's health and to cure sickness when rubbed on the afflicted.

Because the dead have taken on the supernatural condition of "total" beings, relationship with them can no longer be simple. Death enters and even seizes life (while it can also be said that life encompasses death). Death and life irresolvably overrun one another. In the face of this ambivalence *all fundamental distinctions may fail; nothing makes any difference.* This is the state of fearful respect of the beloved dead. Sacrifice, dispatch, and cutting are forms of separation, symbolic acts of discrimination effecting the transition through chaos. They enable mourners to cut through the trying times of ordeal and catastrophe.

CONTESTATION
Ritual contest is another coping mechanism aimed at establishing a difference between two qualities of being. Various forms of ritual strife, funeral sport, games, and antiphonal recitation reflect the conviction that, at this moment above all others, life and death must be made to oppose one another through the deliberate performance of other oppugnant forms (e.g., guessing games, interrogative inquests, tugs-of-war, separation of the sexes or of affinal groups, mudwrestling, food fights, the adversary procedure of trial for the party responsible for the death, battles of the bands, alternating teams of dancers).[103] Only through the effective demonstration of opposition can two modes of being, life and death, be held separate from one another in fruitful tension.

Theoretically, to ensure that they represent reality, funerary games are fair fights or contests. Both death and life exist in full measure. This requires that death be present in some proper way. The soul of a Canelos Quichua, for example, exits through the mouth but stays near the body. In fact, the moment of death merges the world of dead souls and living human beings. While the body lies at its center, the soul journeys throughout the house.[104] Between the chants sung by the man's relatives, people try to pin the blame for his death on a guilty party. Visitors come with gifts of tobacco and chicha. While women retire to keen at the female end of the house, men begin to play games near the body. The first game appears to be quite old.[105] The contestants toss back and forth a toy canoe made of a piece of plantain or manioc with three holes on one side and five on the other.[106] The game is played ostensibly to entertain the dead person's soul since it is "hungry and has sampled the chicha but cannot be satisfied."[107] It is obvious, however, that the point is to keep everyone awake during the night so that their souls do not wander off to merge with the soul of the deceased.[108] The game helps maintain the separation between the living and the dead.

After midnight another game is begun—this time, blindman's buff. Blindfolded and spun around near the corpse, the player enacts the movements of the wandering soul of the dead person, which has come into him. The blindfolded man attempts to grab the people in the room. Another game, the "monkey foot" game, positions a man, tied hands and foot, near the corpse. The dead man's soul enters the bound figure. All during the vigil the dead man's soul promenades invisibly and enters anyone it chooses.[109]

Colonial and contemporary reports from various parts of the Andes describe a game played during a four- or five-night wake and funeral. The game (if indeed it is one game known throughout the region) has several names, including *pichca* and *huairu*, names that may be taken from numbers on the dicelike objects thrown during the game. What precisely the game meant, or what relationship it had with death and the dead is by no means clear. Opinions range from the interpretation that the game is merely a way of passing time during the wake to claiming that it divines the fate of the dead or bespeaks their will.[110]

Music and sonic imagery offer communities other means of demonstrating opposition in the face of death.[111] The Sanemá-Yanoama do this in a subtle way. Ritual weeping begins as soon as someone dies. A brother or sister of the deceased directs the choir of mourners. He or she sings a leadoff solo and the chorus responds antiphonally. The words praise the skills of the dead person and narrate highlights of his or her life story.

Musical contests not only pass the time during funerals; they contend with the reality of death. For this reason they are often dramatic battles of bands. In the province of Pataz (Department of Libertad), Peru, people strike bells of a size and in a pattern correlated with the sex and age of the dead individual. A band accompanies each episode of the funeral with suitable music. "Sometimes there were two bands, each competing with the other in a kind of counterpoint. In the meantime, the most intimate family members raised their voices in a choir of wailing."[112]

Music plays a crucial, contestatory role in Krahó funerals. The Krahó do not cry or lament in the first hours after someone dies (that is, stops breathing). "[The lamentation] would condemn the dead person so that they would never be able to revive and it would send them to the village of the *mekarõ* [dead souls], closing off the return route, and consecrate the break"[113] Finally, women wailers lead the community laments. Mourners strike poses that let their tears and snivel fall freely.[114] The staged contest, replete with somersaults, comes to a climax when the body is taken from its maternal home and separated from blood relatives. The sons-in-law of the deceased, acting in their capacity as gravediggers and pallbearers, pick up the corpse and haul it to the burial site. They enact the role of the dead.[115] Women's dirges reach a crescendo while participants throw themselves on the ground and pound their breasts. The chanted laments arrive at their noisy peak, accompanied by explosions of firecrackers. The competing sounds punctuate the moment of ultimate passage.[116]

THE GREAT WAGER: PLAYING WITH DEATH

The very idea of game and sport within mourning seems to contest the reality of death. Frivolity and gallows humor form part of the strategy to answer death, to respond in kind to the arbitrariness of its appearance and the trivial or absurd nature of its origins. More than that, the specific images of games factor chaos, the experience of total dissolution, into separate symbolic orders. Among the Puinave funeral practices witnessed by Otto Zerries during his 1954–1955 sojourn in southern Venezuela was the game of "blindman's bluff."[117] All the mourners gathered in the home where the corpse was to be buried. They stood around the cadaver, which had been placed on a table, covered with a white sheet, and centered between four burning candles. One man was blindfolded while all the other participants chose the name of a wild animal. Zerries reports,

> The "blind man" touches the dead body with one hand and with the other points to one of the participants while calling out one of the animal names. If the name of the animal chosen corresponds to the person indicated, then it is deemed that the dead man was a good hunter and that the same "blind man" should stay blindfolded and serve as a medium, for the divined animal is symbolically dismembered and the various participants are named after the different parts of the body, such as the head, the tail, the bowels, etc. Thus the game continues.[118]

The game effectively acts out a sacrifice reestablishing separation and order, for the animal designated by "death" is divided into parts, which serve as the generative source of symbolic and classificatory orders (organs, names, things classified by those names).

THE RACE AGAINST DEATH

Competitive sport and athletic spectacle reply to death in a lively way. It has been suggested that log races among the Canela were "a way of practicing bringing home the fallen warrior to his matrilineal family. This training has later become a pure ceremony, a sport. It is a moral duty to bring a dead warrior home."[119] Even without this hypothesis of historical origins, there exists a clear link between competitive log-racing and the contest between life and death. The closing ceremonies of Krahó mourning, for example, consist of both a fixed core of symbolic actions and a discretionary or movable set of symbolic actions that may be added to the rites depending on the status of the dead person. The essential and fixed aspects of the closing ceremonies include actions such as those we have already analyzed. General body painting of all the mourners accomplishes sealing and closure. Acts of division and separation include hair-clipping (the mourners do trim their hair during the mourning period), depilation of body hair, and cutting down trees. These are "rites which mark the full participation in Krahó public life."[120] The period of seclusion ends with public display. The closure of Krahó mourning, signaling the final dispatch of the ceremonial presence of death, also includes dramatic log-races between ceremonially constituted relay teams. Endurance, opposition, and reversal are emphasized in the funerary contests. The evening before the relay races, after the tree trunks have been cut, ritually prepared, and painted, the formal ritual friends of the deceased must sing throughout the night without stopping.[121] In fact, the entire community sings throughout the night. If the rituals are closing the mourning period for a deceased man, women carry the logs in the race. The racers are then offered water by male spectators, who are potential husbands. Every man who offers a young woman water is later given a present. If the deceased person is a woman, the roles are reversed.[122] The logs are then decorated with feathers and brought into the house of blood relatives of the deceased person. A round of ritual lament goes up for the last time. The logs are covered with a new mat and new clothing, which are later removed. Festival food is shared out between the two moieties and consumed.[123]

Carneiro da Cunha points to the fundamental reason for the images of contestation surrounding death. She contends that the fundamental opposition between the living and the dead shapes the identity both of the individual and the society among the Krahó. The dead represent the *other*, and death, therefore, defines the contours of life by grounding all fundamental distinctions of difference. Surrounding the world of the living, the dead circumscribe it, describing its shape while fixing its limits.[124] The dead are seen as opponents, even as enemies, who play a fundamental role in the ritual construction of society: "The three groups which are configured during the funeral rites are consanguines, affines, and the community as a whole. The fourth group is an implied but emphatic presence: it is the group of the dead."[125] Since the living Krahó community pictures itself as "an essentially ceremonial society," the implied opposition in ritual of the dead as a group is an important constitutive presence in the ever-transformative moments of a ritually centered society. The dead, in fact, play the role of the ritual formal friend, whose presence during transition helps reshape and maintain a new identity. "The dead man is the other, and the other is the formal friend. Enemies, affines, and formal friends are some of the many forms which the *other* assumes so that the ego can establish itself."[126]

The theme that the dead constitute a mode of being radically different from that of the living is, according to Carneiro da Cunha, widespread among Brazilian groups. She takes the Krahó as the primary case, citing also the Guayakí of Paraguay and Brazil, the Boróro, and the coastal Tupinambá.[127] It is essential to note that the opposition between the living and the dead is played out ritually — that is, that it bestows its meaning on formal friendships established in ritual — and is reflected in the organization of space and time. Because the dead can be situated and located in the very structures of the cosmos, they can be seen to play an important role in the constitution of human societies and individuals. The myths of the two Krahó demiurges Pëd (sun) and Pëdleré (moon) most clearly reveal the opposition between the dead and the living — or, better, the formal, competitive friendship of death and life. These two supernatural figures not only reveal two different modes of being, they also relate to one another as formal friends. They are responsible for the origin of permanent and irreversible death, of which each reveals a different mode. Whenever the moon died, the sun would place him in the shade of a tree. Soon the moon would resurrect to new life. However, once, instead of placing the expired sun in the shade of a tree, the moon buried him. Ever since then, death has become an irreversible condition.[128] Modeled on the life of the sun and the moon, all life is a contest between modes of death and modes of life. All life makes a difference.

FIGHTING WITH DEATH: FUNERAL FURY

At times the contest with death is no game or wager at all but a battle waged with blind fury. For example, funeral fights between men and verbal duels between women during burial and mourning are part of the ceremonialized combat carried on in Selk'nam funerals.[129] Among the styles of Sanemá-Yanoama mourning noted by Barandiarán, the most dramatic is an expression of violent estrangement or alienation. The mourner, most often a warrior, performs a funeral dance with his bow and arrow or his knife and clubs. With incoherent shouts he attacks the houseposts and the hammocks in a frenzy. Exhausted and foaming at the mouth, the man collapses and is doused with water by women.[130]

The connection between contest and symbolic order is most striking among the Kamayurá. There the hierarchy of importance among the mourners is a rank order of staged rage. The leadoff man is the *'umano(n)yat*, the principal ritual president of the funeral ceremonies. He behaves wildly and can even go so far as to burn down the house of the deceased. Four pallbearers accompany the wild man around in a procession. Behind them comes the head undertaker (*iwikwaraiokat*), who sings to the accompaniment of the noisy rhythm of rattles made from the kidney-shaped seeds of the caryocar tree, which are ritually gathered in bunches and fastened around the legs of flute players.[131] This principal undertaker, who acts as cantor during this procession, must be a shaman.

BATTLING ELEMENTS: THE CONTEST OF FLESH AND BONES
During funerals and mourning, the contest between modes of being centers on the presence of the corpse. The corpse, less than a person but more than an impersonal presence, is drawn into games, interrogations, and divinations of blame. In some cases the corpse itself is the field of battle. The contest is not between live contestants but between elements in the cadaver, which represent different modes of death and life. Flesh and bone show their true colors in a final battle. "Among the Sanemá-Yanoama, death is a kind of brutal violence introduced into the world which it can destroy entirely if life does not prove itself stronger than death."[132] The dead person, absolutely immobilized and decomposing in the funerary fundle, represents a primordial form of violent destruction. On the one hand, the vital elements that took up residence in the deceased's flesh, muscles, and moving blood are now set free. They are by nature aggressive beings. The time of decomposition of personal elements is a return to a time of violent chaos, a time when the outcome, order, and very existence of the world hangs in the balance. On the other hand, the emergent, gleaming skeleton is proof of the fact that the purest spiritual essence, the *noneshí* (the immortal ego of each Sanemá-Yanoama) has overcome the violence and disaster introduced into the world during the long, bloody episodes of human creation and ascent to carnal life.[133] "With the clean bones, corruption, decomposition and sickness engendered by death disappear."[134] The elements contained in bone, the enduring, perfect, and unchanging elements of human creation, have triumphed. Now, through cremation, they may be liberated to assume once again their spiritual condition. Barandiarán writes that

> the final cremation will liberate these spiritual elements in order that they might bring to its end life's final and highest ascent among the Sanemá-Yanoama Indians, the ascension of the Sanemá-Yanoama Immortal Ego to the mansions of

the Supreme Being and the return of the vital force, the *híkola* of that individual, to the Concentrated Unity of all the Sanemá-Yanoama people.[135].

Whatever form the contest takes, the finality of irreversible death is the question to be solved, the adversary to be overcome. Death must be answered and its absoluteness must meet its match, so that even final death can be put to rest as one moment in the creative cycle of periodic existence.[136] Contesting forces, like the imagery of cutting, divide the primordial mode into constituent elements and turn it into a collection of bounded attributes whose meanings are given symbolic identity. Total chaos can be located in the difference between fear and attraction, movement and stasis, male and female, affine and kin, plant and stone, sadness and delight, silence and sound, love and hate, light and darkness, and life and death.[137] But by vying with one another during funerals and mourning, game contestants disclose the oppositions and alternating rhythms that make regenerative life viable.

FOOD, DRINK, DREAMS: FRUITS OF EARTH, LABOR, AND DEATH

Food and consumption figure prominently in funeral symbolism. The bereaved frequently celebrate a last meal with the deceased during the wake or leave food offerings for the dead after the burial. Such is the case among Quechua-speakers in the region of Otavalo, Ecuador, where death and the dead play a primary role in religious life.[138] It is particularly incumbent on all the living to visit the souls of dead relatives during the Día de Difuntos holiday (2–3 November) and to celebrate a ritual meal at the tomb. During the meal, care is taken to satisfy the hunger and thirst of the dead person's soul. In return, the soul of the deceased makes the living relative dream at night.[139]

All norms of conduct among these Quechua-speakers are dictated by their desire to achieve a full state of being in the afterlife. Since one must be "clean" to be accepted by the gods, the living take ritual steps on behalf of the dead in order that the deceased may rest happily for eternity.[140] On the feasts of the dead, during Holy Week, and on the feast of Corpus Christi, people fill the churches with food. They have the food blessed before taking it to the cemetery, where it is ritually offered to the dead. There, during two or three hours of merriment and conversation, the people eat a meal, which is followed by a period of deep drunkenness.[141] The presence of the dead, who are the source of fertility and abundance that comes from the death of seeds or the dismemberment of tubers, looms large in the ritual control over the means of production. However, since they are in the mode of final death, the deceased have no direct access to the regenerative fruits of periodic death, agricultural labor, or the chase. They must obtain food from the living.

For these Quechua-speakers, as for many South American peoples, if the living sustain the dead in the images of memory and with food offerings, the dead give life to the living through dream images that occur during the deathlike state of sleep, which brings home to the living their mortal condition. Death, the final dissolution of the fleshly body, effects the great exchange of material, consumable life-forms for immaterial images. The reciprocal prestations of the living and the dead, trading food for dreams (or shadows, symbolic designs, or invisible sounds, such as names or songs), constitute the total ritual community, the communion of all humanity in its manifest and unmanifest expressions. The dead, having joined the ranks of supernatural beings, become the source of symbolic life.

The exchange of food for images of primordial existence also occurs in funeral drinking. José Toribio Medina, in his study of Araucanian burial practices as these have been described in sources from the Conquest period forward, noted several elements common to most descriptions, the chief one being that the wake and the interment of the body amounted to a three- to four-day drinking bout in which the participants, after pouring out toasts to the dead, drank themselves into a stupor.[142] Among the Quechua-speakers of the Andes, too, during times of disappearance and occultation such as the burial of the dead, the planting of seeds, or the hiding away of potatoes in storerooms, the undertakers, sowers, or storers must force themselves to drink enormous quantities on behalf of the dead and the spirits who have passed from the primordial scene. By tossing down drinks until one is dead drunk, one makes death part of the process of fertile and abundant life. In addition, one is able to see the images of primordial beings (or, at least, *incaychu*, the tiny figurines or stone representations of them) during the alcoholic delirium.[143]

That each form of humanity, living and dead, gives tokens of its own "concrete" existence and offers the very substance of its life to the other is shown in a further illustration. For the Kalapalo, the life of the dead is shadowy and imaginal. When someone in a Kalapalo village dies, kinsmen of the deceased gather in the house to wail. The occultation and enclosure of the body begins when two persons of the same sex as the deceased wash the corpse and decorate it,[144] roll it in mats, and wrap it in a hammock. Before the undertakers place the cadaver in a grave in the center of the village plaza, the mourners stand around the corpse in such a way as to block it from the sun, so that the shadows of living men can embrace the shadow-soul of the dead person. Death allows the living this direct contact with the life of shades. Some ornaments may be taken away from the body at this point; since their shadows accompany the body into the grave, it is not necessary to leave the actual objects with the corpse.

The Akwē-Shavante also think of the substance of the dead as imaginal and shadowy. A small wooden baton suspended over the grave of a dead relative solicits visitations from the deceased, which often occur in dreams, sometimes as a result of techniques of intense concentration. When they appear in dreams, the souls of the dead may communicate important and powerful songs, which bring good fortune. The Akwē-Shavante believe that only the souls of the dead may make the entire journey to the village of the dead.

Funeral hunts often exchange the booty from a life periodically plundered by death for the imaginal life associated with irreversible death. At the death of a relative, the Jívaro make elaborate ritual preparations for the ceremonial hunt to take a *tzantza*, a trophy head. These preparations include not only fasting from meat, abstinence from sexual relations, and the maintenance of a ritual fire over an extended period of time, but also the careful scrutiny of dreams, which are especially valuable during the postmortem period.[145] Another example of the funerary exchange of one life form for another through the ideology of the hunt is the Boróro dance to assist the dead in their ritual hunt for food in the world of shadows and sounds. In return for his assistance to the dead, the young dancer acquires new names. The ritual hunt of the dead is a consumptive act for the Boróro. It slays game and produces food. At the same time, because of the presence or participation of the dead, it produces symbolic life (in the form of names and the spatial icons of social organization associated with them), just as have all deaths and disappearances since the demise of the primordium.

Funeral hunts also fit within the framework of mortuary contestation. Through the ironic logic that answers death in kind, the ritual hunt at funerals frequently takes life in order to prevent the dead from killing. Even while it accomplishes an exchange with the dead, the reciprocity of the funeral hunt aims at breaking ties with the dead and, by providing sustenance for the deceased's journey, dispatching the spirit to another world. A Kaingáng widower is encouraged to hunt many different types of animals. He may not eat them, however. Instead, he washes himself in their blood. He does the same with the honey and bee sugar he gathers, thus purifying himself of all residual contact with his dead spouse, which these very actions brought about when she was alive. The animals' blood washes away the husband-wife bond established through a life of hunting and food preparation.[146] By consuming the forms of this world, death clears the way for new significations of another kind of life.

The fruit of one domain, whether food or phantasm, sustains life in the other. Death is the medium of their mutual consumption. Periodic existence offers fruits of the earth and the work of human hands; the presence of irreversible death concretizes, in symbol, image, shadow, and sounds, the primordial condition of the no-longer-visible. Both kinds of products, taken together, achieve the desired unity of human experience. The exchanges of eating, dreaming, dying, and abundant rebirth accomplish the fullness of human existence.

SARCOPHAGOUS EXISTENCE: TOTAL CONSUMPTION OF THE FLESH

The fate of the cadaver generates images of consumption, the material process resulting from the coincidence of all opposites.[147] As the body decomposes, it exhibits the changing signs of corruption, the ultimate transformation. Human communities have explored this transfiguration in different ways, rendering it reflexive through the symbolic acts by which the corpse is disposed of, whether through burial in the earth, exposure to the air, inundation, cremation, liquidation, or ingestion.

The following pages discuss several ways of disposing of mortal remains: inhumation, cremation, ingesting flesh, and imbibing ashes. In practice, these often overlap. Since a community can dispose of the same corpse in several ways, our separate appraisal of each symbolic process need not suggest that one method (and its significance) excludes any other. Throughout religious life the direct relationship of symbols to the sacred, most fully apparent in the imagination, makes for an economic multivalence of expression in which meanings collide, compete, contradict, or complement one another. To help us discern differences among ways of disposing of the dead we shall, first, note a feature common to them: burial, burning, and eating are all means of consumption.

INHUMATION: CONSUMED BY THE EARTH

THE GRAVEN IMAGE AS MICROCOSM   Excavation of the earth and burial of the corpse resituates human existence. The grave is not an idle setting, for the earth itself is sacred[148] and can image creation. This is why burial often reenacts the cosmogony. The grave centers human death in a perfect world. The Apapocuvá hollow out a cedar trunk to hold the cadaver and bedeck the body with festive ornaments. After an all-night vigil, they accompany the corpse to its burial place and inter it with its face looking toward the rising sun. Using feathers, they decorate a cross, image of the crossbeams upon which the creator built the world at the beginning of time. At the head of the tomb they place a staff, and they set a gourd filled with water on the top of the grave. In this way they surround the corpse in its grave with representations of the entire cosmos as it first appeared.

The impulse to return to the space where life began also underlies the "syntax of space" at work in Krahó burials, which, however, evoke less the origins of the cosmos than the primordial font of the perfect society. If possible, the Krahó individual should die where he or she was born, in the maternal home: the way in and the way out of this life should be through the same passage.[149] The maternal home provides spatial closure to temporal existence. Krahó funeral rites are a choreography drawing the participants through particular symbolic places at specific times. Through the medium of cosmic space centered on the cadaver and represented in the mythic geography of the village, the rites recreate the bonds of communal life.

The Kamayurá construct a microcosmic image of the first world when they set the stage for burial, giving special care to the details of the grave and the disposition of the body in it. Before interment, they lift the corpse and carry it out the door to the center of the plaza, paying extraordinary attention to every move, for wherever it is carried the corpse must remain in perfect alignment with the elementary structures of the house and the cosmos. The cadaver must maintain a proper position within the orders of the social world as well: pallbearers, ritual weepers, and mourners represent key symbolic relationships and fix themselves in patterned arrangements around the moving corpse.

By a circuitous route, the Kamayurá cortege proceeds from the dead person's house to the central plaza, where two burial holes have been dug. The pallbearers lower the corpse, feet first, into the easternmost hole. With the aid of netting, they draw the body into a tunnel that connects the two holes within the earth. They arrange the cadaver so that its head lies in the west, with the face propped up to behold the rising sun. Mats and panels prevent earth from touching the dead body or filling the bottom of the two holes. The gravediggers fill in the trenches and the mourners wash themselves over the gravesite.

The Kamayurá grave depicts death as a permanent state of suspension. The corpse remains eternally in a state of passage deep in the earth. The grave becomes an image of the mythic time of death's origin. At that time, the transformation of the first people from death to life, directed by the mythic figure Mavutsini(n), was suspended before completion. Like the corpse, the process of death itself stopped halfway through its passage. The disposition of the body in the grave represents final death, the state of being stuck irreversibly and invisibly between two clearly defined conditions of being, two openings. Having entered finally and forever the transitory mode, the corpse "sticks in the throat" of the earth in a state of unending but incomplete consumption. Death, a suspended process of transformation, becomes an elemental structure of passage.

THE GRAVE AS A TOTAL SYMBOLIC FACT   Reichel-Dolmatoff's invaluable eyewitness report of the burial of an Ika woman by a Kógi priest[150] illustrates many points made in this chapter, confirming our insistence on the creative uniqueness with which each culture confronts what is sacred. The Kógi funeral highlights the extent to which all the hardware of undertaking carries profound significance. Each gesture, fiber, color, and physical posture reveals meanings of cosmic proportions, which, like all signified realities, originate in the primordial world of the religious imagination and hold in place the structures of the universe. In the ensemble of the burial, the tiniest symbolic acts reconstitute the creative processes of the universe and regenerate life as it passes continually through states of death.

In Reichel-Dolmatoff's report, the Kógi *máma* (priest) first divined the proper place for the burial in the cemetery. Ordering the ground cleared at a certain spot, he took dry coca leaves and held them close to his chest. In the middle of the cleared space he faced south and in a deliberate way lifted the leaves in his right and left hands. He did the same when he faced north, first holding one hand higher than the other and then reversing their positions. Turning to the east, he rubbed the leaves to a fine powder. Letting the flakes fall to the ground, he proclaimed, "This is the village of Death; this is the ceremonial house of Death; this is the house of Death; this is the uterus. I am going to open the house. The house is closed and I shall open it." With a wooden shovel from his ritual bag he scooped up earth from all four sides of the clearing. Declaring "the house is open," he allowed the men to open the grave.[151] The corpse was then tied in a fetal position, with the hands against the chin, and sewn into an envelope of white cotton cloth. White sisal fibers were twisted into a string, which was tied to the dead woman's hair. Women sang dirges while men deposited seashells in the folds of the burial bundle. The shells were "food for the dead."

The *máma* tried to lift the bundle containing the corpse several times, indicating that the corpse felt less heavy at each successive attempt. Finally, on the ninth attempt, "smiling, he picked up the corpse as if it was almost weightless, as if it were something small and light. People looked at each other with relief."[152] After the father of the dead woman put the corpse in the pit, the *máma* spread leaves of green fern over the body. When the grave was half filled with earth, he took from his ritual bag five tiny bundles filled with seeds, white cotton, and small stones. The contents of the first four he arranged at the four cardinal points in the grave. Those of the fifth he spread out at the center of the grave, immediately over the corpse. The sisal rope, one end of which had been attached to the dead woman's hair, was held taut until the grave was completely filled, then it was tied to a thin rod. The rod was plunged vertically into the soft earth and a heavy stone rolled over the grave. The priest now "closed" the grave by reversing the order of the ceremonial shoveling with which he had opened it. All participants left the hillside cemetery by spinning constantly to the left, twirling their way toward their homes in the village. After nine days the priest returned to the grave accompanied by the deceased's parents. He yanked on the rope that had been tied to the dead woman's hair. "The fibers were already rotten and when suddenly the rope broke, they all smiled and nodded and returned to the village."[153]

The significance of these symbolic acts of burial belongs to a larger complex of meaning related to the creation of the universe and its present structures. Dualistic philosophical concepts pervade every level of Kógi life from the individual human body to the social groups that constitute Kogi society. Ritual life achieves the optimal condition of *yulúka*, "agreement" or "equality" between opposed but complementary forces. The priest's "weighing" of the coca leaves in his hands before choosing the proper gravesite reflects this fundamental need to accomplish *yulúka*.

The emphasis in the burial rites on the four cardinal points and the center finds expression at every level of Kógi culture. Associated with the cardinal directions are colors, emotions, particular animals, special mythical beings, the ideal village-plan, the structure of the ceremonial house with its four hearths, the four principal clans of the society, and so on. The center of space, the center of the universe, is the place where the *máma* "speaks with God." In the center of the ceremonial house, itself a representation of the wider cosmos, the priest sits on a small stool and allows the essence of his nature — a humanoid replica of himself — to hear the answers to questions posed during divination.[154] Moreover, the Kógi universe is an immense egg holding nine levels of different-colored earth, which are the nine daughters of the great mother goddess. Uterine symbolism repeats itself in every significant space: the ceremonial house, mountains, the earth itself. From the top of these spaces there descends a rope, the umbilical cord, which offers the

priest access to the supernatural powers inhabiting the space. Reichel-Dolmatoff interprets the symbolism of burial on the basis of these primordial and
cosmic meanings:

> The dead person returns to the uterus, in a flexed foetal position; wrapped in a
> carrying net which represents the placenta, and connected with this world by an
> umbilical cord which is cut after nine days, after which follows rebirth into
> another world. When the *máma* lifts the corpse nine times, he symbolizes by this
> action the return of the uterus, because he makes the corpse return to an embry-
> onic state by leading it through the nine months of intrauterine gestation. At the
> same time, the tomb is the cosmos, the world. Offerings are deposited in the
> seven points of the sacred space: North/South/East/West/Zenith/Nadir/Center,
> and the head of the corpse is oriented toward the east, the direction where the
> sun, the light, life itself are reborn every day. The burial rite then was an act of
> "cosmification."[155]

Not only do the food offerings left at the grave nourish the dead individual's soul, but, in the image of fertilizing male semen, they impregnate supernatural beings and guarantee the fertility and creativity of life in all its forms.
All mythical beings and masters of animals and plants abide in the larger
concept of "death." The offering bundle itself is a uterus. Wrapped in leaves
of maize symbolizing the placenta, the thread binding the offering represents
the umbilicus. "[T]he contents of the bundle have an embryonic character."[156]

A large gastropod shell placed in the young woman's grave symbolically
provides her a husband. This prevents her from calling a young man of the
tribe to serve as her spouse. Since contagious diseases take on the image of a
thread, departing mourners spin in a direction designed to undo the evil
influence and contact of the supernatural threads. They unwind themselves
from the grasp of contagion. Sacred songs also assume the image of threads
that attach a singer to the powerful supernatural being to whom a song is
addressed. One sings one's binding song in silence as one returns home from
the grave. Binding and loosing, enclosing and disclosing, divestiture and
reinvestment become the order of the day for mourners as well as for corpse.
Nine days after the burial (symbolizing the nine months of gestation), the
máma severs the sisal string, the umbilicus. The soul of the deceased now
wanders beyond the grave to the place of new life, where it is reborn to its
new existence.[157]

CREMATION: CONSUMED IN FLAMES

Fire devours. Myths expound on fire's consumptive capacity in two ways. In
the first place, the mythical conflagration, the cosmic fire, utterly transforming whatever it engulfed, destroyed the world. Secondly, primordial jaguars,
birds of prey, or marine monsters (e.g., frogs or snakes) kept fire to themselves. Lodged in their mouth, belly, or unique hearth, fire formed part of
their singular mode of being and remained their exclusive property. After
fire was stolen from these arch-consumers, they devoured flesh raw. Fire still
bears their consumptive stamp even though it was expropriated from them in

the beginning of time. A roaring fire reaches the height of life in a climax of devouring. Because fire expresses these ironic aspects of primal sacrality, it generates social life. From time to time families and ritual groups center themselves around fire to renew life through consumption. A cremation is one such communal gathering; the crematory fire devours dead flesh in order to transform life.[158]

According to the Campa, fire destroys the existence of material and immaterial beings: the purpose of cremation is to destroy the soul of the dead person. Souls that die at the hands of demons become candidates for demonhood. To prevent this outcome, the Campa cremate the dead by the side of the river and allow the ashes to wash away during the rainy season.[159]

Cremation makes the body light, in every sense of the word. Fire helps overcome the undesirable and heavy tendencies of dead flesh or soul. At the moment of death, the dying Waiwai feels his or her body becoming lighter, for the soul is departing. Attendants bring the dying person out of the communal house and place the invalid in a small rain shelter, the same type of lean-to in which he or she was born. Mourners immediately cremate the dead body together with the deceased's personal effects in a clearing far from the village.[160] Relatives remain weeping beside the pyre. Women survivors cut their hair short, men trim off some of their pigtail — acts typical of the symbolic attempt to cut through the chaos of undifferentiation. A few burned bones are taken from the fire for use in fatal revenge-blowing magic, and the rest are covered with leaves and sticks.[161] Until recently, Waiwai funeral burning destroyed not only the container of individual life (the body) but also that of social life: Waiwai funerals included the abandonment and torching of the lifeless village. At the time of Fock's visit, however, the Waiwai totally devastated the locus of social life only at the death of socially prominent people.

For their part, the dead look forward to their transformation through fire. Among the Kaingáng, for example, cremation amounts to liberation, an irreversible step in the life-cycle. The Kaingáng cremate their deceased on a blanket covered with feathers. Mourners fasten broken arrows and a severed bowstring to a broken bow and place these with the body. Undertakers point the corpse's head toward the west, where the kuplêng, a soul-element, will live. The deceased takes viaticum, food for the journey: in one hand meat and in the other wax, symbolic of honey. Furnishing the deceased these provisions, the mourners shout "There! Take it and go and leave me!" Before setting the corpse on fire, they pound its chest and shout, "Leave your animals [souls] to me and go! . . . Leave your children and things to me and go. . . . Speak well of me. I suffered a great deal with you, and so I am putting you in a prepared place."[162] If the corpse does not burn readily it is a sign that the ghost-soul will be vai (supernaturally dangerous) to the living. When the fire dies down, the bones are gathered into bark baskets and carried in procession to their burial place to the accompaniment of a song: "What is being carried? What is being carried? Look, you. Sun's faeces are being carried. Look, you. Under the place where the sun emerges." Like the funeral fire, this song makes the load light and prevents pallbearers from slipping while carrying the basket of bones. The song protects the mourners against death.[163] The bone bearers later wash themselves with clay and scrub their skin with stones, gestures explained by one mourner in these words: "I am going to be like stones that never die. . . . I am never going to die."[164] The cremated bones lie in a grave lined with ferns, over which women construct a little house. No remnant of the cremation fire can remain. Mourners must kindle new fire in their households to ensure that no embers or flames are taken from the cremation, for no remnant of its fire can remain.

HEAVY MOURNING: THE WEIGHT OF DEATH AND THE MALINGERING SOUL Funeral fire lightens the corpse and eliminates the supernatural weight that obstructs optimal postmortem existence. The elements that compose the person must be consumed at death. If they linger untransformed (untouched by some chaotic process such as fire, flood, or consumption), they become increasingly unwieldy. Their presence weighs on the living and threatens to overwhelm the space and imagery of life. The cause of death determines whether or not the Sanemá-Yanoama incinerate the body immediately. In natural death, whose cause is directly apparent, the *híkola* (a spiritual entity in human form — the living force of the dead person) leaves the deceased and enters the body of the nearest relative. The dead person's *híkola* carries tremendous weight, a heaviness that increases constantly from the moment of its entrance into its new habitation. For this reason, the Sanemá-Yanoama incinerate the dead person's body within a short time, usually seven to fifteen days. If death is due to some unknown and occult cause, the *híkola* returns to the assassin who sent him. Not knowing the deadly outcome of the *híkola*'s mission, the murderer does not observe the fasting and other behavioral restrictions that lighten the weight of the *híkola*. As long as the body of the deceased stays intact, the *híkola* accumulates weight inside the body of the spiritual murderer. The supernatural bulk eventually crushes the murderer from the inside. For this reason, the Sanemá-Yanoama do not hurry to cremate the cadaver of a victim of sorcery. They hang it in a funeral bundle in a jar on a tree top or at the top of a forest hut *(troja)* specially made for the occasion and let the lingering life of the dead condemn the killer. Only then is the body burned.[165]

The Sanemá-Yanoama prepare the cadaver for hanging by putting it in a fetal position, wrapping it in its hammock, and rolling it in a mat made of thick lianas. They cover the head with leaves to protect the cadaver from carrion birds. Mourners use resin to attach white feathers of wild birds, the deceased's festival finery, to the mat wrapping. They paint the dead body with *urucú* and *arnotto* sap. A procession brings the bundle from the village to the isolated funeral hut, where the corpse will hang, suspended more than two or three meters above the earth. A shaman places a wad of tobacco in the mouth of the corpse so that the *noneshí*, a spiritual element of the person, can chew tobacco along the trail to the other world. The flesh and muscles decompose, leaving only the bones: a sign that the assassin has died under the weight of the deceased's *híkola*. If flesh still clings to the bones, it indicates that the assassin has overcome the *híkola* and holds fast to life. The clinging flesh may also signal that a deceased man had had relations with women of too close a degree of kinship. This betokens danger and imminent sickness for the entire community. Under such dire circumstances, women beyond childbearing age (or, more precisely, those who have undergone menopause) scrape the remaining flesh from the bones and eliminate the danger to the community. They do so calmly and in silence. The community may now cremate the bones.

The cremation of a Sanemá-Yanoama individual is an essential moment in the life-cycle of personal elements, which make their way back to the primordial space-time of Omao, the supreme being of the sky. In heaven, the elements that constituted an individual achieve a new level of integration. The *híkola* of the dead person reunites itself with the social group by becoming born again in a new child, who may bear the name of the deceased. When the funeral bundle burns, the fire frees the *noneshí*, the diminutive but weighty personal entity identified as the immortal ego of each Sanemá-Yanoama person. The *noneshí*, lightened by flame and buoyed up by the departing breath of the dead person, journeys to heaven along the trail of rising smoke. The *nobolebé* (also called *henboletwan* or *nobolé*), the fiery element that warms and unifies the interior processes of the human individual, loses its heat, as does the breath (*toholilí*), at the moment of death. The *nobolebé* abandons the corpse to wander through the forest in the form of a vaporous jaguar, stiff and cold to the touch. At the moment of cremation, however, the *nobolebé* and *toholilí* unite themselves in communion with the devouring flames. Together with the rising breath, these two elements push the weighty *noneshí* upward "toward the Sky of the Supreme Being and of the Sanemá-Yanoama ancestors who live with him."[166] Without the incineration, there would be no liberation. The dead person would remain decomposed, atomized, and disintegrated. "Never again would he reencounter himself. It would be the supreme tragedy. The greatest threat against a Sanemá-Yanoama is to deny him his post-mortem cremation."[167]

PASSING THROUGH FIRE Crematory fires are not the only fires associated with funerals. Through its capacity to consume, fire can dispose of the dead in ways other than cremation. The Kamayurá ritual leader brings fire from his own home and sets a small blaze near the grave to provide light for his dead relative. Sitting by the flames, the ritual president smokes and cries. When his tobacco is totally consumed, he falls into strict ritual silence.

Putting fire on the grave aids the consumptive process. By passing through fire the deceased succeeds in becoming a spirit. For instance, most reports of Araucanian mortuary customs mention a fire set over the grave for nearly a year after the burial. The fire warms the soul of the deceased as it passes through on its way to the afterlife.[168]

Fire is frequently used to destroy the personal effects of the dead. The fiery destruction of the personal world of the deceased, even without cremation, is reminiscent of the cosmic conflagration. The funeral can reenact the first appearance of human life in the dark afterglow of the world-fire. When a sick Toba man dies, women blacken their faces with ashes and raise a loud lament. Relatives board up the dead man's house with blocks, barricade it with poles, and abandon it. They light a large fire close to a house where the body lies. Another fire crackles beside the corpse. A third fire burns near the dead man's house. Relatives camp for the night around this third fire, surrounding themselves with a fence of arrows. As people walk through the village they carry arrows or big sticks, and female relatives of the dead person paint arrows on their cheeks. After nightfall men seize firebrands from the first fire outside the door of the death house. In acts reminiscent of the emergence of human life at the dawn of time, the men carry the fire far into the forest, into which they disperse in all directions.[169]

At dawn the next day, mourners deposit the corpse in a grave close to the river. It lies naked, in a fetal position, with its head placed between its knees. On top of the grave rests a mound of earth and a large number of thorny tree branches. Relatives light two large fires close to the grave; in these they burn the deceased's clothes and all his personal belongings. When they return home, the kin set the dead man's house ablaze. While the house goes up in flames, men and women engage in separate drinking parties. Close relatives cut off their hair and pare their nails. These acts properly configure the dead in postmortem existence. The life of the community depends on correct relations with its dead members. If their postmortem situation is improperly shaped, the dead may harm the living. Those who die of prolonged illness or old age are most likely to become dangerous beings.[170] Fortunately, living Tobas possess fire to consume what lingers. Cremation and funeral fires prevent the dead from becoming superstitions, the monstrous leftovers or revenants hanging on beyond their time. Fire recreates the existence of the dead and rechannels their destructive propensities.

REFINEMENT: MULTIPLE ENDINGS ACHIEVE A DEFINITE END
Some communities dispose of the dead several times over. Cremation, burial, dispersal, or interment of ashes; immersion in water; or reburial of bones are successively performed. These acts are not redundant but represent steps in a serial process of refinement, each ending a different moment in the spiritual economy. The refinishing process brings the deceased to the final terms of human existence. Finishing off the corpse in multiple ways defines the limits of the dead individual vis-à-vis the universe and the living. By locating the borders where these realities abut one another, the refinement of death lends definition to the cosmos, the community, and the self. The outer reaches of these entities become visible in the deteriorating symbolism of the cadaver as it passes through the terminal processes of fire, earth, water, and human ritual. In this regard, the widespread practice of secondary burial merits special mention.

THE RELIQUARY   Several years after a Goajiro is first buried, family members unearth the bones and hold a second funeral, which, although smaller in scale than the first, is attended with the requisite weeping, eating, and drinking. This rite marks the transition from the individual to the common grave, from a flesh-consuming tomb to an ossuary. A close relative, usually of the same matriline as the deceased, cleans and decorates the bones, and a woman, dressed specially for the occasion, sets the bones in a huge terracotta mortuary urn (*pachisha*), dividing them and distributing them among the bones of the matriclan contained therein. The individual skeleton disappears into the collectivity, and from now on the living pay no individual attention to the dead person.[171]

First and second burial differ markedly in both performance and purpose. Second burial is generally simpler and more serene. Thus, Apinayé primary burial typifies the strategies of wailing, decoration, binding, and eating already examined. At the moment of death, the souls of the dead swarm around the dying person and offer morsels of their own food to the nearly deceased, who is made their permanent companion by eating it.[172] This sharing of food with the dead distinguishes the permanently dead from those who have only temporarily lost their soul during dream, trance, or unconsciousness.[173] Lamentations begin immediately. Shaking a rattle, a cantor sings throughout the night while gravediggers open a hole in the earth. The undertakers are the surviving members of the deceased's *kragéd*, or *kram* ("grandparent," "grandchild"), the formal-friendship unit composed of individuals who have bound themselves to one another ritually by covering one another with ceremonial ornaments during ritual transitions.[174] The ritual friends wash the corpse, paint it red, daub it with black latex, cut its hair, dress it in ceremonial ornaments, and, finally, cover it with a mat and tie it to a pole with two loops of rope. Meanwhile, female relations keen, strike themselves with firewood or rocks, and execute death-leaps (*amni-mõ'ti*), plunging to the ground in a dead fall. After burying the body west of the village, the mourners leave all the ceremonial ornaments of the deceased by the gravesite, and the entire community bathes in a nearby stream. They leave food for the deceased outside of the village so that the soul need not return home to satisfy its hunger. After the deceased eats, the bowl of food may be brought back to the village and its contents shared out among those present.[175] Mourners refrain from sex, body painting, dance, and hair-cutting.

In contrast to the high drama of the first burial, secondary burial, which takes place about a year later, is a quiet, almost casual affair. The ritual friends exhume the body and clean the bones. In front of the dead person's maternal home they wash the bones carefully, dry them in the sun, paint them red, place them in a buriti bag, and rebury them.[176]

Krahó secondary burial presents a more elaborate picture. When the flesh has been consumed by the first grave, the Krahó mark the occasion with a special meal. They extract the body from the primary grave, an earthen tomb fortified with logs, to prevent the armadillo, "the eater of cadavers," from consuming the body. They uncover, clean, and wash the bones before painting them. In the space behind the maternal home the community celebrates a "last supper" that satisfies the last hunger of the dead before the journey to the village of the dead. The meal consists of *khwörgupu*, a ceremonial fare prepared by blood relatives of the dead. The relatives, however, remain enclosed in their house, fearfully abstaining from all food. From outside their container they hear the sounds of musical instruments (the *përiakhö* and *kukhonré*) and the rustling made as the banana-leaf folders, containing the food, are opened. A curer joins the soul (*karō*) in the afterlife banquet held outside the house. The *karō* of the dead person eats only the *karō*, the spiritual essence, of food items, leaving the material food for others to eat (although it consumes cigars totally so that they are useless to anyone else). While blood relatives sing laments inside the house, the village's "outsiders," mostly women, commune with the healer and the dead, consuming the balance of the meal. The meal and reburial terminate obligations between the dead person and the living group.[177]

Through the process of refinement ingredients of the dead person meet successive and different ends. Darkness obscures light; noise or silence envelops sound; earth devours flesh; fire ravages bone; water dissolves ashes. Passing through this succession of elements, the deceased undergoes multiple transformations. The cadaver undergoes refinement by suffering diverse images of total chaos (darkness, petrification, conflagration, flood, utter voracity) in a process that recapitulates the major forms of total transformation. Finish by finish refinement redistributes the deceased human life to the fundamental elements manifest in the primordia—earth, wind, fire, stone, mythic beings, and places. Individuals gradually assume their destiny, their full social and cosmic status.

THE LIVING CONSUME THE DEAD

Ingesting flesh or ashes of the deceased is a definitive moment in the process of refinement. It ends a dilemma. Consumption of the dead is a response to the existential situation I have termed *fearful respect* for the dead. The ambivalence of the situation conditions the response to it. The corpse and the signs of death raise the specter of human life as a supernatural presence.

Death reveals human presence as both a fascinating and dreadful mode of being, a sacred condition. This presence of the sacred under the signs of death poses gripping questions about being human and about the nature of the sacred itself. The coexistence of opposite reactions, such as dread and fascination, arise from the sacrality revealed in human death, a mysterious and profoundly questionable state. Whether the consumer be earth, air, fire, water, or living humans, consuming the dead furnishes a response to the existence of death and the presence of the sacred in deadly guise. By ingesting signs of death, the living thrive on the ambiguity of death even as they dispose of its awe-full traces.

Ambivalence about the sacredness of human death has affected interpretations of eating the dead. The history of reports by explorers and ethnographers betrays the degree to which attraction and repulsion can be inseparable. Any encounter with the sacred empowers the imagination, as is shown by the lurid exaggerations of many of the accounts of foreign visitors. European colonials absorbed the South American customs of consuming the dead into their own myths. Images of savage cannibalism, appearing in the European religious imagination, sparked new cosmologies and demonologies. In many ways, the modern West still locates its identity in the mythic landscape of this New World shaped by the religious experience of the age of discovery. An adequate comprehension of South American funeral ingestion requires new evaluations of traditional Western values concerning death, the body, and ritual performance.

The vivid mythology of the New World obstructs the study of South American funeral practices. "[A]mong the numerous Indian tribes accused of cannibalism in the 16th and 17th centuries, doubtless many of them did no such thing," concludes Pierre Clastres.[178] However, on the basis of historical research and eight months of discussion with the Guayakí, Clastres also criticized an opposite imaginative response: "But the 'mania' of the soldiers, missionaries, explorers and adventurers of past centuries to see a cannibal in every Indian, was answered by a reverse exaggeration on the part of some scholars that drove them consistently to doubt all statements of anthropophagy and thus to reject some reports, extremely valuable due to the personal character of their authors."[179] This caution also characterizes other recent approaches. Neil L. Whitehead concludes that sources do indicate "the existence of cannibalistic practices among the Caribs, as well as other Amerindians, though it would seem that it was the European pre-occupation with this subject, still evident today, rather than its overall sociological significance for Carib peoples that necessitates such a detailed treatment of the topic."[180] The sources define "a limited, ritual act only associated with victory in battle. . . . Undoubtedly, funeral practices which involve the preservation of bones and the consumption of human remains were a fertile source of misinterpretation."[181]

Under these circumstances, it is difficult to understand ingestion of the dead for what it is: a religious response to the ambivalent nature of the sacred. Each culture possesses a unique understanding of what is signified by consuming the dead (either as flesh or bone-ash). Flesh and bone themselves signify different modes of being. The skeleton consists of bones — many, articulated, and well formed; the carnal body is one flesh, formless and indivisible. The disposal of these elements requires that they meet their match in different ways. After extensive comparative study of peoples throughout South America, Zerries predicated a nearly perfect mutual exclusion between the practice of consuming the pulverized bone-ash of close relatives and that of ingesting the flesh of outsiders to one's group. Most groups which imbibe ashes of kinsmen's bone reside in the Upper Orinoco area (e.g., the Shiriana, Waika, Pakidái) or the western and northwestern Amazon (e.g., Siliva, Tukano, Tariana; Cashibo, Conibo, Amahuaca).[182] Eating the flesh of the dead and consuming their ashes are different symbolic processes with separable meanings. They reflect, respectively, the dreadful and attractive aspects of that total condition, respect for the dead. We shall discuss each in turn.

SEEKING SOMEONE TO DEVOUR: THE GNASHING OF TEETH   Consuming the dead reenacts the destructive processes — the slaughter of a water monster, the crushing of the jaguar, the fire or flood — that dispatched primordial beings to an unmanifest mode and closed the mythic world. Ritual ingestion of the flesh[183] makes the human consumer a sacred instrument of closure, or irreversible transformation—like the tomb or pyre. No less than burial and cremation, human sarcophagy, as a symbol of consumption, rewards close examination.

Ritual division and consumption of flesh differs from drinking liquified ashes in that the former subjects cut flesh to bone while the latter subjects bone to the powers of the flesh. The teeth are the only place where the skeleton completely pierces and shows through the flesh. In the form of teeth, bone cuts through the gums and manifests itself. Teeth, relics, and bits of bone betoken the presence of death, for the rest of the skeleton displays itself only in death (either final death after putrefaction or transitory death during hallucination or vision). Glimpses of bare bone in bared fangs, wounds that cut to the bone, or ceremonial ornaments of bones or teeth prefigure death.[184]

DEATH AS THE ENEMY   The act of chewing incises a series of successive divisions on material form, impressing flesh with the marks of death, imitative and effective signs of the primordial destruction, which cut, dismembered, or divided primal realities in order to sustain life in another form. Since the time when mythic jaguars (flesh-eating gluttons) and their ravenous conquerors ruled the day, eating solid foods has been an act of violent aggression, a mode of dispatch imitative of sacred events. By devouring flesh one subjects its inherent formlessness to the sharp divisions made by the rigid form of bone. We have already encountered this symbolic strategy in rites of transition: initiatory ordeals effect transformation through ceremonial piercing, cutting, or breaking the skin with the bones or teeth of birds, monkeys, or rodents.[185] The funeral rite of chewing falls into this symbolic context. It eliminates the independent existence of dreadful beings by dividing and dismembering them.

This symbolic solution to ambivalence finds keenest expression in the ritual ingestion of enemies, especially foreign warriors, as was the practice among the Carib.[186] Eating flesh exploits the domesticating power of consumption exemplified by the devouring of the prepotent primordials who dominated the first world. The disappearance of these plenipotentiaries cleared the way for cosmic life. In the same way, ingesting symbolic fragments of the flesh of foreigners domesticates what is marginal and wild. The transformation of chaos through the symbolic division of formless flesh orders the cosmos and establishes the consumer as its center. Centered on what cultures deem to be genuine humanity (i.e., on ritual consumers), subsistent life in the cosmos remains a symbolic process. Consumption is transformative; it is a religious situation expressed in culinary, political, and economic terms. Basing itself on sacred models, human culture engulfs whatever appears untransformed. Through this ritual process of containment, the unbridled, the unknown, and the insignificant are changed and enter a new quality of space. They become part of the cosmos, a set of relations ordered around the sacred as it appears in the symbols of the religious imagination. Dismemberment through chewing has much in common with blood sacrifices, which cut and divide the body of the victim. Both kinds of symbolic acts divide and conquer chaos, manifest in the physical presence — the foreign body — of an outsider. They suit the cause of an aggressive program of territorial and political expansion, subduing and humiliating the vanquished.[187]

Feeding on the intense ambivalence of death, some cultures describe the ingestion of foreign flesh as a form of "loving" enemies. Foreign warriors remain enemies but become so in controlled, ritual ways. Tupinambá customs studied by Métraux illustrate the point. During the lengthy period of captivity before his execution, a foreign warrior was treated by his Tupinambá captors as one of the family.[188] The care lavished on the prisoner amounted to domestication. For example, the community immediately offered the man a bride from among its women. He fathered a child by this woman. Women, who played a role in the dismemberment of the captive's corpse, showed special affection for the man. He was allowed to come and go freely. He reciprocated the love of the community for him.[189] Few warriors tried to escape; if one did, his home community castigated him and killed him as a coward because he had lacked the courage to endure the death prepared for him by his enemies. The escapee's fault consisted in acting as though his relatives were incapable of avenging his death. In the terms of the present study, he feared that his relatives would fail to effect the closure that would give his death (and, therefore, his life) the meaning of a sacred reality. He brought into question the entire symbolic terminology of his culture.[190]

The Tupinambá explicitly treated their captive as a pet and patronized him with love and kindness. Through ordeals of running gauntlets, periods of confinement, and moments of ritual display before the entire community, the captive underwent an initiation in which the captor (or executioner) played the role of a formal friend bound by parallel ritual restrictions. "In fact, once incorporated into the group of his enemies, the prisoner ceased to be a part of the one into which he was born."[191]

After acculturation through prolonged residence, linguistic adaption, sexual union, production of offspring, and bodily ornamentation, the captive was given the opportunity for consummate transformation through the ultimate ritual death and rebirth into new form: communion through his own substance. In keeping with the ideology of conspicuous consumption associated with death, the victim at the moment of his execution was sumptuously adorned with ceremonial body-paint, ornaments, and full-feathered dress. Thus transfigured, he was paraded throughout the village. Partaking of his body culminated the process of his transubstantiation: he was ingested into the community of his consumers.

In this extreme form, the ingestion of foreign flesh mitigates the ambivalence of death by dispatching the symbolic form of the *other* who threatens life. Through permanent acquisition of what is other than oneself, this sort of imperial consumption expands life. Consuming the flesh of an enemy subjects it to signs (of food and rites of communion) that sustain the life of the consumers by eliminating signs of the alien warriors who take it. What is foreign (the enemy, death) undergoes reevaluation and transignification. The transaction of sacrificial dismemberment and consumption draws foreign flesh and blood, together with all they represent about life and death, into the symbolic currencies sacred to the consumers.[192]

As a religious act, consumption of the flesh of enemies, a process requiring dismemberment and division of the body, bears close affinity with blood sacrifice. The ordering of the fearful chaos of death by dividing the corpse shares its meaning with homologous divisions of territorial space and the cosmogonic sacrifices and destructions that created images of property (in the wide sense of *proper order* in the material universe).[193] Métraux's description of human sacrifice among the Inca finds its place here, if territorial division and cumulative expansion are seen as a response to particular forms of the sacred, including the fear of/fascination with death.[194] In Cuzco, the sacred center of their universe, the Inca performed bodily sacrifice. They cut open the chest and extracted the heart from the center of victims who represented subjugated communities (and who were the tribute paid by these communities to Inca overlords). Here, sacrifice becomes a microcosmic icon of the attempt to cut through chaos, vanquish death, and establish a life-order based on division and conquest of peoples and territories.

Métraux summarizes the "general practice" of Inca human sacrifice, including the regular immolations of men and women at shrines and of children during times of special need (e.g., the end of an old regime and the beginning of a new reign, imperial illness, earthquake, threat of calamity): "The children sent from the outlying lands to imperial temples for sacrifice were part of the tribute the provinces were forced to pay."[195] Because the victims symbolized, *pars pro toto*, the space of the entire empire, every detail affecting their body-space was important. Their corpses would mark life with regenerative signs of final death and signify the irreversible death undergirding the life of the entire empire (the cosmos). Thus even the tiniest bodily mark carried ultimate significance: "The bodies of the little victims had to be flawless; the least skin blemish would disqualify them. Before they were killed the children were well treated. On the day of sacrifice they were fed, or if they were still babies, their mothers suckled them, so that they should not 'enter the presence of the Creator hungry or crying.'"[196]

Following the logic by which occultation encloses the marks of final death, these young victims were often buried alive. But as Métraux writes,

> in certain cases their chests were cut open and the heart torn out. . . . The still-beating heart was offered to the idol, and the idol's face daubed from ear to ear with its blood. The bodies were buried in a special cemetery near the sanctuary. . . . Among the quota of girls that the provinces provided for the Incas there were always some who, sooner or later, would be sacrificed to the gods. Yearly, when a share of the tribute was doled out to the provincial temples, the chief sanctuaries were granted human victims. These were kept in enclosures near the temple until the feast day came when, decked in jewels and wearing their finest clothes, they would be led to the idol to be strangled or slaughtered. First, however, they were benumbed with *chicha*, and told that they were "called upon to serve the gods in a glorious place."[197]

GUAYAKÍ COMMUNION WITH THE DEAD The Guayakí offer us a unique opportunity to examine the practice of disposing of the dead through ingestion. According to Lucien Sebag and Pierre Clastres, the values underlying the consumption of the dead lie at the heart of Guayakí culture, especially that of the Guayakí group at Yñaro. "Every form of conduct and of belief is attached in one manner or another to the consumption of human flesh: the place of hunting activity, the relationship with the animal world, the meaning of the transmission of names, difficulties arising from the duality of the soul."[198] One should analyze these symbolic issues in a complete way in order to understand the Guayakí practice of consuming their dead.

The Guayakí dispose of the corpse in two ways. Sometimes they bury the cadaver until it decomposes, at which point the mourners disinter the head after detaching it from the rest of the skeleton, then smash the skull with blows from hunting bows and burn the splintered remains. Sometimes, though, the dead man's allied relations (or even strangers) eat the flesh of the deceased.[199] Helène Clastres emphasizes that, in both instances, survivors treat the dead person as a mortal enemy. In both processes of disposal, the living behave as supernatural jaguars who devour the deceased's body and soul. Significantly, the dead themselves are considered jaguars (or serpents or vultures), which must be hunted, killed, and devoured.[200] That is, consumption of the dead reenacts the mythical dispensation in which prepotent supernaturals were dispatched to make way for this epoch. The dead appear as primordial animals, sacred beings. Elimination of the dead continues the catastrophic process that accounts for the symbolic order. Disposal of the dead sustains life in the world. The dead are not consumed for their individual qualities but because human death signifies the dreadful sacrality of supernatural life.

According to Pierre Clastres, the Yñaro group of the Guayakí (known also as Aché Gatu) dispose of the flesh of their dead by consuming it in a ritual meal.[201] The Guayakí told Clastres that all of their dead are consumed by eating. "The normal resting place of the dead is the stomach of the living."[202] Clastres provides details of a Guayakí funeral meal held toward the end of July 1963, while researchers were absent.[203] All parts of the dead body are consumed. Only female sex organs are never eaten but, instead, are buried. With the exception of close relatives, all the living commune on the dead. Immediate kin observe restrictions. "[T]he taboo is strictly binding on close relatives of opposite sexes and, . . . in reality, it overlaps the incest prohibitions."[204]

Clastres details the preparation of the body, its distribution in the ritual meal, and the comments of participants. The rite was not secret; other bands were invited to attend. Bones were broken to extract their marrow. To neutralize the pathogenic powers of human fat, the flesh was cooked with the pith or terminal shoot of the *pindo* palm. Those who do not share in the ritual meal of human flesh are subject to attack by the soul (*ianvé*) of the deceased, which especially threatens the close kin who are forbidden to take communion. When the meal ends, the bones are pulverized and burned. In the case reported to Clastres, in which a young child was consumed, the father of the child "beat his wife a little bit with a leather lash" in order to "avenge" the child. In fact, the woman solicited the ritual beating, saying, "Then beat me at the same time as his Chikwagi to avenge him!"[205]

More important than these details, for our purposes, are the Guayakí interpretations of their symbolic acts.[206] The Guayakí hold that groups that do not consume their dead will all die.[207] Ingesting the dead preserves life for two reasons. First, continuity of life depends upon continuity of consumption of the dead. The deceased flesh, abandoned by the soul-ghost, reenters life in the bodies of fellow men and women. The life of the dead person's flesh continues, reabsorbed into the consuming group, which offered it carnal existence in the first place. In a way unique to them, the Guayakí make a point we have met elsewhere: life thrives on containment of death. Continuity of life, in this first sense, encompasses the mortality of the person within the immortal flesh of the group. Death marks a transition that guarantees the continuity of fleshly life, although that concrete life transcends individual experience. In this first sense, immortality is inclusive, dynamic, consumptive, and material.

The second reason for ingesting the dead is exclusive, negative, and defensive. It derives from a familiar, sinister premise: souls of the dead linger in the area after death in order to invade the living. They enter the bodies of survivors to make them sick and die. Continuity of life depends upon an effective method of banishing the postmortem soul.[208] The Guayakí drive off the soul by consuming its abode, the body. "Abolishing the material existence of the cadaver by eating it is to abolish the invisible presence of the soul. The soul is tied to the body; cutting up the body and eating it is to sever the soul from its base in the world of the living, then to expel it and banish it to its distant abode."[209]

Once the body is eaten, the soul no longer has a proper place in this world, and the soul-elements can begin their independent careers as fully supernatural entities. The soul journeys off in two forms: the *ové* travels toward the sun; the *ianvé* wanders in the forest. Consumption of the dead frees the soul for its new existences in accordance with the Guayakí saying, "As long as the body is alive there is no soul. Only at the death of the body do souls begin to exist."[210] The two components of the ghost-soul, *ové* and *ianvé*, can only be said to exist when the body has died. Consumption liberates them so that they can assume their destiny. If the flesh of the dead person is absorbed by living flesh, these soul-elements must make their separate ways beyond the land of the living to enter their appointed realms of sun and forest.[211] By consuming the dead body, the Guayakí redirect the course of supernatural existence. They terminate the soul's hidden career as an unlocatable and unrecognizable ghost. Flesh, which signals death, is recontained and furnished with discernible signs of life in the bodies and names of the living.

It is clear that Guayakí funeral ingestion of the flesh is a response to the ambivalence of supernatural life manifest in death. It is not reducible exhaustively to sociopolitical structures for, as Pierre Clastres takes pains to point out, the dead person is neither a foreign warrior nor a representative of subject peoples. The corpse is a member of the community of ritual consumers. The Guayakí dead are not enemies because they belong to threatening outside groups but rather because — in the images of mythic jaguars, serpents, or vultures — they represent death, a condition of reality utterly different from life.[212] The rite of ingesting carnal remains yields its meaning only in the context of the mythical universe of the Guayakí, for consumption of the dead is a fully symbolic act. Within that imaginal world, ambivalent death is the enemy. Division and consumption of its fleshly signs offers hope of victory over the threat of final death.

IMBIBING THE FERMENTING SPIRIT

Drinking the bone-ash of close kin differs from ingesting the flesh of enemies in that it embraces the other pole of ambivalent respect for the dead, not dread but fascination. Drinking consummates the desire to unite with the dead. Important signs bespeak this unity. Nothing is cut. Neither knives nor teeth divide the ingested substance of death. Under the species of ashes blended in fermented brew, death assumes the formlessness and indivisibility signified by fluid. Ritual preparations force what are otherwise signs of division to signal uniformity. Flames and pounding reduce separate bones to homogeneous ashen powder, a condition offering no basis for distinction. Drinking ashes or pulverized bone, each portion of which is indistinguishable from the next (unlike flesh), effects material union with the dead and communion among the living. Through this ritual channel, the attraction for death nourishes life and regenerates social institutions.

In the earliest reports, consumption of the ashes of the dead appears an intimate family feast. Sir Walter Raleigh reported, "Those nations which are called Arwacas which dwell on the South of Orenoque . . . are dispersed in manie other places, and do use to beate the bones of their Lords into powder, and their wives and friends drinke it all in their severall sorts of drinks."[213] In 1819, Robert Southey used the term "family bread" for the preparation of powdered bone consumed by relatives. Southey reported, "When the body had mouldered they dug up the bones, reduced them to powder and mingling it with maize, composed a sort of cake, which they considered it the strongest mark of friendship to offer and partake."[214] More recent reports confirm that bone-ash consumption has roots in the unity of the social group. Chagnon, for instance, writes, "Endocannibalism, to the Yąnomamö, is the supreme form of displaying friendship and solidarity."[215] The living consume the bone-ash of the dead in order to "see their departed friends and relatives in *hedu*."[216]

The Amahuaca illustrate, in the following event witnessed by Dole, how imbibing bone-ash can be set within the context of the family unit. For a week after death, the body of an Amahuaca infant, wrapped in its mother's skirt, lay buried in a cooking pot with a second pot set over the first. Then the grave was opened and the two pots removed for cremation. Caressing the cooking pot, the mother wailed over the remains of her child. Her husband joined her.

A young man emptied the rotting corpse into a third pot and placed it on a funeral pyre. Fragments of the grinding trough that had belonged to the infant's mother were among the firewood. In accordance with the rubrics of the rite, the father tried to pull the corpse off the fire and was restrained by some of the men. Mourners chanted as they sat around the fire.[217] When fire had completely consumed the flesh, the mother began to extract from the cooking pot the small pieces of bone that remained, while the father of the dead child shared a bowl of cornmeal with the young undertaker. After four hours, when the mother had extracted all the bits of bone, she replaced the cremation pots and ashes in the grave and covered them with dirt. Taking charcoal from the cremation fire, she carried it in a basket to the river and dumped it in the water. During the following days of mourning, one of the grieving mother's sons made her a new grinding trough, in which she ground some corn to make gruel. "Into this she mixed the bone powder and drank the mixture."[218] When the mother had eaten the last of the powdered remains of her infant, she put aside her mourning.

Sigvald Linné was the first to study the consumption of ashes of the dead in South America on a wide comparative basis.[219] In 1960, Otto Zerries carefully sifted the many reports of this practice, mapping the distribution of some thirty-three groups in South America who consume their dead in a fermented beverage. The complex rites surrounding this consumption typically include a first burial (or some other preparation of the body, such as smoking or mummification), an exhumation, cleaning and decorating the bones, incineration of the remains, pounding of the bones to powder, storage of the powder or ashes in specially prepared containers, mixing the ashes or powder with a fermented beverage, and festive consumption of the remains by family members. Ingesting carbonized or pulverized bone is often a component of feasts of ripened fruit and is accompanied by dances, songs, and rituals. Participants often mix some ashes with red paint and apply the decoration to their bodies.[220] Zerries gathers important testimonies, and poses key culture-historical questions. Most importantly, he notes that all rites in which the ashes of the dead are cared for — either by storing them or ritually consuming them — center on the link between human bone and the human soul, which he connects with the widespread idea that bone is a container of the soul, an ancient concept associated with hunting economies. Whether consumption of the ashes intends to reincorporate a personal element of the dead being into the living community or, on the contrary, to prevent the independent existence of a wandering soul, the motive arises from the conviction that bone is the manifest expression of the soul.[221]

The most detailed information on the practice of imibibing remains of the dead comes from the Waika and related groups. The Waika, among whom Zerries lived, consume the ashes of the dead during the festival marking the harvest of *pijiguao* fruit. During the festival they pour the ashes of the dead from storage gourds into a large gourd filled with plantain soup. Hans Becher reported that the Surára and the Pakidái celebrate a similar feast once a year at the time of plantain and *pupunha* harvest. These groups mix bone-ash with plantain soup so that "the soul and power of the dead" might remain with the tribe.[222]

The Yąnomamö cremate their dead on a pyre, burning the corpse until only the large bones remain.[223] Only men are present in the village during cremation. They sift the ashes for bits of bone, which they pulverize in a special log mortar. If the deceased is a man, the men decorate the mortar with white buzzard down; if a woman, they use palm-fiber decorations. They then store the black bone powder for a year in a hollow gourd sealed with wax and buzzard down. After a year has passed, the relatives pour the ashes into a plantain beverage and consume it at a feast. The Yąnomamö reserve some of the ashes for consumption at other ceremonies. Before a raid of revenge, for example, Yąnomamö warriors imbibe ashes of dead kin.[224] Barandiarán throws further light on Yąnomamö practice.[225] He asserts that, for the Yąnomamö, drinking the remains liberates both the living and the dead from the ambivalence made present in death. The path of liberation is through union with bone through material identification with imaginary process which contains souls.

The Sanemá-Yanoama, too, cremate their dead, destroying everything except the calcinated bones. Spectators take carbonized vegetal matter from the pyre and smear it on their faces and over their entire bodies, especially the chest. With great care they gather up the charred remains. Amid the dancing of women and a crescendo of lamentations, mourners sprinkle the remains with banana-leaf sap, red-ochre paste, and a mixture *urucú* and *arnotto*.[226] They place the calcinated bones in a container or wrapper and treat them with utmost veneration. Ordinarily they apportion out the remains to related neighboring groups, who consume the ashes during a feast or before a raid on mutual enemies. No one who has touched the body or bones may wash his or her hands in water lest all water become contaminated. To the accompaniment of songs, dances, and lamentation, men pound the bones to powder and store them in calabash cups sealed with wax. The mortar is painted black on the inside and red on the outside and is decorated with white feathers, as is the red-and-black painted pestle. Both instruments are burned after the bones are milled. At the proper time, a large batch of ripe-plantain beverage is prepared in a ceremonial tub. While dancing and crying, a close relative of the deceased pours the ashes into the drink. Warriors, with bows and arrows, stand at full attention while relatives mix the drink, accompanied by a choir of yells and laments. All present take communion, including toddlers. Only pregnant women abstain. Until the moment of consumption of the bone-ash, the *híkola* of the dead person remains in a suspended state dangerous to relatives and assassins of the dead person. Liberated from the flesh and the cremated bones, the soul lingers as a free spirit. Depositing the ash in fermenting brew and imbibing it brings the autonomous career of the soul to an end. Relatives ingest the *híkola*, reincorporating its vital energy into the human community. The *híkola* had lodged in the marrow of the bones. The marrow, now consumed by fire and ground to powder, offers concrete hope of unity with the fertile and fascinating power of death.[227]

THE LIMITS OF CONSUMPTION: THE TERMINOLOGY

The termination of human life and the disposal of the corpse assume various forms of consumption, challenging one's understanding of the limits of significant existence. In particular, mortuary consumption of human relics questions the nature of symbolic life. These "terminological" questions direct themselves to mourners as well as to scholarly interpreters. Although consumption finds economic and political expression, its basic significance arises from the religious situation of human existence: consumption enacts a disposition toward the sacred in the sense that it reenacts the symbolic process that disposed of the first beings. Whether sacrificial, funereal, imperial, or economic, consumption originates with the undertakings of sacred beings. This is why each form of consumption owes something of its meaning to the others and why no single consumptive process is fully understood without exposing its religious roots.[228]

Mythic beings reached precedent-setting limits as the primordium ended. The cataclysm or the first irreversible death put an end to these beings, and their disappearance or transignification marked a border that closed the paradisal condition and inaugurated a new currency of life. To sustain itself, today's world ceaselessly replays the process that brought the first world to term. Because it imitates the disposal of sacred beings, consumption has the power to establish symbolic limits. Grounded in myth, consumption is the inner dynamic of the cosmos and the principal symbolic strategy with which the life forms of the cosmos confront chaos. Hence all consumptive acts are sacrificial in some measure; that is, they create the symbolic conditions for an experience of what is holy and deeply ambivalent. In generating the symbolic world, however, consumptive processes alienate significant forms from the primordial setting in which their meaning is fully apparent. To evaluate the meaning of their existence, human communities must explore the limits of consumption by revealing the primal locus of these limits and reenacting their original form.

Death offers unique possibilities for this reflection on symbolic terms. Mythic beings suffered transignification when they disappeared from their original context—in the dismemberment of the aquatic dragon, the putrefaction of celestial birds, the bone-crunching demise of the primordial jaguar, the petrification of protohuman ancestors, the cremation of ancients in the cosmic conflagration. The corpse undergoes similar occultation, corruption, and destruction when mourners, imitating the undertaking of sacred beings, dispatch the signs of the cadaver's appearance (flesh, blood, bone) to an unmanifest mode.[229] And in this consumptive process meaning itself suffers the same fate as the corpse (and primordial beings).

The meaning of the consumption of mortal remains is complicated by at least two factors already discussed: contestation and ambivalence. Elements of the person (flesh, hair, nails, blood, bone, belongings, ritual relationships) not only contend with one another, but each element is *in se* a coincidence of opposites. That is, each material constituent of the person can be a symbol representing a sacred reality. Flesh and bone, for example, disclose the coexistence of opposite modes of being. On its own, flesh is one formless mass, and can thus signify the undifferentiated state of the first world. Replicable carnal life in multiple species, however, came into existence in the calamity that divided or scattered the first, fluid realities. When first beings bathed in the blood or feces of the all-engulfing aquatic monster, for instance, they took on the marks of separate carnal species; from the flood that accompanied the monster's slaying and from the blood-bath that ensued came animals whose fleshly forms bear differential body-markings and express distinct sounds. Thus, the life of flesh bespeaks the separation of species while never losing signs of the inherent formlessness of flesh, which promises an eventual return through dissolution to the primordial condition.

By contrast the numerous, various, and well-defined bones of the skeleton represent the temporal and spatial state of the current world, and they make manifest, like so many metronomes set swinging at the same time, the complex polyrhythms of calendrical existence. Festival dances display the syndesmotic state of the skeleton and of transitory life, joined at the points of transition. Ritual dances are physical and cultural ligaments binding together the experiences of a community at the points where it passes from one quality of time to a markedly different one. Funeral cleaning, painting, and dressing of bone also put style and grace on parade. The treatment of bone in secondary burial or bone-ash ingestion exhibits the human capacity to coordinate multiple experiences of time by means of the aesthetic symbolism of the body. Yet, at the same time that bone communicates something about movement through differential times, its hardness and durability give material expression to the eternal and permanent condition of the primordium.

In order to sacrifice death — that is, in order to call out its sacrality and reveal its meaning — funeral practices place each manifest quality of being in the creative presence of its opposite. Thus funerals are ironic exercises, juxtaposing sorrow and festivity, sadness and graveside humor. On one side, the undivided flesh meets its match through dismemberment. Ironically, in the divisive act of chewing the "one" flesh, the separate bodies of consumers become one communion and many territories become one imperial universe under the consumers' hegemony. On the other side, the many bones, well defined and durable, meet a different, opposite sort of end: burned and pulverized beyond distinction, their ashen residue is consumed as an indivisible and formless liquid, and bone is thus subjected to the sucking power of the flesh. The paradoxical reversal here is that by reengulfing bones of individual relatives within the flesh — this time the flesh of the entire community — through the act of drinking, the group reaffirms itself as unique and separate from other self-contained kin groups.

Once sacralized (that is, once viewed as a fully symbolic form) each element of mortal remains includes all possible primordial meanings. That is why the interpreter should not collapse funeral symbolism into a single set of meanings (e.g., life versus death). Rather, one's analysis will be drawn in the opposite direction, from simple to complicated and from singular to multiple expressions of culture as the meaning of death becomes traceable in the elaborate symbolic patterns and hierarchies of territory, kin, enemies, animal and plant taxonomies, dress codes, and food. Since each culture encompasses the fullness of meaning in a unique way, mortuary symbolism provokes reflection on the peculiar limits of each semantic universe, for it confronts the chaos that appears when death threatens to transcend those limits.[230] Whether it functions to dispel the chaos of uninhabitable foreignness or to relocate defunct life within new, fermenting forms, funeral ingestion of the dead signals the existence of a total supernatural process embracing everything and liberating it from the final ambivalence of death. During the consumptive rites of death, the symbolic process, born of terminal situations, turns on itself and attempts to free human language and understanding from the limits of its own terminology.

COSMIC DISTRIBUTION OF THE PERSONALITY

Decomposition of the body and disintegration of the individual personality disclose the principles of distributive justice. That is, the redistribution of personal and physical elements to their postmortem places shows how material, spiritual, individual, cosmic, and moral dimensions of existence interface. Religious imagery reveals how these aspects of reality interdepend as a single, ecumenical economy.

The distribution of the personality after death can be complicated. We can begin, however, with a simple illustration. For the Wakuenai of the upper Río Negro, death is a disintegrative process in which the body and its two life-principles separate. The symbolic elements of the person move through the symbolic universe like pieces in a kaleidoscope. The animal-shaped soul (*lidzaruna*, or *liwaruna*) first travels vertically toward a celestial paradise; then it, or some portion of it, apparently goes to inhabit a newborn sacred animal (*durucubite*).[231] Meanwhile, the human-shaped soul (*likaale*, or *likariwa*) becomes one of the *lidanam*, the transmigrating ghosts of the recently dead. They first move horizontally to the world of *iyarudati*, a limbo where dead souls are purified in fire. The fire bath lightens the soul for its journey to the sky world of Yaperikuli, the creator-transformer. In Yaperikuli's paradise, the purified *lidanam* becomes imbued with light. Brilliant and shining, the *lidanam* live in eternal sunlight and eat clear honey.[232] Once they arrive in heaven, they never return to their bodies on earth.

The Cashinahua offer another case in which the reapportionment of the dead individual is both simple and mystical. For the Cashinahua, death is incomprehensible on any but a spiritual plane, for the cause of death is the definitive departure of the soul from the envelope of the body.[233] The soul of the deceased goes to the "root of heaven" (heaven has the anatomical form of a tree). The root of heaven is the vault of the sky, but it is also esoterically understood to be the same as the farthest reaches of the earth. In other words, the outer limits of the earth and the highest point of the sky are one and the same place, the root of heaven. Therefore, the separation of the body (interred in the earth) and soul (gone to the root of heaven) actually effects their reunion in a mystical existence that transcends the individual's mortal condition. By journeying to different stations in the universe "body and soul find themselves reintegrated."[234]

The disintegration of the individual is linked to material decomposition. The maximal breadth and order are achieved fleetingly in dream, trance, or transition during life and become permanent in death. At the moment of death the Boróro personality begins to fragment, and its constituent parts take on autonomous life-histories.[235] The supernatural being (bope) who formed the fetus in the womb consumes the skin and flesh of the cadaver. Mourners ceremonially clean the bones once the flesh has fallen from them. They paint the bones, array them with feathers, and place them in a mortuary basket. The person's vital force (rakare) is depleted, and the soul-shadow (aroe marigudu) abandons the corpse to inhabit the body of an animal — specifically a carnivore, which takes life from fleshly beings to make up for the consumption of the cadaver's flesh during putrefaction.

Instructed by mourning relatives, a Boróro hunter, representing the deceased, blows on a little gourd. The breath of the defunct thus becomes the breath of an animal, for it is this breath which the hunter has captured in a ritual hunt and now encloses in the little gourd. From then on, the gourd is the voice of the aroe, the soul-shadow that, during the deceased's lifetime, wandered in his dreams in the form of an animal. The gourd is put inside a mortuary hut. During life, a Boróro's soul-shadow voice travels uncontrollably in his dreams at night, but after death, it remains contained in the "voice box" of the funeral hut.[236]

Although the hushed voice resides as a darkened dream-image inside communal space, one no longer hears the name of the deceased. The living do not utter it. One's personal name stays wrapped in silence until the bones have become powder. Instead, survivors use "names of the hunt of the dead" (iebio-mage). Iebio-mage are bestowed not only on the deceased but on the ritual hunter who represents him and on a couple who stand as ritual parents of the deceased. The dead person is always treated as the dead "son" of some pair of ritual parents. The hunter represents not only the dead "son" but the animal into which the dead man's soul transforms itself.[237] The bestowal of death-hunt names follows ceremonial preparations: songs, communal meals, funeral dances, the cleaning and feathering of the bones, the burning of the deceased's effects, and the reburial of his remains. By redistributing the transformed elements of the individual, these symbolic processes project the person into new relations with the social, physical, and supernatural aspects of existence. In fact, because these dimensions present themselves as related aspects of reality, the Boróro person becomes integrated, in death, on a scale not possible during life.

Throughout South America, spiritual elements of the person (perhaps even cosmic or mythic prefigurations of the personality) are believed to reside in material remains after death and putrefaction. That is why the care tendered bones and flesh affects the entire spiritual destiny of an individual. The reconfigured fate of one of its members confirms a group's vision of the interrelatedness of all manifestations of being. The dissolution of the individual exposes the ultimate foundations of communal well-being. This is the case, for instance, when a Krahó person's components dissolve into separate parts at death. Each portion of the Krahó individual returns to the place whence it came. Biological individuality, located in the blood (the flesh), evaporates as the blood dries up. Vital breath, previously governed by the heart, now falls under the rule of the *mekarõ*, the shadowy souls of the dead. No longer entering and exiting the body in the form of breath, it ceases to move.[238] The bones, the locus of the persona with its complex of obligations and responsibilities, remain in the social sphere. They are decorated and interred below the house or at the center of the dance plaza, the epitome of social space within which, during life, the "socialized" aspects of the persona were ceremonially endowed upon the individual. These personal endowments are enclosed in the marrow of his bones, the center of corporeal life. The ceremonial plaza, the center of corporate life in the circular village, reingests the distinctive features it bestowed.[239] This is especially the case for those privileged persons who represent the whole of society. "In reality, it is itself, with its political groups and ceremonials, which the village inscribes in the soil with the bones of its representatives."[240] Death affords a community the opportunity to reappropriate its vision of itself and its place in existence. The secondary burial installs death at the very center of ritual existence, the source of all transformation, reflection, and regeneration. Human being gradually moves itself toward that center throughout its ritual life.

But not all scenarios of the cosmic apportionment of the person are as simple as these. The deadly process of redistributing an individual can be as complicated as the process of life in the universe, for death fulfills and makes visible the individual's involvements in every aspect of reality. Because it draws life from disintegration (from the chaos of destruction or nothingness present in the corpse), death can recapitulate on the scale of the person the cosmogonic process, with its series of failures and advances. When this is the case, creation myths illuminate the process of death and dying.[241]

Sometimes a hero discovers the link between death and the process of universal life. The mythic account of heroic discoveries throws light on the dispersal of human life to the elements. A Goajiro hero, for example, once visited Jepíra, the land of the dead. Taking no part in the social life of the dead (their communal eating and festive dancing), he stayed until he witnessed his dead wife being sexually penetrated through all her orifices while she was dancing. At this, he ran from the land of the dead and tried to find his way home. Unfortunately, he became lost and strayed to the land of the god Juyá ("rain"), where he was put to work obtaining food plants and game animals for Juyá. These bounties eventually benefited humankind.[242] Edible goods are not the only fruits of his servitude, for he also learned the symbolic meanings, the esoteric analogies, used by Juyá in his discourse. Each time the hero was sent to fetch a plant, he was expected to go to the land of Jepíra and kill one of a number of human-looking beings, who then changed into the desired food. To get corn, he shot his arrows into those being who had very hairy pubes; to get melons, he killed "foreigners." On each occasion, the bewildered hero took the slain being home in the form of the food desired by Juyá.[243]

The Goajiro hero's journey, in addition to mapping out postmortem geography, has the more important function of clarifying the cyclic nature of Goajiro existence. The sojourn among the dead enables the Goajiro to relate personal existence to cosmic life. "We die twice. Once here, once in *Jepíra*."[244] Goajiros begin their life on earth as *wayú* (fully human beings). At death they live as *yoluja*, inhabitants of Jepíra, the land of the dead. After a period of time, they pass into a state that is nameless and without specific location and that represents a state of profound crisis, which is resolved when these anonymous beings are assimilated either to Juyá (a male being) or Pulówi (Juyá's wife, the female supernatural associated with earth).[245] The rains that fall under the constellation Arcturus embody Juyá. Consequently, *juyá* is also the word for "year," the annual stellar cycle marked by Arcturus.

It was Juyá's intention that the human soul dwell with him forever. To that end, he admonished the hero not to look at Pulówi. However, the hero espied Pulówi through the window of her house. She wore no loincloth and her legs were spread apart. As soon as the hero glanced at her, he fell dead upon the earth. When Juyá arrived on the scene, Pulówi told him, "He is dead because he looked." In anger, Juyá told his wife, the earth, that she could eat the dead human if she wished. Juyá always carries bottles of human blood for Pulówi to eat as her only nourishment.[246]

The souls of dead Goajiro who are assimilated to Juyá return to earth as rains that bring fruit and food. "The price of rains and pasturelands is the death of the Goajiro and all their animals: humans give their dead and, in exchange, *Juyá* gives rain to the families of the dead."[247] The souls assimilated to Pulówi return to the earth in the form of *wanili*, the spirits of the long-dead, who are reincarnated as nocturnal, pathogenic foreign objects and as foreigners. These foreign objects and peoples are linked with places where vegetation is thick and animal life is abundant.[248]

In either case, the dead Goajiro return to earth as presences that can be both beneficial and harmful. The dead are destined to be essential elements of earthly life: weather, flora, and fauna, which both sicken and strengthen people. Far from the idea that nature can be understood apart from a mythic apprehension of human life in its fullest reach, Goajiro culture implies that "man is finally the essence of beings and things."[249] The Goajiro take the critical view that significant universal processes are a function of the symbolic constitution of human existence. The distributive process of decomposition allows the Goajiro to unravel that constitution and reflect on its cosmic implications. They conclude, as do many South American peoples, that symbolic properties of the person, transformed and redistributed after death, guarantee the truth that the meaning of mortal human life is coextensive with the significance of the wider universe of being. This chapter now turns to images of that larger world, which is thrown into sharper relief by the centrifuge of death.

MYTHIC GEOGRAPHY

Death and afterlife pitch human life into a fully imaginative existence played on a mythic stage. Few human experiences so vividly illuminate the supernatural realm. In tracing the whereabouts of the dead, the no-longer-manifest, one outlines the contours of the invisible world. The Goajiro word *a'iñ* denotes (1) the vital dimension of the heart, (2) the visceral area, and (3) a principal, constitutive of the person, that could best be called the "soul."[250] The *a'iñ* is invisible. At death it leaves the body forever, and the living follow the course of its travels. The person becomes irreversibly dead when the *a'iñ* crosses over the Milky Way (*spïna wayú ouktïsï*, the "path of dead people"). Beyond the path, the soul heads toward the middle of the sea and thence to the outer banks of *Jepíra*, the isle (or peninsula) of the dead. There a bittern stands guard over the drinking waters needed to continue the journey. Jepíra is invisible to living humans, sealed off from this world by an impenetrable stone door.[251] By passing through the stone, a permanent condition, the dead soul assumes its postmortem form, *yoluja*.[252] On the far side of the afterworld, the *yoluja* scurries across moving fields of mud before arriving at the summit of the mountain of the heavenly being Juyá. Since, for the Goajiro, knowledge of mythic geography is knowledge of postmortem life, the study of this geography offers them a measure of confidence in facing death: "At our death, our soul [*a'iñ*] is not lost. Only our bones are lost. Our bones and our skin. Our soul goes on its way, that's all."[253]

In a brief summary of ideas about the other world, Tullio Tentori underlines several important features of South American concepts of the afterlife. The dead inhabit various parts of the cosmos. Trial or judgment condition one's entrance to life after death. Judgments are not made only on the basis of the deceased's moral character but also depend on other personal qualities (e.g., social rank) and on the manner of death. A guide often conducts the dead on their journey. The songs of mourners and pictographs along the route to the afterlife remind the deceased which is the safe road, for various obstacles, especially distracting voices, lie in wait to block the way or to lure the dead from their goal.[254]

The dead do not traverse an unambiguously clear map; ambivalence reappears on the landscape of death, and, indeed, the sparse but multivalent terminology of symbolic space pulls these contradictions into sharper focus. Even the location of life after death is often confused. For instance, there appear to be two residences for the Shipibo dead after life. Some of the dead inhabit the celestial domain in the form of *yoshin* (evil spirits) and reappear as thunder and lightning, while others dwell in the underworld, to which caves, mountains, and deep pools give access.[255]

The complicated geography of the afterlife reflects the complexity of life before death, and the life of the dead is bound up with the history of culture and cosmos. For example, the postmortem existence of the *huanushca runa* (the Canelos Quichua word for the dead) runs parallel to the experience of the living, although the dead inhabit all realms of the universe. Occasionally, they appear to human beings on forest trails at night. A knowledgeable individual may acquire such an ancient soul as a spirit helper.[256] In this way, the dead soul's experience of other spaces and times broadens the knowledge and self-understanding of the living. In an exemplary way the earliest Canelos Quichua shamans, living during the Time of the Grandparents, learned the spatial nature of death by acquiring such souls.[257] Originally, in the Ancient Times before creation, people knew how to send their souls into stones and trees so that they would be reborn in the future. Encapsulated in special spaces, these souls awaited the call of the wise shamans of the Times of the Grandparents. The shamans acquired the ancient souls by awakening them and learned from them that the souls of ordinary folk journey through the underworld or sky after death until, at the bidding of soul-master spirits, they reenter the world in the form of animals and birds. In the meantime, the body, separated from its soul, "continues to exist as a dead soul."[258] Life does not end at death for the body or the soul. The experience of space, however, changes and diverges. For the Canelos Quichua, that experience becomes complex enough to reflect the spiritual and material history of culture and the universe.

Postmortem geography sorts out the confusion of human existence. It discloses the essential relationship between morality and symbolic space.[259] For the Kógi, the soul, after death, follows a trail leading in a particular direction; the course depends on the morality of the deceased's behavior during life. The virtuous head east or south and the immoral travel west or north. Apparently, the disintegration of ancient wisdom traditions and mores is causing the *mámas*, Kógi priests, to worry about the distribution of souls in the afterlife and the maintenance of the balance of the universe, which depends on a right distribution. Indeed, those ignorant of the tradition and its moral norms seem far to outweigh the virtuous, and the *mámas* have developed complicated schemes to accomodate this new situation: "in-between ways" (the northeast, southeast, northwest, and southwest) have also become paths traveled by souls in the afterlife.

The segregation of the dead on ethical grounds reveals how directly the moral valence of human experience is tied to the mythography of cosmic space, a culture's evaluation of the human place in the world. Moral discernment — like ritual combats, contests, and images of cutting or piercing — divides the experience of a sacred reality, especially the fearful respect for the dead, into comprehensible components. Sorting out the experience of death in terms of the value-laden spaces of their cosmos, the Campa root their fear of dead souls in the belief that most Campas are not good enough during their lives to be anything but malign ghosts after death. Malingering souls are not well fixed in space. The dead person who was bad during life becomes a *siréci*, who wanders around the world attacking the living. "This, then, is the anticipated fate of most Campas: they will become malignant ghosts wandering through the forest, perhaps in the form of diseased animals (*peári*)."[260] A more distinguished group of evil spirits, the souls of witches, join the company of their demon teachers in the forest. Some of these demonic souls go to the level of the underworld, *Sarinkavéni*. The souls of good Campas, a minority of those who die, join the "hidden ones" on mountain ridges or in the sky and in fact become "hidden ones" themselves.[261] As they ascend skyward, these good souls encounter ordeals, and only the best arrive at the apex of the sky. That is why there is a hierarchy of good spirits. Life in the celestial sphere is similar to life on earth, but goods abound and there is no suffering. The good soul takes a new spouse. Reproduction occurs without sexual intercourse and without the pain of childbirth.

Because symbolic space is an evaluation of qualities of being that are simultaneously material, moral, historical, and spiritual, the mythic geography of death can organize the living community. Thus, the physical layout of the Boróro village and the social relations inscribed in its architecture are linked with the space of death. Great mythical heroes (*iedaga*) first developed Boróro techniques of burial (as well as body painting and ritual decoration). Caring for the dead recreates a mythical event linked to the *iedaga*, who are supernatural beings who represent the names of mythical places, each of which takes its name from an act that marked mythical space. That is, mythical space is a heroic mode of action transmitted through personal names bestowed on living human beings. Personal names are recycled to the living only when those who once bore the names are long dead. Each *iedaga* therefore unifies a collection of personal names and forms a community based on them. This community, named after a sacred place, cuts across time. Names, as key fixtures in the mythical space-time inhabited by the dead, lend structure and order to the community of the living. A Boróro reckons his rank order and hierarchial place in society according to the circular pantheon of mythical place-names and heroic exploits.[262] The ground plan of the village and the social structure of the living community are symbols from a mythic geography created by heroes and peopled with the dead.

THE ROADS BEYOND DEATH

Since mythic geography makes sense of human and cosmic life, descriptions of postmortem space become elaborate. One report, cited at some length below, will suffice to show how the supernatural panorama of death offers a mythic context for understanding every dimension of being. Warao spatial scenarios of death depict the ways in which human life participates in the most basic processes of the universe. These roads beyond death lead to the fundamental sources of experience: the quintessence of what is sublime, absurd, grotesque, terrifying, and beautiful.

Among the Winikina-Warao the destiny of the soul after life primarily depends on the role of the deceased during life on earth. Souls of ordinary people who have taken no distinctive role during life wander forever in the vicinity of human habitations in the form of dwarflike beings.[263] This is also the fate of about half the children who die in infancy. Depending on the disease that causes their death, the souls of the rest of the children who die in infancy are destroyed either by creatures of the underworld or by the divine beings who live on the mountains at the cardinal points of the horizon at the end of the world. "[T]he Goddess of the Nadir, for instance, is believed to kill the body and steal the souls of babies whose mothers are careless enough to spill their milk on the ground where the goddess can lap it up."[264] The Winikina-Warao view all of life as a gradual process of dying, of returning to the *wa*, the dugout canoe-coffin which is the vagina of Dauarani, mother of the forest. Human life first arrived in this canoe, and life is a process of returning to the womb.[265] The mode of death, which comes through the agency of a shaman or some other supernatural being, is less important than the survival of the soul, *mehokohi*, which is imaged as a light in the chest.[266] Several categories of people die with assurance of an afterlife, notably three classes of shamans and several kinds of artisans. The conditions of postmortem existence of each class are intimately bound up with the conditions of mythic space.

When death comes for the priest-shaman, he rides on a golden horse to the height of heaven and there rests in the home of Yaukware, the god of the center. With the help of Yaukware, the shaman is thence dispatched to the dwelling place of the deity whom he served during life. Furnished with a last cigar and mounted on a winged horse, he speeds like a comet to the far end of the world, where he is received by his patron god, invested with beautiful clothes, and awarded a home bedecked with gold and flowers. He lives peacefully among the other shamans who reside there and receives tobacco from the community of living shamans on earth.[267] The priest-shaman is confident of his arrival in this mythical land after death because he has journeyed there successfully during his ecstasies in life, when the road was much more perilous and unfamiliar.

The light-shaman, another category of specialist, has also often journeyed to his ultimate destination. When, for the last time, his soul climbs to the zenith of heaven, an invisible soul-guide meets him and offers him a cigar. The guide brings him to a bridge made of tobacco smoke and bordered with rows of beautiful flowers, which leads to the white home of Kanobo Amawari, the light-shaman's divine patron. This mountain house is the place of origin of light-shamanism. The songs sung by the light-shaman were originally chanted by the four beings who live in the white house: Black Bee, Wasp, Termite, and Honey Bee.[268] Here, the souls of light-shamans (and those of their wives) live, fed with tobacco smoke offered by their fellow light-shamans on earth.[269]

The soul of the dark-shaman also journeys to the land of its patron, the western land of death governed by Scarlet Macaw, god of the underworld, Ever since the artery of sustenance (the duct through which blood flowed from the heads of sleeping people on earth to the land of the dead in the west) was severed, it has fallen to dark-shamans to provide nourishment for the beings of the underworld. That nourishment consists of human beings who fall victim to the dark-shaman's magical arrows or the sling carried just below his breast. When he dies, the soul of the dark-shaman ascends to the abode of Soul-Hoebo, which is west of the zenith of heaven. There he enters the black house of the Hoebo family, which is furnished with human skin and bones and in which an infant cries in a hammock of coagulated blood. The dark-shaman moves on. He leaves the home of the Hoebo spirit with the long, blood-clotted hair, and, traveling along a slippery road wet with human blood, he descends to the dark underworld home of Scarlet Macaw. A faint white and yellow light and the heavy stench of rotting corpses guide him to his destiny. Along the way, the soul of the dark-shaman smokes a cigar. Macaw plays on instruments made from human skulls and long bones. He welcomes the shaman, offers him a drink of blood from a canoe and some human flesh to eat, and decorates him with a necklace of human ribs. On his arrival, the dark-shaman takes on a new body form: half-parrot and half-human, with the tail of a monkey.[270]

Warao canoemakers who have practiced their craft carefully also succeed in securing a distinguished place in the afterlife. They return after death to the mountain home of the mother of the forest, Dauarani, which they had visited during their initiation journey. Along the way, their souls pass over a bridge formed by the body of a snake, which will devour them if during their lives they have offended the mother of the forest. Guided to the heights of heaven by a psychopomp who provides him with a cigar, the craftsman's soul journeys from the vault of heaven to the southeastern horizon, the home of Dauarani. If, at this point, he hears his wife or other mourners complimenting his artisanry during life, he must not succumb to nostalgia but continue through the body of the sky-snake without looking back. "If he passes his final test and exits at the anus of the snake, he will find there the abode of the Master Spirit of Boat-making."[271] All his life the good artisan has served Dauarani by making dugout canoes in the image of her vagina. Now he takes up residence in her well-lit but windowless house. On entering this permanent home, which is perfumed with incense and filled with flowers that chant the ceremonial songs of his craft, the canoe-maker's soul is invested with new clothes and washed in perfumed waters.[272]

Warao basketmakers also have a special place. Their souls journey to live with the Creator Bird of Dawn on the eastern horizon of the world. This is because the spirit of the reed plant with which baskets are made has appeared to them in dreams, offering them cigars and helper spirits.[273] When women who make hammocks die, they journey to the northeast, to the place where the sun rises at the winter solstice. This is the home of the mother of *moriche*, the woman who was transformed into a *moriche* palm tree and who now provides fruit and flour for her people.[274]

An ordinary Warao individual who dies as a result of the magic arrows of a dark-shaman becomes the sacrificed food of Scarlet Macaw and the other inhabitants of the underworld. "His flesh is to be eaten by the spirit shamans, his blood will be their drink, the god himself will relish his heart and liver, and his bones and skin will serve as raw materials in this sinister world."[275] Apparently, the majority of Waraos suffer the ultimate destiny of complete death of body and soul, serving as nourishment in the land of the dead. Usually they have been killed by pathogenic arrows transported by tobacco smoke that the dark-shaman puffs from a cigar whose lit end he holds in his mouth. The arrow penetrates the victim's ribcage and, seeking out the heart, kills him. At first the victim is transported upside down on the back of the dark-shaman to the zenith, the home of Hoebo. Later the dark-shaman carts the victim off to the land of death, where Scarlet Macaw uses his fierce beak to tear off the victim's head.[276]

Mythic geography expands to accommodate the complexities of material and supernatural life. The destinations of life are inextricably linked to the destiny of space itself. No matter what realities it contains, life remains comprehensible because it falls within the bounds of space. The mythic map that comes alive at death demonstrates this assurance: even if that space is invisible and the powers within it ambivalent or unmanifest, they remain imaginable and, to that degree, significant. In the face of death, such breadth of meaning is attainable only at great cost, and so mythic geographies invariably include portrayals of struggle. The full map of being issues from the ordeal of transcending limits and traveling beyond death.

TRIALS OF THE WEARY TRAVELER

To traverse the mythic map is to move from one mode of being to another in a journey requiring transformation—a thoroughgoing, arduous change of one's fundamental conditions of existence. The ordeals that the dead undergo reflect the difficulty of obtaining experiential knowledge of the full range of being.

On 2 November, the Feast of the Dead, the people of Kaata, a community in the Bolivian Andes, set up a three-tiered table. The table is a map of mythic geography and outlines the space traversed by the dead. Its three levels symbolize the three spatial domains of the universe and of Mount Kaata, where the community resides. The dead person must make a postmortem journey along the underground river that the sun follows during the night. This demanding three-year voyage on subterranean watercourses leads the deceased to the origin of life, the head of the mountain-body, which is both the universe and a divine being. Relatives equip the dead person with clothing, food, alcoholic drink, and coca as well as with a candle for the journey. The dead need these fortifications, for the journey amounts to a series of rigorous festivals that include exhausting dances and ritual deaths.[277] During these three years of trial and uphill progress, the community ritually feeds the dead person, and on 2 November the dead feast on offerings placed on the table-map of the world. Music and fermented brew are the order of the day. Joseph Bastien writes, "The Feast of the Dead expresses to Andeans that the mountain body contains the living and the dead, gives form to their history, and underlies their social and economic structure. It is the conclusive ritual of the Andes."[278]

The progress of the dead along their path to the other world is punctuated by trials that play an initiatory role and mark transitions into new states. Thus, when a Waiwai man once journeyed through the afterlife, he was first split open, and then, having been resuscitated by the medicines of heavenly spirits, he contended with a menacing anaconda, which bridged the river that separates the world of the living from that of the dead. In another ordeal faced by Waiwai souls entering the realm of the dead, stinging wasps strip the dead body of its flesh, making the deceased light and pure.

Familiar initiatory ordeals impede progress on the roads to the other world. The dead must pass through fire or nearly impenetrable barriers, cross tightropes or slippery paths, squeeze through tight passages or tiny holes, remain silent or dance past exhaustion, keep their eyes or ears shut, display extraordinary skill, suffer bizarre multiple deaths, or be swallowed by monsters. After passing through such ordeals, dead souls assume new clothes, bodies, or forms that signal their new condition.

The afterlife of the Baniwa soul, for example, consists of a journey to the highest heaven, where it will live forever near Yaperikuli in this place of plenty where there is no sickness. "To attain heaven, the soul must 'throw off its person' (lipekoka newikika) and be transformed by passing through a 'hole' of flaming tree resin which washes it clean. Then the soul is dressed in 'beautiful clothes,' white garments, before it proceeds onward to Yaperikuli."[279]

In the case of the Kalapalo, the deceased soul must limit his power of vision. At death, the soul-shadow journeys to the east, where he enters the sky. Along the way, other soul-shadows try to waylay the traveler by making him look at them. For the sake of his ultimate well-being, the soul must remain narrowly focused, keeping a steadfast gaze on the upward path. Should he look upon the wandering souls, the spirit would never arrive at his highest destiny. A guide, usually a deceased relative, aids the soul across the final obstacle: a stream bridged by a slippery, moss-covered log.[280]

Through performing rites and obeying restrictions the living help the dead through their time of trial. At the time of the lunar eclipse, the dead Kamayurá soul (a(n)ng) is dispatched with tobacco and song and makes its way to Ìwakakape, the road of heaven (the Milky Way). There it encounters terrible trials of the sort which the mythical hero Kanaratê suffered in obedience to the commands of his sadistic older brother, Karanavarê.[281] These ordeals accomplish the same kinds of death achieved during puberty rites and ceremonial transitions. The soul is slain in several ways and undergoes a process of refinement or distillation, for it must be completely rearranged in order to pass into a world where day is night, night day, and all other conditions reversed: death, ultimately, is life. The soul squeezes itself through a tiny hole in the western end of the Milky Way. Guarding the gate of heaven are two ravenous birds, the two-headed king vulture and the giant harpy eagle.

During this time of test, the living Kamayurá follow the fate of the dead, which is revealed in their dreams. During the lunar eclipse, when the soul travels to heaven along the treacherous Milky Way, the living aid the dead: dance, din, smoke, the cutting of thatch, and the killing of specific animals help the soul (and, for that matter, the cosmos, especially the moon) to effect its passage from one state of being to another. (After the eclipse, mourning assumes a new form, and until the celebration of Kwarìp people neither paint themselves nor utter the name of the dead person.) This assistance from the living may be positive or negative, for death is an ambivalent state and to be installed in its quarters may be seen as a blessing or a curse. The acts of the living can propel the dead through their ordeal and advance them toward final glory, yet they can equally push them toward annihilation by closing off every route of escape from a trial and a destiny that the dead soul resists. The Apapocuvá illustrate both possibilities. The Apapocuvá soul fragments into its component parts at the instant of death, and these elements encounter great difficulties in approaching and arriving at the Land Without Evil. The *ayvúkué* ("the breath that sprouts, the soul that goes forth from the body"), is a tranquil entity that preexists the birth of an infant[282] and accounts for the appetite for vegetable foods.[283] The *ayvúkué* of young, innocent children (who have died without having had contact with animal souls) returns immediately to Yvỹ Naráeỹ, the Land Without Evil. On its journey, it must tiptoe past the sleeping Añay, the supernatural jaguar who stretches his hammock across the path to the other world, for should Añay awaken, he would devour the soul. Once it arrives in the Land Without Evil, the innocent *ayvúkué* lives a life of perfect happiness eating *kaguyiy* (a concoction of maize beer and honey).

Adult *ayvúkué* have had extended contact with animal souls in the form of *asyiguá*, their companion soul-elements, as well as through the handling and consumption of game, and so they are unable to enter the Land Without Evil. They must remain just outside that paradise. A second supernatural jaguar, called Yrukurca keeps them out, alerting the souls of dead relatives and friends should anyone attempt to cross the border into the Land Without Evil. Any soul who oversteps the bounds of its destiny in this way becomes a wandering soul (*tarykué*),[284] who can be dangerous, especially in cases where the person died suddenly, prematurely, or violently. If it is the *ayvúkué* that roams the earth, the community performs the *yoasá*, the dance that "crosses one thing with another." The dance is physically demanding and spiritually dangerous. It fixes the wandering soul in place by marking it off in ordered dance-space and presents it to the god *Tupá*, who takes it to the place of lost souls.[285] If, however, the wandering soul-element is the *asyiguá* (the animal element) the situation is much more dangerous. The *asyiguá* is responsible for violent inclinations and for the desire to consume meat. After death the *asyiguá* transforms itself into an *anguëry*, a dangerous supernatural entity that inspires great fear. The living redress this situation by subjecting the soul to its final ordeal, a ritual hunt. The soul meets its end by becoming the prey of the living. A volunteer, ritually prepared and accompanied by two men and a woman, who serve as ritual-hunt companions, must kill the *an-guëry*. In addition to ceremonial weapons, dress, and ornaments, the ritual hunter is fortified with shamanic song, a *maraka*, and a vision. A shaman chooses the proper place in the forest for the hunt and begins to chant and play his rattle. In addition, he encourages the ritual companions to pound on tree trunks so that the sounds might attract the *anguëry*. The shaman's rattle indicates the center of the hunting arena (that is, the place where the beast is trapped), and the other companions stand at the four cardinal directions to close off the avenues of escape. With the sound of his rattle pinpointing the supernatural presence, the shaman orders the ritual hunter to shoot. Weeping with emotion, the shaman reports that he has made the fantasm vanish.[286]

PSYCHOPOMPS AND JUDGES

When they can, mourners help the dead in their trials. Often, however, the dead are beyond help from the living. The living can neither bring the dead to trial nor assist them in the ordeals that pockmark the roads beyond death. In such circumstances, a psychopomp, a supernatural guide for souls, offers the assistance the living cannot furnish. The psychopomp knows the territory of the other world. For example, a dead kinsman guides the deceased Akwẽ-Shavante soul along its perilous route to the village of the dead. Located at the "root of the sky" far to the east, the village of the dead is a place of abundance, happiness, singing, and dancing. To reach it, however, the soul must contend with the *wazepari'wa*, malevolent spirits who dwell in the west, at the "end of the sky." Apparently the *wazepari'wa* threaten to transform the captured soul into one of their own kind. The dead kinsman knows from experience how to negotiate the road safely.[287]

Often the best thing that the living can do to help the dead through their ordeals is to invoke the intercession of a supernatural guide. Near the moment of death, an Avá-Chiripá shaman sings a funeral song to the rhythm of his rattle. The shaman's song is the sonic presence of a dead shaman, whose power the living shaman acquired in a dream. This sonic power acts as a psychopomp, guiding one soul-element of the deceased (the divine vital-word soul) back to the divinity who sent it into the incarnate world. Among other obstacles in the soul's path are the *añag*, supernatural jaguars who devour souls, and fantastic owls. Guided by the shaman's song and purified of heavy imperfections *(téko-achy)*, the soul arrives at Oka-Vusú, the paradisal home of the deity from whom it first came.

The Yupa count a number of tests administered on the way to the land of the dead.[288] Among them is an ordeal found in many South American scenarios of death: trial by a judge. The Yupa tell of girl who, mourning her lover's death, let him guide her to the afterworld. In the form of a cloud and a gentle breeze, the lover led the girl through a dense forest. She came to the house of Kopecho, the frog grandmother who is mistress of the earth of the underworld. Before her transformation into a frog, Kopecho had put the two primordial suns to a test. She seduced one of them into a pit of fire, thereby transforming that sun into the moon and creating the separate solar and lunar cycles, the day and the night. Now she separates the good from the bad on the path to the underworld. She imposes on the dead soul a test to see what quality of baskets it weaves. Technical competence in basketry includes intimate knowledge of the mythic realities depicted on the baskets. Knowledge, skill, and reflection on supernatural realities are essential to perfection in the art during life, and they determine the destiny of the soul after death. Before arriving in the land of the dead, the Yupa soul must overcome several other obstacles. It must pass along the "path of unworthy people," where wild beasts threaten to devour it.[289] Dead souls must also pass through Taiyáya, a wall that only the righteous (good basketweavers) can penetrate, and they must cross a river. A guide dog helps the good across the water, but the unrighteous and unskilled are forced to try to cross the river on a spinning log filled with dangerous beings.[290]

Ordeals mark off one space in the universe from another. Trial by judge is a particularly noteworthy delineation of mythic space. Like the psychopomp, the judge of the dead is intimately linked to space. While the psychopomp leads the dead soul from one quality of space to another, the function of the judge is more critical. The judge holds one kind of being separate from another and sets up divisions among the newly arrived according to the qualities of their character. He assigns them to the space (that is, the quality of being) from which the criteria for judgment derive.

Many of the trials suffered on the road beyond death are familiar features of rites of passage, especially ordeals of initiation. These tests define the end of an epoch, a state of mind, or a social role. The extraordinary consistency with which trials, judges, and guides appear along the postmortem road, however, reveals something further: death itself is a probative state. The imagery of final death probes the limits that its reality imposes. More dramatic and comprehensive than failure or transition during life, death is the condition that struggles most to explore new possibilities of being. That is, death itself, the ultimate state of trial, provokes an entirely new assessment of reality and initiates new modes of existence for both living and dead.

LIFE IN THE LAND OF THE DEAD

After undergoing trials, the dead gain admittance to their own realm. The land of the dead is like no place on earth; the ways in which it differs from the world of the living vary from one cultural account to another. It may reverse the image of this world (day for night, left for right), for instance, or it may erase distinctions (e.g., of clothing, seasons, lineages) that are important to this world's order. In any case, the land of the dead is utterly strange to the living. Even if at first it resembles life on earth, it soon betrays the signs of a fundamentally different condition of being. For the Kadiuéu, for instance, the realm of the dead seems to be constructed on the same model as the village of the living,[291] but the initial similarities give way to bizarre differences. A Kadiuéu man, mourning the death of his dear friend, once visited the land of the dead. When the visitor slapped the horse he rode, its hide turned to ashes, and the animal became a walking skeleton. In this topsy-turvy world, termites were antelope, and dried leaves replaced living flesh. The living visitor married a woman from the realm of the dead. When they embraced at night to make love, he discovered that she had no flesh at all. For her part she inquired of him, "What is this? Is this a tiny bird?" Upon discovering that in the realm of the dead there is no carnal desire, the man decided to return to the land of the living. After he did, however, he vomited up whatever food he ate. He soon wasted away and died for good.

NEGATION AND REVERSAL

The opposition with which the land of the dead confronts life is seldom a simple matter: the land of the dead confronts life with life's own implicit contradictory conditions. It plays with resemblances and differences and scrutinizes the foundations of analogy and dialectic. Conditions that remain an obscure or imperceptible background in the land of the living, such as shadows or the images reflected in the iris of the eye, come to the fore as substantial entities in the land of the dead. The absolutes of social life (e.g., affinity, marriage, labor) become arbitrary and ephemeral. Thus, the notions of the afterlife among the Krahó reveal "not a simple reflection of society . . . but a reflection upon the conditions of existence."[292] Although the sphere of ritual is maintained unchanged — division into ritual moieties, log races, the playing of ceremonial instruments, and so on[293] — the arrangement of space in the place of the dead is the reverse of that in the living world. The moon takes the place occupied by the sun in the land of the living. The *mekarõ* (shadowy souls of the dead) prefer to live in the forest and avoid the cleared land. They enter homes only through the back door, the *atëkrumpe-harkwa* ("the door towards the direction of the dead").[294] The village of the dead is in the west, except when there are foreigners in the land of the dead (in which case, it is set in the east). Matrilateral kin lead the deceased to the village of the dead and encourage him to stay there, urging him to share food and to socialize with the dead. After death, each group of kin lives in a village of its own. There is no marriage. Husband and wife sleep together for only one night and then separate. For this reason there are no affines. The absence of affines eliminates the need for the social respect and restraint which constitute social norms and social organization.[295] The village of the dead is not round, a quality essential to the space inhabited by the living. It lacks a central plaza or circular path for ceremonial dancing and chanting. "It does not matter where [the dead] gather to sing."[296] Trees surround most of the village, and there is only one planted field, an arrangement that recalls the mythic world of the beginning, which contained only one thing of each kind and did not yet know the multiplicity generated from death and destruction.

The Krahó *mekarõ* have a strange association with water. They either drink constantly and do not wash, or they continually plunge into stagnant water at night. This immersion in stagnant water appears to be the counterpart of the immersion of living youths in running water during initiation. It causes the souls to forget their past and initiates them into the static existence of the dead.[297] The new arrangement of space reflects a change in the physiology of the *mekarō* themselves. Their bodies, too, are static: "Their gaze is fixed, their blood clotted — these being the elements associated with life and movement — and they have no flesh, only skin and bones."[298] The dead make different sounds. They twitter like birds. They merely pick at their insipid food, and they drink stagnant water. Unable to move on their own, they are tossed hither and yon by the wind.

The Krahó village of the dead twists the familiar images of the living village into new shapes, a reshaping common throughout South American depictions of the land of the dead. This refraction of the imagery of passage into another medium unearths analogical and dialectical possibilities of symbolic life not immediately apparent in the land of the living, showing that the dynamic symbolic processes fundamental to life harbor the stasis, immobility, and permanence that signal death. The periphery, a necessary but less highlighted counterimage to the prestigious center in the living village, becomes ubiquitous. In the marginal world of the dead, the meaning of the periphery overshadows that of the center.

The reversals of the land of the dead recast the obvious imagery of life, allowing latencies to challenge what has been blatant. For instance, night and day are reversed in the Campa realm of dead ghosts,[299] a reversal attributed to the contrasting modes of perception among the living and the dead. Weiss writes that his Campa commentator, Sariti, "musing about the strange reversal of day and night in the perceptions of ghosts, suggests that it is analogous to the daylight we see in dreams during the night; i.e., it is the invisible inner light which exists within the substance of all darkness."[300] A parallel reversal subverts the principle of utility. Food and clothing offered to the Campa dead, for instance, must first be cooked (that is, burned) in order to be of use in the land of the dead.[301]

Reversals frequently govern the social life of the dead. Although the political and economic structures of Jepíra, the Goajiro island or peninsula of the dead, appear similar to those of the living society, a closer look shows that "the domains of food and conjugal and sexual morality . . . are the opposite of the earthly world."[302] Food abounds without there being any need to work for it or to cook it. Women refuse their husbands sex and, instead, initiate sexual liaisons with several other "husbands"; women become the active partners in sex, keeping their men immobile and passive. This contrasts with the society of the living, in which Goajiro men are traveling polygynists who serially visit their various wives in their mothers' residences.[303] Reversals affect not only the perceptions of the social and moral world but of every realm of the senses. During one Goajiro man's trip to the underworld, his dead wife refused him sex. He made love to one of the young women lying at the edge of the dance plaza with her legs spread open. "But he felt no sensation of sexual tightness. . . . [T]he woman seemed to have no flesh. She was like a liquid, without friction."[304]

Negativity (for example, the negation of a symbolic center) reveals the strangeness and mystery that hedge the process of symbolic knowledge. Reversal (e.g., evaluating background over foreground, invisible over visible, dream or shadow over concrete form) uncovers the unexamined arbitrariness that marks off and binds all that is familiar. Some quality of otherness and negativity is requisite to knowledge based on symbolism, for the meaning of a symbol points beyond itself toward what it is not. That otherness, hidden in manifestations of this world but evident in the afterlife, defines the meaning of death: an existence without alliances or sharp distinctions, a state without growth or change.[305] Death, as a probative state, interrogates and tries the symbolic processes taken for granted in reproductive life. The ambivalent land of the dead houses obscure principles, which, precisely because they were less visible in the living world, remained in creative tension with its clarity.

THE CEASELESS FEAST

Unbroken entertainment is one curious feature of many descriptions of the afterlife. The Sanemá-Yanoama afterlife provides illustration. The road of ascent to the Sanemá-Yanoama heaven is a dangerous one for the soul-element called the *noneshi*. To regain access to the heavenly realm of the supreme being, Omao, the immortal soul must pass through the neighborhood of the moon, *Pulipulibará*, who devours souls in his house of blood. If the soul-elements *nobolé* and *toholilí*, which carry the soul skyward, are strong enough, the *noneshí* whizzes by the moon like a speeding arrow. If not, Pulipulibará devours it. The second most dangerous obstacle on the road to heaven is the final crossroads, located at the foot of the heavenly mountain. The attractive, flower-strewn path that appears to rise smoothly toward the summit is a deception. It ends in a precipitous fall into the abyss, where souls burn forever in Mominawá (or Shobalí), a lake of fire. The difficult-looking path winds around the steep sides of the mountain but ends in the eternal mansion. One's conduct during life determines whether one will choose the proper path: those who were generous in sharing their goods with others make their way to the heavenly banquet.

Once in heaven, deceased Sanemá-Yanoama wear new ornaments of many beautiful colors. This contrasts directly with life on earth, where, ever since the time of the universal fire and flood, human beings have worn only white and black feathers. Life atop of Omao's heavenly mountain is an unbroken *pijiguao*-fruit feast. But the ceaseless feast is strange. Its uniqueness warps time: all the episodes of preparation, invitation, and celebration are performed simultaneously and eternally. Permanent feasting suppresses the distinctions between diverse qualities of time. Within this eternal praxis, separate kinds of time seem redundant, bizarre, and incomprehensible. There is time for neither death nor disease. All inhabitants remain eternally young.[306]

In the Kalapalo land of the dead, the deceased soul constantly performs in the ceremonial plaza. On their visits to the land of the dead, Kalapalo shamans witness the entire process of initiation into the afterlife. The newly arrived soul-shadow is brought to the center of the village, where it meets Sukufenu, the being from whose body all people come. "Sakufenu has one breast swollen with milk. . . . [T]he newly arrived shadow drinks from her breast or from a gourd dipper into which the milk has been squeezed."[307] The soul enters ritual seclusion for a long time, during which Sakufenu visits the soul to have intercourse with him. (Female souls are visited by the men of the village.) Confinement fortifies the soul, who, strengthened, emerges from ritual seclusion and spends the rest of existence dancing and singing in the central plaza. The dead do not cultivate gardens or work in any way. A limitless supply of manioc, unaffected by the seasons, fills the immense silo standing in the center of the village.

Festival is a time of closure. The eternal feasting so often characterizing the land of the dead signifies the permanent closure of irreversible death. Joyous as it may appear, perpetual ceremony is exhausting. It becomes trying, like so many other aspects of death. The Kamayurá dead, for instance, lead a life of constant struggle in the afterworld. They wage ritual war with supernatural birds. The birds annihilate souls by carrying them to a giant eagle, who devours them.[308] Ritual acts, music, and ornaments protect the dead. (One reason why their celebrations never end is that the dead always wear their finest ceremonial garb, the outfits they took into the grave.) The intensity of festival life lends an air of timelessness to the Kamayurá land of the dead. Since all dances are performed at once, the seasons collapse into simultaneity. There is neither death nor birth.[309] The principal occupation is the cosmic ritual battle that is the root of ceremonial existence. Within the temporal perspective of earthly life, the battle becomes manifest at every eclipse. Equipped with grave goods of weapons and spindles, the souls of the dead battle the birds of heaven. The struggle typifies the ordeal of endless festival.[310]

Life among the dead is a bizarre version of life on earth. Ordinary labor ceases. Holidays become work from which one takes no vacation. Marriage is nonproductive. Directions are reversed. Separate episodes become a simultaneous event. Unending feast becomes a form of unchanging stasis. Food is plentiful but tasteless. Central qualities of being are absent or diffused. Periphery is everywhere. Essential distinctions are lowered.

By exploring the condition of death, the religious imagination critiques its own achievements. Dismantling the established clarities of the spatial, temporal, political, economic, or social orders, it raises questions that carry back to the sources of symbolic life. Death cuts through the dazzling accomplishments of life and exposes them as short-lived, flawed, and failing. In depictions of the land of the dead, the imagination dredges up the latent but everlasting sources of symbolic existence: alienation, hiddenness, and irreversible closure. Human being can never escape the bounds of symbolic meaning. Only within this alienated predicament, a symbolic enclosure or ritual seclusion permanently sealed in death, do humans grasp their own situation and transcend its limits. By caricaturing life on earth through weird resemblance and striking contrast, the life of the dead helps a culture come to grips with the human condition.

Portrayals of the land of the dead are reflections on the arbitary and negative aspects of symbolic life. These fabrications define the shape of culture among the living.[311] Originating in the disruptive character of the sacred, these destructive elements underlie the symbolic process. Briefly apparent in myth, rite, or critical speculation during life, the negative foundations of symbolism come to the fore in the land of the dead, where symbolic configurations of every kind (personality, calendar, social division of labor, choreography) are deconstructed. This capacity for alienation makes symbolic change—the symbolic exchange of one condition of being for another—possible. Ultimately, this negative and dreadful possibility, the experience of *another* mode of being, roots itself in the encounter with sacred beings.

A clear view of postmortem alienation enables humans to recognize death as an integral part of human—that is, symbolic—reality and not just an inappropriate end to life. In facing death, human beings' great hope is that one form of existence can dissolve completely in favor of a new condition of being. The deconstructive forces of symbolic life guarantee this complete dissolution. The life in the land of the dead is fully and inescapably symbolic. In the symbolic exchange of one state for another resides death's sacredness, ambivalence, hope for freedom, and promise of metamorphosis.

TRANSMIGRATION AND METAMORPHOSIS

The migration of the soul to a new dwelling-place after death entails the soul's metamorphosis, its acquisition of a form suited to new conditions. Metempsychosis and reincarnation are the main ways by which this metamorphosis is achieved. In metempsychosis the soul passes into some other form of existence; through reincarnation the dead person is reborn in another fleshly body. Postmortem metamorphosis is not absolutely different from the transformations effected in other, ritual deaths, for like them it produces a new state of being enclosed in new symbolic form. Final death, however, is an unparalleled chrysalis for change. Enwrapped totally in symbolism, death remains penetrable only to the religious imagination, which is why death's imagery offers unmatched freedom for transformation.[312]

Postmortem freedom on this scale is not always a welcome reality. It approaches the wanton freedom of sacred and chaotic beings, who inspire dread as well as awe. The Waiwai, for instance, fear the dead soul, which they see as a vengeful, murderous being.[313] A Waiwai dies when the soul (*ekati*) leaves the body and becomes a ghost (*ekatinho*) reincarnated in animal form.[314] The reincarnate ghost is spatially dislocated. Although based near the gravesite of its former body, it wanders through the forest, especially at night. It also remains unsituated in time, for it has no recollection of its former existence. The surviving relatives of the ghost perceive its frightening process of transmigration.

Transmigration of the deceased soul to the land of the dead helps to eliminate the terror associated with its metamorphosis. Sealed in an environment suited to their totally symbolic condition, the dead experience an eerie freedom of form without unsettling the living. In some cases, the dead take on several different forms. For instance, the first stage of transformation for the Krahó shadow-image (karō; pl., mekarō) is the land of the dead. From the moment when mekarō commune with the dead or join in their ritual activities, they may assume any form. In fact, mekarō shift shape as they undergo the successive deaths and transformations that punctuate their postmortem existence.[315] "[T]hey are believed to be able to die several times and to take on successively first the forms of large animals, then of smaller and smaller animals, . . . and finally to end as stones, roots, or tree stumps."[316]

Such metamorphoses through a series of separate forms signify the fully spiritual condition of the free soul. Apinayé souls also undergo several transformations after death. The recently dead stay on the earth, inhabiting their gravesites.[317] The dead live a life of plenty; their food has a different taste, and so they prefer to commune permanently among themselves rather than return to the food of the living. In this first stage, dead souls appear from time to time, floating above the ground, until they eventually "die of a pain on the left side and are transformed into animals, stumps of trees, or termite hills."[318]

Thus the dissolution of the individual personality liberates personal elements for metamorphosis. Even in cases of reincarnation, the entire individual never reappears in new form, but disintegrates into its constituent parts in such a way that some components are set free to pursue their separate careers of metamorphosis while the individual personality, that unique configuration of symbolic elements, dissolves forever. For the Avá-Chiripá reincarnation occurs when, for one reason or another, a divine soul-element (ñe'eng) fails to complete its initiatory journey to paradise (Oka-Yusú). Reincarnation is the privilege of the ñe'eng; the asyinguá (animal-ghost soul) cannot be reincarnated.[319] Several reasons can account for the ñe'eng's failure to achieve its destiny, foremost among which are inadequate spiritual preparation for the ordeals of the journey, excessive physical weight (which impedes celestial flight), and nostalgia for familiar beings on earth. Reincarnation is the frequent fate of children's divine soul-elements. In fact, during special ceremonies, dreaming shamans visit the land of the divine souls of unborn and stillborn children, where they choose a ñe'eng and transport it back to earth for reincarnation.[320] In the meantime, the asyiguá, weighed down with heavy imperfections, becomes an anguëry, a spirit of death that "roams the earth molesting the living, causing disease, madness, and even death."[321] Unlike the ñe'eng that becomes fully initiated into life in paradise, the animal soul-element undergoes metamorphosis on earth. It takes the form of a possessive ghost, which resides in another human personality and displaces its host's divine soul. The anguëry provokes soul-loss among the living by taking over the locus of the divine soul and forcing a person's *ñe'eng* to flee.

Metempsychosis, the reappearance of human spiritual elements in other material forms, reveals that human spirituality is part of the cosmic economy. The human spirit is at home in the material cosmos and may manifest itself in the world in the form of its fundamental elements (earth, stone, animals, clouds, lightning, wind, rain, stars, plants). More precisely, elements of the human spirit identify with the *meaning* of these cosmic structures and processes. For it is in the *symbolic, primordial, or mythic condition of matter* that elements of the human spirit reappear and not in the world described by geology, chemistry, genetics, or meteorology. In the symbolic dissolution that obliterates or transcends individuality, human existence discovers that its meaning coincides with the mythic history of the cosmos.

The Yąnomamö illustrate how the transmigratory human spirituality manifests itself in cosmic structures whose mythic history is known. The Surára and Pakidái, eastern Yąnomamö tribes, hold that the dead are reincarnated by means of the same substance from which humans originated: the blood of the moon.[322] In the beginning of time, Poré, the lord of the moon, sent Xiapó, a tiny bird, to earth with the souls of the first four men in her leg. This bird was actually a manifestation of Perimbó, the feminine principal of the moon. After the four men were born from her leg, a first woman, named Petá, was born. She had intercourse with the four men, and the son she bore as a result brought about a catastrophic flood of moon-blood when he shot the moon with an arrow. From this blood came all the Yąnomamö tribes.

When a dead Yąnomamö is cremated, his or her two external souls accompany the physical soul on its rise to paradise along the path of smoke.[323] The physical soul (*uwekík*) is located in the bones. The bright physical souls of men (*uwekík aua*) journey to the eastern half of the moon while the darker-colored physical souls of females (*uwekík miritíti*) go to the western half of the moon.

The processual structure of the moon, the relationship of its working parts in space over time, accounts for the process of reincarnation. The moon is an androgynous being comprised of two half-moons joined by Parauke Iniíke, a river of blood that runs from north to south. The male and female principles of the moon are embodied in a central lake of blood, Oxokora Iniíke Porokabö, which is a large vagina (manifesting the feminine principal of Perimbó) in which Poré, the masculine principal of the moon, lives in the form of an enormous snake.[324] The moon has two other lakes of blood, and a river of blood connects all three pools. After the *uwekík*, the physical soul of a human being, has left its bones in the smoke of cremation, it resides in one of the half-moons for two years in peace and prosperity. "After that it is transformed into a little water snake by Poré/Perimbó and it spends the same amount of time in one of the large blood lakes. Here the souls are rejuvenated and prepared for their new existence on earth, which will be entirely different from the previous one."[325] In the next life, males become females and females become males; all the Yạnomamö told Becher that they had previously lived lives as members of the opposite sex.[326]

Regenerated in the central lake of blood, the physical souls are reduced in size and separated once again on the basis of color. The more brilliant souls proceed to the lake of blood connected to the upper part of the moon-river; the darker ones descend to the lower lake. They are now small enough to "fit into a drop of blood" and are ready for reappearance on earth. Becher tells us,

> The double deity then sends blood from these lakes to the earth by shaking the blood-trees (or rain-trees). This blood changes to rain when it strikes the clouds. Many of the drops contain such tiny souls, and in this way they reach a man's penis, which is tied upward. The primary reason why all Yạnomamö men tie up their penises with waist strings is because the foreskins then work as sucking funnels. During intercourse the soul enters a woman's body, in which an infant then develops.[327]

Understanding human metamorphosis depends on knowledge of the mythic history of cosmic form. When the world and humanity are appraised as fully symbolic processes — that is, as charged with the meaning of sacred realities and events — the cosmos becomes the proper context for human freedom. The scenarios of the spirit's transmigration show how freedom and history can terrify as well as exalt. The dissolution of the individual and the total metamorphosis of elements fundamental to human life plunge the religious imagination into processes that transcend individual experience. The open-ended trajectory of human spirituality is both fearful and promising, but, whichever emotion it inspires, the final loss of individuality in favor of a totally spiritual or sacred condition furnishes additional forms of concrete experience and opens avenues to meaning on a new scale.

RENEWING THE FACE OF THE EARTH

Since human life, at death, becomes one with fundamental processes of the cosmos, and since death unleashes life in new forms, human death can recreate the physical and social universe. Reports from the Kamayurá are extraordinary testimony that death not only instigates new careers for the soul but inaugurates new life for lineage, village, seasons, stars, and fruits. The case of the Kamayurá brings a fitting close to these considerations of death in South America, allowing us to review, in a single cultural context, many of the points made in the treatment of the origins of death, funeral practices, and descriptions of the afterlife. Kamayurá strategies of funerary enclosure offset the excessive openness with which death originated; funeral finery, a form of occultation, aids passage from one state to another; ordeals, vigils, contests, games, ritual combats, hunting (or fishing), and funerary meals figure prominently. The Kamayurá demonstrate that each culture can maintain original and authentic traditions of these symbols, for Kamayurá funeral imagery interprets the sacred events of Kamayurá origins.

In addition to these familiar features, however, the ceremonies that, long after burial, the Kamayurá celebrate to commemorate death provoke reflection on the bond between death and memory. Both death and memory are completely symbolic states. Origins are recalled in myth and remembered in rite. Because memory encompasses both creation and death, it reveals the shared symbolic status of beginnings and ends. That is, memory (a species of imaginal existence) demonstrates that the symbolic language that first appears in myths of beginnings is also a terminology disclosing the meaning of ends. Memory is the symbolic medium of the sacred beings who appeared in the creative period and disappeared at the opening of the mortal age. Kamayurá culture is a commemoration of these fundamental acts and the beings who performed them. The Kamayurá can remember the dead because death, too, is fundamental and symbolic; that is, it originates in the beginning. When performed in memory of the deceased, ritual gestures, which reenact origins, disclose the meaning of death.

The Kamayurá funeral, already examined above, is a remembrance of mythic times. It is sufficient to allude here to a few ways in which Kamayurá mourners follow the exemplary acts performed by the heroes Kwat and Yaii when their mother was killed by her mother-in-law. The ritual president organizes a fishing expedition. With actions which recall the heroes and their companions, men and women follow separate routines and move in separate ritual spaces for eating, sitting, and dancing. In careful hierarchical order, men and women wash, paint, and decorate one another. Beginning with the most prestigious, participants cut their hair, paint their shaved heads, and refeather their ear and nose ornaments. Agostinho contends that the reciprocal painting, washing, and decorating is an oratorical form using nonverbal language. People "speak" in precise order and in prescribed ways. This genre of symbolic language amounts to a system of reciprocal prestations and counterprestations that bind together the community of painters and ornamented. This "speaking" in body language goes on over the grave of the deceased, which lies at the center of the village. More precisely, it occurs in the place called Murena, the "center of the world," where life first appeared at the origin of time. The most powerful people in the hierarchy stand closest to the center. The sacred center, visible in the acts remembering Kwat and Yaii sets up a field of forces that ordinarily remain invisible. Like iron filings in a magnetic field, the symbolic acts bring unmanifest meanings into relief. The fundamental powers of Kamayurá existence radiate from the center in the form of vibrant colors, symbolic relations, and the stylized postures of sitting, standing, processing, singing, speaking, ornamentation, and dance. Ironically, the center itself, embodied in the defunct chief buried deep in the earth, is the concrete locus of absence and occultation. On the central plaza, the symbolic life of exchange, reciprocity, and hierarchy displays itself as a terminology, for it centers itself on death and draws life from the meaning of life's end.

The death of a Kamayurá chief revitalizes every level of symbolic life. This is most evident in the Kwarìp, the commemoration of death that takes place long after the funeral has ended. The Kwarìp, one of the great ritual events of the Upper Xingu area, is the great rite of passage celebrated in coordination with death, usually at least a year after the death of someone of chiefly status or lineage. By celebrating the passing of an individual, it effects passage to new life in every realm of being. These reasons warrant a presentation of its outline and principal structures. The Kwarìp recreates individual, social, and cosmic being by symbolically celebrating the passing of life in its previous form. During the Kwarìp, marriages take place, pubescent girls emerge from their initiatory seclusion, relatives of the dead come out of mourning, the community concludes its performance of ritual sadness, and the fate of the dead is settled. The Kwarìp marks the passage of the cosmos from one mode of time to another, from the dry to the rainy season. The falling of ritual tears during the Kwarìp stimulates the onset of rains. Eyes open, tears pass through them, life begins anew with the transition signified by death. The *Kwarìp* coincides with the ripening of *pequi* chestnuts, which manifests the recreation of the cosmos, and with the appearance of abundant fish.

During the Kwarìp, emphasis falls most noticeably on two symbolic processes: remembrance and remoteness (or seclusion). Mavutsini(n), the creator, instituted these two processes at the first celebration of Kwarìp, which occurred at the beginning of time and the center of the earth. "It is performed only in order to remember," the creator reminded the mythical heroes.[328] The symbolism of the Kwarìp festivals is like a protective integument for all the kinds of being that must pass from chaos to structured form. The Kwarìp ceremonies in general and many of their particular features (e.g., dance) form an enclosure at the center of the universe, which revivifies all of symbolic existence.[329] The key to this symbolism of multiple, concentric enclosures is found in Kamayurá myth. The first Kwarìp was celebrated at the beginning; death entered the world in that creative instant because of a failure to safeguard a perfect enclosure. At the crucial moment, while the creator was resurrecting a dead child, someone opened an eye to look, or opened a mouth to speak, or came through an open doorway to peek. The failure to maintain perfect ritual closure resulted in the irreversible presence of transition from one state of being to another. Only memory can return human life and cosmic being to its generative origins, to Murena, the central womb where life was engendered.

During its final days, the Kwarìp advances through four stages, each of which effects the passage of time and the transition from one state to another. In the first stage, the community installs *kwarup*s, cut tree trunks, in the center of the village, and a night-long vigil is held for the *kwarup*s. The second stage is one of *huka-huka*, ritual battle in the form of *yoetikawa* (wrestling), *moitara* (tumultuous exchange of commodities), a ritual ballgame, or competitive dance. In the third stage, young girls emerge from their initiatory seclusion and distribute pequi chestnuts. During the final stage, local women and visiting men dance together.

It is important to keep in mind that the Kwarìp cycle reenacts not only the very first act of creation but also the first narration of the mythic account of those acts. It celebrates mythic memory and ritual symbolism, for it restages the first telling and first performance. One could say that contemporary celebrations are on a third level of reflection. Kwarìp honors symbolic life as the kind of life that triumphs fruitfully over death, even the primordial death that interrupted the first creative process of Kwarìp. Symbolic life incorporates death into the reproductive sequence of life. Life in one form dies to bear fruit in the form of *pequi* chestnuts, new generations of fertile women, and eternal life in heaven. Alienation, in the form of death, guarantees that symbolic life remains concrete and material.

CULTURAL EXISTENCE AS MEMORY: ENCLOSING THE CREATIVE PROCESS

Hiding, enclosure, and remoteness attend the celebration of memory. The myth of the origin of Kwarìp — that is, the myth of the first celebration of Kwarìp as a symbolic exercise performed *after* the first death (not the Kwarìp performed at creation and interrupted by the first death) — makes clear that memory depends upon the installation of the symbolic closure associated with death. The first Kwarìp festival required the construction of a tiny house inside a larger one; in the smaller house's innermost enclosure were placed the two mythical boys, Kwat and Yaiì. To immure them further, their maternal aunt made another enclosure, a vaginal cover (*uluri*), for "she thought that they were women." One notes that the *uluri* is associated with yet another sort of hiddenness: the misunderstanding, misinterpretation, or disguise that accompanies symbolic existence.[330]

Kwat and Yaiì sons of the jaguar, had come to term in and been born from a surrogate womb — another ritual enclosure — because their own mother had been slain by the jaguar's mother. After they were grown, they went to the enclosure where their mother was interred, dug her up, and removed her remains to another enclosure. The creator, Mavutsini(n), encountered the mythical brothers in the center of the world and taught them to perform the activity appropriate to that place; that is, the Kwarìp. At the center of the world, it is only possible to act symbolically, for the very act of recognizing the center is a symbolic one. Mavutsini(n) made clear that the performance would not bring the boys' mother back to the life intended for her at the beginning, but he also revealed that memory is a generative form of resurrected life and of rebirth.[331] "The boys said, 'Will the *Kwarìp* bring her back?' 'No, no it will not bring her back again; it is only in order to remember your mother,' said Mavutsini(n). He taught them how to perform Kwarìp. Afterwards they invited another tribe. All the tribes came their for the feast."[332] The emphasis on memory is of great moment and explains the importance of the Kamayurá cultic commemorations of the dead.

In the Kamayurá view, human existence in multiple generations of symbolic actors is really a form of memory. Human culture is the performed memory of the first creative times and acts. The reality is thicker than this, however, since every performed image is doubly reflective. Each gesture recalls not only the acts of the two culture heroes but also the primordial acts of Mavutsini(n), who, in turn, remembered what he had once done so that the boys could imitate his creativity. Particular acts of remembrance, such as the Kwarìp, take place within mythic existence, the wider symbolic celebration of memory. Festival memory is an enclosure, a deliberate insertion of the community into Mavutsini(n)'s first act of remembrance. Containment is essential to mythic existence because the time of origins is now hidden away in memory. Death is one form of hiding; symbolic action and language are others. The premature disclosure of creative processes at the beginning of time is overcome, in funeral rites, by various sorts of enclosure: burial, mourning, and occultation through body painting and confinement, as well as by submerging the *kwarup* logs in water or hiding them in the forest. Memory is also a form of enclosure. Remembering the time of beginnings requires hiddenness, the hiddenness or distance of symbolic life.[333] Creation is known retrospectively, in symbols and through memory. Memory allows creativity to thrive in hiddenness and recovers its fruits at a later time. Appearing in the Kwarìp, new generations of fertile women and of *pequi* chestnuts are forms of living memory. Their birth, growth, and transitions (including death) reenact the events of the first times. Generative life, symbolic and concrete, is the fruit of death.[334] Imagery must possess the capacity to represent the sources of its limits if it is to be a generative language. Symbolism must be a terminology, capable of describing and discussing the meaning of its own ends, in order to be able to create authentic life on all planes—social, intellectual, musical, and linguistic.

ESCHATOLOGY

THE BITTER END AND THE QUEST FOR NEW BEGINNINGS

Few historians tell the truth about the Conquest and the meaning of its devastation more precisely than do the fantastic legends and myths concerning the end of the world that were created in the wake of the European invasion. Nowhere is the toll of the colonial experience better reckoned than in the native accounts of the eschaton that have been reported since the first moments of the Conquest. The colonial presence, manifest in the cruel signs of overwhelming military might, epidemic disease, and domineering religion, was, for native South Americans, sure proof of the end of the world— created by the gods, fashioned by heroes, and reworked in the image by human beings. Nevertheless, one must resist the temptation to reduce the stunning and elaborate imagery of the end of the universe to political metaphor. Every complete mythology includes a terminal vision. The end is an essential religious element of the integrity to which individual symbols point, and it is the completion for which the symbolic condition as a whole yearns. The end it is the longed-for fulfillment of all the periodic expressions of meaning. Eschatologies do not only comment on immediate social circumstances; they also assess human life and the material universe as states of being defined by constant confrontation with the obliterative condition of cosmic life. The fate of all creation, its status as a religious condition, appears in the signs of its decay, for creation is a terminal condition. The symbolic orders of space, time, color, sound, the food chain, the cycle of prey, social structure, and political hierarchy are the residual effects of the primordial catastrophe.[335] Signs of this world's demise promise hope for a new emergent order.

We must recognize at the beginning of this brief examination of the end that attempts by outsiders to interpret South American religious life are themselves notable symptoms of the end of time. On the one hand, the many studies written from within the historicist mind-set of the modern West carefully scrutinize the political, economic, and military implications of native uprisings, thereby shuttling millenial movements into the loom on which the imperial values of Conquest were woven.[336] Receiving scant attention, on the other hand, are the spiritualities of the end of time themselves, the extravagant symbolic threads and tatters that, against overpowering oppression, whipped up eschatological mass movements and gave people a grip on their own historical meaning, if not on the material forces shaping that history.[337] South American eschatological visions describe the systematic dismantling of their religiously significant world and portray the crumbling of the universe as the climactic and shattering spiritual experience of modern life.[338] The split focus that counterposes political realities against spiritual ones and the imbalance resulting from too much attention being accorded the political reading of reality are primary symptoms of the end of the world. As the Inca chronicler Guaman Poma realized, analysts of South American eschatologies should know that their writings are part of the issue under examination, part of the vision of the end.

The eschaton culminates symbolic life. All powers and techniques become simultaneously active through concurrent display or performance. The end of time summons forth all the total conditions promised by the partial, symbolic appearances of this world. Most dramatically, the eschaton fulfills the total degeneration implied in partiality itself. The advent of its plethora causes symbolic life to collapse under its own concentrated weight, the appearance of the sacred in every form.

This section does not exhaustively account for any single eschatology, still less for eschatological praxis throughout South America. In keeping with the scale of this volume, the following pages select key symbolisms that define the religious profile of South American eschatology. Placing eschatology within the full panorama of South American religious life, the aim of this section is to frame a genuine understanding of the images of imminent universal destruction; the return of the gods, heroes, and the dead; the assembly of believers; the impeachment of worldly powers; and the renewal of native health and power. In a sense this final section of the chapter on the end calls for a detailed review and even revision of all the meanings and symbols discussed from the beginning: creation, water, heaven, origins of a new world, destruction, human constitution, song, dance, food, clothing, shelter, and death. One symptom of the approaching end is that all realities pass in review before one's eyes. This parade of the events of the past, akin to the evaluation of time known in the West as history, sets the stage for the passing away of these manifest forms, which constitute civilization and culture as we know them.

Thus, this volume, for all its thematic treatments, remains history of a certain kind — a presentation of South American peoples' evaluations of their existence in time, and a chronicle that respects their religious conceptualizations of time as well as the rhythms of literary narrative. Like all eschatological and historical views, it tries to hasten the demise of the outmoded perceptions that explain away South American religious realities, and it anticipates new ways of interpreting the religious foundations of culture.

THE DESTRUCTION OF CATASTROPHE

The study of eschatologies must immure itself in historical detail, for millennial dreams and prophetic reforms grapple with the overwhelming particularity of the society's circumstances. Messianic revolts probe irradicable historicity as a religious situation wherein historical events themselves become signs of the sacred. But what do they mean? To this question, South American prophets have made a unanimous reply: the ineradicable significance of history spells destruction, the utter dissolution of symbolic being, for the relentless press of historical circumstance reveals the im-mediacy of the sacred. Because the cumulative weight of "significant events in history" suffocates the creativity originated by sacred beings in myth and exercised in rite, prophetic leaders have interpreted historical details as effective signs of the end of cosmic existence.

Before this chapter goes on to the Campa, Guaraní, Canela, and Quechua cases in some depth, the next few pages outline major concepts that will help us to interpret the religious structure of eschatology. To ferret out eschatologies' themes, such as their common treatment of time and space, imminence, unsealing, dance, and violence, this section will refer briefly to several eschatologies, beginning with those of the Toba and Mocoví of Argentina. From 1905 onward, these groups have diagnosed the breakdown of their leadership, social network, economy, and relationship to their land as a religious situation requiring an ultimate ritual response: the search for salvation in history through the proclamation of the historical end of time.

Leopoldo J. Bartolomé points out that the religious movements of native revitalization among peoples of the Argentine Chaco, which arose in the 1940s and centered themselves on Christian pentecostal beliefs and practices, were actually a manifestation of forces long at work in Toba and Mocoví cultures.[339] Provoked by natural disasters or political conflicts, several millenarian movements, involving entire populations, set themselves in motion between the years 1905 and 1933.

The Toba and Mocoví, originally nomadic hunters and gatherers, had been displaced into the northeastern part of the province of Santa Fe and the easternmost region of the province of Chaco. That they had regrouped their socioeconomic and military organization around the horse allowed them to mount some measure of resistance to foreign encroachment. In the second half of the nineteenth century, however, the Argentine army finally snuffed out the last sparks of hostile opposition in order to promote European settlement in these "uninhabited" areas.[340] The Toba made their last stand against this wave of military campaigns in 1870, at the battle of Napalpí, where they suffered a crushing defeat. These hostilities dampened neither Jesuit enthusiasm for missionary work among the Indians nor lively economic trade between Indians and Europeans throughout the nineteenth century. The establishment of lumber mills provided the Toba and Mocoví the wherewithal to obtain manufactured goods, and rail networks formed the infrastructure for agricultural trade. To this day the Toba and Mocoví depend for their economic livelihood on the cotton industry. After 1878, with the first large contingent of Italian immigrants, there began an influx of outsiders, who colonized Chaco province.

By 1912 the best farmland had been expropriated and the Toba and Mocoví had been forced into reservations for the alleged purpose of learning modern agricultural techniques. Bartolomé summarizes their situation at the time of the 1905 millenarian movement: "(i) an almost absolute dependence for their subsistence on nonindigenous economic activities; (ii) immersion in a population whose ethnic origin was predominantly European; and (iii) exploitation as poorly paid farmworkers, abused by their foremen and swindled by labor contractors."[341] Confidence in the traditional leadership broke down almost completely as it proved helpless in the face of devastation. In these circumstances, movements arose that emphasized traditional shamanic dramas, nostalgia for a time when supernatural powers were common possessions, embodiment of primordial power in religious leaders, and direct communication with ancestors or sacred beings, and that elaborated myths that described a promised return of culture heroes as saviors.[342]

Newspaper coverage of the Mocoví uprising in 1905 reported the appearance of *tata dioses* ("lord gods") — prophets who predicted the immediate end of the world in cataclysm that would annihilate white men and their culture. God would restore the earth to the Mocoví and turn the foreigners into pigs. Signs of the change were already present since many whites, it was rumored, had grown pigs' tails to complement their pig-colored skin. Under the supernatural leadership of the *tata dioses*, the Mocoví would remain invulnerable to rifle fire, since bullets striking the power-filled bodies of native revolutionaries would turn to water or harmless mud, the prime materials from which the new world would be created. Empowered by the command from God, the Mocoví needed no modern arms when they attacked whites to expropriate their fields. They carried spears, arrows, and spoons filled with supernatural force. Swarming in great numbers against the white installations of farms, settlements, and religious missions, the

Mocoví were slaughtered by machine-gun and rifle fire. Settlers carried out punitive massacres after repelling the initial attacks.

The Mocoví also played a central role in the religious uprising at Napalpí in 1924. The skimpy wages they earned by picking cotton were the principal source of income for the native peoples in and around Napalpí. Since the employment was seasonal, workers usually made their way to Salta and Jujuy for the sugar harvests at those localities. However, in 1924 an ordinance enacted by the provincial governor of Chaco (and typifying the mistreatment of indigenous people by local administrators and settlers) prohibited the migration of seasonal laborers to the sugar mills. When the price a harvester could obtain for cotton fell by 30 percent and, on top of that, a 15 percent tax was levied on the reduced value of the picked crop, indigenous leaders declared a general strike. Under the direction of two Tobas (Machado Gómez and Dionisio Dios ["God"] Gómez) and one Mocoví (Pedro Maidana), the movement took on a religious tone and spread across the province. Answering the calls of the prophet God Gómez, Tobas and Mocovís gathered in the Pampa Aguara just north of Napalpí.

God Gómez conducted daily séances in the Pampa Aguara, during which he communicated directly with the spirits of dead ancestors and with God himself. Speaking through his mouth, these beings announced their return to earth and the immediate destruction of white people and their culture. All the goods of the earth and the property of whites would become the possession of the indigenous people. The mythical conditions of ancient ancestors would once again prevail; local peoples would live in absolute power, freedom, and happiness. However, the supernaturals stipulated, if followers wished to see the end come and the golden age dawn, they must observe without exception certain prescribed restrictions. While those who refused to follow the commands of God revealed through the mouth of God Gómez would suffer sickness and death at the hands of the true believers, no enemy could harm those who followed God's commands faithfully. In the center of their encampment devotees built a "temple" with a large plaza for meetings, ceremonies, and soccer games.[343] After months of rising tensions, some 150 armed police attacked the gathering in Pampa Aguara on 19 July 1924. The Tobas and Mocovís gathered there believed they were invulnerable and responded to the onslaught by dancing intensely. Although none of the attackers was wounded, some fifty indigenous people died, including Maidana and God Gómez.

In 1933, in the midst of a devastating drought, the prophet Natochí (also known as Evaristo Asencio, a Toba shaman) proclaimed himself the son of God who was the lord of thunder. Natochí predicted the destruction of oppression, the advent of prosperity, and the end of the world if his disciples would reject the religion of the whites and suspend or terminate all routine activities. Supernatural powers of the past had returned to earth and appeared in the form of batons, which Natochí sold to his followers. Devotees purchased these staffs of power, the traditional ceremonial accoutrements of Toba shamans, as "admission tickets" that enabled them to see the spectacle of the new age.[344] "Under the direction of Natochí there formed a cult whose principal activities seemed to consist of collective dances and songs in honor of the morning star and of *wanika* and *salcheró*, supernatural mountain beings."[345] In response to the expropriation of settlers' livestock, armed police arrested many native leaders. Natochí himself escaped by, some say, causing a violent electric storm or flying away into heaven, whence he will yet return.

Another movement was inspired by the dreams of a leader named Tapenaik, a contemporary of Natochí. While he slept, Tapenaik saw a number of planes land at the foot of a nearby mountain on a landing strip ritually cleared and prepared by his disciples. The planes had taken off from Buenos Aires, the origin place of all the goods of white culture. When a plane landed, its cargo was given to the indigenous people, who had prepared the ceremonial place for ritual distribution. Following his dream, Tapenaik's disciples suspended normal activities and gathered on a nearby hill to dance and sing. Tapenaik handed them staffs of power and enjoined them to purify themselves of all the pollutions of the past, especially those caused by strange clothes and exotic food. The devotees performed ecstatic dances during the day and at night had prophetic dreams whose images brimmed with the abundant goods that would imminently arrive. Eventually, night-dream and day-vision merged during the dancing. "The reigning climate . . . was one of enthusiasm and of unbroken festivity."[346] Many visions included apparitions of the Virgin Mary and of a new supernatural power called Gospel (Evangelio). Tapenaik and other leaders of his movement were ultimately arrested and deported to another region.

These few instances from the Chaco exhibit a host of striking features common to the millennial movements that have erupted across the continent since the Conquest. Since the balance of this chapter treats these factors systematically, a random listing here, in staccato style, will fix some of them[347] in mind: Christian symbolism; political and economic displacement; prophets; imminent catastrophe; reinstallation of paradisal state; suspension of routine; divestiture of foreign clothes, goods, or foods; ceaseless dancing and unbroken festive performance as insignia of admission into the new age; dreams and visions; miraculous abundance; incarnation of gods in material (e.g., staffs) or human form (e.g., the messianic prophet, who becomes god or directly embodies god's voice, power, or will); prominence of celestial powers (e.g., the stars, thunder, the leader's heavenly contacts); reversion of the transformed earth to native control; arduous restrictions (ceaseless dance, vigil, diet); transformation of bodies (through ordeals, believers' bodies become healthy, invulnerable, or even immortal, but enemies become the animals that their skin color, behavior, or other marks already signify).[348]

HEROIC PROPHETS OF DOOM

Certain signals rise above this crowd of symbolic features. The happiness and immortality of the imminent paradise arrive only with the spectacular historical cataclysm that marks the end of the world. Eschatological movements, promulgating visions of physical strength and socioeconomic power, are religious in character. They represent a quest for the virtues and prodigious plenty of paradise and enforce practice of a ritual life-style to achieve their goal. Violence is often a component of the ritual performances designed to hasten the end.

Forceful personalities emerge, delicately balancing the attraction for colonial values and products with the relentless rejection of every semblance of European culture. These prophets recontextualize such goods and values as religion, weapons, education, and money by reconceptualizing their relationship to the sources of creativity that produce them. Such prophets always break the link between valuable goods and the secular processes of industrial production by reconfiguring the products' relationship to the beginning and end of the world. Thus, for example, the newly empowered ritual process of production (e.g., dance) is seen as compelling trade goods, weapons, and foods to fall from the sky (the sacred source of primal creativity) even as eschatological violence guts stores and factories. Alternately, origin myths explain how the routinized patterns of industrial production *excrete* goods because of Western technology's clumsy imitation of the primordial acts of indigenous culture heroes. (Or, alternately Western culture is believed to apply trade secrets revealed by demonic beings who gave away the goods to foreigners at the time of creation.) Now the prophet announces the restoration to his own people of the creative power of the mythic hero. Whether prophets reveal the true origin or the glorious end of material goods, they establish these goods' sacredness, declaring that their sacrality is the source of their value. All the rest is worthless or unworthy and should be rejected before entering the new age.

Prophets among the Baniwa have exemplified this effort to create a cultural posture that both saves and rejects various realities by revealing their origins and destiny (that is, by disclosing the relationship of historical realities to mythic and eschatological time). These prophets make clear that their role has creative power because it was instituted by the forceful heroes or deities who presided during the first creative catastrophes in the mythic world. The Baniwa hold that the world will end again at some undetermined time in the future. "When it happens, a celestial ascension will again occur and the people of the world below this earth will 'be born,' that is, the 'new ones,' the 'others' will arise. It is thus an end in only one sense, for it is followed by the beginning of new life."[349] This theme was portrayed most grippingly in Baniwa history during the 1858 millenial movement led by Venancio Christo, who wished to lead his people, "dancing in circles," to a better life at the moment when, he predicted, fire would destroy this world. The dramatic messianic movements that occurred between 1857 and 1860, among the Indians of the Içana, Vaupés, and Xié rivers were directly related to the myths of Yaperikuli (the supreme being, who destroyed the primordial world through fire), Kuai (from whose burned body grew the cosmic tree whose pieces became ancestral trumpets) and Kaali (from whose burned body issued the first manioc plants).[350] In the shamanic mold, the messiah

Venancio Christo journeyed ecstatically to the highest heavens. He predicted the end of the world through a cosmic fire that would end suffering and usher in an era of happiness. In preparation for this great rite of passage, which was to be provoked by intense ritual dancing and singing, he encouraged disciples to avoid material goods and ideas brought by whites. Similarly, the Baniwa prophet Alexandre Christo highlighted the fact that, when this epoch ended, goods would shower down from the world above and satisfy people on earth. "Manioc from heaven" would feed the Baniwa, who would no longer have to work for their living.[351]

The Baniwa case illustrates that one sign of impending doom is the rise of the individual as interpreter of collective and cosmic reality. Ascendent individualism becomes an omen of what it interprets, namely, the new, more personal, voluntary foundations of creativity. That is, the divine election of the prophet sacralizes personal choice as a source of cultural creativity and as an authentic mode of historical existence. But the messianic prophet usually incorporates a sacred model of individuality; his presence on earth marks the return of the long-awaited mythic hero or ancestor, and his advent reopens the account of creation. His power makes it possible to add a new and final creative episode to cosmic history, one in which believers are privileged to play the part of supernatural or immortal beings. That the prophet-hero now dwells among believers is a sure sign that they are living in a fully mythic reality.[352]

As Baniwa messianism shows, all millenial movements bear the stamp of contact with Christianity,[353] but the effects of that influence are unpredictable. The ties between South American and Christian eschatologies are subtle and complicated. While it is certain that the millennarian foundations of Christianity and its scenario of the return of the dead resonated in South American cultures and provoked a requickening of traditional eschatologies, many messianic movements are outright and bitter rejections of Christianity, even where prophets take biblical or saintly names or even the name of Jesus Christ himself.

Roger Bastide examined several failed millenial movements in an attempt to discover the necessary preconditions for a successful messianism. Strains of messianism in Brazilian society draw their strength from different sources, including the Indian myths of the civilizing hero and the Land Without Evil and the Portugese tradition of Dom Sebastian, the king of Portugal, who according to the legend never died but disappeared during a battle against the Moors in order to return one day in triumph and restore his nation to glory. In the Canudos messianic uprising (1893–1897), Antonio Maciel, known as Antonio the Counselor, preached to crowds of followers in the famine-ridden areas of northeastern Brazil that the end of the world was at hand. He founded a capital at Canudos in the northern part of the state of Bahia and promised that in the year 1896 all significant distinctions would disappear: the interior of the continent would become the seaboard and the seashore would become the interior. He proclaimed that by 1899, "the waters [would] turn to blood and the planet [would] appear in the East with the rays of the sun and the sun [would] crash into the sky and . . . from the waves of the sea [would] emerge Dom Sebastian with his whole army."[354] Another messianic movement, the Contestado revolt (1912–1916), was led by José Maria the Second, an army deserter who led groups who had been dispossesed of their lands, which were expropriated for use as the bed for a railroad running from São Paulo to Uruguay. José Maria claimed to be the messiah, brother of the self-appointed messiah João Maria, a self-styled monk who reportedly wandered throughout Brazil during the nineteenth century. The movement attracted a large number of peasants from Paraná and Santa Catarina states. José Maria at first retreated northward to his waiting place on a sacred mountain. Eventually he was killed in a clash with government and private troops. His followers believed, however, that when the time was ripe he would descend to earth again with an army of heavenly angels. In anticipation of this, believers established a "holy city." In 1914, the sizable communities of believers were set upon by military forces; in these final battles, more than three thousand devotees (including bandits and railroad construction workers) died.[355] Both the Canudos and Contestado movements promised to install a popular Catholicism over and against institutional Roman Catholicism.

Bastide contended that several elements militated against an authentic Afro-Brazilian messianism. African religions in large measure survived in the New World. According to Bastide, they succeeded in "keeping the black attuned to nature, not to a problematical future. [In addition,] the society had no color line and therefore no pariah group."[356] The relationship of African religions to Christianity largely determined the shape of messianism. As a precondition for authentic messianism, thought Bastide, Christianity would first have to diverge radically from the African religions in such a way as to condemn them to extinction and, then, would have to "replace what has been destroyed and to fill the gap [by introducing] the [Protestant] sense of history, the sense of serial time, the Old Testament of the prophecies of the Messiah and the apocalypse in which Christ the Redeemer will return to restore justice."[357]

Bastide attempted to explain why Afro-Brazilian messianism developed more in communities influenced by Protestant Christianity rather than by Roman Catholicism. His desire to attend to the particulars of Christianity is welcome, in that it counters the tendency to regard Christianity as a monolithic ideology rather than a continuum of religious praxis, varying from one place and time to another. But even the distinction between Catholicism and Protestantism is vague and unwieldy.[358] Although Bastide had the important insight that a radical break with Christianity plays an important role in the formation of South American millenarian visions, he misunderstood this disillusionment with Christianity as being provoked by the eschatological hopes that Christian doctrine and South American mythology share. The disenchantment seems rather to stem from tragic dealings with church authorities and from ecclesiastical policy aimed at the extirpation of native religious belief and practice. Most alienating of all was the growing realization that Christians and their priests ignored or openly rejected Christianity's own constitutive vision of an imminent end to time, the very vision that reawakened millenial hopes in native peoples. The presence of Christianity in South America, then, contributed to the eschatological furor and frenzy not only by spreading its own visions of the end and by implicating itself in colonial subjugation, but also by its failure, in the native view, to act religiously and, on account of its canonizations of history as the only reality in which the sacred fully appears, by its incapacity to recognize when others act religiously.

Whatever the intricacies of each case and whatever the possibilities for constructing a general model of the links between Christian and South American realities, Christian complicity in the eschatological catastrophe of South American peoples remains undeniable.

COLLAPSE OF DIFFERENCES AMONG TEMPORAL ORDERS

What is the shape of catastrophe and the nature of the final destruction that puts an end to it? This question leads to an examination of the South American traditions of cataclysm and re-creation.[359] The meaning and imagery of the universe's final end are bound up with the traditional myths and periodic rites that celebrate primordial destruction and renew the world. That is why the Guayakí already know what the final end of the world will be like. The order of the world, which was established at the beginning of time, is threatened constantly by a celestial blue jaguar. During the entire cosmic era, this supernatural beast seeks to devour the sun or the moon. Should he swallow the sun, the world would plunge into eternal darkness. Should he eat the moon, the fire of eternal day would consume the earth. This drama, whose dynamism accounts for the vital movement of cosmic time, began with an event that brought the First Night into being. During that age, there was only day. The sun never moved as it heated the static earth. But an uninitiated boy (who had never crossed the symbolic threshhold of cultural knowledge) broke the clay pot of Baiö in spite of the admonitions of his father. From the pot escaped a flood of ashes, which plunged the world into darkness. Only when perfumed wax was burned did the night retreat to leave room for the day, at least in a regular alternation. Now, when that regular rhythm is threatened by an eclipse (a symptom of the risky dynamic that impels lively cosmic order), men and women set up a terrific din and burn perfumed wax to drive off the ravenous blue jaguar. Fury, pandemoniacal noise, and perfumed smoke also help to renew generations of men during boys' initiation and appear at other transitional moments in cosmic and human life cycles.[360]

The Guayakí accounts typify the vivid imagery of a destruction that collapses the differences that shore up the symbolic structures of the cosmos. In this case, the blue jaguar eliminates the vital contrasts and contradictions between lunar and solar time. In all cases, destruction reunites the chaos of the beginning with the catastrophic present, collapsing them into a single, undifferentiated quality of time. The temporal cosmos thrives on complexity and differentiation. An exclusively historical reading of cosmic and cultural life (that is, a single-strain reckoning of what time is and the refusal to recognize other kinds of histories) devours, in the manner of the blue jaguar, every other quality of time recognized in the myths, rites, and calendars of South American cultures. The corpus of history threatens to ingest and eliminate different evaluations of existence in time.

As a mode of explanation and a symbolic construal of existence, history (in the narrow sense that has prevailed since the Age of Discovery) seeks to extract the vital force from myths, rites, and calendars and thereby to nourish its pretended ability to explain away every other kind of reality through the power of its own substance.[361] The complicated temporal structures and destructive images of religious traditions, rooted as they are in the violent propensities of symbolic existence itself, stave off this all-devouring notion of time. South American eschatologies invoke their traditions of cataclysm to dismantle narrow historical vision.

FORETOLD FROM OF OLD: RESPONSORIAL FORM Destruction is traditional in several senses. Not only do historically ancient traditions of deluge and conflagration exist, and not only do these accounts portray catastrophic events as unfolding in ancient times, but the very expectation of a future end to the world is rooted in the mythic past. Prophets reveal how even the first episodes of creation promised the destruction of recently arrived foreigners and their products. Expectation of the end and hope for renewal, purification, or salvation are fundamental qualities of the beginning.

This expectation of the end casts historical existence into a responsorial mode that amounts to more than mechanical cause-and-effect. In the same way that death meets its match in various contestatory forms (ritual combat or antiphonal style, lamentation, consumption, competitive sports, games of chance), the eschaton provides the long-awaited response to the primordial cataclysm and its historical aftermath. The primordium reached its climax in a catastrophe of destruction; the eschaton heralds the desconstruction of the catastrophic condition that initiated human history as a mode of being.

Eschatological salvation is, by its very nature, something foretold long ago, for it is related directly to a certain historical evaluation of existence in time. Messianism is a particular species of historical experience and an element in a comprehensive view of time which affects the way one reads existence from its beginning to its end. Furthermore, messianic salvation is a response to political history, a prophetic way of reading signs of the vitality or morbidity of cosmic life. From the religious point of view, the germinal hopes of even political salvation must exist at the beginning if they are to be real.

The Makiritare recount that, at the beginning of creation, perfect, good, and immortal people were on the verge of birth from Huehanna, a stonelike egg. At that very instant, night tragically escaped into the world from a medicine pouch because of the treachery of the evil being Odosha, the primordial who was born from the rotting placenta of the spirit-messenger Seruhe Ianadi, an aspect of the creator Wanadi.[362] Odosha governs this world with sickness, death, and the darkness of night, "but he is not eternal."[363] At

the beginning of time, when night first disrupted the paradisal state of unbroken celestial light, a second aspect of the creator hid Huehanna on Mount
Waruma Hidi. From inside Huehanna come the noises, laughter, song, and
screaming of the good people, who wait "for the end of the world, for the
death of Odosha," which will occur "when evil disappears."[364] Then Wanadi
will go back to Waruma Hidi again. "The light from Kahuña ['sky place'] will
shine once more. We'll see Heaven from here like in the beginning. Wanadi
will come looking for Huehanna. The good, wise people who couldn't be
born in the beginning will finally be born. He'll tell his people that the time
has come."[365]

The spatial and temporal orders of the Makiritare world, which came
into existence after the flood, will pass away. After the flood, the stars were
driven into the sky by Kuamachi, the Evening Star, to avenge his mother's
death.[366] Since the stars had consumed Kuamachi's mother, their life is
transitory and marked by the consumption characteristic of this world. Their
life and light are not eternal like the true light of the true Sky. "The stars, the
moon, the sun, they aren't going to live forever. They're going to fall when
this Earth ends. They're going to die along with us, with Odosha. Then Wanadi will return. You'll be able to see the real Sky. Its light never goes out."[367]

The touching mythic episode of Wanadi's farewell foreshadows the end
of the world and the beginning of a new existence. At the feast at which he has
gathered together all the "grandfathers" of human beings, Wanadi explains
that he cannot live on earth any longer since Odosha has dominated it
through sickness, fighting, and death. In fact, Wanadi is crucified by the
fañuru (españoles, Spaniards) and nailed to his cross at the instigation of the
cruel Fadre (from Sp., Padre, "priest") who leads them. But Wanadi promises to return when the epoch of the Earth ends:

> "I'm going. I'll be back soon. Odosha will die. When Odosha dies, the Earth will
> end. Then there will be another one, a good one. The sun, the moon, the stars are
> all going to fall on the Earth. This sky is going to fall. It's a bad sky, a fake one.
> Then you'll see the good Sky (Heaven) again, the real one, like in the beginning.
> When the sun falls, Wanadi's light will come back and shine. I'll return. I'll send
> you my new damodede [spirit double], the new Wanadi. It will be me with
> another body, the Wanadi of the new Earth. I'll go find Heuhanna in the moun-
> tain. The unborn people are waiting for me to be born."[368]

This cosmos, the symbolic existence which only represents true, unseen
realities, will crumble. The symbolic world will exhaust its meaning. Odosha, creature of darkness and disease, becomes an image of the modern
opacity of symbolic meaning, which brings an end to a world that relies upon
the significance of symbols. That is, Odosha becomes an emblem of the
modern incapacity to understand traditional religious life: "Odosha was
watching [Wanadi singing and dancing in ritual]. He saw him. He heard him.
He didn't understand."[369] Before leaving the earth, Wanadi chose twelve
men and revealed to them the location of his own hidden house on earth, a
place where the true light from heaven shines. The twelve moved off to
assemble in this hidden dwelling of Kuchi, the Evening Star. Wanadi prom-

ised to come for them there when he returned in splendor. Then Wanadi drank *iarake* (an alcoholic festival beverage), danced, and sang beautifully. "When the sun rose . . . he went away singing and dancing."[370]

Like so many South American eschatologies, the Makiritare tradition introduces from the very beginning the theme of waiting. The stone egg, hermetically sealed, lies latent with the meanings and sounds of a new kind of life. From its inception this cosmic age exists as an expectant quality of time. For those to whom the signs are not hidden, the temporal world is pregnant and approaching term, when it will open onto a scenario that will complete the one broken off by primordial destruction. Time itself, the time of this world, is giving birth to a new species of being, a new race of immortals or invincibles who will live in new conditions of space and time. But when the new age arrives, it must first pick up where the primordial age left off. Creation reopens with chaos, the unmediated encounter with primordial reality. In the temporal collapse of the eschaton, end meets beginning. Images of total destruction rend the differences between times and render them simultaneous. The old become young, rejuvenated. The time of night and dream overruns the time of day and dance until existence becomes an eternally luminous and beatific vision of mythic reality, as it was for the prophet Tapenaik and so many others.

Powers of the beginning, such as Wanadi, return to postcosmic circumstances. Therefore the end of time is always more than an echo of the first cosmic destruction, and the responsorial form in which eschatological realities reply to primordial ones is always more than rote repetition. The presence of colonial power was a challenge to native religious assumptions about the nature of creation and its mythic beginnings. Native populations responded to the challenge by reinterpreting the devastation of modern history in terms of the mythic cataclysm that destroyed the world in order to bring an end to temporal and spatial conditions of disintegration. The response included two parts. The first claimed that the nature of spiritual existence in the colonial world was such that it had to end. Every aspect of its machinations became a sign of the end of the world it was fashioning. Secondly, the eschaton had to usher in a completely new world of conditions in which the human spirit could in concrete terms recover a meaningful existence.[371] The first insight made sense of the ravages of the Conquest and of the extermination of local peoples, and the second came to grips with the continued demise of the colonial enterprise in revolutions for independence and subsequent civil wars and politicoeconomic crises. In millenial movements across the continent the conviction grew that it was not sufficient for the Conquest to yield to merely neocolonial solutions. To transcend its disintegrative propensities, colonialism had to give way to a completely new mode of being.

RAZING SEPARATE FORMS

Final destruction not only dissolves symbolic times but also dismantles cosmic space. It reunites visible forms — the layers of the universe, the cardinal directions, upstream and downstream, inhabited space and wilderness.

These places parted from one another during the violence of the first destruction. Their boundaries severalized different modes of being and roughed out the frame of cosmic order.[372] Now the modes of being apparent as separate spaces overrun one another once again with a deliberately primordial violence related to the reformation of space.[373] In the Guayakí case, the celestial blue jaguar unites himself with the moon or sun by eating it. The distinction between coastline and interior blurs in the Brazilian messianism of Antonio the Counselor. Among the Makiritare, the invisible sky (eternal light) and the visible sky, sun, and stars (temporal light) reunite with the opaque matter of the earth. When heaven and earth merge in this way, material substance will glow from within like the crystal (wiriki) that is Wanadi himself. In the Toba case, the sky or its elements fall to earth, and for the Baniwa the end of the world comes when the people of one spatial level of the universe rise into the one above. Beings that were once deposed into subterranean space (especially infernal monsters, sealed in caves or stone, and the buried dead) now invade earthly space; creatures of darkness burst out of confinement into the light of day.[374] Mountains fall and valleys fill so that the earth becomes flat. Pieces of the center scatter to the four winds on the periphery.

Collapse of the differences among spaces, especially of the distinction between heaven and earth, is a major theme in South American eschatologies. Being reverts to the undifferentiated state of the first instants of creation. The Wayãpi creation story sets the stage for the dramatic downfall of the world into one spatial heap. Two teams of architects, one taking charge of the earth and the other of heaven, set their respective levels of the universe on four stabilizing columns. As long as the posts stand firm, heaven and earth shall last. However, Yaneya, the Wayãpi creator, himself announced at the very beginning that "if the braces unwedge themselves, it [the sky] will fall."[375] The Wayãpi are convinced that the four supports will come unglued and the sky crash down, bringing an end to time. "The sky will exterminate us all."[376] When the firmament falls, people will "explode" and "cease to exist". "We will be extinguished," they say.[377]

The eschatological image of the falling sky is extremely important. In nearly all millenial visions, the sky tumbles to earth or else the sun, moon, and stars (or other objects, such as food or manufactured goods) plummet from on high. In some way or other the gap between human beings and celestial realities closes: the divinity of the sky swoops down to earth, or prophets and their devotees dance or fly their way into the heights. The end of the world is marked by the proximity and immediacy of the creative powers who withdrew on high at the beginning. The collapse of the sky occasions the possibility of starting creation anew.

The alienation of the sky from the earth interrupted the primordial process. Myths of creation portray the sky as the paradigm of distance and difference.[378] As the first object of real separation, the sky (or the celestial divinity and his or her companions, such as the hunters, animals or children who ascended as stars) betokens the possibility of distance between one kind of reality and another. The sky's continued transcendence and absence from earth throughout the duration of this world guarantees the symbolic vitality and ontological variety that they signify. Visions of the dropping sky dramatize the collapse of symbolic possibilities. If the symbolism of the divine sky no longer stands at a remove, then no kind of symbolic distance is possible, and representational life fails. This extermination of the symbolic differences between places can occur only at the end of cosmic time since cosmic time itself sustains the complex symbolisms of space.[379]

The collapse of spatial difference and the catastrophic deconstruction of symbolic life furnish the staging for true tragedy, the contemporary mode of historical existence. In the case of the Wayãpi, the unseating of the posts that mark the four cardinal points and the subsequent crumbling of the sky graphically signify a complete loss of bearings. As the celestial horizons of the universe (the symbolic condition) sink, so slumps the fundamentally upright and human posture of orientation toward the meaning that upheld it.

The Juruna eschaton likewise identifies with humanity the symbolic process that shores up the sky. The eschaton knocks out the props that undergird the symbolic order that imbues and surrounds the spaces of the human body and of human society. That is why the extinction of authentic humanity (the Juruna) signals the end of the universe. As usual, the end is prefigured in the cataclysm that occurred in the beginning. After the period of reorganization following the flood and fire that destroyed the primordial universe, the Juruna culture hero Sinaá moved far downstream. There he bathed in waters that let him peel his skin off, pulling it over his head to rejuvenate himself. In that distant place in time, Sinaá married an enormous spider, who spun dresses. A Juruna once visited Sinaá there. Sinaá showed the visitor the massive forked stick that holds up the sky and promised, "The day our people die out entirely, I will pull this down, and the sky will collapse, and all people will disappear. That will be the end of everything."[380] The imagery of new skin, new clothing, rejuvenation, and the periodic collapse of the sky are joined together by the power to renew depleted symbolic manifestations. Such imagery pervades the religious assessment of the exhaustion of human and cosmic possibilities. Both the forked stick and human beings (the Juruna) bespeak the separateness and distinction intrinsic to symbolic life, the world condition that their presence effects. Their symbolic character holds one kind of reality (heaven) apart from another (earth). It is the Juruna who know the history of the sacred and the story of its withdrawal. They are the ones who are cognizant of the meaning of the sky's symbolic distance from earth and of Sinaá's absence from the human scene. They know the meaningful mode of being (Sinaá) that established the symbolic differences between upstream, downstream, and the midpoint the Juruna inhabit. The Juruna's (and every other people's) annihilation yanks away the prop, the symbolic experience, that imposes distance between one quality of being and another, especially between the sacred and the profane—those unique significations of meaning particular to each culture and implicated in each culture's creative origins as described in myth. When a people die out, symbols of meaning no longer have their locus, and the experience of space itself comes to an end.

The human drama is central to the eschatological drama in other ways as well. In all the scenarios so far examined the end of the world is a ritual achievement accomplished through dance, music, or the prescribed behavior typical of initiation (festive clothing or ritual nudity; absence of normal work; restrictions on movement, consumption, or sexual relations). Even at the end, human being remains the ritual agent and center of significant change in the universe; the structures of the universe remain interlocked with human perception and human acts. Dance redefines for a specific occasion the meaning of all movement through space and all passage through time.[381] Because dance and music are modeled on the changes of sacred beings as they underwent transformation or destruction, performance effects the passage of time. Cultural creativity, including the power to envision and effect the end of the world as the final passage of space and time, is an orchestrated event. The eschaton is a performance that acts out, in an interpretive way, the meaning of the present predicament of human life.[382]

The removal of the forked stick or the pillars that pry open the symbolic universe can be treated under the important eschatological heading of *removing seals*, those signs and symbolic constructions that mark off one space or mode of being from another. The sense of unsealing lies at the root meaning of the word *apocalypse* (from Gr., *apokalypsis*, an uncovering, a removal of what covers or closes, the freeing of what has been secreted away or contained since the beginning). The theme of unsealing has appeared already in the smashing of the clay pot of Baiö in the Guayakí myth, the collapsing of coast and inland in Brazilian messianism, and the obliteration of the differences between work and rite or miraculous vision and everyday sight among the Toba. The eschatological removal of skin (Juruna), the exploding of the body (Makiritare), the shedding of clothes (various groups), the abandonment or destruction of houses and other buildings containing old forms of life, and the breaking or hatching of the primordial egg (Makiritare) represent the passing of the symbolic devices that confine realities during the cosmic era. It is as if the entire span of cosmic existence were a period of ritual seclusion in which human history and cosmic life were sealed off from direct contact with sacred beings by a veil of symbolism, the very cultural condition that maintained mediated contact with primordial beings. The eschaton, however, dismantles the ritual wrapper (that allowed for ritual transformation) and permits a new humanity to come forth from symbolic confinement. By dissolving the differences among temporal orders and by razing separate spatial forms, the eschaton eliminates all the expressions that mediate between one reality and another. The eschatological destruction, therefore, unseals the symbolic condition, and images of unsealing (opening ancient caves, tombs, gourds, funeral bundles, mountains, or the earth itself) remain important in the cases that follow.

Myths of the beginning end with forms of closure (e.g., the food chain, cycles of prey, repeating calendars, systems of social organization, narrative genres) that make the entire expanse of the cosmic age a period of waiting. The cosmos exists as *an expectant quality of time*, constantly looking toward specific ends — the end of the season, year, generation, meal, individual life span, and the end of the story. Every individual expectation points to the arrival at its end of the cosmos as a whole — a dissolution that is also a fulfillment foretold from the beginning, not only because specific signs (even deliberate prophecies) portend its coming, but also because the fractious and enclosed (finite) nature of symbolic existence signals it. There must be an end. Symbolic existence is predicated on destruction, alienation, and finitude. Meaning can exist in this world only in the alienated condition in which one state of being points to or represents another. The paradigm of this alienation is the manifestation of sacred realities in profane signs. Such circumstances point to the possibility of the exhaustion or depletion of symbolic meaning. In the light of history, meaning appears as a terminal condition, a condition founded on the expectation that cosmic life and historical existence have their limits and that they point to realities beyond their own bounds. By shattering the seals of symbolic closure, the eschaton passes beyond those bounds to a direct, unmediated encounter with primordial sacrality, which returns in order to open up new creative possibilities.

At the close of the creative period, the fullness of creative being entered a state of suspended animation. Because primordial realities withdrew from unmediated manifestation into the spirit-forms or alien spaces, the cosmic epoch represents a period of extended ecstasy. The separation into diverse species or lineages and the separation of spirits from their primordial forms at the catastrophic close of the mythic era occasioned a symbolic world that encounters its own reality only through the symbolic vestiges of an earlier and fuller state of being. There is every indication, however, that this condition will pass away. The mortal separation between a person's bodily form, his shadow, the sound of his voice and name, and the images of his dreams, for example, will pass away so that these realities may reunite to form a more perfect union. The return, in the flesh, of the hero (Makiritare Wanadi, Baniwa prophets modeled on Kuai or Yaperikuli, Toba messiahs incarnating God, and others reembodying the spirits of long-lost saints, heroes, gods, and emperors) is a paradigmatic sign that the spiritual withdrawal of sacred beings from the world has ended. Just as the eschaton fuses mythic and mundane realities, it also closes the gap among spaces, merges times, and melds modes of being (the divine, the human, the demonic, the bestial). Just as the uneven features of the landscape collapse, so does the food chain dissolve and the cycle of economic relations reverse itself.

It is important to distinguish the primordial catastrophe from the eschatological one. Both mark the return of chaos, often under the same signs of flood, fire, darkness, and earthquake, but they differ in meaning, cause, and effect. The primordial world was overwhelmed by the immediate presence of supernatural beings, whose sacrifice freed the world from their totalizing character and offered the possibility of regenerative order in a periodic world. Flood, fire, and sacrifice still offer hope for renewal even when they reappear to destroy the world. At the end of time, however, the immediacy once associated with divine beings is brought back by the press of *history* and the domination of alien paradigms of space evident in the expropriation of native lands or the invasion of native bodies by foreign disease (as well as in the outright physical extermination of peoples). Historical circumstance appears as unmediated reality: unlike symbolic entities and much like primordial ones, history represents nothing but itself.[383] The solution lies in one direction only. To fulfill history requires destroying it, thereby dispatching it to an unmanifest mode. This sacrificial act forces history to become a symbolic reality. To dispatch history by bringing it to full term through ritual violence and ritual dance successfully alienates historical existence and makes it holy. Through visions of the extermination of history, eschatologies yearn for history's fulfillment, the vital redemption of existence in time.

SPECTERS OF HISTORY AND SAVIORS OF TIME

The traditional eschatological visions of the River Campa employ images of unsealing. At the beginning of time, demonic preternaturals roamed the world and devoured human beings. These monsters (*korinto*) inhabited the wild forest and were literally preposterous. They had long trunks with which they heaved victims backwards, eating them through holes in their backsides. These beasts do not now forage over the earth because heroic shamans sealed them in a cave at the headwaters of a river. When the world ends, however, they will burst forth from the cave. People will then need to escape their enclosures, for symbolic containment will become a vulnerability. Even houses, the quintessential image of the settled cosmos, will become wild furies, gorging on their inhabitants.[384] The River Campa also profess another vision of the end of time, this one focusing on abolishing the confines of both personal space (the body) and earthly space bounded by the sky. At the end of time Tasórenci, the creator, will transform the universe into a new world, destroying the life contained in the old one. "When that occurs sky and earth will again be close together, the earth will speak once again, and its inhabitants will be a new race of humanity knowing nothing of sickness, death or toil." In short, the world will return to the conditions it knew before the march of history.[385]

For the Pajonal Campa, white men are the returning demonic monsters that were slain or walled up in darkness by the cultural heroes who founded symbolic existence.[386] These pale monsters unleash themselves by breaking the bonds of the symbolic existence that confined them. In fact, they reverse the generating engines of symbolic life so that its continued activity (money, military exercise, economic procedure) portends only degeneration. Nowhere is this accelerating demise more evident than in the material history of trade and economic exchange. Throughout the cosmic era this highly sacred activity, paradigmatically represented by long-distance trading in salt, had generated networks of social alliances and spiritual relations that brought power and health to the Campa.[387] The process of trade, which had created well-being in every spatial and temporal sphere, now unravels Campa social fabric and spawns rampant disease, impoverishment, and oppression. Bodily spaces filled with disease and earthly space stuffed with rotting corpses signal the need for an end to confinement. Campa messiahs called for a termination of interment, whose end would dismantle the dissolute symbolic process evident in imbalances of trade, unequal distributions of property, and the decay of the physical body.

Stéfano Varese has argued against an exclusively economic or social analysis of messianism in the Andes. Instead, he examines millenarian movements in the context of the visions of history and cosmos possessed by the societies in question. Varese writes,

> It would seem necessary to search out the reasons for a messianic cultural attitude, in the first place, in the doctrinal and mythological contexts of the people in question, in their conception of time, in their ethical and soteriological conceptions, and in the workings of their religious institutions in order subsequently to connect these cultural elements with the deprivations suffered in the economic order.[388]

In the Pajonal Campa worldview, the universe periodically renews itself through cosmic cataclysms. Varese claims that "these may be brought on and accelerated by means of the direct intervention of a divine envoy who carries out what was already described in the mythic tradition: he is the messiah of the heroic tradition who sacralizes history by entering it or giving 'reality' to that which would otherwise remain only a profane temporal flow."[389]

In the beginning, the Campa got trade goods (such as machetes, pots, salt, rifles, gun powder and cartridges, and axes) directly from the supernatural being Pachakamáite through the symbolic indirection of ritual trade. They remained poor but had plenty. As traders picked their way across the face of the earth, they ran a gauntlet of supernatural dangers, including encounters with mythical bats, crabs, and monsters of affliction, especially those generating the diseases of foreigners. Famed shamans and mythical heroes thus journeyed to the realm of Pachakamáite and fetched the goods he freely bestowed on them. Today's Campa are less able to pull off this spiritual ordeal for material benefit. No longer in constant contact with the sacred, traders no longer bring well-being from its source.[390] "The material goods of white men, in this case, constitute a prize not because they are the objects of whites, but because in the impossibility of obtaining them through the traditional means of inter- and extratribal commerce, the Campa behold a symbol of the decay of their sacramental life."[391]

Pokinántzi, the Campa demon responsible for measles and other diseases that native shamans cannot control, now blocks the initiatory trade-route to the generous and benevolent Pachakamáite. "The work of the Virakocha [colonial Europeans] and of the Chori [foreigners from elsewhere in the Andes] have profaned and broken the ancient and divine order. Their presence and that of the obstacles they place on the road obstruct the pilgrimages to God and the sacred trade."[392] In the past, Campa trade and the knowledge gained during that initiatory experience bridged the great gulf between God and human beings, but the coming of foreigners obscured the power of these sacred means and the meaning of symbolic life in general. Ignorance became an insuperable obstacle impeding communication with God and impoverishing society both materially and spiritually. With all its strength, then, Campa society dedicated itself to restoring primordial conditions, beginning with the furious chaos that ended the primordial epoch. Only by returning to the time when contact with the divinity flourished could there blossom a bountiful future of free trade. The past, present, and future were no longer qualitatively distinct moments, as they may have seemed to an historicist mentality. They merged as "an eternal 'time without time' profaned by the appearance of the white man."[393] The purity and intimacy of the divine primordium would restore creative principles and clear all paths taken in time.

The oppressive and unjust distribution of material goods characterizing the present was a sure sign of the collapse of sacred order. From the beginning, material wares had been the free gifts of Pachakamáite, and they sparked a long series of symbolic exchanges beneficial to dynamic social order. By accumulating these goods and locking them in storehouses, whites and foreign Andeans not only blocked the Campa's access to the material goods, but they denied them a creative role in the world by denying them any authentically generative role in the network of trade and economic exchange instituted by supernatural beings at the beginning of time.[394] Hoarding and excessive accumulation deprived material products of the exercise of their spiritual capacity to appear periodically as symbols that reproduce traditional networks of relations and generate new ones.

The Pajonal Campa associate the origins of white people with the monstrous aquatic dragon Nónki, a primordial serpent linked with darkness, death, and the amorphous abyss of the underworld, as well as with the rainbow. "White people emerged from [Nónki's] supernatural lagoon, protomatter *par excellence*."[395] This world has no place for whites since they were not a part of the original creation carried out by the god Oriátziri. "The white man is homologized with Nónki and is symbolically identified with the enemy of humanity who provokes death but who, it is said, has been vanquished by an heroic shaman [named Kontáwo] during the primordium."[396] This assurance of mythic triumph emboldened the Campa to take stock of their historical situation. The guarantee that the very conditions of existence assured their victory over the monster afforded the Campa the courage to seek a sacred renewal of time through material transformation of the universe.

In the second half of the eighteenth century, the Campa carried out a series of rebellions. Juan Santos Atahualpa, an extraordinary individual by any reckoning, led the most significant uprising, which took place in 1742. Juan Santos had studied under the Jesuits at Cuzco, mastered four languages (Inca, Spanish, Latin, and Campa), and apparently visited Europe in the company of a Jesuit companion. During his voyage he may have visited Africa and had contact with the British.[397] To open his campaign he destroyed some twenty-seven Franciscan missions east of Tarma, Peru. Using this zone as a base of operations, he stirred the Amuesha and other tribes of the montane region into a rebellion aimed at the restoration of the Inca empire.[398] From 1742 to 1761, Juan Santos lived the life of a successful revolutionary, never defeated by government troops. Unlike other rebellions of the eighteenth century, his was apparently a personal initiative and not an alliance of caciques. However, like other rebel leaders, he asserted his authority by invoking the religious figures of the mythical past.

At the end of May 1742, just as the dry season was drawing to a close and giving way to the first rains, Juan Santos, then about thirty years old, made a dramatic official appearance at a place called Quisopango on the upper Rio Shimaqui in the Gran Pajonal area.[399] Wearing a traditional short haircut and a red-colored native dress called a *cushma*, he declared that he was Apu Inca, the legitimate heir of the great Inca emperors Atahualpa and Huayna Capac, returned in the flesh. His appearance marked the end of time, for he claimed he would rule as the promised eschatological messiah, leading his sons (Indians, mestizos, and African slaves) out of bondage and into the glorious kingdom. "He declared himself the Son of God and declared he had come to end slavery, the drudgery of plantations and the hard work in the bakeries. . . . [He] promised them big things, a great many tools and all the riches of the Spaniards."[400] The prophetic announcement of liberation drew immediate response from Indians of many tribal backgrounds throughout the forests of east-central Peru.

Juan Santos declared that the messiah had desired to make his appearance for some time but that only now was the time propitious. In this prelude to the end of the world, God granted him permission to undertake his mission. He immediately gathered a following among the Campa, Amuesha, Piro, Simirinche, Conibo, Shipibo, and Mochobo. "The entire central forest area came to his support as though the signal had been passed down silently for years, as if the expectation of it had been transmitted from father to son together with other traditions."[401] In strict accordance with Campa religious tradition, Juan Santos ordered the performance of ritual dances to honor a divinity named Kesha, cosmogonic hero who had survived the universal flood by floating on the trunk of a palm tree. By tossing the seeds of the palm tree into the floodwaters, he eventually dried up the deluge and saved the possibility of cosmic life.[402] Although dance was the preeminent religious instrument hastening the arrival of the new day, Juan Santos also ordered ample use of *masato* (fermented-manioc brew), and he encouraged traditional use of coca, reminding people that it was "the herb of God, not of sorcerors, as the Virakochas [white men] claimed."[403] He prescribed a diet that included beef and sheep but proscribed pork. Since pigs were 'bad', they should be slaughtered. But Juan Santos was not an unreformed traditionalist. He envisioned a native clergy within the framework of the Roman Catholic church, as he claimed to have seen in Africa. After being crowned emperor of Peru he intended to ask the pope to send the bishop of Cuzco to ordain Indian clerics from the forest areas.[404]

Varese divides the rebellion into two periods. From 1742 to 1752 Juan

Santos led a series of successful military campaigns that guaranteed the Indians autonomy and isolation for the rest of the century. By 1752, "the ancient Piro, Amuesha, and Campa territory had been completely recovered by its inhabitants. Not even one mission, not even one Spanish installation had been able to resist the slow but tenacious action of restoration by the rebel tribes."[405] But from then on, the military intensity of the millennium abated. Nonetheless, the messianism of Juan Santos "had created forever a sagacious indigenous consciousness given to protecting its liberty and its independence at any given moment."[406]

Conflicting stories cloud the reports about Juan Santos's death. Although some hypothesize that the messiah died between 1755 and 1756, Rowe and Métraux report that he was assassinated by one of his own men in 1776.[407] Varese contends that nothing certain is known of his death. To the Campa the date of his physical death is of little importance for, according to their accounts, Juan Santos will never really die. He was buried under a destroyed Christian chapel, and his grave was the center of Campa devotion for more than 150 years. "Every year they laid a new tunic over his tomb in the hope, maybe, that he would return and wear it."[408] Although his tomb is on the Cerro de la Sal, marked by a pile of small stones which face toward the east, his body disappeared in a cloud of smoke.

The messianic movement of Juan Santos exemplifies the tenacity of traditional eschatological hopes and the force required to recast these ancient images into forms redemptive of contemporary realities. Visions of the end and millennial movements embody critical theories of history; that is, they interpret specific qualities of existing in time. They can be shrewd, merciless, and unswerving analyses of grim realities. A fundamental negativity pervades every soteriological experience of history. Millennial prophets see clearly the unavoidable violence and destruction required to reimagine competing and incommensurate visions of time so that they may gain a creative footing in existence.

This negative valence of the final end can create frenetic mass movements that are politically volatile. On the one side, political leaders hurry either to defuse them or to fan fears of fanatical reaction against them. On the other side, politicians court their constituency, revolutionaries enlist their might, and institutional churches divert their mystical energies into ecclesial channels. The Juan Santos rebellion illustrates how, at times, only violence and military display give adequate symbolic expression to the frenzied destruction envisioned as the definitive precondition for total change. Juan Santos faced this destruction and even encouraged his followers to invoke it. By embodying sacred beings he became a model of how to act as an authentic human being, facing the end of time with style, grace, and deliberation. He assured his disciples that a culture catches hold of its meaning by grasping the final and catastrophic nature of the human situation, which is most evident in the symbolic separation of sacred and human realities. The time for overcoming that tragic distance was now at hand, as was revealed in his own sacred flesh's uniting of primordial and mundane powers.

Followers could take courage from the knowledge that their fate was not solitary but was open to and shared by cosmic life itself. This identification of human significance with cosmic being established the framework for a mordant critique of Christian culture and of the historical circumstances to which Indians, mestizos, and black slaves had been reduced. Without fear or reservation, Juan Santos, like many South American messiahs, impeached the Western reading of reality. South American messiahs adjudge total dissolution of totalitarian manifestations of time and space as the only sure path toward the regeneration of material and meaningful life.

PARADISE AND APOCALYPSE

While prophets and messiahs see ultimate regeneration in apparently contradictory signs, all agree that the end of the world is at hand. But is this vision of a spring of hope or a winter of despair? Some perceive the end in manifestations of disaster while others behold wonders portending the imminent return of paradise, the original cultural and economic state of mythic beings. Arc the symbols of contemporary life omens of a final apocalypse or miracles indicating that the promised time has already come?[409] It falls to messiahs and their followers to evaluate the relationship between miracle and omen, hope and despair, strength and weakness, perfect righteousness and sinful imperfection, oppression and castigation, justice and peace. These judges exercise this ultimate sort of justice in light of the paradise or apocalypse whose imaged meanings they discern in the rapture of eschatological dance. They assemble all the resources of symbolic life to witness and assist their reflection on the terminal symptoms of disease, distress, and decimation. Their diagnostic visions render a final verdict on contemporary history.

The Avá-Chiripá (and Guaraní-speakers in general) possess two scenarios of the end of the world. One they anticipate with hope and earnest effort; the other they dread. The dreadful end of the world comes through the accumulating weight of imperfections (tekó-achy). Imperfections make human souls heavy and incapable of magic flight to the realms that could renew and revivify them. The Conquest increased the risk of excess weight since, in its wake, human beings more often eat foods not created by gods and enact customs not instituted by cultural heroes. The accumulative weight of these imperfections brings on the end of the world through ará-kañi, the "fleeing of the light."[410] The crushing press of unbroken history becomes evident in the uninterrupted accumulation of faulty individual choices, which increasingly select foreign foods and mime the awkward gestures of foreigners. The bulk eventually will block the light. When that occurs "the sun will disappear and then there will be nothing for us to do on this Earth. This will be the moment of the ará-kañi. This will be our last day, the [last] time that we shall see this Earth"[411]

Guaraní-speakers also maintain visions of a final paradise in which great shamans master special spiritual techniques that lighten their physical weight, provide wisdom, and achieve spiritual perfection to the point where flames spring from their chests. These shamans defy gravity: their lithesome bodies rise lightly above the earth and fly across the great primeval sea to the Land Without Evil. More importantly, these shamans lead migrations of dancers on the same magical flight toward Ywy Mará Ey, an anxiety-free paradise of abundance and wealth. They find true immortality there, for one need not die to enter it. It is a place in this cosmos, a real world that lies far to the east. Only dancing believers dwell there. Their entrance into the new world also spells a change in their personal geography, for faith (in the form of steadfast dance and diet) transforms the space of their bodies into concretely immortal forms.

Once upon a time pilgrims migrated to this land in sacred cedar canoes. Now "cultural saviors" must lead the migrations. By ridiculing sacred rites and impeding the strict observance of religious custom, creoles and whites become obstacles to the onset of the end of time, the final pilgrimage to Ywy Mará Ey. Contemporary accounts of this messianic tradition, consequently, exclude whites and creoles from the Land Without Evil.

Although there was an increase in messianic migrations after the time of the Conquest, Bartolomé concurs with other investigators, most notably Métraux, Nimuendajú, and Egon Schaden, that "these concepts were already present in the tribal religion, so that it was relatively easy to see the Jesuit priests as bearers of a new cult whose eschatology could be identified with the local one."[412] Knowledge of the political and economic plight of the post-Conquest Guaraní helps one understand their pictures of paradise and apocalypse, for these religious visions treat social circumstances as ciphers of sacred realities. But an exhaustively political or economic explanation would continue the colonial pattern of placing creativity only in the hands of the conquerors and vitiating Guaraní attempts to assess and shape reality in their own terms. For the same reason it is important to affirm with Eliade that, whatever it owes to Christianity as a negative force or positive influence,

> Guarani messianism is not the consequence of the cultural shock of the European conquerors and the disorganization of social structures. The myth of and the quest for the Land-without-Evil existed among the Tupi-Guaranis well before the arrival of the Portugese and the first Christian missionaries. Contact with the conquerors exacerbated the search for Paradise, gave it an urgent and tragic — or even pessimistic — character of a despondent flight from an imminent cosmic catastrophe, but it was not the contact with the conquerors that inspired the quest.[413]

The Land Without Evil was neither a land of the dead nor a postmortem abode for the divine soul-element in every human being. These places existed elsewhere in the Avá-Chiripá cosmos. The dead do not make their way to the Land Without Evil. Living humans go there because, explained the Chiripá chief Avá-Nembirá,

> "Our ancestor departed in life without dying, and left no trail for us to follow. It is he who thunders in the east, he who departed with our human body and, while he who went away dances, we too shall dance. . . . Long ago the chief danced and his feet did not touch the Earth. This is why, in order to dance, we must not eat meat but only those things which Nanderú has commanded us."[414]

Kuarahy is the mythic exemplar of ecstatic transport to the other cosmic realms. Kuarahy shook his rattle-gourd and danced until his father, the creator god Nanderú Guazú, finally gathered him into heaven.[415] The mystical value of dance has been an ineluctable element in all the millenarian movements since the sixteenth century. "So great was the power they attributed to dancing that they were convinced that if only they could keep going long enough both they and their ceremonial house would fly to the sky. They often attributed their failure to achieve their aim to the weakness of their bodies."[416]

Myth also offers eschatological chanters a model in the person of Chary Piré, the primordial grandmother who lived at the time of the universal flood. She saved her son from the deluge by constantly beating her rhythm stick while singing a sacred song without cease. "Thanks to her devotion, a pindó (palm tree) sprouted out of the earth and she and her son took refuge in the top of it."[417] This eternal palm now joins earth to heaven.

Dancing like heroes and led by messianic prophets, countless groups of Guaraní followed their millennial dreams and quested for paradise. The earliest mass migration on record was in 1515.[418] The 1540s comprised the most intense decade of pilgrimage among the Tupinambá. Some spectacular expeditions put whole populations on the march — arduous and epic journeys that spanned almost the entire breadth of the continent at its widest point.[419] The motives for these missions lie deep in the origins of creation. Before the creator Ñanderuvusú fashioned the earth, he made firm the *yvý ytá*, the support of the earth. First he set a beam in place, positioning it to run from east to west. On top of that he put a second beam, this one running north to south. The creator set himself in the very center of the wooden cross. Later, when the earth had exhausted itself, the culture hero Ñanderykeý, who lived in the zenith and who was the son of the creator, took charge of the support of the earth.[420] He grabbed the far eastern end of the first wooden crossbeam that held up the earth and slowly withdrew the prop eastward so that the earth lost its underpinning on the western side. As the earth started to crumple from west to east, an enormous fire spread from under the surface of the earth at its western end and gradually consumed the world. At this point a hero named Guyraypotý began to seek the sea. He saved himself from destruction by moving eastward, dancing all along the route and eventually arriving at the dike that held back the eternal waters. At that very instant, the container burst and the waters gushed forth in a flood that spilled across the world. It extinguished the cosmic fire, "refreshed the earth, . . . and permitted the creator *Ñanderuvusú* to establish a new earth on top of the one which had been heated by the fire."[421] While Guyraypotý sang the solemn song (*ñeengaray*) that shamans now intone at the instant of someone's death to accompany the deceased soul to heaven, the house that Guyraypotý built for this cataclysmic occasion floated above the floodwaters and eventually ascended into heaven with all its dancing inhabitants.

After all the creative episodes ended, Ñanderuvusú withdrew into the eternal darkness beyond the highest heights of the zenith, where his son, Ñanderykeý, dwells. The creator hid in darkness in order to "stave off [the] destruction" that his full manifestation would provoke.[422] Surrounded by eternal night, the creator lies in his hammock while primal light beams from his chest. As long as the world exists he does not meddle in it, but he possesses the fatal means (*mbaé-neguá*) to destroy the earth utterly. In his house lives the primal bat (*mbopí rekóypý*) who will devour the sun. Below his hammock lies the blue jaguar (*Yagurový*), who will consume humanity. An enormous serpent stretches out on the threshhold of his house. These agents of the eschaton are beings of the first age, and they may even have preexisted the creator Ñanderuvusú in the time of primordial chaos (*oiogueroá*), during which they fought among themselves.[423]

Not only will darkness swallow the sun, but that black night itself will fall and become exterminated. Existence will be annihilated. Then all the Apapocuvá will "cross over" to the place where "our mother Nandé Cy," who was devoured during the primordium, was restored to life.[424] The newcomers will eat sweet bananas and *kaguyjy*, a sweetened corn pudding fermented with saliva. Their mother *Nandé Cy* will welcome them with tears and greet them with ceremonial weeping while announcing, "You have already died on earth. Don't go back there again; stay here."[425] The threat of extinction, manifest in the dwindling numbers and disappearing lifeways of the Guaraní, lent urgency to their quest for paradise and a bittersweet quality to the image of them folded in their mother's arms in a paradisal embrace transcending fear and death.

Impelled by the hope and anxiety set in motion during creation, masses of people abandoned their homes and set out for the Land Without Evil, located in the center of the universe or at the eastern horizon.[426] Nimuendajú provided details on several groups in which "*paié* [shamans], inspired by visions and dreams, became prophets of the coming destruction of the earth."[427] Before the imminent destruction could swallow them, the Guaraní, led by prophets who were able to foresee universal doom, planned to lighten their bodies by fasting and dance and to ascend, dance-house and all, into the sky along the zenith-bound path taken by Guyraypotý during the deluge. They would enter paradise through the door of heaven (Yráy Rokē), which would keep out the floodwaters.[428]

This Guaraní scenario affords opportunity for comment on a characteristic difference that sets the eschaton apart from life in this world or the primordium. The eschaton locates *both* human and primordial beings at the center of the same universe. That is, the conditions that reign at the end of time collapse radically different world systems (the primordial and the cosmic) into one single ritual space such as Guyraypotý's house, Juan Santos's kingdom, Tapenaik's mountain airstrip, God Gómez's temple-plaza, or the hidden dwelling of Kuchi, to which Wanadi returns with the splendor of true light. The new quality of space and time is occupied simultaneously by the supernatural and human figures who previously had defined the center of their separate, mutually exclusive worlds. This fusion of the primordial and cosmic worlds requires their mutual deconstruction. The divine habitat becomes a human dwelling while the creator or culture hero indwells human space.[429] Thus, in the eschaton, human beings go to live in a primordial being's abode, or returning primordial beings transform the face of the inhabited earth or the living body of a prophet. Above all, the messiah, prophet, or inspired dancer fulfills the best promises of both worlds. These figures embody both the fullness of humanity and the fullness of primordial sacrality and thus realize the new condition of the eschaton. The indomitable physique of the messiah is the surest sign that all qualities of space have collapsed into a new fusion, commingling the mythic with the mundane, the everlasting with the temporal, up with down, matter with light, and the mortal with the immortal. The bodies of prophet and disciple signal the transfiguration of all spaces into mythic geographies through the faith and dancing of believers. The existential knowledge of mythic geography, however, comes only with the realization of a final end and is the privileged experience of the dead and the eschatological elect.

The Guaraní migrated toward the place where divine life would infuse human reality. Gathering disciples around them, Guaraní prophets marched east, toward the sea, amid songs and religious dances. "They thought it was the only way to escape impending doom."[430] Almost invariably they encountered war and disease, which "exterminated them to the last man, before anyone could have understood their plans and purposes."[431] Nimuendajú writes that the "march of the Guaraní to the east [was] due . . . only to the fear of the destruction of the world and to the hope of reaching the 'Land without Evil' before that destruction."[432] Of those who arrived at the shores of the eastern sea, many danced with the expectation of miraculous levitation across the ocean. Alternately, some hoped that their dancing would dry up the sea so that they could pass over the place where it had been. When the incessant dancing failed to achieve the desired effect, some shamans explained that idle nondancers had killed messenger birds sent with essential dance instructions. Others surmised that contemporary Guaraní simply could no longer achieve what powerful ancestors had accomplished in ancient times.[433] The Guaraní, they concluded, had gained insuperable weight by eating European foods.

The Guaraní were sure that the time of destruction (*mbaé meguá*) had returned because "the earth is old; our tribe is no longer multiplying." Nature itself was bloated with imperfections and weary with decay. The dream journeys of shamans graphically clarified this point. They heard the earth cry out to the creator-father, "I have already devoured too many cadavers; I am stuffed and tired; put an end to my suffering, my father."[434] Water, too, pleaded with her creator "that he should let her rest, as did the trees, who give wood and construction materials; as did the rest of nature. They waited daily for *Ñanderuvusú* to lend an ear to their prayers."[435] The theme of the depletion and sterility of the cosmos resounds strongly throughout this story. Human activity and the turbulence of this world, regulated and sustained by the incessant order of periodic times and transitional spaces, had exhausted creation. Creation pined for stasis and longed for the replenishment that comes from the reappearance of chaos. Chaos is the great alternative to every ordered and, therefore, exhaustible expression of time and space.

The ferocious antagonism of universal destruction toward every form of ordered time helps us understand the meaning of *eschatological imminence*. Signs of imminent end are not so much calculations of chronological time. This is clear from the fact that disciples cling to belief in an immediate end even after continued postponements of its chronological arrival. Besides, visions of the end repudiate the value of chronological (that is, purely linear, accumulative) time. Imminence signifies proximity, the immediacy of another quality of time which defies all others and presses in on contemporary existence *at every moment*. Chaos makes its definitive presence and power felt even within the quality of time commonly known as history, the matrix of the political and economic signs of normative reality. Indeed, at any instant, the destructive and renovative time that has "not yet" arrived chronologically is "already" here, manifest in ominous signs and in the miraculous capacity to imagine other kinds of existence.

For the Guaraní, as for so many South American peoples, fear of world destruction created political and aesthetic ripples throughout society. On the one hand, "the *paié* [shaman] rose to the highest level of attention as the unique route to salvation."[436] On the other, every adult sought to possess one or more of the inspired songs and dances through which the whole community hoped to sing and dance its way to paradise, as did the heroes at the beginning of time.

Against devastating odds, the Apapocuvá group led by the renowned shaman-prophet Ñimbiarapony arrived at the sea via the route that follows the Rio Tieté. Ñimbiarapony soon realized the impossibility of crossing over to the Land without Evil from the eastern seaboard and decided to follow an alternate tradition, which located it not on the world's eastern periphery but at its center. He trooped his followers back toward the interior, and all but two people died during the trek. Undaunted, the prophet returned to Iguatemí (Mato Grosso), assembled a new following, and set out across Ivinhema and the state of Paraná in search of the center of the universe. After thirty-five years of mystical wandering across terrestrial geography, Ñimbiarapony died on the march in 1905.[437]

DREAMS DEFERRED

What happened to those Guaraní whose prophecies failed? Did they cling to their dreams of imminent paradise? How did these beliefs change? Schaden set out to answer these questions.[438] Guaraní paradise myths based themselves on the concept of *aguydjê*, the fulfillment of all capacities for happiness and health. *Aguydjê* is the goal of human existence, the very point of being human.[439] The Land Without Evil was the space-time that conditioned the perfectly fulfilled human being. The existence of the Land Without Evil offered the Guaraní hope, security, and courage in the face of the hunger, sickness, and death of normal life. The Conquest, however, changed all that.

The extraordinary suffering of the postcontact period exacerbated the apocalyptic imagery already present in the mythic accounts of the destruction of the world. According to Pierre Clastres's calculations, the Guaraní population was literally decimated in the first two hundred years of European contact. The Guaraní were 1,500,000 strong in 1530, but they wasted away to 150,000 by 1730.[440] In response to this reality, the Guaraní adjusted their vision of the end and the achievement of *aguydjê*. No longer could they escape death and destruction, as had been their hope. Unlike primordial heroes and the great shamans of history, contemporary spiritual leaders no longer knew the dance path to paradise. Now the dance line inevitably threads its way through misery and suffering. Prophets identified the ecstatic "crossing over" in dance with the stumbling death through extermination by contemporary circumstance. The Guaraní revamped their myth so that the wish for eternal life without evil became a wish for death.[441]

Although the social and historical circumstances of particular communities affect their eschatological visions and movements,[442] Schaden nonetheless discerned three motives common to all of them: a deep-rooted indigenous mysticism based on the longing for the Land Without Evil that preexisted this world; a well-articulated theory of world destruction associated with the fear of an imminent end of the world; and devastating social and cultural conditions consequent upon contact with European culture.[443]

After discussing the matter with the Nhandeva, Mbyá, and Kaiová groups, whose forebears had migrated to southern Brazil during the great eschatological quests of the nineteenth century, Schaden outlined the consequences of failed eschatological hopes.[444] In the first place, social units unraveled. Cultural exchange with colonial society bankrupted the repositories of tradition that had previously bound groups together, and displacement and disease diminished community numbers and cohesion. Secondly, the bases of authority eroded. Spiritual leaders grew ignorant and failed in their tasks. Local authorities demeaningly yielded to outsiders whose expertise in the new ways of the world dwarfed their own. Thirdly, the groups increasingly used Christian ideas to explain away the postponement of the eschaton. Legends about the end of time became remote from the course of material history and descriptions of the Land Without Evil were reinterpreted.[445] Finally, these Guaraní groups concluded that no course was open to them. Imperfection surrounded them on every side. Squeezed between the powerlessness of their own symbolic life and the unworthiness of the changes forced on them by others, they found themselves without a creative place in the cosmos. They became demoralized in the true sense of the word. Since their symbolic actions no longer signified the powers of the sacred, their mores were devoid of meaning and reduced to mere routines. They no longer acted as agents of their own destiny. Their malaise "led to a general depression, sense of persecution, disease epidemics and, in some cases, it led to the morbid manifestations of fascination with death and suicide."[446] Despondence and leaden despair confirmed the final Guaraní verdict. On their swift path to paradise, *tekó-achy* had overtaken them. The weight of accumulating imperfections had blotted out the light of the sun, eliminated their shadows, smothered their existence in time, and returned them to their Mother's arms.

UNRAVELING AND REWEAVING THE FABRIC OF THE ONTOLOGICAL IMAGINATION   Keeping in mind the eschatological imagery of the Toba, Mocoví, Baniwa, Guayakí, Makiritare, Juruna, Wayãpi (as well as other Guaraní), Campa, and Brazilian messianisms, one is better able to guage the distance from paradise to apocalypse and to assess their common ground. Paradise and apocalypse are visions of the same reality, the finality of the cosmic condition. They are two estimations of the ambivalence that arises when symbolic being confronts its own end — when human life faces the limit and purpose of imagination. In this sense, paradise and apocalypse are the extremes on a continuum composed of the constant responses of the religious imagination to human experience as viewed in the ambiguous light cast by the mixed outcome of daily intentions and lifetime goals. The preoccupation with terminal imagery hardly ceases, whether awake or asleep, conscious or not, collective or individual. Pleasant and painful images of the end (as climax or cutoff) pervade psychic life in all its manifestations: sweet dreams, nightmares, fantasies, plans for success, delusions of grandeur, haunting memories of failure, neurotic deliria.[447] Climactic and cutting symbolism fills the experiences of liturgical sacrifice, anniversary celebrations, sexual intercourse, obsessive behavior, ritual battle, victory parades, and death marches that memorialize defeat.

Eschatological hope and despair are the most comprehensive and inclusive preoccupations with termination. In paradise and apocalypse the religious imagination *realizes its own end*. Through images of a total end, symbolic being accomplishes its integrity, a sense of entirety needed to assess the meaning and *telos* of symbolic existence.

The mythic world of origins reappears at the end, when the religious imagination comes face to face with the sources of its creativity, the mythic beings on whose actions or passions culture is modeled. The expectation of immersion in the wellsprings of creativity and physical rejuvenation incites a hopeful rush toward paradise. But the primordial resources of the cosmos return at the time of its dissolution as the destructive aliens of the eschaton: strange and absolute beings who inspire terror as well as hope — and the full range of emotions that lie between them. The full manifestation of these sacred beings creates a finalizing experience for cosmic beings, an inescapable awareness of their periodic and terminal nature.

Catching hold of the whole of symbolic being requires the gripping experience of its limits, paradise and apocalypse. In the same instant, the religious imagination grasps the reality of the cosmos at both its terminal points, creation and demise. Eschatology unites the primordial catastrophe that initiated the cosmos with the final destruction that ends it. The closing movement of the cosmos clashes with its opening movement to eliminate any possibility of mediation. The terrifying crash of the sky into the earth and the simultaneous appearance within the imagination of creative and eschatological beings reunite the beginning and end. The clash of symbolic horizons leaves no place for the cosmos, no locus for the interim character of symbolic being. The myths of the end snap shut the book of human history, slamming one end against the other. To examine the limits of the imagination is to discover the end of the cosmos, for the cosmos is a symbolic construction at every level, from beginning to end. Both paradise and apocalypse envision the entanglement of the cosmos in the snarling significations of human history. Each offers a solution that frees the universe from the symbolic constraints imposed by human presence. Human being must recondition itself to new surroundings if it wishes to "cross over" into the new age, the new world.

The sacred possibilities that underlie the creativity and degeneracy of human life rear themselves in unmediated fashion only when the bounds of symbolic existence exhaust their ability to confine meaning; when symbols no longer signify the sacred, the deep ambivalence of reality fully sets in. For the Campa and Guaraní, earth is overstuffed with corpses and other lifeless forms. The incontinent darkness of night seeps out of its own time and blots out the light of day. Every aspect of nature is bloated with meanings it can no longer contain. At the beginning of the cosmos, destroyed or dismissed primordials left only vestigial signs of their passing and reduced their presence in the world to contained signs. Ñanderuvusú closeted himself in primal darkness; the celestial blue jaguar shut his maw, closed his eyes, and slumbered at the foot of the retired creator. The reopening of symbolic closures of the sacred, the reawakening of primordial reality in all its unleashed fury or splendor, inspires both terror and dizzy delight. Eschatological expectation is similar to the admixture of fear and respect for the dead, but on a cosmic scale.

Paradise conditions the simultaneous fulfillment of all the separate and partial signs of this world. The Guaraní concept of *aguydjê* provides a striking illustration. In *aguydjê*, even contradictory possibilities fuse into a heretofore unimaginable union, a single experience of fulfillment, which overcomes all differences without eliminating them. In paradise, nothing significant is left out (although significance is a function of signification and, therefore, rooted in the sacred history and symbolic practice of each culture). The clearest example of paradisal fulfillment is the experience of the elect. Lifted up together, all differences (in age, sex, household, personality, name, bodily feature, dance style) are assembled into a new unity. Paradisal bliss exalts the company of the elect to a level that transcends differences even while it preserves them. The experience of a paradisal end creates a new difference, the unique unit of the saved.

Apocalypse raises relative differences to monstrous heights. Every distinguishing mark and oddity (skin color or texture, body hair, coiffure, gait, footprint, personal quirk) obtains fulfillment in the form of ghoulish fiends and were-animals, who devour one another.[448] The distances between all degrees of difference are filled in by infinite gradients of other differences, which realize themselves so fully and exclusively that there is no longer any hope of relating one gargantuan value to another or of preserving one value without destroying the other. The universe is overwhelmed by indistinguishable differences. That is why apocalyptic visionaries cry out for justice, the judgment that finally sorts out and terminates the catastrophic condition of rampant and meaningless symbolism.[449]

The apocalypse extends primordial catastrophe. The Makiritare serpent of indivisible floodwaters disintegrated into the distinct colors of the rainbow, which also branded the bodies of separate animal species and seasonal styles of festival decoration. The eschatological pursuit of signs preserves the violent character of their origins so that apocalyptic breakdown becomes a form of mercilessly critical analysis. Driven by the ferocious logic of their signs and the distinctness of their premises, barely significant arguments and images come to life as an apparently endless bestiary. Each partial symbolic expression of the cosmos (and they are legion) undergoes an *exaltatio ad absurdam* that fills the imagination with every species of exaggerated caricature and preposterous absurdity.[450] They consume and eliminate one another in a frenzy from which there is no escape. Apocalypse unleashes and unseals all the distinctive powers of symbolic being, and the imagination itself is inundated by the all-consuming character of its creativity.

The clearest image of the apocalyptic elimination of difference is the experience of the damned—the nondieters, nonfasters, nondancers, and nonconformers condemned by the symbols of their constitution. They are excluded as "different" (different race, linguistic group, lineage, style of dress or eating habits) and exterminated in the image of wild beasts or pets. They are "differenced" right out of existence, finessed by the predetermining logic of their own signs.

Paradise and apocalypse are both ways of rendering difference in a time when every fixture of human and cosmic existence has dissolved into an undefinably commingled state betwixt and between all nameable emotions, concepts, and values. Chaotic indetermination is a monstrous condition akin to that in which the malingering presence of sacralities whose time has passed crushes existence with disease. When history is no longer symbolic and human experience no longer signifies some other mode of being, they threaten to become absolute realities. Humans can be pitched into this disorienting chaos, the homogenous state where nothing makes any difference, by the whimsical failures of everyday life as well as by the momentous events of history. At that point human history and cosmic life can and must be cut short. The diverse signs are sorted out on the basis of their perceived destinies: paradise, on the one hand, or apocalypse, on the other.

Paradise and apocalypse give definition to the total experience of life because they bring on a summary end that focuses and defines the meaning and value of terminal experiences. Sky falls to earth. Familiar territory shimmers surreally. The eerie doomscapes of the Makiritare and Guaraní glow with inner light, peopled by radiant heroes or pocked by brooding beasts and dark monsters. Ordinary features of the earth become omens or miraculous signs and betray presences that are "out of this world."

Eschatology subjects the ambivalence of human experience to summary judgment. Paradise is the glorious summation of all significant differences whereas apocalypse is the hellish mutual consummation of all differences. These distinct meanings of termination lend their imagery to fear and fascination, ennui and anxiety, election and rejection. They allow cultures to determine where one meaning leaves off from another. Apocalypse and paradise subsume experiences of time that appear to be endless, pointless, purposeless, or unbroken. By bringing on a reappearance of the end, eschatology renews the terminal condition of symbolic being and gives new meaning and destiny to all the terms that constitute symbolic languages.

Paradise and apocalypse are both solutions to the insolubly symbolic situation of human existence. They allow cultures to articulate the unspeakably horrible or beatific visions of absolute reality before and beyond the cosmos. Based on a prophetic evaluation of monstrous signs, the indistinctions of the present are divided into paradisal or apocalyptic possibilities. But the one always lies latent in the other. Paradise for the elect often involves the extermination of outsiders, enemies, or oppressors. And the purgative ordeals of the end (through fire, flood, earthquake, fearsome dark) purify all those who enter paradise. The sour and explosive realities of apocalypse lie stored within the ferment of paradise, while the dreams of immortal bliss and heavenly freedom defer to the furies that destroy the time of oppression. The intimate relationship of heaven and hell is evident in their equal proximity to the imminent end.

HISTORY AS MESSIANIC MYTH

Myth helps people to face history meaningfully. In order to take an active role in the creation of their fate, cultures draw the signs of their times within the compass of myth. Historical circumstance becomes interpretable in terms of millennial vision as the binding consequences of the inevitable past, seemingly inescapable, submit to a new kind of time. In a stunning reversal of priorities, the quality of time past — a reality that has fully appeared — pales before the time of expectation, a world still undisclosed. "Already" submits to the reality of "not yet" and the searing heat of revelation smelts down accomplished fact. No deed avoids its undoing; no order escapes reversal. Even creation, the work of the gods, is dismantled. To save any semblance of its reality, history, through the symbolic actions of its cultural agents, must take refuge in the mythic times to come.

The millenarian attempts of South American peoples to take history into their own hands were inspired by motives such as these. To offer a recent example, in February 1963, there were reports of a Canela prophetess foretelling the destruction of white rule and the conquering of the cities by Indians. The *civilizados* "would be banished to the woods to hunt animals with bows and arrows while the *indios* would take over the cities, driving the buses and flying the airplanes."[451] While this messianism was not a call to return to Indian tradition (but rather to assume control of white culture and values), a close examination of the movement reveals its faithful adherence to the spirit and letter of myth. It sought to interrupt the course of history by forcing the present to confront the supernatural powers of its primordial beginning and to reverse the consequences of historical order by restoring this strange mode of time to its mythic matrix, the origin myth of the white man. In her analysis of the 1963 movement, Carneiro da Cunha argues that the uprising of the Ramkokámekra-Canela of the state of Maranhão, Brazil, closely followed a preexisting mythic model and that it should therefore be regarded as a ritual act. The revolt enacted the Canela origin myth of the white man "for whose utmost discomfort the myth is literally replayed."[452] An account of the myth in question, the story of Auké, was published by Nimuendajú in 1939.[453] Auké (in the Canela version; Vanmegaprána in the Apinayé account) is identified with the old emperor of Brazil, Dom Pedro II, who ruled from 1831 until 1889. According to the Canela, the story of Auké is as follows.

Once upon a time a wanton woman named Amcokwei became pregnant. The fetal child spoke to her from her womb while she was bathing with her companions and later while she was lying down in her house. The voice of the unborn child was that of a *préa* (a guinea-piglike rodent, *Cavia apearea*). It was difficult to recognize it as coming from within her. The child suggested it was time to come out of its uterine enclosure and designated its own birthday. On the appointed day, Amcokwei entered the forest, covered the ground with leaves to prepare a place, and gave birth to a son. She dug a hole and buried the boy in it (she intended to keep the child if it had been a girl). Eventually, however, Auké frightened his mother into rearing him. She returned to the forest, uncovered the child, washed it, and carried it home, where she nursed the boy at her breast.

The boy was miraculous. He grew at a heroic rate and transformed himself into all kinds of animal shapes, fish and jaguars in particular. Amcokwei's brother was especially frightened by Auké's jaguar form and determined to kill him.[454] While the boy was eating he attacked him with a club and buried him in the earth behind the house, but the boy returned.

The mother's brother organized a foraging trip for honey. Under this pretense, he escorted the boy far away and, on a distant mountaintop, tossed him into an abyss. But Auké took the form of a dry leaf and floated lightly to the ground. He then surrounded his vile uncle with a circle of insurmountable cliffs that he created by spitting. Only five days later did the boy return to demolish the mountains and save his uncle from starvation.[455]

Unmoved, the uncle tried again to kill the boy. He clubbed the boy over the head, burned his body, and, together with the other residents, left the village. After a while, Auké's mother asked that his ashes be brought from the abandoned village. When the two emmissaries arrived there to carry out this mission, they found that Auké had turned into a white man.[456] In their absence, he had freed himself from the grave, constructed an enormous house, and fashioned black people, horses, and livestock from various species of wood. He displayed all his goods to the two messengers and sent them to recall his mother so that she might come to live with him.[457] (Present-day

Canela watch the burning embers and hot cinders of Auké in the Magellanic Clouds, the two small galaxies close to the Milky Way and visible near the south celestial pole.[458])

The essential details of the messianic movement, sketched here in brief outline, follow the course of myth.[459] The prophetess was a married woman named Keekhwei, in her sixth month of pregnancy; she claimed to be empowered by revelations received from the fetus in her womb. The child had exited the womb and appeared in the light of the full moon. She looked like a fully dressed prepubescent girl and predicted that her time of birth would be at sundown on 15 May 1963. By dawn of the following day, she promised, she would be full grown and the Canela would take over the villages of the whites, fly their planes, and drive their buses. In the same instant, the dawn of the new day, whites would change into primitive hunters, chasing game through the forest with bows and arrows.[460] The girl's name was to be *Krää-Kwei* ("dry girl"). She proclaimed that she was the sister of Auké.

The pregnant prophetess Keekhwei encouraged the people to overcome their differences, return to traditional living, and dance and sing for the pleasure of Auké and Krää-Kwei. She gathered up a following of young men and women, who formed choirs and dance troupes. She prescribed songs and styles of dance attuned to specific days of the week. On the three days of the long weekend, she called for the performance of Brazilian-style dances and proscribed sexual relations (a prohibition that held within the village-space even on weekdays). The prophetess declared the imminent coming of a new age: Canela were free to expropriate livestock from nearby ranchers and, indeed, were enjoined to hurry to do so, for whatever amount of goods they offered to the pregnant prophetess would return to them one hundred-fold when the sacred child was born. Little time was left to free the goods of this world from the storehouses and corrals (and thereby save them) before the miraculous infant freed herself from the womb.

The messianic child was born dead. Worse than that, the infant was male. These facts did not blunt the messianic momentum. The dead male child, the devotees learned, was merely an image of Krää-Kwei. The sacred girl, in consultation with her brother Auké, had decided to postpone her arrival. The delay was propitious, in fact, for in the meantime Auké had decided to join her in the womb of her mother. All that Canela had to do to accomplish these wonders was to satiate the two celestial beings with dance.

The delay of the eschaton transformed and complicated social existence. On her side, the prophetess, no longer pregnant, dismissed her husband and married the son of the village chief. Keekhwei encouraged the performance of a new symbolic act designed to effect the age to come, an age already present somehow in the hiddenness and enclosure of her womb, where the prospective but imminent presences of the two divine children dwelled: "She prescribed the breaking of sexual taboos between secondary relatives and even, it seems, between first cousins and between sons-in-law and mothers-in-law on occasion."[461] For their part, the ranchers, upset by the pilfering of their livestock, attacked the village. Although the prophetess guaranteed that all inhabitants were invulnerable to harm, the assailants killed four residents and burned the compound to the ground. Keekhwei attributed the openness to fatal attack to the over-openness of the mouths of certain women who had been heard to curse. The women's cursing not only rendered men vulnerable to death but provoked the unplanned departure of the supernatural beings Krää-Kwei and Auké.[462] Once the beings of the eschaton withdrew, life changed. The prophetess declared that the period of freedom and license had ended. Brazilians suppressed the movement and Indians reckoned the prophecies as lies.[463]

This is not the place to explain this movement in the detail provided by Carneiro de Cunha. What is pertinent to this discussion is that the Canela have not faced their historical circumstances without religious resources. They assess their dismal station in terms that are sacred to them. The terms of their own tradition can account even for the injustice wrought by foreign forces and alien modes of time. Far from relinquishing their mythic foundations, the Canela reassert and enlarge their mythic understanding. They expect their own meanings to prevail through the disastrous experience of the present, and they live in the hope that their own self-understanding gives the true account of their suffering. Their inordinate suffering has a final truth hidden in it, for utter destruction signifies the transformation, burning, and ashes of Auké. Their ordeal raises the expectation that Auké's experience is their own—that, when the time is right, they will manifest his power to overthrow the inequities of this age in favor of a new order. The new economy will conform to the structures of *their* myths of foundation; the future will be a development of *their* sacred history.

The entire cosmos supports the native view. Krää-Kwei ("dry child"), for example, is cosmic dryness. She not only betokens the dry season; she signifies the mythical mode of existence without water.[464] Auké, who speaks for the first time while his mother is bathing in water, represents the primordial condition of rain now signified by the rainy season.[465] Furthermore, Auké and his sister are *mekarō* (deceased souls, shadows, visual images, the visible forms of any realities). *Mekarō* are vital elements in the process of metamorphosis, the transformation of forms through successive deaths. Their essential quiddity as imaginal beings coinvolved with transformation makes the appearances of Krää-Kwei and Auké auspicious signs of a new age.

The messianists take control of cosmic time. Cultural time, evident most clearly in seasonal performances, is made in the image of cosmic time. More precisely, both cosmic periodicities and cultural performances are orchestrated movements modeled on the acts of sacred beings as they stepped out of the primordial world (or were cut out of it) to make room for the cosmos.[466] Humans manipulate expressions of time, especially dance and music, in order to hasten the end. The songs and dances honoring Krää-Kwei and Auké possess their same capacity to effect transitions from dry to wet season and from one state of being to another, which clarifies the meaning of the performances of messianic disciples: "the songs and dances are destined to hasten the time, to make Krää-Kwei, the dry girl."[467] Chanting and dancing on each of the seven days of the week is a way of pulling out all stops. It eliminates the routine and mundane. But that is not all. The dancing and singing that ordinarily effect the passage of time when performed occasionally throughout the course of the year are now crammed together in one period in an intense desire to speed up the passage of time, "advancing in some way the hands of the watch."[468] The two kinds of dance performed, traditional and Brazilian, represent the two kinds of season, thus reducing the cycle of the year to the period of a week.

Incest, metamorphosis, intentional confusion, noise, intense songs and dances of passage, and the arrival of heavenly messiahs all mark the complete destruction of the contemporary world order. Social structures collapse and the fixtures of time are compressed, suppressing or dissolving all the formal but friable conditions of society — "age classes, alliances, political alignment, and the different ritual groups."[469] All these symbolic actions, Carneiro da Cunha concludes, signify the imminent end of time and the transformation of the nature of time itself. Far from denying the mythic realities from which Canela culture arises, they exemplify them. In keeping with the images of the mythic world, the messianic movement set out to annihilate society as it is now known and to recreate a new order intelligible in terms of myth.[470] On the most general level, Canela and other South American eschatologies force us to ponder the possibility that history, in the narrow sense, is a messianic species of time.

TIME SIGNATURES: WRITING AND HISTORY, MYTH AND DANCE

What is the fate of unprecedented events that remain unassimilable to myth? Myth is the condition in which realities never seen before make their first appearance. Historical incidents that occur for the first time but that resist myth create a conundrum. Sacred realities that appear in the mythic imagination are the sources of authentic creativity in culture and cosmos, but the conspicuous absence of historical details in the mythic world casts doubt on history's claim to reality and bodes ill for the future of historical detail. What significance do history and its human authors have in South American visions of the end? Are historical time and its performers utterly obliterated as insignificant? South American eschatologies puzzle out the signs of contemporary existence.[471] To see the kinds of answers provided in such a crisis, the following pages offer a glimpse into the questionable circumstances into which, after the Conquest, the Quechua peoples of the Andes fell without the least warning. The aim is to examine the religio-historical perspective from which these Quechua-speakers viewed the fateful details of their lives, thereby delineating their religious evaluations of history.

Nathan Wachtel details the way in which the history of the Conquest and its aftermath is a messianic tale of royal deaths, cosmic destructions, and expectations of universal renewal. The first instant of the invaders' arrival plunged the social and religious world into chaos. Andean peoples had no chance to recoup the lost order. The fate of the royal *inca*, the sacred center of the universe, most drastically typified the confusing devastation. Atahualpa, bastard son of Huayna Capac, the eleventh *inca*, was the last *inca* to reign before the Conquest. Carried on his ceremonial litter, the holy man went forth in person to greet the strangers.[472] After holding Atahualpa for ransom in exchange for the empire's gold, Francisco Pizarro killed him in cold blood in 1533. Three years later, Manco Inca (one of the sons of Huayna Capac and a brother of Huascar, who was Huayna Capac's legitimate heir and the rival of Atahualpa) led the first great insurrection against the Spaniards. Manco Inca initially had aligned himself with the white invaders because he viewed them as sons of God, the children of Tecsi Viracocha. Their insatiable lust for gold, however, convinced him that they were sons of the Devil.[473]

In their greed for gold the Spaniards took Manco Inca captive in the Inca fortress of Sacsahuaman. They clapped him in irons, exhibited him to his followers in chains, abused him verbally and physically, urinated on him, and raped his wives before his eyes. Using their voracious appetite for gold to his advantage, Manco escaped custody by pretending to set out in search of a golden statue. Once free, he organized an army of some fifty thousand men and attacked the Spaniards when they were weakened by division in their ranks.[474] From March 1536 until April 1537, Manco held the capital, Cuzco, under siege. Manco led the charges on horseback during the full moon. Although his troops extensively damaged the city, they were unable to take it. After the failed battle of Cuzco, Manco pursued a strategy of ambush and skirmish. In the end, he set up headquarters in the mountains of the Inca-empire province of Vilcabamba, with his central command at Vitcos.

From 1537 to 1572, Vitcos was the heart of Inca resistance. It was not only the principal garrison of military force but "the most sacred zone of the ancient empire."[475] Vitcos had always been the inviolable sanctuary of Inca priests and holy women, the so-called Virgins of the Sun. In the eyes of the local population, Manco Inca's kingdom restored the cosmos's order. He reinstituted ritual life and brought the image of the sun god and the sacred mummies of ancestors to the temple precincts in Vitcos. But there was a new element to the traditional religion: it had become a religion of rejection, of deliberate and self-conscious dissent from Christian ideology and practice.

Manco's denial of Christianity centered on the Spaniards' own poor estimation of the efficacy of their religious signs and on the profane nature of their cosmos: "[T]he Christian God was nothing more than a piece of painted cloth that could not speak; on the contrary, the *huacas* [local supernatural beings embodied in specific places, such as stones or springs] made their voices heard to their followers, the Sun and the Moon are gods whose existence is visible."[476]

In 1545 Manco was assassinated. In the eyes of the Spaniards, his successor was his brother Paullu, who collaborated with the Spanish but who died in 1549. Manco himself had designated one of his children as heir, a boy named Sayri Tupac, who died of poison in 1560. Titu Cusi, another son of Manco, fiercely and cleverly resisted the Spaniards during the social and spiritual maelstrom of the 1560s. This was a period festering with millennial ferment, as manifest especially in the Taki Ongo movement, which swept through the Andes from 1565 to 1571.[477]

As history ensnared them, South Americans worried about its religious nature and the meaning of its military, economic, political, aesthetic, and literary signs. Is historical existence finally meaningless? If its linear, progressive, and cumulative mode is in any sense redeemable, *what signs* announce its meaning and which vestiges of historical existence are saved from destruction? The Quechua case offers another example of the scenario in which eschatology musters all the religious resources of culture to grapple with questions that are ultimately troubling because they probe the meaning of the end.

South Americans are not the only ones to raise these questions. We also know ourselves to be historical beings. Our relative meanings and limited understanding are bound by the arbitary assignments of our time, place, language, culture, and personal experiences. We live out the truth that our individuality and culture, fashioned by historical whimsy, possess no absolute, lasting value, and, concomitantly, we sense the real threat of ultimate insignificance. That is why the eschatological beliefs and rebellions of South Americans, suffering under the full weight of historical insignificance, easily fascinate or disturb us. They propose solutions to the enigma of our common historical condition. Until recently, however, millennial dreams and dances were dismissed as infantile sentimentality for the past or futile hysteria about the future. That is, we have used our historical vision of time to eliminate the relevance of our contemporaries by outdating them. Perhaps we shrink from these visions of the end because they relativize history, the mode of time whose imaginal structure licenses the accumulation of the symbolic currencies it generates: wealth, territory, human labor, written word, and "science" and other forms of cumulative knowledge.

HISTORICAL WRITING AS AN EFFECTIVE SIGN OF THE END OF TIME

South American peoples share with their global contemporaries the urgent need to render historical happenstances significant. Above all, they yearn to subject the inexplicable historical accident of the Conquest to signs consonant with its linear and cumulative nature. This is why the native chronicler Felipe Guaman Poma de Ayala sought to cast the tragic events of the Conquest into writing. "To write is to weep," he claimed.[478] *In the act of writing* he reduced the chaos of colonial circumstances to tears and to written lines of consonants and syllables, the signs with which colonial power made its mark and that betoken its entire reality. He literally sought to circumscribe unbounded powers by enclosing their vestiges in a book that the messiah would open and read. The act of reading would provoke a flood; that is, it would contrive, in the manner of millenial ritual, the eschatological confrontation of cleansing primordial power with the effective signs of cosmic corruption. The rites of reading and writing appeared in these last days to bring a just end to the furious reign of the realities they signify, and Guaman Poma divined connections between narrative writing, historical existence, and the messianic condition of time.

Guaman Poma, born sometime between 1526 and 1545,[479] wrote his *First New Chronicle* between 1584 and 1614, a chronological inexactness that already roots it in the other temporal dimensions of history with which it was preoccupied.[480] For this native historian the writing of modern history, the first full appearance of his people in a written chronicle, summarizes the cosmic calamity that is bringing an end to time.[481] *El Primer nueva corónica y buen gobierno* is less a book of historical details than a letter with a manifestly messianic content and function. "In Guaman Poma, history and geography, chronicle and voyages only serve . . . to introduce us to the struggle and to the denunciation of a time of infinite despair."[482] By writing a report that chronicles all the signs of the end of time, the author intended to effect the passing of the abominable age and to usher in a new one. He inscribed a thousand pages of text and three hundred drawings detailing the atrocities.

He did not describe the Conquest as an historically limited event but as "a cosmic cataclysm, a *pachacuti*, to use the Andean term, by means of which the world is overturned and set upside down."[483] With the public beheading of Tupac Amaru (son of Manco Inca), the last *inca*, in 1572, the chaos reigning since the Conquest passed "beyond any human explanation. . . . [T]he presence of the Spaniards in their midst constituted [for the Inca] a constant reminder of the image of chaos."[484] Guaman Poma

> believed that he was the spokesman for the Andean world and he directed his remarks to the sole being capable of ordering the world; that is, the Inca as represented in the form of the King of Spain. This Inca is held up not as an historical personality but as a metaphysical principle capable of resolving the chaos unleashed by extrahuman forces and of restoring order.[485]

In Guaman Poma's view, his written declaration would become a key instrument in the world, sounding a clarion call and summoning the power of the saving king.

Guaman Poma interpreted the writing of history (both in the sense of the writing techniques brought by history and in the sense of a chronicling of disaster) as an effective manifestation of destructive chaos, a chronicle of irresolvable disorder. His scripture and his stirring ethnographic drawings, documenting the horrors of the day, show how the pen gives shape to the tortured time of existence.[486] But historiography was also an instrument of salvation. Guaman Poma grounded this ambivalent estimation of the sacred power of his own scripture on the spatiotemporal structures established in myth and reflected in the social order and the human constitution. For Guaman Poma, the mythic history of the universe consisted of five consecutive ages. *Pachacuti* designates the chaotic transition, the state of cosmic cataclysm, that intervened to dissolve each mythic world.[487] Guaman Poma described two parallel series of cosmic epochs, one for the native world and one for the world of the conquerors. Entirely different beings, the Andean and the Spaniard lived in two different worlds and were reflections of different histories.

For the conquerors, as Guaman Poma outlined their history, existence had passed through (1) the age of Adam and Eve, (2) the age of the flood of Noah, (3) the age of Abraham, (4) the age of David, and (5) the age of Christ. The universe of the Andes had also passed through a five-stage history interrupted by periods of chaos. Each of the five Andean ages breaks down into two moieties. The first half-age ascends toward clarity of the new order, the second half winds down toward chaos. Together they create ten episodes of constant change, of rise and fall.[488] Guaman Poma located himself at the end of the ninth, the penultimate episode. This was the turgid time, the height of the final period of chaos. But it was also the time when salvation, though not yet fully arrived, was already present. Soon the messianic king would appear to usher in the final and everlasting order. The stream of Andean worlds had followed its own separate course, remaining unpolluted and untroubled by the temporal structures of the conquerors' universe until the moment of their tragic coincidence.

Each age offers signs of its meaning and the character of its power. In the prophetic perspective of Guaman Poma, the world-to-be had already come, recognizable in the incipient hopes and eschatological visions of his day. Good government would be the most powerful sign of the messianic age. Dress codes proper to each office would reflect the social hierarchy of perfectly ordered statuses. The costumes of official bodies would outwardly signify the transformation of cosmic space. Every category of officeholder, would represent a territorial jurisdiction in the impeccable order of the new world.[489] Social order had always mirrored cosmic geography.[490] The division of the spatial world into upper and lower halves and into four quarters had been self-evident from the time of the first creation, but the times of *pachacuti* had obscured the differences toward which the cosmos orients itself. The clash of interests in the colonial era had caused *hanan* (the forces, places, and people of the upper world and upper moiety) to fuse with *hurin* (the lower half of the cosmos). The purity of the dawning social order would reestablish the powerful purity of creation as intended at the beginning. Guaman Poma drew a detailed "map of the world," an extraordinary document. At the center of the universe lies Cuzco, presided over by Topa, the tenth *inca*. The crests of the pope and the king of Spain stand to either side, framing the central figure of the *inca*. From Cuzco radiate the important rivers of the earth and the intercardinal axes that divide the world into four quarters. Each quadrant receives the title it held in the Inca empire and is governed by an *apo* (high lord) and his wife.[491]

In Guaman Poma's rendering, the Spanish had also had a land that was ordered at creation and to which there corresponded a hierarchy. The territorial and social hierarchies of value in Spain and the Andes were absolutely irreconcilable, which was why their overlap proved fatal. The imposition of Spanish concepts of space and notions of time on Andean civilization wrought physical and moral havoc on the land and its people. In order to purify and renew the world, the two forms of history would have to separate and free themselves from one another, just as *hanan* and *hurin* would again have to be distinguished. Good government would sort out justly the tangle of historical realities and prevent the confusion of conceptual categories, of proprietorship in land, and of intermarriage.

No human efforts, however, could separate the two cosmic forces of order, *hanan* and *hurin*, for they are the preconditions of human life. Guaman Poma never ceased to lament that "there is no remedy" for the sufferings of the final days. A supernatural power would have to intervene judiciously. While others sought the help of the ancient *huacas* through ritual dance, Guaman Poma summoned the aid of another sacred being, the king of Spain, whose power transcended contingent reality. He approached the king through the ritual medium of historiography in the form of a letter.

Guaman Poma read his own historical experience as an omen signaling the end of time. His nom de plume reveals this. In Andean mythology *guaman*, the falcon, inhabits the sky (*hanan*), while *poma*, the puma, dwells on earth (*hurin*). In keeping with his exaltation of the power of the written word, Guaman Poma's penname joins heaven and earth in the eschatological fusion that marks the end of the world. His experience of this chaotic relapse of primary order, the admixture of the sky and earth, nominated him as spokesman for the entire native population (that is, both moieties). Guaman Poma assumed another name as well: Auki, the "second person of the *inca*." *Auki* is both an exalted title of the official spokesman (to the *inca*) of the Andean peoples and the name of the cosmic force that empowers the officeholder to carry out his charge as medium. Auki was the mediating power that both joined and separated different modes of being in the cosmos in order to regulate their symbolic distance from one another. The process of meaningful communication, unlike the overlap of histories, helped maintain proper order. By assuming this name, Guaman Poma placed himself high on the hierarchy of beings, close enough to the *inca* to intercede directly on behalf of his suffering people. The cosmic principle of *auki*, which he embodied entitled Guaman Poma to the supernatural power of communication, and Guaman Poma activated that power in the ritual of historical writing and invoked it in sending his letter to Philip III, king of Spain.[492]

Whoever he was,[493] Guaman Poma understood that the stylized movements of writing and reading mime the movements of history, the mode of time that had overturned his world. As a modern man of letters, he dutifully recorded both the destructive symptoms of his day and his eschatological vision of good government. He set the historical details of his people's pain into writing so that they would no longer be insignificant in history. His craving to write was fierce, whetted by the miseries of the apocalypse. He writes, "For I say unto you, reader, that this book cost me thirty years of labor and poverty. Leaving behind me my child, my house, and my property, I worked by mingling with the poor."[494] By expressing the meaning of a catastrophic age, he hoped to render a new summary of its terminal signs and effectively hasten its passing. To the just judge he poured out the history of injustices and the last hopes of all his people. There is no historical trace of a response nor is there any indication that the message got through.

GRACEFUL DANCE

Guaman Poma's history, cosmology, and vision of the end coincide in almost every detail with the messianic outlook of the Taki Ongo dance uprising of 1560s.[495] "The only difference is that [Guaman Poma] rejected the cultural forms that the divinity adopted, that is, the *huacas*, and even collaborated in their destruction."[496] This crucial difference led him to hope for the restitution of good government, whereas the *takiongos* foretold apocalyptic destruction. While the writer turned to the sacred center (the reading king who ruled the world), local deities, even the *huacas* fixed in stone, bolted from their central locations to seize and mobilize Guaman Poma's neighbors. The presence of the Spaniards had brought disease and defeat into the midst of the Andean cosmos. These military and bodily infiltrations proved that the boundaries of the world were more than porous; they had in fact given way. The periphery would not hold, and, therefore, the sacrality at the center could be continent no longer.[497] The containments of symbolic life fell apart. Religious fixtures set themselves loose and went on the move. The powers of the *huacas*, the divine sites where all modes of being came together to form "centers," exploded outward, seized helpless victims, and threw them into dancing fits. Dance, like Guaman Poma's historical writing, consists of stylized movements whose significances configure and affect a people's existence in time. Both dance and historical writing can be graceful designations of their own reality and time. By choreographing the end-time, the movements of Taki Ongo dancers literally figured out the time-lines of eschatological force for all to see.

Taki Ongo means the "song, or dance, of the Pleiades."[498] The term came to designate a religious sect, a set of beliefs, and a collection of ritual practices that swept through the provinces of central Peru, especially the region of Huamanga, during the 1560s. The Taki Ongo movement was not only a reaction to the colonial situation; it possessed an autonomous spirituality. This authentic creativity rooted itself in the long prehistory of Andean millennial theories.[499] *Takiongos* were the messengers of Andean divinities. As Steve J. Stern tells us,

> The Andean huacas — no longer confined to rocks, water, or hills — swept down on the natives, literally "seizing" them, entering their bodies and causing the "possessed" to shake, tremble, fall and dance insanely. Taki Ongo literally meant "dancing sickness," and much of its ritual focused on the apparently uncontrollable singing and dancing of those possessed by the "sickness." The seizure spiritually purified the possessed, who renounced Christianity and spoke for the reinvigorated native gods.[500]

Around 1564 these messengers spread the word that the traditional gods of the Andes would unite to overthrow the Christian god and would slay Christ's Spanish representatives with diseases and disasters of local origin.

Through dance and other ritual means, the local deities would bring this dismal world to an end. They would throw the current situation into question and lead society toward liberation from colonial oppression in all its forms,[501] bringing time to a crashing close. A new age would dawn, the gods would be reborn in their fullness, and local custom would triumph once again. The upshot of the divine message was that the *Andean powers of creation* would arise and swamp the world with fever, a sickness that would annihilate the corruption of the immediate historical past. The ocean would flood the earth, obliterating any memory of Spanish dominion. With the *huacas* to lead them through the time of deluge, the indigenous peoples would turn back the invading tide of disease and conquest. They would crush the sickening overlordship, close off the sluices that let it in, and shut off at its divine source the torrent of Christian history that had swept the invasion forward. When the waters receded they would leave a newborn paradise of regenerated abundance, free of disease and inhabited by new people. The new ocean would firmly reestablish the outer perimeters of the world.

Native people who wished to pass safely through the calamity were pressed to return with devotion and vigor to the worship of local deities manifest in the *huacas* (local shrines). The *takiongos* arose to satisfy the hunger of the *huacas*, whose spirits had entered their bodies, because the *huacas* no longer received food offerings or libations of *chicha*. In response, thousands of faithful offered animals, clothing, beer, and other goods. They expected the imminent arrival of a paradise of good health and abundance. More than half the *takiongos* were women.[502] Proclaimed through sermons delivered at *huacas*, the Taki Ongo vision of the end spread like wildfire through every class and social group of Andean peoples. The message was credible because it appealed to the indigenous, cyclical view of history and interpreted contemporary experience within the traditional framework of divinations, which explained misfortune, sickness, and all particular historical incidents as symptoms of particular alignments of forces. Taki Ongo, from this perspective, is a cosmic movement as well as a ritual procedure and a political upheaval. "More exactly, it is a revolution founded upon a cyclic representation of time."[503] At this point, information drawn from two other Andean chroniclers of the period, Cristóbal de Molina and Sarmiento de Gamboa, embellishes the schema of their fellow historian, Guaman Poma.[504] They report that four epochs (*mita*) had preexisted the imperial Inca age. Each *mita* possessed its own form of humanity and was presided over by its own sun. Each lasted for a period of one thousand years, at the end of which there was a universal cataclysm. Wachtel explains:

> According to one version laid out by Sarmiento de Gamboa, the Inca empire had been founded at a date that corresponds to the year 565 of the Christian era; and was destroyed by white-skinned, bearded, foreign beings; and it is in 1565, 1,000 years after the foundation of the great empire, that Cristóbal de Molina situates the apogee of the Taki Onqoy movement. Would not the catastrophe provoked by the Spanish conquest announce the reign of a new sun and the birth of a new humanity? It was, therefore, no accident that Titu Cusi prepared a general uprising of the Indians precisely in the year 1565.[505]

The *Takiongo*s divined time itself, the historical experience of the community since the Conquest, as a noxious condition whose symptoms now surfaced to make diagnosis possible. The epoch itself was diseased. The outbreak of epidemics brought the obscure causes of sickness into the full light of day; rampant pathology became the prelude to imminent cure. The possessed messengers played the role of traditional diviners writ large, such that the mediums themselves became the divine shrines on the temporal landscape of history just as the *huaca*s were the geographic loci of divine power. The *huaca*s had always been the central ritual foci for moral discernment during times of historical crisis and conflicts of value,[506] and now they popped up everywhere, a symptom of the destructive confusion they were perpetrating on the cosmos. The sacred fixtures had come under attack, defiled by colonial inquisitors and their vandals, but now "all the *huacas* of the kingdom, all those that the Christians had destroyed and burned, had resurrected to new life . . . to wage war with [the biblical] God and vanquish him."[507] Now they were mobile, a mode of existence from which they had withdrawn at the dawn of the cosmos. Their movement put all values in flux and called their followers to experience the critical change that would revaluate the past.

In order to cut through the indistinctness of the present chaos, the uprising deities called for renunciation of the Christian god. Devotees learned that continual contact with Spaniards would tow them under the floodwaters of the cleansing deluge. They must abjure European ways and relationships without compromise. Their recantations took shape in the rejection of Spanish names, cuisine, and clothing. Furthermore, they shunned colonial spaces, especially churches. To succumb to the foreign structures of space (clothing, food, architecture, property, dance), sound (names, hymns, language), or time (the Christian calendar of feasts and liturgical performances) perverted and bestialized one's constitution and turned the world topsy-turvy. The apocalypse would heighten distinctions and clarify the grotesque meaning of the differences between Spanish and Andean culture. The natives who would not repudiate Spanish Catholic culture "would die and walk with their heads on the ground and their feet above, and others would be turned into guanacos, deer, vicuñas and other animals."[508] Indians who had entered the waters of Christian baptism became llamas and vicuñas and died of horrible diseases.

To conclude that Taki Ongo was a reversion to the past, however, would be mistaken. Details of the movement and its associate political revolts uncover not only a religious conservatism, upholding traditional values and practice, but a crafty spirit of adaptation. The religious tradition coped with change and even induced it. "In spite of its hostility to Spanish influences it appears that the Taki Onqoy integrated, in the very act of rejection, certain elements of the culture that it combated."[509] Thus, Juan Chocne, one of the principal leaders of the movement, gained the supernatural assistance of Santa María and Santa María-Magdalena during his preaching. In fact, the *takiongo*s did not so much retreat back into the ancient empire, an age that was past and gone, as summon the *re-creation* of ancient imperial realities. They announced the transformation of the past and not its reinstallation. For example, the spatial organization of the new empire would vary from the old form: "[I]t appears to be founded on a dualism and not so much on a quadri-partition. The *huacas* had gathered together in such a way as to form two distinct groups, one surrounding the *huaca* of Pachacamac, the other surrounding the *huaca* of Lake Titicaca."[510] These two sacred places, the mountain and the coast, constitute two poles, marking off a newly negotiated symbolic distance that again props open the cosmos. Between the two poles lies the restructured span of the new world to come. These ancient sacred sites transpose into a new key the movements of *hanan* and *hurin*, the upper and lower worlds of the traditional Andes.

The renovations are still more drastic. The gods themselves undergo transformation. "Traditionally the [*huacas*] were localized in stones, springs, lakes. . . . [N]ow, however, in the Taki Onqoy, the divinity becomes interiorized. The *huacas* incarnate themselves in human beings."[511] During possession-trance, the supernatural powers seized the bodies and personalities of the *takiongos*. The possessed themselves became sacred objects. Their own human presence—their flesh with its grimaces, sickness, and dance—proclaimed the coming of gods to earth. "For two or three days [at a time] the Indians direct[ed] offerings and feasting, replete with dances and singing, to the *huaca* incarnate."[512]

The incarnation of the *huacas* in human flesh brought salvation to those who believed. The element of belief is another profound innovation in Andean religiosity and a direct corollary of the sacralization of the incarnate individual. Participation in the new cult and in the new kingdom was a voluntary affair. One deliberately had to choose to join the movement. Salvation resulted from *conversion*. The conversion experience followed several days of abstaining from salt and colored maize as well as from sex. In short, discipleship in the Taki Ongo movement required a definitive break with the past, with the colonial ambience and mindset but also with the ascribed condition that bound one to ephemeral elements of one's passing culture. As always, culture remained a ritual achievement. Through the innovation of conversion, however, the meaning of cultural rites became rooted in personal human choice, a mode of decision sacralized by the incarnation of *huacas* in individuals and instituted by their divine command.

The ritual revival accompanied, in fact, the birth of a completely new social reality—a pan-Andean solidarity, which transcended affiliation to the local group. "Significantly, major gods of the Incas, who still represented a potential threat to ethnic independence, were not to play a leading role in the armies of Andean gods."[513] People followed the examples set by the *huacas*, who united in a new alliance in order to form a more perfect union. "Just as the *huacas* had buried latent rivalries to make the Andes safe for indigenous gods and peoples as a whole, so should the Indians recognize their common position vis-à-vis the Europeans."[514]

The foundations of faith in the *huacas* lay in revelations about the beginning of time: "The *huacas* had created the Indians, this land, and the provisions which the Indians once enjoyed."[515] Through their ties to the forces of creation and to the subsequent economic vitality of the Andean land, local deities laid irrefutable claim to superiority over foreign gods. In contrast, the Christians' "stick," the wooden cross, would not speak through the *takiongo*s—a mute testimony to its impotence.

The Taki Ongo movement proclaimed chaos and enacted frenzy. Dancers identified with the sacred wellsprings of cosmic confusion. Paradoxically, their stylized performances of disease and dissolution clarified the disjunction between Indian and Spanish histories. While their rites of possessed affliction dramatized the unhealthy mishmash and helter-skelter of the times, they offered both the means and the matter for reflection on existence in time. The ways in which *takiongo*s suffered the symptoms of the pathogenic commingling of two worlds pulled the two histories into direct confrontation. By ritually heightening, and thus sacralizing, the separation of the two cultures, the "dance craze of the Pleiades" passed through the stormy chaos and created something new. The performance of irony—the deliberate reenactment of contradictory appearances and disappearances, differentiations and simultaneities (especially the ironic dances connected with the mythic fate of the cycling stars)—smelted down and recast the social ties and alliances among native communities.[516]

The oppugnant form of this cosmic struggle makes sense of the ironic ritual combats performed to the puzzlement of the Spanish emissary Diego Rodríguez Figueroa.[517] The Spaniard took his life in his hands when, under orders, he visited the Bambacona stronghold of the *inca* Titu Cusi on 13 May 1565. To Figueroa's utter amazement, the enemy chief took him to the theater, where the Indians staged a dramatic spectacle. Titu Cusi wore all his traditional regalia, including a red mask, a feathered headpiece and body work, wooden bells, and a gold shield. After Titu Cusi and his visitor ceremonially exchanged gifts, the host served a large meal. It degenerated into a drinking bout and a competition in which verbal abuse was heaped on the Spaniards by Indians trying to outdo one another in sarcasm and invective.[518] On 14 May, the *inca* himself worked up a violent rage and threatened Figueroa with death. And the following day, Titu Cusi presided over a dance festival in which companies of high-stepping warriors in full costume menaced the visitor in a spirit of aggressive good humor. Figueroa, for his part, reports that he laughed along with them even while, fearing for his life, he commended his spirit to God. The *inca* himself claimed that he was on the verge of rounding up all the Spaniards, killing them, and offering their corpses to wild Indians to eat. "The next day Titu Cusi assured [Figueroa] that the scenes he had witnessed on the previous evening had been performed as a joke."[519] Struggle and combat pervaded every level of reality, from humor to theater to military exercise and dance. In those final days, the cosmos was a stage where contradictory signs played themselves out to the full in order to manifest their creative ironies as intensely as possible. In the juxtaposition of existing contraries, the religious imagination perceived the appearance of a new creation.[520]

We will resume this theme of ironic and creative theater momentarily in a discussion of the staged dramas of the *inca* Atahualpa's death. The point to underscore here, however, is that Taki Ongo and other millennial sects of the period were universal struggles between two kinds of creation and two kinds of creator, Spanish and Indian. The clash exalted the local gods, who would expel the Spaniards and their divinity. *Because of their history* the Spaniards had turned the world upside down and deposed the local gods by burning and destroying them. Now, however, the *huaca*s would rise up to unleash a new quality of time and to right the world. "This time God and the Spaniards would fall victim, the Spaniards would be slain and their cities would be annihilated; the sea would rise up to drown them all and to eliminate any memory of them."[521]

The very weaknesses that the Taki Ongo condemned may have caused its sociopolitical undoing.[522] Its hostility toward the Christian God was accompanied by a sympathy for some of the lesser Christian supernatural beings. In the battle between the divine powers of the traditional Andes and the European overlords, Christian saints, rather than Andean *huaca*s, seized many women *takiongo*s. Possession by the saints drove the *takiongo*s to proclaim messages of remorse and repentance, and these dampened the enthusiastic rage for dance.

Steve J. Stern reminds us that a spiritual crisis created the political and moral impasse facing native Andean society in the 1560s. Millenarian dream and apocalyptic cataclysm responded to the darkness of moral obscurity and the demoralization of spiritual malaise. These visions clarified the sources of crisis and the images of justice in such circumstances. For that reason, Taki Ongo renewed hope for many native people, but it did not release them into final bliss. It "had important economic, political, and military repercussions for society at large,"[523] but its religious and symbolic aspects were stamped out rapidly and effectively. Colonial authorities suppressed devotions at the *huaca*s. They destroyed these shrines, which spoke through the possessed and through the landscape in the symbolic languages of song, dance, clothing, and social alliance, which had descended from the times of creation. The predicted flood of destruction swept across the land, but the faithful were deprived of the symbolic means to escape its devastation. A campaign of punishment by Cristóbal de Albornoz condemned some eight thousand Indians for their part in hastening the dawn of the messianic age. He fined the leaders, put them to the lash, or exiled them far from the *huaca*s of their native land.[524]

RETRACING STEPS: HISTORIANS AND DANCERS
Taki Ongo placed dance at the center of the eschatological stage of history. So did the millennial movements of the Toba, Mocoví, Juruna, Makiritare, Baniwa, Campa, Canela, Wayãpi, Chiripá, Apapocuvá, Nhandeva, Mbyá, Kaiová and other Guaraní groups examined above. Dance is central to messianic movements throughout the native Americas and, indeed, in Africa, Oceania, and other cultures across the globe. The *takiongo*s shed light on the nature of millennial dance. Their *taki* is a song-dance-labor rite performed in

concert with the ultimate harvest, the final germination of the last seed, the terminal afflictions of individual human beings, and the last cycle of the Pleiades. The dancing sickness of the Pleiades is the final round of cosmic time.

The function of eschatological dance does not vary greatly from the general purpose of sacred dance in South American cultures.[525] Dance reenacts mythic movement and joins human movement to the violent, mythic changes that created cosmos and culture, filling the jolting passages of time with grace. As ritual imitation is the proper human response to the creativity of other modes of time and the violent changes they provoke, the polyrhythms of dance are an essential part of festivals that mete out the passages of seasonal times, cultural transitions, and individual life-cycles. Human gestures mime *gesta dei*, the creative acts of the gods and other supernaturals. One by one, each dance festival reenacts the reappearance and then the dismissal of the gods and heroes. Each successive performance brings closure to the old season or life-stage and opens a new unit of time.

The eschaton, however, must become *full* of grace, for it is the time when mythic beings — *all* significant realities — most fully reappear. Each form of being calls for human response. But these powers no longer reappear in accordance with the stately rhythms of cosmic order or the regular rotation of the seasons. Supernatural modes of time break free of their symbolic expressions, the periodicity that contained them. Temporal structures collapse. Time itself is crowded with ominous signs and full of miraculous appearances. In order to contest every appearance, dance must be constant. There is no time left for routine or leisure. All is ritual labor and dance. The grace of eschatological dance merges with frenzy as it juggles the multiform responses called for by the bewildering variety of presences apparent at the end. This final dance contest coordinates the passage of all the powers that had hidden within significant forms. Indeed, dance and song summon forth all supernatural powers at once and, for a long eschatological moment, sustain their terrible pleroma until timely dance once again coordinates their disappearance. Unlike that in ordinary festival performance, the ironic play of differences in eschatological dance (such as beginning and end, hope and anxiety, sky and earth, reaping and sowing) renders the disappearance of all beings simultaneous and final. Marching in step to the just rhythms of ritual music, the entire cast of true and worthy powers exits the spatiotemporal house of history and brings it crashing down (or transports its pure and stylized version to another spatiotemporal mode, as in the case of Guyraypotý's dance hall). During the final cadenza of the cosmos, the sacred sources of its meaning dance free of their symbolic container and abandon the arena where human history unfolded. With them go the saved, who cross over to another space and time through the work of the grace-filled movements of their ceaseless dance.

The connection between dance and time clarifies the intentions and meaning of eschatological dance crazes. In turn, visions of the end add a unique dimension of ultimacy to the significance of dance. A few words are sufficient to recall how dance is a calendric expression.[526] It coordinates diverse cycles of emotion, color, sound, and movement with mythic realities and acts. Because it is a critical element of culture (grounded in the great crises of primordial destruction), dance forms part of the foundation of morality, the model of upright action. It renders the spatiotemporal matrix of culture visible, adjustible, and adjudicable. Because it encapsulates cultural values and profiles the process of their critical reevaluation, dance allows a community to scrutinize the meaning of symbolic experience. Human culture unfolds in a complicated calendar of multiple times. Dance not only keeps pace with the rhythms of these multiple times but intercalates and prioritizes diverse temporal experiences, literally figuring out the various modes of time that impinge on human existence. In moments of crisis, especially during periods when diverse times fuse with one another, there exists a moral imperative to dance as did the mythic founders of temporal modes. That is, to create moral order one must act gracefully. Ritual dance is thus a paradigm of human life in time and a moral cornerstone of calendric existence.

Periodically performed to pass the time (of season, age-set, life-cycle unit, fruiting season, new year), dances celebrate and reshape existence in time. Eschatalogical dance now sends the seasons and the years of the calendar spinning in a single frenzy toward their complete passage, like a film run at fast speed. It is not simply the quantity of times made present, however, nor the compressed velocity of their passing that constitutes the uniqueness of eschatological dance, but the way it synchronizes the transition points of every imaginable cycle of time, forcing them to occur at the same instant and thereby creating an unprecedented passage, a crossing-over that is ultimate in scale and in kind. Eschatological dance becomes the "time when" all differences come together.

Taki Ongo was a frenzied dance composed of such frantic moves. It orchestrated all the moving things that were colliding and collapsing at the end: aeons, courses of history, *huacas*, saints, Andeans, Spaniards, seasons, upper and lower worlds, and all other sacred and profane realities. For both Guaman Poma and the *takiongos*, ritual remained the effective sign and instrument of exclusively Andean values, especially the values of ordeal, death, and termination associated with initiation and world renewal. The Indians who remained faithful to the powers manifest in their own history would take their place in the promised land. But the *takiongos* performed Andean dances, whereas Guaman Poma wrote Andean history. The difference between these two rites points to the important question of style.

Written history and dance are two styles of evaluating existence in time. More precisely, each represents a different effort to *stylize history*. Here we take advantage of the word *style* in the sense of an instrument for writing and for cutting a figure as well as the distinctive manner of executing any symbolic expression. Dance and historiography stylize history in both these senses and they do so in two ways. First, they make pointed remarks. These stylized reenactments of remarkable transitions create symbolic units (years, months, days, volumes, books, chapters) that are recyclable or, in the case of the book, rereadable. By retracing the paradigmatic steps with which time unfolds, seasonal dancers and writing historians cut stylish figures for communal reflection. Dance and handwriting thereby make specific periods of time apprehensible.

There is a second, related sense in which dance and historical writing stylize history. They cast events into conventional forms of symbolic or precedent-setting language such as patterned gesture, body language, dance step, scale of tones, fashionable chant, written letter, word, glyph, ideogram, diagram, literary genre, and historical paradigm. By reducing experiences of time to stylish figures, dancers and historical scribes evaluate events and draw them into line with the meaning manifest in the universe and history that, indeed, first gave rise to their specific written and choreographic forms.

Because they are bound by the limits of their own period, dance and writing suffer constraint as they describe their own times. More interesting than this in the context of eschatological styles, however, is the fact that dance and writing are subject to the *mode* of time in which their signs have meaning. They make no sense outside that fundamental ontological frame. Furthermore, they participate in the mode of time whose steps (symbolic traces) they retrace and reshape. Writing and dance-steps are the visible tracks of the particular human experience of time that they inhabit. That is, they are not only stylish genres delineating what happened during specific times, but they are themselves symbols of existence in specific modes of temporality. As such, historical writing and dance are the finest metastatements about their own temporal mode of existence, pointing toward the meaning of that mode of being in ways that no other medium does as validly.[527]

In order to be effective, the instrument — the *style* in the sense of pen or dance-form — must be a part of the reality it describes or inscribes. It never remains objective and remote from the mode of time it succeeds in interpreting. Eschatological writing and dance are involved in the final reality they create. They are not the only styles of participant observation. By cutting figures of another sort, the sword and other weapons, for example, impose a different style on the fashioning and interpretation of existence in time.

ESCHATOLOGICAL DIVERSION: MILITARY, POLITICAL, AND THEATRICAL ACTS INTERPRET HISTORY AND BRING ON THE END OF TIME   The paradigm of dance and the ritual violence needed to account for change[528] make sense of the millenarian value of military symbolism: especially battle array, the choreographed maneuvers of troops in ritual combat or skirmish, and dramatic acts of terrorism. The eschatological values of dance and ritual violence also explain the prominent place of military victory and defeat within the incisive interpretive style of written history. Eschatological military action settles final historical accounts by dramatizing the terror of the eschatological condition of time. In bloody choreography and in written word, decisive battles enact the meaning of the end, making visible its grisly and summary nature. The power and scope of final battle effectively signal the imminence of the end of an era.

This explains why military action stands with writing and dance as an instrument that shapes history. The eschatological vision of Andean peoples impelled Guaman Poma to write and drove the *takiongos* to dance. The same schemas of history and dreams of the future urged others to mount armed struggle. In the spirit of a ritual response to the imminent eschaton, many — especially the dashing figures of legendary commanders such as Manco Inca, Juan Santos, Juan Chocne, and Titu Cusi — took up sword and gun to stylize history in their own image.

Armed resistance and hope for *final* victory did not die out with Titu Cusi. A number of authors delineate the "conception of the world" that united the classes, social groups, and leaders who participated, for example, in the eighteenth-century "cycle of uprisings." The 1780 rebellion that spread outward from Cuzco under the leader Tupac Amaru II (José Gabriel Tupac Amaru) receives particular attention.[529] In light of the analyses above, it is not surprising that the worldview underlying these revolts rooted itself in the land and its symbolic fate. The uprising of Tupac Amaru II typified the native eschatological movements that created the momentum for national independence movements in Latin America — a liberation that, ironically, further postponed the fulfillment of native peoples' hopes for freedom.

Guaman Poma and the *takiongos* showed how Andean social organization and historical consciousness embedded themselves in the sacrality of the land and its symbolic manifestations. The sources of that sense of integrity remained intact for a while afterward. For nearly two centuries after the Conquest, the territorial wholeness of Tahuantinsuyu, the Inca empire, was respected. Peru's eighteenth-century inhabitants viewed Peru as the historical continuation of the Inca empire.[530] The territory was first dismembered under the Bourbon king Philip V beginning in 1717, and the process continued relentlessly through 1776. Nonetheless, Inca royal genealogies (spurious as well as authentic) descended through Cuzcan families, indicating that Inca traditions were in some way kept intact throughout the eighteenth century.[531] This continuity offered grounds for a rebirth of the glorious Inca world. The return to a golden age, however, was never a simple nostalgia for times gone by. The yearning for direct contact with the sacred sources of tradition always stirred up creative change. As the integrity of the land was demolished, new ideas of territory, jurisdiction, good government, and religious practice filled the millennial dreams. "In the indigenous rebellions of the eighteenth-century we see, then, a series of attempts to restore the dynasty of the Incas. However, the independent Inca state which the rebels proposed to install would not be a simple reconstruction of the empire of Huayna Capac; it would be a monarchy on the model of Spanish government directed, however, by indigenous leaders."[532] Similarly, reassertion of the right to direct their own religious lives came to mean "the formation of an Inca Catholic church corresponding to the Spanish Catholic church," in which Indians would become bishops and priests at all levels of the ecclesiastical hierarchy.[533] Militarists aspired to consummate a dramatic end in order to live the free, blissful existence of mythic beings.

There is no need to detail the symbolic aspects of José Gabriel Tupac Amaru's failed attempt to achieve a final military triumph in 1780. The sentence levied against him after his defeat, however, contains noteworthy details regarding the role of sounds, body space, ornaments, and performance that constitute social and personal identity. The sentence was an apocalyptic document. It deprived the Inca of the right to recognize and declare lines of authentic genealogical descent and placed this power in the hands of the Spanish king alone. It abolished the hereditary character of leadership. It outlawed traditional clothing and proscribed, in particular, the use of the *maskapaycha*, the Inca crown. The sentence called for the confiscation of all portraits of Inca emperors and banned any future images of them. The significance of sound and its connection with memory did not escape the Spanish authorities. "To be outlawed and confiscated are the trumpets and clarinets which the Indians use in their festivals and which they call *pututos* . . . with which they announce the mourning and lamentable remembering of their ancient times."[534] Leaving no obvious symbolic language unattacked, the sentence ordered that local parish priests give intensive instructions in Spanish so that, after four years time, Spanish would replace native languages as the common means of communication.

The terms of Tupac Amaru II's sentence dramatize the clash of symbolic times and spaces and, indeed, of all terminologies — linguistic, behavioral, performative, anatomical, and cosmic. The symbolic languages of the Andes and of Spanish rule derived from different meanings of the end. The written clauses of the sentence, a symbolic form of justice as it exists within a history stylized by writing, gave shape to the apocalyptic monsters who would unravel the symbolic threads of the Andean cosmos. In writing and through martial force, the sentence imposed an unmistakably eschatological climate: it stipulated the end of effective symbolic existence, exterminated the traces of Andean history, and obliterated its significance. Deprived of the symbolic means to stylize their own history, Andeans ran the apocalyptic risk of remaining unremarkable and insignificant. They faced the prospect of cultural annihilation. Deprived of land, religion, hierarchy, military strength, festival calendar, and dance, with what signs could they mark their steps through time and with what stylistic instruments could they retrace these nearly obliterated signs of their existence?

THE FINAL STAGE: THEATER AND POLITICAL ACTION
Although sentenced to death, Inca symbolic life lived on. Symbols of the end instigated political uprisings and instilled a nationalist spirit of hope for the Inca state. Against the overwhelming odds of socioeconomic and cultural disintegration, Andean peoples faced their protracted final ordeal with tenacious strength. They drew strength from the religious meaning of their struggle and created new symbolic vehicles for the meaning of their history. Theater was one such newfound style of interpreting the religious value of historical events, especially political acts. Under colonial suppression many religious performances were recast as secular theater.

On the eve of the 1780 rebellion, Andean playwrights staged a number of popular dramas. These dramas interpreted local traditions and legends that had circulated in the Andes from the time of the Conquest. Antonio Valdez, a Catholic priest and friend of José Gabriel Tupac Amaru, for example, composed the influential play *Ollantay* from popular historical accounts with messianic themes. These theatrical performances tied directly into the military acts of eschatological battle.[535] The connection of *Ollantay* to Tupac Amaru's rebellion recalls the prophetic character of theatrical images already discussed in this section: the ironic and menacing performances that Titu Cusi staged to intimidate Figueroa, the Spanish emissary; Carneiro de Cunha's remark that the Canela messianic uprising of 1963 was a myth dramatized to unsettle the "audience" of white *civilizados*; the messianic troubadours of northeast Brazil; the shamanic batons that Natochí, the Toba prophet, sold as "admission tickets" to the spectacle of the new age; the ubiquitous emphasis on the dramatic performance of dance-chants and ritual combats.

The sentence against Tupac Amaru banned "provincial comedies" and any other public performances that might further the memory of the ancient Incas.[536] But folk theater has proven an irrepressible stylization of Andean history, sustaining a manifestly eschatological content. The history enacted in messianic theater perpetuates the eschatological worldview (so evident in the uprisings from the sixteenth through the eighteenth centuries) and the historical schema that undergirds it. Notwithstanding the demise of Spanish rule, the contradictions imposed by colonial values of time, space, religious experience, and economic order continue to spark millennial hopes for a judgment that will finally sort out symbolic existence.[537] As usual, eschatology adjudicates history by subsuming it into the framework of traditional myth even while it creatively adapts the tradition to new times. Through dramatic representation Andeans preserve and rework their vision of the end even after centuries of deferred dreams. To that theatrical tradition we now turn.

Today, 450 years after the arrival of the Spanish conquistadors, a play entitled *The Tragedy of the Death of Atahualpa* continues to relive the trauma of the Conquest.[538] In 1533 Pizarro executed Atahualpa, the last *inca* to reign before the arrival of the Spanish. Atahualpa's first meeting with the Spaniards and his death at their hands has quickened the creativity of Andean poets, playwrights, and choreographers for centuries. One cycle of such plays dates to the end of the sixteenth century.[539] A brief look at its contemporary version shows how eschatological theater juxtaposes different styles of history: writing, dream, choral dance, and military exercise.

The performance of the play usually coincides with a significant Christian feast day, such as the Sunday and Monday of Carnival week before the onset of Lent or the Feast of the Holy Spirit, a triduum celebrated from 1 to 3 June. The annual reenactment places the historical death of the *inca* (and the Conquest-event, in general) on a par with the mythic disappearance of primordial beings who reappear periodically as the stars, sun, or other temporal signs. The enacted reappearance of Atahualpa and disappearance of the Inca cosmos, like the cyclic appearance of the Pleiades, becomes an event one could set one's watch by.[540] That is, the historical commemoration marks (and makes remarkable and reflective) the appearance of the eschatological kind of time that the tragic event created.

In the central square of the Andean town in which the performance occurs, two masked young men armed with tridents keep spectators at bay. A band of musicians plays indigenous flutes and drums. "The actors are divided into two groups: on one side are the Indians and on the other, about twenty meters away, are the Spaniards."[541] A choir of young girls dressed as Indian princesses sings. Their adornments, which bespeak their privileged status, include gold-color paper crowns, sunglasses, and parasols. The *inca* himself dresses rather outlandishly and sports a royal scepter topped with braids of white wool. The natives who portray Spaniards wear period costumes and bear sabers, clubs, and shotguns.

Atahualpa opens the play on an ominous note. He narrates a recurring nightmare of his to the choir of princesses: "For the second time in his dreams he saw his father the Sun dimmed by dark smoke while the sky and the mountains burned like the red breast of the pillku-birds; a *huaca* had foretold the future through an unmistakably clear dream: the arrival of warriors dressed in iron and coming to destroy his kingdom."[542] In fact, the creator, Viracocha, has himself sent this announcement about the coming of bearded foreigners to Atahualpa. In order to confirm and clarify the meaning of the *inca*'s dreamy presentiments, the royal diviner, Huaylla Huisa, enters deep sleep in his mansion of gold. It becomes almost impossible to awaken this living repository of traditional knowledge. Three times the diviner sleeps on the matter in order to discern from his own dream the truth and consequences of the *inca*'s. Each time the noisy choir must make more racket to call him back to the land of the living. Each time they insistently stir him awake he confirms the hard truth.

The second part of the play proceeds quickly through several dramatic episodes. The Spaniards arrive but cannot talk. In a series of silent conversations, Almagro, the Spanish interlocutor, "speaks" inaudibly by moving his lips (this gesture continues through the play). Little by little, the Spaniards' intentions become clear. A civil interpreter (Felipillo) declares that they want to acquire gold and silver; the priest (Valverde) interrupts to assert that they have come to proclaim knowledge of the true God.[543]

The play turns next to the meaning of writing, offering a profound interpretation of writing as a mode of being in the world. "There unfolds a long series of episodes whose unique theme is the astonishment and incomprehension of the Indians before the mysterious 'cornhusk-leaf' [a written letter] that Almagro sends to the Inca.[544] The actors pass the written sheet of paper from hand to hand, from one Inca to another. Attention dwells on the inability of any Inca sage or royal person to make sense of the unspoken message. The master-diviner Huaylla Huisa tries to decipher the message by plunging into deep sleep and dream. What cosmic realm must his spirit inhabit to decode this symbolic expression? Where can he experience the preconditions of its meaning? In one version of the play, performed in Toco, the diviner's sleep becomes permanent. His attempt to understand reduces him to a condition of death. In the meantime, it becomes clear that the Spaniards partake of the same deadly mode of being as their writing. Their communications are inaudible. When they express themselves they only move their lips in silence, like the silent page. Since these initial exchanges between their emissaries prove ineffectual, Pizarro and Atahualpa decide to meet face to face.

Atahualpa hopes to encounter the king of Spain, his counterpart in the hierarchy of beings in the universe. Pizarro offers Atahualpa safe passage to Barcelona, and so Atahualpa entrusts himself to Pizarro. But the conquistador disregards his mandate from the Spanish king and breaks his promise to the *inca*. Pizarro confines him, subjects him to grave indignities, and threatens him with death. Atahualpa instructs his son, Inkaj Churin, not to die with him but to go to Vilcabamba, whence he must establish a dominion that eventually will expel the bearded foreigners. Atahualpa casts a curse on Pizarro. The choir picks up the malediction and repeats it, fixing the curse as a pivotal point in the drama. The pace of the action picks up.

The priest Valverde insists that the *inca* undergo baptism and confess his sins. The good father holds out the Bible toward the *inca* and urges the holy man to accept it. Atahuallpa declares that it says absolutely nothing to him and knocks the sacred book to the ground. The priest accuses the *inca* of blasphemy. Pizarro draws his sword and runs it through Atahualpa. The *inca* dies.

The choir of Inca princesses begins to wail. Their ritual weeping and lengthy lamentions proclaim that "the whole world participates in the death of Atahuallpa."[545] The hills and stones "sing funeral songs, their tears come together as torrents, the Sun grows dark, the sickly Moon wastes away, everything goes into hiding, everything disappears and time itself is reduced to opening and closing one's eyes."[546]

The rest of the play illustrates the meaning of the Conquest. Most striking is the mutual misunderstanding, or, rather, the lack of shared ground, for understanding symbolic life. The thudding contact of the Bible with native soil gives resonance to the mutual impenetrability of the sacred sources of meaning. The collision of the two worlds that grow from these opposing wellsprings of symbolic life, scripture and Andean earth, occults meaning and necessitates the death of the *inca*. Every species of symbolic language that flows from one of these sources is unintelligible to those rooted in the other. Coming from another history, Spaniards cannot understand the *symbolic* language of gold, while natives are struck by the Spaniards' inability to understand gold in any terms other than material and cumulative. For their part, the Indians possess no basis for understanding the symbolic language of writing. The performance dramatizes the absolute incommensurability of symbolic languages of sacred origin: gold and scripture. The death of the *inca*, the sacred center of meaning, itself resulted from an absolute failure to communicate, the total absence of any symbolic medium. Since there was no ordered space and time in which the two worlds could meet, there could no longer be a center. Wherever Spanish and Andean realities clashed chaos reigned. The *inca*'s death, his absence and occultation, is a truth statement, an assertion of the unintelligible condition into which reality has fallen.[547]

The play builds toward a messianic close, drawn by its own logic toward the end of time and the appearance of a new age. In the end the *inca* will return to the center of the world and restore its lost harmony. The Conquest marked the end of the last age. The present is a time of waiting, of hidden growth, of anticipation. The dead *inca*'s physical disposition sets the tone of the powerful preparations the cosmos undertakes out of sight. Atahualpa's decapitated head enters the secluded enclosure of the fertile earth. From the moment of its burial, however, the head begins to sprout a new body. In this frenzied time that represents the violent decomposition of the seed, an experience the entire world suffers in these last days, the new, magnificent body of Inkarri (fr. *Inca* and Sp. *rey*, "king") grows in the dark. The head itself takes on new and larger proportions. When the germination process is finished, Atahualpa will burst forth from the earth as Inkarri, drive out the conquerors, and reestablish the ancient empire.[548]

For now, until that promised ending can bring the drama to its paradisal fulfillment, the play ends bizarrely and abruptly. The last scene takes place in Spain, at the court of the king. Pizarro presents the monarch with Atahualpa's head and *llautu* (the plaited-cord headpiece that serves as the insignia of the *inca*). The Spanish king is incensed. In fulfillment of Atahualpa's curse, the king condemns Pizarro, who drops dead on the spot. The king then extols Atahualpa, and on this note of praise, the play closes.

THE ESCHATOLOGICAL NEED FOR DIVERSION   Dramatic interpretations of the Conquest grapple with the chaos that came with the Spaniards. Performances display distinctive signs of the colonial presence in order to discover its meaning. *The Tragedy of the Death of Atahualpa*, for example, stylizes remarkable features of physiognomy (facial hair, skin color, build and stride), military might (swords, guns, uniforms, chains of command), writing (paper, lettered characters, genres such as the letter and Bible), reading, foreign speech, and the greedy habit of sequestering what is sacred (hoarding gold, holding the *inca* for ransom, binding the sacred scripture). No attempt is made here to interpret the abundant symbolic detail of the plot and performance, which would require sustained treatment of the dramatic tradition and its many cycles of plays as well as of the varying mythic and social history of the community of performers. The one version of one cycle sketched here, however, suffices to show that drama is a style of moving interpretively through time and, in this respect, is comparable to the kinds of historical writing, dance, and military action that aim to accomplish a final end.

Eschatological drama does not state facts neutrally; it renders them different by interpreting them. It heightens the contradictions of symbolic life and evaluates them as terminologies by relating them to the final end. The *Death of Atahualpa*, for example, opposes two ways of evaluating existence in time, two ways of creating and reckoning one's history. In contrast to the reading of history by reading written words it places the divining of dream by dreaming. Both processes decipher historical events of their own making by means of the symbols derived from their own terms. Both expressions presage the death that their self-defining reality betokens. Both are forms of symbolic closure. The diviner Huaylla Huisa, for example, becomes encapsulated in the reality that gives meaning to dreams. But that world, the sacred source of esoteric wisdom, becomes evermore remote. Finally, the diviner is hermetically sealed in a form of knowledge whose full manifestation has passed away.

The play also differentiates two distinct symbolic languages of gold and money and points to the opposed meanings of disappearance that give rise to these terminologies. On the one side is an economic language of accumulation based on the meaning of "hiding" as "hoarding." In the same way that Western history squirrels away time, the Spaniards impound and heap up material symbols. Compounding gold is a form of hiding symbolic vestiges of sacred reality. Hoarders subject gold to confinement, to the ritual state of seclusion. The symbolic matter, like a corpse or the body of an initiand, is wrapped in shrouds. Incapable of understanding the sacred *quality* displayed in gold, hoarders hide it away. The historical process of cloaking symbols produces incremental, *quantitative* change over time. The symbolic exercise of ritual seclusion transforms the enclosed or invested cosmic material into wealth, a cumulative expression of the mode of time that manifests itself in historical writing.

Atahualpa's head, on the other side, undergoes the form of occultation suffered by all of Andean reality during these last days. The disappearance of symbolic forms is not hoarding; rather, it represents a return to the sacred sources of time. The earth receives Atahualpa's head. His disappearance signals a process of decomposition and germination, a qualitative change that moves toward the display of a new kind of reality. Toward that same end, the Andean cosmos now enters chaotic occultation in order to close its accumulative history and reencounter the enduring, primordial wellsprings of creativity. Andean history has always been a cycle of such disappearances and appearances.

The play shows how different economic symbols base themselves on divergent appreciations of display and hiding. The significance of these processes of revelation and withdrawal derive from modes of time (for example, myth or history) sacralized by the appearance and disappearance of divine beings, saints, ancestors, cultural heroes, prophets, mystics, diviners, messiahs, and saviors of time. The fully manifest forms of these supernatural agents of creativity, whether biblical or Andean, have passed away. Hoarding and hiding both reenact the process of alienation generated and made generative by the disappearance of the gods. That is, occultation restages the sacrificial process through which primordial beings became aliens, "radically other" than the creatures of this world. Conversely stated, disappearance and alienation reenact the process of metamorphosis, which generated the transformative terms and values (money, might, rite, and ornament) that construct a cosmos out of symbolic forms (sounds, sights, textures, temperatures, emotions, movements) that are alienated from their primordial realities.

All performances interpret the quality of time they inhabit. The Andean dramatic cycles performed during this time of the eschaton exhibit ritual trappings: ceremonial musical instruments, festive garments, festal time (of the Christian calendar), ritual division into two antagonistic groups ("Indians" versus "Spaniards"), and the symbolic presence of cosmic, oneiric, and scriptural powers. Symbolic action of this sort, however, is neither rite (an enactment of primordial events) nor historical action (im-mediate behavior that represents only itself). Dramaturgy intends to be something else again, for it bases itself on another experience of time that, like legend, fiction, or fable, is a deliberate diversion from historical experience. That is why so-called secular theater is an eschatological reality. In a profound and captivating way, drama shows that history can be brought to an end. By imaginatively turning away the flow of history, momentary theatrical diversion demonstrates the real, cathartic possibility of acting in other modes of time. Alternate construals of existence in time become concretely imaginable; appear live and on stage *right now*. Atahualpa will come again just as surely as he *now* appears in some way that is not historical in the narrow sense. The experience of a time that is here *now* but not yet fully manifest makes theater an eschatological vehicle. It conveys the imminence of the other modes of time that press against the experience of the historical present.

These dramas are neither rites nor ceremonies. They are spectacles (something to see), in keeping with the secular frame of historical time wherein they appear. The reality they enact, the quality of knowledge on which the performances base themselves, is ultimately questionable. The frame of the action deliberately introduces a question about the nature of reality. Diversion renders existence questionable so that it can be critically reappraised. In eschatological time, when symbolic structures collapse, secular theater reopens history to question, fends off its oppressive immediacy, and thus reintroduces the time and distance conducive to symbolic reflection.

Because they signal the limits of history, dance, written literature, theater, and military exercise can be diversionary tactics. At the end, when symbolic containments (rite, myth) no longer hold meaning, entertainments divide chaos and conquer history. Under eschatological conditions, all these styles work to create remarkable signs of struggle. Irony pervades every cultural and cosmic level as the imagination juxtaposes contraries in the hopes of creating something new. Every form of diversion—military, linguistic, theatrical—attempts to pass the time, to end the terrible expectation. Each takes its cue from religious rites of renewal, which divert recurrent primordial disaster through the ironic symbolic exercise of reenacting the flood, fire, or other catastrophic dismissal of the fully sacred world. The very performance of struggle, the heightened contrast between Spanish and Andean worlds, creates a new cultural reality, a theatrical way of acting in time, which transforms them both.

The eschaton, like death, is an ambivalent experience and provokes the need for diversion. Divergent forms, such as the cutting ironies and tragic ordeals or deaths of eschatological theater, pry apart the realities that have converged at one chaotic point and force them to resume their separate courses. By parading the diversity of their signs, theater shows how divergent Andean and Spanish meanings are. The chaos of their encounter is diversifiable. By turning primordial realities off to one side and historical existence off to the other, diversionary entertainment rends chaos asunder and opens the distance between clashing times. In the eschaton, recreative theater offers a foretaste of re-creation, the hope of prying open once again the ironic distance between sky and earth, beginning and end.

Eschatological performance (acting in the awareness that one is living in the final time) turns one away from the paralyzing experience of chaos. Prophetic action, ceaseless dance, ritual violence, staged performance, and decisive battles steer one in a more positive direction. These styles of action make one the agent of one's new existence. Forms of diversion are both catalysts and prime examples of the creation to come. That their users live in the last days and that they therefore inhabit several divergent modes of time at once, accounts for the close ties among all the stylizing instruments of history. Decisive wars and historic battles become histrionic source-material. Combat in the military theater observes the scripted choreography of tactic and strategem. Written accounts of military action become divertive reading that cast living history into the experience of reading a story. All these entertainments divert one's attention and experience out of one's immediate temporal frame toward other experiences of time.

Eschatological theater thrives on the knowledge that every symbolic closure has an end. Every performance ends. What if one could *perform* the chaos of history with all its grisly signs? Dramatists, Guaman Poma, the *takiongos*, millennial military prophets, and other diversionary stylists shared the same hopeful conviction. There *is* an end, and this end accounts for the symbolic terms of the play. The end of the symbolic universe, its chaotic period of hiding, gives meaning to the bloody end of Atahualpa's life, the accursed end of Pizarro, the end of Andean history. This hope propels actors and audience through the episodes of struggle and of ambiguous overlap of comedy and tragedy toward the inevitable end, however obscure, unexpected, or unwanted that end may be.

The diversionary quality of eschatological acts and styles of history merits discussion at some length because of its connection to symbolic life in general. Through remarkable symbolic action, diversions become historical ruses—that is, re-uses of symbolic traces in order to double back on one's tracks and thereby divert the powers of disaster. Diversion is not only what a symbol helps accomplish. On the most profound level, seen clearly in the final light of the eschaton, diversion is the heart of what a symbol *is*: the sign that effects a negotiated and artful distance from the terrifying, absolute, and sacred sources of reality.

COMING TO TERMS AND COMING TO TERM

Summaries have periodically been offered throughout the course of this chapter on death and eschatology and will be not repeated here. These closing paragraphs make final mention of eight issues that delineate the meaning of the end in South America:[549] ambivalence, imminence, disclosure, assembly, critical judgment, cultural relativity, the demise of Western civilization, and heroic destiny.

Death and the eschaton are trying conditions that probe the farthermost capacities of symbolic being. Both are irreversible transitions, marking the outer limits of individual and cosmic life, punctuated with ordeals, and crowded with dread and fascination. Far from imposing fearful curfew on the imagination, the certain prospect of termination strikes new sparks. Funeral and millennial acts strike hard to contest chaos and cut through confusion. Sports, combat, drama, and irony hit the limits of their meaning as the religious imagination percusses its own terms and sounds out its end.

In death and during the eschaton, symbolic beings confront the primordial sources of new life. Cultures contest the arbitary limits imposed by death and thereby create terminologies that construe the social world and revitalize cosmic life. Pointing toward the absent but sacred sources of meaning, symbolic life centers itself over death and disappearance.

The death of a Kamayurá village leader, for example, opens a new generation of marriageable women, a new wave of human offspring, a new village, new year of fishing, new harvest of *pequi* chestnuts, new lunar cycle, and a new opening in the Milky Way. Ritual regulates all these openings by synchronizing symbolic closures (shrouds, graves, decorations, gourds). Standing atop the new grave at the center of the village, Kamayurá mourners reenact the exemplary performance of the heroes Kwat and Yaiì when their mother died. The meaning of death becomes visible in performed "speech," the symbolic relations that radiate from the center, where the dead leader lies unseen in the earth. The aesthetic and political repercussions of death are stylized in terms of ornaments and dances as well as in terms of the relative differences among those sitting, processing, singing, and speaking. Through cultural terminologies, the grave that marks the chief's significant absence becomes *murena*, the center of the heroic world, where life first appears. Symbolic existence centers itself on death and draws exuberant life from the meaning of life's end.

The experience of the imminent end of the world causes entire communities to rethink every detail of their existence in light of that coming end. The elements of symbolic life — including foods, dress, gestures, and personal economic relations — are judged and adjusted so that communities can reorient their life-styles toward the end. Whatever does not mark itself with the sign of the sacred realities apparent at the end of time becomes unremarkable and invites its own destruction. Historical incidents that appear absolute, particularly the Conquest and its aftermath, risk suffering the same dismissal as totalitarian modes of primordial being. Millennial prophets yearn for the flood that periodically flushes away the accumulating but insignificant residue of history. With hope and fear, disciples follow messiahs who offer salvation from the end they invoke.

Symbolic being (human being) is propelled by the need to grasp its limits and apprehend their meaning, which constantly forces symbolic life to transcend its already-apparent possibilities and to cross over toward what is unmanifest, unclear, or obscure. That opacity is never far away. Death is imminent; it can strike at any time. The imminence of the eschaton is a function of the fragility of any imaginary structure. At any moment another quality of being may flatten the dimensions of the present world. By virtue of its own origins, the imagination awaits these new appearances and hopes for shattering revelations. It reaches toward reality in all its fullness. Without benefit or medium of symbolic props, one comes face to face with the sacred, ambivalent sources of meaning.

Death originates in this excessive openness to meaning, a symptom of the transcendent capacity of symbolic being. By redressing the openness that terminates each life-cycle, the rites of death reseal the closure of symbolic life even while they liberate the individual from its strictures. Shrouded round with wraps, mats, earth, or ornaments, the corpse represents and renews the closed condition of culture and cosmos. The components of the individual are parceled out to cosmic destinations. Cremation, the funerary communion of relics, and food offerings traded with the dead for dreams or fertility renew the cycles of consumption and exchange that underlie symbolic life.

Every form of closure, however, has an end, for closure is itself a limit. In Guaraní eschatology, the earth complains that she is stuffed with cadavers and calls to the creator to bring an end to the cosmic process. The eschaton arrives when the cosmos reaches its limit and openness becomes a general and irreparable condition. The bonds of closure exhaust themselves. Meaning slips its symbolic leash. Mythic realities unseal themselves from caves, wombs, eggs, and darkness — as do the preposterous *korinto* monsters of the Campa, the Makiritare beings inside Huehanna, the messianic child in the womb of the Canela prophetess, and the blue jaguars of Guayakí and Apapocuvá myth. Symbols no longer contain meaning. Among the Makiritare, even the dance of Wanadi, the creator, means nothing to those watching. Renewing the terminal condition and its constitutive terminologies requires the experience of fatal limits. They clarify the purpose of space and time as well as the lesser terms the cosmos contains.

South American millenarian visions show how the sun, moon, darkness, water, sky, and light point toward the end, a fulfillment toward which any symbol impels the culture in which it appears. When every color makes its appearance total, one color overruns another to produce cataclysmic gloom or total darkness. At the death of the *inca* Atahualpa, even the rainbow turned black. Alternately, in the Makiritare vision, every degree of light manifests itself totally to create a blinding brilliance of divine light eclipsing every partial illumination. Every sound becomes a total expression, outshouting all others to produce the ultimate in devastating noise. Alternately, a mystical unison blasts forth from sacred instruments, or an absolute silence, which includes all tonal possibilities, reigns after the passing of creatures constituted by separate sounds. This is the fullness mimed or approximated from time to time in festivals, especially those that mark the new year, the periodic return of the dead, or turning points in time (eclipses, solstices, seasonal changes, fruiting seasons, or initiation). At the eschaton, the final, irreversible passage requires the ultimate release and full manifestation of all the possibilities inherent in symbolic forms. Millennialists aim to relive and re-present the destruction on which all partial passages are modeled. Eschatological dancers, for example, simultaneously manifest all the signs of time's passage. Ceaseless dancing or the simultaneous dance of all significant dances effects the frenzy of the final time.

Symbolic existence as a whole is drawn toward the termination implied by its finite state. In fact, the imagination itself, locus of all symbolic appearances, needs to imagine its end. All South American eschatologies describe the end of human life on earth. The Juruna, for example, foresaw the time when they would cease to exist and the forked stick holding up the far end of the sky would collapse. The end of imaginable being becomes the ultimate expression of human destiny. It must seek liberation from its own limits. The imaginal condition dissolves its symbolic horizons in order to escape its confines, renew its own meaning, and accomplish its own fulfillment.

This is the context in which to understand the symbolism of assembly that is part of every eschatological movement. In response to a prophetic announcement of the end, foretold long ago, people assemble in a ritual space, plaza, soccer field, dance hall, or community residence set apart from others. By reassembling all the symbolic fragments (embodied in their own constitutions) that issued from the first universal destruction, millennialists desire to make that destruction a *total presence* once again. The assembly of the elect runs counter to the accumulation of imperfections. The just or the true believers recongregate symbolic realities in a way that undoes the sequestering of individual symbolism in funeral rites and of cosmic symbolism in history. Display is the purpose of the final gathering of the saved. They muster to parade the significant realities that break free of history. They show off their uprightness by dancing, diet, and fashion in order to demonstrate the powers that destroy the cosmos and liberate the saved from bondage. The fact that the saved constitute a *totality* brings on the end of the world and calls down judgment and condemnation on those not present in the assembly.

Several forms of assembly present themselves at the end:

1. Historiography gathers remarkable features of the past for a final review. The written images of life in time pass before one's eyes to signal that the end is near. Guaman Poma and eschatological theater propose this reading of history.

2. Center and periphery gather unsortably, as in the case of Brazilian messianism, where the coast and interior of Brazil become indistinguishable. In the Taki Ongo, the *huaca*s, sacred fixtures where all modes of being come together, move across the landscape, and then the center appears everywhere, boundless and uncontained, gathering everything within it.

3. Other spatial features gather in similar ways. Sky and earth merge; the horizon and cardinal points conjoin with the center; mountains fall and valleys fill; forest monsters return to center stage; the fires kept at the four points of solstitial sunrise and sunset sweep across the earth to scorch the world.

4. Dance gathers significant moves into simultaneous and perpetual motion, mobilizing all transitions in the hopes of a single, final passing.

5. Incongruent species of time assemble and become coterminous. Night's darkness blends with day's light; signs of the rainy and dry seasons appear within the same week; European and local history merge in the colonial experience of the last days. The simultaneous presence of all finite times signals their end, for their gathering recreates the experience of eternity.

Assembly accompanies the eschatological experience of chaos in which every symbolic detail view for central importance. The momentous and the trivial no longer remain separable. The sacred appears in profane guise while ordinariness engulfs every trace of the miraculous. The assembled seek signs of purity and omens of dangerous imperfection. The pursuit of signs can become an obsessive scrupulosity symptomatic of the imminent breakdown of symbolic order. The gathering of the saved imposes a crucial difference on chaos. Their symbolic constitution offers criteria for judgment; their acts display the norms for salvation. The assembling of the just becomes *the* effective sign of ingathering, the final harvest of symbolic life.

Death and eschatology highlight images of crisis and judgment. Religious expressions of critical existence include funeral consumption, ordeals, games, dance, drama, noise, struggle, sacrifice, self-sacrifice, dedication to ritual causes, and piety. In light of the mythic crisis of primordial destruction, these acts create critical differences in the midst of chaos. Images of cataclysm, performed in rite, theater, public demonstration, and military exercise, serve as wellsprings of change. Strengthened by their knowledge of mythic destructions, messiahs face unprecedented disruption with confidence and direct the imaginations of their people in the quest for primordial forces that will shatter the present world and refashion political, economic, and spiritual existence.[550]

The eschatological crisis is due to the merging of two distinct and irreconcilable orders. The Andean and the Spaniard, for example, are different *kinds* of beings because they take shape in different histories. The infestation of the one by the other generates terminal disorders. South American eschatologies foresee the consequences of cultural relativity and the collision of cultural worlds in mythic terms. Their spiritualities of cosmic extinction provoke "a profound humiliation for Western consciousness. Western man considered himself successively God's creature and the possessor of a unique Revelation, the master of the world, the author of the only universally valid culture, the creator of the only real and useful science, and so on."[551] South Americans and other peoples "discovered" during the Age of Exploration force the West to discover the historical conditioning of every human existence, the plurality of histories, and, consequently, the cultural relativity of all visions of reality. In the estimation of South American eschatologies, such revelations will rock the world to its foundations. "Now [Western man will] discover himself on the same level with every other man, that is to say, conditioned by the unconscious as well as by history — no longer the unique creator of a high culture, no longer the master of the world, and culturally menaced by extinction."[552]

South American eschatologies are not provincial visions but ecumenical positions. They not only predict their own end but promise the demise of Western dominance as well. South American peoples recognize that their reality ends as it becomes legible in terms of modern political history. To subject a culture to rigorous historical or scientific treatment implies that its creativity can be circumscribed objectively and totally accounted for in terms alien to it. Political, economic, and military readings ignore or annihilate the religious foundations that allowed native cultures creatively to manage the meaning of their experiences. Once alien explanations of sacred realities triumph, by dint of the material force that imposes itself with them, the world founded by supernatural events is finished. But South American visions of the end play host to a deeper irony: the "modern" world constructed of these "readings" is a form of disastrous cataclysm. Readers no longer can contain human existence in time within the symbolic categories that derive from Western history. The *very appearance* of South American cultures within the horizons of universal history condemns to oblivion the civilizations founded on histories that give no creative role to South American significations. From their experience of suffering under Western modernity, native millennialists finger the obscure source of its anxiety. Their eschatological visions expose to full view the shrouded premonition that its world is ending and its civilization passing away. Messiahs and prophets revile the signs of corruption (uncritical acceptance of foreign foods, dress, behavior, authorities, rights to land, money). They reject symbolic life as it stands and denounce the Western view of history in favor of a different evaluation of existence in time. They invoke the end in order to prove "history" wrong by calling down the judgment of a renewed experience of time in the form of paradise, apocalypse, or neotraditional utopia.[553]

The end of the world benefits the cosmos and the saved, but the new age is not a perfect return to the primordium. The existence of the cosmos and human history makes that return impossible and undesirable; the primordium could not withstand change. The new world bears the consequences of the prior existence of the primordium and of the cosmic epoch. It combines the best of both worlds. In all the millennial movements, for example, the earth is a primordial instrument of change as well as a cosmic object affected by alteration. Juan Santos, the Campa messiah and son of God, promised that mountains would fall so that landslides would exterminate nonbelievers.[554] In the Andes, the dark night of the seed in Mother Earth makes possible the end of the world. The seed, in the image of Atahualpa's head, lies buried and hidden. The time of its decomposition in the earth is the long and torturous hiatus of colonial existence. However, the earth is always more than an agent of total destruction. She is a sign of its effects.[555] The earth may be mystically flattened, the differentiations of the landscape burned or flooded away and the physical universe thereby transformed into a mythic geography. Equalized in every quarter, the earth becomes a powerful image of the new kind of life to come, including a new social existence. All forms of surviving life obtain equal access to its plenteous vitality.

Eschatological ordeals and stylized performance transform human beings by allowing them to assume the mythic stature and heroic destiny formerly achieved by only a few after death. The initiatory experience of the end of the world subjects them, in their living bodies, to the transformative process suffered by supernatural beings and primordial ancestors. Human beings, however, are constituted by the signs of cosmic time and space; they were born to change. Their presence in the new world makes the eschatological paradise a markedly different existence than the primordial one. The sustaining presence of humans — symbolic, ritual beings — in the new world holds promise. The new humanity retains its symbolic expressions (such as dance and food) but frees itself from the constraints of differential space and time (such as exhaustion, lumbering body-weight, the long cycle of agricultural labor). The transformed religious imagination of humankind encounters everywhere the qualities of being formerly contained at the symbolic center of the cosmos. The cycle of festivals never ends. Drinking, dining, and entertainment escape the periodic rhythms of surfeit and depletion. The qualities symbolized in the cosmic mountain endure even though it is razed, eliminating all need for arduous ascent. When mountains fall, their sacrality spills across the flattened, darkened, or silent earth. The eschatological condition renews itself at every instant. This is the great contribution of symbolic being to the sacred world it now fully enters. There is no need for further periodic destruction. Historic being has not been for nought: the end transforms the *matter* of history and preserves, in transfigured forms, its significant achievement of having suffered change. The new mythical geography, which participates eternally in the transitional condition of immortal human beings, is the final age, a ceaseless feast, a world without end.

CHAPTER 9

SUMMARY CONCLUSIONS

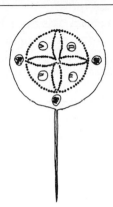

This chapter gathers generalizations from the preceding reflections on South American religious life. Although these summary conclusions at first were inferences drawn from specific cases, and must be reviewed in that light, they now stand as hypotheses about the nature and categories of religion, myth, and symbol, space, time, authority, and death. Thus exiled from South American worldviews, these assessments need new homes; they merit application, as analytic terms, to the study of particular religious traditions and, as edifying concepts, to the constructive task of understanding the general history of religions.

COSMOGONY AND BEGINNING

The order and integrity of religious life take their cue from the imaginary structures displayed in myth. In the imaginal condition, structures of the sacred appear before human awareness as fundamental to existence and as primordial. The first manifestation of these first-order realities discloses their meaningful nature. The experience of a beginning founds the imagination, for the context of beginning makes apparent those imagical qualities that remain determinative influences in culture. Creation myths reveal the passage from nothing to something and the transformation of time and matter into newly ordered forms. Displaying the greatest contrasts in modes of being (even describing the passage from nothingness to extant being), cosmogonies make change recognizable and ground the capacity for reflection on its meaning. The absolute (total darkness, chaotic waters, formless states, divine breath, or preconsciousness of the supreme being) signals the barely imaginable quality of unconditioned being from which all images flow as a spontaneous revelation.

Beginnings are the indispensable prehistory that reveals the meanings of the creative propensities of symbolic life. Myths of creation from nothing, for example, carry human experience back to the brink of sublimity. A mystery of unfathomable nothingness opens up behind every appearance of singular being that emerges from the unknown.

The meaning of nonreferential existence becomes manifest, in a paradoxical way, through the multivocal and ironic symbolism of absolute beginnings: nothingness, chaos, indivisibility, the immediacy of the changeless sky, and the ambivalence of the supreme being, who, though relatively inactive, instigated the entire process of creation. Supreme beings offer a glimpse of the most sublime end of the spectrum of religious forms, the most remote and intangible of primordial powers, and represent the experience of being that most fully transcends the ordinary realm of the senses. To that extent, myths of supreme beings comment instructively on the nature of creativity and on the subtlest possibilities of the religious imagination. The sub-limen of the religious imagination surfaces in the many different forms of supreme being across South America. To make matters more interesting still, South American notions of supreme being, unlike the conscious direction of mainline Western theologies, creatively absorb and reimagine the forms brought from abroad in the course of colonial history. Imagining the absolute beginnings of reality—as ambivalent supreme being or as chaos—sets the cultural process in motion; the extraordinary forces of imagination, made apparent in myth, ripple through the cosmos in the form of the social, economic, political and aesthetic orders.

Most South American creation myths do not begin with a state of absolute nothingness but rather with some prime matter or state of affairs that suffers transformation in the course of "creation." These myths of transformation account for a world where everything is subject to metamorphosis and redefinition. Creation myths make clear the meaning of the world's appearance and the reasons why that meaning is no longer fully apparent. Myth's reality is not grounded in descriptions of the self-evident world that a people now inhabits but on myth's participation in the world of the beginnings. The beginning of reality is a quality of being which is no longer manifest. The real world of meaning, to which all apparent signifiers now point, has disappeared: the mythic farewell of divine beings, heroes, and ancestors engenders imagery that points to primordial, but absent, meaning. The way primordial being absents itself generates the specific features of symbolic and cultural life. Meaning is the omnipresent but always problematic context of existence.

The passion of primordial transformers, the way they suffer existence, indelibly marks the colors, shapes, smells, sounds, languages, and relations of this world. The deaths of heroes and ancestors give rise to botanical taxonomies; to species of birds, marked by mystical blood, excrement, and ash; to orchestrations of festival music; and to patterns of decoration. The immediacy and unreplicability of primordial beings yields to the symbolic strategies that, by miming the adventures and demise of sacred beings, produce and reproduce the cultural, political, social, and economic orders.

The mythic age accounts for the indirection of symbolic life and the present world's distance from reality's sources. Because primordial beings were all that they appeared to be, they were, literally, insignificant. That primordial world of full manifestation and direct relations (exhibited in the incest and voracity of mythic beings) came to an end, however. The bracketing of the mythic age is epitomized by the enveloping structures of the cosmos: the hoisted sky, the periphery as a cosmic house or village-enclosure, the cardinal directions oriented toward the center. The new sky is not only remote and apprehensible as a symbol, but it is peopled with heavenly bodies (sun, moon, stars) that regulate time and space. The cosmogonic preoccupation with hoisting the sky or raising the roof of the first cosmic space emphasizes the urgent need for transcendence, the religious quality of imagination, which upholds the distance between one kind of being and another and makes symbolic life possible. The recognition that separate forms represent fundamentally different modes of being with different meanings is founded upon the possibility of transcendence. Toward that end, myths dramatize the hoisting of the sky and the withdrawal of primordial beings into other, inaccessible realms.

Transformations of this sort construct the cosmos and the vehicles of salvation that help the world survive the destructive tendencies of creative change. When change insinuates itself into a totally apparent world, complete crisis results. Any change in a world of totally manifest meaning must mean total change. The passage from the primordium to the cosmos is depicted as a fall, a deluge, or a conflagration: a catastrophe that leaves only vestiges of the previous world. With the symbolic remnants of the first world the order of a cosmos that tolerates change is construed. Symbolic life appears in the guise of wrappings, enclosures, starry heaven, houses, gateways, clothing, and disguises.

DESTRUCTION AND AGES OF THE WORLD

Symbolic life, based on transcendence, is linked to the experience of awe, and symbolic knowledge to the awesome awareness that the creaturely forms of this world (including forms of human knowledge) are not the only ways of being present. There also exist primordial modes of being, whose full presences transcend this world and whose reappearances would destroy it once again. Furthermore, the destruction of whole universes, replete with their own populations and relationships, witnesses to the power of the religious imagination to transcend any single perspective on reality. The systematization of calamities and multiple epochs leads to a hermeneutics of history (an evaluation of existence in time) based upon discernment of the impact of different modes of time on one another rather than on the chronological unfolding of events. Coming to grips with the meaning of history—interpreting the interpretations of multiple kinds of time—requires the capacity to sort out the complex experience of time that characterizes human culture. The hermeneutics of culture must necessarily be the interpretation of history.

Because each source of a temporal quality (sun, moon, stars, rains) was destroyed in the past, each of these temporal measures has a termination point or a remarkable rhythm based on its punctuating disappearance or absence. The multiple accounts of mythic disasters convey their own message: total disaster is a manifestation of sacred being, and, because primordial devastation is a total event, it can never be wholly accounted for. Its origins are inexhaustible and continue to appear in new mythic variants as well as in the failures of daily life. The inability of any single narrative to exhaustively account for the cosmic destruction suggests an existential dissatisfaction with what is singular and absolute. The myths are reworked and modified; their multiple variants bespeak the interminable need to mull over the events of creation, interpreting them in new ways. The variety of catastrophic myths reveals the uncomfortable but creative situation of human cultures as they confront sacred realities. Recognizing more than one modality of being (celestial or earthy; male or female; proximate or distant; contained or boundless), inevitably leads to crisis. When the symbolic connection or disjunction between them is severed, distinctive qualities of being disappear in a chaotic flood of im-mediacy. The violent transition generates the multiple episodes of reproductive life, a new life obtained by forfeiting immediate relations with old life forms or powers.

Since the deluge effects the passage (between one mode of being and another) it signifies, flood imagery frequently appears during the transition from one age to another, whether cosmic epochs, annual seasons, or stages of the individual life-cycle. First rains, initiatory baths or drinking bouts, the flooding of the womb with semen, the flow of menstrual blood or embryonic fluids—all these inundations periodically mark off the passing of time. Myths of the flood dramatize the real threat of indistinction between forms. Distinctions are regenerated in the passages that symbolic life constitutes: transitions, orifices, the sounds of speech and music. The transitions that overcome the flood of indistinction are represented most blatantly in the images of the cosmic mountain or tree or of canoes or clay vessels, in chants or recited incantations, and in other symbolic vehicles that allow culture to rise above the indistinctions that course below symbolic existence.

Why are there multiple creations interrupted by influxes of cosmic destruction? Why do myths record successive catastrophes? Rather than provide answers to these questions, myths justify the questions. Periodic universal cataclysms disclose a dissatisfaction, rooted in the primordium itself, with any being that appears exhaustive, total or absolute. Though eternal and indestructible, primordial realities are ultimately questionable, and, through the images of cosmic crisis (flood, fire, petrification, occultation of the first universe), primordial realities are made subject to critical thought.

Myths of catastrophe, the most dramatic and widespread myths in South America, furnish South American cultures with imagery and language with which to critique the status of absolute being and meaning. The imagery of disaster proves essential to apprehending all instances of breakthrough. Only through the symbolism of disaster can one come to grips with a completely new mode of being. The myths of catastrophe exhibit the violence of novelty and change — a violence that propels the creativity of symbolic existence and religious experience.

The cosmic fire demonstrates the susceptibility of matter to total spiritualization, the ethereal condition of primordial matter, which is all-consumed and all-consuming. The cosmic fire takes life and form from what it consumes and brings the meaning of sustenance to the new world. Its consumption by fire opened the primordial world to the possibility of extinction. Fire and the theme of openness are linked in myths in which fire is stolen from the belly of a monster whose jaws open or whose belly is ripped open. An instrument of consumption, the mouth "contains" fire (raging appetite, inflammatory ritual speech or curses, and so on) when it is properly controlled. Sound may be a symptom of openness and may be associated with the consumption of cosmic fire. Control over sound, either by observing silence or by making deliberate noise, curbs the total appetite of primordial consumption. Control over other forms of openness associated with body orifices (eyes, anus, nostrils) also restrains the destruction wrought by uncontrolled openness.

That all modes of being are combustible and comestible (a fact amply demonstrated in the myths of conflagration) creates the need for new kinds of time able to stagger the appearance and disappearance of species of being and to protect them from simultaneous extinction through total consumption. Each bodily opening and each source of passage associated with primal fire unleashes a new mode of time. From the time of the catastrophe on, the opening and closing of orifices and moments of passage must be closely regulated and intercalibrated in order to sustain life in this world.

The cosmic fire frequently accounts for the origins of fleshly body forms, the instruments and objects of consumption. Species-specific body markings and new generations of offspring begin with the total, simultaneous manifestation of all consumptive processes in the cosmic fire. In order to generate and sustain the reproductive units of cosmic and cultural life, the fire is divided into partial appearances: sun, hearth, burning fields, cooking fire, kiln, the heat of sexual life and of gestation, the fire that warms the blood, the fire of festivals and of ritual cigars, the body-markings of animals, the body-paint of humans, the periodic hunger of bodily appetite, and the fever of consumptive disease. These processes of partial consumption effect the transformations that make existence dynamic. Their partialness forestalls the total obliteration of existence that occurred during the cosmic conflagration. After the cosmic fire, all subsequent existence is an orderly way of perpetuating the process of spiritualization and of keeping alive the insatiable appetite for other modes of being.

Each of the primordial states of affairs that brings on destruction exhibits a specific image of infinity. Foremost among these images are ones of ferocious arrogance and voracity, eternal light, uncontained darkness, ceaseless rain, unregulated speech, unimpeded promiscuity or disobedience, pandemoniacal din, uncontrolled eavesdropping or peeping curiosity, and indivisibility. All these unbounded or unguarded conditions transcend or ignore limits, and life without limits was a prelude to disaster. Each absolute manifestation demanded infinite expression, but the infinity of primordial being, in multiple modes, could only appear as chaos. The appearance of more than one kind of unbounded being signaled disaster. Infinity, the absence of any limit, became the manifest need for termination, if only to make clear the everlasting meaning of transcendence. Unless new, intermediate expressions appeared and unless true change came into being, transcendent and imminent forms of being exhausted all their possibilities in their very appearance.

The plenipotential beings of the primordium embodied a paradox: although they were full of meaning (full of themselves) and are the precondition for significance, primordial realities remained insignificant. Each primordial reality was all that it appeared to be, an exhaustive expression of its own mode of being. It could neither point beyond itself nor stand as the outward sign of something else. Thus conditioned only by itself, it could generate no significant order of signs, consumptions, or reproductive body forms. Neither could it sustain life through replication or change. This nonsymbolic world had to end in order to make room for the universe in which nothing is beyond symbolic expression and where everything is significant.

Because the significant orders of the cosmos arise from primordial destruction, the world exhibits clear signs of catastrophe. The significant orders of the new world arise from sacrifice, acts of dispatch that cast mundane realities in images of the sacred. The primordial sacrifices that dismissed the first mythic beings help image the conquest of chaos and indistinction. The sites where the deaths occurred or where they are reenacted stand out above others. Destruction leaves indelible marks where being passes from one mode of manifestation to another. What in the primordial age was unique has suffered division. The fractured and periodic state of space and time that human beings inhabit forces them to order their life by imitating the dismissal or demise of the primordial characters.

To sustain itself, symbolic life becomes a sacrificial existence predicated on the acts and images that make life sacred. These signs of change condition the new world of significance, memory, and symbol by scattering eternity and infinity across periodic spaces and times and across the ordered divisions of species, whose reproductive cycles measure off abundant life in this world. By imitating the sacrificial acts that dispatched the primordium and by symbolically recreating those sacrificial places and times, cultures discern the orders of geographic space, pastoral movement, calendric time, animal taxonomy, and social hierarchy. In this way, sacrifice, the climactic exit of primordial beings, effects and conditions the specific colors, smells, shapes, tastes, sizes, sounds, and textures — that is, the appearance — of this world.

The disappearance of absolute beings makes other forms holy. Partial signs indicate the presence of primordial realities in the new world. The destruction of the primordium amounts to the sacrifice (from Lat., *sacer facere*, "to make holy") of insignificance. The religious imagination becomes a sacrificial mode of existence that lends new forms of ordered expression to meaning and power: food chain, cycle of prey, the astronomic procession of the Milky Way, the hierarchy of political offices, the strings of sounds in language, and so on. These new forms of experience and knowledge are intelligible because they are grasped as expressions of sacrifice, the imaginal process that makes them sacred. They are seen as partial, serial, staggered, and symbolic appearances of a meaning fully present at the beginning.

Division, the key mark of catastrophe, impresses its stamp on the cosmos. All primordial reality suffers division so that the consumptive, divisive, and destructive aspects of social and individual life come into being in the form of cuisine, the social divisions of labor, linguistic phonemes, and sexual oppositions. The serial deaths of this world can be ordered and made comprehensible by referring them to the total destructions reported in myth. When they are seen as partial and relative reflections of the great demise of primordial being, they become symbols of a real and sacred event. Here lies the religious foundation of the staggered deaths that constitute the food chain, the cycles of prey, feuding, war, and ritual sacrifice.

All significant orders of the cosmos cohere because they spring from the same universal catastrophe (or set of catastrophes). Symbols point to one another's meaning because each reveals a glimpse of the first mythical reality, the fabulously indistinguishable world of absolute manifestation. Thus, classificatory schemes interdepend and can be analyzed in terms of one another in a manner similar to the way in which the interlocking codes of a single symbolic system might be approached by a structuralist. Since symbolic divisions of classificatory schemes arise from the deluge or fire that forms the great divide, separate taxonomic orders imply one another and suggest that their relationship to one another exists within a whole (defined as something that has had an end put to it). The myths of the primordial world reveal the meaning of that whole and supply the imagery through which it may be apprehended. The breakdown of that imagery and the transformation of primordial realities into the animals of the food chain, spirits, and the components of the human personality make possible the beginning of human history.

Memory, the symbolic repetition or continued repatterning of images from a closed primordial age, makes for historical existence, the self-conscious evaluation that one lives in reflected conditions of time. Self-consciousness and reflection are traits that arise from the nature of the time that humans inhabit: disrupted, symbolic, ordered, periodic, and recurrent. Historical order, like the astronomic and gastronomic cycles, becomes a means of sustenance. Through historical experience, the primordial world becomes recuperable in the fragmentary events of societal epochs and the episodes of the personal life-cycle. The symbolic devices of lineage, sociopolitical order, and division of subsistence and ritual labor periodically subject culture to the absent meanings that are sources of renewal. Historical existence, the cumulative recovery of the experiential knowledge of primordial being, becomes the distinguishing mark of human life. Arising from disaster, the images of historical time signify and sustain a tragic moment of existence that at the same time holds open the hopeful expectation that history will end.

Myths tend to be self-destructive in the sense that their descriptions climax in the passing of the mythic epoch. The end of mythic narrative conveys the goal of myths of extermination: the disappearance of eternity, which leaves the contemporary world pocked with paradox so that death becomes a transition from one life form to another. The paradox of periodic time is that it begins with an ending. Historical existence imposes on human beings the burden of having ceaselessly to decipher a universe in which symbolic conveyances of meaning complicate the process of understanding either by pointing to a range of contradictory significations or by obscuring any clear vision of meaning at all. The cosmos, arisen from crisis, and the human being at its center live out a critical condition. In order to survive, human beings must discover the meaning of incessant change — in the weather, crop cycles, dream life, memory, performances of myth, celebrations of history, quirks of human personality, the infinite generativity of new sentences in a language, symptoms of sickness, and the appearance of new generations. Each appearance can signify many things, the meaning of any single sign can be lost in the chaos of change. Interpretation becomes a state of creative puzzlement in which new and shifting cosmologies are constructed from changing images.

By bringing an end to the unbounded conditions of the primordium, the signs of destruction make all existence re-markable with those same catastrophic symptoms. All life, therefore, is terminable, moving toward a determined end consonant with its meaning. Symbols continue to reveal the meaning whose appearances once created, and now order, the universe. The sacrifice of primordial appearance gives rise to the symbols that make life holy, ambiguous, paradoxical, and significant.

The fragments of the primordial age are rarely equal. They appear, for example, as fractured qualities of light of dissimilar intensity, such as the sun, moon, stars, colored body-paints, and feathers. These give rise to unequal units of time: the solar year, the lunar phases, the astral cycles, and the festival periods marked by distinct seasonal costumes. The orders of inequality that appear after the destruction of the world create hierarchies, the ordered but catastrophic results of violence and tragedy. Hierarchical orders prolong the tragedy of postprimordial existence through the uneven distribution of sacrality, power, and clarity of meaning.

Symbolic existence is the result of the violence and negativity effecting all creation. The crimes carried out by or against primordial beings become the grounds for discrimination, discretion, decrees, and the criteria of order and judgment. The devastation of the primordium creates the possibility of apprehension, in all its senses — understanding, dread, and arrestment. The imagery of primordial crisis furnished South American cultures a foundation for critical thought and for a critical existence that faced change, welcomed renovation, and instigated innovation as part of the religious responsibility for continued creation.

SPACE

Every form of existence is involved with the space appropriate to its nature in such a way that the two realities reveal one another. Spatial expressions make the universe structured, knowable, and viable for a variety of life forms. The universe in which South American cultures dwell usually consists of a number of significant levels, which contain different kinds of beings with different arrangements of relations. The distinctness of separate worlds of imaginable being becomes a spatial expression of the profound spiritual challenge that lies at the heart of human existence: the religious imagination undoes itself in the rich exercise of its powers. The symbolism that offers access to transcendent spheres of experience also functions to separate those worlds from the mundane world. This fragility of communication among cosmic realms and modes of experience becomes symbolized in the myths that described the destruction of the *axis mundi* (the felling of the world-tree, the cutting of the sky-rope, or the severing of a celestial vine). To unify all imaginable existences, the labor of the mythic imagination, which creates a universe, must give constant attention to the full range of symbolic possibilities. The unity of being is able to be entertained because experience of separate kinds of beings is always grasped symbolically, that is, through the meanings they signify. On the other hand, symbolic life generates separation and distinction, for no single symbolic expression exhaustively reveals its own meaning, and as the significance of the sacred changes aspect so also do perceptions of space shift over time.

The heavenly or upper world is unique, for it is inhabited by unreplicable beings who are one of a kind. These primordial beings are not only the first of their kind; their form at any given moment of their appearance is the full manifestation of their complete essence. They have no need to grow or change to reveal the full content of their being. That is why the upperworld nearly transcends imaginable qualities. It is without precedent or analogy; indivisible, infinite, eternal. The upper realm expresses the conditions of existence that prevailed when being was manifest in only one kind of place and time, the primordial world. When unreplicable being reveals itself fully, as it does as soon as it appears, its function is exhausted. The meaning of its appearance may be inexhaustible, but the form of its appearance can only be repeated without change. The beings of the celestial realm possess a mode of activity that is difficult to distinguish from stasis. It is hard to differentiate the inclusion of all creative possibilities in the upper realm from infertile void.

When images or tokens of heavenly realities appear subject to this world's conditions of earthly space (in such manifest forms as light or liquid), they express themselves as fertile forms. Channeled into the symbolic spaces of this world through astronomic movements, seasonal rains, and periodic rituals, the celestial flows of semen or blood become the fertile rains, rivers, garden crops, and lineages or residence-groups with their foods, dreams, and fermented brews. In ritual, art, and technology (e.g., irrigation, beverage brewing, cooking, and the use of hallucinogens), human beings experiment with the unique, heavenly light and liquid, subjecting them to the generative conditions of this world-plane, where multiple forms of reproductive life thrive. Intimate contact with and knowledge of heavenly light or liquid in this world, however, offer more than the promise of generative abundance on this earthly plane. These experiences of light and liquid are tantamount to initiations, altering the meaning of earthly senses and so preparing the initiand for a transported, transcendent, or renewed experience of the world in a new spatial dimension of meaning. The "death" of drunken visions or the blindness brought on by mystical sight provide glimpses of the infinite light or fluid wisdom of another realm to which humans, as symbolic beings, can gain entrance.

Unlike the lightness that aids one in entering the upperworld, access to the lower realms of the universe demands weight. Appetite and the resulting bulk of accumulating weight frequently account for the underworld's inferior position in the cosmos: it fell to its current position during primordial times; insatiable or cannibalistic monsters reside there. The underworld anchors the universe and gives it the force of gravity. Matter tends to descend into its maw. The underworld is subject to its own conditions of time and, for that reason, can never perfectly mirror the conditions of this world.

Human existence occupies the ambiguous center, the middle layer of the universe. Human life (symbolic being) sets things apart into separate modes of being by situating itself ambiguously between one reality and another. By coming to know something of these others, human being constitutes its own specific difference. Human life is the locus, for example, of genuine food and the means of its cultivation and preparation. The earth of human existence is the place of consumption, of incomplete fragments that require puzzling and piecing together, and of space that is carefully arranged to accommodate change in the central world. Puzzling transformations create the possibility of multivalent symbolic links among all conditions of being, including contact with sacred realities that are no longer fully manifest. Contact with supernatural beings is made through the indirection of image and representation.

The different kinds of space in the universe and the statuses of being within them are systematically associated with and dissociated from one another to constitute a whole universe. Disjunction and conjunction become conceptual processes fundamental to the formation of separate spaces and, for that matter, of all separate categories of thought. The knowledge and experience concomitant to ordering and constructing space highlight the role of religious imagination in grasping the distinctness of particular qualities of being in the form of spaces, colors, fluids, metals, or animals. All these distinct forms are related by their original appearance at the center of space in mythic time. As the center becomes the paradoxical locus of the processes of conjunction and disjunction, the manner of appearance and disappearance at the center becomes the main clue in piecing together the puzzle of spatial existence in ritual, dream, songs, labor, and growth through the life-cycle.

Since human beings occupy the center of existence—a position first achieved by primordial beings, who serve as models (or cautionary counter-exemplars) for human behavior—it is encumbent on them to maintain the systematic processes of culture, whether ritual, medical, economic, aesthetic, or political. In the experience of finding and traversing cosmic space through the arduous spiritual ascent of a cosmic mountain, vine, tree, rope, cross, or vessel, human beings draw into a single experience the multiple domains of imaginable being. As symbolic beings *par excellence*, human beings represent the communication between realms of the cosmos, and they center themselves through images of an *axis mundi*. The tendency to replicate images of the *axis mundi* on the multiple spatial scales of cosmos, village, house, ritual arena, body, artistic design, musical instrument, and personal adornment sets every level of space apart from the unimaginable chaos that lies beyond, behind, or outside the universe. At every mundane level, human life maintains vital contact with the reality that manifests itself fully at the center. Moreover, the myths that relate the chopping, slicing, fracturing, or destruction of the *axis mundi* underline the idea that this instrument, which unites all multiple forms of being, is actually a quality of religious experience achieved in the religious imagination. This conjunction of different qualities of being in a unique experience becomes the unifying heart of existence, the center from which the reality of the universe derives.

The relationship of the center to the periphery gives the universe dynamism. The waters or poisons located in the central lake or tree trunk often surround the earth's disk and form its outermost boundary. In other cases, center and periphery are drawn into relationship through astronomic observations and rites that periodically reestablish the relationship of the center to the horizon or of the center to the zenith or nadir. The points on the horizon are not absolute markers but relative ones: the stuff of reflection and introspection, they reveal the meaning of irony and contradiction, as do all boundaries and limits. By contrast, links between places disclose the nature of dynamism, fertility, and consumption and, through the media of ancestors, liquids, ritual movements, and sound, display these effective powers in ways worthy of reflection.

TIME

The dynamism of space—the traffic from one space to another—has temporal consequences. Since time is the way human beings understand their proper place in a world of heterogeneous spaces, temporal existence reflects the complexity of human experience. Marked units of time, such as season, year, month, week, and the day its divisions, bespeak different qualities of time, whose proper meanings, based on sacred realities, become the foundation for evaluating life in the world. The distinctness of times creates an order of variable values in the cosmos, in society, and in the formation of the individual. Each time calls for a response appropriate to its character. The distinction that most sharply marks off one quality of time from another is that between the mythic conditions of being and the periodic kinds of time that flow from the calamities that brought the primordium to a close. For all their distinctiveness, periodic time and mythic time may be linked through the ritual symbolism that reenacts the beginnings, the time before time lines and cycles definitively separated from one another.

A return to the time of unitive being makes the integrity of time imaginable and available to human experience. The religious experience of ritual time becomes normative for aesthetic, intellectual, and moral life because it situates the human imagination within the fullness of time, culturally conceived. It places human experience into conditions where "is" reunites with "ought," freedom exists with history, justice with peace, beauty with truth, and truth with human action. The merging of differential times often takes on a sexual valence, a ritual return to the forbidden unity of all temporal being once effected in, say, the incestuous union of brother sun and sister moon. Ever since that tragic union, the punctuations basic to the temporal rhythms of cosmos and culture (death, destruction, wilting, eclipse, disappearance, the striking-noises of instruments, the movements of dance) have intervened. The first appearance of such markers intruded upon the *status quo entis* and inserted a new condition of existence into the world. Myth is essential to any understanding of the meaning of time because myth describes the events (appearances, withdrawals, transformations) that first punctuated time.

Cycles exemplify the temporal structures that bridge the divide between mythic and periodic existence. Cycles respect the permanent character of mythic being because they eternally return to key recognizable moments (the first flowering of a calendrical fruit-tree, the new moon, the new year). Yet cycles reveal the transient nature of a world that passes through one state after another. Cycles are the produce of the encounter between two unlike temporal modes: earthly transition and mythic fullness. As symbolic instruments, they preserve the best of these two worlds, which can never accommodate one another completely.

Through the structure of the cycle, the dominant symbols of the primordium surrender their singularity and submit to the transitory structures of recurrent existential time. They alternate between appearance and occultation so that a symbol's presence is coextensive with the time proper to it. In this way, every symbol calls its peculiar temporal meaning into cyclic existence and the programmed interweaving of various cycles of time approximates cosmic perfection. Cycles of stars, sounds, fruits, flowers, fragrances, consumption, and decay consist of different moments of time that individually offer access to the primordial modes of being they signify. Hence nothing is lost even though the primordium has passed away. Hence ritual actors become the medium for the merging of qualities of time: through their knowledge and ritual acts, the mythic past reveals the meaning of the present. Each cycle has its own mythic story, unveiling the meaning of the past events whose effects have become the inescapable destiny of the present.

Astral cycles, for example, rhythmically define the cadence of fate. While they foster a sense of security and predictability, their origin myths also account for the unfolding of ironic tragedy. The gradients of celestial light illustrate the varying degrees of darkness to which unmanifest primordial light has become subject. In a world where no form can be totally apparent, the recurrent cycle of stars signals the meaning of abundant life through occasional death. In the same way, sounds become the foundation of recurrent cycles, for no sound in this world is uninterrupted. Sound-specific times are consonant with the sounds that signify them. The sonic cycles that structure the universe force one to recognize that the world is a symphony of powerful and dynamic presences.

Each cycle embraces contradictory states of being, which are distributed in time, allowing mutually exclusive states to coexist in an integral experience. Hunger and satiety and their intermediate moments create the alimentary cycle; ripening and rotting signal the cycle of fruit; birth and death frame the life-cycle of an individual. A cycle requires the recognition that the "same time" has reappeared. Cyclic ceremonies retrieve and relive the meaning of all the human experiences of that "same time" and allow human beings to appraise their existence in a critical and reflective way. The very cycle that ensures continual return to the origins of a given quality of time also induces the realization that one cannot ever return to it fully. Every cycle depends on the recognition of the significance of crisis—that is, of an apparent break in the flow of time. The reflective exercise becomes a critique of one's existence in time and ensures that human nature is cyclical because it encompasses contradictory states of being. The recognition of cycles, an act wrapped up with the very meaning of time, grounds the human condition.

In the constant return to meanings that appeared in the mythic beginnings but that can only be approximated in an ironic way through the cycles of symbolic existence, truth becomes a central human question. The symbolic capacity of human existence makes the relationship of the cosmos to the mythic primordium the central question of truth and explains why mythic time has a privileged role in establishing the foundations of culture, a mode of human existence predicated on verisimilitude and understanding.

Because calendars respect the multiplexity of human experience, their intricate devices are geared to prevent the hegemony of any single quality of time. Although they take their cue from the presence of supernatural realities, they also fend off the unbroken presence of divinities by celebrating their disappearance. By marking moments of closure on specific kinds of sacrality, sacred calendars clear the way for the time of human culture. Calendars reflect the multiple realities that have appeared in the mythic period, at its demise, and in subsequent history. Founded upon mythic events, the calendar of sacred feasts nourishes cultural life with experiences of the real and full. Feast by feast, the calendar reenacts the episodes that created fruitful and consumptive existence. That is why observance of the ritual calendar maintains life in a creative, abundant, and ordered fashion. The symbolic acts that mark time base themselves upon the sacred events that established new temporal orders. Rite and myth become the responsible ways of reacting to symbolic existence, for they maintain critical and reflective awareness of the sacred realities whose first appearances transformed existence in time. The symbolism of those apparitions generates imaginary connections, calendric interweavings of the world's delicate movements. Mythic plot, story line, episode, ritual drama, art, and labor are human acts within a calendrical web of significant interconnections and thus carry cosmic consequences.

Each event or appearance in the mythic world makes time for a new mode of being to which cultures must react creatively. The calendar of feasts coordinates the most significant human reactions into a system, a world. That is, cultures must recall and transmit meanings in the creative manner befitting meaning's sacred character. Even as they keep the experience of the world intact, calendars experiment with sacred realities and redesign the meaning of the universe. Festival calendars are predicated on destruction and disappearance. Dance ornaments, ceremonial space, ritual competition, chaotic noise, song, fire, drink, and ceremonial darkness can refer to the moments of cosmic destruction, the catastrophic foundations of calendric feasts. For example, festivals frequently allude to the sacrifices of primordial beings, whose deaths brought order to life in the world. Such destructions and disappearances signal the end of an episode and become turning points toward new stretches of time. To produce a calendar, cycles conjugate and interlock precisely at the point where each cycle dissolves, a moment that alludes to the great chaos that undid the primordial world. The calendar explores the breaks in every plane of time and logic and thus opens experience to multiple dimensions of time so that the infinitesimal life-moments of an individual human being synchronize with the nearly infinite movements of the outermost cosmos.

One should not exaggerate the astronomic character of calendars. Economic, political, and social units, together with their locations, sounds, and ritual activities, also become coordinates of the calendar, for each unit manifests a distinct quality of time. Myth elevates all these symbolic orders to the rank of determinative realities by providing the fundamental language of spatial meaning and rank order, the marks that evaluate existence in time. Myth describes the original appearance and disappearance of beings associated with particular spaces, genealogies, or politico-economic processes. The power of such sacred events reveals the connections among distinct qualities of time. Joined together in the calendar, these interlocking cycles (solar, lunar, wet and dry season; flower cycles, songs, sounds, the human life-cycle; emotions and colors) express the dialectical relations among differential qualities of existence. Thus, through the calendar, humans live more than one kind of existence. This full experience of being, a serial rotation of alternating, overlapping cycles and temporal moods, accounts for the dynamism and creativity of culture.

The appearance and disappearance of the ephemeral states of being we call emotions also establish cycles. Prescribed festive emotions, such as euphoria, fear, nostalgia, or fury, immerse the community in specific qualities of time and become norms for the evaluation of existence. Emotionalism becomes essential to self-critical moral life. Music and dance are the most striking calendric devices for achieving a full experience of being. Festival music and dance are time-factored arrangements that not only accompany moments of the calendar but actually orchestrate the passage of time. Music returns the community to the conditions that obtained during primordial comings and goings; dance makes primordial movements remarkable. These symbolic performances bring cosmic and social time into alignment with primordial conditions. Too, the manner of musical production becomes a model for social organization and cultural activity. Musical performance organizes the human body and orchestrates symbolic structures, emotions, rhythms, groups of musicians, and audiences. Music and dance often achieve and symbolize the transition into a different state of being first made evident in myth. Through song or instrumental performance, one sings or plays that primordial condition into being once again.

The enchanting music of festivals carries a double valence. It once disrupted the primordium and introduced change; now, however, it returns human beings to moments that are eternally the same. In both instances, sacred music has a disruptive character. It violates the mundane experience of time and reorients experience toward the mythical past, giving evidence of the same destructive capacity that undid the primordium when realities first broke into song or withdrew from the world and left music or sound behind as a vestige of their passing. Because the cutting capacity of music and sound opens the spatial world to the times of abundant life, festival music and revelry render the earth fruitful and multiplicative. Sound penetrates every "womb" of the universe and activates the reproduction of all species of plants and animals.

In festival dance, the human body is transformed into an instrument of calendric time. Festival dances frequently reenact moments of destruction and the violence of change. Body parts, rearranged and moved through space, posture and signal the myriad qualities of time that form the matrix of cosmic life. Because they are calendrical, festive dances exhibit a wealth of religious meaning, evident in the choreography, the participants' order of appearance, dance style, the different roles and movements of the sexes, the type of musical accompaniment and the instruments used, performance times, place, pace, order of dances, costume fabrics, language employed, ornaments, significance of space on the dance floor, and so on. The entire complex of materials, gestures, and sounds composes the significant symbol that is musical dance. Taken together, the powerful dance-signs create a complex species of time: the festival calendar—that is, the time of human culture.

Symbolic existence cultivates the human capacity to see nature and history as signs of sacred life and not just as simple representations of themselves. The ability to look beyond, to understand time symbolically, enables cultures to pull the separate movements and conditions of existence into fruitful relationship with one another. Through festival dance, music, instruments, adornments, motions, foods, and songs, human beings coerce the entire cast of sacred realities to make its symbolic appearance in accord with the performances of human culture.

Sacred dance is not a technocratic response to a moral dilemma. Ritual dance and music are moral and aesthetic answers to the question, How should humans behave in the face of mystery, anomaly, and paradox? One must behave properly and stylishly by scrutinizing and responding to the significance of symbolic experience. The ritual calendar prescribes symbolic experiences that are normative because their meaning has been clearly revealed in their mythic origins. Festive dance and music become moral bench-marks whose symbolic expressions (costumes, movements, emotions) and order help evaluate the more inchoate experiences of mundane time and rational life.

The moral imperatives to dance, to dance in time, and to dance well serve as a reminder that whatever is can only be grasped representationally. That is, reality is literally figured out, or acted out, in this world. Moral life has an aesthetic base. Art must be a forceful enough presentation of what is to compel human existence to conform to what ought to be. By calculating with the stylish figures of dance and music, cultures not only mark off the calendar with feasts but establish guidelines for acting morally throughout one's existence in time. Furthermore, knowledge that mythic events are the proper model for everyday behavior draws all action into the moral sphere and centers quotidian gesture on the paradigmatic acts of mythical beings. Every human move becomes potentially symbolic and sacramental. Community life, insofar as it becomes conscious of these facts—that is, insofar as it becomes powerful and creative—takes on the quality of a performance. Morality is therefore dynamic and based upon the experience of order in motion. Moral life continuously widens the awareness of meaning of a person's everyday acts by evaluating them against those acts that created or destroyed the primordium. When performance is coupled with the full awareness of the meaning of the sacred events that the dancer imitates, song and dance become foundations of moral action.

The human situation is constituted by the recognition of multiple qualities of time. Cultures recognize, adapt to, and manipulate myriad evaluations of temporal existence. Since humans must live in the conjunction of these existential conditions, cultures situate themselves at the center of time, an

achievement of the religious imagination. Because of this religious disposition, human beings are enwreathed within recurrent cycles and human
culture takes its place at the center, between the disappearance and reappearance of all significant realities. The festival calendar parades supernatural beings and fundamental realities, one by one or in coordinated groups,
into the central arena of human culture, the center of time. Thus, mythic
events that interrupted primordial existence continue to intrude upon cosmic life from time to time so that all species of being converge on one
another in the human imagination, where images of destruction play a key
symbolic role in locating the center of time. Sacrifices, offerings, and consumptions reenact the withdrawal of fully manifest primordial beings. For
this reason, sacrifice lies at the heart of the human world and reestablishes
the differentiation of times that is reflected in the calendar.

The temporal complex of cycles, calendars, music, dances, and founding feasts makes sense of festival drinking and violence. Ritual drinking
restages the transformative acts that first marked off time. Drinking festivals
celebrate the origins of separate animal species, whose distinct markings
betoken unique breeding and life-cycles and, in some cases, the unique
patterns of marriage between social groups that are distinguished by their
association with animals as emblems. Temporal cycles are founded on the
rupture, or interruption, of a preexisting temporal condition, the mythic
world. Drinking festivals now celebrate the productive differences between
kinds of people and species. Sometimes, even the plant from which fermented brew is concocted is reported to have emerged from the slain body of
a mythic being. The preparation of drink by crushing or chewing the plant
amounts to sacrifice.

The cosmic catastrophes of cosmic food and primordial darkness provide the backdrop for many drinking festivals. Drink is the reappearance of a
destructive or deadly mode of liquified being, which manifests a unique
temporal condition and marks a cycle of time. Periodic drinking bouts reenact the return of destructive monsters, especially the marine monsters whose
very shape embodies formless chaos. Anomalous and eccentric beings, such
as masters of the forest or of pottery clay, the spirits of the dead, and the souls
of animals, return during drinking festivals. In some cases, the dead are
remembered in a communion through the medium of fermented drink. The
ashen powder of relatives' bones is folded into fermenting brew and consumed. Beer recontextualizes the matter of human death and blends it into
the fruitful and fermenting token of recurrent cosmic time-lines.

Since festivals return the community to a time that is no longer accessible or licit under mundane conditions, the imagery of illicit sex returns the
community to the time before the appearance of the social divisions that
regenerate society and reproduce its values. Festival promiscuity is one such
relaxation of social norms. By ritually abandoning the social norms that
uphold it, society renews itself. The symbolism of incest often becomes the
predominant image for the impossible merging of human being with sacred
being, the transmutation effected in festival performance. The imagery of

incest lets incompatible temporal horizons reconverge within imaginative experience. This explains why words denoting incest are used to describe the metamorphosis that occurs in ritual or during anomalous temporal events such as eclipses of the sun or moon.

The tensions of festival times celebrate the beginnings of change and the excitement of the first rending of differences, which gave rise to symbolic life. Ritual drink is often a metonymic part of the fluids of mythic time, such as heavenly liquid or the waters of the cosmic flood. The eternal waters or the waters of destruction brought new life — of a rushing, fertile, changing kind — to the cosmos. These are the beverages that humans regularly quaff during the life-giving feasts that mark the passage of periodic time. Beer brings back old times and marks the reappearance of ancient presences. Ritual drink effectively symbolizes the capacity to absorb the kind of undifferentiated experience that threatens to drown the senses and blur distinctions that lie at the heart of human existence. In many societies, humans must consume outrageous quantities of ritual drink and force themselves to surpass their capacities in order to demonstrate how human culture holds chaos at bay. The human body, with its senses and appetites, demonstrates the struggle of culture to absorb and channel the boundless meaning of sacred life. Human control over time is manifest in the manipulation of ritual drink and the control of other fluids that are fundamental for abundant life. Irrigation, navigation, and festival brew set humans apart from animals and heavenly beings, neither of which exert symbolic control over fertile fluids.

In a similar way, the violent confrontations of ritual combat, singing, races, dance competitions, or oratorical contests become essential to the renewal of time. Ceremonial violence during seasonal feasts reenacts the violence of change that was occasioned by sacred beings and that is essential to fertility, growth, and health. The abundance and robustness of life forms is at stake in ritual combat. Stylized violence assures the victory of new life of the sort that emerged from the primordial drama of change. Through the symbolism of staged antagonism the social group places itself once again in contact with the powers of the mythical past and renews time. Stylized violence heightens symbolic differences between social actors and groups. Antagonism between males and females, a difference frequently exploited in calendrical combats, is one of the most fruitful antagonisms of culture. The battle of the sexes, like other instances of ritual combat, mimics the act of war, a war that one avoids carrying out. Paradoxically, by demonstrating stylized aggression, the point that war is not intended is made. In fact, the performance instigates relationships, friendships, alliances, courtships, and intercourse that are both sexual and economic.

Masked dance, a widespread example of stylized terror between the sexes, is performed on occasions that mark the passage of time. Women and men (or their representatives, such as women's brothers, who may wage combat with their sisters' future husbands) impersonate the destructive mythical spirits of chaos, or menacing supernatural beings, or the dead. They deliberately set themselves at odds with one another through the imagery of ritual aggression and dance in order to recreate mythic scenarios whose violence effected the first significant change and passage of time. Food fights, eating and drinking contests, rhetorical competitions, and verbal abuse, as well as masked dances and the dramatized attacks of supernatural animals, exhibit festival combat in a variety of forms. Musical ensembles and orchestral arrangements for diverse instruments frequently stage symbolic belligerence in sonic terms.

Ritual combats unite separate modes of being, whose interpenetration is essential to continued life. Ritual combat is frequently a temporal response to the existential dilemma of existing in space. For this reason, symbolic battles are fought over different kinds of spaces—bodies, cult houses, masks, musical instruments, territories—as well as over extensions of those spaces into time, in the form of offspring, abundant yield, and accumulated goods. Human beings attempt to resolve the paradox of spatial existence through their calendric ability to coordinate times into complex rhythms. Incommensurable experiences and oppositions are coordinated in the calendar through the power of festival combat, which configures change, alternation, destruction, withdrawal, and cyclical reappearance. Ritual battle represents the struggle to insert the full experience of time, even the experience of primordial, sacred beings, into one passing moment. For that reason, ritual battle changes the course of history and the cultural meaning of existence in time by marking off new eras and creating new evaluations of them.

Ritual noise also overcomes the separateness of distinct times made present as distinct sounds. Ritual din portrays the clash of meaning signified in sound and represents the attempt to recreate primordial conditions of time. That fullness of time, when all sounds could be significant simultaneously, preexists the serial or narrative existence of this world, where distinction between sounds is essential to their intelligibility. One can distinguish two kinds of ritual noise. The first is racket, an ear-splitting volume of din. The second is babble, the simultaneous utterance or confusion of tongues and sounds. These two kinds of noise may combine and overlap, and both are deliberate sound-effects and intentional symbols of uproar. Ritual clamor is intense, in the sense that it is neither random nor accidental but rather a skillful confusion of sounds, intended to achieve a purpose. The goal is to create a healthy state of soundness and a fullness of being no longer available in mundane, intelligible circumstances. The wholeness achieved through the symbolism of sound is the ultimate reality on which the temporal world is founded. Noise recreates a mythic reality that is wholly concrete and sensual, even if the experience of it is mystical, for the fullness of primordial being in the mythic world is organic. Ritual racket and babble, like the symbolisms of incest and combat, return culture to the inaccessible fullness of being that obtained at the moment when it passed away forever. Through these symbolic strategies, the calendar places human culture in the moment when mythic history left off.

The religious imagination permits human culture to become a continuation of mythic history, such that humans live two qualities of existence, which are reflected in the kinds of time they inhabit. Human history, unfolding in the fragmented cosmos of separate periodic units and prepositional places, is also an elaboration of a mythical story that continues in undiminished, though relatively unmanifest, power through the work of the human imagination and its fertile consequences. The cyclic nature of cosmic time assures that humans live a sacred story even as they mark off their passage through mundane existence. The complex human experience of time enfolds these relatively simple cycles into temporally complex calendars. The calendar reveals that temporal existence has an integrity of the first order, rooted in the primordial condition of the religious imagination that undergirds culture and comes to the fore during feasts. The symbolic actions of calendrical rites make visible and reflexive the specifically human quality of knowledge — the awareness of one's multiplex temporal existence — that underlies the performance of cultural acts. Ritual action puts time on display and postures the reflexive nature of human existence in time. Human beings grasp their own meaning by creatively repeating the acts of the wholly-other sorts of beings who generated the conditions of culture, and therefore one may view calendrical rites as comparative exercises in interpreting contrastive modes of being.

Because primordial realities were nonsymbolic, exhaustively manifesting their own meaning, the primordium exhibited no regular transformations but only total, destructive change. The rites of the calendar return to those destructive moments in reparable and redemptive ways by joining what was separated or dismembered in periodic time, such as the monstrous snake whose severed body-parts became the lineages that descend through time. In reuniting separate species of time at the moment when they broke apart, the calendar manifests the human capacity to relive different modes of being and thus to discover the power that effects true change. Images of anomaly, chaos, monstrosity, or eccentricity once again make available to human experience the forbidden and terrible conditions under which the fractured times of the periodic world reunite.

Within the framework of cosmic periodicity, culture aims at a shuffled perfection, a stylized arrangement of all the possible qualities of being symbolized by diverse times. Toward this end, each mode of primordial reality finds its place on the calendar-round and returns to the center, but only for that calendrical moment that also celebrates it passing. Through the calendar of sacred feasts, the human appetite for being is satisfied in a piecemeal way.

HUMAN CONSTITUTION

A cross-cultural analysis shows that human beings have been created in myriad ways by a variety of supernatural beings or, in more mysterious and vague circumstances, by ill-defined forces and means, but the locus of human origins always stands out as a sacred place of special power. In any case, human life is not a given within the cosmos but is discontinuous with the world around it, having appeared through some independent act of creation or transformation. For that reason, human experience of the world always carries a valence of the strange and the marks of the struggle to be at home in the world. Sensitivity to the strange and the effort to apprehend the meaning of other forms of being constitute the religious disposition of humankind in the cosmos. From the point of view of the cosmos also, human presence intrudes on the nature of existing relations in such a way as to reorder nature. The symbolic constitution of human beings ties in with all manner of cosmic elements: stars, plants, waters, animals, and so on. Culture (art, music, technology, ritual action, play) emerges from the creative imitation and interpretation of the powerful forces toward which symbolic life draws human beings. In origin myths, human beings grasp their original character; that is, they cultivate the capacity to be self-conscious and to fasten upon their unique ability to reproduce sacred meaning in the works of culture.

Two symbolic processes, fabrication and metamorphosis, arrange the images that constitute an individual and produce the human person. On the one hand, deliberate control over the entrance or exit of substances that communicate between the body and the outside world (such as breath, blood, feces, tears, saliva, foods, vomitus, tobacco, urine, semen, milk) fabricates the body in the image of an enclosure and fosters the person's awareness of himself or herself as a being composed of passages. The individual becomes conscious of himself or herself as a person set apart by the imposition of human intention and cultural design on matter. On the other hand, metamorphosis excessively modifies the essence of humanity even to the point of obscuring the boundaries between the human and the supernatural. Metamorphosis reclaims the experiences and powers that one has alienated from oneself in the deliberate, controlled acts of fabrication; it reaches beyond the human, fabricated condition to reappropriate nonhuman possibilities. But because this is done self-consciously, metamorphosis need not undo the carefully constructed human nature itself.

Among the images which compose the human being, that of the soul, with its lineage and mythic history, brings human individuals their fullest experience of time, whether manifest in the biological tempos of pulse and breath, in visits to preexistent or future worlds, or in life after death. In contact with all these complex qualities of time, the soul manifests the fact that human existence is continuous and whole. The soul ensures that individuals are part of a history—the history of mythic ancestors, epic heroes, and the natural elements of the world. Understanding the nature of the human soul is the key to evaluating human existence, which always dwells within multiple temporal frames and levels of reality.

Souls often become more visible at death, and their postmortem history is well charted. By arranging concepts, faculties, tasks, and destinies into coordinated series of spiritual functions and relationships, some cultures are able to develop systematic theories of the soul. The spiritual elements and functions within the individual become systematized along physiological and epistemological lines. The physiological organization of the soul emphasizes the relations and appetites (e.g., for food or sex) that construct the human being. Epistemologies configure the spiritual elements associated with specific human faculties, such as speech, reflection, thought, imagination, memory, and will. But the distinction between physiological and epistemological tendencies lies at the level of the systematization of the soul's properties, and one should not confuse the full range of the soul's experience with the theoretical apparatus that a culture uses to think about it. Physiology and epistemology are typological solutions for ordering the temporal properties of human beings and for organizing spiritual life. They are seldom mutually exclusive. They map the human soul's ability to experience multiple modes of time in their symbolic expression, but it is the soul's contact with the sacred in multiple forms that generates systematic reflection on the human capacity for mental, emotional, and physical experience.

The dream-soul assures continuity between the imagery of dreams and the patterned cultural imagery of rite, myth, and art that constitutes the individual. Whether conscious or unconscious, a person inhabits the same world of meaning, which is explored by the imagination. During dream, the soul wanders into other qualities of time. The images encountered there express both the human attitude toward existence and the sacred realities one meets there. Foremost among those realities are the dream-elements of the human soul itself. In this respect, dream approximates death insofar as it makes the soul visible. Various mythologies of dream show how the significance of the human image (that is, the meaning of the soul's form as seen in dream and after death) generates a spectrum of symbolic analogies that bind together — or, in the case of the analogies that derive from the images arising in the supreme being's dreams, even create — the whole universe. The dream-soul's connection to the faculties of human speech and song highlight how language is rooted in the images that appear in the primordial world. Whether the reality of the world is dreamed up by the creator or called into being by the creator's thought or word, language, dream, thought, speech, and creativity in every form participate in the same nature as the image-soul that constitutes the human being.

Once a person recognizes, in dream or some other visionary episode, the shape of spiritual existence and of the spiritual human image, experience opens to the myriad meaningful forms that can appear within the human imagination. In the primordium, both dream and sound exist as sacred images. Like all images of the sacred, dreams assume specific value in the act of interpreting them. Interpretation is frequently a social event, a public performance that, taking its cues from the dream itself, manifests itself as a ritual chant, a rite, or a change in a person's public role and behavior. Dreams are frequently distintegrative, the personality dissolving so that certain spiritual elements can transcend the normal human condition and obtain vision-knowledge of other realities. During the act of performance, the chants or narrative accounts of visionary experience reintegrate the person and reunite the elements of the soul. The song, rite, or story that analyzes the adventures of the soul-elements (in this sense, one might call them genres of psychoanalytic narrative) casts the images of dreams into the episodic and narrative rhythms consubstantial with the structures of time that condition this world and human culture, transposing primordial realities into the rhythms of this world. Performance and fine arts modulate primordial images into visible and audible expressions of culture. The dream itself can be a species of performance, the ideal performance of the sacred realities whose acts created the world through dreaming. By means of dreams, human beings gain admittance to the creative scenario, and through performance of the song-images heard or seen in dreams, humans punctuate the cadence of culture with creative, momentous acts of power. The dream-song guarantees that human creativity will fashion worlds in the image of the sacred realities that gave rise to the universe and its creatures in the first place. Human culture is a linguistic, intellectual, musical, dramatic, and visual interpretation of those primordial realities.

Projected into time as shadows, souls are the active but relatively separable aspects of being human. One temporal aspect of the soul takes shape over time. This is *character*, the unique set of features that result from the historical process of maturation. Memories and decisions of the will accumulate as images of recollection over time. Furthermore, time spent in reflection throughout life shapes a person's image as he or she perceives it cast as a shadow onto time, especially the time of primordial being. The person grasps his or her likeness in time as projected against a totally other reality, as a shadow cast by or onto what is sacred. The human shadow-soul is a form of darkness that, constituting the human being, assures direct connection to the world of fully manifest light. In their innermost being, however, human beings experience that omniscient and omnipresent light as a dark absence constitutive of their own soul.

The constancy of a person's existence, paradigmatically represented by the soul-elements of dream and shadow, is counterbalanced by other, periodic elements that constitute the human being. Individuality is an interrelationship among several modes of periodic time: the cyclic nature of human attention, the interplay of generations, appetites for food or sex, cycles of health, sickness, and revival, and rhythms of death and rebirth.

Menstruation is an effective sign of the periodic nature of the cosmos embodied by human experience. In cultures where both men and women are said to menstruate, menstruation becomes one of the strongest signals of the periodic nature of incarnate human life. The openness of the human body (seen as a container) from time to time during menstruation creates the temporal conditions generative of relations—between men and women in sex, between parents and child in filiation, between age-groups, between exogamous groups in marriage alliances, between the individual and society, and so on. Similarly, the passing-exchanges of food, body wastes and fluids, words, sounds, and breath enmesh an individual in a unique configuration of crucial cosmic cycles at initiation, childbirth, calendrical feasts, and death.

The ability to relate periodically to diverse realities is a fundament of culture, and the temporal constitution of the person allows culture to orchestrate the periodic rhythms of the cosmos through symbolic manipulation of body passages. From time to time, cultures prescribe the opening or closing of the body (during, for example, toilet training, menses, periods of sexual abstinence or orgy, and festival fasts or forced feedings). In addition, the passage of body parts through defined space and time is controlled in the symbolism of properly timed rites and dances. Avoidances and prescribed expressions of shame or respect set human life into the rhythm of periodic tempos, which are manifest not only in menstrual flow of women and the actions of those related to them but in everything that has a beginning, a time of growth, and an end: plants, stars, animals, sentences, body movements, and so on. So too, inhalation, exhalation, alimentation, evacuation, excretion, lactation, urination, and orgasm and seminal emission during intercourse embody the periodic tempos of incarnate life and generate the kinds of relations that take on rich symbolic value in culture.

A name may be an aspect of the soul or identical to it and, as such, is a statement of a person's specific presence in the world. Since the name is a form of knowledge that bespeaks the shape of the personality, the naming process or the reality of a name often includes death. Receiving a name, capturing the sound-name of another, calling other modes of being, and knowing others by name mold the person's entire being to the shape of a specific sound. The meaning of names and the naming process help compose the significant order of society since by their agency individual and society create one another through the images of sound. The transmission of names can provide a society with an enduring but dynamic image of itself. Names catapult the individual into a specific network of relationships with other human beings, animals, or supernaturals, who nourish and shape the child's personality. Names are always cultural interpretations of the relationship between two kinds of structures, sound and body, and the very act of interpreting the relationships between sound, form, and meaning across time mutually shapes individual and society.

The act of naming as it occurs in the naming ceremony contextualizes a personality by placing the named individual within a specific conjunction of relations. This is why the process of giving names can be more important than the names themselves. Individuals who have undergone the naming ceremony mature because their relationships have been (or henceforth may now be) examined, interpreted, and named. They are socially and self-consciously located. The quality of reflection that must ground all moral action can be based on ordered experiences properly arranged in conformity with the meaning of a person's name. The naming process bears moral weight, for the relations within which it places the person named represent the normative order of experience. The power of a personal name propels the individual into a trajectory of moving relations (with mythic, supernatural, ancestral, and historical powers) at the point in time when the cosmic and social forces are aligned in a way similar to the disposition of forces in the named person's own personality. The act of discerning this configuration of forces guarantees that a person's name is always an interpretation and an act that gives rise to culture. For this reason, naming ceremonies pull into visible focus and audible expression the set of inner correspondences by means of which the universe becomes accessible even to the most idiosyncratic of personalities. Since the bestowal of a name is often a sacramental interpretation of the sacred, the utterance of one's name becomes a species of ritual performance.

Sound arises from a specific presence, whether known or unrecognized, and implies the eventual revelation of a specific being. Sound is pointed and has a bearing, even if that direction cannot always be controlled. For these reasons, sound is always a "vocation," a calling-out of being into specific forms of existence. Sound is the effluvium from passage, the inner content of primordial being excreted through the embodied instruments of change. Therefore, sound provides demonstrable evidence of change brought on by the passage of time. For this reason, festive songs effect the changes they signify; their performance marks the times and places of passage where culture regenerates itself. All sound in this cosmos is distinct, even if the distinctions occasionally overrun one another to become noise. The serial or simultaneous presence of specific beings through their sounds allows for the composition of being, unions of opposites, calendars, and other subtle, symphonic orchestrations of the forms of existence.

Response to the presence announced in sound indicates mindfulness of the meaning of that sound. Such mindfulness never stands apart from the meaningful sound that is being responded to. Already an interpretive act, awareness of meaning brings a reality into cultural life. The presence of the sacred in sound prompts the performed interpretation of its meaning in the significant emotions that shape society. Weeping, for instance, by responding to the nostalgic image of the integrity of being, recreates the meaning of the wholeness for which it longs. Lamentation and weeping are performed responses to the significance of catastrophe or to the furied frenzy that accompanied the primordial destruction. For that reason, weeping frequently accompanies important moments of change, transition, and initiation into a new state by means of symbolic death or destruction.

The ways in which sound, especially music, organizes the body become organizing principles within a society. By clarifying the symbolic value of music, myth renders it referential and revelatory. As a sacred symbol, music enunciates aesthetic and emotional tones of meaning, representing the supernatural mode of being it signifies and serving as model for culture and a template for the symbolic relations that obtain between the forms of animal, plant, human, space, and time. The meaning of sound, as revealed by sacred figures and their music, generates not only the spatial and temporal conditions of culture but the important divisions of the social order as well, often corresponding to the ranking of groups and ritual roles. Since sound is constitutive of individual and society, different musical styles and performative settings inspire alternative social forms and creative strategies for social experiment and change. In addition, the periodic opening and closing of music-producing forms (the orifices of mythic animals' bodies) symbolically orchestrate sounds by bringing them into relationship with specific times of day, night, season, or mythic era.

Human speech is often an alienating process, for its removes the meaning of sound from its original, sacred context and parcels out figures of speech and syllables phoneme by phoneme. In addition, human speech is often appropriated from some other kind of being—a primordial or supernatural being. Ironically, the songs of the masters of animals or other supernaturals, recited exactly as they were at the beginning of time, are performed at feasts that define *human* culture. The difference distinctive of the human performance is that the songs are now symbolic, remembered, or mimed. They become the presence of sacred beings echoed in human reality—deliberate fabrications inflected in the human voice.

Sound and song overcome the confinement of language. Sound ironically negates language. Overwhelming the separateness of phonemes and effacing the staccato rhythm of individual speech, sound can return the personality to such inchoate conditions as babbling, buzzing, murmuring, or inarticulate blather. Sound can mime undifferentiated sonic states, which dissolve the linguistic patterns ordinarily required for human communication. Harmful incantations, for example, annihilate the articulate structures of the victim, who collapses into a dissolute chaos.

Humans conceive of themselves in spatial imagery. Physiological processes and the properties attributed to body substances and fluids comprise an important social idiom. Spatiality permits reflection and draws the human into the meaning of creation revealed in myth, since the physiological language of creation myths applies to all created spaces, including the house, plaza, ceremonial space, and cosmos. In its physiological processes the human body is a specific instance of an extraordinary cosmic process. Arranging and manipulating body forms, fluids, and substances establishes group relations and the ecological network of ties that links humans to the surrounding world through the symbolic values of movement, distance in space, heft, texture, color, and shape.

Physiology highlights the individual as a container whose vital processes initiate relationships organized by the senses, the body's capacities for meaning. Bone and flesh are important physiological instruments. Frequently, bone is seen as having contained the first kind of life. Flesh makes possible blowing and sucking, both of which are essential to speech, song, ingurgitation, woodwind performance, conception, and medical cure. Blowing and sucking, as two manifestations of power over passages, make possible incarnate, dynamic self-control over the spiritual processes of human life. Diet and table manners distinguish groups and qualities of relations within a given society (or between different societies) because the mouth controls contact with the cosmic powers that order one's entire shape and meaning. The meaning of food and the relations entailed in its production, distribution, and consumption mark cultures as unique and distinguish one mode of being from another. Thus, each individual is a finely crafted spatial image containing subtle arrangements of the character traits evaluated within a given culture. These arrangements are reflected in the foods (their mode of preparation and their order of service) that may or may not enter the individual body-container. The habits of space become the marks of taste and distinction.

The body is not only a vessel in the sense of a container but a vehicle that passes through a maelstrom of changing times. Since specific images of space constitute the person, these images must change to make metamorphosis possible, whether at the moment of final death or at the times of symbolic death that make for change and growth. The body, then, is a vessel of spiritual life, a vehicle for transformation. Its symbolic breakdown and reconstruction enable one to understand and, therefore, to effect one's process of spiritual growth. Through mutation, the growing body-figure becomes a cipher of spiritual transition as transfiguration is always an understanding of the spirit. Through ritual control over one's symbolic containments, each individual, each physiological integrity, can become a shrine, a locus of sacred forces and an icon of sacred history. Architecture and interior design, choreography, and sacred space exploit the powers inherent in the symbolism of containment to subject bodies to cultural conditioning and thereby build up a social body for communal experience. In the deliberate shaping of shared social space, a person's experience of himself or herself is made to conform to the meanings manifest in sacred beings at the beginning. Such is the foundation of the sexual orgy, a deliberate imitation of the momentous act that altered the course of historical existence.

The fact that significant action unfolds in relation to spatial imagery (of which the physical body is one kind) indicates that space is a moral situation. In space (a perception of the ordered sets of processual relations symbolized in the cosmos), the actions of the human body are those of a moral actor and so invite understanding and critique. Physiology, as construed or spatially rearranged in dance or medicine, for example, can be the basis of morality because the body's actions and capacities always symbolize and open onto the possibility of meaning.

HUMAN GROWTH AND CREATIVITY

Although change compels the reinterpretation of an individual's meaning, a different perspective on the relationship between meaning and change will help us better to understand human growth and creativity. One becomes what one already means: a person's significations, modeled on mythic precedents set by cosmic change at the beginning of time, draw him or her inexorably through the events that effect what he or she already signifies. Dramatic events of ritual change heighten awareness of the transformative power present in a person's symbolic constitution, revealing the intimacy of change and meaning, an involvement that dates back to the withdrawal of sacred beings into the many significant forms of appearance in this world. Their withdrawal and transformation impels change. The symbolic vestiges of their passing constitute cultural reality. Symbols are themselves material involvements in transformative processes, the powerful changes in states of being.

In the tension between change, which prompts new symbolic expressions of meaning, and significant meaning, which sparks new change, is a dialectic of growth and decay. New life and creativity are part of a violent contest of forces that oppose and contradict one another in every domain of human image, whether sonic, temporal, or spatial. Contradiction of meaning on every level is the spiritual situation of humanity. Within this context, human beings can grow.

Human life is symbolic because it embodies the changes of meaning and of concrete form instituted by mythic beings. Recombinations of the elements in one's symbolic configuration move one in and out of existential, emotional, social, and spiritual states. The propelling symbolisms include special foods, drinks, songs and musical instruments, dance, games, colors, clothing, divisions of labor, and calendrical timing. All transitional moments are supported by spiritual companionship, changes in the states of one's knowledge, and creative labor.

Conception is the outcome of spiritual and carnal processes and, especially, of symbolic acts performed during the initiations and marriage ceremonies of the parents. These include not only the couple's sexual foreplay and intercourse and their avoidance of specific foods and behaviors but also the community's dancing, singing, decoration, hunting, gathering, and eating. A fetus does not fashion its own signifiers. This is done by others, both human and supernatural. The symbolic logic of conception draws attention to the mythic situation of human beginnings, when creator gods or cultural heroes generated human life.

Rites of passage induce change by manipulating symbols of sacred power in order to provoke encounters with supernatural forces, whose presence alters the course of events. The symbolic acts of the life-cycle do not simply move the individual from one reified "state" to another, they *create* (or powerfully reenact the creation of) the significant levels of being into which one is inducted at each of life's stages. The act of birth shows how functional behavior can reveal meanings that affect the texture of existence. The practical movements of the birth process effect life itself. These acts launch the child into a constellation of relationships called into being by the very act of birth.

The acts of birth introduce a child to the new conditions of space and time. A guide, sponsor, or companion may lead the new being out of its old realm and ito the new world, where it takes its place in the situation that defines its relationship to the shaping influences around it. The midwife often plays the role of deliverer in both a physical and a spiritual sense. Sometimes the infant is made to perform the first acts of the first human beings as they appeared on the earth at the beginning of time. The babe immediately becomes a ritual actor and its life in this world a constant performance of sacred moments. Thus, children may be placed on the ground and lifted up again to reenact the emergence of the first human beings from the womb of the earth. Or they may be bathed in ritual waters to restage the emergence of human life at the time of the primordial flood. The ritual performances of midwives, relatives, and sponsors guarantee that the biological functions of human birth are also cultural acts, that is meaningful interpretations of the sacred. The symbolic acts of birth attempt to grasp the meaning of the creative powers present in the form of the new child. Birth is an epiphany of the supernatural forces at work in the life of the parents and the community and embodied in the infant. The rites of birth discern the repercussions that encounters with these forces will have on individuals and groups. The community structures its existence around these powers composed, signified, and revealed in the incarnate form of the newborn babe.

The creative drama of conception, gestation, and birth becomes a model for cultural and spiritual rebirth throughout the life-cycle, where transitions are accomplished through the knowledge associated with the power of symbolic life. Knowledge of symbolism either is simultaneously material and spiritual or actualizes a condition wherein the separation of spiritual and material dimensions is unnecessary or transcended. Such knowledge is essential to the kind of life — human life — that always crosses over ontological threshholds and that first appears in transition.

Initiation is a process coextensive with the human condition. Every initiation rite produces teaching and learning roles for a range of social actors and not only for the initiands. Over a lifetime, the role of the participating individual shifts from that of initiand to parent, sponsor, food preparer, instrumentalist, spectator, or invited guest. Multiple perspectives gradually allow a person to witness mythic and ritual revelations from many different angles, so that initiation never ceases. Nevertheless, the focus often falls on the novices because, during initiation, sacred realities are placed at the disposal of their human understanding for the first time. Initiation consequently serves as a reflexive gathering point for similar moments of breakthrough, when human understanding pierces symbolic expression and gains new insight into meaning. At those moments, the significance of human life changes, and one can embark on a new beginning. Even so, initiation cannot be set apart as a moment separate from all others. Rather, it celebrates an essential quality of being human: the creature's self-awareness of his or her transitory and symbolic condition.

Initiation forces novices to encounter their own symbolic nature and the symbolic foundations of their capacity to understand. They are informed that these symbolic conditions bind them to the realities that empower their world, and they are taught that even the symbolic nature of human life is grasped through its significations. Acting on one level, human beings signify another realm of reality; they live a betwixt-and-between experience of paradox and contradiction, which ensnares them in multiple conditions of existence at any single time. The symbolisms of death and rebirth, so prominent in formal initiations, proclaim that the essential act of human culture is to undergo symbolic existence.

By suffering one's own significations, human beings grow critical and reflective, so that they come to embody the dynamism, change, creativity, and sacredness intrinsic to meaning. Distinctive cultural statements about the nature of human death, for example, account for the nature of human growth and open human reality to other realms. Death is a part of the constitution of mortal beings and so harkens back to the origins of human life, forming the foundation of the symbolic nature of human existence. The union of death with the origins of life places human existence on an initiatory plane. From its beginnings, human life calls for rebirth. Death is not the last instant of life but an integral part of it. Because of death, human life cannot persevere in constant form but continually changes. More positively stated, the human being can be born and grow because it is mortal and transitory. Symbolic existence depends on death in many forms, for no symbolic reality exists on its own as an objective and autonomous reality; rather, symbolic life *subsists*, contingent upon relations, maintained at every level, to all else that is.

During women's initiation, a new locus generative of life is established. On their bodies, initiated girls bear the scars or decorative souvenirs of the time when the world passed through chaos into a state of fertile regeneration. Tattoos, bite marks, painted designs, scarifications, and ornaments often commemorate the teeth, nails, stingers, inner organs, or anatomical designs of the mythical monsters who once flooded the earth or impeded the passage of life through the first birth canal. Women's initiations highlight several symbolic strategies: seclusion, containment of openness and flow, propriety (both hygienic and moral), invisibility, and dazzling display of beauty.

During initiation, the powerful processes that imbue initiands are concealed in secrecy. Seclusions encircle and enshroud the girls in a tomb or womblike environment. At times this encirclement takes the form of a parade or a musical entourage that marks the outer confines of the world. Like the supernatural females who became instruments of closure within which life could thrive, the new woman becomes a vessel for power over processes of physical, social, and economic reproduction. The moment of her initiation offers the community a chance for reflection and control over the meaning of change. Modeling herself on the mythical heroine whose perseverance and strong will saved the possibility of culture, the young girl constructs, in her own body, a more perfect cultural vessel, whose biological openness (manifest in the flow of her menstrual blood) becomes one with the power of her reflective will. Women embody the paradox that, while new life requires openness and flow, cultural life, being a generative and reproductive system, demands closure.

This dilemma dates back to the time of the catastrophic flood that brought closure to the creative primordium in order to initiate the changing conditions of this replicative world. The deluge gave rise to culture as a symbolic system, and symbolic containments (gourds, canoes, stone-eggs, mountain or underground caves, floating logs, clay vessels of refuge) safe-guarded that closure, which was necessary for meaning to survive under conditions within which life is regenerated by periodic flow. Within the space marked off by ritual restrictions and symbolic seclusions, fluids are admitted and emitted according to deliberately observed and symbolically marked periodic schedules, such as the menstrual period, festival cycle, times of conception, gestation, parturition, and other life-passages. Such symbolic controls produce the periodic rhythms of tides, rainy and high-water seasons, lunar cycles, menstruation, and new generations. The fact that symbolic human life is precipitously open to meaning raises questions about the resources that can staunch its flow and contain its utter dissolu-tion. Shame, shyness, and embarassment obstruct the normal flow of events and relationships during passage from one reality into another. They serve as ritual avoidances, which create the ceremonial seclusions that protectively embrace the changing individual. Covered with shame or guilt or hemmed in by restrictions, the initiand is enclosed in a protective mantle of seclusion, which defines the fixed place and time of hidden change. Should these pro-cesses of change not be hidden, their effects and meaning might never be known. At the same time, society protects itself from deliquescence.

By appearing to cover over moments of change, the images of conceal-ment foreshadow the emergence of the new symbolic forms of meaning that appear when the veil is lifted. Through silence, stasis, fixity, and overdress-ing, the ordinarily unseen processes at work in the hidden darkness of women's wombs are made visible through their beautiful and effective bodies and in the products of their craft (such as basketry, pottery, or weav-ing) exercised during initiatory seclusion. The display of these goods and of the new woman who emerges refashioned from her chrysalis reveals the sacredness of women, which undergirds the power of the cultural process.

Men's initiation highlights the distance and alienation interposed be-tween one mode of reality and another. In the symbolic behavior of male initiation, the violence inherent in all symbolic life is particularly visible. Violence and disillusionment becomes tokens of the new and critical con-sciousness needed to understand myth. Drawing one toward disenchant-ment, initiatory death imposes an experience of crisis and introduces the critical distance that separates one mode of being (including the one signi-fied by one's prior estimations of reality) from another. This fundamental awareness of contrast and contradiction, which intrudes upon the maturing young adult, induces a new appraisal of the sacred world.

Regenerative life-processes attach themselves to men through violence and through the dynamism of relating to, or even expropriating, what is strange and foreign. Reproductive processes conjoin with male sacredness only through the violence of the religious imagination, as is reflected in myths in which men steal initiatory masks, musical instruments, magical gourds, or garments from primordial women, the authentic, primordial pos-sessors of the powers of reproduction. This mythic violence represents the force of imagination required to overcome the insignificance inherent in nonsymbolic life. The exhibitionism of male initiation stands in contrast to the hiddenness of female initiation, in which women display the fact that menses, pregnancy, parturition, and other moments of production and reproduction are manifestations of internalized, sacred powers that are consubstantial with their own bodies. Male powers of reproduction, on the contrary, remain an appendage to male sacrality and always appear as if they were a cultural construction, an external, ideological, or instrumental force. For that reason, men's symbolic life is a clearer window on the meaning of the violence that undergirds all the symbolic processes that constitute culture.

The violence associated with men's behavior (when understood as symbolic) relates directly to the discovery of the symbolic nature of life. The critical awareness that the meaning of a sign is not fully present in its appearance but rather points to something absent does violence to existence. Convictions such as these lie at the foundation of men's secret initiatory societies, especially those masked societies that use disguises stolen by males from primordial females in a frenzy of violence and slaughter. The discovery that the first females had defrauded the first males through the manipulation of symbols brought closure to the primordial world. That disillusionment, the discovery of pretense, of fissured time, ended the primordial matriarchy, opened history, and led to the growth of human culture. Secret societies and their masks, musical instruments, or dances bear this history of violence, dissimulation, and disenchantment as inherent symbols of their regenerative power. The act of primordial hoax and disillusionment is restaged for contemporary novices. By thus introducing a critical experience of distance from and immersion in symbolic reality, initiation marks the beginning of a maturing process and not its full achievement. It admits a young man to participation in the ritual life of the community and invites novices, male and female, to pursue a lifelong symbolic existence in which they will gradually unfold the mysteries and puzzle together the pieces exposed as *sacra* during initiation.

Many cultures intend men's and women's initiations to be quite different. Both males and females account for the creation and regeneration of culture in terms of themselves. Consequently, each kind of initiation tends to be totalizing, embodying alternative and sometimes competing claims about the way culture stands toward human reproductive processes. Sex-discriminating secret societies, where each sex's initiation scenario exhaustively accounts for creativity without designating any role to the other sex, often abound with symbolic terrorism aimed at the opposite sex — the terror, that is, of remaining without a creative and essential role in the cosmos. When they reenact their myths of origin, these secret initiatory societies focus on and extend into everyday life the absence (or alienation) of meaning and the meaning of absence (or alienation). Whereas women's initiations climax in momentary display of the individual woman as a manifestation of the hidden powers underlying reproductive processes, men's initiations lead to a protracted ceremonial life that displays the regenerative powers who withdrew into symbolic appearances at the close of the primordium. Women over-come threatening powers, especially aquatic monsters, by embodying them so that they become an imaged part of the amniotic waters of their wombs or the periodic ebb of their hair or menstrual blood; men instrumentalize the threatening powers contained in feathered ornaments, hair-tubes, penis-sheaths, musical instruments, or masks, which are put away in the off-season.

The ceremonies of initiation display virtues—powers, known from myths, that are esteemed because they initiated the very conditions of cul-tural existence. Sustained attention, vigilance, and concentration bring about the alertness they signify. The initiand's vanity of his or her physical prowess or fine appearance define what is meant by beauty, an unimpedable generative power modeled on the gestures of those beings who in mythic times successfully created and transformed the world and its contents. Thus, rituals perform beautiful patterns of dance and song that create harmonious wholes.

The ordeals that find their place in all initiations are not arbitrary inflic-tions of pain but deliberate techniques aimed at developing the critical self-knowledge required for human maturity. An ordeal is a division or appor-tionment, a dealing out of pain, discomfort, or restriction that separates one from one's prior existence in order to configure one's new character. Re-strictions on the sense of touch, custody of the eyes, ritual silence or stasis, and the endurance tests of marathon dancing, exposure to the elements, and nocturnal vigil help one make sense of oneself by keeping individual, cos-mic, and mythic conditions separate and orderable. Such lines, limits, and avoidances are helpful in defining the self, for the very process of becoming, through growth and change, renders being fallible and vulnerable to imma-turity.

Ordeals disclose some truth about the novice's character and about the relationship of that initiand to unseen powers. They divide one reality from another. The novice suffers his or her own pain and bears the indelible marks, both psychic and physical, which prove his or her unique individual-ity. The symbolic pains of growth signify each individual's apportioned lot. Whipping, cutting, and piercing the skin create openings that ironically allow for symbolic closure because these acts mark the outer limits of the body and make life conceivable, in every sense of the word. Ordeals instigate memory, reflection, guilt, history, and other forms of accountability for one's existence in time. The initiate's scars not only commemorate a mo-ment of personal growth but recall the great divide in the history of being itself. These are the cuts that divided chaos during the flood or fire, that dismembered a monstrous or supernatural being, or that felled the world-tree at the beginning of time. Piercing and cutting mark the initiate with every conceivable kind of time and every possible type of change. The trans-formations of being signified in the scars regenerate creation and make it rich with new life.

Existence in time jeopardizes essence and renders it vulnerable and questionable (a questionability underlined by the multiplicity of myths in which the absolute essences of the primordium are destroyed through flood, fire, quake or darkness). By exploiting failures and limits during ordeals and treating them as possibilities for rebirth, initiation overcomes this problem. Mature human growth entails awareness of the conditions of one's growth. The symbols of initiatory discipline, seclusion, and ordeal impose on the individual an awareness of personal limits and help the initiate transcend them through symbolic death and rebirth. Knowledge of one's own symbolic nature is the critical issue, the divisive reality issuing from chaos and separating human culture from other modes of being. Through ordeals, the imposed images of chaos and crisis, the novice comes to grips with his or her own critical symbolic life.

Ordeals commemorate the fact that existence never came to full term and never arrived at its intended destiny. Through some failure, something leaked, spurted, broke out, or was torn from the womb before it was time. The very nature of the temporal conditions required for growth undid the projected perfection of creation. During initiation, the candidate is placed within new symbolic limits, new cultural confinements, in order to continue the interrupted process of primordial gestation. Silence, stasis, and custody of the eyes, for example, render initiands partly "senseless." The supression of the senses of sight, hearing, articulate speech, or touch calls forth extraordinary meanings and new sensitivities, which discern the presence of sacred realities behind everyday appearances. Similarly, fasting and forced eating accomplish the transition from one state to another. The passage of symbolic items of food in and out of the body helps effect the passage of the initiate, as a symbolic item, through the stages of the spiritual economy of culture. Fasts and prescribed consumptions during initiation break the tragic cycle of consumption in which human life is caught and reestablish the conditions of immortality. Culture itself reintroduces the closure required to attain a new level of development, often in the image of a new container.

Opening and enlarging the candidates, peeling off old skin in order to grow new, and changing wardrobes are acts of rebirth and rejuvenation. Men as well as women must bear responsibility for the opening and penetration of sacred enclosures, especially the body-envelope. In due season, one learns to fast, eat prescribed foods, induce vomiting, avert the eyes, or control breath while playing sacred musical instruments.

One can distinguish among three kinds of ritually appointed company provided for initiands and others undergoing the experience of ritual transition from one state to another: supernaturals who serve as ritual friends to humans, human beings who act as ritual friends for supernaturals, and human beings who act as ritual consociates for other humans. Ritual companionship models itself on the performance of mythic beings, who mutually effected one another's transformations during the primordium. During their seclusions, initiates keep touch with social reality through contact with their ritual companions, who are living tokens of social life. In this way, social relationship becomes an essential ingredient of personal transformation.

Ritual ties can be both sensuous and economic. Ceremonial partnerships, trading partnerships, adoptions, and marriage partnerships are among the forms such relations take. The ritual assignment of friends, companions, and adversaries pushes self-awareness beyond the social ties generated only by personal preference, the nuclear family, and subsistence tasks and ensures the breadth of relationship required for spirituality maturity. Ceremonial ties frequently endure outside the ritual, thus underscoring the permanence of growth and the fact that change continues to have social bearing. The foundation of ritual companionship is a bond between the individual and society, established through the symbolic expressions of their sacred origins. Because it is symbolic, the social-personal ligament is intrinsic to being human and, through appointment of ritual company, becomes subject to scrutiny by maturing individuals during their life-cycle rites.

Significant human growth is not limited to formal rites of passage, but occurs during all self-conscious exchanges of body fluids and substances, foods, and sounds and is impelled by symbolic processes on every plane of cultural existence. Myth, rite, and work, for instance, are cultural performances that manifest the same periodic rhythms of symbolic transformation: exertion, rest, accumulation, surplus, consumption, depletion. All acts of growth fall within structured symbolic existence and base themselves on the uniquely human quality of knowledge: awareness of one's existence in time. Hunting, agriculture, and other acts of economic subsistence can be fully ritual performances, transforming the state of human knowledge as well as the physical conditions of human existence. The same is true of special crafts such as pottery, weaving, basketry and canoe making. Manufactured objects, such as tools and weapons, are fruits of the full labor of human hands and imagination. As such, they can become multivalent symbols of all the levels of meaning in human existence. Material objects of labor, which focus human attention for hours on end, become microcosms of force and meaning. Myth and rite make the intimate relationships that humans enjoy with modes of matter available for reflection. The forms of human labor assess and develop that intimacy in a characteristically human way through the symbolic action, creative production, and self-awareness critical to understanding the human situation of the laborer in the cosmos. The techniques of labor become means by which consciousness matures. As spiritual exercises, these techniques lead to a rejection of uncritical perceptions of matter or of the symbolic ways that humans relate to it and disclose the less apparent sources of meaning that they signify. Economic action changes the symbolic composition of individuals, of communities and of the world.

The shared symbolic nature of economic labor and religious ceremony narrows the gap between their diverse ergological expressions: the work of subsistence and that of interpretation, act and thought, knowledge and theory. Interpreting sacred realities is laborious and coextensive with human relations to modes of matter. Myth, liturgy, and all other "urgent" forms (including physical labor) express the human need to be energetic, creative, and productive of culture.

BASES OF SPECIAL AUTHORITY

The practices and beliefs of the religious specialist never account for all the religious expressions of an entire community. Nonetheless, the symbolic life of the specialist orders, from a particular point of view, an ensemble of religious ideas shared by the community. Terms that evaluate special roles, such as images of call, apprenticeship, or initiation, not only form an integral part of a religious tradition but also display a systematic construal of a tradition's reckoning of the sacred in all its forms.

The community recognizes that some human beings experience an extraordinary rapport with the sacred. These specialists embody the outer reaches of the human capacity for religious knowledge and power. A nonexhaustive list of the bases of religious authority would include the following three sources of knowledge: the experience of possession, the mastery of a canon, and the experience of ecstasy. In possession, personalities and bodies become instruments of communication with the spirit world. Musicians and accompanists control the progress of the possessive séance, since the medium is often out of control during the most revelatory moments. In the person of the possessed, the community transcends the human condition and guarantees its spiritual liberation. Authority inheres in the supernatural being who commandeers the human individual in order to communicate with the community.

Priests, herbalists, liturgists, diviners, and confessors often base their authority on the mastery of a canon. Having learned a lexicon of taxa and the procedures for their application, canonical exegetes interpret how these symbolic items coordinate with the symbolic structures of the universe. In this way, they bring herbs or ritual gestures into alignment with the seasons, the cardinal points, the divisions of the sexes and social groups, the coordinated spaces and movements of physiology, the cycles in the life of animals, and so on. The nature of canonical authority lends itself to institutionalization, for it relies upon the revealed wisdom accumulated across the historical tradition. Masters of canons tend to be workaday specialists whose duties are routine when compared to the spontaneity of possession or the drama of ecstasy. Their training is often scholastic. Even if they are designated to serve by the operation of canonical procedures (such as election to office by casting divinatory votes or the unfolding of royal genealogy), canonical authorities function by virtue of their control over protocols, rubrics, and catalogues of plants and animals, symptoms, therapies, moral principles or sins, or rites of communal labor, economy, or warfare.

All three forms of authoritative knowledge are experimental sciences and base themselves on experiential knowledge. Possession and ecstasy are firsthand experiences: Authoritative knowledge flows directly from the individual practitioner's encounter with the sacred. Pathos is the foundation of these bases of authority. They are empathetic sciences whose data are generated in the transactions of the authority's physiology and personality. Canonical mastery, however, is a more objectively informational science whose data need not flow directly from the personal experience of the practitioner. Canonists, instead, become acculturated to the categories of their discipline until all reality appears to reflect the structures of their science. Among canonists, styles of interpretation — rather than the quality and content of canonical knowledge — are what owe their relative adequacy (credibility and persuasive effectiveness) to the experience and personality of the canonist. Authority itself resides in the canon.

During ecstasy, the human soul leaves the body. Ecstatic specialists learn to control the passage of the soul out of the body (unlike its spontaneous and ungoverned exits during dream, fright, anger, sneezing, or coughing). The shaman is the most important and well-known ecstatic specialist in South America. Shamans are experts in the movements of the human soul, for they not only control the ecstasy of their own souls but specialize in the knowledge and care of others' souls. Shamanism arises during the mythic period, and its origins identify human life with the function and destiny of model protoshamans, such as gods, cultural heroes, and primordial ancestors. The apparel, techniques and responsibilities of the shaman first appear during mythic times. Knowledge of the sacred origins of shamanism gives courage to the community and enables its specialists to cope with the dangers of confronting manifest and unmanifest realities.

The training of apprentice shamans dramatizes a world full of supernatural adventure, power, and danger. In their dreams, hallucinations, heightened senses of hearing, or extrasensory perceptions, apprentices manifest a special sensitivity to the world of spirits. They learn to enter the supernatural realm of images under their own control and embody wishes and conflicts at will so that they lend clear conceptual form to the desires or fears of the soul (their own or their prospective client's). The adventures of the shamanic soul are accompanied by the manipulation of his or her body, whose extraordinary physiology has been transformed by the shaman's knowledge of the spiritual world. Shamans emerge from training equipped with techniques for contacting supernatural realities (to cure patients or destroy enemies) and with a fund of practical knowledge regarding music, hunting, cycles of game, astronomic lore, and meteorology.

Shamanic apprenticeship cannot be equated with general education. School for shamans has a mythic structure derived from the accounts of the first shaman's accomplishments. Knowledge is acquired in a manner that befits the shamanic vocation and ecstatic temperament. In many cases, separation from one's natal group is essential to spiritual experiences of a contemplative kind. The solitude of initiatory illness and the psychic isolation brought on by the strange experiences of the shamanic vocation contribute to the disintegration of the individual's social and psychic being. Strange supernatural forms appear to the initiand, who enters other spatial realms of the universe. Magical items and objects of power are inserted into his or her body-space, and substances (vomit, blood, sweat, fat, or mystical objects) are extracted from the novice shaman. The apprenticeship of a shaman essentially takes place on the spiritual plane. Fasting, vigil, and physical trial are symbolic expressions of activities that conform to the ideal patterns of myth, which guarantees that the shaman's experience in ecstasy is neither uncontrolled nor insuperably individualistic.

The presence of a master is essential to shamanic apprenticeship, for novices "die" to their former life, and there is danger that this real death of ecstasy might be permanent. Candidates must prove themselves capable of dealing with the spiritual world and of finding the path that opens to the experiences of resurrection. The master insures an authentic ritual death and, at the same time, prevents the loss or disorientation of the novice's ecstatic soul during that experience. The master not only advises on practical matters such as when to sleep, wake, wash, what to eat, and how to prepare ritual items but offers spiritual direction to guide initiands through strange supernatural terrain. Through the presence of a master, whether dead or alive), novices grasp the meaning of their own experience of the sacred and, through comparison and contrast, examine the nature of their own consciences. The ultimate master is the first mythical shaman.

During apprenticeship, novices survive a series of ordeals, from simple quizzes on matters of fact to demanding physical feats or harrowing psychological episodes. These trials deconstruct fixed patterns of thought and behavior to rearrange the novices' sense of things. Reality is questioned and reconfigured, and candidates' perceptions are placed on trial. The goal of ordeals is to obtain a new spiritual state, and the tests establish the worthiness they signify. They function sacramentally, which is why the path to other worlds is marked off into stages by ordeals. The accomplishment of each test moves the candidate further along the trail of ecstasy and toward knowledge of other conditions of being. The dismemberment of the candidate's body (in delirium, dream, hallucination, vision, or the special effects of staged magical illusion) is the paradigmatic ordeal of shamanic apprenticeship. The candidates' experience of radically different modes of time makes the experience of their own bodies disjointed. When this sense of time is reconditioned, they are reordered and refashioned; they cannot be the same as they once were.

Many shamanic technologies deliberately push the shaman to the brink of disorientation in space and time: tightrope walking, swings, twirling ropes that bring on dizziness or vertigo, songs, fasting, seclusion and social alienation, and sexual abstinence. Shamans leave their accustomed senses of space and time and travel to other supernatural realms by manipulating the powers of magical plants, music, motion, dress, behavior, or mood. Hallucinogens color and shape the visions of sacred realities. The ecstatic's systematic science of the soul not only rearranges the sense of the physical body but reconfigures the social network within which experience takes shape and has meaning. The apprentice's relations with other novices, fellow shamans, the master of initiation, the guardian spirit, other helper spirits, his or her spouse, clients, relatives, neighbors, and enemies determine the success or even the life-or-death outcome of ecstasy. Apprenticeship is the time when the shaman learns to live within the social network created by these new experiences and techniques. Conversely, communities depend upon the shaman's techniques of ecstasy and knowledge of the soul. In some cases, the ecstatic shaman is responsible for transporting souls from other realms of being to their mothers' wombs. Thus every human being represents the success of shamanic technology, and proper social order represents the cumulative shamanic accomplishment of discerning which realm to visit as a soul-source and which spirit to select as the one best suited to the social and historical circumstances of its lineage and parents-to-be.

Shamans move in the company of spirits. Their individual personalities, styles of behavior, physical appearance, and ultimate destiny change, depending on the spirits with whom they develop rapport. The spiritual and physical life of the community hinges upon the supernaturals with whom the shaman keeps ties. Spirits reveal their sacred names, symbolic form, or character to the novice. Such systematic knowledge of the sacred, divulged by supernatural helpers, is itself an extraordinary power. On the one side, spirits often reveal sacred realities to shamans because they must. Many helper spirits find themselves stalled in the midst of a cycle of transformations that began during the mythic period. They seek aid from shamans, masters in the subtle movements of spirits, in order to continue their transmigration. On the other side, some helper spirits are motivated by the will to save humankind or maintain cosmic order in the form of game protection, weather control, or crop growth. In either case, self-revelation on the part of the spirits discloses not only their power but their desires, needs, and vulnerabilities. Helper spirits are frequently ravenous for spiritual food or for the essence (e.g., smoke, alcoholic ether, vapor, or odor) of material food for their spiritual bodies.

Tobacco smoke is a prime object of the craving of helper spirits, since they no longer possess fire as human beings do. Fire has the capacity to "spiritualize" tobacco and other material substances through consumption by flame. The acquisition of spirit help requires familiarity with the meaning of such consumptive processes. As with the mastery of fire, the ability to serve food offerings to spirits rests on knowledge of spiritual appetites. Such knowledge is a goal of shamanic training, disclosing how the desire to consume inheres in the spiritual dynamism governing the cosmos. Spiritual helpers not only need food but are *like* food, often entering and residing in the body of the shaman in the same way that nutrients are ingested and stored in the human body. Meditation on the meaning and nature of their spirit helpers draws novices into reflection on the meaning of their own appetites and on the ways in which those cravings draw them into relationship with all creation. The novice comes to view himself or herself as a consumer of visible and invisible realities and as the outcome of the interpenetrating relations of consumptive processes. The shaman's knowledge of consumptive processes makes the shaman the ideal candidate for the role of curer.

The transmission of knowledge and of spirit helpers is often a visceral and material process in which fasting, special diets, and sexual continence play integral parts. Power may be transmitted by the ingestion of magical substances or by the insertion of darts, thorns, arrows, or other penetrating images of primordial power into the novice's body. The master of ecstatic passage from one realm of being to another must master the passages of his or her own body through controlled diet, regurgitation, the exit of breath during song, or the exit of the soul during dream or ecstasy. The shaman's body and its desires and appetites become identified with helpful or harmful spiritual powers at work in the cosmos. Thus the shamans' physical and social relations express in this life the reality of the supernatural world.

The alienation of spirit and form in this cosmic epoch makes the process of consumption visible as fire, a dynamic most clearly demonstrated in the cosmic conflagration and in the burning of mythic beings, which produced the spiritual and symbolic world. As master of fire, the shaman knows consumptive processes as expressions of the intrinsic relatedness of matter and spirit in the time after primordial wholeness has disappeared. The shaman, as caretaker of souls, must master the consumptive processes that produce transformations of spirit. In some cases, fire (supernatural heat and primordial cooking) produced a number of transformative orders over which the shaman, as master of fire, presides: reproductive physiology seen in menstruation, birth, growth, and death; speech and music related to the separate species of animals and human language-groups; feverish sickness, poison, venom, and their remedies; and symbolic action, especially initiation rites that "cook" candidates or subject them to the heat of incubation. The shamanic master of fire is responsible for the transformative processes that burn at the core of spiritual life: the symbolism at the center or hearth of social units, community groups, all civilized life, and the cosmos itself. Ecstatic specialists also ward off fire by summoning their helper spirits and doing battle with the causes of the cosmic fire that once reduced the earth to cinders.

The ability to endure the heat and light shed by heavenly beings demonstrates the shaman's mastery over fire. Quartz crystals, which embody celestial light and heat, and which glow and simmer inside the shaman's rattle, medicine pouch, or body organs, are emblems of the shaman's relationship to heavenly powers. The shamanic experience of consumption correlates directly with ecstasy. Consumption by fire signifies the death inflicted by supernatural powers during ecstatic trance. Ecstatic death consumes the spiritually awakened or inflamed human being, who is transported to an illumined state of consciousness. This is why the dazzling displays of pyrotechnics that often occur during shamanic demonstrations of power are important cultural spectacles. The shaman's fire-walking, fire-eating, glowing in the dark, and flashing across the sky like a shooting star fasten reflection on the nature of fiery heat and light and on the power of the human specialist who "knows" them intimately.

Through ecstasy, shamans gain authoritative knowledge and experience the supernatural life-conditions of the many strange spaces that the universe comprises. The shaman's soul assumes the physical form of a bird, a beam of light, a lightning bolt, cloud, breeze, or meteor. The metamorphosis invests the shaman with the power of magical flight, by means of which he or she visits diverse cosmic realms. Shamans need not await death to take on the form of free souls who ascend to heaven but may rise to other planes of existence at will. The reachievement of the free-moving and weightless state of the first age is a reminder of the shortcomings of the present human condition and a critique of the status quo. Ordinary mortals free themselves from their present state and fly to celestial existence only when, in death, they transcend the boundaries of human limits, whereas shamans freely pass in and out of all realms, including states labeled "life" and "death." Shamans descend into the underworld or travel to realms on the horizons of the world. In some cases, the entire mythic universe is open to the shaman; in others, types of shamans are distinguished by the cosmic realms they visit or by the worlds from which their spirit helpers come.

The shaman is completely transformed by experiences such as visits to the realm of the dead. Even physical appearance changes, so that, for example, the shaman's countenance radiates with the first celestial light or the shaman's organs become immortal stone or crystals of light. Shamans undergo full existences in different worlds, as is evident in the various physical forms that make possible their different kinds of experience. The ability of shamans to pick their way through the perils of postmortem existence assures their own ultimate destiny and empowers them to serve as psychopomps to guide souls to their destinations or to recover lost souls who have prematurely strayed from their place on earth.

Because shamans can accommodate human existence (their own) to the inaccessible reaches of the universe, they are ideal mediators between incompatible modes of being. The ecstatic's familiarity with spirits and their worlds offers orientation to circumstances that defy the ordinary imagination. Therefore, shamans act as psychopomps, curers who return lost souls, and political leaders who interpret the encounters with colonial beings (whose reality is also shaped by other conditions of time and space).

Shamans possess extraordinary vision, for they see spaces and times no longer fully manifest. Their ecstatic passage enlightens their sight. Shamanic "seeing" is a total experience and not just an exercise of the eyes. Immersed in pure light, the shaman is imbued with the unimaginable colors of sacred realities, which concentrate themselves within him as crystals, visions, or dreams. The supernatural light remakes the eye so that it sees the heart of invisible realities and penetrates the darkness that obscures distinctions between forms. Shamans see reality in its im-mediate state. The shaman's clairvoyance overcomes distance and recovers the condition of knowledge that prevailed before separation of form intervened. The materiality of solid mass presents no obstacle to the penetrating vision of shamans. Concealed objects, such as pathogens hiding inside the body, appear clearly, as do things that have been lost, stolen, or hidden away at enormous distances (such as the soul taken to the forest or underworld).

The reciprocity between supernatural light and the shaman's vision explains the shaman's ability to become invisible. Clairvoyance and invisibility are part of the same process of transformation. As the shaman gains acuity of vision to see the spiritual world, so the shaman's presence, at first invisible and insignificant in the world of spirits, becomes more visible and tangible until the spirits recognize the shaman among their company. In the process, the shaman learns to travel invisibly, like a spirit, in this world. Visions of supernatural realities are often induced by sacred plants. Shamans orchestrate hallucinogenic séances and interpret the luminous images that come during the experiences sparked by ingesting, snuffing, or drinking plant powders and potions. Since sight of this sort is a total existential condition, the shaman's vision effects his intimacy with sacred beings and with the entire unmanifest dimension of existence. The power to discern spirits, which is based on the shaman's transformations during ecstasy, distinguishes this specialist's control over hallucinogenic techniques just as it characterizes control over other forms of knowledge (consumption, fire, sound, initiation). Clairvoyance is a function of shamanic physiology; the material senses are reordered to suit the realm of clear light. The shaman demonstrates the extraordinary human capacity to come to grips and be at home with every imaginable apparition of being. Even in the most sublime realm, where invisible, omniscient beings see all creation, the shaman's glance penetrates the barely imaginable and unmanifest forms of matter with perfect clarity.

Shamans are also masters of sound. The noises of the primordial world — it groans, roars, squeaks, and tinkles — become themes for magical music. In replicating those sounds, the shaman creates variations on primordial themes and evokes new ways of existing. The gourd-rattle is the epitome of the link between sacred sound and shamanic power. Emitted sound, like the shaman's soul, has an ecstatic quality: the sound of primordials assumed a fully autonomous life outside and beyond them and opened up the existence of a new realm of the cosmos. Those sounds are re-presented in the rattle and its noises; they become images of the shaman's own ecstatic soul. The shaman fills the rattle with elements he collects in voyages to other cosmic realms (from which the rattle itself may have come). The rattle contains powers fully present in worlds that normal mortals enter only at death, and hence the rattle may have the power to cause dangerous mystical death. The rattle is frequently a microcosm of active forces, for its construction and the assembly of component elements amount to a creation of the far-flung reaches of the cosmos. By carving mouths or symbols of teeth into the gourd, the shaman reinstigates the cosmic hunger for being and stimulates the appetites of spirits who are fed with tobacco smoke, fire, sound, or the bodies of sick patients consumed by fever or disease.

A similar logic of sound explains the shaman's mastery of music and song. The acquisition of melodies and rhythms and the uses toward which they are put remain consonant with the ecstatic vocation. The formation of aesthetic categories and musical genres cannot stand apart from their religious meaning. Musical categories are not a function of purely acoustical data. The origins of songs and sounds in the realm of space and time visited by the shaman during ecstasy and the symbolism that links those sounds to primordial events are essential features of their aesthetic structure and musical character. Sound is first and foremost an image, an intelligible and communicative expression common to all being.

Every being has a sonic structure that, given certain levels of perceptive awareness, becomes audible. Silence is a sonic form that many potent entities assume, just as invisibility may be their visual form. In ritual blowing and breathing, shamans perform powerful demonstrations of "silent sound." Magical blowing stretches the limits of perceived, meaningful sound. Only spirits and shamans with extremely subtle senses can hear it. The relationship of blowing to spirit-sound allows for interchangeability and creativity along the entire acoustical spectrum. On this spectrum also lie the unintelligible lyrics of shamanic songs and esoteric languages, which are comprehensible only to the initiated. The language that orients one in this life must transcend speech in order to situate one in the presence of creative powers apparent in the imagination. Esoteric speech and arcane liturgical cant make sense in other conditions of existence. Thus, secret language bespeaks the shaman's acculturation to the spirit world.

Shamanic mastery of sound and song sets the ecstatic apart, as do other forms of knowledge. Secrecy and esotericism are not simply methods of hiding information from others. Since mastery of sound requires a fundamental rearrangement of the senses, the sonic dimensions of the experience of ecstasy isolate shamans from the general public, which does not share that experience. In the sound of its shaman, the human community learns that the cosmos makes sense. In the sounds of the shaman's rattle, feathers, leaf bundles, breath, ventriloquism, bird calls, and esoteric languages, the community hears snatches of meaning from the paradisal life that existed before the world's catastrophic division into separate species. The shaman demonstrates how humankind can communicate more freely with all kinds of beings.

Several of the traits discussed above converge to explain the shaman's association with animal forms. Shamans possess intimate knowledge of other kinds of space (that is, they know the secrets of nature) and are expert in the consumptive processes underlying the food chain, which includes animals. The shaman's transformed physiology enables him or her to take on the forms and experiences of primordial animals — life forms conditioned by other kinds of space. South American shamans frequently become jaguars. Shamans and jaguars share many characteristics, including adaptability to all ecological zones, hunting behavior, fearful aggression, sexual prowess, thunderous noise and association with violent weather, and moral ambivalence, but religious reasons account for their identification with one another. Shamanism and jaguar imagery are complex symbolisms that bear the burden of a religious history that goes back to the primordium. The shamans' total transformation in their appearance in jaguar form is an immense spiritual achievement: everything ordinary about the human condition of the shaman is devoured, digested, and left as waste.

Consumption by the jaguar, the consummate consumer, parallels consumption by fire and ecstatic death. All three forms of consumption produce spirit; mastery over them assures control of the changes that compose spiritual life. Through the shaman-jaguar complex, the significations of appetite appear in the symbolisms of food, sex, spirit transformation, fire, light, death, and rebirth. These images are creatively cross-threaded, embellished, and rewoven in unique cultural patterns. They appear in myths about the foundation of social units, the ordering of sexual mores, and economic practices. Embodying the power of consumption on behalf of the community, the shaman guarantees the existence and the viability of spiritual transformation. The prowling spiritual life, embodied in the image of the deadly jaguar, enlivens all social and psychological realities. As master of consumption, the jaguar-shaman directs spiritual life on its proper rotational course (respecting spiritual hierarchies, cycles of prey, systems of avoidances, seasonal change, patterns of shifting political and marital alliance, food chains, and cycles of revenge). The jaguar-shaman counters the tendency of disease to reverse the cycle of consumptions and to exterminate the multiplicative transitional forms of well-nourished life by returning them to a single, all-devouring, unitary state.

The shaman's bodily transformation is connected to cyclic transition through time. By transforming themselves into primordial jaguars, birds, snakes, or other animal forms, shamans recover some of the knowledge lost in past times. The continuity of life and society depends upon this procedure of recovery through animal transformation. Each of the animals with which the shaman identifies has a power and meaning revealed in myth. The power of shamans to assume the bodily shapes of mythic animals relates directly to their power to penetrate and endure the conditions of other forms of cosmic space. Familiarity with changes of form makes the shaman expert in costumery and disguise, transvestism, or homosexual experience. Shamanic management of space through this manipulation of bodily experience, especially through the animal imagery of mythical beasts, situates the entire community in proper relationship to the powers that define its territory and its place in the world.

As a specialist in space, the shaman cares for the health of the human body, the spatial home of the human soul. The shaman restores well-being by reinstating lost souls to the body or by extracting from the body's inner space pathogens that only he or she can see. The curing-shaman directs cosmic traffic, safeguards the good order of cosmic spaces, and polices qualitatively different areas of the universe. The knowledge of physics possessed by the shaman-physician thus guarantees the significance and integrity of human physical space when it is threatened by the disorder of disease.

Sucking is a technique of cure that accompanies the picture of the body as a spatial microcosm. The efficacy of sucking cures relates directly to the shaman's mystical physiology, especially the ability of the shaman's mouth and stomach to engulf, transform, and extrude spirits that appear in the form of physical objects, such as tobacco, hallucinogenic beverages, stones, splinters, snakes, insects, and songs. Swallowing and vomiting are moments of the sucking operation. They highlight a spirituality of cosmic matter centered on the shaman's mouth, which, like the primordial vagina or mouth of mythical heroines, becomes the place of transformation. Mystical channels inside the shaman's chest, legs, arms, hands, or rattle serve as vessels or canals of passage from one state to another. During sucking cures, the shaman opens his or her body and sucks in a pathogen, drawing it into seclusion and into the presence of powerful forces that transform and control the menace. Through the powers of the shaman's mouth (signified in its fleshly power to suck and blow), all afflicting elements are removed from integral space, whether that be the body or the living space of the house or village. The extraction of a pathogen by sucking with the mouth (or the mouths incised on the rattle-gourd) is a cosmic drama in which shamans enlist the aid of all the ecstatic techniques and spiritual powers at their disposal. The shaman's mouth, like the mouths or body-openings of the powerful heroes whose acts are the models for medical practice, contains all the transformative processes that make life in this world possible.

Shamanic cure is theatrical. Public display of the sick and dramatic celebrations of triumphs over the forces of disease are themselves acts that promote health. Illness becomes a sacrament of well-being. Communal reflection focuses on the right order of the cosmos, puzzled out in the face of disorder and disease. This explains why shamanic cure is so often miraculous, in the sense of a deliberate exhibition of normally invisible powers. It seeks to astonish spectators and compel them to admire what is real and, therefore, life-giving. Miracles publicize realities ordinarily housed in unseen realms of the universe or stashed beneath the limen of awareness. Truth-telling in shamanic medical practice requires that the performance amaze the audience with a startling demonstration of that truth. To communicate truths of this kind, shamans must make available to the naked eye what they see in their clairvoyant penetration of the spirit domain. By means of miraculous performances and shamanic miracle plays, the audience is able to see reality reflexively, the way shamans see it. The miraculous apparition of sacred powers moves patient and audience into a healthier state; the appearance of an extracted pathogen, held up for all to see, reestablishes the world order fundamental to wellness. Dramatic curing performances, which reenact the gestures of mythic protoshamans, provide for the public what ecstasy offers the shaman: a visible encounter with the forces at work on other planes of existence. This existential knowledge, mediated by the shaman, sustains public health and well-being.

The possessed medium, the canonist, and the ecstatic are examples of religious specialists who are individual persons. But not all religious authority is personal or individual. Binding contracts and group consensus also have a religious foundation. Such is the case in ceremonial dialogue, where formality, exchange, and antiphonal proceedings may carry on at great length. In some cases, ceremonial chanting is a judicial institution that is used to settle claims or decide requests. At times the aesthetics of ranting outweigh in importance the contents of the arguments. At any rate, performance of the ceremony binds the two implicated parties by creating a new solution of difference.

The parliamentary procedure of ceremonial dialogue observes a mythic structure that echoes the order in the process of creation. Forensics and social contracts derive their efficacy, binding authority, and clausal structures from primordial speech-contests or from other dialectics of creation described in myth and often reflected in the antiphonal cadence of myth-telling performances. Myth-telling and ceremonial speech are both oppugnant, existential stances. By calling present realities into question and by creating new qualities of relations, which contravene everyday existence, they publicize contradictions between different states of being and exhibit, in the center ring of formally ordered society, the combativeness that sustains human culture. Myth and ceremonial dialogue are not only creative refutations of the status quo but persuasive arguments for change. In their very performance, they create motives for credibility and conditions for accepting new lifeways and abandoning old ones. Ceremonial dialogue imitates the creative encounter between entirely different qualities of supernatural being and is, therefore, a suitable ritual behavior for occasions when different social or linguistic groups must creatively merge their cultural perspectives or self-interests.

The religious bases of special, authoritative knowledge should not be equated with their functional applications. Healing and evildoing, for example, may base themselves on any of the forms of knowledge that ground special authority: possession, ecstasy, scholasticism, or faith in the forces of formal argument. All authority depends, in some degree, on public performance, for, even if self-appointed, authorities must gain recognition from some constituency in order to be effective. Performance renders visible for communal scrutiny the alleged basis of a candidate's authority. Legitimate authorities make public appearances to demonstrate symbolically their intimacy with the supernatural powers that embolden them and make them credible. This inevitable connection between staged performance and the practice of a religious specialist opens shamans to the accusation of being shams and authorities in general to the charge of being mere actors. Separating specialists from laypeople requires powerful imagination and authentic performance. To remain apart, authorities must keep their gestures and ornaments vital and their symbolic instruments charged with power. Their own special roles are channels for the sacred, revitalizing sources that influence communal imagination by reimbuing it with images of power.

DEATH AND TERMINOLOGY

The meaning constituting termination — the deliberate attempt to accomplish a proper end — discloses itself through the symbols that surround death and the end of the world. Death and eschatology are the final strain-gages of human and worldly significance. Endings are intrinsically probative. Indeed, ultimate endings test language and try to the limits its capacity to reveal and communicate primordial meanings. The creativity of primordial appearances goes on trial; its significations are subjected to final examination.

Death originates at the dawn of time. Mythic explanations of death do not usually show just cause for death: the triviality of death's causes matches the arbitrariness of death's interruptive presence. Final, irreversible death makes itself a part of the cycle of conception, gestation, and birth. Through death arises regenerative life, the dissoluble condition of mortal being, which reveals a new quality of time. All changing and corruptible matter (blood, flesh, wood, humus) uncovers, at some point in its cycle, an inert, dormant, or decomposed condition fertile with potential. Death is the humiliating consequence of material existence, a moment that turns one to decayed prime matter or humus rich with the possibilities of new life.

Regenerative life takes place in the symbolic world, the partial and fragmentary condition born in the wake of primordial destruction. Nothing is exhaustively what it appears to be and no appearance totally exhausts the meaning it signifies. Under such conditions, emitting the wrong signal at the wrong place or time carries irreversibly fatal consequences. Miscues, premature signals, or incorrect signs all provoke death. In myths of the origins of death, ornaments, clothing, gestures, spoor, smells, tastes, colors, or sounds have deadly effect when they evoke the wrong one of their many possible significations. Significant meaning requires coordination of the symbolic orders of space, time, light, sound, and movement. In this symbolic world of subtle distinctions it expresses itself in fatally complicated ways.

Disobedience, especially the transgression of divine or heroic commandments, caused permanent death. Those commands surrounded existence with the negative assumptions that framed the fully manifest meanings of the primordial world. Proscriptive commands ("Thou shalt not . . . ") directly established negative relationships and imposed absolute distance and separation by explicitly forbidding certain categories of act, sound, time, food, or relationship. Exhortatory commands ("Thou shalt only, totally, or above all . . . ") indirectly imposed a network of negative relations by setting up exclusive ties with only one kind of food, place, being, or activity. Both kinds of negative command would avoid the noise and miscommunication that characterize the condition of meaning in a postcatastrophic world. Both gave priority of value to certain kinds of relations even while they closed off other signal-paths. All important primordial signals could have remained unimpeded, distinct, and unambiguous markers of social, dietary, sexual, and other orders. The commands highlighted the patterns of significant communication and cautioned the creatures of the new world against acting like primordial beings, the nonsymbolic and fully manifest realities who performed acts of unbridled sex, sound, consumption, dance, or travel with blatant disregard for the time, place, and relationships involved. The commands imply that human beings should not perform such acts in the absolute manner of primordials but should confine these performances to their proper symbolic setting. Breach of symbolic closures of this sort figure largely in myths of the origins of death through disobedience. Disobedience loosed the symbolic, paradoxical condition in which contraries overlap and coexist.

The myths of the origins of death demonstrate how the efficacy of signs in this world eventually impedes the clarity of their meaning. As soon as the signs of death are present, through unguarded speech, inadvertent misapplication of body-paint or earrings, or deliberate disobedience, mortality enters the world in the form of interruption, opacity, and noise. Incorrect answers to questions posed by divinities or a mythic character's inability to produce the proper password, countersign, grip, or high sign results in death. These failures are failures to perform successfully the test that demonstrates control over symbolic life. Percussive sounds and loud reports are the most striking symbols in these myths. Final words and curses, yelling, shouting, onomatopoeic noises, and premature crying or weeping become instruments of death in the primordium. Later, in the funeral rites of this world, such noises are instruments of transition to another life.

Even within single communities, differing accounts are made of the origins of death. This variation has a religious meaning that is lost when all are reduced to a single common structure. The religious value of myths appears precisely in their capacity to depict the real and to express its ambivalent, ambiguous, and contradictory guises in this world—in the full significance of their multiplicity and multivalence. In turn, the religious value of mythic variance resides in the imagination that spawns such significant contradictions and clashing images of what is real, along with signals (one might say metastatements) that the full meaning of these symbols transcends any single representation. In mythic variation, the religious imagination creates a perpetual need for new experiences and expressions of whatever is real.

Its origin myths illustrate that the meaning of death, in whatever guise it first appeared (darkness, noise, decay, offspring or generative womb, faulty gesture or decoration), was not sufficiently recognizable as what it was. Its consequences, too, were never entirely clear. Hence, the noise, opacity, and disorder of death continue to obscure the meanings necessary to negotiate one's course through symbolic existence. The self-consciousness of mortals sorts out the process by which meaning is signified in the symbolic world. Self-consciousness depends upon the clear sense that one's existence is symbolic.

Human mortality becomes a key to gaining knowledge of one's own significations. This self-awareness develops in the rites that manipulate alienation and ceremonial death during transition from one state to another. In experiencing the "divide" of symbolic death, cultures separate noise into the distinct sounds of music, language, speech, and other symbolic codes whose meaning is evident; when mortals make sense of their signals (the signs of death and its obscuring effects), cultures glimpse more clearly the primordial meaning that underlies all significant order. In this way, awareness of one's own meaning reestablishes authentic communication in the cosmos. Symbolic languages are, in the full sense of the word, a *terminology* because they include the reality of termination at every turn, thereby making metastements about the ends and purposes of every bounded form (speech units, hand movements, decorative articles, dance patterns, weeping, and so on). Since every symbol is predicated on its finiteness, symbolic expressions must remain true to their end.

The instant of death signifies a profound change whose nature and effects are revealed in the shifting images of the dying body. New relationships with other dimensions of time and space provoke death by recomposing the individual's physiology. At some definable point of no return in the process of dying, the person's body manifests signs of the reconfiguration of its constitutive powers. At death, the elements of personal and social life no longer congregate in the body-space in a viable way. The soul departs, losing its accustomed place in the spatial worlds centered on the body. Consequently, in the presence of the corpse, the spaces of the house, village, and universe signify different meanings. They betoken not life but death. Space becomes an indicator of the changing relationship to the diverse qualities of time. Taking their cue from bodily changes, variations in music or prescribed behavior mark off the ritual of dying into episodes.

The person who certifies death is not merely a medical examiner but a discerner of spirits. Since death conditions the whole being, the expert reads physiological signs as evidence of irreversible spiritual change. Postmortem inquest amounts to a reconstruction of an individual's history, a biographical process that interprets the signs of the deceased's existence in time. Beyond identifying historical facts, however, the inquest evaluates and judges their meaning for the future life of the community. Inquest is a hermeneutics of retrieval motivated by suspicion. It does not seek to create meaning but to interpret what already lurks in the devastating signs of a particular death. If it attributes blame, it only detects a presence announced in the residue of the terminative acts that determined the final state of meaning. Like responsible historiography, the coroner's report is the outcome of a process of recognition. Unlike myth, whose interpretation is tantamount to the repetition or imitation of the beginnings that form the creative foundations of culture, historical inquest interprets the past from its fatal consequences and reconstructs irreversible events in order either to avoid a repetition of their deadly effects or to transcend the signs of their endings.

Burial presents a fleeting opportunity to understand religious life in South America, but burial sites soon fall into the state of being they signify: opacity of meaning to those living in another condition of time. During the ceremonial deaths that take place during rites of transition, ritual seclusions enshroud space in order to define the time of change, and this ambiguous imagery of enclosure attends death to the end, for the dead are often enveloped in containers during their disintegration. Because containers hide signs of life, they can be instruments of transformation and change. Closure is a central achievement of funeral proceedings, which often abound with images of enclosure. In some cases, mourners paint the cadaver, then wrap it in leaves, ferns, or vines, surround it with mats or place it in an urn, coffin, or canoe, which is then inserted in a hole in the ground. They tap up the deceased's body-passages, deliberately shut the mouth and eyes, and fold the hands or arms to signal closure. Clothing also helps accomplish the occultation desired for closure. In its finest hour, death manifests closure through consummate finery. Ceremonial attire, ordinarily used during festivals that mark the closing of seasons or periods of marked time, shrouds the corpse forever as a sign of irreversible closure. The outfitted corpse is hidden away in a condition of perpetual occultation, much as liturgical masks and ornaments are temporarily hidden during the off-season. Sealing the dead from sight in their finest array unveils a fundamental ambivalence toward death. High visibility and conspicuous display cover over a mysterious mode of existence.

The corpse is sometimes returned to a tomb that represents a womb, but while the living womb enveloped one in flesh, containers made of other substances promise a different future condition. Clay pots, vegetal gourds that rot, leaf bundles, vehicles, wreathes of ferns and greens, textile mantles, fiber nets, and wooden crates become vessels of one-way transport to a new world. Funeral enclosures accomplish the complete transfiguration of the dead person. Each mythic image of closure reveals specific values of the death and transmutation of incarnate life. By occluding the significations that marked the deceased in this world (such as physical features, personality traits, signs of change or growth), these final seals foreshadow and make room for a new kind of appearance under utterly new conditions. Death is the ultimate ritual seclusion; its obscuration effects the passage from transitory existence to the domain of postmortem life. Once at home in the symbolic world, human life now mysteriously assumes the unmanifest condition of sacred beings. For this reason, the dead are objects of fear and awe, dread and attraction.

Death-related ambivalence is a religious situation. The fearful respect accorded the dead prompts contradictory behaviors. Even while the dead are mourned with sorrow, funeral proceedings act to guarantee that they will depart this world. In the presence of death, ambivalence reveals itself to be a total condition, like primordial chaos. Ordinarily discrete and opposed to one another, conditions such as fear and fascination, longing and dread, or love and hate, now appear absolute and unbounded. Their unbridled coexistence, an overwhelming and consumptive experience, is imaginable in the guise of universal catastrophe. Cataclysmic fire, flood, darkness, stone, and rot reappear in the forms of funeral pyres, bonfires, memorial stone, durable bone-relics, vigils, heavy drinking during wakes, watery graves, the putrifying corpse, and so on.

The dead take on the supernatural condition of total beings; relationship with them can no longer be simple. In death, death and life irresolvably overrun one another. All fundamental distinctions fail in the face of this ambivalence. Nothing makes any difference. The state of fearful respect for the beloved dead calls for symbolic acts of discrimination, which effect transition through chaos by means of sacrifice, dispatch, cutting, or the contestation of sports and ritual battle. To penetrate the ambivalence of death and to separate fear from fascination and anxiety from hope, mourners manipulate images of mutilation by slicing, biting, scratching, scourging, gashing the skin, gnashing the teeth, tearing out their hair, or rending their garments. Breaking, biting, and cutting the body (or ceremonial foods or sacrificed items) leave impressions and mark fundamental distinctions. These acts reimpress symbolic order on chaos just as, at the beginning of this world's epoch, some form of sacrifice dispelled absolute darkness or deluge and divided the primordial from the mundane mode of being. The mutilations practiced by mourners demonstrate the symbolic process that imposes distinctions on overlapping modes of being. Smashing utensils or destroying personal effects rends differences in the experience of the sacred, a fundamentally seamless reality. In order to dispel the inordinate, irrational, undifferentiated, and indistinct condition of primordial being signified by death, mourning must be impressive.

Through the effective demonstration of opposition (in tugs-of-war, guessing games, food-fights, trials, dance contests, or battles of the bands), life and death are separated from one another and held apart in fruitful tension. The finality of irreversible death is the puzzle to solve, the adversary to overcome. Death must be answered; its apparent absoluteness must meet its match so that even final death may be put to rest as but one moment in the creative cycle of periodic existence. By vying with one another during funerals, contestants disclose the oppositions and alternating rhythms that make regenerative life viable in the face of a chaos that equalizes fear and attraction, movement and stasis, affine and kin, sadness and delight, life and death.

Food and consumption figure prominently in funeral symbolism. Furthermore, the dead (imaged as decomposing seeds, fruit or leaves fallen to the forest floor, or dismembered tubers) become guarantors of fertile abundance. Caught in the clutches of final death, the dead have no direct access to the regenerative fruits of periodic death, agricultural labor, or the hunt. They must obtain food from the living. While the living sustain the dead in memory with food offerings, the dead give life to the living through dream images during the deathlike state of sleep, which brings home the experience of mortality. Death effects the exchange of material, consumable life-forms for immaterial images. Having joined the ranks of unmanifest supernatural beings, the dead become a source of symbolic life. Thus, each form of the human being, living and dead, gives tokens of its own existence to the other and offers the other the very substance of its life. This exchange takes place most dramatically in the ritual hunt performed at (or after) funerals, in which hunt the shadows and sounds of the dead are provided with game, and, in return, the young dancer-hunters (or their children or ritual wards) acquire new names from the dead. Even while they accomplish an exchange with the dead, the funeral hunt and food offering interpose distance between the living and the dead by providing sustenance for the deceased's journey and dispatching the dead spirit to another world. By consuming the forms of this world, death clears the way for the significations of another kind of life. The fruit of one domain, whether food or phantasm, sustains life in the other, and death is the medium of their mutual consumption. The reciprocal prestations of the living and the dead, who trade food for dreams (or shadows, symbolic designs, or invisible sounds such as names and songs), constitute the total ritual community, the communion of all humanity, whether manifest or unmanifest, living or dead.

The fate of the cadaver generates images of consumption, the material process that results from the coincidence of all opposites. The body decomposes as it exhibits the changing signs of corruption and ultimate transformation. The symbolic performances that dispose of the corpse render this transfiguration reflexive through the acts of burial in the earth, exposure to the air, cremation, liquidation, or ingestion. The grave is not an idle setting. It can be an image of creation; the act of burial can reenact an episode of the cosmogony. The grave centers human death in a perfect world. The tomb can be considered a total symbolic fact, representing the process that regenerates life as it passes through states of death and thereby reconstituting the creative processes of the universe.

Cremation fire transforms what it engulfs. In the manner of the mythical conflagration that destroyed the world, fire comes to light while eating and bears the consumptive stamp of ravenous primordial jaguars, birds of prey, or marine monsters who once possessed fire in their bellies or mouths. Crematory fire devours dead flesh to transform life and, in several senses, enlightens the body. Weight obstructs the achievement of optimal postmortem existence. If the elements that compose a person linger untransformed or untouched by a process such as fire, flood, or consumption, they become increasingly unwieldy. Their presence weighs on the living and overwhelms the space and imagery of life. Fire overcomes the undesirable weight of the dead flesh or soul. Hence, cremation is a liberation, an irreversible step in the life-cycle. Not all funeral fires are crematory. Sometimes fires are placed on top of the grave, in the central plaza of the village, or at a crossroads beyond the residence space, so that the deceased will pass through them and become a spirit. Sometimes fires are used to destroy the personal effects of the dead or to warm the soul on its way to the afterlife.

Some communities dispose of the dead several times over, through cremation, burial, dispersal of ashes, immersion in water, or reburial of bones in a secondary grave. These acts are not simply redundancies. They represent different steps in a serial process of refinement in which each ending is a distinct moment in a spiritual economy. This refinishing process brings the deceased to the final terms of human existence. Finishing off the corpse in multiple ways defines the limits of the dead individual vis a vis the society of the living and the elements of the universe. By locating the borders where these realities abut one another, the process of refining death lends definition to the cosmos, the community, and the self. The outer reaches of these entities become visible in the symbolism of the cadaver's deterioration as it passes through the terminal processes of fire, earth, water, and human ritual. Passing through successive elemental qualities, the deceased undergoes multiple transformations; the cadaver undergoes refinement by suffering images of total chaos: darkness, petrifaction, conflagration, flood, utter voracity. These processes recapitulate the major forms of total transformation. Finish by finish, refinement redistributes the deceased human life to the fundamental, primordial elements — earth, wind, fire, stone, mythic beings, mythic places. Deceased individuals gradually take on their destiny, their full social and cosmic status.

The ingestion of some of the flesh or ashes of the deceased is a definitive moment in the process of refinement. By ingesting signs of death, consumers respond to the presence of the sacred in deadly guise. Consuming the dead reenacts the destructive processes that dispatched primordial beings to an unmanifest mode and closed the mythic world. Ingesting relics makes the human consumer a sacred instrument of closure and irreversible transformation, like the tomb or pyre. Thus, the living thrive on the ambiguity of death even as they dispose of its awe-full traces. Flesh and bone signify different modes of being. The skeleton consists of many bones, articulated and well-formed, whereas the carnal body is one flesh, formless and undivided. Appropriate disposal of the elements of flesh and bone requires that they meet their match in different ways. Eating flesh and consuming bone-ash are different symbolic processes with separable meanings. They reflect, respectively, the dreadful and attractive aspects of that total condition called respect for the dead. Ritual division or consumption of flesh differs from drinking liquified bone-ash in that the former subjects cut flesh to bone (especially the teeth), while the latter subjects bone, burned and pulverized, to the sucking powers of the flesh.

The dissection of chaos through the symbolic division of flesh orders the cosmos and establishes the consumer as its center. By devouring flesh, the consumer subjects its inherent formlessness to the sharp divisions made by the rigid form of bone — a symbolic strategy also evident in other rites of transition that pierce or score the skin with the bones or teeth of birds, monkeys, fish, or rodents. As in blood sacrifices in which the body of the victim is cut up, the ritual ingestion of flesh divides and conquers the chaos manifest in the physical presence of outsiders such as the dead (especially enemy dead and foreigners). Ambivalent death is the enemy. Conceived in the image of supernatural jaguars, serpents, vultures, or monsters, the bodies of sacrificial victims become corpses marking life with regenerative signs of final death and signifying the irreversible sort of death that undergirds life of empire or cosmos.

The link between the presence of aliens and the ritual ingestion of flesh also characterizes the colonial situation during the age of European expansion and explains the lurid reports of cannibalistic practices that were disseminated by both sides. Blood sacrifice and the related ingestion of fleshly relics are symbolic processes that can suit aggressive programs of territorial and political expansion. Partaking of the captive's or tributary's body culminates the acculturating process of transubstantiation: the one who is wild, savage, or marginal is ingested into the community of civilizing consumers. The ingestion of foreign flesh, in this extreme form, dispels the ambivalence of death by dispatching the outward form of the "other" who threatens life. The consumed corpse represents death, a condition of reality utterly different from life. Division and consumption of its fleshly signs offer hope of victory over the threat of final death. Through permanent acquisition of what is other than oneself, processes of imperial consumption expand the boundaries of life. The transaction of sacrificial dismemberment and consumption draws foreign flesh and blood, together with all they signify about life and death, into the symbolic currencies sacred to the consumers. Sacrifice becomes a microcosmic icon of the attempt to cut through chaos, vanquish death, and establish a life-order based on division and conquest of peoples and territories. Because human death signifies the dreadful sacrality of supernatural life, consumption of the dead reenacts the mythical dispensation in which prepotent supernaturals were dispatched to make way for this epoch.

Drinking the bone-ash of close kin differs from ingesting the flesh of enemies in that it embraces the other pole of ambivalent respect for the dead: not dread, but fascination. Drinking consummates the desire to unite with the dead. Rites that care for ashes of the dead, either by storing or consuming them, link human bone and the human soul. Drinking bone-ash relics liberates both the living and the dead from the ambivalence present in death.

Terminating human life and disposing of the corpse can be forms of consumption that challenge one's understanding of the limits of significant existence. Mortuary consumption of human relics unsettles mourners as well as scholarly interpreters because of the way it questions the nature of symbolic life. Notwithstanding the economic and political ramifications of consumption, its basic significance arises from the religious situation of human existence. Symbolic life is a disposition toward the sacred, in the sense that it reenacts the process that disposed of the first beings. Whether sacrificial, funereal, imperial, or economic, consumption originates with the undertakings of sacred beings. This is why each form of consumption owes something of its meaning to others and why no single consumptive process is fully understood without exposing its religious roots.

To sustain itself, the cosmos ceaselessly replays the process that brought the first world to term. Grounded in myth, consumption is the inner dynamic of the cosmos and the principle symbolic strategy with which it confronts chaos. Imitating the disposal of sacred beings, the centrifugal or entropic forces of consumption exercise the power to establish symbolic limits and to imagine the edges of order. All consumptive acts are therefore in some measure sacrificial and create the symbolic conditions for the sustaining experience of what is holy and, therefore, deeply ambivalent. To evaluate the meaning of their existence, which is symbolic in every dimension, human communities must explore the limits of consumption by discovering the primal locus of these limits and reenacting their original form. Death is a privileged opportunity for such reflection on symbolic terms.

In order to sacrifice death — that is, in order to call out its sacrality and reveal its meaning — funeral practices place each manifest quality of being in the creative presence of its opposite. Funerals are ironic exercises, juxtaposing sorrow and festivity, sadness and graveside humor. On the one hand, undivided flesh is subjected to dismemberment. But, ironically, in the act of consuming the one flesh, separate bodies of consumers become one communion and many territories become one imperial universe. On the other hand, the many bones, well defined and durable, meet a different end. Burned and pulverized beyond distinction, their ashen residue is consumed as an indivisible and formless liquid. Bone, in the refined form of drink, is thus subjected to the sucking power of the flesh. By reengulfing bones of individual relatives through the act of drinking, each group reaffirms itself as unique and separate from others. During the consumptive rites of death, the symbolic process, born of terminal situations, ironically turns on itself and attempts to free human language and understanding from the limits of its own terminology.

Elements of the personality unravel after death and components of the body and psyche are redistributed to their various postmortem abodes. The disintegration of the individual discloses principles of distributive justice and clarifies how the material, spiritual, individual, cosmic, social, and moral dimensions of existence interface with one another. The process of decomposition prompts reflection on the cosmic implications of the human constitution. The reconfigured fate of its deceased member confirms a group's vision of the interrelatedness of all manifestations of being. Death recapitulates, on the scale of the person, the cosmogonic process of the universe (with its series of failures and advances over aeons of time), and the life of the dead is involved with the entire history of culture and cosmos. Transformed and redistributed after death, the symbolic properties of the person guarantee that the meaning of mortal human life is coextensive with the significance of the wider universe of being.

The complicated geography of the afterlife reflects the complexity of mythic, cosmic, and cultural life before death. In tracing the whereabouts of the dead, the no-longer-manifest, one outlines the contours of the invisible world. Postmortem geography sorts out the confusion of human existence and discloses the essential relationships between morality and symbolic space. Trial by judge, for example, is a noteworthy postmortem ordeal through which one space of the universe is marked off from another. The judge holds one kind of being separate from another and sets up divisions among the newly arrived according to the qualities of their character. The judge assigns them to that quality of being, that space, from which the criteria for judgment derive. Only malingering souls are not well fixed in space. The segregation of the dead on ethical grounds, including the ethos-fashioning performance of kinship, ceremonial, and linguistic patterns, reveals how the moral valence of human experience is bound to a mythography of cosmic space, a cultural evaluation of the human place in the world. Moral discernment, like ritual combat, contest, and cutting, divides the experience of a sacred reality, especially the fearful respect for the dead, into imaginable components. Moral judgment sorts out the experience of death in terms of the value-laden spaces of the cosmos.

Symbolic space is an evaluation of qualities of being which are simultaneously material, moral, historical, and spiritual. The mythic geography of death therefore organizes the living, historical community. Social relations, architecture and village layout, and naming patterns all take their cues from the dead. The roads beyond death lead to fundamental sources of experience, the quintessence of what is sublime, absurd, grotesque, terrifying, and beautiful. No matter what supernatural realities life may grow to contain, it remains comprehensible because it falls within the bounds of space. The mythic map, which comes alive at death, demonstrates that space remains imaginable and significant even when invisible or when powers within it are ambivalent and unmanifest. Such assurance is achieved only at great cost.

Mythic landscapes are dotted with portrayals of struggle, for the full map of being issues from the ordeal of transcending limits and traveling beyond death. To traverse the mythic map is to move from one mode of being to another, journey requiring arduous changes in one's fundamental conditions of existence. The ordeals that the dead undergo reflect the difficulty of obtaining experiential knowledge of the full range of being. Initiatory trials punctuate the progress of the dead along their path to the otherworld and mark transitions into new states. The dead pass through fire or impenetrable barriers, cross tightropes or slippery paths, squeeze through tiny cracks or holes, remain silent or dancing, keep custody of their eyes or ears, display extraordinary skill, suffer bizarre multiple deaths, or are swallowed by monsters. The living often help the dead through their time of trial by performing rites and observing restrictions. Care tendered the material remains and spiritual elements of the deceased can affect the entire spiritual destiny of the individual. At times, however, the dead are beyond the help of the living. Often the best that the living can do is to invoke the intercession of a supernatural guide, or psychopomp, who will lead the dead across the unfamiliar territories, pockmarked with trials, of the otherworlds. After passing through their ordeals, dead souls don new clothes, assume new bodies, or take on new forms that signal their transformed condition.

The land of the dead confronts life with its own implicit, assumed conditions; its opposition to the world of the living is seldom simply that of a mirror image. As a probative state, death interrogates and tries the symbolic processes most taken for granted in reproductive life. In the land of the dead, essential distinctions are lowered, directions are reversed, separate episodes occur as simultaneous events, food is plentiful but tasteless, central values are absent or diffused, and the periphery is everywhere. Through these contradictions and reversals, the religious imagination, exploring the condition of death, critiques its own achievements and deconstructs the certitudes of the spatial, temporal, political, economic, or social orders.

The land of the dead plays with resemblances and dissimilations and scrutinizes the underpinnings of analogy and dialectic. Conditions that remain an obscure or invisible background in the land of the living, such as shadows or images reflected in the iris of the eye, come to the fore as substantial agents in the land of the dead. Conversely, the absolutes of social life, such as affinity, marriage, or labor, become arbitrary and ephemeral. Reversals in the land of the dead (day for night, right for left, motion for stasis) allow latencies to challenge and subdue the blatant imagery of life. Refraction of the imagery of deathly passage into another medium unearths aspect of symbolic life that are not immediately apparent in the land of the living. The dynamics of life in this world invisibly harbor the stasis, immobility, and permanence of death. Reversals expose the unexamined arbitrariness that marks off and binds all that is familiar. The negativity simulated in the absence of a symbolic center in the afterlife, for example, reflects the strangeness and mystery that hedge the process of symbolic knowledge in this world. Existence without affines, alliances, sharp distinctions, growth or change is an expression of the otherness that defines death and afterlife. Hidden in manifestations of this world but more evident in the bizarre afterworld is the quality of strangeness and mystery that is requisite to knowledge based on symbolism, for the meaning of a symbol points beyond itself toward that which it is not.

In the land of the dead, imagination dredges up the latent but everlasting sources of symbolic existence: alienation, hiddenness, and irreversible closure. Eternal feasting signifies the permanent closure of irreversible death. The unbroken entertainment that so often is a feature of the afterlife contrasts directly with earthly life, where ceremonial celebrations occur only from time to time. Joyous as it appears, perpetual ceremony is exhausting and trying, like so many other aspects of death. Endless festival exemplifies the ordeal, the struggle to bring on an end or create a new and fitting boundary.

Human being never escapes the bounds of symbolic meaning. Within this alienated predicament, a symbolic enclosure or ritual seclusion permanently sealed in death, human beings grasp their own situation and transcend its limits. By caricaturing life on earth through weird resemblance and striking contrast, the life of the dead brings a culture to grips with the human condition and the fulfillment of its destiny. A clear view of postmortem alienation enables human beings to recognize death and its meaning as integral parts of human, symbolic reality and not just an inappropriate end to life. In facing death, human beings' great hope is that one form of existence can dissolve completely in favor of a new condition of being. The deconstructive forces of symbolic life guarantee this complete dissolution.

The migration of the soul to a new place after death implies metamorphosis, the acquisition of a form suited to its conditions. Metempsychosis and reincarnation are the main forms of metamorphosis. Postmortem metamorphosis is not absolutely distinct from the transformations effected in all ritual deaths, for, like them, it produces a new state of being enclosed in new symbolic form. But the chrysalis of final death is unparalleled. Wrapped totally in symbolism, death remains penetrable only to the religious imagination. That is why its imagery offers unmatched freedom for transformation —a liberation that is not always welcome, since it approaches the wanton freedom of sacred and chaotic beings, who inspire dread as well as awe. But the transmigration of the deceased soul to its proper final abode helps eliminate the terror associated with metamorphosis. Sealed within an environment suited to their totally symbolic condition, the dead experience their eerie freedom of form without overly unsettling the living.

Metempsychosis, the reappearance of human spiritual elements in various material forms, reveals that human spirituality is part of the cosmic economy. In the dissolution that accompanies death, human existence discovers that its meaning coincides with the mythic history of the cosmos and its components. After undergoing the transformation of death, the human spirit is at home in the world and even manifests itself in the material form of fundamental elements (earth, stone, animals, clouds, lightning, wind, rain, stars, plants). Elements of the human spirit identify with the *meaning* of these cosmic structures and processes; these elements reappear in the symbolic, primordial, or mythic condition of matter and not in the abstract world described by modern scientific geology, chemistry, genetics, or meteorology. Understanding human metamorphosis, then, depends on knowledge of the mythic history of cosmic forms. When the world and humanity are appraised as fully symbolic processes, charged with the meaning of sacred realities and events, the cosmos becomes the proper context for human freedom.

Since human life, especially at death, becomes one with the fundamental processes of the cosmos, and since death unleashes life in new forms, human death can recreate the physical and social universe. Symbolism incorporates death into the reproductive sequence of life. In the form of death, alienation guarantees that symbolic life will remain concrete and material and that it will bear fruit in the form of food, new generations of human beings, and extended life in another world. Through its intimate link with death and passage, symbolism proves itself to be a terminology capable of describing and discussing the meaning of its own ends and, therefore, a language creative of authentic life on any plane, whether social, intellectual, musical, or linguistic.

ESCHATOLOGY

Every complete mythology includes a terminal vision, for the end is an essential element of the integrity to which individual symbols point and the completion for which the symbolic condition as a whole yearns. The escha-

ton culminates symbolic life. Eschatologies assess humanity and the material universe as they are defined by their constant subjugation to the obliterative tendencies of cosmic life. The fate of all creation appears in the signs of
its decay, because it is a terminal condition. The symbolic orders of the
universe are the residues of the primordial catastrophe. At the end of time,
the powers that make passing appearances in this world are recalled all at
once for a final, concurrent display. The end of the world summons forth all
the total conditions betokened in the partial symbolic appearances of this
world. In the most dramatic apocalypses, the eschaton fulfills the total degeneration that is implied in partiality itself. The advent of the fullest expression of partiality, limit, erosion, shortcomings, failure, and fault collapses
symbolic life under its own concentrated weight: the appearance of the
sacred in every symbolic form.

Because millennial dreams and prophetic reforms grapple with the
overwhelming particularity of a society's historical circumstances, studies of
eschatology must immure themselves in historical details. Heroic prophets
of doom interpret historical details as signs of the end of cosmic existence
and quest for the virtues and abundance of paradise as they practice a ritual
life-style designed to achieve their goal. Violence is one form of such ritual
performances designed to hasten the end. In messianic revolts, irradicable
historicity is a religious situation, and historical events themselves become
signs of the sacred; that is, the relentless press of historical circumstance
reveals the im-mediacy of the sacred and portends the utter dissolution of
symbolic being. The cumulative weight of significant historical events suffocates the creativity originated by sacred beings in myth and exercised in rite.

Messianism is one kind of response to political history, a prophetic way
of reading signs of the vitality or morbidity of cosmic life. If they are to be
real, the germinal hopes of even political salvation must have existed at the
beginning. Expectation of the end and hope for renewal, purification, unbroken health, and salvation point to fundamental qualities of the beginning.
They harken back to ancient traditions of deluge and conflagration. The
eschaton offers the long-awaited response to primordial cataclysm and its
historical aftermath. This cosmos, this symbolic existence that only *represents* true, unseen realities, will crumble. The symbolic world will exhaust its
possibilities for expressing primordial meaning.

Prophets exemplify the effort to create a cultural posture that both saves
and condemns historical realities by disclosing the relationship of historical
realities to mythic and eschatological qualities of time. Prophets can reveal
the true origins or the glorious end because prophecy was instituted by
forceful heroes or deities who presided over the first creative catastrophes in
the mythic world. One sign of impending doom that is both pointed to and
embodied by the prophet is the rise of the individual as interpreter of collective and cosmic reality. Individualism becomes an omen of what it interprets: the new, more personal and voluntary foundations of creativity. The
prophet sacralizes personal choice as a source of cultural creativity and
historical existence. The messianic prophet embodies a sacred model of

individuality, for the presence of the prophet on earth marks the return of the long-awaited mythic hero or ancestor, and his coming reopens the account of creation.

Apocalyptic accounts swell with pandemoniacal noise, final fury, smoke, terror, and confusion, signaling a destruction that will collapse the differences that shore up the symbolic structures of the cosmos. Lunar and solar time cave in on one another and no longer sustain their vital contrasts and contradictions. Destruction merges the chaos of the beginning with the catastrophic present, heaving them together as a single, undifferentiated quality of time with no time-in-between, no cosmos separating them. Whereas the temporal existence of the symbolic cosmos thrived on complexity and differentiation, an exclusively historical reading of cosmic and cultural life (that is, a single-strain reckoning of what "real" historical time is) devours every other evaluation of time recognized in the myths, rites, and calendars of South American cultures. The corpus of history (as evident in mainline European, colonial, and national history and, as depicted by native historians, in the body-image of a wild beast threatens to ingest and eliminate different qualities of existing in time. In response, South American prophets and eschatologies invoke their traditions of cataclysm to blind narrow historical vision. The complicated temporal structures and destructive images of religious traditions, rooted in the violent propensities of symbolic existence itself, stave off this all-devouring notion of historical time and put it to an end.

The presence of colonial power was a religious challenge to native assumptions about the nature of creation and its mythic beginnings. Native populations responded to the challenge by reinterpreting the devastation of modern history in terms of the mythic catastrophe that destroyed the world in order to end the temporal and spatial conditions of disintegration. Spiritual existence in the colonial world demanded that this world end, too. Each of its signs pointed to the end of the world that colonialism was fashioning. This made sense of the ravages of the Conquest and of the extermination of local peoples. But the matter did not stop there. The human spirit would recover a meaningful existence in concrete terms only in a completely new world. This vision accounts for the continued demise of the colonial enterprise in revolutions for independence, civil wars, and politico-economic crises. Millennial movements across the continent affirm the conviction that neocolonial solutions are not sufficient to overcome the history of the Conquest. The present historical situation must give way to a completely new mode of being, a new set of world conditions, in order to transcend its own disintegrative propensities.

Final destruction not only dissolves symbolic time but also dismantles cosmic space by reuniting separate forms (layers of the universe, the cardinal directions, upstream and downstream, inhabited space and the wilds, the differently shaped phonemes of distinct tongues), which parted during the violence of the first destructions. Now, separate spaces overrun one another once again with a primordial violence. Heaven and earth pass away as distinct layers; mountains fall and valleys fill so that the earth becomes flat.

Beings once deposed into subterranean space (especially infernal monsters sealed in caves or stone and the buried dead) invade earthly space. Creatures of darkness burst out of confinement into the light of day. Pieces of the center scatter to the four winds or spill across the landscape. Being reverts to the undifferentiated state of the first instance of creation.

In nearly all millennial visions, the sky tumbles to earth, or the sun, moon, stars, or objects (food or manufactured goods) plummet from above. The gap between humans and celestial realities closes when the sky swoops to earth or prophets fly to the heights. The end of the world is marked by the proximity of the creative powers who withdrew on high at the beginning. The fall of the sky makes re-creation possible.

The collapse of spatial difference and the catastrophic deconstruction of symbolic life furnish the staging for tragedy, the contemporary mode of historical existence. Drama becomes a central eschatological action. The end of the world is a ritual achievement accomplished through dance, music, theater, prescribed behavior, festive clothing or ritual nudity, the absence of normal work patterns, and restrictions on movement, consumption, or relationships. The eschaton is an orchestrated event, a performed interpretation of current realities, based on primordial moments of change when the appearance of sacred beings underwent transformation or destruction. Against this backdrop of mythic beginnings, eschatological performances act out the meaning of the present predicament of human life.

Myths of the beginning end with forms of closure: the food chain, the cycle of prey, the repeating calendar, the system of social organization, and narrative genres. The entire cosmic age is a period of waiting, an expectant quality of time constantly looking forward to specific ends: the end of the season, year, generation, meal, individual life-span—and the end of the story. These single expectations, when taken as a whole, point to the arrival of the cosmos at its end, a fulfillment foretold from the beginning by the fractious nature of symbolic existence. Unlike the symbolic entities of the cosmos, and much like the primordial ones, history represents nothing but itself. The solution to this impasse of meaning lies in one direction only. Fulfilling history requires that it be destroyed, dispatched to an unmanifest mode, as were the gods. This sacrificial act forces history to become a symbolic reality. Dispatching history by bringing it to full term through ritual violence, dance, and drama successfully alienates historical existence and its fruits from their exclusive this-worldly existence and makes them holy. Through visions of the extermination of history, eschatologies yearn for history's fulfillment, the vital redemption of existence in time.

Visions of the end unveil the tenacity of traditional eschatological hopes and the power of the force that recasts these ancient images into forms that redeem contemporary realities. Millennial movements are critical theories of history, and millennial prophets can be shrewd, unswerving analysts of grim realities. They see clearly the unavoidable violence and destruction required to reimagine competing and incommensurate visions of time. The negativity that underlies prophetic soteriology of history can be politically volatile, fanning the fears of fanatical followers or rousing the ire of politicians who wish to defuse the revolutionary challenge to the status quo. The violence of messianic dance and the choreography of riot, procession, and revolution unfold within the context of world-recreation as signified in the changes of eschatological space, time, prophecy, and economy. The end of the world is at hand, and only messiahs, prophets, and eschatological judges may evaluate correctly the relationship between miracle and omen, hope and despair, strength and weakness, perfect righteousness and sinful imperfection, oppression and castigation, justice and peace. These judges decide whether paradise or apocalypse is on the horizon. Their diagnostic visions render a final verdict on contemporary understandings of history.

The social and historical circumstances of particular communities affect eschatological visions and movements. The extraordinary suffering of the postcontact period exacerbated apocalyptic imagery already present in the mythic accounts of the destruction of the world. Disease and displacement diminished community strength and numbers. Social units unraveled; repositories of tradition went bankrupt. The authority of spiritual leaders eroded as, ignorant and failure-ridden, they yielded to outsiders whose expertise in the new ways of the world dwarfed their own. Squeezed between the powerlessness of their own symbolic life and the unworthiness of changes forced on them by outsiders, local groups and their prophets found themselves without a creative place in the cosmos. They became demoralized in the root sense of the word: their symbolic acts no longer signified the powers of the sacred and their mores became devoid of meaning, reduced to mere routines. In some cases, such malaise led to depression and morbid fascination with death and suicide.

Preoccupation with terminal imagery never ceases. Pleasant and painful images of the end, whether imagined as a climax or as a cutting-off, pervade sweet dreams, nightmares, fantasies, plans for success, delusions of grandeur, haunting memories of failure, horror stories, and neurotic deliria. The religious imagination grasps the reality of the cosmos at both its terminal points, creation and demise. Paradise and apocalypse are polar extremes on a continuum of response of the religious imagination to the human experience of the ambiguity manifest in the outcome of daily intentions and lifetime achievements. Eschatological hope and apocalyptic despair are the most comprehensive and inclusive of these constant preoccupations with termination. In paradise or apocalypse, the religious imagination realizes its own end and accomplishes its integrity, a sense of entirety needed to assess the meaning and *telos* of symbolic existence. The destructive aliens of the eschaton inspire terror, hope and the full range of emotions between these poles. They are the strange and absolute beings of the primordium, the wellsprings of creativity and rejuvenation. The full manifestation of these sacred beings creates a finalizing experience for cosmic beings, an inescapable awareness of their periodic and terminal nature. Catching hold of symbolic being as a whole requires the gripping experience of its limits. Paradise and apocalypse appear at the outermost margin of imaginable life.

Eschatology unites the primordial catastrophe with the final destruction. This closing movement of the cosmos smashes beginning against end, like crashing cymbals, and eliminates any possibility of mediation. The clash of symbolic horizons or the terrifying crash of the sky into the earth collapses space and time and leaves no place for the cosmos, no locus for the interim character of symbolic being. The book of human history snaps shut; the opening mythic verses slam against the final mythic chapter. Since the cosmos is a symbolic construction at every level, the experience of the limits of the imagination implies the end of the cosmos. When history is no longer seen as symbolic and human experience no longer signifies some other mode of being, history and personal experience threaten to become absolute realities. At that point, human history and cosmic life must be cut short and ended, lest the cosmos, like the nonsymbolic primordial world, become a homogeneous state where nothing makes any differen‹e. Chaotic indetermination is a monstrous condition akin to the malingering presence of sacralities whose time has passed but whose continued presence crushes existence with disease and dread.

Paradise and apocalypse provide two ways of envisioning the entanglement of the cosmos in the snarling significations of human history. Paradise is the set of conditions that allow for the simultaneous fullfillment of all the separate and partial signs of this world. In paradise, nothing significant is left out. Even contradictory possibilities fuse into an unimaginable union, a single experience of fulfillment that overcomes all differences without eliminating them. At the same time, paradise creates a new difference, the unique unit of the saved, who are lifted up together and assembled as a people set apart.

Apocalypse, on the other hand, raises relative differences to monstrous heights. Each partial symbolic expression of the cosmos is exalted to its absurd extreme so that the imagination fills with every species of exaggerated caricature. Every odd distinguishing mark, every coarse hair or colored blemish, stretches toward its eccentric fulfillment as a ghoulish fiend or were-animal. These heightened differences devour one another and overwhelm the universe. When every gradient of difference realizes itself fully and takes on ludicrous proportions, no value preserves itself. These preposterous absurdities consume and eliminate one another in a frenzy from which there is no escape. The imagination itself is overwhelmed and inundated by the all-consuming character of its creativity. Driven by the ferocious logic of signs and distinctions, the critical analysis that undergirds culture and mature spirituality unleashes a violent bestiary in pursuit of signs. Apocalypse calls out for justice, the judgment that will succeed in sorting out and terminating the catastrophic conditions of rampant symbolism. Apocalypse eliminates difference in its treatment of the damned. These nondieters, nonfasters, nondancers, and nonconformers are condemned by the symbols of their own constitutions. In the image of wild beasts or pests they are exterminated or are excluded from the experience of the saved because they are "different" in race, linguistic group, lineage, style of dress, dance, rite, or diet. They are finessed by the predetermining logic of their own signs.

Apocalypse and paradise are both ways of rendering difference at a time when every fixture of human and cosmic existence dissolves into an undefined state betwixt-and-between all nameable emotions, concepts, and values. At this point, the destinies of diverse signs are sorted out as paradisal, on the one hand, or apocalyptic, on the other. Each gives definition to the total experience of life by defining the meaning of the past and the value of all terminal experiences. The ambivalence of human experience is brought to trial and subjected to summary judgment. Paradise and apocalypse are both solutions to the insolubly symbolic situation of human existence: paradise being the glorious summation of all significant differences, apocalypse the hellish mutual consummation of all differences. The intimate relationship of heaven and hell is expressed in their equal proximity to the imminent end. Paradise for the elect involves extermination for outsiders or enemies. The purgatorial ordeals of the end of the world purify the just so that they may enter paradise. With these symbolic complexes, cultures articulate horrible or beatific visions of the absolute reality that lies before and beyond the cosmos. Using the remarkably different imagery of heaven and hell, cultures put an end to experiences of time that seem endless, pointless, purposeless, or unbroken and attempt to discern how one meaning in life leaves off from another. By bringing on the end, eschatology renews the terminal condition of symbolic being and lends new meaning and destiny to all the terms that constitute symbolic languages.

South American eschatologies cause us to ponder whether history is a messianic species of time. Historical incidents that occur for the first time, but that resist myth, create a conundrum, for myth is the condition in which realities never seen before make their first appearance. What is to be the fate of unprecedented events that remain unassimilable to myth? South American cultures draw the signs of their times within the compass of myth, interpreting historical circumstances in terms of millennial vision. Thus, the seemingly inescapable consequences of the inevitable past are forced to submit to a new kind of time. The fully manifest time of history pales before the expected time to come, a world still undisclosed. Even creation, the work of the gods, is dismantled. Attention turns to the possibility of salvation. To be saved, any semblance of reality, cosmos and history must take refuge in the mythic time to come and be redeemed through the symbolic action of its cultural agents: prophets, messiahs, final-battle militarists, and saviors.

If history is not finally meaningless, what signs announce its meaning and which vestiges shall be saved from destruction? This question does not only weigh on South American peoples and their prophets. The realization dawns on all of us that historical whimsy fashions our individuality and the particularity of our culture. The arbitrary assignments of our time, place, language, sexual gender, culture, and personal experiences constrain our relative meanings and limit our understanding. The threat of ultimate insignificance weighs on all historical beings unable to locate sources of absolute and lasting value. That is why the eschatological beliefs and rebellions of South Americans who suffer under the full weight of historical insignificance could easily fascinate or disturb us. But our own historical visions of time have often served to eliminate the relevance of our contemporaries' proposed solutions to the enigma of our common historical condition. We shrink from these visions of the end because they relativize history, the mode of time that has licensed the accumulation of symbolic currencies in the forms of wealth, land, labor, written word, and science.

Various South American peoples, however, have scrutinized Western history as it impinges on their own existence in time and shrewdly analyzed its signs, such as writing and literacy. They perceive a relationship between narrative writing, historical existence, and the messianic condition of time. Historiography becomes an instrument of salvation, for scripture offers the power to assemble all the signs at work in social order, human constitution, cosmic process, and divine plan. Writing becomes a way of stylizing existence in time, recording remarkable signs of its meaning, and remembering the character of its power. Writing and reading mime the movements of history and literally describe the mode of time that overturns this world. Historical writing is a form of ritual to bring on the eschaton. The fact that outsiders introduced writing and, in written word, describe exhaustively the life and times of South American cultures, is a sure sign of their end. South Americans are no longer the sole agents of their own cultural meaning and historical consciousness. At the same time, however, the writing of signs prevents one from becoming insignificant in history. Consequently, for some native chroniclers, to write became a fierce craving, whetted by the miseries of apocalypse. Through eschatological writing, South American scribes hoped to bind up the history devouring them. By rendering a new summary of this catastrophic age and its terminal signs, they would effectively hasten its passing.

Many South American peoples situate dance on the central stage of the eschaton. Dance consists of stylized movements whose significations, like historical writing, configure and affect a people's existence in time. Dances are usually performed periodically at moments of transition, their rhythms meting out the periodicity of season, year, cultural fashion, and individual life-cycle. Through dance, human movement joins in the violent, mythic changes that generated cosmos and culture. By reenacting mythic movements, dance fills the jolting passages of time with grace. During the eschaton, when temporal structures collapse, frenetic or constant dancing juggles the multivariate responses to the bewildering array of presences apparent at the end. This last dance coordinates the passage of powers hidden behind every significant form. Eschatological song and dance summon forth all supernatural forces at once, display their terrible pleroma, and stage their simultaneous disappearance. Synchronizing the transition-points of every imaginable cycle of time and forcing them to occur at the same calendric instant, eschatological dance creates an unprecedented passage, a crossing-over that is ultimate in both scale and kind. Eschatological dance orchestrates the single, simultaneous dismissal that becomes the final cadenza of the cosmos, when all sacred sources of its meaning dance free of their symbolic containers and abandon the arena where human history unfolded.

All reality passes over to another space and time. Through the grace-filled movements of ceaseless dance, the saved cross over as well.

Dance and writing make specific periods of time apprehensible by casting events into conventional forms of symbolic language. By retracing the paradigmatic steps in which time unfolds, seasonal dancers and writing historians cut stylish figures for communal reflection. Both reduce experiences of time to stylized shapes, and both are subject to the mode of time in which their signs have meaning. Historical writing and dance are metastatements about their own temporal mode of existence. They are not objective realities that stand apart from the world they inscribe but are implicated in the final order they create.

The violence underlying ritual dance and historical writing makes sense of the millenarian value of military symbolism, battle maneuvers, choreographed combat, and dramatic acts of terrorism, as well as of eschatological theater. Both militarism and theater are forms of eschatological diversion designed to interpret history and bring on the end of time. Military weapons and theatrical props impose a style different from that of dance or writing on the fashioning and interpretation of existence in time.

Eschatological military action settles final historical accounts by dramatizing the terror of the eschatological condition of time. In bloody choreography, decisive battles enact the meaning of the end, making visible its grisly and summary nature. The power of final battle signals the imminence of the end of an era. Thus, military action stands with writing and dance as an instrument that shapes history.

Theater is a newfound style of interpreting the religious value of historical events, especially political acts, and a vehicle for conveying the meaning of history. In some prophetic movements, the new age is a spectacle, a dramatic performance of dance, chant, and ritual combat to which the saved will gain admission. The history stylized in messianic theater perpetuates the eschatological worldview so evident in military uprisings. Often, historical theater is commemorative, making remarkable and reflective the military defeat or political revolution that caused the appearance of eschatological time.

Eschatological dramas never state facts in a neutral way but heighten the contradictions of symbolic life and evaluate them as terminologies related to the final end. All such performances interpret the quality of time they inhabit. Dramatists share the hopeful or apocalyptic conviction that one might perform the chaos of history with all its grisly signs and thus bring it to the end that would properly account for the symbolic terms of the play. After all, every performance ends. That hopeful or fearful expectation propels actors and audience through the episodes of struggle, of ambiguous overlap of comedy and tragedy, toward the inevitable end. Although eschatological theater exhibits the trappings of a rite, symbolic action of this sort is neither ritual (a deliberate reenactment of sacred events) nor historical action representing only itself.

Eschatological theater is a deliberate diversion from historical experience. In a profound and captivating way, drama shows that history can be brought to an end. By imaginatively turning away the flow of history, momentary theatrical diversion demonstrates the imminence of the other modes of time that press against the historical experience of the present as well as the real, cathartic possibility of acting in other modes of time. Alternate construals of existence in time appear on stage and become concretely imaginable in the here and now. By fending off its oppressive immediacy, eschatological theater reopens history to question and reintroduces the time and distance conducive to symbolic reflection.

Each form of diversion — military, scriptural, choreographic, or theatrical — attempts to pass the time, to end the quality of terrible expectation. Taking their cue from religious rites of renewal, warfare, writing, dance, and drama divert recurrent primordial disaster through the ironic symbolic exercise of reenacting or miming the catastrophic flood, fire, or other violent dismissals of the fully sacred world. *By turning primordial realities off to one side and historical existence off to another, diversionary entertainment rends chaos asunder and stretches open the distance between clashing times.* In this light, one can reevaluate Enlightenment sciences as forms of diversionary entertainment that arose during the same period as colonial theater in South America and were designed to confront the same eschatological situation. This is true especially of the human and social sciences, which base themselves, in part, on data from contact with cultures in the New World. These forms of knowledge think of themselves as sorting out the collision of contemporary life with archaic prehistory as the latter re-presents itself in archaeological sites and in the multiple historical consciousnesses of cultures encountered during the Age of Discovery. Enlightenment sciences not only determined, in their consciously objective way, the differences between civilized historical peoples and primitive archaic cultures. They unwittingly involved themselves in the distinction, setting themselves up as judges whose scientific verdicts about history were *the* distinguishing marks, the ultimate historical achievements, of the rational, reflective order distinguishing modern from primal reality. Such divisions of science (in the wide sense of all human forms of knowledge) by science (in the narrow sense of the Enlightenment rationalizations of contact with new worlds) diverted attention from the eschatological chaos into which clashing times — the "discovery" of myriad, different historical consciousnesses — plunged the Western views of humanity, cosmos, and history.

The diversionary quality of eschatological acts, styles of history, and forms of knowledge relates directly to symbolic life in general. Diversion is not only what a symbol helps accomplish. On the most profound level, seen in the light of the eschaton, diversion is the heart of what a symbol is: the sign that effects an artful distance from the sacred sources of realities that are terrifying and absolute. Particularly in this sense, many of the scientific and philosophical theories developed since the sixteenth century have been diversionary symbolic languages and styles of cultural analysis. And the contemporary self-understandings of which modern sciences are symptomatic can be seen as responses to the presence of South Americans (and others) in these last times, which bring to an end, through the symbolic terms of the sciences, the unenlightened existence of "recently discovered" peoples.

Enlightenment sciences, like the eschatological diversion of theater, have aimed at indirectness. They have avoided outright the sacred sources of reality in the cultures that have come to the attention of the West since the Age of Discovery. Rather, the human sciences preferred to dislocate primordial qualities of reality by treating them as neurotic dreams, infantile desires, prescientific or precognitive fantasies, fictions, disguised social relations, or economic false consciousness. Such symbolic indirections have provided fruitful stimuli for entirely new sciences to take their places in the modern academy. At the same time as Enlightenment sciences have viewed historical behavior as immediate reality, they have imputed ahistorical primordiality to the peoples of South America and to their cognitive capacities and technical skills. In passing from late medieval religiosity to modern enlightenment, Western historical consciousness has put cultural others on its own mythic, primordial stage. In their rendering of human history, Enlightenment sciences have cast the Empirically Other or Different in the role of primordial being, a fossilized, irrational, technologically backward, and superstitious creature whose lingering presence in this world represents something absolutely other than the historical consciousness that characterizes Western humanity.

But the historical, cultural, and behavioral sciences are diversions that hasten their own end. In delimiting the relevance of the cultural meaning of peoples around the world and in denying to sacred sources of reality their fundamental role in the human imagination, the sciences unleash a logic that demythologizes their own culture-bound terminology. The logic of their signs forces sciences to meet their ends (both cognitive and existential) and to confront both the relativity of their scientific judgments and the finiteness of their dominance in time. Only by passing through its limits and confronting, in a reflective way, the boundaries of its own forms of knowledge, can modern history, as defined by the intellectual categories of the West, give way to a new spiritual horizon, wider in scope and more profoundly real in cultural diversity. The varied spiritualities of South Americans are experiments of the human spirit with the sacred sources of creativity. Their long-enduring and creative existence in time warrants a fundamental role for South American religions in the coming horizon, the new rendering of world history that is being defined by the multiple cultures that now encounter one another as historical agents. Transformed through understanding, South American religions help orient the new world to its cardinal sources of meaning.

NOTES

Abbreviations

AA	*American Anthropologist* (Menasha, Wisconsin)
AAAB	Acta Academiae Aboensis (Abo)
AAE	*Archivio per l'Antropologia e la Etnologia* (Florence)
AASF	*Annales Academiae Scientiarum Fennicae*
ACAR	*Antropológica* (Caracas)
AFV	*Archiv für Völkerkunde* (Vienna)
AGEM	*Annals Göteborgs Ethnografiska Museum* (Göteborg)
AI	*América Indígena* (Mexico City)
AL	*América Latina* (Moscow)
ALIM	*Anthropológica* (Lima)
AM	*Américas* (Washington, D.C.)
ANT	*Anthropos* (St.-Augustin)
AP	*Amazonia Peruana* (Lima)
APA	*Apacheta* (Lima)
APAMNH	*Anthropological Papers of the American Museum of Natural History*
APH	*Allpanchis Phuturinqa* (Cuzco)
ARW	*Archiv für Religionswissenschaft* (Freiburg and Leipzig)
AUC	*Anales de la Universidad de Chile*
BA	*Baessler-Archiv* (Berlin)
BANH	*Boletín de la Academia Nacional de la Historia* (Caracas)
BBEW	*Bulletin of the Bureau of American Ethnology* (Washington, D.C.)
BCA	*Boletín del Centro Argentino de Estudios Americanos* (Buenos Aires)
BELC	*Boletín de Estudios Latinoamericanos y del Caribe* (Amsterdam)
BIV	*Boletín Indigenista Venezolano* (Caracas)
BMPEG	*Boletim do Museu Paraense Emilio Goeldi-Antropologia* (Belem)
BMN	*Boletim do Museu Nacional* (São Paulo)
BSAB	*Bulletin de la Société des Américanistes de Belgique*
BSSA	*Bulletin de la Société Suisse des Américanistes* (Geneva)
BTLV	*Bijdragen tot de Taal-, Land- en Volkenkunde* (Leiden)
CA	*Current Anthropology* (Chicago)
CDAL	*Cahiers des Amériques Latines* (Paris)
CES	*Comparative Ethnographical Studies* (Göteborg)
CHS	*Cultura, Hombre, Sociedad* (Temuco, Chile)
CPAAE	University of California Publications in American Archaeology and Ethnology (Los Angeles)
CSSH	*Comparative Studies in Society and History* (Cambridge)
CZ	*Ciba Zeitschrift* (Basel)
EA	*Estudios Andinos*
EAI	*Études Américanistes Interdisciplinaires* (Paris)
EJ	*Eranos-Jahrbuch* (Zurich)
EOR	*The Encyclopedia of Religion* (New York, 1987)
ES	*Ethnologiska Studier* (Göteborg)
ETH	*Ethnohistory*

ETM	*Ethnomusicology* (Middletown, Conn.)
ETS	*Ethnos* (Stockholm)
ETY	*Ethnology* (Pittsburgh)
EZ	*Ethnologische Zeitschrift Zürich* (Zurich)
FO	*Folk: Dansk Etnografisk Tidsskrift*
H	*L'Homme* (Paris)
HR	*History of Religions* (Chicago)
HSAI	*Handbook of South American Indians*
I	*Indiana* (Berlin)
IAE	*Internationales Archiv für Ethnographie* (Leiden)
ICA	*Proceedings of the International Congress of Americanists*
JAFL	*Journal of American Folklore* (Boston and New York)
JLAL	*Journal of Latin American Lore* (Los Angeles)
JRAI	*Journal of the Royal Anthropological Institute* (London)
JSAP	*Journal de la Société des Américanistes* (Paris)
LAIL	*Latin American Indian Literatures* (Pittsburgh)
MN	*Man*
MAGW	*Mitteilungen der anthropologischen Gesellschaft in Wien* (Vienna)
MGVK	*Mitteilungen der Gesellschaft für Völkerkunde* (Leipzig)
MI	*Mitológicas* (Buenos Aires)
MMVH	*Mitteilungen aus dem Museum für Völkerkunde Hamburg* (Hamburg)
MSCNL	*Memoria de la Sociedad de Ciéncias Naturales La Salle* (Caracas)
N	*Numen* (Leiden)
NP	*Ñawpa Pacha*
NS	*New Scholar* (Santa Barbara)
RAM	*Revista do Arquivo Municipal* (São Paulo)
RASP	*Revista de Antropología* (São Paulo)
RCA	*Revista Colombiano de Antropología*
RFC	*Revista de Folklore Chileno*
RGA	*Revista Geográfica Americana* (Buenos Aires)
RHR	*Revue de l'Histoire des Religions* (Paris)
RA	*Revista Andina*
RI	*Revista Inca*
RIEB	*Revista do Instituto de Estudos Brasileiros*
RIEN	*Revista del Instituto Etnológico Nacional* (Bogotá)
RIHGB	*Revista do Instituto Historico Geographico Brasileiro*
RJBP	*Revista del Jardin Botánico y Museo de Historia Natural del Paraguay*
RLEE	*Revista Latinoamericana de Estudios Etnolingüísticos* (Lima)
RMLP	*Revista del Museo de La Plata* (La Plata, Argentina)
RMN	*Revista de Museo Nacional* (Lima)
RMP	*Revista do Museu Paulista* (São Paulo)
RPC	*Revista Peruana de Cultura* (Lima)
RSAA	*Relaciones de la Sociedad Argentina de Antropología* (Buenos Aires)
RSI	*Annual Report of the Smithsonian Institution* (Washington, D.C.)
RSR	*Revue des Sciences Religieuses*
RU	*Runa* (Buenos Aires)
SA	*Suplemento Antropológico* (Asunción, Paraguay)
SAA	*Sociedad Argentina de Antropología* (Buenos Aires)
SE	*Scripta Ethnológica* (Buenos Aires)
SJ	*Staden Jahrbuch* (São Paulo)
SMSR	*Studi e Materiali di Storia delle Religioni* (Rome)
SSFCHL	Societas Scientiarum Fennica. Commentationes Humanarum Litterarum (Helsinki)
T	*Tribus* (Stuttgart)
TA	*Terra Ameriga* (Genoa)

TMHR	*Timehri* (Georgetown, Guiana)
TMIE	*Travaux et Mémoires de l'Institute d'Ethnologie* (Paris)
WBKL	*Wiener Beiträge zur Kulturgeschichte und Linguistik (Vienna)*
WVM	*Wiener Völkerkundlich Mitteilungen* (Vienna)
YIMR	*Yearbook of Inter-American Musical Research* (Austin, Texas)
ZFE	*Zeitschrift für Ethnologie* (Berlin)
ZMR	*Zeitschrift für Missionskunde und Religionswissenschaft* (Berlin)

CHAPTER ONE

1. "We" are secular, or carefully compose our religious life with selective acts of faith or reason, whereas "they" are uncritically religious in the extreme (inheriting animism or polytheism); we are civilized, they are savage and wild; we are literate (biblically formed, book-based), they are oral-aural and unlettered; we are free-thinkers, they are tradition bound; we are a voluntary society, they are born into ascribed social states and roles; we are pluralists, they are homogeneous; we are complicated and reflect on contradictions, they are simple and untroubled by inconsistency. I call these kinds of claims misunderstandings not because they are wrong, as they may be when viewed from certain premises, but because they are inadequate in the face of the experiences and understandings that constitute our own current situation. They misconstrue the relationships of the peoples, histories, and ideas that compose our world. These and other contrasts are brought forward as defining features of modern civilization in Hans Peter Duerr, *Traumzeit. Über die Grenze zwischen Wildnis und Zivilisation* (Frankfurt am Main, 1978).
2. See the bibliographic essay of Juan Adolfo Vázquez, "Central and South American Religions," in Charles Adams, ed., *A Reader's Guide to the Great Religions*, 2d ed. (New York, 1977).
3. Pierre Bourdieu, *Outline of a Theory of Praxis* (Cambridge, 1977); Daniel Sperber, *Rethinking Symbolism* (Cambridge, 1974); Rodney Needham, *Belief, Language, and Experience* (Chicago, 1972) and *Reconnaissances* (Toronto, 1980); George W. Stocking, Jr., ed., *Observers Observed: Essays on Ethnographic Fieldwork* (Madison, Wis., 1983); Curtis M. Hinsley, Jr., *Savages and Scientists: The Smithsonian Institution and the Development of American Anthropology 1846– 1910* (Washington D.C., 1981); George E. Marcus and Michael M. J. Fischer, *Anthropology as Cultural Critique: An Experimental Moment in the Human Sciences* (Chicago, 1986); Victor Turner, *At the Edge of the Bush: Anthropology as Experience*, edited by Edith L. B. Turner (Tucson, 1985). Furthermore, some investigators fear that scientific fieldwork easily degenerates into a new kind of tourism that transforms local peoples into curiosities, photographic subjects, and sources for the acquisitive, well-funded traveller; see Richard Chapelle, *Os Índios Cintas-largas* (Belo Horizonte, Brazil, 1982), p. 14.
4. The ranks of such historians include Marshall Hodgson, who wrote his monumental *The Venture of Islam*, 3 vols. (Chicago, 1974), within the context of what he termed "historical humanism." He acknowledges that "historians' questions are concerned ultimately with the dated and placed" but insists that they must "ask questions that are undatable within the historical context" (vol. 1, p. 23). In order to lead "to better understanding of things that matter to us humanly," the field of historical studies (a single enterprise inquiring into the nature of human history and not merely an agglomeration of disparate, area-specific historical studies) must be "nothing less than the whole body of questions about human cultural development, about human culture in its continuity over time; and here we cannot rule out a potential need to develop relatively dateless generalizations, for instance about what may be possible in cultural change, such generalizations are not simply derivable from any other discipline as such, yet they are necessary for studying what is timelessly important about the dated and placed events of human culture" (ibid.). Included also is Fernand Braudel, whose "History and the Social Sciences," in Peter Burke, ed., *Economy and Society in Early Modern Europe: Essays from Annales* (London, 1958), pp. 11–42, argues that one can organize history around three species of social time—event, *conjoncture*, and *longue durée*—and insists that the historian must be aware of multiple modes of temporal existence. Reflecting on the experience of clandestinely writing *La Méditeranée et le monde méditerranéen à l'époque de Philippe II* (Paris, 1949) while a prisoner of war at Lübeck prison, where he was subjected to the propagandist historiography of his jailors as well as to the historical circumstances to which they had reduced his contemporaries, Braudel has written, "Down with occurrences, especially vexing ones! I had to believe that history, destiny, was written at a much more profound level" ("Personal Testimony," *Journal of Modern History* 44 (1972): 454). For yet another example of a perspective on universal human history see Geoffrey Barraclough, *Turning Points in World History* (London, 1979).
5. Mircea Eliade, *Ordeal by Labyrinth* (Chicago, 1982), p. 137.
6. "Whoever struggles on behalf of the land of indigenous peoples, struggles equally for the

basic conditions of their religion" (Mário Juruna (with the assistance of Antonio Hohlfeldt and Assis Hoffmann), *O Gravador do Juruna*, Porto Alegre, Brazil, 1982). Juruna is quoting Paulo Suess.

7. Richard Shutler, Jr., in R. Shutler, ed., *Early Man in the New World* (Beverly Hills, Cal., 1983), pp. 11–12, has conservatively summed up the most significant advances in Paleoindian research during the decade 1973–1983: "We can now place the minimum time for the first occupation of North America at 20,000 years ago, with some probability of this important event having occurred 30,00) years ago, and the possibility that it occurred as long ago as 50,000 years." Most early sites in South America date from fourteen thousand to twelve thousand years ago but some quartz implements discovered in Brazil in 1983 may date to twenty-two thousand or twenty-six thousand years ago, says Juan Adolfo Vázquez, "South American Religions. Mythic Themes," in Mircea Eliade, ed., *The Encyclopedia of Religion* (New York, 1987; hereafter referred to as *EOR*). The provenience and history of aspects of South American culture have long been difficult problems. The uniqueness of South American culture largely lies locked in its prehistory. In *Origins of the Indian Civilizations in South America* (Göteborg, 1931), Erland Nordenskiöld published results of a lengthy comparative study of cultural traits, dealing with (1) South America when juxtaposed with those in North America—especially southwest North America—and Northern Asia; (2) Central America, Colombia, the Amazon, and parts of Peru juxtaposed with similar traits in Oceania; (3) the distribution of indigenous American metallurgical technology; and (4) the distinctive cultural features of each of the Americas (South, Central, North). He concluded that "most S. American culture elements that are of fundamental importance to the Indians in the struggle for existence were invented in that continent, or common [sic] to South and North America" (p. 76). For a concise statement of theories concerning the prehistory of South America, including extensive recent bibliographies, see the essays in Jesse D. Jennings, ed., *Ancient South Americans* (San Francisco, 1983). Stephen C. Jett summarizes the evidence and hypotheses concerning transoceanic influences in Jennings, ibid., pp. 337–393. Gordon R. Willey, *An Introduction to American Archaeology*, vol. 2, *South America* (Englewood Cliffs, N.J., 1971), remains a valuable foundational study.

8. André-Marcel d'Ans, *Le Dit des vrais hommes: Mythes, contes, légendes et traditions des indiens cashinahua* (Paris, 1978), p. 22.

9. Juan Adolfo Vázquez, "The Present State of Research in South American Mythology," *N* 25 (1980): 240. See Arthur P. Sorensen, Jr., "South American Indian Linguistics at the Turn of the Seventies," in Daniel R. Gross, ed., *Peoples and Cultures of Native South America* (Garden City N.Y., 1973), pp. 312–341. To make even rough estimates of American Indian populations proves to be a difficult and controversial endeavor. P. Chaunu, "La Population de l'Amérique indienne. Nouvelles recherches," *Revue historique* 1 (1963): 111-118, estimated that there were some eighty to one hundred million American Indians on the eve of the Conquest and that, in the American Indian death toll alone, the "microbial shocks of the 16th century annihilated one quarter of humanity" (cited in P. Clastres, "Éléments de Démographie Amérindienne," *H* 13 January-June 1973, pp. 23–36; Clastres also cites references that contravene his and Chaunu's figures). Regarding Indian populations and demography, see Magnus Mörner's review of William Denevan's pre-Columbian population estimates in *LAIL* 3 (1979) as well as his review of attempts to estimate present populations in *LAIL* 4 (1980): 46ff. In particular, Mörner criticizes Enrique Mayer and Elio Masferrer, "La población de America en 1978," *AI* 39 (1979): 217–337, for understating the drastic conditions of contemporary peoples and for overestimating their population growth. Regarding the population of Amazonian groups in Peru between 1900 and 1975, see Darcy Ribeiro and Mary Ruth Wise, *Los Grupos Étnicos de la Amazonia Peruana* (Lima, 1972).

10. Jorge A. Suárez, "South American Indian Languages," in *Encyclopedia Brittanica*, 15th ed., vol. 17, p. 106.

11. The eight groups are Arawakan, Cariban, Macro-Chibchan, Macro-Ge, Macro–Pano-Tacanan, Quechumaran, Tucanoan, and Tupian. A glance at the color-coded map in Suárez's article for *Encyclopedia Brittanica* reveals, even in spatial terms, what the article's author calls the "various and undetermined levels of relationship" and cross-reference among them. Many

of the colors overrun one another, all over the map. In addition to overlaps, the author is forced to mark large sections "other language areas, " " unrecorded languages," and "areas unaccounted for."

12. The fourteen groups in Rowe's linguistic classification are Tupí-Guaraní, Ge, Arawak, Carib, Pano, Catuquina, Takan, Aymará, Chibcha, Barbacoas, Sáliva, Guahibo, Tucano, and Guaycurú. I am referring to the 1973 revised edition of the map, copyrighted by Rowe in 1974, that accompanies Patricia A. Lyon, ed., *Native South Americans: Ethnology of the Least Known Continent* (Boston, 1974).

13. Juan Adolfo Vázquez describes this scheme as provisional and uncertain ("South American Religions. Mythic Themes," in *EOR*). For further classifications see the bibliography in Suárez, op. cit., and also the following: Čestmír Loukotka, *Classification of South American Indian Languages*, Johannes Wilbert, ed. (Los Angeles, 1968), which surveys the evidence from the whole continent; Joel Scherzer and Greg Urban, eds., *Native South American Discourse* (The Hague, 1985); Desmond C. Derbyshire and Geoffrey K. Pullum, eds. *Handbook of Amazonian Languages*, vol. 1 (The Hague, 1985), the first of a projected three-volume set; and Harriet E. Manelis Klein and Louisa R. Stark, eds., *South American Indian Languages: Retrospect and Prospect* (Austin, 1985).

14. Thus Otto Zerries, "South American Religions: An Overview," in *EOR*, opens by delineating six such areas (he joins Tierra del Fuego with Patagonia and the Pampas but then separates the southern Andes from the northern Andes). However, he quickly points out that religious ideas and practices make extremely permeable the boundaries between these groups, and he immediately abandons the geographic presentation in favor of specific phenomena (deities, heroes, rites) found throughout the continent. Basing himself on the system of culture-geographic regions used by Julian H. Steward in the *Handbook of South American Indians*, 6 vols. (Washington, D.C., 1946–1950; hereafter referred to as *HSAI*), Peter G. Roe, *The Cosmic Zygote* (New Brunswick, N.J., 1982), pp. 22–25, proposes some eighteen areas he believes are significant for the study of myth and religion: Montana, Northwest Amazon, Venezuela, Brazilian Highlands, Central Amazon, Ecuador, Lower Amazon, Guianas, Colombia, Xingú, Mato Grosso, Gran Chaco, Eastern Brazil, Panama, Antilles, Andes, Costa Rica, and Coastal Peru. The existence of so many areas helps Roe avoid the anomalies (but not the redundancies) into which Steward was led (one whole volume of *HSAI*, volume 1, is entitled *The Marginal Tribes*). The difficulties of employing culture-area hypotheses in the study of religion are discussed in Juan Adolfo Vázquez, "The Religions of Mexico and of Central and South America," in Adams, ed., *A Reader's Guide to the Great Religions*, pp. 78–89 (pp. 86–89 touch on the Andes and the peoples "beyond the Andes"), and in his "The Present State of Research in South American Mythology," cited above.

15. In regard to the self-designation "South American Indian," it is noteworthy that the First South American Indian Congress met in and about Cuzco, Peru, only in late February 1980. It was funded by grants from Scandinavian countries, the Canadian movement Development and Peace, and the World Council of Churches and was organized with the support of the World Council of Indian Peoples. The tense atmosphere climaxed in the meetings of the Committee on Indian Philosophy, wherein delegates denounced the history written by the conquerors, who tried to justify their invasion: "For us the Occident means destruction" (Flavia de Faria Castro, "No umbigo do mundo os indios se encontraram para aprender sobre si memos," *Jornal do Brasil*, Rio de Janeiro, 17 March 1980, p. 9, as reported in "News and Notes," *LAIL* 5 (Spring 1981): 78–79.

16. Charles H. Long writes, "As such the phrase itself raises a constitutive methodological issue. It is as much a cultural methodological category of the modern West as it is a way of describing certain kinds of religious data" ("Primitive Religion," in Adams, ed., *A Reader's Guide to the Great Religions*, pp. 1–39.) Here Long's reference to the category "primitive" (p. 1) is made to apply to the term "South American religions." See how Paul Kirchhoff wrestled with the parallel question of what constitutes "Mesoamerica" as an object of knowledge and the relationship of this geographic-cognitive category to lived historical (urban) experience ("Mesoamérica: Sus límites geográficas, composición étnica y carácteres culturales," *Acta Americana* 1 (1943). 92–107).

17. In a letter dating from late in his life, Christopher Columbus wrote, "God made me the messenger of the new heaven and the new earth of which he spoke in the Apocalypse of Saint John after having spoken of it through the mouth of Isaiah, and he showed me the spot where to find it. . . . I undertook a voyage to the new heaven and earth, which land, until then, remained concealed." The letter is quoted in G. B. Spotorno, *Memorials of Columbus* (London, 1823) pp. 224–225, and cited in Pauline Moffitt-Watts, "Prophecy and Discovery: On the Spiritual Origins of Christopher Columbus's 'Enterprise of the Indies,' " *American Historical Review* 90 (February 1985): 73–102. Moffitt-Watts concludes, "In [Columbus's] mind, then, the New World was identified with the end of the world—the first heaven and earth were passed away. There was no more sea—and the journey of the *viator*, which had begun in the deserts of the Old Testament prophets, was surely almost over" (ibid., p. 102). Columbus's messianism and the eschatological framework within which the European exploration of the New World was carried out are delineated in Alain Milhou, *Colón y su mentalidad mesiánica en el ambiente franciscanista español* (Valladolid, 1983). Regarding the "invention" of America there is a large and growing literature. For a sample, see Edmundo O'Gorman, *The Invention of America* (Bloomington, Ind., 1961); Francis Jennings, *The Invasion of America* (Pittsburgh, 1976); and Gilbert Chinard, *L'Amérique et le rêve exotique dans la littérature française au XVII et XVII siècles* (Paris, 1934).
18. David Carrasco, *Quetzalcoatl and the Irony of Empire: Myth and Prophecies in the Aztec Tradition* (Chicago, 1983), pp. 6–7, referring to the symbols of the pre-Columbian city and the conquest of Mexico.
19. Charles H. Long, "Other Times, Other Places: Myths and Cities in Meso-American Religion," *HR* 23 (1984): 383. On the Enlightenment impulse to classify and its parallels and consequences, see Rodney Needham, *Symbolic Classification* (Santa Monica, Cal., 1979); J.A. May, *Kant's Concept of Geography and Its Relation to Recent Geographical Thought* (Toronto, 1970); and Jonathan Z. Smith, *To Take Place: Toward Theory in Ritual* (Chicago, 1987), pp. 27ff. For a broader perspective, see Bruce Lincoln, *The Tyranny of Taxonomies*, University of Minnesota Center for Humanistic Studies, occasional paper 1 (Minneapolis, 1985).
20. I am preparing a volume-length history of the study of religion that evaluates choices of methods and the relationshiip of those choices to cognitive forms and social experience.
21. Ruth Benedict, foreward, to Jules Henry, *Jungle People: A Kaingáng Tribe of the Highlands of Brazil* (New York, 1941), p. xi.
22. Julian H. Steward, ed., *HSAI*, vol. 3, *The Tropical Forest Tribes*, p. xxi.
23. Steward, ibid., p. xxi. See also Steward, "South American Cultures: An Interpretative Summary," in *HSAI*, vol. 5, *The Comparative Anthropology of South American Indians*, pp. 669–772.
24. Lyon, *Native South Americans*, p. xiv.
25. This pattern has been pointed up by an increasing number of scholars who are notable exceptions to it. For example, Egon Schaden, *Aculturação indígena* (São Paulo, 1969), pp. 3ff.; Johannes Wilbert, *Folk Literature of the Yamana Indians* (Los Angeles, 1977), p. vii; Gerardo Reichel-Dolmatoff, *Amazonian Cosmos* (Chicago, 1971), pp. xv–xvi; Stephen Hugh-Jones, *The Palm and the Pleiades: Initiation and Cosmology in Northwest Amazonia* (Cambridge, 1979). The complaint is that field investigators are schooled to discern fine distinctions in kinship and social patterns in a manner that transcends their ability to sketch even the gross features of religious systems. For a forceful statement of this position, see the essays written by a number of Brazilian scholars, "A construção da pessoa nas sociedades indigenas," *BMN* n. s. (antropologia) 32 (May 1979): 1–51. Mention of the works of Schaden, Reichel-Dolmatoff (especially his early studies of the Kogi), and the Brazilian scholars who contributed to this special issue on the construction of the person brings to mind another serious problem, attested to by Lyon: "Works published in South America and in Spanish or Portuguese frequently fail to have the impact on the anthropological world that they should. . . . [A]ny work not published in English is likely find itself doomed to obsurity . . ." (*Native South Americans*, p. 289).
26. Egon Schaden, "Les Religions indigènes en Amérique du Sud," in Henri-Charles Puech, ed., *Histoire des Religions*, vol. 3 (Paris, 1976), p. 837.
27. This effort should not be mistaken for romanticism or democracy. There is here no nostalgia for primitivism or hankering after simpler ways of life. On the contrary, the aim is to *understand* the complexity of human experience and existence. That is, interpreting South American reli-

gions must also be a project of *self-understanding*, for these cultures are part of the diversity of being human. Only by acquainting oneself deeply with the highest aspirations and basest fears —an entire value system of meaning—can one slowly gain a sense that another people's history and the experiences shrouded in its imagery illumine the meaning of being human, that is, what it means to become *ourselves*.

28. Alicia M. Barabas and Miguel A. Bartolomé, "The Mythic Testimony of the Mataco," *LAIL* 3 (Fall 1979): p. 77.

29. Claude Lévi-Strauss, *La Potière jalouse* (Paris, 1985), p. 197.

30. Examples of such exploratory documents are Gaspar de Carvajal [1542], *Descubrimiento del Río de Orellana*, edited by Jorge A. Garcés G. (Quito, Municipal, 1958); Hans von Staden [1557], *Captivity of Hans Stade of Hesse, 1547-55: Among the Wild Tribes of Eastern Brazil*, edited by R. F. Burton and translated by A. Tootal (Philadelphia, 1964); Jean de Léry [1557], *Journal de bord de Jean de Léry, en la terre de Brésil*, edited and commented upon by M. R. Mayeux (Paris, 1957); Anthony Knivet [1591], *The Admirable Adventures . . . of Master Antoine Knivet, which with Master Thomas Cavendish . . . to the South Seas, 1591*, in book 4 of *Purchas his Pilgrimes: Contayning a History of the World in Seas Voyages and Lande Travells by Englishmen and Others*, by Samuel Purchas, B.D. [1625], (reprint, Glasgow, 1905–1907); Juan de Betanzos [1551], *Suma y narración de los Incas* (Lima, 1924); Pedro Cieza de León [1550], *La crónica del Perú* (Madrid, 1922), and [1553] *Segunda parte de la crónica del Perú, que trata del señorio de los Incas Yupanquis y de sus grandes hechos y governación* (Madrid, 1980); Cristóbal de Molina (of Cuzco) [1575], *Relación de las fábulas y ritos de los Incas* (Lima, 1916); and Claude d'Abbeville [1614], *Histoire de la mission des peres capucins en l'Isle de Maragnanet terres* (Graz, 1963).

31. Often written by priests trained in revamped and intellectually rigorous seminary curricula, theologically grounded studies of religion could be careful and orderly. Systematic studies include such works as José de Acosta [1590], *The Natural and Moral History of the Indies*, 2 vols, edited and translated by Clements R. Markham (Philadelphia, 1970); Cristóbal de Albórnoz [1582], "Instrucción para descubrir todas las cuacas del Pirú y sus camayos y haciendas," edited by Pierre Duviols, *JSAP* 56 (1967): 7–39; Francisco de Avila [1598], *Dioses y hombres de Huarochirí*, for which see Jorge L. Urioste, ed., *Hijos de Pariya Qaqa. La Tradición oral de Waru Chiri: Mitología, ritual, costumbres*, 2 vols., Syracuse, N. Y., 1984); Pablo José de Arriaga [1621], *La Extirpación de la idolatría en el Perú*, edited by Horacio H. Urteaga (Lima, 1920); Bernabé Cobo [1653], *Historia del nuevo mundo* (Madrid, 1956); Martin Dobrizhoffer [1784], *An Account of the Abipones, an Equestrian People of Paraguay*, 3 vols. in 1 (1822; New York, 1970). Often such studies were part of wider attempts at systematization—efforts to assess and then suppress indigenous religious life. Examples of native chronicles, whose value increases as we learn to appreciate different imagery and perspectives, include Felipe Guaman Poma de Ayala [from 1584 to 1614], *El Primer nueva corónica y buen gobierno* (Paris, 1936); Inca Garcilaso de la Vega [1609], *Royal Commentaries of the Incas and General History of Peru*, translated by Harold V. Livermore 2 vols, (Austin, 1965); Joan Santa Cruz Pachacuti Yamqui Salcamaygua, *Relación de antigüedades desde reyno del Pirú* [about 1613] (Lima, 1927). Regarding these and other documents see Rolena Adorno, ed., *From Oral to Written Expressions: Native Andean Chronicles of the Early Colonial Period* (Syracuse, N.Y., 1982), especially the article by Frank L. Salomon, "Chronicles of the Impossible: Notes on Three Peruvian Indigenous Historians," pp. 9-40.

32. W. H. Brett, *Mission Work Among the Indian Tribes in the Forests of Guiana* (London, 1852) and *The Indian Tribes of Guiana, Their Condition and Habits* (London, 1868); Martin Gusinde, *Die Feuerlandindianer* (Mödling bei Wien, 1931); Antonio Colbacchini and Cesar Albisetti, *Os Bororos orientais* (São Paulo, 1942); Anton Lukesch, *Bearded Indians of the Tropical Forest: The Asurini of the Ipiacaba* (Graz, 1976); Luis Cocco, *Iyewei-teri: Quince años entre los Yanomamos* (Caracas, 1972). See also the series on Shuar culture presented by Siro M. Pellizzaro: *Shakáim: Mitos de la selva y del desmonte* (Sucúa, Ecuador, 1977), *Cantos de amor de la esposa achuar* (Sucúa, Ecuador, 1978), *Mitos de la sal y ritos para obtenerla: Wee* (Sucúa, Ecuador, 1979), *La Reducción de las cabezas cortadas: Ayumpúm* (Sucúa, Ecuador, 1980).

33. Johannes Fabian, *Time and the Other: How Anthropology Makes its Object* (New York, 1983), uses the term *allochronology* to describe the willful and highly imaginative endeavour of assigning one's contemporaries to another period or quality of time. By denying the coeval existence

of the other, one manipulates images of time in order to deny them their full humanity or at least keep the different mode of humanity at bay. Fabian traces how the idea shapes modern cultural studies. George W. Stocking, Jr., *Race, Culture, and Evolution: Essays in the History of Anthropology* (New York, 1968) reviews the relationship of the natural sciences, concepts of evolutionary time, and the growth of theories concerning culture and race in the nineteenth-century sciences. Arthur O. Lovejoy and George Boas, *A Documentary History of Primitivism and Related Ideas* (Baltimore, 1935), treat theories of "chronological primitivism," which envisioned the temporal and progressive accumulation of good (knowledge, wealth, political virtue), as a kind of philosophy of history that provided grounds for moral judgement and hierarchies of value in a world shaken by its own discoveries. On the other hand, the theory of "cultural primitivism," which romanticized the pristine virtues of "natural man," represents, according to these writers, "the discontent of the civilized with civilization. . . . It is the belief of men living in the relatively highly involved and complex cultural condition that a life far simpler . . . is a more desirable life" (p. 7). The presentation of religious practices and beliefs was often a mere by-product of the naturalists' descriptive accounts of their field surveys. See, for example, Edward Bancroft, *An Essay on the Natural History of Guiana, in South America; Containing a Description of Many Curious Productions in the Animal and Vegetable Systems of that Country; Together with an Account of the Religion, Manners and Customs of Several Tribes of it Indian Inhabitants* . . . (London, 1769); Alexander von Humboldt and Aimé Bonpland, *Personal Narrative of Travels to the Equinoctial Regions of America During the Years 1799–1804*, 3 vols. (London, 1852–1853); Gaetano Osculati, *Esplorazioni delle regioni equatoriali lungo il Napo ed il fiume delle Amazzoni; frammento di un viaggio fatto nelle due Americhe negli anni 1846–1847–1848* (Milan, 1850); Francis de Castelnau, *Expédition dans les partes centrales de l'Amérique du Sud* . . . , 6 vols (Paris, 1850–1851); Charles Darwin *The Origin of Species by Mean of Natural Selection; or, The Preservation of Favored Races in the Struggle or Life; and, The Descent of Man and Selection in Relation to Sex* (1859, 1871; New York: The Modern Library, 1936); Henry Walter Bates, *The Naturalist on the River Amazons. A Record of Adventures, Habits of Animals, Sketches of Brazilian and Indian Life, and Aspects of Nature Under the Equator, During Eleven Years of Travel*, 2d ed. (London, 1864); Manuel de Almagro, *Breve descripción de viajes hechos en América por la comisión enviada por el gobierno de S. M. C. durante los años de 1862 a 1866* . . . (Madrid, 1866); Carl Friedrich Philipp von Martius, *Beiträge zur Ethnographie und Sprachenkunde Amerika's zumal Brasiliens*, 2 vols. (Leipzig, 1867); Charles Wiener, *Viaje al Río de las Amazonas y a las Cordilleras, 1879–1882*, in *America pintoresca: Descripción de viajes al nuevo continente, por los más modernos exploradores* (Barcelona, 1884) pp. 1-112; Henri Anatole Coudreau, *La France équinoxiale*, 2 vols. (Paris, 1886–1887).

34. For example, H. Schaaffhausen, "Die Menschenfresserei und das Menschenopfer," *Archiv für Anthropologie* (Braunschweig) 4 (1870): 245–286; Richard Andrée, *Die Anthropophagie. Eine Ethnographische Studie* (Leipzig, 1887); Rudolf S. Steinmetz, "Endokannibalismus," *Mitteilungen der anthropologischen Gesellschaft in Wien* 26 (1894): 1–60; Alés Hrdlicka, "Cannibalism," in Frederick Webb Hodge, ed., *Handbook of American Indians North of Mexico* (Washington, D.C., 1911), pp. 200–201; Theodor Koch-Grünberg, "Die Anthropophagie der südamerikanischen Indianer," *IAE* 12 (1899): 78–110; Ricardo Eduardo Latcham, "La capacidad guerrera de los Araucanos: Sus armas y métodos militares," *Revista chilena de historia y geografía* (Santiago, Chile) 15 (1915): 22–93; Alfred Métraux, "Warfare, Cannibalism, and Human Trophies," *HSAI*, vol. 5, pp. 383–409.

35. See, for example, the special section entitled "Guerre, société et vision du monde dans les Basses Terres de l'Amérique du Sud," in *JSAP* 71 (1985): 129–208, which issue contains six articles on warfare, vengeance, human sacrifice, the exchange of teeth, and consumption of the dead.

36. See James A. Boon, *Other Tribes, Other Scribes: Symbolic Anthropology in the Comparative Study of Cultures, Histories, Religions and Texts* (New York, 1982); Marvin Harris, *The Rise of Anthropological Theory: A History of Theories of Culture* (New York, 1968); George W. Stocking, ed., *Observers Observed*, cited above; Talal Asad, ed., *Anthropology and the Colonial Encounter* (New York, 1973). On recent trends in anthropological research and reporting see Sherry B. Ortner, "Theory in Anthropology Since the Sixties," *CSSH* 26 (1984): 126–166; Dan Rose,

"Occasions and Forms of Anthropological Experience," in Jay Ruby, ed., *A Crack in the Mirror: Reflexive Perspectives in Anthropology* (Philadelphia, 1982); Dan Sperber, "Ethnographie interpretative et anthropologie théoretique," in *Le Savior des anthropologues* (Paris, 1982); Marc Auge, *The Anthropological Circle: Symbol, Function, History*, translated by Martin Thom (Cambridge, 1982; and Stephen Tyler, "Post-modern Ethnography: From Document of the Occult to Occult Document," in James Clifford and George E. Marcus, eds., *Writing Culture: The Poetics and Politics of Ethnography* (Berkeley, 1986): Marcus and Fischer, in *Anthropology as Cultural Critique* (cited above), treat questions about the adequacy of ethnographic reporting as a symptom of a general crisis of representation in the human sciences (pp. 7–16).

37. In his study of Bororo religion, *Vital Souls: Bororo Cosmology, Natural Symbolish, and Shamanism* (Tucson, 1985), Jon Christopher Crocker rendered this verdict on the monographic program: "Just how an anthropologist presents an understanding of another society used to be straightforward. A volume on the practical verities of economics and politics, another on the intricacies of domestic life, and a final effort to explain the 'religion,' a progression from the 'necessary' to the 'possible' to the 'imaginary.' Now that we have understood just how thoroughly each of these domains permeates the other, no such facile divisions seem possible. The Bororo seemed especially difficult to present in terms of a technology-to-ideology format, because . . . the latter permeates the former just as much as the inverse. The Bororo live their daily, momentary existences very much in the domains of what can only be called the 'really imagined' . . . " (p. 13).

38. The seminal formulation of this view remains Emile Durkheim and Marcel Mauss, "De qualques formes primitives de classification: contribution a l'étude des representations collectives," *Année sociologique* 6 (1903): 1–72. For an update, see Serge Tcherkézoff, *Le Roi Nyamwezi, la droite et la gauche. Revision comparative des classifications dualistes* (Cambridge, 1983).

39. See, for example, María Rostworowski de Diez Canseco, *Estructuras andinas del poder: Ideología religiosa y política* (Lima, 1983).

40. The fact that classification became the predominant social scientific goal now receives negative reviews. "The predicament of modern social and cultural anthropology, then, is that it settled for the primary function of systematically describing cultural diversity across the world, which the encompassing project of achieving a generalized science of Man had effectively withered . . ." (Marcus and Fischer, *Anthropology as Cultural Critique*, p. 19). Moreover, as Bruce Lincoln writes, "Interest has shifted from the social implications of taxonomy to the formal principles by which taxonomies are constructed" (*The Tyranny of Taxonomies*, p. 2). Lincoln sees the anthropological preoccupation with taxonomy as a power play and not a neutral exercise, because "taxonomy is . . . not only a means for organizing information, but is also — as it comes to organize the organizers — an apparatus for the classification and manipulation of society" (ibid.). These issues are typified by two special issues of *Social Compass* (Louvain): vol. 14, *Religious Sociology in Latin America*, and vol. 26, *Politics and Religion in Latin America*. The inability to speak of religiousness in a language appropriate to the subject affects Latin American theology as well. Even liberation theologians, dedicated to reflection on the reality of the "popular masses," prove incapable of uncovering the religious intentions and premises of indigenous religious history in anything other than politico-economic terms. See, for example, Leonardo Boff and Virgil Elizondo, eds., *La Iglesia Popular. Between Fear and Hope*, (New York, 1984). The concepts "popular," "people," and "mass" are defined by liberation theologians in economic and class terms (as in "the church of the poor") in such a way that the distinctive cultural traits, especially local religious beliefs and practices, disappear before the authors' own political-economic language, concerned as it is with the critique of ecclesiastical structures. Theology has been unable to sustain any interest in South American religions, although there is a passing reference to the fact that "the élite speak a European language, the mass use native languages and dialects. . . . The élite is opposed to popular religious practices which are called 'animist,' 'magical,' or 'superstitious'!" (Pedro Ribeiro de Olivera, "An Analytical Examination of the Term 'People', in Boff and Elizondo, ibid., p. 82). But see Gonzalo Castillo-Cárdenas, *Theology from Below: The Life and Thought of Manuel Quintín Lame* (Maryknoll, New York, 1987) for a new attempt.

41. Egon Schaden, "Les Religions indigènes en Amérique du Sud," in Puech, ed., *Histoire des Religions* vol. 3, p. 836.

42. Obviously, linguistic research as such falls into this category and includes works such as the following: John Alden Mason, "The Languages of South American Indians," *HSAI*, vol. 6, pp. 157–317; Aryon Dall'Igna Rodrigues, "Die Klassifikation des Tupí-Sprachstammes," *ICA*, 32d Congress (Copenhagen, 1958), pp. 679–684; Aryon Dall'Igna Rodrigues, "Über die Sprache der Surára and Pakidái," *Mitteilungen aus dem Museum für Völkerkunde in Hamburg* 26 (1960): 134–138; Aryon Dall'Igna Rodrigues, "Os Estudos de lingüistica indígena no Brasil," *RASP* 11 (1963): 9–21; Zdanek Salzmann, review of Čestmir Loukotka, "Klassifikation der südamerikanischen Sprachen" (whose original version appeared in *ZFE* 74, 1942, pp. 1–69), *International Journal of American Linguistics* 17 (October 1951): 259–266; Sol Tax, "Aboriginal Languages of Latin America," *CA* 1 (1960): 430–436; Antonio Tovar, *Catálogo de las lenguas de América del Sur* (Buenos Aires, 1961); Charles F. Voegelin and Florence M. Voegelin, "Languages of the World: Native America Fascicle Two," *Anthropological Linguistics* (Bloomington, Ind.) vol. 7, no., 7, part 1 (October 1965); Arthur P. Sorensen, Jr., "South American Indian Linguistics at the Turn of the Seventies," in Gross, ed., *Peoples and Cultures of Native South America*, pp. 312–341; Norman A. McQuown, "The Indigenous Languages of Latin America," *AA* 57 (1955): 501–570; Harriet E. Manelis Klein and Louisa R. Stark, eds., *South American Indian Languages: Retrospect and Prospect* (Austin, 1985); and Loukotka, *Classification of South American Indian Languages*, cited above. But the category also includes most Anglo-American and French ethnography that views culture in the linguistic mode and seeks to unearth through analysis the grammar, rules, codes, or deep structures of the "language" that lies beneath the surface features of cultural expression; see the arguments presented in Dell Hymes, *Foundations in Sociolinguistics: An Ethnographic Approach* (Philadelphia, 1974) and in Anthony Wilden, *System and Structure: Essays in Communication and Exchange*, 2d ed. (London, 1980). Examples of such works would include most of the culture-specific (i.e., language-specific) studies cited in the course of this book. In general these ethnographers think that they eschew broad comparison, but they overlook the fact that even the application of kinship terms and the nomenclature of social organization, for example, compares the ideas of the people they study with the social scientific ideas from the anthropologist's cultural environment. Nowhere has the linguistic turn of Enlightenment science been more stimulatingly directed toward the comparison of South American materials than in Claude Lévi-Strauss's four-volume *Mythologiques* (Paris, 1964–1971; trans. by John Weightman and Doreen Weightman as *Introduction to a Science of Mythology*, 4 vols., New York, 1970–1983), which has renewed comparative study and reawakened an interest in myth. See Lawrence E. Sullivan, "Lévi-Strauss, Mythologic, and South American Religions," in Robert L. Moore and Frank E. Reynolds, eds., *Anthropology and the Study of Religion* (Chicago, 1984), pp. 147–176. Nevertheless, the call for a halt to the rampant application of linguistic theory to every symbolic expression and intelligible form comes from several quarters. For instance, see W. J. T. Mitchell, ed., *The Language of Images* (Chicago, 1980); Mitchell, ed., *Against Theory: Literary Studies and the New Pragmatism* (Chicago, 1985); and Mitchell, *Iconology: Image, Text, Ideology* (Chicago, 1986).

43. Erland Nordenskiöld, "The Origin of the Indian Civilizations in South America," *Comparative Ethnographical Studies* (Göteborg) 9 (1931): 1–153; Walter Krickeberg, "Beiträge zur Frage der alten kulturgeschichtlichen Beziehungen zwischen Nord-und Südamerika," *ZFE* 66 (1934): 287–373; Karl Gustav Izikowitz, *Musical and Other Sound Instruments of the South American Indians: A Comparative Ethnographical Study* (Göteborg, 1935); Junius Bird, "The Archaeology of Patagonia," in *HSAI*, vol. 1, pp. 17–24; Max Uhle, "Procedencia y origen de las antiguas civilizaciones americanas," *ICA*, 27th Congress (Lima, 1942), pp. 355–368; Stig Rydén, "A Study of South American Indian Hunting Traps," *RMP* 4 (1950): 247–352; Otto Zerries, *Wild- und Buschgeister in Südamerika. Eine Untersuchung jägerzeitlicher Phänomene im Kulturbild südamerikanischer Indianer* (Wiesbaden, 1954); Sven Henry Wassén, "On Dendrobates-Frog-Poison Material among Emperá (Chocó)-speaking Indians in Western Caldas, Colombia," in *Etnografiska Museet, Göteborg Arstryck fór 1955 och 1956* (Göteborg, 1957), pp. 73–94; Donald W. Lathrap, "The 'Hunting' Economies of the Tropical Forest Zone of South America: An Attempt at Historical Perspective," in Richard B. Lee and Irven De Vore, eds., *Man the Hunter* (Chicago,

1968), pp. 23–29, and Lathrap, "Our Father the Cayman, Our Mother the Gourd: Spinden Revisited, or a Unitary Model for Emergence of Agriculture in the New World," in C. A. Reed, ed., *Origins of Agriculture* (The Hague, 1977), pp. 713–751; William Maxfield Denevan, "The Aboriginal Population of Western Amazonia in relation to habitat and subsistence," *Revista geográfica* (Rio de Janeiro) 72 (June 1970): 61–86; William H. Isbell, "Cosmological Order Expressed in Prehistoric Ceremonial Centers," *ICA*, 42d Congress, vol. 4 (Paris, 1977), pp. 269–298; Andrzej Krzanowski, *The Cultural Chronology of Northern Andes of Peru (the Huamachuco-Quiruvilca-Otuzco Region)* (Warsaw, 1983); and Johannes Wilbert's forthcoming volume on tobacco and mystical death.

44. In Schmidt's opinion, different combinations of these and other items configured the patterns of group contact and separation. He hypothesized about the historical relations of five cultural-linguistic groups whose migrations and present habitats he could locate on the map even though they overlapped considerably: (1) primary cultures, (2) patrilineal, totemic cultures, (3) exogamous matrilineal cultures (two-class societies), (4) free matrilineal cultures (cultures of the bow), and (5) a zone of Austronesian cultural influences. See Wilhelm Schmidt, *Etnologia Sul-Americana. Circulos culturães e estratos culturães na America do Sul* (São Paulo, 1942); see also Schmidt, "Kulturkreise und Kulturschichten in Südamerika," *ZFE* 45 (1913): 1014–1124.

45. Jacques Lizot, "Histoire, organisation et évolution du peuplement yanõmami," *H* 24 (April-June 1984): 5-40. Lizot takes issue with other culture-historical hypotheses, notably M. Layrisse and J. Wilbert, *Indian Societies of Venezuela: Their Blood Type Groups* (Caracas, 1966). The central difficulties in constructing culture areas were touched on by John Howland Rowe, review of "Outline of South American Culture" (the scheme used to organize Yale University's "Human Relations Area Files" research project), *American Antiquity*" 18 (1953): 279–280.

46. Lizot, "Histoire," p. 5.

47. Ibid., p. 37.

48. Marshall S. Chrostowski, "The Eco-geographical Characteristics of the Gran Pajonal and Their Relationships to Some Campa Indian Cultural Patterns," *ICA*, 34th Congress, vol. 4 (Lima, 1973), pp. 145–160; Juan V. Murra, "El 'control vertical' de un máximo de pisos ecológicos en la economía de las sociedades andinas," in John V. Murra, ed., *Visita de la Provincia de León de Huánuco en 1562, Iñigo Ortíz de Zuñiga*, vol. 2 (Huánuco, Peru, 1972); Joseph W. Bastien, *Mountain of the Condor: Metaphor and Ritual in an Andean Ayllu* (Saint Paul, Minn., 1978); Billie Jean Isbell, *To Defend Ourselves: Ecology and Ritual in an Andean Village* (Austin, 1978); Eric Barry Ross, "Food Taboos, Diet, and Hunting Strategy: The Adaptation to Animals in Amazon Cultural Ecology," *CA* 19 (1978): 1–36; Gary Urton, *At the Crossroads of the Earth and the Sky: An Andean Cosmology* (Austin, 1981).

49. Egon Schaden, "Les Religions indigènes en Amérique du Sud," in Puech, ed., *Histoire des Religions*, vol. 3, p. 836. Schaden's own systematic overview of South American religions (ibid.) generally follows a phenomenological breakdown (supreme beings and astral divinities, pp. 839–849; mythic brothers and civilizing heroes, pp. 849–854; the world of spirits, pp. 854–861; the human soul, pp. 861–867; shamanism, pp. 868–875; religious feasts and masked dances, pp. 875–878) with a separate treatment of the Andes geographical region (Quechua and Chibcha speakers, pp. 879–885). In the same volume, Åke Hultkrantz presents Inca religion, "Les Religions des grandes civilisations précolombiennes," pp. 803–835; Roger Bastide describes Afro-American religions of the Caribbean and South America (pp. 1027–1050); and, in a separate article, Schaden appraises messianic movements by geographic region, by tribe, and by selected reports of messianic incidents among "rural" populations (pp. 1051–1109). Pierre Grenand, *Introduction a l'étude de l'univers wayãpi: Ethnoécologie des indiens du Haut-Oyapock (Guyane Français)* (Paris, 1980), and Françoise Granand, *Et l'homme devint jaguar: Univers imaginaire et quotidien des indiens wayãpi de Guyane* (Paris, 1982) admirably overcome the centripetal force of ecological studies of religion to include wide comparative treatment of mythical themes.

50. See the account of the indigenist movement as it affected studies of Andean religion in Luis Millones Santa Gadea, *Las Religiones nativas del Peru. Recuento y evaluación de su estudio*, (Austin, 1979). Examples of such scholarship include Julio C. Tello, "Wirakocha," *RI* 1 (1923): 583–606; Julio C. Tello and Prospero Miranda, "Wallallo," *RI* 1 (1923): 475–548; Julio C. Tello,

Chavín: Cultura matriz de la civilización andina (Lima, 1961); Jorge A. Lira, *Diccionario Kke-chuwa-Español* (Tucumán, Argentina, 1944); Jorge A. Lira, *Farmacopea tradicional indígena y prácticas rituales* (Lima, 1946); José María Arguedas, *Cuentos mágico-religiosos quechuas de Lucanamarca* (Lima, 1961); Rudolfo Kusch, *America profunda* (Buenos Aires, 1968); and Juan Victor Nuñez del Prado B., "The Supernatural World of the Quechua of Southern Peru as Seen from the Community of Qotobamba," in Lyon, ed., *Native South Americans*, pp. 238–250.

51. See Deborah Poole, "South American Religions: History of Study," in *EOR*, for a fine and different rendering of religious studies in South America from the one I have offered here.

52. An example of the toolbox approach to method (and, in this case, toward the study of myth) is Martin S. Day, *The Many Meanings of Myth* (Lanham, N.Y., 1984).

53. Joachim Wach, *Das Verstehen: Grundzüge einer Geschichte der hermeneutischen Theorie im 19. Jahrhundert*, 3 vols. (1926–1933; reprint Hildesheim, 1966) examines the foundation of modern theories of interpretation by arguing that understanding is not a theoretical question but a uniquely human capacity (a primordial human fact) and, correctly viewed, the purpose of human existence as well as a practical necessity for social formation. Because understanding is not a simple task but one fraught with constant failure, human existence is a problematic condition whose elusive meaning necessitates a hermeneutic of one's existence in time (history). Adequacy of understanding depends on the interpreter's awareness of assumptions that ground the process of interpretation and, therefore, on the constant subjection of one's premises and categories to the light of one's ongoing engagement with the object of understanding. Although such a stance is more familiar in the humanities, especially among historians and textual critics, the social-scientifically oriented students of culture are not total strangers to hermeneutics, but informed practitioners are generally few and new; see Marcus and Fischer, *Anthropology as Cultural Critique*, pp. 30f. Exoticism (the naturalist's ideology of "field" work wherein one "collects raw materials," reimposes, in the initiatory experience of each new generation, the dated divisions between "nature" and "culture" that reproduce themselves in anthropological theories) and the lure of models from the natural sciences generally stunt the growth of cultural studies that would place investigators under the same interpretive lens as the cultural forms of knowledge they seek to explain. Robert C. Ulin, *Understanding Cultures. Perspectives in Anthropology and Social Theory* (Austin, 1984), reviews the state of hermeneutical questions in social anthropology and synthesizes positions taken by Boas, Habermas, Gadamer, Ricoeur, Althusser, Winch, Jarvie, Lukes, MacIntyre, Hindess, Hirst, Horton, E. P. Thompson, and Raymond Williams. Some hermeneutical concerns are creeping into the social sciences with the realization that "anthropology does not transcend history. . . . Every methodology is also a vision of life and of the world" (Ariosvaldo Figueiredo, *Enforçados: O Índio en Sergipe*, [Rio de Janeiro, 1981], p. 11). Critical literary theory often has brought self-conciousness that approximates hermeneutical sensitivity. See, for instance, Tzvetan Todorov, *The Poetics of Prose* (Ithaca, N.Y., 1977); Terry Eagleton, *Literary Theory: An Introduction* (Minneapolis, 1983), and Eagleton, *The Function of Criticism: From the Spectator to Post-Structuralism* (London, 1984); Jonathan Culler, *Structuralists Poetics: Structuralism, Linguistics and the Study of Literature* (Ithaca, N.Y., 1975) and *The Pursuit of Signs: Semiotics, Literature, Deconstruction* (Ithaca, N.Y., 1981); the anthology edited and commented upon by Jerome Rothenberg and Diane Rothenberg, *Symposium of the Whole: A Range of Discourse Toward an Ethnopoetics* (Berkeley, 1983); James A. Boon, *Other Tribes, Other Scribes: Symbolic Anthropology in the Comparative Study of Cultures, Histories, Religions, and Texts* (Cambridge, 1982). See also Paul Ricoeur, *Interpretation Theory* (Dallas, 1979).

54. On the development of the general history of religions as a field of study see Pierre Daniël Chantepie de la Saussaye, *Lehrbuch der Religionsgeschichte*, 2 vols. (Freiburg, 1887–1889), as well as the third edition of the *Lehrbuch*, edited by Chantepie in 1905; Louis Jordan, *Comparative Religion: Its Genesis and Growth* (Edinburgh, 1905); Gerardus van der Leeuw, *Einführung in die Phänomenologie der Religion* (Munich, 1925); Joachim Wach, "Development, Meaning and Method in the Comparative Study of Religion," chapter 1 of his *Comparative Study of Religions* (New York, 1958); Mircea Eliade, "The History of Religions as a Branch of Knowledge," appendix to *The Sacred and the Profane* (New York, 1961). *Religion* 5 (August 1975), a special issue entitled "The History of Religion, An International Survey," chronicles on a global scale the

development of the study of history of religions. See also Joseph M. Kitagawa, ed., *The History of Religions: Essays in the Problem of Understanding* (Chicago, 1967); Joseph M. Kitagawa and Charles H. Long, eds. *Myth and Symbol* (Chicago, 1969); Joseph M. Kitagawa, ed., *History of Religions: Retrospect and Prospect* (New York, 1985); Michel Meslin, *Pour une science des religions* (Paris, 1973); Michel Meslin, "L'Histoire des religions," in Puech, ed., *Histoire des religions*, vol. 3, pp. 1279-1328; Raffaele Pettazzoni, "Il Metodo comparativo," in Pettazzoni, *Religione e Società* (Bologna, 1966), pp. xvii–xlviii; Ugo Bianchi, *The History of Religions* (Leiden, 1975); Eric Sharpe, *Comparative Religion: A History* (London, 1975); Henri Pinard de la Boullaye, *L'Etude comparée des religions*, 2 vols. (Paris, 1925); Gustav Mensching, *Die Religion* (Stuttgart, 1959); Jan de Vries, *Perspectives in the History of Religions*, translated by Kees Bolle (Berkeley, 1967); Jan G. Ploetvoet, *Comparing Religions: A Limitative Approach* (The Hague, 1982); Mircea Eliade, "Myth: Nineteenth and Twentieth Centuries," in Philip P. Wiener, ed., *Dictionary of the History of Ideas*, vol. 3 (New York, 1973), pp. 307–318; Angelo Brelich, *Introduzione alla storia delle religioni* (Rome, and *Storia delle religioni. Perchè?* (Naples: Liguori Editore, 1979); G. Lanczkowski, ed., *Selbstverständnis und Wesen der Religionswissenschaft* (Darmstadt, 1974); Hubert Seiwert, "Systematische Religionswissenschaft. Theoriebildung und Empiriebezug," in *ZMR* 61 (1977): 1–18, and Seiwert, " 'Religiöse Bedeutung' als wissenschaftliche Kategorie," *Annual Review for the Social Sciences of Religion* 5 (1981): 57–99; Reiner Flasche, *Die Religionswissenschaft Joachim Wachs* (Berlin, 1978); Peter Antes, "Systematische Religionswissenschaft: Zwei universöhnliche Forschungsrichtungen?" in *Humanitas Religiosa. Festschrift für Haralds Biezais zu seinem 70. Geburtstag* (Stockholm, 1979), pp. 213–221; Lauri Honko, ed., *Science of Religion: Studies in Methodology* (The Hague, 1979); Donald A. Crosby, *Interpretive Theories of Religion* (The Hague, 1981); Olof Petterson and Hans Akerberg, *Interpreting Religious Phenomena: Studies with Reference to Phenomenology of Religion* (Stockholm, 1981); Aldo Natale Terrin, *Spiegare o comprendere la Religione? Le Scienze della religione a confronto* (Padua, 1983); Burkhard Gladibow and Hans G. Kippenberg, eds., *Neue Ansätze in der Religionswissenschaft* (Munich, 1983); Ursula King, "Historical and Phenomenological Approaches to the Studies of Religions: Some Major Developments and Issues under Debate Since 1950," in F. Whaling, ed., *Contemporary Approaches to the Study of Religion*, vol. 1, *Humanities* (New York, 1984), pp 29–164; Peter Antes, "Religion in den Theorien der Religionswissenschaft," in Walter Kernk, Hermann J. Pottmeyer and Max Seckler, eds., *Handbuch der Fundamentaltheologie*, vol. 1, *Traktat Religion* (Freiburg, 1985), pp. 34–56, with concise bibliography on pp. 54–56; Jacques J. Waardenburg, *Classical Approaches to the Study of Religion: Aims, Methods, and Theories of Research*, 2 vols. (The Hague, 1973–1974); Waardenburg, "Religionswissenschaft in Continental Europe," *Religion* 5 (1975): 27–54; Waardenburg, "Religionswissenschaft in Continental Europe Excluding Scandinavia: Some Factual Data," *N* 23 (1976): 219–238; Waardenburg, "Religionswissenschaft New Style: Some Thoughts and Afterthoughts," *The Annual Review of the Social Sciences of Religion* 2 (1978): 189–220; Waardenburg, *Religionen und Religion. Systematische Einfuhrung in die Religionswissenschaft* (Berlin, 1986); see also the various articles on the history of the study of religion in *EOR*.

55. These authors squarely faced enduring problems in the history of religions. For example, see James G. Frazer, *The Belief in Immortality and the Worship of the Dead*, 3 vols. (London, 1913–1924), and *The Worship of Nature* (London, 1926); Carl C. Clemen, *Die Reste der primitiven Religion im ältesten Christentum* (Giessen, 1916), *Das Leben nach dem Tod im Glauben der Menschheit* (Leipzig, 1920), and *Urgeschichtliche Religion. Die Religion der Stein-, Bronze-, und Eisenzeit*, 2 vols. (Bonn, 1932–1933); Raffaele Pettazzoni, *La Confessione dei peccati*, 3 vols. (Bologna, 1929, 1935–1936); Gerardus van der Leeuw, *In den hemel is eenen dans . . . over de religieuze beteekenis van dans en optocht* (Amsterdam, 1930); Mircea Eliade, *A History of Religious Ideas*, 3 vols. (Chicago, 1978–1985). The list of historians of religions instrumental in the development of cultural studies could be longer than the one here. For example, E. B. Tylor, the founder of modern anthropology, was president of the International Association of the History of Religions in the first decade of this century.

56. Scholars have long pointed out the need for general theoretical works on American Indian religions. In his introduction to the one-thousand-page volume *Tropical Forest Tribes* in *HSAI*, Julian H. Steward underlined the need for "comparative studies . . . permitting a synthesis of

these data in terms of ecological, historical, and configurational factors" (p. xxi). The absence of such configurational comparisons of religion is not due primarily to lack of ethnographic material. In *Religions of the American Indians* (Berkeley, 1979), Åke Hultkrantz writes, "Among South Americans Indians religious life is in many respects imperfectly known . . . Consequently they have been less appealing to scholars of religion . . . and yet the literature on the religions of the American Indians is almost beyond reckoning it its quantity" (p. ix). Egon Schaden fingers the problem in this way: "In all these works, one cannot discover any unity of method or theoretical point of view" (*Aculturação indigena*, p. 3). The inability to confront Amerindian religion runs deep into the ground of modern culture. In part, the refreshment that emboldens one to take a new tack on cultural and religious issues comes from investigations of intelligible forms other than narrative language and its analogs. See, for instance, Susan Kent, *Analyzing Activity Areas: An Ethnoarchaeological Study of the Use of Space* (Albuquerque, 1984); Peter Seitel, *See So That We May See: Performances and Interpretations of Traditional Tales from Tanzania* (Bloomington, Ind., 1980); Jean-Pierre Vernant et al., *Divinazione e razionalità: I procedimenti mentali e gli influssi della scienza divinatoria* (Turin, 1974); Claude Meillassoux, *Maidens, Meal and Money: Capitalism and the Domestic Community* (Cambridge, 1981); Pierre Bourdieu, *Distinction: A Social Critique of the Judgement of Taste* (Cambridge, Mass., 1984); Frederick K. Errington, *Manners and Meaning in West Sumatra: The Social Context of Consciousness* (New Haven, 1984); Christopher Hookway and Phillip Pettit, eds., *Action and Interpretation* (Cambridge, 1980; Bernth Lindfors, ed., *Forms of Folklore in Africa: Narrative, Poetic, Gnomic, Dramatic* (Austin, 1976).

57. Regarding the images that justify and motivate the atrocities and obliterations, see W. Dostal, ed., *The Situation of the Indian in South America: Contributions to the Study of Inter-ethnic Conflict in the Non-Andean Regions of South America* (Geneva, 1972), wherein some twenty academic researchers describe the destruction of South American groups, assess government policies, summarize demographic surveys, and furnish critical bibliographies. The volume is the result of a symposium held in Bridgetown, Barbados, from 25–30 January 1971, and was originally published as *La Situación del indígena en America del Sur. Aportes al estudio de la fricción interétnica en los indios no-andinos* (Montevideo, 1972), which includes a "Declaration of Barbados" for the liberation of Indians. See also Roberto da Matta, "Notas sôbre a contato e a extinção dos índios Gavioes do médio rio Tocantins," *RMP* 14 (1963): 182–202, and also José Barreiro and Robin M. Wright, eds., *Native Peoples in Struggle: Russell Tribunal and Other International Forums* (Boston, 1982).

58. See Charles H. Long, "Freedom, Otherness, and Religion: Theologies Opaque," a chapter in his *Significations: Signs, Symbols, and Images in the Interpretation of Religion* (Philadelphia, 1986), for development of the meaning and value of such opacity in religious history.

59. Gilbert Durand, *Structures anthropologiques de l'imaginaire* (Paris, 1982), pp. 499–500. On this point, Durand owes an intellectual debt to Henry Corbin who studied the concept of imagination in esoteric schools of Islamic spirituality, where the "Imagination is creative . . . because its activity defines it essentially as a theophanic Imagination. It assumes an unparalleled function, so out of keeping with the inoffensive or pejorative view commonly taken of the 'imagination,' that we might have preferred to designate this Imagination by a neologism and have occasionally employed the term *Imaginatrix*" (Corbin, *Creative Imagination in the Sufism of Ibn 'Arabi* (Princeton, 1969, p. 6). Corbin explains how the angelology of Avicenna and Suhrawardi (as well as of the popular mystical romances of Persian literature) grounds a view of the imagination as a state of intimacy with revealed realities. Such a perspective on imaginary life makes possible the cultivation of a contemplative intellect that Corbin also calls the *intellectus sanctus* (ibid., p. 11). One need not view the imagination mystically to appreciate its creative and ameliorative possibilities. Michael T. Taussig, *The Devil and Commodity Fetishism in South America* (Chapel Hill, N.C., 1980), lauds art because it "fights the amnesia of reification by making the petrified world speak and sing against a repressive reality. . . . [M]iners' art is informed by their history extending back through peasant life to pre-conquest times" (p. 155). Taussig's conclusion about religious imagery is similar to Durand's: "As art, these rites and statues dramatize and mold the meaning of the present in the hopes of liberation from it" (ibid.). For additional studies of imagination, see Chapter 2, note 1.

60. Myths are always historical documents coming from specific situations in time, a point made by historians of religions and anthropologists since the founding of their disciplines and well illustrated by David M. Guss, "Historical Incorporation among the Makiritare: From Legend to Myth," *JLAL* 7 (1981): 23–35. But, underneath this truth repeated from the times of Euhemerus to the present, there often lurks the pathetic need to use a narrow notion of history or so-called ethnohistory to demonstrate the reality of myth, and, therefore, the humanity of myth-telling peoples. This effort to set all cultures on the historical foundations of a humanity whose essence is taken to be "historical," in the narrow sense, precludes learning about the symbolic and mythic foundations of a humanity whose experience of time and "reality" is more broadly conceived.

61. The historical character of religion is undeniable and must underlie our study of it. "As Raffaele Pettazzoni and other scholars have noted, the meaning and significance of religious structures can only become apparent from the study of their relation to historical context. Although this is a valid requirement, it is also clear that the possibility of making a theoretical definition of the relation between historical context and religion depends upon an adequate knowledge of the temporal model of social fact. 'Historical context' should not be taken simply to refer to a 'frame' for religious facts; nor may an explanation adequate to the problem be derived from the application of an explanatory model which relates, in terms of external causality, context and religious function" (Dario Zadra, " Victor Turner's Theory of Religion: Toward an Analysis of Symbolic Time," in Moore and Reynolds, eds., *Anthropology and The Study of Religion*, p. 92). For another exploration of what it means to say that significations can be studied within their explanatory social framework, see Roger Bastide, *The African Religions of Brazil: Toward a Sociology of the Interperetration of Civilizations*, translated by Helen Sebba (Baltimore, 1978), p. 391, where interpretation is related to the desire to redefine symbolic life.

62. Claude Lévi-Strauss puts the matter this way: "The fact that myths belonging to very different tribes reveal an obscure knowledge of customs, evidence of which is only to be found outside their traditional habitat, proves that the distribution and state of these tribes in recent times tells us little or nothing about their past. The analysis of South American myths shows that the various communities, unconsciously no doubt, know too much about each other for us not to conclude that their present distribution was preceded by different distributions, which were the results of innumerable mixings of races and cultures occurring throughout the ages. The differences we can observe between cultures and the geographical remoteness from each other of the inhabitants are not facts possessing any intrinsic significance; still less do they offer evidence in support of any historical reconstruction. These superficial differences merely reflect a weakened image of a very ancient and complex process of development, at the point where it was suddenly arrested by the discovery of the New World" (*Introduction to a Science of Mythology*, vol. 2, *From Honey to Ashes*, New York, 1973, p. 437. Roger Bastide states things more concisely and profoundly by viewing symbolic life as a token of the complexity of the experience of being human: "The interpenetration of civilizations is not a new problem arising from nineteenth-century European expansion. On the contrary, it might be said that the whole history of humanity has been one of cultural struggles, migrations, and fusions" (*African Religions of Brazil* p. 12).

63. Few intellectuals who hold to a ferocious relativism of cultural ideas would claim that the sum total of their own ideas are relevant only to the socioeconomic matrix from which they spring (or that one must carry out fieldwork in French neighborhoods in order to understand the thoughts of, for example, Jacques Lacan or Jean Piaget in any fruitful way). Few would concur that the imaginative paradigms of the hard and the social sciences (such as atomic and molecular structure, physiological systems, kinship structures, and theories of social organization) are irrelevant to any human circumstances save the Western cultures that gave rise to them. David Bloor, *Knowledge and Social Imagery* (Boston, 1976), explores the status, imagery, and implications of notions of relativity in the social sciences.

64. Mircea Eliade, *The Quest: History and Meaning in Religion* (Chicago, 1969), p. 53. Regarding the relationship between historical circumstance and the meaning of religious existence, Edward Sapir ("The Meaning of Religion," *The American Mercury* 15, 1928, pp. 72–79) remarked, "It is sometimes said that it is impossible to disentangle religious behavior among primitive peoples from the setting in which it is found. For many primitives, however, it seems almost

more correct to say that religion is the one structural *reality* in the whole of their culture and that what we call art and ethics and science and social organization are hardly more than the application of the religious point of view to the functions or daily life" (p. 78).

65. The last words of Roger Bastide's monumental study of *The African Religions of Brazil* try to distill what is distinctive about religion: "[W]hat distinguishes religious values from other values is the utilization of 'the sacred,' transcendence in respect to the social, the participation of the human in something that goes beyond it" (p. 402). "Religious ideology can be differentiated from other forms of ideology—political ones, for instance—by the fact that, however much these other forms may degrade the sacred, they can never completely obliterate its distinctive character. Mystic values may bear the obvious scars of social tensions, but inasmuch as they are mystic, not political, values, they always retain a certain specificity that the sociologist is obliged to describe or at any rate to acknowledge" (p. 405). In using the term "sacred" we do not wish to overdetermine its meaning too rashly, because it epitomizes the multivocality of symbolic life. See the range of meanings of the term "sacred" in Enrico Castelli, ed., *Le Sacré: Etudes et recherches* (Paris, 1974), and as chronicled by Robert A. Nisbet, *The Sociological Tradition* (New York, 1966), pp. 221-263; Nisbet studies the concept of "the sacred" as "a unit-idea of sociology."

66. Gary Urton, "Animal Metaphors and the Life Cycle in an Andean Community," in Urton, ed., *Animal Myths and Metaphors in South America* (Salt Lake City, 1985) p. 272. Jonathan Culler's comments about the episodes of a *fabula* apply to the efficacy of symbols used to realize the power and meaning they signify. Culler observes that the events themselves are "compelled by meaning. . . . Instead of saying, therefore, that there are events which took place and which the play reveals in a certain order and with certain detours, we can say that the crucial event itself is a product of the demands of signification. Instead of determining meaning and meaning being the result or effect of a crucial event, it turns out that meaning is the cause of the event, the cause of its cause, in a tropological operation that can be assimilated to metonymy ('substitution of cause for effect or effect for cause')" ("Fabula and Sjuzhet in the Analysis of Narrative," *Poetics Today* 1 3, 1980, p. 30). Culler doubts that there is any common ground between these two mutually exclusive logics constructive of symbolic life. The first gives primacy to events; the second sees events as the outcome of meanings (ibid., p. 31).

67. At times I describe the meanings of South American symbols in the terms of Western physics, psychology, anthropology, philosophy, aesthetics, sociology, and theology. This is not because South Americans use words translatable as "transcendence," "space-time," "mind," "symbol," or "culture." My perspective on South American religions is not a native one; I do not pretend simply to clarify the native view, a presumption as pretentious as it is impossible. The issue is not one of speaking equivalent words but of talking about equivalent realities. Understanding South American religions obliges one to talk about the ultimate structures of reality as well as the status and power of the languages used to address them, because the symbols of South American religious life describe the real standing of being in the world.

68. Alfred Métraux, "Religion and Shamanism," *HSAI*, vol. 5, p. 563. Pierre Clastres, "Eléments de démographie amerindiennes," *L'Homme* 13 (1973): 23–36, also argues that the separation of the Andean high cultures from "the rest" was unjustifiable. It darkened the horizon of understanding South American realities by acting as if the myriad societies of the forests, savannahs, and pampas were "all similar to one another, monotonous repititions of the same things that appeared to make no difference" (p. 23).

69. Anthony F. Aveni, "The View from the Tropics," in E. C. Krupp, ed., *In Search of Ancient Astronomies* (Garden City, N.Y., 1978), pp. 286–87. On the rebirth of comparison in cultural studies, especially comparative history, see the opening discussion in Cristiano Grottanelli, "Tricksters, Scapegoats, Champions, Saviors," *HR* 23 (November 1983): 117–139.

70. Jacques Lizot represents one extreme and negative view of broad comparison; see Lizot's review of Johannes Wilbert, *Survivors of Eldorado: Four Indian Cultures of South America* (New York: Praeger, 1972) in *L'Homme* 13, (October-December 1973): 163–164. Lizot even criticizes Johannes Wilbert's comparison of various Yanōmamɨ. subgroups. "To describe the social organization . . . by using the works of N. A. Chagnon on the *samatāri* (southern Yanōmamɨ), and then to pass on to a discussion of ritual and death by relying on D. Barandiarán's studies of the

Sanemá (northern Yanõmamɨ) is to construct a monster, for these two groups are too different: . . . one should not juxtapose cultural traits borrowed alternately from the one or the other of these diverse sub-groups" (p. 164). John V. Murra, "Andean Societies," *Annual Review of Anthropology* 13 (1984): 119–142, offers a more sanguine but still negative summary of the current evaluations of comparison: "[A] careful comparison between these two regions [Mesoamerica and the Andes] at the time of the European invasion will convey many more contrasts than similarities. . . . It is probable that the Andean achievement may well be better understood once comparisons are made further afield. Once studies of Tibetan management of high altitudes or African statecraft become a routine part of anthropological endeavour in the Andes, we can expect substantial parallels to apply, but until then, a tactical stress on Andean 'exceptionalism' will continue to be productive" (p. 119). For a view that encourages the kinds of comparison that Murra would postpone, see Pedro Carrasco, "The Political Economy of the Aztec and Inca States," in G. A. Collier, R. I. Rosaldo, and J. D. Wirth, eds., *The Inca and Aztec States 1400–1800* (New York, 1982), pp. 13–40.

71. Napoleão Figueiredo, "Religiões mediúnicas na Amazônia: O Batuque," *JLAL* 1 (1975): 183.

72. See, for example, the conflicts and contradictions in cosmological descriptions provided by Bernard Mishkin, "Cosmological Ideas Among the Indians of the Southern Andes," *JAFL* 53 (October-December 1940): 225–241. The diversity staggers and frustrates the investigator and prods Mishkin to conclude, "Naturally, in every society in which the problem of cosmology is selected for special study, markedly differing views will be found among different individuals, but I am speaking here of something beyond normal differences. Rather, this is a situation of chaotic heterogeneity" (p. 238).

73. "The process of comparison is a fundamental characteristic of human intelligence . . . [and] is the omnipresent substructure of human thought. Without it, we could not speak, perceive, learn, or reason." Jonathan Z. Smith, "Adde Parvum Parvo Magnus Acervus Erit," *HR* 11 (1972): p. 67.

74. Notable examples of works that delineate the orders of meaningful religious symbolic complexes are Victor Turner, *Forest of Symbols* (Ithaca, N.Y., 1967); Claude Lévi-Strauss, *Mythologiques*, cited above; Clifford Geertz, *Interpretation of Cultures* (New York, 1973); James W. Fernandez, *Bwiti: An Ethnography of the Religious Imagination of Africa* (Princeton, 1982). Each of these studies differs from the others in its estimate of what meaning is, how it is generated, and where it is located.

75. This does no more than place comparative religious studies on a par with comparative linguistics, comparative literature, comparative law, comparative philosophy, and so on. Because of the strange position religion occupies in the Enlightenment imagination, however, the equal footing has been hard won. See Jonathan Z. Smith, *Imagining Religion: From Babylon to Jonestown* (Chicago, 1982), especially pp. xvi–35; and the appreciation of Georges Dumézil in Chapter 2 of J. Z. Smith, *To Take Place* (Chicago, 1987).

76. See Marcus and Fischer, *Anthropology as Cultural Critique*. By way of example, the doctrine of the arbitrariness of the sign—a postulate that has plagued symbolic studies during the last generations—comes under attack in Paul Friedrich, *Language, Context, and the Imagination* (Palo Alto, Cal., 1979), pp. 1–62. Friedrich challenges the degree to which one can generalize theories of analysis constructed on axioms of the semantic vacuity of formal systems.

77. Michel Meslin, *Pour une science des religions* (Paris, 1973), p. 146. For further description and discussion of morphological method in the study of religion see Charles H. Long, "From History to Phenomenology," in Mircea Eliade and Joseph M. Kitagawa, eds., *The History of Religions: Essays in Methodology* (Chicago, 1959), and Long, "Prolegomenon to a Religious Hermeneutic," *HR* (February 1967): 254–264; Angelo Brelich, "Prolégomènes à une histoire des religions," in Puech, ed., *Histoire des religions*, vol. 1, pp. 3–59; J. Bottéro, "Les Histoire des religions," in H. Desrouche and J. Seguy, eds., *Introduction aux sciences humaines des religions* (Paris: Cujas, 1970), pp. 99–127; James S. Helfer, "On Method in the History of Religions," in *History and Theory*, vol. 8 (Middleton, Conn: Wesleyan University Press, 1968), pp. 1–30; and S. A. Tokarew, "Principles of the Morphological Classification of Religions: Part I," in George H. Nadel, *Soviet Anthropology and Archaeology* 5 (1966): 3–10.

78. The morphological stance stems from Goethe's approach to the study of life sciences. I have assessed the way a morphology of symbolic forms relates to the recounting of their history in "A History of Religious Ideas," *Religious Studies Review* 9 (1983): 13–22. Morphological method has been applied successfully to single religious forms in the study of South American cultures; see, for example, Otto Zerries, *Wild- und Buschgeister in Südamerika* (Frankfurt-am-Main, 1954); Hildegard Matthäi, *Die Rolle der Greifvogel, insbesondere der Harpye und des Königsgeier, bei ausserandinen Indianern Südamerikas* (Hohenschäftlarn, 1977); and Ana Maria Mariscotti de Görlitz, *Pachamama: La santa tierra* (Berlin, 1978). It has not been applied to a general study of South American religions. The most pathbreaking and widely known application of morphology to the study of religion is Mircea Eliade, *Patterns in Comparative Religion* (New York, 1977). The present volume reevaluates morphology in light of a generation of significant advances in hermeneutics.

79. In his *Imagining Religion*, Jonathan Z. Smith identifies structuralism as a functionalist subspecies of morphology and thus accounts for the rash first impression that the two approaches to symbolism are similar. Adrian Marino, *L'Herméneutique de Mircea Eliade* (Paris, 1981), correctly locates comparative morphology in relation to contemporary philosophical, aesthetic, semiological, semiotic, literary-critical, and cultural-linguistic schools of interpretation. Julien Riès, *Il Sacro nella Storia Religiosa dell'Umanità* (Milan, Editoriale Jaca, 1981), pp. 53–78, uses the terms *comparative phenomenology* and *comparative hermeneutics* to describe the way the morphological method juxtaposes various cultural interpretations of reality.

80. With a few exceptions, I have refrained from taking a typological approach toward the religious symbols of South America. "Typology [is] a branch of hermeneutics which had figured in doctrinal development from the church fathers through the Reformation, which had informed the major creative works of medieval and Renaissance Europe—*Pilgrim's Progress* and *Paradise Lost* no less than the *Divine Comedy*—and which, from the Enlightenment into our own times, had been the subject of religious controversy and of literary, philological, and historical analysis" (Sacvan Bercovitch, *Typology and Early American Literature* [Boston, 1972], p. 3). But typology is no longer the sole possession of Christian theology. By 1980 Rodney Needham could speak of "an inveterate inclination among anthropologists to the elaboration of typologies" (*Reconnaissances*, p. 68).

81. See, for example, Joachim Wach, *Types of Religious Experience Christian and Non-Christian*, where he tries to sort out the relationship of church, denomination, and sect (pp. 187-208), and Wach's *Sociology of Religion* (1931; Chicago, 1971), which constructs types of religious experience, expression, cult-group, religious organization, religious society or state, and religious authority. Wyatt McGaffey, "African Religions: Types and Generalizations," in Ivan Karp and Charles S. Bird, eds., *Explorations in African Systems of Thought* (Bloomington, Ind., 1980), pp. 301–328, discusses the creative tension between endogenous concepts that respect the meaning of the subjects of study and the categories that satisfy scientific criteria for typology. Subtle types may be established by even one distinctive feature. One finds the use of such monothetic taxons applied successfully to the taxonomy of plants and animals. See the discussion of monothetic and polythetic taxons in Rodney Needham, "Polythetic Classification: Convergence and Consequences," *Man* n.s. 10 (1975): 349-69, and Neeham, *Symbolic Classification*, cited above.

82. I zero in on this unfolding quality of symbols. Contemplating the dynamic significance of one symbolic complex permits one to recognize that meaning in other elaborated forms. In morphological interpretation, each set of images draws attention to itself as a momentary center of gravity in the imagination. Symbolic constellations, such as images of cosmic destruction, are arranged so as to set up later reflection on their rearrangement when they reappear as ritual battle, ordeal, or drinking in another complex symbolic form (e.g., initiation, entrance into the afterlife, passage into the eschatological age).

83. Raffaele Pettazzoni, "Il Metodo Comparativo," in his *Religione e Società*, warned against the degeneration of morphology into a "purely extrinsic and formal phenomenological comparison without any historiographic consistency" (p. 107). In constructing a morphology, says Pettazzoni, the religious symbol must be understood as an appearance, revelation, or experi-

ence of the sacred which presupposes a process of development. Each symbolic form bears the history of change behind it (ibid.). On the distinctions among morphological, typological, and phenomenological comparison see Smith, "Adde Parvum Parvo Magnus Acervus Erit" and *Imagining Religion.* The difference between comparative morphology and comparative phenomenology, on the one hand, and essentialist phenomenology (as practiced by van der Leeuw, Friedrich Heiler, or Rudolf Otto), on the other, is underestimated or ignored by analysts of religious hermeneutics such as Douglas Allen, *Structure and Creativity in Religion* (The Hague, 1978) and Guilford Dudley III, *Religion on Trial* (Philadelphia, 1978). On the ordering power of visible significations see Long, *Significations.*

84. That is why this morphology, a method that always deals with the genesis of forms, relies on myth and chronicles the origins *(naissance)* of imaginal forms without which there can be no fully human relationship to reality. The morphology also maps the relationship *(connaissance)* of these images to one another and surveys the location *(reconnaissance)* of their metamorphoses in mundane life and the reappearance *(renaissance)* of archaic images in the forms of knowledge and experience which constitute mature human existence in each generation.

85. Mircea Eliade, *Myths, Dreams, and Mysteries* (New York, 1975), p. 118.

86. Understanding religion as an integral dimension of human experience is crucial to interpreting historical existence. Failure to do so has stunted the interpretive possibilities of the human sciences during this century. Geoffrey W. Conrad and Arthur A. Demarest make this point in *Religion and Empire* (Cambridge, 1984), a comparative study of the Inca and Aztec (Mexica) empires. "In Mexica and Inca culture religious, political, and philosophical thought formed an integrated whole united by belief in a supernatural order. Sometimes subdivisious of that whole into discrete categories can result in misleading impositions of modern Western ideology on native systems of belief. Therefore, analyses of the Precolumbian ideologies must proceed with extreme caution and a constant awareness of the continuity and unity of Precolumbian belief systems" (p. 5). "In the end, the Aztec and Inca Empires can only be understood if religious and political ideas and behaviors are viewed as an integrated whole" (p. 9).

87. Curt Nimuendajú, *Los Mitos de creación y de destrucción del mundo como fundamentos de la religión de los Apapokúva-Guaraní* (Lima, 1978), p. 90.

88. Developments in the study of South American myth aid the present task. Such works as Raffaele Pettazzoni, *Miti e leggende,* vol. 4, *America Centrale e Meridionale* (Turin, 1959); Theodor Koch-Grünberg, *Indianermärchen aus Südamerika* (Jena, 1920); Harald Schultz, "Lendas dos índios Krahó," *RMP* 4 (1950): 48–163; and Herbert Baldus, *Die Jaguarzwillinge* (Kassel, 1958) demonstrate both the value and the shortcomings of anthologies of myth taken from across the continent. These works contributed to a new wave of interest in myth, resulting in more careful and detailed collection of myths as well as in the publication of excellent compilations that include information about the myths' transcription and sources (e.g., biographies, genealogies, circumstances of their transmission). Examples of recent works include Nunes Pereira, *Moron Buēta: Um Decameron indígena,* 2 vols. (Rio de Janeiro, 1967); Marcelo Bórmida and Alejandra Siffredi, "Mitología de los Tehuelches meridionales," *RU* 12 (1969–1970): 199–245; Bórmida, "Problemas de heurística mitográfica," *RU* 12 (1969–1970): 53–65; Bórmida, "Mito y Cultura. Bases, para una ciencia, de la conciencia mítica y una etnología tautegórica," *RU* 12 (1969–1970): 9–52; Maria E. Grebe, "Cosmovisión mapuche," *Cuadernos de la realidad nacional* (Santiago, Chile) 14 (1972): 46–73; Hugo Nino, *Literaturas de Colombia aborigen: En pos de la palabra* (Bogotá, 1978); Cesáreo de Armellada and Carmen Bentivenga de Napolitano, *Literaturas indígenas venezolanas* (Caracas, 1975); Mario Califano, *Análisis comparativo de un mito maschco* (Jujuy, Argentina, 1978); Marjorie Crofts, trans., *Aypapay'ūm'ūm ekawēn. Lendas mundurukús* (Brasilia, 1978); Manuel García-Renduelas, *'Duik Múum'. Universo mítico de los aguarunas,* 2 vols. (Lima, 1979); Henrique Urbano, *Wirachocha y Ayar: Héroes y funciones en las sociedades andinas* (Cuzco, 1981); Françoise Grenand, *Et l'homme devint jaguar,* previously cited. A series of volumes edited by Johannes Wilbert of the Latin American Studies Center, University of California–Los Angeles, has been published since 1968; each volume presents myths from a particular cultural-linguistic group (e.g., the Warao [1970], Yupa [1974], Selknam [1975], Yamana [1977], Ge [1978], Mataco [1982], Toba [1982], Bororo [1983], Tehuelche [1984], Chorote [1985], Goajiro [1987]) and includes multiple variants of myths, elaborate

critical apparatuses (such as indexes of motifs), and a bibliography, which prove indispensable for comparative study. Susan A. Niles, *South American Indian Narrative. Theoretical and Analytical Approaches: An Annotated Bibliography* (New York and London, 1981) helpfully gathers a large number of sources, although the introduction and annotations are not as valuable as the collection of materials. See the survey of thirty years of postwar research into South American myth presented by Juan Adolfo Vázquez, "The Present State of Research in South American Mythology," *N* 25 (1978): 240–276. Vázquez geographically maps the scholarly study of South American myths, especially those studies that have examined the northern and central parts of the continent. Vázquez has also presented a thematic treatment of South American mythology (creation of the world, levels of the cosmos, heavenly bodies, universal destruction, high gods, and myths of the origins of human beings, plants, fire, death, and rites). This article cuts across geographic and linguistic boundaries and makes separate mention of what he calls "modern" myths or legends generated in colonial times ("South American Religions: Mythic Themes," in *EOR*). He notes that a large number of these mythic themes are found not only among countless South American peoples but also in other continents of the world. The study of South American myth, therefore, opens onto larger questions about the origin, history, and meaning of such mythic motifs.

89. This is why, in the theories of the past centuries, myth, imagination, and religious symbolism—as a threesome—have suffered mistreatment and trivialization. Kurt Hübner, *Die Wahrheit des Mythos* (Munich, 1985), takes a critical hermeneutical approach to theories about myth and methods applied to the study of myth. Mircea Eliade, *Myth and Reality* (New York, 1963) remains a penetrating delineation of the issues at stake in the estimation of the nature of myth. In addition, see R. J. Siebert, *The Critical Theory of Religion: The Frankfurt School* (The Hague, 1985); Roman Jakobson, *Selected Writings*, vol 7, *Contributions to a Comparative Mythology: Studies in Linguistics and Philology, 1972–1982* edited by Stephen Rudy (The Hague, 1985); William G. Doty, *Mythography: The Study of Myths and Rituals* (University, Ala., 1986); Bruce Lincoln, *Myth, Cosmos, and Society: Indo-European Themes of Creation and Destruction* (Cambridge, Mass, 1986); Percy S. Cohen, "Theories of Myth," *Man* 4 (1969): 337–353.

90. Historians of religions will feel the absence in the notes of scholars whose views are pertinent to many discussions in the text: R. Pettazzoni, A. Brelich, U. Bianchi, Å. Hultkrantz, M. Eliade, G. Tucci, H. Corbin, A. K. Coomaraswamy, J. Z. Smith, P. Mus, G. Van der Leeuw, K. Bolle, N. Söderblom, W. C. Smith, N. Smart, Ch. H. Long, J. M. Kitagawa, G. Widengren, G. Dumézil, R. Stein, W. Heissig, E. Goodenough, W. Burkert, M.-P. Vernant, H. Biezais, H. Klimkeit, J. Ploetvoet, M. Meslin, J. Pentakaïnen, and others. Although I decided to give as much space as possible to South American materials that are unknown and ignored, my considerable debt to the formative thinkers of my discipline will be evident to those who know the literature of my field. I am now preparing a full volume on the history of the field.

91. I suppose that this fathoming of ordinary language falls under what Paul Ricoeur, the father of "second naiveté," calls metapoetics (from Greek, *poietikos*, "to make creative, to create artistically"), a reflection on the nature of creativity, especially as it appears in the language used to speak of imagery and the imagery at work in language.

CHAPTER TWO

1. Hermeneutics of culture that insist that interpretation requires creative expressions of culture (and that specifically call for a re-creation of the interpreter's culture) come from many different intellectual persuasions. The point made here is that "the meaning of culture can be grasped only when a common interchange of ideas and interpretations is possible. A body of critical cultural theory is needed which incorporates not only the praxis of human culture but its telos as well." David M. Rasmunssen, *Cultural Hermeneutics* (Dordrecht, 1973), pp. 31–32. Critical to the cultural interpretation referred to in this paragraph is a prominent role for imagination. "It is imagination *(Phantasie)* that is the decisive function of the scholar," writes Hans-Georg Gadamer, "The Universality of the Hermeneutic Problem," in David E. Linge, ed., *Philosophical Hermeneutics* (Berkeley, 1976), p. 12. The precise nature and function of the

imagination in the interpretation of religion is being analyzed from various points of view. See, for example, Long, *Significations*; Smith, *Imagining Religion*; David Tracy, "Creativity in the Interpretation of Religion: The Question of Radical Pluralism," *New Literary History* 15 (Winter 1984): 289–309; Tracy, *The Analogical Imagination* (New York: Crossroad, 1981); and Leopoldo José Bartolomé, "La experiencia estética ante la narración mítica," *RU* 12 (1969–1970): 407–412.

2. Anthony F. Aveni and Gary Urton, eds., *Ethnoastronomy and Archaeoastronomy in the American Tropics* (New York, 1982), p. vii. The ways in which comparative and historical studies can overcome our "fragmentary" knowledge are well illustrated in the contrast between two works by Gerardo Reichel-Dolmatoff: *Amazonian Cosmos* is based on one informant's view, whereas *The Shaman and the Jaguar* (Philadelphia, 1975) casts a wider comparative net over its thematic subject matter.

3. Based on his exhaustive studies of cosmogony throughout the world, Mircea Eliade offered the following classification:

> 1. Creation *ex nihilo* (a High Being creates the world by thought, by word, or heating himself in a steam hut, and so forth); 2. The Earth Diver Motif (a God sends aquatic birds or amphibious animals, or dives, himself, to the bottom of the primordial ocean to bring up a particle of earth from which the entire world grows); 3. Creation by dividing in two a primordial unity (one can distinguish three variants: a. separation of Heaven and Earth, that is to say, of the World-Parents; b. separation of an original amorphous mass, the "Chaos"; c. the cutting in two of a cosmogenic egg); 4. Creation by dismemberment of a primordial Being, either a voluntary, anthropomorphic victim (Imir of the Scandinavian mythology, the Vedic Indian Purusha, the Chinese P'an-ku) or an aquatic monster conquered after a terrific battle (the Babylonian Tiamat). . . . [and] speculative cosmogonic texts. (Eliade, *From Primitives to Zen: A Thematic Sourcebook of the History of Religions* [San Francisco, 1977], p. 83)

The analysis that follows in this chapter makes no attempt to produce an exhaustive typology of creation accounts and, consequently, does not employ Eliade's schema. See also Charles H. Long, *Alpha: The Myths of Creation* (New York, 1963).

4. Aureliano Oyarzún, "Los Onas o Selknam de la Isla Grande de Tierra del Fuego," *Anales del Instituto de Etnografía Americana* (Mendoza) 2 (1941): 20–21.

5. Manuel Llaras Samitier, "Primer ramillete de fábulas y sagas de los antiguos Patagones," *RU* 3 (1950): 187. Kóoch is also known as *Weq.on*, "the truthful one." The fragmentary knowledge of Tehuelche myth is admirably summarized and evaluated in Marcelo Bórmida and Alessandra Siffredi in their articles "Mitología de los Tehuelches meridionales," *RU* 12 (1969–1970): 199–245, and "Hierofanías y concepciones mítico-religiosas de los Tehuelches meridionales," *Runa* 12 (1969–1970): 247–271. In general, creation appears to be carried out in several stages. In the beginning there is nothing but watery chaos. Then Kóoch (or Weq.on), the ageing high god, creates essential elements and orders them. However, the most dramatic events of creation are carried out by Elal, a robust and young god who transforms earthly order and creates humanity and human society and economy. Siffredi points out that, among the seventy or so Tehuelche surviving today, the name Kóoch is no longer identified with a divinity but simply means sky. See the materials collected in Johannes Wilbert and Karin Simoneau, eds., *Folk Literature of the Tehuelche Indians* (Los Angeles, 1984). Although Llaras Samitier provides the most detailed cosmogonic material, the texts he gathered are difficult to place in context.

6. Llaras Samitier, "Primer Ramillete," p. 188. On Elal, see Juan Adolfo Vázquez, "Nacimiento e infancia de Elala, mitoanalisis de un texto tehuelche meridional," *Revista iberoamericana* (University of Pittsburgh) 95 (April–June 1976): 201–216.

7. The Kogi myth of creation, for example, begins with a formless sea that lies in total darkness. Without the light of the sun, moon, or stars, and without the life of people, animals, or plants, the sea was the total expression of primordial being. It was everywhere. The name of the sea was Gaulchovang, the Mother manifest through every formless expression of liquid and darkness. She was *alúna*, the spirit of the deep, which would give rise to all substances and forms, especially thought and memory. She would give birth to the nine separate worlds and would

make the first man from a hair of her body by rubbing it with menstrual blood. The Mother lived in the center of darkness, in Nyiduluma, the "foam of the seawater, the heart of total darkness." See Gerardo Reichel-Dolmatoff, *Los Kogi, una tribu de la Sierra Nevada de Santa Marta, Colombia*, vol. 2 (Bogotá, 1951), pp. 20ff.

8. Nimuendajú, *Mitos de creación*, p. 50. Unfortunately, Nimuendajú does not provide the Guaraní version of this statement.

9. The Apapocuvá-Guaraní creation myth was collected by Curt Nimuendajú and published in "Die Sagen von der Erschaffung und Vernichtung der Welt als Grundlagen der Religion der Apapocuvá-Guaraní," *ZFE* 46 (1914): 284–403. The entire text has been translated and reassembled with further commentary in *Los Mítos de creación y de destrucción del mundo como fundamentos de la religión de los Apapokuvá-Guaraní*, ed. Jurgen Riester G. (Lima, 1978). One should see the important linguistic and interpretive commentary provided by Juan Francisco Recalde, "A Criação du mundo e o dilúvio universal na religião dos primitivos Guaraní," *RAM* 136 (September 1950): 100–111. Recalde (p. 101) considers the myths of *iñypyrũ* ("the beginnings") and Guyraypoty̆ (the name of the being who escapes the cosmic flood) essential to understanding the foundations of Guaraní thought.

10. Nimuendajú, *Mitos de creación, p. 155.*

11. Ibid., pp. 155ff.

12. For an interpretation of myths in which supernatural beings disappear and leave a symbolic residue in this world, see Marcelo Bórmida, "Ergon y mito: Una Hermenéutica de la cultural material de los Ayoreo del Chaco Boreal. Primera Parte," *SE* 1 (1973): 9–68. It gives special attention to the *nanibaháde* (mythical ancestors) and interprets their meaning in the light of the consciousness that imbues material culture, especially tools and cultural artifacts used in labor, including ritual. The disappearance of the creative beings is complicated and various. The Lengua report, for example, that the world was created by a beetle. The first man and woman he made were abortive attempts, for he fashioned them from clay but joined them together in a way that set them at a definite disadvantage and immobilized them in the face of their enemies. The beings of the first world disappeared and became disembodied. "The beetle then ceased to take any active part or interest in the governance of the world." Wilfred Barbrooke Grubb, *An Unknown People in an Unknown Land; An Account of the Life and Customs of the Lengua Indians of the Paraguayan Chaco*, 4th ed. (1911; London, 1925), pp. 114–115.

13. Paul Radin, *Monotheism Among Primitive Peoples* (Basel, 1954), pp. 13–14. Radin is drawing on the reports of Konrad Theodor Preuss, *Religion und Mythologie der Uitoto*, vol. 1 (Göttingen, 1921), pp. 27, 166–168.

14. For comparative discussion of the figures of supreme beings, their symbolic forms, and the history of theories concerning their nature and importance for the study of religion, see Lawrence E. Sullivan, "Supreme Beings," in *EOR*.

15. Reichel-Dolmatoff, *Amazonian Cosmos*, p. 23. Reichel-Dolmatoff bases this account primarily on conversations held with one Desana man who had migrated to Bogotá. For a wider comparative treatment of the themes of this narrative in the context of the entire continent, see Mircea Eliade, "South American High Gods," part 1, *HR* 8 (1969). 338–354, and part 2, *HR* 10 (1971). 234–266.

16. Reichel-Dolmatoff, *Amazonian Cosmos*, p. 25.

17. Ibid., p. 41.

18. Ibid., p. 25.

19. Ibid., p. 41.

20. Ibid., p. 25.

21. Ibid., pp. 47–48.

22. Ibid., pp. 30, 41.

23. Ibid., pp. 30ff.

24. Ibid., pp. 41–42.

25. Ibid., p. 28.

26. Ibid., pp. 26, 57.

27. Mbyá, the southern Guaraní creator, made the world by crossing sticks together. Not only did they form the ordered foundation of the world, structured by cardinal points and a central

axis, but they came together in such a way as to make a vital sound that generated change and new life. Egon Schaden contends that the crossed sticks used as ritual noisemaking instruments are symbolic of the primordial percussion-sound made by the creator. See Schaden, "Caracteres específicos da cultura Mbuá-Guaraní," *RASP* 11 (1963): 83–94.

Even apart from the scenes where supreme beings create by power of their word, sound is often an instrument of creation from nothing. The Kari'ña contend, for example, that invisible sounds generated all the physical aspects of the world, every kind of being coming from a different sound. "We believe that the *aula* [word, speech] of every *wala* [species of being] has existed from the very beginning, and that it created the physical aspect. Every *wala* in the visible world is the physical counterpart of a flowing *wala* [melody] which gives it life." C. H. de Goeje, "Philosophy, Initiation, and Myths of the Indians of Guiana and Adjacent Countries." *IAE* 44 (1943): 4. Every sound a creature makes is the imitative expression of the invisible power that created it. Because they are embodiments of the same eternal principle, created beings that make the same sound (such as creaking tree branches, running waters, animals of the same species, and so on) participate in the same continuously creative mode of being.

28. Ewald Boening, *Der Pillánbergriff der Mapuche* (Buenos Aires, 1974), p. 175 and passim.

29. These facts, essential to understanding religions on a culture-by-culture basis, tempted generations of scholars to ignore or downplay the importance of these symbolic expressions of so-called high gods. By foreshortening the range of divine forms to include only what they considered important or pristine according to the theological canons of evolutionary history or noble savagery, investigators risked distorting the data and stunting the appraisal of religion. Worse than that, by concentrating investigation only on the religious symbolism of so-called concrete forms of action, such as ritual, social organization, and economic behavior, scholars of culture arbitrarily sheared off whole areas, sometimes the most striking and unique ones, of the cultural creativity of the peoples in question.

30. See the wide range of images of South American supreme beings assembled by Mircea Eliade, "South American High Gods," cited above. Comparative study of South American supreme beings has often centered on the extent of the diffusion or overlap of specific divine forms. See, for example, Albert Kruse, "Purá, das Höchste Wesen der Arikéna," *ANT* 50 (1955): 404–416, which is a study of the divine being who existed (together with his companion Mura) at the beginning of the world. Protásio Frikel, in "Zur linguistisch-ethnologischen Gliederung der Indianerstämme von Nord-Pará (Brasilien) und den anliegenden Gebieten," *ANT* 52 (1957): 509–563, continued and corrected Kruse's study and hypothesized that Pura was the primal, invisible Sun. Using the Arikena descriptions of Pura as a starting point, Josef Haekel undertook a comparative study of the name and of other high gods exhibiting similar features: "Purá und Hochgott, Probleme der südamerikanischen Religionsethnologie," *AFV* 13 (1958). Hans Becher, in *Pore-Perimbo. Einwirkungen der lunaren Mythologie auf den Lebensstil von drei Yanonami-Stammen-Surára, Pakidái und Ironasiteri* (Hanover, 1974), then offered a detailed study of the concept of a supreme being named Pore, a lunar divinity, among the Brazilian Yanonami.

For a discussion of the nature of Omao, the celestial cultural hero of the Sanemá-Yanoama, who lives on high and who is associated with the indestructible and very hardwood tree of black wood named Polí, the cosmic axis, see Daniel de Barandiarán, "Vida y muerte entre los indios sanemá-yanoama," *ACAR* 21 (1967): 4ff. This perfect and immortal tree trunk of Omao is not to be confused with the nice-looking but faulty tree Tókoliwán, which is associated with the tricksterish counterpart Soao, who saw to it that human beings were made of inferior wood.

For further reports and interpretations of some South American high gods, see the following works. Arthur A. Demarest, *The Nature and Antiquity of the Andean High God* (Cambridge, Mass., 1981) is an essay that gathers together the complicated history and structure of the Inca upper pantheon, capped by Viracocha, the sublime creator god. The essay admirably demonstrates the complexity of any divine form and the diverse forces of the history of political, social, and imaginative life that it carries in its symbolism. Regarding the most rarified and sublime figures of the Mataco, especially the celestial high god Nilataj but also astronomic and meteorological divinities, see Celia Olga Mashnshnek, "Seres potentes y heroes míticos de los Mataco del Chaco Central," *SE* 1 (1973): 105–154. And on the Mapuche, see Else Maria Waag, "El ser supremo de los Mapuches neuquinos," *SAA* n.s. 9 (1975): 147–154.

31. For an account of the ways in which scholarly attitudes to the concept of supreme being have influenced the study of religion, see Sullivan, "Supreme Beings," in *EOR*.

32. Pierre Clastres, *Le Grand parler. Mythes et chants sacrées des indiens guaraní* (Paris, 1974), p. 55.

33. David Maybury-Lewis, *Akwẽ-Shavante Society* (Oxford, 1967), pp. 285–286. There seems to be no clear or coherent heroic tradition in the accounts gathered by David Maybury-Lewis.

34. Ibid., p. 286.

35. Alfred Métraux, "Ensayos de mitología comparada sudamericana," *AI* 8 (1948): 10.

36. Alfredo Jiménez Núñez, *Mitos de creación en Sudamérica*, vol. 3 (Seville, 1962), p. 27. See treatment of this question in Umúsin Panlon Kumu and Tolaman Kenhíri, eds., *Antes o mundo não existia. A mitología heróica dos indios desâna* (São Paulo, 1980). Dick Edgar Ibarra Grasso, *Cosmogonía y mitología indígena americana* (Buenos Aires, 1980), is less reliable in its use and interpretation of the many valuable mythic sources it gathers together on this point.

37. Johannes Wilbert and Karin Simoneau, eds., *Folk Literature of the Toba Indians* vol. 1 (Los Angeles, 1982), p. 101.

38. The account is taken from a report by Edgardo J. Cordeu, "Aproximación al horizonte mítico de los Tobas," *RU* 12 (1969–1970): 126.

39. Wilbert and Simoneau, eds., *Folk Literature of the Toba*, vol. 1, p. 103.

40. The epiphanic quality of existence is often an explicit mythological theme. See, for example, the Andean term *Nayjama*, the "epiphany" associated with cosmogonic beings and times, as considered in Fernando Diez de Medina, *La Teogonia andina: Pacha, Wiracocha, Thunupa, Nayjama* (La Paz, Bolivia, 1973).

41. The subtleties of these points are not lost on South American societies. On the contrary, they engage these questions in profound and original ways. See, for example, Diez de Medina, *La Teogonia Andina*, in which the author delineates the Andean concept of *pacha* ("world") as a condition of coming-into-being whose meaning is grasped through myth (pp. 113–198).

42. Robin Michael Wright, "History and Religion of the Baniwa Peoples of the Upper Rio Negro Valley," 2 vols. (Ph.D. diss., Stanford University, 1981), p. 382. Now *"whenever* the jaguar-song occurs in myth or shaman-song, it indicates a transformation—*Ipadámawa*—is being made" (p. 382).

43. Ibid., p. 564.

44. Ibid., pp. 537–538; see the diagram on p. 473.

45. Marcos Fulop, "Aspectos de la cultura tukana: Cosmogonía," *RCA* 3 (1954): 115.

46. Ibid., p. 116.

47. Gerald Weiss, "World of a Forest Tribe in South America," *APAMNH* 52 (1975): 407.

48. Ibid., pp. 340–342.

49. Ibid., p. 309.

50. Ibid., p. 310.

51. Ibid., p. 311.

52. Ibid., p. 313.

53. Ibid., pp. 314–315. On Avíreri's creation of night by dancing and panpipe music, see also the myth of Ya'viveri reported in Gerhard Baer, *Die Religion der Matsigenka Ost-Peru: Monographie zu Kultur und Religion eines Indianervolkes des Oberen Amazonas* (Basel, 1984), pp. 430–434.

54. Ibid., p. 315.

55. Ibid., p. 319ff.

56. Ibid., p. 324. Regarding the Machiguenga myth in which Pačákama stablizes the earth, see Baer, *Die Religion der Matsigenka*, pp. 426ff.

57. Ibid., pp. 554–565. For consideration of the Machiguenga and Campa myths of the transformation of primordial earth and excrement and the relationship to the death and disappearance of primordial humanity, see Lévi-Strauss, *La Potière jalouse*, pp. 232ff. and passim.

58. Weiss, "World of a Forest Tribe," p. 328.

59. Ibid.

60. Fock, *Waiwai: Religion and Society of an Amazonian Tribe* (Copenhagen, 1963), p. 48. This contributes to a theme we will meet elsewhere, in those cases where the earliest times have a strong female valence. Here, in the case of the Waiwai, this primordial femininity is present both in the main protagonist of the creation myth, the heroic *wayam-yenna* (tortoise) woman, and

through the protective "grandmothers" who offer themselves so that the foundational items of culture might appear and endure: manioc from the bones of the jaguar grandmother, fish poison-plants from another self-sacrificing *chacha*, and so on. See, for example, pp. 39–42, 48, 65.

61. Ibid., pp. 64–65.

62. Ibid., pp. 74–75.

63. Ibid., pp. 79–82.

64. Ibid., p. 81.

65. Weiss, "World of a Forest Tribe," p. 370. See also Lévi-Strauss, *La Potière jalouse*, p. 234.

66. Weiss, "World of a Forest Tribe," p. 370.

67. Fock, *Waiwai*, p. 23.

68. Ibid., p. 101.

69. Ibid., pp. 38ff.

70. Ibid., p. 39.

71. Note the similarity between this episode and the Canelos Quichua myth of the pregnant woman among wild jaguars. Also noteworthy here is the fact that a large clay vessel is placed over the remains of a cremated corpse. For this, see ibid., p. 164.

72. Note again the similarity between this myth and the Canelos Quichua myth wherein the pregnant woman's children are extracted by the ancient jaguar and placed in a large clay vessel.

73. Ibid., p. 40.

74. Ibid., p. 41.

75. Ibid., pp. 38–43.

76. Norman E. Whitten, Jr., *Sacha Runa: Ethnicity and Adaptation of Ecuadorian Jungle Quichua* (Urbana, Ill., 1976), p. 51.

77. Ibid., p. 51.

78. Ibid, pp. 51–52.

79. Weiss, "World of a Forest Tribe," pp. 406, 412. Kientibákori is linked, through his material form, to the earth's bowels, a dark and gelatinous tangle of indistinct organic masses. He himself has a remarkable heap of intestines that resemble half-formed tadpoles. See Lévi-Strauss, *La Potière jalouse*, pp. 30–31, and F. M. Casevitz-Renard, "Les Matsiguenga," *JSAP* 61 (1972). 249f.

80. Rafael Karsten, *The Toba Indians of the Bolivian Gran Chaco*, (1923; Oosterhout, The Netherlands, 1970), p. 101.

81. Ibid., p. 103.

82. Marc de Civrieux, *Watunna: An Orinoco Creation Cycle*, ed. and trans. David M. Guss (San Francisco, 1980). The introduction to this work points out that the cycle is not a collection of the solemn and relatively fixed-form sacred texts sung during festivals but rather of popular versions, collected in fragments and episodes and told in everyday language as anecdotes prompted by mundane circumstances of the moment (pp. 16–17).

83. Ibid., p. 21.

84. Ibid.

85. Ibid., p. 22.

86. Ibid., p. 23.

87. Ibid., pp. 24, 180.

88. Ibid., p. 180.

89. Ibid., p. 24. It is significant that the hallucinogenic drink contained in the egg in heaven allows visions of realities that can only be seen, but not heard, when Huehanna descends to earth. The sights of one dimension seen in vision are the sounds of invisible beings heard on earth. For a discussion of this theme in the context of the South American quest for a dream-song, see Lawrence E. Sullivan, "La persona y la sociedad como composiciones musicales," *Cuadernos internacionales de historia psicosocial del arte* 3 (December 1983): 9–17.

90. Civrieux, *Watunna*, p. 27. The eschatological functions of these two kinds of creations, each embodying a different concept of time (finite and infinite), are found throughout religious history. Another striking and well-studied instance may be found in the Iranian Bundahishn whose first chapter describes the tension between Menok and Getik; see Gherardo Gnoli, "Osservazioni sulla dottrina mazdaica della creazione," *Annali dell'Istituto di Napoli* n. s. 13 (1963): 180ff.

91. Civrieux, *Watunna*, p. 28.

92. Ibid., pp. 29–30.

93. Ibid., p. 29.

94. Ibid., pp. 186, 192. As in so many cases, the shaman here plays a salvific role where even aspects of the gods cannot succeed in overcoming destructive intentions and dreams. Attawanadi's eventual success depends upon his mastery of the shamanic skill of assuming different forms.

95. Ibid., p. 31.

96. Ibid., p. 31.

97. Ibid., p. 32.

98. The Barasana provide a typical illustration. In some of their most fundamental myths about the origins of the world, they recount how the sky fell. The disaster recurred again and again, but eventually the mythic age did achieve the distance between heaven and earth that brought the epoch to a close and opened the way for a symbolic cosmos. As summarized in Stephen Hugh-Jones, *The Palm and the Pleiades*:

> *Romi Kumu* [shaman woman] makes the world. 1. In the beginning the world was made entirely of rock and there was no life. *Romi Kumi* . . . took some clay and made a cassava griddle. She made three pot-supports and rested the griddle upon them. The supports were mountains holding up the griddle, the sky. She lived on top of the griddle.
>
> 2. She lit a fire under the griddle. The heat from the fire was so intense that the supports cracked and the griddle fell down upon the earth below, displacing it downwards so that it became the Underworld; the griddle became the earth. . . . Then she made another griddle which is the layer above this earth, the sky." (p. 263)

That sky also fell when the earth caught fire again.

99. Grenand, *Et L'homme devint jaguar*, p. 47ff.

100. Ibid., p. 50.

101. Ibid., p. 48. Grenand calls attention to a similar conception recorded by Clastres: "The firmament rests on four columns. (Our father) first set it up on three columns, but the firmament was still moving." When it was set on four posts, the world became firm. Clastres, *Le Grand parler*, p. 34; cited in Grenand, *Et L'homme devint jaguar*, p. 50.

102. Ibid., p. 55.

103. Angelo Brelich, "Dreams in the Religious World Concept of the Greeks," in G. E. Von Gruenebaum and Roger Caillois, eds., *The Dream and Human Societies* (Los Angeles, 1966), p. 301. "The temporal anticosmos," continues Brelich, "is always the origin of the cosmos, and as such, it has a supernatural value." (ibid.). The foundational value of images of chaos need not be restricted to religion nor to the study of religion. Making sense of a reality, of whatever kind, can be aided by grasping it as a whole. On one extreme, that of modern social sciences, such apprehension of a total fact has recently expressed itself in the image of a system, a set of dialectical relations, an organic whole, or a configuration. Many different schools of anthropological thought share some such notion of culture as a totalizing concept. Less numerous are the scholarly approaches that begin with chaos as the originative holistic image. But see the discussion of such a possibility in Paul Friederich, "Linguistic Relativity and the Order-to-Chaos Continuum," in Jacques Maquet, ed., *On Linguistic Anthropology: Essays in Honor of Harry Hoijer 1979* (Malibu, Cal., 1980), pp. 89–139.

104. Miguel Alberto Bartolomé, "Shamanism among the Avá-Chiripá," in David L. Browman and Ronald A. Schwartz, eds., *Spirits, Shamans, and Stars: Perspectives from South America* (The Hague, 1979), p. 107.

105. Ibid., p. 107. The Chiripá version of this myth varies only in that the sun alone is born from Nandé Cy. The sun then creates his brother the moon.

106. Ibid., p. 108. During its early history, the world has suffered cataclysmic destructions through fire, water, or the creator's violent overthrow of the eternal wooden cross that supports the world. During these times of crisis, the conditions of human culture were saved by Chary Piré, "the grandmother."

107. Weiss, "World of a Forest Tribe," pp. 389–390.

108. Ibid., p. 470.

109. Ibid.

110. The flip side of the question regarding the meaning and motives of cosmic destruction is, Why do so many South American cultures bother to go through the exercise of describing a world that, by their own accounts, no longer exists (i.e., the primordial world that existed before the cataclysm?) Why treasure the images of a world that has disappeared? What is the meaning of the interpretive archaeology carried out by myth? Answers to these questions must address several levels of concern. On an ontological plane, descriptions of the primordial world offer assurance that being has fully appeared and, consequently, that the fullness of being is real. To know that being has exhibited an integrity means that, under some conditions of time, that entirety had been achieved and that, under similar conditions, it might be reachieved. Furthermore, there seems to be a cognitive value to myths of the lost primordium: by appearing in the primordium, reality has made itself known. Its guises and disguises have been made manifest. Since myths reveal the forms that primordial being took, accounts of the beginnings have an existential dimension: one can recognize the experience of sacred beings in the symbolism of social, economic, aesthetic, cosmic, and political life. Since myth reflects the realities of the primordium and participates in their power to reveal being in manifest imagery, the recounting and reliving of myth gives human life a reflexive dimension, immerses it in reality, and reveals how it participates in the history of the sacred.

111. Enrique Palavecino, "Notas sobre la mitología chaquense," in *Homenaje a Fernando Márquez Miranda* (Madrid, 1964), pp. 284–285.

112. Ibid., p. 286. See also Sara Josefina Newbery, "Los Pilagá: Su religión a sus mitos de origen," *AI* 33 (1973). 757–769. For a description of Selk'nam creation, which begins in an absolutely simple and amorphous state (smooth, flat, and lacking any differentiation such as mountains, valleys, rivers, or seas, so that Kenós, the creator, could walk in a straight line in all directions without interruption), see Martin N. Gusinde, *Los Indios de Tierra del Fuego. Los Selk'nam*, 2 vols. (Buenos Aires, 1982), pp. 650–670. The process of creation is the process of development of permanent structures of order, which give replicable form and numerical value to reality.

113. Palavecino, "Notas . . . chaquense," p. 290.

114. Civrieus, *Watunna*, p. 158. See the quite different myths of successive abortive creations in the Sanemá-Yanoama tradition in Barandiarán, "Vida y muerte," pp. 7ff.

115. Civrieux, *Watunna*, p. 158.

116. Symbols become the best way of dealing with absences, the best representations of a meaning that is no longer fully present or fully known but whose existence is powerfully real. Creation always appears in the passing away of some primordial condition. In the accounts provided in the first sections of this chapter, the first world appeared in several different ways. In some versions, absolute nothingness, chaos, or unconsciousness gave way before the awareness of the supreme being's thought, word, dream, or emotion. In others, creation appeared in its current form when the eternal supreme being withdrew into less obvious circumstances by retreating on high or by absconding behind symbolic disguises. Alternately, tricksters, culture heroes, demiurges, or ancestors remodeled or messed up the preexistent material order to put a new face on creation. Then these architects and artisans of separation, collision, or contradiction underwent transmogrifications, especially dramatic deaths. Their disappearing acts signified the meaning of the creative existence they had wrought. For a discussion of the way in which appearances are related and evaluated in terms of "reality" or "unreality" among the Cashinahua, see Kenneth Kensinger et al., *The Cashinahua of Eastern Peru*, vol. 1, (Providence, R.I., 1975), pp. 18–23. For interpretations of the ways in which material culture, examined in the light of disappearing mythic beings, construes realities in symbolic terms, see Marcelo Bórmida, "Ergon y mito," *SE* (1973): 9–68.

By definition, an act of creation cannot leave reality the same. When something new appears, reality must appear in a new way; preexisting reality must, in some measure, disappear or change appearance. Change presents a special difficulty for the primordial world, the real world. Myths of catastrophe dramatize that any change in reality, the unique world of the beginning where each mode of being is already fully apparent, must be a total change with never-ending effects. Mythic disasters prove essential to understanding all moments of breakthrough. Only through disaster can some completely new mode of being, that of the changing world, make an appearance. Myths of catastrophe portray the violence of novelty and creativity, which must never cease to run throughout symbolic existence, especially religious experience.

117. Stéfano Varese, *La Sal de los cerros* (Lima, 1968), p. 135.

118. Ibid.

119. Fock, *Waiwai*, p. 36. For further discussion of the mythical figure named Mawári (in the context of Warao myth), see Johannes Wilbert, "The House of the Swallow-tailed Kite: Warao Myth and the Art of Thinking in Images," in Urton, ed., *Animal Myths and Metaphors*, pp. 147ff.

120. Allan R. Holmberg, *Nomads of the Long Bow: The Siriono of Eastern Bolivia* (Chicago, 1960), p. 46.

121. Roe, *Cosmic Zygote*, p. 127.

122. Llamas Samitier, "Primer Ramillete," pp. 175–176.

123. Whitten recognizes that the Canelos Quichua have heavily historicized the category called Times of Destruction by speaking of it variously as the age of rubber exploiters, Republican Times, times of slave raids, and so forth (*Sacha Runa*, p. 47). However, he notices that conceptually, and without fail, images of a time of near total destruction always intervene between Ancient Times and Times of the Grandparents.

124. Núñez del Prado B., "Supernatural World of the Quechua," p. 239.

125. Rosalind Gow and Bernabe Condori, *Kay Pacha* (Cuzco, Peru, 1976) p. 21.

126. Ibid., p. 22.

127. Ibid., p. 24.

128. Ibid., p. 24. Additional materials may be found in Juan M. Ossio, "Los Mitos de origen en la comunidad de Andamarca (Ayacucho-Peru)," *Allpanchis* (Cuzco) 10 (1977): 105–113.

129. Roe, *Cosmic Zygote*, p. 68.

130. Weiss, "World of a Forest Tribe," p. 309.

131. Ibid., p. 309.

132. Whitten, *Sacha Runa*, p. 62. Whitten holds that the notion of a flood and a time before creation were introduced by missionaries. However, an account he gives of the Canelos Quichua conception of the earliest mythic time seems to account quite easily for the primordial flood in terms of the tragedy of incest between the moon and his wife-sister or daughter. When the children of this union, the stars, weep incessantly, rains fall and rivers swell to flood the earth and to sweep people into the sea. It is after this episode that the "creation" of men and women is discussed (see pp. 51–52).

133. Ibid., p. 48.

134. Fock, *Waiwai*, p. 23.

135. Roe, *Cosmic Zygote*, pp. 128–129.

136. The following sections concentrate on scenarios of flood and fire. Since modes and accounts of destruction often overlap and interweave, other forms of catastrophe receive oblique reference. However, no special treatment is given to the myths of universal petrification and putrefaction. This latter is seen among the Gran Pajonal Campa who, according to Varese in *La Sal de los cerros*, say that the world once began to smell foul with the stench of rotting flesh because buried bodies filled the earth. The most developed instances of petrification occur in Andean myths. As the sun rose for the first time, ancient beings, petrified with fear, turned to stone while trying to escape from the dark center of the universe. They now appear as the *huacas*, the sacred sites scattered across the Andean landscape. The petrified motion of their escape helps to organize the spatiotemporal cosmos, accounting for its dynamism, order, and relatedness to the center and to the rhythmic procession of heavenly light and darkness in the stars and planets; see R. T. Zuidema, *The Ceque System of Cuzco: The Social Organization of the Capital of the Inca* (Leiden, 1964). In other cultural cases, the primordial catastrophe of petrification leaves different effects. After the Makiritare universal flood, for example, the twin heroes sift the mud on earth looking in vain for the souls of the powerful primordial beings who killed the twins' mother by rending open her dark womb while the twins were still inside it. At first it appears that these protean beings (giant protoshamans) had escaped the destruction. A few other beings (e.g., the woodpecker and water hen) also were saved because they hid in mountains, i.e., in gourds (Civrieux, *Watunna*, p. 82). What the boys find instead are *wiriki*, small

quartz crystals, the very same substances from which Shi, the true invisible Sun, had created Wanadi, the creator of the world and its beings. *Wiriki* are used by shamans as wisdom and power stones. The boys do not recognize the fact that the primordial beings of light have been petrified, and they throw the crystals away as worthless. That is why other tribes (e.g., the Maku) have more powerful shamans today. The twins keep a couple of the less powerful stones because they taste sweet. The *wiriki* are *tahuanohonato* ("shaman's wisdom stones"), obtained in an ecstatic flight to heaven during initiation. Placed in the shaman's maraca during his lifetime, the *wiriki* return to heaven after the shaman's death (ibid., p. 194). The *wiriki* are "filled with the wisdom of the Sky," the essential expression of the first world, and are consubstantial with the eternal light, the creator Wanadi (ibid., p. 81). In effect, the crystals of light are the petrified material substance of the primordial creator himself. See the analysis of such Makiritare myths of destruction by fire and flood presented by Daniel de Barandiarán, *Introducción a la cosmovisión de los indios ye'kuaná-makiritare* (Caracas, 1979), pp. 806ff. The author locates the Makiritare myths of universal destruction within the comparative context of Tupí, Guaraní, and Carib myths. He notices that the myths center on the twin brothers, heroes in the epic cycle (for further treatment of this cycle, see also ibid., pp. 963–985).

137. Bartolomé, "Shamanism among the Avá-Chiripá," p. 108.

138. Karsten, *Toba Indians*, p. 107.

139. Fulop, "Aspectos: Cosmogonía," p. 119.

140. The ontological tension between order and chaos is not restricted to battles between the creator and the flood monster. The creator himself or herself may bring on the flood, as in the case of the Barasana creator Romi Kumu, mother of the sky or day *(Ʉmʉari hako)*. Before she withdrew on high in the form of the Pleiades (Nyokoaro), Romi Kumu "made a door in the edge of the earth, the Water Door, in the east. There was lots of water outside and when she opened the door the waters came in and flooded the earth" (Hugh-Jones, *The Palm and the Pleiades*, p. 263). There is some suggestion that Romi Kumu floods the world with her urine which is the rain (p. 264) or with her menstrual flow when she changes her skin, the sky. Neither is the flood the only kind of destruction to highlight the struggle between order and chaos. The Barasana report that Romi Kumu, who contains fire in her vagina, set fire to the earth (pp. 263–264). A creation cycle from the Peruvian coast, to mention a different sort of example, reports that Con, the boneless creator of the first world and the first people, destroyed everything by turning his creation into a desert. Bernard Mishkin, "Cosmological Ideas Among the Indians of the Southern Andes," *JAFL* 53 (October/December 1940): 235–236.

141. Rodolfo M. Casamiquela, "The Deluge Myth in Patagonia," *LAIL* 6 (Fall 1982): 91.

142. Ibid. Casamiquela believes that this mythic structure comes from northern Patagonia, specifically from the area near the Valdés Peninsula. Here, he says, there is evidence of an ancient sea-flood. Furthermore, "there is on Valdés Peninsula the only colony of sea-elephants on the Atlantic coast" (p. 95). Casamiquela believes that these sea-elephants are the basis for the aquatic monster Caicai. "from the Peninsula Valdés [the deluge myth] probably migrated, on the one hand, to the interior of Chubut and Santa Cruz, Río Negro and Neuquén, and on the other to the province of Buenos Aires" (p. 96).

143. Curt Nimuendajú, *The Apinayé* (Washington, D.C., 1939) pp. 139, 177–179, 183.

144. Ibid., p. 183. The importance of the deluge can hardly be overstated for many South American cultures. The authors of the *Enciclopédia Boróro*, for example, felt that the event of the universal flood was so fundamental to Boróro life and thought that they began their mammoth volume on legends with accounts of the universal flood. See César Albisetti and Ângelo Jayme Venturelli, *Enciclopédia Boróro*, vol. 2, *Lendas e Antropônimos* (Campo Grande, Brazil, 1969), pp. 3ff.

145. See Fock, *Waiwai*, pp. 49–50, 53.

146. Ibid., p. 49. The question of boundedness and its link to the deluge can be explored from many angles. For example, the Yabarana flood was brought on by opening a mysterious basket containing a songbird; see Johannes Wilbert, "Mitos de los indios yabarana," *ACAR* 5 (1958): 58–67. Before the flood, the sun had remained fixed at the zenith, but afterwards it moved through the sky.

147. Civrieux, *Watunna*, pp. 53–54.

148. León Cádogan, *Como interpretan los Chiripá (Avá-Guaraní) la dansa ritual* (Asunción, 1959), p. 18; Bartolomé, "Shamanism among the Avá-Chiripá," p. 108.

149. Janice Krugh, "The Mythology of the Pemón Indians of Venezuela: A Survey of the Work of Father Cesáreo de Armellada," *LAIL* 4 (Spring 1980): 29–35. The story of Makunaima typifies those South American myths that have inspired creative writers of the twentieth century. See, for example, the influential novel (published in 1928) by the Brazilian writer Mário Andrade, *Makunaíma*, trans. E. A. Goodland (New York, 1984).

150. Ibid., p. 30.

151. Krugh is drawing from the myths presented in Cesáreo de Armellada, *Tauron panton: Cuentos y leyendas de los índios pemón* (Caracas, 1964), pp. 54–57. Krugh underlines the similarities between this event and the mythic episodes reported by the Arekuna, or Kamara-koto, in which brothers, who were descended from the sun, chopped down the central tree, Wazaca. In this case she draws upon Walter E. Roth, *An Inquiry Into the Animism and Folklore of the Guiana Indians* (1915; reprint, New York, 1970), pp. 147–148, which recounts a narration from an unknown "Carib" group concerning the cosmic tree Allepantepo. A parallel account from the Makiritare is provided in Civrieux, *Watunna: Mitología Makiritare*, (Caracas, 1970), pp. 117–124.

152. Aureliano Oyarzún, "Los Onas o Selknam," p. 25. Another Selk'nam account of the deluge may be found in Gusinde, *Los Indios de Tierra del Fuego. Los Selk'nam*, pp. 600f.

153. Casamiquela, "The Deluge Myth," pp. 91–92.

154. German M. A. Fernandez G., "The Araucanian Deluge Myth," *LAIL* 6 (Fall 1982): 102–113.

155. Pierre Clastres, *Chronique des indiens guayakí: Ce que savent les Aché, chasseurs nomades du Paraguay* (Paris, 1972), pp. 34, 43.

156. Ibid., pp. 187–188.

157. Napoleon A. Chagnon, *Yąnomamö: The Fierce People* (New York, 1968), p. 47.

158. Maybury-Lewis, *Akwë-Shavante Society*, pp. 248–249.

159. Ibid., p. 248.

160. Ibid., p. 249.

161. Marc de Civrieux, *Religión y magia kari'ña* (Caracas, 1974), pp. 78–79.

162. Wright, "History and Religion of the Baniwa," p. 506.

163. Ibid., p. 506.

164. Nimuendajú, *The Apinayé*, p. 160.

165. Ibid.

166. Ibid., p. 161.

167. Ibid. This myth provides a variation on the theme of "instruments of darkness." As in this case, such instruments are often gourds, which, when opened, release darkness and din into the world. Here, creative accommodation is made for the important role of the sun in the religious world view of the Apinayé. The event also establishes a foundation for the ritual relationship of the moieties, which model their interrelations on the sacred acts of the sun and the moon. The moon's desire to steal fire, or at least to play with fire (i.e., to have a flaming headdress like the sun and to dance with it at night), destructively transforms the world through ceremony. Like fire, ceremonial life exhibits forms of consumption, both conspicuously ornamental and culinary.

168. Many myths of the origin of cooking fire, for example, associate fire, consumption, and the mouth/container of some celestial predator, such as the jaguar or the vulture. In other cases the inherently chaotic form of fire is associated with consumption and containment because the fire is extracted from the mouth or belly of a mythical being of the water domain, such as a frog or alligator.

169. Karsten, *Toba Indians*, pp. 105–106.

170. Irving Goldman, "Cosmological Beliefs of the Cubeo Indians," *JAFL* 53 (1940): 244-25.

171. Alicia M. Barabás and Miguel A. Bartolomé, "Mythic Testimony of the Mataco," *LAIL* 3 (Fall 1979): 76–85.

172. Wilbert and Simoneau, eds., *Folk Literature of the Toba*, vol. 1, pp. 68–78.

173. Civrieux, *Watunna*, p. 25.

174. Ibid., p. 26.

175. Alfred Métraux, *Religions et magies indiennes d'Amérique du Sud* (Paris, 1967), p. 146.

176. Ibid., p. 128. The association of the great fire with food underlines the fact that the cosmic fire that destroys the earth makes the whole world both combustible and comestible. The cosmic fire bestows on the cosmos its consumable character: it has been, and therefore can be, devoured; that is, it has a spiritual value, for it sustains life, even through the disappearance of its present material form. During this epoch, the cosmic fire waits eternally on the horizon at "the end of the world."

177. See, for example, the myths described in Métraux, *Religions et magies*, pp. 127–129.

178. According to some traditions, all warm-bodied beings possess living forms of consumptive fire in their blood. Blood consumes the body from within and in this way constantly offers it spiritual existence. The Juruna appear to make this identification of blood with fire. In the Juruna myth of destruction (through flood, actually), one mythic brother rekindles the life of his dead brother by cutting off the latter's legs and arms and blowing on the blood that flows from the stumps. See Orlando Villas Boas and Claudio Villas Boas, *Xingu: The Indians, Their Myths* (New York, 1973), p. 233.

The heat of the body, evident not only in blood but in breath and body temperature, may be a continuation of the transformative heat processes of cosmic fire. This would bring into relationship (as parallel spiritualizing processes) the procedures of magical breathing or transformative blowing and the complex of magical heat and mastery of fire. In addition, without denying a possible connection between red ochre and blood, Robert Lehmann-Nitsche long ago wished to address the possibility of a mystical connection or a correlation between red ochre, found so frequently in prehistoric graves, where it was used to dust the skeletons of the dead, and fire. See Lehmann-Nitsche, "El Revestimiento con ocre rojo de tumbas prehistóricas y su significado," *RMP* 30 (1927): 321–327. Thus far, however, the possibility that such symbolic avenues extend the transformative properties of cosmic fire, the fullest manifestation of consumption and spiritualization, has received little comparative exploration. In *Wild- und Buschgeister*, Otto Zerries has studied the conjoined symbolic meanings of fire, sun, blood, and red body-paint in connection with rituals for hunting consumable game. A worthwhile study would include also the ceremonial practices of burning incense and tobacco, especially long-lasting cigars.

179. Wilbert and Simoneau, eds., *Folk Literature of the Toba,*, vol. 1, pp. 68ff.

180. Wright, "History and Religion of the Baniwa", pp. 537–541.

181. Ibid., p. 532; see the myth of Kuai on pp. 478–515.

182. Ibid., pp. 276–349.

183. Mishkin, "Cosmological Ideas among the Indians of the Southern Andes," 235–236.

184. Clastres, *Chronique des indiens guayakí*, pp. 126–127.

185. Mercedes López-Baralt, "The Quechua Elegy to the All-Powerful Ínka Atawallpa," *LAIL* 4 (Fall 1980): 79–86.

186. "The convulsion of nature points to the cosmic nature of the cataclysm brought about by Atahualpa's death. This is not an elegy on the decease of a historic figure but a mythic poem on the destruction of a cosmic era" (ibid., p. 85). For fuller discussion of the meaning and symbols of Pachakuti, the dark end of the world, see chapter eight.

187. Ibid., pp. 83–84.

188. Ibid., p. 79.

189. Fulop, "Aspectos: Cosmogonía," p. 131.

190. Goldman, "Cosmological Beliefs of the Cubeo Indians," p. 244.

191. Chagnon, *Yąnomamö*, pp. 47, 38.

192. Núñez del Prado B., "Supernatural World of the Quechua," p. 239.

193. Fock, *Waiwai*, pp. 54–55.

194. "Listening" seems to be a power peculiarly characteristic of demons and monsters. See Reichel-Dolmatoff, *Amazonian Cosmos*, p. 34.

195. Ibid., p. 34.

196. Darrell A. Posey, "The Kayapó Origin of Night," *LAIL* 5 (Fall 1981): 59–63. Johannes Wilbert and Karin Simoneau, eds., *Folk Literature of the Gê Indians*, vol. 1 (Los Angeles, 1978) provides several variants of this Kayapó myth. The version reported by Métraux, which appears on pages 88–91, for example, centers on Dyoibekro's daughter and emphasizes the invasion,

under cover of darkness, of other domains of being by men with exorbitantly long penises. The men want darkness in order to make love without being seen. Other images of penetration are particularly violent (slitting with blades, cutting throats, puncturing with fishes' teeth). In addition there figures the penetrating noise of a parrot. A calabash, topped by a lid tied on with cotton thread, contains darkness in the form of a scorpion, which bites when released. Dyoi-bekro's daughter is also the protagonist in the version recorded by Anton Lukesch (pp. 92–94). Men seek the dark in order to sleep. The daughter obtains darkness in a gourd that is tied shut with lianas. When loosed, the scorpion of darkness jumps out and bites the hand of the culprit-liberator, who becomes an owl. Only with great effort, then, did people manage to separate night from day. Norman J. Girardot has raised important questions about the connections between gourds and the penetrating openings that appear in the myths of primordia and chaos. See his *Myth and Meaning in Early Taoism: The Theme of Chaos (Hun-Tun)* (Los Angeles, 1983), esp. pp. 169–256. Regulating penetrating darkness is also a primordial preoccupation; this motif is especially evident in Cashinahua myths that resolve the problem another way, that is, by inventing separation of times. Originally, the sun, the morning, and the night were kept in three separate holes, which were watched over by three different groups of people. Regulating the quantity of darkness and finding a way of containing it (eventually, through time) took some doing. See Alfred Métraux, "Tribes of the Western Amazon Basin," *HSAI*, vol. 3 (Washington, D.C., 1948), p. 683.

197. Núñez del Prado B., "Supernatural World of the Quechua," p. 239.

198. Wright, "History and Religion of the Baniwa," p. 400.

199. After his destruction through fire, according to Wright's analysis, the slain animal's divided parts come to 1) define the various periodic temporal orders; 2) delineate the socioeconomic orders; and 3) embody reproduction and generativity, especially in the idea of shadow relations existing among animals, spirits, and humans (ibid., p. 400).

200. The unwillingness or inability of primordial being to be bound returns in the theme of binding and clothing as a symbolic exploration of multiple limits and, therefore, as a strategy to reachieve an experience of infinity, or at least of countable infinity, which transcends the mundane differences between sexes, ages, humans, animals, and supernaturals. See, for example, chapter 5 of this book on the manipulation of the limits of bodily space through scarification, clothing, cross-dressing, body painting and masks. See chapter 4 for a discussion of the attempt made, in recreational drinking and the noisy pendemonium of festival din, to recreate the infinite fullness of being that is associated with the openness that leads to the flood.

201. The coexistence of unbroken darkness and unbroken light in some myths (which describe the primordium as an eternal twilight or perpetual eclipse) never proves wholly satisfactory to the demand that each condition reveal itself fully and without restraint.

202. Sacrifice plays an important role in Wayãpi accounts of the primordial ordering of the universe. The sky is raised up when a mythical shaman orders specific species of birds (the harpy eagle, the red ara, the king vulture, and others) to be killed in order that their feathers may be used for a night-long ceremonial dance. The feathers are placed on a long dance baton. After a night of dancing, the sky is made to climb on high (Grenand, *Et L'homme devint jaguar*, p. 128). As in the Makiritare accounts, the colors that mark differentiated bird species also derive from the sacrifice of a primordial anaconda. The anaconda was invincible until a hummingbird masterminded a plot to induce the monster to stick out its tongue. Dance was the instrument of change. The birds, the great ancestors, danced and sang until their dances forced the laughing anaconda to expose his tongue, which provided an entrée to his innards. The hummingbird shot the anaconda's tongue with an arrow. The tongue was pulled out by the roots, and the anaconda was slain. The primordial beings bathed in his blood and in the even more brilliant colors of his excrement. Thus, they assumed the colors of their separate species. The soul of the anaconda climbed into heaven with his colors and became the rainbow (ibid., pp. 128, 150–163).

203. Civrieux, *Watunna*, p. 54.

204. Ibid., p. 61. In many instances the domestication of fire, especially through its "division" into replicable units, can be directly related to the ordering of the food chain and, therefore, to the development of the social world, that is, to the regulation of consumption and the formation of community (in the sense of gathering together to eat in an ordered or ritual way). The Baniwa

link fire and consumption in an origin of fire myth which bears some similarity to the Makiritare story. In the Baniwa version, fire was originally the possession of Jawari, the mother of fire, who kept fire in her belly. Whenever she had need of it, she would spit the fire out of her mouth. It was the culture hero Inapirikuli who succeeded in obtaining fire from the mouth of Jawari. In fact, in his quest to obtain fire, the culture hero had to extract the fire from an ordered series of mythical beasts who attempted to swallow it. See Wilhelm Saake, "Mythen über Inapirikuli, den Kultur-heros der Baniwa," *ZFE* 93 (1968): pp. 272f.

205. Civrieux, *Watunna*, p. 68.

206. Ibid., p. 69. The bones of an enormous dismembered being who had dominated the pri-mordial scene can play an important role in the order of the actual universe. The Baniwa universe, with its multiple layers, for example, has the shape of a human body. Its parts are the different spheres of being presided over by different supernaturals (for example, Yaperikuli, the creator himself, presides over the sky, which is the primordial world of the head). How the world came to be this way is not directly reported since the Baniwa are more interested in their own origins and the transformations of their own habitat, which lying at the center of the universe, is the torso presided over by the culture hero Kuai. However, the narratives that report the origins of the creator-transformer Yaperikuli suggest the shadowed outlines of a primordial cosmo-gony-through-dismemberment. "The name Yaperikuli is derived from *Niape-*, bone, *-riku-*, inside of, *-li*, masculine singular. . . . This bone came from the remains of a person who had been eaten by the animal-tribe called *Doimeni*. This bone was thrown into the river and was fished out by a grandmother. She carried the bone inside of a gourd with a hole at one end" (Wright, "History and Religion of the Baniwa," p. 536).

207. Whitten, *Sacha Runa*, pp. 55–56.

208. Villas Boas and Villas Boas, *Xingu*, pp. 99–104.

209. Casamiquela, "The Deluge Myth," p. 91.

210. Fernandez G., "The Araucanian Deluge Myth," pp. 109, 110.

211. Ibid., p. 109. Similar is the Araucanian deluge, in which a young girl was sacrificed, her heart removed, and her body thrown into the water to make the waters recede and dry land appear. See M. Inez Hilger, with the assistance of Margaret A. Mondloch, *Huenun Namku. An Araucanian Indian of the Andes Remembers the Past* (Norman, Okla., 1966), pp. 60–61.

212. Fernandez G., "The Araucanian Deluge Myth," p. 111.

213. Fock, *Waiwai*, p. 64.

214. Ibid., p. 72.

215. The passing of primordial being into multiple forms of fruit and food at the moment of death betrays the logic of reincarnation: "[T]he way here passes through death. In reality this is merely a figurative description of the ideas held about people who at death are reincarnated as animals and the continued existence of the ekati, via ekatinho to ekatinho-kworokjam" (ibid., p. 78).

216. See R. T. Zuidema, *Ceque System of Cuzco*, cited above; "La imágen del sol y la huaca de Susurpuquio en el sistema astronómico de los Incas en el Cuzco," *JSAP* 43 (1974–1976). 199–230; and "The Inca Calendar," in Anthony F. Aveni, ed., *Native American Astronomy*, (Austin, 1977), pp. 219–259. See also Zuidema's discussion of *quespi* (crystal, translucent stone, or the petrified clear water that fell into the primeval water before the emergence of the sun) in "Catachillya: The Role of the Pleiades and of the Southern Cross and α and β Centauri in the Calendar of the Incas," in Aveni and Urton, eds., *Ethnoastronomy and Archaeoastronomy* pp. 203–229, esp., pp. 216–217 and n. 26 on p. 228. A quite different case is the Mapuche story of the petrification of Manquian, an ancient primordial being who lived on shellfish, recorded in Louis C. Faron, *The Hawks of the Sun. Mapuche Morality and Its Ritual Attributes* (Pittsburgh, 1964), pp. 78–79. From the feet up, the ancestor was, by degrees, turned to stone. He told his people to burn the meat of sacrificed animals so that the smoke would nourish his spirit in the sky. He gave these instructions just before he completely turned to stone and died. He is the lord of the sea.

217. Bórmida in "Ergon y mito, Tercera Parte," traces the origins of various forms of creative and destructive power in contemporary Ayoreo society to the murders and sacrifices of the mythic period.

218. Antonio de la Calancha, *Coronica moralizada*, p. 554; cited in Mishkin, "Cosmological Ideas among the Indians of the Southern Andes," p. 227.

219. Gary Urton, "El Sistema de orientaciones de los Incas y de algunos Quechuahablantes actuales tal como queda reflejado en su concepto de la astronomía y del universo," *ALIM* 1 (1983): pp. 209–238. Aveni and Urton, eds., *Ethnoastronomy and Archaeoastronomy* is an important set of essays that are devoted to delineating a number of tropical Amerindian astronomic systems, whose fine details cannot be reproduced in this section. Let me simply point out the consistent presence of the point made in this section: astronomic order emerges through chaos, mayhem, dismemberment, death, and destruction of primordial beings.

Stephen M. Fabian, "Ethnoastronomy of the Eastern Boróro Indians of Mato Gross, Brazil," in Aveni and Urton, ibid. (pp. 283–301), gathers together much of what is known about Boróro astronomy. The origins of various constellations center around the mythic adventures of the Meri-doge, the brothers sun (Meri) and moon (Ari). They are propelled by fans of fire through the red, white, and blue planes of the heavens. During the course of their epic westward journey, they frighten away species of animals (hierarchically ordered jaguars, pumas, ocelots, eagles, herons, parakeets, monkeys, and caimans) in about a dozen encounters before returning to the point where their travels began (pp. 292–295). Further investigation is needed to link these animals to the known animal constellations.

In "Astronomical Models of Social Behavior Among Some Indians of Colombia," (in Aveni and Urton, ibid., pp. 165–181) Gerardo Reichel-Dolmatoff remarks on key similarities in the mythic imagery of the Desana, Kogi, and Muiska astronomic systems. All three involve the petrification of light in the form of hexagonal crystals or stones. In the Kogi case, the light is born in the form of an emerald that emerges from the primeval waters (the womb of the sun's daughter) after acts of incest. In all cases, the chaotic images of underdifferentiation (such as the unbroken coitus of primordial serpents, of incest) or running amok (death, castration, or dismemberment) give way to the appearances of important constellations, especially Orion (which, among other images, is identified in the Desana view with the master of animals, who is gamekeeper and master hunter, or with a flayed tapir hide, a castrated penis, or the excised tongue of a hanged and burned primordial jaguar).

In "The Pleiades and Scorpius in Barasana Cosmology," (in Aveni and Urton, ibid., pp. 183–201), Stephen Hugh-Jones points out that the Barasana primordial beings (*umuari masa*, "universe people"), who are the heavenly bodies of the sun, the sky, the moon, and the stars, died when humans were created. Some were dismembered; for example, Rihoa Mangu ("headless one," decapitated by his daughter Nyoko Anya, "star snake") is the corpse of an eagle called Wekomi, who was the father-in-law of Busuri Nyoko ("Morning Star"). Masa Hoti, "corpse bundle," i.e., *Delphinus*) "is the body of a Star Woman killed by a swarm of wasps sometimes identified with the Pleiades" (p. 188). Those primordials reappeared in new form in the world of space and time. "[I]n myth, dead stars buried in the sky fall to earth to marry living mortals and dead people buried in the house fall to the underworld, where they become living spirits. By their very presence, the sun and stars unite the past with the present and their movements in space and time unite a series of opposed principles upon which the fertility and continuity of the universe depend" (p. 184). Important Barasana constellations include egrets, vultures, snakes, a caterpillar, a jaguar, a spider, a scorpion, a crayfish, otters, an ant, fish, and an armadillo. "Notably absent are any stars named after the game animals that are hunted for food," which are classed with creatures of the earth (p. 189).

In an article entitled, "Astronomy, *Cosmovisión*, and Ideology in Pre-Hispanic Mesoamerica" (in Aveni and Urton, ibid., pp. 81–110), Johanna Broda points out the centrality of chaos as a preconditioning image of order in a new age; throughout the breadth and depth of Mesoamerican history also, there runs the leitmotiv that astronomic order (as well as the related formal orders of architecture, calendrics, historical chronology, and ritual) imposes itself on chaos. "A truly 'new order' was created as a unique structure of time and space" (p. 102) in which "religion is conceived as a whole with the universe" (p. 103).

220. Mario Califano, "A Tapuí Myth of the Izozog Region, Bolivia," *LAIL* 3 (Spring 1979): 25–26. One might remark that the act which causes the ascent of the stars into the sky is, here, one of ingestion through eating. Elsewhere myths recount the event as an ingestion into the body through sex.

221. Ibid., p. 26. The association with music, the passing of the primordial age, and transition in time marked by the presence of multiple generations and by the withdrawal of celestial beings

into the sky is explored in Lawrence E. Sullivan, "Sacred Music and Sacred Time," *The World of Music* (Berlin) 26 (1985): 33–52.
222. Califano, "A Tapuí Myth," p. 26.
223. Edwin C. Krupp, *Echoes of the Ancient Skies: The Astronomy of Lost Civilizations* (New York, 1983), pp. 84–88. Krupp is rendering an interpretation of myths collected and analyzed by Hugh-Jones in *The Palm and the Pleiades*.
224. Saake, "Mythen über Inapirikuli," pp. 270f.
225. Urton's *Crossroads of Earth and Sky*, best demonstrates how the procession of animal constellations is coordinated with the biological rhythms of animal species on earth. See also Urton, "Astronomy and Calendrics on the Coast of Peru," in Aveni and Urton, eds., *Ethnoastronomy and Archaeoastronomy*, pp. 231–247, for suggestions as to ways in which astronomic cycles may correlate with environmental cycles of major resource zones along the coast (e.g., blooming of various plants, fish cycles) as well as with subsistence activities, pilgrimages, and trading relationships linking the coast to the highlands.
226. Robert Lehmann-Nitsche, "Mitología sudamericana: X, La Astronomía de los Tobas (segunda parte)," *RMLP* 28 (1925): 181–209. See the earlier studies of Toba astronomy by the same author: "Mitología sudamericana: VI, La Astronomía de los Tobas (primera parte)," *RMLP* 27 (1923): 253–266, and "Mitología sudamericana: VI, La Astronomía de los Tobas," *RMLP* 27 (1923): 267–285. Many of the myths important to Lehmann-Nitsche's study of Toba astronomy appear in Wilbert and Simoneau, eds., *Folk Literature of the Toba*. Also presented in that volume are astral myths recorded by Alfred Métraux and Buenaventura R. D. Terán. Pages 25–67 concentrate on star lore; pages 68–100 focus on universal catastrophes.
227. Lehmann-Nitsche, "Mitología sudamericana: X," p. 195f.
228. Ibid., p. 203. Dionisio Schoo Lastra, in *Indio del desierto, 1535–1879* (Buenos Aires, 1928), reports that for the Ranqueles also the Milky Way was a hunting ground where mythic ancestors, specific constellations, chased after rheas. Clouds were feathers of the birds taken in the hunt (p. 149).
229. Lehmann-Nitsche, "Mitología sudamericana: X," p. 206. See also Robert Lehmann-Nitsche, "Der Ziegenmelker und die beiden Grossgestirne in der südamerikanischen Mythologie," in *ICA*, 24th Congress (Hamburg, 1930).
230. See the index in Lehmann-Nitsche, "Mitología sudamericana: XV," p. 209. All of these myths are drawn from the eastern Toba. In an earlier study, Lehmann-Nitsche studied the astronomy of the Toba in the more westerly Pilcomayo region. For this latter, see "Mitología sudamericana: VI (primera parte)" in the series of studies published in *RMLP*. Attention should also be drawn to the fact that some of the major heavenly bodies—most of the outstanding ones born of flood and fire or hunt—have string figures associated with them. Just as order, composed of fragments and divisions, is made in space and time by stars, which are born of the infinity of chaos, so too the "string without end" can be shaped into a variety of forms by human fingers. Lehmann-Nitsche provides a bibliography on this string game and its astronomic associaitons in "Mitología sudamericana: V," p. 264. To this should be added L. Lutz, "String-figures from the Patomana Indians of British Guiana," *APAMNH* 12 (1912). 1–14, and W. E. Roth, "An Introductory Study of the Arts, Crafts, and Customs of the Guiana Indians," *Annual Report to the Bureau of American Ethnology* 38 (1916–1917; publ. Washington, D.C., 1924): 500–550.
231. Villas Boas and Villas Boas, *Xingu* pp. 171–173. For comparative treatment of the astronomic myths of the tapir, see Lévi-Strauss, *La Potière jalouse*, pp. 220ff. where the tapir is associated with the origins of stars through the mutilation of primordial bodies. Lévi-Strauss draws attention to several other places in his studies of South American myths where he has dealt with these questions of bodily mutilation and origins of the periodic heavenly bodies. See also his discussion of meteors, excrement, and dismemberment (ibid., pp. 169–187).
232. Civrieux, *Religión y magia kari'ña* pp. 76–77; W. E. Roth, "An Inquiry into the Animism and Folklore of the Guiana Indians," *Annual Report of the Bureau of American Ethnology* 30 (1908–1909; publ. Washington, D.C., 1915): 135, 147–48. Regarding the origins of the Hyades, Pleiades, and Orion, see Claude Lévi-Strauss, *Le Cru et le cuit* (Paris, 1964), pp. 225–232; *Du Miel aux cendres* (Paris, 1966), pp. 257ff.; and *L'Origine des manières de table* (Paris, 1968), pp. 67 and passim. These passages generally touch upon the theme of the tapir as the owner of a secret food source in the form of a miraculous tree.

233. Civrieux, *Religion y magia kari'ña*, p. 110.
234. Ibid.
235. Ibid., pp. 111, 187.
236. Ibid., p. 111.
237. Ibid., p. 112.
238. Ibid., p. 114.
239. Great care is given to the order of appearance in the sky:

> The seven Wlaha shot another arrow and then another and then another. Seven arrows in all. They hung there in space, seven rungs tied to that big vine. It was the ladder, the road to Heaven. That Troupial and that Frog built it. Ahishama and Kutto. They climbed up without a ladder. When they built it, there was no road.
>
> They were the first ones to arrive. Right away they changed. They started shining. They were the first two stars in the black night. The very first was Ahishama, then Kutto. Now that Troupial named Ahishama burns orange (Mars). He built the ladder in space. That's what they say.
>
> Now Wlaha leapt up; first one rung and then another and another. He climbed right up and called down to the others. "Come on!" he told them. They followed him. He was the guide for everyone.
>
> He arrived at the top as seven men. They turned into stars, the seven *damodede*, always together (the Pleiades). Now they shine up there as a sign of union, peace and friendship. When they hide over in one side of the sky (in May) they bring the rains. When they come out from the other side again (in July), they bring the summer, the dry time.
>
> Wlaha's son climbed up with him too. His name is Wlaha Nakomo. He turned into three stars. Monetta, the scorpion, went up too. He turned into many stars (the Big Dipper). Then Ihetta went up, slowly creeping, bleeding, carrying his cut-off leg (Orion's Belt). Now Amaduwakadi, the Morning Star, went up. He shines very bright, but only in the early morning. Others went up too: Waramidi, Warerata, the sloth, Wachedi Chato, the tapir, and others, many, many others.
>
> Kuamachi watched them as they fled up the ladder. He thought: "I'm going to go up. I want to go too" (Civrieux, ibid., p. 114)

Then the ladder to heaven was destroyed so that no one else could ascend to join the stars.
240. Ibid., pp. 114–115.
241. Robert Lehmann-Nitsche, "Mitología sudamericana: VII, La Astronomía de los Mocovi," *RMLP* 28 (1924): 68–69. In addition to those presented in the text, astral origin myths in which emphasis often falls on gruesome themes of disfiguration and dismemberment may be found in Celia Olga Mashnshnek, "Texto Míticos de los Chulupi del Chaco Central," *SE* 3 (1975): 151–189. Along the same lines, the star Venus, according to the Chamacoco of Paraguay, is a woman who was half burned by curious girls who desired to make love to a handsome man who had been sealed in a gourd. In another myth the star's husband is badly burned before they both ascend into the sky. See Alfred Métraux, "A Myth of the Chamacoco Indians and Its Social Significance," *JAFL* 56 (April-June 1943): 118. Such themes are found throughout South America. The Yabarana, for instance, recount that the stars were once the beloved son of their hero Mayowoca. When the sun was devoured by an aquatic monster named Payare, the lord of water, the child's heroic father cut open the monster's entrails and transformed his partially eaten son into the stars of heaven. Johannes Wilbert, "Mitos de los índios yabarana," *ACAR* 5 (1958). 58–67.
242. Anne M. Chapman, "Lune en Terre de Feu. Mythes et rites de Selk'nam," *Objets et mondes* 12 (Summer 1972): 148, 150–151. For a lenthy description of the origins of periodicity in multiple forms, (e.g., the separation of the sun and the moon, the lunar phases, the solar and lunar eclipses) among the Selk'nam, see Gusinde, *Los Indios de Tierra del Fuego. Los Selk'nam*, pp. 576–581.
243. Roe, *Cosmic Zygote*, p. 68.
244. Reichel-Dolmatoff, *Amazonian Cosmos*, p. 30.
245. Wright, "History and Religion of the Baniwa," p. 370.

246. Ibid., pp. 354–355. As masters of fire, shamans are masters of these various transformative orders produced by the primordial burning.

247. After the cosmic destruction of the Apinayé primordium through fire, even consumptive relations become life-sustaining. The fire was brought on by fiery ornaments, which in later symbolic form become the ceremonial dress of human culture. After the conflagration, the sun collects and prepares to eat the burned game. The moon, on the other hand, had game that was lean and rotting, full of maggots. The sun transformed the moon's carcasses into many species of consumable game and birds.

248. Henry, *Jungle People*, pp. 145–146.

249. Pierre-Yves Jacopin, *La Parole generative de la mythologie des indiens yukuna* (Neuchâtel, 1981), p. 99.

250. Ibid., p. 101. Several birds eventually averted the disastrous rain (p. 101f.). The tapir's dance originates the dances performed to effect marriage alliances (p. 101).

251. Civrieux, *Religión y magia kari'ña*, pp. 11–12. Carib speakers of Guiana also recount the origins of benefits such as peppers and other plants from primordial murders that are avenged by further taking of life. See Roth, *An Inquiry . . . Guiana Indians*, p. 231.

252. P. Grenand, *Introduction . . . Wayãpi*, pp. 41–42. Giovanni Raul, *Santo Tanbem Come. Estudio socio-cultural da alimentação cerimonial em terreiros afro-brasileiros* (Recife, 1979), to cite another kind of case, focuses on the consumptive imagery prevalent in Afro-Brazilian spirituality.

253. Alicia M. Barabás and Miguel A. Bartolomé, "Mythic Testimony of the Mataco," *LAIL* 3 (Fall 1979): p. 79.

254. Ibid., p. 84.

255. Ibid., p. 79.

256. Regarding the catastrophic origin of plants and botanical taxonomies, see Otto Zerries, "Entstehung oder Erwerb der Kulturpflanzen und Beginn des Bodenbaues im Mythos der Indianer Südamerikas," *Paideuma* 15 (1969): 64–124. The origin of the first fruit trees from the body of a young woman who was eaten and dismembered, part by part, by her lascivious, caressing, and belching brother is related by Arawak peoples of Guiana in Roth, *An Inquiry . . . Guiana Indians*, pp. 146–147.

257. Civrieux, *Watunna*, p. 78.

258. Ibid., p. 80.

259. Here we see something of the inverse of the earth-diver myth. The twins dive to the bottom of the river to bring back the bottom of the *water* to earth, causing earth to be inundated (earth can only be found underneath the bottom of the waters that now cover it), whereas the earth-diver dives to the bottom of the cosmic ocean to bring back the matter from which the earth is formed.

In any case, once the twins returned to land with samples of deep water, the entire earth was flooded. There was nothing left standing except two *moriche* palm trees along which the boys ascended into heaven. Gradually, as the twins ate fruit on high in the tree, the Sea receded so that now it begins at the place "where our Earth ends." Civrieux, ibid., p. 81.

260. Ibid.

261. Reichel-Dolmatoff, "Training for the Priesthood among the Kogi of Colombia," in Johannes Wilbert, ed., *Enculturation in Latin America: An Anthology* (Los Angeles, 1976), p. 267. A quite different system of ordered values can be seen in an essay by Alejandra Siffredi that discloses the mythical bases of the food chain, the cycles of social reciprocities, and their relationship to hierarchies of rank (e.g., chief, shaman, elders, various social segments) among forest-dwelling groups of the western Chaco. See Alejandra Siffredi, "La Noción de reciprocidad entre los Yojwaha-Chorote," *SE* 3 (1975): 41–70.

262. Reichel-Dolmatoff, "Training," p. 267.

263. Thekla Hartmann, "Zur botanischen Nomenklatur der Boróro-Indianer," *ZFE* 96 (1971): 240–242.

264. Albisetti and Colbachinni were so convinced that the flood was the essential explanation for the coming into being of the Boróro world that they defined it as the fundamental reality and presented it at the opening of their massive volume of Boróro myths and legends; see *Enciclopédia Boróro*, vol 2., pp. 2ff.

265. Various studies seem to point to this same conclusion. See, for example, León Cádogan, *Breve contribución al estudio de la nomenclatura guaraní en botanica* (Asunción, 1955); Carlos Brumond, *Contribuição do Boróro à toponîmia brasilica* (São Paulo, 1965); C. Fiebrig-Gertz, "Guarany Names of Paraguayan Plants and Animals," *RJBP* 2 (1930): 2–20; Franz Muller, "Drogen und Medikamente der Guaraní (Mbyá, Paí und Chiripá) Indianer im östlichen Waldgebiet von Paraguay," in Wilhelm Koppers, ed., *Festschrift Publication D'Hommage au P. W. Schmidt* (Vienna, 1928). Two authors bring out clearly that the connections between these different realms of symbolic classification are achieved in the transcendent order that supernatural beings bring about through their powerful actions: Otto Zerries, *Wild- und Buschgeister in Südamerika*, e.g., pp. 225ff., and Egon Schaden, *A Mitología heroica de tribos indigenas do Brasil* (Rio de Janeiro, 1959). Louis Girault, in *Kallawaya: Guérisseurs itinérants des Andes* (Paris, 1984), shows how Andean peoples have classified some 880 plants according to local symbolic codes that embrace other life forms as well. For a recent discussion of the nature of perceptions, cognitions, intentions, and argumentative reassessments involved in forging and maintaining taxonomies of plants, with passing special mention of the Aguaruna Jívaro (pp. 309–310), see Scott Atran, "The Nature of Folk-Botanical Life Forms," *AA* 87 (June 1985): 289–315, which offers an ample bibliography.

266. Villas Boas and Villas Boas, *Xingu*, p. 177.

267. Ibid., p. 178.

268. Ibid., p. 179.

269. Ibid., p. 243ff.

270. Ibid., p. 244.

271. Ibid., p. 246.

272. For theories of phonetic dismemberment, see chapter 5 of this work. For ceremonial destructuration of sound into syllables where the separation is performed as a dramatic binary opposition between two orators, see chapter 7.

273. Civrieux, *Religion y magia kari'ña*, pp. 78–79.

274. Ibid., p. 80.

275. Ibid., p. 77. Variations on this theme of species-sound-separation-flood abound. According to the Wayãpi, sonic conditions changed dramatically on account of the deluge. Before that time, Yaneya, the creator, lived among the beings he created. "But when he climbed into heaven, he took with him all the languages, except those of animals which he had previously bestowed on them" (F. Grenand, *Et l'homme devint jaguar*, p. 52). In particular, the jaguar, the spider monkey, the howler monkey, the wild sapajou, and the red brocket have, like humans, a primordial language. At that early time, the land tortoise was also a great musician, "but one day, he swallowed his flute and for that reason is mute today" (ibid.). Incidentally, the first kind of humanity was destroyed in the Wayãpi deluge. A second kind of human condition was created after the flood (ibid.; see also text no. 10 in chapter 2). The Yabarana offer yet another rendering of these issues. In the very beginning of time there was a closed, mysterious basket containing a symphony of sounds and songs made by an unseen bird. When the basket was opened, it flooded the world with water, darkness, movement, and change. It brought on the generation of all the separate species. See Johannes Wilbert, "Mitos de los indios Yabarana," *ACAR* 5 (1958): 58–67.

276. Ellen B. Basso, " A 'Musical View of the Universe': Kalapalo Myth and Ritual as Religious Performance," *JAFL* 94 (1981): 273–291; Basso discusses the liminal character of these songs, which is reflected in the time of their singing as well as their internal symbolic structure. On the values of Kalapalo sound, see also Basso's *Musical View of the Universe: Kalapalo Myth and Ritual Performance* (Philadelphia, 1985), passim.

277. Basso, "A 'Musical View of the Universe'," p. 285. Says Basso,

> It is our own 20th-century understanding of music—that it is essentially a matter of entertainment—that does injustice to the theoretical power of our anthropological understanding of religious symbolism, and contributes, of course, to our misunderstanding of other people's musicality. It also prevents us from clearly seeing the possibility of a musical religion." (ibid., p. 291)

278. Ibid., p. 275.

279. Civrieux, *Watunna*, p. 82.

280. This variant of the myth of Inkarrí and Qollari was reported by the people of Q'ero, Peru (Department of Cuzco, Province of Paucartambo).

281. Some ñawpas, supernatural hangovers from the age of primordial darkness, linger on in this world and seek to destroy Inkarrí and to thwart his plans of founding a great city. Nonetheless, Inkarrí succeeds with tools provided by the apus, the mountain spirits. He traverses the world, founds Cuzco, teaches wisdom to human beings and disappears into the jungle (Núñez del Prado B., "Supernatural World of the Quechua," p. 241). In the version recorded from the community at Qotobamba, the first couple created by God, or Roal, are called Arran and Iwa (probably variations of Adam and Eve). They are driven out of the primordial fertile garden after Iwa has encouraged Arran to eat of a forbidden fruit.

282. To be sure, all beings have forms, often animal-body forms, but not all of these beings were mortal in the same way from the beginning. Absolute forms of the "immortals" suffered absolute eclipse. Ironically, this is not the way with mortals. It is the kind of death to which one is subject that makes the difference. For a discussion of human mortality see chapter 5 of this work, on human origins, and chapter 8, on the origins of human death and on beliefs surrounding human death and life after death.

283. Fock uses the term "the Fall" to describe the act that brought on the flood because the improper behavior that brings on the catastrophic flood is a free and personal act that deliberately disobeys the warning of the chacha not to let one's eyes wander (Waiwai, p. 53).

284. Ibid., p. 50.

285. Note, for example, the economically expressed but symbolically elaborate repeopling of the earth by Con Tici Viracocha described in the account by the chronicler Juan de Betanzos [1551], Suma y narración de los Incas (Madrid, 1880).

286. This summary is provided by Mishkin, "Cosmological Ideas among the Indians of the Southern Andes," p. 228.

287. See Sarmiento de Gamboa, History of the Incas (London, 1907), pp. 33–37. The Inca had varying accounts describing the origin of human beings after primordial chaos. In one version, the period of chaos from which human life emerges is variously referred to as purum-pacha ("wild, savage, untamed or unconquered space-time"), ccallac-pacha (the time when something is destroyed, broken down, or punctured; the beginning of time), and tutayac-pacha (the "time of night" when hapi-nunus, unbridled primordial beings, ravaged the land and its primordial inhabitants). However, in the middle of the night the hapi-nunus began to disappear with mournful cries, exclaiming, "We are conquered, we are conquered." It was after this time that the Inca were created. See Juan de Santa Cruz Pachacuti-Yamqui Salcamayhua, An Account of the Antiquities of Peru, in Narratives of the Rites and Laws of the Yncas, trans. and ed. with notes and an introduction by Clements R. Markham (1873; reprint, New York, n.d.), pp. 70–78. Eventually each group of people created chose some lake, spring, rock, hill, or ravine from which to emerge.

288. Charles Wagley, Welcome of Tears (New York, 1977), p. 176f.

289. Ibid., pp. 104–112, regarding the Bird societies; pp. 115–117 describe the "eating groups," a term used by Herbert Baldus, Tapirapé: Tribo tupí no Brasil central (São Paulo, 1970), pp. 330ff.

290. Wright, "History and Religion of the Baniwa," pp. 557–560.

291. In this respect it comes to resemble the kaltakí, the ceremonial drum made from a clay pot partially filled with water.

292. Karsten, Toba Indians, p. 108.

293. Chagnon, Yąnomamö, p. 48.

294. Ibid.

295. Otto Zerries, "Schöpfung und Urzeit im denken der Waika-Indianer des Oberen Orinoco (Venezuela), ICA, 32d Congress (Copenhagen, 1958), pp. 280–288. An old woman caused the flood to recede by painting her body red and diving into the floodwaters as they were about to cover the last mountain. She became the mythical crocodile Lahala. On another drastic occasion, when the sky fell (this earth is a portion of the upper sky, which fell), a young maiden saved the possibility of culture by observing a perfect ritual seclusion (p. 282). Zerries argues that the soul-constructs associated with a single lord of the animals (described in the holonama legends recounted by old women) may be theoretically distinguished from the hekula system of spirit

masters of individual species of edible fauna reflected in the food chain. Although both these symbolic orders, as well as the hierarchy of spirits, take their origin from a cataclysmic event, Zerries believes that they are separate mythic complexes with separate culture histories. The *hekula* system, in his opinion, is the more recent of the two. It is more closely linked with shamanic specialists (Zerries, ibid., pp. 286–288).

296. Diverse images of history can derive from the breakup of preformal or inchoate beings of the primordium (e.g., the serpentine monsters of watery chaos). For an idea as to what extent the meanings and organizing principles of human history can be signified by bodily form and processes see, for example, Irving Goldman, "Time, Space, and Descent: The Cubeo Example," *ICA*, 42d Congress, vol. 2 (Paris, 1977), pp. 163–74, and Christine Hugh-Jones, "Skin and Soul. Social Time and Social Space in Piraparana Society," *ICA*, 42d Congress, vol. 2 (Paris, 1977), pp. 185–204. Like peoples of the northwestern Amazon, Carib speakers of Guiana place their origins in the fragments of a dismembered serpent. Some months after the mythic brothers chopped the snake into pieces, they heard "a great noise and the sound of voices." They found "four houses in the identical spot where they had cut up [the snake] all occupied by Indians who had grown out of the fragments of the snake"; see Roth, *An Inquiry . . . Guiana Indians*, p. 144. But the idea of sociogony from dismembered parts is widespread. It serves as a basis for social history—the evaluation of the relations among social groups over time. See Edgardo J. Cordeu, "Textos míticos de los Angaite (Chenanesma) y Sanapana," *SE* 1 1 (1973). 199–234, which presents myths of the origins of ethnic groups (from Puerto Casado, Paraguay) in connection with the narratives of mythic dismemberment. And see also the special issue of *L'Uomo* (Rome) 9 (1986), entitled *Divisione delle carni: Dinamica sociale*.

297. Women are originally celestial beings, stars. Two stars descend to earth in the form of white grubs. These two sisters live in logs or in the earth until one of them becomes a lovely woman and marries a man on earth. Men begin as mushrooms (Whitten, *Sacha Runa*, p. 52).

298. Ibid., p. 57.

299. The fact that history can sustain tragic existence opens the hopeful expectation that history will end. Cultures often look forward to the annihilation of the residue and consequences of historical life in the celebrations of the new year or on occasional feasts of purification, exorcism, healing, and obliteration of time, when chaos is momentarily ushered into the center of the world and then dispelled (see, for examples, the discussion of drinking bouts and festival din in chapter 4.) Alternately, dissatisfaction with the epoch sustained by history may become so complete that a culture longs for the extermination of time altogether. Such circumstances, discerned as the return of the chaos of flood, fire, or darkness, build toward the hope for the end of the world. See the treatment in chapter 8.

300. Mario Califano, "La Incorporación de un elemento cultural entre los Mashco de la Amazonía peruana," *RSAA* n.s. 9 (1977): 185–201.

301. Fulop, "Aspectos: Cosmogonía," p. 119.

302. Wright, "History and Religion of the Baniwa," p. 371.

303. Robert Lehmann-Nitsche, "Folklore argentino," *JAFL* 48 (1935): 179–185.

304. François Berge, "Conclusions d'une étude comparative des légendes de déluges," *Actes du IVe Congrès International des Sciences Anthropologiques et Ethnologiques* vol. 2 (Vienna, 1955), pp. 60–62.

305. Ibid.

306. Through conflagration and deluge, as well as through the other forms of universal catastrophe, death and destruction insinuate themselves into every aspect of existence. One is reminded of the modern existentialist view expressed by Nicholas Berdyaev in *The Destiny of Man* (London, 1960): "Life, not in its weakness but in its strength, intensity and super-abundance, is closely connected with death" (p. 251).

307. Jacopin emphasizes that Yukuna myth recounts acts that generate irreversible differentiations between kinds of beings (e.g., groups of animals, of fruits, of humans, of distinct behaviors). Ironically, the myths themselves *are* reversible because they are fully symbolic and imaginary (Jacopin, *La Parole generative*, p. 367). Full of internal redundancies, myths themselves are constantly reduplicated as they are retold. Myths provide the imagery of an interpretative life for which they are themselves the prime image.

308. Whitten, *Sacha Runa*, p. 46.

309. Ibid., p. 53.

310. Lajos Boglár, "Creative Process in Ritual Art: Piaroa Indians, Venezuela," in David L. Browman and Ronald A. Schwarz, eds., *Spirits, Shamans, and Stars: Perspectives from South America* (The Hague, 1979), pp. 233–239.

311. Ibid., p. 234.

312. Jacopin, *La Parole generative*, p. 79.

313. Ibid., p. 112 and passim.

314. Fernandez G., "The Araucanian Deluge Myth," p. 110. See Gerardo Reichel-Dolmatoff, "Tapir Avoidance in the Colombian Northwest Amazon," in Urton, ed., *Animal Myths and Metaphors* pp. 107–144, for consideration of myths of the tapir and their connection with disease among Tukano speakers.

315. Roe, *Cosmic Zygote*, p. 127.

316. For instance, the organization of space in the Inca universe followed on the heels of several periods of absolute catastrophe and chaos. The first royal Inca and his wife wandered through the world, instructed by their father, the sun. The places where they stopped and the actions they performed there marked the space of the universe and gave it a discernible order and meaning. See Garcilaso de la Vega, *Royal Commentaries of the Incas and General History of Peru* vol. 1, pp. 43–45.

But the point that symbolic life is a centered one and that a centered life has religious foundations can be made in a more general way. Mario Juruna, the leader of the Xavante community of Namunkurá and well known for his role in the Russell Tribunal convoked in Rotterdam, Holland, to judge crimes against the native peoples of the Americas, made explicit the connections between the symbolic organization of the earth's space, the division of labor, the social organization of a people, and religious life. The earth and its symbolic order form the religious axis, the symbolic center, where social, political, economic, territorial, and material dimensions of life coincide. That is why various bureaucratic programs of " 'civilization,' 'integration,' 'emancipation,' 'legalization,' 'education,' 'militarization' of the Indians must be studied in the light of this coincidence! Whoever struggles on behalf of the land of indigenous peoples, struggles equally for the basic conditions of their religion" (Juruna, *O Gravador do Juruna*, p. 111).

317. Chagnon, *Yąnomamö*, pp. 47, 38.

318. Ibid., pp. 44–45. The Canelos Quichua also see history or historical-time-in-unfolding as a process of analysis, a breakdown of spaces and domains as well as a dichotomization of times. (Whitten, *Sacha Runa*, pp. 55–56). The first Canelos Quichua woman separates the forest domain of hunting from the soil domain of manioc gardens. This historical "creation," in the form of separation and differentiation, is accomplished and directed by Nunghuí, the female soul-master spirit of the fields.

319. The Canari people of the kingdom of Quito at the time of the Conquest, for example, reported that a very high mountain, named Huaca-ynan, stood high above the flood. It was there that two brothers escaped the deluge and from there that all life regenerated itself. Cristobal de Molina, *Fables and Rites of the Yncas*, in Markham, trans. and ed., *Narratives of the Rites and Laws of the Yncas*, pp. 8–9.

320. Civrieux, *Religión y magia kari'ña*, pp. 53–54. This dialectic of center and periphery, collision and distant repulsion, takes on many expressions. For example, the Selk'nam acknowledge the increasing differentiation of geographic space in the wake of the demise of the primordium. In one myth, the cardinal directions of south and north battle one another. Once Táita, the fearful supernatural monster who slayed people in great number, was dispatched, her blood went everywhere so that the rivers and streams could not be kept free from it. People took up arms and began to fight one another to the point of extermination. Eventually, K'aux divided the earth into separate territories and distributed them to the various lineages. Gusinde, *Los Indios de Tierra del Fuego. Los Selk'nam*, pp. 582–599.

321. Whitten, *Sacha Runa*, p. 48.

322. Ibid., p. 51.

323. Wright, *History and Religion of the Baniwa*, p. 98.

324. For further consideration of this theme see Anthony Seeger, "Porque os índios Suyá cantam para suas irmãs," in Gilberto Velho, ed., *Arte e sociedade* (Rio de Janeiro, 1977), pp. 39–64, and Seeger, "What Can We Learn When They Sing? Vocal Genres of the Suyá Indians of Central Brazil," *ETM* 23 (1979): 373–394.

325. Ibid., p. 393.

326. Ibid.

327. "He ascended from the Great Fire, *in the fire* he ascends . . . (singing) 'HeeHeeHee--eey-teyteytete . . . ' until today" (Wright, ibid., p. 393).

328. This point is developed by Jonathan Z. Smith in several places; see, for example, *Map is Not Territory* (Leiden, 1978), pp. 97–98. Summing up reviews of comparative studies of mythic chaos, N. J. Girardot concluded,

> The mythic chaos, however, is never just equivalent to nothingness, profanity, neutrality, unreality, nonbeing, death, or absolute disorder. Despite the fact that chaos constantly threatens the cosmic order, frequently becoming synonymous with the demonic, a comparative assessment of creation mythology generally affirms that the cosmos originally came from, and continually depends on, the chaos of the creation time. The logic of myth claims that there is always, no matter how it is disguised, qualified, or suppressed, a "hidden connection" or "inner law" linking chaos and cosmos, nature and culture (*Myth and Meaning in Early Taoism*, p. 3)

329. Jean E. Jackson, *The Fish People: Linguistic Exogamy and Tukanoan Identity in Northwest Amazonia* (Cambridge, 1983), emphasizes the connections that Tukanoan peoples observe among sacrality, hierarchy, and meaning:

> Whether something is sacred or not depends on which of several levels is being conceptualized. At a very profound level, everything is sacred, because behind what is perceived by humans as everyday reality, including the most prosaic of events or situations, lies an extraordinary reality or realities. . . . The symbolism pervarding all levels of Tukanoan life also explains and makes sense of the universe and Tukanoans' place in it." (p. 208)

330. Civrieux, *Religión y magia kari'ña*, p. 13.

331. Ibid., p. 14.

332. Structural studies of many versions and variants of the myth of Manco Capac from the sixteenth to the eighteenth centuries may be found in three articles with the same title — "¿Qué es el Mito?" — by José Pérez Mundaca, Alvaro Diez Astete, and Rodolfo Sanchez Garrafa, all of which appeared in *ALIM* (1983). In her article, "De los hermanos Ayar a Inkarrí," *ALIM* 1 (1983): 37–50, Maria Burela stresses, in her structural analysis of several variants, that symbols and meaningful ideas (relationships between signs and symbols) are directly related to the systematic differentiation of orders that occurs after the destruction of "constitutive unities" (p. 47).

333. Mishkin, "Cosmological Ideas among the Indians of the Southern Andes," pp. 228–229. The Inca kingship was created to bring order to the chaotic world:

> [I]n olden times the whole of this region . . . was covered with brush and heath and people lived . . . like wild beasts, with no religion or government and no towns or houses, and without tilling or sowing the soil, or clothing or covering their flesh, for they did not know how to weave cotton or wool . . . and even in their intercourse with women they behaved like beasts, for they knew nothing of having separate wives. (ibid.)

For that reason the Father Sun sent emissaries to subdue the peoples, plants, and animals of the earth. The first two emissaries, children of the Sun, made their way from Titicaca to Cuzco, "which was then a wilderness." They became the first Inca and his wife, the queen. See Garcilaso de la Vega *Royal Commentaries of the Incas and General History of Peru*, vol. 1, pp. 40–43.

334. For a consideration of the ways in which the succession of Andean mythic epochs, interrupted by destruction and reinitiated with new creations, generates classificatory orders of colors, clothing, social organization, and historical categories and arranges them in orders according to the geographic disposition of *huaca*s and the location of places of emergence (*puqyo*s) after cosmic destruction, see John Earls and Irene Silverblatt, "La Realidad física y

social en la cosmología andina," *ICA* 42d Congress (Paris, 1978), pp. 299–325. Pierre Duviols, in "Un Symbolisme andin du double: La Lithomorphose de l'ancetre," *ICA*, 42d Congress, pp. 359–364, clarifies the mythic history and the paradoxical character of the Andean *huaca*s that appear in the moment when one age gives way to another. They represent mediations between modes of being: primordial and mundane, supernatural and human, eternal and historical, darkness and light, death and the fertility that generates new life, and so on.

Afro-Brazilian religions, bearing the history of African royal states, also display the connection of sacrality to ranked power. In *A Morte Branca do Feiticeiro Negro* (Petropolis, Brazil, 1978), Renato Ortiz summarizes the attempts to categorize the many spirits and the divine forms manifest in Umbanda. Their elaborate symbolic accoutrements appear in ritual even though they lived in an age now past. Beneath the supreme being Qlórun (a.k.a. Zambie or Deus) there follows a trinity formed by Qbàtálá (the Father), Qṣalá (the Son), and Ifá (the *òrìṣà* of destiny, the Holy Spirit). Below Qlórun also stand a number of armies of spirits. Each army obeys its chief, an òrìṣà. All the spirits are entrusted with specific duties and functions in the spatial world. Each army (*linha* or *vibração*) is directed by one of the seven òrìṣà, each one of which corresponds to an astral body: Qṣalá to the sun, Yemọnja to the moon, Ṣàngó to Jupiter, Ògún to Mars, Ọ̀ṣọ̀ọ̀si to Venus, Crianças to Mercury, and Pretos-Velhos to Saturn. Each of these seven leaders has seven followers who comprise the *linha*. In addition, each legion is divided into seven phalanxes; every phalanx is divided into seven subphalanxes. The bottommost rung of the hierarchy is occupied by spirits called "guides" or "protectors." Unlike their African religious counterparts, the Afro-Brazilian òrìṣà themselves never descend into their devotees. Rather, "they transform themselves into sacred essences which transmit their attributes to other agents, for example, the guides" (p. 76).

335. Varying theories of the ages of the world, from Hesiod's ages of metals to the *yuga*s and *kalpa*s of the Hindu and Buddhist worlds, abound in religious outlooks throughout history. The cultures of South America are no exception. What is important to note is that systematizations of ages of the world, imaginative construals of space-time contingencies, become central to discussions of the nature of being, creativity, order, destiny, division of labor, accumulation of time and its fruits, and other issues of utmost importance. To see the fundamental importance of theories of aeons, one need only glance at the ways in which they have aided theologians and philosophers to speak of divine substances. For example, the Christian church father Tertullian described two distinct views held by Valentinus, on the one hand, and Ptolemy, on the other. Ptolemy, said Tertullian, provided each age of the world (*aeon*) with a separate name and number because he viewed them as personalized substances that stood apart from God. Valentinus viewed the *aeon*s as emotional states or thoughts of the fullness of divinity itself (Tertullian, *Adversus Valentinianos* 4.2). In South America as well, careful and subtle differences exist between one culture and another and from one mythic account of primordial ages to another. These differences give rise to wholly different philosophical, psychological, economic, and political interpretations of primordial realities.

CHAPTER THREE

1. See chapter 2 , above.
2. This observation has been made for many Amerindian cultures. See, for example, Åke Hultkrantz, *The Religions of the American Indians*, trans. Monica Setterwall (Berkeley, 1979), pp. 27ff., which presents materials from North and South America. The universality of such spatial patterns suggests to Hultkrantz that "a three-layered world picture predominates. Sometimes there are even more levels, all developed from the basic pattern heaven-earth-underworld, . . . [a] pattern common to most archaic societies affected by the so-called Neolithic Revolution . . . and [which] may have even a higher age, as Siberian and American data suggest" (p. 27). Peter Furst has also studied the similarity of spatial concepts found throughout the Americas, in "The Roots and Continuities of Shamanism," *Artscanada* 184–187 (December 1973/January 1974): 33–60, in which he contends that the underlying structure is that of an underworld and upperworld connected by an *axis mundi* passing through this world (p. 40). As

is the case with the works by Hultkrantz and Furst, most comparative studies of the spatial organization of the universe into layers acknowledge their debt to the precedent-setting research of Mircea Eliade, especially in *Shamanism: Archaic Techniques of Ecstacy* (Princeton, 1974). (A smaller version of this work was first published in French in 1951.) See esp. pp. 259–287 for consideration of the spatial world views. Roe, in *Cosmic Zygote*, investigates the question of the multiple planes in the universe among South American cosmologies. Roe's interpretations lack interpretive subtlety and methodological sophistication, but his work is valuable for the bibliography of materials it draws together on this mythic theme. In the section entitled "The Cosmic Layer Cake," he discusses the spatial conceptions of spatial arrangements in three, four, five, eight, nine, ten, and eleven tiers (pp. 127–136).

3. Krugh, "Mythology of the Pemón" p. 30. A cosmos of three levels can become more complicated than it at first appears. According to Barandiarán, the three worlds of the Yekuana-Makiritare are further subdivided. For example, the upper or heavenly world contains some eight different levels. See the details as they are laid out, with further bibliographic suggestions, in Barandiarán, *Introducción . . . ye'kuaná-makiritare*, pp. 796ff.

4. Baldus, *Tapirapé*, p. 357; Wagley, *Welcome of Tears*, p. 169.

5. Fock, *Waiwai*, pp. 43, 73.

6. Ibid., p. 101.

7. Johannes Wilbert, "Eschatology in a Participatory Universe: Destinies of the Soul Among the Warao Indians of Venezuela," in Elizabeth P. Benson, Ed., *Death and the After-Life in Pre-Columbian America* (Washington, D.C., 1975), p. 168.

8. See the figures in Wilbert, "Eschatology," pp. 164, 165.

9. Jacopin, *La Parole generative*, p. 79.

10. Anthony F. Aveni, "The View from the Tropics," in E. C. Krupp, ed., *Archaeoastronomy and the Roots of Science* (Boulder, 1984), p. 286. Aveni constructs a diagram of the Kogi cosmos based on data reported by Reichel-Dolmatoff but does not cite the specific sources he draws upon. In his report of 1949–1950, Reichel-Dolmatoff said that the egg-shaped Kogi universe has nine layers, of which the earth is the central level. Above the earth are good layers; below it are evil places. The universe is extremely heavy and is supported by two large beams, which rest on the shoulders of four men who stand two in the east and two in the west. Below the world there is water. Floating on the surface of the water is an enormous, flat, and beautiful rock. On this rock the great mother sits naked. She feeds the four men water and food and massages their shoulders so that they never tire. Once in a while one of the men changes the beam from one shoulder to the other, causing an earthquake. Each of the world's nine layers has a great mother, sun, moon, stars, and people. See Gerardo Reichel-Dolmatoff, "Los Kogi, Una tribu de la Sierra Nevada de Santa Marta-Colombia," part 1, *Revista del Instituto Etnologico Nacional* (Bogotá) 4 (1949–1950): 241–247.

11. Weiss, "World of a Forest Tribe," p. 256. In this study of Campa culture, Weiss points out the many similarities between the Campa and their neighbors on the east and south, the Machiguenga, an Arawakan-speaking group whose language bears great similarity to Campa. The Machiguenga also believe in a universe consisting of several relational levels in which each level is seen to be the sky of the level below. The Campa and Machiguenga view exemplifies a truth that lies at the constitutive center of any construal of the world. This truth can be correlated with the most important concept of quantam mechanics: the status of an object is determined by the act of perception of an observer, and the nature of the observer determines the conditions of an object.

12. Bartolomé, "Shamanism Among the Avá-Chiripá," p. 107.

13. For brief discussion of the symbolism of *axis mundi* and for bibliography of its comparative study, see Mircea Eliade and Lawrence E. Sullivan, "Axis Mundi," in *EOR*.

14. Roe, *Cosmic Zygote*, p. 119.

15. The myth of the crumbling, tumbling, or disintegration of the *axis mundi* accounts for more than the tenuousness of the integrity of symbolic spaces. It frequently accounts for the separateness of other symbolic expressions of significance as well: for example, the appearance of multiple languages, races, eco-niches, fauna, times, and artistic expressions. See chapter 2, above. This imaginative strategy is not limited to South American religions. Even the suppressed

mythology of the Hebrew Bible continues to use the same dramatic symbolism to make similar points; see the account of the tower of Babel in *Genesis* 11:1–9. In Christian accounts, the dispersion of Babel into disconnected symbolic systems (cultural practices and languages of separate races) would be brought together in the church (Greek, *ekklēsia*, a "gathering together") just as the first disciples of Jesus were a union of "devout men" from "every nation under heaven" in the Temple in Jerusalem (Acts 2:46) by speaking the sound of all their languages (*Acts* 2:1–47). See also the accounts of similar Hebrew religious experiences on Mount Horeb (*Exodus* 34:28 for Moses; *1 Kings* 19:8ff. for Elijah) and the discussion in J. Lust, "A Gentle Breeze or a Roaring Thunderous Sound," *Vetus Testamentum* 25 (1975): 110–115.

16. See the diagram in Reichel-Dolmatoff, *Amazonian Cosmos*, p. 44. The parallels between the conception of the Milky Way as a seminal river among both the Desana and the people of Misminay near Cuzco are quite remarkable. In this case, it should be recalled that Reichel-Dolmatoff believes that the Desana underwent strong Andean influence in prehistoric time. He accounts in this way for Desana myths having to do with metallurgy (pp. 24, 253). For the conception of the Milky Way in Misminay see Urton, *Crossroads of Earth and Sky*.

17. Núñez del Prado B., "Supernatural World of the Quechua," p. 250. He concludes further that "the structure of the supernatural world that I have described is susceptible to generalization over an extensive area of Southern Peru. . . . It must be emphasized that the generalization applies to the structure and organization of the religious system and not to the local variations in form to which it is subject." (p. 249).

18. Ibid., pp. 249–250.

19. Núñez del Prado B. recognizes that, after long exposure to Christianity, the Quechua have received many Christian ideas into their cosmology. He attributes this absorption to parallelisms between the two religious systems and also to a desire to complement one or another of the systems with ideas from the second. See the careful analysis of the Inca post-Conquest universe as a spatial system in Juan M. Ossio, "Guaman Poma: Nueva corónica o carta al rey. Un Intento de aproximación a las categorías del pensamiento del mundo andino," in Ossio, ed., *Ideología mesiánica del mundo andino* (Lima, 1973), pp. 155–213. For a presentation of Andean concepts of space that confirms the viewpoint of Núñez del Prado B. (although the data are drawn from communities in Bolivia), see Diez de Medina, *La Teogonia andina*, pp. 13–98. Basing his view on a comparison of Andean folktales, Federico Aguilo argues that the Andean cosmos contains four different qualities of mythic space: 1) vertical space, the domain of the condor, is unlimited but cold, solitary, and dark; 2) horizontal space, the domain of the fox, is fractured, penetrable, and hollowed by passages; 3) ambiguous space is the locus of water, rivers, and lakes, and no being succeeds in dominating it perfectly; 4) domestic space is found in the mother's womb, the refuge, and the primordial mythic *ayllu* and is the space of the dog, the cat, and other domestic animals. See Federico Aguilo, *Los Cuentos, ¿Tradiciones o vivencios?* (La Paz-Cochabamba, Bolivia, 1980), pp. 114–119.

20. For instance, André-Marcel D'Ans, *Le Dit des vrais hommes* (Paris, 1978), pp. 16ff., provides a schematic description of the structures of the Cashinahua universe, replete with boundaries, heavens, horizons, mythic figures, and moving parts. D'Ans points out that the conception is so clear that an artist could do an exact rendering of the structures of the cosmos. He also reckons that the Cashinahua would recognize their world in the depiction, at the same time as they admired the ingenuity of the design. However, the Cashinahua would remain "crestfallen before the absolute and rigid character of such a representation" (p. 17). The reason for this is that the cosmos, according to their conception of it, is neither a structure nor a mechanism like a timepiece.

> For them, the world is a magic entity where life is diffused. By its very essence, that entity is absolutely irreducible to a geometric figure or to a unique, functional or mechanical schema. . . . [Such a schema] is intuitively perceived by the Cashinahua as a dangerous limitation of the *meaning* of the cosmos which emanates from myths and, above all, from the esoteric texts of the tradition. (p. 17)

See also pp. 109–123 for myths recounting the primordial events that gave rise to the spatial structures and processes of the cosmos.

21. See chapter 5 of this work for an explanation of the way in which both the sound and the visible image of heavenly beings are held to be the same structure. For a further consideration of the significance of the rustling sound of feathers, see chapter 7, and for treatments of the sounds that effect death and the end of time, see chapter 8.

22. Fock, *Waiwai*, p. 101.

23. Roe, *Cosmic Zygote*, p. 118.

24. Chagnon, *Yąnomamö*, p. 44.

25. The plane below that, Hedu Kä Misi (level of the sky) has two surfaces. Its top side possesses terra firma where spirits of human beings, the souls of the dead, carry on the same activities as they did once on earth. The undersurface of Hedu is the sky one sees from earth (ibid., p. 45).

26. Weiss, "World of a Forest Tribe," p. 254.

27. Ibid., p. 254.

28. Ibid. Weiss here relies on Secundino García, "Mitología machiguenga," *Missiones dominicanas Peru* 17 (1935): 170–172. Baer (*Die Religion der Matsigenka*, pp. 345–346, n. 1249) discusses the etymology of the Milky Way River, spelled by Baer as *meshi'ari(-nt)*, along with the meaning of its symbolism and the bibliography relevant to its analysis. Regarding the Machiguenga cosmograph, see ibid., pp. 221–237.

29. Weiss, "World of a Forest Tribe," p. 257; Secundino García, "Mitología machiguenga," pp. 171–172.

30. Barandiarán emphasizes the singularly important role that the heavenly waters of Lake Akuena play in ordering the space of the universe; see Barandiarán, *Introducción . . . ye'kuaná-makiritare*, pp. 738–748.

31. Fulop, "Aspectos: Cosmogonía," passim.

32. Núñez del Prado B., "Supernatural World of the Quechua," pp. 238–239.

33. Reichel-Dolmatoff, *Amazonian Cosmos*, p. 42.

34. Fock, *Waiwai*, p. 102. Fock attributes this alternative cosmology to a late borrowing from Wapishana Indians. One will notice the similarity between this view of the unvierse and that of the Barasana. The Barasana see life as a griddle and the sky (the supreme being, Romi Kumu) as the source of moisture. "In the beginning the world was made entirely of rock and there was no life. *Romi Kumu*, Woman Shaman, took some clay and made a cassava griddle. She made three pot-supports and rested the griddle upon them. The supports were mountains holding up the griddle, the sky. She lived on top of the griddle" (Hugh-Jones, *The Palm and the Pleiades*, p. 263). Eventually Romi Kumu flooded the earth. Her urine is the rain (p. 264). During her menses she changes her skin, the sky, and rejuvenates herself.

35. Urton, *Crossroads of Earth and Sky*, passim.

36. Such was the end of time hoped for in several Guaraní messianic movements. See Métraux, *Religions et magies*. See also the symbolism of Warao eschatology in Wilbert, "Eschatology in a Participatory Universe."

37. Civrieux, *Watunna*, pp. 28, 180, 182.

38. Weiss, "World of a Forest Tribe," p. 257, reporting from Secundino García, "Mitología machiguenga," *Missiones dominicanas Peru* 17 (1935): 172. Baer (*Die Religion der Matsigenka*, pp. 94–95 and 221ff.) provides different nomenclature for the levels of vertical space in the Machiguenga universe.

39. Weiss, "World of a Forest Tribe," p. 255.

40. See chapter 5 of this work for a discussion of the meaning of physiological appetites, body contents (food, blood, semen, excrement), openings, and weight.

41. See the discussion entitled "The Two Senses of the River" in Joseph W. Bastien, *Mountain of the Condor*, pp. 155–159. The river flowing throughout all levels of the universe has a creative sense because it originates in the time and place of the creative origins of the universe. Its flowing waters can always restore existence to the fullness it enjoyed at the beginning of time. On the other hand, its death-dealing power is also inherent. This negative sense of the world-river is made clear in the association of the river with the destruction of the cosmic flood (p. 159).

42. Whitten, *Sacha Runa*, p. 45.

43. Roe, *Cosmic Zygote*, p. 117.

44. Chagnon, Yąnomamö, p. 45. See also Hugh-Jones, The Palm and the Pleiades, p. 263, where appears a Barasana account that describes the fall of the lower world-levels associated with food. They are clay griddles, which crack as they are heated over fire and plummet with their own weight. The cosmologic of space and its relation to food is further explored in Thomas Allen Langdon, Food Restrictions in the Medical System of the Barasana and Taiwano Indians of the Colombian Northwest Amazon (Ann Arbor, 1983), pp. 67ff. and pp. 81–132.

45. Johannes Wilbert, "Navigators of the Winter Sun," in Elizabeth P. Benson, ed., The Sea in the Pre-Columbian World (Washington, D.C., 1977), pp. 17–46, esp. pp. 39–44.

46. Ibid., p. 41.

47. "To give an example, we may cite the following here: gahkí is a synonym for penis, ahpíri is the breast or womb; ahpiritó are the testicles; nyahpí is the sweet potato whose fruit is compared with a female breast; gahsiro is the placenta" (Reichel-Dolmatoff, Amazonian Cosmos, p. 46).

48. Ibid.

49. Fock, Waiwai, p. 101.

50. Núñez del Prado B., "Supernatural World of the Quechua," pp. 238–239.

51. See Gregory Bateson's discussion of the similarity between play and ritual frames and the "double bind" of ambiguous situations, including schizophrenia, in Steps to an Ecology of Mind (New York, 1972).

52. The exact arrangement varies with the ethnographic reports. Roe was told there are two levels above this world and two below.

53. Roe, Cosmic Zygote, p. 113.

54. Ibid., p. 114.

55. Núñez del Prado B., "Supernatural World of the Quechua," pp. 238-239.

56. P. Grenand, Introduction . . . Wayãpi, p. 322.

57. Reichel-Dolmatoff, Amazonian Cosmos, p. 42.

58. Ibid.

59. Ibid., p. 49.

60. Chagnon, Yąnomamö, p. 45.

61. Wilbert, "Navigators of the Winter Sun," pp. 21–22.

62. James Fernandez, "Edification by Puzzlement," in Ivan Karp and Charles S. Bird, eds., Explorations in African Systems of Thought (Bloomington, Ind., 1980), pp. 44–59.

63. Civrieux, Watunna, p. 28.

64. Ibid.

65. Bartolomé, "Shamanism among the Avá-Chiripá," p. 103.

66. Wilbert, "Navigators of the Winter Sun," p. 166.

67. Jules Henry, Jungle People, p. 5.

68. Whitten, Sacha Runa, p. 38.

69. Ibid., p. 41.

70. Regarding the forms of thought, knowledge and experience that accompany the ordering and construction of space, see Joseph Rykwert, On Adam's House in Paradise: The Idea of the Primitive Hut in Architectural History (New York, 1984). The relationship of thinking and doing, necessity and convention in the rites that construct a separate space as a proper house for the soul are discussed in comparative and historical perspective. Rykwert pursues a similar set of issues in regard to the construction of urban space in The Idea of a Town (Princeton, 1980). See also the detailed descriptions of the mythic worlds that comprise the Tacana universe, in Karin Hissink and Albert Hahn, Die Tacana, vol. 1, Erzählungsgut (Stuttgart, 1961), pp. 41ff., esp. pp. 83ff. (the heavenly world) and pp. 86ff. (the earthly landscape and the underworld). The mythic chima palm tree is a central cosmic structure (pp. 75ff.). And for the systematics of the spatial universe of the Krahó, see Julio Cezar Melatti, Ritos de Uma Tribo Timbira (São Paulo, 1978), pp. 94–99.

71. Gabriel Martínez, "Toponimos de Chuani: ¿Organización y significación del territorio?" ACAR 1 (1983). 71. Martínez associates this complex with what he has called a "uterine configuration" in which creations come to gestate in an enclosure.

72. Ibid., p. 77.

73. Bastien, Mountain of the Condor, passim, and J. Bastien, "Qollahuaya-Andean Body Concepts: A Topographical-Hydraulic Model of Physiology," AA 87 (September 1985): 595–611.

74. Wright, "History and Religion of the Baniwa," pp. 471–474.

75. Pierre Clastres, "L'Arc et le panier," *H* 6 (1966): p. 15. Although the distinction may be held by the Guayakí, Clastres may be overlooking the economic aspects of the physical production of children, which takes place in the space of women in the domestic unit. For other cultural expressions of sexualized space, see the following papers, published in *ICA*, 42d Congress (Paris, 1976). Hans Dietschy, "Espace social et 'affiliation par sexe' au Brésil central (Karajá, Tapirapé, Apinayé, Mundurucú)," pp. 297–308; Christine Hugh-Jones, "Skin and Soul: The Round and the Straight, Social Time and Social Space in Pirá-Paraná Society," pp. 185–204; Jean-Paul Dumont, "Le Sens de l'espace chez les Panare," pp. 47–53; and Kenneth M. Kensinger, "Cashinahua Notions of Social Time and Social Space," pp. 233–244.

76. Clastres, *Chronique des indiens guayakí*, pp. 19–20.

77. Bartolomé, "Shamanism among the Avá-Chiripá," p. 103.

78. Whitten, *Sacha Runa*, p. 172.

79. Ibid.

80. See Mircea Eliade and Lawrence E. Sullivan, "Center of the World," in *The Encyclopedia of Religion*, for fuller comparative treatment of this point and for bibliography.

81. Johannes Wilbert, "Eschatology," p. 163.

82. Lux Vidal, *Morte e vida de uma sociedade indigena brasileira. Os Kayapó-Xikrin do Rio Cateté* (São Paulo, 1977), pp. 18ff. For a consideration of the ways in which Kayapó notions of vertical space in myth affect the shape of household, village, and family relations throughout the course of human life-cycle, see Terence S. Turner, "Animal Symbolism, Totemism, and the Structure of Myth," in Urton, ed., *Animal Myths and Metaphors*, pp. 49–106, esp. pp. 65ff.

83. Weiss, "World of a Forest Tribe," p. 251.

84. Mark Münzel, "Zwischen den Steinen. Die Übergangssituation einer Maku-Gruppe in Nordwest-Brasilien," *EZ* special supplement number 1 (1974): 287–308.

85. Jacopin, *La Parole generative*, p. 79.

86. Ibid., pp. 77ff. This example is a striking parallel to the act of orientation in the myth of the founding of the city of Rome. See, for example, the comparative study by Werner Müller, *Die heilige Stadt: Roma quadrata, himmlisches Jerusalem und die Mythe vom Weltnabel* (Stuttgart, 1961). See also Müller's application of his studies to Amerindian materials in "Raum und Zeit in Sprachen und Kalendern Nordamerikas und Alteuropas," *ANT* 57 (1962). 568–590. For a comparative consideration of the meaning and imagery of orientation in a global perspective, see the article and bibliography in Mircea Eliade and Lawrence E. Sullivan, "Orientation," in *EOR*.

87. For more extended treatment in comparative perspective and for bibliography on *axis mundi*, see Lawrence E. Sullivan, "Axis Mundi," in *EOR*.

88. The knowledge obtained by ecstatic specialists in their ascents to heaven is widely documented. See, for example, Ernst Arbman, *Ecstasy or Religious Trance*, ed. Åke Hultkrantz, 3 vols. (Uppsala, 1963–70), esp. vol. 2, pp. 275–630, on the notion of mystical union with beings from other realms. Their experiences there serve as resources for the imagery of art, narrative, and ritual as well as for the sciences that cultures use to make sense of their world. See Tullio Tentori, "South American Ideas of the Other World," *ICA*, 30th Congress (London, 1955), pp. 199–201. Also of interest regarding journeys to the underworld are Åke Hultkrantz, *The North American Indian Orpheus Tradition* (Stockholm, 1957), and Eliade, *Shamanism*, pp. 198ff and 305ff. Knowledge of the relations among the powers and possibilities which reside in worlds that lie along the vertical axis of the universe is not only mystical but economic. The visualization and evaluation of space as a manifestation of sacred being goes hand in hand with the development of a social system of relations to the economic and sacred resources within the space of the land. This theme is developed in several essays edited by José R. Sabogal Wiesse, *La Communidad Andina* (Mexico City, 1969). For example, see the article in that volume by Héctor Martínez, "Tierra y desarrollo de la comunidad en Canas y Canchis," esp. pp. 207ff., which shows how the relationship of humans to land is built around the images of sacred places and of the body of the earth mother, Pachamama. Antoinette Fioravanti-Molinié, "Multi-levelled Andean Society and Market Exchange: The Case of Yucay (Peru)," in David Lehman, ed., *Ecology and Exchange in the Andes*, pp. 211–230, examines the images of verticality as they relate to mythical images of incest, monstrosity, foreigners, supernaturals, disease, and so on (pp. 228–230). In the same volume, Olivia Harris sorts out the impact of images of center and vertical axis on productive

labor relations; see her essay "Labour and Produce in an Ethnic Economy, Northern Potosí, Bolivia," pp. 70–96. In the same vein, Frank Salomon, *Los Señores etnicos de Quito en la epoca de los Incas* (Otavalo, Ecuador, 1980) studies variations in the imagery of vertical space and the practices that surround such spatial concepts (e.g., pp. 57ff. and passim). See also Herbert Baldus, "Vertikale und horizontale Struktur im religiösen Weltbild südamerikanischer Indianer," *ANT* 63/64 (1968–1969): 16–21, for a general consideration of images of verticality. The exchange between realms of being carries economic ramifications and bears material consequences.

89. Whitten, *Sacha Runa*, p. 61. *Allpa* also designates productive soil and clay used for pottery.

90. Ibid., p. 67.

91. Carol E. Robertson-DeCarbo, "Lukutún: Text and Context in Mapuche Rogations," *LAIL* 1 (1977): 77. See also Rodolfo M. Casamiquela, *Estudio del Nillatun y la religión araucana* (Bahia Blanca, Argentina, 1964). Thérèse Bouysse-Cassagne and Philippe Bouysse, "Volcan indien, volcan chrétien. A propos de l'éruption du Huaynaputina en l'an 1600 (Pérou méridional)," *JSAP* 70 (1984): 43–68, looks at a set of volcanic mountains as they appear, not only in geographic and social space, but in the religious imagination through the times of pre- and post-Christian existence in the Andes. The mountain becomes the center of sacrality in all its dimensions (autochthonous and Inca cults and the meaning of historical events; terrestrial and celestial sacred fires; the axis of aquatic sacrality; the center of horizontal axes; the locus of the vertical axis, and so on).

92. Weiss, "World of a Forest Tribe," p. 482.

93. "[F]or the Cashinahua, Marinahua, Cuniba, Jívaro, Canelo, Quijo, Yagua, Witoto, Warrau, Guiana Arawak, Taulipáng, Cayapó, Bacaïri, Umotina, Boróro, Mosetene, and Tiatinagua; it is also reported for the Lengua, Mataco, Toba, and Vilela of the Chaco region" (ibid., p. 482). Weiss also lists the many groups that hold a belief that the sky was once close to the earth and the communities that report that a sky-ladder or a sky-tree connect the earth and the celestial realms. In the same place he charts the distribution of the idea of a chain of arrows connecting the earth to the sky. He also traces the belief that a rope connects the earth with the underworld.

94. Krugh, "Mythology of the Pemón," p. 30. See the stimulating analysis of the cosmic tree among the Mashco in Mario Califano, "El Mito del arbol cósmico wanamei de los Mashco de la Amazonía sud Occidental," *ANT* 78 (1983): 739–769.

95. The significant connection between the *axis mundi*, the wandering quest, the merging of figures from disparate world-planes, and the image of the vessel is not unique to South American religions, although nuances and applications are unique to each culture in which the complex appears. See, for example, the fascinating study of the connection between the symbolism of the vessel in Iranian esoteric traditions and medieval literature of Christian gnosticism in Henry Kahane and Renée Kahane, *The Krater and the Grail: Hermetic Sources of the Parzival* (Urbana, Ill., 1965).

96. See chapter 7, below, on the symbolism of the rattle.

97. Civrieux, *Watunna*, pp. 135, 143.

98. Ibid., p. 143.

99. Ibid., p. 178.

100. Ibid., p. 41.

101. Ibid., p. 135.

102. Ibid., p. 185.

103. Ibid., pp. 152–153.

104. Ibid., p. 35.

105. Wright, "History and Religion of the Baniwa," p. 474.

106. Johannes Wilbert, "Geography and Telluric Lore of the Orinoco Delta," *JLAL* 5 (1979): 148.

107. Aveni, "View from the Tropics," p. 285.

108. Ibid., p. 276. Aveni emphasizes that zenith stars are important perhaps because the declination of a star passing the zenith parallels the observer's geographic latitude. Consequently, every site could situate itself in relationship to the celestial equator by associating itself with its own zenith-passing guide star (ibid., p. 283). In this connection, see also Guillermo Illescas Cook, *Astrónomos en el antiguo Peru: Sobre los conocimientos astronómicos de los antiguos pueblos del*

Peru (Lima, 1976). Through an examination of pottery, art, and architecture, Illescas Cook has attempted to highlight the astronomic value of spatial designs—the famous lines of Nazca, which, he contends, were part of an astronomic education. The lines not only helped to locate certain stars, they represented specific constellations. Also pertinent to this discussion is Eloy Linares Malaga, "La Estrella de ocho puntas en la arqueología del area meridional andina," in Hartmann and Oberem, *Amerikanistische Studien*, pp. 16–23.

109. Reichel-Dolmatoff, *Amazonian Cosmos*, p. 42.

110. Gerardo Reichel-Dolmatoff, "Desana Shamans' Rock Crystal and the Hexagonal Universe," *JLAL* 5 (1979): 117–128.

111. The sacred significance of space is extended to a number of hexagonal shapes, including the honeycomb, the design on the shells of certain tortoises, spiderwebs, and marriage relationships (which are visualized in terms of a hexagon). See Krupp, *Echoes of Ancient Skies*, pp. 317–319.

112. Gow and Condori, *Kay Pacha*, p. 61.

113. Roe *Cosmic Zygote*, p. 118.

114. Fulop, "Aspectos: Cosmogonía," p. 118.

115. Ibid., p. 120. The same point has been made very clearly by Christine Hugh-Jones in her article "Skin and Soul."

116. Whitten, *Sacha Runa*, p. 42. Near Canelos, Whitten was told that stones and rocks were once people who inhabited the world "before creation" and "before the flood." He tentatively judged this conception to be the result of missionary work. However, from the internal evidence supplied in his own study, it seems as though this opinion warrants reconsideration. See Whitten's discussion of the *tayaj rumi* (stone-souls) on p. 62. When the soul-stone opens, like a flower, it "brings to itself insects and birds, their continuous noise and motion."

117. Fock, *Waiwai*, pp. 114–115.

118. Ibid., p. 67. Origin myths in which an anaconda swallows a human being, gives up the victim's bones, and is then dismembered in such a way as to bring the multiplicity of different peoples into existence, draw this celebration into an arc that would include the myth of origin of the Barasana sibs. These latter are all transformations of body parts of the original ancestor anaconda, who, after having swum to the middle of the universe, broke into pieces along the river that runs to the center of the earth. Also noteworthy is that the Shodewika flutes and bark trumpets are played in imitation of those once played in mythical times by the macaw spirits. When the celebration was first performed by animal-human beings, they were unadorned. Contemporary festival costumes are worn only to imitate the beautiful, but unadorned, people whose integral beauty comprised both human and animal aspects. It was only at the festival's end that these beings were transformed into separate species of animals and human tribes (p. 63).

119. Reichel-Dolmatoff, *Amazonian Cosmos*, pp. 116–177.

120. In his studies of pilgrimage, Victor Turner had the opportunity to apply his theories of "liminality" and frame to the symbolism of space. See his "The Center Out There: Pilgrim's Goal," *HR* 12 (1973): 191–230. For further bibliography, see Lawrence E. Sullivan, "Victor Turner," *HR* 24 (November 1984): 160–163. Turner developed the field theories of Kurt Lewin. For other approaches to the impact of center and periphery on the formation of social and urban space, see Edward Shils, *Center and Periphery: Essays in Macro-Sociology*, vol. 2, (Chicago, 1975); Paul Wheatley, *The Pivot of the Four Quarters* (Edinborough, 1971); Jonathan Z. Smith, *To Take Place* (Chicago, 1987); and David Carrasco, *Quetzalcoatl and the Irony of Empire* (Chicago, 1982).

121. In the most general terms this is discussed in Douglas R. Hofstadter, *Gödel, Escher, Bach: An Eternal Golden Braid* (New York, 1979). James W. Fernandez, "Reflections on Looking into Mirrors," in Barbara A. Babcock, ed., *Signs about Signs: The Semiotics of Self-Reference*, a special issue of *Semiotica* 30 (1980): 27–40, offers a glimpse into the depth of reflection on this image in cultures without academic traditions of philosophy.

122. Apinayé space, by way of illustration, is essentially concentric, but, since it is bounded, its design includes diametric aspects. Roberto da Matta concludes, "It is as if the concentric dualism conceptualizes gradations while the diametric divides the world in a more extreme

way" (*A Divided World: Apinayé Social Structure*, Cambridge, Mass., 1982, p. 37). The concentric structures, beginning at the center, are fire, the plaza for ceremonial, the ring of houses, the outer limits of the village, the area of garden plots, civilized Indians, the realm of water, untamed Indians, Brazilians, the outer edge of the earth, the sky, and the village of the dead. Beyond that is the realm of the sun and the moon. Da Matta finds these reflexive contradictions at work in the organization of closed and bounded space of the universe: "Man/woman, raw/cooked, women and children/men, water/fire, and sun/moon" (p. 37). What is fascinating, from our perspective in discussing the importance of a boundary and a reflexivity that close the system of space and make it symbolic, is the judgment of the Apinayé about the differences between their own villages and the nonindigenous Brazilian settlements. "The Indians see the Brazilian settlement pattern as open and their own as closed" (p. 39). It becomes clear in da Matta's discussion of the relationship system that space is actually a way of grasping the world of personal and powerful relationships in a systematic and coherent way (pp. 100–130). This realization is not limited to South American cultures. See, for example, Robert Nozick's chapter, "The Identity of the Self," in his *Philosophical Explanations* (Cambridge, 1981); Kent Bloomer and Charles Moore, *Body, Memory, Architecture* (New York, 1977); or, in a more anthropological vein, Gregory Bateson, "A Theory of Play and Fantasy," in his *Steps to an Ecology of Mind*.

123. Whitten, *Sacha Runa*, p. 44. The relative indistinction of northern and southern horizons holds true elsewhere. For Northern Kayapó (Xikrin), for instance, "North and South are referred to by a single phrase which means 'the edge of the sky' [koy-kwa-nhirê-a]. Gestures or references to landmarks are necessary to indicate whether North or South is meant." Terence S. Turner, *Social Structure and Political Organization Among the Northern Cayapó* (Ph.D. diss., Harvard University, 1965), p. 31.

124. Whitten, *Sacha Runa*, p. 44.

125. Wilbert, "Eschatology," p. 165.

126. Roe, *Cosmic Zygote*, p. 113.

127. For a thoughtful description of the ways in which the Aztecs of Mesoamerica, through tribute, offering, capture and sacrifice, symbolically tried to "incorporate the edges of their world into the center of the unvierse" in the form of valued objects from the periphery (shells, masks, swordfish, jewelry and clothing from the frontier provinces), see Davíd Carrasco, "City as Symbol in Aztec Thought: The Clues from the Codex Mendoza," *HR* 20 (February 1981): 199–223, esp. 220f., and Johanna Broda, "El tributo en trajes guerreros y la estructura del sistema tributario Mexica," in Pedro Carrasco and Johanna Broda, eds., *Economía, política e ideología en el Mexico prehispánico* (Mexico City, 1978). (The question of tribute is taken up again in chapter 8, below, in connection with images of consumption associated with death). On the relationship of peripheral peoples as symbols vital to ceremonial and political centers, see S. J. Tambiah, "The Galactic Polity: The Structure of Traditional Kingdoms in Southeast Asia," *New York Academy of Sciences* 293 (1977): 69–98.

128. Wilbert, "Eschatology," p. 166.

129. Whitten, *Sacha Runa*, p. 35.

130. For a discussion of the Inca case, see R. T. Zuidema, "The Inca Calendar," in Anthony F. Aveni, *Native American Astronomy* (Austin, 1977). On contemporary Andean cosmologies that coordinate the contrasting movements of water (descending from west to east) and sun (rising east to west), see Bastien, *Mountain of the Condor*, and Billie Jean Isbell, *To Defend Ourselves* (Austin, 1978). A similar opposition of water and sun motions is fundamental to the cosmology of the Barasana of the northwestern Amazon; cf. Christine Hugh-Jones, *From the Milk River* (Cambridge, 1979).

131. Lévi-Strauss discusses this image in *The Origin of Table Manners*.

132. See chapter 2, above.

133. Urton, *Crossroads of Earth and Sky*. Isbell, in *To Defend Ourselves*, also describes the flow of celestial waters from the upper-mountain spirits, through the irrigation canals, into the fertile valleys of mother earth as a flow of semen. She suggests that this contemporary idea has a long history in the Andes. Juan M. Ossio, "El Simbolismo del agua y la representación del tiempo y del espacio en la fiesta de la acequia de la comunidad de Andamarca," *ICA*, 42d Congress, vol. 4, (Paris, 1976), pp. 377–396, concurs with Isbell's interpretation but points out, first, that the

identification of the irrigation waters with semen is not explicit among Andean populations. Rather, they see the mountain waters as a form of fertile blood from above (p. 380). Second, water has many meanings, which should not be reduced to one single denotation. The meaning highlighted in each context embellishes the rich symbolic content of the whole complex of meanings (pp. 318, 389). The symbolism of water in the Andes signals a wide and complex range of conditions of being, grasped as images of space. River and irrigation water is literally central to the community of Andamarca, which is transected by the Negromayo River. Ossio, in analyzing the feast of the cleaning of irrigation canals in August, points out the distinctions made in qualities and meanings of water: blood of the male mountain beings, fluid associated with the female serpent of the underworld, secular water, metaphysical water, the water of the flood in primordial times, semen (although he seems to suggest that semen should be interpreted as a form of blood coming from the heart of the mountain gods, the *wamanis*); water is also a young child whose presence is discerned principally through the sound of ceaseless crying. In particular, Ossio points out that water acquires and leaves off its many multivalent possibilities of meaning depending on the spatial context in which it appears. He also points out that water makes its way through all the temporal conditions, most notably through the trinity of ages of existence: the "epoch of the father," which preceded this age; the "epoch of the son," in which human beings now live; and the "epoch of the Holy Spirit," which is that of the world to come (p. 383). The meanings of water, as a symbolic form, can bring one into living contact with the powers of these spaces and times.

134. Weiss, "World of a Forest Tribe," p. 257, reporting from Secundino García, "Mitología machiguenga," *Misiones dominicanas Peru* 17 (1935): 171–172.

135. For the people of the community of Chuani in Bolivia (Province of Camacho, Department of La Paz), for example, every color is a mediate expression of light that originally derived from a single source, the primordial totality of light called *achachila-wak'a*. *Achachila-wak'a* is a mythical complex of sacred space, a nearly unimaginable (now unmanifest) "all-color" located at the center of the world's space. See Gabriel Martínez, "Topónimos de Chuani: Organización y significación del territorio?" *ALIM* 1 (1983): 71.

136. Reichel-Dolmatoff, *Amazonian Cosmos*, p. 49: "Between the visible world and the invisible there is sexual contact."

137. Weiss, "World of a Forest Tribe," p. 255.

138. Whitten, *Sacha Runa*, p. 45.

139. Ibid., p. 44.

140. Ibid., p. 38.

141. See Arthur A. Demarest, "Illapa/Thunupa: The Substratum of the Upper Pantheon," in his *Viracocha: The Nature and Antiquity of the Andean High God* (Cambridge, Mass., 1981), pp. 35–39, which discusses the history of the Aymara thunder deity. See also Ana Maria Mariscotti de Görlitz, "Die Stellung des Gewittergottes in den regionalen Pantheen der Zentralanden," *BA* n.s. 18 (1970): 427–436, and "La Posición del señor de los fenómenos meteorológicos en los panteones regionales de los Andes centrales," *Historia y Cultura* (Lima) 6 (1973): 207–215. In *Pachamama: Santa Tierra*, Mariscotti de Görlitz gathers a useful collection of source materials, from historic chronicles to ethnographies, on meteorological beings in the central Andes (pp. 333–340).

142. Gow and Condori, *Kay Pacha*, p. 61.

143. For a consideration of the ways in which myth serves as a map, "an ethnoecological blueprint of residence, subsistence, and territoriality patterns," see Wilbert, "Geography and Telluric Lore of the Orinoco Delta."

144. Wright, "History and Religion of the Baniwa," p. 591.

145. Ibid., pp. 591–592.

146. Religious processions and pilgrimages mediate between qualities of space in the cosmos and frequently are associated with changes in physical or social reality (e.g., healing or rebellion). See Pierre Arnold, "Pèlerinages et processions comme formes de pouvoir symbolique des classes subalternes: Deux cas péruviens," *Social Compass* 32 (1985): 45–56. David Carrasco summons investigators to examine the plastic elaborations of the supernatural and social forces organized in symbols of the center and periphery. Dance, design, ritual, and architecture repre-

sent the cosmic struggle or divine drama of holding terrestrial space in the image of celestial archetypes. The two homologies of heavenly and earthly order "are related by the exact sequences of ritual and worship. . . . Aztec cities were great theaters of motion, color, sound, and gesture. . . . [M]uch more needs to be done to understand the relationship of space and ceremonial motion" (Carrasco, "City as Symbol," p. 214).

147. Whitten, *Sacha Runa*, p. 67.

148. Fock, *Waiwai*, p. 128.

149. Waldeloir Rego, "Mitos e ritos africanos da Bahia," in Carybé (Artist), *Iconografia dos deuses africanos no Candomblé da Bahia* (São Paulo, 1980); the book is not paginated—Rego's essay is found, with several others, at the back of the book. The opposition between the meaning of street and house as religious spaces is further explored in Roberto da Matta, "Carnival in Multiple Planes," in John J. MacAloon, ed., *Rite, Drama, Festival, Spectacle* (Philadelphia, 1984), pp. 208–240. Regarding the practice of ritual *desfile*, "symbolic wandering," through the streets at the time of Carnival, da Matta remarks, "What is basic is how one goes, never where one arrives" (p. 238). In the same article, da Matta discusses the opposition between Amazonian spatial categories of *mato* (scrubland) and *floresta* (forest).

150. B. J. Isbell, *To Defend Ourselves*; William H. Isbell, "Cosmological Order Expressed in Prehistoric Ceremonial Centers," *ICA* 42d Congress, vol. 4 (Paris, 1977), pp. 269–298.

151. Wilbert, "Warao Cosmology and Yekuana Roundhouse Symbolism," *JLAL* 7 (1981): 179.

152. Ibid.

153. Garardo Reichel-Dolmatoff, "The Loom of Life: A Kógi Principle of Integration," *JLAL* 4 (1978): 5–27, and "Templos kógi: Introducción al simbolismo y a la astronomía del espacio sagrado," *RCA* 19 (1977): 199–246.

154. Krupp, *Echoes of the Ancient Skies*, p. 239.

155. Ibid., p. 241.

156. Ibid.

157. Weldell C. Bennett surveyed the variety of religious architectural structures. He concentrated on the building compounds, pyramids, ceremonial centers, and altars of the central Andes. Only passing mention was made of initiation lodges, ceremonial plazas, and men's clubhouses found in the areas outside the Andes.

158. Juana Elbein Dos Santos and Deoscoredes M. Dos Santos, "Ancestor Worship in Bahia: The Égun-Cult," *JSAP* 58 (1969): 93.

159. Rego, "Mitos e ritos africanos da Bahia."

160. Ibid.

161. Renato Ortiz provides a comparative analysis of the organization of sacred space for Afro-Brazilian cult practices. He shows how the social history and structures of particular groups and communities are reflected in the organization of ritual space. He makes a distinction between the more complicated and less westernized *terreiros* of Candomblé as opposed to the more westernized *tendas*. See Ortiz, *A Morte branca do feiticeiro negro: Umbanda, integração de uma religião numa sociedade de classes* (Petropolis, Brazil, 1978), pp. 89–95. Ortiz remarks that the differences in the arrangement and structures of sacred space are reflected in the attitudes, emotions, gestures, dances, musical combos, and clothing of the participants. All of these symbolic differences can reflect the social realities as well as the religious aspirations of the devotees. Ortiz' study compares the cultic spaces in the cities of Rio de Janiero and São Paulo. The first is the origin place of Umbanda; the second, in Ortiz' opinion, is the place where Afro-Brazilian cults are growing most intensely.

162. Daniel de Barandiarán, "El habitado entre los Indios Yekuana," *ACAR* 16 (1966): 3–95. For a brilliant exposition of the house as microcosm, see Barandiarán, *Introducción . . . ye'kuanamakiritare*, pp. 937–949. The immediate and concrete cultural living space of human beings, their communal house, becomes the central symbolic system of their religion and philosophy. It is a symbolic system consubstantial with the structures, the powers, of the universe created by the divinity. See also David M. Guss, "The Atta," *New Wilderness Letter* (New York) 2 (1980): 14–15. See also Meinhard Schuster, *Dekuana: Beiträge zur Ethnologie der Makiritare* (Munich, 1976), pp. 55, 88, 164.

163. Johannes Wilbert, "Warao Cosmology," p. 69. "In other words, the roof of the modern Warao house relates to the solstitial rectangle within the circular ground plan of the cosmos (and, one should add, the *mesa* to the circular floor plan of the House of Tobacco Smoke), as the rectangular tie beam structure to the circular ground plan of the Yekuana roundhouse" (pp. 68–69). Wilbert points out the calendrical function of the spatial structures (p. 65). In his article "The House of the Swallow-Tailed Kite: Warao Myth and the Art of Thinking in Images" (in Urton, ed., *Animal Myths and Metaphors*, pp. 145–182), Wilbert shows how all these connections are clarified in the imaginative labor of myth. The Warao myths associated with *bahana* (a type of Warao shamanism specialized in knowledge of human reproduction and its physical, psychological, and social ramifications) make the transcendental, social, and physical worlds parallel to one another in structure, meaning, and function. The wide cosmos (serpentine underworld, terrestrial disk, and celestial vault) is isomorphic to the cosmic egg, which serves as model for the traditional stilt house (inhabited by an anaconda and suspended over water), as well as to the human body (whose intestines and reproductive organs of the abdominal cavity represent the serpentine imagery of the world processes and whose thoracic regions and head participate in the processes and matters of the upperworlds; see pp. 178–179). In an entirely different context of meaning, Alejandra Siffredi examines the meaning of the Tehuelche house as it is revealed in myth; see her "Aspectos mitico-religiosos de los Tehuelches meridionales (Aonikenk): El Habitat," *BCA* 1 (January-April 1968): 49–54. Arturo Jiminez Borja, *Puruchuco* (Lima, 1973), examines and interprets the structures of the pre-Conquest house in the valley of Lima, Peru. See also Theodor Koch-Grünberg, "Das Haus bei den Indianern Nord-Westbrasiliens," *Archiv für Anthropologie* (Braunschweig) 35 (1908): 37–50.

164. Civrieux, *Watunna*, p. 177.

165. Gerardo Reichel-Dolmatoff, "Brain and Mind in Desana Symbolism," *JLAL* 7 (1981): 73–98. He writes,

> The wider cosmic image is this: the isomorphic chain formed by the human brain, the longhouse, and the hills continues in the celestial vault. This, too, is an immense brain; the Milky Way is the great fissure which separates the two hemispheres and is called Trail of the Master of Animals, because the constellations and all other stars are the animals and people, the butterflies and flowers which occupy the brain compartments. In another image, the Milky Way and its swaying motion represent the same two intertwined serpents: the female anaconda and the male rainbow boa.
>
> Beyond the Milky Way lies space, and cosmic space is said to be a womb; it is called *ëmësée paa toré*, an expression that can be glossed as "time-seat-abdominal-cavity." This cosmic womb is a limitless hexagonal rock crystal. The entire chain, from the cosmic crystal to the human brain, is linked together by a steady flow of solar energy *(bogá)* which forms a line of conduction that pulsates in synchronization with the human heartbeat. In this way, the material and the immaterial world come to constitute a single whole. (p. 97)

Such a series of isomorphic spatial systems is widespread and can be well developed. Among Qollahuaya communities of the Bolivian Andes, for example, the body, the mountain, and the cosmos are three forms of physiological processes carried on in space. All three processes can be understood in terms of the movement of fluids to and from the center and periphery. The body has three levels (head, trunk, and members) situated along a vertical axis. Fluids mingle together at the heart *(sonco)*,

> a distillation center that includes digestive, respiratory, reproductive, and circulatory processes, in an inward spiral. The fluids are broken down, distilled into other fluids, and dispersed throughout the body in an outward spiral. Distillation is the compressed movement of fluids to the center: this separates fluids, such as fat, from the food. Dispersal is the circulating of the fluids to the parts of the body for storage, release of energy, and elimination." (Bastien, "Qollahuaya-Andean Body Concepts," p. 608)

Land, body, cosmos, and society become analogs of one another. These spatial systems and their interrelationships are represented on *mesas* (ritual tables) which are constructed "to feed the earth shrines of the *ayllu* [the community and its land] when they are sick" (Bastien, ibid., p. 608). Although the terms of the analogy conjoin on the *mesa*,

> the analogies are never one to one: the body metaphor never corresponds completely to the communities, earth shrines, ecology, and physiology. The analogies involve imagination, ability to understand meanings of Andean languages, embellishment by oral traditions, and most of all, the external application of the metaphor in ritual. The mountain and its people change with the seasons, sickness, natural catastrophes, migrations, and conquest. When the terms change, diviners gather the people together to match the body metaphor with the land and communities. (Bastien, ibid., p. 609).

Antoinette Molinié-Fioravanti, "Tiempo del espacio y espacio del tiempo en los Andes," *JSAP* 71 (1985): 97–114, demonstrates the homologous spatial structures of myth, cosmos, village, society, and human body in Yucay, Peru. Moreover, she contends, an examination of rites, myths, toponyms, and astral configurations reveals that space and time share similar elementary forms. In particular, she traces the meaning of the constellation Cruz Calvario through Andean history to the present day as a marker of space, time, and transition.

166. Gow and Condori, *Kay Pacha*, p. 61. See also Molinié-Fioravanti, "Tiempo del espacio," for the ways in which the symbolic space of the land is healthful or harmful.

167. Grenand, *Introduction . . . Wayãpi*, p. 324.

168. Peter Kloos, "The Akuriyo Way of Death," in Ellen B. Basso, ed., *Carib-Speaking Indians, Culture, Society, and Language* (Tucson, 1977), p. 121.

169. Ibid.

170. Gow and Condori, *Kay Pacha*, pp. 61–62.

171. Enrique Palavecino, "The Magic World of the Mataco," *LAIL* 3 (1979): 67.

172. Wagley, *Welcome of Tears*, pp. 215, 217.

173. Conrad and Demarest, *Religion and Empire*, p. 84. Regarding the interpenetrability of Andean space and time, see Molinié-Fioravanti, "Tiempo del Espacio," pp. 97–114.

174. Mercedes López-Baralt, "La Persistencia de la estructúras simbólicas andinas en los dibújos de Guamán Poma de Ayala," *JLAL* 5 (1979): 83–116. The very name of the famous chronicler upon whose work López-Baralt bases her analysis is a conjunction of spatial opposites, for "in the Andean mythology Guamán (the falcon) generally appears in association with the celestial sphere (Hanan), while Poma (puma, American mountain lion) possesses a telluric character (Hurin)" (Ossio, "Guamán Poma," p. 211).

175. Not only did the organization of space provide the framework for ritual and political hierarchies, but

> the political structure of the empire was visibly interlocked with astronomical thought. The city of Cuzco was divided into a northern and southern sector, callen Hanan-Cuzco and Hurin-Cuzco, respectively. Everything that transpired in the northern half of the domain was governed or cared for by the people who inhabited that ward of the city. The same held for the south, and their duties evidently included even the procurement of astronomical observations along the jagged horizon that framed their isolated world. (Aveni, "The View from the Tropics," p. 279)

The body-politic of Cuzco is spoken of, in several chronicles, as a mountain lion, puma, or jaguar. The arguments have been summarized by R. T. Zuidema, "The Lion in the City: Royal Symbols of Transition in Cuzco," in Urton, ed., *Animal Myths and metaphors*, pp. 183–250. The following chroniclers and scholars contend that the city was actually laid out in the shape of a puma. First, Pedro Sarmiento de Gamboa [1572], in his *Historia de los Incas* (Buenos Aires, 1947), chapter 53; Zuidema argues that the motives for this report were political—that is, Sarmiento de Gambia's intent was to extol Topa Inca Yupanqui by showing how he built the "head," the fortress of Sacsahuaman (lit., "eagle's head"). Next, Garcilaso de la Vega (El Inca) [1609] uses the body-image metaphorically in his *Comentarios reales de los Incas* (Buenos Aires, 1945): see book 7, chapter 8; book 2, chapter 11; and book 1, chapter 16. John H. Rowe, in "What Kind of Settlement Was Inca Cuzco?" *Ñawpa Pacha* 5 (1967): 59–76, argues that the physical city was built in the form of a puma lying on its side; in his counterargument, Zuidema remarks that Rowe's "unfounded opinion has been generally accepted by archaeologists and historians of architecture" ("The Lion in the City," p. 239). William H. Isbell, "Cosmological Order Expressed in Prehistoric Ceremonial Centers," *ICA*, 42d Congress, vol. 4 (Paris, 1978), pp. 269–298, does comb the sources and, on the basis of physical and textual data, concurs with Rowe. Also agreeing with Rowe are Graziano Gasparini and Luise Margolies in their *Arquitectura inca* (Caracas, 1977). Zuidema, who compares Betanzos, Garcilaso, and Sarmiento, concludes,

> 1. There is no evidence that the shape of Cuzco was seen as an animal (in this case, a puma), lying on its side. 2. Betanzos's and Garcilaso's understanding of Cuzco as a puma or a human was completely metaphoric; only Sarmiento's erroneous conclusion that Sacsayhuaman represents the puma's head suggests that Cuzco has the shape of a puma. . . . As Rowe does not understand the metaphoric quality of the comparison, he completely misinterprets the element of symmetry in the metaphor which refers to the totality of Cuzco society. ("The Lion in the City," p. 239)

The northern Inca capital of Quito was guided by different spatial particulars, but its space was nonetheless centered on powerful modes of being from other realms of the vertical cosmos. Ricardo Descalzi, *La Réal audiencia de Quito claustro en los Andes* (Quito, 1978), recounts several versions of myths of the origins of Quito. In all of them, a rock of sacred origin (falling from heaven as a falling star or taken from the volcano of Cotopaxi as a heated stone) is thrown down from the heights of a mountaintop. The city of Quito is constructed where the heavenly stone lands (pp. 22–23).

176. Aveni, "The View from the Tropics," p. 275.

177. Ibid., p. 277. Responsibility for observing the lunar cycle and its tasks may have fallen more directly on inhabitants of one moiety of the capital's space than on the other, thus continuing the homology between kinds of space, kinds of being, and kinds of time.

178. Ibid.

179. Turner, "Liminality and the Performative Genres," p. 19. For an example of the ways in which the meaning of space pervades South American languages even at the level of grammatical structure, see Francisco Queixalos, "L'Orientation spatiale dans la grammaire sikuani," *JSAP* 71 (1985): 115–128.

CHAPTER FOUR

1. See the following articles, which appear in *ICA*, 42d Congress, Vol. 2 (Paris, 1976):Irving Goldman, "Time, Space, and Descent: The Cubeo Example," pp. 175–183; Mireille Guyot, "Structure et évolution chez les indiens bora et miraña, Amazonie colombienne," pp. 163–173; Patrice Bidou, "Naître et être Tatuyo," pp. 105–120; Pierre Y. Jacopin, "Quelques effets du temps mythologique," pp. 217–232; Stephen Hugh-Jones, "Like the Leaves on the Forest Floor: Space and Time in Barasana Ritual," pp. 205–215; Lux Vidal, "As Categorias de idade como sistema de classificação e controle demografico de grupos entre os Xikrin do Catete e de como são manipulados em diferentes contextos," pp. 361–367; Anthony Seeger, "Fixed Points on Arcs in Circles: The Temporal, Processual Aspect of Suya Space and Society," pp. 341–359; and Jean Lave, "Eastern Timbira Moiety Systems in Time and Space: A Complex Structure," pp. 309–321. See also Miguel Chase-Sardi, "Cosmovisión mak'a," *SA* 5 (1970): 239–246; Miguel Chase-Sardi, "La Concepción nivaklé del mundo," *SA* 7 (1970): pp. 121–141; and Herbert Baldus, "O Conceito do tempo entre os indios do Brasil," *RAM* 71 (1940): 87–94.

2. For considerations that unearth the temporal assumptions of moral existence and ethical judgment, see works as different as Stanley Hauerwas, *Truthfulness and Tragedy* (Notre Dame, Ind., 1977), which illustrates the effect of determined notions of memory, story, and history on moral decision, guilt, and moral reform; Lévi-Strauss, *The Origin of Table Manners*, which shows how images of cosmic periodicity, the proper relations of time and space, form the foundation for propriety in general (hygiene, etiquette) and good moral order in particular; and Peter Rigby, "Some Gogo Rituals of 'Purification': An Essay on Social and Moral Categories," in Edmund Leach, ed., *Dialectic in Practical Religion* (Cambridge, 1968).

3. Without some attention to the religious meanings attached to the symbolism of cosmic rhythms, investigators find it difficult to fathom the depth of a people's evaluation of their existence in time. According to Holmberg, for instance, since the Siriono possessed no time-reckoning calendar, their accounting of the passage of time was limited to the empirical observations that the dry season was distinct from the wet one and the day distinct from the night, and to identifying some eight positions of the sun during its daily round, as well as to vague references to past events (childhood, a good hunt). Holmberg, *Nomads of the Long Bow*, p. 48.

4. See the discussion concerning the different but coherent shapes of local history in Marshall Sahlins, *Islands of History* (Chicago, 1985). Charles M. Sherover, ed., *The Human Experience of Time: The Development of Its Philosophic Meaning* (New York, 1975), is both an anthology of essays about time in the Western philosophical tradition from Heraclitus to Minkowski and a less attractive argument (on Sherover's part) about the development of temporal consciousness and its relationship to the human experience of the world. The materiality of time was recognized early in the sociological studies by Marcel Mauss and Henri Beuchat, *Seasonal Variations of the Eskimo: A Study in Social Morphology*, trans. James J. Fox (Boston, 1979), researched between 1903 and 1905. This work influenced later studies of time, such as that contained in E. E. Evans-Pritchard's *The Nuer* (Oxford, 1940). See Godfrey Lienhardt, *Social Anthropology* (Oxford, 1964), pp. 44–51, for an account of the connection between Mauss and Evans-Pritchard. The insight of Mauss remained unnoticed, however, in regard to the material expressions of time and was treasured more for its analysis of the systemics of economics, productivity, and ecology as they impinge on complex social phenomena and vice versa. See the translator's foreword in Mauss and Beuchat, *Seasonal Variations*, esp. pp. 11ff. For a recent study of the materiality of the temporal structures of society, see Georges Condominas, *L'Espace social. A propos de l'Asie du Sud-Est* (Paris, 1980).

5. This argument is presented by Claude Lévi-Strauss, *The Savage Mind* (Chicago: University of Chicago Press, 1973), pp. 217–244 on "Time Regained," and pp. 245–269 on "History and Dialectic." On entirely different grounds, and to a different end, Mircea Eliade also argues for the contemporary need to confront the authentic notions of time found in "primitive" societies; see Eliade, *The Myth of the Eternal Return: Cosmos and History* (Princeton, 1974). See also Michel Meslin, *La Fête des kalendes de janvier, un rituel de nouvel an* (Brussels, 1970).

6. Johannes Fabian, *Time and the Other: How Anthropology Makes its Object* (New York, 1983), chronicles the uses of temporal constructs underlying ethnographic discourse. Fabian argues that they define and maintain hierarchical relations of political power and that "allochronic devices" even manipulate the ranked ontological status of investigators (living in the "here and now") and their subjects, the "others" who are denied an existence fully coeval in time (i.e., reality) with their academic interpreters. Peter Rigby, "Time and Historical Consciousness: The Case of Ilparakayo Maasai," *CSSH* 25 (1983): pp. 428–456, reviews and analyzes the treatment of time in ethnographic studies (see esp. pp. 428–441) and provides a helpful bibliography.

7. Wendell C. Bennett, "Numbers, Measures, Weights, and Calendars," in *HSAI*, vol. 5, pp. 601–610.

8. Bennett doubted that there was ever a very formalized concept of the month; ibid., p. 606.

9. Ibid., p. 607.

10. Gow and Condori, *Kay Pacha*, p. 82.

11. Ursula Wiesemann, "Time Distinctions in Kaingáng," *ZFE* 99 (1974): 121–123.

12. Ibid., p. 120.

13. Ibid., p. 129. Wiesemann points out, however, that once contact was made with Western cultures, which evaluated their experience in time by recounting "history," "the terminology was developed, partly by adopting words from the contact language and partly by developing new words by fusion" (ibid.). In short, just as economic needs that reshaped systems of value and behavior were created, so too existential needs were created calling for new modes of evaluating existence in time.

14. Maybury-Lewis, *Akwẽ-Shavante Society*, p. 156.

15. Ibid.

16. Ibid., p. 41.

17. Rego, "Mitos e ritos."

18. Civrieux, *Religión y magia kari'ña*, p. 29.
19. Whitten, *Sacha Runa*, p. 46.
20. Else Waag, *Tres entidades wekufu en la cultura mapuche* (Buenos Aires, 1982); Casamiquela, *Estudio del Nillatun; Miguel Angel Olivera*, "Mapuche Religion," in *EOR*.
21. Carol E. Robertson-DeCarbo, "Lukutún" p. 68.
22. Ibid., p. 77.
23. For a treatment of the role of primordial imagery and ritual experience as a basis for moral action, see Lawrence E. Sullivan, "Above, Below, or Far Away: Andean Cosmogony and Ethical Order," in Frank E. Reynolds and Robin W. Lovin, eds., *Cosmogony and Ethical Order: New Studies in Comparative Ethics* (Chicago, 1985), pp. 98–132.
24. Jean-Paul Dumont, "Not in Ourselves, But in Our Stars," in David L. Browman and Ronald A. Schwarz, eds., *Spirits, Shamans, and Stars: Perspectives from South America* (The Hague, 1979), p. 253.
25. Chapter 2 discusses the destruction of the hegemony of primordial symbols.
26. Gow and Condori, *Kay Pacha*, p. 5. The Andean calendar is a complex of autochthonous historical conceptions of time combined with ideas imported by conquerors, both Inca and Spanish. The various pantheons of divinities reveal a complicated range of modes of time. See the discussion of the ceremonial calendar of feasts associated with the goddess Pachamama in Mariscotti de Görlitz, *Pachamama Santa Tierra*, pp. 117–120. Details of Andean festivals, seen from the perspective of the cult of Pachamama, are recounted and their symbolism interpreted in ibid., pp. 149–189. For further consideration of the ancient Peruvian calendar, with special reference to the cult of the earth mother Pachamama, see Lucia Kill, *Pachamama: Die Erdgöttin in der Altandinen Religion* (Bonn, 1969), pp. 104–116.
27. Gow and Condori, *Kay Pacha*, p. 5.
28. Weiss, "World of a Forest Tribe," p. 318.
29. William C. Farabee, *Indian Tribes of Eastern Peru*, (Cambridge, Mass. 1922), p. 16; quoted in Weiss, "World of a Forest Tribe," p. 254.
30. Nimuendajú, *The Apinayé*, p. 139.
31. Several stars found in the Panare dry-season sky are named and considered related to one another. By contrast, the "lonely star" (Antares), the only named star of the rainy season, makes its isolated appearance after the disappearance of Sirius (the last of the named dry-season stars).
32. Dumont, "Not in Ourselves," p. 242.
33. Ibid., p. 243.
34. Ibid., p. 246.
35. See also the origin myths of star-cycles presented in chapter 2 of this work, which deals not only with incest associated with flood but with maiming, dismemberment, consumption, and slaying of game in conjunction with a celestial hunt.
36. Hernan Gallardo Moscoso, *Fisonomía de Loja: Paltas, Incas y Virachochas* (Loja, Ecuador, 1964), p. 40. The role of the predictable cycle of stars in discerning the tragic and ironic meanings of historical fate appears elsewhere in the Americas. The nature of the Mesoamerican divinity Quetzalcoatl highlights the function of star-based principles of predictability in grounding evaluations of the ironic and tragic character of historical time. See Carrasco, *Quetzalcoatl*, esp. pp. 148–204, in which Carrasco draws out the place of the divinity in the ironic histories of Mesoamerican empires. José López Portillo, Demetrio Sodi, and Fernando Diaz Infante, *Quetzalcoatl in Myth, Archeology and Art* (New York, 1982), esp. pp. 205–229, clarify the calendrical meanings of the tragedies associated with Quetzalcoatl, as do Laurette Séjourné, *El Pensamiento nahuatl cifrado por los calendarios* (Mexico City, 1981), passim, and Miguel Leon-Portilla, *The Broken Spears: Aztec Account of the Conquest of Mexico* (Boston, 1966).
37. Urton, *Crossroads of Earth and Sky*, p. 17.
38. It should be clear that "deliberately controlled sounds" are prescriptive. For example, [T]he *pichiko*, which—although I have often heard its distinctive call during the daytime—is *said* to call only at dawn and dusk. Thus, the sound of the *pichiko* is 'appropriate,' or recognized, only at these transitional (twilight) times" (Urton, ibid., p. 18).
39. Ibid., p. 31.
40. See also William P. Mitchell, "Irrigation Farming in the Andes: Evolutionary Implication,"

in Rhoda Halperin and James Dow, eds. *Peasant Livelihood* (New York, 1977), pp. 36–59, esp. pp. 52–53, which describes the use of drum and flute music during the feasts of the cleaning of irrigation canals at the opening of the rainy season. Cited in Urton, *Crossroads of Earth and Sky*, p. 31. For another description of the cleaning of the irrigation canals and cisterns, see Kill, *Pachamama* pp. 165ff.

41. Eva Krener and Niels Fock, "Good Luck and the Táita Carnaval of Cañar," *FO* 19–20 (1977–1978): 152, 156.

42. Walter J. Ong, S. J., "World as View and World as Event," *American Anthropologist* 71 (August 1969); p. 634.

43. Walter J. Ong, S. J., *The Presence of the Word* (New Haven, 1967), p. 112.

44. Ong, "World as View," p. 638.

45. Wright, "History and Religion of the Baniwa," p. 385.

46. Since the moon promotes growth, a Čwųl-Krō ceremony was celebrated by the Apinayé at the appearance of that new moon when plants first began to grow. See Nimuendajú, *The Apinayé*, pp. 89, 138.

47. Ibid., pp. 89–90. Women are especially attached to gourds. Human beings were created by the sun and the moon from bottle-gourds (*Lagenaria*); see ibid., p. 164.

48. Ibid., p. 90. Although it is true that, altogether, Nimuendajú spent almost eight months among the Apinayé, his research was spread over five different visits, ranging from one week to, at most, two months, over a ten-year period. It is understandable, then, that his picture of the annual cycle is incomplete (ibid., pp. 8, 15).

49. Lucrecia Vidal Arias, *Oro para el rescate: Costumbres, cuentos, anécdotas, supersticiones y leyendas de la Provincia de Pataz* (Lima, 1979), pp. 66–71.

50. Ibid., p. 68.

51. Ibid.

52. The connection of feasts to the fruit cycle allows Zerries to construct a culture-historical argument based upon the paleobotanical history of the fruit plants in question. The heart of Zerries' thesis is expressed already in one of his early reports, "Some Aspects of Waica Culture," *ICA*, 31st Congress (São Paulo, 1955), pp. 73–88. There Zerries points out that the Waica today are horticulturalists who mainly cultivate plaintains and bananas. When did this begin? He cannot be sure but supposes, along with Carl O. Sauer, that these plants came from southeast Asia.

> "Furthermore, it is of great interest that the Waica depend seasonally largely on the fruits of the peach palm (*Guilelma utilis*) and cultivate this tree by planting sprout cuttings, because the plant has lost the capacity to produce fertile seeds in many cases. The palm is said to be unknown in a truly wild state. But, unlike the plantain, the peach palm originated in South America itself, probably on the eastern side of the Andes in valleys of limited rainfall. The location of its cultivation may identify it with the proto-Arawak and proto-Chibcha areas as a quite old cultigen—according to Sauer's opinion [in "Cultivated Plants of South and Central America," *HSAI*, vol. 6, pp. 525–527]. In any case, the peach palm appears to be older in South America than the introduced plantain. . . . The *le ahuno* feast of the Waica is so directly connected with the peach palm . . . that it can be compared to the Guilelma palm feast which the Witoto celebrate during the harvest of this fruit. In my opinion, the peach or *pijiguao* palm, as it is more commonly named, has, in its uncultivated state already played a fundamental role in the past of Waica economic life, when the tribe lived only as hunters and gatherers, and was not familiar with the plantain tree. Although the plantain became afterwards the principal foodstuff of the Waica, the *pijiguao* palm maintains its outstanding position in the socio-religious life of the tribe. (ibid., p. 79).

Zerries further develops and refines this culture-historical hypothesis in *Waika: Die kulturgeschichtliche Stellung der Waika-Indianer des oberen Orinoco im Rahmen der Völkerkunde Südamerikas* (Munich, 1964), pp. 29–36 and pp. 53–84.

53. Weiss, "World of a Forest Tribe," p. 253.

54. Farabee, *Indian Tribes of Eastern Peru*, p. 16; cited in Weiss, "World of a Forest Tribe," p. 254.

55. See especially Lévi-Strauss, *The Raw and the Cooked.*

56. See chapter 2 for the ways in which the disappearance of primordial beings gave rise to the replicable orders of symbolic life.

57. See chapter 2 for a presentation of South American destructive scenarios creating marked times and spaces.

58. Urton, *Crossroads of Earth and Sky*, p. 32.

59. Dumont, "Not in Ourselves," p. 246.

60. Jürg Gasché, "Recherches ethnographiques dans les bassins des Rios Caqueta et Putumayo (Amazonie colombienne)," *JSAP* 58 (1969): p. 275. For a comparative discussion of the cycles of important feasts among the Tukano-speaking groups, and for a synthesis of their most prominent features, see Ute Bödiger, *Die Religion der Tukano in nordwestlichen Amazonas* (Cologne, 1965), pp. 59–65 and 161–188.

61. Civrieux, *Watunna*, p. 33.

62. Fock, *Waiwai*, pp. 49, 170.

63. Robertson-DeCarbo, "Lukutún" pp. 67-78. The ceremony may be called *Kamarrikún* in southeastern Neuguén.

64. Ibid., p. 71.

65. Ibid., p. 70.

66. Whitten, *Sacha Runa*, p. 173.

67. Ibid., p. 177. Such women's ceremonies, centered on crafts, are not uncommon. See, for example, Mircea Eliade, "History of Religions and 'Popular Cultures'" *HR* 20 (1980): 1–26.

68. Nimuendajú, *The Apinayé*, pp. 159–160.

69. Rego, "Mitos e ritos."

70. The episodic and processual structure of these rites conforms to the narrative structures of the divine drama. The festival opens with the ritual called Fogueira de Ayra, which is followed, the next day, by the rites of Ajèrè and Àkárá. The next episode is known as the "three days of Şàngó" (Éta Qdún Şàngó). On its heels comes a block of time called the "six days of Şàngó" (Éfà Qdún Şàngó). The closing day is given over to a procession in honor of Ìyá Mase. This is the way the festival is carried off in Bahia at Ase ợpợ Àfònjá, a place that maintains quite ancient forms of honoring Şàngó Àfònjá. See the treatments of this provided by Vivaldo da Costa Lima, *Uma Festa de Xangô no Opo Afonjá* (Salvador, Brazil, 1959), and Deoscoredes Maximiliano dos Santos, *Axé Opo Afonjá: Noticia histórica de um terreiro de santo da Bahia* (Rio de Janeiro, 1962).

71. When cultures reenact the sounds and acts of the primordium, they must do so in a creative way. Faithfulness to the "script" does not consist in the literal verbatim repetition of a text, as may be the case for written drama. As Dennis Tedlock writes,

> In an oral poetics, actual performance is not the imperfect realization of a playwright's lofty intentions by lowly actors, nor is it an incomplete obedience to the rules set forth in an imaginary mental handbook of the poetic act. Instead, if I may paraphrase Richard Bauman, performance is *constitutive* of verbal art, and each performance has the potential for making changes, large or small, in the constitution of future verbal art. (Tedlock, *The Spoken Word and the Work of Interpretation*, Philadelphia, 1983, pp. 16–17).

72. The catastrophic foundations of feasts extend beyond Amerindian cultures. For instance, the study of folkloric festivals held along the north coast of Brazil (especially in the areas of São Sebastião, Caraguatatuba, and Ubatuba) indicates that the cycle of feasts honoring the King of the Congo and Saints Benedict, Francis, Gonçalo, and Sebastião commemorate various disasters due to legendary attacks by enemies of the past or by destructions brought on by plague, earthquake, attacks of the devil, and so on. The festival music betrays an Afro-Brazilian structure. See Rossini Tavares de Lima, *Folclore do litoral norte de São Paulo* (Rio de Janeiro, 1981), a work that includes words and music notations of songs, descriptions of musical accompaniment, and detailed choreographic figures.

73. Civrieux, *Watunna*, p. 78.

74. Fock, *Waiwai*, p. 181.

75. Bennett, "Numbers, Measures, Weights, and Calendars," p. 605.

76. See the following works by R. T. Zuidema: "The Inca Calendar," in Aveni, ed., *Native*

American Astronomy, pp. 219–259; "El calendario inca," *ICA*, 36th Congress, Vol. 2 (Seville, 1966) pp. 25–30; "Kinship and Ancestor Cult in Three Peruvian Communities: Hernández Príncipe's Account in 1622," *Bulletin Institut Français des Études Andines* (Lima) 2 (1973); 16–33; "Calendars: South American Calendars," in *EOR*.

77. Joseph H. Howard, *Drums of the Americas* (New York, 1970), writes, "If the variety of instrumental types and skillful fabrication sufficiently index their musical cultures, then the Incas outstripped any of the aboriginal groups of Mexico and Central America" (p. 70).

78. Juan M. Ossio, "The Idea of History in Felipe Guamán Poma de Ayala" (Bachelor of Letters thesis, Oxford University, 1970). Ossio remarks on the intimate relationship between time and space in the Inca cosmology. They are, in fact, both expressions of one another:

> The most outstanding feature about these ages is that they are ordered in a quinquipartite structure, . . . conceiving the past as the succession of four "suns" whereas the present was being illuminated by a fifth one. This fixed character of the "suns" is also shared by the years of duration for the period in between them which are given in the form of a round number. (p. 198)

This fivefold quality of being finds expression not only in the five cosmic ages and in the conditions of space in the universe (the four quarters and the center), but also

> this quinquepartite organization seems to have been operating with the Inca Society. This fact leads Zuidema to derive a model by which he tries to explain the Inca ideas about kinship, social organization and hierarchy, military organization, ancestral, religious, and cosmological systems, their Calendar System, and History. This model, according to Zuidema, was expressed in the form of a man representing a marriage from whom descended one patriline of four men only and one matriline of four women only. . . . [F]or any individual there always were four generations of ancestors, and it is this type of organization which seems to have been projected onto the arrangement of the Five Ages of the World, where the living generations were eternally placed within a Fifth Age. . . . Guamán Poma was still dominated by an idea of eternal time whose structure was deeply embedded in Andean thought. (pp. 202–203)

For a description of the temporal epochs as they were systematized in the post-conquest Andes, see Ossio, "Guamán Poma: Nueva corónica o carta al rey," pp. 155–213. The matter of Guaman Poma's history is taken up again in chapter 8 of the present work.

79. Zuidema, "El Calendario Inca," pp. 25–30.

80. See the detailed and closely argued presentation in Zuidema, "The Inca Calendar." As usual, Zuidema examines the fine details coming from a large number of colonial chronicles and subsequent reports. His argument carefully sifts and accumulates tiny pieces of evidence that are geographical, social, astronomic, mathematical, artistic, historical, and linguistic in nature.

81. For the degree to which Inca individual and social life was constituted by multiple time scales, including the number of epochs (punctuated by cosmic destructions) of the entire universe, periodicities manifested by the two moieties, the decimal organization of the population, the genealogy of royal Incas, the divisions of historical time and the time of various tasks of labor, and so on, see Zuidema, *The Ceque System*, pp. 228ff.

82. The Raymi feasts exemplify the tenacity of the modes of calendrical time that constitute culture. The feast of Inti Raymi was abolished in 1572 by Viceroy Don Francisco Toledo. Faustino Espinoza Navarro, *Guión para la escenificación del "Inti Raymi" en la ciudad sagrada de los Inkas* (Cuzco, Peru, 1977), recounts the history of the feast, the contemporary program of its activities, and its revival in 1944. Today "its production is the responsibility of . . . Cusco school children and the Infantry Battalion No. 9" (p. 54), who perform it on the esplanade of the fortress of Sajsay Waman. The author directed the festival for fourteen years in Cuzco and one year in Lima.

83. This is why Bennett's restriction of calendars to the Andes is overly narrow. It does not help in understanding the temporal existence of other South American peoples. The Kógi calendar, for instance, is based on observation of the solstices and equinoxes, that is, the times when the

sun "is in his house," "going out the door," or "taking a walk" (as well as other terms indicating precise positions of the sun during the course of the year). The calendar is marked off into eighteen months of twenty days each, and the year begins with the spring equinox. The episodes of the year are broken into the times when different constellations appear on the horizon at dawn. Only the *mamas*, the specialized priests, have full knowledge of the calendar, which information is considered to be highly secret. It is interesting to note that the calculation of time and its meaning should be kept enclosed. See Reichel-Dolmatoff, "Los Kogi," part 1, pp. 254f. Even keeping in mind Bennett's distinction between simple time divisions and true calendrical systems, it appears he underestimated the possibility of intercalating symbolic orders and codes that are more than mathematical abstractions (e.g., sounds, foliage, winds, rainbows, social structures). See Anthony F. Aveni and Gordon Brotherston, eds., *Calendars in Mesoamerica and Peru: Native American Computations of Time* (Manchester and Oxford, 1983), and also Guillermo Illescas Cook, *Astrónomos en el antiguo Peru: Sobre los conocimientos astronómicos de los antiguos pueblos del Peru* (Lima, 1976).

84. Maybury-Lewis, *Akwẽ-Shavante Society*, p. 48.

85. Ibid., p. 17. For a description of the way in which Krĩkatí rites enfold various marked periods and cycles in time, including the annual calendar, the dry and rainy seasons, the life cycle of humans, the structures of social and ecological time, and the units of time within day and night, see Jean Carter Lave, "Trends and Cycles in Krĩkatí Naming Practices," in Maybury-Lewis, ed., *Dialectical Societies*, pp. 16–44. Other kinds of conditions are also interwoven into the ritual cycles and, therefore, temporalized calendrically. They include sonic structures of names and the symbolic codes of moisture and dryness (a "ripe" child, i.e., a child who is ready to receive a name, is considered "moist"). Light is also made subject to proper time, brought onto a cycle, and therefore made available for coordination with other conditions of being. The Akwẽ-Shavante and Krĩkatí cases demonstrate that a lack of historicist interest can accompany a great sensitivity to the quality, tone, importance and evaluation of time. Chronological history, then, proves to be only one way of living in time. The issue was taken up some time ago in A. I. Hallowell, "Temporal Orientations in Western Civilization and in a Preliterate Society," *AA* 39 (1937): 647–670.

86. Nimuendajú, *The Apinayé*, p. 134.

87. Ibid.

88. Clastres, *Chronique des indiens guayakí*, p. 163.

89. Ibid., p. 174.

90. Ibid., pp. 163–164. See also Manuela Carneiro da Cunha and Eduardo B. Viveiros de Castro, "Vingança e temporalidade," *JSAP* 71 (1985): 191–208.

91. Rego, "Mitos e ritos." Afro-Brazilian calendars allow for adaptation to change. For a discussion of the variety of ways in which structures of time allowed blacks from Africa to relocate themselves in the ecology and society of the New World by variously incorporating seasonal and festival cycles of many sorts, see Bastide. *African Religions of Brazil*, pp. 272–277. Dance, music, song, ritual gesture, manipulation of spatial areas, and the presence or absence of vegetal and animal substances help "localize ceremonies linked to a certain rhythm of nature and society in a country having different seasonal rhythm" and represent "the synchronization of the Christian and Yoruba time frames" (ibid., p. 274).

92. Bartolomé, "Shamanism Among the Avá-Chiripá," p. 137.

93. Whitten, *Sacha Runa*, p. 167.

94. Karsten, *Toba Indians*, p. 60.

95. Ibid., pp. 106ff.

96. Ibid., p. 61.

97. Hans Buechler, *The Masked Media: Aymara Fiestas and Social Integration in the Bolivian Highlands* (The Hague, 1980), pp. 358–359. In Irpa Chico, a highland community some thirty kilometers south of La Paz, there exists a complex cycle of many wind instruments (including the *tarka, pinquillo, llaquita, kena-kena, chokela, julu julu, waca waca, chuncho, llano, sicuri,* and *pusi p'iya*), whose performance is coordinated with seasons of the year, points in the life-cycle, and the timing of specific dances (ibid.).

98. For a description of a calendar in a contemporary Andean community, see Ossio, "El

Simbolismo del agua," especially the schematic presentations on pp. 390–395. Note that different forms of water (blood, semen, primordial floodwaters, etc.) are particularly important temporal expressions of being. For a detailed description of the current festival calendar in the contemporary Quechua-speaking community of Otavalo (Iambabura Province), Ecuador, see Anibal Buitron, Táita imbabura: Vida indígena en los Andes (La Paz, Bolivia, 1964), pp. 69–76. Replete with dances, music, and ritual battles, the calendar and its symbolic actions, in the opinion of Buitron, has maintained itself intact in the face of hundreds of years of foreign influence.

99. B. J. Isbell, *To Defend Ourselves*, pp. 137–145. According to Isbell, "the condor is one of the mediators between the Real World (Kay Pacha) and the Upper World (Hanan Pacha)" (p. 214). I have already alluded above to the *pingullo* fashioned from a condor bone and played in the community at Juncal in the highlands of southern Ecuador. A mythic being first played the condor-bone instrument to open mountains in the upperworld in order to distribute goods contained there to the people in the human world; See Krener and Fock, "Good Luck," pp. 152, 156. In the community of Chuschi, a different set of musical instruments, the *waqrapuku*s (trumpets fashioned from coiled cattle horns), mark the formal drinking ceremonies of the harvest festival, the feast of Santa Cruz held in early May (ibid., pp. 145–151).

100. Zuidema, "Calendars: South American Calendars."

101. Clastres, *Chronique* p. 168.

102. Boglár, "Creative Process in Ritual Art."

103. Weiss, "World of a Forest Tribe," p. 470.

104. Jonathan Hill, "Kamayurá Flute Music," *ETM* 23 (1979); 429. The same argument may be made for dance. For a careful analysis, in great choreographic detail, of Kamayurá dances, especially those performed in connection with the cycle of the Kwaríp ceremonies, see Pedro Agostinho, *Kwaríp: Mito e ritual no alto Xingu* (São Paulo, 1974), pp. 109–34. Agostinho considers these dances a kind of symbolic language, a generative form of communication which takes place at Murena, the center of the world. Dances are the actions of those beings who existed at the beginning of time, the time when the first Kwaríp was celebrated. These are the symbolic acts which generated the structures of the social and cosmic universe.

105. Whitten, *Sacha Runa*, p. 51.

106. Wagley, *Welcome of Tears*, p. 215.

107. Ibid., pp. 213–214.

108. Reports of sacred songs having unintelligible lyrics are common. The experience has vexed investigators who care to ascertain the meaning of songs. See, for instance, references to Siriono song in Holmberg, *Nomads of the Long Bow*, p. 38.

109. Basso, "A 'Musical View of the Universe,'" p. 288.

110. Ibid. On *itolotepïgï* ("birding"), see Basso's book *A Musical View of the Universe*, appendix 3 and pp. 245–246, 305, and 308.

111. Basso, "A 'Musical View of the Universe,'" p. 288. Regarding the *itseke*, see Basso, *A Musical View of the Universe*, pp. 69–71, 248, 252f.

112. Lawrence E. Sullivan, "Sound and Senses: Toward a Hermeneutics of Performance," *HR* 26 (1986); 1–33, uses examples of sacred sound to probe the quality of knowledge underlying performance and setting it apart from behavior.

113. Civrieux, *Watunna*, p. 12. Young men and women are initiated in separate moments of this festival: "there is an exclusively female portion of the *Adahe ademi hidi*, taking place several months after the initial [phase at which boys are initiated] just before the rains at the end of March" (p. 16).

114. Ibid., p. 13.

115. Ibid., pp. 132–137.

116. Ibid., pp. 136–137. In the absolute beginning of creation, heaven and earth were indistinct from one another; they were the same realm until darkness flooded the earth and the true light of the sky withdrew on high. The two realms were connected by the unique tree-mountain Marahuaka, the "little gourd" that grew from a splinter stolen from the unique "tree of life" located in the center of heaven. Now, in this moving world, the ephemeral forms of water, chaos, and flood (i.e., the *symbols* of the water domain, viz., the visible rainbow) connect this world with the world above.

117. A variation of the origin myth of the great Makiritare garden festival is associated with the adventures of the supernatural twins. It replaces the retrieving function of song with the instrument of dream. For some time, the twins had been separated on account of an argument concerning the younger one's wife. The festival is said to be modeled on the occasion of their reconciliation and reunion (Civrieux, Watunna, p. 78). It was for this feast of reconciliation that vegetal food first came into existence: "Iureke [the younger of the twins] just sat there thinking in silence. . . . [H]e was sitting, thinking, dreaming food. . . . [N]ow food [trees, fruit, gardens] sprang up there, when Iureke dreamed it" (ibid.). For a consideration of the ways in which the images of song and dream merge in human existence, see chapter 5 of this work.

118. Civrieux, *Religion y magia kari'ña*, p. 15.

119. Ibid., p. 38.

120. Ibid., p. 29.

121. Ibid.

122. Calendars that incorporate diverse cycles of sounds, stars, and species rhythms of breeding, birth, and bodily change are widespread, complicated, and culturally rich in their expressions. Urton has described such a calendar for the Andean community of Misminay in *Crossroads of Earth and Sky*. Jonathan Hill, "Wakuenai Society: A Processual Structural Analysis of Indigenous Cultural Life in the Rio Negro (Guainía) Region of Venezuela" (Ph.D. diss., University of Indiana, 1983), emphasizing the metaperformative role of festival sounds, reports the existence of a similar calendar among the Wakuenai:

> The *molitu* frog is referred to as one of Kaali's [the mythical originator of cultivated crops] children (*kaalieni*) and is also the name of an important musical instrument played in *kwepani* ceremonies [held in order to play flutes made from the body of the hero Kuwai and to exchange fruit]. The high-pitched singing of the *molitu* frogs provided the Wakuenai with a year-round schedule for agricultural activities. It sings in September and October, "telling" the men to go cut new gardens. It stops singing in November and does not start up again until late March and April, when it is believed to tell people to go burn and plant in the gardens. It stops singing during the heavy rains of late April and May until the slightly drier months of June and July when it is interpreted as telling people to go weed and clean their gardens. In August, the *molitu* frogs stop singing until the beginning of the short dry season in middle or late September. According to traditional beliefs, when people work in synchrony with the "orders" of Kaali's sons, their agricultural activities proceed smoothly and quickly, but if they ignore the mythical calendar of the *molitu* frog's singing their labor is slow and difficult. (pp. 53–54)

The Wakuenai coordinate the cycle of *molitu* frog songs with the movements of some constellations, river water levels, weather patterns, and economic tasks. The *molitu* flute may be modulated to produce the phonemes of speech. It is used by players to pronounce other men's names so as to hide their identity from overhearing women. Ironically, once a man masters the calendric sounds of the flute (i.e., once he can successfully disguise his identity while "speaking" through the flute), he may serve as a diviner whose words are invariably true.

123. Robertson-DeCarbo, "Lukutún," p. 70.

124. Ibid.

125. Carol E. Robertson, "'Pulling the Ancestors': Performance, Practice and Praxis in Mapuche Ordering," *ETM* 2 (September 1979): 395–416. Robertson contends that the *tayil* consists of four episodic "tenses," consisting of temporal worlds set one atop the other. During the performance one ascends to the top of the temporal heights, to the time of origins and mythic beings. One breaks through, or ruptures, the plane between temporal worlds by performing certain "time-crossing tones" (p. 409).

126. Ibid., p. 408.

127. Ibid., p. 407.

128. Wright, "History and Religion of the Baniwa," passim. The phenomenon is not limited to South America. The aboriginal Australian celebrations of the Kunapipi (Gunabibi) rites, to cite only one example from elsewhere, bear some fundamental resemblances to the performances in the northwestern Amazon. In particular, in northeastern Arnhem Land, the Dua moiety members reenact the Djanggau (Djanggawul) mytho-ritual cycle. During these rites, *rangga*,

sacred posts decorated with ochred designs and feathers, attract the deity, who temporarily occupies them during the rites. The *rangga* are carried to a special hut, representing the uteri that once held all the first unborn children inside the two primordial sisters. There the *rangga* revitalize all aspects of nature. See William Lloyd Warner, *A Black Civilization: A Study of an Australian Tribe* (New York, 1964), pp. 238–281, and Ronald M. Berndt, *Kunapipi* (Melbourne, 1951).

129. For a discussion of the place of music and instruments in negotiating connections and separations of the sexualized spaces and shapes of the universe, see K. A. Gourlay, "Sound-producing Instruments in Traditional Society: A Study of Esoteric Instruments and their Role in Male-Female Relations," *New Guinea Research Bulletin* (Canberra), 60 (1975): vii–133.

130. Hugh-Jones, *The Palm and the Pleiades*, pp. 265–266. Barasana men, the only ones allowed to play the instruments, "menstruate" when they play the trumpets at initiation periods. This opens them, enabling them to give birth to a new generation of their patriline. The Barasana attribute similar ideas to the Cubeo and Siriano (p. 265). See also Fulop, "Aspectos:Mitología," p. 366.

131. Jacopin, *La Parole generative*, p. 120, n. 8.

132. Ibid., pp. 132ff. The dance is an imitation of the first dance, which the hero shared with cranes and an anaconda. The homology of drum, house, and world, which is established through the symbolism of sound emitted by similarly structured spatial images, is noted elsewhere as well. The Catuquinaru used an idiophone plank- or hollow-log–drum, the latter consisting of a partially filled earth pit "into which a hollow trunk of hard palm wood is placed on end and partially filled with many different things. A small space is left empty in the center of the trunk—the pit and the upper end of the trunk are covered with a slab of hard rubber or rawhide which is struck with a large club" (Howard, *Drums in the Americas*, p. 79; includes a diagram of the Catuquinaru drum). See also Karl Gustav Izikowitz, *Musical and Other Sound Instruments of the South American Indians* (Göteborg, 1935), p. 14.

133. See the fascinating interpretations of the nature of myth in Jacopin, *La Parole generative*, pp. 165–370.

134. *Maloca* cultures are not the only ones to model their calendrical feasts after the creative pilgrimages of primordial divinities and heroes. The wandering of primordials through space serves as the model for human ritual processes through time even in the urban societies of the Andes. For example, after bringing forth the sun on the island of Titicaca, Viracocha, the Inca creator god, travelled along the Andean ridge to the region of present-day Ecuador, from which he turned to head out into the ocean. In the course of his travels near Cuzco, Viracocha made his way along the Villcanota River. As a consequence, during the periods of the solstices the citizens of Cuzco processed out of the city on their two most important calendric pilgrimages. These pilgrimages out of the city were coordinated in the same moment with the arrival of *acllas* ("chosen ones," elected as victims for sacrifice), who travelled in a straight line from their home communities to the center of Cuzco, where they presented themselves as potential victims for *capac hucha*, "the obligation to the king." By these direct comings and goings in June and December, the citizens of Cuzco not only recreated the creative travel of Viracocha, but, by returning to the moments and movements of their own origins, they knit together the Andean structures of time and space into a calendar. See Zuidema, "Calendars: South American Calendars." Zuidema here relies on Maria Rostworowski Diez de Canseco and Pierre Duviols. See also Michael Sallnow, "La Peregrinación andina," *Allpanchis Phuturinqa* 7 (1974): 101–142. We look forward to the publication of Deborah A. Poole, "Rituals of Movement, Rites of Transformation: Pilgrimage and Dance in the Highlands of Peru," in *Latin American Pilgrimage*, eds. N. Ross Crumrine and E. Alan Morinis (in press).

135. Each seasonal feast not only takes place in a season of the calendar but, because it is a ritual, celebrates the origin of at least one other time line as well. Along with the process, item, or social unit that appeared for the first time (manioc, puberty, house or residence group, sun, lineage), a mythic event celebrates the *kind* of time which came into existence with it (e.g., crop-cycles, adolescence, generation, affinal alliances, day, descent). Each feast becomes remarkable; that is, it not only celebrates a successive point in the passing year but marks once again the discovery, invention, or recognition of a wholly different kind of time (i.e., a mode of

being with a concomitant set of relations). Each feast is a unique time consisting of all the temporal qualities and relations which are indispensable to one another.

136. Herbert Baldus, "As Danças dos Tapirapé," *ICA*, 31st Congress (São Paulo, 1955), p. 93.

137. Pierre Verger, "Relations commerciales et culturelles entre le Brésil et le Golfe du Bénin," *JSAP* 53 (1969): pp. 31–56, esp. pp. 39–44.

138. K. J. Hye-Kerkdal, "Tanz als soziale Funktion bei den Timbira Brasiliens," *ICA*, 32d Congress (Copenhagen, 1958), pp. 263–270. For a description of the Timbira calendar as a coordinated system of transfigurations of relationships (past to present, family to family, in-group to out-group, individual to individual, one condition of the individual to another), see Julio Cezar Melatti, *Ritos de uma tribo timbira* (São Paulo, 1978), passim, esp. pp. 345–360. In connection with the power of dance to coordinate seasons, fruits, colors, sounds, and labor, see the description of Yanoama ritual dance in Otto Zerries and Meinhard Schuster, *Mahekodotedi. Monographie eines Dorfes der Waika-Indianer (Yanoama) am oberen Orinoco (Venezuela)*. Ergebnisse der Frobenius-Expedition 1954/55 Nach Südost-Venezuela, vol. 2 (Munich, 1974), p. 94.

139. Nimuendajú, *Mitos de Creación*, p. 99.

140. Ibid., p. 95.

141. See n. 15, by Juan Francisco Recalde, ibid. The affinities between prayer and dance are reflected linguistically as well; for example, the word *ieroky*, means "prayer" among the Guaralu of Bolivia but "dance" in Paraguay.

142. Fock, *Waiwai*, p. 170.

143. The background of destruction, violence, change, and contrast between "before" and "after" states of being accounts for the frequently oppositional structure of calendric dances. The oppugnant nature of festive dance takes many forms: paired partners, dancing teams, contests, serial divisions of squads of dancers (by age, by sex), and so on. Often, there is an ironic contrast between the stated reasons for actions and the action themselves, whose symbolism implies contestation and opposition. For example, there are several important categories of nocturnal dances performed by Toba men alone or with a few elderly women who, like the men, possess guardian spirits. These dances, which heighten the opposition between men and women, are said to protect and honor women, who are the only persons in Toba society to be formally initiated. In fact, the dances imply a combat with a supernatural being known as Nahót, an evil spirit (in the Mataco language from which people the dance is borrowed). In *nahotti*, ring dances, men hold hands and encircle the women who are to be protected from evil (Karsten, *Toba Indians*, p. 64). Dances often achieve stated goals of unity by heightening opposition in various ways: separation, stylized combat, alternation. For a discussion of the nature of polarities and contradictions between states of being, especially the contrast between "reality" and "unreality" in regard to animals, supernaturals, humans, and other discreet categories conjoined in festivals among the Cashinahua, see Kenneth Kensinger et al., *The Cashinahua of Eastern Peru* (Providence, 1975), pp. 18–23.

144. Luis Millones S. G., "Un Movimiento nativista del siglo XVI: El Taki Onqoy," and "Nuevos aspectos del Taki Onqoy," in Ossio, ed., *Ideología Mesiánica*, pp. 85–94 and 97–101, respectively; on Obera see Métraux, "Messies indiens," in his *Religions et magies*, esp. pp. 23–27. See chapter 8, below, on the Taki Ongo movement

145. Boglár, "Creative Process in Ritual Art."

146. Izikowitz, *Musical and Other Sound Instruments*, p. 109. For detailed descriptions of the symbolism of Boróro musical instruments and their religious meaning, see Albisetti and Venturelli, *Enciclopédia Boróro*, vol. 1, *Vocabularios e etnografía* (Campo Grande, Brazil, 1962), pp. 47–63. In general, the Boróro showed an extraordinary interest in precision in vocal and instrumental music. They manifest a deep concern for "impeccable execution," especially as regards tuning, pitch, and rhythm in large ensembles (ibid., p. 62).

147. Rafael Karsten, "Indian Tribes of the Argentine and Bolivian Chaco," *SSFCHL* 4 (1932): 159. The Mataco ceremony designed to hurry the ripening of *algaroba* fruit took its origin from the behavior of Icanchu, one of the birds surviving the cosmic fire. Actually, Icanchu had been burned to death, but when his cadaver passed through fire it was transformed into a bird that danced and danced, pounding away on a piece of charcoal left over from the destruction. His dancing and playing gave strength to the tree at the center of the world, which sprouted by

degrees and gave birth to every form of plant. See Alicia M. Barabás and Miguel A. Bartolomé, "Un Testimonio mítico de los Mataco," *JSAP* 66 (1979): 127. Destruction and regeneration are part of the same sacred drama reenacted in festival music.

148. Alfred Métraux, "Religion and Shamanism," in *HSAI*, vol. 5, p. 584.

149. Anya Peterson Royce, *The Anthropology of Dance* (Bloomington, Ind. 1977), p. 163. Cited in Stanley H. Brandes, "Dance as Metaphor: A Case from Tzintzuntzan, Mexico," *JLAL* 5 (1979): 25–43.

150. Brandes, ibid., p. 25

151. Some investigators have explored the possibility that ritual dance also serves as a paradigm for physical existence in time. For example, Marcel Mauss suggested the possbility that even bodily gestures are the cultural-historical residue of collective rituals; see Mauss, "Les Techniques du corps," in Claude Lévi-Strauss, ed., *Marcel Mauss:Sociologie et anthropologie* (Paris, 1966), pp. 365–386. Alan Lomax has put forward similar hypotheses connecting dance and the gestures of everyday life in *Folk Song Style and Culture* (New York, 1968), p. xv. However, he reverses the emphasis so that ritual movement reinforces cultural patterns of daily gesture. See, however, the criticism of Lomax in Adrienne Kaeppler, "Dance in Anthropological Perspective," *Annual Review of Anthropology* 7 (1978): 31–49.

152. The word "figure" is not used casually. It carries the weight of meaning given it in Dario Zadra, *Tempo simbólico: Liturgia della vita* (Brescia, Italy, 1985) where *figura* is a recurrent rhythmic movement of religious time that repeats in ritual form an original and central temporal structure. The performance of a *figura*, for Zadra, is both a memorial to and an anamnesis of the foundational intention that binds one to existence in time. Also see Zadra's "Victor Turner's Theory of Religion: Toward an Analysis of Symbolic Time," in Reynolds and Moore, eds. *Anthropology and the Study of Religion* (Chicago, 1984), pp. 77–104, especially those sections in which Zadra discusses the "mental character of the symbolic performance" (p. 89), the "function of awareness" (pp. 90–91) and "performance and epigenesis" (pp. 95–103).

153. See Bateson's essay on style and grace in *Steps to An Ecology of Mind*.

154. Herbert Baldus, "Some Aspects of Tapirapé Morals," in Vergilius Ferm, ed., *Encyclopedia of Morals* (New York, 1956), p. 607.

155. Karl Gustav Izikowitz, "Rhythmical Aspects of Canella Life," *ICA*, 31st Congress, (São Paulo, 1955), p. 195. Izikowitz refers not only to the obvious temporal rhythms of seasons, stars, and life cycles but also to the structural rhythms of social organization itself (the age classes, the moieties, the marriage alliances and kinship structures), as well as to the temporal manifestations of supernatural entities.

156. Ibid., pp. 208–209.

157. Whitten, *Sacha Runa*, p. 46.

158. This is intended in the sense put forward by Georg Gurvitch, *The Spectrum of Social Time* (Dordrecht, 1964), whose analysis is fuller than that contained in Evans-Pritchard's chapter on "social time" in *The Nuer*. Evans-Pritchard's influential essay may be considered a detailed affirmation of one small part of the project outlined by Gurvitch. Regarding intercalations of cultural constructions of times revealed in cosmic appearances (rain, various crops, drought, breeding cycles), see Harold C. Conklin, *Ethnographic Atlas of Ifugao: A Study of Environment, Culture and Society in Northern Luzon* (New Haven, 1980), as well as Conklin's other works (cited in the bibliography to *Ethnographic Atlas*) on systems of shifting cultivation, ethnobotany, and folk taxonomies. See also Eviatar Zerubavel, *Hidden Rhythms: Schedules and Calendars in Social Life* (Chicago 1981), and Paul Bauschatz, *The Well and the Tree: World and Time in Early Germanic Culture* (Amherst, Mass., 1982).

159. Clastres, *Chronique des indiens guayakí*, p. 165.

160. In particular, the custom of naming, orchestrated by the mother-to-be, enlarges the circle of relations to includes "strangers" who hunt game for the pregnant mother. The mother names her child after the preferred game, thus drawing into a tightly knit circle of relations the unrelated hunter of the name-game.

161. Maybury-Lewis, *Akwé-Shavante Society*, p. 156.

162. See the presentation of kinship terms by Wagley, *Welcome of Tears*, pp. 313–315, which is based on Baldus, *Tapirapé* p. 308, and on Judith Shapiro, "Tapirapé Kinship," *BMPEG* 37 (1968):

1–20. For the examination of the role of myth in revealing the nature of time involved in the following articles in *ICA*, 42d Congress, vol. 2 (Paris, 1977): descent, lineage, and generation, see Irving Goldman, "Time, Space, and Descent," pp. 175–183; Stephen Hugh-Jones, "Like the Leaves on the Forest Floor . . . Space and Time in Barasana Ritual," pp. 205–216; and Christine Hugh-Jones, "Skin and Soul," pp. 185–204. Barbara Bradby, "'Resistance to Capitalism' in the Peruvian Andes," in David Lehman, ed., *Ecology and Exchange*, pp. 97–122, treats kinship as the social memory of exchange relations (p. 113) and studies the effect of time on exchange (p. 115), especially the relationship between qualities of time and the impersonality of exchange (p. 115).

163. Wagley, *Welcome of Tears*, pp. 101–102, 104. See the various interpretations of this organization in Baldus, *Tapirapé* pp. 320f., and Shapiro, "Tapirapé Kinship," p. 26.

164. Wagley, *Welcome of Tears*, p. 108. These masks represent spirits (*anchunga*) or spirits of slain enemies (*upé*) (p. 110). The divisions of the Bird Societies also serve as competitive teams in collective labor and hunting (p. 112). See the descriptions of Bird Society feasts, ibid., pp. 62–63.

165. Ibid., pp. 115–117.

166. Bartolomé, "Shamanism Among the Avá-Chiripá," p. 138.

167. Gow and Condori, *Kay Pacha*, p. 83. *Apu* is a title meaning "great lord" and may refer to a high judge, first chief, or king as well as to the indigenous divinity of a mountain. *Apu* can also be the mountain, the community, or its residence space. All of these are symbolic expressions of a particular *apu*'s supernatural power. See Zuidema, *The Ceque System of Cuzco*, p. 87; Isbell, *To Defend Ourselves*, pp. 67, 74–76; Sharon, *Wizard*, pp. 60, 76–80; Bastien, *Mountain of the Condor*, passim.

168. Gow and Condori, *Kay Pacha*, p. 83.

169. Ibid., p. 84.

170. Ibid., p. 85.

171. Alexander Marshack, *The Roots of Civilization: The Cognitive Beginnings of Man's First Art, Symbol and Notation* (New York, 1972), discusses the concept of suddenness as an obstacle to understanding in cultural and historical sciences:

> Searching through the historical record for the origins of the evolved civilizations, I was disturbed by the series of "suddenlies." Science, that is, formal science, had begun "suddenly" with the Greeks; in a less philosophically coherent way, bits of near-science, mathematics and astronomy, had appeared "suddenly" among the Mesopotamians, the Egyptians, the early Chinese, and much later, in the Americas. . . . [A]griculture, the economic base of all the evolved civilizations, had apparently begun "suddenly" some ten thousand years ago with a relatively short period of incipience. . . . [T]he calendar had begun "suddenly" with agriculture. . . . Coming fresh to the archaeological evidence and interpretations, and asking new questions, I now felt uneasy about the "suddenlies." . . . Art, agriculture, science, mathematics, astronomy, the calendar, writing, the growth of cities — these things that make up civilization — could not, it seemed to me, have happened 'suddenly.' (pp. 11–12)

172. Lawrence E. Sullivan, "Astral Myths Rise Again: Interpreting Religious Astronomy," *Criterion* (Winter 1983): 12–17, explores the way in which predominantly astronomic calendars depend upon other symbolic evaluations of time and the ways in which these multiple modes of time are drawn together by religious symbolism.

173. This is the argument made in Dell Hymes, *"In Vain I Tried to Tell You": Essay in Native American Ethnopoetics* (Philadelphia, 1981), p. 81ff. Hymes develops an earlier analysis of content and style of oral delivery made in Melville Jacobs, *The Content and Style of an Oral Literature: Clackamas Chinook Myths and Tales* (Chicago, 1959), p. 7.

174. Hymes, *In Vain I Tried"*, p. 81.

175. Fock, *Waiwai*, p. 169. This remark, together with the celebration of this feast in the light of the new moon, draws it into comparison with Shipibo, River Campa, Canelos Quichua, and Cubeo drinking festivals. But there is a long and steady testimony to the religiosity of drinking festivals. In 1845, for example, Ignacio Domeyko reported that the principal festival honoring

the supreme being Pillán, the creator of the Araucanians, was a drinking festival in which people joined together, offered sacrifices, and "got themselves drunk with profane screaming and howling" in such a way as to drive away the rainstorms which threatened the harvest. Ignacio Domeyko, *Araucanía y sus habitantes: Recuerdos de un viaje hecho en las provincias meridionales de Chile* (Buenos Aires, 1971), pp. 131ff.

176. Fock, *Waiwai*, p. 177.

177. Whitten, *Sacha Runa*, pp. 165–167.

178. Ibid., p. 167.

179. Ibid., p. 180.

180. Ibid., p. 191. For detailed descriptions of the importance of symbolic drinking in the Jiña festival of the Yagua people, the best source is Esther Powlison and Paul Powlison, *La Fiesta yagua, Jiña: Una Rica herencia cultural*, trans. Hilda Berger (Lima, 1976), pp. 17–25 and passim. See also Gunther Tessman, *Die Indianer Nordost-Perus, Grundlegende Forschungen für systematische Kulturkunde* (Hamburg, 1930), p. 468. Rafael Girard, *Índios selváticos de la Amazonía peruana* (Mexico City, 1958), pp. 41–44, provides some observations of the drinking festival, and Bertrand Flornoy, *Iawa, le peuple libre* (Paris, 1953), p. 113, mentions the connection of this drinking feast to girls' initiation, the killing of animals in a ritual hunt, and the performance of a rather complicated musical "concert" (pp. 137–140) with serpentine dances and snake-songs. As is the case with many rituals, drinking feasts can symbolically heighten the sexual division of labor. Siriono women, for example, maintain separate drinking feasts for themselves in which song is the principal element (Holmberg, *Nomads of the Long Bow*, p. 38). Much needed in South America studies are investigations like Caroline Walker Bynum's *Holy Feast and Holy Fast: The Religious Significance of Food to Medieval Women* (Berkeley, 1987). On pages 190–193 and 221–227, for example, Bynum shows how women's control of food in sacred feasts and festivals is a source of personal and social creativity.

181. The propensity of South American cultures to celebrate their feasts by drinking fermented brew in enormous quantities also proved to be a problem for missionaries spreading other religious evaluations of time and consumption; see, for example, Dionisio Ortiz, O.F.M., *Las Montañas del Apurimac, Mantaro y Ene* vol. 2 (Lima, 1976), p. 437.

182. Weiss, "World of a Forest Tribe," p. 468. In fact, the moon occupies an ambiguous place in Campa mythology. It is clear that the Campa ascribe primacy as a supernatural being to the moon and yet rank it as inferior (in both power and moral quality) to the sun.

183. Dumont, "Not in Ourselves," p. 246.

184. Nimuendajú, *The Apinayé*, pp. 118–119. However, Nimuendajú never witnessed such an event and could provide no details. We have no way of knowing, therefore, whether these ceremonial deaths of animal imitators are comparable to the Waiwai or Shipibo ritual "deaths" of "animals" at the hands of women.

185. Fock, *Waiwai*, p. 67. Origin myths in which an anaconda, after having swallowed a human being and after having given up the victim's bones, is dismembered in such a way as to cause the multiplicity of different peoples to come into existence, draw this celebration into an arc that includes, for example, the myth of origin of the Barasana sibs. The sibs of the Barasana are all transformations of body parts of the original ancestor anaconda, who, after having swum to the middle of the universe, broke into pieces along the river that runs to the center of the earth. It is also notable that the Shodewika flutes and bark trumpets are played in imitation of those once played in mythical times by the macaw spirits. When the celebration was first performed by animal-human beings, those beings were unadorned. Contemporary festival costumes are worn only to imitate the beautiful, but unadorned, people whose integral beauty comprised both human and animal aspects. It was only at the festival's end that these beings were transformed into separate species of animals and human tribes. See ibid., p. 63.

186. Ibid., pp. 179–181. This behavior draws the Waiwai festival into comparison with the Shipibo "killing of pets," which takes place during the drinking festival marking a girl's initiation. Among the Shipibo, when the men fail to kill the animals, women come out and beat the animals to death in order to put them out of their misery. The result is a bloodbath.

187. Ibid., pp. 179–180.

188. Holmberg, *Nomads of the Long Bow*, p. 44.

189. Grenand, *Et l'homme devint jaguar*, p. 43. Grenand, believing that the plants and manioc

beer had "issued from man in order to be consumed by man" believed that this was "a cleverly disguised form of endocannibalism." This, in his opinion, made sense of a statement made to a child who was about to eat papaya: "You're going to eat the breast of the grandmother" (ibid.). In the light of myth, then, cultivated plants are spoken of as meat.

190. Bartolomé, "Shamanism Among the Avá-Chiripá," p. 138.

191. Enrique Palavecino, "The Magic World of the Mataco," trans. and ed. by Juan Adolfo Vázquez, *LAIL* 3 (Fall 1979): 61–75, provides a description of an entire ceremony that took place in February 1935. On p. 71, the translator, J. A. Vázquez, provides several other references which describe a similar ceremony.

192. Ibid., p. 67.

193. Karsten, *Toba Indians*, p. 69.

194. Ibid., p. 104.

195. Ibid., pp. 65, 66, 67, 69, 104–106.

196. Civrieux, *Religión y magia kari'ña*, p. 22.

197. Ibid., p. 22. A similar myth is found among the Makiritare of Ño'mo concerning the mistress of poisonous snakes; see Civrieux, *Watunna*, p. 185.

198. Whitten, *Sacha Runa*, pp. 193–194.

199. Ibid., p. 194.

200. Henry, *Jungle People*, p. 69.

201. Karsten, *Toba Indians*, p. 70.

202. A large number of cases of consumption of the ashes of the dead in a fermented drink are gathered in Otto Zerries, "El Endocannibalismo en la América del Sur," *RMP* 12 (1960): 125–175.

203. Clastres, *Chronique des indiens guayakí*, p. 171. *Proaä* is a large bean, something like the fava, which is the product of pod-bearing liana in the forest.

204. Guayakí marriages are inaugurated by the mutual consent of both young people. The young husband builds a *tapi*, a shelter in which the new couple will live. When the hut has been built, the young man goes to the home of his in-laws and "captures" his bride. In order to revenge the offense, the father of the bride beats his own wife. After the festival camp is broken, the couple almost always follows the band of the woman, although this is not prescribed.

205. Ibid., p. 172.

206. Ibid.

207. Nimuendajú, *The Apinayé*, pp. 123–124.

208. Maybury-Lewis, *Akwẽ-Shavante Society*, p. 304.

209. Ibid., p. 76.

210. Ibid.

211. Ibid., pp. 248–251.

212. Dumont, "Not in Ourselves," p. 246.

213. Ibid.

214. Reichel-Dolmatoff, *Beyond the Milky Way*, p. 6.

215. Ibid., pp. 49–142.

216. Whitten, *Sacha Runa*, p. 59.

217. Ibid., p. 59.

218. Ibid., pp. 165–204.

219. Ibid., p. 167.

220. In these rites in which women force *chicha*, made from starter mash taken from their mouths, down men's throats, we may see overtones of a female counterpart to that process by which a male shaman regurgitates spirit darts from his own belly and offers them to a novice, who swallows them. Both processes sometimes imitate birds coughing up their food to nourish their dependents.

221. Ibid., p. 181.

222. Ibid., p. 183.

223. Ibid., p. 187. The drinking, dancing, singing, and vigils of the Canelos Quichua feast become techniques for dreaming and vision, for people "actually dream on their feet while dancing and playing."

224. Ibid., pp. 185–186.

225. Irving Goldman, *The Mouth of Heaven: An Introduction to Kwakiutl Religious Thought* (New York, 1975); see esp. pp. 104–107, which discuss the simulation and impersonation of primordial supernaturals as inescapable counterparts of incest symbolism:

> The inescapable counterpart of the incest taboo is the sacred obligation to retain connections by endowing them with deep significance. The Garden of Eden is never again to be reentered, and never to be forgotten. . . . Simulation, however, is no casual matter. It seeks identity [with earlier pristine conditions], even through danger, but dares not make identity absolute. The initiate enters the realm of the supernaturals, but as a differentiated human being. (p. 106)

226. For this reason, drinking, violation of sexual mores, and images of the flood feature prominently in eschatological visions of the end of time. The Mbya-Guaraní, for example, celebrate raucous drinking bouts in the Land Without Evil. The first being to enter that eschatological world as Jeupie, whose act of incest brought on the flood. See Hélène Clastres, *La Terre sans mal: Le prophétisme tupi-guarani* (Paris, 1976): p. 83.

227. Günther Hartmann, "Destillieranlagen bei südamerikanischen Naturvölkern," *ZFE* 93 (1968): 225–232. In the pre-Columbian period, alcoholic beverages used in festivals were fermented. A comparative study of reports of distilled alcohol finds little ground for the contention that there was an indigenous distillation of alcohol carried on in South America before the Conquest.

228. Carole Daggett, "Las Funciones del masato en la cultura chayahuita," *ALIM* 1 (1983): 301–310.

229. This schematic account presented in this and the following paragraph draws on a large corpus of mythic materials already presented in chapter 2 (concerning the primordial flood) and in chapter 3 (on space).

230. The Shipibo offered no explanation of the fact that the drinking feasts are coordinated with the phases of the moon. Ambiguity also surrounds the role and meaning of the moon in the drinking feasts of the River Campa, which are celebrated at the full moon. Weiss's explanation of the timing of River Campa manioc beer-drinking festivals need not be exhaustive: "the Campas prefer to have their masato festivals at night, thereby avoiding the heat and distractions of the day. It is also true that they can be expected to prefer a night when there is enough moonlight so that they can see what they are doing. . . . [T]he masato festival is primarily a recreational activity" (Weiss, "World of a Forest Tribe," p. 468). The Pajonal Campa also celebrate drinking feasts timed to coincide with the lunar cycle; see Varase, *La Sal de los cerros*, p. 22.

231. Peter Kloos, *The Maroni River Caribs of Surinam* (Assen, 1971), p. 229.

232. Ibid., pp. 69–70. Kloos relates these drinking feasts to the Jari festivals of the Bush Negroes, which were held on plantations to mark the end of each year; see August Kappler, *Zes Jaren in Suriname* (Utrecht, 1854), p. 58, and *Hollandisch-Guiana. Erlebnisse und Erfahrungen während eines 43 jährigen Aufenthallts in der Kolonie Surinam* (Stuttgart, 1881), p. 395. For the mythological origins of *oki*, a Yabarana alcoholic drink made from yuca and sweet potato, see Johannes Wilbert, "Mitos de los indios yabarana," *ACAR* 5 (1958), pp. 58–67. *Oki* was created by Mayowaca, the twin who created the new earth and new humanity after the flood, and was used to celebrate the first festival of the new age of human beings.

233. Udo Oberem, "Einige ethnographische Notizen über die Canelo Ost-Ecuadors," *EZ*, special supplement number 1 (1974): 327f.

234. See chapter 3, above, on liquid in heavenly space compared to the liquid (rains, flood, channeled rivers) of this world. Lévi-Strauss draws together a number of mythic and ritual allusions to heavenly liquid in connection with din and the noise of rattles in *From Honey to Ashes*, esp. pp. 435ff.

235. F. S. Gilij, *Saggio di storia americana*, vol. 2 (Rome, 1781), p. 284f. The return of snakes to dance and bring liquid refreshments is drawn into the complex of feasts employing spiral-twisted bark trumpets; see ibid., p. 260. For a comparative treatment, see Izikowitz, *Musical and Other Sound Instruments*, pp. 222–227.

236. Nimuendajú, *Mitos de Creación*, pp. 59, 97.

237. Ibid., p. 97.

238. Regarding the mythic origin of the cooking fire, see the sources gathered by Lévi-Strauss in

The Raw and the Cooked. In offering a different interpretation of one version of this myth, Terence S. Turner demonstrates the degree to which the tiniest symbolic details of fire symbolism can relate to the meaning of psychic and social processes. See Turner, "Animal Symbolism, Totemism, and the Structure of Myth," in Urton, ed., *Animal Myths and Metaphors*, pp. 49–106, and Turner, "Le Dénicheur d'oiseaux en contexte," *Anthropologie et Sociétés 4* (1980): 85–115.

239. For a discussion of the notion of distance needed for symbolic life, see the comments on myths of the raising of the sky in chapter 2. Myths of the withdrawal of the sky and the receding of the primal waters, among others, provide images of transcendence and symbolic distance.

240. Fock, *Waiwai*, p. 177. Indeed, one has the distinct impression that the men are drinking up the flood brought on by the women.

241. The way festive time sets its mark on space (in the form of the branded bodies of livestock) becomes visible in the configurations of space as reflected in the symbols of social organization, shrines, residences, and ritual positions of participants in the Herranza ceremony (the branding ceremony). These concerns are detailed in Ultiano Quispe M., *La Herranza en Choque Huarcaya y Huancazancos, Ayacucho* (Lima, 1969), e.g., pp. 24f., 53, 59, 65f., 72.

242. Men's tattoo patterns carry the same fatal cutting ability, for they are powerful aids to taking game in the hunt and to butchering it for consumption.

243. Audrey J. Butt, "The Mazaruni Scorpion," *Timehri* 36 (October 1957): 40–54.

244. See the sources drawn together by Butt (ibid.), including James Gillin, *The Barama River Caribs* (Cambridge, Mass., 1936), p. 30; Walter Edmund Roth, *Arts and Crafts of the Guiana Indians* (Washington, D.C., 1924) pp. 91 and 420–422; W. C. Farabee, *The Central Arawaks* (Philadelphia, 1918), pp. 81–82; W. C. Farabee, *The Central Caribs* (Philadelphia, 1924), pp. 64, 167.

245. Wright, "History and Religion of the Baniwa," pp. 551–557.

246. Civrieux, *Watunna*, pp. 88–90. De Barandiarán provides an analysis of drinking festivals in which he emphasizes the role of sacrifice, communion, and women's initiation. His principal interest is to explain the worldview of the Makiritare, but he does provide a comparative context. See his *Introducción ye'kuana-makiritare*, pp. 816–822.

247. Civrieux, *Watunna*, p. 91.

248. The spatial meaning of channel, vessel, and vehicle have been touched upon in chapter 3. A different rendering of the connection between drink, flood, destructive death, and vessels of salvation (which set humanity apart through unique control over water) can be found in the documents from Huarochiri that describe how the cosmic deluge arrived because of the first drinking festival. At that time, Pariacaca, the divinity who wandered through the earth during the primordium, came upon a drinking festival. He was passing in the guise of a poor beggar asking for a drink, but no one gave it to him. A young girl, however, did offer him a large *putu* (a white calabash gourd), and he forewarned her of the coming flood, which he would send in his rage. She and a few of her chosen friends escaped the flood of heavy rain, hail, and yellow or white stones, which drove the village into the sea and killed everyone. People were still drinking when they were pushed into the drink. See Francisco de Avila [1608], "A narrative of the errors, false gods and other superstitions and diabolical rites in which the Indians of the Province of Huarachiri, Mama and Chaclla lived in ancient times, and in which they even now live, to the great perdition of their souls," in Markham, trans. and ed., *Narratives of the Rites and Laws of the Yncas.*

249. Bastien offers an analysis of the ways in which irrigation canals in the Andes become important fixtures for evaluating several incompatible senses of time with repercussions for supernatural beings, human individuals, and society as a whole. More than that, he makes clear that liquid of this sort offers a means of evaluating human existence in time. See his *Mountain of the Condor*, esp. "The Two Senses of the River," pp. 155–169. Like those of ritual drink (a connection not made in this section by Bastien), the temporal meanings of river and canal are body-linked:

> As a metaphor, the river is associated with different geographical places, periods of time, and social groups, as well as sickness, feuds, and loss of land. Another set of meanings is, however, attached to the river in the form of a continuous stream originating from and flowing to the original time and place (*uma pacha*). The river makes the body [the primor-

dial mountain-body on which the community lives] complete not only by washing it but by defining its boundaries and by forever returning what has been removed. Kaatan geography, society, time, and history have two dimensions, which coincide with the river. The particular levels of land, ecological zones, distinct communities, ordered time, and layered history is one dimension. The other is understood in terms of a complete geographical body, social and cultural *ayllu* unity, and an original time and place. This original time and place is self-contained, cyclical, and constitutive of everything else. These two dimensions are of one body. (p. 169)

250. The control over the passage of symbolic items in and out of the body amounts to a system of exchange, a kind of micro-economy. This system of relations has important temporal aspects for constructing and deconstructing individuals and societies over time (cosmogonic, cosmologic, eschatological). See Lawrence E. Sullivan, "Personal Political Economy: Symbolic Control over Integration and Disintegration," (in press).

251. For the Selk'nam, ritual combat is an important component of the festival of Pesére, during which shamans (*xon*) gather together for a spectacular ceremony that renews their number by discovering new candidates for their profession; see Gusinde, *Los Indios de Tierra del Fuego. Los Selk'nam*, pp. 762–777. Ritual combat frequently is directed toward the replication or numerical increase of a quality of existence.

252. Holmberg, *Nomads of the Long Bow*, p. 38. In a similar vein, the Yanoama practice several styles of ritual combat, including chest-pounding duels and club fights, open warfare and raiding, stealing women, axe fights, and musical battles. See Otto Zerries and Meinhard Schuster, *Mahekodotedi*, vol. 2 pp. 215–222.

253. Nimuendajú, *The Apinayé*, pp. 150–160.

254. See Urton's fascinating article "Animal Metaphors," in which he analyzes the role of *ararihua* in the contemporary community of Pacariqtambo (near Cuzco), pp. 264ff.

255. Palavecino, "Magic World of the Mataco," p. 72.

256. Ibid., p. 65.

257. Alfred Métraux, "Ethnography of the Chaco," in *HSAI*, vol. 1, p. 354. This reference is provided by Vázquez, the editor and translator of Palavecino, "The Magic World of the Mataco," on p. 71 of that article.

258. Wagley, *Welcome of Tears*, pp. 198–211. A shaman must guide a child-spirit from another realm so that its soul will take up lodging in the womb of a woman and conception take place. With the whole community of shamans "dying" and journeying to the prized realm of Thunder, it stands to reason that many women could become pregnant at this time. See also Charles Wagley, "World View of the Tapirapé Indians," *JAFL* 53 (1940): 252–260.

259. Roswith Hartmann, "Otros datos sobre las llamadas 'batallas rituales,'" *ICA*, 39th Congress, vol. 6 (Lima, 1972), pp. 125–135. Gow and Condori, *Kay Pacha*, point out that drinking large quantities of *trago* is an essential element of festival in Quechua-speaking communities wherein disputes can escalate into fights between communities (p. 84). See also Catherine Allen Wagner, "Coca, Chicha, and Trago: Private and Communal Rituals in a Quechua Community" (Ph.D. diss., University of Illinois, Urbana-Champaign, 1978).

260. Krener and Fock, "Good Luck."

261. Ibid., p. 153.

262. "According to accounts the Incas literally went underground with all their property and gold at the Spanish conquest. It was only intended to be a short stay, but they have not yet had the possibility of emerging again. That is why the Juncal concept of 'inside the mountain' is identical with the concept of 'back to the time of the Inca'" (ibid., p. 166).

263. Ibid., p. 155.

264. Ibid., p. 163.

265. Ibid.

266. Ibid., p. 161. Hartmann reports that the ritual fights at Ludo/Quingo must end in the wounding or death of a combatant, otherwise the following year will bring ill luck for the participants in both teams. See Hartmann, "Otros datos sobre las llamadas 'batallas rituales.'" Krener and Fock describe several alternatives to the ritual battle with the stone-bola. Among them is the ritual contest in which men compete to tear apart a cock that is suspended from a

crossbeam. Ossio, "El Simbolismo del agua" may prove relevant in explaining the emphasis on timely flow of blood.

267. Clastres, *Chronique des indiens guayakí*, p. 168.

268. Ibid.

269. Bateson has fruitfully explored this dimension of symbolic action.

270. Alfred Métraux, "Religion and Shamanism," *HSAI*, vol. 5, pp. 573–574. The Chamacoco report their own variation of the theme of violence and primordial matriarchy. An incestuous son told his mother that the spirits of the Anaposo feast were only masked men. When the men discovered that they were discovered,

> they decided to slaughter all the women lest everyone die. This they did, but one escaped in the shape of a deer. Men then performed all the women's tasks in a state of depression and loneliness. The last woman was finally chased into a tree and raped. She instructed her attackers to cut her into small pieces which fell on their sperm, clinging to the tree. Each man took an inseminated piece of the matrix. From the pieces of flesh soaked in sperm grew women and children of each area. Each Chamacoco obtained a woman whose appearance corresponded to the morsel which he had picked up. Those who had brought home pieces from the woman's thighs had fat wives, those who had taken fingers were provided with lean ones." (Alfred Métraux, "A Myth of the Chamacoco Indians and Its Social Significance," *JAFL* 56, April–June 1943, p. 116)

271. Theodor Koch-Grünberg, *Zwei Jahre bei den Indianern Nordwest-Brasiliens* (Stuttgart, 1923), p. 248.

272. Métraux, "Religion and Shamanism," p. 574.

273. Karsten, *Toba Indians*, p. 73.

274. Ibid., pp. 26ff. and p. 43.

275. Whitten, *Sacha Runa*, p. 186.

276. Ibid., p. 190.

277. Ibid., p. 193.

278. Ibid., p. 198. Indeed, this would seem to make sense of a ritual that builds up (or degenerates) into a climax of chaos and ritualized hostility without resolution. Indeed, the abrupt and incomplete termination of an otherwise elaborate and lengthy ceremony has necessitated a time of follow-up and readjustment that often seems to involve fighting and feud; see ibid., pp. 194–199. The Jívaro origin myth of the first victory feast prepares the way for their dramatic symbols of the fullness of being. The feast celebrates the cosmic battle between people and the great water serpent, Pangi. A fantastic din went up during the chaotic struggle. Today men still shout *"histi histi histi"* in imitation of the primordial bird (*mashu*). Women, in a sort of battle of choirs that is also a battle of the sexes, repeat incessantly, "oa-a-ao, oa-a-ao," an imitation of the black monkey (*washi*). The whole event is based on the episode of the deluge and enacts the sacrifice, the flowing of blood, and the tunneling through the earth that allowed people to escape; see Rafael Karsten, *The Head-hunters of Western Amazonas. The Life and Culture of the Jibaro Indians of Eastern Ecuador and Peru* (Helsinki, 1935), pp. 527–532.

279. Whitten, *Sacha Runa*, p. 196.

280. Hill, "Kamayurá Flute Music," p. 418. The antagonism finds its origin in the mythic account that tells of a society originally governed by women until men stole the flutes from them. See the very detailed analysis of ritual combat held during the Kwarìp ceremonial cycle of the Kamayurá of the upper Xingu in Agostinho, *Kwarìp*, 128–134. The ritual combat takes the form of wrestling, antagonistic dancing between competitive teams of men and women or individuals, intense prestation of economic goods, ritual sports such as the ballgames, and commodities trading. This stylized combat forms part of a ritual aimed to accomplish not only the initiation of girls (the moment of their emergence) but also the transition of the dead person to the next, heavenly, life, the transition from dry to wet season, the transition from single married life, and the transition from one mode of economic production to another (this is the time for ritual gathering of *pequi* chestnuts, for ritual fishing, and for the first planting of manioc).

281. Wilhelm Saake, "Die Juruparilegende bei den Baniwa des Rio Issana," *ICA*, 32d Congress (Copenhagen, 1956), pp. 271–279.

282. Inapirikuli is the being named Yaperikuli in the accounts provided by Wright, *History and Religion of the Baniwa*, pp. 535ff. The being is also referred to as Jesu Cristo.

283. Melville J. Herskovitz, "The Social Organization of the Candomblé," *ICA*, 31st Congress (São Paulo, 1955), p. 529. For more general discussion of ritual combat in Afro-Brazilian religion and for consideration of ritual inversion as a symbolic vehicle for the presence of the holy, see Yvonne Maggie Alves Velho, *Guerra de orixá: Um Estudio de ritual e conflito* (Rio de Janeiro, 1977). African religious sects of Brazil take full advantage of rivalries, jealousies, hatreds, and personal ambitions by interweaving them, through ritual, and transforming them "into a new element of social cohesion" (Bastide, *African Religions of Brazil*, p. 235). The same point is made by René Ribeiro, *Cultos afro-brasileiros de Recife: Um Estudo de adjustamento social* (Recife, 1952), p. 118. Disagreements between and within groups are performed and interpreted as supernatural battles: "The gods cease to be mere collective representations and become Homeric forces working alongside mortals — to the point where in studying the history of individual sects it is hard to tell whether one is dealing with a battle of men or a battle of gods" (ibid., p. 235). For example, the struggle between two candidates for the office of supreme priesthood "was interpreted on the level of reality in terms of the dramatic struggle between the *orixás* [the Yoruba mortals] and *eguns* [the souls of the dead]" (ibid., p. 236). The dance floor became a battleground where supernatural beings and spirits of the dead took advantage of the ceremonies, entered the bodies of the initiates, and battled with one another.

284. Gerardo Reichel-Dolmatoff, "Desana Shamans' Rock Crystals and the Hexagonal Universe," *JLAL* 5 (1979): 117–128.

285. Karl Gustav Izikowitz, "Rhythmical Aspects of Canella Life," *ICA*, 31st Congress (São Paulo, 1955), p. 207. The same principle is reflected in the "names of the rainy season – moieties . . . sun and moon, fire and firewood, dry and rainy season, east and west, earth and water, day and night, and so forth. It may be that such a thought or principle is usual with many people" (p. 207).

286. Michel Perrin, *Le Chemin des indiens morts: Mythes et symboles goajiro* (Paris, 1976), p. 211.

287. Ibid., pp. 140–150, 210–213.

288. Irving Goldman, *The Cubeo: Indians of the Northwest Amazon*, 2d ed. (Urbana, Ill. 1979), pp. 235–237. Goldman writes,

> The point of view is of symbolic frenzy rather than of sheer unrestraint. The mastery of this mood is surely a difficult one, because the women, who are a laity, are under no compulsion to discipline their feelings. . . . This interplay between emotional form and substance, so to speak, adds spontaneity and emotional spice to the ceremony but always within the framework of form. (p. 236)

289. The meaning of silence, another symbolic lowering of distinctions between sounds, can also imply the confusion and simultaneous coexistence of all sounds so as to make present all the significant powers that sonic symbols represent. The issue is taken up in chapter 7, below.

290. Palavecino, "Magic World of the Mataco," p. 64.

291. Ibid., p. 65. We frequently see the synchronous performance of uniquely individual songs at the height of ceremonies in which a multitude — or better, a plethora — of spirits is convoked.

292. Ibid.

293. Karsten, *Toba Indians*, p. 65. Comment has been made on this attempt to use noise as an efficacious symbol that makes present a plenitude of powers.

294. Fock, *Waiwai*, p. 177.

295. Whitten, *Sacha Runa*, p. 191.

296. Basso, "A 'Musical View of the Universe,'" p. 290.

297. Ibid. Among others, Basso is calling upon the analyses of the meaning of musical experience made by Victor Zuckerkandl in two books: *Man the Musician*, (Princeton, 1976), pp. 24–25 and *Sound and Symbol* (Princeton, 1956), p. 219, 374. In the latter work, the author describes the role of the meaning of music as a symbol in creating a sense of "space without distinction of places" and "time in which past and future coexist within the present." This space and time form

a state of being for the performer which is symbolized effectively by the very movements of tones in the music itself.

298. Wright, "History and Religion of the Baniwa," p. 586.

299. Ibid.

300. Ibid., p. 587.

301. Mircea Eliade, "Prologomenon to Religious Dualism: Dyads and Polarities," in *The Quest*, p. 174. This view drives home the argument that ritual combat is intrinsically related to cyclic time that is based on polarities of appearance and disappearance: "Antagonism becomes the 'cipher' through which man unveils both the structures of the universe and the significance of his own existence" (p. 174).

302. In her analysis of theoretical discourses used to talk about ritual, Catherine Bell offers this conclusion: "Ritual is a window on culture because it is also a model of the very generation of a concept of culture and of a level of cultural analysis" (Bell, Discourse and Dichotomies: The Structure of Ritual Theory," *Religion*, Vol. 17, 1987, pp. 95–118). Bell's approach explains both the reflexive function of ritual in a culture's calendar as well as the ease with which reflexive categories find their way into performance theory.

303. Throughout this chapter, the attempt was made to show how pervasive in ritual can be the imagery of disjunction. Bell points out that images of disjunction can be typical also of the theoretical discourse used to discuss ritual: "There is an interesting tendency to cast ritual as a type of critical juncture wherein some pair of opposing cultural forces meets to be integrated. Examples have come to include the relationships between tradition and change, the individual and the group, subjectivity and objectivity, nature and culture, the real and the imaginative idea" (ibid., p. 12). According to Bell a singularly important pair conjoined in ritual are thought and action (or, referred to on another level, theory and practice): "[T]heories of ritual are often designed to join what we simultaneously wish to separate—or be separated from" (ibid., p. 15).

304. At the same time, however, ritual calendars can be interpreted as setting aside maximum amounts of time for mundane and trivial behaviors by restricting paradigmatic moments of festival to a relatively small proportion of time during the year. Ritual calendars invent and maintain profane time by celebrating the moments of its origin, the demise of the primordium. From this point of view, ritual underscores the impossibility of consciously controlling life in the same way and to the same degree that one can manage the symbolic variables of a rite. The fact that ritual is contained and has closure reveals the religious conviction that human life is not meant to unfold totally within the supernatural world, a temporal condition whose manifestation has also been made subject to closure. The contrast cultures maintain between ritual and mundane action also requires that humans must labor mostly in the comparatively pale light of historical circumstance.

305. The trivialization of events without mythic paradigm need be interpreted neither as an outright rejection of history, in the narrow chronological sense of that word, nor as a futile attempt to escape one's specific situation in time, even if that is an oppressed status in "modern" history. Rather, the religious calendar systematizes the effort to understand that historical situation in the light of what is permanent, i.e., to grasp its fragmented experiences in terms of the whole of which it is a transitory part. The whole of time, the proper context to evaluate one's historical situation in time, is a primordial condition, a state of supernatural affairs. It is accessible in the acts symbolic of sacred beings and events (the recollection of primordial appearances and disappearances). Those creative manifestations and destructions recur periodically, thus forming the cycles of time through which human culture apprehends its own meaning and that of the cosmos.

306. Ritual life, coming to grips with the different qualities of temporal existence, is an important element in the process of reflexive life. For the Canelos Quichua, for example, life in the present is a process of *yacha*, a "learning process" with temporal aspects: the goal of learning is to approximate or regain the kind of knowledge possessed by beings in Ancient Times (Whitten, *Sacha Runa*, p. 46). In relation to another festival described in this chapter, Bartolomé calls the Chiripá Prayer of the Forest a "collective act of self-knowledge" during which the community returns to "the world of sacred things" in order to restore the social order (Bartolomé, "Shamanism Among the Avá-Chiripá," p. 139).

CHAPTER FIVE

1. The point is that, as Mircea Eliade writes,

> our historical moment forces us into confrontations that could not even have been imagined fifty years ago. On the one hand, the peoples of Asia have recently reentered history; on the other, the so-called primitive peoples are preparing to make their appearance on the horizon of greater history (that is, they are seeking to become *active subjects* of history instead of its *passive objects*, as they have been hitherto). But if the peoples of the West are no longer the only ones to "make" history, their spiritual and cultural values will no longer enjoy the privileged place, to say nothing of the unquestioned authority, that they enjoyed some generations ago. These values are now being analyzed, compared, and judged by non-Westerners. On their side, Westerners are being increasingly led to study, reflect on, and understand the spiritualities of Asia and the archaic world. These discoveries and contacts must be extended through dialogues. But to be genuine and fruitful, a dialogue cannot be limited to empirical and utilitarian language. A true dialogue must deal with the central values in the cultures of the participants. Now, to understand these values rightly, it is necessary to know their religious sources. For, as we know, non-European cultures, both oriental and primitive, are still nourished by a rich religious soil." (Eliade, "A New Humanism," in *The Quest*, p. 2)

See also Eliade, *Ordeal by Labyrinth*, p. 78.

2. Louis-Vincent Thomas, *Anthropologie de la mort* (Paris, 1976), is a comprehensive study of the place that the significance of death occupies in the formation of a culture's anthropology. Among the most fascinating considerations is Thomas's investigation of the way in which death structures the human imagination, including its semiology (pp. 397–432).

3. Wilbert, "Eschatology," p. 168. The Warao myth of human origins also describes how the first human being was, in a sense, "born dead." Unlike all the other creatures of the world, the human being refused to shout when encouraged to do so by Kanobo, the "old one" who called beings into existence; see Johannes Wilbert, *Textos folklóricos de los indios waraos* (Los Angeles, 1969), pp. 27–30.

4. Ibid., p. 169.

5. Richard Huntington and Peter Metcalf track the history of important scholarly attempts to study the "death" that occurs in moments of transition through the cultural life-cycle. See their *Celebrations of Death: The Anthropology of Mortuary Ritual* (Cambridge, 1981), pp. 44–120, especially the discussion of rites of passage and the meaning of death as it shapes society's life values on pp. 93–120. See also Peter Metcalf, *A Borneo Journey into Death: Berawan Eschatology from its Rituals* (Philadelphia, 1982), pp. 33–70 and pp. 233–258 for discussion of the way in which the meaning of death shapes the concept of the individual and the cosmos.

6. A new father, observing couvade by lying on a mat, needed to ritually procure honey. During his hunt, a singing bird attracted his attention. He began to dig a hole in the earth in order to get closer to the bird. In fact, he emerged onto the face of the earth, where he found fruit. He brought the food back to his people to taste. "They found it very good and wanted to come out" (William Lipkind, "Carajá Cosmography," *JAFL* 53, 1940, p. 248). They emerged in a particular order. The last one to emerge, having eaten well, was too fat to pass through the emergence hole. He got stuck, saw a dead leaf, said, "There is death there," and returned to the ground. In fact, a young boy soon fell from a tree and died, precipitating the first rituals of mourning and the first funeral songs (ibid., p. 249).

7. Clastres, *Chronique des indiens guayakí*, p. 227.

8. The irreversibility of death, making it the closing moment of life, is usually attributed to some tragic or absurd accident; see chapter 8.

9. Chapman, "Lune en Terre de Feu," p. 152. Taking the surviving young girls with them, the male beings journeyed to the east, remaining there during a period of mourning. When the young girls matured into women, the *howenh* began the centuries-long journey of return, passing through the other cardinal points along the way. During the course of this voyage, in the pattern of an inclined plane spiraling back to the center of the world, the mighty primordial

beings left this earth and took on a new existence, transformed into constellations or stars or other elements of nature. Only after the transformation of the primordial beings was the first human being created from a clod of earth.

10. Fire is a reality taken from the belly of the primordial toad, Kawao. It is the center of a being from the water domain.

11. For examples of mortality and destruction contained in the form of fire as a material constituent of trees, see Civrieux, *Watunna*, pp. 55–61, and Curt Nimuendajú, "Sagen der Tembé-Indianer," *ZFE* 47 (1915): 289. See also Charles Wagley and Eduardo Galvão, *The Tenetehara Indians of Brazil* (New York, 1949), p. 133, and Egon Schaden, "A Origem e a posse do fogo na mitología guaraní," *ICA*, 31st Congress (São Paulo, 1955), pp. 217–225.

12. Kamayurá myths describe how the creator, Mavutsinim, made the first humans from logs, which he cut in the forest, brought to the center of the world, and painted and ornamented in a ceremonial way. Unfortunately, the process of their transformation was interrupted and, in some sense, human beings were "born dead." For origin accounts of peoples in the Upper Xingu, especially the Kamayurá, see the texts and interpretations in Agostinho, *Kwarìp*, pp. 16–23 and 161ff. See the accounts also provided in Villas Boas and Villas Boas, *Xingu*, pp. 53ff., for descriptions of the simultaneous creation of humanity, symbolic existence and the origins of death.

13. Fock, *Waiwai*, p. 15.

14. The view is by no means limited to the Warao nor even to South America. For a presentation of a range of variations, see Hans-Peter Hasenfratz, *Die toten Lebenden: eine religionsphänomenologische Studie zum sozialen Tod in archäischen Gesellschaften* (Leiden, 1982).

15. In her study of the Senufo of West Africa's Ivory Coast, Anita J. Glaze draws an essential connection between the cultural meaning of death and the creative symbolism that makes art possible. The periodic occultation of human understanding of the rhythmic ritual "deaths" experienced in initiations and in funerals maintain the alternating existence of symbolic consciousness. She writes, "One of the definitive characteristics of Senufo art could be said to lie precisely in this quality of art in time, art as an appearance and a display that is temporal and ephemeral" (Glaze, *Art and Death in a Senufo Village*, Bloomington, 1981, p. 198).

16. The concept of frame varies with interpretive tradition and purpose. In the context of ritual action, Victor Turner, in *Dramas, Fields, and Metaphors: Symbolic Action in Human Society* (Ithaca, N.Y., 1974), makes fruitful use of Bateson's *Steps to An Ecology of Mind*, of Erving Goffman's *Frame Analysis* (New York, 1976), and of Mihaly Csikszentmihalyi's *Beyond Boredom and Anxiety* (San Francisco, 1975). In this particular consideration the study of Alfred Schutz, "Multiple Realities," (in his *Collected Papers*, vol. 1 (The Hague, 1962), pp. 207–259), is most helpful. There Schutz distills the thoughts of Franz Brentano and William James in regard to the character of the "paramount reality" that empowers social knowledge. The South American appraisals of death in human origins and growth is quite different from Freud's appreciation of the link between ego and death (see, e.g., *The Ego and the Id*) or John Dewey's articulation of the connection between growing consciousness and death in *Human Nature and Conduct* (New York, 1922). The origin myths do not make the individual ego the basis of reflection on the nature of human mortality. Instead, the reality of death links humans to sacred beings and to events outside human autonomy. For the same reason, the South American view has little in common with the German Romantic notion (or its later extensions in works like those of Otto Rank) that consciousness requires a kind of killing and that self-consciousness implies a self-sacrifice.

17. Reichel-Dolmatoff, *Amazonian Cosmos*, pp. 32–33. The first Desana marriage and first sexual intercourse were celebrated at the first feast held by men. The feast was invoked at a time when only men existed. However, the Daughter of Aracú Fish emerged from the water to copulate with the first Desana man. The first earth-born Desana was their son. The sun trapped the Mother of Snakes and bit off her head. The snake was called *pirú se'e* ("gull snake") because these birds, which now represent the snake, possess the same white, black, and dark gray coloring.

18. Peter Rivière, *Marriage Among the Trio: A Principle of Social Organization* (Oxford, 1969), p. 264. In the Trio conception of things, all creation comes through water. This is true also of the

waters of birth when born from a woman. The association of birth, waters, and woman goes back to the period of myth when "not simply the first woman (a fish) but also culture came from out of the water . . . " (ibid.).

19. Such is the view of the Barasana, the Yąnomamö, the Campa, the Mochica, the Cubeo. The life of this world, especially since the cosmic conflagration, has the character of "cooked" food. Outside the field of South America studies, some especially fine investigations of this theme have been carried on. For example, see Marcel Detienne and Jean-Pierre Vernant, eds., *La Cucina del sacrificio in terra greca* (Turin, 1982), especially the articles by Jean-Louis Durand, "Bestie greche: Proposte per una topología dei corpi commestibili," pp. 90–120, and Vernant, "Mangiare nei paesi del sole," pp. 164–170.

20. Otto Zerries, "Schöpfung and Urzeit." Zerries believes it possible to distinguish between two historically different accounts of the origin of the component parts of humans. Barandiarán, "Vida y muerte," offers a number of accounts of the origin of human beings from the pregnant calves of primordial beings and from the blood of the moon. Barandiarán attempts to systematize these different kinds of accounts into a single developmental process, which he calls "the progressive emergence and perfection of life" in four stages. Man was created from a tree, but not a tree hard enough to endure forever. The creation of woman was first attempted by pulling her out of the water like a fish. When that failed, the first woman was sculpted by a pecking bird from the calf of Ila, a primordial male whose name means "large jaguar." The jaguar and the woman that were fashioned from his calf were bloodless. In the second stage of the ascent of human life, blood appeared when a primordial shaman mixed water with the sap of the *arnoto* tree. The shaman was a woman named Waipilishomá; she prepared the concoction in order to bring her pregnancy to full term (she needed blood to do it). She gives birth to the busy heroic twins, one male, one female, who marry one another and give birth to children. In most mythical accounts, blood was obtained by shooting the moon with an arrow. Barandiarán collects several versions and offers a rather lengthy one that he himself obtained from the Sanemá (pp. 10–12). The third stage of the ascent of human life is distinguished by its violence. Here originated the festival habits of dueling by pounding one's opponent's chest and flanks with fists or clubs. Spilling blood and causing the chest cavity to resound (giving up the sound of the *híkola* that is housed there) instigates growth by creating a microcosm of world processes within the human body (pp. 13–25). The Yanomami offer another version of the creation of human beings. In the beginning there existed only one group of human beings, the Pariwa. There were no women. The lonely men fashioned a woman by cutting a hole in the thigh of their leader. From this opening a woman was born, and through the body of this young girl humankind came into existence. As they wandered on and time went by, people grew more numerous and had to split into village-sized groups. See Gottfried Polykrates, *Wawanaueteri und Pukimapue Zwei Yanomami*-Stämme Nordwe (Copenhagen, 1969), p. 185. For a consideration of the way in which concepts and experiences of primordial death and its meaning pervade Yanoama life, see Zerries and Schuster, Mahekodotedi, pp. 127f. The Yanoama are not unique in recounting multiple, fatal tragedies in the course of human creation. Two attempts to create humanity were aborted by the catastrophes of fire and universal flood. In the meantime, the Wayãpi earth, created by Yaneya as a life-space intended for humanity, continued to endure (F. Grenand, *Et l'homme devint jaguar*, p. 28).

21. Weiss, "World of a Forest Tribe," p. 426.

22. Fock, *Waiwai*, p. 151.

23. This is the thrust of a number of essays in Maurice Bloch and Jonathan Parry, eds, *Death and the Regeneration of Life* (Cambridge, 1983); see esp. pp. 1–44, 74–110, and 211–230.

24. Weiss, "World of a Forest Tribe," p. 269.

25. This fact has encouraged Lévi-Strauss to apply a theory of alienation drawn from reflections upon the natural history and political economy of postindustrial West. However, it seems as though the cultures of South America have considered the question of alienation in the light of a different network of recognized relations, in a world united by another quality of dialectic and motivated by dissimilar causes and effects.

26. Several examples were presented in chapter 2, above. Although his interpretative framework is now quite dated, Alfredo Jiménez Núñez compiled a number of interesting mythic accounts of the origin of human life in his *Mitos de creación en Sudamérica* (Seville, 1962).

27. Nimuendajú, *The Apinayé*, p. 164.

28. Ibid., pp. 133, 164ff.

29. Ibid., p. 164.

30. Weiss, "World of a Forest Tribe," p. 407. There are countless variations on the theme. According to Métraux, the Machiguenga attributed the creation of other human beings from ants to a demonic being, the Devil of the missionaries, whereas authentic human beings, namely the Machiguenga themselves, were created when Tasórenchi blew on a stick of balsa wood; see Alfred Métraux, "Ensayos de mitologia comparada sudamericana," *AI* 8 (1948): p. 12. Julian Steward, "Tribes of the Peruvian and Ecuadorian Montaña," *HSAI*, vol. 3 (1948), pp. 535–656, reports that the balsawood people were antediluvian and nonreplicating; that is, they were not fully human. They partook of the one-of-a-kind mode of being typical of the primordium. Each one of the balsawood people was created by a separate *tasórenchi* blowing on a separate piece of wood (ibid., p. 550).

31. Holmberg, *Nomads of the Long Bow*, p. 46.

32. Henry, *Jungle People*, p. 91. Some of them emerged from that ocean in the east. Other human beings entered the world by passing over the mountains located in the west. They meet in the center of the universe, the arena of human action.

33. Chagnon, *Yąnomamö*, pp. 47–48.

34. Fock, *Waiwai*, p. 42.

35. Clastres, *Chronique des indiens guayakí*, pp. 14–15.

36. Karsten, *Toba Indians*, pp. 105–106.

37. "The women were beautiful, with nice mantles and other clothes, but their vulva was [*sic*] very hard" (ibid., p. 106). In fact, in Toba society women are the only people to be initiated in a formal ceremony. The cycle of dancing feasts is said to be celebrated in their honor and praise, and women are the beings who most often are transformed into supernatural jaguars after death.

38. For a description of the origins of Mataco women, who descended from on high when a parrot heard the arriving sounds of their voices, see Alfred Métraux, *Myths and Tales of the Matako Indians, Gran Chaco, Argentina* (Göteborg, 1939), pp. 49–52. These women had toothy vulvas. The trickster Tawkxwax made the mistake of attempting sex with them and lost his penis. He replaced it with a bone. He threw a stone between the legs of a woman to break out the teeth in her vagina and cleared the way for the rest of men. Sherente women descended to earth from on high. During the primordial period, men were homosexual animals until they spotted the first woman in a tree. They gnawed different pieces from the woman's body, cut her into little bits, wrapped them in leaves, and stuck them in the grass walls of their homes. Then they went off hunting. Each slice became a woman with distinct physical features. These were the first wives. The men went off hunting on the first trek with their wives; see Robert H. Lowie, "Serente Tales," *JAFL* 57 (July-September 1944); 186.

39. Reichel-Dolmatoff, *Amazonian Cosmos*, pp. 25, 30.

40. Zuidema, *The Ceque System of Cuzco*.

41. Nimuendajú, *The Apinayé*, pp. 162–163.

42. Ibid.

43. Johannes Wilbert, *Yupa Folktales* (Los Angeles, 1974), pp. 86–89. This myth of the origin of dwarfs opens up a complicated culture-historical question as to possible influences established during the trans-Pacific Manila Galleon trade (1565–1815). See the discussion and sources concerning the possible historical connection between pygmoid components of Yupa culture and the pygmy peoples of Mountain Luzon (Pinatubo Negritos) and Interia Formosa (ibid., pp. 14–20).

44. Ibid., p. 22.

45. Ibid., pp. 22, 92–95.

46. Ibid., p. 75.

47. One version recounts how the varieties of people began to fight one another. Monkey solved the problem by sending some of the peoples far away beyond the sea. In another version, the white people of the earth attempt to steal the magic wand of Monkey, but he sends Riko the parrot and Kurugo, the opossum, to fetch it back. These two versions are brought together by Charles R. Marsh, Jr., "The Indians and the Whites: Two Boróro Texts," *LAIL* (Spring 1977):

34–36. The texts were first published in Antonio Colbacchini, *Os Boróros orientais* (São Paulo, 1942), p. 242; the second text appeared in Albisetti and Venturelli, *Enciclopédia Boróro*, p. 595.

48. The transmission of female souls is bound up with Nunghuí, the supernatural figure who presides over garden soil and pottery clay. "From the female standpoint the culture will live as long as the rock- and clay-dye soul designs endure" (Whitten, *Sacha Runa*, p. 11). Regarding the myths of origin that set human beings apart from nature, Reichel-Dolmatoff's 1975 Huxley Memorial Lecture, published as "Cosmology as Ecological Analysis: A View from the Rain Forest," *Man* n.s. 2 (1976): 307–318, prevents us from exaggerating the claims made (in conclusions 1 and 2 in the text) that humankind intervenes in the cosmos and remains alien to it: "Nature [in the Tuakano worldview] is not a physical entity apart from man. . . . [H]e never stands apart from it" (ibid., p. 318).

49. Ibid., pp. 11, 52.

50. Fock, *Waiwai*, p. 40. Mawári and his wife eventually left the earth on a chain of arrows.

51. Henry, *Jungle People*, p. 197.

52. Civrieux, *Watunna*, p. 143.

53. Ibid., p. 28.

54. Ibid.

55. Ibid., p. 143.

56. Ibid.

57. Ibid. Wanadi himself was created in a similar manner by Shi, the invisible Sun. However, Wanadi was not fashioned from earthly clay, the material embodiment of the earth, but from *wiriki*, yellow quartz crystals, the material embodiment of pure light which comprises heaven, Kahu.

58. Ibid., p. 144.

59. Ibid., p. 145.

60. Arnold Van Gennep, *The Rites of Passage*, (1909; Chicago, 1960), p. 183.

61. This restrictive application to social structure and relations is best exemplified in the works of Max Gluckman and Meyer Fortes. In contradistinction to the approach of van Gennep, these two social scientists

> perceive changes in status as the *raison d'être* of the ritual itself. The change in emphasis is a subtle one. Instead of seeing the human mind as being prone to ritualize a change in the state of being—as Van Gennep saw it—the reinterpretation sees the change in status as generating the ritual and . . . gives causal primacy to the social structure. . . . The structure of social relations is seen as determining cultural expressions and as being, therefore, logically antecedent to it." (Igor Kopytoff, "Revitalization and the Genesis of Cults in Pragmatic Religion: The Kita Rite of Passage among the Suku," in Ivan Karp and Charles S. Bird, eds., *Explorations in African Systems of Thought*, Bloomington, Ind. 1980, p. 184)

Examples of the more restrictive approach to rites of passage may be seen in Max Gluckman, "Les Rites de Passage," in Max Gluckman, ed., *Essays on the Ritual of Social Relations* (Manchester, England, 1962), pp. 1–52. In the same volume (pp. 53–88) is the essay by Meyer Fortes, "Ritual and Office in Tribal Society." In his study of the Suku of southwestern Zaire, Kopytoff studies states of being that are socially and culturally constituted but that do not involve social statuses. Each case is a rite of passage between states of being that cannot be logically antecedent to the ritual itself because "it is the ritual itself that defines the transition and the states of being" (p. 185). Kopytoff goes on to say that the "transition that it marks is the one that it has itself created" (p. 197). The religious meaning that the rite defines for itself "links into ideas about the nature of society and its revitalization—and not into those about social statuses and social structure" (ibid.).

62. These processes are constant religious experiences of human existence. However, through symbols they surface in ritual to appear as separate moments. There they become evidently visible in the episodes of ritual that van Gennep labeled the "rites of separation" and the "rites of aggregation."

63. Eduardo B. Viveiros de Castro, "A Fabricação do corpo na sociedade xinguana," *BMN* n.s. 32 (May 1979); 40–49.

64. "For the Yawalapíti, transformations of the body and of social position are one and the same thing" (ibid., pp. 40–41).

65. Ibid., p. 41.

66. Ibid.

67. Maybury-Lewis, *Akwē-Shavante Society*, pp. 75–76.

68. Viveiros de Castro is probably appealing to a political-economic portrayal of the relationship of labor to its many forms of value. Parallel to the process of alienation of labor power is the process of fabrication; and parallel to the process of the metamorphosis of value into the transforms of capital, rent, profit, wages, taxes and so on, is his use of metamorphosis leading to superstructures that transcend their material base. The symbolism of metamorphosis has high profile in the reproductive processes of a society. Metamorphosis leads to transcendence, an order of the reproduction of culture. Both processes are necessary to understand what constitutes the specific difference of being human vis-à-vis all other things. It does not appear necessary to found the existence of these two processes on exclusively Marxian grounds. For instance, they may be seen as manifestations of the dialectic of human existence, which is constantly interrupted and reinitiated. This general condition of being is most highly visible in the symbolic religious moments called rites of separation and aggregation by van Gennep. South American religious worldviews tend to look upon these processes not as political-economic dynamics of exchange- and use-value but as the consequences of cataclysm, which creates a yearning for primordial wholeness. In other words, fabrication and metamorphosis are essentially ways of experimenting with sacred realities by decomposing and recomposing their images.

69. Earlier consideration of the calender underscored the astronomic correlates of the person and the periodic nature of human society oriented toward the heavens.

70. Anthony Seeger, *Nature and Society in Central Brazil: The Suyá Indians of Mato Grosso* (Cambridge, Mass., 1981), p. 92.

71. Ibid., p. 93. "Odor classification is also central to the analysis of curing chants, myths, dreams and omens" (ibid.). Pierre Grenand succeeds, after five years of fieldwork, in detailing how the Wayãpi use fragrance to complement vision in establishing taxons of plants and animals. In the case of plants, fragrance replaces marked sound, the primary distinctive feature of animals. See Grenand, *Introduction . . . wayãpi*, and André-Marcel d'Ans, *La Verdedera Biblia de los Cashinahua (mitos, legendas y tradiciónes de la selva peruana)*, (Lima, 1975) pp. 136f., for a description of the origin of the intimate smells that characterize a Cashinahua individual. Particular attention is paid to the smells of sexual substances and other body fluids. A whole series of smells distinguish and constitute the identify of specific individuals (distinguishing whites from natives, men from women, one age group from another, one dietary group from another, one emotional state from another, one ritual state from another, and so on).

72. Seeger, *Nature and Society*, p. 106.

73. Neither temporal nor spatial constructs are excluded from one another. Each has expressions of the other.

74. Gerardus Van der Leeuw, *Religion in Essence and Manifestation*, vol. 1 (1933; New York, 1963), p. 275. That is why, in van der Leeuw's point of view, the soul is easily perceived as a speck of eternity, a divine element within the human: it remains constant even in the encounter with other rhythms of life and modes of being. The soul *is* human continuity, often ill at ease with (although, somehow, generated in) the inherently transitional condition of human life in the body.

75. See, for example, Ernst Arbman, *Untersuchungen zur primitiven Seelenvorstellung mit besonderer Rucksicht auf Indien*, 2 parts (Uppsala, 1926–1927), and also his "Seele und Mana," *Archiv für Religionswissenschaft* 29 (1931): 293–394. For a general consideration of theories of the soul, see Jehan Vellard, "La Conception de l'ame et de la maladie chez les indiens americains," *Travaux de l'Institut Français d'Études Andines* Vol. 6 (1957-58), pp. 5-35; and "Die Vorstellung von der Seele bei den südamerikanischen Indianern," *Kairos* (1959), pp. 145–48.

76. Métraux, "Religion and Shamanism," p. 570.

77. Ibid.

78. Karsten, *Toba Indians*, p. 89.

79. Jürgen Riester, "Medizinmänner und Zauberer der Chiquitano-Indianer," *ZFE* 96 (1971); 261.

80. The light and smoke from a cigar help to render the power of these evil beings ineffective; see ibid. For a detailed description of the imagery of Ayoré souls and spiritual elements, an extensive knowledge of which is essential to medical practice, see Ulf Lind, *Die Medizin der Ayoré-Indianer* (Bonn, 1974), pp. 118–128.

81. Civrieux, *Religion y magia kari'ña*, p. 71.

82. The soul is rooted in a form of being expressed as *personal* existence. For instance, the Campa word for soul only exists in a possessive form that is, as *nošíre* ("my soul"), *pišíre* ("your soul"), and so on. A soul must be associated with a living being. Otherwise it is expressed by the nonpossessive form *širéci*, meaning "ghost"; see Weiss, "World of a Forest Tribe," p. 428.

83. Ibid., p. 431.

84. The Mapuche possess such a concept of lineage-soul. The Kaingáng present an example of the extension of the human spirit into nature. Since so much of nature threatens human existence with destruction, the Kaingáng achieve security through extension of their body and psyche by the process *kalêlê nyá* ("to live in someone else"). The result is an extensive social personality, extended through the means of divination into nature itself; see Henry, *Jungle People*, p. 87. In another case, plants—especially psychotropic plants—are often believed by the Campa to have spirits or souls of their own. If any of these plants are abused, their souls may travel to the sun (Pává) to complain; see Weiss, "World of a Forest Tribe," p. 264. In this connection, see also the description of the Selk'nam soul in Gusinde, *Los Indios de Tierra del Fuego. Los Selk'nam*, vol. 2, pp. 512–515.

85. Civrieux, *Watunna*, p. 176.

86. Ibid.

87. Civrieux, *Watunna*, p. 178.

88. Whitten, *Sacha Runa*, p. 57.

89. Ibid., p. 95.

90. Ibid.

91. Ibid., p. 67.

92. The multiple temporal frames, the "multiple realities" within which human experience, especially religious experience, is embedded may be illustrated by tracing the career of the Canelos Quichua souls. In addition to their inherited male or female souls, which reside in the right shinbones, young Canelos Quichua children often involuntarily pick up spirit-helpers, which are animal souls lying around the house. They enter children's mouths and live in children's *shungus* (the stomach-heart-throat area) see Whitten, *Sacha Runa*, p. 142. Eventually, in order to mature, a growing child will have to acquire additional souls. A Canelos Quichua man obtains increasing numbers of souls through hunting. The skins of the heads of monkeys and sloths are removed from the skull and shrunk. Monkey skins are containers of the human souls of foreigners. Bird souls may also be acquired and kept (ibid., p. 80).

Since all rocks may contain ancient souls, the destiny of human beings and of Canelos Quichua society is closely involved with stone. A soul-stone, *aya rumi*, is described in the same terms as a human being, especially a maturing shaman, as a "flower bud, a hard, silent enclosure which, when opening, brings to itself insects and birds with their continuous noise and motion" (ibid., p. 42). As is usual with enclosures of mystical substances, stones are the locus of transformative processes. Men are given these stones by Amasanga. They use them in attracting game during a hunt for converting monkey skin into drumheads, whose resonations bring contact with spirit souls. Women obtain their stones from Nunghuí via the stomachs of peccaries. These stones carry the songs of women to Nunghuí (ibid.). Hairballs found in the stomachs of tapirs are considered gifts to men from Amasanga. Hairballs found in the stomachs of white-lipped peccaries are gifts to women from Nunghuí (ibid., pp. 79–80).

People may also acquire additional souls and knowledge through visions induced by *ayahuasca* (ibid., pp. 40–41) or *Datura*, through acquisition of the souls of monkey-people (foreigners) who possess human souls (ibid., p. 41), or directly from the dead who died long ago (ibid., p. 42).

93. Fock, *Waiwai*, p. 15.

94. Ibid., p. 16.

95. Ibid., p. 19.

96. Ibid. The eye has a tremendous power manifest not only in seeing but in being seen. Once, in mythical times, an adolescent girl glanced into the middle of the river, causing the uprising of anaconda-people and bringing on a cosmic flood when they saw her looking at them.

97. Fock, *Waiwai*, p. 20.

98. Arrows frequently occupy a special place of value and are associated with the soul. For example, in the Kaingáng scheme of things, arrows can perceive when a man is threatened with death. They have this capacity to see "all the time" and may warn the threatened man by falling from their appointed place in his house (Henry, *Jungle People*, p. 86). Each arrow possesses a soul, called a *kuplêng*. When arrows become lost on hunting expeditions they weep ceaselessly. Eventually, if they are not retrieved, their soul will come and kill the hunter who lost them (ibid., pp. 14, 86).

99. Clastres notes that the *ové* of a deceased person threatens to become possessive of the body of a living person. The result of such possession would be disastrous. As a result, in order to prevent the *ové* from taking up residence in the bodies of the living, the body-envelope of the deceased, where the *ové* lingers, is consumed by the living in a cannibal ritual (Clastres, *Chronique des indiens guayakí*, p. 248). By depriving the *ové* of its body-home, one obliges it to hasten on its high road to heaven, "recognizing itself irrevocably for that which it is: a phantom without substance which no longer has anything to do with the living (ibid.).

100. Ibid., p. 250.

101. It is not clear what repercussions that possession of the *ové* of a deceased person carries with it. The *ové* does not affect the personality of the individual, nor his or her sex. Clastres surmises that it does not in any way transform the living person.

102. Ibid., p. 224.

103. Their bodies are covered with hair, a modulation of light. They are silent, though when they fall from the sky at night, they make loud noises through their anuses—sounds that possess a religious value.

104. Clastres, *Chronique des indiens guayakí*, p. 94.

105. Ibid.

106. Ibid., p. 246.

107. Ibid. However, the issue is far from clear since one person told Clastres that when the dead are eaten, "there is no more *ianvé*, *ianvé* flutters away" (ibid.). In general, there seems to be some inability on the part of Clastres' hosts to distinguish clearly and consistently between these two elements of the soul, the *ové* and the *ianvé*.

108. Ibid., p. 247.

109. Chagnon, Yąnomamö, p. 48. The most complete discussion of Yanoama concepts of soul, including souls of the dead, heavenly spirits, and spirits of other worlds, shadows, and alter-egos, occurs in Zerries and Schuster, *Mahekodotedi*, pp. 152–164.

110. Chagnon, *Yąnomamö*, p. 48.

111. Ibid., p. 50. The Yąnomamö recognize the audible sounds of their voices as this second soul-element; later on, as we shall see, they label the images of themselves in photographs as representatives of a third soul-constituent part, the *noreshi*.

112. Chagnon, *Yąnomamö*, pp. 49–50.

113. Napoleon A. Chagnon, "Yąnomamö Warfare, Social Organization and Marriage Alliances" (Ph.D. diss., University of Michigan, 1966); cited in Zerries and Schuster, *Mahekodotedi*, p. 160.

114. Ibid., p. 164.

115. Ibid., pp. 152–155.

116. Ibid., pp. 157–162.

117. Ibid., pp. 162–163.

118. Otto Zerries, "Die Vorstellung der Waika-Indianer des oberen Orinoko (Venezuela) über die menschliche Seele," *ICA*, (Copenhagen, 1958), pp. 105–113.

119. Zerries and Schuster, *Mahekodotedi*, p. 163.

120. It should be clear, however, that there is no question of a Cartesian solipsism. Even the autonomous faculties have an origin that relates them to another mode of being in another time; that is, the "divine soul" of speech may be relatively autonomous from the objects it speaks about, but it is nonetheless viewed by Guaraní groups (see below) as a shadow cast by the being

who is the source of celestial light in the world above and, therefore, the source of the shadow-life of the faculties here below.

121. Bartolomé, "Shamanism among the Avá-Chiripá," p. 112.

122. See León Cádogan, "El Concepto guaraní de alma," *Folia Lingüística Americana* 1 (1952): 1–4. See also Bartolomé, "Shamanism among the Avá-Chiripá," p. 111.

123. Ibid. Once again we find animal nature accounting for the imperfections and/or faults without which existence would not be what it is. However, the Guaraní situate this animal nature not so much in the mythical events at the beginning of time but within the human personality itself.

124. Ibid., pp. 111–112. We see here a striking example of orientation to the center of human space. The personality is ordered on the spatial planes and dimensions of the human being itself. The vertical axis, source of the light that brings shadows into existence, defines the state in which one gains a conscious grasp of oneself.

125. Pierre Bourdieu has suggested the possibility of analyzing rituals across time by employing a notion of *habitus* descended from the Augustinian tradition; see Bourdieu, *Outline of a Theory of Practice* (Cambridge, 1977). The analysis of social performance and meaningful behavior by the Apapocuvá is based on a similar strategy, although the history of French and Apapocuvá ideas of appetite, consumption, and habit are clearly unrelated.

126. Nimuendajú, *Mitos de creación*, pp. 51–67, 137–38.

127. The next two sections of this chapter will deal with commonly recognized temporal images, the dream and the shadow-soul, which are epistemologically important elements of the person. The final paragraphs of this section speak of temporal constitutents of the person expressed in the physiology of menstruation.

128. Hultkrantz, *Religions of the American Indians*, p. 131. Hultkrantz makes clear that his generalization applies most fully to North America (except the Southwest) and conjectures that "there are in South America many instances of soul-representations of a different structure" (p. 131). See also Åke Hultkrantz, *Conceptions of the Soul among North American Indians* (Stockholm, 1953), esp. pp. 52–53 and 272–273, which fruitfully develop the seminal investigations of Ernst Arbman. A helpful distinction should be maintained between the nature of the spiritual elements and the nature of the basis for their systematization. These two levels of categories are conceptually distinct.

129. This scholarly view extends back to the time of E. B. Tylor, who founded his entire theory of religion on the existence of two intellectual puzzles in "Primitive culture": death and dream. According to Tylor, two concepts of the souls were crafted to explain, on the one hand, the life-quickening element that exited the body at death but that could appear as a postmortem ghost and, on the other, the capacity that allowed the consciousness to wander far away while the body lay sleeping.

130. Such a confusion of levels of category is endemic in philosophical discussions surrounding logical typologies from Aristotle to Kant and from Frege to Russell.

131. Theodor Koch-Grünberg, *Vom Roroíma zum Orinoco*, vol. 3, *Ethnographie* (Berlin, 1923), pp. 170–172.

132. Roger Bastide, "The Sociology of the Dream," in G. E. von Grünebaum and Roger Caillois, eds., *The Dream and Human Societies* (Los Angeles, 1966), p. 199. This is not to say that dreams were held unimportant but only to point out that their significance could not be of the same sort as the value of conscious, social action. For example, Maurice Halbwachs, in his study of the rudimentary importance of social memory, deemed dream the example of pure memory itself. Ironically, for that very reason, he was forced to place dream imagery outside of the frame of social analysis; see Halbwachs, *Les Cadres sociaux de la mémoire* (Paris, 1914).

133. Dorothy Eggan, "Hopi Dreams in Cultural Perspective," in von Grünebaum and Caillois, eds., *The Dream and Human Societies*, pp. 240–241. Eggan was fascinated with the linguistic theses of Benjamin Whorf at the time she wrote this article. Compare, for example, Benjamin L. Whorf, "The Relation of Habitual Thought to Language," in Leslie Spier, A. Irving Hallowell, and Stanley S. Newman, eds., *Language, Culture and Personality: Essays in Memory of Edward Sapir* (Menasha, Wis., 1941), pp. 75–93, and Whorf, *Language, Thought and Reality: Selected Writings of Benjamin Lee Whorf*, ed. J. B. Carroll (Cambridge, Mass., 1956). It does not seem

necessary to accept Whorf's hypotheses about the nature and use of language in order to entertain the usefulness of Eggan's hypothetical premises, which, in this general form, apply also to South American views of dreaming. Eggan's works of Hopi dreaming are highly suggestive. See, for example, "The Significance of Dreams for Anthropological Research," *AA* 51 (1957): 1036–1045; "The Manifest Content of Dreams: A Challenge to Social Science," *AA* 54 (1952): 469–485; "The Personal Use of Myth in Dreams," in Thomas A. Sebeok, ed., *Myth: A Symposium* (Bloomington, Ind., 1965), pp. 107–121; and "Dream Analysis," in Bert Kaplan, ed., *Studying Personality Cross-Culturally* (Evanston, Ill., 1961), pp. 551–577. Of course, the connection between dream, myth, and ritual symbolism has been made often in the scholarly study of culture. Usually, however, the connection has served to trivialize both dream and myth as infantile or prelogical. The religious value of the imagination cannot be successfully extricated from the entire symbolic universe that humans inhabit during ecstasy, vision, dream, delirium, and hallucination. This is why even interpreters of high intellectual merit, such as Bernard Lonergan, fail to construct a convincing anthropology when they separate the conscious life of thought from the unconscious life of the dream-state. This continuity of myth and dream is asserted in South American cultures at the level of humankind's sacred nature, the nature of the soul, which assures continuity of the structure and meaning of human nature in all its states. Lonergan, to stay with him as an example, has little to say of value about the thoroughly human expression of myth. By degrading the imagery of human life in its "unconscious" state, Lonergan and others cannot be persuasive when they resurrect the value of the imagination in myth. For whatever cultural reasons, this trivialization of imagery in dream and myth does not carry over to symbols in purported rational and conscious exercises of the intellect in math, physics, logic, philosophical and theological doctrine, and so on. Lonergan's erudite anthropology, in short, is founded on a more stunted view of human insight than is the anthropology of the tribal peoples of South America. In comparison with South American views, Lonergan's analyses are exasperatingly lucid. This is decidedly not the case with such works as Kenelm Burridge, *Mambu: A Melanesian Millennium* (London, 1960), which contends that the concept of "myth-dream" among the Kanaka is a reality "which spans generations—not the momentary crises, physical expressions in a local cultural idiom, the symptoms. [The myth-dream] is the significant phenomenon" (p. 245). It is located "in myths, in dreams, in the half-lights of conversation, and in the emotional responses to a variety of actions. . . . [The myth-dream is] not private to any particular individual but . . . is shared by many. A community day-dream as it were" (p. 148).

Instead of basing culture theory on dream, contemporary theories of culture tend to form themselves on language (*langue* vs. *parole*). The patterned arrangement of images in language, as opposed to dream, serves as the generative template for cultural theories in vogue today.

134. This continuity does not exclude the images of social structure, even though its importance and meaning may be rearranged. As Bastide points out, "[W]ith us as with the traditional societies, the dream always takes its place in a social framework. But the anthropologist is able to achieve for the primitive a direct reading of the sleeping world from his observations of the waking world, because with him whether he sleep or work, he is the same man, and one continues in the same myth-based world" (Bastide, "Sociology of the Dream," p. 210). Recognizing the place that social structure occupies and the impermanent meanings it assumes in dreams, myths, and rites may be a first step in bringing into better perspective its exaggerated importance in contemporary social science. As the matter now stands, the illusion that social structures of "life on the ground"—the imagic concepts of western social science—are more concrete than dream imagery turns them into, in Victor Turner's words, "reinforced concrete." Eggan comments on the concept of continuity of existence and identity underlying Hopi dreams and contrasts it with "the burden [of discontinuity and the struggle for identity] that our concept of time imposes on us" (Eggan, "Hopi Dreams in Cultural Perspective," p. 253). She was told by a Hopi friend,

"When you ask a *bahana* [white] if he is hungry or sleepy he looks at his watch; you wear your God on your wrists." And now we can understand that this Hopi feeling of timelessness in our sense, of the continuity, or more exactly of the coexistence of events (the *manifesting* and *manifested*) through time . . . give validity to Hopi dream experience which we, with our linguistically circumscribed concepts of time and space, cannot know. . . . Dream action for all men unites past and future in the present, and in dreams space is absent. (ibid., pp. 253–254).

135. "A more thorough exploration, not only of native dreaming and dreams, but also of native dream theory and of its influence upon both dreaming and waking thought, is one of the most urgent tasks of psychologically oriented anthropology" (George Devereux, "Pathogenic Dreams in Non-Western Societies," in von Grünebaum and Caillois, *The Dream and Human Societies*, p. 226).

Myth, dream and song occupy an ambivalent position in the contemporary academic rendering of reality. However, across the sweep of time they have been valued as powerful and significant bases for the interpretations of culture. Although dream, in certain contemporary theories, may be privileged in assessing "pathological" views of reality, it rarely forms the basis for a general theory of culture and history as it has in other civilizations. For example, in the Islamic tradition, among the Isfahan metaphysical schools, the concept of *'álam al-mithal*, the "realm of images," became one of its most distinct and creative contributions to philosophy. Suhravardi defines it as the personal and individual realm of knowledge and experience upon which history and culture is based, for it avoided the exaggerated notion of intellectual abstraction from sense perception put forward by Aristotle as well as the exaggerated universalism of Platonic Ideas. Like time, the frame within which history and culture develops, the "realm of images" extended itself in a concrete way but, like a reflection in a mirror, was not material in the ordinary sense of spatial extension. In this way Suhravardi situated the study of history and culture over the central question of human meaningfulness made accessible through the symbolic imagination. He considered this to be more in keeping with the existential experience of human beings throughout time than any scholarly search for structures and rules of causality. The realm of symbolic imagination furnished concrete form for human significance. Long before Dilthey, Suhravardi argued that the meanings of these forms could only reveal themselves to investigators whose subjectivity, not merely logical analyses, penetrated their meanings. His ideas were refined and extended by Mir Damad and by Mulla Sadra. Mulla Sadra used *'álam al-mithal* as the foundation for his cognitive theory, his doctrine of the mutability of essences, his ontology of light, and his theory of history. See Henry Corbin, "The Visionary Dream in Islamic Society," in von Grünebaum and Caillois, eds. *The Dream and Human Societies*, pp. 381–408, and Corbin, *Terre céleste et corps de résurrection: De l'Iran mazdéen a l'Iran shiite* (Paris, 1960), which makes clear the relationship between devotional angelology and *'álam al-mithál*. See also Fazlur Rahman, "Dream, Imagination, and *'álam al-mithál*," in von Grünebaum and Caillois, *The Dream and Human Societies*, pp. 409–419, and Rahman, *The Philosophy of Mulla Sadra* (Albany, 1975).

For a discussion of a South Asian dream theory, which is a particular cultural construction of the judgment that "there is no impermeable boundary between dream and reality" (p. 61), see Wendy O'Flaherty, *Dreams, Illusions and Other Realities* (Chicago, 1984). In particular, O'Flaherty systematically analyzes the theory of dream contained in the *Yogavāsiṣṭha*, a Kashmiri text compiled between the sixth and twelfth centuries, by focusing on specific aspects of the theory: the shared dream (pp. 61–79), the myths of passage between reality and illusion (pp. 81–126), the myths about successive dreams within a dream (pp. 127–205), and the myths of the dreamer dreamt (pp. 206–259, esp. pp. 252–259). O'Flaherty decides that the approach to dream is fundamental to culture because it guides experience toward three kinds of truth: self-referential insights into the nature of dream (pp. 61–79), myth, and culture; truths about particular human experiences of love, children, and death (pp. 140–164), which become elaborated into a general understanding of the physical (pp. 174–188) and emotional (pp. 221ff.) universe; and speculative truths (293ff.) about "the relationship between our dreams of God and God's dream of us" (p. 304).

136. Waud H. Kracke, *Force and Persuasion: Leadership in an Amazonian Society*, (Chicago, 1978), p. 19.

137. Ibid. Of course the dreams not only signify different tenses, or different temporal modes (e.g., of the future or of the dead), but are different spatial worlds as well.

138. Holmberg, *Nomads of the Long Bow*, pp. 91ff.

139. Renate Brigitte Viertler, "A Noção de pessoa entre os Bororo," *Boletim do Museu Nacional* (Rio de Janeiro) n.s. 32 (May 1979); 24.

140. For example, bad dreams involving episodes of having one's hair cut may predict calamities. These associations are based on the mythology of the monsters Butoriku and Jure. Regarding the *aroe*, see Crocker, *Vital Souls*, esp. pp. 265–332.

141. Whitten, *Sacha Runa*, p. 58.

142. Ibid., p. 59.

143. Ibid., p. 67.

144. Ibid.

145. Manuela Carneiro da Cunha, "Eschatology Among the Kraho: Reflection Upon Society, Free Field of Fabulation," in Sally Humphreys and H. King, eds., *Anthropology and Archaeology of Death* (New York, 1981), p. 162.

146. Ibid.

147. Ibid., p. 163.

148. Nimuendajú, *The Apinayé*, p. 140.

149. Ibid. For another discussion of the meaning of the Apinayé word *me-karon* (images), see Matta, *A Divided World*, pp. 23, 55, 153. "Since everything has an 'image,' everything has a *me-karon*. The idea here is that there are two worlds, a real world and a world of images. But the Apinayé, not being Platonists, say that the real world is better than the image world since images are weaker and more ephemeral than their real counterparts" (ibid., p. 171).

150. See chapter 2, above. The personality of the creator may not be important or well delineated. Instead, the dream of existence may emanate from a vague creative power or barely described and mysterious primordial force, whether that first reality is the divine mind, a primordial sound, or beings now existing in the form of supernatural animals or natural elements.

151. Lawrence C. Watson, "Dreaming as World View and Action in Guajiro Culture," *JLAL* 7 (1981): 241.

152. Ibid., pp. 240–242.

153. Ibid., p. 241.

154. Ibid.

155. Civrieux, *Religion y magia kari'ña*, p. 23.

156. The similarities of the process should not blind us to the differences in the qualities of the imagery of thought, of language, and of reverie. These distinct kinds of image allow for quite different cultural appraisals about the nature of creation's meaning. The matrix of creative being within which images arise may be a supernatural divinity. For example, in the case of the Witoto, "In the beginning there was nothing but mere appearance, nothing really existed. It was a phantasm, an illusion that our father touched; something mysterious that he grasped. Nothing existed. Through the agency of a dream our father, He-who-is-appearance-only, Nainema, pressed the phantasm to his breast and then was sunk in thought" (Konrad T. Preuss, *Religion und Mythologie der Uitoto*, vol. 1, Göttingen, 1921, pp. 166–168, as presented in Paul Radin, *Monotheism among Primitive Peoples*, Basel, 1954, pp. 13–14). Alternately, the creative matrix for the images of existence may be preternatural animals or even formless forces of being.

157. Weiss, "World of a Forest Tribe," p. 428.

158. Ibid., p. 356.

159. Ibid.

160. Ibid., p. 390.

161. By looking at what he calls linguistic deep structures, Lévi-Strauss has examined only the surface features of the shared nature of myth and music:

> If we try to understand the relationship between language, myth, and music, we can only do so by using language as the point of departure, and then it can be shown that music on the

one hand and mythology on the other both stem from languages but grow apart in different directions, that music emphasizes the sound aspect already embedded in language, while mythology emphasizes the sense aspect, the meaning aspect [i.e., the formal set of logical relations] which is also embedded in language. (Claude Lévi-Strauss, *Myth and Meaning*, New York, 1978, p. 53)

Because he bases his analysis on linguistic methods derived from the study of phonetic structures of words rather than from the semantic structures of images, Lévi-Strauss mistakes surface for depth and form for meaning; see Lawrence E. Sullivan, "Lévi-Strauss, Mythologic, and South American Religions," in Moore and Reynolds, eds, *Anthropology and the Study of Religion*, pp. 147–176.

162. Contemporary Western hermeneutics has not emphasized the heuristic value of performance. Nonetheless, recent studies of the creative imagination and of the importance of the "audience" of the interpreter open themselves up to a full-blown performative hermeneutics; see Sullivan, "Sound and Senses"

163. The period that Akwẽ-Shavante initiates spend in the bachelors' hut is one marked by an insistence on sharing. Understanding the role of performance in interpretation helps explain why the sharing is true not only of food and of work preparatory to ceremonies but also in the matter of the songs acquired during dreams. These songs are sung at night to give evidence of the fact that the young boys are vigilant and thus fulfilling the ideal of the Shavante man (Maybury-Lewis, *Akwẽ-Shavante Society*, p. 113).

164. Bartolomé, "Shamanism among the Avá-Chiripá," p. 128.

165. Ibid.

166. Ibid., p. 131.

167. Ibid., p. 112.

168. Ibid. See also Miguel Alberto Bartolomé, "Notas sobre etnografía apyteré," 4 (1969): 63–75.

169. See, for example, Paul Ricoeur, *Interpretation Theory* (Fort Worth, Tex., 1976), pp. 71–89, and Ricoeur, "Explanation and Understanding: On Some Remarkable Connections Among the Theory of the Text, Theory of Action, and Theory of History," in Charles E. Reagan and David Stewart, eds., *The Philosophy of Paul Ricoeur: An Anthology of His Work* (Boston, 1978). The problem of arriving at authentic interpretation without sterile tautology threads its way throughout the history of hermeneutics. See, for example, Richard Palmer, *Hermeneutics: Interpretation Theory in Schleiermacher, Dilthey, Heidegger and Gadamer* (Evanston, Ill., 1969). The problem is by no means restricted to philosophical hermeneutics; for an example taken from professional anthropology, see Clifford Geertz, *The Interpretation of Cultures* (New York, 1973), esp. pp. 93–123, where Geertz discusses religious life as both a model *of* and model *for* society and interpretation. The problem is similar in the debates over proper interpretation of art, literary texts, and music: viz., that of setting the meaning of reality expressed in one set of images within the context of the interpreter's reality. One of the keys to finding a solution lies in the appraisal of the nature of the distance between one expression of reality and another. For the cultures of South America, myth offers increasingly concrete and imagic language to use as one approaches the world of being where these two dimensions of reality intersect (within the image-/dream-soul as well as in the primordium). Western hermeneutics, on the contrary, seems to reach the climax of its struggle for adequate language when it attempts to measure out and define the nature of the distance between the "world of the text" and the "world of the reader." For example, David Tracy offers this summary of "the common subject matter expressed through the form in the text which provokes the questions for the preunderstanding of the interpreter":

> Both text and reader, moreover, are not static but process realities: the identity of each is an identity-in-difference. The major "difference" occurs when a genuine conversation occurs between text and interpreter. Then the classic becomes a classic provoking a genuine (as different) interpretation. And the reader becomes a genuine reader of the classic provoked into a new self-understanding. These constantly shifting horizons of both text and reader in conversation head toward some new "fusion of horizons" (in Gadamer's justly famous

phrase)—a fusion of the horizons (in my language) of the identity-in-difference of the text and the identity-in-difference of the reader into a new identity-in-difference: an interpretation that will recognize itself as "understanding differently" insofar as it understands at all. (Tracy, *Analogical Imagination*, p. 136)

Although the problems facing interpreters in native South America and contemporary academia are similar ones, the overreliance on "text" as the genre privileged with unique intelligibility severely restricts the applicability of the academic hermeneutics when trying to deal with the realities of dream, sound, performance. Properly understood, they should not be viewed as "text," a species of expression which is already an arrangement of images constraining its proper interpretation; nor even should they be viewed as language, if by language is meant ordered sound or deep-structural grammar used in expressing thoughts in words. They are meaningful images expressed in significantly different modes of human activity. They are stylized semantic fields whose specific forms of expression are themselves symbolic and significant. The mode of activity (dream, dance, song, performance) has a direct bearing on understanding and cannot be reduced to the mode of action called "text" of spoken language without losing part of its unique meaning in the translation. See Adrian Marino, *L'Herméneutique de Mircea Eliade*, trans. Jean Gouillard (Paris 1980).

170. Paul Ricoeur, *Time and Narrative* (Chicago, 1984). Among the many fascinating considerations, Ricoeur views psychoanalysis as casting the images (metaphors) of unconscious life into the rhythms of conscious narrative.

171. The continuity between reality peripheral to attention and the dream-reality is not a perception unique to traditional societies. For an example of that connection in the psychological theory of Western science, see Charles Fischer and I. H. Paul, "The Effects of Subliminal Visual Stimulation on Images and Dreams: A Validation Study," *Journal of American Psychoanalytic Association* (1959). However, the emphasis that dream life and the world peripheral to attention are temporally related because they both relate to sacred realities manifest as primordial images is not shared by the current scientific approach. The continuity of the two realms of image-realities is an emphasis variously interpreted in different religious systems. For example, the ancient Greeks' negative view of myth found its way into their judgment of the value of dream as well as the images peripheral to full consciousness. "To archaic Greek consciousness, dreams belonged to the spatial and temporal peripheries of the cosmos, to the antiworld that surrounds the world, to the antireality that is found outside real time and real space. . . . [But that antiworld] has supernatural value: Chaos is not only the reverse of cosmos, it is also its condition and foundation" (Angelo Brelich, "Dreams in the Religious World Concept of the Greeks," in von Grünebaum and Caillois, *The Dream and Human Society*, pp. 300–301).

172. Victor Turner, drawing upon insights from Freud's analysis of the processual structure of dream patterns, argued that the same quality was present in symbolic social action, especially ritual. See Turner, *The Ritual Process* (Chicago, 1969). The implications of the term *processual structure of ritual* were described in a review of Turner's work by Charles Keyes, *Journal of Asian Studies* 36 (1977): 283. For an example of Freud's treatment of the dream as a patterned processual structure, see Freud, *The Interpretation of Dreams* (1899; New York, 1927). Most important is Freud's stimulating suggestion that the process is imaged at two levels: one casts experience and emotion into images, the second recasts the meaning of those already translated images into further disguised form. Bastide, along with Freud and Turner, has stated that the spiritual continuity in the encounter with every appearance of reality includes social reality, for "sociological structure does indeed find its place in oneiric images," albeit in changed and inverted form. Bastide contends that biased obstinacy shrinks those sciences and disciplines that insist on dealing only with structures that conform to their narrow view of authentic human reality. See Bastide, "Sociology of the Dream," p. 210. Peter Homans, "Once Again, Psychoanalysis East and West," *HR* 24 (November 1984); 133–154, underlines, in connection with dreams, the need to study all images as part of the infrastructure (of developmental processes) that constitute the human imagination and cultural systems (pp. 148f.).

173. A clear example has been presented above for the case of the Canelos Quichua. During their nocturnal dreams, rites, and sexual acts performed at the center of the house-universe they

bring together the realms of forest, water, and garden soil with the primordial images of Ancient Times.

174. Gabriel Martínez, "Topónimos de Chuani," *ALIM* 1 (1983); 51–84.

175. The Baniwa formulate a system of resemblances which operates on many levels thus: visual, sonic, social, individual, linguistic, narrative. In his criticism of structuralist notions of metaphor underlying several contemporary theories of resemblances, Ricoeur calls for a phenomenology of imagination that would provide access to the semantic fields (not just bundles of formal relations) that lie beyond the "frontiers" of verbal expression. "Bachelard," says Ricoeur, "has taught us that the image is not a residue of impression, but an aura surrounding speech: 'the poetic image places us at the origin of the speaking being.'" In the end, however, Ricoeur finds it impossible to step behind spoken language to find meaning, for, following Bachelard, Ricoeur, philosopher of narrative text in a culture based on the Book, is convinced that "the poem gives birth to the image"; see Paul Ricoeur, *The Rule of Metaphor: Multidisciplinary Studies in the Creation of Meaning in Language* (Toronto, 1981), p. 214. Ricoeur is quoting Gaston Bachelard, *The Poetics of Space*, trans. Maria Jolas (Boston, 1969), p. xix. See also Bachelard, *The Poetics of Reverie*, trans. Daniel Russell (New York, 1969), pp. 1–26, for a helpful statement of Bachelard's position on the matters at hand in this and the previous section.

176. Wright, "History and Religion of the Baniwa," pp. 404ff.

177. Civrieux, *Religión y magia kari'ña*, p. 70.

178. Ibid.

179. Ibid., p. 72.

180. Ibid., p. 74.

181. Ibid., p. 75.

182. See, for example, the relationship of image to memory in the Desana epistemology outlined by Reichel-Dolmatoff in *Amazonian Cosmos*, pp. 64, 93–97, 126. Reflection is a process of relationship between the soul (*simporá*), located in the heart, and *ka'í* (the mind), located in the brain. Their relationship over a lifetime accumulates in the form of a residual image, a shadow (also *ka'í*) which lives eternally after the death of the body. The *ka'í* allows the Desana to reflect (*pesi d'ranyearí*, a word based on the verb *peri*, "to hear") At the same time the process of reflection is a contemplation of visual images (existing in the form of remembered sounds — that is, images that comprise the essential structures of sound, and not the noises themselves). The vision of reflection is *tularí*, a "penetrating glance." The soul of a shaman is said to be "a fire whose light penetrates obscurity and makes things visible" (ibid., 126). Among the Kógi as well, the penetrating glance (*sojorín*) of reflection makes shadow-images visible. See Reichel-Dolmatoff, *Los Kogi* vol. 2, p. 134. Kógi dreams penetrate time as well, linking the individual to his or her future through the symbolic signs that appear in dreams. The significations apparent in dream are efficacious, for their very appearance effects the conditions of the future. For a list of typical symbols and their interpretations, see Reichel-Dolmatoff, "Los Kogi," part 1, pp. 288ff. For another example, see the way the Yąnomamö related image-souls (*noreshi*, visual animal image; *no uhudibo*, aural image) to will (*buhii*, the "self" that exists as a postmortem *no borebö* — an ethereal being — in the celestial realm of the primordium), described in Chagnon, *Yąnomamö*, pp. 48–50.

183. This is a summary statement of the South American views presented in this section. Crocker suggests that one is never so much oneself and the meaning of one's identity is never so clear as when one is a significant *other*; see Jon Christopher Crocker, "Selves and Alters among the Eastern Boróro," in David Maybury-Lewis, ed., *Dialectical Societies* (Cambridge, Mass., 1979), pp. 249–300. Self-possession is the fruit of seeing one's image in another, a process that implies identification with the other to some degree. This seems to be the point of the communication theory and relational theories of, for example, R. D. Laing in *The Divided Self* (New York, 1969) and *The Facts of Life: An Essay in Feelings, Facts, and Fantasy* (New York, 1976). Mark Kline Taylor suggests that the discipline of cultural anthropology may provide the same base for a new self-understanding of Western cultures. He analyzes the perception of the "ethnographic other" in Lévi-Strauss. Taylor suggests that Lévi-Strauss's perception of the "otherness" of culture is homologous to the encounter with the "radically other" mode of being that underlies certain theories of religious experience (that of Rudolf Otto, for example). Taylor implies that

ethnographers' experience, expressed in their theories, can serve as a source of reflection for theologies of culture wishing to interpret the religious qualities of modern secular experience. See Mark Kline Taylor, "Religion among the Anthropologists," *Papers in Comparative Studies* (Ohio State University) 3 (1984): 55–70. More intriguing would be the reflecting on the ethnographies themselves, the reports of the religious worlds of aboriginal Oceania, Asia, Africa, and the Americas. Theology might interpret them not only as encounters with "others"— encounters that serve as sources of personal self-understanding for certain modern anthropologists—but as confrontations with "ultimate reality" as humans perceive it in "other" cultures. Here lies the foundation of a new theology of culture.

184. It is fascinating to contrast the Kari'ña shadow-soul with Jean-Paul Sartre's use of the images of the face as the basis of a kind of consciousness that constructs the magical (as opposed to determined) world of emotion. Both sorts of reflection constitute a world. However, the distinct values assigned to the worlds situate the human being within a different orientation toward the self and reality. See Sartre, *Esquisse d'une théorie generale des émotions* (New York, 1948), pp. 83–85. Alphonse de Waelhens, *Une Philosophie de l'ambiguité* (Louvain, 1967), esp. pp. 61–152, reviews the notion of ambiguity as it relates to space, the body, the physical senses, and language in Merleau-Ponty's philosophy; see also the discussion of "the ethics of the face" in Emmanuel Levinas, *Totality and Infinity* (New York, 1969).

185. The techniques of spirituality aid in the process of seeing the distinctive features of shadow existence. The lengthy process is sometimes circumvented with magic (e.g., by using a mirror), in which case the value of the process is altered.

186. It should be clear that resemblance based on a *contiguity* between the soul-shadow and the dark distinctions marking the features of all earthly reflections of primordial light is decidedly different from the concept of resemblance based on *metaphor* (substitution) as the primary trope. See Paul Ricoeur, "The Work of Resemblance," in *The Rule of Metaphor*, pp. 173–215.

The facile conclusion that these views are Platonic could only come from a superficial glance at them. Many religious systems utilize the contrasts between light and shadow; however, they apply them in the service of vastly different systems of value and meaning. Plato's exposition of the theory of the recollection of Ideas (e.g., *Meno* 81 a–e) and of soul (e.g., *Gorgias* 493; *Phaedo* 107e; *Republic*, bk. 7) does not exhaust all coherent meanings assigned to polar dyads of light and darkness. For a sample of the wide variety of religious meanings of light and shadow, see Mircea Eliade, "Experiences of the Mystic Light," in *Mephistopheles and the Androgyne* (New York, 1965), pp. 19–77, which discusses the Iglulik Eskimo light-concept of *qaumaneq*, the "solidified light" of Australian aboriginal thought, the Tibetan myth of the Man of Light and the light of the *bardo*, South Asian concepts of light in relation to *ātman* as well as to yogic mystical practice, the experience of light in the Chinese alchemical text *The Secret of the Golden Flower*, and the role of light in the Hebrew Bible and in Eastern Christian mysticism.

187. Civrieux, *Religión y magia kari'ña*, p. 18. In fact, depending on the primordial image of one's soul, meanings of the world, even in the same culture, may be quite different. For example, because of the separate histories of male and female souls and the different images in which they once existed, the Canelos Quichua world has different meanings from female and male points of view. Both males and females were once stars, for example, but the star-people are reckoned to have become white grubs or larvae from the female point of view, whereas they became white mushrooms from the male point of view. Even the concept of "present" does not exist in a unified abstract form. Rather, a series of "now times" vary according to the images of place, time, age, sex, and degree of knowledge of the speaker (Whitten, *Sacha Runa*, p. 46).

188. The continuity of the soul, ironically, allows for understanding spontaneous spiritual experiences since it represents the contact with that eternal creative world from which, for example, the soul's image derives or to which it travels in dream. Spontaneity represents the unforeseen interruption of primordial creativity into everyday space and time. The above discussion of the dream-soul and its spontaneous journeys into the primordial and "eternal" time brings out the close relationship enjoyed between constancy and spontaneity.

189. Reichel-Dolmatoff, *Amazonian Cosmos*, p. 28.

190. Menstruation is not the only image of periodic time comprising the person. Just as dream was only one kind of imagery composing the individual (in addition to ritual imagery, delirium,

ecstasy, vision, peripheral attention, sound), menstruation is the clearest example of the periodic flow of time manifest in the imagery constructing the person.

191. Weiss, "World of a Forest Tribe," pp. 376ff. Weiss also provides parallel information from the Machiguenga (pp. 567–569). There, too, bathing is a source of life through impregnation. Perhaps this serves as a kind of model for the bathing that, in the Machiguenga conception, rejuvenates one and helps one to shed one's skin.

192. Bastien, *Mountain of the Condor*, p. 161. Blood (*yawar*) of different qualities circulates throughout the mountain-body on which the community lives. Their life is essentially one with the manifest and unmanifest life of the mountain whose heart (*sonqo*) pumps blood to its residents, relating them to one another through their *yawar masikuna* ancestral line (literally, "blood neighbors"); see pp. 45–46.

193. Mariscotti de Görlitz, *Pachamama Santa Tierra*, pp. 117–120 and 292–295, discusses the symbolism of these ritual acts at the feast of Citua (Situa, Sitowa, Cithua) and gathers together the principal sources describing the feast in Inca and pre-Incaic culture.

194. For a discussion of some of the ways in which symbolically controlled exchange, in relation to the body, is a temporal punctuation mark, a caesura creating periodic rhythms, see Jean Baudrillard, *L'Echange symbolique et la mort* (Paris, 1976). Baudrillard discusses the symbolism of the political economy of death as it appears in such body-related actions as burial, strip-tease, transvestism, and speaking.

195. Roe, *Cosmic Zygote*, p. 106.

196. Ibid., p. 105.

197. Ibid., pp. 105–106.

198. That is why Lévi-Strauss is able to analyze the embeddedness of these social relations in myths that feature the periodic elements of nature—the sun, the moon, the zodiac, the seasons; see, for example, *The Origin of Table Manners*. Lévi-Strauss is never more brilliant than when he points out the interconnection of many different periodic "codes." He also shows that they are associated with female menstrual periods. Control over periodicity is the basis of morality, for Lévi-Strauss, because it regulates right (i.e., morally as well as temporally proper) relations. For a discussion of Lévi-Strauss' approach to these matters, see Sullivan, "Lévi-Strauss, Mythologic, and South American Religions."

199. See the discussion of this question by Sherry Ortner, "Is Female to Male as Nature is to Culture?" in H. R. Rosaldo and Louise Lamphere, eds., *Women, Culture and Society* (Palo Alto, Cal., 1974), pp. 67–88. The article has provoked fruitful discussion of the terms and issues in its title and is valuable, above all, for the discussion it has engendered concerning the value and usefulness of the dichotomy. Several authors identify women with nature on various grounds; for example, see Luce Irigaray, "Women's Exile," *Ideology and Consciousness* 1 (1977): pp. 62–76; Julia Kristeva, *About Chinese Women* (London, 1977); Susan Lipshitz, ed., *Tearing the Veil: Essays on Femininity* (London, 1978); M. Montrelay, "Inquiry into Femininity," *m/f* 1 (1978): 83–101. Olivia Harris and others, however, hesitate to endorse this direction of thought:

> [T]o identify certain structures of masculine dominance cannot of itself lead to the conclusion that culture in its entirety is the domain of men. This would be to make the mistake, in Bourdieu's words, of privileging "the *structure* of signs, that is, the relations between them, at the expense of their *practical functions*, which are never reducible, as structuralism tacitly assumes, to functions of communication or knowledge." . . . [I]t is all too easy for anthropologists using the dominant discourse of European culture to universalize our own categories of male and female, nature and culture, and thus render ourselves deaf to alternative ways of structuring the world. (Harris, "The Power of Signs: Gender, Culture, and the Wild in the Bolivian Andes," in Carol P. MacCormack and Marilyn Strathern, eds., *Nature, Culture, and Gender*, London, 1980, p. 93; the article contains a helpful bibliography on the issue)

Harris argues that "[M]any of the resonances attached to these English terms are not applicable to Andean representations, and to use them as a shorthand would preclude a full understanding of what associations are actually being made" (ibid., p. 71). See also Olivia Harris, "Complementarity and Conflict: An Andean View of Women and Men," in J. LaFontaine, ed., *Sex and Age* as *Principles of Social Differentiation* (London, 1978), pp. 21–40. Katherine Arnold, "The Introduction of Poses to a Peruvian Brothel and Changing Images of Male and Female," in John Blacking, ed., *The Anthropology of the Body* (New York, 1977), pp. 179–197, emphasizes the fluid relationship between images of masculinity and femininity as they are affected by changes in culture, society, technology, and economy. Irene Marsha Silverblatt, *Moon, Sun, and Devil: Inca and Colonial Transformations of Andean Gender Relations*, is a more extensive historical study of the shifting images of gender and the transformation of their meaning. The following works criticize the very notion of a "status" of women: Penny Schine Gold, *The Lady and the Virgin: Image, Attitude, and Experience in Twelfth-Century France* (Chicago, 1985); Michelle Zimbalist Rosaldo, "The Use and Abuse of Anthropology: Reflections on Feminism and Cross-Cultural Understanding," *Signs: Journal of Women in Culture and Society* 5 (1980): 401; Martin King Whyte, *The Status of Women in Preindustrial Societies* (Princeton, 1978); Naomi Quinn, "Anthropological Studies on Women's Status," *Annual Review of Anthropology* 6 (1977): 181–183; and Bynum's *Holy Feast and Holy Fast*, cited above. Bynum calls "generalizations about '*the* status of women'—statements to which historians have sometimes been tempted—presumptuous and ill-advised" (p. 22).

200. In an article sharply critical of anthropology's unwillingness to examine its temporal foundations, Kees Bolle underscores the fact that the "history" of the "ethnographic present" has little to do with any philosophically grounded idea of history. He writes,

> Both synchronic and diachronic manners of examining materials, expressions, rituals, symbols, are just that: manners of looking. They are instruments used. Without facetiousness, one might imagine an even greater sharpening of anthropological tools in the future. After all, one might have, next to synchrony and diachrony, also achrony (looking at things without even thinking of time), or even antichrony (looking at things while violently resenting time). These terms have nothing whatever to do with history. . . . History is something other than diachrony, it is something other than evolution or development. (Kees W. Bolle, "The History of Religions and Anthropology: A Theoretical Crisis," *Epoche: Journal of the History of Religions at UCLA* 7, 1980, p. 7)

201. See the stimulating review of this problem, from a quite different angle, in Johannes Fabian, *Time and the Other: How Anthropology Makes its Object,* (New York, 1983). Even the pioneering work of Georges Gurvitch failed to move sociology from its skinny temporal foundations to considerations of other notions of time and history. In addition to the cognitive dissonance of Gurvitch's views in his day, he was less than persuasive perhaps because he left time unassailable by regnant social analysis when he posited a plurality of qualities of social time that were essentially relativist and unanchored in social roles and statuses. In the face of the numberless kinds of social time that he makes plausible by his argument, Gurvitch's simplistic division of them into two general types ("promothean," the historical time governing modern societies, and all other "ethnographic" societies generally unconcerned over precise reckoning of time) was of little use to anyone. For a look at various social-scientific attempts to come to grips with multiple modes of social time, see Fritz Kramer, "Über Zeit, Genealogie and solidarische Beziehung," in Fritz Kramer and Christian Sigrist, eds., *Gesellschaften ohne Staat,* vol. 2, *Genealogie und Solidarität* (Frankfurt, 1978), pp. 9–27; Victor Gioscia, "On Social Time," in Henri Yaker, Humphrey Osmond, and Frances Cheek, eds., *The Future of Time* (Garden City, N.Y., 1971), pp. 73–141; David Turton and Clive Ruggles, "Agreeing to Disagree: The Measurement of Duration in a Southwestern Ethiopian Community," *CA* 19 (1978): 585–600; and D. N. Malz, "Primitive Time-Reckoning as a Symbolic System," *Cornell Journal of Social Relations* 3 (1969); 85–111, which contains an extensive bibliography on the history of the study of time in social science. These and other works are critically discussed in chapter 2, "Our Time, Their Time, No Time: Coevalness Denied," of Fabian, *Time and the Other.* For a discussion of this question in the context of an application of anthropological approaches to the Christian liturgical calendar, see Dario Zadra, "Victor Turner's Theory of Religion: Toward an Analysis of Symbolic Time," in Moore and Reynolds, eds., *Anthropology and the Study of Religions,* 77–104.

202. "Blood," for example, has been central to kinship studies from their inception to the present. Early kinship studies sensed the connection between blood, avoidances, relations, and

time in generation and descent. However, the incapacity to deal with the local systems of time, which would have allowed a fully symbolic consideration of "blood," made early studies cele-brated failures of materialist literalism. See, for example, Lewis Henry Morgan, *Ancient Society or Researches in the Lines of Human Progress from Savagery through Barbarism to Civilization*, edited with an introduction and annotations by Eleanor Burke Leacock (1877; Gloucester, Mass., 1974), esp. pp. 410–432 of systems of consanguinity. For a contemporary attempt to study the fully symbolic value of "blood" in contemporary North American kinship see David M. Schneider, *American Kinship: A Cultural Account* (Englewood Cliffs, N.J., 1968), pp. 23ff. and pp. 111ff., which emphasizes the cultural *depiction* of blood, as a symbol invested with meaning in a cultural system of ideas, emotions, and motives. Blood becomes a feature in distinguishing sets of relations. Says Schneider, "Kinship is *not* a theory about biology; but biology serves to formulate a theory about kinship" (p. 115). In general, Schneider does not treat either the material or symbolic construct of blood as inherently rhythmic, related to a species of time (the images and tempos of descent). "Relatives by blood" he claims, "are linked by *material* sub-stance . . . blood is a *permanent* tie" (p. 37). Schneider presents an essentially static set of distinctive features in the "ethnographic present," which is simply perpetuated across time as a system of relations as though it had no intrinsic relationship to the quality of history (the set of relations called descent) that it creates. For lucid commentary on the temptation to materialist and biological reductionism inherent in the very categories used to study social structures, see Marshall Sahlins, *Culture and Practical Reason* (Chicago, 1976), esp. pp. 57–60, 73, 87, 98, 121.
203. Sahlins points out the thinness and nonexistence of theories of meaning in anthropology, which conceives of culture as an intervention in nature, in chapter 3, "Anthropology and Two Marxisms: Problems of Historical Materialism," of *Culture and Practical Reason*, pp. 126–165, esp. pp. 151, 164.
204. Sahlins calls this "the founding disagreement over the nature of the anthropological object. . . . If these oppositions [e.g., "history/science," "culture/society," "diachrony/synchrony"] succeeded in generating a development from one theoretical moment to the next, it was only to reproduce at each stage the unresolved contradiction at the base" (ibid., p. 73).
205. Bolle harshly attributes the persistence of the dogmatic distinction between "conscious" and "unconscious" meaning to

> the psychological satisfaction of being in charge. Religious folks, so this mechanism oper-ates, do not really know what makes them tick. Fortunately, the anthropologist does know. What has only an unconscious basis among these people, the trained observer is capable of figuring out consciously at last. The *very meaning* of these people's traditions, their religion, their memories, the stories they tell, the significance of all this *is not known to them but is known to the anthropologist*. Their own expressions, *their* images, *their* stories, *their* asser-tions, *their* beliefs, *their* history will yield their real significance only when the anthropolo-gist applies his bag of tricks to make the meaning consciously realized at last. (Bolle, "History of Religions and Anthropology, pp. 8–9).

In quite a different tone, I assess the appeal of the dichotomies hypothetically existing in the "deep structures" of linguistic codes manifest in myth; see Sullivan, "Lévi-Strauss, Mythologic, and South American Religions," pp. 161–163. See Charles H. Long, "Primitive/Civilized: The Locus of Problem," *HR* 20 (1980); 43–61, for a discussion of the ways in which existing catego-ries of value (e.g., medical and religious dichotomies) of European thought were applied to ethnographic realities during the encounter of cultures in exploration and colonial expansion.
206. "Most of anthropology's borrowed (should I say: stolen?) vocabulary is scientifically inap-propriate, not relevant to the subject studied; but its very arrogance makes it contagious. It makes the user feel powerful" (Bolle, "History of Religions and Anthropology," p. 9).
207. See "Essay in Protest Anthropology," by the Ethiopian anthropologist Asmaron Legessee in his excellent book *Gada: Three Approaches to the Study of African Society* (New York, 1973).
208. See Sullivan, "Lévi-Strauss, Mythologic, and South American Religions," pp. 161–163.
209. The problem is twofold: how to craft a language for the study of religion that is not in itself religious discourse (theology), and, second, how to speak, on a general and comparative level, of meanings specific to cultural systems. See a lengthy treatment of this question in Leszlek Kolakowski, *Religion* (New York, 1982).

210. The fact that many cultures use these concepts to evaluate the sacrality of gender is quite a different sort of conclusion; see, for example, the case of the Barasana presented in Christine Hugh-Jones, "Skin and Soul," and *From the Milk River*, pp. 235–275. See also Stephen Hugh-Jones, "Like the Leaves on the Forest Floor."

211. See, for example, the case of the Bororo parents who abstain from certain foods during pregnancy. Which foods are avoided depends on the knowledge of which particular *bope*, the supernatural being who shapes the foetus, inhabits the expectant mother's womb. Familiarity with the sacred allows one to recognize the *bope* who enters a woman's womb during the period of pregnancy. Such knowledge of the supernatural is reflected in the periodic abstentions from the foods associated with that *bope*. In the Bororo view, periodic avoidances of food, which take their cue from the character of sacred beings that periodically enter the body, set humans apart from animals.

212. The sound of falling fruit becomes one of the most striking and efficacious images of the passage of time when the eternity of the primordium passes into the transitional mode of time conditioning human life. This widespread symbolism is largely ignored in scholarly interpretation. Chapter 2, above, discusses how the sound of falling fruit marks off the otherwise measureless and formless chaos of the flood; see Sullivan, "Sacred Music and Sacred Time," pp. 33–52, as well as Civrieux, *Watunna*, passim, and Wright, "History and Religion of the Baniwa," passim, for illustrations of the extensive application of this sound-image in myth and rite. Furthermore, for a myth linking sound and fruit to the passage of time marked off by human generations see Hugh-Jones, *The Palm and the Pleiades*, pp. 270–271, for a summary of the myth of the Ayawa and the Tree-Fruit Jaguar. The Ayawa, children of the eternal sky, are the three Thunders who literally help pass the time in two ways: first, by ejaculating their sperm into *kanea* (*Chrysophyllum caimito*) fruit to create their younger brother, and, second, by obtaining night. To end the first catastrophic night, the younger brother discovers the dawn while the Ayawa make the croaking sound of *umamu* (*Hyla* sp.) frogs. Sound is a key marker establishing the periodic orders (older/younger generations, day/night) that condition human existence. The periodic ripening of fruit is viewed as a sign of the changing of the soul, a condition of this world. In the primordial world fruit did not ripen and rot since it had a different, "shamanized" nature, which kept it from becoming exhausted. Today, however, since the disappearance of the primordial shaman-beings, there is less fruit, and it must renew its appearance periodically so that it does not become exhausted and stop.

213. See the considerable mass of comparative materials illustrating an inherent connection between three kinds of periodic existence: the seasonal ripening of fruit (pp. 63–79), the life-cycle changes of the body viewed as a container of forces constituting different kinds of relations (pp. 197–199, 237–273), and the generative knowledge obtained during the celebrations of initiation (pp. 292ff.) in Zerries, *Waika*. See also Zerries and Schuster, *Mahekodotedi*, passim, but especially the section entitled "Die Pijiguao-Palme und ihre Rolle in Mythos und Kult," pp. 285–290, which discusses the role of palm fruit both in relation to the times of dance and initiation as well as in the myths of origin.

214. Clastres, *Chronique des indiens guayaki*, p. 135.

215. The notions of "shame" and "respect" are discussed in relation to the seclusions of rites of passage chapter 6, below.

216. Hugh-Jones, *The Palm and the Pleiades*, p. 132; see pp. 112 and 127–132 for discussion and references to important mythic materials in the appendices.

217. Fock, *Waiwai*, p. 129.

218. Ibid., p. 140.

219. Nimuendajú, *The Apinayé*, pp. 23, 27. See the detailed and lucid discussion of Apinayé names and name-giving in da Matta, *A Divided World*, especially chapter 3. da Matta extends and clarifies the data provided by Nimuendajú. da Matta bases his analyses on his own field work.

220. A variety of conclusions are drawn about the nature of names throughout the considerable linguistic, ethnographic, philosophical, theological, and scriptural literature on names. In regard to scriptural and theological treatment see, for example, Martin Noth, "Israelitischen Personennamen," *Beiträge zur Wissenshaft vom Alten und Neuen Testament* 3rd series 10 (1928): 10, and James Barr, *The Semantics of Biblical Language* (New York, 1961), pp. 107–109. For an examination of the social and cognitive power of naming from the point of view of

contemporary theology, see Phyllis Trible, *God and the Rhetoric of Sexuality* (Philadelphia, 1978), p. 17ff. For a discussion of the importance of the cultural process of naming in the rise and development of theological doctrine, see Martin Hengel, *The Son of God: The Origin of Christo-logy and the History of Jewish-Hellenistic Religion* (Philadelphia, 1976). Miguel de los Rios, "Hacía una hermeneutica del nombre en la etnía mataco," *SE* year 3, no. 3, part 2 (1976): 68–88, analyzes instances of name-giving, and, through a close reading of associated myths and inter-preting the role of supernatural figures, he suggests that the understanding of names could be a gateway to a total hermeneutics of culture.

221. Nimuendajú, *Mitos de creación*, pp. 52–53.

222. Ibid., p. 53; see pp. 51–67 for a fuller treatment of this theme.

223. Ibid., p. 53.

224. Civrieux, *Religion y magia kari'ña*, p. 27.

225. Ibid.

226. In other words, the father makes the sound "his own." Concerning the eradicable associa-tion of voice with individual identity, which makes this procedure possible, see Paul Friedrich, "Speech as a Personality Symbol: The Case of Achilles," in his *Language, Context, and the Imagination* (Palo Alto, Cal., 1979), pp. 402–440. Friedrich intends the article to be a follow-up to Edward Sapir, "Speech as a Personality Trait," *American Journal of Sociology* 32 (1927); 892–905.

227. Civrieux, *Religión y magia kari'ña*, p. 28.

228. "Names are not fictions, labels, or signs, but evocations of some kind of social order" (Hugh Dalziel Duncan, *Communication and Social Order*, Oxford, 1970, p. 320). As we have had occasion to point out before in regard to other scholarly interpreters, Duncan views names as primarily a function of language (p. 163), specifically the function of identifying motives. In this respect Duncan is following Kenneth Burke, *A Rhetoric of Motives* (New York, 1950), e.g., p. 6. Frank Salomon and Sue Grosboll, "Names and Peoples in Incaic Quito: Retrieving Undocu-mented Historic Processes through Anthroponymy and Statistics," *AA* 88 (June 1986); 387–399, demonstrates how human names continue to be constitutive of society, even for contemporary historians. Knowledge of names and naming patterns across time permits historians to recon-struct "social and cultural processes no less important than those recorded in the overt content [of historical chronicles or tributary census]" (p. 397). Jacques Lizot gives evidence of this ability to analyze social constitution through names. His "Onomastique Yanomami," *H* 13 (July–September 1973); 60–71 is based on the systematic collection and analysis of 1,300 proper names from fifteen distinct local groups (p. 61). He ferrets out the systems of organized relations embedded within the names. They are legion: phonetic and grammatical systems, vegetal and animal taxonomies, sexual codes, physical features, degrees and styles of decora-tion, comparative anatomies of humans and animals, social categories, states of the living and the dead. For all that, he chooses to skirt "the fundamental question. . . . Why is indigenous thought convinced that naming a dreaded object necessarily brings about its manifestation, whereas naming a desired object threatens it with disappearance?" (p. 70). The divers customs and beliefs that converge in names have, says Lévi-Strauss, a "family atmosphere" about them such that the various classificatory systems create correspondences and mutually illumine one another. Because names effect the ensemble of so many elements constituting an individual and, in some direct way, *create* the personality, Lévi-Strauss could point to the sacred character of personal names; see Lévi-Strauss, *The Savage Mind* (Chicago, 1966), pp. 172–216.

229. Carneiro da Cunha, "Eschatology Among the Krahó," p. 169.

230. It should be noted that Emile Durkheim's view of the sexual division of labor in society applies to the Krahó view only if the latter is stunted and circumscribed by an arbitrary line drawn around "empirical" social action on the ground; see Emile Durkheim, *The Division of Labor in Society*, trans. George Simpson (New York, 1933). Specifically, the basis, in Durkheim's view (pp. 39–49), of the moral value of the division of labor is utterly strange to the Krahó basis of the moral value of sexual division of labor. This should have repercussions for the applicabil-ity of notions of mechanical solidarity (pp. 70–110) and organic solidarity (pp. 111–132) in social science. In particular, Durkheim underestimated the subtlety of a theory of resemblances in what he calls "primitive" societies (pp. 133–138), something we have had occasion to touch

upon above. This same mistake underlies his analysis of the social origin of logical and conceptual thought in *The Elementary Forms of The Religious Life*, trans. Joseph Ward Swain (1912; New York, 1965), passim (e.g., pp. 235ff. on totemism, pp. 273–304 about the soul, pp. 330ff. on gods), but he especially misconceives the origins of the categories of individual thought and of conception in general (e.g., pp. 463–496). The Krahó simply do not distinguish the individual from society in the way that Durkheim does. Durkheim is nervous that if one affirms the individual as the origin of value for thought and meaning, society and its logic will continue their pale, *merely nominal* existence. This is how he concludes his brilliant analysis and monumental hypothesis:

> Thus sociology appears destined to open a new way to the science of man. Up to the present, thinkers were placed before this double alternative: either explain the superior and specific faculties of men by connecting them to the inferior forms of his being, the reason to the senses, or the mind to matter, which is equivalent to denying their uniqueness; or else attach them to some super-experimental reality which was postulated, but whose existence could be established by no observation. What put them in this difficulty was the fact that the individual passed as being the *finis naturae* — the ultimate creation of nature; it seemed that there was nothing beyond him, or at least nothing that science could touch. But from the moment when it is recognized that above the individual there is society, and that this is not a *nominal being* created by reason, but a system of active forces, a new manner of explaining men becomes possible. (ibid., p. 495)

The sociological appraisal of the relationship between individual and society must be different from Durkheim's for at least two reasons pertinent to this section: (1) philosophers of science have pointed out that constructs such as "social structure" and "organic solidarity" are "super-experimental realities," which are equal in their conditional existence as mental images to the imaginative constructs of myth, although each set of images certainly attempts to safeguard a different evaluation of the reality of its respective self-image. (2) The appraisal of individual and society must now differ from Durkheim's also because we realize that cultures like the Krahó offer sophisticated and finely tuned reflections on the question. *Nominal* existence has totally different meaning for the Krahó than it does for Durkheim and his disciples. For the Krahó, nomination is essential to the shared reality of individual and society because it is a sacred process. That is why the power of names and their circulation through time can configure both individual and society, at one and the same time (although each marks its own tempo), into unique individualities and specific societies. Neither one can achieve definition without the other. In his analysis of the Kwakiutl concept of name (*tleq*), Irving Goldman makes the point succinctly: "The name is the essential ingredient of religious worth. The basic social division is between those who possess real names from a power-granting donor, and those whose names are . . . made up" (Goldman, *The Mouth of Heaven: An Introduction to Kwakiutl Religious Thought*, New York, 1975, p. 56). See ibid., pp. 56–62, for a discussion of why name acquisition is a "spiritual obligation" — viz., because, taken collectively, all 658 Kwakiutl names "would seem to sum up Kwakiutl character" since they represent the powers of original ancestors.

231. Stanley Walens elucidates the connection between orality (in consumption and speech) and the sustenance of supernatural relations in his *Feasting with Cannibals: An Essay on Kwakiutl Cosmology* (Princeton, 1981), esp. pp. 21–45. The connection with names is made especially clear on pp. 63–66. Pages 135–138 and 162–163 discuss orality as a basis for morality, when both are understood in the power of their imaged relations.

232. Clastres, *Chronique des indiens guayakí*, p. 189. Clastres does not make this point in so many words. However, these are the only examples of name acquisition that he provides.

233. This resolves the semiotic dilemma in distinguishing the denotation of proper names versus the denotation of purely syntactic entities. According to Umberto Eco, the crucial point is to decide whether or not the sign is *interpreted* (and not merely *interpretable*, as in the case of mere signal systems); see Eco, *A Theory of Semiotics* (Bloomington, Ind. 1976), pp. 86–90. If names are interpreted, as appears to be the case in the choice and ceremonial bestowal, then they may be seen as truly "semiotic," that is, as having the fully symbolic nature of what Louis Hjelmslev called a "biplanar" system; see Hjelmslev, *Prolegomena to a Theory of Language*

(Madison, Wis. 1961), pp. 99–100. It should be noted, in this connection, that Eco bases his "compositional theory of sememes" partly on the difference between the denotation of proper names and the purely syntactic signs of music, which appear to have no semantic depth. For Eco, "music offers another example of a semiotic system in which each situation could be differently *interpreted*." However, such does not seem to be the view of music in many South American tribes. Perhaps Eco confuses the unpredictability of notes in specific musical solutions (even though they are foreshadowed by the structures of each tonal situation in a musical piece) with the culturally interpreted symbolic meaning of the music and musical event. See, for example, Anthony Seeger, "Porque os índios suyá cantam para as suas irmãs," in Gilberto Velho, ed., *Arte e sociedade* (Rio de Janeiro, 1977), pp. 39–64; and Seeger, "What Can We Learn When They Sing? Vocal Genres of the Suyá Indians of Central Brazil," *ETM* 23 (1979): 373–394. See also Jonathan Hill, "Wakuenai Society: A Processual-Structural Analysis of Indigenous Cultural Life in the Upper Rio Negro (Guainia) Region of Venezuela" (Ph.D. diss., University of Indiana, 1983). Hill underscores that specific ritual music is symbolic. As such it not only is always a *performance*, but it always enjoys the status of a metaperformative statement of interpretation of social reality precisely because it has a meaning of its own.

234. Maybury-Lewis, *Akwē-Shavante Society*, p. 232.

235. Ibid., p. 233.

236. Ibid., pp. 74, 233.

237. David Maybury-Lewis, "Name, Person, and Ideology in Central Brazil," in Elisabeth Tooker, ed., *Naming Systems*, (Washington, D.C., 1984), p. 5.

238. Ibid.

239. Ibid., p. 235.

240. Mireille Guyot, "Le Bora," *JSAP* 58 (1969): p. 280. This is generally the case for the children of the head of the *maloca*. The Siriono present a variation on the acquisition of multiple names. Each time a Siriono parent bestows a name on a new child, the parent's name also changes to the same name as that of the new child. It is "possible for an Indian to have as many as fifteen or twenty names during the course of a lifetime" (Holmberg, *Nomads of the Long Bow*, p. 51).

241. No longer traditional ballgames but, by 1970, a soccer game.

242. Ibid., p. 281.

243. This point is made clearly and at length by both Goldman, *The Mouth of Heaven*, and Walens, *Feasting with Cannibals*, in their treatments of Kwakiutl names.

244. See the description provided in Herbert Baldus, "Das Dualsystem der Kaingáng-Indianer," in *Actes du IV Congrés International des Sciences Anthropologique* (Vienna, 1955), pp. 376–378.

245. Ursula Wiesemann, "Time Distinctions in Kaingáng," *ZFE* 99 (1974): 120–130. See also Weisemann's "Semantic Categories of 'Good' and 'Bad' in Relation to Kaingáng Personal Names," *RMP* n.s. 12 (1960): 177–184.

246. Although morality is ritually based, only a caricaturist would say that moral action is the thoughtless replication of a static ritual model. The process of reflection on one's normative ritual experience and the process of discernment always intervene between brute action and moral choice. In short, it is the religious meaning of one's experience that is normative. See Lawrence E. Sullivan, "Above, Below, or Far Away: Andean Cosmogony and Ethical Order," in Frank E. Reynolds and Robin Lovin, eds., *Cosmogony and Ethical Order: New Studies in Comparative Ethics* (Chicago, 1985), pp. 98–132. In such a construal, contemporary ethics, whether rules-oriented or deontologically inclined, is also based on ritual, the ritual of "rational procedures." Reason is acted out as a properly ordered procession of reflections guided by the symbolic order of axioms, premises, and the other symbolic moments of the process of adjudication. The practice and experience of "rational" (i.e., properly ordered; from Latin, *ratio*, "order") procedure is the ritual performance and quality of knowledge grounding moral choice. Ronald Green, *Religious Reason: The Rational and Moral Basis of Religious Belief* (New York, 1978), offers not so much a presentation of this view as a demonstrable working example of the ritual qualities of the rational process.

247. As we have seen, the personal name renders the order of this experience social, supernatural, and individual.

248. Thus, for example, Boróro clans may be more fruitfully viewed as name-base corporations than matrilineal descent groups. See Jon Christopher Crocker, "Selves and Alters among the Eastern Boróro," in Maybury-Lewis, ed., *Dialectical Societies*, pp. 249–300. Crocker develops his analysis in *Vital Souls*, pp. 31f., 84–89, 344–346, 353–354.

249. The naming ceremony emphasizes that relations of blood must be transcended in favor of the symbolic correlations of culture. Through the naming process one becomes a correlative conjunction for a unique network of coparents, ritual filiations, ceremonial groups based on name, spirit-helper ties and so on. "Names then are what distinguish humans from animals. It is the names bestowed on a human that give that person his/her social persona and link him/her to other people" (Maybury-Lewis, "Name, Person, and Ideology," p. 5).

250. See, for example, John Algeo, *On Defining the Proper Name* (Gainesville. Fla., 1973). Gregory Bateson attempts to situate the philosophical discussions surrounding logical typology and the nature of classes in rational thought within the ethnographic forum by considering the process of naming. He calls "this section . . . the most difficult and perhaps the most important part of the book," *Mind and Nature: A Necessary Unity* (New York, 1979), p. 176. Although he does use the word "interpretation," Bateson also sees the process of naming as an act of interpretation of the relationship between two kinds of stochastic systems, analogic and digital:

> But *naming* is itself a process and one that occurs not only in our analyses but profoundly and significantly within the systems we attempt to analyze. Whatever the coding and mechanical relation between DNA and the phenotype, DNA is still in some way a body of injunctions demanding—and in this sense, naming—the relations which shall become apparent in the phenotype. And when we admit naming as a phenomenon occurring in and organizing the phenomena we study, we acknowledge *ipso facto* that in those phenomena, we expect hierarchies of logical typing. (pp. 184–185)

Instead of the word "interpretation," Bateson says, "to get from the *name* to the *name of the name*, we must go through the *process* of naming the name. There must always be a generative process whereby the classes are created before they can be named" (p. 185). Arguing against Bertrand Russell's theoretical treatise on the nature of logical types, Bateson contends that the interpretive act of naming in culture deals not only with the assignment of labels to digital sets (the "naming of names of names" or the discussion of "classes of classes of classes" possible in the "empty world" of pure-math games) but also with the analogic steps required to bestow names in a semantically loaded world (one in which "the process of naming is itself nameable"). See the section of *Mind and Nature* called "From Classification to Process," in which Bateson criticizes the obsolete notions of "physicalism," best typified in attempts to understand the nature of names, which underlie academic explanations of mental phenomena, thereby installing dualistic premises, an "unconscious epistemology," as the basis for both "hard" and "social" sciences (pp. 189–223). Until recently, most philosophical discussion of the nature of names and naming has been carried on only in relation to some Indo-European examples. See, for example, John Stuart Mill, *A System of Logic* (New York, 1843), chapter 2, and P. Strawson, "On Referring," *Mind* 49 (1950): 320–344. Without specifically treating the question of name, John Skorupski, *Symbol and Theory: A Philosophical Study of Theories of Religion in Social Anthropology* (London, 1976) examines the relative adequacy of contemporary philosophical appraisals of the nature of definition, denotation, language, and meaning to the analysis of other cultural cosmologies.

251. The relationship of personal names to categories is problematic. See, for example, the discussion stemming from Charles Cooke's collection of some 6,000 Mohawk and Iroquois personal names in Cooke, "Iroquois Personal Names: Their Classifications," *American Philosophical Society Proceedings* 96 (1952): 426–438. Most instructive is Marianne Mithun, "Principles of Naming in Mohawk," in Elisabeth Tooker, ed., *Naming Systems*, pp. 40–54; Mithun points out that the distinction between proper and common nouns in Mohawk is semantic rather than formal (p. 41) and that most Mohawk proper names referring to persons and places are verbs. They pertain to such natural things as trees, grass, flowers, rivers, mountains, meadows, islands, the sky, stars, the mind, voice, or events or activities somehow associated with the person or place named" (p. 46). Confirming the idea that names are an interpretation of

the meaningful relationship between the structure of the person and a particular configuration of cosmic forces rather than *a priori* social categories, Mithun adds,

> Personal names, now disappearing from use as fewer people use Mohawk, were not traditionally given randomly. Each clan owned a set of names, which no one outside of the clan had the right to bear. The clan to which a name belonged could not be inferred from the name itself, by any regular principle, but was rather a fact learned with the name. . . . Among all groups, one should not simply choose any name at random, but, rather, consult the child's maternal grandmother or the clan "keeper of names" for an appropriate free name. Often this would be the name of an ancestor, but not necessarily. The name might be somehow associated with some circumstances surrounding the child's birth, or not. Certain names are only for women, others for men, and others may be for either, perhaps with an appropriate change of pronoun. (p. 46)

For a fascinating portrayal of local accounts of the cognitive bases of names and categories, see Gabriel Martínez, "Topónimos de Chuani: Organización y significación del territorio?" *ALIM* 1 (1983): 51–84.

252. Jean-Paul Dumont, "From Dogs to Stars: The Phatic Function of Naming among the Panare," in Ellen B. Basso, ed., *Carib-speaking Indians* (Tucson: 1977), p. 89.

253. Ibid., p. 94

254. Ibid., p. 96.

255. There is an extensive and interesting literature dealing with the toponymous dimension of names. See, for example, Ernest Negre, *Les Noms de lieux en France* (Paris, 1963); Ward H. Goodenough, "Notes on Truk's Place Names," *Micronesica* (Guam) 2 (1966): 95–129; Renato Rosaldo, "Where Precision Lies," in Roy Willis, ed, *The Interpretation of Symbolism* (London, 1975), pp. 1–22; Raymond Firth, *We, the Tikopia: Kinship in Primitive Polynesia* (Boston, 1957), esp. pp. 69–71 on village names and pp. 82–87 on house names; and Ivan Lind, "Geography and Place Names," in Philip L. Wagner and Marvin W. Mikesell, eds., *Readings in Cultural Geography* (Chicago, 1962), pp. 118–128. The relation of name to space is actually a part of a larger discussion of the aspectual character of language; see Roman Jakobson and Linda R. Waugh, *The Sound Shape of Language* (The Hague, 1985).

256. Maybury-Lewis, "Name, Person, and Ideology," p. 5.

257. Renate Brigitte Viertler, "A Noção de pessoa entre os Boróro," *Boletim do Museu Nacional* (Rio de Janeiro) n.s. 32 (May 1979): p. 21.

258. As a person matures, his or her individual life-cycle is understood in terms of theories surrounding the body, the soul, the meanings attached to particular social contexts, magico-religious practices surrounding health, and notions of physical growth and sickness and death (ibid.).

259. Ibid., pp. 22–23.

260. Ibid., p. 28; Crocker, *Vital Souls*, pp. 90–97 and passim.

261. Viertler, "A Noção de pessoa," p. 28.

262. Ibid., p. 29. The expression "I am Jerigi Otojiwu!" carries with it an enormous and profound reality. In the accounts of several Boróro subclans, this hero was the sole survivor of the great flood. As an heroic chief, Jerigi Otojiwu exhibited his persistence in his ceremonial shouting and in his wearing of his feathered headdress at dawn. It was this persistence that was responsible for reestablishing the center of the world and for repopulating the universe with human beings, the Boróro. For several versions of these accounts, see Albisetti and Venturelli, *Enciclopédia Boróro*, vol. 2: *Lendas e antropônimos*, pp. 4, 15–23, 271–99.

263. In this connection see also Jean C. Lave, "Cycles and Trends in Krĩkatí Naming Practices," in Maybury-Lewis, ed., *Dialectical Societies*, pp. 16–44.

264. Viertler, "A Noção de pessoa," p. 24.

265. Together with the penis sheath, a growing Boróro man receives a hunting name associated with the men's organizations. The hunting name has associations with the monster *aíje* (*zunidor*), which has connections with body painting and the absence of plumage. This ceremonial complex heightens the separation of the sexes (ibid., p. 25).

266. Ibid., p. 26.

267. See, for example, Hymes, *"In Vain I Tried,"* pp. 116, 220, 282–283, 373–378.

268. "Proper" not in the sense of the exclusive *property* of an individual, a concept which may be absent from some cultures, but in the sense that it correctly interprets the proper arrangement of social, cosmic, and supernatural relations that give the individual specific meaning.

269. The Chiripá process of naming pulls together these summary points in a concrete way. Every Chiripá possesses two names. One is a "Christian" name used with strangers. People change this name frequently. However, the first name that a Chiripá individual possesses is called *re'ra kaa'güy* ("forest name"), which is the sacred name of his or her soul. This name is used only in ritual, for "the name *is* the person." A person's truest being is invisible, a sound. The use of name only in ritual highlights the Chiripá conviction that people are most fully themselves when their souls' attributes are most completely realized; that is, in ritual. For the Chiripá, the utterance of one's name is always a species of ritual performance. The sacred "forest name" is vitally bound up with the divine element of an individual's soul, the "vital word" *(ñe'eng).* Together they comprise a single entity. The *ñe'eng* is provided by divine beings. Since these "vital words" may come from the celestial realm of the gods or from the country of the dead *(ñe'eng-güery),* a "shaman [must] decide which deity it is who is sending the new essence of life which will take shape and become incorporated into humanity." In the season of fair weather from November to March, the Chiripá shaman conducts the Mitá-mbó-ery, the "naming of children." Aided by his repertoire of powerful songs and dreams, he dispatches his spirit-helpers in the form of messenger birds who fly away to the time of the mythic past. On their return, the sound of their beating spirit-wings bears a forest name, whose provenance and meaning the shaman must identify before he bestows it on the child (Bartolomé, "Shamanism Among the Avá-Chiripá," pp. 112–113).

270. Wright, "History and Religion of the Baniwa," pp. 407, 480.

271. Ibid., pp. 408, 480.

272. Ibid., p. 408.

273. In their own imagery, the Baniwa appear to be wrestling with the same issues raised by Pierre Bourdieu, *Outline of a Theory of Practice* (Cambridge, 1979).

274. Marcelo Bórmida, "Ayoreo Myths," *LAIL* 2 (Spring 1978): 2.

275. Bórmida (ibid.) provides examples of the transformation of the South Wind, the North Wind, the Woman of Salt, the Rain, the Turtle, the little frog named Mi, the tree named Gesnusná, and the Gray Butterfly. Each one of these myth-beings is associated with a magical curing song. In addition, the myth of the separation of sky and earth is the source of very powerful medicinal chants. "Chants about the Sky cure any kind of infirmity. Those about the Earth cure serious illnesses. If one says a chant about the Sky without there really being someone ill, there will be a long drought. By the same token, a chant about Earth under those circumstances will cause illness" (p. 11). Unfortunately, because of taboos *(puyák)* restricting their ritual performance, *saúde* were not recorded by any investigators. Bórmida, in "Ergon y mito, Primera Parte," interprets the relationship between material existence and "the metatemporal and transtemporal nature of the *nanibaháde,"* especially, the power of their names and sounds.

276. Bórmida, "Ayoreo Myths," p. 2.

277. Ibid., p. 4.

278. Ibid.

279. For similar views of musically induced change, see Anthony Stocks, "Tendiendo un puente entre el cielo y la tierra en alas de la canción," *AP* 2 (1978): 71–100; Jorge Novati, "Música y marco temporal en los Shipibo del Rio Maputay," *SE* 4, part 2 (1976–1977): 6–30; Rafael José de Menezes Bastos, *A Musicológica kamayurá: Para uma antropología da comunicação no Alto-Xingu* (Brasilia, 1978); Jorge Novati, "Las Expresiones musicales de los Selk'nam," *RU* 12 (1969–1970): 393–406; Jurgen Riester, "Acerca de la canción de los Chimane," in Roswith Hartmann and Udo Oberem, eds., *Amerikanistische Studien: Festschrift für Hermann Trimborn* (St. Augustin, 1979), pp. 199–206.

280. Pierre Laromiguiere, *Leçons de philosophie sur les principes de l'intelligence, ou sur les causes et sur les origines des idées,* 4th ed. (Paris, 1826), vol. 1, p. 86.

281. See, for example, the tragic misdirection of sound in the myths of the origin of death related in chapter 8, below. Because sound is always pointed, its power results in tragedy when it

falls on the wrong ears (spatial misdirection) or if it is uttered inappropriately (temporal misdirection).

282. Civrieux, *Religión y magia kari'ña*, p. 9.

283. Ibid., p. 10.

284. *Tamu* is a word strictly associated with *tamutu*, one of the secret names of tobacco.

285. Seeger, *Nature and Society*, p. 388.

286. Ibid.

287. For example, Inca social divisions, land holdings, calendars of feasts, and geographic layout as well as the coordination of space with astronomic time were musically orchestrated. For instance, the *panaca* was a royal *ayllu*, a residence-based descent group that functioned as a key unit in all these orders. The *panaca* associated with Yahuar Huacac, the seventh ancestor-king in mythic genealogy, was named Ancailli, also the name of a category of songs performed during the ritual processions of the harvest. See Zuidema, "Calendars: South American Calendars," in *EOR*

288. Songs, sounds, specific melodies, and sex-specific music associated with one's gender, occupation, or helper-spirits compose the identity of an individual at any one time. See the information recorded by Kurt Reinhard in Zerries and Schuster, *Mahekodotedi*, pp. 95–124. The tone and texture of the voice and its ability to mimic or capture the sounds of spirits manifest through animal language are especially important (p. 111).

289. The term "affecting presence" is drawn from the work of Robert Plant Armstrong, *The Affecting Presence: An Essay in Humanistic Anthropology*, (Urbana, Ill., 1971). He suggests that the relationship between beings cannot be reduced to a series of data compiled from the reports of the body's senses and faculties. Thus, for example, the religious performances of culture are not performed as spectacles to be "observed," sacred music is not performed to be "heard," meanings are not demonstrated emotionally in order to be "perceived." Affecting presence (a disposition of cultural understanding that is normally abstracted for study under the heading called "art") is an existential stance in the world. It is a "witness" in specific symbolic expression to being in its fullest meaning. For all that, Armstrong contends that the meaning of feeling can be analyzed as it witnesses to being in specific cultural forms. Armstrong thereby hopes to lay the theoretical groundwork for an aesthetics of being in cross-cultural expression; see also Armstrong, *Wellspring: On the Myth and Source of Culture* (Berkeley, 1975). For Armstrong, aesthetics is the study of the symbolic forms incarnating feelings as it witnesses to the meaning of being (ibid., pp. 11–20). Walter J. Ong has also founded an aesthetics of the spoken word on a notion of sound as presence; See his *The Presence of the Word: Some Prolegomena for Cultural and Religious History* (New Haven, 1967). The symbolic study of sound itself (apart from word or song) as a meaningful symbol has been studied by Victor Zukerkandl in *Sense of Music* (Princeton, 1959), and in his *Sound and Symbol*, vol. 1, *Music and the External World*, trans. Willard R. Trask (Princeton, 1956), and *Sound and Symbol*, vol. 2, *Man the Musician*, trans. N. Guterman (Princeton, 1973). For another view of sounds, especially the sounds of language, see Tzvetan Todorov, "Le Sens des sons," *Poétique* 11 (1972): 446–461.

290. Roe, *Cosmic Zygote*, p. 115. The meaning of the loud report that brings death is discussed in chapter 8, below.

291. Ibid., p. 115.

292. Nimuendajú, *The Apinayé*, pp. 144–146.

293. Whitten, *Sacha Runa*, p. 59.

294. Giselle Cossard-Binon, "La Fille de Saint," *JSAP* 58 (1969); p. 77.

295. Gerardo Reichel-Dolmatoff, "Brain and Mind in Desana Shamanism," *JLAL* 7 (1981): 83.

296. Ibid., p. 91.

297. This point has been made persuasively by the ethnomusicologist Steven Feld when he describes his stay among the Kaluli of Papua New Guinea:

> Whatever [the Kalulis'] perception of my musical abilities, they were much more impressed when they saw me weep openly after receiving a letter. . . . If making music, talking about it, and being moved by it are not extraordinary things for Kaluli, it is because these behaviors are so deeply related to the sound and the emotions surrounding weeping. For Kaluli,

weeping is a measure and an indicator of one's emotional nature as a person. . . . [T]he sight of me weeping went a lot further to establish for them just what sort of person I might be. (Feld, *Sound and Sentiment: Birds, Weeping, Poetics, and Song in Kaluli Expression*, Philadelphia, 1982, p. 233)

It should be clear that in citing this instance from Papua New Guinea, the suggestion is not made that weeping sends the same signal everywhere. Throughout this work an effort has been made to emphasize the importance of the meanings of the sacred in each local culture. The fact that weeping can be a ritual and proper response to the meaning of emotion does not in any way predetermine the specific meanings that that emotion takes in specific cultures. That specificity, together with the peculiarity of stylized forms of ritual weeping, always lies in the particular religious imagery that forms the foundations of a given culture.

298. The question of ritual weeping, "the welcome of tears," and lamentations will be treated below. Here weeping serves as an example of sound constituting human being because its meaning evokes a response that creates the specific forms of individuals and cultures.

299. Wagley, *Welcome of Tears*, pp. 212–213. The energy of the Siriono in this regard is extraordinary. They invariably start the day with at least two hours of impromptu singing before dawn. Unfortunately, the songs were unintelligible to Holmberg. In any case, the words of the songs did not convey their deepest significance. When asked the meaning of their aubade, they explained that "they were like the birds who bring on the day by greeting it with song" (Holmberg, *Nomads of the Long Bow*, p. 44). On the morning song of the Siriono, see also Heinz Kelm, "O canto matinal dos Siriono," *RASP* 15–16 (1967–1968): 111–132.

300. James Howe and Lawrence A. Hirschfield, "The Star Girls' Descent: A Myth About Men, Women, Matrilocality, and Singing," *JAFL* 94 (1981): 318.

301. Howe and Hirschfield provide an interesting set of contrasts between women's and men's songs in which the former are seen to be more spontaneous, improvised, personal, expressive, unrestrained, and general in purpose, and less instrumental than the latter.

302. Maybury-Lewis, *Akwẽ-Shavante Society*, pp. 270–271. See also Laura Graham, "Three Modes of Shavante Vocal Expression: Wailing, Collective Singing, and Political Oratory," in Joel Sherzer and Greg Urban, eds., *Native South American Discourse* (Berlin, 1986), pp. 83–118.

303. Ibid., p. 271. On weeping as a rite of passage, see also William A. Christian, Jr., "Provoked Religious Weeping in Early Modern Spain," in J. Davis, ed., *Religious Organization and Religious Experience* (London, 1982), pp. 97–114, and Ernesto De Martino, *Morte e pianto rituale nel mondo antico. Dal lamento pagano al pianto di Maria* (Turin, 1958).

304. Clastres, *Chronique des indiens guayakí*, p. 128. A strident ritual song is performed, in the form of a ritual lamentation called *chenga ruvara*, by Guayakí women. As soon as one woman intones the chant, all women present take up the cry, and, consequently, it is never sung by a lone individual. It is performed as a weeping greeting to welcome visiting guests or group members returning home after a long absence. It is also sung whenever circumstances are "a little bit exceptional" (ibid., p. 32). During the boys' initiation rite, the women's chant is sung on the night when the young men fast from food and drink for the first time. This is the day on which the young boys have their lips pierced. The initiates strike up a special song that is taken up by the rest of the men. In response, the mothers of the young initiands intone the *chenga ruvara*. The singing becomes a noisy and violent contest that lasts throughout the entire night. The young men sing aggressively; the mothers wail in song. Later in the initiation ceremony, when perfumed wax is burned, a larger group of women join together to chant the *chenga ruvara*. Squatting on the ground and hiding their faces in their hands, they cry out loud. The fathers of the candidates for initiation throw themselves on the women, cuffing and kicking them. The men are said to be in a state in which their names or "nature" (*by*) has left them. All the women run to the defense of the mothers of the candidates. "They hang on the men's arms and on their shoulders. They try to calm them down. They immobilize the men and, with the marrow of a palm tree they rub the face and torso of the men. 'Do not strike!' Forcefully they blow in the ears of the men as if there was a need to have something put back there" (ibid., p. 128). Eventually, in spite of the efforts of the women, the mature men pass completely into a fury of violence. The

chenga ruvara is also performed at the girls' initiation rite, when the novices are ceremonially scrubbed from head to toe (ibid., p. 137). Frequently, the *chenga ruvara* is performed in honor of slain game animals brought home as booty from the hunt. In one case, women chanted this dramatic wailing chant in honor of a jaguar (*baipu*) while the hunter who had bagged the animal was massaged by the men with the bark of the *piry* tree. Of course, the *chenga ruvara* is performed in ceremonies associated with death—for example, at the time when a grave is prepared (ibid., p. 220). It could be said that the hysterical intensity and basic significance of the wailing event derive from the moment of death. In each case cited by Clastres, death is at issue, albeit death in symbolic terms: at initiation, at the death of a game animal, as a memorial for those who have died during the visitor's absence. "The *chenga ruvara* is a last-ditch attempt to hold onto time; it is also the first song of separation. It celebrates a break" (ibid., p. 121). As is so often the case with sacred music, the *chenga ruvara* celebrates and effects transition from one state of being to another; it marks a time of passage. See Lawrence E. Sullivan, "Sacred Music and Sacred Time," *The World of Music* 26 (1984): 33–52.

305. Ibid., p. 121. The musical din created by these three separate choirs, who sing stimultaneously throughout the night, continues the theme of cacophony used in ritual to make simultaneously present separate powers associated with particular songs. Here, the Guayakí limit the variety of simultaneous musical sounds to three: the hunting songs of men, the attempted songs of the young initiates, and the songs of the women. Instead of demonstrating chaos in sound, the Guayakí emphasize through their behavior the dissolution of order: their singing contest degenerates into aggressive violence.

306. Civrieux, *Religión y magia kari'ña*, p. 31. It might be fruitful to consider this concept of dance-existence as a parallel to the current Western term "history": that is, as a certain evaluation that is given to existence in time, of which the time-space linear chronology is only one expression.

307. Ibid.

308. Ibid., p. 32.

309. It is at this level of thought and meaning of symbolic sound and transformation that one may fruitfully consider the points raised by Jonathan Z. Smith in "I Am a Parrot (Red)," *HR* 11 (1972); 391–413, which traces the tragic and demeaning attempts of Western scholars to interpret bird-human identifications and transformations. The problem lies in the inability to accept the symbol as anything more than a metaphor and the inability to explore with a scholarly imagination the ways in which these symbolic acts and statements have ontological value.

310. John Blacking, "The Study of Man as Music-Maker," in John Blacking and Joann W. Kealiinohomoku, eds., *The Performing Arts: Music and Dance* (The Hague, 1979), pp. 6–7.

311. Anthony Seeger, "Can We Learn When They Sing?" p. 392. Regarding Suyá musical form, see also Seeger's "Oratory Is Spoken, Myth Is Told, and Song Is Sung but They Are All Music to My Ears," in Sherzer and Urban, eds., *Native South American Discourse* (Berlin, 1986), pp. 59–82.

312. "What Can We Learn When They Sing?" p. 392.

313. Fulop, "Aspectos: Cosmogonía," p. 130.

314. Hugh-Jones, *The Palm and the Pleiades*, pp. 195ff, 284–285. Hugh-Jones has assembled a number of myths dealing with this theme from several cultures. Lévi-Strauss has brilliantly illuminated various kinds of orders that are regulated through their symbolic correspondences with the meanings of sound: gradations of temperature, change of seasons, measures of height, shifts of weather, degree of degrading filth, intensity of darkness. See Claude Lévi-Strauss, "Résumé de cours de 1964–1965," *Extrait de l'Annuaire de Collège de France* 65, (1965–1966): 269–270; cited in Hugh-Jones, *The Palm and the Pleiades*, p. 195. See also Lévi-Strauss, *From Honey to Ashes*, p. 429. Hugh-Jones summarizes the organizing effects of the exchange of music and voices between the sloth and the howler monkey in this way:

> The howler monkey is a producer of filth literally as a proverbial shitter and metaphorically as a producer of loud noise which is correlated with corruption. As such it is opposed to the sloth which produces a tiny whistle at night and defecates only occasionally, coming down to the ground to do so. . . . [Lévi-Strauss] also points out that both the howler monkey and

the sloth are "barometric animals," for the howler monkey howls when there is a change in weather and the sloth comes down to the ground and shits when it is cold. (Hugh-Jones, *The Palm and the Pleiades*, p. 195)

315. Norman E. Whitten, "Personal Networks and Musical Contexts in the Pacific Lowlands of Colombia and Ecuador," in Norman E. Whitten, Jr., and John F. Szwed, eds., *Afro-American Anthropology: Contemporary Perspectives* (New York, 1970), pp. 203–218.

316. Civrieux, *Religión y magia kari'ña*, p. 15.

317. Ibid., p. 16.

318. Clastres, "L'Arc et le panier," p. 19.

319. Ibid., pp. 27–30.

320. Fock, *Waiwai*, p. 104.

321. Ibid., p. 105.

322. Revenge-blowing requires observation of special diets during the period between the blowing and the downfall of the intended victim. In practice, this amounts to a two-month period of dietary restriction after the cremation of one's relative. Revenge-blowing is considered an obligation of honor (ibid., pp. 107–108). When the two-month period of fasting has ended (and presumably the intended victim has died), the avenger purifies himself by heating a stone and bathing himself in the steam that arises when he pours water on it.

323. Ibid., p. 107. Another method is to build a fire over the buried bamboo tube-container.

324. For discussion of the *vagina dentata* theme in connection with Amerindian ethnopoetics, see Pat Carr and Willard Gingerich, "The Vagina Dentata Motif in Nahuatl and Pueblo Mythic Narratives: A Comparative Study," in Brian Swann, ed., *Smoothing the Ground: Essays on Native American Oral Literature* (Berkeley, 1983), pp. 187–203. The authors are more interested in the culture-history of the idea than in providing an interpretation of it. For a consideration of its meaning in relation to initiation, see Mircea Eliade, *Rites and Symbols of Initiation: The Mysteries of Birth and Rebirth*, trans. Willard Trask (New York, 1965), pp. 62–63. Eliade does not consider any linguistic dimensions of the motif.

325. Civrieux, *Religión y magia kari'ña*, p. 28.

326. Fulop, "Aspectos: Cosmogonía," pp. 125–128. This account continues the theme of a *dema* origin for this important plant.

327. For accounts of the Pishtaco, who roam the areas near contemporary Lima, see José Maria Arguedas and Francisco Izquierdo Rios, *Mitos, legendas y cuentos peruanos*, 2d ed. (Lima, 1970), pp. 163–167. Takahiro Kato is preparing a bibliography and analysis of the Pishtaco.

328. For example, in the case of Kúwai, cited above, the transition is from the primordial mode of being to the existence of multiple and changing forms. A closer look at the origin myths of sound would provide a better understanding of the aesthetic underlying the universal ritual use of percussion instruments. The mistake of many cultural studies investigating this phenomenon is the attempt to bypass the religious imagery of local cultures in seeking an adequate "scientific explanation," (i.e., an interpretation lodged only within the narrow strictures of value that are operative in one institutional segment of a few modern societies). The faulty approach is based upon a social anthropology that would separate the role physiology plays in the formation of society from the meaning it has in human culture. For example, see Andrew Neher, "A Physiological Explanation of Unusual Behavior in Ceremonies Involving Drums," *Human Biology* 34 (1962): 151–160. More promising is the interesting puzzle Rodney Needham poses when he pays minimal attention to only the most general level of cultural detail, in "Percussion and Transition," *MN* 2 (1967): 606–614. There, after reviewing psychoanalytic, psychological, and neurological considerations (which merely lead him to conclude that percussion involves "aurally generated emotion" and is widespread because "percussive sounds are the easiest to make"), Needham notices that percussion "instruments are identified with events . . . rites and ceremonies which are distinguished by sounds. What is it that these events have in common? Obviously that they are *rites de passage*." This glance at the veneer of cultural symbolism already permits Needham to advance an intriguing hypothesis: "there is a significant connexion between percussion and transition. This, I suggest, is the definitive relation, and the nature of the connexion is the real problem." At this point, however, Needham veers away from the cultural

symbolism, which has constituted the source of his only inspiration, by concluding, "There is certainly no intrinsic relationship between the phenomena, yet the association is too firm for the answer to be sought in the contingent particulars of cultural tradition." Needham's disregard of the seriousness of answers provided by cultural traditions is grounded in the unexamined presumption that answers of firm value are forthcoming only from "science," as though science were not also an institutionalized evaluation of knowledge composed of "the contingent particulars of a cultural tradition." This exclusive but implicit truth-claim is clearly in evidence in a response to Needham by William C. Sturtevant, "Categories, Percussion and Physiology," *MN* 3 (1968): 133-134. More recent works on the question of percussion, trance, and transition include Evon Z. Vogt, "On the Symbolic Meaning of Percussion in Zinacanteco Ritual," *Journal of Anthropological Research* 33 (1977): 231-244; Bruce M. Knauft, "On Percussion and Metaphor," *CA* 20 (March 1979): 189-190; Barbara Lex, "The Neurobiology of Ritual Trance," in Eugene G. d'Aquili and Charles D. Laughlin, Jr., eds., *The Spectrum of Ritual: A Biogenetic Structural Approach* (New York, 1979), pp. 117-152; and Brenda E. F. Beck, "Reply (to 'On Percussion and Metaphor')," *CA* 20 (March 1979); 190-191.

329. In a sense, spoken language is one significant spatial expression, produced by the deliberate rearrangement of body space (tongue, lips, teeth) and its excretions (breath, saliva). Paul Friedrich, "On the Meaning of The Tarascan Suffixes of Space: Meaning and Morphotactics," in his *Language, Context, and the Imagination* (Stanford, Cal., 1979), examines the place of space, shape, and aspect, especially as they relate to the idiom of corporeality and affect the relationship of form and meaning. Perhaps language is aspectual and tied to shape-categories because language is a body-based symbolic behavior and the body is a spatial entity. See Paul Friedrich, "Shape Categories in Grammar," *Linguistics* 48 (1972): 742-747.

330. Anthony Seeger, Roberto da Matta, and E. B. Viveiros de Castro, "A Construção da pessoa nas sociedades indígenas brasileiras," *BMN* n.s. 32 (May 1979); p. 3.

331. Ibid., p. 16. The authors also feel that this language of corporeality would require a rewriting of the traditional anthropological categories of kinship, social organization, and economy in order to rethink anthropology through the eyes of Brazilian Indians.

332. On that plane, Seeger, da Matta, and Viveiros de Castro argue, order and meaning derive from conceptions about names, body substances, blood, and soul rather than abstract political language or social obligations, statuses, and roles (ibid., p. 14). The interactive relationship of a few basic substances, for example, accounts for the Apinayé theory of physiology. The most significant substances are sperm (*hôko*), blood (*kābrô*), water (*kó*), and mother's milk (*kó-kagô*, "white water"). The body organs transform water into blood. Robust drinkers and healthy people have moist skin and lots of blood. Food is seen to be a material form of water and blood; see Matta, *A Divided World*, p. 49. Functions of the various organs differ, but, in general, the upper organs (heart, lungs, liver, stomach, and pancreas) are classified as a group needing lots of water in order to purify the blood. Blood and soul are in many ways equated (ibid., p. 52). One's diet and the volume of one's intake affect the soul directly in terms of its color and smell. Da Matta provides an illuminating discussion of the interweaving meanings of physiological parts, colors, smells, textures, and conditions in relation to social processes and the social meanings of ageing, intercourse, menstruation, murder, and seclusion (pp. 48-58). Growth and ageing are considered processes of continued loss of blood and desiccation. Menstruation is considered to be the consequence of intercourse with a male.

333. Seeger, Matta, and Viveiros de Castro, "A Construção da pessoa," p. 14.

334. Ibid., p. 13.

335. Ibid.

336. Theories of the transmission of souls, along with concomitant theories concerning the transmission of names and of substantial fluids, point out that the physical body does not comprise the totality of the body any more than the body comprises the totality of the person (ibid.). The meaning of the body, the semantic basis that allows it to serve as a symbolic language, depends upon its relationship to worlds of being that transcend it.

337. Ibid., p. 12. See the degree to which physiology of the Warao organizes the house, cosmos, and cosmic egg, as well as the four kinds of selves contained in them, in Wilbert, "House of the Swallow-Tailed Kite," esp. pp. 178-180. Another extraordinary example of the way physiologi-

cal processes govern the cosmos and make it understandable is detailed in Bastien, "Qolla-huaya-Andean Body Concepts." Bastien writes, "A principal informant, Marcelino Yanahuaya, explained the mountain/body metaphor this way, 'I am the same as the mountain, *Pachamama*. *Pachamama* has fluids which flow through her, and I have fluids which flow through me. *Pachamama* takes care of my body, and I must give food and drink to *Pachamama* [holy mother earth]'" (ibid., 597).

338. Seeger, da Matta, and Viveiros de Castro, "A Construção de pessoa," p. 11. Such generalizations need not be limited to central Brazilian societies. For descriptions of Yanoama aesthetics of body space and decoration, see Zerries and Schuster, *Mahekodotedi*, pp. 68–93; for an interpretation of physical ornaments and decorative hardware, see pp. 350–354.

339. Seeger, da Matta, and Viveiros de Castro, "A Construção de pessoa," p. 11.

340. Ibid., p. 10.

341. Victor Turner demonstrated the weakness of an overzealous structuralism, which reduces all oppositions to equivalents of one another, in, his essay "Planes of Classification in a Ritual of Life and Death," in Turner, *The Ritual Process* (Harmondsworth, England, 1974), pp. 1–39, esp. pp. 34–39. Turner isolates a number of significant dyadic relations between symbolic elements in an Ndembu procreation ritual. But he notes that the dyads cannot be seen as isomorphic without ignoring their exegetical meaning in Ndembu culture:

> These sets of pairs of opposed values lie along different planes in ritual space. The first set is *longitudinal* and is spatially polarized by the "*ikela* [hole] of life" and the "*ikela* of death." The second set is *latitudinal* and is spatially bounded by the male fire on the right and the female fire on the left. The third set is *altitudinal* and is spatially bounded by the surface of the ground and the floor of the combined *makela* [holes] and connecting tunnel. These oppositions are made by the Ndembu themselves in exegesis, in practice, or in both. In terms of spatial orientation, the main oppositions are: animal-made hole/manmade hole; left/right; below/above. These correspond respectively to the paired values: death/life; female/male; candidates/adepts. But, since these sets of values transect one another, they should not be regarded as equivalent. In *Isoma* [the procreative ritual], the Ndembu are not saying, in the nonverbal language of ritual symbols, that death and femininity, and life and masculinity, are equivalent; nor are they saying that candidates are in a feminine role in relation to adepts (though they are certainly in a passive role). Equivalences may be sought *within* each set, not *between* them. (ibid., pp. 34–35)

342. Reichel-Dolmatoff, *Amazonian Cosmos*, pp. 47–51.

343. Ibid., p. 51.

344. The local rendering of natural history is inextricably bound up with social organization. The categorization and manipulation of geography, animals, plants, sounds, colors, and movements as they are represented symbolically are closely tied to the symbolic appreciation of human physiology. Reichel-Dolmatoff refers to this nexus of relations as a "biotope." For example,

> The rivers of this area are often interrupted by large or small rapids or falls. When fish run yearly to their places of ovulation, certain species advance only to the limits established by certain rapids, while other species advance farther upstream. In the Indians' mind, some species of fish are intimately associated with certain categories of women, in terms of potential spouses or forbidden marriage partners. It follows then that, if certain fish should not be eaten by the people living on a stretch of the river, the reason for this prohibition is that their consumption of fish obeys exogamic rules. Moreover, the fish that run are associated with certain fruit, insects, or the smaller fish they feed upon, and these too are echeloned along the river, as are certain birds which, in their turn, feed upon fish and/or fruit. We have here then larger and smaller ecological zones upon which not only is the social structure projected but which also form an integral part of an intricate and highly meaningful web of man-animal-plant relationships, combined with certain characteristics of the river, "black" or "white" waters, rapids, currents, and so forth. . . . The key importance of this approach is obviously not limited to the study of social organization but

includes other aspects as well. Economic activities, cult and ritual, culture contact, and the diffusion of ideas or objects can all be geared to this particular use and interpretation of the natural environment and should therefore be understood in this manner.

345. Dumont, "Not in Ourselves."
346. Karsten, *Toba Indians*, p. 55.
347. Ibid., p. 53. See also Ulf Lind, "Einige Notizen zu den Vorstellungen über Physiologie bei den Lengua-Indianern (Maskoi) im Gran Chaco," in Hartmann and Oberem, eds., *Amerikanistiche Studien*, pp. 24–29. For further treatment of the ways in which the mythic geography of the body serves the procedures of therapy, see the special issue of *International Journal of Psychology* 19 (1984) on symbol and symptom inscribed in bodily space-time, edited by R. Devisch and A. Gailly, as well as R. Devisch, *Se recréer femme: Manipulation sémantique d'une situation d'infécondité chez les Yaka du Zaire* (Berlin, 1984).
348. Whitten, *Sacha Runa*, pp. 53, 142. Because of the different origins of men and women, the kinds of souls they inherit and the manner in which subsequent souls are acquired are quite different.
349. Ibid. See also Roe, *Cosmic Zygote*, p. 315.
350. The *ové*, a transformative spiritual element of the Guayakí person, may continue its shape-changing after death, passing from *barendy*, a postmortem state, to the form of a jaguar (*baipu*) or even a venomous snake.
351. Clastres, *Chronique des indiens guayakí*, p. 226.
352. Ibid., p. 92.
353. Ibid., p. 95.
354. In describing the rite of breaking the skull, one mourner declared, "I am an orphan. I have seen the skull of my mother broken and rebroken . . . the bones and the skull . . . which the jaguar has smashed and smashed again" (ibid., p. 95). At the death of a courageous leader or notable hunter, the dead man's valor is honored with a duel carried out between two mourners. The duel consists of striking the skull with a piece of wood. In a clearing set aside especially for the purpose, two ritual duelists face one another. One squats on the ground in a comfortable position; the other remains standing facing him with a club. A blow is delivered to the head of the seated man. Then, if he so wishes, the seated man stands and in his turn delivers a blow to the head of the man who had just struck him. Then the duel is over. The blood that flows and the scars that result from the blows are signs of *kyrymba* (courage). The ritual duel is carried out in silence.
355. Inapirikuli's name is built around the word root *iñapi*, meaning "that which has its origin in bone." See Saake, "Mythen über Inapirikuli."
356. Ibid., p. 262.
357. Special consideration of sucking and magical blowing is given in chapter 7.
358. According to Jules Henry, the mouth is an important symbolic locus for the Kaingáng. Oral functions and images in myth are often destructive. However, this destructive valence of mouth symbolism, in Henry's opinion, is characteristic only of the realm of fantasy. In actual practice, oral functions are positive and constructive: cherishing and healing. For example, the mouth functions positively in curing by spitting, blowing, and biting. In other instances, people who are too sick to eat by themselves are fed by loved ones, who "cough up" their food after chewing it and force it into the sick person's mouth. Women often chew food for husbands as a sign of affection (Henry, *Jungle People*, p. 86). These uses of food increase in significance when we consider that "food and sex have become so closely interwoven in the Kaingáng mind that they even use the same term for eating as they do for coitus" (ibid., p. 35).
359. Conception and birth can be species of sucking and blowing, respectively. See the discussion of the Desana word *uhúri* ("to suck"), above.
360. Holmberg, *Nomads of the Long Bow*, p. 86.
361. Bartolomé, "Shamanism Among the Avá-Chiripá," p. 132.
362. Viertler, "A Noção de pessoa," p. 25.
363. Henry, *Jungle People*, p. 86.
364. Initiation to a new stage of raw economic power does not exhaust all applications of this

symbolic act of control over the mouth. For instance, a maturing Canelos Quichua man will apprentice himself to a shaman who "coughs up" spirit-helpers in the form of spirit darts, which both protect a human being from attack and allow for a counterattack. When the shaman coughs up these darts from his own stomach, the novice swallows them. The novice should avoid the temptation to bring them out of his stomach by "blowing" them at an enemy. This requires control over one's evil intentions (Whitten, *Sacha Runa*, p. 146).

365. The point is made in several different ways in Lévi-Strauss, *The Raw and the Cooked*, and, especially, *The Origin of Table Manners*.

366. Their different relations to food frequently distinguish humans from primordial beings. Human generativity and the meaning of food in human culture is consistent with the unique meaning of humanity's control over all body passages. For instances, in Makiritare myth, before the creation of human beings, the primordial beings celebrated a cassava meal with food brought directly from heaven. At this first cassava meal, Odosha, the trickster who brought death and disease, taught the primordial beings how to perform sexual intercourse. While the creator was away in heaven getting more food, Odosha appeared in the guise of the creator. Since those early beings didn't know how to grow cassava, and since the heavenly being who transported it from on high was repulsed by intercourse, he stopped bringing the food from heaven. The beings began to die. Others of them tried to survive by eating the earth directly (Civrieux, *Watunna*, p. 29).

367. Ellen B. Basso, "The Kalapalo Dietary System," in Basso, ed., *Carib-speaking Indians*, pp. 98–105; see the table of taxa of living beings on p. 99 and the list of cosmological features on p. 102.

368. Ibid., p. 105. Although the Kalapalo, like many members of Upper Xingu society, avoid eating most species of land animals as food, their principle of defining categories of being by what they eat places them back on common ground with other tropical-lowland tribes of South America. See the more lengthy discussion in Ellen B. Basso, *The Kalapalo Indians of Central Brazil* (New York, 1973), pp. 9–42.

369. Wagley, *Welcome of Tears*, pp. 65, 67, 69, 70; see also Baldus, *Tapirapé* pp. 209–225.

370. Wrote Wagley in 1977, "I still do not entirely understand the basis for their elaborate classification of and taboos regarding meat" (*Welcome of Tears*, pp. 21–22).

371. Ibid., p. 65.

372. Time is an important dimension of arks and temples. See the discussion "Templum-Tempus" in Mircea Eliade, *The Sacred and the Profane* (New York, 1959), pp. 73–76. On the homology of the body and spatial vessels embodying the temporal dimensions of the cosmos, see Lima de Freitas, *O Labirinto* (Lisbon, 1975). The isomorphism between body and cosmic space-time is not an inference drawn by scholars but often an explicit interpretation offered by cultures. For example, in South Asia, the *vástupuruṣa maṇḍala*, symbolically arranged in the base of temples, assures that the space of the temple and its festival cycle of time are identified with the Cosmic Man, whose body parts are the deities and planets.

373. Carneiro da Cunha, "Eschatology Among the Krahó," p. 164. Carneiro da Cunha makes clear that the Krahó possess alternative views of individual destiny in the afterlife.

374. Weiss, "World of a Forest Tribe," p. 291. The Machiguenga are more explicit in their statements of reincarnation. However, exactly how such metempsychosis is carried on does not seem to be clearly systematized; see ibid., p. 304.

375. Rites of passage make ample use of symbolism derived from the biology of death and decay to effectively illustrate that an individual has died to what he or she once was. By a principle of economy, the very same symbols manifest the possibility of renewed life in a changed form. The issue is discussed in Victor W. Turner, *The Forest of Symbols: Aspects of Ndembu Rituals* (Ithaca, N.Y., 1967), esp. pp. 93–111 Turner writes,

> In so far as [initiates] are no longer classified, the symbols that represent them are, in many societies, drawn from the biology of death, decomposition, catabolism, and other physical processes that have a negative tinge. . . . In so far as a neophyte is structurally "dead," he or she may be treated, for a long or short period, as a corpse is customarily treated in his or her society. (ibid., p. 96)

376. For an interpretation of the symbolic meaning of the body in Kógi culture, see Reichel-Dolmatoff, "Los Kogi," part 1, pp. 271ff. It is essential to view all the organs, functions, openings and processes of the body as symbolic. This manner of viewing the body (alúna) is what distinguishes humans from animals. It enables the human to think with his or her head and heart. In fact, the head and heart are the same organ united by body fat. The material form of human being allows it to also be a symbolic being: for example, human sperm is the "blood of the head" and breathing in the human manner is a constant series of initiatory deaths or ecstasies, for "when respiration goes, life goes and alúna goes" (ibid., p. 273).

377. Reichel-Dolmatoff, "Brain and Mind in Desana Symbolism," p. 81.

378. Edison Carneiro, "The Structure of African Cults in Bahia," JAFL 53 (October-December 1940): 273.

379. Ibid.

380. Ibid., p. 275.

381. Rego, "Mitos e ritos."

382. Ibid.

383. Ibid.

384. This should not imply that South American cultures contend that an impersonal culture or social ideology shapes individuals; nor do they insist that culture is an agglomeration of individual shapes. Neither one is a derivative of the other. Neither one has a mode of reality that dwarfs the ultimate reality of the other. Rather, both culture and individual are real because they take shape in response to sacred "givens." In relating to the meanings of the sacred manifest in the beginning of time, cultures and individuals shape themselves by interpreting the sacred symbolically. Understanding the sacred and conforming to its manifest meanings always requires creativity.

385. Civrieux, Religión y magia kari'ña, p. 17.

386. Chapter 6, below, shows how costume, masks, and enclosures deliberately shape experience by symbolically rearranging body parts.

387. Goldman, The Cubeo, pp. 219–252. It may be of interest to note that the conjunction of sexual orgy and mourning is not limited to the northwestern Amazon. For instance, "in England the London synod of 1342 put an end to love-making at wakes" (Elémire Zolla, The Androgyne: Fusion of the Sexes, London, 1981, p. 90).

388. Goldman, an astute observer and sensitive interpreter, realizes that "the sexual attack [with masks and phallic effigies] as the Cubeo dramatize it is, after all, symbolic and abstract" (Goldman, The Cubeo, p. 239). The symbolic character of the action is clear because it has "the appearance of a dance and not an orgy" (ibid.). He is less able to assign the same symbolic quality of knowledge to the basis for the physical orgy that terminates the second phase of the ceremony. But the orgy is also a symbolic act. Because Goldman takes the physical acts of sex only in their literal sense, he is able to elucidate only some social and psychological aspects of their meaning, but he does not emphasize the fundamentally religious meaning, which, for the Cubeo, grounds the value of their action:

> One month [after the ritual coitus that concludes the first phase of the ceremony] the mourning series is completed at a two-hour dance, at the end of which the masks are burned and, as the ultimate act, men take women, the wives of their phratry mates, into the bush and copulate, couples changing partners as often as they like. . . . The final sexual event in this ritual sequence is to be understood as somewhat more than sexual consummation. It is also an act of mass adultery, as the Indians are only too well aware. In this act, the adulterous longings of the people are given expression without any real suppression of the stormy feelings of jealousy that adultery provokes among them. The adulterous act adds still another modality of sexual passion. (ibid.)

Here Goldman grounds the meaning of Cubeo actions on the tenets of the behavioral science of psychology, a set of beliefs about truth and value that have but recently arisen in European and American culture. But the Cubeo are not middle-class Viennese patients of clinical psychiatrists. They are performing the normative symbolic acts of their culture during mourning. The Cubeo ground their knowledge of the meaning of their acts on religious understandings, which must also be taken into serious account in any rendering or interpretation of their reality. The orgy is a religious act with a sacred meaning unique to the Cubeo culture.

389. Goldman, *The Cubeo*, pp. 230–231.

390. "By contrast to the sexual emphasis, the ritual of dealing with the spirit of the deceased seems almost minor and anticlimactic. It is only at the very end, when most guests have departed, that the ghost is dispatched" (ibid., p. 232). Although he mentions the mythic event that founds such activity, Goldman does not in general emphasize that the Cubeo are reenacting the entire first sequence of death, including sex, which occurred at the beginning of time. Since the kind of knowledge one brings to performance is essential to its interpretation, the founding myth of the *óyne* rite distinguishes it from promiscuity and marks it off as a religious activity imitative of sacred beings.

391. Ibid.

392. Roe, *Cosmic Zygote*, p. 324.

393. Ibid.

394. The mechanist assumptions of neo-Kantian and post-Kantian deontological and rule-governed ethics emerge in the light of studies of the spatial assumptions underpinning cosmology. See Robin Lovin's article on William Paley in Frank E. Reynolds and Robin W. Lovin, *Cosmogony and Ethical Order* (Chicago, 1985). For a presentation of a range of ethical theories sharing the ethos of a specific view of detached and value-free space, see Tom L. Beauchamp and James F. Childress, *Principles of Biomedical Ethics*, 2d ed. (Oxford, 1983), or Tom L. Beauchamp and LeRoy Walters, eds., *Contemporary Issues in Bioethics*, 2d ed. (Belmont, Cal., 1982). For a discussion of the spatial and temporal cosmology underlying medical knowledge, see Larry Dossey, *Space, Time and Medicine* (Boulder, 1982), esp. the sections on "Biodance," pp. 72–81, and on the "implicate order" of space and time, pp. 181–189. For quite different reasons, Heinz R. Pagels discusses the role of human creativity as it relates to the physics of space and its symbolic understanding in *The Cosmic Code: Quantum Physics as the Language of Nature* (New York, 1982), passim, esp. pp. 57–61, 339–340.

CHAPTER SIX

1. Chapter 4 discusses the images of festival violence and contestation needed to impel cultures through time and effect change or foster fertility, growth, and abundance: promiscuity (incest), drunkenness, gluttonous consumption, ritual combat, and noisy din.

2. Etta Becker-Donner, "Notizen über die Huanyam, Territorium Rondonia, Brasilien," *EZ*, special supplement 1 (1974): 96–97. For a brief overview of the range of symbolic practices and institutions celebrating rites of passage in the South American life-cycle, see Gerhard Baer, *Südamerikanische Indianer* (Basel, 1965), pp. 24–28. Other examples: for a description of the ritual acts propelling the individual Krahó personality through the episodes of his or her life-cycle, see Julio Cezar Melatti, *Ritos de uma tribo timbira* (São Paulo, 1978), pp. 100–126; for the symbolic transitions through the Cashinahua life-cycle, including the dramatic passage at death, see André-Marcel d'Ans, *La verdedera biblia de los Cashinahua (Mitos, leyendas, y tradiciones de la selva peruana)* (Lima, 1975), pp. 16ff; for the Macuna life-cycle and its transitions, including death, see Kaj Arhem, "Vida y muerte en la Amazonía columbiana: Un relato etnografico macuna," *ANT* 79 (1984): 171–189. For a description of Waika life-cycle rituals, see Otto Zerries, *Waika. Die kulturgeschichtliche Stellung der Waika-Indianer des Oberen Orinoco im Rahmen der Völkerkunde Südamerikas* (Munich, 1964), pp. 197–200. For a number of action photos depicting people dressing for and celebrating rites of passage and festivals for growth, and practicing artisanry, see Harald Schultz, *Hombu: Indian Life in the Brazilian Jungle* (New York, 1962), which provides descriptions and explanations of the activities from the Javahé, Karajá, Cashinahua, Krahó, Makú, Suyá, Tukuna, Umutina, and Uruku peoples.

3. Udo Oberem, "Geburt, Hochzeit und Tod bei den Quijos-Indianern Ost-Ecuadors," *ICA*, 32nd Congress (Copenhagen, 1958), pp. 232–237.

4. Other kinds of transitions are examined elsewhere throughout this volume; for example, chapter 7 deals with the call to the vocation of a religious specialist, and chapter 8 looks at the symbolism of the transition effected by death.

5. Rafael Karsten gathered comparative data regarding theories of conception in his *The Civilization of the South American Indians with Special Reference to Magic and Religion* (London, 1926), pp. 414–435. Significantly, the conception of life, in Karsten's opinion, is often tied to theories of metempsychosis, reincarnation, and the exit of the soul from the body (of animals, plants, the dead, or the entranced). That is, the origins of individual life are bound up with forms of death.

6. Melatti notes that, for example, the conception and bringing to successful birth of a child actually constitute the final moment of the initiatory transformation of a young person into a mature adult. Up until that time, he or she still is, in a sense, in seclusion, for it is only after the birth of a child that a mature Krahó male perambulates through the village, liberated from the childish relationship of care given him by his mother; see Melatti, *Ritos de uma tribo timbira*, p. 338. For the ritual behaviors surrounding Krahó procreation, see ibid., pp. 103ff.

7. Wright, "History and Religion of the Baniwa," p. 386.

8. Wagley, *Welcome of Tears*, pp. 134–135.

9. Abel Adrian Ambía and Rodolfo Sánchez Garrafa, *Amaru: Mito y realidad del hombre* (Lima, 1970), p. 16.

10. Susan C. Bourque and Kay Barbara Warren, *Women of the Andes: Patriarchy and Social Change in Two Peruvian Towns*, (Ann Arbor, Mich., 1981), p. 89. Bourque and Warren's fieldwork extended from 1965 to 1980, with special attention given from 1974 on to the role and ideologies surrounding women's roles. The two towns were Chiuchin and Mayobamba in the districts of Checras and Santa Leonor, Department of Lima, Peru.

11. Ibid., p. 112.

12. Ibid.

13. Ibid., p. 90.

14. Ibid., p. 112.

15. Ibid., p. 90.

16. Ibid., p. 113.

17. Ibid. Although such explanations are used to explain behavioral and personality traits in young children, however, they do not seem to have provoked a strict set of behavioral prohibitions for pregnant women.

18. Igor Kopytoff presents a plausible argument for the view that "ritual itself defines the transition and the states of being" on page 185 of his "Revitalization and the Genesis of Cults in Pragmatic Religion: The Kita Rite of Passage among the Suku," in Ivan Karp and Charles S. Bird, eds., *Explorations in African Systems of Thought* (Bloomington, Ind., 1980). He also sketches the history of the theoretical view that "the human ritualizing mind . . . insists on marking with ritual the transitions between states of being" (p. 185) whose "essence is not structural but existential" (p. 198), "a transition between purely 'invented' states of being" (p. 198).

19. Maybury-Lewis, *Akwẽ-Shavante Society*, p. 63.

20. The expectant mother continues her rounds unrestrictedly (ibid., p. 64). Symbolic interventions and acquired imagery continue to define the new individual's physical and psychic shape. As we shall see in the discussion of initiation, the symbolic apparatus defining a person is made increasingly available to the subject through the mediating instrument of cultural knowledge. At about the age of six, an Akwẽ-Shavante boy is given a name and a cotton necklet by his mother's brother (ibid., p. 73).

21. Fock, *Waiwai*, p. 141.

22. Ibid., p. 136.

23. Holmberg, *Nomads of the Long Bow*, pp. 65–66.

24. Clastres, *Chronique des indiens guayakí*, p. 96.

25. See, for example, the descriptions of Yanoama practices surrounding birth, including couvade, food avoidances, the image of the tapir as a mythical figure, and those practices associated with the images of cutting the umbilicus, in Zerries and Schuster, *Mahekodotedi*, vol. 2, pp. 128ff.

26. José Luis Jordana Laguna, *Mitos e historias aguarunas y huambisas de la selva del Alto Marañon* (Lima, 1974), pp. 107–110. In the beginning of time the Cashinahua, to cite another example, could conceive children but did not know how to make them pass successfully through the transition of birth. They learned the ritual procedures that make birth possible from

the mythical Inca, but the Inca used to eat the children born of the Cashinahua. Finally, a small rat taught a pregnant Cashinahua woman how to give birth. See d'Ans, *La verdedera biblia de los Cashinahua,* pp. 136–139.

27. Wright, "History and Religion of the Baniwa," p. 465.

28. Kaj Arhem, "Observations on Life-Cycle Rituals among the Makuna: Birth, Initiation, Death," Annals of the Ethnographical Museum of Göteborg. Annual Report for 1979 (1980): 10–47. See also the symbolic beliefs and practices surrounding birth among the Selk'nam as described in Gusinde, *Los Índios de Tierra del Fuego. Los Selk'nam,* vol. 2, pp. 340–368.

29. Nimuendajú, *The Apinayé,* p. 100.

30. Waldeloir Rego, "Mitos e ritos africanos da Bahia."

31. Bartolomé, "Shamanism Among the Avá-Chiripá," p. 113.

32. P. Clastres, *Chronique des indiens guayakí,* pp. 14–15.

33. Ibid., pp. 12–13. The concept is widespread that birth is a fall, not only from the womb but from a prior state of being from which one must exit precipitously in order to make the transition into this state of affairs. It is not unusual to find the idea reflected in language. For instance, *aán,* in the Tapirapé language, means both "I fall" and "I am born." (Baldus, *Tapirapé,* p. 156.)

34. Clastres, *Chronique des indiens guayakí,* p. 14.

35. Ibid., pp. 14–16.

36. Ibid., p. 18.

37. Ibid., p. 23.

38. Ibid., p. 31.

39. Ibid., p. 29.

40. Ibid., p. 28.

41. Ibid., p. 32.

42. Ibid., p. 33. Regarding Guayakí birth and naming, see Friederich C. Mayntzhusen, "Über Gebräuche bei der Geburt und die Namengebung der Guayakí," *ICA,* 18th Congress, part 1 (London, 1913), pp. 408–412.

43. B. J. Isbell, *To Defend Ourselves,* and Mariscotti de Görlitz, *Pachamama Santa Tierra.* For a description of the rituals surrounding birth in the Aymara-speaking community of Kaata, Bolivia, see Bastien, *Mountain of the Condor,* pp. 85–102. The Mallkuta Qukuy is a ritual to assign the newborn a place (a shrine) on the earth. "At this rite of passage, the Indian passes from inside to the outside of Mount Kaata. According to Andean cosmology, the infant originates from the summit of Mount Kaata and travels on its slopes during life" (Bastien, p. 85). The mountain represents the entire universe and the stages of life's way represent "different theological states" (ibid.).

44. Bourque and Warren, *Women of the Andes,* p. 92. One woman's explanation for preferring birth at home underlines the insignificance of the birth-event as it is carried out in modern hospitals. Her description emphasizes how privatized the event has become, obscuring any links to wider social processes or cosmic values:

> "They leave you with nothing to cover yourself and they don't take care of you. You could drown in your own blood and they wouldn't change the sheets. They give you nothing to eat. Once when I was giving birth, all of a sudden I became very cold and asked for an herb tea to warm me. They wouldn't even give me that. They won't bring you a bedpan. The nurses sit in another room, laughing and gossiping. The doctor comes but he just looks at you and tells the nurses to carry on with the delivery. It [childbirth] is much better in the *Sierra.* You have someone to help, to bring you something to eat and drink, to take care of you." (p. 91)

In Mayobamba, men are present at a delivery if the mother is having serious difficulty in giving birth. Otherwise, they are asked to stay outside of the house lest they "suspend the birth" and make labor more difficult. In Chiuchin, men (especially husbands and close male relatives) are more easily brought into the birth process.

Bourque and Warren have produced a study that, from the outset, set itself the goal "to show how women's subordination is institutionally structured, yet negotiated, disputed, and changed through the conscious actions of women and men" (ibid., p. 4). Among the central questions they used to focus their work they single out these as most important: "How do women and men perceive sexual subordination? Do women act on their consciousness of sexual hierarchy? Do women's perceptions contribute to their oppression? Do women formulate strategies for change based on their understandings of subordination?" (ibid.). They conclude, "Our study shows that women are not silent or inactive victims in the face of the serious economic consequences of sexual subordination" (p. 214).

45. Ambía and Garrafa, *Amaru*, p. 18.

46. Ibid.

47. Henry, *Jungle People*, p. 194.

48. Ibid.

49. Baer once remarked, "One could call South America the classical land of the couvade" (*Südamerikanische Indianer*, p. 25). The ritual behaviors of the husband, the wife, and the other assistants who deal with the spiritual processes that produce a child are described for the Sanemá-Yanoama in Barandiarán, "Vida y muerte," pp. 36–39. For a description of the restrictions that parents observe among the Apinayé, see da Matta, *A Divided World*, pp. 55f. Newborns cannot see, know nothing, and have little blood and weakly attached souls. What their parents eat affects them directly. "It is clear that *both* the father and the mother observe the food prohibitions and they do so because the child has not yet eaten those kinds of foods" (ibid., p. 55). "Human beings are formed by the mixture of the vital fluids of the parents: mother's blood and father's sperm. The family is a veritable factory of social production and reproduction. In cosmological terms one might say that the nuclear family is the domain that transforms natural products (food, blood, sperm) into potential human beings" (p. 56). Couvade and food avoidances "restore order by separating domains that have been brought into a dangerous conjunction" (ibid.). They are social mechanisms used to classify objects, groups, and relationships.

50. Fock, *Waiwai*, p. 110.

51. Ibid., p. 111.

52. Karsten, *Toba Indians*, p. 22.

53. Holmberg, *Nomads of the Long Bow*, p. 68.

54. Ibid., p. 70. For a comparable discussion of Tehuelche birth practices, including diet restrictions, the father's ceremonial hunt for a rhea, the sacrifice of a mare by slitting its throat, the washing of the child, the dances at the naming festival, the placing of the newborn into the stomach or heart cavity of the sacrificed mare, and the association of the newborn with heavenly stars, see Alejandra Siffredi, "Hierofanías y concepciónes mitico-religiosas de los Tehuelches meridionales," *RU* 12 (1969–1970): 263–264.

55. Bruce Lincoln, *Emerging From the Chrysalis: Studies in Rituals of Women's Initiation* (Cambridge, Mass., 1981), offers a lucid comparative treatment of women's initiation and provides an ample bibliography of general and case-specific materials. He suggests a fourfold typology of women's initiations: bodily mutilation (the simplest means of transforming the entire female being), identification with a mythic heroine or goddess in order to benefit the whole world (radically transforming the temporal context that conditions the candidate's meaning), the reenactment of a cosmic journey (liberating the girl from the confines of domestic or local space and offering her the entire universe as her proper sphere of influence), and the play of opposites (which permits her a total existence by providing the symbolic means of overcoming oppositions such as male/female, line/circle, birth/death, past/future, inside/outside, naked/clothed, and so on). Lincoln does not intend the types to exclude one another. He also distinguishes three morphological complexes underlying the symbolic processes of women's initiations: enclosure, metamorphosis, and emergence. Throughout his work Lincoln provides cases to illustrate these points. He draws his conclusions together most succinctly on pages 91–109.

56. Wright, "History and Religion of the Baniwa," p. 597.

57. Ibid., p. 499.

58. Ibid., p. 511.

59. For descriptions of related rites in the northwest Amazon that are timed with ripe-fruit cycles and aimed at achieving openness through music and whipping, see Henri A. Coudreau, *Voyage a travers les Guyanes et l'Amazonie*, vol. 2, *La France equinoxiale* (Paris, 1887); Alexander von Humboldt and Aimé Bonpland, *Personal Narrative of Travels to the Equinoctial Regions of America during the Years 1799–1804*, 3 vols. (London, 1907); Theodor Koch-Grün-

berg, *Zwei Jahre unter den Indianern Reisen in Nordwest-Brasilien, 1903–05* (Vienna: 1907), e.g., pp. 185–188; A. B. de Amorim, "Lendas em Nheengatú e em Portugues," *RIHGB* 100 (1926–1927): 9–475; and Stephen Hugh-Jones, *The Palm and the Pleiades*, which contains an ample bibliography.

60. Wright, "History and Religion of the Baniwa," p. 387. South American qualities of space created during female initiation become relevant to investigations such as Julia Kristeva's development of the idea of *chora:* a maternal condition that is both "a state of language anterior to the word" and a "receptacle, the place before the space which is always already named" (p. 216). See Julia Kristeva, "The Speaking Subject," in Marshall Blansky, ed., *On Signs* (Baltimore: Johns Hopkins University Press, 1985).

61. The Baniwa are by no means unique in this regard. Curt Nimuendajú, in *The Tukuna* (Berkeley, Cal., 1952), pp. 73–92, abundantly testifies to the fact that Tukuna girls' initiation requires travel throughout a mythic geography of the universe. The ways in which Tukuna ritual space symbolically maps the universe and the importance during women's initiation of parading with instruments and masks to its separate domains is vividly described in Bruce Lincoln's chapter "Festa das Moças Novas: The Cosmic Tour," pp. 50–70 of *Emerging From the Chrysalis*.

62. Eduardo B. Viveiros de Castro, "A fabricação do corpo na sociedade xinguana," *BMN* n.s. 32 (1979): 42.

63. Ibid.

64. Ibid.

65. The designation *Itsatí* refers not only to the funerary feast but also to the demiurge who instituted it. This supernatural being is considered to be the artificer *par excellence* because of his ability to extract culture from primordial nature, now manifest in the powers of death. Human beings are to model their behavior on this artisan of culture. Pedro Agostinho, "Estudo preliminar sobre os mito de origens xinguano. Comentario a uma variante aweti," *Universitas: Revista de cultura da Universidade Federal de Bahia* 6–7 (1970): 457–519, also shows how myth links the ritual enclosure used in initiation and funerals with all life-sustaining containers. Even calabash containers for ordinary domestic use possess the same properties (indeed, *are* the same) as the ones in which the great Kamayurá heroes Kwat and Yaí were incubated and from which they were reborn, as from a surrogate womb, after they were torn prematurely from the womb of their slain mother.

66. Viveiros de Castro, "A fabricação do corpo," p. 43.

67. Peter Kloos, "Female Initiation Among the Maroni River Caribs," *AA* n.s. 71 (1969): 898–905. The initiate undergoes a series of ordeals, including holding fire in her hands and having her arms bitten by ants, before her coming out.

68. As we shall see below in a discussion of initiatory cutting, sometimes the first flow of blood is deliberately provoked. Among the Cubeo, for example, a prepubescent girl is made into a woman when she has intercourse with the moon, who causes her first menses. (The defloration is actually accomplished digitally.) Before menses the girl is called *paúnwe bebíko* ("one who has not yet copulated with the moon"). Menstrual blood is not human blood but the moon's blood. The moon's sexual penetrations bear no fruit. He returns each month. See Goldman, *The Cubeo*, pp. 179–181.

69. Bartolomé, "Shamanism Among the Avá-Chiripá," p. 142.

70. For a description of Tehuelche female initiation and first menstruation, see the descriptions of Casa Bonita ("beautiful house"), a musical ceremony and dance with food restrictions and tattooing rites, in Siffredi, "Hierofanías y concepciones," pp. 265–265. A Sanemá-Yanoama girl's initiation, held at her first menses, is considerably more elaborate than the one held for a boy. See the descriptions in Barandiarán, "Vida y muerte," pp. 39–42.

71. Civrieux, *Watunna*, p. 16.

72. Deliberate bodily mutilation, a form of containment, is a cultural device that brings a number of spontaneously "flowing" temporal features of change into the same orbit. Among such symbols of time evident in flow from the body, hair is of the first order. The logic of containment applies also to the symbolism of flowing hair. Some societies (the Barasana, for example; see Hugh-Jones, *The Palm and the Pleiades*, p. 205) explicitly link hair and menstruation, as transformed expressions of one another. Containment of flow in such circumstances

can reflect various tactics for circumscribing the space within which hair flows. On the one hand, the strategy of seclusion encompasses free-flowing hair inside a container, such as the ornamental tube that binds the hair of a mature man among the Barasana and the Waiwai; cf. Paul Riviere, "Myth and Material Culture: Some Symbolic Inter-relations," in R. F. Spencer, ed., *Forms of Symbolic Action* (Seattle, 1969), pp. 151–166. By their presence, absence, length, and design, hair-containers—spatial images to be sure—differentiate the times and stages of growth of individuals and society. On the other hand, deliberate mutilation of the body, this time through cutting (or ripping out) the hair, imposes outer spatial limits to flow and instigates a marked time of growth. The Siriono offer an example. They observe no initiation for young boys. Only young girls are initiated, before marriage. At about the time she reaches puberty, a girl's initiation rites are celebrated near a stream about a day's journey from home. Several girls are initiated at one time. The principle symbolic manipulation involves their hair: it is completely shaved off. They sit for the better part of two or three days on a specially constructed platform of poles, and they are made to bathe repeatedly. During this time they must observe food restrictions; see Holmberg, *Nomads of the Long Bow*, pp. 80ff. Older participants in the ceremony dance and sing. When an initiated girl's hair has grown out to the length of her chin, a process that takes about a year, she is able to have intercourse and marry. In another case, Bastien shows in what way clothing, the embodiment of the woof and warp of the loom, reflects the reality of the social world, which is linked by vertical and horizontal ties among human individuals and between human beings and the divine mountain body. Fittingly enough, these ties are highlighted at the time of the first haircutting ceremony, when godparents from different levels on the mountain community (different spatial domains of the divine body) "strengthen their ties with godchildren when they clothe them for the first time"; see Bastien, *Mountain of the Condor*, p. 111. The head is linked to the summit of the world mountain, and the hair to grass, the food of the grazing animals that produce wool. It is at the summit, the origin of life, that hair and wool merge as one and become interchangeable (ibid., pp. 112–113).

Gananath Obeyesekere, in his exploration of the religious life of Sri Lanka, *Medusa's Hair: An Essay on Personal Symbols and Religious Experience* (Chicago, 1981), offers a stimulating review of theoretical perspectives on the interpretation of hair symbolism, an antidote to Edmund R. Leach, "Magical Hair," *JRAI* 88 (1958): 147–164. See also the article and bibliography provided in C. R. Hallpike, "Hair," in *EOR*.

73. Roe, *Cosmic Zygote*, p. 94.
74. Ibid.
75. Ibid., p. 96
76. Ibid., p. 321.
77. Ibid., p. 97.
78. Ibid., p. 323.
79. Ibid., p. 324.
80. Roe's witnesses state that the clitoris was in fact amputated and buried; ibid., p. 325.
81. Ibid.
82. Ibid., p. 109.
83. Ibid., p. 104.
84. Indeed, Lincoln singles out exaggerated investiture as one of the most conspicuous features of women's initiations in general, as opposed to the emphasis on nakedness, singled out by Victor Turner, as a general feature of men's initiations. See Lincoln's *Emerging From the Chrysalis*, pp. 102ff., where he interprets excessive adornment with finery as a process of ontological magnification, or amplification. Ultimately, in order for her to become a woman (as opposed to assuming the sociopolitical status aimed at in men's initiation), a girl's powers, capabilities, and experiences must be expanded, even "cosmicized." "The general tendency in women's rites seems to be toward an additive process (clothes put on) rather than a subtractive one (clothes taken off)" (ibid., p. 103).

The meaning of exorbitant decoration should also be interpreted in light of the desire to seclude by hiding with ornaments, a process of occultation through decoration closely aligned with the symbolic death that underlies all processes of clothing, especially masking. All these symbolic manipulations of space find their places on the spectrum of symbolic confinement designed to redefine cosmic and social realities while transforming individual persons. See the discussions linking symbolic space, clothing, and death in chapters 5 and 8. The importance of body decoration and the symbolic rearrangement of body space is so important in South American cultures that one could easily construct an interpretation of religious life using bodily ornamentation and the meaning of physiology as the organizing principle. Indeed, this is nearly what Karsten did in his *Civilization of the South American Indians;* see, for example, his treatments of body painting (pp. 1–40); of hair, nails, head, and skin (pp. 43–72); of feather ornaments (pp. 75–100); of ear-, lip-, and nose-ornaments and of necklaces, bracelets, and anklets (pp. 102–130); of body coverings that manifest a sense of shame (pp. 131–150); of bodily mutilations, tattoos, and scarifications (pp. 153–197); and of the arts associated with ritual ornamentation (pp. 198–263). Extraordinary detail on Boróro body decoration is offered in Albisetti and Venturelli, *Enciclopédia boróro*, vol. 1, *Vocabularios e etnografía*, e.g., pp. 2097ff. et passim. The Waika decorate and dress themselves to arrange the significations of human body space to conform to personality, age, and other physical and spiritual (as well as economic and political ones) situations. See Zerries, *Waika*, pp. 103–124, which gives special attention to body painting, haircutting (the tonsure is shaved in phases that not only respect the life-cycle but imitate the mythic history of the moon), the decorative deformation of the face, the penis sheath, and other decorations, such as sashes, waistbands, armbands and so on.

85. Human clothing (most particularly ritual dress) and animal bodies share this in common: they are the discarded remains of primordial beings. According to the Campa, humans and animals, like the sacred beings of the first times, discard their "clothing" (bodies) when they move from one state of being into another. For example, when a Campa shaman dies, it is said that he leaves his former clothing, his skin, on earth. What ascends into the heights is his soul. This concept may help to open paths for interpreting the meaning of the ritual episode called the "killing of pets" performed during Shipibo girls' initiation. For a comparative discussion of the ways in which the human body is ceremonially outfitted to assume the supernatural powers of primordial birds, see Hildegard Matthai, *Die Rolle der Greifvögel ins besondere der Harpye und des Königsgeiers, bei ausserandinen Indianern Südamerikas* (Munich, 1977), pp. 54–89 and 135ff.

86. Roe, *Cosmic Zygote*, pp. 99 and 328.

87. Once again the idea is driven home that ritual adornments, beautiful clothes *par excellence* (serving, in fact, as the definitive criteria for beauty in dress), are directly linked to death, especially the sacrifice or withdrawal of primordial beings whose departure left animal forms on earth as symbolic tokens of their former full presence. Cross-dressing with the beasts and decorating the girl reinstall the primordial state of affairs. Elsewhere, see Otto Zerries, "Das Federdiadem—Ein Sonnensymbol bei südamerikanischen Indianern," in Hartmann and Oberem, eds., *Amerikanistische Studien*, pp. 314–321, and Johannes Wilbert, "Vestidos y adornos de los indios warao," *ACAR* 12 (1964), pp. 6–26. Descriptions of the function and religious value of clothing among the Selk'nam can be found in Gusinde, *Los Indios de Tierra del Fuego. Los Selk'nam* vol. 1, pp. 190–200. Gusinde gives particular attention to body painting and ornamentation, including bows, arrows, slings, scrapers, baskets, and other instruments of labor (ibid., pp. 201–240). According to Alana Cordy-Collins, figures appearing in Chimu and Moche ceramics are normally clothed and wear head coverings. The two exceptions are captured prisoners, who wear no hats or other clothing, and supernatural figures; see Alana Cordy-Collins, "Andean Area," in E. K. Land, ed., *Pre-Columbian Art from the Land Collection* (San Francisco, p. 211. See also the discussion of the symbolism of clothing worn by ceramic figures in Elizabeth P. Benson, *The Mochica: A Culture of Peru* (New York, 1972), figs. 2–18, and Christopher B. Donnan, *Moche Art and Iconography* (Los Angeles, 1976), figs. 66 and 67. John Rowe points to the important role traditional dress played in conserving the religious culture of the Inca. Official court and imperial religion and the speculative religious philosophies of the elite schools crumbled under Spanish hegemony. However, dress became a focus for traditional art, symbolism, social relations and work relations in production, and identity because the shapes, colors, flowers, geometric designs, and so on were laden with cosmological significance. Clothing carried this cosmology across the centuries (Rowe, "El Movimiento nacional inca del siglo XVIII," in Alberto Flores Galindo, ed., *Tupac Amaru*, pp. 22–24.

88. Lévi-Strauss, *The Raw and The Cooked*, pp. 158–160, draws together a number of cases in which confined female initiates, modeling their behavior on the models set by mythic heroines, could be said to be in a state of fermentation effecting the transformations of puberty.

89. See, for example, the lucid discussion of *piâm*, the prescribed shame, or respect, that imposes social distance between affines and ritual relatives among the Apinayé, in da Matta, *A Divided World*, pp. 41, 47, and, especially, pp. 50–51, which discuss the relationship of shame to mystical influence, seclusion, and flowing blood. For another sort of example, see Maria Helena Farelli, *Os rituais secretos de magia negra e do Candomblé* (Rio de Janeiro, *Pallas*, 1981).

90. Fock, *Waiwai*, p. 157.

91. Ibid., pp. 48–53. Fock was never present at a Yamo festival, and, consequently, we have no way of knowing from his account whether a girl's initiation is connected to the festival in any way other than in myth. Fock's reports indicate that a girl's initiation begins from the moment of menarche. However, see the comparable Shipibo materials for a similar drinking and dancing festival, held when a girl first menstruates; Roe, *Cosmic Zygote*, pp. 94–104. In the Shipibo case, it appears that the menses is provoked or sustained, culturally, through the bleeding that results from clitoridectomy.

92. Fock, *Waiwai*, p. 158.

93. Karsten, *Toba Indians*, pp. 26ff.

94. Clastres, *Chronique des indiens guayakí*, p. 133.

95. Ibid., p. 135.

96. See the discussion of the relationship between closure (including the convention of "secrecy") and the cultural currency signified by money in Daniel L. O'Keefe, *Stolen Lightning: The Social Theory of Magic* (New York, 1983), p. 475.

97. For descriptions of Yanoama girls' puberty rites, which prescribe eating parts of the head of an animal; impose restrictions on contact with the earth; include ritual seclusion, washing, painting, adornment, and piercing of lips and ears; enforce the girls' avoidance of contact with their own skin; and so on, see Zerries and Schuster, *Mahekodotedi*, pp. 134ff.

98. An explanation of the spectacular display of the woman initiate when she emerges from seclusion is provided for the case of the Makiritare women's initiation by Barandiarán, *Introducción a la Cosmovisión de los Indios Ye'kuana-Makiritare*, pp. 820–821. Barandiarán also explains and describes the mechanism of drunken stupor and vomiting that the initiate is subjected to. These become violent devices of ritual death. The presiding shaman watches for any signal that will allow him to say that the girl has died: *"nëumai!"* However, this ritual death is only a precondition, a prelude to her resurrection, for as soon as she awakes from her drunken stupor, she receives her first purifying bath. In effect, her ritual death and resurrection at the center of community life identify her with the Tree of Life (the Central Pillar of the universe), symbolized by the center post of the community house (pp. 820–822).

99. Eliade draws conclusions of this sort in his widely comparative study of initiation, *Rites and Symbols of Initiation: The Mysteries of Birth and Rebirth* (1958; New York, 1965). Among other conclusions, Eliade calls attention to several widespread and frequently overlapping patterns of initiation:

> (a) the simplest pattern, comprising only the neophyte's separation from his mother and his introduction to the sacred; (b) the most dramatic pattern, comprising circumcision, ordeals, tortures, that is, a symbolic death followed by resurrection; (c) the pattern in which the idea of death is replaced by the idea of a new gestation followed by a new birth, and in which the initiation is expressed principally in embryological and gynecological terms; (d) the pattern whose essential element is individual withdrawal into the wilderness and the quest for a protecting spirit; (e) the pattern peculiar to heroic initiations, in which the emphasis falls on victory gained by magical methods (e.g., metamorphosis into a wild beast, frenzy, etc.); (f) the pattern characteristic of the initiations of shamans and other specialists in the sacred, comprising both a descent to Hell and an ascension to Heaven (essential themes: dismemberment of the body and renewal of the viscera, climbing trees); (g) the pattern that we may call "paradoxical," because its principal feature is ordeals that are inconceivable on the level of human experience (ordeals of the Symplegades type). (p. 130)

Victor W. Turner took note of the sociological implications of the initiatory condition, which an individual occupies two orders of existence at the same time. Turner characterized this "liminal" state as one in which the initiate is *both* a child *and* an adult but, at the same time, is *neither* a child *nor* an adult. The novice is "betwixt and between" and, as such, is defined by the paradox inherent in all multivalent symbolism of marginal conditions. For example, with the symbolic gesture of nakedness novices depict the state of a corpse and of a newborn child; the seclusion hut can symbolize a tomb and a womb at the same time. It is in this paradoxical state, a time when normal social relations are suspended or even countered in order to create a new social being, that the revelation of the sacredness of everyday realities can be revealed. See Turner's analysis of Ndembu initiation in his *The Forest of Symbols: Aspects of Ndembu Ritual* (Ithaca, N.Y., 1967), pp. 93–112. Because initiation is a statement of the human condition as such, as argued in this chapter of the present volume, Turner thought it fitting to analyze many other human experiences and "social dramas" in terms of the liminality most clearly expressed during rites of passage. See Lawrence E. Sullivan, "Victor W. Turner," *HR* 24 (1984): 160–163.

100. Civrieux, *Watunna*, pp. 13–14.

101. Ibid., p. 15.

102. Similarly, the aim of Sanemá-Yanoama initiation is to destroy unconscious identities and thereby "begin [in the psyche of the candidate] the lucid consciousness of his or her personal, mystical participation"; Barandiarán, "Vida y muerte," p. 42. Details of Yanoama male initiation can be found in Zerries and Schuster, *Mahekodotedi*, pp. 134ff.

103. Interpreting the myths of a primordial matriarchy has proven difficult and controversial. Discussion has revolved around whether or not the myths represent an actual historical situation, in the narrow sense of the word *history*. Do the myths of prior female possession of instruments or masks now associated with men's initiatory fraternities, clubhouses, and political confabs point to a period when women governed sociopolitical life? In spite of the lack of evidence, this question has endured in scholarly and popular literature ever since the hypothesis was forwarded by Johann J. Bachofen. Though Bachofen died in 1887, his studies of myth, religion, and mother right were first published in 1926: see Bachofen, *Das Mutterrecht und Urreligion*, 2 vols. (Basel, 1948). Surveys and critiques of contemporary interpretations may be found in Carolyn Fleuhr-Lobban, "A Marxist Reappraisal of the Matriarchate," *CA* 20 (1979): 341–460, and in Sally R. Binford, "Myths and Matriarchies," in Elvia Angeloni, ed., *Anthropology 81/82* (Guilford, Conn., 1981), pp. 150–153. For treatments of South American materials, particularly men's initiation and exclusive ritual clubs in the Amazon, see Yolanda Murphy and Robert F. Murphy, *Women of the Forest* (New York, 1974); Joan Bamberger, "The Myth of Matriarchy: Why Men Rule in Primitive Societies," in Rosaldo and Lamphere, eds., *Woman, Culture, and Society*, pp. 263–280; and S. Hugh-Jones, *The Palm and The Pleiades*, pp. 127 ff. and passim. C. Hugh-Jones, in *From the Milk River*, points to a parallel between male regenerative rites and female activities associated with manioc among the Barasana and in the Vaupés River area generally. The parallel includes a mythic scenario in which women take over the implements of food preparation (tripod, pounding sieves), which primordially belonged to males:

> Thus, instead of the set of instruments which can be united to draw upon ancestral power, they got the power to separate the three manioc constituents which can be united to nourish the community. The opposition between female manioc separation and male *He* [the musical instruments which embody the ancestors during male initiation and which once belonged to females] is echoed in versions of 'the rule of women' myth collected from different Pirá-paraná groups. In these, it is mentioned that when the women had Yurupary, men had white arms up to their elbows from the pounding of manioc in the tripod sieve. (p. 184)

104. See Wright, "History and Religion of the Baniwa," pp. 582–599, for a description of the initiation rites. Initiation and the burning of Kuai in myth are considered to be the same moment to such an extent that, when Wright asked about contemporary practices, his hosts recounted the myth of Kuai:

> I will only note [says Wright] that the switch or jump from "now" to "long ago" can be made so easily because initiation rites are times when the world of long ago becomes alive.

Initiates are shown the sacred flutes; and everything the elders tell them emphasizes that what they do with the flutes and to the initiates is "as it was made" in the beginning. (p. 368)

Wright provides a summary of important elements common to the rites and the myth on pp. 428ff.

105. Ibid., p. 441.
106. Ibid., p. 413.
107. Fulop, "Aspectos: Cosmogonía," p. 124.
108. Villas Boas and Villas Boas, *Xingu*, p. 138.
109. C. Hugh-Jones, *From the Milk River*, pp. 115ff., 134 ff., and passim.
110. Terence S. Turner examines the concept of a social skin in regard to the Northern Kayapó in Turner, "Social Skin," in *Not Work Alone*, pp. 112–140 (Beverly Hills, Calif., 1980); see also his "Tchikrin: A Central Brazilian Tribe and Its Symbolic Language of Bodily Adornment," *Natural History* 78 (1969). According to Simone Dreyfus, among the Northern Kayapó "the human body is the sole material on which the imagination and sense of beauty can be applied"; see Dreyfus, *Les Kayapó du nord. Etat de Para-Brésil: Contribution à l'étude des Indien-Gé* (The Hague, 1963), pp. 39f. The body-paint markings are apparently not associated with the social group to which one belongs; rather, they have a "magical significance: they assure the fruitful execution of the hunt or the fishing expedition, victories in war or, for a woman, they impede procreation" (ibid., pp 39–40). For a detailed description and analysis of body painting and other ornamental decoration of the body among peoples of the Upper Xingu area (especially the Kamayurá), see Agostinho, *Kwarìp*, esp. pp. 135–144, on body painting, and pp. 145–151, on ceremonial ornaments.
111. S. Hugh-Jones, *The Palm and the Pleiades*, p. 120.
112. Ibid.
113. That is, the Barasana initiatory skin-change is different from that among the Inca, for example. The Inca *ararihua* were young ritual warriors who donned fox skins, notably in October and March, to battle furiously with Thunder, Hail, and varmints who tried to destroy crops; see Guaman Poma de Ayala, *El Primer Nueva Corónica*, edited by J. V. Murra and R. Adorno (Mexico City, 1980), pp. 1138, 1159. Urton writes that

The male fox takes on familial responsibilities similar to those the *ararihua* assumes. . . . [T]he merging of the agricultural cycle with the transformation of the status of the *ararihua* and his wife through reproduction is metaphorically compared to a similar transformation [mating, reproducing, and shedding] that foxes undergo at the same time [October and March]; the two are juxtaposed when the *ararihua*, along with his wife and child, move into the puna to oversee the potato plants. In Guaman Poma's drawings, the juxtaposition is carried one step further when the *ararihua* covers himself with the skin of a fox. ("Animal Metaphors and the Life Cycle in an Andean Community," in Urton, ed., *Animal Myths and Metaphors*, p. 267).

114. S. Hugh-Jones, *The Palm and the Pleiades*, p. 154.
115. Ibid., p. 179.
116. Ibid., p. 264.
117. Ibid., p. 182.
118. Ibid., p. 264.
119. Ibid., p. 183.
120. C. Hugh-Jones, "Skin and Soul: The Round and the Straight. Social Time and Social Place in Pirá-Paraná Society," in *ICA*, 42d Congress, vol. 2 (Paris, 1977), pp. 185–204.
121. S. Hugh-Jones, *The Palm and the Pleiades*, p. 273.
122. Ibid., p. 61.
123. Ibid., p. 63.
124. Ibid., p. 68.
125. Ibid., p. 73. Hugh-Jones notes that, properly speaking, the initiates flee from the house at this point, along with the women. He also remarks that during the particular instance of initiation that he witnessed, the initiates did not do so but came into the house with the ceremonial procession.

126. Ibid., p. 77.

127. Ibid., p. 151.

128. Ibid., p. 79.

129. Although Hugh-Jones did not witness this rite, he was informed that it is part of the ritual.

130. Ibid., p. 82.

131. Deconstruction of sacred objects and replacement in hiding so that they disappear from plain sight play a significant role in many men's initiations. They constitute the strategem of disillusionment, a form of revelation in its own right.

132. Ibid., p. 85.

133. Ibid., p. 84.

134. The origin myth of the Kína ceremony of the Yamana may be found in Louis Ferdinand Martial, *Mission scientifique du cap Horn 1882–83*, vol. 1, *Histoire du voyage* (Paris, 1888), p. 214, and in Gusinde, *Die Feuerland-Indianer. Die Yamana*, vol. 2, pp. 1337–1342. Myths of the origin of the Klóketen may be found in Gusinde, *Die Feuerland-Indianer. Die Selknam*, vol. 2, pp. 859–879, and in E. Lucas Bridges, *Uttermost Part of the Earth* (London, 1948), pp. 412ff. See also Carlos Keller, "Der Ursprungsmythus der Klóketen-Feier der Selknam-Indianer auf Feuerland," *ANT* 57 (1962): 524–528. The Selk'nam provided a lengthy mythic account explaining the origins of the Klóketen ceremony, which once belonged to women (primordial animals directed by Kra, the female divinity who is the moon) but which now is the exclusive secret institution of men (who slaughtered the women at the direction of Kran, the sun). See Johannes Wilbert, ed., *Folk Literature of the Selknam Indians: Martin Gusinde's Collection of Selknam Narratives* (Los Angeles, 1975), pp. 147–171. The Yahgan report that women once ruled men and performed all the ceremonial duties. The women had power in those days because they controlled the Kína ceremonies, body-painting marks, masks, and songs. Anuxa, the moon, led them. All the women were slaughtered. Anuxa escaped, but bruises can still be seen on her face. The sun also rose into the sky, and the sun's father became Venus and his brother the rainbow. See Samuel Kirkland Lothrop, *The Indians of Tierra del Fuego* (New York, 1928), pp.177–178.

135. This is not to say that divestiture, investiture, or ritual fury are *a priori* the prerogative of either male or female initiation. In fact, display, symbolic violence, and disillusionment are likely to be present in both male and female initiation, as well as in many other ritual performances. For instance, Sam D. Gill, in "Disenchantment," *Parabola: Myth and The Quest for Meaning* 1, (1976): 6–13, discusses several cases in which initiation rites,

> which should germinate relationships with the holy, focus upon the intentional destruction or defamation of sacred objects in the presence of the initiates. It would seem in these cases that the symbolic blow of death is dealt to the gods or the sacred rather than to the initiates. . . . [T]he adepts of the society often go to great lengths to deceive the initiates, to set them up for the disillusionment they will suffer. (p. 7)

Gill's cases include both male and female initiations. The point at issue is to locate them within the logic and goals of the entire complex of symbolic forms associated with male and female maturation and to note the relatively different ways in which violence, disillusionment, display, and liquefaction are highlighted in male and female growth.

136. Ibid., p. 11.

137. Ibid.

138. When it comes to offering finely tuned interpretations of masks, Goldman's observations hold true: "The use of ceremonial masks is common enough in South America, . . . but we have as yet little information as to their meaning, nor do we know their full distribution. What is certain, though, is that masked cults have different significances in different tribes" (*The Cubeo*, pp. 222–223). Goldman relies on descriptions of masked rites in the following works: Karl von den Steinen, *Unter den Naturvolkern Zentral-Brasiliens* (Berlin, 1894); Fritz Krause, "Tanzenmaskennachbildungen vom Mittleren Araguaya," *Jahrbuch des Städtischen Museums für Völkerkunde zu Leipzig* 3 (1910): 97–122; Theodor Koch-Grünberg, "Die Maskentanze der Indianer des oberen Rio Negro und Yapura," *Archiv für Anthropologie* 4 (1906): 293–298, and *Zwei Jahre unter den Indianern*, 2 vols. (Berlin, 1909); Gunter Tessmann, *Indianer Nordost-Perus*, vol 2, (Hamburg, 1930); and Alfred Métraux, "The Hunting and Gathering Tribes of the Rio Negro Basin," in *HSAI*, vol. 3, pp. 861–868. Goldman offers a brief outline of the distribution of

mask-styles and their ritual functions for the central Amazon, northwest Amazon, and northeast Peru. The Cubeo themselves, however, center boys' initiation, replete with terrifying ceremonial whipping, around the presence of ancestors embodied in flutes taken from primordial females (*The Cubeo*, pp. 190–202) and reserve emphasis on masking for the Óyne, the mourning rite festival, which celebrates the incestuous act that brought death and new generations into the world (pp. 221–252). New information on masks continues to gather. Gerhard Baer's "The Pahotko-Masks of the Piro (Eastern Peru)," *BSSA* 38 (1974): 7–16, and "Masken der Piro, Shipibo, und Matsigenka (Ost-Peru)," *Verhandlungen der Naturforschenden Gesellschaft in Basel* 87–88 (1976–1977): 101–116, provide examples of the rich religious meaning of masks in areas where the very existence of masks had been in doubt not long ago. Compare Baer's information with Julien H. Steward, "Tribes of the Montaña and Bolivian East Andes," in *HSAI*, vol. 3, pp. 507–533, especially pp. 507–508 for the measure of how mask data and interpretation have changed. See also the four essays on masks in South America in N. Ross Crumrine and Marjorie Halpin, eds., *The Power of Symbols: Masks and Masquerade in the Americas* (Vancouver: University of British Columbia Press, 1983); Guillermo Delgado-P., "The Devil Mask: A Contemporary Variant of Andean Iconography in Oruro," pp. 128–145; R. T. Zuidema, "Masks in the Incaic Solstice and Equinoctial Rituals," pp. 146–153; J. Christopher Crocker, "Being an Essence: Totemic Representation Among the Eastern Bororo," pp. 154–173; and Angelina Pollak-Eltz, "Masks and Masquerades in Venezuela," pp. 174–190.

139. Maybury-Lewis, *Akwẽ-Shavante Society*, pp. 290–291.

140. See the dates in ibid., pp. 115, 123.

141. Ibid., p. 141.

142. Ibid., pp. 113–114.

143. Ibid., pp. 116–120.

144. Ibid., p. 124.

145. Ibid., p. 125.

146. Ibid., p. 129.

147. As Terence Turner has pointed out, in regard to the Northern Kayapó, the myth of the origin of fire is closely associated with the processes and powers of human growth and maturation. Turner relates the process of initiation to the myth of the jaguar and his wife, the possessors of primal fire, and to the establishment of the cooking fire, the center of the social unit (and the generative center for processes of reproduction at every social, material, biological, and ideological level). See T. Turner, "Animal Symbolism, Totemism, and the Structure of Myth," in Urton, ed., *Animal Myths and Metaphors*, pp. 49–106.

148. Maybury-Lewis, *Akwẽ-Shavante Society*, pp. 132–134.

149. Ibid., p. 140.

150. Ibid., pp. 142, 248–252.

151. Ibid., pp. 178–179.

152. Ibid., p. 240.

153. Ibid., p. 251.

154. Nimuendajú, *The Apinayé*, pp. 32ff. Roberto da Matta observed that the Apinayé of the 1960s no longer practiced their formal initiation ceremonies. Nonetheless, da Matta has offered insightful analyses of the initiatory data from earlier reports among the Apinayé (*A Divided World*, pp. 65–66; 91–97).

155. Nimuendajú, *The Apinayé*, p. 56. Da Matta distinguishes between three kinds of Apinayé seclusion. The first is undertaken by a killer in order to separate him from the soul, especially the powerful smell, of the dead man. The second kind of seclusion is observed by menstruating women. This may even involve her partner since they are linked by blood. The third and most elaborate seclusion is observed by both husband and wife after the birth of their child. It lasts some two months for the woman and some four months for the father (this was the case in the 1960s). The reason for the third kind of seclusion is "to safeguard the child's blood, which is still very weak" (da Matta, *A Divided World*, p. 53).

156. Nimuendajú, *The Apinayé*, p. 59.

157. See the discussion of this relationship in ibid., pp. 30ff., and da Matta, *A Divided World*, pp. 74–77, 85–93.

158. Nimuendajú, *The Apinayé*, p. 177.

159. Ibid., pp. 154–156.

160. Wagley, *Welcome of Tears*, p. 153.

161. Ibid., p. 155.

162. Ibid., p. 156. This is considered the "high point" of a man's life. It is the most highly decorated moment of his existence, for "from this time on men discard decorations progressively as they grow older. At middle age and later, they decorate their bodies hardly at all" (ibid., p. 157).

163. Fock, *Waiwai*, p. 159.

164. Douglas Sharon, "The Inca *Warachikuy* Initiations," in Johannes Wilbert, ed., *Enculturation in Latin America*, pp. 213–236. The rites of initiation go along with another series of rites of fertility in which the ears of the boys are pierced, the fields are pierced to receive rain, and sacrifices of llamas are made to guarantee increase. It is also the time of the summer solstice, the time of passage from one year to the next and from the dry season to that of the fertile rains. See the summary of information and sources on Inca initiation in John H. Rowe, "Inca Culture at the Time of the Spanish Conquest," in *HSAI*, vol. 2, pp. 283–284, 308–311.

165. Clastres, *Chronique des indiens guayakí*, p. 124.

166. Ibid.

167. Ibid., p. 125. The fact that a tibia bone is used at this moment cannot be overlooked, although Clastres presents no particular interpretive details on its meaning. We cannot speculate on the meaning that this particular instrument of perforation has for the Guayakí. We can, however, note that elsewhere the tibia is seen as a container of the soul.

168. Ibid.

169. Ibid., p. 128.

170. It is interesting to observe that, in taking the part of the initiates against the mature men, the master of the ceremonies of initiation places himself in a position on the side of the women, the birth-givers. This idea is only implied in Guayakí ritual action, but it is drawn explicitly by such groups as the Barasana, who equate the shaman-initiators with menstruating and birth-giving women.

171. In fact, most cultures intend men's and women's initiations to be quite different. Even more than that, both male and female initiations tend to be totalizing. Each accounts for the creation and regeneration of culture in its own way. They are, from one viewpoint, alternative claims about the way human culture stands in relation to reproductive processes. Insofar as they are contrasting total views, it is not surprising to find in them the symbolism of terrorism, especially in connection with sex-discriminating secret societies and in initiation scenarios in which creativity is exhaustively accounted for in terms of one of the sexes without remainder left to the other. This is the terror of remaining without a creative and essential role in the cosmos. The present discussion dovetails with that in the preceding chapter concerning the analogy "nature is to culture as female is to male." Nicole-Claude Mathieu, "Homme-Culture et Femme-Nature," *H* 13 (1973): 101–112, focuses less on the sexual divisions in societies studied by ethnographers than on the divisions of data as they are cloven by the categories of ethnography itself. See also Mathieu's "Notes pour une définition sociologique des catégories de sexe," *Epistémologie sociologique* 2 (1971): 19–39.

172. Alfred Métraux, "Religion and Shamanism," p. 581.

173. Wright, "History and Religion of the Baniwa," p. 504.

174. Ibid.

175. Ibid.

176. Ibid., p. 435.

177. Ibid.

178. For further information on the Yurupary initiation rites among the Baniwa, see the bibliography cited ibid., pp. 582, 598–599. In particular, see C. Pinheiro, "Rio Negro, Villa São Gabriel, curiosidades naturais, costumes dos Indios," *Revista da sociedade geographica* 13 (1900): 29–35; Koch-Grünberg, *Zwei Jahre unter den Indianern*, pp. 185–188; A. B. de Amorim, "Lendas em Nheengatú e em Portugues," *RIHGB* 100 (1926–1928): 9–475. On Baniwa girls' initiation, see Jean Chaffanjon, *L'orénoque et le Caura: Relation de voyages exécutées en 1886–7* (Paris, 1889),

pp. 213–216, and Eduardo Galvão, "Aculturação indígena no Rio Negro," *BMPEG* 7 (1959): 1–60, especially pp. 50–51. S. Hugh-Jones comments on the reports about Yurupary in the Northwest Amazon:

> It can also be argued that the classic Yurupary myths can be taken as stories about how Yurupary was initiated by being opened up. When he was born, he had no mouth and could neither speak nor eat and had to be fed with tobacco smoke that was blown over him. . . . [O]ther myths describe a progression from having no holes at all to a body full of holes. . . . [W]hen asked questions he replied by shaking his head. According to Magalhães [cited in J. Bolens, "Mythe de Jurupari: Introduction à une analyse," *H* 7 (1967): 51], *Yurupary* can be translated as "to hold one's hand over one's mouth." He grew very rapidly and at "the age of six" a mouth was cut in his face whereupon he let out a terrible roar and soon after ate up the disobedient initiates in his cave-like mouth (W. Saake, "Die Juruparile-gende"). (*The Palm and the Pleiades*, p. 201)

179. Clastres, *Chronique des indiens guayakí*, p. 138.
180. Villas Boas and Villas Boas, *Xingu*, p. 261.
181. Ibid., pp. 98ff.
182. Ibid., pp. 103f.
183. Clastres, *Chronique des indiens guayakí*, p. 131. No other reason is provided for the suitability of one stone as opposed to another. From all that we have seen, however, regarding the mythology of stones and soul-stones that have existed from primordial times and that contain the spirits of ancestors or powerful supernatural beings, and given the difficulty and care exercised by the Guayakí in finding the proper stone (as well as the fact that the boy is endowed with a new power at this point by the cutting that the stone will do), we might want to remain sensitive to a possibility that the meaning of the stone may go beyond its purely functional sharp edge.
184. Ibid., p. 132.
185. Ibid., p. 133. Later on, Clastres reflected on the relationships among ideas of order, writing, cutting the body, body language (rite), and the ritual nature of links between ordeal and torture as well as between painful ordeal and memory (keeping in mind that the marked body, written on and scarred by torture, is the locative instrument as well as one expressive form of memory). See Clastres, "De la torture dans les sociétés primitives," *H* 13 (1973): 114–120.
186. Wagley, *Welcome of Tears*, pp. 152, 163–168.
187. Ibid., p. 168. A boy's lip is pierced at birth and his earlobes may be pierced at initiation.
188. Audrey J. Butt, "The Mazaruni Scorpion," *Timehri* 36 (1957): 40–54. The meaning of cuts and the significance of filling the wounds should be examined afresh in each cultural context. Local theories of physiology have a large role in decoding the significance of symbolic wounds. The meanings attached to the substances used to fill wounds will also depend on the cultural context, especially the myths of origin and the other uses of the substance as a symbol of the sacred. Fruitful comparison might be made, for example, between the Akawaio case of scarification of women's faces (the wounds being then smeared with honey) and the Apinayé case of men's legs being cut during initiation without our having to depend exclusively on structural analysis. After a period of several days during which Apinayé initiates run a series of log races, the novices are inspected to see whether a superfluity of blood is causing their knees to tremble with exhaustion. If this is the case, the candidates' thighs and lower legs are scratched with rats' teeth so that they bleed. The charcoal from an ant's nest is rubbed into the cuts (Nimuendajú, *The Apinayé*, p. 63).
189. For example, in an apologetic book consisting of answers to questions "that Christians frequently ask concerning Umbanda," an explanation is provided for the initiatory cutting of the head and of the tattoos that are sometimes cut into the face or body. The marks vary in size, depending upon the place in the hierarchy occupied by the Orixá, who descends into the head of the initiate; see Silvio Pereira Maciel, *A vida dos orixás e a Umbanda: Cristianismo* (Rio de Janeiro, 1979). Among the Tehuelche, *sháin* (wrist tattoos) are an absolute prerequisite to eternal life in heaven. Sésom, the judge of the dead, examines the deceased for the proper tattoo; see Siffredi, "Hierofanías y concepciónes," p. 251.

190. For instance, R. T. Zuidema, "Catachillay: The Role of the Pleiades and of the Southern Cross and alpha and beta Centauri in the Calendar of the Incas," pp. 203–29, in Aveni and Urton, eds., *Ethnoastronomy and Archaeoastronomy*, esp. pp. 225ff., connects the Inca ear-piercing ceremonies and the prescribed weeping of sacrificial llamas with the first flow of waters in the primordial flood. That was the occasion on which the first women and llamas emerged from a spring. A constellation appeared to drink up the deluge. When the constellation called Mother Llama gave birth to the constellation Baby Llama, amniotic fluids were released into the stream of the Milky Way. Zuidema suggests that the motif of gestation and birth unites all these diverse images.

191. Métraux, "Religion and Shamanism," p. 582.

192. Alfred Métraux, "Warfare, Cannibalism, and Human Trophies," in *HSAI*, vol. 5, p. 397. Similarly, a Jívaro man who had slain an enemy and taken a trophy head observed dietary restrictions for six months and remained sexually continent during that time. Métraux also reports that

> Sherente warriors refrained from bathing for a period of time. Tupinamba and Sherente braves incised themselves with a sharp instrument and rubbed the wounds with ashes and genipa. Apinayé and Cashinawa killers ate large quantities of pepper. In addition, the Apinayé killer was not allowed to speak to anyone for a time, and no one could drink out of his cup. Even while the party was returning from the raid he remained segregated from his companions both on the march and in camp. (ibid., p. 397)

193. Fulop, "Aspectos: Cosmogonía," p. 125.

194. Clastres, *Chronique des indiens guayakí*, p. 135.

195. Marathon dancing as an instrument of change has been discussed in chapter 4 and will be discussed again below in connection with Toba marriage.

196. Maybury-Lewis, *Akwẽ-Shavante Society*, pp. 248–249.

197. Villas Boas and Villas Boas, *Xingu*, pp. 207–210, p. 259.

198. Ibid., p. 253.

199. Ibid., p. 174.

200. This relation has been discussed in Chapter 5, under metamorphosis and fabrication, as well as in the treatment of the soul. In his "Dramatistic View of the Origins of Language," Kenneth Burke describes the intrinsic relation between negative language, on the one side, and property and personality, on the other. He concludes that the personality itself is "compounded of negatives"; see Burke, *Language as Symbolic Action* (Berkeley, 1973), p. 472. In regard to the development of distinctive tastes that characterize an individual, Pierre Bourdieu remarks,

> Objective limits become a sense of limits, a practical anticipation of objective limits, a "sense of one's place" which leads one to exclude oneself from the goods, persons and so forth from which one is excluded.
>
> The *sense* of limits implies *forgetting* the limits. One of the most important effects of the correspondence between real divisions and practical principles of division, between social structures and mental structures, is undoubtedly the fact that primary experience of the social world, far from being a simple mechanical reflection, is always an act of cognition involving principles of construction that are external to the constructed object grasped in its immediacy; but at the same time it is an act of miscognition implying the most absolute form of recognition of the social order. . . .
>
> The system of classificatory schemes is opposed to a taxonomy based on explicit and explicitly connected principles in the same way that the dispositions constituting taste or ethos (which are dimensions of it) are opposed to aesthetics or ethics. (Bourdieu, *Distinction*, p. 471)

201. In the Inca case, for instance, the *tarpuntay* ("priests of the Sun," from *tarpuy*," to plant") abstained from sex, coca, and peppers during the two months when new maize shoots germinated and grew to a viable height. The retention of seed within the priests' body-space, synchronized with the expulsion of pathogens and evil from civic space by ritual warriors, aided Mother Earth *(Pachamama)*. The symbolic control of bodies harnesses generative power of new growth

at every level of the cosmos. Even the sun grows a beard of white rays for the season—like the white llamas that grow the long wooly hair that makes them the appropriate victims for the season's sacrifices. See R. T. Zuidema, "Calendars: South American Calendars," in *EOR*.

202. In addition to the discussion in chapter 2, see the treatment of vengeance and time in Manuela Carneiro da Cunha and E. B. Viveiros de Castro, "Vingança e temporalidade," *JSAP* 71 (1985): 191–208.

203. Initiations deliberately create experiences of inversion and reversal at their center in order to make visible the paradoxical state of mature symbolic existence, which lives aware of the subtle and multivalent, even contradictory, referents of all its signifiers. At the heart of every religious initiation is the awareness that symbolic participation in a sacred world is the primary reason for the generative power of cultural life (including the generation of conflict and confusion). That symbols are not only concrete signs of a primordial existence but also vestiges of its passing sets up the conditions just enumerated, to wit, the ontological dilemma of symbolic life; the collapse of action and passion; the simultaneous coexistence of contrastive states that can also be experienced as recurrent cycles; and the coincidence of opposites, which allows death to become the germ of rebirth. This spiritual condition of human culture, wherein the significance of a single symbolic experience forms one complex with all its reversals, contrasts, and contradictions (because symbolism in itself constitutes a meaningful existence), is the reason that various forms of structuralism can be so illuminating. Structuralism lays out many of these transformations, which essentially are refractions of the human spiritual condition, as systematic series of permutations; it illustrates that a single symbol not only implies the meaning (or at least the form) of all others but that symbolic life is inescapably ordered and ordering. The very fact of symbolic existence orients human life; self-conscious knowledge of its regenerative order orients adult life in a mature way.

204. Da Matta, *A Divided World*, passim; Maria Manuela Carneiro de Cunha, "De Amigos, formais e pessoa; de companheiros, espelhos e identidades," *BMN* n.s. 32 (1979): 31–39; Jacques M. Chevalier, *Civilization and the Stolen Gift: Capital, Kin, and Cult in Eastern Peru* (Toronto, 1982), passim.

205. One consequence of this chain of relationships is that when a hunter arrives with game, a woman almost always sends up a plaintive wail in memory of someone to whom the game animal is related as an *ijagi* ("companion"); see Clastres, *Chronique des indiens guayakí*, p. 198.

206. Wilbert, "Eschatology," p. 169. If Warao can successfully initiate themselves to the perilous journeys throughout the mythic universe while in ecstasy during life, they can obtain the expertise, ritual items, and divine patronage necessary to assure themselves a successful journey to a happy abode with that deity in the afterlife. Thus, for example, the goddess Daurani provides six chest-abiding helper spirits to a soul that succeeds in journeying to and from Daurani's abode on the world's horizon. A human being who feeds and shelters the supernaturals in his chest ultimately joins his divine patroness after death (Wilbert, "Eschatology," p. 171).

Similarly, the *genios*, spirits who help a Pajonal Campa healer in his curing performance, stand to gain something from the ritual. Chevalier calls this "the importance of 'faith' as a value of exchange sought by spirits in shamanistic rituals" (*Civilization*, p. 374, n. 13).

207. Chapter 7 discusses helper spirits, their tutelage, and their dependence upon human partners for ritual assistance.

208. Whitten, *Sacha Runa*, pp. 110, 139. Whitten contends that the Canelos Quichua *gumba* system of mystical coparents is an ego-centered system of addresses indigenous to tropical forest peoples (p. 139). He cites Goldman's description of ceremonial friendship in *The Cubeo*, pp. 130–133, as a similarly authochtonous system. The Cubeo refer to the relationship as *híkü-híko* (from *hi*, "to give," *híkü*, "giver"), for the relationship is built on ceremonial exchanges (of desirable goods, as we shall see). Varese, in describing the *ayúmpari/niyúmpari* relationship of the Pajonal Campa, perceptively touches the heart of the matter for many ceremonial partnerships ostensibly based on exchange. That the acts involve reciprocal exchange of material goods has not deterred him from seeing that they are form of "sacred commerce which, far from being of interest only to the economic and social sphere, must be understood as an eminently religious accomplishment" (*La sal de los cerros*, p. 22), ultimately a form of communion entered into only with other *ashaninka*, fully human beings who share the same sacred

origins. This excludes whites and Andean peoples. In particular, salt was a most important element in this ceremonial association; see also ibid., p. 107. J. H. Bodley, "Deferred Exchange among the Campa Indians," *ANT* 68 (1973): 586–596, however, refers to instances of whites considered as *niompari*. Chevalier not only provides various descriptions of the social, historical, and economic ramifications of the *ayompari/niompari* relationship among the Pajonal Campas (*Civilization*, pp. 114, 198–199, 204, 212) but provides some mythic background explaining why trade carries with it such awesome spiritual responsibilities, with repercussions not only on the social but cosmic scale. Trade regulates distance. "The initial failure to keep all beings at a certain distance from one another can thus lead to no other outcome than a total rupture of the universe, the impossibility of reuniting the opposite and complementary ingredients of a healthy life" (ibid., p. 428). Sacred traders exchange the "culturally indispensable wealth" obtained in dangerous journeys to other realms (of the dead, of blood-sucking and body-snatching monsters, of foreign manufacturers and merchants). They maintain the dynamism necessary for continued life. Following the mythic model, the trader must be "always on the move. . . . To stop moving would be tantamount to an abuse of identity, namely, between man and his other-worldly benefactor; it would also constitute a threat to the basic objective of such a sacred commerce, which is the distribution of natural gifts to mortal men through the hazardous transactions of valiant intermediaries" (p. 429). Regarding ritual partnerships, see the review of theories about Andean barter in Benjamin S. Orlove, "Barter and Cash on Lake Titicaca: A Test of Competing Approaches" *CA* 27 (1986): 85–98, with comments on pp. 98–106.

209. Carneiro da Cunha, "De amigos, formais e pessoa," pp. 31–39. Krahó initiation at puberty is described in detail in Melatti, *Ritos de uma tribo timbira*, pp. 203–342. The myths that underlie the processes of initiation and its formal friendships are presented and interpreted on pp. 234ff and pp. 294ff.

210. Carneiro da Cunha, "De amigos, formais e pessoa," p. 34.

211. Ibid., and Carneiro da Cunha, *Os mortos os outros*, pp. 74–82.

212. Sun and moon also provide the model for Apinayé formal friendship. Da Matta provides stimulating analyses throughout *A Divided World*, esp. pp. 82–99. Essentially, formal friendship among the Apinayé succeeds in recreating the individual because it embodies the relationship of the sun and moon, whose dialectic collaboration created the world (ibid., p. 157) by producing not only differentiating characters but also their opposites and complements, which interact to generate new possibilities. Da Matta explains how formal friendship functions to maintain the individual as a social, relational, and living being. He says it is "the ultimate social link" (p. 94), and that

> the relationship between formal friends is activated whenever one of those involved finds himself in a critical situation regarding the community as a whole: when a person dies and has to be segregated from the society; when a person wants to leave the village; when he needs encouragement to endure a physical ordeal, as during initiation rites; when he is reintegrated into the community after a period of marginality, such as those following rites of passage or periods of mourning. (pp. 94–95)

Naming and formal friendship both draw individuals into relationships with one another in socially structured ways. They create a social system. However, naming among the Apinayé remains circumscribed by the limits of the bilateral system of kin relationships. Formal friendship transcends these limits.

213. Carneiro da Cunha, "De amigos, formais e pessoa," p. 35.

214. Ibid., p. 37. Among the Apinayé the placenta *(krati)* is the fetal child's ritual companion in the seclusion of the womb, the ritual enclosure of transformation. This "child's companion" is buried at birth (da Matta, *A Divided World*, p. 49). Carneiro da Cunha points out that Crocker has made a similar point in regard to the Boróro, for whom the person is ironically or paradoxically consituted in such a way that one is never so much oneself as when another person represents him; see Christopher Crocker, "Les Reflexions du Soi," in Lévi-Strauss, ed., *L'Identité* (Paris, 1977), pp. 157–184. Among the Krahó another ritual bond is established between a boy initiate and his *keti*, someone from the category of kinsmen (mother's brother, mother's father, and father's father) from which a boy's name-giver is chosen. The *keti* helps to bring back his

itamtxua (the reciprocal term applied to the boy in the ritual) to the community of the living (Carneiro da Cunha, "Eschatology," p. 169). This discussion does not intend to do justice to the subtle complexity and sociological precision of ritual ties. Da Matta, *A Divided World*, pp. 100–130, admirably illustrates for the Apinayé (by way of comparison with the Krahó, Krīkatí, Canela, and Northern Kayapó) the degree of exactness and intricacy assumed by networks of ritual ties.

215. Similarly, a human companion helps a supernatural being make the transition into human society if the spirit wishes to assume the benefit of the human condition (food, corporeality, containment, song, etc.). In all three types of ritual company, the companion acts as a herald of new social conditions. As token of a new social reality to come, the companion becomes a sort of minister to a new condition of public affairs for the person undergoing passage into a new social network.

216. Nimuendajú, *The Apinayé*, pp. 107–108. Once again, da Matta offers helpful clarification of the technical aspects of such a relationship as it functions in the larger system of Apinayé domestic and social relations. See chapter 4, "The Relationship System," in his *A Divided World*, esp. pp. 108ff., 116–117, 124–127.

217. Wright, "History and Religion of the Baniwa," p. 71.

218. Jacopin, *La Parole generative*, p. 71.

219. Ambía and Garrafa, *Amaru*, p. 76.

220. Chevalier, *Civilization*, p. 311. Footnote 13 on page 311 gathers together a number of sources on the subject of *compadrinazgo*. For mention of the *corte de ombligo*, during which the *madrina*-midwife not only cuts the cord with new scissors but donates alcoholic beverages and clothes, see ibid., p. 312.

221. The *ajibona (agibonan, jibonan)* is also known as the *mãe pequena* ("little mother"). In the cult, she exercises the priestly role of *iya kêkêrê*, functioning as an assistant to the high priest *(yalorixá, babalôrixá)*. In the structural hierarchy, she occupies the office of deputy director of the *candomblé*. See, for example, Bastide, *African Religions of Brazil*, p. 195. For a discussion of an alternative set of Afro-Brazilian godparental relations, expressed in the idiom of Catholicism, which establishes ceremonial links in the hierarchy of color and class, see Bastide's analyses on pp. 40, 80, 283.

222. Edison Carneiro, *Candomblés da Bahia* (Bahia, Brazil), p. 75. From the perspective of an inside leader of an Umbanda religious tradition, the religious goal of transforming the personality (p. 146f.) is achieved and signaled by the transformations of the body that occur under the direction and influence of divinities and spirits. The glossary of terms provided by the cult leader are in large part African names for body parts (over half the terms are body parts and body substances) or animals (virtually the rest of the list except for the term for "death" is given over to the names of animals); see Babalaô José Paiva de Oliveira, *Mistérios da Umbanda e do Candomblé* (Rio de Janeiro, 1980), p. 144.

223. Melville J. Herskovitz, "The Social Organization of the Candomblé," *ICA*, 31st Congress (São Paulo, 1955), pp. 526–527. See also Roger Bastide, *African Religions of Brazil*, pp. 198–210, 230, 288–289.

224. Maybury-Lewis, *Akwẽ-Shavante Society*, pp. 105–108.

225. Ibid., p. 108.

226. Ibid., p. 251.

227. Goldman, *The Cubeo*, p. 131.

228. Ibid., p. 133. Other body-centered intimacies normally performed by immediate family members can also signal ceremonial friendship: such is the case with "picking lice, or removing insect-bite scabs from the body" (ibid.).

229. Ibid., p. 131. For example, one exchange between *hiku* and *hiko* ran like this:

> A man of a Bahúkiwa subsib took a sib sister as his hiko. He gave her, immediately, cloth for two petticoats, two boxes of matches, two decorative combs, two small hand mirrors, thread and needles, two tins of brilliantine hair dressing, and a bar of soap. In return she gave him four big chicha serving calabashes, two balls of miriti twine, and a valuable necklace of silver triangles known as "butter-flies." In addition, her father gave her two fishing bows to give to her ceremonial friend. (ibid.)

230. S. Hugh-Jones, *The Palm and the Pleiades*, p. 80. "Two men should do the painting, one for the lower body, one for the upper body" (ibid.).

231. Ibid., p. 96.

232. Ibid.

233. Ibid., p. 112.

234. Hugh-Jones writes,

> For an initiate, these are as follows: between the initiates and the officiating shamans *(guga-biaga)*; between the initiate and the ritual guardian *(masori-masorio)*; between the initiate and the elder who carries him into the house at the start of *He* House *(umari-umari)*; between the initiate and the woman who paints him and to whom he gives basketry *(henyeri-henyerio)*; between the initiate and those who paint him with black paint during *He* House *(sɨtori-sɨtori)*; and between all the initiates who go through *He* House together *(kamokɨkɨ-kamokɨkɨ)*. The initiate's guga, masori and umari are all said to be like fathers or father's brothers and his masorio like a mother. . . . The henyerio is compared to a sister and the sɨtori and kamokɨkɨ are both compared to brothers. (ibid., p. 114)

235. Ibid., pp. 114–115.

236. Henry, *Jungle People*, pp. 113–114.

237. Bartolomé, "Shamanism Among the Avá-Chiripá," p. 142.

238. S. Hugh-Jones, *The Palm and the Pleiades*, p. 113 n., referring to P. G. Riviere, "Marriage: a Reassessment," in R. Needham, ed., *Rethinking Kinship and Marriage* (London, 1971), pp. 57–74. See also Raul Iturra, "Marriage, Ritual and Profit: The Production of Producers in a Portuguese Village," *Social Compass* 32 (1985): 73–92. Kenneth M. Kensinger, ed., *Marriage Practices in Lowland South America* (Urbana, Ill., 1984), offers eleven essays surveying a wide range of marriage customs, practices, and symbolism and provides an ample bibliography on important theoretical materials concerning marriage in South America. In the volume's overview essay, Judith R. Shapiro points out how some of the essays

> show how an understanding of cosmological beliefs enables us better to interpret marriage rules and preferences. . . . These studies come at a time when the anthropological investigation of social organization has been moving beyond its traditional boundaries to include the kind of material that was often, in standard monographs, treated under separate rubrics as "religion," "ideology," or "world view." . . . What remains to be seen more clearly is how analyses like these can figure in comparative investigation. (p. 13)

Carneiro da Cunha, *Os mortos os outros*, pp. 49–53, prompts the question whether Krahó spouses can be considered formal friends, parallel to funeral friends. Affines, at least, are bound in similar sorts of social ties in their marriages alliances, and the bonds derive from the same mythic models (sun and moon) as ritual friendships. Carneiro da Cunha also suggests that the Xikrin (Kayapó) may have the strictest association between formal friendship and spouses (see her "Put-karôt, grupo indígena do Brasil Central," Ph.D. diss., University of São Paulo, 1972). From time to time, some cultures acknowledge the ritual nature of the bond between husband and wife. In Warao culture, at the time of the Dance of the Little Rattle,

> the affinal kin ties between spouses become suspended and replaced by ritual bonds known as *mamuse*. Husbands agree to exchange wives, and upon payment of a substantial price, called *horo amoara*, "skin payment," the partners are free to engage in dancing and sex. *Mamuse* relationships are considered honorable and are believed to exercise a fortifying influence on the woman's offspring. (Wilbert, "The House of the Swallow-Tailed Kite," p. 158)

239. The entire spatio-temporal ensemble (manifest, for example, in the origins of social organization and descent) enters into the calculation of the features distinguishing these three ritual relations. Included are the nature of the blood (that of consanguines, affines, or primordial beings represented in body-paint) relating them and the restrictions on the time and spatial extent of their physical contact. For example, there are no sexual connotations to the *henyerio* relationship for, in fact, those women usually come from the same exogamous group, whereas a man's wife hails from a different one. Throughout his *Origin of Table Manners*, Lévi-Strauss

illustrates that the calculus of cosmic space and time enters into any consideration of marriage partnerships in which the normatively correct symbolic "distance" or "proximity" is observed. He shows how this matter greatly preoccupied the beings of the mythic era. Only after disastrous failures on a cosmic scale was the heroic adventure of marriage alliance properly achieved. Significantly enough, the ventures that failed to generate successful marriage did produce many other kinds of symbolic relationships, partnerships, and antinomies associated with periodicity, change, and regeneration (of time, space, and society). For further illustration, see the Selk'nam view of marriage and its cosmic repercussions, in Gusinde, Los Indios de Tierra del Fuego. Los Selk'nam, vol. 2, pp. 287–338. Yanoama marriage symbolism and its interpretation are discussed in Zerries and Schuster, Mahekodotedi, pp. 136–144.

240. "What I am saying is that the henyerio relationship introduces the initiates to a general form of socially approved and recognised relationship between men and women, of which marriage is a particular case" (S. Hugh-Jones, The Palm and the Pleiades, p. 113).

241. Karsten, Toba Indians, p. 18.

242. Civrieux, Watunna, pp. 97–98.

243. The myth does not end there. The girl's father is slain by ants for having attempted to kill the boy in the first place with the fish trap. A tiny drop of the father's blood turns into Mado, the first supernatural jaguar. When the father dies, the jaguar's body appears (ibid., p. 99). In fact, the transformation of the heroes succeeds in generating a whole series of fruitful ritual relationships among human beings and supernaturals. Together they constitute the foundations of contemporary culture.

244. Chapter 7 discusses the symbolism of oppugnant relationships between ritually appointed adversaries who are charged with publically negotiating important public transitions and exchanges.

245. The sacred nature of the bond need not be rendered in terms of Durkheimian sociology. Taking his cue from Marxian political economy, Chevalier concludes a lengthy comparative treatment of ritual sponsorship in eastern Peru:

> a godparent appears as a complex mediator endowed with the overdetermined attributes of parenthood, holiness, and material wealth, and with the ritual power of attenuating the profound differences that separate men from gods and men from men. This ritualized mending of a highly divided world is performed by means of an elaborate condensation process that brings together—within a single relationship—divergent elements of social life, while effectively concealing the implicit contradictions that may exist between such positions as that of a biological parent, a powerful bourgeois, and a charitable benefactor. (Civilization, p. 336)

In Chevalier's view, the mediation of ritual sponsorship lends itself to comparison with shamanism which also struggles against all forms of evil in "a cultural and natural universe of its own making" (ibid.). The point is that the symbolic representations of both kinds of social bonds are coextensive with the symbols of the sacred in which they ground themselves.

246. Chapter 5, above, discusses these and other symbolic processes that compose and recompose the imagery of the human person.

247. For the Cashinahua view that hunting constitutes the sacred axis of masculine life, see d'Ans, La Verdedera Biblia, pp. 30–33.

248. Farabee, The Central Arawaks, p. 49. In fact, the remote preparations for successful hunting may be an explicit part of the initiation itself. Such was the case, for example, among the Cariri, who made cuts in boys' skin as part of their initiation rites at puberty. While the boys were advised in the art and lore of hunting and compelled to exercise their new knowledge, the ashes of burned fish and animal bones were placed in the wounds of the candidates, who also drank off a beverage with the same ashes in it; see Métraux, "Religion and Shamanism," pp. 377f.

249. The Boróro case (western Boróro, near Descalvados) is recounted in Julio Koslowsky, "Algunos datos sobre los Indios Boróros," RMLP 6 (1895): 12–13. The Tupinamba material is mentioned in Alfred Métraux, La Religion des Tupinamba et ses rapports avec celle des autres tribus tupí-guaraní (Paris, 1928), pp. 174–175. Métraux is evaluating the report of André Thevet, Cosmographie universelle (Paris, 1575), f. 937R. These and other cases are cited in Zerries, "Primitive South America," pp. 270f., 327.

250. Etta Becker-Donner, "Notizen über die Huanyam," p. 99. In some instances the hunting dances are performed to open or close the hunting seasons for specific game or are performed periodically rather than for each hunt. Such seems to be the practice of the Lengua; see Hans von Becker, "Lengua und Kaiotugui: Indianerstudien im Chaco Boreal," ZFE 73–74 (1944): 400.

251. The mythical past is not the only temporal dimension operative in rituals of the hunt. In relation to human beings, different animal species reflect diverse modes of the future. The network of hunting prohibitions that a hunter must respect is geared, after all, to protect his offspring and to ensure the survival of his line of descent, just as is the meat and spirit of the game taken in the hunt. At the same time, to assure himself and his family of daily life-sustenance in the form of game, the hunter must jeopardize his immediate future in this life and run the spiritual risk characteristic of this world of transition. Acts of subsistence bear essential affinities in form and function to other symbolic acts that regenerate or sustain life because they all involve "death." The matter is put in a striking and dramatic way in a Wayāpi myth that recounts the origin of different social groups from the worms that appear in the rotting corpse of an ancient slain monkey; see P. Grenand, Introduction . . . Wayāpi, p. 320.

252. Jean Chaffanjon, L'Orénoque et le Caura (Paris, 1889), pp. 203ff.

253. For a collection of comparative materials on hunting rites see Zerries, Wild- und Buschgeister in Südamerika. See also Zerries' summary descriptions of hunting ceremonies and the supernaturals associated with them in "Primitive South America," esp. pp. 258–276. For an interpretation of the religious meaning of Yanoama hunting, see Zerries and Schuster, Mahekodotedi, pp. 265–277, which discuss the origins of animals and hunting techniques, the supernatural master of animals (Holonama), the helper-spirits of hunters, the relationship of each animal species to spiritual entities, ritual hunting songs, the division of game and restrictions of its consumption, the care of bones of game animals, and so on.

254. Holmberg, Nomads of the Long Bow, p. 91.

255. Ibid., p. 33.

256. Herbert Baldus, "Supernatural Relations with Animals among Indians of Eastern and Southern Brazil," in ICA, 30th Congress (London, 1952), pp. 195–198. For the ways in which, in the Yanomami view, hunting locates itself in the context of war and alliance not only between human groups, and not only with the animal world, but in the confrontation, struggle, violence, and alliance with the world of sacred beings, see Lizot, Le Cercle des feux, pp. 185–203.

257. Baldus, "Supernatural Relations," p. 197.

258. Ibid. Among the Kaingáng of Rio Grande do Sul, similar steps were taken to protect the young person who found a beehive in the forest or who extracted honey, which was brought home and delivered to the mother's father or to the father-in-law.

259. Clastres, Chronique des indiens guayakí, pp. 23–24.

260. Ibid., p. 25.

261. Ibid., p. 26.

262. For a description of the imaginal world in which agricultural labor takes place and within which labor itself has ritual value in ancient Peru, see Lucia Kill, Pachamama: Die Erdgöttin in der altandinen Religion (Bonn, 1969), pp. 145–172, which locates fertile labor in relationship to the sacrality of mother earth, Pachamama.

263. Weiss, "World of a Forest Tribe," pp. 269, 279.

264. Whitten, Sacha Runa, p. 74.

265. "Whether Nunghuí is best viewed as a class of crop fairies or as a goddess appears to be a difficult matter to decide. On the one hand, the Jívaro usually speak of Nunghuí in the singular, but they deny that there is just one, saying that there are 'many,' although all are identical in their attributes. For convenience, Nunghuí will be referred to here in the singular" (Michael J. Harner, The Jívaro: People of the Sacred Waterfalls, Garden City, N.Y., 1973, p. 70; see also the descriptions of the goddess's relationship to agricultural processes on pp. 70–76). For Aguaruna concepts of Nunkui and the origin of yuca and plantains, see José Luis Jordana Laguna, Mitos e historias aguarunas y huambisas de la selva del Alto Marañon (Lima, 1974), pp. 31ff.

266. As for the male aspect of agriculture and plants, it is presided over by Shakaema, Nunghuí's husband. For example, banana plants possess masculine souls. They are planted and tended by men who observe a number of ritual procedures and restrictions in the process.

267. Harner, The Jívaro, p. 70.

268. Zerries, "Primitive South America," p. 277. Zerries is drawing upon Julian H. Steward and Alfred Métraux, "Tribes of the Peruvian and Ecuadorian Montaña—The Peban Tribes," in *HSAI*, vol. 3, p. 620; Günter Tessmann, *Die Indianer Nordost-Perus* (Hamburg, 1930), pp. 356, 746; and Métraux, "Religion and Shamanism," in *HSAI*, vol. 5, p. 620.

269. Civrieux, *Watunna*, pp. 132ff.

270. Ibid., p. 134.

271. Ibid., p. 135.

272. Ibid., p. 136.

273. Ibid., p. 136.

274. Eliade, *A History of Religious Ideas*, vol. 1, p. 34. For a description of the way in which silver was worked to produce ornaments for the Araucanians, see Günther Hartmann, *Silberschmuck der Araukaner, Chile* (Berlin, 1974), which offers photographs, detailed descriptions, and cultural commentary on the techniques of silverworking. On artistic metalwork see also *Pre-Columbian Gold Sculpture* (New York, 1958); Reichel-Dolmatoff, *Tears of the Moon*, on goldworking; and Reichel-Dolmatoff's *Basketry as Metaphor: Arts and Crafts of the Desana Indians of the Northwest Amazon* (Los Angeles, 1985). For a study hypothesizing the continuity of religious themes across various artistic material media (metal, featherwork, woodcarving, painting), see Luis Alberto Acuña, *El arte de los indios colombianos* (Mexico City, 1942); for illustrations of pre-Conquest art (in several media) from the Argentine area, see Giancarlo Puppo, *Arte argentino antes de la dominación hispánica* (Buenos Aires, 1979). Most of the materials are ceramic ware or stone carvings. For an examination of material forms in artistic expression and for an interpretation of their meaning, see John Howland Rowe, *Chavin Art: An Inquiry into Its Form and Meaning* (New York, 1962). In this connection, see also Garth Bawden and Geoffrey W. Conrad, *The Andean Heritage: Masterpieces of Art from the Collections of the Peabody Museum* (Cambridge, Mass., 1982). Hernan Jaramillo Cisneros, *Inventario de diseños en tejidos indígenas de la Provincia de Imbabura*, 2 vols. (Otavalo, Ecuador, 1981) provides some 850 designs used in weaving (of some two thousand surveyed designs) that testify to the antiquity and constancy of certain artistic themes in weaving throughout Andean history. The 850 designs were chosen because they demonstrated, in a way no other medium was able to, the persistence of specific cultural themes in that region (vol. 1, p. 19).

275. Johannes Wilbert, "To Become a Maker of Canoes: An Essay in Warao Enculturation," in Wilbert, ed., *Enculturation in Latin America: An Anthology* (Los Angeles, 1976), p. 349.

276. Wilbert, "Navigators of the Winter Sun," p. 40.

277. Ibid., p. 41.

278. Ibid., p. 44. The link between boatsmen and religion is made clear in a series of articles on the Gaan Gadu cult, which appeared around 1890 among Djuka villagers of Surinam and spread throughout the Surinamese Maroon population. Religious ideas and practices center on the chief means of production: boat transport. See H. U. E. Thoden van Velzen, "Affluence, Deprivation and the Flowering of Bush Negro Religious Movements," *BTLV* 139 (1983): 99–139, and "The Gaan Gadu Cult: Material Forces and the Social Production of Fantasy," *Social Compass* 32 (1985): 93–109.

279. Civrieux, *Watunna*, p. 87.

280. Ibid.

281. Whitten, *Sacha Runa*, p. 104. The association of clay with souls, according to the neighboring Jívaro, originates at the beginning of time. The clay from which women make the vessels used in feasts has its origin "in the woman Aoho, having emanated from her soul, and wherever this clay is now found it has been scattered by the woman Aoho, who was afterwards changed into the bird of that name." The clay scattered when she fell to the ground while climbing to heaven on a liana deliberately cut by the moon; see Rafael Karsten, *The Head-hunters of Western Amazonas. The Life and Culture of the Jíbaro Indians of Eastern Ecuador and Peru* (Helsinki, 1935), pp. 519–520.

282. Whitten, *Sacha Runa*, pp. 172–177.

283. Ibid., p. 177.

284. Reichel-Dolmatoff, "Los Kogi," pp. 258–260.

285. "What I intended by way of the Yecuana and Warao examples is to show that basketry may

be so highly valued in native lore that at least in some societies it is actually the degree of skill and artistry applied to this craft that determines man's final destiny after death" (Johannes Wilbert, *Yupa Folktales*, Los Angeles, 1974, pp. 24–25). See also Reichel-Dolmatoff, *Basketry as Metaphor*.

286. Whitten, *Sacha Runa*, p. 143. This odd assortment of substances includes

> the brilliant blue wings and body of the *cantarica* beetle, a "secret" female substance called yutu papa (literally "quail potato," possibily a small, wild sweet potato), balls of hair from the stomach of the tapir, a cooked red achiote mixture, bark from the red *mindal* tree and a leaf also yielding a red dye, carahuira (bark or husk of the wind), boa brain, fer-de-lance rattle, scrapings of porpoise tooth, dried and pulverized bat, brains and bones of several small birds, and fungus . . . (p. 143)

287. Ibid. This process bears remarkable similarities to the conceptual structures underlying alchemy, wherein the soul of the worker is transformed by his own "opus." Rolf Stein discusses similar beginnings for the origins of Chinese alchemy in *Les Jardins en miniature d'Extrême-Orient: Le Monde en Petit* (Hanoi, 1943), pp. 56ff. Stein writes, "There appears to be an unbroken continuity of folklore traditions, Taoism and alchemy: the Taoist alchemist is the successor of the hunter of medicinal remedies, who, from time immemorial, went off into the mountains with a calabash to collect magic seeds and plants" (quoted in Mircea Eliade, *The Forge and the Crucible: The Origins and Structures of Alchemy*, 2nd ed. (Chicago, 1978) p. 214.)

288. See Marcelo Bórmida, "Ergon y mito. Una hermenéutica de la cultura material de los Ayoreo del Chaco Boreal. Primera parte," *SE* 1 (1973): 9–70; "Ergon y mito. Segunda parte," *SE* 2 (1974); "Ergon y mito. Tercera parte," *SE* 3 (1975): 73–130. See also Celia Olga Mashnshneck, "Aportes para una comprensión de la economía de los Mataco," *SE* 3 (1975): 7–39, which uncovers the mythico-religious meaning of economic production among the coastal Mataco of the Misión San Andrés area. Zerries details the symbolic richness of labor in all its forms among the Waika, in his *Waika*, pp. 125–152. Regarding technology as a demonstrable reflection on the full range of cultural and cosmic creativity, see the articles in Heather Lechtman and Ana Maria Soldi, eds., *Runakunap kawsayninkupaq rurasqankunaqa: La Tecnología en el mundo andino*, Vol. 1 (Mexico City, 1981); and also Rogger Ravines, *Tecnología andina* (Lima, 1978).

289. Reichel-Dolmatoff, "Training for the Priesthood," p. 269.

290. P. Grenand, *Introduction . . . wayãpi*, pp. 41–42.

291. Ibid., p. 31.

292. Ibid.

293. Ibid., p. 32.

294. For another instance, see the description of the importance and forms of knowledge among the Selk'nam (intelligence, reason, memory, mimesis, fantasy, sensual perception, adaptation to change, language, judgment, numeric value, temporal perception, astronomic and meteorological knowledge, geographic conceptions, botanical categories and zoological taxonomies, curing, etc.) in Gusinde, *Los Indios de Tierra del Fuego. Los Selk'nam*, vol. 2, pp. 1060–1102.

295. P. Grenand, *Introduction . . . wayãpi*, pp. 34–41. Perceiving "the whole" is also a tenet of Kofan learning and knowledge, the very core of human and spiritual existence. One probes the meaning of symbolism through ritual behavior, botanical knowledge, and, most importantly, hallucinogenic experience under the effects of the magical drink *yagé*. It is *yagé* that helps a person learn to see "every kind of thing there, the punishment of God, how life is in this world, everything, all of it, everything can be seen" (Scott Studebaker Robinson, "Towards an Understanding of Kofan Shamanism," Ph.D. diss. Cornell University, 1979, p. 188). The universe is a set of open ciphers revealing the meaning of everything because there is "a systematic quality to life as perceived with the aid of *yagé*. . . . [There is] a notion of totality or cosmos. The shaman, and other *yagé*-drinkers to a lesser degree, then, are given access to this totality" (ibid., p. 189).

296. P. Grenand, *Introduction . . . wayãpi*, p. 41.

297. Ibid.

298. For example, among the Tapirapé, as among many other South American peoples, only myth makes a large number of songs *(kaó)* intelligible, for the songs are sung with meaningless

"words" or sounds or without any texts at all. The myth of the song's origin makes clear and intelligible the symbolic sounds that comprise the song. In this way, the performance of song serves as a good paradigm for all cultural action, which, from an ignorant point of view, could always pass as meaningless, idle behavior. In the light of myth, however, human behavior becomes symbolic, intelligible, and even a form of knowledge itself; see Wagley, *Welcome of Tears*, pp. 212–217.

299. Weiss, "World of a Forest Tribe," pp. 407–408.

300. Ibid., p. 260.

301. Fulop, "Aspectos: Cosmogonía," p. 114.

302. Henry, *Jungle People*, pp. 50–51.

303. Ibid., p. 50.

304. John M. Schechter, "The Inca *Cantar Histórico:* A Lexico-historical Elaboration on Two Cultural Themes," *ETM* 23 (1979): 196.

305. Ibid., pp. 191–204.

306. Ibid., p. 198.

307. Ibid.

308. Schechter, following Jerome Bruner, draws the connection between music and memory by linking them with metaphor, which connects "previously unconnected domains of experience, producing an initial 'shock of recognition' followed by acceptance . . . and . . . brings continuity into culture, transforming disparate experiences into meaningful wholes" (ibid., p. 196). Schechter indicates that music, like the performance of myth, is symbolic on both the level of language and the level of gesture. On the level of language one takes seriously the metaphors used or found in the semantic roots of the names and descriptions of musical genres. These are native figures of speech, which operate as textual metaphors. On the level of the gesture, music itself may be a communicative symbol with social meaning. Following Wilson W. Coker, Schechter distinguishes two ways in which musical gesture is a significant symbol. The first way is internal to the structures of music and sound: "the sonorous, rhythmic, or gestural configurations of music may operate as iconic and non-iconic signs for congeneric objects (i.e., *other* musical materials)." In the second case, musical gestures serve as meaningful symbols for nonmusical objects—extrageneric objects. Here the range of symbolic valences is virtually unlimited: "affective states, attitudes, concepts, value-properties, physical things and events, the character of objects" (p. 202). In fact, the internal (congeneric) symbols come to stand for a wide range of nonmusical (extrageneric) meanings. Coker emphasizes the way in which music stands as a symbol for social action. John Blacking offers a different emphasis by pointing out that "music is a metaphorical expression of feelings and experiences" that are, after all, social facts. See Schechter, ibid., p. 202; Jerome Bruner, "The Conditions of Creativity," in H. E. Gruber, G. Terrell, and M. Wertheimer, eds., *Contemporary Approaches to Creative Thinking* (New York, 1962), pp. 3–5; Wilson W. Coker, *The Roots of Musical Meaning with Special Reference to Leonard B. Meyer's Theory* (D.M.A. thesis, University of Illinois, 1965), pp. 66–67, 97–102 (cited in Schechter, p. 202); and John Blacking, "Ethnomusicology as a Key Subject in the Social Sciences," *In Memoriam António Jorge Dias* (Lisbon, 1974), vol. 3, pp. 71–93, especially p. 83, and "Can Musical Universals Be Heard?" *The World of Music* 19 (1977): 14–22, especially pp. 17–18.

309. Whitten, *Sacha Runa*, p. 59.

310. Ibid., p. 141. Whitten recommends comparison of this experience with the Jívaro encounter with Arutam or Arutam Wakani ("ancient specter soul"), described in Harner, *The Jívaro*, pp. 135–143. Whitten notes that the Canelos Quichua recognize that the Arutam is equivalent to the *huandujta upisha muscuna*, a datura-induced vision (Whitten, *Sacha Runa*, p. 104). Whitten notes that the Canelos Quichua put more emphasis on knowledge of ancient souls, whereas the Jívaro express an overwhelming desire to kill. In a related matter, Whitten believes that the way in which the Canelos Quichua relate *muscuna* (dream or vision) experiences to the acquisition of souls from animals and birds suggests comparison to the Jívaro *muisak*-complex of the "avenging soul" (see Harner, *The Jívaro*, 143–149). For lengthy and detailed treatment of the Jívaro concepts, see *Mundo Shuar* (Sucua, Ecuador), volumes 1 (1976), entitled *Arutam*, and 3 (1980), entitled *El Uwishin*.

311. Whitten, *Sacha Runa*, p. 141.

312. Ibid.

313. Ibid., p. 100.

314. Ibid., p. 141.

315. Ibid., p. 48.

316. Ibid., p. 56.

317. Ibid., p. 50.

318. Ibid., p. 35.

319. See the discussion in Norman E. Whitten, Jr., "Quechua Religions: Amazonian Cultures," in *EOR*.

320. For treatment of male shamanism and female pottery as related aspects of the process of human knowledge see Norman E. Whitten, Jr., *Sicuanga Runa: The Other Side of Development in Amazonian Ecuador* (Urbana, Ill., 1985).

312. Reichel-Dolmatoff, *Amazonian Cosmos*, p. 65.

322. It should be noted, however, that the mind bears relation to light. Force of mind *(ka'i)* depends on knowledge that light provides. "He *[ka'i]* can only act in a field already explored by the light. He is a part of the light of the Sun" (Reichel-Dolmatoff, ibid., p. 127). For example, the *ka'i* of a mad person is lost in the darkness of a jungle thicket (p. 184). Here there is little or no light, an inchoate condition similar to that of the womb, from which one must be led into the light to begin to accumulate one's personal experiences.

323. Ibid., p. 94.

324. Ibid.

325. Ibid.

326. See Alejandra Siffredi, "La Autoconciencia de las relaciones sociales entre los Yojwaha-Chorote," *SE* 1 (1973): 71–103, and Darcy Ribeiro, *Kadiwéu: Ensaios etnologicos sobre o saber, o azar e a beleza* (Petropolis, Brazil, 1979).

327. Melatti shows how the various ways in which human beings control symbolic items passing in and out of their bodies serve as principles for distinguishing between social groups in postcolonial history as well. The Krahó, for example, do indeed distinguish between Catholics and "believers" (Protestants) but not on doctrinal grounds concerning the theology of grace, justification, predestination, or salvation. Rather, they consider these two distinct modes of living:

> The Catholics smoke, drink alcoholic beverages, indulge in extramarital sex, use weapons and swear-words; the believers don't do any of this; furthermore, the Catholics observe Sundays and holy days, but the believers show respect only for Sundays. For the Krahó, the distinction between Catholics and Protestants . . . has been assimilated to the distinction between members of opposing moieties, each one of which possesses its own symbolic behavior" (Melatti, *Ritos de Uma Tribo Timbira*, p. 94.)

CHAPTER SEVEN

1. Familiar and long in use in a variety of applications, for example, are the types of legitimate religious authority presented by Max Weber in his *Theory of Social and Economic Organization* (1922). These types of authority base themselves on: 1) rational grounds "resting on belief in the 'legality' of patterns of normative rules," 2) traditional grounds "resting on an established belief in the sanctity of immemorial traditions," and 3) charismatic grounds "resting on devotion to the specific and exceptional sanctity, heroism or exemplary character of an individual person" (Weber, *On Charisma and Institution Building: Selected Papers*, S. N. Eisenstadt, ed. (Chicago, 1968), p. 46. In *The Sociology of Religion*, (Boston, 1964), pp. 20–30 and 46ff., Weber uses these three ways of legitimating authority to make analytic distinctions among the roles of priest, magician, and prophet. Weber's types serve the needs of sociology. Many alternatives to Weber have also been put forward. In his *Sociology of Religion* (Chicago, 1944), Joachim Wach, for example, attempted to delineate a typology of religious specialists better suited to inquiry into the history of religions. He envisioned a larger set of religious authorities distinguished by the quality of their religious experiences: founders, reformers, prophets, seers, magicians, diviners,

saints, priests, the "religiosus," and the audience (pp. 331–374). The variety of religious specialists can be a complicated matter. For a description of the variety of specialists and special tasks (offerings, sacrifices, cures, divinations, ritual presidency, etc.) associated with one cultural base, the cult of the earth mother in the Andes, see Mariscotti de Görlitz, *Pachamama Santa Tierra*, pp. 121–148.

2. For a discussion of the ways in which musicians govern and control the possessed medium, see Gilbert Rouget, *La Musique et la transe: Esquisse d'une théorie generale des relations de la musique et de la possession* (Paris, 1980), pp. 103–184, esp. pp. 166–169. For a discussion of the role of music in Afro-Brazilian states of possession, see Gisèlle Cossard (Gisèlle Binon-Cossard), "Musique dans le Candomblé," in Tolia Nikiprowetsky, ed., *La Musique dans la vie* (Paris, 1967), pp. 159–207. A typology of cultic structures found in possessive cults of Afro-Brazilian tradition is attempted in Reiner Flasche, *Geschichte und Typologie afrikanischer Religiosität in Brasilien* (Marburg, 1973). Flasche calls particular attention to the symbolic structures of instrumental music, song, esoteric speech or babbling in tongues, and dance in controlling possessive trance (pp. 146–149, 157ff.). These structures can serve several functional goals, including most particularly divination and healing.

3. Ann Q. Tiller contends that Umbanda, the possession-based "Brazilian cult," is a symbolic complex centered on healing, *cura*. This, she argues, is true of all its major forms: Candomblé (the most African form, found especially in Bahia), Pajalença (the most Indianized form found in the Amazon; its name comes from the word *pajé*, "shaman"); Kardecism; and Batuque, a cult prevalent in Belém; see Ann Q. Tiller, "The Brazilian Cult as a Healing Alternative," *JLAL* 5 (1979): 255–272. Tiller defines *cura* as healing "in a broad sense such as treatment of an illness or disease, attempts to obtain employment, or efforts to bring back a wandering spouse or lover" (ibid., pp. 256–257). In this way, Tiller consciously relates *cura* to the principle of health articulated by the World Health Organization as "a state of complete physical, mental, and social well-being and not merely the absence of disease or infirmity" (World Health Organization, *Basic Documents*, Geneva, 1974, cited in Tiller, p. 257). Tiller thereby includes the central motifs of the religion outlined, for example, as three sets within the fortune-misfortune complex by Mary Karasch: 1) the "fecundity constellation" (childbearing, hunting, abundant crops, wealth); 2) security and protection from attack and punishment; 3) the amelioration of social status; see Karasch, "Central African Religious Tradition in Rio de Janeiro," *JLAL* 5 (1979): 236. Karasch is calling upon the theoretical analysis of Central African religious cults made by Willy de Cramer, Jan Vansina, and Renée C. Fox, "Religious Movements in Central Africa: A Theoretical Study," *CSSH* 18 (1976): p. 469. Roger Bastide details the way in which control over possession, especially violent possession, devolves on musicians, the ritual president, or fellow dancers in Afro-Brazilian ritual (Bastide, *African Religions of Brazil*, pp. 190–193) and even on the police (p. 209).

4. See the discussion of the relationship between vestments, masks, possession, and self-possession in chapter 6, above.

5. There exists a wide variety of applications. Among the Guayakí, for example, a pregnant woman is believed to make an especially fine healer because the child in her womb directs the therapy. The woman's saliva—a powerful curing substance—is applied to the afflicted areas of the patient's body. "Being cared for by pregnant women is almost a guarantee of cure" (Clastres, *Chronique des indiens guayakí*, p. 183). The powers of a pregnant woman are not limited to healing. The child in her womb may be consulted on many different topics, including inquiries concerning the location of game, knowledge of enemy attacks, and foreseeing the future, especially death. Clastres believes that a Guarani myth makes clear the reason for the existence of such powers. In the myth that recounts the origin of Guarani tribes, divine twins spoke to their mother while still in her womb. When their mother and other supernatural beings refused to take their advice, the divine twins fell silent. As a result, their mother lost her way and was devoured by supernatural jaguars. In fact, all the ills found in the world came into existence because supernatural beings refused to take into account the great wisdom of these unborn children (Clastres, ibid., pp. 183–184).

6. Giselle Cossard-Binon, "La Fille de Saint," *JSAP* 58 (1969): p. 78. Cossard-Binon is speaking of the *yawo*, the possession-based specialist of Afro-Brazilian tradition. The *yawo* is the human

being chosen by an *òrìṣà* and inhabited by this divine being during trance. The possessed human medium allows divine beings to descend to earth. This possessed medium, often a young woman called the "daughter of holiness (or sainthood)," undergoes a rigorous initiation and life-style that is demanding in spiritual, physical, and financial terms. However, the role is one of high prestige, for the *yawo* is an essential element in communicating with the divine world.

7. For example, the Kógi, who, together with the Ika and Sanha, are contemporary descendants of the ancient Chibcha-speaking Tairona of the Sierra Nevada area of Colombia, maintain a tradition of specialists who interpret, transmit, and carry out their religious principles. These specialists, called *mama*, are elders of impeccable character and years of religious training. "These men are not shamans or curers, but constitute a class of tribal priests who are highly respected" (Reichel-Dolmatoff, "Funerary Customs and Religious Symbolism among the Kogi," p. 290). Because of their powerful knowledge of traditional rituals, the sun stays on its course, the seasons pass in their yearly round, and the world and its elements remain fertile and alive. In short, the *mama* "guarantee the order of the universe" (ibid.). The *mama* are also sought out to preside over the celebrations of an individual's life-cycle. Masters of canons tend to be workaday specialists. Generally, their work is routine when compared to the spontaneity of possession or the drama of ecstasy. That is not to say that canonical authority is without social consequence. In fact, the nature of canonical authority, intimately related to the revealed wisdom accumulated across the historical tradition, easily lends itself to institutionalization.

8. Reichel-Dolmatoff, "Training for the Priesthood," pp. 265–288. For a description of priesthood in ancient Peru, with special reference to the cult of the earth mother (Pachamama), see Lucia Kill, *Pachamama: Die Erdgöttin in der altandinen Religion* (Bonn, 1969), pp. 48–52. John Rowe depicts the history of distinction between religious elite lore and religious folklore among the Inca and their descendants and stresses that the distinct segments of social tradition formed part of a single whole. See John Rowe, "El Movimiento nacional inca del siglo XVIII," in Alberto Flores Galindo, ed., *Tupac Amaru II – 1780* (Lima, 1976), pp. 11–66, esp. pp. 21ff.

9. Reichel-Dolmatoff, "Training for the Priesthood," p. 273.

10. Ibid., p. 275.

11. Ibid., p. 279.

12. Ibid., p. 284.

13. Ibid.

14. A less powerful office than the Andean *altomisa* is that of *pampamisa*, still occupied today by individuals chosen on 1 August by the *apu* Ausangate. The office is more commonly referred to as *paqo*, of which there are three categories: "those who cure human sickness"; those who make offerings to supernatural beings for the fertility of animals and fields; and evildoing *paqo*s, called "*layqa*s," or witches, who carry out rituals in which the normal actions of offering are intentionally reversed in order to cause harm to enemies (Gow and Condori, *Kay Pacha*, p. 72). Because the *paqo* is unable to communicate directly with supernatural beings (he must divine their will through the reading of coca leaves), and because his powers endure for a short time only, the fate of the world and its inhabitants remains uncertain. In spite of his diminished powers, the *paqo* is the most respected authority in the community.

The fact that a diviner can base authority on mastery of a canon should not be confused with the supernatural calling to assume that kind of authority. Prior to training, the diviner may be drawn to practice through some extraordinary experience of the sacred. Gow and Condori, for example, were provided an account of the calling of a *paqo* by Ausangate. The individual was still quite young when he went, in the company of his older brother, to "learn his destiny" (Gow and Condori, ibid., pp. 76–77). On 1 August they went to Ausangate carrying their ritual items. Arriving at the place at the end of the day, they bathed ceremonially in a lake. The older brother, who was already a *paqo*, prepared his younger brother by bathing him in the smoke of incense. They then prepared a burnt offering to Ausangate. Eventually, during the moonlit night, they returned to bathe in the lake. At this point they heard a cry followed by the sound of a falling stone. The older brother tried to divine what was happing by reading coca. Eventually, two beings dressed in white rode by on a white horse. The older brother determined that the younger one was called to be a *paqo*. If his vocation would have been to become an *altomisa*, the two beings would have stopped. The brothers looked for sacred stones and then returned home to have a meal which included *chicha* and *trago*. Then they offered a burnt offering to *apu* Ausangate (ibid., p. 77). In spite of this extraordinary signal to assume the vocation of diviner, the candidate's authority and reputation will depend on his competent application of canonical knowledge learned over the course of time. Antoinette Fioravanti Molinié points out that, in the valley of Cuzco, both types of medical specialist—the less powerful herbalist *(pampamisayoc)* and the *altamisayoc*, who cures through ritual contact with the *apu* during the darkest obscurity of night—are experts in reestablishing the correct mode of relationship between the space of the human body and the symbolic space of the cosmos. See Molinié, "Cure magique dans la vallée sacrée du Cuzco," *JSAP* 66 (1979): 96.

The symbolic systems of correspondence in divinatory practices embrace a variety that defies the imagination. Isomorphism, the structural principle licensing the discernment of the larger meanings of the cosmos from close examination of the structure or movements of its smaller parts, leaves almost nothing without universal significance. The Kaingáng, for example, place great emphasis on various kinds of divination. Divination allows one to "live in someone else" *(ka lele nya,* a process of extending one's body and psyche into a larger social personality, which helps one to achieve a sense of security; Henry, *Jungle People,* p. 87). Divination is achieved by belching, by reading the movements of insects found in the ashes of a funeral cremation, and by watching burning charcoal. Divination by belching is used to avoid threat of death. However, in the course of this life-threatening divination, great insights may be obtained of a more general sort. Drinking *matte,* the diviner belches in answer to questions regarding the chances of death, the prospects of hunting, the location of lost articles, and so on. The belches are then interpreted as answers to the question. Divination by insects *(kumbedn)* has its origins in the ancient period when human beings first appeared on the earth. In addition to the body paint and personal names characteristic of each of the five groups that emerged at that time, particular insects were peculiar to each group as well. When an insect appears in the funeral ashes after a cremation, the position and condition of the insect reveals the fate of the dead person (Henry, ibid., p. 89).

Kôplegn, divination with charcoal, requires a special relationship with the deer spirit. The size and location of sparks from burning charcoal reveal the game's location and the kind of game that will be taken in hunting. Human death may also be seen in the sparks. However, no one may foresee his or her own death (Henry, ibid., pp. 90–91).

See also the account of the vocation and practice of the diviner Eduardo, whose power resides in his control over the power objects of his *mesa,* his mastery of their "accounts," and his exegetical skills in applying them to the specific situations of his clients, in Douglas Sharon, *Wizard of the Four Winds.*

15. Kenneth M. Kensinger, "Cashinahua Medicine and Medicine Men," in Lyon, ed., *Native South Americans,* p. 284. The Cashinahua, a Panoan-speaking group of four hundred people in seven villages of southeastern Peru, live along the Curanja and Purus rivers. They recognize two types of religious medical specialist. The distinction between them rests upon the methods, materials, and manner in which specialists obtain the power to cure. The *huni dauya,* the herbalist, uses *dau bata* ("sweet medicine") to cure diseases that the patient "has" *(haya;* swellings, dysentery, boils) or "feels" *(tenei;* nausea, sleeplessness, poor luck in hunting, anger, lassitude, etc.). *Dau bata* consists of herbs, the excretions of animal glands, and ornaments worn during rituals. Although all initiated people may use such medicines, the *huni dauya* is recognized as someone especially competent in their use. For every symptom, there is a medicine. The *huni dauya* learns the value of the lists of symptoms, corresponding medicines, and methods of diagnosis from an older herbalist. The herbalist does not treat the patient directly but provides materials and instructions so that another may cure the patient. If the prescribed therapy fails, "the medicine was improperly given or taken, the diagnosis was incorrect, or the disease has a supernatural cause" (Kensinger, ibid., p. 285). The medicine itself is always effective. The coordination of relations within and among the canonical lists of symbols (symptoms, medicinal properties, personal case histories) accounts for successful application. Among Qollahuaya of the Bolivian Andes, "herbalists are primarily concerned with the circulation, distillation, dispersal, and elimination of fluids" (Joseph W. Bastien, "Qollahuaya-Andean Body Concepts: A Topographical-Hydraulic Model of Physiology," *AA* 87, 1985, p. 608). This is because

Qollahuaya etiology . . . attributes diseases to the following causes: (1) fluids dispersing from the body to the land (*susto*, diarrhea, V.D.), (2) loss of blood and fat *(liquichado)*, (3) too much wind *(mal de aire)*, (4) improper circulation of fluids and blockage of ducts, (5) accumulation of noxious fluids, (6) upsetting distillation processes by improper mixing of fluids, and (7) skewed relationships with the land." (ibid., p. 608)

The different species of herbs are the variously combined fluids that issue from the body of Pachamama, the earth mother. That is why the herbalist is a religious specialist in hydraulics. Louis Girault, *Kallawaya: Guérisseurs itinérants des Andes* (Paris, 1984) shows how the Qollahuaya classify some 880 plants according to local symbolic codes. See also Enrique Oblitas Poblete, *Cultura callawaya*, 2d ed. (La Paz, 1963), as well as Bastien, *Mountain of the Condor*. 16. Gusinde reported that most Araucanians understood the healing properties of more than 250 species of plants (Gusinde, "Der Medizinmann bei den Indianern Südamerikas," *CZ* 4, 1936, pp. 1302–1306). The Araucanian herbalist's knowledge of literally countless numbers of plants, their properties, and the symptoms they addressed far transcended that of the common person. According to Wilbert, the Yupa of Venezuela possess the most extensive knowledge of medicinal plants in South America outside of the Andean Highlands (Wilbert, *Yupa Folktales*, pp. 18–19). Any Yupa man or woman "can name and describe hundreds of plants and explain their utility to man" (ibid., p. 19). However, some individuals possess exceptional herbal knowledge. They are known as *tuano, tuanu,* or *tuwano:* the etymology of this word involves an important question in culture history and, in particular, the influence of the Spanish galleon trade on the Americas. Wilbert draws together sources that indicate that the word is cognate with *ani-tuwan,* a word used by the pygmies of Luzon in the Philippines to designate an herbal curing session. The word may also be linked to the Indonesian-Malayan word applied to a learned person of distinction: *tuan* (among the Sea Dayak), *tuwan* (in Java), *tuwani* (Galela, Halmahera), *tuan* (in standard Malay). Wilbert indicates that the learned occupation of those who have exceptional knowledge of healing herbs is highly unusual among the societies of lowland South America. He notes that it is an unprecedented office among the Carib. At the same time, he points out that it was a common and important office among the pygmies of Luzon, whose experts could describe "specific or descriptive names of at least 450 plants" (Wilbert, ibid., p. 19, citing Robert B. Fox, "The Pinatubo Negritos: Their Useful Plants and Material Culture," *The Philippine Journal of Science* 81, 1952, p. 188).
17. For discussion of shamanism as a phenomenon, see Åke Hultkrantz, "A Definition of Shamanism," *Temenos* 9 (1973): 25–37; Vilmos Diószegi, *Tracing Shamans in Siberia: The Story of an Ethnographical Research Expedition* (Oosterhout, Netherlands, 1968); Vilmos Diószegi and Mihaly Hoppál, eds., *Shamanism in Siberia* (Budapest, 1978); Mihaly Hoppál, ed., *Shamanism in Eurasia, Part One* (Gottingen, 1984); Carmen Blacker, *The Catalpa Bow: A Study of Shamanistic Practices in Japan* (London, 1975); Sudhir Kakar, *Shamans, Mystics and Doctors: A Psychological Inquiry into India and Its Healing Traditions* (New York, 1982); Hans Peter Duerr, ed., *Sehnsucht nach dem Ursprung* (Frankfurt am Main, 1983); and Hans Peter Duerr, ed., *Alcheringa oder die beginnende Zeit. Studien zu Mythologie, Schamanismus und Religion* (Frankfurt am Main, 1983). All these works contain essays that critically examine the categories used during recent decades to study shamanism. For good general discussion of shamanism in the context of specific South American societies, see Miguel Alberto Bartolomé, *Shamanismo y religión. Entre los Avá-Katú-Eté* (Mexico City, 1977); Crocker, *Vital Souls;* Daniel de Barandiaran, "Mundo espiritual y shamanismo sanema," *ACAR* 15 (1965): 1–28; Gerhard Baer, "Religion y chamanismo de los Matsigenka (este Peruano)," *AP* 2 (1978): 101–138; Peter Kloos, "Becoming a Piyei: Variability and Similarity in Carib Shamanism," *ACAR* 24 (1968): 3–25. For a brief but dense inventory of shamanic tasks and hardware, see Gerhard Baer, *Südamerikanische Indianer: Wildbeuter und Pflanzer* (Basel, 1965), pp. 28–30.
18. Fulop, "Aspectos: Cosmogonía," p. 115.
19. Bartolomé, "Shamanism Among the Avá-Chiripá," p. 132.
20. Janice Krugh, "Mythology of the Pemon Indians of Venezuela," p. 32.
21. Julio Cezar Melatti, "Myth and Shaman," in Lyon, ed., *Native South Americans*, p. 275.
22. Wilbert, "Eschatology," p. 173.
23. Gow and Condori, *Kay Pacha*, p. 71.

24. Ibid.
25. Ibid.
26. Ibid.
27. Métraux, "Religion and Shamanism," p. 589.
28. Ibid.
29. Gusinde, "Der Medizinmann," pp. 1302–1306. For a description of the call to become a Yanoama ecstatic healer, see Zerries and Schuster, *Mahekodotedi*, vol. 2, pp. 307–309.
30. Douglas Sharon described the apprenticeship of a shaman in northern Peru in the 1960s and 1970s. It follows the typical vocation of the "sickness vocation," and is a highly individual experience. Sharon uses the case of Eduardo to point out that Peruvian shamanic practices of the northern coast are holding their own in the setting brought on by "modernity." See Sharon, "Becoming a *Curandero* in Peru."
31. Bartolomé, "Shamanism Among the Avá-Chiripá," p. 132.
32. Lyon, *Native South Americans*, p. 266.
33. Martin Gusinde, "In der Medizinmannschule der Yamana-Feuerlander," *CZ* 4 (1936): 1307–1310.
34. Ibid., p. 1309.
35. Métraux, "Religion and Shamanism," p. 590.
36. Ibid., p. 592.
37. Mario Califano, "El Chamanismo mataco," *SE* 3 (1976): 7–60, examines the mythic basis of the crises of shamanic initiation among the riverine Mataco of northeast Argentina. The shaman aspires to the *aját* condition (a theophanic state) by incorporating divine power *(la-ka-ayáj)*. Apprenticeship to become a Yanoama shaman is described in Zerries and Schuster, *Mahekodotedi*, vol. 2, pp. 308–310. Symbolic behavior bears much in common with the behavior of initiands, especially girls undergoing the rites of their first menstruation (ibid., pp. 135f., 309). Mark Münzel, *Medizinmannwesen und Geistervorstellungen bei den Kamayurá (Alto Xingu-Brasilien)* (Wiesbaden, 1971), pp. 244–259, describes the period of seclusion and initiation among the Kamayurá.
38. Melatti, "Myth and Shaman," p. 272.
39. Ibid., p. 273.
40. Ibid., p. 268.
41. See, for example, the details of shamanic initiation among the Ayoré in Lind, *Die Medizin der Ayoré-Indianer*, pp. 183–192. The normatively mythic structure of shamanic initiation and ecstatic experience is not peculiar to South America. It follows a pattern found in Asia and North America. See Eliade, *Shamanism*, and Louise Backman and Åke Hultkrantz, *Studies in Lapp Shamanism* (Stockholm, 1978), which provides several comparative typologies and phenomenologies of shamanism. Hultkrantz offers four constituents of shamanism: "the ideological premise, or the supernatural world and the contacts with it; the shaman as the actor on behalf of a human group; the inspiration granted him by his helping spirits; and the extraordinary, ecstatic experiences of the shaman" (*Studies in Lapp Shamanism*, p. 11). "[S]hamanism must be regarded as a continuous historical complex. Until recent times it has existed in three interrelated areas, South America, North America and Northern Eurasia (with Central Asia, and in isolated fields as South-East Asia, Australia and Oceania" (ibid., p. 28). See also Hultkrantz, "A Definition of Shamanism," and the works of Hoppál, Diószegi, and Duerr cited above.
42. This is the judgment of Audrey Butt Colson, "The Akawaio Shaman," in Ellen B. Basso, ed., *Carib-Speaking Indians: Culture, Society and Language* (Tucson, 1977), pp. 43–65.
43. See also Audrey Butt, "Réalité et idéal dans la pratique shamanique," *H* 2 (1962): 5–52.
44. Colson, "The Akawaio Shaman," p. 63.
45. "The true *piai'can* (shaman) is said to be *eneoge*" ("The Akawaio Shaman," pp. 43, 48).
46. Ibid., p. 58.
47. Ibid., p. 51.
48. Ibid., p. 52.
49. Ibid., pp. 56–57.
50. Ibid., p. 59.
51. Ibid., p. 62. See Wilbert's forthcoming volume on mystical death, ethnobotany, and the pharmacology of tobacco.

52. Typical is the Chapacura case. The Chapacura shaman is called to his vocation through dreams and afterwards lives as an apprentice to a master shaman for "a long period of time" (Becker-Donner, "Notizen über die Huayam," p. 99). The master shaman brings his apprentice into contact with helper-spirits and, at the same time, teaches the novice the songs he will use in his religious practices. The mature Chapacura shaman lives away from the village, in the sole company of his wife. He needs the peace and quiet in order to maintain constant intimacy with the spirit world. He commands knowledge of a large number of medicinal plants; uses tobacco in the form of cigars as well as snuff to help cure the sick. Since he is the only one who can pick his way in and out of the supernatural world at will, he is the only one among his people who uses powdered *parica* to induce ecstasy and hallucination (Becker-Donner, ibid., p. 99).

53. Civrieux, *Religión y magia kari'ña*, p. 50.

54. Ibid., p. 62. For example, all that remains of the fermented or distilled drink is plain water.

55. Ibid., p. 67.

56. Palavecino, "Magic World of the Mataco."

57. Ibid., p. 70.

58. Wilbert, "Eschatology," p. 171.

59. Audrey Butt, "The Birth of a Religion," *JRAI* 90, (1960): pp. 77, 103 n. 13.

60. Alfred Métraux, "Le Shamanisme chez les indiens de l'Amérique du Sudtropicale," *Acta Americana* (Mexico) 2 (1944): p. 208. See the techniques collated from a number of sources in Friedrich Andres, "Die Himmelsreise der caraibischen Medizinmänner," *ZFE* 70 (1939): 331– 342, and the interpretation of these techniques as ways of reorganizing sensory experience offered by Eliade, *Shamanism*, pp. 127–131.

61. Gerhard Baer and Wayne W. Snell, "An Ayahuasca Ceremony Among the Matsigenka (Eastern Peru)," *ZFE* 99 (1974): 68–69.

62. Wagley, *Welcome of Tears*, pp. 180–197. Wagley reports that

> A novice sat upon the ground near a panché, his mentor, and swallowed smoke from his mentor's pipe until violent vomiting occurred. When the novices were too ill to hold the pipe, the shaman held it for them, forcing them to continue "eating smoke." Generally the neophytes fell backwards in a trance and ill from the smoke; during this state they might dream. In any case, when they regained their senses the pipe was again placed in their mouth until they fell backwards, ill and unconscious once more. The process might be repeated several times over a period of two or three hours. (p. 198)

The period of apprenticeship intensified in the weeks before the Thunder ceremony, during which period of preparation the novice refrained from bathing and observed strict restrictions on food and sex (ibid.).

63. Ibid., p. 192.

64. See chapter 5, above, for discussion of dream-souls.

65. Bartolomé, "Shamanism Among the Avá-Chiripá," p. 119.

66. Ibid., p. 128.

67. Kensinger, "Cashinahua Medicine," p. 287.

68. Ibid., p. 288.

69. Fock, *Waiwai*, pp. 26–27.

70. Ibid., pp. 113, 126. Such rocks represent helper-spirits on *earth*. The shaman addresses these rocks as "my pet" or "my son." One is reminded of the forms of address that Warao shamans direct to their shrine-stones. The stone may be acquired when it descends in a dream into the shaman's mouth, the place where souls may enter and exist freely (ibid., p. 127).

71. Ibid., p. 126.

72. Ibid., p. 123. The hut is reminiscent of the hut used by adolescent girls during the two months of seclusion at their initiation. In the case of the shaman's hut, if the wrong leaves are used as a covering, the shaman will fall from on high during his ecstatic ascent into the heavens.

73. Ibid., p. 124.

74. Kloos, *Maroni River Caribs*, pp. 211–212.

75. Barbara Chesser, "The Anthropomorphic Personal Guardian Spirit in Aboriginal South America," *JLAL* 1 (1975): 107–126. Chesser's main goal is to interpret these helper-spirits in the terms of Carl Jung [e.g., in terms of anima/animus figures, the Self ("often represented as a

stone, a crystal, or an animal" — p. 122), and the Shadow ("a person of the same sex as the perceiver and usually a personification of his bad traits" — ibid.).

76. Alfred Métraux, "Religion and Shamanism," *HSAI*, Vol. 5, pp. 592–593. Various examples of spirit-helpers are offered throughout this chapter. Métraux was surely correct to insist on the wide divergence of spirit-helpers. The Chiripá, Toba, and Kaingáng provide a sample of this diversity of types and of the difficulty of classifying them. The two principal sources of divine power and knowledge for the Chiripá shamanic candidate are the same beings who reveal the "divine vital word soul element" of every individual human being: either the messengers of Nanderú Guazú (Tupá and Kuarahy) or the beings in the "country of the dead." No matter the source, both illuminations take place during sleep-dreams at night through the medium of helper-spirits who transmit sacred songs (Bartolomé, "Shamanism Among the Avá-Chiripá," p. 128). The principal religious specialist of the Toba is the *yeyátten* ("the one who knows"). This religious specialist enjoys a particularly close relationship with a helper-spirit called *peyák nótta*, the "good spirit" (Karsten, *Toba Indians*, p. 51). Karsten remarked that the special knowledge based on this spiritual alliance is a "real art" that is "acquired through learning" (ibid., p. 52). The power of the Kaingáng shaman derives from his "strong, enduring, emotional relations" with his spirit-helper, a supernatural being (Henry, *Jungle People*, p. 78). After death, this relationship endures. Consequently, the name of the dead shaman was invoked after his death by those who encountered forces that, through the aid of his helper-spirit, the deceased shaman had been able to "see" and control during his lifetime.

77. Fock, *Waiwai*, p. 123.

78. The *yaskomo* has these powers because mythical shamans performed such powerful tasks. Two mythical *yaskomo* once helped the sun to shine with the aid of the sun's father, Warakoimo. They removed the black-feather headdress of clouds and rain and replaced it with a brilliant crown of red toucan feathers (Fock, ibid., p. 33). Just as other species of beings have their life-source-father, the sun is known as the Father of Yaskomo (p. 35).

79. Ibid., pp. 12, 22.

80. On the other hand, since blood makes a Waiwai *yaskomo* weak, he must avoid seeing or contacting adolescent girls, menstruating women, and pregnant women. Ibid., p. 155.

81. Alicia M. Barabás and Miguel A. Bartolomé, "Mythic Testimony of the Mataco," p. 84.

82. Barabás and Bartolomé, "Mythic Testimony of the Mataco," pp. 79, 84.

83. Baer and Snell, "An Ayahuasca Ceremony," p. 66f.

84. Johannes Wilbert, *La Metafísica del tabaco entre los indios de Suramérica* (Caracas, n.d.).

85. Riester, "Medizinmänner und Zauberer," pp. 251, 259.

86. See Chapter 2.

87. Whitten lists such spirit darts as including "chonta splinter, small frog, living hair, small snake, stinging caterpillar, spider, machaca moth, blood-sucking insects, bees, stinging ants, chonta soul stone, and also sentient scissors and Gillette razor blades" (*Sacha Runa*, p. 146).

88. Ibid., p. 146.

89. Ibid., p. 147.

90. Ibid., p. 149.

91. Ibid.

92. Michael J. Harner, "The Sound of Rushing Water," in Lyon, ed., *Native South Americans*, p. 278.

93. Chagnon, *Yąnomamö*, p. 52. Zerries and Schuster, *Mahekodotedi*, pp. 325–326, present a long list of the spirit-helpers that the Yanoama shaman calls upon in time of need. The village of Mahekodotedi, during the visit of the ethnographers, used spirit songs to call upon some 55 different, distinguishable and important helper-spirits *(hekula)*, mostly associated with the powers of nameable plants. The relationship of Yanoama helper-spirits to ecstatic healers during their apprenticeship is described on pp. 305–307, 310ff.

94. Wilbert, "Eschatology in a Participatory Universe," p. 172.

95. I do not mean to say that the imagery of flight is without philosophical value. In many cultures, the experience of flight becomes a foundation for discussions of truth. See the descriptions in Plato's *Phaedrus*, for example, where the human being "beholds the beauty of this world, is reminded of true beauty, and his wings begin to grow" (*Phaedrus* 249e) because

"aforetimes the whole soul was furnished with wings" (*Phaedrus* 251b). For a glimpse of how this philosophical application of flight imagery endured and developed, see Antonio Orbe, "Variaciones gnósticas sobre las alas del alma," *Gregorianum* 35 (1954): 24–35. South American shamanism takes wing in different ways and for different motives.

96. Gerhard Baer, "Ein besonderes Merkmal des südamerikanischen Schamanen," *ZFE* 94 (1969): 284–292.

97. Palavecino, "Magic World of the Mataco," p. 72. Juan Adolfo Vázquez notes in this connection a report from Lehmann-Nitsche in which the word *yulo* in northern Argentina denotes birds of the stork family. Furthermore, he remarks that *yulo* is a constellation that figures in Mataco mythology. He also notes a report from Métraux that describes how the leg bone of a *yulo* was used as a kind of ritual whistle to help curing specialists into an ecstatic state during which they would "send their souls in the form of *yulo* birds to the other world." Palavecino, "Magic World of the Mataco," p. 72; R. Lehmann-Nitsche, "La astronomía de los Matacos, Mitología sudamericana V," *RMLP* 27 (1923): p. 261; Alfred Métraux, "Ethnography of the Chaco," in *HSAI*, vol. 1, p. 361. This information is helpful in understanding the religious dynamic behind the dream-song quest and the process of the use of dream-songs in curing and ecstasy. For further details of the Mataco shaman's magic flight, including precise information on the disintegration of the elements of the shaman's soul (*otichunayaj*, the head-based source of reason, will and assertion; *onechetayaj*, the body-based source of dreams and imagination; *jûsek*, the heart-based capacity for language and emotion, the strongest of the souls), see Alicia M. Barabás and Miguel A. Bartolomé, "Un Testimonio Mítico de los Mataco," *JSAP* 66 (1979): 125–131.

98. Wright, "History and Religion of the Baniwa," p. 418.

99. Eliade, *Shamanism*, p. 481. A shaman knows what is in other kinds of space, and he experiences the rupture of planes of being. When this fact is juxtaposed with the realization that the different kinds of space are born of catastrophe (see chapter 2, above), we can see the connection that some have drawn between shamanism as presented here and the assessments of shamanism that appeal to catastrophe theories developed by pure mathematicians, such as R. Thom, *Modèles mathématiques de la morphogénèse* (Paris, 1981); R. Thom, *Paraboles et catastrophes* (Paris, 1983); and R. Thom, C. Lejeune and J.-P. Duport, *Morphogénèse et imaginaire* (Paris, 1978). A proposal to apply such mathematical models to the study of Guajiro shamanic initiation and the development of the shaman's therapeutic role may be found in Michel Perrin, "Une Interpretation morphogénètique de l'initiation chamanique," *H* 26 (1986): 107–124. The relationships of Yanoama shamanic healers to other domains of the universe (heaven, marginal areas, the inner earth, mountains, water realms, forest) are described in Zerries and Schuster, *Mahekodotedi*, pp. 312–320. Regarding the ecstatic visit to other worlds, see Mark Münzel, *Medizinmannwesen und Geistervorstellungen*, pp. 198–214. In his ecstatic travels, the Wayāpi shaman, guided by his helper-spirit, undertakes once again the great mythic voyage once accomplished by a supernatural chief. The voyage began at the outermost edge of the earth. The chief was the brother-in-law of Yaneya, the creator. The sacred traveler encounters a panoply of primordial beings subsequently known only through their much-reduced animal images, left on earth at the time of their withdrawal (F. Grenand, *Et L'homme devint jaguar*, pp. 102–109; see also Clastres, *Le Grand parler*, p. 34). For an account of the travels of the Makiritare shamans through the eight levels of heaven, see Barandiarán, *Introducción . . . ye'kuana-makiritare*, pp. 867ff.

100. Wilbert, "Eschatology," p. 171.

101. Ibid., p. 172.

102. Carlos Mariani Ramírez, "Machitún: Ceremonia magico-religiosa mapuches," in Carlos Alberto Seguin and Ruben Ríos Carrasco, eds., *Anales del tercer congreso latinamericano de Psiquíatria* (Lima, 1966), p. 374f.

103. Wilbert "Eschatology," p. 173.

104. Bartolomé, "Shamanism Among the Avá-Chiripá," p. 129.

105. Whitten, *Sacha Runa*, p. 149, 155–156.

106. Charles Wagley, "World View of the Tapirapé Indians," *JAFL* 53 (1940): 253.

107. Wright, "History and Religion of the Baniwa," p. 62.

108. Gerhard Baer and Gisela Hertle, "Zwei Matsigenka-Mythen, Versuch einer Annalyse," *EZ*

special suppl. no. 1 (1974): 33–75. On the South American "Orpheus" traditions, see Maria Susana Cipoletti, "Motivo del Orfeo y el viaje al reino de los muertos en América del Sur," *Indiana* (Berlin) 9 (1984): 421–431.

109. Ibid., p. 72.

110. See, for instance, the description of the Makiritare shaman as psychopomp in Barandiarán, *Introducción . . . ye'kuana-makiritare*, pp. 892–895.

111. Carneiro da Cunha, "Eschatology Among the Krahó," p. 162.

112. Wilbert, "Eschatology," p. 171.

113. Ibid., p. 174.

114. See chapter 2, above.

115. The Baniwa, for example, illustrate the way in which their most sacred symbols (flutes, sounds, ritual songs, languages) come from the burning body of Kuai. See Wright, "History and Religion of the Baniwa."

116. The link between spirit and fire can be quite direct. They may even be identical processes. For example, according to a report of Jacopin, the Yukuna use the same term to indicate spirit and fire. Thus, the terms "spirit of my father" and "fire of my father" are interchangeable. See Jacopin, *La Parole generative*, p. 77; see also p. 75.

117. Egon Schaden, "A Origem e a posse do fogo na mitología guaraní," *ICA*, 31st Congress (São Paulo, 1955), p. 218. Fire must be stolen or furnished as a gift for humankind since fire is not, in the very beginning, a constitutive element of the human person and human society. Schaden points out that human being undergoes a transformation parallel to the one that trees undergo when fire is placed within them as a material element constituting their own being.

118. Ibid., especially pp. 223–227.

119. Alfred Métraux, *Myths of the Toba and Pilagá Indians of the Gran Chaco* (Philadelphia, 1946), p. 36. In other variants of this myth, jaguars (spirits of the dead) provoke the cosmic fire; see ibid., pp. 33–34.

120. Wright, "History and Religion of the Baniwa," p. 399. In this way, for example, Yaperikuli burned the world to rid it of dangerous beings and prepare a place for humans; he provided the origin of cooking fire from his tongue *(ienene)*.

121. Ibid., pp. 354–355, 360, 364–367.

122. Villas Boas and Villas Boas, *Xingu*, p. 242.

123. Barabás and Bartolomé, "Mythic Testimony of the Mataco," pp. 79, 84.

124. Ibid., p. 83. Other accounts are offered in Alfred Métraux, "Myths and Tales of the Matako Indians," *Ethnological Studies* (Gothenburg) 9 (1939), and Enrique Palavecino, "Algo sobre el pensamiento cosmológico de los indígenas chaquenses," *Cuadernos* (Instituto Nacional de Investigaciónes Folklóricas, Buenos Aires) (1961): 93–95.

125. During his ecstasy, for example, the Tapirapé shaman journeys close to the sun, an old man with no hair. The red parrot feather headdress of the sun radiates tremendous heat. Only the shaman can endure it. See Wagley, "World View of the Tapirapé," p. 255.

126. Association with the unbearable heat of celestial beings not only manifests the specialist's transformed character, it may bespeak the privileged condition of his ultimate destiny. After his death, for instance, the beneficent Carajá shaman takes the Milky Way road through the villages of the supernatural beings of the sky. There he takes up residence "in the heat of the sun with his inexhaustible pot of food and gourd of water in front of him and his shamanistic rattle in his hand, held up to shade his eyes from the glare of the sun"; see William Lipkind, "Carajá Cosmography," *JAFL* 53 (1940): p. 249.

127. Johannes Wilbert, "The Calabash of the Ruffled Feathers," *Artscanada* 30 (December 1973/January 1974): 90–93. *Wishi* is the pain brought on by poison, a substance that the Warao contend possesses fire within it.

128. Ibid., pp. 92–93.

129. Ibid., p. 92, and Johannes Wilbert, "Secular and Sacred Functions of the Fire Among the Warao," *ACAR* 19 (1967): 3–23.

130. The symbolism linking the shaman to the consumptive processes central to the cosmos varies widely. For example, by keeping a poisonous sap-spirit in his throat, the Shipibo shaman approximates himself to the world-tree. The Yanomamö shaman becomes homologous to a

cosmic mountain because *hekura,* the spirits of edible fauna who can devour souls, dwell in his chest. Kari'ña shamanic rattles with consuming mouths become the preserves of life-forms.

131. Jürgen Riester, "Medizinmänner und Zauberer," p. 254.

132. Baer and Snell, "An Ayahuasca Ceremony among the Matsigenka," p. 71. During his ecstasy, the shaman's soul exits his body. The exit for the soul is the crown of the head, now ringed with the light of his crown. As his soul leaves his body, it passes through the fiery light.

133. Métraux, "Religion and Shamanism," p. 597.

134. Weiss, "World of a Forest Tribe," pp. 255, 263. A Campa warrior, a second category of Campa religious specialist, may also reveal his power and intentions in lightning. When a warrior is to attack another community, he first blow-spits in the direction of the people he will attack. This action culminates in the appearance of thunder and lightning to the community under attack (ibid., p. 257).

135. See Wilbert, *Metafísica del tabaco,* passim.

136. Günther Hartmann, "Zigarrenhalter Nordwest-Brasiliens," *EZ* special suppl. no. 1 (1974): 177–189.

137. Ibid., p. 182. See also Otto Zerries, "Tierbank und Geistersitz in Südamerika," *EZ* 1 (1970): 47ff.

138. Nimuendajú, *The Apinayé,* p. 150.

139. Baer and Snell, "An Ayahuasca Ceremony Among the Matsigenka," p. 69.

140. Ibid., p. 69.

141. Melatti, "Myth and Shaman," p. 268.

142. Métraux, "Religion and Shamanism," p. 590.

143. John Gillin, *The Barama River Caribs of British Guiana.* Papers of the Peabody Museum of Archaeology and Ethnology. Harvard University (1936), Vol. 14, No. 2, pp. 1–274; p. 173.

144. Métraux, "Religion and Shamanism," p. 598.

145. Ibid.

146. Ibid., p. 597.

147. E. Lucas Bridges, *The Uttermost Part of the Earth* (New York, 1948), pp. 284ff.

148. Karsten, *Toba Indians,* p. 52.

149. Wagley, *Welcome of Tears,* p. 192.

150. Henry, *Jungle People,* p. 76.

151. P. Grenand, *Introduction . . . wayãpi,* p. 45.

152. Krugh, "Mythology of the Pemón Indians," p. 32.

153. Ibid. Mircea Eliade has drawn attention to this mythic structure, in which the shaman conquers chaos in order to give the world and its creatures more concrete form and order. See Mircea Eliade, "The Dragon and the Shaman: Notes on a South American Mythology," in Eric J. Sharpe and John R. Hinnells, eds., *Man and His Salvation: Studies in Memory of S. G. F. Brandon* (Manchester, England, 1973), pp. 99–106. As we have seen, the coloring (and therefore the body-forms from which taxonomies of species derive) of birds and animals deriving from the blood of a primordial being is a very common theme. The Warao report that birds received their various colors when they penetrated a primordial tree-woman (Wilbert, *Folk Literature of the Warao Indians,* pp. 247–248 and 377–379; cited in Krugh, "Mythology of the Pémon Indians," p. 32).

154. Wagley, *Welcome of Tears,* pp. 179–185. The battles that contemporary shamans wage with spirits in their dreams are described in the same terms.

155. Carlos Mariani Ramírez, "Personalidad del hechicero indígena. El Machi o hechicero mapuche," in Seguin and Ríos Carrasco, eds., *Anales,* pp. 377–383.

156. Peter T. Furst, "The Roots and Continuities of Shamanism," *Artscanada* 30 (December 1973/January 1974): 57.

157. Ibid.

158. See Alfred Métraux, *La Religion des Tupinamba et ses rapports avec celle des autres tribues tupi-guaraní* (Paris, 1928).

159. Bartolomé, "Shamanism among the Avá-Chiripá," p. 118. Also relevant to the issue of shamanism in the presence of colonial power is Michael T. Taussig, *Shamanism, Colonialism, and the Wild Man: A Study in Terror and Healing* (Chicago, 1987).

160. Antonio R. de Montoya, *Conquista espiritual* (Bilbão, Spain, 1892), p. 112; see Bartolomé, "Shamanism among the Avá-Chiripá," p. 121.
161. Ibid., p. 140.
162. Ibid., p. 143. For a description of the ways in which shamans negotiate the outermost frontiers of culture, in both its cosmic and territorial and linguistic expressions, see Lucien Sebag, "Le Chamanisme ayoreo," *H* (1965): 7–32, (1965): 92–122. Just as the Kofan shaman is the master of all spaces and times, he is also the "adaptive mechanism whereby individuals resolve their conflicts, cure their illnesses, and continue to adapt to changing social conditions. When there cease to be practicing shamans, there will be in effect no more Kofan." The shaman provides access to reality; without that encounter with sacred beings, the order of generative life unravels. See Scott Studebaker Robinson, "Towards an Understanding of Kofan Shamanism" (Ph.D. diss., Cornell University, 1979), p. 250.
163. Bartolomé, "Shamanism among the Avá-Chiripá," pp. 144–145.
164. Regarding the ecstatics' experience and power of vision, see Ernst Arbman, *Ecstasy or Religious Trance in the Experience of the Ecstatics and from the Psychological Point of View*, esp. vol. 1, *Vision and Ecstasy*, ed. by Åke Hultkrantz (Norstedts, Sweden, 1963). Arbman treats vision comprehensively, from mystical ecstasies and hallucinations to meditative and intellectual visions.
165. Henry, *Jungle People*, pp. 74–75.
166. Audrey J. Butt, "The Birth of a Religion," *JRAI* 90 (1960): 66.
167. The founder is named variously: his English name is Eden, his Makusi name is Bichiwng or Ara'opö. He is from the Kanuku Mountains of the Rupununi Savannah.
168. In short, "Abel's attempted entry into heaven is reminiscent of a typical shamanistic task" (Butt, "Birth of a Religion," p. 82). The forest spirits, and the archangels, instead of singing the traditional shamanistic songs, were singing and dancing Hallelujah. The prophet saw God, saw the dances, and heard the songs. He brought them back to teach the people. Since

> spirit flight was achieved by means of prayer and song, . . . for this purpose the stress is placed on getting the right words from God or from some important spirit. The early Hallelujah prophets were shamans by training and the method of seeking spirit contact with God and the type of spirit flight and revelation envisaged are obviously reflections of the traditional shamanistic procedures. (ibid., pp. 101–102)

169. Michael J. Harner, "The Sound of Rushing Water," in Lyon, ed., *Native South Americans*, p. 278.
170. Melatti, "Myth and Shaman," p. 269–270.
171. Carneiro da Cunha, "Eschatology Among the Krahó," p. 162.
172. Civrieux, *Religión y magia kari'ña*, p. 47.
173. Ibid., p. 48. Civrieux was able to obtain reports about initiation even though he was not able to witness one. He obtained this information from a fellow (a rather exceptional case) who became a shaman after he was forty-five years old. All other *puidei* remained absolutely silent in the face of his inquiries.
174. Ibid., p. 49.
175. Ibid.
176. Palavecino, "Magic World of the Mataco," p. 70.
177. Georg J. Seitz stresses the ritual control and care that surround the use of magical plants used to stimulate dreams and visions. He provides a description of a number of hallucinogenic agents with powerful optic and acoustic effects, arguing that they were originally used only in cult situations that permitted their safe experimentation; see Seitz, "Die Waikas und ihre Drogen," *ZFE* 94 (1969): p. 283. See also Vera Penteado Coelho, ed., *Os Alucinógenos e o mundo simbólico: O Uso dos alucinógenos entre os índios da América do Sul* (São Paulo, 1976).
178. Gerardo Reichel-Dolmatoff, *Beyond the Milky Way*, pp. 11–12.
179. Ibid., pp. 151–152. Because of his ability to see and to hear other realities, having traveled to the realms where they exist, the shaman becomes the center of Tukano hallucinogenic meaning.
180. Ibid., p. 34. For a comparative discussion of the role of hallucinogens among the western

Tukano-speakers, see Ute Bödiger, *Die Religion der Tukano in nordwestlichen Amazonas* (Cologne, 1965), pp. 41–58. Weston La Barre, "I Narcotici del nuovo mondo. Riti sciamistici e sostanze psicotrope," *TA* 12 (1976): 31–40, offers more general considerations of the place and practice of vision-inducing plants in the Americas. For a detailed description of a hallucinogenic ritual and a symbol-by-symbol exegesis by a Kofan shaman, see Robinson, "Towards an Understanding of Kofan Shamanism," pp. 152–180 and pp. 182–221, respectively.

181. Alana Cordy-Collins discusses the same issue in "Chavin Art: Its Shamanic/Hallucinogenic Origins," in Alana Cordy-Collins and Jean Stern, eds., *Pre-Columbian Art History: Selected Readings* (Palo Alto, Cal., 1977).

182. Harner, "Sound of Rushing Water," p. 276.

183. For example, in a normal state the Jívaro bewitching shaman can see his unique spirit helper, *pasuk*, a supernatural being who appears near the victim in the form of an insect or forest animal. However, under the influence of hallucinogenic *natema*, the *pasuk* appears in true human form, covered with a protective shield of iron. Only its eyes remain vulnerable (Harner, ibid., p. 278).

184. Nevertheless, in some South American cultures the mastery of hallucinogenic plants is a *sine qua non* of the shaman's technology of ecstasy. In the opinion of Baer and Snell, for example, visions under the influence of *ayahuasca* are essential to the vocation of Matsigenka shamanism. See Baer and Snell, "An Ayahuasca Ceremony Among the Matsigenka." The authors interpret the ceremony as an instruction session for a novice. For a slightly different description and interpretation of the ceremony among the neighboring River Campa, see Gerald Weiss, "Shamanism and Priesthood in Light of the Campa Ayahuasca Ceremony," in Michael J. Harner, ed., *Hallucinogens and Shamanism* (New York, 1973), pp. 40–48.

185. For detailed descriptions and illustrations of Boróro rattles, for example, and their religious meaning and functions, see Albisetti and Venturelli, *Enciclopédia Bororo*, vol. 1, *Vocabularios e etnografia*, pp. 47–63. A detailed presentation of the types of Warao rattles, including two kinds of sacred maracas, and photographs and detailed drawings of the decorations that appear on the instruments, may be found in Johannes Wilbert, "Los Instrumentos musicales de los indios Warrau (Guarao, Guarauno)," *ACAR* 1 (1956): esp. pp. 13–17. The place of the shaman's rattle in South America contrasts with the primacy of the shaman's drum elsewhere. See Eliade, *Shamanism*, pp. 168–180. Eliade writes,

> The drum has a role of the first importance in shamanic ceremonies. Its symbolism is complex, its magical functions many and various. It is indispensable in conducting the shamanic séance, whether it carries the shaman to the "Center of the World," or enables him to fly through the air, or summons and "imprisons" the spirits, or, finally, if the drumming enables the shaman to concentrate and regain contact with the spiritual world through which he is preparing to travel. (p. 168)

In South America, the shaman's drum does not have wide use. However, for a discussion of the way in which the Mapuche shaman's drum is a microcosm of the universe and its construction a reenactment of the cosmogony, see Maria Ester Grebe, "El Kultrún mapuche: Un Microcosmo simbólico," *Revista musical chilena* 27 (1973): 3–42.

186. Métraux, "Religion and Shamanism," p. 573.

187. Eddie W. Wilson, "The Gourd in Magic," *Western Folklore* 23 (Berkeley, Cal., 1954), pp. 113–124; for treatment of the South American rattle, see pp. 123f.

188. Carl O. Sauer, "Cultivated Plants of South and Central America," in *HSAI*, vol. 6, p. 506. The paleobotanical history of the bottle gourd as a pre-Columbian cultigen forms a piece in a larger culture-historical puzzle concerning the influence of "Old World" cultures on the Americas. See, for example, Thomas W. Whittaker, "Endemism and Pre-Columbian Migration of the Bottle Gourd, *Lagenaria Siceraria* (Mol.) Standl.," in Carroll L. Riley et al., eds., *Man Across the Sea: Problems of Pre-Columbian Contacts*, (Austin, 1971), pp. 320–327.

189. Eugenio Yacovleff and Fortunato L. Herrera, "El Mundo vegetal de los antiguos Peruanos," *RMN* 3 (1934–1935): 241–322, and *RMN* (1935): pp. 29–102; esp. vol. 3, p. 314.

190. Sauer, "Cultivated Plants," p. 506.

191. Lathrap, "Our Father the Cayman," p. 719. Mildred A. Konan and Raymond W. Konan, "El

Arte tradicional de la calabaza Peruana," *AM* 31 (1979): 41–45, illustrates the modern revival of traditional art forms using gourds. The authors make the case that these art forms extend back some three thousand years.

192. Lathrap, "Our Father the Cayman," p. 719. In addition to his assertions that the gourd is the basis of "the record of man's utilization of plants" and that it shows the "progressively greater importance to the technology, economy, and art of the people who cultivated it" (pp. 722–723), Lathrap postulates a path of expansion of *Lagenaria* cultivation coming from West Africa through the Amazon Lowlands, thus spreading with the first "Neolithic revolution" in the New World to Mesoamerica and the Andes. He has drawn together and summarized a large number of valuable sources on the history of the gourd (pp. 745–751).

193. The origin of the ceremonial rattle is variously accounted for. Zerries, following C. H. de Goeje, links the rattle to the idea of the disembodied-head image of spirits. Zerries postulated an Eastern Tupí origin for the head-rattle complex. See Zerries, "Kürbisrassel und Kopfgeister in Südamerika," *Paideuma* 5 (1953): pp. 328, 334–335. This conclusion ran contrary to Izikowitz's claim that the gourd rattle came from Central America; see Izikowitz, *Musical and Other Sound Instruments*, pp. 116 and 125. Rafael Girard, basing his investigations on an analysis of the rattle-complex of features described in the *Popol Vuh*, an epic of the Quiché Maya of Guatemala, agrees with Izikowitz. Girard insists that the rattle be seen as part of a set of meaningful symbols including supernatural beings, religious specialists, fruits and seeds, lexical items, ceremonial ornaments, and so on; see Girard, "Mito guatemalteco de origen de la sonaja," *ICA*, 31st Congress (São Paulo, 1955), pp. 41–53.

194. See also Berthold Laufer, "Insect-Musicians and Cricket Champions of China," Field Museum of Natural History, Department of Anthropology, leaflet no. 22 (Chicago, 1927).

195. Karl Izikowitz, "Calabashes with Star-shaped Lids in South America and China," *CES* 9 (1931): 130–133. For a semiotic study of the meaning of gourds in cross-cultural perspective and in literature, Ralf Norrman and Jon Haarberg, *Nature and Language: A Semiotic Study of Cucurbits in Literature* (Boston, 1980).

196. S. Henry Wassén, "A Medicine-man's Implements and Plants in a Tiahuanacoid Tomb in Highland Bolivia," *Etnologiska Studier* (Göteborg) 32 (1972): 8–114; see dating on p. 29ff and gourd description on p. 42. After examining colonial chronicles, John Rowe suggests that highland Indians received these gourds in trade from other, warmer regions of the lowlands; see Rowe, "Inca Culture at the Time of the Spanish Conquest," in *HSAI*, vol. 2, p. 245.

197. Karsten, *Civilization of the South American Indians*, p. 225.

198. Alfred Métraux, *Ethnography of the Chaco*. Bureau of American Ethnology Bulletin 143 (Washington, D.C., 1946), I, p. 353.

199. Nimuendajú, *Mitos de creación*, p. 99.

200. Ibid.

201. Bartolomé, "Shamanism among the Avá-Chiripá," p. 122. Bartolomé follows Schaden (*Aspectos Fundamentais*, p. 120) by explaining the common term for a shaman, *paí* (as derived from *maír* and *mbai*), meaning "the solitary one, the one set apart, he who lives far away" (Bartolomé, p. 123).

202. Bartolomé, ibid., p. 122. The use of spirit-seeds in rattles is common. For example, the Toba *yeyátten's* rattle-gourd houses spirits, as do the seeds within it (Karsten, *Toba Indians*, p. 52).

203. Wright, "History and Religion of the Baniwa," p. 68.

204. Barandiarán, "Mundo espiritual y shamanismo sanemá," *ACAR* 15 (1965): p. 12.

205. Wagley, "World View of the Tapirapé," p. 257.

206. In a similar way, because of his special power in the face of celestial heat and light, the Tapirapé shaman handles the headdress of red parrot feathers, which are said to be dangerous because they are "hot like fire"; see Wagley, *Welcome of Tears*, p. 208. The sun is hot because he (the sun) wears a similar kind of red feather headdress. The ceremonial headdress handled by shamans "infuriates Thunder and attracts his creatures to the wearer" (p. 114).

207. Civrieux, *Religión y magia kari'ña*, p. 21.

208. Ibid., p. 53.

209. For the Makiritare also, mountain-spirits inhabit the *maraka*. The reason for this becomes

clear in the cycle of myths of creation (Civrieux, *Watunna,* passim), in which the tree that housed life was also a mountain as well as a gourd: it was, in short, the archetypical container of life.

210. Civrieux, *Religión y magia kari'ña,* p. 54.

211. Ibid.

212. The curative power of the shaman's rattle finds different foundations in the religious life of each culture. For example, in the case of the Baniwa cited above, the rattle cures because, like the shaman's soul, it sucks out supernatural pathogens from the body. Like the Kari'ña shaman, the Wayãpi *paye* intervenes to ward off harm when all other attempts at cure fail. He does so with the help of a spirit he keeps housed in his rattle (Pierre Grenand, *Introduction à l'étude de l'univers wayãpi,* p. 45.

213. A similar report of the structure, meaning, and practice of the rattle among the Carib (Kaliña) of the Manawarin River in Surinam was provided by Walter E. Roth, *An Inquiry into the Animism and Folklore of the Guiana Indians,* p. 349. See also Peter Kloos, "Becoming a Pïyei: Variability and Similarity in Carib Shamanism," *ACAR* 22 (1968): 8, which discusses the *maraka* and its meaning.

214. Wilbert, "Calabash of the Ruffled Feathers," p. 90.

215. Ibid., p. 92.

216. Carlos Mariani Ramírez, "Prácticas y ceremonias magico-religiosas mapuches," in Seguin and Carrasco, eds., *Anales,* pp.363–376. All sacred sounds have an integrity, a fullness of manifestation that cannot be broken down or divided. This seems to underlie the difficulty of interpreting sacred vocal performances accompanied by music. For example, Mapuche shamans simply could not bring themselves to repeat the words or melodies of sacred songs. The words, the phonetic structures, were inseparable from the melodic structure. Together, the whole sonic integrity comprised the *ül,* the sacred sound that we might call a song. It is a primordial entity, a residue of the time before the separations and distinctions of this world set in. See Bertha Koessler-Ilg, *Tradiciones Araucanas,* vol. 1 (Buenos Aires, 1962), pp. 3ff.

217. Ernesto Moesbach, *Vida y costumbres de los indígenas Araucanos en la segunda mitad del siglo XIX* (Santiago, Chile, 1936), and E. Robles Rodríguez, "Ñeicurehuén. Baile de Machis," *Revista de Folklore Chileno* 2 (1911) and, by the same author, "Machiluhún, Iniciación de Machis," *Revista de Folklore Chileno* 3 (1912).

218. Mariani Ramírez, "Prácticas y ceremonias," p. 365.

219. The Machitún diagnostic ceremony also makes use of music as a controlled technique for ecstasy. In particular, it makes use of delicate lamentations sung by women; songs sung by men are not considered suitable in tone to constitute the ceremony. The moment of sacrifice is marked by a change of song as well as of the style of singing, which becomes more confused when the lamb's heart is extracted (Mariani Ramírez, ibid., p. 368).

220. Wilbert, "Calabash of the Ruffled Feathers," p. 174.

221. Dale A. Olsen, "Music-Induced Altered States of Consciousness among Warao Shamans," *JLAL* 1 (1975): 21.

222. Ibid., p. 19.

223. Ibid., p. 20.

224. Ibid., p. 24; see also Dale A. Olsen, "The Function of Naming in the Shamanistic Curing Songs of the Warao Indians of Venezuela," in *Yearbook of Inter-American Musical Research, 1974,* (Austin, 1975).

225. Olsen, "Music-Induced Altered States," p. 29. Olsen cites sources studying this phenomenon across a range of cultures: see Peter Crossley-Holland, ed., "Panel Discussion (Microtonal Inflection)," in *Proceedings of the Centennial Workshop on Ethnomusicology,* University of British Columbia, Vancouver, 19–23 June 1967 (Vancouver, 1968), p. 114.

226. Karsten, *Civilization of South American Indians,* p. 52.

227. The belief in the healing power of music is widespread in Amerindian cultures; see Frances Densmore, "The Use of Music in the Treatment of the Sick by American Indians," in *Annual Report of the Smithsonian Institution* (Washington, D.C., 1953), pp. 439–454. According to Densmore, music is a nearly indispensable therapy of Amerindian medicine. It derives its power

from supernatural beings, who usually teach the practitioner the songs during dreams or visions. This is true whether the songs are used in private cures by an individual doctor or in public ceremonies conducted by numbers of doctors over several days.

228. Palavecino, "Magic World of the Mataco," p. 70.

229. Ibid.

230. Ibid.

231. Boglár, "Creative Process in Ritual Art: Piaroa Indians, Venezuela," in Browman and Schwarz, eds., *Spirits, Shamans, and Stars*, pp. 233–239.

232. Ibid., pp. 234–235. Boglár reports that a *menyerua* was expelled when he could not sing the magical chants properly. An exceedingly good memory is required. The exercise of good memory is directly related to good health, for in ancient times the culture hero Wahari afflicted people with diseases carried by animals so that those who ate the game would not forget Wahari.

233. Note the nexus of consumptive themes: the shaman attracts game to the stone held in his mouth; the game is slain; he can't consume it; others do. Many of the same connections between consumption and powerful sound are found among the Kari'ña. The Kari'ña singing voice *(saka)*, captured from an animal during the ritual hunt for one's name at birth, is like a piece of food-bait lodged permanently in the human throat. Never totally consumed, it attracts beings. The shaman's voice can call an exceptionally large range of beings. His voice has the power to induce them to dance, just as primordial animals brought about creation in response to their sounds. By forcing a victim to dance, enchantment controls the shape of an enemy's existence *(uba* means both "dance" and "existence") and renders the enemy vulnerable to capture by the singer.

234. Henry, *Jungle People*, p. 79.

235. Montoya, *Conquista espiritual*, p. 112; see Bartolomé, ibid., p. 121.

236. Bartolomé, "Shamanism among the Avá-Chiripá," p. 131.

237. Throughout South America, the shaman's mastery of sound is nowhere more apparent than in the control over powerful names. Chevalier provides a "typical account" of a *Banisteriopsis* session in the Peruvian selva. After ingesting the *ayahuasca,*

> the master started to sing the names of the various strong trees, such as the *shihuahuaro* and others. . . . After that, he called [the patients] one by one and started to cure them. When it came to my turn, he magnetized *(icarar)* his cigar with the *shihuahuaro* tree and blew it on me. He did this so that the evil done to me would never enter my body. This was done simply by pronouncing the name of the tree. (Chevalier, *Civilization,* p. 403)

238. Such is the opinion of León Cádogan, *Como interpretan los Chiripá (Avá-Guaraní) la dansa ritual* (Asunción, 1959), p. 13.

239. Bartolomé, "Shamanism among the Avá-Chiripá," p. 130.

240. Civrieux, ibid., p. 35.

241. This is the conclusion reached by Audrey J. Butt, who has made a special study of the subject in "Ritual Blowing: *Taling*—A Causation and Cure of Illness among the Akawaio," *MN* 61 (1956): 49–55. Butt suggests that one unique feature of Akawaio blowing may be its ubiquity: "the practice of blowing permeates all aspects of the society. It enters into the economic, legal, structural, and religious spheres of society; it enters, in fact, into almost every department of thought and into nearly every social activity" (p. 55).

242. Ritual blowing, then, in the view of the Akawaio, bears very close affinity to theories of ecstasy in which a person detaches his own spirit from his body and sends it forth, under control, to perform certain tasks. This is precisely the explanation that the Akawaio offered Butt to clarify the operation of ritual blowing (ibid., p. 50).

243. Ibid., p. 51.

244. Ibid., p. 54.

245. Colson, "The Akawaio Shaman," p. 60.

246. Ibid. *Malik,* the songs of primordial spirit-birds, manifest themselves as wings, transporting the shaman into ecstasy, and also as the sound of those wings and other rustling spirits, including the rustling leaves. They also manifest themselves visibly as the ceremonial ornaments which the shaman wears on his arms and ears. These are called *činik,* "flowers."

247. Boglár, "Creative Process in Ritual Art," p. 234. For a discussion of *pakarin*, the esoteric language used in Cashinahua song (especially initiatory chants), see d'Ans, *Le Dit des vrais hommes*, pp. 11ff. *Pakarin* cannot be understood as a discursive language; "it's a question of 'divining' the meaning" (ibid., p. 11). Paulo de Carvalho-Neto, *Folklore Poético. Apuntes de Sistemática, Propuesta de Clasificación y Archivo de los Versos Tradicionales y Aporte al Cancionero Ecuatoriano* (Quito, 1966), offers a classificatory scheme for several different kinds of esoteric language forms, including *embololalias*, which distort normal language in intelligible ways; *glossalalias*, which consist of unintelligible neologisms; *mnemotecnias*, which are nomenclatures used as frameworks for popular wisdom speech; and so on.

248. Johannes Wilbert, "The Metaphoric Snare: Analysis of a Warao Folktale," *JLAL* 1 (1975): 15.

249. Ibid.

250. Everard F. Im Thurn, *Among the Indians of Guiana, Being Sketches, Chiefly Anthropological, from the Interior of British Guiana* (London, 1883), p. 336; cited in Eliade, *Shamanism*, p. 97.

251. Kloos, *Maroni River Caribs*, p. 211.

252. Civrieux, *Religión y magia kari'ña*, p. 15.

253. Ibid., p. 17.

254. Ibid., pp. 9–10.

255. Ibid., p. 11.

256. Ibid., p. 18.

257. Ibid., p. 13.

258. Ibid., p. 18.

259. Ibid., p. 19. The theme of wisdom associated with the sharp tooth of the mouth, whose passage one must master in order to have wisdom, reappears in the mythic theme of the toothy vagina *(vagina dentata)*. The mouth as the locus of transformative passage is an image extended in a different way through the Desana concept of sucking, which expresses both feminine fecundity and the curative power of the shaman's mouth; see chapters 5 and 6 of this work.

260. In fact, in the Kari'ña view, the spiritual life of every human being depends upon the slain sound placed within the person as his or her voice at the time of naming. One's voice is the sound taken as game in a ritual hunt at the time of one's birth.

261. Capturing pets for their sound, especially pet birds, is a strong manifestation of a Kari'ña hunter's *aka* (strength, acumen of spirit). The process is said to parallel the way in which a shaman calls spirit-helpers to cure. The captured pet is called *eki* ("spirit"), and a child may be named after its sound *(saka)*. The child and the pet then become *aska* (spirit companions). *Aka* is the word for a free spirit; *aska* refers to a dominated, or domesticated spirit (i.e., a familiar or a helper-spirit). These noisy pet birds or insects serve as mascots through the magic power of their voices. They efficiently call the congeners to the hunter and to the family with whom they are associated through the deepest kind of tie in reality: sound. "In this way they help men establish ties with the various *wara* [sound, a species composed of beings that make that sound, the true invisible form of each animal species] and overcome them in their hunts" (Civrieux, ibid., p. 25). For this reason, noisy birds, animals, and insects are preferred as pets. Civrieux provides an extraordinarily fascinating discussion of bird-calling and the techniques used to achieve religious and magical ends (pp. 25ff.), sexual seduction, attraction of spiritual powers, killing, defense, and exorcism. Certain kinds of birds are bird-shamans because they too are ventriloquists who imitate the sounds of other animals and "throw" their sound-realities into distances in a disturbing and mysterious way (p. 26). Ventriloquist birds are captured as especially prized pets, not only for their own sounds but for the various languages of the other species of animals that they have mastered by capturing their sound and names. The woodpecker has a special distinction since, by pecking on a tree, it forces the tree to give out its sound (its name) and thereby dominates it (p. 26). *Machi*, Araucanian shamans, also communicated with several species of birds from whom they obtained wisdom, art, and dance forms, as well as songs, names, and diagnostic information; see Oreste Plath, *Lenguaje de los pájaros chilenos: Avifauna folklórica* (Santiago, Chile, 1976), pp. 151ff. et passim.

262. Civrieux, *Religión y magia kari'ña*, p. 128.

263. Ibid., p. 127.

264. Ibid., p. 39.

265. Ibid., p. 40. Civrieux recorded a conversation held in *derumpuo* between two *puidei* from different locations. It was later translated by a third *puidei* from the tape recording.

266. Ibid., p. 39.

267. Ibid.

268. Ibid., p. 42.

269. Ibid., p. 43.

270. Ibid. The word for possession is *senae*, meaning control or dominion (p. 46). It is not entirely clear, however, who is in control or possession of whom, the shaman or the spirit of cure, *kurano*. Neither is it clear where the union is taking place (within the shaman's body or in a spirit realm).

271. Ibid., p. 44.

272. Ibid., p. 46.

273. See ibid., the chapter on Kari'ña "neomythology."

274. For an analysis of the shaman as a master musician, whose performance is analyzed in terms of the differences between the person "musiquing" and the one "musiqued," see Gilbert Rouget, *La Musique et la transe: Esquisse d'une théorie générale des relations de la musique et de la possession* (Paris, 1980), p. 185–196.

275. Reichel-Dolmatoff, *The Shaman and the Jaguar*, pp. 43–44.

276. See ibid., pp. 43–54, for a survey of materials in the northern part of the subcontinent. Reichel-Dolmatoff concludes that "these reports cover the entire Colombian territory, from the Caribbean Coast to the Andean highlands, and from the Orinoco Plains to the Western Cordillera" (p. 48). For the imagery of the jaguar in connection with shamanism among west Tukano-speaking groups, see Bödiger, *Die Religion der Tukano in nordwestlichen Amazonas*, pp. 41–48. For wider geographic coverage of the theme see Peter T. Furst, "The Olmec Were-Jaguar Motif in the Light of Ethnographic Reality," in Elizabeth P. Benson, ed., *Dumbarton Oaks Conference on the Olmec* (Washington, D.C., 1968), pp. 143–178, esp. pp. 154–164, and Furst, "Shamanism: South American Shamanism," in *EOR*. For myths and interpretations linking the death or disappearance of the jaguar from the primordial scene with the origins of self-consciousness, see Karin Hissink and Albert Hahn, *Die Tacana*, vol. 1, *Erzählungsgut* (Stuttgart, 1961), pp. 249ff. and 328ff. See also an interpretation of the Tacana jaguar mythology in Karin Hissink, "Der Jaguar im Erzählungsgut der Tacana," *Miscellania Paul Rivet Octogenario Dicata*, Vol. 31. (Mexico City, 1958), pp. 249–267.

277. Many of these ideas are ably presented and amply illustrated in Reichel-Dolmatoff, *The Shaman and the Jaguar*, pp. 43–60, 108–132.

278. According to the Timbira, among many others, fire is a property of the primordial jaguar, the great devourer. Obtaining fire, obtaining power over all the experience and knowledge that fire symbolizes, is bound up with the spiritualizing process of initiation. See Curt Nimuendajú, *The Eastern Timbira*, trans. by Robert H. Lowie (Berkeley, Cal., 1946), p. 243. The jaguar's link to consumptive processes of spiritualization is even broader than its connection with fire. In Guaraní myths, for example, the mother of the divine twins and of all humankind is devoured so that she is caused to die—that is, to take on a purely spiritual existence, in which she awaits all those beings who will join her after the transformation of death. For this reason supernatural jaguars and their shamanic expressions become masters of the soul's destiny in the future life. Passage through the jaguar's body betokens the spiritual passage that transforms being. The shaman-jaguar becomes the caretaker of the transforming soul.

279. See Heinz Walter, "Der Jaguar in der Vorstellungswelt der südamerikanischen Naturvölker" (Ph.D. diss., University of Hamburg, 1956); cited in Reichel-Dolmatoff, *The Shaman and the Jaguar*, p. 271.

280. Weiss, "World of a Forest Tribe," p. 289.

281. Ibid.

282. Ibid.

283. Ibid.

284. Civrieux, *Religión y magia kari'ña*, p. 65.

285. Ibid., pp. 68–69.

286. For a consideration of shamanic bird symbolism in cultures throughout South America, see Otto Zerries, "Die Vorstellung zum zweiten Ich und die Rolle der Harpyie in der Kultur der Naturvölker Südamerikas," *ANT* 57 (1962): 889–914, and Hildegard Matthäi, *Die Rolle der Greifvögel, insbesondere der Harpye und des Königsgeier, bei ausserandinen Indianern Südamerikas* (Hohenschäftlarn, 1977), esp. pp. 104–178. Shamanic art often reflects shamans' birdlike experiences. The *tayucunchi*, the pectoral ceremonial ornament worn by Shuar and Jívaro shamans, was a magnificent artifact composed primarily of the tiny bones of the *tayo* bird *(Steatornis sp.)*. The *tayo* is especially well adapted to the dark inner chambers of caves, and, like a bat, it hangs by its feet from the ceiling of a cave when it rests. Each of the tiny bones used in the large ceremonial ornament is perfectly straight. Only a tiny bone from the wing is used. It is estimated that a single *tayucunchi* requires the sacrifice of some 320 birds! Along the border of the ornament was set a fringe of tiny, iridescent feathers and wings from cave-dwelling, iridescent scarabs and other insects. The cave of the *tayos* plays an integral part of the mythology and religious ceremonial life of the Shuar, as it did for the unknown civilizations, unrelated to the contemporary populations, who left their ceremonial objects and ceramics for teams of archaeological investigators to find. See Pedro I. Porras G., *Arqueología de la cueva de los tayos* (Quito, 1978), pp. 73–79. It was believed that Nunkui, a primordial being, moved into the cave at the beginning of time, bringing samples of the perfect life-forms that existed in the primordial age. Today those forms and ornaments exist as treasures that ought not to be disturbed by mortal humans.

287. Whitten, *Sacha Runa*, p. 141.

288. Ibid., p. 148.

289. Ibid.

290. This is reminiscent of a process which Carneiro de Cunha describes for the Krahó.

291. Whitten, *Sacha Runa*, p. 142. Instead of the stones remaining enclosed, inactive, and immobile until a knowledgeable shaman could bring about a proper awakening of their contained souls, these lost living souls of the dead began to outnumber the living (ibid., p. 149). Today, contemporary shamans acquire the ancient souls enclosed in stone.

292. Nimuendajú, *The Apinayé*, p. 148.

293. The role of biting insects and snakes in shamanic practice is widely reported. In his study of shamanism among groups in the Gran Chaco area, Métraux reported that among the Kaskihá, on a given day toward the end of a lengthy novitiate, "the master pulled out of his disciple's mouth a cricket, a small serpent, and a tarantula and gave them to the novice to eat." The novice would later specialize in curing snakebite; see Alfred Métraux, "Le Chamanisme chez les indiens du Gran Chaco," in his *Religions et magies indiennes d'Amérique du Sud* (Paris, 1967), p. 108. Toba-Pilagá shamans may be bitten by snakes and spiders, whose substances (teeth, heart, eyes) the shamans subsequently "see" in their sick patients. If the shaman, because of his personal experience with the snake, recognizes it, he will sing its song to cure the patient. The personal song of the snake (or noxious stinging insect) is an irresistible call which forces the animal to dialogue with the curer. Eventually, its spirit is persuaded to leave the patient and its pathogenic remains are sucked out of the patient's body (ibid., pp. 131–133).

294. Kari'ña shamans never pronounce the word *ako.du* ("snake"), preferring the esoteric euphemism *a.kato* ("companion spirit").

295. Civrieux, *Religión y magia kari'ña*, p. 21.

296. Ibid., p. 19.

297. Ibid., p. 22.

298. Jacopin, *La Parole générative*, p. 72.

299. Boglár, "Creative process in Ritual Art," p. 236.

300. Gusinde, "Der Medizinmann mit dem umgekehrten Geschlecht," pp. 1323–1324.

301. Here we find an allusion to "houses" in the other worlds that are made so much of in Tukano and Warao mythical geography. In the Waiwai case, however, the houses are described as if they were only artifacts of culture revealed to the primordial shaman. Contemporary people build these kinds of house-spaces on the model that exists in another plane, seen in another time (Fock, *Waiwai*, pp. 37, 75). The idea that earthly buildings are constructed on heavenly models revealed to human beings or to an architect is a variation of the *imago mundi*.

302. Fock, ibid., p. 64.

303. Ibid., pp. 113–114.

304. Ibid., p. 114.

305. Ibid., p. 116.

306. P. Grenand, *Introduction . . . wayãpi*, p. 45.

307. Civrieux, *Religión y magia kari'ña*, pp. 24, 31.

308. Ibid., p. 24.

309. Métraux, "Religion and Shamanism," p. 594.

310. Civrieux, *Religión y magia kari'ña*, pp. 55–56; see also James Gillin, *The Barama River Caribs of British Guiana*, Papers of the Peabody Museum of Archaeology and Ethnology, vol. 14, no. 2 (Cambridge, Mass., 1936), which discusses the concept of the "strong arm" among the Carib and Kalinye of the Rio Barama area.

311. Civrieux, *Religión y magia kari'ña*, p. 55.

312. The Ayoré healer begins the diagnosis and outlines the choices of therapy by locating the agents of illness in corporeal and cosmic space. See Lind, *Die Medizin der Ayoré-Indianer*, pp. 227–240.

313. Claude Lévi-Strauss, "The Use of Wild Plants in Tropical South America," in *HSAI*, vol. 6, p. 468.

314. Stig Rydén, *Andean Excavations I–II*, Statens Etnografiska Museum, monograph series no. 4 and no. 6 (Stockholm, 1957–1959).

315. Eskil Hultin, "The Accuracy of the Radiocarbon Dating," *ES* 32 (1972): 185–196.

316. S. Henry Wassén, "A Medicine Man's Implements and Plants in a Tiahuanacoid Tomb in Highland Bolivia," *ES* 32 (1972): p. 13f.

317. Villas Boas and Villas Boas, *Xingu*, pp. 144ff.

318. P. Grenand, *Introduction . . . wayãpi*, p. 45.

319. Bartolomé, "Shamanism Among the Avá-Chiripá," p. 134.

320. Palavecino, "Magic World of the Mataco," p. 71. Needless to say, the shaman knowledgeable in plant lore does not always side with cure in the battle of disease. Occasionally, for example, the Jívaro bewitching shaman practices his power to strike down enemies with disease by attempting to afflict a tree. He casts a *tsentsak* (spirit dart) through the thickest part of the trunk. Only under the influence of *natema* can the magical dart be seen passing through the tree. The most powerful bewitching shamans can shoot the *tsentsak* clear through the tree just as they would cast the magical dart clean through the body of their victim, leaving nothing for the healing shaman to suck out (Harner, "Sound of Rushing Water," p. 280).

321. It is important not to confuse the role of curer with the vocation of shaman. The one does not define the other. Although the shaman's knowledge gained from ecstasy offers the community advantages for health care, it need not be the only option. For instance, among the Kaingáng, anyone could try to summon the lost soul of the sick person, using its name and food as attractions (Henry, *Jungle People*, p. 79). Specialist techniques of cure did not involve the summoning of a lost soul. Although not greatly developed or emphasized, a Kaingáng shaman did possess special abilities to cure the sick. However, the shaman only cured within his extended family. For description of healing scenarios conducted by ecstatics, see Münzel, *Medizinmannwesen und Geistervorstellungen*, pp. 259ff. For a summary of the ecstatic healing techniques and symbolism of Tukano-speaking shamans, see Bödiger, *Die Religion der Tukano in nordwestlichen Amazonas*, pp. 150ff. According to some Arawak speakers, ecstatics can cure with gourd music and tobacco because this is the way that Harliwanli first created human beings: "Thus was the beginning of men (Arawaks) knowing the medicine-art"; see C. H. de Goeje, *The Arawak Language of Guiana* (Amsterdam, 1928), p. 275.

322. Bartolomé, "Shamanism Among the Avá-Chiripá," p. 135. "Suggestion is too simplistic a formula to designate a process in which the actors are aware of a cosmos in which the correspondences to themselves are direct" (p. 136).

323. Ibid., p. 133

324. Ibid.

325. In retrieving the lost soul, the shaman must frequently do battle with the soul's adversaries on their own turf. For instance, the Chiquitano can be made sick unto death if elements of their

souls, which are able to wander at night and in trance, are captured and forced to drink the water or swim in the water of another cosmic realm. In such cases, the services of shamans are needed to survey the mystical landscape with their heightened vision, diagnose the problem, and liberate the soul (Riester, "Medizinmänner und Zauberer," p. 261).

326. Wright, "History and Religion of the Baniwa," pp. 63, 415.

327. Ibid., p. 426.

328. As evidenced in the examples presented here, blowing tobacco smoke is an important shamanic therapy. The practice is a reminder that the shaman's ability to cure is a by-product of his specialized knowledge of the spirit world. As master of fire and as one knowledgeable in the consumptive habits of spirits, the shaman frequently deals with tobacco and with the food and, at times, the "flesh" of spirits. The entire cure may center on manipulation of tobacco through fire. For example, the Matsigenka shaman cures soul-loss by puffing tobacco smoke onto the crown of the patient's head, the place where the soul passes in and out of the body (Baer and Snell, "An Ayahuasca Ceremony Among the Matsigenka," p. 66). See the abundant case material presented in Wilbert, *Metafísica del tabaco*, passim.

329. Roe, *Cosmic Zygote*, p. 122.

330. Ibid., pp. 121–122.

331. Ibid., p. 330.

332. Ibid., p. 123.

333. Ibid., p. 124.

334. Ibid.

335. Nimuendajú, *The Apinayé*, p. 146.

336. Ibid., p. 144. Nimuendajú believes that, along with tobacco, this practice was imported from the Tupí. He notes that the practice is lacking among the Eastern Timbira and the Sherente.

337. Erwin H. Ackerknecht, "Medical Practices," in *HSAI*, vol. 5, p. 633.

338. Many ethnographies attest to the cure by sucking. Descriptions of these acts are generally spare, as these two examples show. During curing sessions, the Yǫnomamö *shobori* chants and dances in front of the patient's home. Chanting songs to the afflicting *hekura*, the shaman massages his patient and draws the *hekura* into an extremity. There he extracts the *hekura* by sucking and then regurgitating the afflicting spirit (Chagnon, *Yǫnomamö*, p. 52). Often sickness among the Apinayé is caused by the shadow-soul of a plant or animal which the patient has consumed. This shadow-soul produces pathogenic sensations analogous to the properties of the animal or plant itself; for example, deer when consumed may cause the pulse to quicken, and so on. In such cases, the *vayaṅgá*, the healing shaman who communicates with the dead (his helper-spirits), massages the patient's body until he isolates the intruding shadow-soul in one part of the body. Then he sucks it out. Next, he must apply an antidote *(gandé)* since every plant and animal has a particular antidote in the form of another plant or animal (Nimuendajú, *The Apinayé*, p. 142). The sparseness of descriptions of the detailed symbolic actions of sucking cures and, more importantly, of the meanings attached to these gestures and images, often obscures the cosmic dimension of these performances. Sucking cures can culminate in the ecstatic talents of the healer and the spiritual history of the universe. But these larger aspects of therapy appear only in the light of the fully religious meaning of sucking.

339. Métraux, "Religion and Shamanism," p. 595. Métraux writes,

> The cure consisted essentially in massaging, blowing, and sucking the patient. Very often the shaman rubbed him with saliva and blew tobacco smoke on him. After some time he removed that cause of the evil: sticks, thorns, or insects. If the agent was a magic substance, he made gestures as though he were removing some sticky but invisible mass. In cases of soul-loss, the shaman sent his own soul after it; if it succeeded in recapturing the victim's soul, the shaman placed it back in its bodily envelope. (p. 595)

340. Henry, *Jungle People*, p. 84. Henry offers this typical case. Performing a cure on her son, who was afflicted with snakebite, a Kaingáng shaman named Thalú blew on the child and ran around him singing an unintelligible song that imitated the sound of the *macuca* while eating (ibid., p. 79). After singing, Thalú summoned her husband, who came and massaged the child and blew on him. The husband made loud cries imitative of the howler monkey and then spat on

the child. The husband then declared himself to be a supernatural being, the Howler Monkey. The father ordered the boy to be washed, after which the boy vomited blood and opened his eyes. "Chu [the father] had thrown all the poison out of him" (ibid.). Although Henry insists on the centrality of sucking, he does not describe its performance in the cases he provides. From accounts provided by Métraux it would seem that cure by sucking is often a tandem performance of a man-woman team. One party acts as the masseur or masseuse who locates and isolates the noxious object; the other sucks the pathogen out of the body. See, for example, the cure of snakebite among the Toba-Pilagá, in Métraux, "Entretiens avec Kedoc et Pedro," in his *Religions et magies indiennes*, pp. 130–131.

341. Since the time of the Conquest, the literature of travelers, administrators, and professional ethnographers in South America is sprinkled with startling descriptions of sucking cures as religious events. The bond between religion and cure is remarkably durable, located as it is in the mouth-powers of the shaman. The late-twentieth-century Pemón view the *piache* (shaman) primarily as an intermediary with the supernatural world who uses his communicative powers toward medical ends and specializes in sucking cures (Krugh, "Mythology of the Pemón Indians," p. 31). One hundred seventy years earlier (in 1801–1804), based on his investigations of what was then the Captain-Generalship of Carraccas, François Depons also reported that in all the native traditions in the provinces of Venezuela, Maracaybo, and Cumana, "religion was united to the healing art" since the principal religious functionary, the *Piache*, was also a physician; see F. Depons, *Travels in Parts of South America During the Years 1801, 1802, 1803, and 1804* (London, 1806), pp. 50ff. "After having been taught the elements of medicine and magic, which were regarded as inseparable, they submitted to a seclusion of two years in caverns, situated in the deepest recesses of the forests. During this period they ate no animal food; they saw no person, not even their parents. The old *Piaches*, or doctors, went and instructed them during the night" (ibid., p. 50). The practices of cure consisted in "licking and sucking the affected part . . . to eliminate the peccant humour. When the fever or pain increased, suction of the joints, as well as friction over all the body with the hand, was employed" (ibid.). These actions were accompanied by "dreadful exclamations" and the howling of unintelligible words, together with shaking, gyrations and contortions of the curer's body. Understanding the spirituality of the mouth would be a key to knowing the relationship between religion and medicine in the history of South American cultures.

342. Wagley, *Welcome of Tears*, p. 191.

343. Métraux, "Religion and Shamanism," p. 593.

344. Ibid., p. 595.

345. It may be fruitful to look upon shamanic sucking as a miniature parallel of the shaman's own initiatory "death" through dismemberment, evisceration, and extraction of organs or innards. Rethinking sucking as a variation of the process of opening and drawing out the internal parts of the apprentice's body sets it in the context of symbolic death. The relationship of sucking and sacrifice is not unprecedented among Amerindians of Latin America. Among the Maya of the Classic period, one form of sacrifice, called *chuch* (or *chuchuncil*), involved extracting the heart. *Chuch* is a word meaning "to suck, to nurse." Cf. Linda Schele, "Human Sacrifice Among the Classic Maya," in Elizabeth P. Benson and Elizabeth H. Boone, eds., *Ritual Human Sacrifice in Mesoamerica* (Washington, D.C., 1984), pp. 7–48. Jacqueline Duvernay draws attention to similarities in female and shamanic initiation, centered on the transformative powers of a newly made opening (mouth, vagina, mystical channels in the body, cuts). The sexual imagery pervades therapeutic sucking and blowing:

> In effect, when the shaman sucks in a pathogenic object, in some manner he opens his body in the image of nubile girls who are pierced at the moment of puberty. And in this case, the ropes of vegetable fibre which the girls plait during their seclusion guarantee communication with the supernatural world in the same way as the ladder that is described in shaman's rites. In the second place, when the shaman begins to blow on his sick patient, he represents a phallic agent who pierces the envelope of the sickness, in the image of the cosmic cylinder piercing the levels of the world. (Duvernay, "Les Voies du Chamane," *H* 13, 1973, p. 92)

346. Harner, "Sound of Rushing Water," p. 280.

347. Ibid.
348. Ibid., p. 281.
349. Ibid.
350. Ibid.
351. Hill, "Wakuenai Society," p. 223.
352. Whitten, *Sacha Runa*, p. 155.
353. Ibid.
354. Ibid., p. 156.
355. Ibid.
356. Ibid.
357. Ibid., p. 157.
358. Ibid., p. 157–158.
359. Ibid., p. 158.
360. Bartolomé, "Shamanism Among the Avá-Chiripá," p. 132.
361. In the northwest Amazon this sort of myth forms the basis for the equation of sucking and being blown over with sacred musical instruments during initiation. The instruments are actually parts of the body of a mythical being or anaconda. The equation, replete with other accompanying symbolic details, is found elsewhere around the world. For example, sucking and being blown over with musical instruments are equated in the great Wawalag cycle of northeastern Arnhem Land, in Australia. Male novices are painted in the same manner as mythic women. Then a drone pipe *(didjeridu)* is blown over their heads. The sound and the action mean that the great python Yulunggul is devouring them. Later they are vomited up again (i.e., resurrected). Cf. Warner, *A Black Civilization*, chaps. 8–13.
362. Wright, "History and Religion of the Baniwa," p. 424.
363. Ibid., p. 426.
364. Ibid., p. 68.
365. The fact that curative processes aim for publicity underlines the extent to which good health rests upon clear knowledge of the cosmos and one's place in it. Visibility of sacred powers and clarity about their meaning lay the foundations for good health. This truth stands out against its opposite: hiddenness fosters disease. Shamans work for health or sickness by disclosing or veiling the presence of sacred realities that impinge on the community. For example, one of the two categories of Cashinahua medical specialist is the *huni mukaya*, who cured through the use of *muka dau* ("bitter medicine, supernatural power obtained from spirits). The last specialist of this sort had died some fifteen years before Kenneth M. Kensinger's visit to the Cashinahua in 1966. Consequently, little was known about the subject. The *huni mukaya* acted as a shaman, diviner, sorcerer, and prophet. Since the *huni mukaya* had special rapport with supernatural beings, he acted as a seer to clarify, in conversation with his spirit familiars, information and communication that villagers had seen in the spirit world during *ayahuasca* visions. He cured sickness caused by supernatural power. Under the influence of tobacco snuff and in a state of ecstasy, he passed his hands over the patient's body. He perceived the hidden pathogen and removed it from the sufferer's body by sucking it out of the affected body part.

However, this category of Cashinahua specialist who deals with supernatural beings also served as a sorcerer who inflicted harm on other individuals. Such deleterious acts were cloaked in secrecy. (The secrecy redoubles itself since, unknown to his victim, the sorcerer conceals powerful realities in the body of the sufferer. Hiding is a major factor instigating disease.) The *huni mukaya* was able to accomplish all this because he had been given *muka* by spirit beings whom he encountered during his dreams. Whether he chose to reveal this power to the other members of the community or conceal it from them had immediate consequences for bodily health and the common weal; see Kensinger, "Cashinahua Medicine," p. 285.
366. Karsten, *Toba Indians*, p. 53.
367. Ibid.
368. Ibid., p. 55. This moment parallels the introduction of saliva into fruit mash, a magical process essential to the enlivening fermentation of intoxicating liquors, which is construed as the birth process of a supernatural being.
369. This stage of cure for disease that is essentially possessive falls perfectly in line with the

stereotype of expulsion of spirits: the importance of the voice, the interrogation of the inhabiting and possessing spirit, the specific questions put to the spirit concerning what it wants so that it might be appeased and leave the afflicted person, the provision by the possessing spirit of the information needed to expel him, and finally, the expulsion using the powerful name of the helper-spirit.

370. Ibid., p. 57.

371. Ibid., p. 59.

372. The Cashinahua, among others, expect a dramatic spectacle to take place during shamanic cure. The most important shamans fill the bill nicely. "There is a sharp sense of show; but not of show business. . . . The shaman would be considered the complete comedian: an admirable prestidigitator pulling out from the aching areas of the body thorns, nails, needles, little pebbles, fish hooks, and pieces of razor blades which *are* the pains of the patient" (d'Ans, *La Verdedera Biblia de los Cashinahua*, p. 20).

373. Civrieux, *Religión y magia kari'ña*, p. 49.

374. Jacopin, *La Parole générative*, p. 104.

375. Ibid., p. 70. Thus, for example, the gift of shamanic clairvoyance derives, in Yukuna accounts, from certain mythical birds.

376. James G. Frazer, *The Golden Bough: A Study in Magic and Religion*, vol. 1; cited in Lessa and Vogt, *A Reader in Comparative Religion*, 4th ed., p. 340.

377. See above for an examination of the role of disease as a signal to the calling of shaman. Often the episodes of illness and cure constitute a shamanic initiation.

378. Since the experience of ecstasy has a structure of its own, shamans can be confused with other functionaries whose technical knowledge derives from the flight of their soul to other realms. Warao canoe-makers provide a good case in point. A lengthy look at the symbolic details of their vocation clarifies the ways in which distinct ecstatic specialties can overlap in regard to initiations that include ecstatic voyage, apprenticeship under a master, acquisition of helper-spirits, and so on. Nevertheless, the canoe-maker's practice, when contrasted with the functions of shamanic ecstasy, brings into relief the unique dedication of shamans to the perfection of ecstatic techniques and the care of the human soul.

Warao canoe-makers are asked to make a successful journey of ecstasy to the house of the Mother of the Forest, Dauarani, before beginning their trade. A canoe-maker must be called to his vocation by Dauarani in a vision, which he reports to his father-in-law, the headman of the local group. During initiation as an artisan, the neophyte fasts and feeds the goddess tobacco smoke. In a dream trance, he visits the goddess on her world-mountain at the point of the winter sun's sunrise.

After fasting and smoking, the soul of the aspiring artisan climbs to the zenith of the universe. There a black leader of souls indicates the bridge that joins the zenith to the mountain home of Dauarani, at the end of the world. The journey to the goddess's residence is perilous. In the dome of the celestial vault the soul guide shows the artisan a snake-bridge awaiting him with an open, hissing mouth:

> The bridge is an enormous snake, the male companion spirit of the goddess. The huge reptilian head rests close to the zenith, and the tip of the tail reaches to the roots of the tree-mountain in the southeast. The snake never closes its mouth. . . . It has eight horns, four in front and four at the rear. The two pairs on the right side of the body are red and green; those on the left are yellow and blue. Flowers of the same color decorate each horn and chant the ceremonial songs peculiar to the profession of builders of dugout canoes. (Wilbert, "Eschatology," p. 175)

The snake never coils. It remains straight and smells lovely. The novice must tread upon the head of the snake, give its horns a shake, "and then either pass through it to exit and return through its anus, or walk over its head and body" (ibid.). If the candidate successfully completes the ordeal of walking through the body of the serpent and emerging from its anus (or passing through the horns and across the back of the snake's body), he is allowed to take a true measure of the perfect canoe by passing his hands along the sides of the snake's body; see Wilbert, "Navigators of the Winter Sun," p. 25.

During his state of intense ecstasy, the initiate for the office of master canoe-maker is devoured by a serpentine, half-excavated hull, a treelike water monster from whose body the candidate must emerge:

> Being enclosed in the darkness of the boat is analogous to being inside the womb of the *cachicamo* [tree-spirit-female] woman. Canoes and hollow logs are used by the Warao as coffins in which the corpse is reduced to a skeleton. The bones are reburied. Lying in the hollow envelope of his tomb, the novice contemplates his own death and his own skeleton. He has reentered the womb of his primordial life in the expectation of mystical rebirth. Only if he successfully clears the Symplegadian passage through the serpent's jaws will the novice be regenerated in the germinal darkness of the monster. Within he faces annihilation. But he hopes to emerge as before through a "knothole" in the boat, this time through the rectal opening, and to proceed from one world into a new world. (Wilbert, "To Become a Maker of Canoes," p. 348)

Eventually, the neophyte arrives in a house of dazzling and blinding light, the house of the Great Mother Dauarani. He is blinded by the experience of the "spark of the same creative energy" needed for the construction of canoes. The candidate sees the house of the goddess and hears songs coming from the flowers that decorate the roof. The songs are absolutely crucial to the successful career of the artisan. A master craftsman will correct any failure to imitate the flowers' chants correctly (Wilbert, "Navigators," p. 26). For the rest of his life, the canoe-master will construct vessels in the hope of recapturing that deathly moment of ecstatic sound and light (Wilbert, "To Become a Maker of Canoes," p. 349).

The craftsman must carefully observe the rules laid down for his trade. It is believed that he fashions his boats in the image of the great goddess's vagina. If he observes the restraints placed upon him in his trade—sex and food restrictions, obligations to offer flour and tobacco, and other rules—the boatmaker may be assured that his soul will successfully pass over (or through) the snake bridge when it comes time to make his final voyage to the abode of the Mother of the Forest after death.

Because the Warao consider the dugout canoe an article of culture that preceded the existence of people on the earth, the canoe-maker must work under radically different conditions of space and time. Haburi, the ancient culture hero, designed the first canoe, which transformed itself into the goddess Dauarani [Wilbert, "Navigators," pp. 16–46]. All canoes are now made in her image and from her tree-daughters. At the present time, Dauarani's soul inhabits the point of sunrise of the winter sun and her body its point of sunset. At the beginning of time, the paddle was the male companion of the canoe.

The paddle-canoe relationship becomes the model of the relationship of master craftsman to the goddess (ibid., p. 23). Following in the model of Haburi, the master canoe-makers *(moyomutuma)* transform trees into canoes. In ancient times, Haburi led two sisters (one of whom was his mother) in an escape from a murderous ogre and the house of a tree-frog woman named Wauta. In the course of the escape, Haburi inadvertently committed incest. After several unsuccessful attempts, Haburi finally fashioned a canoe out of the *cachicamo* tree, in which canoe he and his mothers escaped to the northernmost point of the earth. Here, at the world-mountain known as the Father of the Rivers, they remain to this day (ibid., pp. 22–23). This remarkable mythical canoe and paddle transform themselves into the primordial couple of the center of the earth: the goddess Dauarani, Mother of the Forest, and her male companion. The goddess is the first priest-shaman *(wishiratu)*, and her body and soul remain separated at different points of the horizon in a kind of eternal ecstasis.

Given the centrality of the canoe in Warao material culture, and the importance of the canoe in the supernatural world, it is less surprising that "primarily, therefore, canoe-making is a divine service at which the artisan officiates. It connects him and his society with the remote mythological past at the same time that it assumes eschatological import for the future of the individuals concerned" (ibid., p. 21).

Making a canoe may take from three to four months. The master craftsman observes sexual continence, food restrictions, and other behavioral restrictions. The correct construction of a canoe involves dangerous experimentation and transformation of the supernatural world (ibid.,

p. 27). The master craftsman must control these changes, especially through his chants. The felling of the tree and its transformation into a canoe is understood to be a sacrifice of one of the daughters of Dauarani, the mother of the forest trees. She and her daughter must consent to this sacrifice. A priest-shaman is called in to arrange these negotiations. With a cycle of songs the master craftsman signals that he has received the awaited permission in a dream. A bisexual horse carries the craftsman and his crew through the forest air. A straight road appears, "white as cotton," which leads to a girl-shaped tree, adorned and smiling. The maiden transforms herself into a tree "adopting on its eastern half the sex of a man and on its western half the sex of a woman" (ibid., p. 33). Actually, the tree is viewed as a set of twins. During his chanting, the master craftsman also assumes the role of both men and women. While the tree is sacrificed and hollowed out, its restless spirit is placated by the night chants of the master craftsman. The celestial serpent-bridge comes to view the work. It must not be found wanting. After the canoe is roughed out, it is floated back to the home of the master craftsman. Here, using an adze that "works by itself, 'eating the insides of the tree'" (ibid., p. 36), the craftsman finishes off the inside and outside of the canoe. The body of the canoe is now open. Frequently, at this point, the master craftsman is swallowed by the hull. If the man has been a worthy craftsman, he is led out of this magical death-womb when a psychopomp shows him an escape hole. If, on the other hand, the artisan has transgressed the many restrictions of his craft, he remains imprisoned in this dark coffin. He will stir from this dream-trance of death only to awaken and die (ibid., p. 36). In fact, the dead are buried in canoes. The triangles found at the bow and stern of the canoe are called vaginas. The thwarts that push the walls of the hull apart are called penises. As the canoe is fired, the chanting craftsman impersonates the female being:

> My little brothers, do with me as you please, . . .
> Now with this very sun,
> My grandfather, and
> With this virgin fire,
> You have arisen
> To warm my body. My time has arrived.
> (Ibid., p. 38)

When the canoe is launched, the priest-shaman once again presides. A meal is provided for Dauarani and her spirit companions. They are then asked to leave the land of the living.

Warao basketmakers may also ply their trade by virtue of their ecstatic experience. They achieve a status similar to that of a light-shaman. During a basketmaker's dream, the spirit of the plant used to make baskets offers the dreamer a cigar and a set of helper-spirits:

> It is believed that the maggot that can be seen in the pithy core of the reed burrows a tunnel leading from the artisan's chest, where the nascent tutelary spirits reside, through each arm to the opening in each hand. In other words, the weaver is aware that the reed spirit is at work in his body, and one day, upon noticing the supernatural holes in his hands, he knows that the transformation from ordinary person to light-shaman has been accomplished. (Wilbert, "Eschatology," p. 177)

If the artisan abides by the same kinds of rules that bind the light-shaman in his office, the artisan's soul will take up residence, after death, with the Creator Bird of the Dawn in the east.

379. Maybury-Lewis, *Akwē-Shavante Society*, p. 145.
380. Lucio Mansilla, *Excursion*, pp. 182ff.
381. Ibid., pp. 172–174, 177.
382. Ibid., p. 182.
383. Fock, *Waiwai*, p. 216.
384. Ibid., p. 218.
385. Ibid., pp. 303–316.
386. Ibid., p. 219. Pajonal Campa contractual speech dramatizes the need for oppugnant ritual gestures. The spoken word thereby acquires a "mysterious force" or violent "power" that imposes itself on the issues in order to impel them toward a decisive outcome; see Varese, *La Sal de los Cerros*, p. 24.

387. Ibid., p. 228. Fock is relying on research done by Métraux in *La Religion des Tupinamba*, p. 180, and "Mourning Rites and Burial Forms of the South American Indians," *AI* 7 (1947): 40. The only overlapping case, in Fock, is that of the Jívaro. See also Joel Sherzer and Greg Urban, "Introduction," in their *Native South American Discourse*, pp. 1–14.

388. Fock, *Waiwai*, p. 229.

389. Henry, *Jungle People*, p. 126. For some time scholars have studied the particular form of stylized redundancy found in ceremonial dialogue. Roman Jakobsen addressed it under the heading of "parallelism" (the pairing of couplets) in Finnic and Russian oral traditions in "Grammatical Parallelism and its Russian Facet," *Language* 42 (1966): 398–429. An important follow-up is James J. Fox, "Roman Jakobsen and the Comparative Study of Parallelism," in Fox, *Roman Jakobsen: Echoes of his Scholarship* (Lisse, the Netherlands, 1972). Fox illustrates how widespread is the occurrence of "canonical parallelism" around the world:

> What is of particular interest to us is that parallelism is a pervasive device and idiom of formal speaking, chanting, singing, and of greetings, farewells, petitions, and courtship overtures. Especially throughout the world's oral traditions it is a speech form or language stratum reserved for special situations: for the preservation of past wisdom, for the utterance of sacred words, for determining ritual relations, for healing, and for communication with spirits. (pp. 127–128)

On the canonical form of ceremonial dialogue, see Greg Urban's discussion of Kaingáng materials in "The Semiotic Functions of Macro-Parallelism in the Shokleng Origin Myth," in Joel Sherzer and Greg Urban, eds., *Native South American Discourse*, pp. 15–57; and also Maurizio Gnerre, "The Decline of Dialogue: Ceremonial and Mythological Discourse Among the Shuar and Achuar," in ibid., pp. 307–341.

390. For example, the Makiritare carry on an oppugnant and formalized speech when welcoming guests. The formal welcome may include speeches that openly insult and provoke those present. Plaintiffs lodge their complaints and defendants answer the charges. All this is accompanied by the sounds of drums and two mythic flutes, which make the noise of a male and female mythical toad. Eventually things calm down, and the hosts and visitors, having thus maintained their dignity, can encounter one another with their honor intact. The solemnities of departure are just as rigorous and formal. See Barandiarán, *Introducción . . . ye'kuana-makiritare*, pp. 960–961.

391. Basso, "A 'Musical View of the Universe': Kalapalo Myth and Ritual as Religious Performance," p. 282. On ritual dialogue among the Kalapalo material, see also Ellen Basso, "Quoted Dialogues in Kalapalo Narrative Discourse," in *Native South American Discourse*, pp. 119–168, ed. Joel Sherzer and Greg Urban (Berlin, 1986).

392. The essential role of the "yes-man," or back-bencher, and the antiphonal interjection of the congregational "amen" is a widespread component of both parliamentary rhetoric and myth-telling in South America. For example, in telling myths and providing explanations based on myth, the Baniwa narrator usually works in tandem with an "active listener." In this way, the telling of myth usually becomes a kind of performance in which the hearer repeats word-phrases and prods the tale-teller by punctuating the narrative with one-word questions (Wright, "History and Religion of the Baniwa," p. 416).

393. Basso, "A 'Musical View of the Universe,'" p. 283.

394. Ibid.

395. This function of the dialogue is found elsewhere, although the social effects linking it to feud have not been so thoroughly explored. The Tapirapé, for example, maintained an institution of stylized dialogue with which they carried out formalized quarrels. During the heated arguments, the opponents avoided direct conflict. "They had to remain hidden from one another and not interrupt the speech of their antagonist, but only reply when he had finished" (Herbert Baldus, "The Fear in Tapirapé Culture," in Anthony F. C. Wallace, ed., *Men and Cultures: Selected Papers of the Fifth International Congress of Anthropological and Ethnological Sciences, Philadelphia, September 1–9, 1956*, Philadelphia, 1960, p. 397). Each quarreling party remains in his house, out of sight of the other. From there he rails violently and loudly against his opponent. The speaker gesticulates with a club and speaks in a loud and monotonous voice.

When he stops speaking, the respondent replies in the same manner. Baldus observed that the same stylized quarrels were held between women. Furthermore, he gathered together other instances of the same sort of stylized dialogue during quarrels. See, for example, Amilcar A. Botelho de Magalhães, *Pelos Sertões do Brasil*, 2d ed. (São Paulo, 1941), pp. 497–498, and Gusinde, *Die Feuerland-Indianer*, vol. 1, *Die Selk'nam*, pp. 456–458.

396. The fundamental meaning of stone is drawn from the Trio myths of the origin of human death. During mythic times, a Trio man was instructed to respond only to stone when he wandered. "In the forest he heard a tree fall and thought it was a rock calling to him, so he answered it; ever since then the Trio have been like trees or wood (same word for both, *wewe*) both in terms of softness and ephemerality. People, i.e., the Trio, die like trees" (Peter Rivière, *Marriage Among the Trio*, Oxford, 1969, pp. 262–263; the various levels of ceremonial dialogue are outlined in Peter Rivière, "The Political Structure of the Trio Indians as Manifested in a System of Ceremonial Dialogue," in T. O. Beidelman, ed., *The Translation of Culture* (London, 1971), pp. 293–311. Building upon Rivière's and Fock's "correlational hypotheses" that link social distance (potential social conflict) to linguistic form (see Rivière, "Political Structure of the Trio Indians," and Fock, *Waiwai*), Greg Urban analyzes ceremonial speech in his "Ceremonial Dialogue in South America," *AA* 88 (1986): 371–386. He eschews the "semantic content" of the discourse ("what has been said") in favor of the "form of linguistic interaction," which he deems "meaningful" (pp. 383–384).

397. Roberto Cortez, "Diálogo ceremonial e diálogo mitológico entre os Tiriyó," *Boletim do Museu Goeldi (Belém)* n.s. 61 (1975): 1–25.

398. Ibid., pp. 60–61.

399. There is some question that Pereperewa is perhaps "the old one of heaven *(Kapú-tamu)* who made the world"; see Protásio Frikel, "Os Tiriyó (notas preliminares)," *BMPEG* n.s. (Anthropología) 9 (1960): 17. In order to see the degree to which the ritual structure of dialogue is used on many different levels in culture, see Peter Rivière, "The Political Structure of Trio Indians as Manifested in a System of Ceremonial Dialogue." The Tiriyó are a Carib-speaking group living on both sides of the Tumucumaque Range on the Brazil-Surinam border. In Surinam, the group is called the Trio. The form of ceremonial dialogue between mythic beings can sustain itself as a poetic genre. See, for example, Nelson Estupiñan Bass, *Timaran y Cuabu: Cuaderno de poesia para el pueblo* (Quito, 1956), in which a story appears of two fighting cocks who square off in a duel of song and poetry which neither wins; in the course of their vocal combat, however, they create a poem and a cultured people.

400. Gary H. Gossen draws the same conclusion in his "To Speak With a Heated Heart: Chamula Canons of Style and Good Performance," in Richard Bauman and Joel Sherzer, eds., *Explorations in the Ethnography of Speaking* (London, 1974), pp. 389–416. "[F]rom the point of view of performative efficacy the structure of the entire recursive recitation may be seen as an iconic analogue of the cycles of creations of the cosmic order in their temporal and spatial regularity and cumulative effect" (p. 416).

CHAPTER 8

1. Fulop, "Aspectos: Cosmogonía," p. 114.

2. There exists an abundant cross-cultural literature on death. Some works are cited in this chapter, but no exhaustive account of the comparative materials is attempted. Cultural studies increasingly demonstrate the powerful sweep and value of symbolic aspects of death that heretofore were quickly passed over. Examples of such study are Louis-Vincent Thomas, *Cinq essais sur la morte africaine* (Dakar, Senegal, 1968), and *Anthropologie de la morte* (Paris, 1980); Olof Pettersson, *Jabmek and Jabmeaimo; A Comparative Study of the Dead and of the Realm of the Dead in Lappish Religion* (Lund, 1957); and a series of articles by Jacques Lemoine: "L'Initiation du mort chez les Hmong. I. Le Chemin," *H* 12 (1972): 105–134; "L'Initiation du mort chez les Hmong. II. Les Thèmes," *H* 12 (1972): 85–125; and "Culte des ancêtres et réincarnation offensive," *H* 13 (1973): 147–150. Other good examples of such study are Jeannine Koubi, *Rambu solo', "la fumée descend." Le Culte des Morts chez les Toradja du Sud* (Paris, 1982); Elizabeth P. Benson, ed., *Death and the Afterlife in Pre-Columbian America* (Washington, D.C.,

1975); Thomas O'Shaughnessey, *Mohammed's Thoughts on Death* (Leiden, 1969); Frank E. Reynolds and Earle H. Waugh, eds., *Religious Encounters with Death: Insights from the History and Anthropology of Religions* (University Park, Penn., 1977); Georges Bataille, *Death and Sensuality: A Study of Eroticism and the Taboo* (New York, 1977).

3. For example, several Boróro myths illustrate that, at the beginning, death was never a final condition but a reversible end. See Albisetti and Venturelli, *Enciclopédia Boróro*, vol. 2, *Lendas e antropônimos*, pp.1019–1115.

4. Reichel-Dolmatoff, *Amazonian Cosmos*, pp. 35–36.

5. Mothers are not the only sources of regenerative life who experience the first death. Fruit and fathers are often the signs of regenerative life whose consumption or fall signals death. According to the Kaingáng, for instance, death originated in the world when the father of Pathí, a supernatural being who cleared the paths for the wandering ancestors when they first danced their way across the world, climbed a tree in search of food for his son. The father fell and died (Henry, *Jungle People*, p. 151).

6. Bartolomé, "Shamanism among the Avá-Chiripá," p. 114. Today the Chiripá shaman carries the soul of each newborn child to the moon for inspection. The moon chooses a suitable name for the child based on the child's image and reveals it to the shaman. Every human being continues to be mortal because the moon continues to preside over their sonic structure, the fundamentally periodic mode of organized presence in the world. See discussion in chapter 5, above.

7. Civrieux, *Watunna*, pp. 21–22.

8. Ibid., p. 23.

9. Ibid., p. 25. In many communities in South America, specific sounds, especially the calls of birds, serve as omens of death. The Araucanians, for example, contended that the *mero* bird *(Dasycephala livida)* made a sound that announced to the community the impending death of one of its members; see José Toribio Medina, *Los Aborígenes de Chile* (Santiago, Chile, 1952), pp. 239, 259–269. Sounds are also frequently identified as the original cause of death.

10. Civrieux, *Watunna*, pp. 27, 163ff.

11. Antonio Colbacchini and Cesar Albisetti, *Os Boróros orientais Orarimogodógue do Planalto Oriental de Mato Grosso* (São Paulo, 1942), pp. 233–235. The myth was republished in German translation in Herbert Baldus, ed., *Die Jaguarzwillingen: Mythen und Heilbringergeschichten, Ursprungssagen und Märchen brasilianischer Indianer* (Eisenach, 1958), pp. 64–67.

12. Villas Boas and Villas Boas, *Xingu*, pp. 55–56.

13. See chapter 2 of this work for a discussion of the birth of symbolic order from the fragments of destruction or from the residue and vestiges (spatial, temporal, sonic, etc.) remaining after the withdrawal of primordial beings.

14. Wilbert, *Folk Literature of the Selknam Indians*, pp. 23–25.

15. Ibid., p. 37.

16. See chapter 2 on the origins of symbolic existence through the destruction or withdrawal of primordial reality (raising the sky, dismemberment of monsters, dismissal of prepotent and plenipotential beings such as the jaguar). The supernaturals of the mythic worlds were the only fully manifest meanings; they were, exhaustively and uniquely, what they appeared to be.

17. Wright, "History and Religion of the Baniwa," p. 390.

18. Saake, "Mythen über Inapirikuli," p. 269.

19. Bórmida, "Ayoreo Myths," p. 6.

20. For example, the choice between a banana and a stone.

21. "In the beginning there was only Mavutsinim. No one lived with him. He had no wife. He had no son, nor did he have any relatives. He was all alone"(Villas Boas and Villas Boas, *Xingu*, p. 53). For a set of commandments that are quite different from the examples that follow but that instantiate the connection of disobeying commands, death's origins, and regenerative life of food crops, see Zerries and Schuster, *Mahekodotedi*, Vol. 2, pp. 276ff., which presents Yanoama commandments and interprets them in terms of subsistence. Karsten, *Civilization of the South American Indians*, pp. 468–497, also details the sorts of commandments that are associated with the origins of death as well as the ritual purifications and confessions that restore a modicum of health and order to the world.

22. Villas Boas and Villas Boas, *Xingu*, p. 55.

23. Ibid., p. 56.

24. Ibid.

25. Ibid.

26. Michel Perrin, *Le Chemin des indiens morts: Mythes et symboles goajiro* (Paris, 1976), p. 42. For further details on ritual lamentations among the Goajiro, see José António Polanco, "Noticias guajiras por un Guajiro: Los Velorios o 'Lloros' (Arapaja y Ayaraja)," *BIV* 3–4 (1956): 197–204.

27. Perrin, *Le Chemin des indiens morts*, p. 43. For treatment of the "Orpheus" motif in South America, see Maria Susana Cipolletti, "Motivo del Orfeo y el viaje al reino de los muertos en América del Sur," *Indiana* 9 (1984): 421–431. The issue was also treated in the section on psychopomps in chapter 7.

28. Even the term *disobedience*, an English word used to express a theme figuring prominently in origin of death myths, appeals to sonic imagery. In its Latin root (from *oboedire*, "to listen to") "disobedience" means to give an effective sign of not listening to a sound (literally, to hear incorrectly; to listen in a distorted way; or to be unwilling or unable to listen effectively).

29. Wilbert, *Folk Literature of the Yamana Indians*, pp. 58–61.

30. Johannes Wilbert and Karin Simoneau, eds., *Folk Literature of the Mataco Indians* (Los Angeles, 1982), p. 79.

31. Ibid., p. 89.

32. Ibid., p. 90.

33. See chapter 4, above, for a discussion of ceremonial dialogue and parliamentary speech procedures based on mythic models in which oppugnant speech resulted in creation and death.

34. Johannes Wilbert, ed., *Folk Literature of the Gê Indians*, vol. 1 (Los Angeles, 1978), pp. 172–175.

35. Ibid., p. 174.

36. Ibid. See also Nimuendajú, *The Apinaye*, p. 156.

37. See chapter 5 (including especially note 304) on sound during the transitions of human growth (i.e., the sonic constitution of the person), and on sound's role in initiation, see chapter 6, above. Regarding deliberate markers of controlled transition of time, see chapter 4.

38. Wilbert, *Folk Literature of the Warao Indians*, p. 192, transcribes the text recorded by Basilio Maria de Barral, *Guarao Guarata lo que Cuentan los Indios Guaraos* (Caracas, 1959), p. 149; see also C. H. de Goeje, "The Inner Structure of the Warao Language of Guiana," *JSAP* 22 (1930): 66–72.

39. Basilio de Barral, *Guarao A-Ribu: Literatura de los indios guaraos* (Caracas, 1969), p. 158.

40. Wilbert, *Folk Literature of the Warao Indians*, p. 98. A quite different myth recounting the origin of death also links it to female reproductive physiology. It also associates the origin of death with the curse of a primordial being (as was the powerful and mortal curse of the father of the water spirit). In this variant a boy sees the earth-world when he penetrates the floor of the sky with an arrow. Contrary to instructions, pregnant women try to lower themslves to earth and follow the young boy on his expedition. The boy's older brother curses them with mortality. Then the hole between the sky and earth closes forever (ibid., p. 310–311).

41. Ibid., p. 193. The Warao are not the only South Americans to link the openness of female reproductive physiology with sound and the origins of death. For the Tukuna, death originated when a young girl, going through the seclusion period of her puberty festival, made a mistake by answering the wrong call. She invited into her cell the spirit of old age rather than the spirit of immortality. The old age spirit stripped off his own skin and, after stripping off the girl's skin in the same way, he coated her with the shriveled and wrinkling complexion of the aged. Then old age, newly rejuvenated, whistled sharply through his fingers so that the girl remained a decrepit old woman, who would die irreversibly. Curt Nimuendajú, *The Tukuna*, ed. Robert H. Lowie, trans. William D. Hohenthal (Berkeley and Los Angeles, 1952), p. 135.

42. André-Marcel d'Ans, *Le Dit des vrais hommes*, pp. 146–157; the final citation is from p. 157.

43. Chapter 5, above, discussed the negative aspects of a self-consciousness produced through the two symbolic processes of alienation (the maintenance of symbolic boundaries separating inside from outside, what can be ingested or excreted from what cannot, what can be done from

what cannot) and metamorphosis (the symbolic reunification or reidentification of the self-aware one with formerly alienated modes of being through transformation and transmutation). The point made here is that the experience of being centered in a web of negative relations underlies self-consciousness, a mode of being well suited to symbolic existence.

44. The relationship between symbolic existence and the finite existence that comes into being with the end of the primordium is discussed in chapter 2.

45. As is made clear in the treatment of each topic in this volume, the specific meanings of each community's actions, nuanced and creative in each setting, disclose themselves in the context of each culture. No effort is made to study exhaustively the specifics of any single cultural speech as, for example, in Karl-Heinz Plitek, *Totenkult der Ge und Bororo* (Hohenschäftlarn, 1978). The attempt is to appraise a mode of discourse, the religiousness of symbolic life in South America. For a glimpse at the range of customs, see Hannes Stubbe, "Zum Trauerverhalten der südamerikanischen Indianer," *Ethnologia Americana* (Düsseldorf) 17 (1981): 977–981.

46. Chapter 5, above, discusses some of the temporal, spatial, and sonic elements which constitute the person and presents ways in which the composition of the person is constantly rearranged to produce transition through the physical stages of the life-cycle through the process of knowledge.

47. Barandiarán, *Introducción . . . ye'kuaná-makiritare*, pp. 961–962. Regarding the abandonment of the dead, including the destruction of their goods and the leaving of the village where they once lived, see Ricardo E. Latcham, *Costumbres mortuorias de los indios de Chile y otras partes de América* (Santiago, Chile, 1915), pp. 8ff., 23ff.

48. Chapter 6, above, discusses the controlled movement of symbolic items (food, sweat, blood, semen, urine, feces, tears, hair, vomit, smoke, sound, etc.) in and out of the body in the processes of life-sustaining and growthful transition.

49. Carneiro da Cunha, *Os Mortos e os outros*, pp. 10–11.

50. The curer uses the *khôt*, a tobacco-pipe that has the "light of a star," to smoke himself into a trance during which he falls "dead" beside the "dead" body of the sick person. Their two souls then journey together, eventually returning home from the village of the *mekarō*. "When the curer moves his foot, the dead one moves his foot . . . when the curer opens his eyes, the dead person opens their eyes" (ibid., p. 11).

51. Maria Carneiro da Cunha, "Espace funeraire, eschatologie et culte des ancêtres: Encore le problème des paradigmes africains," in *ICA*, 42d Congress, vol. 2 (Paris, 1976), p. 283. Carneiro da Cunha argues that, whereas the Krahó once followed the custom of a double burial, over the course of recent history the handling of the cadaver has been condensed and relocated. She forwards the hypothesis that the body was first deposited in a space quite close to the maternal home, perhaps even within the maternal home (ibid., p. 284). Later, there took place a second burial in which the bones, painted and decorated, were interred either in the plaza of the village or in the maternal domestic space (ibid.).

52. For a discussion of sound as an effective sign of passage and of the excretion of one mode of being into another see chapter 5.

53. Nimuendajú, *Mitos de creación*, p. 57.

54. Ibid., pp. 57–58.

55. C. Onelli, *Trepando los Andes* (Buenos Aires, 1904), p. 149; cited in Siffredi, "Hierofanías y concepciones mítico-religiosas de los Tehuelches meridionales," p. 267.

56. Maybury-Lewis, *Akwē-Shavante Society*, p. 276–277.

57. Karsten, *Toba Indians*, pp. 51, 91.

58. Don de M. le Marquis de Wavrin, "Simples notes sur la tribu des Jívaro," *BSAB* 4 (1930): 6–7.

59. The Selk'nam inquiry into the circumstances and causes of death is described in Gusinde, *Los Indios de Tierra del Fuego. Los Selk'nam*, vol. 2, pp. 518–521. For a description of the Krahó inquest and its connection to the significance of space (the space of the territorial world as well as the cadaver, the space of a person), see Carneiro da Cunha, *Mortos e os outros*, pp. 14–19.

60. Henry, *Jungle People*, p. 93.

61. Ibid., p. 21.

62. Ibid., p. 31.

63. Consequently, the living ask ghosts to depart (ibid., p. 67). These ghost-souls are remembered in a special way during honey-beer drinking feasts (p. 69).

64. Ibid., p. 80–81.

65. José Maria Cruxent, "Hallazgo de vasijas funerárias en el Rio Vigirimita (Guacara.-Edo. Carabobo)," *Acta Venezolana* (Caracas) 3 (1948): 138–141. He is unable to date the period in question. Even where graves are more elaborate and their history better known, they testify only in an obscure way to the meaning they held for mourners and undertakers. Archaeology offers countless cases. From 1945 to 1950, for instance, Peruvian investigators explored some 1,570 ancient tombs in one district. See the detailed reports of twenty-eight of these burial sites in Rogger Ravines, "Prácticas funerárias en Ancón," *RMN* 43 (1977): 327–396. The reports reconstruct the physical disposition of cadavers, clothing, wraps and bundles, grave-goods, offerings, and art objects. What remains ungathered is the world of meaning in which those who made the graves lived. Francisco L. Cornely, *Cultura diaguita chilena y cultura de el Molle* (Santiago, Chile, 1966) offers ample descriptions of archaeological materials from Diaguita burial, especially of the "El Olivar" cemetery, a group of some twenty burial sites found two kilometers north of La Serena (pp. 68–86). Most fascinating is the report of six burial sites from what Cornely calls El Molle culture, not far from La Serena (pp. 179–222). The elaborate placement of colored stones, arranged by size and color in the form of two circles, flanks the grave. The head of the corpse is oriented to the east in a grave containing pottery, smoking pipes, copper bracelets and rings, and so on. Cornely has been unable to date the El Molle finds. The same opacity cloaks the religious meaning of ancient life-taking weapons; see, for example, Ernesto Salazar, *Talleres prehistóricos en los altos Andes del Ecuador* (Cuenca, Ecuador, 1980). On archaic weapons and grave-goods outside the Andes, see Peter Paul Hilbert, *Archäologische Untersuchungen am mittleren Amazonas* (Berlin, 1968); or *Catalogo de Colección Vela (Prehistoria Americana)* (Valencia, 1964).

66. Chapter 5 discusses the way in which the human body, with self-controlled symbolic passages, proves to be the proper enclosure for human life; chapter 6, under women's initiation, presents several images and meanings of the cocoon of culture itself which helps to apprehend and, therefore, contain change and dissolution. For a list of various kinds of containers in which groups in South America bury the dead, see Latcham, *Costumbres mortuorias*, pp. 31ff., which describes the coffins, baskets, canoes, boxes, and urns of various kinds. Pages 245ff. describe the way groups in Chile (Conchales, Changos, Atacameños, and others) dispose of the dead in wells, trenches, or stone cists. Each culture may offer a range of symbolic vehicles for ritual passage at death. For detailed descriptions of the manifold types of Jívaro funerary enclosures (e.g., burial inside an abandoned house, beer-brewing jar or cooking pot, two vessels sealed with clay, *chonta*-palm-stave covering, bamboo-splint wrappers, hollowed-out balsa logs), see Harner, *The Jívaro*, pp. 166ff. Even in the case of platform burial, the corpse is heavily adorned with new kilt, necklaces, paint, weapons or tools, and so on.

67. Agostinho, *Kwarìp*, p. 50.

68. Ibid., p. 50 and pp. 161ff., as well as Agostinho, "Estudo preliminar sobre o mito de origens xinguano. Comentario a uma variante awetì," *Universitas: Revista de cultura da Universidade Federal da Bahia* 6–7 (1970): 494–497, 512–513. Regarding the myths of Kwat and Yaì, see Agostinho, *Mitos e outros narrativas kamayurá* (Bahia, 1974), esp. texts nos. 1–8.

69. The relation of hands to death warrants special study. The motifs of "in manus tuas, domine . . ." and of death taking one by the hand (e.g., in dance or in sexual seduction) deserve to be seen as instances of the imagery of transformative enclosure.

70. Until this point, when the individual's personal effects are abandoned, the Guayakí burial rite is like most Guaraní funeral rites. However, the removal and destruction of the skull (by smashing it with hunting bows) and the consumption of the flesh of the dead are features unique to the Guayakí.

71. Medina, *Los Aborígenes de Chile*, pp. 259–269.

72. Agostinho, *Kwarìp*. For reports of other groups in the Xingu area, see Robert Murphy and Buell Quain, *The Trumaí Indians of Central Brazil* (Locust Valley, N.Y., 1955); Kalervo Oberg, *Indian Tribes of Northern Mato Grosso, Brazil* (Washington, D.C., 1953); Roque de Barros Laraia, "O Sol e a lua na mitología xinguana," *RMP* n.s. 17 (1967): 7–36; and Villas Boas and Villas Boas,

Xingu, which provides ample mythical background from several different groups. The range of decoration that the corpse undergoes in South America is described in Latcham, *Costumbres mortuorias,* pp. 131–158. The effort to enclose and occlude the corpse is not limited to its decoration. The Selk'nam corpse is not decorated in any way, neither washed nor combed, nor are the eyes or mouth closed. The body receives no body-painting, not even on the face. Instead, the cadaver is placed inside a circle of upright posts, rather stout trunks of wood. Inside this enclosure, the corpse is stretched out on a hide that is suspended fur-side up. Leather straps are then wound around the posts in such a way as to completely enclose the cadaver. The body itself is bound up with strips of leather. Then another enclosure is built around the first one, lashing the corpse with spirals of leather from head to toe. The feet and face are covered with special care; see Gusinde, *Los Indios de Tierra del Fuego. Los Selk'nam,* vol. 2, pp. 522ff. The ambivalent irony of display and closure in the symbolism of death is brought out when the corpse is laid out on a platform or catafalque. The body is frequently *covered over* while it is "on display." See Latcham, *Costumbres mortuorias,* pp. 31–54.

73. Agostinho uses the term *morerekwat* generically to refer to both men and women, although, strictly speaking, women who are direct descendants of the lineage in which the hereditary authority of the *morerekwat* descends are called *noitu,* or *morerekwara Kunyā* (Agostinho, *Kwarìp,* pp. 27, 31).

74. Villas Boas and Villas Boas, *Xingu,* p. 268.

75. Strictly speaking, then, funeral rites form the preparatory stage for the *Kwarìp* only in the cases of the death of leaders in the hereditary group.

76. There are several different kinds of graves. A single hole may be dug in the ground and the body may be placed in it, feet first, in a vertical position. Alternately, depending on the status of the person being buried and the practices and mythic traditions of the community, two holes may be dug, a tunnel made underground between them, and the corpse suspended in a net in the middle of the tunnel in a seated position. The net is suspended from two posts set vertically inside the two holes. There is a suggestion that the mythical twins killed a mythical toad in this way, suspending it with its belly down. For the various kinds of burial and the mythic foundations underlying them, see Oberg, *Indian Tribes of Northern Mato Grosso, Brazil,* p. 68, cited in Agostinho, *Kwarìp,* pp. 46–47.

77. Agostinho points out that his information on the first part (the funeral rituals) of the Kwarìp is based entirely on interviews, since he was never present at a death or funeral (ibid., p. 45).

78. Gertrude E. Dole, "Endocannibalism among the Amahuaca Indians," in Lyon, *Native South Americans,* pp. 302–308.

79. For example, the Tehuelche cadaver, together with special weapons and ornaments, was wrapped in the hide of a young colt. Pressed into a fetal position with some of the upper vertebrae of its spinal column exposed, the body was carried by two women to a grave dug by two men. They put water in the grave with the body, which faced the mountain range, and covered everything with earth. During the following year, mourners, clad only in white clothing, visited the grave every two weeks. The meaning of these many enclosures only comes to light in the full scope of Tehuelche religious life. See Onelli, *Trepando los Andes,* p. 149, cited in Siffredi, "Hierofanías y concepciones mítico-religiosas de los Tehuelches meridionales," pp. 268–269. For a survey of the types of body-wrappings found in Andean graves, see Vicente Norero, "El Culto de los muertos entre las poblaciones aborígenes de la costa ecuadoriana," *TA* 2 (1966–1967): 5–9. For a sample of the kinds of symbolic containers in some Brazilian burials, see Charles Frederik Hartt, "The Indian Cemetery of the Gruta das Mumias, Southern Minas Geraes, Brazil," *American Naturalist* 9 (1875): 205–217. Georg Eckert, *Totenkult und Lebensglaube im Caucatal,* (Braunschweig, 1948) collects the history of burial practices among some nineteen groups (see map, p. 57) of the Cauca valley, lying between the western and central cordilleras of Colombia. He contends that the material surrounding the cadaver represents, in each case, a specific "kind of transfiguration" related to the particular symbolism employed (p. 17, 28ff. and passim).

80. Whitten, *Sacha Runa,* p. 138.

81. Roe, *Cosmic Zygote,* p. 116.

82. Ibid.

83. Henry, *Jungle People*, p. 181.

84. Ibid., p. 107.

85. Ibid., p. 184.

86. Mario Califano, "El Concepto de enfermedad y muerte entre los Mataco-costañeros," *SE* 2 (1974): 32–73, provides the most penetrating analysis of the comprehensive fear that "centers one's being in the world" (p. 65). The fear that stems from the manifestation of supernatural forms, notoriously visible in sickness and death, affects Mataco concepts of shape (and morphology in general), smell, color, sound, temperature, sex, hierarchy and space (pp. 61–65). Fear of this sort is an existential structure. Califano's explication is bound up with close examination of Mataco language for sickness and well-being as it describes the situation of *noésl* (human being) confronting *wichi* and *ajat*, two polar aspects of the sacred.

87. Weiss, "World of a Forest Tribe," p. 431.

88. Ibid.

89. Ibid., p. 433.

90. Ibid.

91. Ibid., p. 434.

92. Ibid.

93. Ibid.

94. Ibid., p. 442.

95. Ibid.

96. The ideas presented in this section on overcoming the chaotic ambivalence of total states through the rending of differences are elaborations of themes discussed in chapter 2, above, on the origins of the differential orders of symbolic life through sacrificial acts of division and separation.

97. Orestes Araujo, *Etnología salvaje, historia de los Charrúas y de mas tribus indígenas del Uruguay* (Montevideo, 1911), pp. 95–100.

98. Holmberg, *Nomads of the Long Bow*, p. 88.

99. Siffredi, "Hierofanías y concepciones mítico-religiosas de los Tehuelches meridionales," pp. 268–269.

100. Holmberg, *Nomads of the Long Bow*, p. 87. The last words of a good Siriono hunter are treasured. The last sounds often have special value. Regarding the last words of the Krahó dying person, for example, see Carneiro da Cunha, *Mortos e os outros*, pp. 19ff.

101. Holmberg, *Nomads of the Long Bow*, p. 87.

102. Ibid., p. 89.

103. The contest is not always manifest as a competition between teams or individuals. At times the contestants compete with unseen forces present in images of death (sleep, fatigue). In keeping vigil, for example, participants must fight off sleep; marathon dancers must fight off exhaustion. Female mourners among the Sanemá-Yanoama, for instance, must take on both these images of death when they dance the night away during the funeral.

104. Whitten, *Sacha Runa*, p. 136.

105. Whitten (ibid.) cites ethnographic parallels and archaeological evidence.

106. In other cultures' versions of this game, the canoe (which the Canelos Quichua refer to as *aya tullu*, "soul-bone") is called a *huairu*. This information helps enrich a pattern that exists here and elsewhere relating the long bones-canoe-tree-cayman (bench-flute) as vehicles of the soul. Here we see the ironic juxtaposition, tragic-comic as the funeral game, of the durable "stone-like" vehicle of the soul opposed to the rotting "food" vehicle of the mortal being. See Whitten, *Sacha Runa*, pp. 136–137 and 140.

107. Ibid., p. 137.

108. Ibid.

109. Ibid., p. 138.

110. For a collection of sources, interpretations, and explanations of the manner in which the game was played, see Roswith Hartmann and Udo Oberem, "Beiträge zum 'Huairu-Spiel,'" *ZFE* 93 (1968): 240–259.

111. In this regard, see the lengthy descriptions of Selk'nam lamentations in Gusinde, *Los Indios de Tierra del Fuego. Los Selk'nam*, vol. 2, pp. 529–539.

112. Lucrecia Vidal Arias, *Oro para el Rescate: Costumbres, cuentos, anécdotas, supersticiones y leyendas de la Provincia de Pataz* (Lima, 1979).

113. Carneiro de Cunha, *Os Mortos e os outros*, p. 26.

114. Ibid., pp. 26–29.

115. Ibid., p. 32.

116. Similar noise and musical contestation accompanies Krahó initiation rites. Cf. ibid.

117. Otto Zerries, "Algunas noticias etnológicas acerca de los indígenas Puinave," *BIV* 9 (1964): 33–34.

118. Ibid. Zerries calls attention to reports of similar funeral games played during wakes for the dead in which a "blind man," impersonating the dead person, attempts to grab mourners, thus recruiting new victims from among the living. See Rafael Karsten, "Zeremonielle Spiele unter den Indianern Südamerikas," *Acta Academiae Aboensis Humaniora* (Abo) 1 (1920): 92–94. Zerries also alludes to card games played in front of the mortuary house (p. 34). Because the dead person is a participant in the game; strangers and foreigners — people not related closely to the dead person — are invited to sit in on the game to stave off death for the relatives.

119. This information is provided by Carl Gustav Izikowitz, "Rhythmical Aspects of Canella Life," *ICA*, 31st Congress (São Paulo, 1955), p. 207.

120. Carneiro da Cunha, *Os Mortos e os outros*, p. 60. Melatti witnessed four funerals during his visits with the Krahó and describes the symbolic actions in some detail in *Ritos de uma tribo timbira*, pp. 106–114.

121. Carneiro da Cunha, ibid., p. 70.

122. Ibid., p. 67.

123. Ibid., p. 71. The last supper of the Krahó soul of the dead is described in Melatti, *Ritos de uma tribo timbira*, pp. 114ff. There is some doubt as to how healthy it is for participants to partake of the meal (p. 116).

124. Carneiro da Cunha, *Os Mortos e os outros*, p. 145.

125. Ibid., p. 143.

126. Ibid., p. 145.

127. Hélène Clastres, "Rites funeraires guayakí," *JSAP* 62 (1968): 72. J. Christopher Crocker, "The Social Organization of the Eastern Boróro," (Ph.D. diss., Harvard University, 1967), pp. 152–154 and p. 120, n. 1. The coastal Tupinambá materials are found in Hélène Clastres, "Les Beaux-frères ennemis. À propos du cannibalisme tupinambá," *Nouvelle revue du psychanalyse* (1972): p. 73. All cited in Carneiro da Cunha, *Os Mortos e os outros*, pp. 142–145.

128. Carneiro da Cunha, ibid., pp. 20–21.

129. Gusinde, *Los Indios de Tierra del Fuego. Los Selk'nam*, vol. 1, pp. 417–431.

130. Close relatives of the dead person usually carry on a different style of mourning. Holding her dead husband's bamboo container against her heart, a widow weeps over it, imploring her husband to arrive and take his quiver of arrows from her. She falls on the cadaver and appeals to the dead man to go hunting. Similarly, the father of a dead child implores it to go and play with the tiny arrows and bow he has made for it. "Wake up!" pleaded one father. Barandiarán points out that the speeches of this kind are formulaic.

131. The Kwarìp ceremonies that are allowed to take place after the death of an important chief or blood relative of the chief are timed to coincide with certain cosmic rhythms, including the abundance of fish and the season of *pequi* chestnuts. The coordination with the chestnut season is particularly complicated since the chestnuts in question must be gathered as the fruit matures during the rainy season following an individual's death (the "fruit of death" gathered during the "time of Kwarìp"). The chestnuts are gathered during a ritual trek. The *caryocar* tree is cultivated for its large, grapefruit-sized fruit, which becomes a staple during the first part of the rainy season. The trees can reach a height of 50 feet. Inside, an oily pulp surrounds the kidney-shaped seed, from which oil can be taken. In this case, however, the seeds are extracted, dried, and kept for many months until the end of the following dry season, when the Kwarìp ceremonies may be held. At that time, the seeds may be split open and the kernels eaten. The entire fruit is actually a ritual item, from its planting, to its gathering, to its processing and use. The oil extracted from the pulp becomes the base for body paints used in ceremonies; see Agostinho, *Kwarìp*, pp. 42–43. See also Villas Boas and Villas Boas, *Xingu*, pp. 262–263. The timing of the ritual

gathering and preparation of the *pequi* chestnuts means that the Kwarìp festivals are held at least a year after a person's death.

132. Barandiarán, "Vida y muerte," p. 30.

133. Ibid., pp. 30–31. For another version of the Yanoama origins of death myth, see Zerries and Schuster, *Mahekodotedi*, vol. 2, pp. 66f.

133. Barandiarán, "Vida y muerte," p. 31.

135. Ibid.

136. Contestation may be a helpful context in which to consider certain tit-for-tat practices of revenge. The *lex talonis* that evens the score with death by exacting the proverbial eye for an eye and tooth for a tooth fits the contestatory mode of symbolic behavior treated here. For example, the death of a Waiwai person is almost always considered due to magical "blowing" by an enemy. Blowing sends a magical, fluidlike substance (similar to that of the soul) into an intended victim. Evil is blown by making animal sounds and by singing magical songs that project the deadly process into the victim. When a person dies, a relative, obliged to respond in kind, must perform *parawa*, revenge blowing. In that way, no individual's death is absolutely final.

137. Purification rites at funerals, like contests, cut through the contrariety associated with irreversible mortality. They sort out the opposing attributes of existence, which overrun one another at death. By refactoring a confused state into the separate categories of an ordered existence, purification leads the community through chaos to its proper place in the cosmos. The coexistence of opposites that occurs at death is not limited to social or cognitive planes. For that reason purification addresses every level of experience. To achieve this end, purification employs images of total catastrophe. In particular, symbolic fire, flood, and cutting redivide the qualities of being that fuse homogeneously with one another in the experience of death. As they did in the beginning, images of destruction sweep the total and, therefore, overwhelming manifestations of sacred beings from the world. For an example of the imagery of fire (and charcoal), water (for washing, for beer, and for body-paint), and cutting (of ferns, hair, and nails) in funerary purification aimed at cleansing the world of the deceased's *nyanggli* ("dirt," as in unclean and forbidden food) and frightening away the *kuplêng* (deceased soul), see Ursula Wiesemann, "Purification Among the Kaingáng Indians Today," *ZFE* 95 (1970): 104–114. The widow is cleansed so that her dead husband will no longer recognize her; that is, she is destroyed and remade in a new image, covered with feathers. For a different kind of purification, the seven years of Egun rites which deliver a Candomblé cult-house and its community from the power of death associated with their decreased cult leader (*pai-de-santo* or *babalorisha* if male; *mãe-de-santo* or *iyalorisha* if female), see Melville J. Herskovitz, "The Social Organization of the Candomblé," *ICA*, 31st Congress (São Paulo, 1955), pp. 505–532, esp. pp. 510–511. For a discussion that places Yanoama revenge and other restrictions surrounding mourning and funerals in the context of other forms of aggressive contestation (chest-pounding duels, club fights, the capture of women, open warfare, musical battles with hymns, and so on), see Zerries and Schuster, *Mahekodotedi*, vol. 2, pp. 215–225. For details on Jívaro practices of revenge, feud, war and their religious underpinnings as manifest in the taking of a trophy head and the celebration of the *tsantsa* festival *(numpeng)*, see Harner, *The Jívaro*, pp. 170–193, esp. pp. 146f. It is interesting that revenge and acts of symbolic consumption lead toward involvement in political and economic systems since the *tsantsa* is commonly later sold by the head-taker (although illegally according to Ecuadorian law) to a *mestizo* in one of the communities on the western periphery of the tribal territory (p. 146). For a consideration of the links that the Boróro establish between death, vengeance, and occultation as definitive forms of closure, see Albisetti and Venturelli, *Enciclopédia Boróro*. vol. 1, *Vocabularios e etnografía*, p. 71 (*ána* and *anági*), 270ff. (*bí*, "death"; *bía*, "occultation"; etc.), and 834ff. (*ókwa*, "occultation, absence, loss, death").

138. Roswith Hartmann, "Creencias acerca de las Almas de los Difuntos en la región de Otavalo/Ecuador," *EZ* special Suppl. no. 1 (1974): 201–227. See also Hartmann, "Conmemoración de muertos en la Sierra Ecuatoriana," *I* 1 (1973): 179–197.

139. Hartmann, "Creencias," p. 202.

140. Ibid., pp. 203–204.

141. Ibid., p. 205. Hartmann draws extensively on Gladys Villavicencio R., *Relaciónes interétnicas en Otavalo-Ecuador* (Mexico City, 1973), esp. pp. 180–188. See also the descriptions of

these rites in Bastien, *Mountain of the Condor*, which describes the Day of the Dead, and interprets the table set for them in the cemetery, the food offerings, feast, and drinking.

142. Medina, *Los Aborígenes de Chile*, pp. 259–269.

143. Catherine Allen Wagner, "Coca, Chicha and Trago: Private and Communal Rituals in a Quechua Community" (Ph.D. diss., University of Illinois, 1978). For a description of the importance and details of funeral drinking in the Quechua-speaking community of Otavalo, Ecuador, see Anibal Buitron, *Táita Imbabura: Vida indígena en los Andes* (La Paz, Bolivia, 1964), pp. 97–99.

144. Ellen B. Basso, *The Kalapalo Indians of Central Brazil* (New York, 1973), pp. 56ff.

145. Le Marquis de Wavrin, "Simples Notes sur la Tribu des Jívaro," pp. 6–7.

146. Henry, *Jungle People*, p. 182.

147. For descriptions of the first consumptions and their relationship to the chaos that reigned when different qualities of absolute being manifested themselves totally, see chapter 2. That chaos marked the first appearance of real change.

148. Lévi-Strauss, *La Potière jalouse*, surveys the range of chthonic sacralities in the forms of earth, mud, slime, soil, clay, and so on. Latcham, *Costumbres mortuorias*, pp. 159–178, provides an overview of the kinds of inhumation in South America.

149. Carneiro da Cunha, *Os Mortos e os outros*, p. 23.

150. Reichel-Dolmatoff, "Notas sobre el simbolismo religioso de los Indios de la Sierra Nevada de Santa Marta," pp. 55–72. Both the Kogi and Ika descend from the ancient Chibcha-speaking Tairona of the Sierra Nevada area of Colombia.

151. Reichel-Dolmatoff, "Funerary Customs and Religious Symbolism Among the Kogi," p. 292.

152. Ibid., p. 293.

153. Ibid., p. 294.

154. Ibid., p. 297.

155. Ibid., p. 298.

156. Ibid.

157. Ibid., p. 299.

158. For a survey of cremation practices throughout the Amerindian populations, see Latcham, *Costumbres mortuorias*, pp. 179–246.

159. Weiss, "World of a Forest Tribe," p. 435. Cremation is not the only way Campas dispose of a corpse. One Campa informed Weiss that they bury a corpse so that it faces the setting sun. Apparently, the sun acts as a psychopomp and carries off the dead person's soul (ibid., p. 443).

160. Fock, *Waiwai*, p. 163.

161. Fock contends that the Waiwai once covered the bones with a large clay vessel, as is now the case in the cremation of children (ibid., p. 164).

162. Henry, *Jungle People*, p. 186.

163. Ibid., p. 187.

164. Ibid., p. 184; see also p. 187.

165. Barandiarán, "Vida y muerte," pp. 28–29.

166. Ibid., p. 32.

167. Daniel de Barandiarán, "Mundo espiritual y shamanismo sanemá," *ACAR*, 15 (1965): p. 4.

168. Medina, *Los Aborígenes de Chile*, pp. 259–269.

169. This fire purification ceremony, Koyadänattí, plays an important part in the ceremonial rites preventing and curing diseases in women. It appears to be based on the myth of emergence of the first Toba man from the earth. As soon as he emerged he took a brand of fire from the cosmic conflagration that had destroyed the world and carried it to all parts of the inhabited earth. Karsten, *Toba Indians*, pp. 104–106.

170. As a result, according to Karsten's report, the Toba prefer to kill young children who become seriously ill, dispatching them with a blow from a club (ibid., pp. 40–41). The Choroti kill old men by shooting them with an arrow. Then they destroy their property. If an old man should die a natural death, "he will be changed into an evil demon who will rage in the village and kill the whole people." Karsten adds that evil spirits among the Choroti have the shape of old men just as among the Toba the harmful spirits look like young boys (ibid.).

171. Perrin, *Le Chemin des indiens morts*, p. 186.

172. Nimuendajú, *The Apinayé*, p. 150.

173. Ibid., p. 146.

174. Ibid., pp. 35–36, 151.

175. Ibid., p. 153.

176. Ibid.

177. Carneiro da Cunha, *Os Mortos e os outros*, pp. 40–41. See Melatti, *Ritos de uma tribo timbira*, pp. 114–118, for a consideration of the Krahó ceremonial offering of food, which definitively locates the decreased in the realm of the dead, and Carneiro da Cunha, *Os Mortos e os outros*, pp. 95–111. See also Audrey J. Butt, "Secondary Urn Burial Among the Akawaio of British Guiana," *TMHR* (Georgetown) 37 (1958): 74–88.

178. Pierre Clastres, "Guayakí Cannibalism," in Lyon, ed., *Native South Americans*, p. 309.

179. Ibid., pp. 309–310.

180. Neil L. Whitehead, "Carib Cannibalism. The Historical Evidence," *JSAP* 70 (1984): 81.

181. Ibid. Regarding connections between images of cannibalism and the fear of colonials, see Michael Taussig, *Shamanism, Colonialism, and the Wild Man: A Study in Terror and Healing* (Chicago, 1987), esp. pp. 104ff.

182. Clastres provides basic data and definitions often used to discuss these issues: (1) *exocannibalism* is the practice of consuming roasted flesh, but not the bones, of an enemy; (2) *endocannibalism* is the consumption of the pulverized bone or bone ashes of dead relatives, in the form of a liquid drink that is frequently a fermented beverage; (3) the two practices appear to exclude one another; see Clastres, "Ethnographie des indiens guayakí," *JSAP* 57 (1968): 34. In general, I avoid the term *cannibalism*. The term *cannibal* derives from Carib (or Caniba) peoples, as seen by French and Spanish explorers; cf. Alexander von Humboldt, *Personal Narrative of Travels to the Equinoctial Regions of America during the Years 1799–1804* (London, 1852–1853), vol. 3, p. 214, and Roque Barcia, *Primer diccionario general etimológico de la lengua española* (Madrid, 1881–1883). The notion of cannibalism is linked to the religious response of Europeans to utterly strange, unknown realms. The word awakens a range of meanings particular to the mythology of the New World, the mythic horizon of European cultures in the age of discovery and imperial expansion, and it conjures up imagery that dislocates or obscures the South American meanings of disposing of the dead through ingestion. Regarding the mutual exclusiveness of the two ingestive practices, Zerries cites some possible exceptions: the Cocama, the Maué and the Tapajo. See Zerries, "El Endocanibalismo," pp. 143f. P. Clastres suggests that the Guayakí are also an important exception: see "Ethnographie des indiens guayakí," p. 34.

183. In addition to works cited in the following discussion (and appearing in their bibliographies), the following studies plot the distribution of ingesting flesh as a means of disposing of the dead in South America and elsewhere: Hermann Schaaffhausen, "Die Menschenfresserei und das Menschenopfer," *Archiv für Anthropologie* (Braunschweig) 4 (1870): 245–286; Richard Andrée, *Die Anthropophagie. Eine ethnographische Studie* (Leipzig, 1887); Rudolf S. Steinmetz, "Endokannibalismus," *MAGW* 26 (1896): 1–60 of which pp. 15–19 deal with South America; Theodor Koch-Grünberg, "Die Anthropophagie der südamerikanischen Indianer," *IAE* 12 (1899): 78–110; William Graham Sumner, *Folkways: A Study of the Sociological Importance of Usages, Manners, Customs, Mores, and Morals* (Boston, 1906); Northcote Whitbridge Thomas, "Cannibalism," in *Encyclopedia Britannica*, 11th ed.; Edwin M. Loeb, "Cannibalism," in *Encyclopedia of the Social Sciences* (New York, 1930); Alfred Métraux, "Warfare, Cannibalism, and Human Trophies," in *HSAI*, vol. 5, pp. 383–409; Florestan Fernandes, "La Guerre et le sacrifice humain chez les Tupinambá," *JSAP* 41 (1952): 139–220. Ewald Volhard, *Kannibalismus* (Stuttgart, 1939), surveys South American practices on pages 334–361. His approach typifies a problem with this literature. He assembles the available information about the mainland Carib and their neighbors (pp. 334–338), Peru (pp. 339–340), the Upper Amazon (pp. 340–350), the Tupí (pp. 350–356), the Ge-speaking peoples (pp. 356–360), and Araucanians (pp. 360–361), briefly dismissing the importance of reports for peoples in Tierra del Fuego (p. 361). These tidbits serve to build an argument for a postagricultural origin of the practices of consuming the dead. There is no attempt at critical checking of the reliability of each source. In some instances, the evidence is quite scanty, indirect, or even circumstantial (e.g., a display of human body parts—

such as fingers—as trophies of war). In any case, Volhard reports on more than 108 groups, plotting their distribution on a map (pp. 336–337). He considers the various Chibcha tribes and their relatives (or those influenced by them) to be most given to the practice of what he calls cannibalism.

184. The meanings of such deaths vary widely. One can apprehend them through the full range of bone and tooth symbolism apparent in myth and rite: the fate of the bones of primordial jaguars, birds, and other beasts; the primordial female with the toothy vagina; in the ceremonial extraction of teeth during initiation; in the ceremonial piercing or scratching with bone instruments; in the use of bones as musical instruments; and so on. Yanomami myths, for example, describe how the jaguar's teeth and voice were altered at the beginning of time. See Jacques Lizot, *El Hombre de la pantorrilla preñada y otros mitos yanomami* (Caracas, 1974), pp. 53ff. The jaguar's teeth become a principal theme in many mythologies throughout South America. He is either hiding them, trading them, or showing them off. The jaguar's conversations with his victims or with those who outwit him often include allusions to his teeth. Jean Pierre Chaumeil, "Echange d'énergie," *JSAP* 71 (1985): 143–158, especially pp. 149–155, connects the symbolism of teeth, especially as viewed in the thought of the Yagua of the Peruvian Amazon, to the imagery of group limits and the boundaries of the territory proper to each species and cultural group: the capture and exchange of human teeth, extraction of the teeth from a deceased chief, taking of teeth in connection with ingestion of the dead, the girdle of teeth worn by warriors at seed-time, the teeth as the seat of vital force, the role of teeth in the exchange and circulation of powers among diverse spatial domains of the universe.

185. In his comparative study, *Civilization of the South American Indians*, Karsten drew the connections between scarifications, mutilations of the body, and ways of coping with death during funerals or mourning as well as death during ceremonies of initiation or rites of passage (pp. 153–197). He also pointed out the widespread connection between death and tattoos (e.g., practiced during mourning, or after the slaying of an enemy, or during puberty initiation, or presentation of the scars of tattoos as part of the examination of the soul on its way to the otherworld after death).

186. See the sources and analysis provided in Whitehead, "Carib Cannibalism," pp. 69–88.

187. See ibid. for a discussion of the relationship between ritually ingesting flesh of slain warriors and political expansion. In her comparative study "Endocannibalism Among the Amahuaca Indians," pp. 302–308, in Lyon, ed., *Native South Americans*, Gertrude Dole alleged that warfare was most intense in areas where communities ingested flesh (p. 307). For the connection between blood sacrifice and political expansion programs see, for example, Alfred Métraux, *The History of the Incas* (New York, 1973), pp. 140ff., and Florestan Fernandes, "A Análise funcionalista de guerra: Possibilidades de aplicacão à sociedade tupinambá. Ensaio de análise crítica da contribuicão etnográfica dos cronistas para o estudo sociológico da guerra entre populacões aborígenes do Brasil seiscentista," *RMP* 3 (1949): 7–128. The question is pursued in a set of studies of Mesoamerican sacrifice in Elizabeth H. Boone, ed., *Ritual Human Sacrifice in Mesoamerica* (Washington, D.C., 1984).

The relationship between forms of sacrifice, ideology, the sacred, disposal of the dead, and the eating of flesh is explored in works that cannot be reviewed here. Recent examples, offering further bibliographic suggestions, are Cristiano Grottanelli, "Cosmogonia e sacrificio. I: Problemi delle cosmogonie 'rituali' nel Rg Veda e nel vicino oriente antico," *Studi Storico Religiosi* 4 (1980): 207–235, and "Cosmogonia e sacrificio. I: Death as the Supreme God's Beloved Son and the Founding Myth of Human Sacrifice," *Studi Storico Religiosi* 5 (1981): 173–196; Bruce Lincoln, "The Indo-European Myth of Creation," *HR* 15 (1975): 121–145, and "The Lord of the Dead," *HR* 20 (1980): 224–241; Bruce Lincoln, "Sacrificio, macellai, e filosofi," *Studi Storici* 25 (1984): 859–874, suggests that the contradictions inherent in ritual sacrifice give rise to speculations and metaphysical systems linked to the specific forms of praxis that political expansion and repression assume; Marcel Détienne and Jean-Pierre Vernant, eds., *La Cucina del sacrificio in terra greca* (Turin, 1982); Walter Burkert, *Homo Necans: The Anthropology of Ancient Greek Sacrificial Ritual and Myth* (Berkeley, 1983), esp. pp. 50ff.; Jonathan Parry, "Sacrificial Death and the Necrophagous Ascetic," in Maurice Bloch and Jonathan Parry, eds., *Death and the Regeneration of Life* (Cambridge, 1982), pp. 74–110, which delineates how blood sacrifice and consumption of flesh are "two opposing ways in which the problems of temporality and man's mortality are handled within Hinduism" (p. 74); Peter Metcalf, *A Borneo Journey into Death: Berawan Eschatology from its Rituals* (Philadelphia, 1982), esp. pp. 90–109, 121–131; and Mircea Eliade, "Mythologies of Death: An Introduction," in Eliade, *Occultism, Witchcraft, and Cultural Fashions: Essays in Comparative Religions* (Chicago, 1976), pp. 32–46, which discusses the mythic choice of consumptive strategies (e.g., stone versus banana) that humans must make when confronting the sacred in the form of the ambivalent images of death and life, which are dialectically related (p. 44). See also the special issue of *L'Uomo* (Rome) 9 (1985), dedicated to the way divisions of meat organize cosmic and social dynamics.

188. Alfred Métraux, "L'Anthropophagie rituelle des Tupinambá," which forms chapter 2 of *Religions et magies indiennes* (pp. 43–78) and which earlier appeared as a part of a *La Religion des Tupinambá et ses rapports avec celle des autres tribus tupí-guaraní.* (Paris, 1928). "Many [prisoners] considered their captors as equal to their relatives. That affection was reciprocal" (*Religion et magies*, p. 51).

189. Ibid.

190. Ibid., p. 52.

191. Ibid.

192. For consideration of ways in which violence underlying a symbolic system passes from overt expressions of consumption of the dead and intertribal warfare to the disguised historical expressions of political economy in the production and consumption of "sacred things," see Mireille Guyot, "La Historia del mar de Danta, el Caqueta: Una fase de la evolución cultural en el noroeste Amazónico," *JSAP* 66 (1979): 99–123. A full treatment of the question of forms of sacrifice, territorial expansion, and the religious evaluation of space should be set in the light of such distinctions as the centripetal and centrifugal images of imperial life evident in foundation myths of urban capitals. For example, a myth told by the common people of Peru, according to the chronicler Garcilaso de la Vega, reports that the first man, the royal *inca* Manco Cápac and his wife, the queen, emerged immediately after the flood at Tiahuanaco, south of Cuzco. Cuzco is a word that means "navel," says the reporter, the place of the cutting of the umbilicus. It was Manco Cápac who "was so powerful that he divided the world into four parts and gave them to four men he called kings . . . [T]hey say that this division of the world was the origin of that which the Incas made of their kingdom called Tahuantinsuyu" (Garcilaso de la Vega, el Inca, *Royal Commentaries of the Incas and General History of Peru*, part 1, 2 vols., trans. Harold V. Livermore, Austin, 1966, vol. 1, pp. 47–49). The Huarochiri documents offer another example of the imperial universe and its immediate division in coming-to-being. Pariacaca, the primordial divine being, comes forth from five eggs, together with his four brothers. Their very birth is a species of primordial division. Pariacaca decides to order the earth by taking on the prepotent being Caruyuchu Huayallo, to whom people were sacrificing children. See Francisco de Avila, *A Narrative of the Errors, False Gods and Other Superstitions and Diabolical Rites in which the Indians of the Province of Huarochiri, Mama and Chaclla Lived in Ancient Times, and in which They even now Live, to the Great Perdition of Their Souls* [1608], in Clements R. Markham, trans. and ed., *Narratives of the Rites and Laws of the Yncas* (London, 1873; reprint, New York, n.d.), vol. 43, pp. 142–44. See also Davíd Carrasco, "City as Symbol in Aztec Thought: The Clues from the Codex Mendoza," *HR* 20 (1981): 199–223, and *Quetzalcoatl and the Irony of Empire: Myths and Prophecies in the Aztec Tradition* (Chicago, 1982), esp. pp. 117–33, 170–191. Also helpful in pursuing the question is a distinction between locative and diasporic views of concrete geography. These views bespeak different appraisals of the nature of symbolic life and of the sacred itself; cf. Jonathan Z. Smith, "The Wobbling Pivot," *The Journal of Religion* 52 (1972): 146–149.

193. See the comparative data compiled in Karsten, *Civilization of the South American Indians*, pp. 377–413, which links sacrifice and funerals.

194. Rudolfo Kusch, *America Profunda* (Buenos Aires, 1962).

195. Métraux, *History of the Incas*, p. 140. The connection between Inca sacrifice and the conquering of territorial chaos is also reflected in a report by the chronicler José de Acosta, *Historia Natural y Moral de las Indias* (1590; Madrid, 1954), book 5, chapter 18, p. 160, which says "The People of Peru sacrificed birds of the Puna—as the desert was called there—when they went into battle in order to reduce the powers of the *huaca* of the opponent. This sacrifice was

called *cuzcovicza* or *contevicza* or *huallvaciza* or *sopavicza.*" These are all territorial terms referring either to mountains, *huacas*, ceremonial enclosures, or sanctuaries attached to specific social groups or categories of social beings. "The birds in the sacrifice were killed in substitution for the enemy. They were linked with the puna, the plains or desert outside the inhabited world" (Zuidema, *Ceque System of Cuzco*, p. 175, where Acosta is cited and translated). The confusion that is dissected in sacrifice is both geographic and social and, indeed, affects every plane of existence. For consideration of ways in which divisions of geographic space around Cuzco, marked by sacred sanctuaries, or *huacas*, gave visible form and clear, divisible structure to fluid formlessness, see Jeanette Sherbondy, "Les Réseaux d'irrigation dans la géographie politique de Cuzco," *JSAP* 66 (1979): 45-66. The fields and water supplies of each community and residence space tend to form one single irrigation district and catchment area, within which each tiny fragment of land fits into a more global network. Not only do the sources of water supply become marked by sacred places of sacrifice but they are often cared for as sacred manifestations in their own right (Sherbondy, ibid., p. 62). It is the eruption of the sacred into space, formless and fluid, that makes territories demarcatable, divisible, and conquerable. The history of sacrifice in the Andes should be coordinated not only with imperial expansion across foreign territories, but also with other forms of taking life, such as the "two types of hunting practiced during Inca hegemony." The first type was the spectacular great drive called the royal hunt *(chaco)*. The second type, smaller in scale, used traps, lassos and spears, bows and arrows, slings and bolas. Both were highly stylized ritual activities. They both also effected the pattern of conservation and harvesting of game and the management of wilderness territories and their resources. That is, they were symbolic manifestations of attitudes toward, evaluations of, and uses of the produce of specific territories as well as of the reproductive patterns used to regenerate life in those spatial areas. See the fuller implications of the link between the mode of taking life and the mode of extension and existence in space in Glynn Custred, "Hunting Technologies in Andean Cultures," *JSAP* 66 (1979): 7-19.

196. Métraux, *History of the Incas*, p. 140.

197. Ibid., pp. 141-2. The sacredness of consumption, reflected in the sacrifice of outsiders' flesh and the division of territory in the process of imperial expansion, would be the proper context to evaluate the mummification of Inca nobility. The sacred bodies of the royal *incas* defined the center. Mummified corpses of the kings signified a state that transcended the limits and corruption brought on by separation from primordial life (just as, in their brother-sister marriages, their bodies transcended the incest taboo and represented the unfallen primordial condition). Pierre Duviols, "Un Symbolisme de l'occupation de l'aménagement et de l'exploitation de l'espace: Le Monolithe 'huanca' et sa fonction dans les Andes préhispaniques," *H* 19 (1979): 7-31, sheds light on this nexus of symbolic issues. A *huanca* is the "mineral double of a sacred cadaver [*mallqui*: seed, mummy] and it quickly becomes clear that this cadaver-monolith pair is at the center of the cosmological and ritual preoccupations of Andean societies" (Duviols, ibid., p. 8). Duviols sees a direct link between the body at the center and the history of territorial expansion, urbanization, and state formation. *Huancas* are sites of sacrifice and tribute-offerings and mark off divisions of territory (just as conquering ancestors used the stone to demarcate newly occupied territory, pp. 13-14). The term *huanca* designates several related realities: the central valley of Mantaro (Jauja) and its people; the stone or stone statue; and a chanted dance *(taki)* performed during the collective agricultural labors of sowing and harvesting (see below for discussion of the *Taki Ongo* eschatological dance craze). For the Inca, each *huanca* represented the sacrificed body of an ancestral hero turned to stone (p. 16). Cuzco, for example, represents the place where Ayar Auca, brother of Manco Capac, turned to stone. These series of sacrificed bodies, preserved indivisibly as stones and as mummies, became sites for the sacrifice of the animals of conquered pastoralist communities (*ayllus*). Mummification was a widespread pre-Conquest practice in the Andes and Peruvian coast; see Aidan Cockburn and Eve Cockburn, eds., *Mummies, Disease and Ancient Cultures*, (Cambridge, 1980), pp. 135-176, for description and bibliography regarding mummies in Peru.

198. Pierre Clastres and Lucien Sebag, "Cannibalisme et mort chez les Guayakís (Achén)," *RMP* n.s. 14 (1963): 181.

199. H. Clastres, "Rites funéraires Guayakí," pp. 66, 69.

200. Ibid., p. 72. Similar themes appear elsewhere. Tacana myths, for instance, link the origins of death and the transformation of the dead through dismemberment into little pieces with the death of the primordial jaguar and his wife. See Karin Hissink and Albert Hahn, *Die Tacana I: Erzählungsgut* (Stuttgart, 1961), pp. 532ff.

201. P. Clastres, "Guayakí Cannibalism."

202. Ibid., p. 313. Even pieces of rotting corpses are cut off and consumed.

203. The absence of the anthropologists is important when we keep in mind criticisms such as those by W. Arens, *The Man-Eating Myth: Anthropology and Anthropophagy* (Oxford, 1979). Arens wants to impeach second-hand testimony and scrutinize the character of witnesses claiming to see consumption of the flesh with their own eyes.

204. P. Clastres, "Guayakí Cannibalism," p. 314. "To exogamy on the matrimonial plane corresponds an excuisine on the anthropophagic plane, and this latter is practically the only limitation to generalized endocannibalism" (ibid.). Aside from the case of kin, the prohibition against consuming human flesh arises also in relation to murder. "The 'killer' does not eat his victim (any more than the hunter eats his own game)" (p. 321).

205. Ibid., p. 320. "The term Chikwagi is applied by an individual to the hunter who, shortly before that individual's birth, provided his mother with the animal that provided the name and 'nature' of the child after the pregnant woman ate it. The Chikwagi thereafter stands in a special relationship to the child" (ibid., p. 321). Funeral beating of the mother by the father should also be studied alongside the same actions, needed to effect ritual transition from one state to another, during Guayakí boys' initiation. At that time, in response to mothers' lamentations, fathers enact a ritual fury (i.e., they become *by-iä*, "nameless") in order to change their child's nature (*by:* "nature, name").

206. Whatever the ultimate judgment of historians regarding the factual details of ritual consumption of the dead, it must be underscored that the Guayakí regard the action as symbolic, and the powerful meanings it conveys are fully coherent with the Guayakí vision of life and being in the world.

207. Ibid., p. 316.

208. This second aspect of continuity of life is prophylactic and negative. "It is, thus, static in its effects" (ibid.).

209. Ibid., p. 317.

210. Ibid.

211. Ibid., pp. 317–318. Clastres compares the Guayakí notion with a Guarani dualism recognizing two soul-elements, the *ayvukué* (which accounts for the "form" of a living entity) and *asyiguá* (which is the source of a person's uniqueness, and which is located in the nape of the neck).

212. Clastres makes the point by using social-psychological terms: "The act of eating one's relatives is a kind of defense mechanism of the group threatened by the souls of the dead and the ritual ends with a separation between the worlds of the dead and the living" (ibid., p. 320). Because Clastres seeks to stay within the frame of sociopolitical explanation he views the Guayakí as an exception to the rule that those who ingest flesh consume enemies from outside their social group. This approach underestimates the power of religious imagination to overflow the bounds of social realities. In fact, the Guayakí speak of their dead kinsmen as their enemies on supernatural grounds. The dead are primal jaguars, vultures, or serpents, the archenemies of life in this world. The dead Guayakí relative enlivens the same evaluative imagery of death as do foreigners in other funeral contexts. "The dead relative [among the Guayakí] is treated among his own people as the enemy is among exocannibals" (ibid., p. 320). In fact, within a perspective that gives full weight to the religious imagination, the Guayakí are no exception: when they consume the flesh of the dead they consume an enemy whose threatening mien derives from the fact that the state of death itself, manifest in the corpse, is the enemy. The same may be said for the Remo and Cashinahua, for whom "eating the flesh was clearly a duty and a disagreeable one" (Dole, "Endocannibalism among the Amahuaca," p. 307). Consumption of flesh rid the world of a supernatural enemy, the ominous soul of the dead, who subsequently flew away to the west.

213. Walter Raleigh, *The Discoverie of the Large, Rich, and Beautiful Empire of Guiana Performed in the Year 1595* (London, 1848), p. 53.

214. Robert Southey, *History of Brazil*, (London, 1819), vol. 3, p. 204.

215. Chagnon, *Yąnomamö*, p. 51.

216. Ibid.

217. The paradoxical acts of the moment typify the ambivalence of dealing with the dead. The father acts as though he would save the body from fiery consumption but allows men to restrain him. In the early stages of the ceremony the elaborate wailing aims to "appease the spirit of the deceased." When the body has been burned, however, the soul of the deceased ought to disappear. If it does not depart, it may linger in the area to kill someone.

218. Dole, "Endocannibalism among the Amahuaca," p. 305. The Amahuaca mother consumes the powdered bones of her child in order to banish the independent existence of its soul. This intention is consonant with those of other Panoan-speakers in the Ucayali Valley region: the Conibo cremate to "prevent the spirit from reoccupying the body" and consume ashes "to forget the dead"; other groups consume the ash to make the soul live anew in the consumer (Tapuya); to preserve the spirit of the deceased in a most dignified way (Tapuya); to return the spirit of a dead child to its mother's body (Camacan); to absorb the virtues of the dead person (Cubeo). Cf. ibid., p. 307.

219. S. Linné, "Darien in the Past," *Göteborgs Kungl. Vetenskaps och Vitterhets Samhalles Handlingar, Femte Foljden*, series A, 1 (1929): 227–235.

220. Volhard, Boglár, and Zerries have suggested that the funeral rites of consuming bone-ash of the dead are linked with religious celebrations of the collection of wild fruits or cultivated plants. See the discussion and sources in Zerries, "El Endocannibalismo en la América del Sur," especially the distribution map on pp. 166–167. Zerries questions the conclusion of Volhard in *Kannibalismus*, pp. 334–361, who argued that cannibalism developed only after the discovery of agriculture. Zerries also takes issue with Boglár, "Ein endokannibalischer Ritus in Südamerika," in *Miscellanea Paul Rivet Octogenario Dicata II* (Mexico City, 1958), pp. 67–86. Boglár extended Volhard's thesis and contended that endocannibalism in South America was primarily associated with slash-and-burn agriculture (p. 83). Zerries points out, however, that many of the festivals during which ashes of the dead are consumed mark the harvest or ripening of wild forest fruits, not cultivated ones.

221. Zerries hypothesizes that consuming bone-ash arose in the oldest level of agricultural economy in the tropical forest. He associates it with the Pano and Tukano groups of the western Amazon. From there it spread to areas where the Waica and Shiriana now live. The custom is mostly observed by Arawak-speakers, who, Zerries contends, influenced the Caribs of the Guianas. This explains why the Arawak and Carib practice the custom only in relation to important chiefs or extraordinary religious specialists. Zerries points to the Arawakan Tariana and Tukano myths of a primordial being whose death by fire causes fruit trees and palm trees to sprout from his ashes. Zerries sees a logical connection between drinking the ashes and drinking the beverage made from fruit trees that have grown from the ashes of the burned culture hero. In these later areas, Zerries points out, the bones of the culture hero are identified with these plants (from which musical instruments are often fashioned). Zerries argues that some of these ideas may be traced back to the economy of hunter-gatherers.

222. Hans Becher, "Bericht über eine Forschungsreise nach Nordbrasilien in das Gebiet der Flusse Demini und Araca," *ZFE* 82 (1957): 115–116. For still another detailed report of the entire process of disposal of remains, see Clastres and Lizot, "La Muerte y la idea del canibalismo entre los Yanomamɨ." For their part, the Guaharibos painted their faces and bodies with a mixture of ashes of the dead and red paint so that they would increase in number; see Alain Gheerbrant, *Welt ohne Weisse* (Wiesbaden, 1953); cited in Zerries, "Endocanibalismo," p. 128.

223. Chagnon, *Yąnomamö*, p. 50. See also José Maria Cruxent, "Indios Guaika: Incineración de cadáveres," *BIV* 1 (1953): 149–151.

224. Chagnon, *Yąnomamö*, pp. 50–51.

225. Barandiarán, "Vida y muerte." For additional narrative descriptions and interpretations of events surrounding death among the Yanomami, including the consummation of the ashes of the dead in a compote of banana beer, see Lizot, *Le Cercle des feux*, pp. 17–43, which highlights the symbolism of ashes and tears; Zerries, *Waika*, pp. 213–236, which interprets Waika and Schiriána ash ingestion in the context of similar customs throughout South America; and Schuster and Zerries, *Mahekodotedi*, vol. 2, pp. 144–151.

226. Barandiarán, "Vida y muerte," p. 32.

227. Ibid., p. 34.

228. For an exemplary description of the ways in which the nature of sacred life and supernatural being is coinvolved with images and realities of consumption at every level and in every image, see the reports regarding the Yanomami in Lizot, *Le Cercle des feux*, pp. 166–182 on "the devourers of souls."

229. H. Clastres and J. Lizot suggest that this is why the procedures of funeral consumption are so complicated: "There is an *excess* of rules . . . which perhaps is opposed to the excess of voracity of the mythic jaguar." See their "La Muerte y la idea del canibalismo entre los Yanomami," p. 142.

230. Memory plays a key role here since it is both a form of reflection and of the ambivalent transcendence that provokes reflection. Consumption of the dead is a mode of remembrance more concrete than dream, recollected image, or name. The bodies of consuming survivors become living memorials to the dead. The body becomes the preeminent sign of death (the corpse) and life (the communicant). The point to underline is that, in the presence of death, all images become similarly ambivalent. Recollection, dream, memory—the whole of imaginative existence—signal contradictory messages at the same time. Memory itself becomes not only a sign of the past (recollecting the dead person) but a reminder of one's own future. By ingesting the remains of the dead, one not only sustains life as a memorial of the dead person but reinforces one's own mortal condition, filling oneself with the substantial sign of death. Just as memory, the body of the consumer, and the corpse emit contradictory signals, symbolic languages of all sorts show signs of strain. Funerary customs forbid some sounds (e.g., names of the dead, songs, or speech itself) and heighten others (lament, din, noisy salutes to the dead). Some body decorations (such as paint, clothing, hairstyles) become unsuitable for the occasion while other signs of dress and closure become normative. Death refigures reality. Lying at the bottom of the examined life, death provokes a reassessment of the value of symbolic existence.

Many indications suggest that such a reevaluation is essential to active membership in community life. Funeral performances transform the community. In order for absent members to make the transition into the new reality, they also should undergo a death-centered performance. For example, when an Apinayé traveler returns to a village after a lengthy period of time, older female relations greet him. Seated beside the traveler, the women weep vehemently to remember those who died during the traveler's absence. This weeping greeting lasts half hour or more. Cf. Nimuendajú, *The Apinayé*, p. 113.

231. Robin Wright and Jonathan Hill, "From History to Myth: 19th Century Millenarian Movements in the Northwest Amazon," (Unpublished MS., 1984), pp. 6–7, citing and confirming Martin Matos Arvelo, *Vida Indiana* (Barcelona, 1912), p. 95.

232. Wright and Hill, "From History to Myth" pp. 6–7.

233. d'Ans, *Le Dit des vrais hommes*, p. 25. Cashinahua and Amahuaca burials are described on pp. 23f.

234. Ibid., p. 23.

235. Renate B. Viertler, "A Noção de pessoa entre os Bororo," *BMN* n.s. Antropologia 32 (1979): 20–30.

236. Ibid.

237. Ibid., p. 28.

238. Carneiro da Cunha, *Os Mortos e os outros*, pp. 110–111.

239. Carneiro da Cunha treats the reingestion of bones, persona and name by the lineage as a kind of endocannibalism: the metaphorical consumption of the dead individual by the kin group. "In fact, what is cannibalism other than a form of burial?" (Carneiro da Cunha, "Espace funéraire," p. 292). In this case, however, the bones are not consumed directly by the kin group but by the sacred powers that originated and sustain it through appearances at the center of the community (or, in some cases, the maternal home). Like all other death-transformations happening in that place (e.g., initiation), the consumption effects a new state of being. The Canela also buried their dead in front of the home until the bones had becomes clear of all flesh. Then they reburied the bones in the center of the village (Nimuendajú, *The Eastern Timbira*, p. 98; cited in Carneiro da Cunha, "Espace funéraire," p. 285).

240. Carneiro de Cunha, ibid., p. 284. Melatti looks upon the complexity of funeral behaviors as an outcome of the complex constitution of the human being, both physically and as a personality. The ties that link various elements of flesh, bone, soul, names, property, social relationships, and so on, must be dissolved each in their proper way. See Melatti, *Ritos de uma tribo timbira*, pp. 126–128.

241. Barandiarán, for example, shows how the history of creation and the complicated process of Sanemá-Yanoama human origins bear directly on the progress of the death process signaled by the disintegration of personal elements; see Barandiarán, "Vida y muerte," esp. pp. 26–35.

242. Perrin, *Le Chemin des indiens morts*, pp. 35–37.

243. Johannes Wilbert analyzes such analogic languages as elitelore.

244. Perrin, *Le Chemin des indiens morts*, p. 28.

245. Ibid., pp. 137ff.

246. Ibid., p. 40.

247. Ibid., p. 97. "*Juyá*, the Rain, is none other than the Goajiro who are long dead" (p. 98, p. 179).

248. Ibid., pp. 137ff.

249. Ibid., p. 184.

250. The Goajiro *a'iñ*, although invisible, is "like a tiny bit of white cotton, like a wisp of smoke" (ibid., p. 25). It follows the person everywhere, "like a shadow." The soul wanders from the body during sickness and dreams. Death may be viewed as an eternal dream-state in several ways. The soul not only exits the body as it usually does during dreaming, but also the person dreams that he is dead and, therefore, never awakens. In this way the *a'iñ* is captured by an entirely spiritual reality.

251. Ibid., p. 171.

252. Ibid., p. 172. Incidentally, the stone-door opened for the living hero, who visited his wife in the underground. Since he did not pass through the irreversible condition of stone, he never succumbed to the mode of being called final death. Through this and other heroic achievements, he preserved his ability to return to the land of the living. For further details on the symbolism of the Goajiro door to the land of the dead, see Johannes Wilbert, "Puertas al Averno," *MSCNL* 19 (1959): 161–175. Wilbert looks at doors to the otherworld in Goajiro, Yupa, and Ica (of the Sierra Nevada de Santa Marta), as well as the otherworld of the Warao, which is inhabited by river beings.

253. Ibid., p. 27.

254. Tullio Tentori, "Ideas of the Other World," *ICA*, 30th Congress (London, 1955), pp. 199–201. For a brief survey of similar ideas among several groups in the Gran Chaco, see Wanda Hanke, "Costumbres y creéncias indígenas relacionadas con la muerte," *RGA* 2 (1939): 363–368.

255. Roe, *Cosmic Zygote*, p. 117.

256. Whitten, *Sacha Runa*, p. 42.

257. Ibid., p. 149.

258. Ibid., p. 39.

259. I delineate links between symbolic space and moral action in Lawrence E. Sullivan, "Above, Below, or Far Away: Andean Cosmogony and Ethical Order," in Frank Reynolds and Robin Lovin, eds., *Cosmogony and Ethical Order* (Chicago, 1985), pp. 98–129.

260. Weiss, "World of a Forest Tribe, p. 437.

261. Ibid.

262. Viertler, "A Noção de pessoa entre os Bororo," pp. 23, 28.

263. Wilbert, "Eschatology," p. 180.

264. Ibid., p. 182.

265. Ibid., p. 169. The self-designation, *Warao*, means "boat people" (Wilbert, "The House of the Swallow-Tailed Kite," p. 145). The name sums up the origins and destiny of human life as well as the material and mythic vehicles (*wa* in the sense of "death" and of "canoe") that transport one through the stages on life's way.

266. Wilbert, "Eschatology," p. 169.

267. Ibid., p. 170.

268. Ibid., p. 172. Regarding this ecstatic scenario and other Warao depictions of houses in mythic geography, see the detailed analysis in Wilbert, "The House of the Swallow-Tailed Kite."
269. Wilbert, "Eschatology," p. 172.
270. Ibid., p. 174.
271. Ibid., p. 176.
272. Ibid.
273. Ibid., p. 177.
274. Ibid.
275. Ibid., p. 174.
276. Ibid., p. 173.
277. Bastien, *Mountain of the Condor*, pp. 174–175.
278. Ibid., p. 186. The feast gathers together all sorts of temporal expressions: historical, diurnal, seasonal, and agricultural (it is the seed time), as well as cycles of reciprocal exchange and ritual obligations among natural and ritual kin. For additional details on the mythic geography of the mountain body and its relationship to the trials and ills of the physical and social body see Joseph W. Bastien, "Qollahuaya-Andean Body Concepts: A Topographical-Hydraulic Model of Physiology," *AA* 87 (1985): 595–611.
279. Wright, "History and Religion of the Baniwa," p. 391. Baniwa funeral symbolism derives from the myth of Kuai, the culture hero who was burned so that his spirit ascended to the middle sky and his life passed through his body orifices, making sounds and songs of the ancestors and festivals. For a general discussion of funerals in the Vaupés area see Alves da Silva Brüzzi, "Os Ritos fúnebres entre as tribos do Uaupés (Amazonas)," *ANT* 50 (1955): 593–601, which gives special attention to elegies, forms of burial, and the elaborate feast celebrated after burial.
280. Basso, *The Kalapalo Indians*, p. 57. The Kalapalo soul-shadow prepares for this journey on the first evening after burial of the body. On that night the soul-shadow eats a last supper in the family house. The day after the burial, surviving relatives shoot arrows into the air "signifying the movement of the dead person's shadow from the grave to the village of the dead" (ibid.). The arrows carry the dead soul into the heavens. While the dead soul undergoes its way of trials, the surviving spouse enters ritual seclusion (after burning the deceased's possessions over the grave). In fact, mourning subdues the entire village for this one- to two-month period. Ceremonial signs are kept from sight. A communal washing ceremony *(itsongitsa)* marks the end of the seclusion. Afterwards, people resume the customary body-painting.
281. Villas Boas and Villas Boas, *Xingu*, pp. 213–225. The soul had lived in the eyes of the living person but now is made to leave the land of the living in peace. Apparently, the soul hangs around the residence space, hopefully at some distance from it, until the first lunar eclipse after its death. Its continued presence on earth is a liability, especially for spouse and kin. Should it appear to someone (it looks just like the living person), it would cause the viewer to disappear into heaven.
282. Nimuendajú, *Mitos de creación*, p. 51.
283. Ibid., p. 55.
284. Ibid., p. 60.
285. It is the *ayvúkué* which reincarnates itself *(oikové yevý)* after death. The deceased's desire to complete unfinished business impels its rebirth. Often, moved by the tears of his mourners, a man reincarnates himself immediately in a woman of his own lineage. These are called *tuiá* ("old ones") and are considered to be their own grandfathers. See ibid., pp. 65ff.
286. Ibid., pp. 64–65.
287. Maybury-Lewis, *Akwẽ-Shavante Society*, p. 291. The village of the dead is one of unique unity, for all affinal relations, the basis of factiousness, have been expunged. Once the dead kinsman's soul is installed in the village of the dead, its benevolent aid is sought by the living. It can travel freely between the village of the dead and the village of the living.
288. Wilbert, *Yupa Folktales*, pp. 80–84.
289. Wilbert (ibid., p. 25) points out that in other mythologies of the afterlife, such as the Tacana, the Toad Grandmother herself devours the dead (as does Tlaltecuhtli, the Aztec mistress of the earth).
290. Wilbert (ibid.) notes that in Guarayu tradition the dead must balance themselves on the

trunk of a floating tree that shuttles back and forth at tremendous speed across the river to the land of the ancestors. See Alfred Métraux, "Tribes of Eastern Bolivia and the Madeira Headwaters," in *HSAI*, vol. 3, p. 437. In any case, the images of a treacherous crossing into the afterworld are widespread, ancient, and diverse in South America. In the Andean region of Cuyo in Argentina, for example, a number of petroglyphs in the southwestern section are found at altitudes from 2,300 to 3,100 meters above sea level (e.g., those of La Fortuna and Los Difuntos on the western slopes of the Cordillera of Ansilta). Juan Schobinger contends that they are magico-religious works "associated with the symbolism of the road crossing a mountainous zone. They are probably linked to initiation (and the use of hallucinogens) and funerary rites"; see Schobinger, "Rock Art in Western Argentina: The Andean Region of Cuyo," *LAIL* 4 (1980): p. 66. Schobinger develops his argument in "Experiéncias psíquicas y cultos esotéricos reflejados en el arte rupestre sudamericano," in *Valcamonica Symposium II: Les Religions de la Préhistoire* (Capo di Ponti, Italy, 1975), pp. 491–498.

291. Darcy Ribeiro, *Religião e mitología kadiuéu* (Rio de Janeiro, 1950), pp. 89–92, 155–56.

292. Carneiro da Cunha, "Espace funéraire," p. 291.

293. Ibid., p. 290.

294. Carneiro da Cunha, "Eschatology among the Krahó," p. 165.

295. Ibid., p. 167. One of Carneiro da Cunha's informants reports, "The dead have no brains: that's why they don't marry, although they work (i.e., copulate)." Carneiro da Cunha interprets: "The point is summed up in the unanimous affirmation that the dead 'don't think,' 'live just anyhow,' or, in a word are *pahamnõ*, shameless, lacking *paham*. . . . The 'shameless' dead do not know how to behave, have no idea of etiquette, and above all do not recognize the fundamental principle of appropriate conduct toward affines" (p. 167).

296. Ibid.

297. Carneiro da Cunha summarizes reports from two Krahó concerning the land of the dead. The first, an old man, named Davi, said,

> The mekarõ do not live in a circular village, but instead, in a dark place in the forest. . . . Their families are not located as they would be in a village: those who have no daughters live alone on the outskirts of the village, they move around all the time, they never rest. They have no central place in their village. It does not matter where they gather to sing. They don't sleep in their own houses, but in other people's. The mekarõ don't bathe, they only drink lots of water. . . . [T]hey don't sing in the central place. (ibid.)

The second reporter, a healer, described the Land of the Dead as consisting of two villages. In one, the *mekarõ* spend the nighttime swimming in stagnant water. The water makes them forget the past. They never bathe in fresh or running water. When daylight comes the *mekarõ* go to sleep in the second village. "The mekarõ have no central place or circular path in their village; everything is privately owned, round the village there is nothing but trees, lots of them. There is one road leading to a single large field" (ibid., p. 168). For an even more detailed description of the Krahó afterlife, including the metamorphoses of the soul, the spatial arrangements of life among the dead, the absence of affinal alliances (with their concomitant respect-avoidance relations *(paham)*, see Carneiro da Cunha, *Os Mortos e os outros*, pp. 112–130.

298. Carneiro da Cunha, "Eschatology Among the Krahó," p. 170.

299. Weiss, "World of a Forest Tribe," p. 447.

300. Ibid. Here is a penetrating insight into the nature of consciousness as well as into the imagination's involvement with concrete form. Sariti does not speak of absolute conditions of night or day as they inhere in the physical universe but as outward expressions of a reality whose manifest form are interlinked with consciousness in its various states.

301. Ibid., p. 448. The dead recognize themselves as "cooked." When a living Campa sighted the Land of the Dead, he was seen to be living because he could spit; that is, he was still raw. The Campa dead are characteristically thin. Their bones protrude. Their clothing is in tatters.

302. Perrin, *Le Chemin des indiens morts*, p. 172.

303. Ibid., p. 173.

304. Ibid.

305. The lack of distinction makes life in the land of the dead quite bland. This vague indistinc-

tion often pervades descriptions of the land of the dead. In the reports of Henry, for instance, the Kaingáng concept of the afterlife is not well articulated or elaborated. In general, the afterlife appears a sombre place similar in many ways to present existence. However, life is tasteless and without excitement. Honey is tasteless; there is no meat. People eat only grubs from rotten wood (Henry, *Jungle People*, p. 95).

Chapter 6, above, on human growth and change, describes the symbolic process of fabrication, a negative process of knowledge that constructs the personality and society through conscientious avoidances, restrictions, and controls. Life in the land of the dead is a total fabrication.

306. Omao, on the other hand, stretches to the limit the symbolic processes with which one apprehends the distinctions in space. Omao himself keeps apart from the community of the dead in a house surrounded by flowers called *holholí*. The garden of white flowers forms a barricade that no one may cross. Inside the garden, Omao cultivates sacred trees. Paradoxically, his powerful presence is everywhere. He may not be seen, lest one die. He may only be heard. Omao never moves. Nevertheless, he keeps close track of affairs, listening to everything, looking things over while people sleep, and giving orders through his messengers (Barandiarán, "Vida y muerte," p. 36).

307. Basso, *The Kalapalo Indians*, p. 58.

308. Villas Boas and Villas Boas, *Xingu*, p. 134.

309. Agostinho, *Kwarìp*, pp. 161ff. The heavenly village of the Kamayura dead is a clear, clean, and open place, free of tangled undergrowth and dense jungle. Spatial closure is nevertheless absolute since, although there is a sky, heaven has no opening, as does the celestial vault of the earth. Similarly, human bodies remain closed spaces, without the passage effected in sexual penetration.

310. According to reports of Medina, Araucanians separated into two groups after death. One group waged ritual warfare; the other feasted. The Araucanians lived in several different realms after death. Brave warriors, whose fallen bodies were cremated on the battlefield, became lightning and thunderbolts. At the instigation of the celestial divinity Pillan, they continued to do battle in the afterlife. Common folks, on the other hand, crossed over to the far shore of the sea where they ate tasteless food grown in stingy fields. Nonetheless, their toil made possible the cycle of drinking feasts and dances. Medina gathered some reports which stressed that one realm of the afterlife yielded good food with no labor. In no case do dead Araucanians propagate children, although they live as couples in the land of the dead. See Medina, *Los Aborígenes de Chile*, pp. 241–245. In connection with these themes see the description of the Selk'nam afterlife in Gusinde, *Los Indios de Tierra del Fuego. Los Selk'nam*, vol. 2, pp. 515–517.

311. See chapter 6, above, for a discussion of the process of fabrication—a mode of symbolic praxis and human consciousness that establishes boundaries between human behavior, on the one side, and material and supernatural life on the other.

312. See Karsten, *Civilization of the South American Indians*, pp. 414–435, for data on reincarnation, metempsychosis, and regeneration after death gathered from around the continent.

313. Fock, *Waiwai*, p. 19.

314. Ibid., p. 17.

315. Carneiro da Cunha, "Eschatology Among the Krahó," pp. 162–163.

316. Ibid., p. 163.

317. Nimuendajú, *The Apinayé*, p. 140.

318. Ibid., p. 141.

319. Bartolomé, "Shamanism among the Avá-Chiripá," p. 115.

320. Leon Cadogan reports that a secondary burial of bones could not take place until the community was certain that the *ñe'eng* would remain in the land of the dead and not become reincarnate. Until that moment, surviving relatives kept the bones, cleaned of all flesh, in baskets and sung over them; see Cadogan, "Mitología de la zona guarani," *AI* 11(1951): 195–207; cited in Bartolomé, "Shamanism among the Avá-Chiripá," p. 116.

321. Bartolomé, ibid., p. 115.

322. Hans Becher, "Moon and Reincarnation: Anthropogenesis as Imagined by the Surára and Pakidái Indians of Northwestern Brazil," in Agehananda Bharati, ed., *The Realm of the Extra-Human: Ideas and Actions* (The Hague, 1976), pp. 339–345.

323. During the fourth year of life, the moon sends the external souls to the individual. At that time the individual is named after an animal or a plant. The two external souls are called Petáxibe, "the free soul," and Petánuahi, "the shadow soul." "Both names . . . contain the name of Petá, that first woman from the myth of creation." (Becher, ibid., p. 341).

324. Ibid., p. 340.

325. Ibid., p. 342.

326. The deity sorts out the souls by sex, indicated by their brightness. The brighter male souls on the eastern half-moon are distinguished from the darker souls of females on the western half. Women's blood is darker than men's and is also more magically powerful (ibid., pp. 341–42). Keeping the souls separated by color and sex is essential to the process of successful reincarnation: "If a child dies during or shortly after birth, it is because its soul was mistakenly located again in a body of the same sex" (p. 342).

327. Ibid., pp. 342–343.

328. Agostinho, Kwarìp, p. 165.

329. Ibid., p. 154.

330. Ibid., p. 164.

331. Ibid., p. 165.

332. Ibid.

333. This discovery is not unique to the Kamayurá nor to South America. See, for instance, Jean-Pierre Vernant, "Aspects mythiques de la mémoire," in Mythe et pensée chez les Grecs (Paris, 1965), pp. 51–78.

334. See Yolanda Lhullier dos Santos, "A Festa do Kwarup entre os indios do alto Xingu," RASP 4 (1956): 111–116, for additional brief details, as well as Jorge Ferreira, "Kuarup," O Cruzeiro (Rio de Janeiro) vol. 29, no. 15 (26 January 1957): 58–71.

335. The ways in which symbolic orders originated from cataclysm are detailed in chapter 2, above.

336. Kenelm Burridge scans and evaluates many of the terms emerging from these studies. In general, he criticizes them for being pseudoanalytical since they are, in fact, descriptive or even "impressionistic and subjective characterizations." Some of the terms are nativistic (Ralph Linton, "Nativistic Movements," AA 45, 1943, pp. 230–240); syncretic (Peter Lawrence, Road Belong Cargo, Mancester, England, 1964); adjustment (Ralph Piddington, An Introduction to Social Anthropology, London, 1967, vol. 2, pp. 735–744); accomodative (Fred W. Voget, The American Indian in Transition: Reformation and Accomodation," AA 58, 1956, pp. 249–263, and Peter Worsley, The Trumpet Shall Sound, London, 1957); militant (Marian W. Smith, "Toward a Classification of Cult Movements," MN 2, 1959); denunciatory (H. G. Barnett, Indian Shakers: A Messianic Cult of the Pacific Northwest, Urbana, Illinois, 1957); revitalization (Anthony F. C. Wallace, "Revitalization Movements," AA 58, 1956, pp. 264–281, and Julius Gould and William L. Kolb, A Dictionary of the Social Sciences, London, 1964); vitalistic (Linton, op. cit.; Wallace, op. cit.; Smith, op. cit.); dynamic (Voget, op. cit.); reformative (Smith, op. cit.; Voget, op. cit.). Burridge illustrates his objections in this way: "If for example we were to call the Pai-marire [the nineteenth century "good and peaceful" movement of the Maori of New Zealand] a militant movement, is there any good reason why we should not also call it a reformative or dynamic or vitalistic or denunciatory or accommodative movement? It was all of these things, and the choice between one term rather than another can only be subjective and confusing"; see Burridge, New Heaven, New Earth: A Study of Millenarian Activities (Oxford, 1980), p. 103. Similarly, Burridge points out, "There is no need to say much about the words 'messiah', 'hero', 'prophet', 'chiliastic', 'millenarian', 'messianic', 'cult', 'movement', 'activities'. To think that each term refers to a distinct person or situation obscures rather than clarifies, closes rather than opens the sociological problem" (ibid., p. 11).

337. A growing literature has taken up the religious nature of eschatologies and millennial visions. See the bibliographical references in Burridge, New Heaven, New Earth, and Lincoln, ed., Religion, Rebellion, and Revolution. Egon Schaden, "Le Messianisme en Amérique du sud," in Puech, ed., Histoires des Religions, vol. 3, pp. 1051–1109, reviews South American messianic materials and furnishes helpful suggestions for reading as do Alicia M. Barabás, "Movimientos étnicos religiosos y seculares en América Latina," AI 46 (1986): 495–529; and Robin M. Wright and Jonathan D. Hill, "History, Ritual, and Myth: Nineteenth Century Millenarian Movements in

the Northwest Amazon," *ETH* 33 (1986): 31–54 raises questions about the nature of prophecy and its relation to history. In addition we may call attention to J. Z. Smith, *Imagining Religion*, especially the chapter on Jonestown; Bruce Lincoln, " 'The Earth Shall Become Flat'—A Study of Apocalyptic Imagery," *CSSH* 25 (1983): 136–153, and "Notes Toward a Theory of Religion and Revolution," in Lincoln, ed., *Religion, Rebellion, Revolution*, pp. 266–292; Daniel L. Overmyer, "Folk-Buddhist Religion: Creation and Eschatology in Medieval China," *HR* 12 (1972): 42–70; Vittorio Lanternari, *La Grande Festa. Storia del Capodanno nelle civiltà primitive* (Milan, 1959), *Movimenti religiosi di libertà e di salvezza dei popoli oppressi* (Milan, 1960), *L'Incivilimento dei barbari* (Bari, 1983), and "Messianism: Its Historical Origin and Morphology," *HR* 2 (1962): pp. 52–72; Bernard McGinn, *Visions of the End: Apocalyptic Traditions in the Middle Ages* (New York, 1979); Leon Festinger et al., *When Prophecy Fails: A Social and Psychological Study of a Modern Group that Predicted the Destruction of the World* (New York, 1956); Sylvia L. Thrupp, ed., *Millennial Dreams in Action* (The Hague, 1962); James Mooney, *Ghost-Dance Religion and the Sioux Outbreak of 1890*, ed. by Anthony F. C. Wallace (Chicago, 1965); Anthony F. C. Wallace, *The Death and Rebirth of the Seneca* (New York, 1972); E. J. Hobsbawm, *Primitive Rebels: Studies in Archaic Forms of Social Movement in the 19th and 20th Centuries* (Manchester, England, 1959); Peter Worsley, *The Trumpet Shall Sound: A Study of 'Cargo' Cults in Melanesia* (1957; London, 1968); Max G. Gluckman, *Rituals of Rebellion in South-East Africa* (Manchester, England, 1954); David F. Aberle, *The Peyote Religion Among the Navaho* (New York, 1966); Susan Naquin, *Millenarian Rebellion in China: The Eight Trigrams Uprising of 1813* (New Haven, 1976); Ernesto de Martino, *La Fine del mondo* (Turin, 1977); Norman Cohn, *The Pursuit of the Millennium*, rev. ed. (New York, 1970); Guglielmo Guariglia, *Prophetismus und Heilserwartungsbewegungen als völker-kundliches und religionsgeschichtliches Problem* (Horn, 1959); Georges Balandier, "Messianismes et nationalismes en Afrique Noire," *Cahiers internationales de sociologie* (Paris) 14 (1953); Jean Guiart, "Cargo Cults and Political Evolution in Melanesia," *Mankind* 4 (1951): pp. 227–229; Judy Inglis, "Cargo Cults: The Problem of Explanation," *Oceania* 27 (1957): pp. 249–263; I. C. Jarvie, "Theories of Cargo Cults: A Critical Analysis," *Oceania* 34 (1963): 1–31 and 109–136; Bengt G. M. Sundkler, *Bantu Prophets in South Africa* (London, 1948); and Bryan Wilson, *Sects and Society* (London, 1961).

338. Among others who have made this point, see Varese, *La Sal de los cerros*, p. 22 and passim.

339. For a description of the evangelical uprisings of the 1940s, see Elmer Miller, "The Argentine Toba Evangelical Religious Service," *ETY* 10 (1971): 149–159. The prehistory of the movements is described in Leopoldo J. Bartolomé, "Movimientos milenaristas de los aborígenes Chaqueños entre 1905 y 1933," *SA* 7 (1972): 107–120. Professor Gilberto Mazzoleni of the University of Rome has told me that he continues research of Christian eschatology among the Toba. The recent visit of Pope John Paul II has been taken by many Christian Toba as a sure sign of the imminent end of the world.

340. Bartolomé, ibid., p. 108.

341. Ibid., p. 109.

342. Ibid., p. 110.

343. Ibid., p. 112.

344. Ibid., p. 114.

345. Ibid.

346. Ibid., p. 115.

347. These and other prominent features of eschatological movements are not limited to South America. See the works cited in notes 336 and 338, above.

348. Extravagant symbolism of the body looms large in eschatologies and produces a host of fantastic bestiaries. By means of the ultimate initiation accomplished by the end of time, believers' bodies are transfigured into perfect, indestructible bodies seldom, if ever, seen before. The bodies of nonbelievers and nonpractitioners, on the other hand, now are transformed fully into the bodies of the phantasmagorial beasts that hidden signs always intimated they really were all along. These spatial, temporal, and sonic signs were part of their quasi-human constitution but betrayed animaloid propensities evident in their different diets, table manners and hygiene, places and manner of excretion, body color, coiffure, body hair, clothing styles and colors, body shape, gestures and gait, songs, sounds, names, and language. These different signs set them

apart from the "authentic" humanity. Now, at the end, these partial signs and differences become total and definitive. They define the "others" whose acts and signals do not conform to the authentically eschatological humanity and so condemn them to the condition of consumable reality in the image of huntable wild beasts, consumable domestic livestock, or unclean pests fit for extermination. See chapter 5 regarding the religious evaluation of the human constitution and chapter 6 on change and transformation of the body through its signs. Eschatological bestiaries and evaluations of nonbelievers as animals are developments of theories of ritual physiology.

349. Wright, "History and Religion of the Baniwa," p. 395.

350. Ibid., pp. 276–333.

351. On Baniwa and other messianic movements in the upper Rio Negro area see Robin M. Wright and Jonathan D. Hill, "History, Ritual, and Myth: Nineteenth Century Millenarian Movements in the Northwest Amazon," *ETH* 33 (1986): 31–54; Schaden, "Le Messianisme en Amérique du sud," pp. 1081–1085, and Eduardo Galvão, "Aculturação indígena no Rio Negro," *BMPEG* n.s., Antropologia, 7 (1959): 1–60. In connection with the image of abundance in northwestern Amazon eschatology, see Mauricio Vinhas de Queiroz, "Cargo Cult no Amazonia: Observações sobre o milenarismo tukuna," *AL* 6 (1963): 43–61.

352. "New assumptions which predicate the creation of a new man, a new culture, society or condition of being are being wrought, . . . [and they] meet in the hero and his (divine) revelation, and almost always refer to a 'prosperity and prestige' that are consistent with and even define, the new conditions of being, the new man" (Burridge, *New Heaven, New Earth*, p. 11).

353. "The largest number of recorded instances [of millenarian movements] are surely to be found in Europe, and in European developments overseas. . . . The literature leaves no doubt that the vast bulk of millenarian activities are European in origin." (Burridge, *New Heaven, New Earth*, p. 32). But Burridge adds that the European millennialisms must be traced back "to the first civilizations in the fertile crescent in the Middle East" (p. 32). What connection millennialism has to chronicling and recording history, Burridge does not venture to say. The topic is taken up again below.

354. Bastide, *African Religions of Brazil*, p. 359; see also Schaden, "Le Messianisme en Amérique du Sud," pp. 1099ff., as well as Abelardo F. Montenegro, *Antônio conselheiro* (Fortaleza, Brazil, 1954), and the important study of another important and related Brazilian messianic movement, the Padre Cicero movement (1889–1934), in Ralph della Cava, *Miracle at Joaseiro* (New York, 1970).

355. Bernard J. Siegel, "The Contestado Rebellion, 1912–1916: A Case Study in Brazilian Messianism and Regional Dynamics," in Raymond D. Fogelson and Richard N. Adams, eds., *The Anthropology of Power: Ethnographic Studies from Asia, Oceania, and the New World* (New York: Academic Press, 1977), pp. 325–336, gathers the best sources, especially Herculano Teixeira d'Assumpçao, *A Campanha do Contestado*, 2 vols. (Belo Horizonte, Brazil, 1917). See also Maria I. Pereira de Queiroz, "O Movimento messianico do Contestado," *Revista brasileira de estudos politicos* 9 (1960), pp. 118–139.

356. Bastide, *African Religions of Brazil*, p. 361.

357. Ibid. See the complete analysis on pages 357–365, and see also Bastide, "Les Cultes afro-américains," in Puech, ed., *Histoire des religions*, vol. 3, pp. 1027–1050. Other analyses of Afro-American uprisings make little appeal to religious ideology. See, for example, Julio Pinto Vallejos, "Slave Control and Slave Resistance in Colonial Minas Gerais 1700–1750," *Journal of Latin American Studies* (Cambridge) 17 (1985): 1–34. But religious visions of cosmic destruction may have been operative on all sides of the colonial equation. On 18 July 1725, for example, the Governor of Rio de Janeiro wrote to the King: "[I]t was the confusion of tongues that brought down the Tower of Babel and for this very reason it seems to me that the mines should be worked with slaves from all nations" (Pinto Vallejos, ibid., p. 33).

358. Candido Procópio Ferreira de Camargo, et al., *Catolicos, protestantes, espiritas* (Petrópolis, Brazil, 1973), illustrates the inadequacy of these institutional categories in accounting for religious life in Brazil and criticizes institutional and geographic typologies by showing how they make it difficult to examine common motives (e.g., healing, messianism) as well as ritual frameworks that defy analysis along standard denominational lines (pp. 18, 159–179). The

variable ways Christianity is absorbed is studied in another setting (southern Colombia and the Andes) by Joanne Rappaport, "Mesianismo y las transformaciones de símbolos mesiánicos en Tierradentro," *RCA* 23 (1980): 365–413.

359. Traditions of destruction are presented in chapter 2; analysis of renewal through reenactment of primordial destruction can be found in chapter 4.

360. Clastres, *Chronique des indiens guayakí*, p. 127. For the same ritual gestures taken as precautionary measures at birth ceremonies see, pp. 32–35.

361. That is why historical research, including especially the "contextual" behavioral and social sciences, feed and thrive on the exuberant mythic diversity of cultures. But this celebrated dogma of cultural relativity, which safeguards a single canonical vision of time, excretes traditional religious forms (especially the myriad cultural renderings of time) as so many empty husks: disvalued dreams, wild visions, mere fantasms, fancies, or deliria. To become intelligible, the argument goes, the "surface features" of religious evaluations of time must first be recast in terms of the "deeper structures" of transformational grammar, economic classes, political hierarchies, mythico-logical relations, and social or psychological structures. In this way they disappear, swallowed up by fanciful constructs. These voracious categories, emerging with the centuries of conquest, conform to the accumulative rhythm of a history imagined as a singular and progressive amassing over time of facts, scientific knowledge, statistical data, and material wealth. South American eschatologies are another of the modern modes of inquiry and praxis that challenge history and probe it in order to understand and reshape it. On the academic scene, scholars wrestle with the nature of history in many ways. See Arnaldo Momigliano, *Essays in Ancient and Modern Historiography* (Middletown, Conn., 1977); Frank Manuel, *The Eighteenth Century Confronts the Gods* (Cambridge, Mass., 1967); Hayden White, *Metahistory: The Historical Imagination in Nineteenth Century Europe* (Baltimore, 1974); Karl Löwith, *Meaning in History* (Chicago, 1957); Isaiah Berlin, *Vico and Herder: Two Studies in the History of Ideas*, new ed. (New York, 1976); Gaston Bachelard, *La Formation de l'esprit scientifique: Contribution à une psychanalyse de la connaisance objective*, 10th ed. (Paris, 1977); Michel Foucault, *The Archaeology of Knowledge*, trans. A. M. Sheridan Smith (London, 1974); Marshall D. Sahlins, *Islands of History* (Chicago, 1985); Jan Vansina, *Kingdoms of the Savannahs* (Madison, Wis., 1966); Ekkehart Malotki, *Hopi Time* (The Hague, 1983); Dean MacCannell and Juliet Flower MacCannell, *The Time of the Sign: A Semiotic Interpretation of Modern Culture* (Bloomington, Ind., 1982); A. I. Hallowell, "Temporal Orientations in Western Civilization and in a Preliterate Society," *AA* 39 (1937): 647–670.

362. Civrieux, *Watunna*, pp. 25–27.

363. Ibid., p. 27.

364. Ibid.

365. Ibid.

366. Ibid., pp. 115–116.

367. Ibid., p. 116.

368. Ibid., p. 161.

369. Ibid., p. 162.

370. Ibid.

371. For their part, colonists also conceived of their encounter with a new material and cultural reality in eschatological terms. Many of these colonial visions of the end of the Old World and the beginnings of the New World have received scholarly attention. Arguably, these religious visions generated fundamental images in terms of which the contemporary secular societies of the Americas still think of themselves: a New Race, La Raza, a Pilgrim People, a New Frontier, a people set apart for a new destiny. See, for example, Edmundo O'Gorman, *The Invention of America* (Bloomington, Ind., 1961); Antonelli Gerbi, *The Dispute About America* (Pittsburgh, 1976); Francis Jennings, *The Invasion of America: Indians, Colonialism and the Cant of Conquest* (Chapel Hill, N.C., 1975); Charles L. Sanford, *The Quest for Paradise* (Urbana, Ill., 1961); George H. Williams, *Wilderness and Paradise in Christian Thought* (New York, 1962); H. Richard Niebuhr, *The Kingdom of God in America* (New York, 1937); Gilbert Chinard, *L'Amérique et le rève exotique dans la littérature française au XVII et XVIII siècles* (Paris, 1934); W. Clark Gilpin, *The Millenarian Piety of Roger Williams*, (Chicago, 1979). See also the works of Milhou and Moffitt-Watts mentioned above in chapter 1 note 17.

372. Regarding the ontological character of spaces and the ways in which their contrasting imagery and relationships empower the dynamisms of the cosmos, see chapter 3, above.

373. Examples of strictly eschatological violence described below should not be held too separate from the disruptive civil violence that acts out the collapse or radical critique of oppressive spatial existence. See, for example, Roberto da Matta, "As Raízes da violência no Brasil: Reflexões de um antropôlogo social," in Roberto da Matta, Maria Célia Paoli, Maria Victoria Benevides, and Paulo Sérgio Pinheiro, *Violência brasileira* (São Paulo, 1982), pp. 11–44, which examines the relationship of staged, institutional, and "spontaneous" violence to the symbolic values associated with the meanings of heterogeneous and fragmented spaces, especially the *house* versus the *street*. These spaces represent two "modes" and two "directions" that violence may assume. Space and violence play a crucial role in individual and group identity. See also Maria Célia Pinheiro Machado Paoli, "Violência e espaço civil," in ibid., pp. 45–55, which shows how, even in secular society, the ideas of space are bound up with practices that express the cultural meaning of secrecy, repression, public discourse, privacy, private property, and power. Eschatologies imagine the unsealing of the separate spaces, secrets, privacy, and exclusive exercises of power that constitute current civil and individual orders.

374. The process is similar to the one that exhumes or disinters remains for secondary burial.

375. F. Grenand, *Et L'homme devint jaguar*, p. 49.

376. Ibid.

377. Ibid.

378. On withdrawal or fixture of the sky on high see chapter 2, above.

379. The manner in which symbolic times intercalate the modes of being represented in cosmic spaces is presented in chapter 4, above.

380. Villas Boas and Villas Boas, *Xingu*, p. 249.

381. The case for this interpretation of ritual dance is argued in chapter 4, above.

382. Although this section examines some of the most outstanding, community-wide millennial movements, the expectation of the end, the hope for a prophetic messiah, and the expectation of an imminent paradise or apocalypse enjoy a wider range of expression. These themes of regenerative destruction pervade revolutionary as well as romantic traditions of poetry, art, song, and folk theatre disseminated by wandering minstrels, troubadors, pilgrims, and traders. For example, in the account provided by Manoel Matusalém Sousa, the literature of the Cordel in northeastern Brazil is a form of popular messianism transmitted primarily by troubadours and popular musicians or poets roaming the countryside. Matusalém examines the poetry and lyrics of the messianic songsters and isolates the ironic juxtaposition of two themes: hope in an immediate arrival of a new day of God and apocalypse, since the day of God will be a judgment rending the world asunder; see Manoel Matusalém Sousa, *Cordel, fé e viola* (Petrópolis, Brazil, 1982), pp. 48–54.

383. There is a danger that nothing lies hidden in history. One purchases no other meaning from its signs except that "it has happened." Through a narrow historical reading of signs (i.e., seeing history as a series of factual events and as nonsymbolic "reality"), one neither gains distance from history nor pries open its hermetic closure on other forms of meaning. It appears to contain everything. The directness of its reality crushes any hope that it might point to a fuller condition of being beyond itself. That concluding hopelessness becomes the premise of a vicious circle confirming that historical events themselves are exhaustively real manifestations that expose the irreality and relative worthlessness of imaginal existence manifest as dream, vision, myth, rite, dance, drama, poetry and art. The monorealism and monotemporalism inherent in a narrow construction of history, based on univariate renderings of time that anathematize South American constructions of mythic history, are the heart of the life-threatening situation that eschatologies must face and overcome.

384. Weiss, "World of a Forest Tribe," p. 286.

385. Weiss attributes this paradisal scenario of the River Campa to missionary influence (Weiss, ibid., p. 407). The presence of Christian influence, already previously noted and further confirmed in the cases that follow, is as ubiquitous in South American eschatologies as it is in many other aspects of religious life. Ramon Aranda de los Rios, *Marankiari: Una comunidad de la selva peruana* (Lima, 1978) also investigated the impact of Christian missionary influence on the reformation of Campa eschatology. In particular, Aranda de los Rios studied the effects of the

introduction of Seventh Day Adventism into the Campa community. The author discerns a state of dramatic disorientation wherein the Campa community imagines itself living in a terror (ibid., 63–64) based on imported ideologies: on the one hand, a new national ideology, and, on the other hand, a recently arrived Christian worldview of imminent messianic eschatology. The people reckon themselves as existing in the time between a secure mythic period and the triumphal end of time. The contemporary period is one of "holy waiting" in an environment of exploitation, sickness, and hunger, which, nonetheless, should not preoccupy true believers because they will be vindicated as soon as the end dawns. In Weiss's report it would appear that Christianity fostered the image of a golden age and, in Aranda de los Rios's, that it impelled a specter of dark doom. In fact, there is no reason to doubt that South American religions and eschatologies were complex outcomes of complicated and plural histories long before the introduction of Christianity. That the encounter with Christianity was accompanied by unparalleled devastation is undeniable. This is the point made by many South American visions of the end. But South Americans were already equipped to recognize the signs of radical cultural change and of the end of the symbolic world. They had eschatologies of their own. The tragic and destructive imagery or the pictures of a golden age from their own mythical tradition helped them face change and renewal creatively. The ways in which native religious paradigms absorbed and transformed Christian eschatologies remain the unpredictable fruit of their creative history of involvement with the sacred. Native eschatology is too complex to attribute comprehensive spiritualities to any single, recent reaction to mission theology.

386. Varese, *La Sal de los cerros*, pp. 129–130.

387. Regarding the sacredness of Campa trading partnerships and on other sacred notions of exchange, see chapter 6.

388. Varese, ibid., p. 138.

389. Ibid., p. 140.

390. Ibid., p. 141.

391. Ibid.

392. Ibid., p. 143.

393. Ibid.

394. Ibid., p. 144.

395. Ibid., p. 129.

396. Ibid., p. 130.

397. Alfred Métraux, "A Quechua Messiah in Eastern Peru," *AA* 44 (1942): 721–725; Schaden, "Le Messianisme en Amérique du Sud," pp. 1071f.

398. Rowe, "El Movimiento nacional inca," pp. 40–42.

399. Métraux, "Quechua Messiah," p. 722 mentions that Juan Santos may have come to the territory of Campa chief Mateo Santabangori in order to seek asylum because he had killed someone (his Jesuit master?) in Guamanca.

400. Ibid., p. 723. Juan Santos's attitude toward blacks and mestizos was ambiguous, for he bitterly resented them as a sign of Spanish presence (they also served as policemen, the agents of Spanish secular power) but counted them as allies. Antonio Gatico, for example, a Negro slave, was his brother-in-law and most trusted aid.

401. Varese, *La Sal de los cerros*, p. 68.

402. Ibid.

403. Ibid. Regarding the connection of traditional beer-drinking with the rains and with the deluvial destruction that gave birth to a new world, see chapter 4.

404. Métraux, "Quechua Messiah," p. 723.

405. Varese, *La Sal de los cerros*, p. 82.

406. Ibid., p. 85.

407. Rowe, "El Movimiento nacional inca," pp. 40–42; Métraux, "Quechua Messiah," p. 724, offers no date but says that a companion mortally wounded the leader in a mock battle.

408. Métraux, ibid., p. 725.

409. For a general discussion of these issues and for an account of how scholars have coped with them, see Burridge, *New Heaven, New Earth*, pp. 3–14, 97–140. For a penetrating depiction of this *crise de conscience* that is at once a querulousness about the status of knowledge and a

tendency toward the paralyzing remorse of bad conscience, see Carrasco, *Quetzalcoatl and the Irony of Empire.*

410. Bartolomé, "Shamanism among the Avá-Chiripá," p. 118. H. Clastres translates *tekó-achy* as "life *[teko]* sick *[achy]*" and notes that it "connotes everything that is imperfect, mortal" (H. Clastres, *La Terre sans mal,* p. 114). The situation of humans is constantly tense. *Tekó-achy kue,* according to the Mbya, is the spirit of foods (especially raw meat), which enters one's blood and tends to compete with the forces of the *ñe'ë,* the divine word-soul. As *tekó-achy* accumulates and triumphs, it annihilates the sacred power manifest in human speech, with the result that its victims make animal noises (ibid., pp. 116ff. and passim). *Tekó-achy* designates imperfect existence in general but also the particular components of historical existence (e.g., *teco açi* was translated as "work" in Montoya's seventeenth century *Tesoro de la lengua guaraní,* as cited in H. Clastres, ibid., p. 114). Regarding other expressions of supernatural dead weight of imperfection and catastrophe, see the earlier section on "heavy mourning," in this chapter; see also Michel Perrin, "Chamanisme et morphogénése," *H* 26 (1986): 107–124.

411. Bartolomé, "Shamanism among the Avá-Chiripá," p. 118.

412. Ibid., p. 121. For arguments in a similar vein, see Curt Nimuendajú, "Die Sagen von der Erschaffund und Vernichtung der Welt als Grundlagen der Religion der Apápocuvá-Guaraní," *ZFE* 46 (1914): 284–403; Alfred Métraux, "Migrations historiques des Tupí-Guaranís," *JSAP* n.s. 19 (1927): 1–45, and "The Guarani," in *HSAI,* vol. 3, pp. 69–94; Egon Schaden, "Messianisme en Amérique du Sud," pp. 1051–1070, and *Aspectos fundamentais da cultura guarani* (São Paulo, 1954). But see also Wolfgang H. Lindig, "Wanderungen der Tupi-Guarani und Eschatologie der Apapocuva-Guarani," in Wilhelm E. Mühlmann, *Chiliasmus und Nativismus: Studien zur Psychologie, Soziologie und historischen Kasuistik der Umsturzbewegungen* (Berlin, 1961), which argues against this hypothesis, first put forward by Nimuendajú (e.g., in *The Apinayé,* pp. 335ff.), that Guaraní eschatologies are fundamentally indigenous concepts. Lindig calls attention to Christian input (Lindig, p. 37); see also H. Clastres, *La Terre Sans Mal,* esp. pp. 99–103.

413. Mircea Eliade, "Paradise and Utopia: Mythical Geography and Eschatology," in *The Quest,* p. 111, relying primarily upon Schaden, *Aspectos,* p. 199. Since, throughout this volume, symbolism has been seen as a critical human condition originating in the crises of primordial destruction or dismissal, Eliade's more general conclusion that "the example of the Tupi-Guaranis demonstrates that entire collectivities have been brought to seek Paradise, and to search for centuries, without social crises as a stimulus" (ibid., p. 111) would need qualification.

414. Bartolomé, "Shamanism Among the Avá-Chiripá," p. 118.

415. Ibid., p. 122.

416. Métraux, "Religion and Shamanism," p. 584.

417. Bartolomé, "Shamanism Among the Avá-Chiripá," p. 108.

418. Egon Schaden, "Der Paradiesmythos im Leben der Guaraní-Indianer," *SJ* 3 (1955): p. 151.

419. Alfred Métraux, "Les Messies de l'Amérique du Sud," *Archives de sociologie des religions* 4 (1957): p. 109; *Religions et magies,* pp. 11–41; and "The Tupinambá," in *HSAI,* vol. 3, pp. 95–133.

420. In 1914 Curt Nimuendajú published Apápocuvá creation myths together with a reconstruction of the nineteenth century messianic migrations of three Guaraní groups (the Apapocuvá, led by the prophets Guyrakambit and Nimbiarapoñy; the Oguaíva; and the Tanygua, led by the feared shaman Ñanderykynī); see Nimuendajú, "Die Sagen," and also the commentary and retranscription of Nimuendajú's Guaraní texts by Juan Francisco Recalde in Nimuendajú, *Mitos de creación;* descriptions of the culture hero Ñanderykeý are found on pp. 170f. of *Mitos de creación.*

421. Ibid., p. 88; among the Mbya-Guaraní, the first being to enter the Land Without Evil was Jeupie, a perpetrator of incest with his paternal aunt. He brought on the flood that destroyed the world and originated the drinking festival (H. Clastres, *La Terre Sans Mal,* p. 83).

422. Nimuendajú, *Mitos de creación,* pp. 69, 169–170, 201–202.

423. Ibid., p. 70.

424. In addition to Nimuendajú's report, see the treatment given in Schaden, "Le Messianisme en Amérique du Sud," pp. 1062ff; Schaden relates Nimuendajú's data to information he obtained from messianic groups migrating toward the Land Without End in the late 1940's (pp.

1067f). Regarding the millennial image of "crossing over," see the remarks of J. Z. Smith in the essay "The Devil in Mr. Jones," in his *Imagining Religion*.

425. Nimuendajú, *Mitos de creación*, p. 172; Recalde provides this transcription of the Guaraní text: *"Yvype pemanombama. Nda-pehó-veichéne. Ko'āgā pepytá ko'arupí!"* in Nimuendajú, ibid., p. 214.

426. Nimuendajú argued that indigenous traditions of creation motivated the messianic migrations (see ibid., pp. 29–39), and Recalde's comments affirm this (ibid., passim).

427. Ibid., p. 31; see also H. Clastres, *La Terre Sans Mal*, pp. 40–64 for discussion of the types (*pagé* and *caraïbe*) of Guaraní messianic leadership.

428. Nimuendajú, *Mitos de creación*, p. 116.

429. See Bourdieu, *Outline of a Theory of Practice*, and *Distinction*, for treatment of the dialectical relationship of *habitus*, a mode of praxis, to the imaginative and material processes that structure space.

430. Nimuendajú, *Mitos de creación*, p. 31.

431. Ibid., p. 37.

432. Ibid., pp. 121–122.

433. Ibid., p. 123.

434. Ibid., p. 91.

435. Ibid.

436. Ibid., p. 149.

437. Ibid., p. 38. H. Clastres, *La Terre Sans Mal*, passim, emphasizes that wandering is an element constitutive of the Guaraní messianic leader. It is possible that other cultures carry on regenerative meanderings that reenact the destruction and renewal of the world through processions or parades that stay within more constrained physical territory but that reenact equally wide-ranging mythical journeys. Several examples were treated earlier in this volume: the Barasana procession at the He House initiation of boys, and the Baniwa parade for initiation, which imitates the worldwide wandering of Amaru and her followers at the time of the enlargement of the earth. But it is possible to examine in this light even the rather subdued processions of urban liturgies and passion plays. See, for instance, Pierre Arnold, "Pèlerinages et processions comme formes de pouvoir symbolique des classes subalternes: Deux cas péruviens," *Social Compass* 32 (1985): 45–56, and Joanne Rappaport, "History, Myth, and the Dynamics of Territorial Maintenance in Tierradentro, Colombia," *American Ethnologist* 12 (1985): pp. 27–45.

438. Schaden, "Der Paradiesmythos im Leben der Guaraní-Indianer," *ICA*, 30th Congress (London, 1952), pp. 179–186.

439. Ibid., p. 181; H. Clastres, *La Terre Sans Mal*, pp. 121–131, depicts *agüyjé* as conceptualized by the Mbya, especially as it relates to the physiology of the body (blood, bone, breath, organs) and corporal accomplishments (dance, song). In this life, bone especially approximates the state of *agüyjé* in store for the rest of the concrete physiology in the eschaton (Clastres, ibid., p. 131).

440. Pierre Clastres, "Eléments de démographie amérindienne," *H* 13 (1973): p. 34. Clastres cites studies, notably those of Angel Rosenblatt, that set the first figure lower. Pierre Chaunu, "La Population de l'Amérique indienne. Nouvelles recherches," *Revue historique* 1 (1963): 111–118, argues that the deaths of American Indians of the sixteenth century amounted to the obliteration of one quarter of the world population of the day (p. 117). Demographics of native peoples, especially attempts to ascertain and compare pre- and postcontact population figures, are hotly debated. See Magnus Mörner's review of Enrique Mayer and Elio Masferrer, "La población de America en 1978," *AI* 39 (1979): 217–337 in *LAIL* Vol. 4, no. 2 (1980), pp. 46ff. Several demographic surveys are recommended or criticized in Walter Dostal, ed., *The Situation of the Indian in South America* (Geneva, 1972), pp. 385–453. Statistics barely convey the chilling reality of catastrophe that leveled Amerindian societies. See Robert V. Morey, "A Joyful Harvest of Souls: Disease and Destruction of the Llanos Indians," *ACAR* 52 (1979): 77–108, and Johannes Wilbert, "Warao Ethnopathology," *Journal of Ethnopharmacology* 8 (1983): 357–361, for South American imagery of this devastation.

441. Schaden, "Der Paradiesmythos," p. 186.

442. Schaden's works, especially *Aspectos fundamentais*, testify to the impact of social particularities on the shape of millennial dreams and practices. See also Maurício Vinhas de Queiroz, *Messianismo e conflicto social* (Rio de Janeiro, 1966); Maria Isaura Pereira de Queiroz, "L'Influence du milieu social interne sur les mouvements messianiques brésiliens," *Archives de sociologie des religions* 5 (1958): 3–30, and "Brazilian Messianic Movements: A Help or Hindrance to 'Participation'?" *Bulletin. International Institute for Labour Studies* 7 (1970): 93–121; Rene Ribeiro, "Movimentos messianicos no Brasil," *AL* (1960): 35–56, and "Brazilian Messianic Movements," in Sylvia L. Thrupp, ed., *Millenial Dreams in Action* (The Hague, 1962), pp. 55–69; Roger Bastide, "Messianisme et développement économique et social," *Cahiers internationaux de sociologie* 31 (1961): 3–14; and Udo Oberem, "Die Aufstandsbewegung der Pende bei den Quijo Ost-Ekuadors im Jahre 1578," in Wilhelm E. Mühlmann, ed., *Chiliasmus und Nativismus* (Berlin, 1961), pp. 750–780.

443. Schaden, "Der Paradiesmythos," p. 186; see also Schaden's general assessment of the "profound causes of messianism" throughout South America in "Le Messianisme en Amérique du Sud," pp. 1104–1107.

444. Jürgen Riester, *Die Pauserna-Guaraŝug'wä. Monographie eines Tupi-Guaraní-Volkes in Ostbolivien* (St. Augustin bei Bonn, 1972) also offers an immense and richly detailed study of a Tupi-Guaraní group whose forebears left Paraguay for eastern Bolivia (in the Campo Grande savannah between the Paragua, Itenes, and Pauserna rivers). They had been reduced to some fifty persons at the time of Riester's stay (August 1964 to February 1965). He carefully delineates the economic and political transformations they suffered and helps set this analysis within the Guaraní world of meaning by presenting dozens of myths carefully cross-referenced to the mythology of other Guaraní groups. They longed to return to Janeramai ("our grandfather"), who created humans from gourds and who is the source of eternal light. It was to Janeramai's Land Without Evil — a land of plenty where souls feast on abundant meat, manioc, and honey — that *karaiúhu*, spiritual leaders, led them on their epic migrations. Even in their reduced circumstances the group maintained their creative view of the world. See also Riester, "Zur Religion der Pauserna-Guaraŝug'wä in Ostbolivien," *ANT* 65 (1970): pp. 466–479.

445. Thus, for example, Max Schmidt concluded in 1936 that nothing of the authentic Pauserna-Guarayú religious vision remained; all one could learn from them was Christian; see Schmidt, "Los Guarayú," *Revista Social Científica de Paraguay* (Asunción) 6 (1936): 175. The works of Riester, Schaden, Cadogan, and others proved that Schmidt's judgment, which correctly perceived the all-pervasive influence of Christianity, underestimated the religious creativity of Guaraní people, even in their miserable conditions.

446. Schaden, "Der Paradiesmythos," p. 186.

447. Kenelm Burridge, *Mambu: A Melanesian Millennium* (London, 1960), pp. 147–245, esp. pp. 165ff., 209ff., and 222ff., demonstrates, the restless connection of creative dream and myth (as well as all imaginal forms) to preoccupations with termination and change.

448. See the drawings of the native Andean chronicler Guaman Poma for graphic depiction of the apocalyptic convergence of devouring beasts (Guaman Poma de Ayala, *Nueva corónica*, Paris, 1936, p. 694). Guaman Poma's history is discussed below.

449. Academic presentations of the symbolic condition described in myth are not immune to the need for apocalyptic judgments. Lévi-Strauss's monumental analysis of the contradictions he cumulatively uncovers at increasingly subtle levels of South American myth may predetermine the apocalyptic ending of the fourth and final volume of *Mythologiques*. The section that he calls the "finale" portrays the eclipse of the universe and of human history in the poetic terms of modern physics (not South American eschatologies) but it derives from the analytic quality of his earlier dissections of South American myth and on the exclusive quality of his own premises that leave no room for any other mode of being but the binary opposition of logico-linguisticism. That Lévi-Strauss renders this apocalyptic judgment on the cosmic condition, a final rendering called for by the structures of his own mytho-logic, is a tribute to the integrity (in the sense of eschatological entirety discussed above) of Lévi-Strauss's *opus*. For an assessment of the connection of moral judgment, justice, spatial differentiation, sorting, and cleaning (the ultimate

version of which is the sweeping judgment of apocalypse), see Peter Rigby, "Some Rituals of 'Purification': An Essay on Social and Moral Categories," in E. R. Leach, ed., *Dialectics in Practical Religion* (Cambridge, 1968).

450. Victor Turner used William James's term "consecutive discordances" to describe this process of creative abstraction at work in initiatory experience. In eschatologies the abstractive powers of symbolic existence itself come under reflection. See the section entitled "Betwixt and Between," in V. Turner, *Forest of Symbols* (Ithaca, N.Y., 1967).

451. William H. Crocker, "The Canela Messianic Movement," in *Reunião Brasileira de Antropologia* (Belem, 1966), p. 41.

452. Manuela Carneiro da Cunha, "Logique du mythe et de l'action. Le Mouvement messianique canela de 1963," *H* 13 (1973): 5. See also William H. Crocker, "The Canela Messianic Movement: An Introduction," in *Atas do simpósio sôbre a biota amazônica*, vol. 2, *Antropologia* (Rio de Janeiro, 1967), pp. 69–83. Egon Schaden also summarizes the episode in "Le Messianisme en Amérique du Sud," pp. 1091–1093.

453. A version of the myth of Auké was published by Nimuendajú in *The Apinayé*, pp. 167–168, and later in his *The Eastern Timbira*, pp. 246. Harald Schultz, "Lendas dos indios krahó,"*RMP* n.s. 4 (1950): 49–164, records Krahó versions of the same myth on pp. 86–93.

454. The story of the frightening boy whose mother's brother decides to kill him on a trip into the forest is a common mythic scenario associated with initiation and frequently linked with stories of the mythic jaguar.

455. In this episode, the boy joins together the two common eschatological themes of falling mountains and of unsealing. He "returns" to release his uncle from confinement by making the mountains in which he was walled up disappear.

456. In the Apinayé version, the mother's brother takes the boy from the arms of his crying mother and grandmother and throws him down onto the earth. However, Vanmegaprána "turned into a dry leaf, which slowly circling floated down to earth. [The mother's] brother chased the leaf, looked till he found it, kindled the fire, and threw it in before the eyes of the weeping mother and grandmother. . . . [B]ut he arose from the ashes in the shape of a white man. . . . [H]e put up a big house and made everything now in the possession of Christians" (Nimuendajú, *The Apinayé*, p. 168). At this point the myth plays with the strategy that we called *funeral refinement* (see above), that is, the ritual process of finishing off a being many times over by subjecting the being to multiple kinds of destructive ends.

457. Nimuendaú, *The Eastern Timbira*, pp. 245–246; cited in Carneiro da Cunha, "Logique du mythe," pp. 9–10.

458. Nimuendajú, *The Eastern Timbira*, p. 234; cited in Carneiro da Cunha, "Logique du mythe," p. 11.

459. Crocker, "The Canela Messianic Movement: An Introduction," provides a large number of symbolic details that Carneiro da Cunha, "Logique du mythe," pp. 6ff., selects for a stimulating analysis that not only illumines the meaning of the myth and of the symbolic actions of this messianic movement but provides insight into the relationship of myth, ritual, and history in general. Carneiro da Cunha (p. 37) emphasizes that this messianic movement occurred during a time of "relative abundance" and offers it as a counter-case to those who link messianism with deprivation (on which see, for example, David F. Aberle, "A Note on Relative Deprivation Theory as Applied to Millenarian and Other Cult Movements," in Thrupp, ed., *Millenial Dreams in Action*, pp. 209–214.

460. Reversals of this kind are common features of the end of time and have appeared in examples already mentioned in this chapter. The Kaiová group of Guaraní-speakers, for example, described the eschaton as full of fantastic animals (e.g., flying monkeys and horses) who not only take control from humans but who hunt men down with fiery arrows (Schaden, *Aspectos fundamentais*, p. 187). Tupinambá groups foresaw a time when arrows, shovels, and other tools would perform work by themselves and restore the means of production to the material world. Humans would no longer labor; old folks would become young (Métraux, "Les Messies," p. 108).

461. Carneiro da Cunha, "Logique du mythe," p. 9.

462. The openness that brings death and dismisses immortal beings in the myths of the origins of death was discussed at the opening of this chapter.

463. William H. Crocker, "The Canela Messianic Movement," *Reunião Brasileira*, p. 42.

464. Carneiro da Cunha, "Logique du mythe," pp. 12–13.

465. Ibid., p. 12. Carneiro da Cunha shows how the philological breakdown of the name *Auké* links him to the rainy season, *atuk*.

466. See chapter 4, above, for a presentation of this view of cultural and cosmic time, especially as evident in dance, frenzy, liquid, orgy, incest, and violence.

467. Carneiro da Cunha, ibid., p. 25.

468. Ibid., p. 29.

469. Ibid., p. 32.

470. Carneiro da Cunha believes that the tenacious strength of myth lies in the intelligibility it brings to historical circumstance. The mythic reading of history, even of the historical situation of incredible inequality, is intellectually satisfying and permits the Canela to understand the meaning of their total situation.

471. The enigma centers on the encounter of historical and mythic reality. The disturbing coincidence of these two modes of being within the religious imagination raises urgent questions, for their meeting ends in destruction. Indeed, final destruction liberates a cosmos increasingly entangled in the historic mode of being. When the regulating rhythms of the cosmos no longer signify primordial sacrality, the eschaton eliminates every insignificant form by uncovering the unending sources of creativity.

472. George Kubler, "The Behavior of Atahuallpa, 1531–33," *The Hispanic American Historical Review* 12 (1945): 411–427.

473. Nathan Wachtel, *La Vision des vaincus: Les Indiens du Pérou devant la conquête espagnole 1530–1570* (Paris, 1971), pp. 255ff, and Wachtel, "Rebeliones y milenarismo," in Juan Ossio, ed., *Ideologiá mesiánica del mundo andino* (Lima, 1973), p. 107. In connection with gold and the Devil, see also Michael Taussig's thoughts on Andean messianism in *The Devil and Commodity Fetishism*, pp. 187ff.

474. See the detailed accounts in John Hemming, *The Conquest of the Incas* (New York, 1970), esp. pp. 169–255.

475. Wachtel, "Rebeliones y milenarismo," p. 109; Wachtel, *La Vision des vaincus*, pp. 259ff.

476. Wachtel, "Rebeliones y Millenarismo," p. 110.

477. Ibid., p. 113. See also Franklin Pease G. Y., *El Dios creador andino* (Lima, 1973), pp. 69–81, for a discussion of Taki Ongo (treated below).

478. Wachtel, *La Vision des Vaincus*, p. 246. The image of ritual tears and stylized weeping is important in South American conceptions of transition, especially temporal passage, and have been treated in several places in this volume in connection with cycles of stars, generations of initiands, drinking feasts, New Year ceremonies, funeral laments, transitions from night to day, and greetings of visitors. Tears and weeping recur as important images in the text and drawings of Guaman Poma: see, for example, *Nueva corónica* (Paris, 1936), vol. 2, p. 260, and Vol. 3, p. 300, in the text, and the tears and flowing blood that streak the physiognomy of Indians in his drawings.

479. Wachtel, *La Vision des vaincus*, gives the birth date of 1526 (p. 29) but also of 1545 (p. 244). Guaman Poma himself gives his year of birth as 1525 and also 1533. G. Lobsiger discusses the question and suggests 1545 as the correct date in "Felipe Guamán Poma de Ayala," *BSSA* 19 (1960); cited in Wachtel, *Vision des vaincus*, p. 244.

480. Felipe Guaman Poma de Ayala, *El Primer nueva corónica y buen Gobierno* [1584–1614] (Lima, 1966). Two other native chroniclers of Andean culture who wrote in the sixteenth and seventeenth centuries are Titu Cusi Yupanqui and Santa Cruz Pachacuti. See Titu Cusi Yupanqui (as written down by Diego de Castro), *Relación de la Conquista del Perú y Hechos del Inca Manco II* [1570] (Lima, 1946). Titu Cusi reigned as royal *inca* in Vilcabamba from 1557 to 1570. It remains a serious question how much of the rebel leader's thought and recitation survive in the narration recorded by the Spanish missionary Diego de Castro. See also Joan Santa Cruz Pachacuti Yamqui Salcamaygua, *Relación de antigüedades desde reyno del Pirú* [about 1613] (Lima,

1927). See also the anonymous document, probably dating from soon after 1533, *Apu Inca Atawallpaman. Elegía quechua anónima*, trans. J. M. Arguedas, in Miguel León-Portilla, *El Reverso de la conquista* (Mexico City, 1964), pp. 181–186. Frank L. Salomon, "Chronicles of the Impossible: Notes on Three Peruvian Indigenous Historians," in Rollena Adorno, ed., *From Oral to Written Expression: Native Andean Chronicles of the Early Colonial Period* (Syracuse, N.Y., 1982), pp. 9–40, brings welcome light to the study of such documents.

481. Juan M. Ossio, "Guaman Poma: Nueva Corónica o Carta al Rey. Un Intento de Aproximación a las Categórias del Pensamiento del Mundo Andino," in Ossio, ed., *Ideología mesiánica*, pp. 155–213.

482. José Tamayo Herrera, *Historia del indigenismo cuzqueño: Siglos XVI–XX* (Lima, 1980), p. 83.

483. Ossio, "Guaman Poma," p. 157.

484. Ibid., pp. 206–207.

485. Ibid., p. 157.

486. For a reflection on Guaman Poma's sketches, see Jean Philippe Husson, "Art poétique quechua dans la chronique de Felipe Waman Poma de Ayala," *Amérindia* (Paris) 9 (1984): 79–110. The three hundred detailed and shocking drawings of Guaman Poma (and the sketches of Santa Cruz Pachacuti and other native chroniclers) can be restudied in the light of religious appraisals of the power of writing. In another context, Nordenskiöld wondered why his hosts insisted on drawing pictures to accompany the words and notation of shamanic songs. He concluded that "picture writing *per se* carries a magic import. . . . The virtues of the medicinal incantations are enhanced by the fact of their being expressed in picture writing"; see Nordenskiöld, *Picture-Writing and Other Documents by Néle and Ruben Pérez Kantule* (Göteborg, 1928), p. 19. Aside from the label of magic, thinkers wrestle with the meaning of *inscription* and not simply its discursive "content." This places Guaman Poma in the same orbit as, for example, Erwin Panofsky, *Meaning in the Visual Arts*, new ed. (Chicago, 1983); Ernst Gombrich, *Art and Illusion: a Study in the Psychology of Pictorial Presentation* (Princeton, N.J., 1961), Rudolf Arnheim, *Visual Thinking* (Berkeley, 1969), and Rudolf Arnheim, *Art and Visual Perception: A Psychology of the Creative Eye*, rev. ed. (Berkeley, 1974). The issue of pictorial representation becomes an eschatologically pertinent way of chronicling reality in time. Visual arts become the center of contention later, in the eighteenth century, when Túpac Amaru II and his officers had numerous paintings made of themselves. Production of these pictures was proscribed in the sentence (treated below) levied against the leaders of this uprising; see Jorgé Cornejo Bouroncle, *Túpac Amaru*, 2d ed. (Cuzco, 1963), p. 342.

487. In Quechua, the term *pachacuti* means "the world is transformed" according to José Imbelloni, *Pachakuti IX (El Indario Crítico)* (Buenos Aires, 1946). In Aymara, the term *pachacuti* means "like a time of war," especially the state of affairs surrounding the Final Judgment, according to Ludovico Bertonio, *Vocabulario de la lengua aymara* (Juli, 1612), p. 242. Both sources are cited in Ossio, "Guaman Poma," pp. 187–188. A number of different chroniclers presented the same portrait of successive epoch-worlds. See the materials gathered and analyzed by Imbelloni, *Pachakuti IX*, and Ossio, "Guaman Poma," pp. 187–191. Guaman Poma's schema is fascinating because he sets up two parallel sets of ages, one for the native world and one for the world of the Spanish conquistadors.

488. See chapter 2, above, for a discussion of the meaning of successive ages of the world as they connect with destruction and chapter 4 for fuller exposition of the movements of cosmic or calendrical time in the Andes, especially as embodied in actions of various ritual groups from the two social moieties.

489. Ossio, ibid., pp. 157–163.

490. For more on the links of Andean moral and social order to the expressions of space see Lawrence E. Sullivan, "Above, Below, or Far Away: Andean Cosmogony and Ethics," in Reynolds and Lovin, eds., *Cosmogony and Ethical Order*, pp. 98–130.

491. Guaman Poma, *Nueva corónica* (1936), pp. 993–994. See G. Lobsiger, "Une Curieuse carte du Pérou dressée au 1614," *Globe* (Geneva) 103 (1963) ("Memoires"): 33–69. This remarkable map (which appears inside the cover of this volume) should be studied alongside other Andean cosmographs, such as the Coricancha drawing of Santa Cruz Pachacuti, and Andean mesas,

quipus, and textiles, as well as architectures. See Sullivan, "Above, Below, and Far Away," for a study of the pervasive influence of the principles embodied in such spatial schemes.

492. "[H]e turned toward the only possible sources of order which he could conceive of as legitimate, that is, the Inca, who, however, appeared in his day in the guise of Philip III, King of Spain" (Ossio, "Guaman Poma," p. 204).

493. On the life of Guaman Poma see the descriptions and sources in Herrera, *Historia del indigenismo*, pp. 83ff., and Wachtel, *La Vision des vaincus*, pp. 245ff. An Indian who reckoned paternal descent from kings of Yarovillca and maternal descent from Topa Inca (the tenth royal emperor), Guaman Poma lived mostly in Huamanga and Arequipa, was dispossessed of his properties, and wandered through the inferno of post-Conquest Peru.

494. Guaman Poma, *Nueva corónica* (1936), p. 259.

495. Regarding the dates of Taki Ongo activities see Wachtel, *La Vision des vaincus*, p. 271. Wachtel estimates that the movement was vibrant from 1560 to 1570 but wonders whether or not the millenarian activities of the seventeenth and eighteenth centuries were a continuation of the Taki Ongo movement (p. 276).

496. Ossio, "Guaman Poma," p. 204. For a description of the Taki Ongo messianic dance craze led by Juan Chocne, see Luis Millones, "Un Movimiento nativista del siglo XVI: El Taki Ongoy," *RPC* 3 (1964): 134–140; reprinted in Ossio, ed., *Ideología mesiánica*, pp. 83–94; Millones, "Nuevos aspectos del Taki Ongoy," in Ossio, ed., *Ideología mesiánica*, pp. 95–102; Wachtel, "Rebeliones y milernarismo"; Michael Taussig, *The Devil and Commodity Fetishism*, touches on the Taki Ongo on pp. 171–173, and 198. For additional descriptions and sources of the Taki Ongo, see Pierre Duviols, *La Destrucción de las religiones andinas* (Mexico City, 1977), pp. 133–145.

497. The connection of maintaining frontiers and boundaries to the symbolic containments established and renewed in ritual (ceremonial space, mythic geography) is discussed, along with ideas about their eschatological porousness, in Joanne Rappaport, "Mesianismo y las transformaciones de símbolos mesiánicos en Tierra Dentro," *RCA* 23 (1980): 365–413, (for example, on p. 402), which gathers the relevant observations of Sherbondy, Zuidema, and Deborah A. Poole. As for the physical invasion by fatal disease, see Wachtel, *La Vision des vaincus*, pp. 134–152. Through the "murderous oppression" (Wachtel, ibid., p. 145) of war and abuse and through the biological factor of disease, Wachtel hypothesizes, the population of the Inca Empire was reduced from eight million in 1524 to 1.3 million in 1590. "This fall of at least 80 percent would have completely disorganized the traditional cadres of the society" (p. 152), especially the decimal structure that based itself on mobilizations of groups of ten, one hundred, one thousand, and ten thousand men and which played so important a role in the social order of the empire. In the light of the earlier mention of weighty imperfections that brought on the Guaraní cataclysm, it is noteworthy that questionnaires of native peoples surveyed in the years 1582 to 1586 attribute increased demise of the native population to "eating and drinking more than before, having more vices, more freedom" (less regulated life), in addition to disease, war, and work. Wachtel associates the first several reasons with the vacuum left by the disintegration of traditional life of social customs and religious rites (ibid.). "The Indian escapes [e.g., in alcoholism] a world that no longer has meaning for him." (ibid.). See also ibid., pp. 325ff.

498. Wachtel, *La Vision des vaincus*, p. 270, and "Rebeliones y milenarismo," p. 136. *Taki Ongo* is the most common 16th century spelling. See, for example, Cristóbal de Molina (de Cuzco), *Relación de las fábulas y ritos de los incas* [1575] (Lima, 1916), pp. 96–101. *Taki* is actually a quite specific form of chant-dance performed during agricultural labor of harvest and seedtime. (See Urton, *Crossroads of Earth and Sky*, passim, for the relationship of the beginning and end of the agricultural cycle of the central Andes to the rising and setting of the Pleiades; see chapter 4, above, for a discussion of the way in which disappearance and reappearance create cycles and calendars.) *Taki* is one of the three forms of *huanca*, a spatial form of sacrality linked to the mummified bodies (*mallqui*, "mummy or seed") of ancient ancestors. The *huanca* is the ancestral cadaver's mineral-double, of which the *Taki* dance, sacred monoliths, and the valley of Mantaro (Jauja) together with its inhabitants are the visible expressions. See Pierre Duviols, "Un Symbolisme de l'occupation de l'aménagement et de l'exploitation de l'espace: Le Monolithe 'huanca' et sa fonction dans les Andes préhispaniques," *H* 19 (1979): 7–31. For more extensive

discussion of the definitions of the term *Taki Ongo* see Pierre Duviols, *La Destrucción de las religiones andinas* (Mexico City, 1977), p. 134 note 66.

499. The Taki Ongo movement was not the only millennial cult of its day. For example, Wachtel calls attention to a sect centered on the resurrection of the god Pachacamac, lord of the earth ("Rebeliones y milenarismo," p. 115).

500. Steve J. Stern, *Peru's Indian Peoples and the Challenge of Spanish Conquest: Huamanga to 1640* (Madison, Wis., 1982), p. 52. See also R. T. Zuidema, "Observaciones sobre el Taki Onqoy," *Historia y cultura* 1 (Lima, 1965); Cristóbal de Albornoz, "Instrucción para descubrir todas las Guacas del Pirú y sus camayos y haciendas," ed. by Pierre Duviols, in *JSAP* 56 (1967): 17–39; and Pease, *El Dios creador andino*, pp. 69–81. Wachtel, *La Vision des vaincus*, p. 275, offers further description and documents archival sources regarding the behavioral details of the possessed. It seems that the royal *inca* Titu Cusi coordinated his rebellious activities with the rhythms of the Taki Ongo. His emissaries apparently played a part by helping to incite further the millennial fever (see Wachtel, ibid., pp. 270ff), but "the *Taqui Ongo* also manifested autonomy" (p. 271).

501. Wachtel, "Rebeliones y milenarismo," p. 118.

502. Stern, *Peru's Indian Peoples*, p. 55.

503. Wachtel, "Rebeliones y milenarismo," p. 120, and *La Vision des vaincus*, pp. 272ff.

504. Cristóbal de Molina (El Cuzqueño), "Fábulas y ritos de los Incas" [1575], in F. A. Loayza, ed., *Las Crónicas de los molinas* (Lima, 1943), and Pedro Sarmiento de Gamboa [1572] *Historia de los Incas* (Buenos Aires, 1947).

505. Wachtel, "Rebeliones y milenarismo," p. 120. Zuidema, "Observaciones sobre el Taqui Ongoy," discusses the half-millennial epicycle mentioned in connection with Guaman Poma's history; see also José Imbelloni, "La 'Weltanschauung' de los Amautas reconstruida. Formas peruanas de pensamiento templario," *ICA*, 27th Congress (Lima, 1942); and Franklin Pease, "El Mito de Inkarri y la visión de los vencidos," in Ossio, ed., *Ideología mesiánica*, pp. 441–458, esp. pp. 450ff.

506. Stern, *Peru's Indian Peoples*, p. 57. Sullivan, "Above, Below, or Far Away," explains how sacred places and the rites associated with them become the focus of moral life, especially in times of conflict.

507. Cristóbal de Molina, *Relación de las fábulas*, pp. 97–98; cited in Wachtel, *La Vision des vaincus*, p. 272.

508. Luis Millones, ed., *Las Informaciones de Cristóbal de Albornoz: Documentos para el estudio del Taki Onqoy* (Cuernavaca, 1971), vol. 2, p. 109; cited in Stern, *Peru's Indian Peoples*, p. 53.

509. Wachtel, "Rebeliones y milenarismo," p. 121, and *La Vision des vaincus*, p. 274.

510. Wachtel, "Rebeliones y milenarismo," p. 121, and *La Vision des vaincus*, pp. 274–275.

511. Wachtel, "Rebeliones y milenarismo," pp. 121–122, and *La Vision des vaincus*, p. 275.

512. Wachtel, "Rebeliones y milenarismo," p. 122, and *La Vision des vaincus*, p. 275.

513. Stern, *Peru's Indian Peoples*, p. 53.

514. Ibid., p. 59.

515. Cristóbal de Molina, *Relación de las fábulas*, p. 80; cited in Stern, *Peru's Indian Peoples*, p. 60.

516. On the relationship of irony, dance, and cycles of stars based on the myths of their tragic disappearance and periodic reappearance, see the relevant sections in chapters 2 and 4 above.

517. See chapter 4, above, for a discussion of ritual combat and chapter 7 for treatment of the creativity of oppugnant forms used in making contracts and resolving dilemmas, including the reception of foreigners into one's own cosmic space.

518. See chapter 4 for treatment of the ritual symbolism of excessive drinking and rowdiness.

519. Wachtel, "Rebeliones y milenarismo," p. 117.

520. Stern calls the Taki Onqoy millenarianism "and inward-looking moral drama" (*Peru's Indian Peoples*, p. 69).

521. Wachtel, "Rebeliones y milenarismo," p. 120, citing the chronicler Cristóbal de Molina, *Relación de los fábulas*, pp. 97–98.

522. Stern writes,

In condemning Hispanicizing Indians who bound themselves to colonial power, together with those internal antagonisms which traditionally divided ayllus and ethnic groups, and generally collaborative adaptations toward the colonials and their gods, Taki Onqoy pinpointed precisely the forces which eroded its own capacity to challenge colonial society. Incipient class dynamics, ethnic division, and collaborationism all loomed over Huamanga's popular heresy, and confined its effective scope to spiritual issues. The first made links between the elite and the movement ambiguous and contradictory; the second weakened the natives' capacity to organize a truly united force or strategy; the third tormented natives sensitive to Taki Onqoy's moral command to purify themselves of ties to the Hispanic world. (*Peru's Indian Peoples*, p. 67)

523. Ibid., p. 70.

524. Ibid., p. 51; Zuidema, "Observaciones sobre el Taki Onqoy," p. 137; Pierre Duviols, *La Lutte contre les religions autochtones dans le Pérou colonial* (Lima and Paris, 1971); and Luis Millones, "Introducción al estudio de las idolatrías," *Aportes* (Paris) 4 (1967): 47–82.

525. These concluding paragraphs concerning eschatological dance depend on earlier treatment of the nature of time and dance as they connect to the cycles of appearance and disappearance that began with cosmic destruction. See chapter 4, above.

526. On the relationship of dance to periodic expressions of time and, in turn, to distinct qualities of being, see chapter 4, above.

527. Contemporary Andean messianic myths continue to probe the eschatological nature of writing and the historical nature of scripture. See, for instance, Jorge Flores Ochoa, "Inkariy y Qollariy en una comunidad del Altiplano," in Ossio, ed., *Ideología mesiánica*, e.g., pp. 319, 321, 334f.; see also Alejandro Ortiz Rescaniere, "El Mito de la escuela," in Ossio, ed., *Ideologiá mesiánica*, pp. 239–250, where the origin of written scripture is attributed to the moon. In answer to the pleas of Jesus Christ, the moon causes a page of scripture to fall to earth and teaches Christ how to read. With this power, Christ overcomes his older brother, the *inca*, in their rivalled courtship of Mother Earth (pp. 241, 246). Such notions fall into the same interpretive ambit as Paul Ricoeur, *Time and Narrative* (Chicago, 1985), and Ronald Grimes, "Of Words the Speaker, of Deeds the Doer," *Journal of Religion* 66 (1986): pp. 1–17.

528. On the ritual violence associated with change see chapter 2 on the world-destructions; chapter 4, regarding the violence staged to pass the time from one period to the next; and chapter 6, on initiation.

529. See, for example, Alberto Flores Galindo, *Tupac Amaru II–1780: Sociedad colonial y sublevaciones populares* (Lima, 1976), p. 8. See also Carlos Daniel Valcárcel, ed., *La Rebelión de Tupac Amaru*, 2 vols., (Lima, 1971–1972); Jorge Cornejo Bouroncle, *Túpac Amaru*, 2d ed. (Cuzco, 1963); Juan José Vega, *Túpac Amaru* (Lima, 1969); Luis Durand Florez, *Independencia e integración en el plan político de Túpac Amaru* (Lima, 1973). Herrera, *Historia del indigenismo cuzqueño*, pp. 100–107, conveys how Tupac Amaru II summed up the historical visions of the Andes and created a new reality.

530. Rowe, "El Movimiento nacional," p. 19.

531. Ibid., p. 20.

532. Ibid., p. 33.

533. Ibid., pp. 33–34, citing Francisco A. Loayza, ed., *Juan Santos, El Invencible (Manuscritos del año de 1742 al año de 1755)* (Lima, 1942), p. 163.

534. Pedro de Angelis, *Documentos para la historia de la sublevación de José Gabriel de Tupac-Amaru, cacique de la provincia de Tinta, en el Peru* (Buenos Aires, 1836), pp. 48–51; cited in Rowe, "El Movimiento nacional," pp. 35–36.

535. Valdez also leaves us the only documentary painting of the rebellion (Herrera, *Historia del indigenismo*, p. 99).

536. Bouroncle, *Tupac Amaru*, p. 343.

537. Flores Galindo, *Tupac Amaru II*, p. 10; see also Manuel Burga and Alberto Flores Galindo, "La Utopía andina," *Allpanchis* (Cuzco) 18 (1982): 85–102, and Marco Curatola, "Mito y milenarismo en los Andes: del Taqui Onqoy a Inkarri," *Allpanchis* 10 (1977): 65–92.

538. Wachtel has studied the messianic and eschatological messages in Andean folk theater; see Nathan Wachtel, *The Vision of the Vanquished: The Spanish Conquest of Peru through Indian Eyes, 1530–1570* (New York, 1977), and Wachtel, "La Visión de los Vencidos: La Conquista Española en el Folklore Indígena," in Ossio, ed., *Ideologiá mesiánica*, pp. 37–81. Wachtel

compares the folk tragedy describing the death of Atahuallpa with other plays that celebrate the conquest by the Spanish, such as the "Dance of the Conquest" from Guatemala and the "Great Conquest," or "The Dance of the Feather," from Mexico. These theatrical interpretations of the history of the Conquest have been performed from the sixteenth century to the present day. Wachtel poses himself this question: "Why do the Indian populations feel the need, even four centuries later, to relive their disaster?" (*Vision of the Vanquished*, p. 39). This is one of the questions addressed throughout this section of this volume, which has attempted to show that the answer lies in the traditional reenactments of mythical disaster (flood, fire, sacrifice, disappearance) performed to effect renewal. Efficacious symbols, arising from the catastrophic and sacrificial condition that gave order to the cosmos, bring closure to a condition of time. That is why festive decoration, costume, and noise are brought out at the appropriate moment in order to pass the time of each season. The conspicuous display of catastrophic symbolism in the eschatological age should hasten the end of a cosmos already partly consumed by its own symbolic logic.

539. Jesus Lara, ed. and trans., *Tragédia del fin de Atawallpa* (Cochabamba, Peru, 1957). Wachtel calls attention to comparable theatrical cycles of the conquest; viz., Clemente Hernando Balmori, ed. and trans., *La Conquista de los Españoles. Drama indígena bilingüe Quechua-Castellano* (Tucumán, Argentina, 1955). See also Mario Unzueta, *Valle* (Cochabamba, Peru, 1945), pp. 132–146, which describes "La Fiesta del Señor de Kanata," and Eduardo Fernandez, "La Muerte del Inca," *ALIM* 2 (1984): 201–208.

540. See Robert Randall, "Qoyllur Rit'i, an Inca Fiesta of the Pleiades," *Bulletin de l'Insitut Francais d'Etudes Andines* (Lima) 11 (1982): pp. 37–81. Obviously, "setting one's watch" is figurative here since chronometric time is not so much the issue as the regular cyclic reappearance of a *quality* of time, no matter "when" it appears on the watch or calendar. For a list of other annual Christian feasts on which this tragedy is enacted, see Wachtel, *La Vision des vaincus*, pp. 67–68.

541. Wachtel, "La Vision de los vencidos," p. 41, and *La Vision des vaincus*, p. 68.

542. Wachtel, "La Vision de los vencidos," p. 41, and *La Vision des vaincus*, p. 68.

543. Wachtel, *La Vision des vaincus*, p. 69.

544. Wachtel, "La Visión de los vencidos," p. 42.

545. Ibid., p. 44.

546. Ibid. Cf. the anonymous *Apu Inca Atawallpaman. Elegía Quechua Anónima*, apparently composed shortly after Atahuallpa's death in 1533 and translated by José María Arguedas, republished in Miguel Leon-Portilla, ed., *El Reverso de la Conquista* (Mexico City, 1964), pp. 181–186.

547. Wachtel, "La Visión de los vencidos," p. 48. The meaning of writing is, of course, raised outside of South America from many interesting points of view, from the study of aphasiology (especially dysgraphia and dislexia) to the study of scripture and the historiography of writing. See, for example, Ignace J. Gelb, *A Study of Writing*, rev. ed. (Chicago, 1963), esp. pp. 221ff. Alfred Bertholet, "Die Macht der Schrift in Glauben und Aberglauben," in *Abhandlungen der Deutschen Akademie der Wissenschaften zu Berlin* (Berlin, 1949), looks at the religious power of scriptures; see also William A. Graham, "*Qur'ān* as Spoken Word: An Islamic Contribution to the Understanding of Scripture," in Richard C. Martin, ed., *Approaches to Islam in Religious Studies* (Tucson, 1985), pp. 23–40; Jacques Derrida, *Of Grammatology* (Baltimore, 1976) and *Writing and Difference* (Chicago, 1980), also wrestles with issues similar to the eschatological ones raised in Guaman Poma and Andean theater. On the absence, silence, and separation inherent in writing, for example, see the treatment (Derrida, *Writing and Difference*, pp. 69ff.) of *la parole soufflé*, the word that is spirited away but that *leaves some trace* behind in writing (a form of sacrificial exchange); on the similitude of the movements of theatrical acting and writing (pp. 169–195); and on Freud and the scene, the theater, of writing (pp. 196–231). Michel de Certeau, *L'Ecriture de l'histoire* (Paris, 1975), also offers a rendering of some of these issues as do B. Stock, *The Implications of Literacy: Written Language and Models of Interpretation in the Eleventh and Twelfth Centuries* (Princeton, 1983), and M. V. David, *Le Débat sur les écritures et l'hieroglyphique aux xviie et xviiie siècles et l'application de déchiffrement aux écritures mortes*

(Paris, 1965). René Girard, *Des Choses cachées depuis la fondation du monde* (Paris, 1978) likewise grapples with the conjoined issues of scripture, history, writing, and finality (death, sacrifice, judgment, the ends and purpose of mimesis). Girard's and Derrida's works illustrate how differently this concatenation of themes can be evaluated since their conclusions bear little in common with those of Andean theater and historiography (cf. Wachtel, *La Vision des vaincus*, pp. 227ff.). Regarding the connection between written history and eschatology, see Santo Mazzarino, *La Fin du monde antique. Avatars d'un thème historiographique* (Paris, 1972).

548. Wachtel, "La Visión de los vencidos," p. 49. See also José María Arguedas, "Puquio: Una cultura en proceso de cambio," *RMN* 25 (1956): 184–232; Alfred Métraux, *The History of the Incas* (New York, 1970), p. 196. Franklin Pease G. Y., "Las Versiones del mito de Inkarri," *Revista de la Universidad Católica* n.s. 2 (1977): 25–41, and *El Dios creador andino*, pp. 82–93 and 115–140, gathers a number of myths of Inkarrí, the restored Inca king *(rey)*. Pease underlines that "Inkarrí lives in the subsoil; he is chthonic. . . . [H]is body will be reconstructed deep within the earth where dwell the riches identified with the Incas. . . . [I]n the subsoil dwell also the powers of fertility, including human fertility" (p. 90). From this eradicably native subsoil, the body of the local divinities, the Inca will be reborn:

> [T]his dialectical tension of dismemberment and eventual restoration to wholeness of the king's body is the motif standing for the eventual triumph of the dismembered Indian world over Spanish dominion. Likewise, the various parts of the *huacas* and mummies may lie broken and scattered by the Spanish, but the potential for reunification lives on within this structure of tension-filled space. In Arriaga's formulation the devil oversees this tensed pattern the inner force of which predetermines resolution. Spanish and Indian understandings had to cope with one another on points such as these, forming a complex language of cross-cultural communication and dissension that constituted the new culture of imperialism. (Michael T. Taussig, *The Devil and Commodity Fetishism in South America*, Chapel Hill, N.C., 1980, p. 174)

Understandably, the myths of Inkarri have proven a fertile set of images for intellectuals, literati, and scholars studying the social and cultural history of the Andes. Henrique O. Urbano, "Representaciones colectivas y arqueología mental en los Andes," *Allpanchis* 20 (1982): 33–84, tries to unearth how and why the Inkarri materials attract scholars. Whatever the reasons, an abundant literature exists. In addition to Pease and Ossio, a major contributor to the discussion is Alejandre Ortiz Rescaniere, *De Adaneva a Inkarri* (Lima, 1973). For further examples, see Francois Bourricaud, "El Mito de Inkarri," *Folklore Americano* 4 (1965): 178–187; Thomas Muller, "Mito de Inkarri-Collari," *Allpanchis* 20 (1984): 125–144; Juan M. Ossio, "El Mito de Inkarri narrado por segunda vez diez años después," *ALIM* 2 (1984): 169–194; Henrique O. Urbano, "Del Sexo, incesto y los ancestros de Inkarri. Mito, utopía e historia en las sociedades andinas," *Allpanchis* 17–18 (1981): 77–103; Alejandro G. Vivanco, "Una Nueva versión del mito de Inkarri," *ALIM* 2 (1984): 195–200; and Takahiro Kato, "Una Interpretación mas abierta de Incarri," *ALIM* 3 (1985): 295–305, which suggests opening a middle way between Ossio's histories and Pease's historical typologies of Andean messianisms, on the one side, and Rescaniere's analyses of the formal structures of mytho-logic, on the other. In Ossio, ed., *Ideología mesiánica*, one finds several versions and interpretations of the myths of Inkarri offered by Oscar Nuñez del Prado, Franklin Pease, Jorge Herrera Alfonso, Jorge Flores Ochoa, Abraham Valencia Espinoza, Raúl León Caparó, and others.

549. The generalizations throughout this book apply to the South American materials presented. They may apply more widely, however, to the religious condition of peoples elsewhere and, therefore, this volume locates itself within the general study of religion. The conviction that death and the end of the world have an impact on the shape and meaning of significant terminologies is a notion shared variously by many religious and philosophical traditions; see Frank E. Reynolds and Earl H. Waugh, eds. *Religious Encounters with Death: Insights From The History and Antropology of Religions* (University Park, Penn., 1977). The Russian existentialist Nicholas Berdyaev, for example, sounded a tone similar to one heard in some South American eschatologies and myths of death (although each has its unique modulations):

The fact of death alone gives true depth to the question as to the meaning of life. Life in this world has meaning just because there is death; if there were no death in our world, life would be meaningless. The meaning is bound up with the end. If there were no end, i.e., if life in our world continued forever, there would be no meaning in it. Meaning lies beyond the confines of this limited world and the discovery of meaning presupposes an end here. (*The Destiny of Man*, London, 1960, pp. 250–251)

Berdyaev developed these themes in *The Beginning and the End* (1931; New York, 1952). South American views lend an additional and interesting voice to the worldwide human conversation concerning the meaning of the end. For a Yanoama explanation of how central death is to the celebration of the life-cycle and its punctuations, see Zeries and Schuster, *Mahekodotedi*, pp. 127f. Other cases have appeared earlier, including that of the Warao who have no word for "life" except cognate forms of *wa*, a word used to refer to death, the coffin, and a kind of canoe (modeled on the vagina–birth canal of the goddess Dauarani). These examples testify to a creative understanding of death. In so many societies, important moments of life are grasped in terms of the act of dying. Conversely, the most vibrant episodes of life explore and rehearse anticipated existence in the imaginary worlds of death, whose images of darkness, dazzling light, vertigo, shadowy strangers, or exotic travel people our experiences of dream, relaxation, anxiety, delirium, rapture, and conscious deliberation. The constant materiality of death-in-life disvalues the concept of disembodied spirit just as the irrepressible images of new forms of life-in-death depreciates the reality of spiritless matter.

550. One of the great disservices to our understanding of South American religions has been the perception of tribal peoples as slavishly dedicated to an unchanging order revealed in the images of myth and handed down unquestioned and unmodified from one generation to the next. This attitude accompanies the evaluation of "myth" as a banal and inane narrative. Tribal peoples (representing "archaic" modes of thought) childishly cling to their myths, infantile fantasies, whereas mature contemporaries jettison myths with the passage of "historical time" and the "entrance" into "modernity." It would be fascinating to study these and other justifications proffered for avoiding a serious encounter with the reality of myth and symbolic acts of dance, crisis, chaos, and religious performance. This is not the place to carry out a history of the "modern" ideas of myth and religion. It is enough to suggest that the Western cultural imagination turned away when it encountered the stunning variety of cultural worlds that appeared for the first time in the Age of Discovery. Doubtless this inward turn sparked the appearance of all sorts of imaginary realities. The Enlightenment, the withdrawal of Western thinkers from the whirling world of cultural values into an utterly imaginary world of "objective" forms of knowledge, and its intellectual follow-up coined new symbolic currency. These terms brought new meanings and new self-definition to Western culture: "consciousness/unconsciousness," "primitive/civilized," "ethics/mores," "law/custom," "critical or reflective thought/action." Many categories bear the stamp of this negative reaction to the influx of cultures: "science," "reason," "religion," "art," "culture," "society," "history," "belief," "individual," "nature," "law," "behavior," "survival." See, for example Robert A. Nisbet, *The Sociological Tradition* (New York, 1966), and Tom Bottomore and Robert Nisbet, eds., *A History of Sociological Analysis* (New York, 1978); Norbert Elias, *The Civilizing Process* (New York, 1978); Stanley Diamond, *The Tangled Bank* (New York, 1962); J. Z. Smith, *Imagining Religion;* Foucault, *Archaeology of Knowledge*, esp. pp. 178–211; Rodney Needham, *Belief, Language and Experience* (Chicago, 1972); Charles H. Long, "Primitive/Civilized: the Locus of a Problem," *HR* 20 (1980): 43–61; and Kees W. Bolle, "Reflections on the History of Religions and History," *HR* 20 (1980): 62–80. See also Frank E. Manuel, *The Changing of the Gods*, (Hanover, N.H., 1975), especially the essays entitled "The Triadic Metaphor" and "Theodicy of a Pietist." These terms, whose first appearance was mentioned in the first pages of this volume, still function as fenders or containers; they objectify and keep at a remove the realities they encounter and strive to contain. In the face of threatening chaos, these terminologies cut analytical distinctions and attempt to impose order. They shore up a crumbling worldview, the symbolic construction of the "enlightened" Western world. The logic dictating the verdict that South American peoples lived in static or equilibrious societies is easy to understand. Unchanging cultures have no place

in a world where only the adaptive and fittest survive to carry forward the progress of history. See George Stocking, *Race, Culture, and Evolution* (Chicago, 1982), and Stocking, ed. *Observers Observed: Essays on Ethnographic Fieldwork* (Madison, Wis., 1983); and Arthur O. Lovejoy and George Boas, *A Documentary History of Primitivism and Related Ideas* (Baltimore, 1935); Robert F. Berkofer, Jr., *The White Man's Indian* (New York, 1978); Benjamin Keen, *The Aztec Image in Western Thought* (New Brunswick, N.J., 1971); Philip D. Curtin, *The Image of Africa* (Madison, Wis., 1964). These works discuss the formative influence of the developmental historical schemas underlying the natural sciences upon the construction of symbolic worlds inhabited by the cultural sciences. In the end, the scientific paradigms employed to understand myth may be proving more resistant to change than myths themselves.

551. Mircea Eliade, "The Quest for the 'Origins' of Religion," in *The Quest*, p. 51.

552. Ibid.

553. The rejection of "history" in the narrow senses known in the "modern" "West" (see note 361 above for reference to the works of Manuel, Löwith, Momigliano, H. White and others), often left South Americans vulnerable to the simplistic and hasty charge that they possessed no sense of history proper to themselves. The word "history" still carries an uncertain charge of meaning. It should be clear by now that South Americans do indeed possess very subtle and complex histories, if by that term one intends to say "awareness and evaluation of existence in time." The term *ethnohistory* has come into vogue and has merits to recommend it. But use of the term avoids confronting Western historiographers with the fact that their universal historical conceptions are also culturally conditioned; that is, they also write ethnohistory. Among the many works that recommend themselves in this connection see R. T. Zuidema, "Myth and History in Ancient Peru," in Ino Rossi et al., eds. *The Logic of Culture* (New York, 1982); and Joanne Rappaport, "History, Myth, and the Dynamics of Territorial Maintenance in Tierradentro, Colombia," *American Ethnologist* 12 (1985): pp. 27–45. Thierry Saignes, "La Guerre contre l'histoire: Les Chiriguano du xvie au xixe siècle," *JSAP* 71 (1985): 175–190, shows how war acts as a temporalizing response (in this case to the invasion of colonial pioneers). Even as it marks the rejection of a kind of History brought on by colonial expansion and enslavement, war (especially in its manifestations of revenge, consumption of dead enemies, the taking of trophy heads, the territorial dispossession of the conquered, and the subsequent migration of victors and vanquished) came to blend the traditional Chiriguano evaluation of time as a pursuit of the Land Without Evil with the nostalgia for a paradise accessible only beyond historical death. For more general considerations see Emmanuel Le Roy Ladurie, *Le Territoire de l'historien* (Paris, 1978).

554. Métraux, "Quechua Messiah," p. 721.

555. See the fascinating materials regarding the sufferings of Mamapacha (Mother Earth) and the lack of fruitful dialogue (in the form of harvests, land use, fertility, knowledge of genealogy, contact with the dead) with her in Alejandro Ortiz Rescaniere, "El Mito de la escuela," in Ossio, ed., *Ideología Mesiánica*, pp. 238–250, esp. pp. 246–247.

SELECTED
BIBLIOGRAPHY

This bibliography contains a selection of works that bear on the South American beliefs and practices treated in this volume, and does not touch on related issues in the general history of religions, for which the reader may consult *The Encyclopedia of Religion*, ed. Mircea Eliade (New York: Macmillan, 1987).

Acosta, José de. *Historia Natural y Moral de las Indias*, 2nd ed. Mexico City: Fonda de Cultura Económica, 1962.

Acuña, Luis Alberto. *El Arte do los Indios Colombianos*. Mexico City: n.p., 1942.

Adams, Patsy. *Cerámica culina*. Yarinocoha: Centro Amazónico de Lenguas Autóctonas Peruanas "Hugo Pesce," 1976.

Adams, Patsy. "Textos culina," *Folklore Americano* 10, No. 10 (n.d., n.p.).

Adorno, Rolena. *From Oral to Written Expression: Native Andean Chronicles of the Early Colonial Period*. Foreign and Comparative Studies, Latin American Series, Vol. 4. Syracuse, N.Y.: Syracuse University Press, 1982.

Adrián Ambía, Abel, and Sánchez Garrafa, Rodolfo. *Amaru: Mito; Realidad del Hombre*. Lima: Ediciones Pukara, 1970.

Agostinho, Pedro. "Estudo preliminar sobre o mito das origens xinguano: Comentário a una variante aweti," *Universitas: Revista de Cultura da Universidade Federal da Bahia* 6–7 (1970):457–519.

Agostinho, Pedro. *Mitos e Outros Narrativas Kamayura*. Coleção Ciência e Homem. Bahia: Universidade Federal da Bahia, 1974.

Agostinho, Pedro. *Kwarìp: Mito e Ritual no Alto Xingu*. São Paulo: Editora Pedagógica e Universitária and Editora da Universidade de São Paulo, 1974.

Aguilo, Federico. *Los Cuentos, Tradiciones o Vivencias*. La Paz-Cochabamba: Editorial Los Amigos del Libro, 1980.

Akuts Nugkai, Timias. *Yana najanetnumia augmatban. Historia Aguaruna: Primera Etapa*. Yarinacocha, Peru: Centro Amazónico de Lenguas Autóctonas Peruanas "Hugo Pesce," 1977.

Akuts Nugkai, Timias. *Initik Augmatban. Historia Aguaruna. Primera Etapa, Segunda Parte*, Vol. 1. Lima: Ministerio de Educación and Summer Institute of Linguistics, 1978.

Akuts Nugkai, Timias. *Initik Augmatban. Historia Aguaruna: Primera Etapa, Segunda Parte*, Vol. 2. Yarinacocha, Peru: Pucallpa and the Summer Institute of Linguistics, 1979.

Akuts Nugkai, Timias. *Initik Augmatban. Historia Aguaruna: Primera Etapa, Segunda Parte*, Vol. 3. Lima: Ministerio de Educación and the Summer Institute of Linguistics, 1979.

Albisetti, César, and Venturelli, Ângelo Jayme. *Enciclopédia Boróro*. Vol. 1: *Vocabulários e Etnografia*. Museu Regional Dom Bosco Publicação No. 1. Campo Grande, Brazil: Faculdade Dom Aquino de Filosofia Ciências e Letras. Instituto de Pesquisas Etnográficas, 1962. Vol. 2: *Lendas e Antropônimos*. Campo Grande, Brazil: Faculdade Dom Aquino de Filosofia Ciências e Letras, 1969.

Alegre, F. Pascual. *Tashorintsi; Tradición Oral Matsiguenka*. Lima: Centro Amazónico de Antropología y Aplicación Práctica, 1979.

Alegría, Ricardo E. *Las primeras representaciones gráficas del Indio Americano, 1493–1523*. San Juan: Centro de Estudios Avanzados de Puerto Rico y el Caribe, 1978.

Alegría, Ricardo E. *Apuntes en torno a la mitología de los indios taínos de las Antillas Mayores y sus orígenes suramericanos*. San Juan: Centro de Estudios Avanzados de Puerto Rico y el Caribe, Museo del Hombre Dominicano, 1978.

Alves Velho, Yvonne Maggie. *Guerra de orixá*. Rio de Janeiro: Zahar Editores, 1977.

Amado, Jorge. *Iconografia dos deuses africanos no candomblé da Bahia*. São Paulo: Fundação Cultural de Educação da Bahia, Instituto Nacional do Livro, Universidade Federal da Bahia, 1980.

Amano, Toshitaro. *Diseños precolombianos del Perú*. Lima: Museo Amano, 1981.

Amich, José. *Compendio histórico de los trabajos, fatigas, y muertes que los ministros evangélicos de la seráfica religión han padecido por la conversión de las almas de los gentiles en las montañas de los Andes pertenecentes a los provincias del Perú*. Paris, 1854.

Amorim, A.B. de. "Lendas em Nheengatú e em Português," *Revista do Instituto Histórico Geográfico Brasileiro* (Rio de Janeiro) 100 No. 154 (1926/8):9–475.

Angles Vargas, Victor. *Cacique Tambohuacso. Historia de un proyectado levantamiento contra la dominación española*. Lima: Industrialgráfica, 1975.

Aranda de los Rios, Ramón. *Marankiari. Una comunidad campa de la selva peruana*. Lima, 1978.

Araújo, Orestes. *Etnologia salvaje, historia de los Charrúas y demás tribus indígenas del Uruguay*. Montevideo: Librería Cervantes, 1911.

Arguedas, José María. "Puquio. Una Cultura en Proceso de Cambio," in *Estudios sobre la Cultura actual del Perú*. Lima: U.N.N.S.M., 1964.

Arguedas, José María, and Ríos, Francisco Izquierdo. *Mitos, Leyendas y Cuentos Peruanos*, 2nd ed. Lima: Casa de la Cultura del Perú, 1970.

Arguedas, José María. *Notas elementales sobre el arte popular religioso y la cultura mestiza de Huamanga*. Huancayo: Instituto de Estudios Andinos, 1977(1958).

Arguedas, José María. *Nuestra música popular y sus interpretes*. Lima: Industrialgrafica, 1977.

Arhem, Kaj. "Observations on Life-Cycle Rituals Among the Makuna: Birth, Initiation, Death." *Göteborgs Etnografiska Museum Arstryck* (1980):10–47.

Arhem, Kaj. *Makuna Social Organization: A Study in Descent, Alliance, and the Formation of Corporate Groups in North-Western Amazon*. Uppsala Studies in Cultural Anthropology, vol. 4. Stockholm: Libertryck, 1981.

Arhem, Kaj. "Vida y Muerte en la Amazonia Columbiana: Un Relato Etnográfico Macuna," *Anthropos* 79, (1984):171–189.

Armellada, Cesáreo de. "Exploración del Paragua." *Boletín de la Sociedad Venezolana de Ciencias Naturales* (Caracas) 8, No. 53 (1945):38–60.

Armellada, Cesáreo de. *Como son los indios pemones de la Gran Sabana. Estudio etnográfico*. Caracas: Editorial Elite, 1946.

Armellada, Cesáreo de. *Taurón Pantón: Cuentos y leyendas de los indios pemón*. Caracas: Biblioteca Venezolana de Cultura, 1964.

Armellada, Cesáreo de. *Pemonton Taremuru: Invocaciones mágicas de los indios pemón* Serie Lenguas Indígenas de Venezuela, Vol. 2. Caracas: Universidad Católica Andrés Bello, 1972.

Armellada, Cesáreo de. *Literaturas indígenas venezolanas*. Caracas: Monte Avila, 1975.

Arnold, Pierre. "Pèlerinages et processions comme formes de pouvoir symbolique des classes subalternes: Deux cas péruviens," *Social Compass* 32 (1985):45–56.

Atran, Scott. "The Nature of Folk-Botanical Life Forms," *AA* 87 (1985):289–315.

Aveni, Anthony F. *Skywatchers of Ancient Mexico*. Austin: University of Texas Press, 1980.

Aveni, Anthony F. "The View from the Tropics." In *Archaeoastronomy and the Roots of Science*, ed. E. C. Krupp. American Association for the Advancement of Science, Selected Symposium 71. Boulder, Colo.: Westview Press, 1984.

Aveni, Anthony F., ed. *Native American Astronomy*. Austin: University of Texas Press, 1977.

Aveni, Anthony, and Brotherston, Gordon, eds. *Calendars in Mesoamerica and Peru: Native American Cumputations of Time*. Oxford: BAR International Publications, 1983.

Aveni, Anthony F., and Urton, Gary, eds. *Ethnoastronomy and Archaeoastronomy in the American Tropics*. New York: New York Academy of Sciences, 1982.

Avila, Francisco de. *A Narrative of the Errors, False Gods and Other Superstitions and Diabolical Rites in which the Indians of the Province of Huarochiri, Mama and Chaclla Lived in Ancient Times, and in which they even now Live, to the Great Perdition of the Their Souls* [1608]. In *Narratives of the Rites and Laws of the Yncas*, trans. and ed. Clements R. Markham. Hakluyt

Society First Series, Vol. 43. London: The Hakluyt Society, 1873; reprint ed., New York: Burt Franklin, n.d.

Avila, Francisco de. *Dioses y hombres de Huarochirí. Narración quechua recogida por Francisco de Avila (¿1598?)*, trans. José María Arguedas; bibliography by Pierre Duviols. Lima: Instituto de Estudios Peruanos, 1966.

Ayrosa, Plinio. *Apontamentos para bibliografia da lingua tupi-guarani*. Faculdade de Filosofia, Ciências e Letras, Boletim No. 33. São Paulo: Universidade de São Paulo, 1943.

Baer, Gerhard. *Südamerikanische Indianer: Wilbeuter und Pflanzer*. Basel: Museum für Völkerkunde und Schweizerisches Museum für Volkskunde, 1965.

Baer, Gerhard. "Ein besonderes Merkmal des südamerikanischen Shamanen," *Zeitschrift für Ethnologie* 94, No. 2 (1969):284–292.

Baer, Gerhard. "Reise und Forschung in Ost-Peru," *Verhandlungen der Naturforschenden Gesellschaft in Basel* 80 (1969):327–386.

Baer, Gerhard. *Peru—Indianer gestern und heute*. Basel: Museum für Völkerkunde und Schweizerisches Museum für Volkskunde, 1971/1972.

Baer, Gerhard. "Was Mythen aussagen; Das Beispiel der Matsigenka, Ost-Peru," *Paideuma* (Frankfurt) 22 (1976):189–198.

Baer, Gerhard. "Masken der Piro, Shipibo und Matsigenka, Ost-Peru," *Verhandlungen der Naturforschenden Gesellschaft in Basel* 87–88 (1976–1977):101–115.

Baer, Gerhard. "Religión y Chamanismo de los Matsigenka (Este Peruano)," *Amazonía Peruana* (Lima) 2, No. 4 (1979):101–138.

Baer, Gerhard. "Religion and Symbols: A Case in Point from Eastern Peru. The Matsigenka View of the Religious Dimension of Light," *Scripta Ethnológica* 6 (1981):49–52.

Baer, Gerhard. *Die Religion der Matsigenka Ost-Peru: Monographie zur Kultur und Religion eines Indianervolkes des Oberen Amazonas*. Basel: Wepf & Co., 1984.

Baer, Gerhard, and Hertle, Gisela. "Zwei Matsigenka-Mythen, Versuch einer Analyse," *Ethnologische Zeitschrift Zürich* 1 (1974):33–75.

Baer, Gerhard, and Snell, Wayne W. "An Ayahuasca Ceremony among the Matsigenka (Eastern Peru)." *Zeitschrift für Ethnologie*, 99, Nos. 1 and 2 (1974):63–80.

Baldus, Herbert. "La 'Mère Commune' dans la mythologie de deux tribus sudaméricaines (Kágaba et Tumerehâ)," *Revista* (Tucumán) 2 (1932):471–479.

Baldus, Herbert. "O Conceito do Tempo entre os Índios do Brasil," *Revista do Arquivo* (São Paulo) 71 (1940):87–94.

Baldus, Herbert. *Lendas dos Índios do Brasil*. São Paulo: Editôra Brasiliense Limitada, 1946.

Baldus, Herbert. "Supernatural Relations with Animals Among Indians of Eastern and Southern Brazil." International Congress of Americanists, 30th Session, Cambridge, 1950, pp. 195–198.

Baldus, Herbert. "Kanaschiwuä und der Erwerb des Lichtes. Beitrag zur Mythologie der Karajá-Indianer," *Beiträge zur Gesellungs- und Völkerwissenschaft*, pp. 20–35. Berlin, 1950.

Baldus, Herbert. "As Danças dos Tapirapé." ICA, 31st Congress, August 1954. São Paulo: Editôra Anhembi, 1955, pp. 89–98.

Baldus, Herbert. "Some Aspects of Tapirapé Morals." In *Encyclopedia of Morals*, ed. Vergilius Ferm. New York: Philosophical Library, 1956.

Baldus, Herbert. *Die Jaguarzwillinge: Mythen und Heilbringergeschichten, Ursprungssagen und Märchen brasilianischer Indianer*. Eisenach and Kassel: Erich Röth-Verlag, 1958.

Baldus, Herbert. *The Tapirapé, A Tupi Tribe of Central Brazil*, trans. Ariane Brunel. New Haven, Conn.: Human Relations Area Files, 1960.

Baldus, Herbert. "The Fear in Tapirapé Culture." In *Men and Cultures: Anthropological and Ethnological Sciences, Philadelphia Sept. 1–19, 1956*, ed. Anthony F. C. Wallace. Philadelphia: University of Pennsylvania Press, 1960.

Baldus, Herbert. "Vertikale und horizontale Struktur im religiösen Weltbild südamerikanischer Indianer," *Anthropos* 63–64, Nos. 1–2 (1968–1969):16–21.

Baldus, Herbert. *Tapirapé: Tribo Tupí no Brasil Central*. São Paulo: Editôra da Universidade de São Paulo, Companhia Editora Nacional, 1970.

Baldus, Herbert. *Ensaios de Etnologia Brasileira*, 2nd ed. São Paulo: Nacional, 1979.

Barabás, Alicia M. "Movimientos étnicos religiosos y seculares en América Latina," *América Indígena* 46 No. 3 (1986):495–529.

Barabás, Alicia M., and Bartolomé, Miguel A. "Un Testimonio Mítico de los Mataco," *JSAP* 66 (1979):125–131; "The Mythic Testimony of the Mataco," *LAIL* 3, No. 2 (1979):76–85.

Barandiarán, Daniel de. "Mundo Espiritual y Shamanismo Sanema," *Antropológica* (Caracas) 15 (Dec. 1965):1–28.

Barandiarán, Daniel de. "El Habitado entre los Indios Yekuana," *Antropológica* (Caracas) 16 (1966):3–95.

Barandiarán, Daniel de. "Nota bibliográfica," *Boletín Indigenista Venezolano* (Caracas) 10, Nos. 1–4 (1966):213–216.

Barandiarán, Daniel de. "Vida y Muerte entre los Indios Sanemá-Yanoama," *Antropológica* (Caracas) 21 (Dec. 1967):3–65.

Barandiarán, Daniel de. *Introducción a la Cosmovisión de los Indios Ye'kuana-Makiritare*. Caracas: Prensas Venezolanas de Editorial Arte, 1979.

Bardales Rodríquez, Cesar. *Quimisha Incabo Ini Yoia. Leyendas de los Shipibo-Conibo sobre los tres Incas*. Yarinococha: Centro Amazónico de Lenguas Peruanas "Hugo Pesce," 1979.

Barral, Basilio María de. *Guarao Guarata. Lo que Cuentan los Indios Guaraos*. Caracas, 1959.

Barral, Basilio María de. *Los Indios guaraúnos y su cancionero: Historia, religión y alma lírica*. Madrid: Consejo Superior de Investigaciones Científicas, Departamento de Misionología Española, 1964.

Barral, Basilio de. *Guarao A-Ribu (Literatura de los Indios Guaraos)*. Serie Lenguas Indígenas de Venezuela, vol. 1. Caracas: Universidad Católica Andrés Bello, 1969.

Barreiro, Jose, and Wright, Robin M., eds. *Native Peoples in Struggle: Russell Tribunal and Other International Forums*. Boston: Anthropology Resource Center, 1982.

Barrett, S. A. *The Cayapa Indians of Ecuador*, Part 2. New York: Museum of the American Indian and Heye Foundation, 1925.

Barriales, Joaquín, and Torralba, Adolfo. *Los Mashcos Hijos del Huanamei*. Lima: Santiago Valverde, S.A., 1970.

Barrionuevo, Alfonsina. *Los dioses de la lluvia*. Lima: Editorial Universo, n.d.

Barrionuevo, Alfonsina. *Cusco Mágico*. Lima: Editorial Universo, 1980.

Barroso, Gustavo. *Mythes, Contes et Légendes des Indiens: Folk-Lore Brésilien*. Paris: Librairie des Amateurs, 1930.

Bartolomé, Leopoldo J. "La experiencia estética ante la narración mítica," *Runa* 12, Nos. 1–2 (1969–1970):407–412.

Bartolomé, Leopoldo J. "Movimientos Milenaristas de los Aborígenes Chaqueños entre 1905 y 1933," *Suplemento Antropológico* (Universidad Católica, Asunción del Paraguay) 7, Nos. 1–2 (1972):107–120.

Bartolomé, Miguel A. "El Shamán Guaraní Como Agente Inter-Cultural," *Sociedad Argentina de Anthropología* (Buenos Aires), n.s., 5, No. 2 (1971):107–114.

Bartolomé, Miguel A. "Shamanism Among the Avá-Chiripá." In *Spirits, Shamans, and Stars: Perspectives from South America*, ed. David L. Browman and Ronald A. Schwarz. The Hague: Mouton, 1979.

Basso, Ellen B. *The Kalapalo Indians of Central Brazil*. New York: Holt, Rinehart & Winston, 1973.

Basso, Ellen B. "A 'Musical View of the Universe': Kalapalo Myth and Ritual as Religious Performance," *Journal of American Folklore* 94, No. 373 (1981):273–291.

Basso, Ellen B. *A Musical View of the Universe: Kalapalo Myth and Ritual Performances*. Philadelphia: University of Pennsylvania Press, 1985.

Basso, Ellen B., ed. *Carib-Speaking Indians: Culture, Society and Language*. Tucson: University of Arizona Press, 1977.

Bastide, Roger. "The Sociology of the Dream." In *The Dream and Human Societies*, ed. G. E. Von Grunebaum and Roger Caillois. Berkeley: University of California Press, 1966.

Bastide, Roger. *The African Religions of Brazil: Toward a Sociology of the Interpenetration of Civilizations*, trans. Helen Sebba. Baltimore: Johns Hopkins University Press, 1978.

Bastien, Joseph W. *Mountain of the Condor: Metaphor and Ritual in an Andean Ayllu.* St. Paul, Minn.: West Publishing Co., 1978.

Bastien, Joseph W. "Qollahuaya-Andean Body Concepts: A Topographical-Hydraulic Model of Physiology," *AA* 87 (1985):595–611.

Bastos, Rafael José de Menezes. *A Musicológica kamayurá: Para uma antropología da comunicação no Alto-Xingu.* Brasília: Fundação Nacional do Índio, 1978.

Bawden, Garth, and Conrad, Geoffrey W. *The Andean Heritage: Masterpieces of Peruvian Art from the Collections of the Peabody Museum.* Cambridge, Mass.: Peabody Museum Press, 1982.

Becher, Hans. *Xelekuhahé. Das Stockduell der Surára und Pakidái-Indianer. Ein Beitrag zum Problem der "Nilotenstellung" und der Tonsur in Südamerika.* Mitteilungen aus dem Museum für Völkerkunde Hamburg, vol. 25. Hamburg: Kommissionsverlag Ludwig Appel, 1959.

Becher, Hans. "Algunas notas sobre a religião e a mitologia dos Surára," *Revista do Museu Paulista,* n.s., 11 (1959):99–107.

Becher, Hans. *Beiträge zur Völkerkunde Südamerikas: Festgabe für Herbert Baldus zum 65. Geburtstag.* Hannover: Kommissionsverlag Münstermann-Druck, 1964.

Becher, Hans. "Herbert Baldus," *Zeitschrift für Ethnologie* 95, No. 2 (1970):157–163.

Becher, Hans. "Moon and Reincarnation: Anthropogenesis as Imagined by the Surará and Pakidái Indians of Northwestern Brazil." In *The Realm of the Extra-Human: Ideas and Actions,* ed. Agehananda Bharati. The Hague: Mouton, 1976.

Becker-Donner, Etta. "Notizen über die Huanyam, Territorium Rondonia, Brasilien." In *Ethnologische Zeitschrift Zürich.* Special Supplement No. 1. (1974):93–106.

Beltrão, Luiz. *Indio, Um Mito Brasileiro.* Petrópolis: Vozes, 1977.

Bendezu Neyra, Roger Albino. *Puquio y la fiesta del agua.* Lima: Imprenta "El Carmen," 1980.

Bennett, Wendell C. "Architecture and Engineering: Religious Structures." In *HSAI,* vol. 5, ed. Julian H. Steward. Washington, D.C.: Smithsonian Institution, 1949.

Bennett, Wendell C. "Numbers, Measures, Weights, and Calendars." In *HSAI,* vol. 5, ed. Julian H. Steward. Washington, D.C.: Smithsonian Institution, 1949.

Benson, Elizabeth P., ed. *Death and the Afterlife in Pre-Columbian America.* Washington, D.C.: Dumbarton Oaks Research Library and Collections, 1975.

Benson, Elizabeth P., ed. *The Sea in the Pre-Colombian World.* Washington, D.C.: Dumbarton Oaks Research Library and Collections, 1977.

Benton, Dilson. *Malungo: Decodificação da Umbanda. Contribuição à história das religiões.* Rio de Janeiro: Civilização Brasileira, 1979.

Berdichewsky, Bernardo. *The Araucanian Indian in Chile.* Copenhagen, 1975.

Berge, François. "Conclusions d'une étude comparative des légendes de déluges," *Actes du IVe Congrès International des Sciences Anthropologiques et Ethnologiques. Vienna, 1–8 Septembre 1952,* vol. 2, pp. 60–62. Vienna, 1955.

Bernand-Muñoz, Carmen. *Les Ayoré du Chaco Septentrional. Etude critique à partir des notes de Lucien Sebag.* The Hague: Mouton, 1977.

Bidou, Patrice. "Naître et être Tatuyo," *ICA,* 2 (1976):105–200.

Biocca, Ettore. *Viaggi tra gli Indi del alto Rio Negro—Alto Orinoco,* 4 vols. Rome: Consiglio Nazionale delle Ricerche, 1966.

Biocca, Ettore. *Yanoáma: The Narrative of a White Girl Kidnapped by Amazonian Indians.* New York: E. P. Dutton & Co., 1971.

Blacking, John. "Ethnomusicology as a Key Subject in the Social Sciences." *In Memoriam António Jorge Dias,* vol. 3, pp. 71–93. Lisbon, 1974.

Blacking, John. "Can Musical Universals Be Heard?," *The World of Music* 19, Nos. 1–2 (1977):14–22.

Blacking, John. "The Study of Man as Music-Maker." In *The Performing Arts: Music and Dance,* ed. John Blacking and Joann W. Kealiinohomoku. The Hague: Mouton, 1979.

Blomberg, R. *Chavante: An Expedition to the Tribes of the Mato Grosso.* London, 1960.

Bödiger, Ute. *Die Religion der Tukano im nordwestlischen Amazonas.* Kölner Ethnologische Mitteilungen, vol. 3. Cologne: Kölner Universitäts-Verlag, 1965.

Boff, Leonardo, and Elizondo, Vigil, eds. *La Iglesia Popular: Between Fear and Hope.* Special Issue of *Concilium.* Third World Theology Series, vol. 176, No. 6 (1984).

Boglár, Lajos. "Ein endokannibalischer Ritus in Südamerika." In *Miscellanea Paul Rivet Octogenario Dicata II*. Mexico City, 1958.

Boglár, Lajos. "Zur kulturgeschichtlichen Stellung der Nambikuara-Indianer," *Zeitschrift für Ethnologie* 96, No. 2 (1971):266–270.

Boglár, Lajos. "Creative Process in Ritual Art: Piaroa Indians, Venezuela." In *The Realm of the Extra-Human: Indians and Actions*, ed. Agehananda Bharati. The Hague: Mouton, 1976.

Boglár, Lajos. "Creative Process in Ritual Art: Piaroa Indians." In *Spirits, Shamans, and Stars: Perspectives from South America*, ed. David L. Browman and Ronald A. Schwartz. The Hague: Mouton, 1979.

Bórmida, Marcelo. "Mito y Cultura. Bases, para una ciencia, de la conciencia mítica y una etnología tautegórica," *Runa* (Buenos Aires) 12, Nos. 1–2 (1969–1970):9–52.

Bórmida, Marcelo. "Problemas de Heuristica Mitográfica," *Runa* (Buenos Aires) 12, Nos. 1–2 (1969–1970):53–65.

Bórmida, Marcelo. "Ergon y Mito. Una Hermenéutica de la Cultura Material de los Ayoreo del Chaco Boreal. Primera Parte," *Scripta Ethnológica* (Buenos Aires) 1, No. 1 (1973):9–68.

Bórmida, Marcelo. "Ergon y Mito. Una Hermenéutica de la Cultura Material de los Ayoreo del Chaco Boreal. Segunda Parte," *Scripta Ethnológica* (Buenos Aires) 2, No. 2 (1974):20–45.

Bórmida, Marcelo."Ergon y Mito. Una Hermenéutica de la Cultura Material de los Ayoreo del Chaco Central. Tercera Parte," *Scripta Ethnológica* (Buenos Aires) 3, No. 3 (1975):73–130.

Bórmida, Marcelo. *Etnología y fenomenología*. Buenos Aires: Edición Cervantes, 1975.

Bórmida, Marcelo."Ergon y Mito. Una Hermenéutica de la Cultura Material de los Ayoreo del Chaco Boreal. Cuarta Parte," *Scripta Ethnológica* (Buenos Aires) 4, No. 1 (1976):29–44.

Bórmida, Marcelo. "Ayoreo Myths," *LAIL* 2, No. 1 (Spring 1978):1–13.

Bórmida, Marcelo. "Ergon y Mito. Una Hermenéutica de la Cultura Material de los Ayoreo del Chaco Boreal. Quinta Parte," *Scripta Ethnológica* (Buenos Aires) 5, No. 1 (1978–1979):6–25.

Bórmida, Marcelo. "Como una cultura arcaica concibe su propio mundo," *Scripta Ethnológica* (Buenos Aires) 8 (1984):13–161.

Bórmida, Marcelo, and Califano, Mario. *Los indios ayoreo del Chaco Boreal. Información básica acerca de su cultura*. Buenos Aires: Fundación para la Educación, la Ciencia y la Cultura, 1978.

Bórmida, Marcelo, and Siffredi, Alejandra. "Mitología de los Tehuelches meridionales," *RUNA* (Buenos Aires) 12, Nos. 1–2 (1969–1970):199–245.

Boudin, Max H. *Dicionário de Tupi Moderno*, 2 vols. São Paulo: Conselho Estadual de Artes e Ciências Humanas, 1978.

Bourque, Susan C., and Warren, Kay Barbara. *Women of the Andes: Patriarchy and Social Change in Two Peruvian Towns*. Ann Arbor: University of Michigan Press, 1981.

Bouysse-Cassagne, Thérèse, and Bouysse, Philippe. "Volcan indien, Volcan chrétien: à propos de l'éruption du Huaynaputina en 1'an 1600 (Pérou Méridional)," *JSAP* 70 (1984):43–68.

Bradby, Barbara. " 'Resistance to Capitalism' in the Peruvian Andes." In *Ecology and Exchange*, ed. David Lehmann. Cambridge: At the University Press, 1982.

Brandes, Stanley H. "Dance as a Metaphor: A Case from Tzintzuntzan, Mexico," *JLAL* 5, No. 1 (1979):25–43.

Braunstein, José A. "Dominios y jerarquías en la cosmovisión de los Mataco Tewokleley," *Scripta Ethnológica* (Buenos Aires) 2, No. 2 (1974):7–30.

Braunstein, José A. "Los *wichi*. Conceptos y sentimientos de pertenencia grupal de los Mataco," *Scripta Ethnológica* (Buenos Aires) 4, No. 1 (1976):131–144.

Braunstein, José A. "Cigabi va a la matanza. Historia de guerra de los Ayoreo," *Scripta Ethnológica* (Buenos Aires) 4, No. 2 (1976–1977):32–51.

Braunstein, José A. "La passion amoureuse chez les Mataco: *Kyutislí*," *JSAP* 69 (1983):169–176.

Briggs, Lucy T. "Mururata: An Aymara Text," *LAIL* 2, No. 1 (Spring 1978):14–22.

Briggs, Lucy T., and Chana, Domingo Llanque. "Humor in Aymara Oral Narrative," *LAIL* 3, No. 1 (Spring 1979):1–10.

Brody, Eugene. *The Lost Ones: Social Forces and Mental Illness in Rio de Janeiro*. New York: International Universities Press, 1973.

Browman, David L., ed. *Advances in Andean Archaeology*. The Hague: Mouton, 1978.

Browman, David L., and Schwarz, Ronald A., eds. *Spirits, Shamans, and Stars: Perspectives from South America*. The Hague: Mouton, 1979.

Brown, Dianna de Groat. *Umbanda: Policies of an Urban Religious Movement*. Ann Arbor, Michigan: University Microfilms, 1974.

Brown, Michael F. *Tsewa's Gift: Magic and Meaning in an Amazonian Society*. Smithsonian Series in Ethnographic Inquiry. Washington, D.C.: Smithsonian Institution Press, 1986.

Brühl, Gustav. *Die Kulturvölker alt Amerikas*. New York: Verlag von Benziger Bros., 1875–1887.

Bruner, Jerome. "The Conditions of Creativity." In *Contemporary Approaches to Creative Thinking*, ed. E. H. Gruber, G. Terrell, and M. Wertheimer. New York: Atherton, 1962.

Brüzzi Alves da Silva, Alcionilio. "Os Ritos fúnebres entre as tribos do Uaupés (Amazonas), *Anthropos* 50, Nos. 4–6 (1955):593–601.

Bryan, Alan L. "South America." In *Early Man in the New World*, ed. Richard Shutler, Jr. Beverly Hills, Calif.: Sage Publications, 1983.

Buechler, Hans C. *The Masked Media: Aymara Fiestas and Social Interaction in the Bolivian Highlands*. The Hague: Mouton, 1980.

Buitron, Anibal. *Taita Imbabura: Vida Indígena en los Andes*. La Paz, Bolivia: n. p., 1964.

Burela, Maria. "De los Hermanos Ayar a Inkarrí," *Antropológica* (Lima) 1, No. 1 (1983):37–50.

Busto Duthurburu, José Antonio del. *José Gabriel Tupac Amaru antes de su rebelión*. Lima: Pontificia Universidad Católica del Peru, Fondo Editorial, 1981.

Butt, Audrey J. "Ritual Blowing: *Taling*—a Causation and Cure of Illness Among the Akawaio," *Timehri* (Georgetown, Guiana) 35 (Oct. 1956):37–52.

Butt, Audrey J. "The Mazaruni Scorpion." *Timehri* (Georgetown, Guiana) 36 (Oct. 1957):[40]–[54].

Butt, Audrey J. "Secondary Urn Burial Among the Akawaio of British Guiana," *Timehri* (Georgetown) 37 (1958):[74]–88.

Butt, Audrey J. "The Birth of a Religion," *Journal of the Royal Anthropological Institute of Great Britain and Ireland* 90 (1960):66–106.

Butt, Audrey J. "Réalité et idéal dans la pratique chamanique," *L'Homme* 2, No. 3 (1962):5–52.

Butt, Audrey J. "Akawaio Charm Stones," *Folk* (Cophenhagen) 8–9 (1966–1967):69–81.

Butt Colson, Audrey. "Binary Oppositions and the Treatment of Sickness Among the Akawaio," in *Social Anthropology and Medicine*, ed. J. B. Loudon. A. S. A. Monographs 13, London, 1976.

Butt Colson, Audrey. "The Akawaio Shaman." In *Carib-Speaking Indians*, ed. Ellen B. Basso. Tucson: University of Arizona Press, 1977.

Cacciatore, Olga Gudolle. *Dicionário de cultos afro-brasileiros*. Rio de Janeiro: Forense Universitária, 1977.

Cadogan, León. "El Culto al Árbol y los Animales Sagrados en el Folklore y las Tradiciones Guaraníes," *América Indígena* 10, No. 4 (1950):20–45.

Cadogan, León. *Breve Contribución al Estudio de la Nomenclatura Guaraní en Botánica*. Boletin no. 194. Asunción: Servicio Técnico Interamericano de Cooperación Agrícola, 1955.

Cadogan, León. *Apuntes de medicina popular guaireña*. Publicación del Centro de Estudios Antropológicos del Paraguay. Asunción: Imprenta Nacional, 1957.

Cadogan, León. *Ayvu Rapyta. Textos Míticos de los Mbyá-Guaraní del Guairá*. Boletim No. 227, Anthropology Series No. 5 São Paulo. Universidade de São Paulo. Faculdade de Filosofia, Ciências e Letras, 1959.

Cadogan, León. *Literatura de los Guaranies. Versión de textos guaranies*. Legado de la América Indígena, 3rd ed. Mexico City: Editorial Mortiz, 1978.

Calderón, Eduardo and Richard Cowan, Douglas Sharon, and F. Kaye Sharon. *Eduardo el Curandero: The Words of a Peruvian Healer*. Richmond, Calif.: North Atlantic Books, 1982.

Califano, Mario. "El Ciclo de Tokjwáj: Análisis fenomenológico de una narración mítica de los Mataco costaneros," *Scripta Ethnológica* 1 (1973):156–186.

Califano, Mario. "El Concepto de Enfermedad y Muerte entre los Mataco-costaneros," *Scripta Ethnológica* (Buenos Aires) 2, No. 2 (1974):32–73.

Califano, Mario. "El Chamanismo mataco." *Scripta Ethnológica* 3, No. 3 (1976):7–60.

Califano, Mario. "El Mito de la luna de los Sirionó de Bolivia Oriental," *Scripta Ethnológica* 3, No. 4 (1976–1977):100–127.

Califano, Mario. "La Incorporación de un Elemento Cultural Entre los Mashco de la Amazonia Peruana," *Relaciones de la Sociedad Argentina de Antropología* 9 (1977):185–201.

Califano, Mario. "El Complejo de bruja entre los Mashco de la Amazonia sudoccidental (Perú)," *Anthropos* 73 (1978):401–433.

Califano, Mario. *Análisis comparativo de un mito mashco*. Jujuy, 1978.

Califano, Mario. "A Tapuí Myth of the Izozog Region, Bolivia," *LAIL* 3, No. 1 (Spring 1979):25–26.

Califano, Mario. *Etnografía de los Mashco de la Amazonia Sud Occidental del Perú*. Buenos Aires: Fundación para la Educación, la Ciencia y la Cultura, 1982.

Califano, Mario. "El Mito del Arbol Cósmico Wanamei de los Mashco de la Amazonia Sudoccidental," *Anthropos* 78, Nos. 5–6 (1983):739–769.

Camargo, Cándido Procópio. *Kardecismo e umbanda: Uma interpretação sociológica*. São Paulo: Livraria Pioneira Editora, 1961.

Carmargo, Cándido Procópio Ferreira de, et al. *Católicos, Protestantes, Espiritas*. Petrópolis: Editora Vozes, 1973.

Capistrano de Abreu, J. *Rà-txa hu-ni-ku-î: A lingua dos Caxinauás*. N.p.: Sociedade Capistrano de Abreu and Livraria Briguiet, 1941.

Carneiro, Edison. "The Structure of African Cults in Bahia," *JAFL* 53, No. 210 (Oct.–Dec. 1940):271–278.

Carneiro, Edison. *Candomblés da Bahia*. Rio de Janeiro: Civilização Brasileira, 1977.

Carneiro, Robert L. "The Amahuaca and the Spirit World," *Ethnology* 3 (1964):6–11.

Carneiro, Robert T. Review of *Studies in the Religion of South American Indians East of the Andes*, ed. R. Karsten, Arne Runeberg, and Michael Webster. *American Anthropologist* 68, no. 2 (1966):557–558.

Carneiro, Souza. *Mitos Africanos no Brasil*. São Paulo: Bibliotéca Pedagógica Brasileira, 1937.

Carneiro da Cunha, Manuela. "Logique du mythe et de l'action. Le mouvement messianique Canela de 1963," *L'Homme* 13, No. 4 (1973):5–37.

Carneiro da Cunha, Manuela. "Espace funéraire, eschatologie et culte des ancêtres: Encore le problème des paradigmes africaines," *ICA* (Paris) 2 (1976):277–295.

Carneiro da Cunha, Manuela. *Os Mortos e os Outros: Uma Análise do Sistema Funerário e da Noção de Pessoa Entre os Índios Krahó*. São Paulo: Editora Hucitec, 1978.

Carneiro da Cunha, Manuela. "De Amigos Formais e Pessoa: De Companheiros, Espelhos, e Identidades," *Boletim do Museu Nacional*, n.s. Antropologia No. 32 (May 1979):31–39.

Carneiro da Cunha, Manuela. "Eschatology Among the Krahó: Reflection upon Society, Free Field of Fabulation," in *Mortality and Immortality: The Archaeology and Anthropology of Death*, ed. Sally Humphreys and H. King. New York: Academic Press, 1981.

Carneiro da Cunha, Manuela, and Viveiros de Castro, E. B. "Vingança e Temporalidade," *JSAP* 71 (1985):191–208.

Carrasco Hermoza, Juan R. "La Tribu Machiguenga: Algunos Aspectos de su Cultura." *Zeitschrift für Ethnologie* 95, No. 2 (1970):231–274.

Carvalho, Neto. *Folklore Poético: Apuntes de Sistemática*. Quito: Editorial Universitaria, 1966.

Carybé, Hector Julio Paride Bernabo, and Amado, Jorge. *Iconográfia dos deuses africanos no candomblé da Bahia*. São Paulo: Fundação Cultural do Educação da Bahia, Instituto Nacional do Livro, Universidade Federal da Bahia, 1980.

Casamiquela, Rodolfo M. *Estudio del Nillatun y la religión araucana*. Bahia Blanca, Argentina: n.p., 1964.

Casamiquela, Rodolfo M. "Posibles Raíces Patagónicas en Creéncias Araucanas. I. Las Piedras Sagradas 'Con Ojos'," *Relaciones de la Sociedad Argentina de Antropología*, n.s., 9 (1977):107–114.

Casamiquela, Rodolfo M. "The Deluge Myth in Patagonia," *Latin American Indian Literatures* 6, No. 2 (1982):91–101.

Caspar, Franz. "Clothing Practice of the Tuparis (Brazil)," *ICA*, 30th Session (1950):155–159.

Caspar, Franz. *Tupari: Unter Indios im Urwald Brasiliens*. Braunschweig: Friedr. Vieweg & Sohn, 1952.

Castillo Castro, Gonzalo. *Liberation Theology from Below: The Life and Thought of Manuel Quintín Lame.* Maryknoll, N.Y.: Orbis Books, 1987.

Catálogo de la Colección Vela (Prehistoria Americana). Valencia: Servicio de Investigación Prehistoria, 1964.

Cereceda, Verónica. "De los colores de un pájaro," in *Enciclopedia del Mundo Aymara.* Javier Albo Company and Unesco (in press).

Cesar, Antonio de Oliveira. *Curandeiro: Revelacões dos misterios do candomblé.* Belo Horizonte: Editora Gráfica e Papelaria, 1981.

Chaffanjon, Jean. *L'Orénoque et le Caura: Relation de voyages exécutées en 1886–87.* Paris, 1889.

Chagnon, Napoleon A. *Yanamamö: The Fierce People.* New York: Holt, Rinehart & Winston, 1968.

Chapman, Anne M. "Lune en terre de feu. Mythes et rites des Selk'nam," *Objets et Mondes* 12, No. 2 (1972):145–158.

Chappelle, Richard. *Índios Cintas-Largas,* trans. David Járdim Júnior. Coleção Reconquista do Brasil. Belo Horizonte: Editora Itatiáia, 1982.

Chase-Sardi, Miguel. "Avaporu. Algunas fuentes documentales para el estudio de la antropofagia guaraní," *Revista del Ateneo Paraguayo* (Asunción) 3 (1964):35–70.

Chase-Sardi, Miguel. "Cosmovisión Mak'a," *Suplemento Antropológico* (Asunción del Paraguay, Universidad Católica) 5, Nos. 1–2 (1970):239–246.

Chase-Sardi, Miguel. "La Concepción nivaklé del mundo," *Suplemento Antropológico* (Asunción del Paraguay) 7, Nos. 1–2 (1972):121–141.

Chaumeil, J., and Chaumeil, J. P. "Chamanismo yagua," *Amazonía Peruana* (Lima) vol. 2, no. 3 (1978):159–72.

Chaumeil, J., and Chaumeil, J. P. *Voir, savoir, pouvoir: Le chamanisme chez les Yagua du nord-est péruvien.* Recherches d'histoire et de sciences sociales, vol. 8. Paris, 1983.

Chesser, Barbara. "The Anthropomorphic Personal Guardian Spirit in Aboriginal South America," *JLAL* 1, No. 2 (1975):107–126.

Chevalier, Jacques M. *Civilization and the Stolen Gift: Capital, Kin, and Cult in Eastern Peru.* Toronto: University of Toronto Press, 1982.

Chiara, Vilma. *Notes sur quelques categories religieuses des indiens: Waura du Haut-Xingu.* Microfiche. Paris: Institut d'Ethnologie Museé de l'Homme, 1979.

Chumap Lucia, Aurelio, and Renduelas, Manuel García. *Duik múum: Universo mítico de los Aguaruna.* Lima: Centro Amazónico de Antropología y Aplicación Práctica, 1979.

Civrieux, Marc de. *Religión y Magia Kari'ña.* Caracas: Universidad Católica "Andrés Bello." Instituto de Investigaciones Históricas, 1974.

Civrieux, Marc de. *Watunna: An Orinoco Creation Cycle,* ed. and trans. David M. Guss. San Francisco: North Point Press, 1980.

Civrieux, Marc de. *Caribes y la conquista de la Guayana Española: Etnohistoria Kariña.* Caracas: Instituto de Investigaciones Históricas, Facultad de Humanidades y Educación. Universidad Católica "Andres Bello," 1976.

Clastres, Hélène. "Rites funéraires Guayaki," *JSAP,* n.s., 57 (1968):63–72.

Clastres, Hélène. *La Terre sans mal. Le prophétisme Tupi-Guarani.* Paris: Editions du Seuil, 1976.

Clastres, Hélène, and Lizot, Jacques. "La Muerte y la Idea del Canibalismo entre los Yanomami," *Boletín Indigenista Venezolano* 18, No. 14 (1978):107–142.

Clastres, Pierre. "L'Arc et le panier," *L'Homme* 6, No. 2 (1966):13–31.

Clastres, Pierre. "Ethnographie des Indiens Guayaki," *JSAP* 57 (1968):8–61.

Clastres, Pierre. *Chronique des Indiens Guayaki.* Paris: Plon, 1972.

Clastres, Pierre. "De la Torture dans les sociétés primitives," *L'Homme* 13, No. 3 (July–Sept. 1973):114–120.

Clastres, Pierre. "Guayaki Cannibalism." In *Native South Americans: Ethnology of The Least Known Continent,* ed. Patricia J. Lyon. Boston: Little, Brown, 1974.

Clastres, Pierre. *Le Grand Parler: Mythes et chants sacrées des Indiens Guarani.* Paris: Editions du Seuil, 1974.

Clastres, Pierre. "Archéologie de la violence: La Guerre dans les sociétés primitives," *Libre* (Paris) 1 (1977):137–173.

Clastres, Pierre, and Sebag, Lucien. "Cannibalisme et mort chez les Guayakis (Achén)," *Revista do Museu Paulista*, n.s., 14 (1963):174–181.

Coelho, Vera Penteado, ed. *Os Alucinógenos e o mundo simbólico: O uso dos alucinógenos entre os índios da América do Sul*. São Paulo: Editora Pedagógica e Universitaria and the Editora da Universidade de São Paulo, 1976.

Colbacchini, P. Antônio, and Albisetti, P. Cesar. *Os Boróros Orientais*. São Paulo: Companhia Editora Nacional, 1942.

Colson, Audrey Butt. "The Akawaio Shaman." In *Carib-Speaking Indians*, ed. Ellen B. Basso. Tucson: University of Arizona Press, 1977.

Combès, Isabelle. "Être ou ne pas être: A propos d'*Araweté: Os deuses canibais* d'Eduardo Viveiros de Castro," *JSAP* 72 (1986):211–220.

Conrad, Geoffrey W., and Demarest, Arthur A. *Religion and Empire: The Dynamics of Aztec and Inca Expansionism*. Cambridge: At the University Press, 1984.

Consuegra, David. *Ornamentación Calada en la Orfebrería Indígena Precolombina (Muisca y Tolima)*. Bogotá: Ediciones Testimonia, 1968.

Cooksey, P. C. "El Espiritú Maligno Comegente," *Venezuela Misionera* 479 (June 1979):188–189.

Cooper, John M. "Fuegian and Chonoan Tribal Relations," in *Proceedings of the Nineteenth International Congress of Americanists*, pp. 445–453. Washington, D.C.: 1917.

Cooper, John M. *Analytical and Critical Bibliography of the Tribes of Tierra del Fuego and Adjacent Territory*. Bureau of American Ethnology, Bulletin 63. Washington, D.C.: Smithsonian Institution, 1917.

Cooper, John M. "Areal and Temporal Aspects of Aboriginal South American Culture." In *Annual Report of the Smithsonian Institution, 1943, pp. 429–461*. Washington, D.C.: Smithsonian Institution, 1943.

Cooper, John M. "The Chono." In *HSAI*, Vol. 1, pp. 47–54, ed. Julian H. Steward. Washington, D.C.: Smithsonian Institution, 1946.

Cooper, John M. "A Cross-Cultural Survey of South American Indian Tribes. Fire-Making." In *HSAI*, Vol. 5, pp. 283–292, ed. Julian H. Steward. U.S. Bureau of American Ethnology Bulletin No. 143. Washington D.C.: Smithsonian Institution, 1949.

Cordeu, Edgardo J. "Aproximación al horizonte mítico de los Tobas," *Runa* (Buenos Aires) 12, nos 1–2 (1969–1970):67–176.

Cordeu, Edgardo J. "Textos Míticos de los Angaité (Chenanesma) y Sanapaná," *Scripta Ethnológica* 1, No. 1 (1973):199–234.

Cordy-Collins, Alana. "Chavín Art: Its Shamanic/Hallucinogenic Origins." In *Pre-Columbian Art History: Selected Readings*. Palo Alto, Calif: Peek Publications, 1977.

Cornejo Bouroncle, Jorge. *Tupac Amaru. La revolución precursora de la emancipación continental*. Cuzco, 1963.

Cornely, Francisco L. *Cultura Diaguita Chilena y Cultura de el Molle*. Santiago de Chile: Editorial Del Pacifico, 1966.

Cortez, Roberto. "Diálogo Ceremonial e Diálogo Mitológico entre Os Tiriyó," *Boletim do Museu Goeldi-Antropologia* (Belém-Pará) 61 (Nov. 1975):1–25.

Cossard, Giselle. "Musique dans le Candomblé." In *La Musique dans la vie*, ed. T. Nikiprowetsky. Paris: O.C.O.R.A, 1967.

Cossard-Binon, Giselle. "La Fille de Saint," *JSAP* 58 (1969):57–78.

Costa Lima, Vivaldo da. *Uma Festa de Xangô no Opô Afonjá*. Salvador, Brazil: Universidade da Bahia/Unesco, 1959.

Coudreau, Henri A. *Voyage à travers les Guyanes et L'Amazonie*. Vol. 2 of *La France Equinoxiale*. Paris, 1887.

Coudreau, Henri A. *Chez nos Indiens. Quatre années dans la Guayane française*. Paris, 1887–1891.

Coudreau, Henri A. "Vocabulaires de dialectes indigènes de l'Amérique équatoriale (Chargé d'une mission scientifique dans les territoires de la Guyane Centrale)," *Archives de la Société Américaine de France* (Paris) 4, No. 1 (1889):4-52.

Crocker, J. Christopher. "The Mirrored Self: Identity and Ritual Inversion Among the Eastern Bororo," *Ethnology* 16 (1977):129-145.

Crocker, J. Christopher. "Selves and Alters Among the Eastern Bororo." In *Dialectical Societies: The Gê and Bororo of Central Brazil*, ed. David Maybury-Lewis. Cambridge, Mass.: Harvard University Press, 1979.

Crocker, Jon Christopher. *Vital Souls: Bororo Cosmology, Natural Symbolism, and Shamanism.* Tucson: University of Arizona Press, 1985.

Crocker, William H. "A Preliminary Analysis of Some Canela Religious Aspects," *Revista do Museu Paulista*, n.s., 14 (1963):163-173.

Crocker, William H. "The Canela Messianic Movement: An Introduction," *Atas do Simpósio sobre a Biota Amazônica* 2 (1963):69-83.

Crocker, William H. "The Canela Messianic Movement," *Reunião Brasileira de Antropologia*, pp. 41-42. Belem, 6-11, June 1966. Sumário das Communicações apresentadas. Belem: Imp. Universitaria, 1966.

Crofts, Marjorie, trans. *Aypapayu'üm ekawēn. Lendas Mundurukús*, Vol. 2. Brasília: Summer Institute of Linguistics, 1978.

Cruxent, José María. "Hallazgo de vasijas funerarias en el Rio Vigirimita (guacara-edo carabobo)," *Acta Venezolana* (Caracas) 3 (1948):138-141.

Cruxent, José María. Indios Guaika: Incineración de cadáveres," *Boletín Indigenista Venezolano* (Caracas) 1, No. 1 (1953):149-151.

Cruxent, José María, and Rouse, Irving. *An Archeological Chronology of Venezuela*, 2 vols. Washington, D.C.: Unión Pan America, Organization of American States, 1958.

Cunninghame-Graham, R. B. *A Brazilian Mystic: Being the Life and Miracles of Antonio Conselheiro.* New York: Dodd, Mead, 1920.

Custred, Glynn. "Hunting Technologies in Andean Culture," *JSAP* 66 (1979):7-19.

Daggett, Carole. "Las Funciones del Masato en la Cultura Chayahuita," *Antropológica* (Lima) 1, no. 1 (1983):301-310.

Da Matta, Roberto. "Myth and Anti-Myth Among the Timbira." In *Structural Analysis of Oral Tradition*, ed. Pierre Maranda and Elli Köngäs Maranda. Philadelphia: University of Pennsylvania Press, 1971.

Da Matta, Roberto. *A Divided World: Apinayé Social Structure*, trans. Alan Campbell. Cambridge, Mass.: Harvard University Press, 1982.

Da Matta, Roberto. "As Raízez da Violência no Brasil: Reflexões de um Antropólogo Social." In *Violência Brasileira*, ed. Roberto da Matta, Maria Célia Paoli, Maria Victoria Benevides, and Paulo Sêrgio Pinheiro. São Paulo: Editora Brasiliense, 1982.

D'Ans, André-Marcel. *Materiales para el estudio del grupo linguistico pano.* Lima: Mosca Azul Editores, 1970.

D'Ans, André-Marcel. *Problemas de clasificación de lenguas no-andinas en el Sur-Este peruano.* Lima: Mosca Azul Editores, 1973.

D'Ans, André-Marcel. *Le Dit des vrais hommes: Mythes, contes, légendes et traditions des indiens Cashinahua.* Paris: Union Générale d'Editions, 1978.

Daus, Ronald. *Epische Zyklus der Cangaceiros in der Volkspoesie.* Berlin: Colloquium Verlag, 1969.

Della Cava, Ralph. *Miracle at Joaseiro.* New York: Columbia University Press, 1970.

De Los Rios, Miguel Angel. "Vida y muerte en el cosmos mataco," *Cuadernos Franciscanos* (Salta) 35 (August 1974), unpaginated.

De Los Rios, Miguel Angel. "Presencia y distancia del tiempo primordial en la etnía Mataco," *Scripta Ethnológica* 3, Part 1 (1976):89-128.

De Los Rios, Miguel Angel. "Hacía una hermenéutica del nombre entre los Mataco," *Scripta Ethnológica* 3, Part 2 (1976):63-88.

De Los Rios, Miguel Angel. "Contribución al estudio de la organización del tiempo entre los Yohwaha: el ciclo anual," *Scripta Ethnológica* 4, Part 2 (1976-1977):52-77.

Demarest, Arthur A. *Viracocha: The Nature and Antiquity of the Andean High God.* Cambridge, Mass.: Peabody Museum of Archaeology and Ethnology, 1981.

Densmore, Frances. "The Use of Music in the Treatment of the Sick by American Indians." In *Annual Report of the Smithsonian Institution*, pp. 439–454. Washington, D.C.: Smithsonian Institution, 1953.

Depons, François Raymond Joseph. *Travels in Parts of South America During the Years 1801, 1802, 1803, and 1804.* London: Richard Phillips, 1806.

Derbyshire, Desmond C., and Pullum, Geoffrey K. *Handbook of Amazonian Languages.* The Hague: Mouton, 1985.

Descalzi, Ricardo. *La Real Audiencia de Quito Claustro en los Andes.* Quito: Consejo de Promoción, 1978.

Desmadryl, Jorge Dowling. *Religión, chamanismo y mitología mapuche.* Santiago, Chile: Editorial Universitaria, 1971.

De Wavrin, Don de M. le Marquis. *Les derniers indiens primitifs du bassin du Paraguay.* Paris, 1926.

De Wavrin, Don de M. le Marquis. "Simples notes sur la tribu des Jivaro," *Bulletin de la Société des Americanistes de Belgique.* 4 (Dec. 1930):5–21.

Dietschy, Hans. "La Structure des amitiés formelles dans la société Canella," *ICA*, 31st Session (São Paulo, 1955), pp. 211–216.

Dietschy, Hans. "Espace social et 'affiliation par sexe' au Brésil central (Karajá, Tapirapé, Apinayé, Mundurucú)," *ICA*, vol. 2, pp. 297–308. Paris, 1976.

Díez Astete, Alvaro. "¿Qué es el Mito?" *Anthropológica* (Pontificia Universidad Católica del Peru, Lima) 1, No. 1 (1983):5–18.

Díez de Medina, Fernando. "Legends of the Aymara: The Strange Religion of Bolivia's Highland People," *Américas* (Washington, D.C.) 5, No. 9 (1953):21–23, 42–44.

Dobkin, Marlene. "Fortune's Malice: Divination, Psychotherapy, and Folk Medicine in Peru," *JAFL* 82, No. 324 (April–June 1969):132–141.

Dobrizhoffer, Martin. *An Account of the Abipones, an Equestrian People of Paraguay*, 3 vols. Translated from the 1784 Latin edition by Sara Coleridge. London, 1822.

Dole, Gertrude E. "Endocannibalism Among the Amahuaca Indians." In *Native South Americans: Ethnology of the Least Known Continent*, ed. Patricia J. Lyon. Boston: Little, Brown, 1974.

Domeyko, Ignacio. *Araucania y sus Habitantes: Recuerdos de un Viaje Hecho en las Provincias Meridionales de Chile.* Buenos Aires: Editorial Francisco de Aguirre, 1971.

Dos Santos, Juana Elbein, and Dos Santos, Deoscoredes M. "Ancestor Worship in Bahia: The Égun Cult," *JSAP* 58 (1969):79–108.

Dostal, W., ed. *The Situation of the Indian in South America: Contributions to the Study of Inter-ethnic Conflict in the Non-Andean Regions of South America.* Veröffentlichungen des Seminars für Ethnologie der Universität Bern, Vol. 3. Geneva: World Council of Churches, 1972.

Dreyfus, Dina. *Ethnographie bororo: Objets provenant du village de Kejara (Brésil).* Microfiche. Paris: Museé de l'Homme, 1936.

Dreyfus, Simone. *Les Kayapo du Nord. Etat de Pará-Brésil. Contribution à l'étude des Indiens Gé.* The Hague: Mouton, 1963.

Drumond, Carlos. *Contribuição do Bororo à Toponîmia Brasílica.* São Paulo: Instituto de Estudos Brasileiros, 1965.

Dumézil, Georges, and Duviols, Pierre. "Sumaq T'ika: La Princesse du village sans eau," *JSAP* 63 (1974–1976):15–198.

Dumont, Jean-Paul. "Espacements et déplacements dans l'habitat Panare," *Journal de la Société des Americanistes* 61 (1972):2–30.

Dumont, Jean-Paul. *Under the Rainbow.* Austin: University of Texas Press, 1972.

Dumont, Jean-Paul. "Le sens de l'espace chez les Panare," *ICA*, 42nd Congress, vol. 2, pp. 47–53. Paris, 1976.

Dumont, Jean-Paul. "From Dogs to Stars: The Phatic Function of Naming Among the Panare." In *Carib-Speaking Indians*, ed. Ellen B. Basso. Tucson: University of Arizona Press, 1977.

Dumont, Jean-Paul. "Not in Ourselves, But in Our Stars." In *Spirits, Shamans, and Stars: Perspectives from South America*, ed. David L. Browman and Ronald A. Schwarz. The Hague: Mouton, 1979.

Dundes, Alan. "The Sherente Retellings of Genesis." In *Structural Analysis of Oral Tradition*, ed. Pierre Maranda and Elli Köngäs Maranda. Philidelphia: University of Pennsylvania Press, 1971.

Duvernay, Jacqueline. "Les Voies du Chamane," *L'Homme* 13, No. 3 (July–Sept. 1973):82–92.

Duviols, Pierre. "La visite des idolatries de Concepción de Chupas (Pérou, 1614)," *JSAP* 55 (1966):497–510.

Duviols, Pierre. *Francisco de Avila y la narración quechua de Huarochirí* Lima, 1966.

Duviols, Pierre. "Un inédit de Cristóbal de Albornoz: La instrucción para descubrir todas las guacas del Pirú y sus camayos y haziendas," *JSAP* 56 (1967):7–40.

Duviols, Pierre. "Un procès d'idolâtrie au Pérou: Arequipa, 1671," from *Colloque d'études péruviennes*, pp. 101–119. Publications des Annales de la Faculté des Lettres (Aix-en-Provence). New Series No. 61 (1967).

Duviols, Pierre. "The Inca Garcilaso de la Vega: Humanist Interpreter of the Inca Religion," *Diogènes* 47 (1970):36–52.

Duviols, Pierre. *La Lutte contre les religions autochtones dans le Pérou colonial*. Lima and Paris, 1971.

Duviols, Pierre. "Une petite chronique retrouvée: Errores, ritos, supersticiones y ceremonias de los yndios de la prouincia de Chinchaycocha y otras del Piru," *JSAP* 63 (1974–1976):275–297.

Duviols, Pierre, ed. *Ethnohistoire religieuse du Pérou colonial: Documents édités par Pierre Duviols*. Paris: Ophrys, 1971.

Duviols, Pierre, and Guevara, Nicolas de. "La idolatría en cifras: una relación peruana de 1619," from the *Colloque d'études péruviennes*, pp. 87–100. Publications des Annales de la Faculté des Lettres (Aix-en-Provence). New Series No. 61 (1967).

Earls, John. "The Organization of Power in Quechua Mythology," *Journal of the Steward Anthropological Society* 1, No. 1 (1969):63–82.

Earls, John, and Silverblatt, Irene. "La Realidad física y social en la cosmología andina," *ICA* 4, 42nd Congress (Paris, 1978), pp. 306–310.

Eckert, Georg. *Totenkult und Lebensglaube im Caucatal*. Kulturgeschichtliche Forschungen, Vol. 1. Braunschweig: Albert Limbach, 1948.

Eggan, Dorothy. "Hopi Dreams in Cultural Perspective." In *The Dream and Human Societies*, ed. G. E. von Grunebaum and Roger Caillois. Los Angeles: University of California Press, 1966.

Ehrenreich, Jeffrey, ed. *Political Anthropology of Ecuador: Perspectives from Indigenous Cultures*. Albany, N.Y.: Society for Latin American Anthropology and The Center for the Caribbean and Latin America, 1985.

Ehrenreich, Paul. "Die Mythen und Legenden der südamerikanischen Urvölker und ihre Beziehungen zu denen Nordamerikas und der alten Welt," *Zeitschrift für Ethnology*, supplement to Vol. 17 (1905).

Ehrenreich, Paul. *Studien zur südamerikanischen Mythologie*. Hamburg: Friedericksen & de Gruyter, 1939.

Eliade, Mircea. "Paradise and Utopia: Mythical Geography and Eschatology." In Eliade, *The Quest: History and Meaning in Religion*. Chicago: University of Chicago Press, 1969.

Eliade, Mircea. "The Dragon and The Shaman: Notes on a South American Mythology." In *Man and his Salvation: Studies in Memory of S. G. F. Brandon*, ed. Eric J. Sharpe and John R. Hinnells. Manchester: Manchester University Press, 1973.

Equazini, Melchor, and Herrera, José Tamayo. *Oración funebre de Tupac Amaru*. Lima: Biblioteca Nacional, 1981.

Erikson, Philippe. "Altérité, tatouage et anthropologie chez les Pano: la belliqueuse quête du soi," *JSAP* 72 (1986):185–210.

Espinoza Navarro, Faustino. *Guión para la Escenificación del "Inti Raymi" en la Ciudad Sagrada de los Inkas*. Cuzco, Peru: Academia Peruana de la Lengua Quechua, 1977.

Estrella Odicio, Gregorio. *Cuentos del hombre cacataibo (Cashibo)*. Yarinacocha: Summer Institute of Linguistics, 1977.

Estupiñan Bass, Nelson. *Timaran y Cuabu: Cuaderno de poesia para el pueblo.* Quito: Editorial Casa de la Cultura Ecuatoriana, 1956.

Falkner, Thomas, S.J. *A Description of Patagonia and the Adjoining Parts of South America.* Hereford, England, 1774; reprinted, Chicago: Armann & Armann, 1935.

Farabee, William Curtis. *The Central Arawaks.* Anthropological Publications 9. Philadelphia: University of Pennsylvania, University Museum, 1918.

Farabee, William Curtis. *Indian Tribes of Eastern Peru.* Peabody Museum of American Archaeology and Ethnology Papers, No. 10. Cambridge, Mass.: Harvard University, The Peabody Museum, 1922.

Farabee, William Curtis. *The Central Caribs.* Anthropological Publications 10. Philadelphia: University of Pennsylvania, University Museum, 1924.

Farelli, Maria Helena. *Os Rituais Secretos da Magia Negra e do Candomblé.* Rio de Janeiro: Pallas, S.A., 1977.

Faron, Louis C. "On Ancestor Propitiation Among the Mapuche of Central Chile," *AA* 63 (1961):824–830.

Faron, Louis C. *Hawks of the Sun: Mapuche Morality and Its Ritual Attributes.* Philadelphia: University of Pennsylvania Press, 1964.

Fejos, Paul. *Ethnography of the Yagua.* Viking Fund Publications in Anthropology, Vol. 1. New York: Viking Fund, 1943.

Fernandes, Florestan. "A Análise Funcionalista da Guerra: Possibilidades de Aplicação à Sociedade Tupinambá. Ensaio de Análise Crítica da Contribuição Etnográfica dos Cronistas para o Estudo Sociológico da Guerra entre Populações Aborigenes do Brasil Seiscentista," *RMP* 3 (1949):7–128.

Fernandes, Florestan. "La Guerre et le sacrifice humain chez les Tupinamba," *JSAP*, N.S., 41, No. 1 (1952):139–220.

Fernández, Eduardo. "Quienes nos Enseñaron a hacer Fuego. Mitología Ashaninca," *Anthropológica* (Lima) 1, no. 1 (1983):85–98.

Fernández G., Germán M.A. "The Araucanian Deluge Myth," *LAIL* 6, no. 2 (1982):102–113.

Fiebrig-Gertz, C. "Guarany Names of Paraguayan Plants and Animals," *Revista del Jardín Botánico y Museo de Historia Natural del Paraguay* 2 (1930).

Figueiredo, Ariosvaldo. *Enforcados: O Índio em Sergipe.* Coleção estudos Brasilieros, Vol. 52. Rio de Janeiro: Paz e Terra, 1981.

Figueiredo, Napoleao. "Religiões Mediúnicas na Amazônia: O Batuque," *JLAL* 1, No. 2 (1975):173–184.

Fioravanti-Molinié, Antoinette. "Cure magique dans la vallée sacrée du Cuzco," *JSAP* 66 (1979):85–98.

Fioravanti-Molinié, Antoinette. "Multi-Levelled Andean Society and Market Exchange: The Case of Yucay (Peru)," in *Ecology and Exchange in the Andes,* ed. David Lehmann. Cambridge: At the University Press, 1982.

Flasche, Rainer. *Geschichte und Typologie afrikanischer Religiosität in Brasilien* (Marburg an der Lahn: Universitäts-Bibliothek Marburg-Lahn, 1973).

Flores Galindo, Alberto, ed. *Tupac Amaru II-1780: Sociedad colonial y sublevaciones populares.* Lima: Retablo de Papel Ediciones, 1976.

Flornoy, Bertrand. *Iawa, le peuple libre.* Paris: Amiot-Dumont, 1953.

Fock, Niels. "The 'OHO' Institution Among the Waiwai," *ICA* (1956), pp. 136–140. Copenhagen, 1958.

Fock, Niels. *Waiwai: Religion and Society of an Amazonian Tribe.* Nationalmuseets Skrifter, Etnografisk Raekke, Vol. 8. Copenhagen: National Museum, 1963.

Fock, Niels. "Regulation of Conflicts in Amerindian Societies." In *Conflict Control and Conflict Resolution,* ed. Bengt Höglund and Jorgen Wilian Ulrich. Interdisciplinary Studies from the Scandinavian Summer University, Vol. 17. Copenhagen, 1972.

Frikel, Protásio. "Os Tiriyó (Notas Preliminares)," *Boletin da Museu Paraense Emílio Goeldi.* N.S. Antropologia, 9 (1960):1–19.

Frikel, Protásio. *Dez Anos de aculturação Tiriyo: 1960–70.* Bolem, Paraguay: Instituto Nacional de Pesquisas da Amazonia, 1971.

Fulop, Marcos. "Aspectos de la Cultura Tukana: Cosmogonía." *Revista Colombiano de Antropología* 3 (1954):99–137.

Fulop, Marcos. "Notas sobre los Términos y el Sistema de Parentesco de los Tukano," *Revista Colombiana de Antropología* (Bogotá) 4 (1955):121–164.

Fulop, Marcos. "Aspectos de la cultura tukana: mitología," *RCA* 5 (1956):335–373.

Furst, Peter T. "The Roots and Continuities of Shamanism," *Artscanada* 30, Nos. 5–6 (Dec. 1973/Jan. 1974):33–60.

Furst, Peter T., ed. *Flesh of the Gods: The Ritual Use of Hallucinogens.* New York: Praeger, 1972.

Furst, Peter T.; Keller, Peter C.; Lee, William B.; Ruddle, Kenneth; Reichel-Dolmatoff, Gerardo; Schultes, Richard Evans; and Bright, Alec. *Sweat of the Sun, Tears of the Moon: Gold and Emerald Treasures of Colombia.* Los Angeles: Natural History Museum of Los Angeles County, 1981.

Gallardo Moscoso, Hernan. *Fisionomía de Loja: Paltas, Incas y Viracochas.* Loja, Ecuador: Casa de la Cultura Ecuatoriana, 1964.

Galvão, Eduardo. "Aculturação Indígena no Rio Negro," *Boletim do Museu Paraense Emílio Goeldi*, Antropologia, 7 (1959):1–60.

Galvão, Eduardo. "Indians and Whites in the Brazilian Amazon," *Zeitschrift für Ethnologie* 95, No. 2 (1970):220–230.

García, Secundino. "Mitología Machiguenga," *Misiones Dominicanas Peru*, Vol. 17, pp. 95–99, 170–179, 220–228; Vol. 18, pp. 2–13, 86–97, 121–139, 166–176, 212–219; Vol. 19, pp. 11–17 (1935–1937).

García-Renduelas, Manuel, and Lucia, Aurelio Chumap. *Duik Múum: Universo Mítico de los Aguarunas*, 2 vols. Lima: Centro Amazónico de Antropologia y Aplicación Práctica, 1979.

Garcilaso de la Vega, el Inca. *Royal Commentaries of the Incas* and *General History of Peru*. Part One, 2 vols. Translated by Harold V. Livermore. Austin: University of Texas Press, 1966.

Garr, Thomas M., S.J. *Cristianismo y Religión Quechua.* Cusco: Instituto de Pastoral Andina, 1972.

Gasché, Jürg. "Recherches ethnographiques dans les bassins des Rios Caqueta et Putumayo (Amazonie Colombienne), *JSAP* 58 (1969):267–275.

Giaccaria, Bartolomeu. *Jeronimo Xavante Sonha: Contos e sonhos.* Campo Grande, Brasil: Mato Grosso, 1975.

Giaccaria, Bartolomeu, and Heide, Adalberto. *Xavante (Auwe Uptabi: Povo Autêntico); Pesquisa Histórico-etnográfica.* São Paulo: Editorial Dom Bosco, 1972.

Gibson, Gordon D. "A Bibliography of Anthropological Bibliographies: The Americas," *Current Anthropology* 1, No. 1 (1960):61–73.

Gilij, Filippo Salvadore. *Saggio di Storia Americana, o sia Storia Naturale, Civile, e Sacra de Regni, e delle Provincie Spagnuole di Terra-ferma nell'America Meridionale*, 4 vols. Rome: Luigi Perego Erede Salvioni, 1780–1784.

Gillin, James. *The Barama River Caribs of British Guiana.* Papers of the Peabody Museum, Vol. 14, No. 2. Cambridge, Mass: Peabody Museum of Harvard University, 1936.

Girard, Rafael. *Indios Selváticos de la Amazonia Peruana.* Mexico City: Libro Mexico Editores, 1958.

Girard, Rafael. "Los Mitos y su dramatización entre los selvaticos de la Amazonia peruana," offprint from *A William Cameron Townsend en el XXV Aniversario del I. L. V.* No date, publisher, or location indicated.

Girault, Louis. *Kallawaya: Guérisseurs itinérants des Andes.* Mémoires de l'Institut Français de Recherche Scientifique pour le Développement en Cooperation, Vol. 107. Paris: ORSTOM, 1984.

Goeje, C. H. de. *The Arawak Language of Guiana.* Amsterdam: Koninklijke Akademie van Wetenschappen, 1928.

Goeje, C. H. de. "The Inner Structure of the Warao Language of Guiana," *JSAP* 22, no. 4 (1930):66–72.

Goeje, C. H. de. "Philosophy, Initiation and Myths of the Indians of Guiana and Adjacent Countries," *Internationales Archiv für Ethnographie* (Leiden) 44 (1943):vi–xx, 1–136.

Goldman, Irving. "Cosmological Beliefs of the Cubeo Indians," *JAFL* 53, no. 210 (Oct.-Dec. 1940):242–247.

Goldman, Irving. "The Structure of Ritual in the Northwest Amazon." In *Process and Pattern in Culture: Essays in Honor of Julian H. Steward,* ed. Robert H. Manners. Chicago: Aldine, 1964.

Goldman, Irving. *The Cubeo: Indians of the Northwest Amazon,* 2nd ed. Urbana: University of Illinois Press, 1979.

Goldman, Irving. "Time, Space and Descent: The Cuebo Example," *ICA,* 42nd Congress, 2, pp. 175–184. Paris, 1976.

Goulet, Jean-Guy. "El Universo social y religioso guajiro," *Montalban* (Universidad Católica Andrés Bello, Instituto de Investigaciones Históricas, Centro de Lenguas Indígenas in Caracas) 11 (1979–1981):3–458.

Gow, Rosalind, and Condori, Bernabe. *Kay Pacha.* Cuzco: Centro de Estudios Rurales Andinos "Bartolomé de las Casas," 1976.

Grebe, Maria Ester. "El Kultrun Mapuche: Un Microcosmo Simbólico," *Revista Musical Chilena* 27, Nos. 123–124 (1973):3–42.

Greenberg, Joseph H. "The General Classification of Central and South American Languages." In *Men and Cultures: Selected Papers of the Fifth International Congress of Anthropological and Ethnological Sciences, Philadelphia, September 1–9, 1956.* Philadelphia: University of Pennsylvania Press, 1960.

Gregor, Thomas. *Mehinaku: The Drama of Daily Life in a Brazilian Indian Village.* Chicago: University of Chicago Press, 1977.

Grenand, Françoise. *Et l'Homme devint jaguar: Univers imaginaire et quotidien des indiens Wayãpi de Guyane.* Paris: Editions l'Harmattan, Collection Amérindienne, 1982.

Grenand, Pierre. *Relations intertribales en Haute Guyane du XVIIIeme siècle à nos jours.* Microfiche. Paris: Institut d'Ethnologie Museé de l'Homme, 1972.

Grenand, Pierre. *Introduction à l'étude de l'univers Wayãpi: Ethnoécologie des indiens du Haut-Oyapock (Guyane Français).* Paris: Société d'Etudes Linguistiques et Anthropologiques de France, 1980.

Grieder, Terence. *Origins of Pre-Columbian Art.* Austin: University of Texas Press, 1982.

Gross, Daniel R., ed. *Peoples and Cultures of Native South America.* Garden City, N.Y.: Doubleday/Natural History Press, 1973.

Grossa, Dino J. "Una Visita a los Indios Yaruros de Riecito," *Boletín Indigenista Venezolano* (Caracas) 10, Nos. 1–4 (1966):67–79.

Grubb, Wilfred Barbrooke. *An Unknown People in an Unknown Land: An Account of the Life and Customs of the Lengua Indians of the Paraguayan Chaco,* 4th ed. London, 1925(1911).

Grubb, Wilfred Barbrooke. *A Church in the Wilds,* ed. H. T. Morrey Jones. New York: E. P. Dutton, 1914.

Guaman Poma de Ayala [Waman Puma], Felipe. *El Primer nueva corónica y buen gobierno,* ed. John V. Murra and Rolena Adorno; trans. Jorge L. Urioste. Mexico City: Siglo Veintiuno, 1981.

Guffroy, J. *Bibliographie critique et état des connaissances sur la Patagonie argentine.* Microfiche. Paris: Institut d'Ethnologie, Museé de l'Homme, 1979.

Gusinde, Martin. *Die Feuerlandindianer,* 4 vols. Mödling bei Wein, 1931–1974; translated into Spanish by a team under direction of Werner Hoffman, as *Los Indios de Tierra del Fuego,* 3 vols. Buenos Aires: Centro Argentino de Etnología Americana. Consejo Nacional de Investigaciones Científicas y Técnicas, 1982–1983.

Gusinde, Martin. "Der Medizinmann mit dem umgekehrten Geschlecht," *Ciba Zeitschrift* (Basel) 4, No. 38 (1936):1323–1324.

Gusinde, Martin. "In der Medizinmannschule der Yamana-Feuerlander," *Ciba Zeitschrift* (Basel) 4, No. 38 (1936):1307–1310.

Gusinde, Martin. "Der Medizinmann bei den Indianern Südamerikas," *Ciba Zeitschrift* (Basel) 4, No. 38 (1936):1302–1306.

Guss, David M. "The Atta," *New Wilderness Letter* (New York) 2, No. 8 (1980):14–15.

Guss, David M. "Historical Incorporation Among the Makiritare: From Legend to Myth," *JLAL* 7, No. 1 (1981):23–35.

Guyot, Mireille. "Les Bora," *JSAP* 58 (1969):275–284.

Guyot, Mireille. "Structure et évolution chez les indiens bora et miraña, Amazonie colombienne," *ICA*, 42nd Congress, vol. 2, pp. 163–173. Paris, 1976.

Guyot, Mireille. "La Historia del Mar de Danta, el Caqueta: Una Fase de la Evolución Cultural en el Noroeste Amazónico," *JSAP* 66 (1979):99–123.

Haekel, Josef. "Jugendweihe und Männerfest auf Feuerland. Ein Beitrag zu ihrer kulturhistorischen Stellung," *Mitteilungen der Anthropologischen Gesellschaft* (Vienna) 73–74 (1947).

Haekel, Josef. "Zur Problematik des Heiligen Pfahles bei den Indianern Brasiliens," *ICA*, 31st Session (São Paulo, 1955), pp. 230–243.

Hanke, Wanda. "Costumbres y Creéncias Indígenas Relacionadas con la Muerte," *RGA* 11 (1939):363–368.

Hardoy, Jorge E. *Pre-Columbian Cities*. New York: Walker & Company, 1973.

Harner, Michael J. "Jivaro Souls," *AA* 64, No. 2 (1962):258–272.

Harner, Michael J. "The Sound of Rushing Water." In *Native South Americans*, ed. Patricia J. Lyon. Boston: Little, Brown, 1974; reprinted from *Natural History Magazine* (June-July 1968), pp. 28–33, 60–61.

Harner, Michael J., ed. *Hallucinogens and Shamanism*. London: Oxford University Press, 1973.

Harner, Michael. *The Way of the Shaman*. New York: Harper & Row, 1980.

Harner, Michael J. *The Jívaro: People of the Sacred Waterfalls*. Garden City, N.Y.: Anchor Books, 1982.

Haro Alvear, Silvio Luis. *Atahualpa duchicela*. Ibarra, Ecuador: Imprenta Municipal, 1965.

Haro Alvear, Silvio Luis. *Paruha: Nación guerrera*. Quito: Editoria Nacional, 1977.

Haro Alvear, Silvio Luis. *Mitos y cultos del reino de Quito*. Quito: Editora Nacional, 1989.

Harris, Olivia. "Labour and Produce in an Ethnic Economy, Northern Potosi, Bolivia." In *Ecology and Exchange in the Andes*, ed. David Lehmann. Cambridge: At the University Press, 1982.

Harth-Terre, Emilio. *Símbolo verbal en los mantos de Paracas*. Lima: Editorial J. Mejia Baca, 1976.

Hartmann, Günther. *Masken südamerikanischer Naturvölker*. Berlin: Museum für Völkerkunde, 1967.

Hartmann, Günther. "Destillieranlagen bei südamerikanischen Naturvölkern," *Zeitschrift für Ethnologie* 93, no. 2 (1968):225–232.

Hartmann, Günther. "Zigarrenhalter Nordwest-Brasiliens," *Ethnologische Zeitschrift Zürich*. Festschrift Otto Zerries. Special Supplement no. 1 (1974), pp. 177–189.

Hartmann, Günther. *Silberschmuck der Araukaner, Chile*. Berlin: Museum für Völkerkunde, 1974.

Hartmann, Roswith. "Otros Datos sobre las Llamadas 'Batallas Rituales'," *ICA*, 39th Congress, 6 (Lima, 1972).

Hartmann, Roswith. "Commemoración de Muertos en la Sierra Ecuatoriana," *Indiana* (Berlin) 1 (1973):179–197.

Hartmann, Roswith. "Creencias Acerca de las Almas de los Difuntos en la Región de Otavalo/Ecuador," *Ethnologische Zeitschrift Zürich*. Festschrift Otto Zerries. Special Supplement No. 1 (1974), pp. 201–227.

Hartmann, R., and Oberem, Udo. "Beiträge zum 'Huairu-Spiel'," *Zeitschrift für Ethnologie* 93, no. 2 (1968):240–259.

Hartmann, Roswith, and Oberem, Udo. *Amerikanistische Studien: Festschrift für Hermann Trimborn anlässich seines 75. Geburtstages*. St. Augustin: Haus Völker und Kulturen, 1979.

Hartmann, Thekla. *Nomenclatura Botânica dos Borôro*. São Paulo: Instituto de Estudios Brasileiros, 1968.

Hartmann, Thekla. "Zur botanischen Nomenklatur der Bororo-Indianer." *Zeitschrift für Ethnologie* 96, no. 2 (1971):234–249.

Hartt, Charles Frederik. "The Indian Cemetery of the Gruta das Mumias, Southern Minas Geraes, Brazil," *American Naturalist* 9, No. 4 (1875):205–217.

Hasler, Juan A. *Bibliographía Americanística Brevis*. Medellin, Colombia: Universidad de Antioquia, 1973.

Hassler, Wiley A. *Nguillatunes del Neuquen: Costumbres araucanas*. Buenos Aires: Editorial Siringa, 1979.

Hemming, John. *The Conquest of the Incas*. New York: Harcourt Brace Jovanovich, 1970.

Hemming, John. *Red Gold: The Conquest of the Brazilian Indians*. Cambridge, Mass.: Harvard University Press, 1978.

Henry, Jules. *Jungle People: A Kaingang Tribe of the Highlands of Brazil*. New York: Vintage Books, 1964(1941).

Henry, Jules, and Henry, Zunia. *Doll Play of Pilagá Indian Children*. New York: Vintage Books, 1974.

Herskovitz, Melville J. "Drums and Drummers in Afrobrazilian Cult Life," *The Musical Quarterly* 30 (1944):477–492.

Herskovitz, Melville J. "The Social Organization of the Candomblé," *ICA*, 31st Session (São Paulo, 1955), pp. 505–532.

Hilbert, Peter Paul. *Archäologische Untersuchungen am mittleren Amazonas*. Berlin: Dietrich Reimer, 1968.

Hilger, M. Inez. *Huenun Namku: An Araucanian Indian of the Andes Remembers the Past*. With the Assistance of Margaret A. Mondloch. Norman: University of Oklahoma Press, 1966.

Hilger, M. Inez, and Mondloch, Margaret A. "The Araucanian Weaver," *Boletín del Museo Nacional de Historia Natural* (Santiago de Chile) 30 (1967):291–298.

Hill, Jonathan. "Wakuenai Society: A Processual-Structural Analysis of Indigenous Cultural Life in the Upper Rio Negro (Guainía) Region of Venezuela." Unpublished Ph.D. dissertation. Indiana University, 1983.

Hill, Jonathan. "Kamayura Flute Music," *Ethnomusicology* 23, No. 3 (1979):417–432.

Hissink, Karin. "Das Gürteltier im Weltbild der Tacana-Indianer," *ICA*, (Copenhagen, 1958), pp. 155–164.

Hissink, Karen, and Hahn, Albert. *Die Tacana. Ergebnisse der Frobenius-Expedition nach Bolivien 1952 bis 1954*. Volume One: *Erzählungsgut*. Veröffentlichung des Frobenius-Instituts an der Johann Wolfgang Goethe-Universität, Frankfurt am Main. Stuttgart: W. Kohlhammer Verlag, 1961.

Hocquenghem, Anne Marie. *Code pour l'analyse des représentations figureés sur les vases mochicas*. Microfiche. Paris: Institut d'Ethnologie, Museé de l'Homme, 1976.

Hocquenghem, Anne Marie. *Textiles et les vêtements dans la culture mochica (Perou)*. Microfiche. Paris: Institut d'Ethnologie, Museé de l'Homme, 1977.

Holmberg, Allan. "The Siriono," *HSAI* 3 (1948):455–463.

Holmberg, Allan R. *Nomads of the Long Bow: The Siriono of Eastern Bolivia*. Chicago: University of Chicago Press, 1960; originally issued as Publication No. 10, Smithsonian Institution, Institute of Social Anthropology, Washington, D.C., 1950.

Howard, Joseph H. *Drums in the Americas*. New York: Oak Publications, 1967.

Howe, James, and Hirschfeld, Lawrence A. "The Star Girl's Descent: A Myth About Men, Women, Matrilocality, and Singing," *JAFL* 94, No. 373 (1981):292–322.

Hugh-Jones, Christine. *From the Milk River: Spatial and Temporal Processes in Northwest Amazonia*. Cambridge: At the University Press, 1979.

Hugh-Jones, Christine. "Skin and Soul, the Round and the Straight: Social Time and Social Space in Pirá-Paraná Society," *ICA*, 42nd Congress (Paris, 1977), pp. 185–204.

Hugh-Jones, Stephen. "Like Leaves on the Forest Floor: Ritual and Social Structure Amongst the Barasana," *ICA*, 42nd Congress (Paris, 1977), pp. 205–215.

Hugh-Jones, Stephen. *The Palm and the Pleiades: Initiation and Cosmology in Northwest Amazonia*. Cambridge: At the University Press, 1979.

Hugh-Jones, Stephen. "The Pleiades and Scorpius in Barasana Cosmology." In *Ethnoastronomy and Archaeoastronomy in the American Tropics*, ed. Anthony F. Aveni and Gary Urton. Annals of the New York Academy of Sciences, Vol. 385. New York: New York Academy of Sciences, 1982.

Humboldt, Alexander von, and Bonpland, Aimé. *Personal Narrative of Travels to the Equinoctial Regions of America during the Years 1799–1804*, 3 vols. ed. and trans. Thomasina Ross. London: Henry G. Bohn, 1907 (1852–1853).

Hurault, Jean. *Les Indiens Wayana de la Guyane Française. Structure sociale et coutume familiale*. Office de la Recherche Scientifique et Technique Outre-Mer. Memoires O.R.S.T.O.M., Vol. 3, Part 5. Paris: 1968.

Hye-Kerkdal, K. J. "Tanz als Soziale Funktion bei den Timbira Brasiliens," *ICA*, Copenhagen, 1958, pp. 263–270.

Ibarra Grasso, Dick Edgar. *Cosmogonía y Mitología Indígena Americana*. Buenos Aires: Editorial Kier, 1980.

Idoyaga Molina, Anatilde. "Matrimonio y pasión amorosa entre los Mataco," *Scripta Ethnológica* 4, Part 1 (1976):47–67.

Idoyaga Molina, Anatilde. "Aproximación hermenéutica a las nociones de concepción, gravidez y alumbramiento entre los Pilagá del Chaco Central," *Scripta Ethnológica* 4, Part 2 (1976–1977):78–98.

Illescas Cook, Guillermo. *Astrónomos en el Antiguo Perú: Sobre los Conocimientos Astronómicos de los Antiguos Pueblos del Perú*. Lima: Kosmos Editores, 1976.

Imbelloni, J. "Medicina y Culturas," *Revista Geográfica Americana* 7 (1937):327–336.

Im Thurn, Everard F. *Among the Indians of Guiana, Being Sketches Chiefly Anthropologic from the Interior of British Guiana*. London: Kegan Paul, Trench, & Co., 1883.

Inojosa, Mario Franco. *Fábulas Orales Aymaras*. Juli, Peru, 1975.

Instituto Nacional de Folklore. *Diablos Danzantes de Venezuela*. Caracas: Fundación La Salle de Ciéncias Naturales, 1982.

Irarrazaval, Diego. *Religión del pobre y liberación en Chimbote*. Lima: Centro de Estudios y Publicaciones, 1978.

Isbell, Billie Jean. *To Defend Ourselves: Ecology and Ritual in an Andean Village*. Latin American Monographs, No. 47. Austin, Texas: Institute of Latin American Studies, 1978.

Isbell, William H. "Cosmological Order Expressed in Prehistoric Ceremonial Centers," *ICA*, 42nd Congress (Paris, 1977), Vol. 4, pp. 269–298.

Iturra, Raul. "Marriage, Ritual and Profit: The Production of Producers in a Portuguese Village," *Social Compass* 32, No. 1 (1985):73–92.

Izikowitz, Karl Gustav. "Calabashes with Star-Shaped Lids in South America and China." *Comparative Ethnographical Studies* 9 (1931):130–133.

Izikowitz, Karl Gustav. "Les Instruments de Musique des Indiens Uro-Chipaya," *Revista* (Universidad Nacional. Instituto de Etnología. Tucumán) 2 (1932):263–291.

Izikowitz, Karl Gustav. *Musical and Other Sound Instruments of the South American Indians: A Comparative Ethnographical Study*. Göteborg: Elanders Boktryckeri Aktiebolag, 1935.

Izikowitz, Karl Gustav. "Rythmical Aspects of Canella Life," *ICA*, 31st Session (São Paulo, 1955), pp. 195–209.

Izquierdo Gallo, Mariano. *Mitología Americana: Selección de los Mitos Aborígenes de América*. Madrid: Ediciones Guadarrama, 1956.

Jackson, Jean E. *The Fish People: Linguistic Exogamy and Tukanoan Identity in Northwest Amazonia*. Cambridge: At the University Press, 1983.

Jacopin, Pierre-Yves. "Quelques effets du temps mythologique," *ICA*, 42nd Congress (Paris, 1977), Vol. 2, pp. 217–232.

Jacopin, Pierre-Yves. *La Parole générative de la mythologie des indiens Yukuna*. Doctoral Dissertation. Université de Neuchâtel. Faculté des Lettres, 1981.

Jaquith, James R. "Bibliography of Anthropological Bibliographies of the Americas," *América Indígena* (Mexico City) 30, No. 2 (1970):419–469.

Jaramillo Cisneros, Hernan. *Inventario de Diseños en Tejidos Indígenas de la Provincia de Imbabura*, 2 vols. Otavalo, Ecuador: Instituto Otavaleño de Antropología, 1981.

Jett, Stephen C. "Precolumbian Transoceanic Contacts." In *Ancient South Americans*, ed. Jesse D. Jennings. San Fransisco: W. H. Freeman & Co., 1983.

Jiménez Núñez, Alfredo. *Mitos de Creación en Sudamérica*. Publicaciones del Seminario de Antropología Americana, Vol. 3. Seville, 1962.

Jiménez Borja, Arturo. *Puruchuco*. Lima: Editorial Juridica, 1973.

Jordana Laguna, José Luis. *Mitos e Historias Aguarunas y Huambisas de la Selva del Alto Marañón*. Lima: Retablo de Papel Ediciones, 1974.

Juruna, Mário. *Gravador do Juruna*. Porto Alegre, Brazil: Mercado Aberto Editora, 1982.

Kaplan, Abraham. "Cosmology as Ecological Analysis: A View from the Rain Forest," *Man* 11 (1976):307–318.

Kappler, A. *Zes Jaren In Suriname*. Utrecht: Dannefelser, 1854.

Kappler, A. *Holländisch Guiana. Erlebnisse und Erfahrungen während eines 43 jährigen Aufenthalts in der Kolonie Surinam*. Stuttgart: Kohlhammer, 1881.

Karasch, Mary. "Central African Religious Tradition in Rio de Janeiro," *JLAL* 5, No. 2 (1979):233–253.

Karsten, Rafael. *Contributions to the Sociology of the Indian Tribes of Ecuador: Three Essays*. Acta Academiae Aboensis. Humaniora, Vol. 1, No. 3. Helsinki, 1920.

Karsten, Rafael. *The Toba Indians of the Bolivian Gran Chaco*. Acta Academiae Aboensis. Humaniora 4. (Abo, Finland, 1923); reprinted Oosterhout, the Netherlands: Anthropological Publications, 1970.

Karsten, Rafael. *The Civilization of the South American Indians with Special Reference to Magic and Religion*. London: Kegan, Paul, Trench, Trubner & Co., 1926.

Karsten, Rafael. *Indian Tribes of the Argentine and Bolivian Chaco*. Commentationes Humanarum Litterarum. Vol. 4, No. 1. Helsinki: Societas Scientiarum Fennica, 1932.

Karsten, Rafael. *The Head-Hunters of Western Amazonas: The Life and Culture of the Jibaro Indians of Eastern Ecuador and Peru*. Commentationes Humanarum Litterarum, Vol. 8, No. 1. Helsinki: Societas Scientiarum Fennica, 1935.

Karsten, Rafael. *Studies in the Religion of the South American Indians East of the Andes*, ed. Arne Runeberg and Michael Webster. Commentationes Humanarum Litterarum Vol. 29, No. 1. Helsinki: Societas Scientiarum Fennica, 1964.

Kato, Takahiro. "Una interpretación más abierta de Incarrí," *Anthropológica* (Lima) 3 (1985):295–305.

Keller, Carlos. "Der Ursprungsmythus der Kloketen-Feier der Selknam-Indianer auf Feuerland," *Anthropos* 57 (1962):524–528.

Kelley, David. "Calendar Animals and Deities," *Southwestern Journal of Anthropology* 16, No. 3 (1960):317–337.

Kelm, Heinz. "Einige Bemerkungen zur Frage der sogenannten Kurúkwa in Ostbolivien," *Anthropos* 56, nos. 3–4 (1961):501–518.

Kelm, Heinz. "O canto matinal dos Sirionó," *Revista de Antrepología* (São Paulo) 15–16 (1967–1968):111–132.

Kensinger, Kenneth M. *"Banisteriopsis Usage Among the Peruvian Cashinahua."* In *Hallucinogens and Shamanism*, ed. Michael J. Harner. New York: Oxford University Press, 1973.

Kensinger, Kenneth M. "Cashinahua Medicine and Medicine Men." In *Native South Americans: Ethnology of the Least Known Continent*, ed. Patricia J. Lyon. Boston: Little, Brown, 1974.

Kensinger, Kenneth M. "Studying the Cashinahua." In *The Cashinahua of Eastern Peru*, ed. Jane Powell Dwyer. Providence, R.I.: Haffenreffer Museum of Anthropology, 1975.

Kensinger, Kenneth M. "Cashinahua Notions of Social Time and Social Space," *ICA*, 42nd Congress (Paris, 1976), Vol. 2, pp. 233–244.

Kensinger, Kenneth M., ed. *Marriage Practices in Lowland South America*. Urbana: University of Illinois Press, 1984.

Key, Mary Ritchie. *The Grouping of South American Indian Languages*. Ars Linguistica: Commentationes Analyticae et Criticae, Vol. 2. Tübingen: Günter Narr Verlag, 1979.

Kill, Lucia. *Pachamama: Die Erdgöttin in der altandinen Religion*. Bonn: Rheinische Friedrich-Wilhelms-Universität, 1969.

Klaiber, Jeffrey L. *Religión y revolución en el Peru, 1824–1976*. Lima: Universidad del Pacifico/Departamento de Humanidades, 1980.

Klein, Harriet E. Manelis, and Stark, Louisa R., eds. *South American Indian Languages: Retrospect and Prospect*. Austin: University of Texas Press, 1985.

Kloos, Peter. "Becoming a Píyei: Variability and Similiarity in Carib Shamanism," *Antropológica* (Caracas) 24 (Dec. 1968):3–25.

Kloos, Peter. "Female Initiation Among the Maroni River Caribs," *AA* 71 (1969):898–905.

Kloos, Peter. *The Maroni River Caribs of Surinam*. Assen, the Netherlands: Van Gorcum, 1971.

Kloos, Peter. "The Akuriyo Way of Death." In *Carib-Speaking Indians, Culture, Society and Language*, ed. Ellen B. Basso. Tucson: University of Arizona Press 1977.

Koch, Theodor. "Die Anthropophagie der südamerikanischen Indianer," *Internationales Archiv für Ethnographie* (Leiden) 12 (1899):78–110.

Koch-Grünberg, Theodor. "Die religiösen Maskentänze der Indianer des oberen Rio Negro und Yapurá," *Anthropologische Gesellschaft, Sitzungsberichte* (Vienna) 3 (1905–1906):66.

Koch-Grünberg, Theodor. "Das Haus bei den Indianern Nordwestbrasiliens," *Archiv für Anthropologie* (Braunschweig) 35 (1908):37–50.

Koch-Grünberg, Theodor. *Zwei Jahre unter den Indianern. Reisen in Nordwest-Brasilien, 1903–1905*, 2 vols. Berlin: Ernst Wasmuth, 1909–1910; reprinted in Vienna: Akademische Druck und Verlagsanstalt, 1967.

Koch-Grünberg, Theodor. *Vom Roroima zum Orinoco: Ergebnisse einer Reise in Nordbrasilien und Venezuela in den Jahren 1911–1913*, 5 vols. Volume 1, Berlin: Dietrich Reimer; Volumes 2–5, Stuttgart: Strecker & Schröder, 1917–1928.

Koessler-Ilg, Bertha. *Tradiciones Araucanas*, Vol. 1. Buenos Aires: Instituto de Filología. Facultad de Humanidades y Ciéncias de la Educación, Universidad Nacional de la Plata, 1962.

Konana, Mildred A., and Konan, Raymond W. "El Arte Tradicional de la Calabaza Peruana," *Américas* 31, Nos. 6–7 (1979):41–45.

Kracke, Waud H. *Force and Persuasion: Leadership in an Amazonian Society*. Chicago: University of Chicago Press, 1978.

Kracke, Waud H. "Dreaming in Kagwahiv: Dream Beliefs and their Psychic Uses in an Amazonian Indian Culture." In *Psychoanalytic Study of Society*, ed. Werner Muensterberger and L. Bryce Boyer. New Haven, Conn.: Yale University Press, 1979.

Krener, Era, and Fock, Niels. "Good Luck and the Taita Carnaval of Cañar, " *Folk: Dansk Etnografisk Tidsskrift* 19–20 (1977–1978):152–170.

Krickeberg, Walter. "Beiträge zur Frage der alten kulturgeschichtlichen Beziehungen zwischen Nord- und Südamerika," *Zeitschrift für Ethnologie* (Berlin) 66, Nos. 4–6 (1934):287–373.

Krickeberg, Walter. *Mitos y leyendas de los Aztecas, Incas, Mayas, y Muiscas*. Mexico City: Fondo de Cultura Económica, 1971.

Krickeberg, Walter; Trimborn, Hermann; Müller, Werner; and Zerries, Otto. *Pre-Columbian American Religions*. London: Weidenfeld & Nicolson, 1968.

Krisólogo B., Pedro J. "Antropología Cultural del Pueblo Panare," *Boletín Indigenista Venezolano* (Caracas) 9, No. 4 (1965):161–186.

Krugh, Janice. "The Mythology of the Pemón Indians of Venezuela: A Survey of the Work of Father Cesáreo de Armellada," *Latin American Indian Literatures* 4, No. 1 (Spring 1980):29–35.

Krupp, Edwin C. *Echoes of the Ancient Skies: The Astronomy of Lost Civilizations*. New York: Harper & Row, 1983.

Krupp, Edwin. *Archaeoastronomy and the Roots of Science*. Boulder, Colo.: Westview Press, 1984.

Kumu, Umúsin Panlõn, and Kenhíri, Tolamãn. *Antes o mundo não existia: A mitologia heróica dos índios desâna*. São Paulo: Livraria Cultura Editora, 1980.

Kunike, H. "El Jaguar y la luna en la mitología de la altiplanicie andina," *Revista Inca* 1, No. 3 (1923):561–578.

Kusch, Rodolfo. *América profunda*. Buenos Aires: Hachette, 1962.

Kutscher, Gerdt. *Nordperuanische Keramik*. Berlin: Mann, 1954.

La Barre, Weston. "I Narcotici del Nuovo Mondo. Riti sciamanistici e sostanze psicotrope," *Terra Ameriga* (Genoa) 12, Nos. 37–40 (1976):31–40.

Land, E. K., ed. *Pre-Columbian Art from the Land Collection*. San Francisco: California Academy of Sciences, 1979.

Landes, Ruth. "Fetish Worship in Brazil," *JAFL* 53, no. 210 (1940):261–270.

Langdon, Thomas Allen. *Food Restrictions in the Medical System of the Barasana and Taiwano Indians of the Colombian Northwest Amazon*. Ann Arbor, Mich.: University Microfilms International, 1983.

Langguth, A. J. *Macumba: White and Black Magic in Brazil.* New York: Harper & Row, 1975.

Lanning, Edward P. *Peru Before the Incas.* Englewood Cliffs, N.J.: Prentice-Hall, 1967.

Latcham, Ricardo E. *Costumbres Mortuorias de los Indios de Chile y Otras Partes de América.* Santiago de Chile: Sociedad Imprenta-Litografía "Barcelona," 1915.

Lathrap, Donald W. "The 'Hunting' Economies of the Tropical Forest Zone of South America: An Attempt at Historical Perspective." In *Man the Hunter,* ed. Richard Lee and Irven DeVore. Chicago: Aldine, 1968.

Lathrap, Donald W. *The Upper Amazon.* New York: Praeger, 1970.

Lathrap, Donald W. "The Tropical Forest and the Cultural Context of Chavín." In *Dumbarton Oaks Conference on Chavín,* ed. Elizabeth P. Benson. Washington, D.C.: Dumbarton Oaks Research Library and Collections, 1971.

Lathrap, Donald W. "Our Father the Cayman, Our Mother the Gourd: Spinden Revisited, or a Unitary Model for Emergence of Agriculture in the New World." In *Origins of Agriculture,* ed. C. A. Reed. The Hague: Mouton, 1977.

Lave, Jean. "Eastern Timbira Moiety Systems in Time and Space: A Complex Structure," *ICA,* 42nd Congress (Paris, 1976), Vol. 2, pp. 309–321.

Lave, Jean C. "Cycles and Trends in Krĩkatí Naming Practices." In *Dialectical Societies,* ed. David Maybury-Lewis. Cambridge, Mass.: Harvard University Press, 1979.

Leacock, Seth, and Leacock, Ruth. *Spirits of the Deep: A Study of an Afro-Brazilian Cult.* Garden City, N.Y.: Anchor Press/Doubleday, 1975.

Lehmann, David, ed. *Ecology and Exchange in the Andes.* Cambridge: At the University Press, 1982.

Lehmann-Nitsche, Robert. "La Pretendida Existencia Actual del Grypotherium," *RMLP* 10 (1902):269–280.

Lehmann-Nitsche, Robert. "La cosmogonía según los Puelches de Patagonia: Mitología sud-americana II," *RMLP* 24 (1919):182–204.

Lehmann-Nitsche, Robert. "Las Constelaciones del Orión y de las Híades y su pretendida identidad de interpretación en las esferas eurasiática y sudamericana," *RMLP* 26 (1921):17–68.

Lehmann-Nitsche, Robert. "La Astronomía de los Matacos: Mitología sudamericana V," *RMLP* 27 (1923):253–266.

Lehmann-Nitsche, Robert. "Mitología Sudamericana: VI, La Astronomía de los Tobas (Primera Parte)," *RMLP* 27 (1923):267–285.

Lehmann-Nitsche, Robert. "Mitología Sudamerica: VII, La Astronomía de los Mocoví," *RMLP* 28 (1924):66–80.

Lehmann-Nitsche, Robert. "Mitología Sudamericana: VIII, La Astronomía de los Chiriguanos," *RMLP* 28 (1924–1925):80–102.

Lehmann-Nitsche, Robert. "Mitología Sudamericana: X, La Astronomía de los Tobas (segunda parte)," *RMLP* 28 (1924–1925):181–209.

Lehmann-Nitsche, Robert. "El Revestimiento con Ocre Rojo de Tumbas Prehistóricas y su Significado," *RMLP* 30 (1927):321–327.

Lehmann-Nitsche, Robert. "Der Ziegenmelker und die beiden Grossgestirne in der südameri-kanischen Mythologie," *ICA,* 24th Congress (Hamburg, 1930), pp. 221–224.

Lehmann-Nitsche, Robert. "Folk-Lore Argentino," *Journal of American Folklore* 48, No. 187 (1935):179–185.

Lehmann-Nitsche, Robert. *Studien zur südamerikanischen Mythologie. Die ätiologischen Mo-tive.* Hamburg: Friederichsen, De Gruyter & Co., 1939.

Lévi-Strauss, Claude. "The Use of Wild Plants in Tropical South America," *HSAI* 6 (1950):465–486.

Lévi-Strauss, Claude. *Introduction to a Science of Mythology,* 4 vols. trans. John Weightman and Doreen Weightman. Vol. 1: *The Raw and the Cooked* (1969); Vol. 2: *From Honey to Ashes* (1973); Vol. 3 *The Origin of Table Manners* (1978); Vol. 4 *Naked Man* (1982). New York: Harper & Row, 1969–1982.

Lévi-Strauss, Claude. *La Potière Jalouse.* Paris: Librairie Plon, 1986.

Lewin, Boleslao. *La Rebelión de Túpac Amaru y los orígenes de la independencia hispanoamericana.* Buenos Aires, 1967.

Lewis, Ioan M. "What Is a Shaman?" *Folk: Dansk Etnografisk Tidsskrift* (Copenhagen) 23 (1981):25–35.

Lima, Rossini Tavares de, et al. *Folclore do Litoral Norte de São Paulo.* Rio de Janeiro: Ministério da Educação e Cultura, 1981.

Linares Málaga, Eloy. "La Estrella de Ocho Puntas en la Arqueología del área meridional Andina." In *Amerikanistische Studien,* ed. Roswith Hartmann and Udo Oberem. St. Augustin: Haus Völker und Kulturen, 1979.

Lind, Ulf. *Die Medizin der Ayoré-Indianer.* Inaugural dissertation. Bonn: Rheinische Friedrich-Wilhelms-Universität, 1974.

Lind, Ulf. "Einige Notizen zu den Vorstellungen über Physiologie bei den Lengua-Indianern (Maskói) im Gran Chaco." In *Amerikanistische Studien: Festschrift für Hermann Trimborn anlässich seines 75. Geburtstages,* ed. Roswith Hartmann and Udo Oberem. St. Augustin: Haus Völker und Kulturen, 1979.

Lindig, Wolfgang, H. "Wanderungen der Tupi-Guarani und Eschatologie der Apapocuva-Guarani." in *Chiliasmus und Nativismus,* ed. Wilhelm E. Mühlmann. Berlin, 1961.

Lipkind, William. "Carajá Cosmography," *JAFL* 53, No. 210 (1940):248–251.

Lira, Jorge A. *Farmacopea tradicional indígena y prácticas rituales.* Lima, 1946.

Lizot, Jacques. "Onomastique Yanomami," *L'Homme* 13, No. 3 (1973):60–71.

Lizot, Jacques. *El Hombre de la Pantorrilla Preñada y Otros Mitos Yanomami.* Monografía No. 21. Caracas: Fundación la Salle de Ciencias Naturales, 1974.

Lizot, Jacques. "Histoire, organisation, et évolution du peuplement Yanomami," *L'Homme* 24, No. 2 (1984):5–40.

Lizot, Jacques. *Le Cercle des Feux: Fais et Dits des Indiens Yanomami.* Paris: Editions du Seuil, 1976.

Llaras Samitier, Manuel. "Primer Ramillete de Fábulas y Sagas de los Antiguos Patagones," *Runa* (Buenos Aires) 3 (1950):170–199.

Lobsiger, G. "Une Curieuse carte du Pérou dresseé au 1614," *Globe* (Geneva) 103 (1963):33–69.

López-Baralt, Mercedes. "La Persistencia de las Estructuras Simbólicas Andinas en los Dibujos de Guamán Poma de Ayala," *JLAL* 5, No. 1 (1979):83–116.

López-Baralt, Mercedes. "The Quechua Elegy to the All-Powerful Inka Atawallpa," *LAIL* 4, No. 2 (1980):79-86.

Losonczy, Anne-Marie. "Le destin des guerriers. Agression chamanique et agression guerrière chez les Embera du Choco," *JSAP* 72 (1986):157–184.

Lothrop, Samuel Kirkland. *The Indians of Tierra del Fuego.* New York: Museum of the American Indian, 1928.

Loutkotka, Čestmír. *Classification of South American Indian Languages.* Reference Series, Vol. 7. Los Angeles: Latin American Center, University of California, Los Angeles, 1968.

Lowie, Robert H. "Cosmology and Cosmogony: Mexico and South America," in *Encyclopedia of Religion and Ethics,* ed. James Hastings. Philadelphia, 1923.

Lowie, Robert H. "Serente Tales," *JAFL* 57, No. 225 (1944):181–187.

Lozano, Eduardo. "Recent Books on Indian Literatures," *LAIL* 1, No. 1 (1977):41–60.

Lozano, Eduardo. "Recent Books on South American Indian Languages," *LAIL* 1, No. 2 (1977):97–122.

Lukesch, Anton. *Mythos und Leben der Kayapo.* Acta Ethnologica et Linguistica No. 12. Vienna: Institut für Völkerkunde der Universität Wien, 1968.

Lutz, L. "String Figures from the Patomana Indians of British-Guiana," *Anthropological Papers of the American Museum of Natural History* 12, No. 1 (1912):1–14.

Lyon, Patricia J., ed. *Native South Americans: Ethnology of the Least Known Continent.* Boston: Little, Brown, 1974.

Lyon, Patricia J. "Female Supernaturals in Ancient Peru," *Ñawpa Pacha* 16 (1979):27–34.

Maciel, Sílvio Pereira. *Vida Dos Orixás e a Umbanda: Cristianismo.* Rio de Janeiro: Editora Espiritualista, 1979.

Magalhaes, Amilcar A. Botelho de. *Pelos Sertões do Brasil*, 2nd ed. São Paulo, 1941.

Mangeot, C. *Tissage quechua contemporain (Region de Cuzco, Perou)*. Microfiche. Paris: Institut d'Ethnologie, Museé de l'Homme, 1982.

Marcondes de Moura, Carlos Eugenio, trans. *Olóòrísá: Escritos sobre a religião dos orixás*. São Paulo: Agora, 1981.

Margolies, L., and Suárez, María Matilde. "Historia de la etnología contemporánea en Venezuela," *Montalban* 6 (1978):703-705.

Mariani Ramírez, Carlos. "Personalidad del Hechicero Indígena. El Machi o Hechicero Mapuche." In *Anales del Tercer Congreso Latinoamericano de Psiquiatría, 25-31 October 1964*, ed. Carlos Alberto Sequin and Ruben Rios Carrasco. Lima: Asociación Psiquiátrica de América Latina, 1966.

Mariani Ramírez, Carlos. "Prácticas y Ceremonias Mágico-Religiosas Mapuches." In *Anales del Tercer Congreso Latinoamericano de Psiquiatría, 25-31 October 1964*, ed. Carlos Alberto Sequín and Ruben Ríos Carrasco. Lima: Asociación Psiquiátrica de América Latina, 1966.

Mariátegui Oliva, Ricardo. *Chan Chan. La Milenaria ciudad de barro con enigmáticos relieves*. Lima: Editorial Gráfica "La Confianza," 1980.

Mariscotti de Görlitz, Ana Maria. *Pachamama Santa Tierra: Contribución al Estudio de la Religión Autóctona en los Andes Centro-Merdionales*. Beiträge zur Völker- und Anthropologie des Indianischen Amerika, Vol. 8. Berlin: Gabriel Mann Verlag, 1978.

Marsh, Charles R., Jr. "The Indians and the Whites: Two Bororo Texts," *LAIL* 1, No. 1 (1977):34-36.

Martínez, Gabriel. "Topónimos de Chuani: ¿Organización y Significación del Territorio?" *Anthropológica* (Lima) 1, No. 1 (1983):51-84.

Martínez, Gabriel. "Los dioses de los cerros en los Andes," *JSAP* 69 (1983):85-116.

Martínez, Hector. *Bibliografía indígena andina peruana (1900-1968)*. Lima: Centro de Estudios de Población y Desarrollo, 1969.

Martins, Edilson. *Nossos índios, nossos mortos*, 4th ed. Rio de Janeiro: Editora Codecri, 1982.

Marzal, Manuel Maria. *Estudios sobre religión campesina*. Lima: Pontificia Universidad Católica del Peru Fondo Editorial, 1977.

Mashnshnek, Celia Olga. "Algunos Personajes de la Mitología Chorote," *Sociedad Argentina de Antropología. Relaciones* (Buenos Aires), n.s., 6 (1972):109-144.

Mashnshnek, Celia Olga. "Seres Potentes y Héroes Míticos del Chaco Central," *Scripta Ethnológica* 1, No. 1 (1973):105-154.

Mashnshnek, Celia Olga. "Aportes para una comprensión de la economía de los mataco," *Scripta Ethnológica* 3, No. 3, Part 1 (1975):7-39.

Mashnshnek, Celia Olga. "Textos Míticos de los Chulupí del Chaco Central," *Scripta Ethnológica* (Buenos Aires) 3, No. 3, Part 1 (1975):151-189.

Mashnshnek, Celia Olga. "El mito en la vida de los aborígenes del Chaco Central. Presencia y actuación de las teofanías," *Scripta Ethnológica* 4, No. 4, Part 1 (1976):7-27.

Mason, J. Alden. *The Ancient Civilizations of Peru*, Rev. ed. New York: Penguin Books, 1968.

Matteson, Esther. "Piro Myths," *Kroeber Anthropological Society Papers* 4 (1951):37-87.

Matthäi, Hildegard. *Die Rolle der Greifvogel, insbesondere der Harpye und des Königsgeier, bei ausserandinen Indianern Südamerikas*. Hohenschäftlarn: Klaus Renner Verlag, 1977.

Maximiliano dos Santos, Deoscoredes. *Axé Opô Alfonjá: Noticia Historica de Um Terreiro de Santo da Bahia*. Rio de Janeiro: Instituto Brasileiro de Estudos Afro-Asiáticos, 1962.

Maybury-Lewis, David. *Akwẽ-Shavante Society*. Oxford: Clarendon Press, 1967.

Maybury-Lewis, David. "Name, Person and Ideology in Central Brazil." in *Naming Systems*, ed. Elisabeth Tooker. Washington, D.C.: American Ethnological Society, 1984.

Maybury-Lewis, David, ed. *Dialectical Studies*. Cambridge, Mass.: Harvard University Press, 1979.

Mayntzhusen, Friederich C. "Über Gebräuche bei der Geburt und die Namengebung der Guayaki," *ICA*, 18th Congress (London, 1913), Part 1, pp. 408-412.

McGregor, Pedro. *The Moon and Two Mountains: The Myths, Ritual and Magic of Brazilian Spiritism*. London: Souvenir Press, 1966.

Medina, Fernando Diez de. *La Teogonía Andina: Pacha, Wiracocha, Thunupa, Nayjama*. La Paz, Bolivia: Municipalidad de La Paz, 1973.

Medina, José Toribio. *Los Aborígenes de Chile*, 2nd ed. Santiago de Chile: Fondo Histórico y Bibliográfico José Toribio Medina, 1952.

Mejía Xesspe, Toribio. "Cultura Pukina," in *Amerikanistische Studien*, ed. Roswith Hartmann and Udo Oberem. St. Augustin: Haus Völker und Kulturen, 1979.

Melatti, Júlio Cezar. *Indios e criadores: A situação dos Krahó na area pastoril do Tocantins*. Rio de Janeiro: Instituto de Ciências Sociais da UFRJ, 1967.

Melatti, Júlio Cezar. *Messianismo Krahó*. São Paulo: Herder/EDUSP, 1972.

Melatti, Júlio Cezar. "Myth and Shaman." In *Native South Americans: Ethnology of the Least Known Continent*, ed. Patricia J. Lyon. Boston: Little, Brown, 1974.

Melatti, Júlio Cezar. *Ritos de Uma Tribo Timbirá*. São Paulo: Editora Ática, 1978.

Mercader, Antonio. *Tupanaros: Estrategia y acción*. Barcelona: Editorial Anagrama, 1970.

Métraux, Alfred. "Migrations historiques des Tupi-Guaranis," *JSAP*, n.s., 19 (1927):1–45.

Métraux, Alfred. *Myths and Tales of the Matako Indians, Gran Chaco, Argentina*. Göteborg: Elanders Boktryckeri Aktiebolag, 1939.

Métraux, Alfred. "A Quechua Messiah in Eastern Peru," *AA*, n.s., 44 (1942):721–725.

Métraux, Alfred. "A Myth of the Chamacoco Indians and Its Social Significance," *JAFL* 56 (April-June 1943):120–145.

Métraux, Alfred. "Twin Heroes in South American Mythology," *JAFL* 59, no. 232 (1945):114–123.

Métraux, Alfred. *Myths of the Toba and Pilagá Indians of the Gran Chaco*. Memoirs of the American Folklore Society, Vol. 40. Philadelphia, 1946.

Métraux, Alfred. "Ethnography of the Chaco," *HSAI* 1, pp. 197–370. Washington, D.C.: Smithsonian Institution, 1946.

Métraux, Alfred. "Mourning Rites and Burial Forms of the South American Indians," *América Indígena* (Mexico City) 7, No. 1 (1947):7–44.

Métraux, Alfred. "The Guarani," *HSAI* 3, pp. 69–94. Washington, D.C.: Smithsonian Institution, 1948.

Métraux, Alfred. "The Tupinamba," *HSAI* 3, pp. 95–133. Washington, D.C.: Smithsonian Institution, 1948.

Métraux, Alfred. "Warfare, Cannibalism and Human Trophies," *HSAI* 5, pp. 383–409. Washington, D.C.: Smithsonian Institution, 1949.

Métraux, Alfred. "Religion and Shamanism," *HSAI* 5, pp. 559–599. Washington, D.C.: Smithsonian Institution, 1949.

Métraux, Alfred. "Ensayos de Mitología Comparada Sudamericana," *AI* 8, No. 1 (1948):9–30.

Métraux, Alfred. "Les Messies de l'Amérique du Sud," *Archives de Sociologie des Religions* 4 (1957):108–112.

Métraux, Alfred. *Religions et magies indiennes d'Amérique du Sud*. Paris: Gallimard, 1967.

Métraux, Alfred. *The History of the Incas*. New York: Schocken Books, 1969.

Mieli, F. *Canti e narrazioni degli indiani d'America*. Milan: Guanda, 1977.

Milhou, Alain. *Colón y su Mentalidad Mesiánica en el Ambiente Franciscanista Español*. Cuadernos Colombinos, Vol. 11. Valladolid: Casa-Museo de Colón y Seminario Americanista de la Universidad, 1983.

Miller, Elmer S. "The Argentine Toba Evangelical Religious Service," *Ethnology* 10, No. 2 (1971):149–159.

Miller, Elmer S. *A Critical Annotated Bibliography of the Gran Chaco Toba*, 2 vols. HRAFlex Books, Bibliography Series, Vol. SI 12-002. New Haven: Human Relations Area Files, 1980.

Millones, Luis. *Introducción al proceso de aculturación religiosa indígena*. Lima: Instituto Indigenista Peruano, 1967.

Millones [Santa Gadea], Luis. *Las Religiones del Peru. Recuento y Evaluación de su Estudio*. Special Publication of the Institute of Latin American Studies. Austin: University of Texas Press, 1979.

Minnaert, Paul. "Le Lancement d'une arme ou d'une pierre en signe de prise de possession." *Bulletin de la Société des Américanistes de Belgique* 9 (Dec. 1932):116–117.

Mishkin, Bernard. "Cosmological Ideas Among the Indians of the Southern Andes," *JAFL* 53, No. 210 (1940):225–241.

Mishkin, Bernard. "The Contemporary Quechua," *HSAI* 2 (1946):411–470.

Moesbach, E. *Vida y Costumbres de los Indígenas Araucanos en la Segunda Mitad del Siglo XIX.* Santiago de Chile: Imp. Universitaria, 1936.

Molina, N. A. *Despachos e trabalhos de Quimbanda.* Rio de Janeiro: Espiritualista, 1980.

Müller, Franz. "Drogen und Medikamente der Guarani (Mbyá, Pai und Chiripá) Indianer im östlichen Waldgebiet von Paraguay." In *Festschrift Publication d'Hommage au P. W. Schmidt,* ed. Wilhelm Koppers. Vienna, 1928.

Münzel, Mark. *Medizinmannwesen und Geistervorstellungen bei den Kamayurá (Alto Xingu-Brasilien).* Arbeiten aus dem Seminar für Völkerkunde der Johann Wolfgang Goethe-Universität. Frankfurt am Main, Vol. 2. Wiesbaden, 1971.

Münzel, Mark. *Erzählungen der Kamayurá, Alto Xingú-Brasilien.* Studien zur Kulturkunde, Vol. 30. Wiesbaden: Franz Steiner Verlag, 1973.

Münzel, Mark. "Zwischen den Steinen. Die Übergangssituation einer Makú-Gruppe in Nordwest-Brasilien," *Ethnologische Zeitschrift Zürich.* Festschrift Otto Zerries. Special Supplement No. 1 (1974), pp. 287–308.

Murphy, Robert, and Quain, Buell. *The Trumaí Indians of Central Brazil.* Monograph of the American Ethnological Society, Vol. 24. Seattle: University of Washington Press, 1955.

Murphy, Robert F. "Mundurucu Religions," *University of California Publications in American Archaeology and Ethnology* 49, No. 1. Los Angeles: University of California Press, 1958.

Murphy, Yolanda, and Murphy, Robert F. *Women of the Forest.* New York: Columbia University Press, 1974.

Murra, John V.; Wachtel, Nathan; and Revel, Jacques. *Anthropological History of Andean Polities.* New York and Cambridge: Cambridge University Press, 1986.

Najlis, Elena L. *Lengua Abipona,* 2 vols. Buenos Aires: Universidad de Buenos Aires, Centro de Estudios Lengüisticos, 1966.

Newbery, Sara Josefina. "Los Pilagá: Su religión a sus mitos de origen," *AI* 33, No. 3 (1973):757–769.

Niles, Susan A. *South American Indian Narrative: Theoretical and Analytical Approaches. An Annotated Bibliography.* New York: Garland Publishing, 1981.

Nimuendajú, Curt. "Die Sagen von der Erschaffung und Vernichtung der Welt als Grundlagen der Religion der Apapocuva-Guarani," *Zeitschrift für Ethnologie* 46 (1914):284–403; edited and translated by J. F. Recalde as *Leyenda de la Creación y Juicio Final del Mundo,* São Paulo, 1944; reedited by J. Riester, retranslated by Joseph Barnadas, and annotated by Friedl Gruenberg as *Mitos de Creación y de Destrucción del Mundo como Fundamentos de la Religión de los Apapokuva-Guaraní.* Lima: Centro Amazónico de Antropología y Aplicación Práctica, 1978.

Nimuendajú Curt. "Sagen der Tembé Indianer," *Zeitschrift für Ethnologie* (Berlin) 47 (1915):130–170.

Nimuendajú, Curt. "Bruchstücke aus Religion und Überlieferung des Sipáia-Indianer," *Anthropos* 14–15 (1919–1921):1002–1039.

Nimuendajú, Curt. "Bruchstücke aus Religion und Überlieferung der Sipaia-Indianer," *Anthropos* 16–17 (1921–1922):367–406.

Nimuendajú, Curt. *The Apinayé.* The Catholic University of America, Anthropological Series, no. 8. Washington D.C.: Catholic University, 1939.

Nimuendajú, Curt. "The Eastern Timbira." *University of California Publications in American Archaeology and Ethnology* 41. Los Angeles: University of California Press, 1946.

Nimuendajú, Curt. "Social Organization and Beliefs of the Botocudo of Eastern Brazil," *Southwestern Journal of Anthropology* 2 (1946):93–115.

Nimuendajú, Curt. "The Tukuna." *University of California Publications in American Archaeology and Ethnology* 45. Los Angeles: University of California Press, 1952.

Nordenskiöld, Erland. *Indianerleben: El Gran Chaco.* Leipzig, 1912.

Nordenskiöld, Erland. *Picture-Writing and Other Documents by Néle and Ruben Pére Kantule.* Göteborg, 1928.

Nordenskiöld, Erland. "Origin of the Indian Civilizations in South America," *Comparative Ethnographical Studies* (Göteborg) 9 (1931):1-153.

Nordenskiöld, Erland. "An Historical and Ethnographical Survey of the Cuna Indians," *Comparative Ethnographical Studies* (Göteborg) 10 (1938):1-683.

Norero, Vicente. "El Culto de los Muertos entre las Poblaciones Aborígenes de la Costa Ecuadoriana," *Terra Ameriga* 2, No. 8 (1966-1967):5-9.

Novati, Jorge. "Las expresiones musicales de los Selk'nam," *RUNA* (Buenos Aires) 12, nos. 1-2 (1969-1970):393-406.

Novati, Jorge. "Musica y marco temporal en los Shipibo del Río Maputay," *Scripta Ethnológica* 4, Part 2 (1976-1977):6-30.

Nuñez, Carmen. "Asái, un personaje del horizonte mítico de los Ayoreo," *Scripta Ethnológica* 5, Part 1 (1978-1979):102-114.

Nuñez, Carmen Estela. "Asái, a Mythic Personage of the Ayoreo," *LAIL* 5, No. 2 (1981):64-67.

Nuñez del Prado B., Juan Victor. "The Supernatural World of the Quechua of Southern Peru as Seen from the Community of Qotobamba." In *Native South Americans*, ed. Patricia J. Lyon. Boston: Little, Brown, 1974.

Nuñez del Prado C., Oscar. "Versión del Mito de Inkarri en Q'eros." In *Ideología Mesiánica del Mundo Andino*, ed. Juan Ossio. Lima: Ignacio Prado Pastor, 1973.

Oberem, Udo. "Geburt, Hochzeit und Tod bei den Quijos-Indianern Ost-Ecuadors," *ICA*, Copenhagen, 1958, pp. 232-237.

Oberem, Udo. "Einige ethnographische Notizen über die Canelo Ost-Ecuadors," *Ethnologische Zeitschrift Zürich*. Festschrift Otto Zerries. Special Supplement No. 1 (1974), pp. 319-336.

Ochoa, Jorge Flores. "Inkariy y Qollariy en una comunidad del Altiplano." In *Ideología Mesiánica del Mundo Andino*, ed. Juan Ossio. Lima: Ignacio Prado Pastor, 1973.

O'Gorman, Frances. *Aluanda: A Look at Afro-Brazilian Cults*. Rio de Janeiro: Livraria Alves Editora, 1977.

O'Leary, Timothy J. "Ethnographic Bibliographies." In *A Handbook of Method in Cultural Anthropology*, ed. Raoul Naroll and Ronald Cohen. New York: Natural History Press, 1970.

Oliva de Coll, Josefina. *A Resistência indígena: Do México à Patagonia, a história da luta dos índios contra os conquistadores*. São Paulo: L & PM Editores, 1986.

Oliveira, Jose Paiva de. *Misterios da Umbanda e do Candomblé*. Rio de Janeiro: Editora Espiritualista, 1980.

Oliveira, Roberto Cardoso de. *O índio e o Mundo dos Brancos: A Situação dos Tukúna do Alto Solimões*. Corpo e Alma do Brasil, Vol. 12. São Paulo: Difusão Européia do Livro, 1964.

Oliver-Smith, Anthony. "The Pishtaco: Institutionalized Fear in Highland Peru," *Journal of American Folklore* 82 (1969):363-368.

Olsen, Dale A. "The Function of Naming in the Shamanistic Curing Songs of the Warao Indians of Venezuela," *Yearbook of Inter-American Musical Research, 1974* 10 Austin: University of Texas Press, 1975.

Olsen, Dale A. "Music-Induced Altered States of Consciousness Among Warao Shamans," *JLAL* 1, No. 1 (1975):19-34.

Orlove, Benjamin S. "Barter and Cash on Lake Titicaca: A Test of Competing Approaches," *Current Anthropology* 27, No. 2 (1986):85-106.

Ortiz, Dionisio. *Montañas del Apurimac, Mantaro y Ene*, 2 vols. Lima: Imprenta Editorial San Antonio, 1976.

Ortiz, Renato. *Morte Branca do Feitiçeiro Negro: Umbanda, Integraçao de Uma Religião Numa Sociedade de Classes*. Petrópolis, Brazil: Editora Vozes, 1978.

Ortiz Rescaniere, Alejandro. "El Mito de la Escuela." In *Ideología Mesiánica del Mundo Andino*, ed. Juan Ossio. Lima: Ignacio Prado Pastor, 1973.

Ortiz Rescaniere, Alejandro. *Huarochiri, 400 años despues*. Lima: Pontifica Universidad Católica del Peru, 1977.

Osborne, Harold. *South American Mythology*. Feltham, Middlesex: Paul Hamlyn, 1968.

Ossio, Juan M. "The Idea of History in Felipe Guaman Poma de Ayala." Unpublished bachelor's thesis, Oxford University, 1970.

Ossio A., Juan M., ed. *Ideología Mesiánica del Mundo Andino*. Lima: Ignacio Prado Pastor, 1973.

Ossio, Juan M., and Herrera, Jorge. "Versión del Mito de Inkarri en el Pueblo de Andamarca (Ayacucho-Peru)." In *Ideología Mesiánica del Mundo Andino*, ed. Juan Ossio. Lima: Ignacio Prado Pastor, 1973.

Ossio, Juan M. "El Simbolismo del Agua y la Representación del Tiempo y el Espacio en la Fiesta de la Acequía de la Comunidad de Andamarca," *ICA* 4, pp. 377–396. Paris, 1976.

Ossio, Juan M. "Los Mitos de Origen en la Comunidad de Andamarca (Ayacucho-Perú)," *Allpanchis* (Cuzco) 10 (1977):105–113.

Otter, Elisabeth den. *Music and Dance of Indians and Mestizos in an Andean Valley of Peru*. Delft, the Netherlands: Eburon, 1985.

Overing, Joanna. "Images of Cannibalism, Death and Domination in a 'Nonviolent' Society," *JSAP* 72 (1986):133–156.

Oyarzún, Aurelio. "Los Onas o Selknam de la Isla Grande de Tierra del Fuego," *Anales del Instituto de Etnografía Americana* (Mendoza) 2 (1941).

Pagés Larraya, Fernando. "Entre los últimos Siriono del Oriente de Bolivia," *Acta Psiquiátrica, Psicológica de America Latina* (Buenos Aires) 23 (1977):247–266.

Pagés Larraya, Fernando. "Textos de la tradición oral alacalufe," *Mitológicas* (Buenos Aires) 1 (1985):9–45.

Palanco, José Antonio. "Noticias Guajiras por un Goajiro: Los Velorios o 'Lloros' (Arapaja y Ayaraja)," *Boletín Indigenista Venezolana* (Caracas) 3–4 (1956):197–204.

Palavecino, Enrique. "Breves noticias sobre algunos nuevos elementos en la cultura de los indios del Chaco," *ICA* (Paris and Lima, 1943), pp. 313–314.

Palavecino, Enrique. "Algo sobre el pensamiento cosmológico de los indígenas chaquenses," *Cuadernos del Instituto Nacional de Investigaciones Folklóricas* (Buenos Aires, 1961), pp. 93–95.

Palavecino, Enrique. "Notas sobre la mitología Chaquense." in *Homenaje a Fernando Márquez Miranda*. Madrid: Universidades de Madrid y Sevilla, 1964.

Palavecino, Enrique. "Mitos de los indios tobas," *Runa* (Buenos Aires) 12, nos. 1–2 (1969–1970), pp. 177–198.

Palavecino, Enrique. "The Magic World of the Mataco," trans. and ed. J. A. Vázquez, *LAIL* 3, No. 2 (1979):61–75.

Pané, Fray Ramón. *Relación de Acerca de las Antigüedades de los Indios*, ed. José Juan Arrom. Mexico City: Siglo Veintiuno, 1974 [1498?].

Paoli, Maria Célia Pinheiro Machado. "Violência e Espaço Civil," in *Violência Brasileira*, ed. Roberto da Matta et al. São Paulo: Editora Brasiliense, 1982.

Paredes-Candia, Antonio. *Diccionario mitológico de Bolivia: Dioses, símbolos, héroes*. La Paz, Bolivia: Ediciones Puerta del Sol, 1972.

Parsons, Elsie Clews. "Cosmography of Indians of Imbabura Province, Ecuador," *JAFL* 53, No. 210 (1940):219–224.

Pease G. Y., Franklin. "El Mito de Inkarrí y la Visión de los Vencidos." In *Ideología Mesiánica del Mundo Andino*, ed. Juan Ossio. Lima: Ignacio Prado Pastor, 1973.

Pease G. Y., Franklin. *El Dios creador andino*. Lima: Mosca Azul Editores, 1973.

Pease G. Y., Franklin. "Una versión ecológica del mito de Inkarri." In *Amerikanistische Studien*, ed. Roswith Hartmann and Udo Oberem. St. Augustin: Haus Völker und Kulturen, 1979.

Pease G. Y., Franklin. *El Pensamiento Mítico*. Lima, 1982.

Pellizzaro, Siro M. *La reducción de las cabezas cortadas: Ayumpúm*. Sucúa, Ecuador: Mundo Shuar, 1977.

Pellizzaro, Siro M. *Shakáim: Mitos de la Selva y del Desmonte*. Sucúa, Ecuador: Mundo Shuar, 1978.

Pellizzaro, Siro M. *Celebración de uwi*. Quito: Museos del Banco Central del Ecuador, 1978.

Pellizzaro, Siro M. *Cantos de Amor de la Esposa Achuar*. Sucúa, Ecuador: Mundo Shuar, 1979.

Pellizzaro, Siro M. *Mitos de la sal y ritos para obtenerla: Wee*. Sucúa, Ecuador: Mundo Shuar, 1980.

Peñaherrera de Costales, Piedad, and Costales Samaniego, Alfredo. *El Quishihuar o el árbol de Dios*. Quito: Instituto Ecuatoriano de Antropología y Geografía, 1966.

Peñaherrera de Costales, Piedad, and Costales Sameniego, Alfredo. *Huayana Capac.* Cuenca, Ecuador: Casa de la Cultura Ecuatoriana, 1964.

Penteado Coelho, Vera. "Um eclipse do sol no aldeia waurá," *JSAP* 69 (1983):149–168.

Pérez Diez, Andrés A. "Textos míticos de los Mataco del Chaco Central. Notas al ciclo de Ka'o'o (Ajwuntséj ta jwáj)," *Scripta Ethnológica* 4, Part 1 (1976):159–189.

Pérez Mundaca, José. "¿Qué es el mito?" *Anthropológica* (Lima) 1, No. 1 (1983):33–36.

Perrin, Michel. "Introducción a la literatura oral de los Indios guajiros," *Economía y ciencias sociales* (Caracas) 3 (1970):5–20.

Perrin, Michel. "La littérature orale des Guajiro, compte rendu de mission," *L'Homme* 11, no. 2 (1971):109–112.

Perrin, Michel. "Mythes et rêves, rituel et chamanisme chez les Indiens goajiro, compte rendu de mission," *L'Homme* 15, No. 2 (1975):109–112.

Perrin, Michel. "Une interprétation morphogénétique de l'initiation chamanique," *L'Homme* 26, Nos. 97–98 (1986):107–124.

Perrin, Michel. *The Way of Dead Indians: Myths and Symbols Among the Goajiro.* Austin: University of Austin Press, 1987.

Petrullo, Vincenzo. "The Yaruros of the Capanaparo River, Venezuela," Bureau of American Ethnology, Bulletin 123, Anthropological Papers No. 11, pp. 161–290. Washington D.C.: Smithsonian Institution, 1939.

Pettazzoni, Raffaele. *Miti e legende.* Vol. 4: *America Centrale e Meridionale.* Turin: Unione Tipografico-Editrice Torinese, 1959.

Pinheiro, C. "Rio Negro, Villa São Gabriel, Curiosidades Naturais, Costumes dos Índios," *Revista da Sociedade Geográfica* 13 (1900):29–35.

Plath, Oreste. *Lenguaje de los Pájaros Chilenos: Avifauna Folklórica.* Santiago, Chile: Editorial Nascimento, 1976.

Plitek, Karl-Heinz. *Totenkult der Ge und Bororo.* Münchner Beiträge zur Amerikanistik. Hohenschäftlarn: Klaus Renner Verlag, 1978.

Ploetz, Hermann, and Métraux, Alfred. "La Civilisation matérielle et la vie sociale et religieuse des Indiens Zé du Brésil méridional et orientale," *Revista del Instituto de Etnología de la Universidad Nacional de Tucumán* (Tucumán) 1, No. 2 (1930):107–238.

Polanco, José Antonio. "Noticias guajiras por un Guajiro: El aútshi o piachi guajiro," *Boletín Indigenista Venezolano* (Caracas) 2, Nos. 1–4 (1954):55–60.

Polanco, José Antonio. "Noticias Guajiras por un Guajiro: El Casamiento (Schikü Keéchinwaa)," *Boletín Indigenista Venezolano* 8, Nos. 1–4 (1963):103–114.

Pollak-Eltz, Angelina. "Der Egungunkult der Yoruba in Afrika und in Amerika," *Zeitschrift für Ethnologie* 5, No. 2 (1970):275–293.

Polykrates, Gottfried. *Wawanaueteri und Pukimapueteri. Zwei Yanomami-stämme Nordwestbrasiliens.* Publications of the National Museum, Ethnological Series, Vol. 13. Copenhagen: National Museum of Denmark, 1969.

Poole, Deborah A. "South American Religions: History of Study," *Encyclopedia of Religion,* New York: Macmillan, 1987.

Poole, Deborah A. "Rituals of Movement, Rites of Transformation: Pilgrimage and Dance in the Highlands of Cuzco, Peru." In *Latin American Pilgrimage,* ed. N. Ross Crumrine and E. Alan Morinis. (forthcoming).

Porras Garcés, Pedro Ignacio. *Arqueología de la Cueva de los Tayos.* Quito: Pontificia Universidad Católica del Equador Publicaciones, 1978.

Posey, Darrell A. "The Kayapó Origin of Night," *LAIL* 5, No. 2 (1981):59–63.

Pottier, Bernard. *América Latina en sus lenguas indígenas.* Caracas: Monte Avila Editores, 1983.

Powlison, Paul S. "Tendencias épicas en la mitología yagua," *Folklore Americano* 17 (1971–1972):66–85.

Powlison, Esther, and Powlison, Paul. *La Fiesta Yagua, Jiña: Una Rica Herencia Cultural,* trans. Hilda Berger. Comunidades y Culturas Peruanas, Vol. 8. Lima: Instituto Lingüístico de Verano, 1976.

Preuss, Konrad Theodor. *Religion und Mythologie der Uitoto: Textaufnahmen und Beobachtun-*

gen bei einem Indianerstamm in Kolumbien, Südamerika. Göttingen: Vandenhoeck & Ruprecht, 1921.

Price, Richard, ed. *Maroon Societies: Rebel Slave Communities in the Americas.* Baltimore: Johns Hopkins University Press, 1979.

Price, Richard, and Price, Sally. "Saramaka Onomastics: An Afro-American Naming System," *Ethnology* 11 (1972):341–367.

Price, Richard, and Price, Sally. "Secret Play Languages in Saramaka: Linguistic Disguise in a Caribbean Creole." In *Speech Play*, ed. Barbara Kirschenblatt-Gimblett. Philadelphia: University of Pennsylvania Press, 1976.

Price, Richard, and Price, Sally. *Afro-American Arts of the Suriname Rain Forest.* Los Angeles: University of California Press, 1980.

Puppo, Giancarlo. *Arte argentino antes de la dominación hispánica.* Buenos Aires: Haulfin Ediciones, 1979.

Queiróz, Maria Isaura Pereira de. "L'Influence du milieu social interne sur les mouvements messianiques brésiliens," *Archives de Sociologie des Religions* 5 (1958):3–30.

Queiróz, Maria Isaura Pereira de. *O Messianismo no Brasil e no Mundo.* São Paulo: Dominus Editora, Editora da Universidade de São Paulo, 1965.

Quispe M., Ulpiano. *La Herranza en Choque Huarcaya y Huancasancos, Ayacucho.* Lima: Instituto Indigenista Peruano, 1969.

Rappaport, Joanne. "Mesianismo y las Transformaciones de Símbolos Mesiánicos en Tierradentro," *Revista Colombiana de Antropología* 23 (1980):365–413.

Rappaport, Joanne. "History, Myth, and the Dynamics of Territorial Maintenance in Tierradentro, Colombia," *American Ethnologist* 12, No. 1 (1985):27–45.

Raul, Giovanni. *Santo Tambem Come, Estudo Sócio-Cultural da Alimentação Cerimonial em Terreiros Afro-Brasileiros.* Recife: Instituto Joaquim Nabuco de Pesquisas Sociais, 1979.

Ravines, Rogger. "Prácticas funerárias en Ancon (Primera Parte)," *Revista del Museo Nacional* (Lima) 43 (1977):327–396.

Recalde, J. F. "A Criação do Mundo e o Dilúvio Universal na Religião dos Primitivos Guarani," *Revista do Arquivo Municipal* (São Paulo) 36 (Sept. 1950):100–111.

Rego, Waldeloir. "Mitos e ritos africanos da Bahia." In Carybé (artist), *Iconografia dos Deuses Africanos no Candomblé da Bahia.* São Paulo: Rabizes, 1980, unnumbered pages.

Reichel-Dolmatoff, Gerardo. "Los Kogi: Una Tribu Indígena de la Sierra Nevada de Santa Marta, Colombia," 2 vols. Vol. 1 appeared in *Revista del Instituto Etnológico Nacional* (Bogotá) 4, Nos. 1a–2a (1949–1950):1–320; Vol. 2: Bogotá: Editorial Iqueima, 1951.

Reichel-Dolmatoff, Gerardo. *Amazonian Cosmos: The Sexual and Religious Symbolism of the Tukano Indians.* Chicago: University of Chicago Press, 1971.

Reichel-Dolmatoff, Gerardo. "Funerary Customs and Religious Symbolism Among the Kogi." In *Native South Americans: Ethnology of the Least Known Continent*, ed. Patricia J. Lyon. Boston: Little, Brown, 1974.

Reichel-Dolmatoff. Gerardo. *The Shaman and the Jaguar: A Study of Narcotic Drugs Among the Indians of Colombia.* Philadelphia: Temple University Press, 1975.

Reichel-Dolmatoff, Gerardo. "Training for the Priesthood among the Kogi of Colombia." In *Enculturation in Latin America: An Anthropology.* ed. Johannes Wilbert. UCLA Latin American Studies, vol. 37. Los Angeles: UCLA Latin American Center Publications, 1976.

Reichel-Dolmatoff, Gerardo. "Cosmology as Ecological Analysis: A View from the Rain Forest," *Man*, n.s., 11 (1976):307–318.

Reichel-Dolmatoff, Gerardo. "Desana Curing Spells: An Analysis of Some Shamanistic Metaphors," *JLAL* 2, No. 2 (1976):157–219.

Reichel-Dolmatoff, Gerardo. "Templos kogi: Introducción al simbolismo y a la astronomía del espacio sagrado," *RCA* (Bogotá) 19 (1977):199–246.

Reichel-Dolmatoff, Gerardo. "Desana Animal Categories, Food Restrictions, and the Concept of Energies," *JLAL* 4, No. 2 (1978):243–291.

Reichel-Dolmatoff, Gerardo. *Beyond the Milky Way: Hallucinatory Imagery of the Tukano Indians.* UCLA Latin American Studies, vol. 42. Los Angeles, UCLA Latin American Center Publications, 1978.

Reichel-Dolmatoff, Gerardo. "The Loom of Life: A Kogi Principle of Integration," *JLAL* 4, No. 1 (1978):5-27.

Reichel-Dolmatoff, Gerardo. "Desana Shamans' Rock Crystals and the Hexagonal Universe," *JLAL* 5, No. 1 (1979):117-128.

Reichel-Dolmatoff, Gerardo. "Brian and Mind in Desana Symbolism," *JLAL* 7, No. 1 (1981):73-98.

Reichel-Dolmatoff, Gerardo. "Algunos Conceptos de Geografía Chamanística de los Indios Desana de Colombia," in *Contribuicões a Antropología em Homenagem ao Profesor Egon Schaden*, pp. 255-270. São Paulo: Universidade de São Paulo, Fondo de Pesquisas de Museo Paulista, 1981.

Reichel-Dolmatoff, Gerardo. "Tapir Avoidance in the Colombian Northwest Amazon." In *Animal Myths and Metaphors in South America*, ed. Gary Urton. Salt Lake City: University of Utah Press, 1985.

Reiss, Wilhelm, and Stübel, Alphons. *Peruvian Antiquities: The Necropolis of Ancon in Peru. A Series of Illustrations of the Civilisation and Industry of the Empire of the Incas*, 8 vols. New York, 1880-1887.

Renard-Casevitz, France-Marie. *Arawak de l'Ucayali*. Microfiche. Paris: Institut d'Ethnologie, Museé de l'Homme, 1979.

Renard-Casevitz, France-Marie. *Su-acu: Essai sur les Cervidés de l'Amazonie et sur leur signification dans les cultures indiennes actuelles*. Travaux de l'Institut Français d'Etudes Andines, Vol. 20. Lima and Paris, 1979.

Ribeiro, Darcy. *Religião e Mitologia Kadiuéu*. Serviço de Proteção aos Índios, Publicação No. 106. Rio de Janeiro: Ministério da Agricultura, Conselho Nacional de Proteção aos Índios, 1950.

Ribeiro, Darcy. "Notícia dos Ofaié-Chavante," *RMP* 5 (1951):105-135.

Ribeiro, Darcy. *Kadiwéu: Ensaios etnológicos sobre o saber, o azar a beleza*. Petrópolis: Vozes, 1980.

Ribeiro, José. *Dicionário africano de Umbanda: Africano e portogues; portogues e africano*. Rio de Janeiro: Editora Espiritualista, 1972.

Ribeiro, Rene. "Brazilian Messianic Movements." In *Millennial Dreams in Action*, ed. Sylvia L. Thrupp. The Hague: Mouton, 1962.

Riester, Jürgen. "Zur Religion der Pauserna-Guarašug'wä in Ostbolivien," *Anthropos* 65, Nos. 3-4 (1970):466-479.

Riester, Jürgen. "Medizinmänner und Zauberer der Chiquitano-Indianer," *Zeitschrift für Ethnologie* (Braunschweig) 96, No. 2 (1971):250-270.

Riester, Jürgen. *Die Pauserna-Guarašug'wä. Monographie eines Tupi-Guaraní-Volkes in Ostbolivien*. Collectanea Instituti Anthropos, Vol. 3. St. Augustin: Verlag des Anthropos-Instituts, 1972.

Riester, Jürgen. "Acerca de la canción de los Chimane," *Amerikanistische Studien*, ed. Roswith Hartmann and Udo Oberem. St. Augustin: Haus Völker und Kulturen, 1979.

Rivero, Juan. *Historia de las Misiones de los Llanos de Casanare y los Río Orinoco y Meta. Escrita el año de 1763*. Bogota, 1883.

Rivet, Paul. "La Influencia Karib en Colombia," *Revista del Instituto Etnológico Nacional* (Bogotá) 1, No. 1 (1943):55-93.

Rivière, Peter. *Marriage Among the Trio: A Principle of Social Organisation*. Oxford: Clarendon Press, 1969.

Rivière, Peter. "The Political Structure of the Trio Indians as Manifested in a System of Ceremonial Dialogue." In *The Translation of Culture*, ed. T. O. Beidelman. London: Tavistock, 1971.

Robertson, Carol E. " 'Pulling the Ancestors': Performance, Practice and Praxis in Mapuche Ordering." *Ethnomusicology* 23, No. 3 (1979):395-416.

Robertson-DeCarbo, Carol E. "Lukutún: Text and Context in Mapuche Rogations," *LAIL* 1, No. 2 (1977):67-78.

Robinson, Scott Studebaker. "Towards an Understanding of Kofan Shamanism," Ph.D. dissertation, Cornell University, 1979.

Robles Rodriguez, E. "Ñeicurehuén. Baile de Machis," *Revista de Folklore Chileno* 2 (1911). Also published in *Anales de la Universidad de Chile* 128 (1911).

Robles Rodriguez, E. "Machiluhún, Iniciación de Machis. Travún, una Reunión Pública," *Revista de Folklore Chileno* 3 (1912).

Robles Rodriquez, E. "Costumbres i Creencias Araucanas," *Anales de la Universidad* (Santiago de Chile) 130 (Jan. – Feb. 1912):343 – 369.

Roe, Peter G. *The Cosmic Zygote: Cosmology in the Amazon Basin.* New Brunswick, N.J.: Rutgers University Press, 1982.

Rosen, E. V. *The Chorotes Indians in the Bolivian Chaco.* Stockholm, 1904.

Ross, Eric Barry. "Food Taboos, Diet, and Hunting Strategy: The Adaptation to Animals in Amazon Cultural Ecology," *Cultural Anthropology* 19, No. 1 (1978):1 – 36.

Roth, Walter Edmund. *An Inquiry into the Animism and Folk-Lore of the Guiana Indians.* Thirtieth Annual Report of the Bureau of American Ethnology, 1908 – 1909, pp. 103 – 386. Washington D.C.: Smithsonian Institution, 1915; reprinted New York: Johnson Reprint Corporation, 1970.

Roth, Walter Edmund. "An Introductory Study of the Arts, Crafts and Customs of the Guiana Indians," *Annual Report of the Bureau of American Ethnology* 38 (1916 – 1917). Washington, D.C.: Smithsonian Institution, 1924.

Roth, Walter Edmund. *Additional Studies of the Arts, Crafts, and Customs of the Guiana Indians, with Special Reference to Those of Southern British Guiana.* Bureau of American Ethnology, Bulletin 91. Washington D.C.: Smithsonian Institution, 1929.

Rouget, Gilbert. *La Musique et la transe: Esquisse d'une théorie générale des relations de la musique et de la possession.* Paris: Editions Gallimard, 1980.

Rowe, John H. "Inca Culture at the Time of the Spanish Conquest," *HSAI* 2 (1946):183 – 330.

Rowe, John H. *Chavin Art: An Inquiry into Its Form and Meaning.* New York: University Publishers, 1962.

Rowe, John H. "What Kind of Settlement was Inca Cuzco?" *Ñawpa Pacha* 5 (1967):59 – 76.

Rowe, John H. "An Account of the Shrines of Ancient Cuzco," *Ñawpa Pacha* 17 (1979):1 – 80.

Rudolph, Ebermut. "Indianische Tierherrenvorstellungen — Ein Beitrag zur Frage der Entstehung von Wildgeist- und Eignerwesen," *Zeitschrift für Ethnologie* 99, Nos. 1 and 2 (1974):81 – 119.

Ryden, Stig. *A Study of the Siriono Indians.* Göteborg: Elanders Boktryckery Aktiebolag, 1941.

Saake, Wilhelm. "Die Juruparilegende bei den Baniwa des Rio Issana," *ICA*, Copenhagen, 1958, pp. 271 – 279.

Saake, Wilhelm. "Mythen über Inapirikuli, den Kulterheros der Baniwa," *Zeitschrift für Ethnologie* 93, No. 1 (1968):260 – 273.

Sabogal, Wiesse. *Comunidad Andina.* Mexico City: Instituto Indigenista Interamericano, Dept. de Antropología, 1969.

Salazar, Ernesto. *Talleres Prehistóricos en los Altos Andes del Ecuador.* Cuenca, Ecuador: Universidad de Cuenca Dept. de Cultura, 1980.

Sallnow, Michael. "Le Peregrinación Andina," *Allpanchis Phuturinqa* 7 (1974):101 – 142.

Salomon, Frank L. *Los Señores Étnicos de Quito en la Época de los Incas.* Otavalo, Ecuador: Instituto Otavaleño de Antropología, 1980.

Salomon, Frank L. "Chronicles of the Impossible: Notes on Three Peruvian Indigenous Historians." In *From Oral to Written Expression: Native Andean Chronicles of the Early Colonial Period,* ed. Rolena Adorno. Foreign and Comparative Studies, Latin American Series, No. 4. Syracuse, N.Y.: Syracuse University Press, 1982.

Salomon, Frank L., and Grosboll, Sue. "Names and Peoples in Incaic Quito: Retrieving Undocumented Historic Processes Through Anthroponymy and Statistics," *AA* 88, No. 2 (1986):387 – 399.

Sanabria Fernández, Hernando. *Apiaguaiqui-Tumpa. Biografía del pueblo chiriguano y de su ultima caudillo.* La Paz and Cochabamba: Editorial Los Amigos del Libro, 1972.

Sánchez Garrafa, Rodolfo. "¿Qué es el mito?" *Antropológica* (Lima) 1, no. 1 (1983):19 – 32.

Santa Cruz Pachacuti Yamqui Salcamayhua, Juan de. *An Account of the Antiquities of Peru.* In

Narratives of the Rites and Laws of the Yncas, trans. and ed. Clements R. Markham. Hakluyt Society First Series, Vol. 43. London: Hakluyt Society, 1873; reprinted New York: Burt Franklin, n. d.

Santos, Juana Elbein dos, and Santos, Deoscoredes Maximiliano dos. "Ancestor Worship in Bahia: The Egun-Cult," *JSAP* 58 (1972):78–108.

Sas, Andrés. "Ensayo sobre la música nasca," *Revista del Museo Nacional* (Lima) 8, No. 1 (1939):20–28.

Sauer, Carl O. "Cultivated Plants of South and Central America," *HSAI* 6, pp. 487–543. Washington, D.C., 1950.

Schaden, Egon. "Der Paradiesmythos im Leben der Guarani-Indianer," *ICA,* 30th Congress, London, 1952, pp. 179–186.

Schaden, Egon. *Aspectos Fundamentais da Cultura Guarani.* Faculty of Philosophy, Sciences, and Literature Bulletin No. 188. São Paulo: Universidade de São Paulo, 1954.

Schaden, Egon. "A Origem e a Posse do Fogo na Mitología Guaraní," *ICA,* 31st Session, São Paulo, 1955, pp. 217–227.

Schaden, Egon. "Der Paradiesmythos im Leben der Guarani-Indianer," *Staden-Jahrbuch* (São Paulo) 3 (1955):151–162.

Schaden, Egon. *Aculturação Indígena. Ensaio sôbre Fatôres e Tendências da Mudança Cultural de Tribus Índias em Contacto como Mundo dos Brancos.* São Paulo, 1965.

Schaden, Egon. "Notas Sobre a Vida e a Obra de Curt Nimuendajú," *Revista do Instituto de Estudos Brasileiros* 2 (1968):7–19.

Schaden, Egon. "Le Messianisme en Amérique du Sud." In *Histoires des Religions,* Vol. 3, ed. Henri-Charles Puech. Paris: Gallimard, 1976.

Schechter, John M. "The Inca *Cantar Histórico:* A Lexico-Historical Elaboration on Two Cultural Themes," *Ethnomusicology* 23, no. 2 (1979):191–204.

Schermair, Anselmo. *Sirionó-Texte.* Innsbruck, 1963.

Schindler, Helmut. "Warum kann man den Itutari mit dem Gwaruma erschlagen?" *Zeitschrift für Ethnologie* 98, No. 2 (1973):246–276.

Schindler, Helmut. "Carijona and Manakïnï: An Opposition in the Mythology of a Carib Tribe," In *Carib-Speaking Indians: Culture, Society and Language,* ed. Ellen B. Basso. Tucson: University of Arizona Press, 1977.

Schmidel, U. *Reise nach Süd-Amerika in den Jahren 1534–1554.* Tübingen, 1889.

Schmidt, Wilhelm. *Ethnología sul Americana: Círculos Culturães e Estratos Culturães na America do Sul.* Bibliotheca Pedagógica Brasileira. Brasiliana, Series 5, Vol. 218. São Paulo: Companhia Editôra Nacional, 1942.

Schobinger, Juan. "Rock Art in Western Argentina: The Andean Region of Cuyo," *LAIL* 4, No. 2 (1980):64–69.

Schoo Lastra, Dionisio. *Indio del Desierto, 1535–1879.* Buenos Aires: Agencia General de Librería y Publicaciones, 1928.

Schultes, Richard Evans. "An Overview of Hallucinogens in the Western Hemisphere." In *Flesh of the Gods,* ed. Peter T. Furst. New York, 1972.

Schultz, Harald. *Hombu: Indian Life in the Brazilian Jungle.* New York: Macmillan, 1962.

Schuster, Meinhard. *Dekuana: Beiträge zur Ethnologie der Makiritare.* Munich: Klaus Renner Verlag, 1976.

Sebag, Lucien. "Analyse des rêves d'une indienne Guayaki," *Les Temps Modernes* (Paris) 19, No. 217 (1964):2181–2237.

Sebag, Lucien. "Le chamanisme Ayoreo," *L'Homme* (January-March 1965):7–32; and (April-June 1965):92–122.

Seeger, Anthony. "Fixed Points on Arcs in Circles: The Temporal, Processual Aspect of Suyá Space and Society," *ICA,* vol. 2, pp. 341–359. Paris, 1976.

Seeger, Anthony. "Tractatus Esthetico-Semioticus: Model of the Systems of Human Communication." In *Current Thought in Musicology,* ed. John W. Grubbs. Austin: University of Texas Press, 1976.

Seeger, Anthony. "Porque os Indios Suya Cantam Para as Suas Irmas." In *Arte e Sociedade,* ed. G. Velho. Rio de Janeiro: Zahar, 1977.

Seeger, Anthony. "What Can We Learn When They Sing? Vocal Genres of the Suya Indians of Central Brazil," *Ethnomusicology* 23, No. 3 (1979):373–394.

Seeger, Anthony. *Nature and Society in Central Brazil: The Suya Indians of Mato Grosso.* Cambridge, Mass: Harvard University Press, 1981.

Seeger, Anthony; da Matta, Roberto; and Castro, Eduardo B. Viveiros de. "A Construção da Pessoa nas Sociedades Indígenas Brasileiras," *Boletim do Museu Nacional,* n.s. 32 (May 1979):2–19.

Seguín, Carlos Alberto, and Carrasco, Rubén Ríos, eds. *Anales del Tercer Congreso Latinamericano de Psiquiatría. 25–31, October 1964.* Lima: Asociación Psiquiátrica de América Latina, 1966.

Seitz, Georg J. "Die Waikas und ihre Drogen," *Zeitschrift für Ethnologie* 94, No. 2 (1969):266–283.

Shady, Ruth. *Enterramientos en Chullpas de Chota (Cajamarca).* Lima: Museo Nacional de Antropología y Arqueología, 1976.

Shapiro, Judith. "Tapirapé Kinship," *Boletim do Museu Paraense Emílio Goeldi* (Belém) 37 (1968):

Shapiro, Judith. "Ceremonial Redistribution in Tapirapé Society," *Boletin de Museo Paraense Emílio Goeldi,* 38 (1968):pp. 1–20.

Sharon, Douglas. "The Inca *Warachikuy* Initiations." In *Enculturation in Latin America: An Anthology,* ed. Johannes Wilbert. UCLA Latin American Studies, vol. 37. Los Angeles: UCLA Latin American Studies Center Publications, 1976.

Sharon, Douglas. "Becoming a *Curandero* in Peru." In *Enculturation in Latin America: An Anthology,* ed. Johannes Wilbert. UCLA Latin American Studies, vol. 37 Los Angeles: UCLA Latin American Studies Center Publications, 1976.

Sharon, Douglas. *Wizard of the Four Winds: A Shaman's Story.* New York: Free Press, 1978.

Sharon, Douglas G., and Donnan, Christopher B. "Shamanism in Moche Iconography." In *Ethnoarchaeology,* ed. Christopher B. Donnan and C. William Clewlow, Jr. Archaeological Survey Monograph, Vol. 4. Los Angeles: Institute of Archaeology, University of California, 1974.

Shaver, Harold. "Los Campa-Nomatisiguenga de la Amazonía Peruana y su Cosmología," *Folklore americano* 20 (1975):49–53.

Sherbondy, Jeanette. "Les Réseaux d'irrigation dans la géographie politique de Cuzco," *JSAP* 66 (1979):45–66.

Sherzer, Joel, and Urban, Greg, eds. *Native South American Discourse.* The Hague: Mouton, 1985.

Siffredi, Alejandra. "Hierofanías y Concepciones Mítico-Religiosas de los Tehuelches Meridionales," *Runa* (Buenos Aires) 12, Nos. 1–2 (1969–1970):247–271.

Siffredi, Alejandra. "La Autoconciencia de las relaciones sociales entre los Yojwaha-Chorote," *Scripta Ethnológica* 1, No. 1 (1973):71–103.

Siffredi, Alejandra. "La Noción de Reciprocidad entre los Yojwaha-Chorote," *Scripta Ethnológica* 3, No. 3, Part 1 (1975):41–70.

Silverblatt, Irene. "The Evolution of Witchcraft and the Meaning of Healing in Colonial Andean Society," *Culture, Medicine and Psychiatry* 7, No. 4 (1983):413–427.

Silverblatt, Irene. *Moon, Sun, and Witches: Gender Ideologies and Class in Inca and Colonial Peru.* Princeton, N.J.: Princeton University Press, 1987.

Skar, Haral. *The Warm Valley People.* New York: Columbia University Press, 1982.

Snethlage, Emil Heinrich. "Unter nordostbrasilianischen Indianern," *Zeitschrift für Ethnologie* 62 (1930–1931):111–205.

Sousa, Manoel Matusalem. *Cordel, Fé e Viola.* Petrópolis, Brazil: Editora Vozes, 1982.

Stable, Very Dagny. *Klotzrennen brasilianischer Indianer.* Frankfurt: Goethe-Universität, 1969.

Staden, Hans. *Zwei Reisen nach Brasilien 1548–1555,* 4th ed. Marburg, 1981.

Steinen, Karl von den. *Unter den Naturvölkern Zentral-Brasiliens. Reiseschilderung und Ergebnisse der Zweiten Schingú-Expedition 1887–1888.* Berlin: Geographische Verlagsbuchhandlung von Dietrich Reimer, 1894.

Stern, Steve. *Peru's Indian Peoples and the Challenge of Spanish Conquest; Huamanga to 1640.* Madison: University of Wisconsin Press, 1982.

Steward, Julian H. "South American Cultures: An Interprative Summary," *HSAI* 5 (1949):669– 772.

Steward, Julian H., ed. *The Marginal Tribes: Handbook of South American Indians,* Vol. 1. Bureau of American Ethnology Bulletin 143. Washington, D.C.: U.S. Government Printing Office, 1946.

Steward, Julian H., ed. *The Andean Civilizations: Handbook of South American Indians,* Vol. 2. Bureau of American Ethnology Bulletin 143. Washington, D.C.: U.S. Government Printing Office, 1947.

Steward, Julian H., ed. *The Tropical Forest Tribes: Handbook of South American Indians,* Vol. 3. Bureau of American Ethnology Bulletin No. 143. Washington D.C.: U.S. Government Printing Office, 1948.

Steward, Julian H., ed. *The Circum-Caribbean Tribes: Handbook of South American Indians,* Vol. 4. Bureau of American Ethnology Bulletin 143. Washington D.C.: U.S. Government Printing Office, 1948.

Steward, Julian H., ed. *The Comparative Anthropology of South American Indians: Handbook of South American Indians,* Vol. 5. Bureau of American Ethnology Bulletin 143. Washington, D.C.: U.S. Government Printing Office, 1949.

Stocks, Anthony. "Tendiendo un puente entre el cielo y la tierra en alas de la canción," *Amazonia Peruana* 2, No. 4 (1978):71–100.

Sullivan, Lawrence E. "History of Religions: The Shape of an Art." In *What Is Religion?,* ed. Mircea Eliade and David Tracy, New York: Seabury Press, 1980.

Sullivan, Lawrence E. "The Irony of Incarnation: The Comedy in *Kenosis,*" *Journal of Religion* 62, No. 4 (1982):412–417.

Sullivan, Lawrence E. "Multiple Levels of Religious Meaning in Culture: A New Look at Winnebago Sacred Texts," *Canadian Journal of Native Studies* 2, No. 2 (1982):221–247.

Sullivan, Lawrence E. "Astral Myths Rise Again: Interpreting Religious Astronomy," *Criterion* 22, No. 1 (1983):12–17.

Sullivan, Lawrence E. "A History of Religious Ideas," *Religious Studies Review* 9, No. 1 (1983):13–22.

Sullivan, Lawrence E. "La Persona y la sociedad como composiciones musicales," *Cuadernos Internacionales de Historia Psicosocial del Arte* (Barcelona) 3 (Dec. 1983):9–17.

Sullivan, Lawrence E. "Lévi-Strauss, Mythology, and South American Religions." In *Anthropology and the Study of Religion,* ed. Robert L. Moore and Frank E. Reynolds. Chicago: Center for the Scientific Study of Religion, 1984.

Sullivan, Lawrence E. "Creative Writing and *Imitatio dei:* The Book and the Fall," *Unirea: Revista Asociației Culturale Internationale a Etniei Române* (Toronto) 2 (March 1984):20–24.

Sullivan, Lawrence E. "Sacred Music and Sacred Time," *World of Music* (Berlin) 26, No. 3 (1984):33–52.

Sullivan, Lawrence E. "Above, Below, or Far Away: Andean Cosmogony and Ethical Order." In *Cosmogony and Ethical Order: New Studies in Comparative Ethics,* ed. Robin Lovin and Frank Reynolds. Chicago: University of Chicago Press, 1985.

Sullivan, Lawrence E. "Sound and Senses: Toward a Hermeneutics of Performance," *History of Religions* 26, No. 1 (1986):1–33.

Sullivan, Lawrence E. "Watunna: An Orinoco Creation Cycle," *New Scholar* 10 (1986):291–294.

Sullivan, Lawrence E. Articles in *The Encyclopedia of Religion,* s.v. "Axis Mundi," "Center of the World," "Deus Otiosus," "Diseases and Cures," "Earth," "Healing," "Hierophany," "Nature: The Worship of Nature," "Orientation," "Supreme Beings," "Tricksters: An Overview," "Tricksters: Mesoamerican and South American Tricksters." Edited by Mircea Eliade. New York: Macmillan, 1987.

Sullivan, Lawrence E. "Noise, Nakedness, Flood, and Fire: Purification Rites for a Healthy New Year in Modern Japan," *Second Opinion* 4 (1987):68–91.

Sullivan, Lawrence E. "Religious Foundations of Health and Medical Power in South America."

In *Caring and Curing: Health and Medicine in the World's Religious Traditons*, ed. Lawrence E. Sullivan. New York: Macmillan, forthcoming.

Tamayo Herrera, José. *Historia del Indigenismo Cuzqueño, Siglos XVI-XX*. Lima: Instituto Nacional de Cultura, 1980.

Tamayo Herrera, José. *Historia del monumento a Tupac Amaru*. Lima: Comisión Nacional del Bicentenario de la Rebelión Emancipadora de Tupac Amaru, 1980.

Tangol, Nicasio. *Chiloé: Archipiélago Mágico*, 2 vols. Santiago: Empresa Editora Nacional Quimantu, 1972.

Tastevin, Constant. "Le Fleuve Murú. Ses Habitants--Croyances et moeurs *Kachinaua*," *La Géographie* (Paris) 43, Nos. 4–5 (1925): 403–422; 44, No. 1 (1925):14–35.

Taussig, Michael T. *The Devil and Commodity Fetishism in South America*. Chapel Hill: University of North Carolina Press, 1980.

Taussig, Michael T. *Shamanism, Colonialism, and the Wild Man: A Study in Terror and Healing*. Chicago: University of Chicago Press, 1987.

Tax, Sol. "Indian, Latin American," *Encyclopaedia Britannica*, 15th ed. 1974.

Taylor, Kenneth I. "Body and Spirit Among the Sanumá (Yanoama) of North Brazil." In *Spirits, Shamans and Stars: Perspectives from South America*, ed. David L. Browman and Ronald A. Schwarz. The Hague: Mouton, 1979.

Tedlock, Dennis. *The Spoken Word and the Work of Interpretation*. Philadelphia: University of Pennsylvania Press, 1983.

Tello, Julio C. "Wira Kocha," *Inca* 1, No. 1 (1923):93–320; 1, No. 3 (1923):583–606.

Tentori, Tullio. "South American Ideas of the Other World," *ICA*, 30th Congress London, 1955, pp. 199–201.

Tentori, Tullio. "Il viaggio nell' <<al di là>> nelle credenze degli indigeni sud-americani." In *Scritti americanistici*, ed. Tullio Tentori. Rome: Edizioni Ricerca, 1968.

Tessmann, Günther. *Die Indianer Nordost-Perus: Grundlegende Forschungen für eine systematische Kulturkunde*. Veröffentlichung der Harvey-Bassler-Stiftung. Hamburg: Friedrichsen, de Gruyter & Co., 1930.

Thoden van Velzen, H. U. E. "Affluence, Deprivation, and the Flowering of Bush Negro Religious Movements," *Bijdragen tot de Taal-, Land- en Volkenkunde* 139, No. 1 (1983):99–139.

Thoden van Velzen, H. U. E. "The Gaan Gadu Cult: Material Forces and the Social Production of Fantasy," *Social Compass* 32, No. 1 (1985):93–109.

Tiller, Ann O. "The Brazilian Cult as a Healing Alternative," *JLAL* 5, No. 2 (1979):255–272.

Tomasini, Alfredo. "Señores de los animales, constelaciones y espíritus en el bosque en el cosmos mataco-mataguayo," *Runa* (Buenos Aires) 12, nos. 1–2 (1969–1970):427–444.

Tomasini, Alfredo. "Dapitchi, un alto dios uránico de los Toba y los Pilagá," *Scripta Ethnológica* 4, Part 1 (1976):69–87.

Tomasini, Alfredo. "La narrativa animalística entre los Toba de Occidente," *Scripta Ethnológica* 5, Part 1, (1978–1979):52–81.

Tooker, Elizabeth, ed. *Naming Systems*. Edited from the Proceedings of the 1980 American Ethnological Society. Washington, D.C.: American Ethnological Society, 1984.

Torre Lopez, Fernando. "Fenomenología religiosa de la tribu anti o campa," *Amazonia Peruana* 31 (1969):20–47.

Torres Laborde, Alfonso. *Mito y cultura entre los Barasana: Un grupo indígena tukano del Vaupés*. Bogotá: Universidad de los Andes, Departamento de Antropología, 1969.

Tovar, Antonio. *Catálogo de las Lenguas de América del Sur*. Buenos Aires: Editorial Sudamericana, 1961.

Trimborn, Hermann. "Der Kannibalismus im Cauca-Tal," *Zeitschrift für Ethnologie* 70, Nos 3–5 (1939):310–330.

Trimborn, Hermann. "Zur Symbolik der Farbe in Mythen des alten Peru." In *Der Mensch und die Künste: Festschrift für H. Lützeler zum 60. Geburtstag*, pp. 316–320. Düsseldorf, 1962.

Trimborn, Hermann. "Schriftenverzeichnis von Hermann Trimborn: Lista de Publicaciones," in *Amerikanistische Studien. Festschrift für Hermann Trimborn anlässlich seines 75. Geburtstages*, ed. Roswith Hartmann and Udo Oberem. St. Augustin: Haus Völker und Kulturen, 1979.

Trimborn, Hermann. *El Reino de Lambayeque en el antiguo Peru*. St. Augustin: Haus Völker und Kulturen, 1979.

Trupp, Fritz. *Mythen der Makuna*. Acta Ethnologica et Linguistica no. 40. Series Americana 8. Vienna: Institut für Völkerkunde der Universität Wien, 1977.

Turner, Terence S. "Tchikrin, A Central Brazilian Tribe and Its Symbolic Language of Bodily Adornment," *Natural History* 78, No. 8 (1969):50–59.

Turner, Terence S. "Narrative Structure and Mythopoesis: A Critique and Reformulation of Structuralist Concepts of Myth, Narrative, and Poetics," *Arethusa* 10, no. 1 (1977):103–163.

Turner, Terence S. "Kayapó of Central Brazil," in *Face Values*, pp. 245–278. London: British Broadcasting Corporation, 1978.

Turner, Terence S. "The Txukahamae Kayapó are Alive and Well in the Upper Xingu," *Survival International Review* (London) 3, No. 2 (1978):18–21.

Turner, Terence S. "Kinship, Household, and Community Structure Among the Kayapó." In *Dialectical Societies*, ed. David Maybury-Lewis. Cambridge, Mass.: Harvard University Press, 1979.

Turner, Terence S. "The Gê and Bororo Societies as Dialectical Systems." In *Dialectical Societies*, ed. David Maybury-Lewis. Cambridge, Mass.: Harvard University Press, 1979.

Turner, Terence S. "The Social Skin," in *Not Work Alone*, pp. 112–140. Beverly Hills, Calif.: Sage Publications, 1980.

Turner, Terence S. "Le dénicheur d'oiseaux en contexte," *Anthropologie et Société* 4, No. 3 (1980):85–115.

Turner, Terence S. "Animal Symbolism, Totemism, and the Structure of Myth." In *Animal Myths and Metaphors in South America*, ed. Gary Urton. Salt Lake City: University of Utah Press, 1985.

Txibae, Ewororo. "A Voz dos que não tinha voz," *Revista de Cultura* (Rio de Janeiro) 70, No. 4 (1976):35–48.

Uhle, Max. *Estudios sobre historia incaica*. Lima: Universidad Nacional Mayor de San Marcos, 1969.

Urban, Greg. "Ceremonial Dialogue in South America," *AA* 88, No. 2 (1986):371–386.

Urbano, Henrique. *Wiracocha y Ayar: Héroes y Funciones en las Sociedades Andinas*. Cuzco, 1981.

Urioste, George L. trans. *Hijos de Pariya Qaqa: La Tradición Oral de Waru Chiri (Mitología, Ritual y Costumbres)*, written by Francisco de Avila, 2 vols. Translated, edited, and noted by George L. Urioste. Foreign and Comparative Studies Program, Latin American Series, No. 6, Vol. 2. Syracuse, N.Y.: Maxwell School of Citizenship and Public Affairs of Syracuse University, 1983.

Urton, Gary. *At the Crossroads of the Earth and the Sky: An Andean Cosmology*. Austin: University of Texas Press, 1981.

Urton, Gary. "Astronomy and Calendrics on the Coast of Peru." In *Ethnoastronomy and Archaeoastronomy in the American Tropics*, ed. Anthony F. Aveni and Gary Urton. New York: New York Academy of Sciences, 1982.

Urton, Gary. "El Sistema de Orientaciones de los Incas y de Algunos Quechuahablantes Actuales tal como Queda Reflajado en su Concepto de la Astronomía y del Universo," *Antropológica* (Lima) 1, no. 1 (1983):209–238.

Urton, Gary, ed. *Animal Myths and Metaphors in South America*. Salt Lake City: University of Utah Press, 1985.

Uscamaita Huaman, Teófilo. *Historia y odisea del primer monumento a Tupac Amaru II*. Lima: Editorial Universo, 1981.

Valcárcel, Carlos Daniel. *La rebelión de Túpac Amaru*. Colección Tierra Firme, Vol. 31. Mexico City: Fondo de Cultura Económica, 1947.

Valcárcel, Carlos Daniel. *Rebeliones indígenas*. Lima: Editorial PTCM, 1946.

Vallejos, Julio Pinto. "Slave Control and Slave Resistance in Colonial Minas Gerais, 1700–1750," *Journal of Latin American Studies* (Cambridge) 17 (1985):1–34.

Van Kessel, Johan. *Danseurs dans le désert: Une étude de dynamique sociale*. The Hague: Mouton, 1980.

Varese, Stéfano. *La Sal de los Cerros: Notas Etnográficas e Históricas sobre los Campa de la Selva del Perú*. Lima: Universidad Peruana de Ciencias y Tecnología, 1968.

Varese, Stéfano. "Pachacamaite." In *Ideología Mesiánica del Mundo Andino*, ed. Juan Ossio. Lima: Ignacio Prado Pastor, 1973.

Vázquez, Juan Adolfo. "On the Oral Literature of the Araucanians," *Latin American Literary Review* 1, No. 2 (1973):59–63.

Vázquez, Juan Adolfo. "Nacimiento e Infancia de Elal. Mitoanálisis de un Texto Tehuelche Meridional," *Revista Iberoamericana* 95 (April-June 1976):201–216.

Vázquez, Juan Adolfo. "The Religions of Mexico and of Central and South America." In *A Reader's Guide to the Great Religions*, ed. Charles J. Adams, 2nd ed. New York: Free Press, 1977.

Vázquez, Juan Adolfo. "The Present State of Research in South American Mythology," *Numen* 25 (1978):240–276.

Vázquez, Juan Adolfo. "Reflexiones Finales." In *From Oral to Written Expression: Native Andean Chronicles of the Early Colonial Period*, ed. Rolena Adorno. Latin American Series No. 4. Syracuse, N.Y.: Maxwell School of Citizenship and Public Affairs, Syracuse University, 1982.

Vázquez, Juan Adolfo. "The Field of Latin American Indian Literatures," *LAIL* 1, No. 1 (1977); reprinted in Latin American Reprint Series, No. 14 (April 1978). Center for Latin American Studies. Pittsburgh: University of Pittsburgh, University Center for International Studies, 1978.

Vega, C. *Los instrumentos musicales aborígenes y criollos de la Argentina*, 2nd ed. Buenos Aires, 1950.

Velho, Yvonne Maggi Alves. *Guerra de Orixá: Um Estudio de Ritual e Conflito*. Rio de Janeiro: Zahar Editores, 1977.

Vellard, Jehan. "La Conception de l'âme et de la maladie chez les indiens américains," *Travaux de l'Institut Français d'Etudes Andines* 6 (1957–1958):5–35.

Vellard, Jehan. "Die Vorstellung von der Seele bei den südamerikanischen Indianern," *Kairos* (1959):145–148.

Velthem, Lucia Hussak van. "Reprentações Gráficas Wayâna-Aparaí," *Boletim do Museu Paraense Emílio Goeldi*, n.s., 64 (July 1976):1–19.

Verger, Pierre. *Fiestas y danzas en el Cuzco y en los Andes*. Buenos Aires: Editorial Sudamericana, 1945.

Verger, Pierre. "Orixás da Bahia," In Carybé (artist), *Iconografia dos Deuses africanos no Candomblé da Bahia*. São Paulo: Rabizes, 1980.

Verger, Pierre. "Relations commerciales et culturelles entre le Brésil et le Golfe du Bénin," *JSAP* 53 (1969):31–56.

Vidal, Lux. *Morte e Vida de uma Sociedade Indígena Brasileira: Os Kayapó-Xikrin do Rio Cateté*. São Paulo: Editora Hucitec/Editora da Universidade de São Paulo, 1977.

Vidal, Lux. "As Categorias de idade como sistema de classificação e controle demográfico de grupos entre os Xikrin do Cateté e de como são manipulados em diferentes contextos," *ICA*, 42nd Congress, Paris, 1978, vol. 2, pp. 361–367.

Vidal, Lux Boelitz. *Morte e vida de uma sociedade indígena brasileira*. São Paulo: Editora Hucitec and Editora da Universidade de São Paulo, 1977.

Vidal Arias, Lucrecia. *Oro Para el Rescate: Costumbres, Cuentos, Anécdotas, Supersticiones y Leyendas de la Provincia de Pataz (Dpto. de la Libertad)*. Lima: Impresiones "SA" Librería, 1979.

Viertler, Renate. *Aldeias bororo. Alguns aspectos de sua organização social*. Serie de Etnologia, Vol. 2. São Paulo: Museu Paulista, 1976.

Viertler, Renate. "A Noção de Pessoa entre os Bororo," *Boletim do Museu Nacional* (Rio de Janeiro), n.s., 32 (May 1979):20–30.

Vignati, Milcíades Alejo. "Los dueños del mar según los Patagones de Santa Cruz," *Anthropos* 57 (1962):857–860.

Villas Boas, Orlando, and Villas Boas, Claudio. *Xingu: The Indians, Their Myths*. New York: Farrar, Strauss & Giroux, 1973.

Villavicencio R., Gladys. *Relaciones Interétnicas en Otavalo-Ecuador*. Ediciones Especiales 65. Mexico City: Instituto Indigenista Interamericano, 1973.

Vinhas de Queiróz, Maurício. "Cargo cult na Amazônia: Observações sobre o Milenarismo Tukuna," *América Latina* 6, No. 4 (1963):43–61.

Vivante, Armando, and Chiappe, D. H. *Introducción a la Cartografía de los Indígenas.* Rosario: Departamento de Antropología, Facultad de Filosofía, Universidad Nacional del Lidate, 1968.
Viveiros de Castro, Eduardo B. "A Fabricação do Corpo na Sociedade Xinguana," *Boletim do Museu Nacional,* n.s., 32 (May 1979):40–49.
Viveiros de Castro, Eduardo B. *Awareté: Os deuses canibais.* Rio de Janeiro: Jorge Zahar, Editor/Anpocs, 1986.
Volhard, Ewald. "Südamerika," in Volhard, *Kannibalismus. Studien zur Kulturkunde,* Vol. 5, pp. 334–361. Stuttgart: Strecker & Schröder, 1939.
Von Humboldt, Alexander, and Bonpland, Aimé. *Personal Narrative of Travels to the Equinoctial Regions of America During the Years 1799–1804.* 3 vols., trans. and ed. Thomasina Ross. London, 1907.
Waag, Else María. "El ser supremo de los Mapuches neuquinos," *Sociedad Argentina de Antropología. Relaciones* (Buenos Aires), n.s., 9 (1975):147–154.
Wachtel, Nathan. "La Visión de los Vencidos: La Conquista española en el Folklore Indígena." In *Ideología Mesiánica del mundo andino,* ed. Juan Ossio. Lima: Ignacio Prado Pastor, 1973.
Wachtel, Nathan. "Rebeliones y Milenarismo." In *Ideología Mesiánica del Mundo Andino,* cd. Juan Ossio. Lima: Ignacio Prado Pastor, 1973.
Wachtel, Nathan. *The Vision of the Vanquished: The Spanish Conquest of Peru Through Indian Eyes, 1530–1570.* New York: Barnes & Nobles, 1977.
Wagley, Charles. "World View of Tapirapé Indians," *JAFL* 53 (1940):252–260.
Wagley, Charles. "Xamanismo tapirapé," *Boletim de Museu Nacional* (Rio de Janeiro), n.s., 3 (Scpt. 1943).
Wagley, Charles. "Tapirapé Shamanism," In *Readings in Anthropology,* Vol. 2, ed. Morton H. Fried. New York, 1959.
Wagley, Charles. "Champukwi of the Village of the Tapirs." In *In the Company of Man,* ed. Joseph B. Casagrande. New York, 1960.
Wagley, Charles. "Time and Tapirapé," *ICA,* 47th Congress (Paris, 1977), pp. 369–378.
Wagley, Charles. *Welcome of Tears: The Tapirapé Indians of Central Brazil.* New York: Oxford University Press, 1977.
Wagley, Charles, and Galvão, Eduardo. "The Tapirapé," *HSAI* 3 (1948), pp. 167–178.
Wagley, Charles, and Galvão, Eduardo. "The Tenetehara," *HSAI* 3 (1948), pp. 137–148.
Wagley, Charles, and Galvão, Eduardo. *The Tenetehara Indians of Brasil.* Contributions to Anthropology, No. 35. New York: Columbia University Press, 1949.
Wagner, Catherine Allen. "Coca, Chicha, and Trago: Private and Communal Rituals in a Quechua Community," Ph.D. dissertation, University of Illinois, 1978.
Walter, Heinz. *Der Jaguar in der Vorstellungswelt der südamerikanischen Natürvölker.* Ph.D. dissertation, Universität Hamburg, 1957.
Warren, Donald, Jr. "Portuguese Roots of Brazilian Spiritism," *Luso-Brazilian Review* 12 (Winter 1968):3–18.
Wassén, S. Henry. "Notes on Southern Groups of Chocó Indians in Colombia." In *Etnologiska Studier,* Vol. 1, pp. 35–182. Göteborg: Etnografiska Museet, 1935.
Wassén, S. Henry. "Algunos Datos del Comercio Precolombino en Colombia," *Revista Colombiana de Antropología* 4 (1955):87–109.
Wassén, S. Henry. "On Dendrobates-Frog-Poison Material among Emperá (Chocó)-Speaking Indians in Western Caldas, Colombia," *Göteborg Arstryck för 1955 och 1956,* pp. 73–94. Göteborg: Etnografiska Museet, 1957.
Wassén, S. Henry. "A Medicine-Man's Implements and Plants in a Tiahuanacoid Tomb in Highland Bolivia," *Etnologiska Studier* Vol. 32, pp. 8–114. Göteborg: Etnografiska Museet, 1972.
Watson, Lawrence C. "Dreaming as World View and Action in Guajiro Culture," *JLAL* 7, No. 2 (1981):239–254.
Wegner, Richard N. "Die Quruçg'ua und Siriono," *ICA,* 24th Congress, Hamburg, 1934, pp. 161–184.
Wegner, Richard N. *Indianerrassen und vergangene Kulturen.* Stuttgart, 1934.
Weilbauer, Eugen. "Kannte das alte Amerika das Rad?" In *Amerikanistische Studien,* ed. Roswith Hartmann and Udo Oberem. St. Augustin: Haus Völker und Kulturen, 1979.

Weiss, Gerald. "Campa Cosmology." In *Native South Americans: Ethnology of the Least Known Continent*, ed. Patricia J. Lyon. Boston: Little, Brown, 1974; reprinted from *Ethnology* 11 (April 1972):157–172.

Weiss, Gerald. "Shamanism and Priesthood in the Light of the Campa *ayahuasca* ceremony." In *Hallucinogens and Shamanism*, ed. Michael J. Harner. New York: Oxford University Press, 1973.

Weiss, Gerald. *The World of a Forest Tribe in South America*. Anthropological Papers of the American Museum of Natural History, Vol. 52, Part 5. New York: American Museum of Natural History, 1975.

Weiss, Gerald. "Rhetoric in Campa Narrative," *JLAL* 3 (1977):169–182.

Whitehead, Neil L. "Carib Cannibalism: The Historical Evidence," *JSAP* 70 (1984):69–88.

Whitten, Norman E. "Personal Networks and Musical Contexts in the Pacific Lowlands of Colombia and Ecuador," in *Afro-American Anthropology: Contemporary Perspectives*, ed. Norman E. Whitten, Jr., and John F. Szwed. New York: Free Press, 1970.

Whitten, Norman E., Jr. *Sacha Runa: Ethnicity and Adaptation of Ecuadorian Jungle Quichua*. Urbana: University of Illinois Press, 1976.

Whitten, Norman E., Jr. "Jungle Quichua Ethnicity: An Ecuadorian Case Study." In *Western Expansion and Indigenous Peoples: The Heritage of Las Casas*, ed. Elias Sevilla-Casas. The Hague: Mouton, 1977.

Whitten, Norman E., Jr. "Structure and Transformations of Contemporary Canelos Quichua Spirit Relationships." In *Amerikanistische Studien*, ed. Roswith Hartmann and Udo Oberem. St. Augustin: Haus Völker und Kulturen, 1979.

Whitten, Norman E., Jr. *Sicuanga Runa: The Other Side of Development in Amazonian Ecuador*. Urbana: University of Illinois Press, 1985.

Whitten, Normal E., Jr. "Quechua Religions: Amazonian Cultures." In *Encyclopedia of Religion*, ed. Mircea Eliade. New York: Macmillan, 1987.

Wiesemann, Ursula. "Semantic Categories of 'Good' and 'Bad' in Relation to Kaingáng Personal Names," *RMP*, n.s., 12 (1960):177–184.

Wiesemann, Ursula. "Time Distinctions in Kaingáng," *Zeitschrift für Ethnologie* Nos. 1–2 (1974):120–130.

Wiesemann, Ursula. "Purification Among the Kaingáng Indians Today," *Zeitschrift für Ethnologie* 95, No. 1 (1970):104–114.

Wilbert, Johannes. "Los Instrumentos musicales de los indios Warrau (Guarao, Guaraúno)," *Antropológica* (Caracas) 1 (1956):2–22.

Wilbert, Johannes. "Mitos de los Indios Yabarana," *Antropológica* (Caracas) 5 (1958):58–67.

Wilbert, Johannes. "Puertas del Averno," *Memoria de la Sociedad de Ciéncias Naturales la Salle* (Caracas) 19, No. 54 (Sept.–Dec. 1959):161–175.

Wilbert, Johannes. "Vestidos y adornos de los indios Warao," *Antropológica* (Caracas) 12 (1964):6–26.

Wilbert, Johannes. "Secular and Sacred Functions of the Fire Among the Warao," *Antropológica* (Caracas) 19 (1967):3–23.

Wilbert, Johannes. *Textos Folklóricos de los Indios Waraos*. Los Angeles: UCLA Latin American Center, 1969.

Wilbert, Johannes. *Folk Literature of the Warao Indians: Narrative Material and Motif Content*. Los Angeles: UCLA Latin American Center, 1970.

Wilbert, Johannes. "Tobacco and Shamanistic Ecstasy among the Warao Indians of Venezuela." In *Flesh of the Gods*, ed. Peter T. Furst. New York: Praeger, 1972.

Wilbert, Johannes. "The Calabash of the Ruffled Feathers," *Artscanada* 30, Nos. 5–6 (1973–1974):90–93.

Wilbert, Johannes. *Yupa Folktales*. Los Angeles: UCLA Latin American Center, 1974.

Wilbert, Johannes. "Eschatology in a Participatory Universe: Destinies of the Soul Among the Warao Indians of Venezuela." In *Death and the After-life in Pre-Colombian America*, ed. Elizabeth P. Benson. Washington, D.C.: Dumbarton Oaks Research Library and Collections, 1975.

Wilbert, Johannes. "Magico-Religious Use of Tobacco among South American Indians." In *Cannabis and Culture*, ed. Vera Rubin. The Hague: Mouton, 1975.

Wilbert, Johannes. *Warao Basketry: Form and Function.* Los Angeles: UCLA Museum of Cultural History, 1975.

Wilbert, Johannes. "The Metaphoric Snare: Analysis of a Warao Folktale," *JLAL* 1, No. 1 (1975):7–17.

Wilbert, Johannes. "To Become a Maker of Canoes: An Essay in Warao Enculturation." In *Enculturation in Latin America: An Anthology,* ed. Johannes Wilbert. Los Angeles: UCLA Latin American Center, 1976.

Wilbert, Johannes. "Navigators of the Winter Sun." In *The Sea in the Pre-Colombian World,* ed. Elizabeth P. Benson. Washington, D.C.: Dumbarton Oaks Research Library and Collections, 1977.

Wilbert, Johannes. "Geography and Telluric Lore of the Orinoco Delta," *JLAL* 5, No. 1 (1979):129–150.

Wilbert, Johannes. "Gaukler-Shamanen der Warao." In *Amerikanistische Studien,* ed. Roswith Hartmann and Udo Oberem. St. Augustin: Haus Völker und Kulturen, 1979.

Wilbert, Johannes. "The Temiche Cap," *Principles* 24, No. 3 (1980):105–109.

Wilbert, Johannes. "Warao Cosmology and Yckuana Roundhouse Symbolism," *JLAL* 7, No. 1 (1981):37–72.

Wilbert, Johannes. "Warao Ethnopathology and Exotic Epidemic Disease," *Journal of Ethnopharmacology* 8 (1983):357–361.

Wilbert, Johannes. "The House of the Swallow-Tailed Kite: Warao Myth and the Art of Thinking in Images." In *Animal Myths and Metaphors in South America,* ed. Gary Urton. Salt Lake City: University of Utah Press, 1985.

Wilbert, Johannes. "The Warao Lords of Rain." In *The Shape of the Past: Studies in Honor of Franklin D. Murphy,* ed. Giorgio Buccellati and Charles Speroni. Los Angeles: Institute of Archaeology and Office of the Chancellor, University of California, Los Angeles, n.d.

Wilbert, Johannes. *Metafisica del tabaco entre los indios de Suramérica.* Caracas: Universidad Católica Andres Bello, n.d.

Wilbert, Johannes, ed. *Folk Literature of the Selknam Indians. Martin Gusinde's Collection of Selknam Narratives.* Los Angeles: University of California Press, 1975.

Wilbert, Johannes, ed. *Folk Literature of the Yamana Indians: Martin Gusinde's Collection of Yamana Narratives.* Los Angeles: UCLA Latin American Center, 1977.

Wilbert, Johannes, ed. *Folk Literature of the Gê Indians,* Vol. 1 Los Angeles: UCLA Latin American Center, 1978.

Wilbert, Johannes, and Simoneau, Karin, eds. *Folk Literature of the Mataco Indians.* Los Angeles: UCLA Latin American Center, 1982.

Wilbert, Johannes, and Simoneau, Karin, eds. *Folk Literature of the Toba Indians,* Vol. 1. Los Angeles: UCLA Latin American Center, 1982.

Wilbert Johannes, and Simoneau, Karin, eds. *Folk Literature of the Bororo Indians.* Los Angeles: UCLA Latin American Center, 1983.

Wilbert, Johannes, and Simoneau, Karin, eds. *Folk Literature of the Tehuelche Indians.* Los Angeles: UCLA Latin American Center, 1984.

Wilbert, Johannes, and Simoneau, Karin, eds. *Folk Literature of the Chorote Indians.* Los Angeles: UCLA Latin American Center, 1985.

Wilbert, Johannes, and Simoneau, Karin, eds. *Folk Literature of the Gê Indians.* Vol. 2. Los Angeles: UCLA Latin American Center, 1986.

Wilbert, Johannes, and Simoneau, Karin, eds. *Folk Literature of the Goajiro Indians, 2 vols.* Los Angeles: UCLA Latin American Center, 1987.

Wilson, Eddie W. "The Gourd in Magic," *Western Folklore* 23 (1954):113–124.

Wistrand, Lila M. "Music and Song Texts of Amazonian Indians," *Ethnomusicology* 13, No. 3 (1969):469–488.

Wright, Robin M. *History and Religion of the Baniwa Peoples of the Upper Rio Negro Valley,* 2 vols. Ph.D. dissertation, Stanford University, 1981.

Wright, Robin M., and Barreiro, José, eds. *Native Peoples in Struggle: Russell Tribunal and Other International Forums.* Boston: Anthropology Resource Center, 1982.

Wright, Robin M., and Jonathan D. Hill. "History, Ritual, and Myth: Nineteenth Century Millenarian Movements in the Northwest Amazon," *Ethnohistory* 33, No. 1 (1986):31–54.

Wulff, Juan Hartwig. *Totenkult der Naturvölker des südlichen Südamerika.* Ph.D. dissertation, Universität Hamburg, 1969.

Yacovleff, Eugenio, and Herrera, Fortunato L. "El Mundo Vegetal de los Antiguos Peruanos," *Revista de Museo Nacional* (Lima) 3, No. 3 (1934):241–322; 4, No. 1 (1935):29–102.

Yaranga Valderrama, Abdón. "La Divinidad Illapa en la Región Andina," *América Indígena* 39 (1979):697–720.

Yauri Montero, Marcos. *Ganchiscocha: Leyendas, cuentos y mitos de Ancash.* Lima: Ediciones "Piedra y Niev," 1961.

Zelenka, Georg. "*Safa Casa*--Nur ein Brauch und Nichts Andres?" In *Amerikanistische Studien,* ed. Roswith Hartmann and Udo Oberem. St. Augustin: Haus Völker und Kulturen, 1979.

Zerries, Otto. "Sternbilder als Ausdruck jägerischer Geisteshaltung in Südamerika," *Paideuma* (Bamberg) 5 (1950):220–235.

Zerries, Otto. "Algunas Noticias Etnológicas acerca de los Indígenas Puinave," *Boletin Indigenista Venezolano* (Caracas) 9, Nos. 1–4 (1951):29–36.

Zerries, Otto. "Krankheitsdämonen und Hilfsgeister des Medizinmannes in Südamerika," *ICA,* 30th Congress, London, 1952, pp. 162–178.

Zerries, Otto. "Die kulturgeschichtliche Bedeutung einiger Mythen aus Südamerika über den Ursprung der Pflanzen," *Zeitschrift für Ethnologie* 77, No. 1 (1952):62–82.

Zerries, Otto. "Kürbisrassel und Klopfgeister in Südamerika," *Paideuma* (Bamberg) 5, No. 6 (1953):323–339.

Zerries, Otto. *Wild- und Buschgeister in Südamerika. Eine Untersuchung jägerzeitlicher Phänomene im Kulturbild südamerikanischer Indianer.* Studien zur Kulturkunde, Vol. 11. Wiesbaden, 1954.

Zerries, Otto. "Die Vorstellung der Waika-Indianer des Oberen Orinoko (Venezuela) über die menschliche Seele," *ICA,* 32nd Congress, Copenhagen, 1958, pp. 105–113.

Zerries, Otto. "Schöpfung und Urzeit im Denken der Waika-Indianer des Oberen Orinoco (Venezuela)," *ICA,* 32nd Congress, Copenhagen, 1958.

Zerries, Otto. "El endocanibalismo en la América del Sur," *RMP* 12 (1960):125–175.

Zerries, Otto. "Die Vorstellung zum zweiten Ich und die Rolle der Harpyie in der Kultur der Naturvölker Südamerikas," *Anthropos* 57 (1962):889–914.

Zerries, Otto. *Waika: Die kulturgeschichtliche Stellung der Waika-Indianer des oberen Orinoco im Rahmen der Völkerkunde Südamerikas,* Vol. 1. Frankfurt am Main: Klaus Renner Verlag, 1964.

Zerries, Otto. "Primitive South America and the West Indies." In *Pre-Colombian American Religions,* ed. Walter Krickberg, Hermann Trimborn, Werner Müller, and Otto Zerries. New York: Holt, Rinehart & Winston, 1968.

Zerries, Otto. "Entstehung oder Erwerb der Kulturpflanzen und Beginn des Bodenbaues im Mythos der Indianer Südamerikas," *Paideuma* (Bamberg) 15 (1969):64–124.

Zerries, Otto. "Tierbank und Geistersitz in Südamerika," *Ethnologische Zeitschrift Zürich* 1 (1970).

Zerries, Otto. "Das Federdiadem—Ein Sonnensymbol bei südamerikanischen Indianern." In *Amerikanistische Studien,* ed. Roswith Hartmann and Udo Oberem. St. Augustin: Haus Völker und Kulturen, 1979.

Zerries, Otto. "Kalebassenmasken und Idole bei ausserandinen Indianern Sudamerikas," *Scripta Ethnológica* 6 (1981):173–186.

Zerries, Otto. "Yanoama," in *Menschenbilder früher Gesellschaften: Ethnologische Studien zum Verhältnis von Mensch und Natur,* pp. 143–177. Edited by Klaus E. Müller. Frankfurt: Campus Verlag, 1983.

Zerries, Otto, and Schuster, Meinhard. *Mahekodotedi: Monographie eines Dorfes der Waika-Indianer (Yanoama) am oberen Orinoco (Venezuela).* Frankfurt am Main: Klaus Renner Verlag, 1974.

Zuidema, R. T. *The Ceque System of Cuzco: The Social Organization of the Capital of the Inca.* Leiden: E. J. Brill, 1964.

Zuidema, R. T. "Kinship and Ancestor Cult in Three Peruvian Communities: Hernandez Principe's Account in 1622," *Bulletin Institut Français des Etudes Andines* (Lima) 2, No. 1 (1973):16–33.

Zuidema, R. T. "La imágen del sol y la huaca de Susurpuquio en el sistema astronómico de los Incas en el Cuzco," *JSAP* 43 (1974–1976):199–230.

Zuidema, R. T. "The Inca Calendar." In *Native American Astronomy*, ed. Anthony F. Aveni. Austin: University of Texas Press, 1977.

Zuidema, R. T. "El Puente del Rio Apurimac y el origen mitico de la villca *(anadenanthera colubrina)*," in *Amerikanistische Studien*, ed. Roswith Hartmann and Udo Oberem. St. Augustin: Haus Völker und Kulturen, 1979.

Zuidema, R. T. "Myth and History in Ancient Peru." In *The Logic of Culture: Advances in Structural Theory and Methods*, ed. Ino Rossi. South Hadley, Mass.: Bergin & Garvey Publishers, 1982.

Zuidema, R. T. "The Sidereal Lunar Calendar of the Incas." In *Archaeoastronomy in the New World*, ed. Anthony F. Aveni. Cambridge: At the University Press, 1982.

Zuidema, R. T. "The Inca Observations of the Solar and Lunar Passages through Zenith and Anti-Zenith at Cuzco." In *Archaeoastronomy in the Americas*, ed. R. A. Williamson. Los Altos, Calif.: Ballena Press, 1982.

Zuidema, R. T. "Catachillay. The Role of the Pleiades and of the Southern Cross and α and β Centauri in the Calendar of the Incas." In *Ethnoastronomy and Archaeoastronomy in the American Tropics*, ed. Anthony F. Aveni and Gary Urton. New York: New York Academy of Sciences, 1982.

Zuidema, R. T. "The Lion in the City: Royal Symbols of Transition in Cuzco." In *Animal Myths and Metaphors in South America*, ed. Gary Urton. Salt Lake City: University of Utah Press, 1985; reprinted from *JLAL* 9, No. 1 (1983):39–100.

Zuidema, R. T. and Urton, Gary. "La Constelación de la Llama en los Andes Peruanos," *Allpanchis Phuturinqa* 9 (1976):59–119.

NAME INDEX

Abačikwaia, 292
Abel, 423
Aberle, David F., 868n, 876n
Achachila-wak'a, 257
Achagua, 462
Aché, 62, 175–76, 296, 310, 342, 343, 348, 517
  rites of passage, 310, 348–49
Achuar, 845n; see also Shuar
Ackawoï, 102
Ackerknecht, Edwin H., 451, 839n
Acosta, José de, 690n, 858n, 859n
Acuña, Luis Alberto, 816n
Adahe Ademi Hidi, 181, 371
Adam and Eve, 589
Adams, Richard N., 869n
Adorno, Rolena, 690n, 804n, 878n
Africa, 596
Aganju, 299
Age of Destruction, 100
Age of Discovery, 513, 559
Age of Exploration, 613
Age of Grandparents, 100, 103
Agostinho, Pedro, 488, 546, 746n, 761n, 799n, 804n,
  850n, 851n, 866n, 867n
Agua de Osala, 169
Aguaruna, 308, 721n, 796n
Aguilo, Federico, 728n
Ahpikondiá, 30, 122, 138, 235, 290
Ahpikon-vi'i, 122
Ahpikon-yéba, 122
Akawaio, 210, 349, 396–98, 400, 423, 435, 808n, 834n
Akerberg, Hans, 696n
Akodumo, 444
Akuriyo, 150, 738n
  cosmology, 150
Akwě-Shavante, 33, 63, 64, 156, 174, 175, 191, 202,
  203, 270, 281, 307, 337–39, 352, 360, 461, 484,
  501, 707n, 713n, 745n, 750n, 753n, 772n, 787n,
  796n, 806n, 812n, 844n, 849n, 864n
  and time 156
  calendar of festivals, 175
  cosmogony, 63–64
  death beliefs and practices, 501, 536
  feasts of, 202
  rites of passage, 337–39, 360
Alapá, 331
Albisetti, César, 690n, 712n, 720n, 749n, 764n,
  784n, 801n, 831n, 847n, 854n
Albórnoz, Cristóbal de, 596, 690n, 880n
Alemán, 378
Alexandre Christo, 556
Algeo, John, 783n
Allen, Douglas, 702n
Allepantepo, 713n
Alves Velho, Yvonne Maggie, 758n
Amahuaca, 489, 513, 519, 851n, 860n, 861n, 862n
Amahuaca
  death beliefs and practices, 519–20
Amaru, 106, 144, 183, 184, 217, 275, 276, 305, 308,
  309, 316, 317, 329, 330, 347, 359, 874n

Amasanga, 55, 126, 127, 143, 195, 196, 200, 204,
  236, 380, 381, 407, 446, 766n
Amazon region, 329
Ambía, Abel Adrian, 796n, 798n, 812n
Amcokwei, 582
American Indians, 25, 513
Amorim, A. B. de, 799n, 807n
Amuesha, 569
Añay, 535
Ancailli, 786n
Ancient Times, 106, 168, 169, 380, 443, 529
Ancón, 850n
Andes
  cosmogony, 53–54, 72–73, 74, 77, 96
  death beliefs and practices, 533–34
  divinities, 591
Andes, 53, 70, 82, 305, 311, 359, 495, 533, 567, 594,
  612
Andrade, Mário, 713n
Andres, Friedrich, 825n
Angaite, 723n
Angelis, Pedro de, 881n
Ani Shrëati, 320, 321
Antares, 161
Antes, Peter, 696n
Antonio the Counselor, 556, 562
Anuxa, 805n
Aónik'enk: see Tehuelche
Apamama Grandmother, 100, 103
Apapocuvá, 186, 208, 248, 267, 419, 428, 483, 503,
  535, 574, 576, 596, 610, 705n, 768n, 873n
Apapocuvá
  death beliefs and practices, 483, 503, 535–36
  eschatology, 571–76
Apayaya, 80
Apinayé, 58, 66, 160, 164, 169, 175, 179, 196, 202,
  212, 233, 235, 237, 252, 266, 267, 279, 309, 356,
  359, 395, 418, 444, 451, 476, 511, 543, 582,
  712n, 713n, 720n, 733n, 734n, 741n, 742n,
  752n, 763n, 771n, 779n, 790n, 798n, 806n,
  807n, 808n, 809n, 811n, 812n, 829n, 837n,
  839n, 848n, 862n, 876n
  and time 160, 179
  calendar of festivals, 175
  ceremonies of, 164, 202
  cosmogony, 58, 66–67
  death beliefs and practices, 511
  feasts of, 169, 212
  myths of, 235
  rites of passage, 309, 339–40
Apu Inca, 569
Apus, 53
Apusanai, 252
Apyteré, 255, 379, 772n
Aranda de los Rios, Ramon, 871n
Arapaja, 848n
Araucanian, 156, 445, 453, 488, 501, 732n, 752n,
  816n, 823n, 833n, 835n, 847n, 866n
  cosmogony, 58
  time, 156

933

God the Holy Spirit, 54
God the Son (Dios Churi), 54
Goddess of the Nadir, 531
Goethe, Johann W., 701n
Goffman, Erving, 761n
Gogo, 739n
Gold, Penny Schine, 777n
Goldman, Irving, 205, 300, 713n, 714n, 723n, 739n,
    751n, 754n, 758n, 781n, 794n, 795n, 805n, 812n
Gombrich, Ernst, 878n
Gómez, Dionisio Dios ("God"), 554, 574
Gómez, Machado, 554
Goodenough, Ward H., 784n
Gorgias, 775n
Gospel, 554
Gossen, Gary H., 846n
Gould, Julius, 867n
Gourd of Night, 76, 77
Gourlay, K. A., 748n
Gow, Rosalind, 54, 711n, 733n, 735n, 738n, 740n,
    741n, 751n, 821n, 823n
Graham, Laura, 787n
Graham, William A., 882n
Gran Pajonal, 694n; *see also* Campa; River Campa;
    Pajonal Campa
Grandfather of Deer, 442
Grandfather of the Earth, 259
Grebe, Maria Ester, 702n, 831n
Green, Ronald, 782n
Grenand, Françoise, 694n, 702n, 715n, 721n, 752n,
    762n
Grenand, Pierre, 198, 376, 694n, 720n, 730n, 738n,
    765n, 817n, 815n, 827n, 829n, 833n, 838n, 871n
Grimes, Ronald, 881n
Grosboll, Sue, 780n
Grottanelli, Cristiano, 699n, 857n
Grubb, Wilfred Barbrooke, 705n
Guaharibos, 861n
Guahibo, 688n
Guajajara, 417
Guajiro, 252, 771n
Guaman Poma de Ayala, Felipe, 211, 350, 550, 587,
    588, 589, 590, 591, 592, 598, 600, 608, 611,
    690n, 738n, 744n, 804n, 875n, 877n, 878n, 879n
Guaralu, 749n
Guaraní, 27, 32, 247, 248, 267, 402, 421, 422, 427,
    428, 434, 571, 572, 574, 575, 576, 577, 579, 580,
    596, 610, 705n, 707n, 712n, 729n, 767n, 721n,
    761n, 768n, 828n, 829n, 836n, 850n, 858n,
    860n, 873n, 875n
  Christian influence on, 873n
  cosmogony, 27–28
  eschatology, 571–78
Guarašug'wä, 875n
Guarayú, 864n, 875n
Guariglia, Guglielmo, 868n
Guayakí (Aché), 62, 72, 129, 175, 176, 178, 190, 202,
    215, 231, 234, 244, 245, 265, 269, 270, 281, 282,
    285, 291, 292, 307, 310, 311, 324, 347, 351, 356,
    367, 368, 487, 498, 513, 517, 558, 562, 564, 610,
    731n, 753n, 820n, 787n, 788n, 792n, 797n
    807n, 808n, 850n, 856n, 860n, 870n; *see also*
    Aché
  myths, 234
  cosmogony, 62, 72
  cosmology, 129
  death beliefs and practices, 517–19
  eschatology, 72, 588
  feasts, 175, 191, 202

Guayakí (Aché) *(cont.)*
  myth of human origins, 231
  rites of passage, 310–11, 341–43, 347
  rituals, 215
Guaycurú, 688n
Guessal, 99
Guiana Arawak, 732n
Guiart, Jean, 868n
Gurvitch, Georg, 750n, 777n
Gusinde, Martin N., 392, 393, 394, 445, 690n, 710n,
    724n, 756n, 766n, 797n, 801n, 805n, 814n,
    817n, 823n, 824n, 837n, 846n, 849n, 850n,
    852n, 853n 866n
Guss, David M., 736n
Guyot, Mireille, 739n, 782n, 858n
Guyrakambit, 873n
Guyraypotý, 573, 574, 597, 705n

Haarberg, Jon, 832n
Haburi, 125, 372, 843n
Haekel, Josef, 706n
Hahn, Albert, 730n, 836n, 860n
Hahuba, 122, 372
Halbwachs, Maurice, 768n
Hallowell, A. I., 745n, 870n
Hallpike, C. R., 800n
Halperin, Rhoda, 742n
Halpin, Marjorie, 806n
Hananerite, 117
Hanaqpacha, 118
Handbook of South American Indians, 9
Hanke, Wanda, 863n
Hánuxa, 336
Harliwanli, 838n
Harner, Michael J., 408, 425, 426, 454, 815n, 826n,
    830n, 831n, 838n, 840n, 850n, 854n
Harris, Marvin, 691n
Harris, Olivia, 731n, 776n
Hartmann, Günther, 417, 733n, 754n, 816n, 829n
Hartmann, Roswith, 756n, 785n, 852n, 854n
Hartmann, Thekla, 93, 720n
Hartt, Charles Frederik, 851n
Hasenfratz, Hans-Peter, 761n
Hauerwas, Stanley, 739n
He, 184
He House initiation, 331, 332, 333, 334, 335, 874n
Hebu, 430, 432
Hedu, 122
Hedu Kä Misi, 729n
Hei Kä Misi, 125
Hei Tä Bebi, 122
Hekoapi, 128
Helfer, James S., 700n
Hemming, John, 877n
Hengel, Martin, 780n
Henry, Jules, 200, 237, 294, 362, 422, 423,433, 452,
    689n, 763n, 766n, 792n, 829n, 830n, 834n,
    840n, 852n, 855n, 866n
Heraclitus, 158
Herrera Alfonso, Jorge, 883n
Herrera, Fortunato L,, 831n
Herrera, José Tamayo, 878n, 879n, 881n
Herskovitz, Melville J., 758n, 812n, 854n
Hertle, Gisela, 413, 827n
Hilbert, Peter Paul, 850n
Hilger, M. Inez, 716n
Hill, Jonathan D., 179, 746n, 747n, 757n, 782n,
    841n, 862n, 867n, 869n
Himabaka, 372

SUBJECT INDEX

SUBJECT INDEX

α and β Centauri, 85, 86; *see also* constellations
Abačikwaia, 292, 494
Abandonment, 117, 202, 850*n*; *see also* funeral
Abortion, 368; *see also* fetus; gestation; infanticide; killing; murder; sacrifice
Absence, 117, 336, 353, 616, 710*n*; *see also* disappearance; dispatch; occultation; sacrifice; withdrawal
  inherent in writing, 882*n*
  meaning of, 344, 646
Absolute beginnings, 31; *see also* primordium
Absolute value, 678
Absoluteness, 615
Abstinence, sexual, 372; *see also* avoidances; continence; restrictions, ritual; sex, abstention from
Abuhuwa, 74
Abundance, 121, 213, 214, 869*n*; *see also* accumulation; reproduction; periodicity
Acaan-guaá, 391
Accommodative movement, 867*n*; *see also* millenarian movements
Accounts, apocalyptic, 674; *see also* apocalypse; eschatology
Acculturation, 118; *see also* initiation
Accumulation, 587, 673; *see also* abundance; currency, symbolic; economics; hoarding; periodicity
  and historical time, 870*n*
  and knowledge, 870*n*
  and science, 870*n*
  of goods, 568; *see also* economics
  over time, 633
Acllas, 748*n*
Act, 375, 485; *see also* performance
Action
  and passion, 810*n*
Action, cultural, 227; *see also* interpretation
Action, human, 189, 302, 564
Action, ritual, 225
Action, symbolic, 167, 170, 220, 225
Activity and passivity, conflation of, 355
Adahe ademi hidi, 436, 437, 746*n*
Adaptability, 115, 885*n*
Adjustment movement, 867*n*; *see also* millenarian movements
Adoption, 362
Adornment: *see* decoration
Adultery, 794*n*
Adventurers, 513
Adversary, 359; *see also* enemies
Aeon, 726*n*; *see also* ages of the world
Aesthetics, 339, 786*n*; *see also* art; beauty; consciousness; creativity; dance; imagination; knowledge; music; song
Affecting presence, 786*n*; *see also* emotion
Affinal ties, absence of, in death, 538, 865*n*
Affine, 202, 204, 220, 247, 360, 498; *see also* kinship; marriage; social organization

Afflictions, terminal, 597; *see also* terminology
African influence on South America
  Afro-Brazilian religions, 185, 279–80, 299; *see also* Candomblé; Umbanda
  Colombia and Ecuador, 284
African religions, 557
African slaves, 569
Afro-American religions, 694*n*, 726*n*, 736*n*, 743*n*, 794*n*, 797*n*, 812*n*, 820*n*, 869*n*; *see also* Candomblé; Umbanda
Afro-Brazilian religion, 557, 720*n*, 758*n*
Afterlife, 468, 469, 528, 864*n*, 865*n*, 866*n*; *see also* death; geography, mythic; geography, postmortem
Afterlife, geography of, 528–42, 529, 866*n*; *see also* geography, mythic
Age group, 156, 342
Age of Destruction, 100; *see also* Name Index
Age of Discovery, 681, 682, 884*n*; *see also* Name Index
Age of the Grandparents, 100, 103
Age-grades, 339; *see also* life-cycle
Ages of the world, 735*n*, 744*n*; *see also* aeon; destruction; deconstruction
Ages of the world
  Guaman Poma's, 878*n*
  theories of, 726*n*
Age-set system, 156, 342
Aggression, stylized, 632; *see also* combat, ritual
Agouti, 131
Agriculture, 385; *see also* labor; urgent forms
  as a ritual activity, 368–71, 374–75
Aguydjê, 576, 577, 579, 874*n*; *see also* fulfillment; happiness
Ahistorical primordiality, 682; *see also* primordium
Aiawu, 198, 399, 409, 425, 432, 449
Ail, 222
A'iñ, 528
Ajat, 852*n*
Ajèrè, 743*n*
Ajibona, 359, 812*n*
Àkárái, 743*n*
Akato, 242, 243
Akia, 278, 283
Akolo-cwudn, 451
Akragaikrit, 413
Akurù, 437
Akwa, 423, 435
Akwalu, 397, 423, 435
'álam al-mithal, 770*n*
Alchemy, 817*n*
Alcohol, 561, 754*n*; *see also* beer; beverage; Big Drink; fermentation; liquid; fluids
Ale:mi, 436
Algaroba beer, 324
Algaroba fruit, 198, 749*n*
Alien explanations, 613

955